THE MAKING

MW01230791

PEOPLES AND CULTURES

A CONCISE HISTORY

Volume II: Since 1340

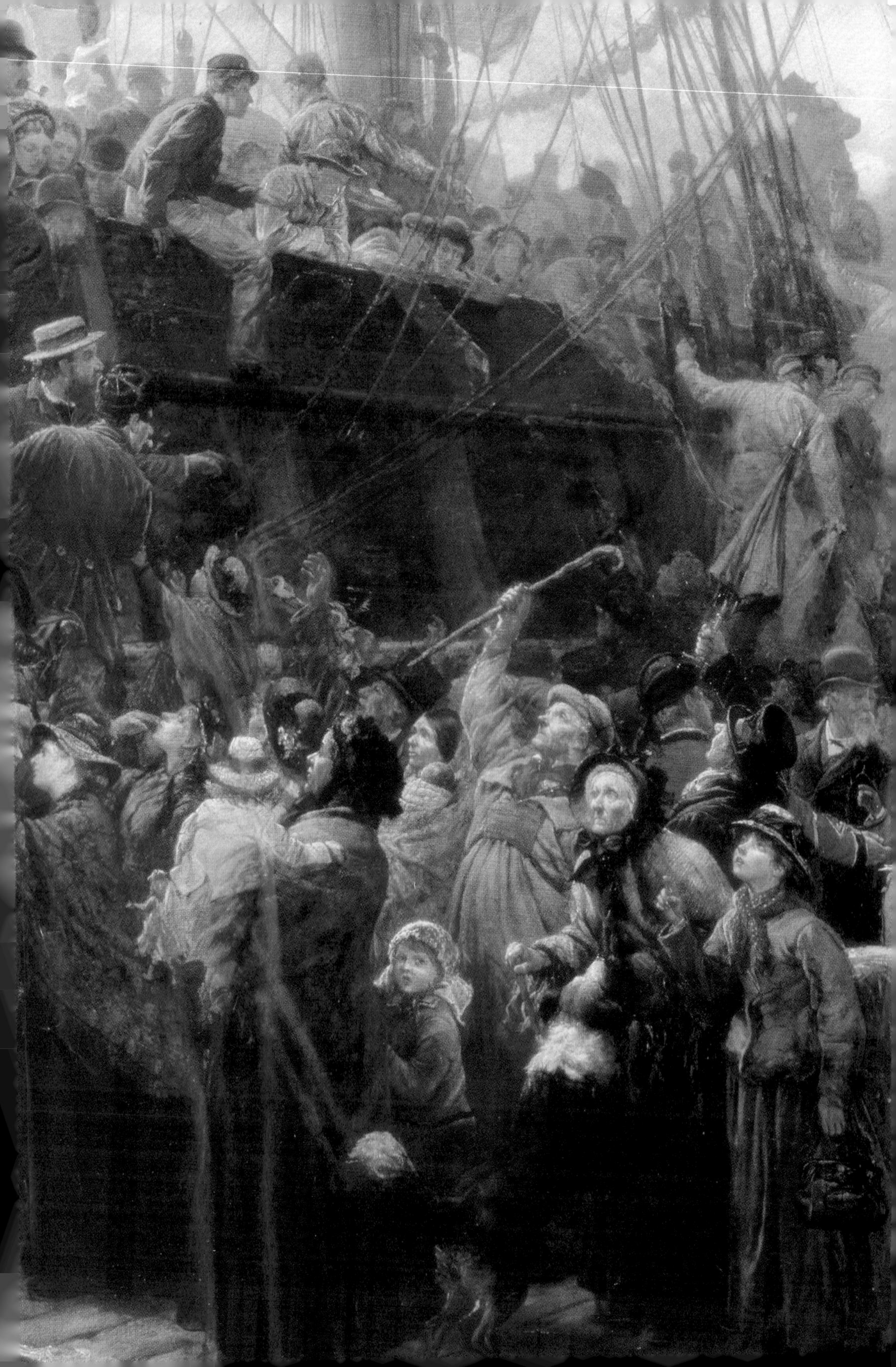

THE MAKING OF THE WEST

PEOPLES AND CULTURES

A CONCISE HISTORY

Volume II: Since 1340

LYNN HUNT
University of California at Los Angeles

THOMAS R. MARTIN
College of the Holy Cross

BARBARA H. ROSENWEIN
Loyola University Chicago

R. PO-CHIA HSIA
Pennsylvania State University

BONNIE G. SMITH
Rutgers University

BEDFORD/ST. MARTIN'S   Boston   ◆   New York

FOR BEDFORD/ST. MARTIN'S

Publisher for History: Patricia A. Rossi
Director of Development for History: Jane Knetzger
Executive Editor for History: Elizabeth M. Welch
Production Editor: Lori Chong Roncka
Production Supervisor: Maria R. Gonzalez
Marketing Manager: Jenna Bookin Barry
Editorial Assistant: Brianna Germain
Production Assistants: Thomas P. Crehan, Kendra LeFleur, Courtney Jossart
Copyeditor: Patricia Herbst
Proofreaders: Mary Lou Wilshaw-Watts, Janet Cocker
Text Design: Wanda Kossak
Indexer: Maro Riofrancos
Cover Design: Donna Lee Dennison
Composition: TechBooks
Cartography: Mapping Specialists Limited
Printing and Binding: R.R. Donnelley & Sons Company

President: Joan E. Feinberg
Editorial Director: Denise B. Wydra
Director of Marketing: Karen Melton
Director of Editing, Design, and Production: Marcia Cohen
Managing Editor: Elizabeth M. Schaaf

Library of Congress Control Number: 2002102840

Copyright © 2003 by Bedford/St. Martin's

All rights reserved. No part of this book may be reproduced, stored in a retrieval system, or transmitted in any form or by any means, electronic, mechanical, photocopying, recording, or otherwise, except as may be expressly permitted by the applicable copyright statutes or in writing by the Publisher.

Manufactured in the United States of America.

7   6   5   4   3   2
f   e   d   c   b   a

For information, contact: Bedford/St. Martin's, 75 Arlington Street, Boston, MA 02116
(617-399-4000)
www.bedfordstmartins.com

ISBN: 0–312–39538–8 (paperback complete edition)
       0–312–40207–4 (paperback Volume I)
       0–312–40208–2 (paperback Volume II)

Cover and Title Page Art: *The Emigrant Ship (c. 1880)*, by Charles J. Staniland. (Bradford Art Galleries and Museums, West Yorkshire, UK/The Bridgeman Art Library International Ltd.)

Preface

M

UCH OF OUR EXCITEMENT ABOUT THIS PROJECT arose from its very nature: textbook writing requires constant revision and updating to keep it fresh and make it better. Since publication of the full-length version of our textbook, *The Making of the West: Peoples and Cultures,* we have had the opportunity to hear from many teachers and students who have used it in their classrooms. Their comments have gratified us considerably and deepened our commitment to the project's basic goal and approach. At the same time, we learned that a shorter book would be appropriate for those instructors who need to cover the entire introduction to Western civilization in a single semester, who wish to assign extensive supplementary readings, or who find a comprehensive textbook by definition too detailed and daunting for their students.

This book—*The Making of the West: Peoples and Cultures, A Concise History*—is intended to meet their needs. We shortened our original narrative by 35 percent, combining some chapters while reducing others. For example, we rethought and rewrote two chapters on the ancient Near East and Greece and two on the French Revolution and Napoleonic era as single chapters, and we condensed and combined thematically related sections throughout the text. The result, we believe, is a concise edition that preserves the narrative flow, balance, and power of the full-length work.

Central Themes and Approach

Our title, *The Making of the West: Peoples and Cultures,* tells much about the themes and approach that we sought to preserve, and indeed strengthen, in *A Concise History.* We focus on the contributions of a multitude of peoples and cultures to the making of Western values and traditions while we show that the history of the West is the story of a process that is still ongoing, not a finished result with a fixed meaning. To understand the historical development of the West and its position in the world today, it is essential as well to place the West's emergence in a larger, global context that reveals the cross-cultural interactions fundamental to the shaping of the Western identity. Our task as authors, moreover, was to integrate the best of recent social and cultural history with the enduring developments of political, military, and diplomatic history, offering a clear, compelling narrative that sets all the key events and stages of the West's evolution in broad, meaningful context.

From our own teaching, we have learned that introductory students need a solid chronological framework, one with enough familiar benchmarks to make the material readily assimilable, but also one with enough flexibility to incorporate the new varieties of historical research. That is one reason why we present our account in a straightforward chronological manner. Each chapter treats all the main events, people, and themes of a period of time in which conditions of life in the West significantly changed; thus students are not required to learn about political events in one chapter, then backtrack to concurrent social and cultural developments in the next. The chronological organization also accords with our belief that it is important, above all else, for students to see the interconnections among varieties of historical experience—between politics and cultures; between public events and private experiences; between wars and diplomacy, on the one hand, and everyday life, on the other. Our chronological synthesis allows students to appreciate these relationships while, we hope, capturing the spirit of each age and sparking their historical imagination. For teachers, it ensures a balanced account, the flexibility to stress themes of one's own choosing, and perhaps best of all, a text that reveals history not as a settled matter but as a process that is constantly alive, subject to pressure, and able to surprise us. If we have succeeded in conveying some of the vibrancy of the past, we will not be satisfied with what we have done—history does not sit still that long—but we will be encouraged to start rethinking and revising once again.

Pedagogy and Features

To engage and inform students, we retained many of the study aids that we learned contribute to the success of the parent text. Each chapter begins with a vivid anecdote that draws readers into the atmosphere and issues of the period and raises the chapter's major themes, supplemented by a full-page reproduction of an artwork that similarly reveals the temper of the times. Chapters conclude with brief summaries that tie together the thematic strands and point the reader onward. A list of important dates at the end of each chapter helps students review key events of the period, while topic-specific timelines appear where useful to assist students' grasp of particular themes and processes. An annotated list of suggested references that combine print works and Web sites appears for each chapter to aid in research of particular topics, and an unusually comprehensive index incorporates a pronunciation guide.

We also drew on the experience of teachers throughout the United States and Canada to fashion our approach to primary sources. Learning that many instructors require a short edition with documents while others either do not elect to ask their students to work with primary sources or prefer their own choices of readings, we carefully selected three or four substantive documents per chapter that put a human face on a development central to the period and illuminate the relationship between narrative history and original sources. To preserve the narrative flow of the text and to allow teachers the flexibility to pick and choose sources, all documents appear in a separate reader, *Sources of* THE MAKING OF THE WEST: PEOPLES AND CULTURES, *A* CONCISE HISTORY, with cross-references in the textbook to ensure easy access.

A new full-color design and trim format give *A Concise History* the look and feel of a trade book, reinforcing visually the strong story line of the historical narrative and encouraging students to turn the page. We retain, however, many of the illustrations of the parent text, which have proved so important to the book's effectiveness in the classroom, to provide the most extensive map, graph, and artwork programs available in a brief survey. Each chapter includes, on average, three or four full-size maps showing major developments and one to three "spot maps," a first in this brief edition, intended to aid the student's understanding of single but crucial issues ranging from the structure of Old Kingdom Egypt to German reunification. "Mapping the West" summary maps, also unique, at the end of each chapter individually provide a snapshot of the West at the close of a transformative period and collectively help students visualize the West's changing contours over time. In addition to the over 160 maps, numerous graphs and charts visually support the narrative, including innovative "Taking Measure" statistical features in every chapter that introduce students to the skill of quantitative analysis by revealing how individual facts add up to broad trends. In common with all maps and graphs, "Taking Measure" features are cited in the text to prompt close study and carry informative captions.

We are proud as well of the over 240 illustrations, most in full color and all contemporaneous with the period under discussion, that directly reinforce or extend the narrative. Carefully chosen to reflect the text's broad topical coverage and geographic inclusion, the illustrations combine classics that are important for students to encounter with images new to brief texts. Unusually substantive captions accompany each picture, helping students to unlock the image and encouraging them to analyze artwork as primary sources. Together with the maps and documents, they provide instructors with a trove of teaching materials and allow students to enter the life of the past to see it from within.

Ancillaries

Because textbook ancillaries take on special importance in classrooms in which a brief survey text is assigned, we have taken care as well to assemble a comprehensive set of print and electronic resources for students and instructors. Reinforcing or extending *A Concise History,* these supplements offer a host of practical learning and teaching aids.

For Students

Sources of THE MAKING OF THE WEST: PEOPLES AND CULTURES, *A* CONCISE HISTORY—Volumes I (to 1740) and II (since 1340)—by Katharine J. Lualdi, University of Southern Maine. For each chapter in *A Concise History,* this companion sourcebook features three or four important political, social, or cultural documents that amplify the discussion in the textbook, where they are cross-referenced to ensure easy access and to encourage students to understand the connection between narrative history and primary sources. Chapter introductions and headnotes further contextualize the wide array of sources and perspectives represented in the documents, while discussion questions guide students' reading and promote historical-thinking skills.

Online Study Guide for THE MAKING OF THE WEST: PEOPLES AND CULTURES, *A* CONCISE HISTORY at www.bedfordstmartins.com/huntconcise. Thoroughly revised to correspond to *A Concise History,* the free Online Study Guide is a uniquely personalized learning tool that offers multimedia activities to help students master the ideas and information in the textbook. For each chapter in *A Concise History,* the Guide offers an initial multiple-choice test that allows students to assess their comprehension of the material and a Recommended Study Plan that suggests specific exercises on the subject areas students still need to master. Two follow-up multiple-choice tests per chapter help students judge their mastery of the material. Additional exercises, including map and visual activities keyed directly to images in the textbook, encourage students to think about chapter themes as well as help them develop skills of analysis. Results of multiple-choice tests can be e-mailed to instructors.

LINKS LIBRARY. Students can conduct their own online research through our comprehensive Links Library, a database of more than 350 carefully reviewed and annotated history Web links searchable by topic or by textbook chapter.

A Student's Guide to History, **Eighth Edition,** by Jules R. Benjamin, Ithaca College. This brief yet comprehensive introduction to the study of history discusses the discipline, reviews basic study, research, and writing skills, and describes the most common history assignments. A thoroughly class-tested bestseller through eight editions, the text has been revised to give students even more help with writing and with conducting research online. The online edition at www.bedfordstmartins.com/benjamin contains abbreviated content from the print version and is accessible to students wherever they have a connection to the Internet.

Research and Documentation Online by Diana Hacker, Prince George's Community College, at www.bedfordstmartins.com/resdoc. This online version of Diana Hacker's highly regarded handbook provides clear advice across the disciplines on how to integrate outside material into a paper, how to cite sources correctly, and how to format in MLA, APA, CPE, or Chicago style.

Research Assistant HyperFolio.   Delivered on CD-ROM, this tool for conducting research helps students collect, evaluate, and cite sources found both online and off.

After September 11: An Online Reader for Writers at www.bedfordstmartins.com/ september11.   This free collection of more than 100 annotated links provides social, political, economic, and cultural commentary about the terrorist attacks on the United States of September 11, 2001. Thoughtful discussion questions and ideas for research and writing projects are included.

For Instructors

Instructor's Resource Manual for THE MAKING OF THE WEST: PEOPLES AND CULTURES, *A CONCISE HISTORY* by Michael D. Richards and Lynn M. Laufenberg, both of Sweet Briar College. Thoroughly revised to correlate with *A Concise History*, this well-received Instructor's Manual offers extensive teaching information for each chapter in the textbook: outlines of chapter themes, lecture and discussion topics, in-class exercises for working with maps and illustrations, writing and classroom presentation assignments, and research topic suggestions. The manual also includes eight essays for instructors, such as "What Is 'The West'?," "Teaching Western Civilization with Computers," and "Literature and the Western Civilization Classroom," and over a dozen frequently assigned primary sources for easy access and distribution.

Computerized Test Bank developed by Tamara Hunt, Loyola Marymount University, and Angela A. Kurtz, University of Maryland at College Park. User-friendly software lets instructors create and administer tests on paper or over a network, and a grade management function helps keep track of students' progress. Teachers can write their own tests or generate exams and quizzes from the test bank provided. Conversion utilities allow instructors to create exams in WebCT and Blackboard formats. In addition to twenty fill-in-the-blank, forty multiple-choice (labeled by difficulty), ten short-answer, and four essay questions, this thoughtfully designed test bank includes for each chapter in *A Concise History* a relationship-causation exercise, which asks students to place five events in chronological order and to explain a common theme that runs through them, and four map and document exercises that test students' comprehension of chapter material and their ability to use sources. An answer key is provided.

Instructor's Resource CD-ROM.   This CD-ROM includes visual materials from *A Concise History* in an easy-to-use format for PowerPoint™ and other classroom presentations.

The Bedford Series in History and Culture—Advisory Editors: Natalie Zemon Davis, Princeton University; Ernest R. May, Harvard University; David W. Blight, Amherst College; and Lynn Hunt, University of California at Los Angeles. Any of the volumes from this highly acclaimed series of brief, inexpensive, document-based supplements can be packaged with *The Making of the West: A Concise History* at a reduced price. The fifteen European history titles include *Spartacus and the Slave Wars, Utopia, The Enlightenment, The French Revolution and Human Rights,* and *The Communist Manifesto.*

Using The Bedford Series with THE MAKING OF THE WEST by Maura O'Connor, University of Cincinnati. This short guide gives practical suggestions for using the volumes for Western civilization in The Bedford Series in History and Culture in conjunction with *The Making of the West.* Available online as well as in print, the guide not only supplies links between the textbook and the supplements but also provides ideas for starting discussions focused on a single primary-source volume.

Map Transparencies.   Full-color transparencies of over 145 maps in the parent textbook broaden the map program of *A Concise History* while helping instructors present the materials and teaching students important map-reading skills. A correlation guide that shows how the transparencies align with the brief text appears in the Instructor's Resource Manual and on the book companion Web site.

Map Central at www.bedfordstmartins.com/mapcentral.   Map Central is a searchable database of over 450 maps from Bedford/St. Martin's major history textbooks. Instructors can download maps for lectures using PowerPoint™ or other presentation software, browse maps by chapter within a specific text, or search for maps by keyword across several textbooks to find all maps related to a given topic.

E-Content for Online Learning allows teachers using *A Concise History* to develop custom Web sites with WebCT or other course-building systems.

Book Companion Web Site at www.bedfordstmartins.com/huntconcise.   The companion Web site for *A Concise History* gathers all the new media resources for the text at a single address.

Acknowledgments

The scholars and teachers who reviewed *The Making of the West: Peoples and Cultures* made suggestions that we gratefully incorporated into *A Concise History.* Our thanks to the following instructors, whose comments often challenged us to rethink or justify our interpretations and always provided a check on accuracy down to the smallest detail: Dorothy Abrahamse, California State University at Long Beach;

F. E. Beeman, Middle Tennessee State University; Martin Berger, Youngstown State University; Raymond Birn, University of Oregon; Charmarie J. Blaisdell, Northeastern University; Keith Bradley, University of Victoria; Paul Breines, Boston College; Caroline Castiglione, University of Texas at Austin; Carolyn A. Conley, University of Alabama; William Connell, Seton Hall University; Jo Ann H. Moran Cruz, Georgetown University; John P. Daly, Louisiana Tech University; Suzanne Desan, University of Wisconsin at Madison; Michael F. Doyle, Ocean County College; Jean C. England, Northeastern Louisiana University; Steven Epstein, University of Colorado at Boulder; Steven Fanning, University of Illinois at Chicago; Laura Frader, Northeastern University; Alison Futrell, University of Arizona; Gretchen Galbraith, Grand Valley State University; Timothy E. Gregory, Ohio State University; Katherine Haldane Grenier, The Citadel; Martha Hanna, University of Colorado at Boulder; Julie Hardwick, Texas Christian University; Kenneth W. Harl, Tulane University; Charles Hedrick, University of California at Santa Cruz; Robert L. Hohlfelder, University of Colorado at Boulder; Maryanne Horowitz, Occidental College; Gary Kates, Trinity University; Ellis L. Knox, Boise State University; Lawrence Langer, University of Connecticut; Keith P. Luria, North Carolina State University; Judith P. Meyer, University of Connecticut; Maureen C. Miller, Hamilton College; Stuart S. Miller, University of Connecticut; Dr. Frederick Murphy, Western Kentucky University; James Murray, University of Cincinnati; Phillip C. Naylor, Marquette University; Carolyn Nelson, University of Kansas; Richard C. Nelson, Augsburg College; John Nichols, University of Oregon; Byron J. Nordstrom, Gustavus Adolphus College; Maura O'Connor, University of Cincinnati; Lawrence Okamura, University of Missouri at Columbia; Dolores Davison Peterson, Foothill College; Carl F. Petry, Northwestern University; Carole A. Putko, San Diego State University; Michael D. Richards, Sweet Briar College; Barbara Saylor Rodgers, University of Vermont; Sally Scully, San Francisco State University; Jane Slaughter, University of New Mexico; Donald Sullivan, University of New Mexico; Victoria Thompson, Xavier University; Sue Sheridan Walker, Northeastern Illinois University; John E. Weakland, Ball State University; Theodore R. Weeks, Southern Illinois University at Carbondale; and Merry Wiesner-Hanks, University of Wisconsin at Milwaukee.

We thank as well the many colleagues, friends, and family members who have helped us develop this work. We also wish to express our gratitude to the publishing team who did so much to bring this book into being. Patricia A. Rossi, publisher for history, guided our efforts throughout publication. Joan E. Feinberg, president, and her predecessor, Charles H. Christensen, shared generous resources, mutual vision, and best of all, confidence in the textbook and in us. Special thanks are due to many other individuals: Lori Chong Roncka, our production editor, who with great skill and professionalism pulled all the pieces together with the help of Maria R. Gonzalez, John Amburg, Thomas P. Crehan, Courtney Jossart, and Kendra LeFleur; Carole Frohlich and Martha Shethar, who contributed their imagination and research to make possible the outstanding art program; Jenna Bookin Barry, marketing manager for history, whose strong efforts helped ensure the success of the full-length work; William J. Lombardo, associate new media editor, who ably shepherded numerous electronic supplements to completion with the help of Coleen O'Hanley and Denise Wydra; Louise Townsend, Sarah Barrash Wilson, and Brianna Germain, who helped in myriad ways on many essential editorial tasks; and our superb copyeditor, Patricia Herbst. Last and above all, we thank Elizabeth M. Welch, executive editor for history, who provided just the right doses of encouragement, prodding, and concrete suggestions for improvement. Her intelligence, skill, and determination proved to be crucial at every step of the process.

Our students' questions and concerns have shaped much of this work, and we welcome all our readers' suggestions, queries, and criticisms. Please contact us at our respective institutions or through our Web site: www.bedfordstmartins.com/ huntconcise.

L.H.   T.R.M.   B.H.R.   R.P.H.   B.G.S.

Brief Contents

Contents

CHAPTER 11

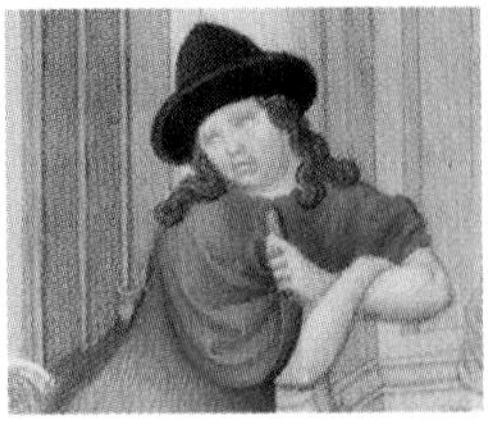

CHAPTER 12

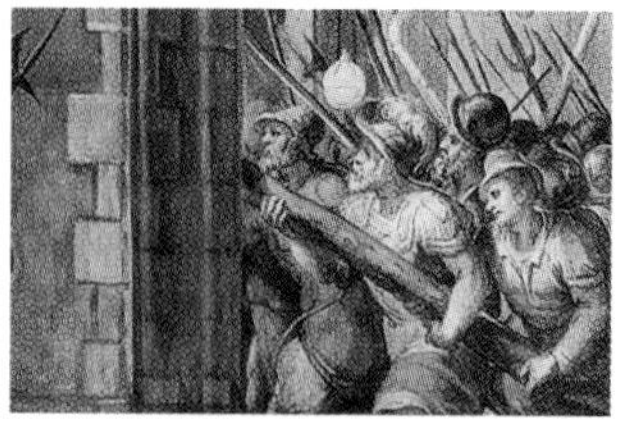

Struggles over Beliefs, 1500–1648 475

CHAPTER 13

State Building and the Search for Order, 1648–1690   527

CHAPTER 14

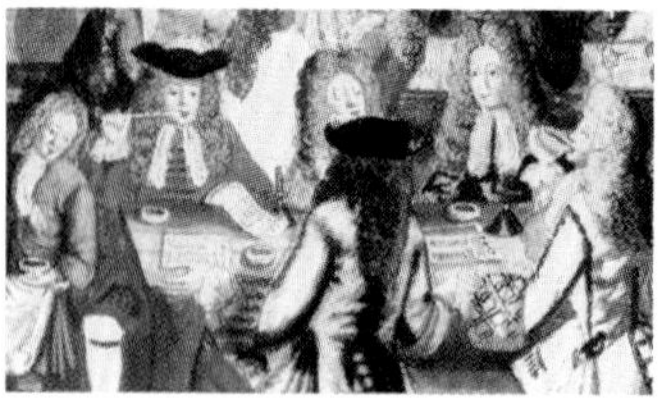

The Promise of Enlightenment, 1740–1789   611

CHAPTER 16

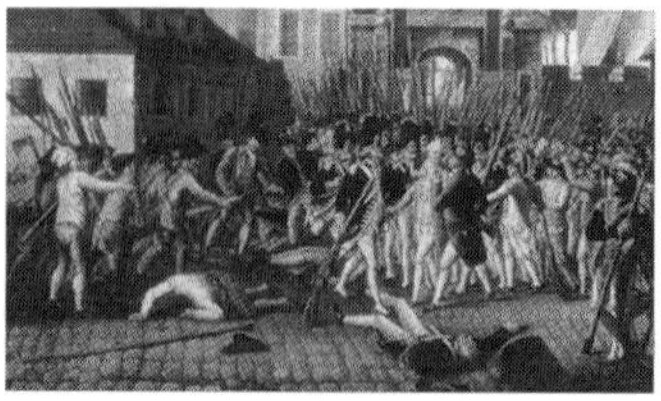

The French Revolution and Napoleon, 1789–1815 653

Industrialization and Social Ferment, 1815–1850   703

Constructing the Nation-State, c. 1850–1880   755

CHAPTER 19

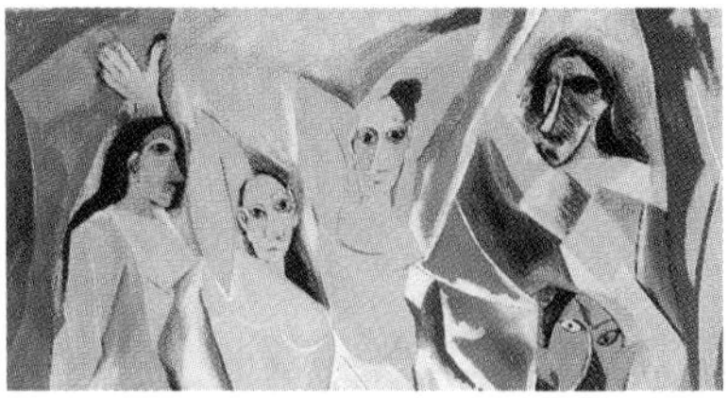

War, Revolution, and Reconstruction, 1914–1929   863

CHAPTER 21

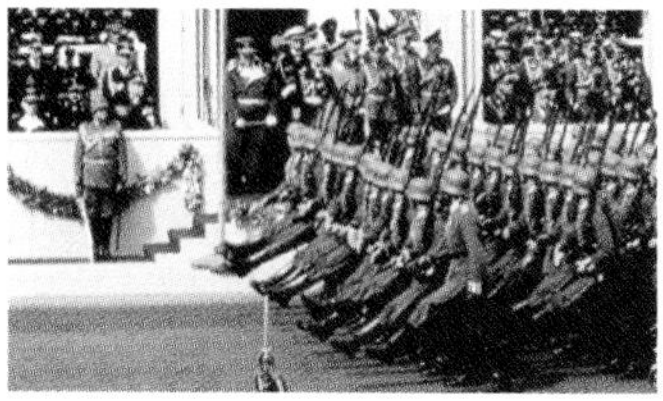

An Age of Catastrophes, 1929–1945 907

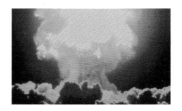

The Atomic Age, c. 1945–1960   951

Challenges to the Postindustrial West, 1960–1980   991

The New Globalism: Opportunities and Dilemmas, 1980 to the Present   1029

Documents

The primary-source collection that accompanies this textbook—*Sources of The Making of the West: Peoples and Cultures, A Concise History*—provides the following documents.

Maps and Figures

MAPS

Chapter 15

Chapter 16

Chapter 17

Chapter 18

Chapter 19

Chapter 20

Chapter 21

Chapter 22

Chapter 23

Chapter 24

FIGURES

About the Authors

LYNN HUNT, Eugen Weber Professor of Modern European History at the University of California at Los Angeles, received her B.A. from Carleton College and her M.A. and Ph.D. from Stanford University. She is the author of *Revolution and Urban Politics in Provincial France* (1978); *Politics, Culture, and Class in the French Revolution* (1984); and *The Family Romance of the French Revolution* (1992). She is also the coauthor of *Telling the Truth about History* (1994); coauthor of *Liberty, Equality, Fraternity: Exploring the French Revolution* (2001, with CD-ROM); editor of *The New Cultural History* (1989); editor and translator of *The French Revolution and Human Rights* (1996); and coeditor of *Histories: French Constructions of the Past* (1995), *Beyond the Cultural Turn* (1999), and *Human Rights and Revolution* (2000). She has been awarded fellowships by the Guggenheim Foundation and the National Endowment for the Humanities and is a fellow of the American Academy of Arts and Sciences. She is president of the American Historical Association in 2002.

THOMAS R. MARTIN, Jeremiah O'Connor Professor in Classics at the College of the Holy Cross, earned his B.A. at Princeton University and his M.A. and Ph.D. at Harvard University. He is the author of *Sovereignty and Coinage in Classical Greece* (1985) and *Ancient Greece* (1996, 2000) and is one of the originators of *Perseus: Interactive Sources and Studies on Ancient Greece* (1992, 1996; www.perseus.tufts.edu), which, among other awards, was named the EDUCOM Best Software in Social Sciences (History) in 1992. He also wrote the lead article on ancient Greece for the revised edition of the electronic *Encarta Encyclopedia*. He serves on the editorial board of STOA (www.stoa.org) and as codirector of its DEMOS project (online resources on ancient Athenian democracy). A recipient of fellowships from the National Endowment for the Humanities and the American Council of Learned Societies, he is currently conducting research on the history and significance of freedom of speech in Athenian democracy.

BARBARA H. ROSENWEIN, professor of history at Loyola University Chicago, earned her B.A., M.A., and Ph.D. at the University of Chicago. She is the author of *Rhinoceros Bound: Cluny in the Tenth Century* (1982); *To Be the Neighbor of Saint Peter: The Social Meaning of Cluny's Property, 909–1049* (1989); *Negotiating Space: Power, Restraint, and Privileges of Immunity in Early Medieval Europe* (1999); and *A Short History of the Middle Ages* (2001). She is the editor of *Anger's Past: The Social Uses of an Emotion in the Middle Ages* (1998) and coeditor of *Debating the Middle Ages: Issues and Readings* (1998) and *Monks and Nuns, Saints and Outcasts: Religion in Medieval Society* (2000). A recipient of Guggenheim and National Endowment for the Humanities fellowships, she is currently working on a history of emotions in the early Middle Ages.

R. PO-CHIA HSIA, Edwin Erle Sparks Professor of History at Pennsylvania State University, received his B.A. from Swarthmore College and his M.A. and Ph.D. from Yale University. He is the author of *Society and Religion in Münster, 1535–1618* (1984); *The Myth of Ritual Murder: Jews and Magic in Reformation Germany* (1988); *Social Discipline in the Reformation: Central Europe, 1550–1750* (1989); *Trent 1475: Stories of a Ritual Murder Trial* (1992); and *The World of the Catholic Renewal* (1997). He has edited *The German People and the Reformation* (1998); *In and Out of the Ghetto: Jewish-Gentile Relations in Late Medieval and Early Modern Germany* (1995); *Calvinism and Religious Toleration in the Dutch Golden Age* (2002); and *The Blackwell Companion to the Worlds of the Reformation* (forthcoming). An Academician at the Academia Sinica, Taiwan, he has also been awarded fellowships by the Woodrow Wilson International Society of Scholars, the National Endowment for the Humanities, the Guggenheim Foundation, the Davis Center of Princeton University, the Mellon Foundation, the American Council of Learned Societies, and the American Academy in Berlin. Currently he is working on the cultural contacts between Europe and Asia between the sixteenth and eighteenth centuries.

BONNIE G. SMITH, Board of Governors Distinguished Professor of History at Rutgers University, earned her B.A. at Smith College and her M.A. and Ph.D. at the University of Rochester. She is the author of *Ladies of the Leisure Class* (1981); *Confessions of a Concierge: Madame Lucie's History of Twentieth-Century France* (1985); *Changing Lives: Women in European History since 1700* (1989); *The Gender of History: Men, Women, and Historical Practice* (1998); and *Imperialism* (2000). She is also the coeditor and translator of *What Is Property?* (1994); editor of *Global Feminisms since 1945* (2000); and coeditor of *Objects of Modernity: Selected Writings of Lucy Maynard Salmon* (2001) and the forthcoming Oxford series in world history and *Oxford Encyclopedia of Women in World History.* She has received fellowships from the Guggenheim Foundation, the National Endowment for the Humanities, the National Humanities Center, the Davis Center of Princeton University, and the American Council of Learned Societies. Currently she is studying the globalization of European culture and society since the seventeenth century.

THE MAKING OF THE WEST

PEOPLES AND CULTURES

A CONCISE HISTORY

Volume II: Since 1340

Tandē p̄ stragem loim maximā luct̄ ieiunia et
pīnas grau̅es ꝓ pꝛocessionale eunti p̄ romā cum
inuicta plebe et clero appaꝛet angelus sanguino
lenti ensē inagina reponēs sup pꝛalacii magi

Crisis and Renaissance

1340–1500

I N 1453, THE CANNONS OF OTTOMAN RULER MEHMED II breached the walls of Constantinople. A Byzantine historian mourned "the city deserted, lying lifeless, naked, soundless, without either form or beauty." The pope at Rome preached a crusade against the Turks. There was a clear sense of crisis. Yet a very few years later, Mehmed was writing to the *signore* of Rimini, asking the Italian prince to lend him the Rimini court painter and architect Matteo de Pasti. The Ottoman sultan was planning to build a new palace at Constantinople (modern Istanbul), as a fitting symbol of his imperial dominion, and he had heard of Matteo de Pasti's reputation. When Pasti was unable to help him, Mehmed turned to several Venetian painters instead. The palace came to be called the Topkapi Saray and still stands today looking across the Bosporus, the strait that divides European and Asian Turkey.

Mehmed sums up in one personage the twin themes of the period 1340–1500. His conquest of Constantinople was one of many crises that rocked the West from the Bosporus to the Atlantic: his age saw disease, war, economic contraction, and religious upheaval. At the same time, his tastes and culture aligned him with the Renaissance, a movement that was rediscovering the arts and worldview of classical antiquity. His interest in Italian art reflected the connection between power and culture characteristic of his era. In the fourteenth and fifteenth centuries, much new

■ **The Last Days of the Plague**
This scene from Les Très Riches Heures du Duc de Berry *(the book of hours of the duke of Berry) depicts the burial of Roman victims of the plague. Books of hours were prayer books for individual use. They contained prayers appropriate for the months of the year, days of the week, and hours of the day. This scene reminds Christians of the imminence of death and the importance of leading a pious life: sudden death does not spare even those in the holy city of Rome. The miniature paintings in this book of hours were created for the duke of Berry around 1415 by the Limbourg brothers, three Flemish miniaturists.*
(The Metropolitan Museum of Art, The Cloisters Collection, 1954. [54.1.1] Photograph © 1987 The Metropolitan Museum of Art [detail].)

artistic, architectural, and musical work was created in praise of personal and public lives. Portraits, palaces, and poetry commemorated the glory of the rich and powerful, while a new cultural movement called *humanism* advocated classical learning and argued for the active participation of the individual in civic affairs. Family, honor, social status, and individual distinction—these were the goals that fueled the ambitions of Renaissance men and women.

Their quest for glory duplicated on a smaller scale the enhanced power of the state, shored up by new military technologies—firearms, siege equipment, fortifications, and well-equipped soldiers. Commoners, criminals, and adventurers often joined the ranks of the fighters. To maintain their social eminence, many nobles were forced to take on new roles as officials or officers in the service of the state. By appointing nobles to the royal household, as military commanders and councilors, kings and princes consolidated their power.

Like individuals, these states, too, competed for wealth, glory, and honor. While warfare and diplomacy channeled the restless energy of the Italian states, monarchies and empires outside of Italy also expanded their power through conquests and institutional reforms. The European world changed dramatically as new powers such as the Ottoman Empire and Muscovy rose to prominence in the east, while the Iberian kingdoms of Portugal and Spain expanded European domination to Africa, Asia, and the Americas.

A Multitude of Crises

Beginning in the fourteenth century and extending to the middle of the fifteenth, Europeans confronted crises of both nature and human design. The plague wracked the cities and hurt the countryside. The Hundred Years' War devastated France. To the east, the rise of the Ottomans had a cataclysmic impact on the politics of eastern and central Europe. Everywhere economic contraction made for material hard times, while spiritual well-being seemed threatened by a long papal schism. Minorities—religious dissenters, heretics, Jews, and Muslims in Spain—suffered the effects of pent-up anxieties.

The Black Death and Its Consequences

Bad weather and overpopulation contributed to a series of famines at the beginning of the fourteenth century. Having cleared forests and drained swamps, peasants divided their plots into ever smaller parcels and farmed marginal land; their income and the quality of their diet eroded. In the great urban centers, where thousands depended on steady employment and cheap bread, a bad harvest, always followed by sharply rising food prices, meant hunger and eventual famine. A cooling of the European climate also contributed to the crisis in the food supply. Modern studies of tree rings indicate that fourteenth-century Europe entered a colder period, with a succession of severe winters beginning in 1315 and extending to 1317. Crop failures were widespread. In many cities of northwestern Europe, the price of bread tripled in a month, and thousands starved to death. Some Flemish cities, for example, lost 10 percent of their population. Many who survived were badly weakened, prime quarry for disease.

In midcentury, the bubonic plague passed from its breeding ground in central Asia eastward into China, where it decimated the population and wiped out the remnants of the tiny Italian merchant community in Yangzhou. Bacteria-carrying fleas living on black rats transmitted the disease. They traveled back to Europe alongside valuable cargoes of silk, porcelain, and spices. In 1347, the Genoese colony in Caffa in the Crimea contracted the plague. Fleeing by ship in a desperate but futile attempt to escape the disease, the Genoese in turn communicated the plague to other Mediterranean seaports. By January 1348, the plague had infected Sicily, Sardinia, Corsica, and Marseille. Six months later, it had spread to Aragon, all of Italy, the Balkans, and most of France. The disease then crept northward to Germany, England, and Scandinavia, reaching the Russian city of Novgorod in 1351 (Map 11.1).

Nothing like the Black Death, as this epidemic came to be called, had struck Europe since the great plague of the sixth century. The Italian writer Giovanni Boccaccio (1313–1375) reported that the plague

> *first betrayed itself by the emergence of certain tumors in the groin or the armpits, some of which grew as large as a common apple, others as an egg. . . . From the two said parts of the body this . . . began to propagate and spread itself in all directions indifferently; after which the form of the malady began to change, black spots or livid making their appearance in many cases on the arm or the thigh or elsewhere, now few and large, now minute and numerous.*◆

Inhabitants of cities, where crowding and filth increased the chances of contagion, died in massive numbers. Florence lost almost two-thirds of its population of ninety thousand; Siena, like most cities visited by the plague, lost half its people. Rural areas suffered fewer deaths, but regional differences were pronounced. (See "Taking Measure," page 433.) Nor was the toll over after 1350. Further outbreaks of the plague occurred in Europe in 1361, 1368–1369, 1371, 1375, 1390, and 1405; they continued, with longer dormant intervals, into the eighteenth century.

Although the Black Death took a horrible human toll, the disaster actually profited some people. In an overpopulated society with limited resources, massive death opened the ranks for advancement. For example, after 1350, landlords had difficulty acquiring new tenant farmers without making concessions in land contracts,

---

◆ For further contemporary accounts of the plague, see Document 33, "The Black Death."

1347
Jan. 1348
June 1348
1349
1350
1351 and later
Few or no plague deaths
Center of urban revolt
Rural uprisings
NORWAY
SWEDEN
SCOTLAND
IRELAND
ENGLAND
North Sea
DENMARK
Baltic Sea
RUSSIAN STATES
Novgorod
LITHUANIA
POLAND
Lübeck
Hamburg
Brunswick
Bruges
Ghent
Liège
London
Calais
Rouen
Paris
Ypres
Cologne
Rhine R.
Elbe R.
Thuringia
HOLY ROMAN EMPIRE
Strasbourg
ATLANTIC OCEAN
FRANCE
Alsace
Savoy
Zurich
Vienna
HUNGARY
Caffa
Black Sea
Milan
Venice
VENICE
Genoa
Po R.
Danube R.
Albi
Marseille
Florence
PAPAL STATES
Rome
Naples
Ebro R.
CASTILE
ARAGON
Barcelona
Corsica
Sardinia
PORTUGAL
Seville
Constantinople
Thessalonika
OTTOMAN EMPIRE
Sicily
Mediterranean Sea
Crete
Cyprus
0 200 400 miles
0 200 400 kilometers
N
E
S
W

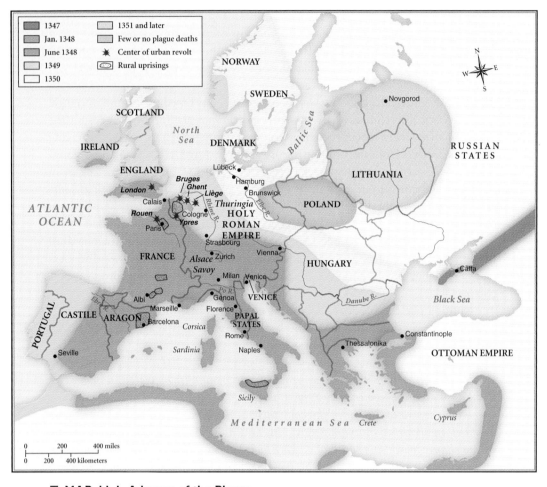

■ **MAP 11.1 Advance of the Plague**

The gradual but deadly spread of the plague followed the roads and rivers of Europe. Note the earlier transmission by sea from the Crimea to the ports of the Mediterranean before the general spread to northern Europe.

www.bedfordstmartins.com/huntconcise See the ONLINE STUDY GUIDE for more help in analyzing this map.

fewer priests competed for the same number of benefices (ecclesiastical offices funded by an endowment), and workers received much higher wages because the supply of laborers had plummeted. The Black Death and the resulting decline in urban population meant a lower demand for grain relative to the supply and thus a drop in cereal prices.

All across Europe noble landlords, whose revenues fell as prices dropped, had to adjust to these new circumstances. Some revived seigneurial demands for labor

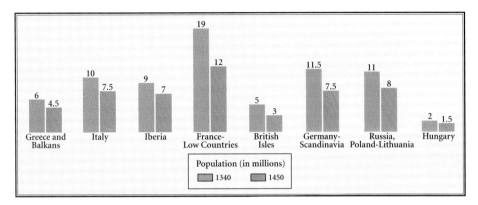

■ **TAKING MEASURE** Population Losses and the Plague, 1340–1450
The bar chart represents dramatically the impact of the Black Death and the recurrent plagues be-
tween 1340 and 1450. More than a century after the Black Death, none of the regions of Europe
had made up for the losses of population. The population of 1450 stood at between 75 and 80 per-
cent of the pre-plague population. The hardest-hit areas were France and the Low Countries,
which also suffered from the devastations of the Hundred Years' War.
(From Carlo M. Cipolla, ed., *Fontana Economic History of Europe: The Middle Ages* [Great Britain: Collins/Fontana Books, 1974], 36.)

services. Others looked to their central government for legislation to regulate wages. Still others granted favorable terms to peasant proprietors, often after bloody peasant revolts. Many noblemen lost a portion of their wealth and a measure of their autonomy and political influence. Consequently, European nobles became more dependent on their monarchs and on war to supplement their incomes and enhance their power.

For the peasantry and the urban working population, higher wages generally meant an improvement in living standards. To compensate for the lower demand and price for grain, many peasants and landlords turned to stock breeding and grape and barley cultivation. As European agriculture diversified, peasants and artisans consumed more beer, wine, meat, cheese, and vegetables, a better and more varied diet than their thirteenth-century forebears had eaten.

Because of the shrinking population and decreased demand for food, cultivating marginal fields was no longer profitable, and many settlements were simply abandoned. By 1450, for example, some 450 large English villages and many small hamlets had disappeared. In central Europe east of the Elbe River, where German peasants had migrated, large tracts of cultivated land reverted to forest. Estimates suggest that some 80 percent of all villages in parts of Thuringia (Germany) vanished.

In the cities, production shifted from manufacturing for a mass market to a highly lucrative, though small, luxury market. The drastic loss in urban population had reduced the demand for such mass-manufactured goods as cloth. Fewer people

■ Deserted Fields

Aerial photography in many areas of northern Europe has revealed the outlines of cultivated fields and old settlements not visible from the ground. These are signs marking the expansion and contraction of human settlement and cultivation in fourteenth-century Europe before and after the Black Death. As the plague swept through the land, and as whole populations of small settlements died off, villages were deserted and cultivated fields reverted back to nature. In England, for example, more than 225 of about 900 medieval churches were abandoned, and nearly 250 were in ruins in the second half of the fourteenth century. This photograph shows the former cultivated fields of the village of Tusmore, Oxfordshire, whose inhabitants all died of the plague.
(Copyright reserved Cambridge University, Collection of Air Photographs.)

now possessed proportionately greater concentrations of wealth. In the southern French city of Albi, for example, the proportion of citizens possessing more than 100 livres in per capita income doubled between 1343 and 1357, while the number of poor people, those with less than 10 livres, declined by half.

Faced with the possibility of imminent and untimely death, some of the urban populace sought immediate gratification. The Florentine Matteo Villani described the newfound desire for luxury in his native city in 1351. "The common people . . . wanted the dearest and most delicate foods . . . while children and common women clad themselves in all the fair and costly garments of the illustrious who had died." Those with means increased their consumption of luxuries such as silk clothing, hats, doublets (snug-fitting men's jackets), and expensive jewelry. Whereas agricultural prices continued to decline, the prices of manufactured goods, particularly luxury items, remained constant and even rose as demand for them outstripped supply. The middle class sought new material comforts, such as fireplaces and private latrines, beds, chests, and curtains. Members of the new peasant elite must have lived in simpler style, but perhaps they no longer shared their house with animals, as they had in the thirteenth century.

The long-term consequences of this new consumption pattern spelled the end for the traditional woolen industry that had produced for a mass market. Diminishing demand for wool caused hardships for woolworkers, and social and political unrest shook many older industrial centers dependent on the cloth industry, such as Flanders. At Ypres, for example, production figures fell from a high of ninety thousand pieces of cloth in 1320 to fewer than twenty-five thousand by 1390. In Ghent, where 44 percent of all households were woolworkers and where some 60 percent of the working population depended on the textile industry, the woolen market's slump meant constant labor unrest.

The new labor market tended to undermine women's economic position. In the German city of Cologne, for example, more and more artisan guilds excluded women from their ranks. Everywhere, fathers favored sons and sons-in-law to succeed them in their crafts. Daughters and widows resisted this patriarchal regime in the urban economy, but they were most successful in industries with the least regulations, such as beer-brewing.

The Hundred Years' War, 1337–1453

In France, the misery wrought by the plague was compounded by the devastation of war. Conflicting French and English interests in southwestern France sparked the Hundred Years' War. As part of the French royal policy of centralizing jurisdiction, Philip VI in 1337 confiscated the southwestern province of Aquitaine, which had been held by the English monarchs as a fief of the French crown. To recover his lands, Edward III of England in turn laid claim to the French throne. Some of his soldiers were nobles and knights, who brought with them the expectations of chivalry. But many were yeomen (free farmers) eager for booty, hostages, and amorous conquests. Mercenary companies came to replace levies of freemen archers in the English army, remaining to wreak havoc on the French countryside when not employed in war.

Ruling over a more populous realm and commanding far larger armies than the English, the French kings were, nevertheless, hindered in the war by the independent actions of their powerful barons. Against the accurate and deadly English freemen archers, the French knights met repeated defeats. Yet the French nobility despised their own peasants, perhaps fearing them and the urban middle classes more than they feared their noble English adversaries.

The war may be divided into three periods: the first was marked by English triumphs, the second saw France slowly gaining the upper hand, and the third ended in the English expulsion from France (Map 11.2). The final, most important phase saw two key developments: the rise of Burgundy, a hodgepodge of territories held together only by the political machinations of its dukes; and the rise of France as a distinct nation. This phase began when the English king Henry V (r. 1413–1422) launched a full-scale invasion of France and crushed the French at Agincourt (1415). Three parties then struggled for domination in France. Henry occupied Normandy and claimed the French throne; the dauphin (heir apparent to the French throne), Charles VII of France (r. 1422–1461),* ruled central France; and the duke of

*Although the dauphin was not crowned until 1429, he assumed the title Charles VII in 1422, after the death of his father.

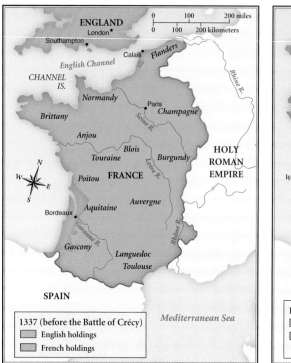

1337 (before the Battle of Crécy)
- English holdings
- French holdings

1360 (after the Battle of Poitiers)
- English holdings
- French holdings
- ✶ Battle

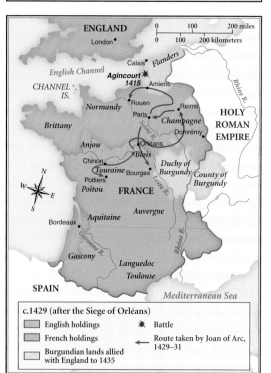

c.1429 (after the Siege of Orléans)
- English holdings
- French holdings
- Burgundian lands allied with England to 1435
- ✶ Battle
- ← Route taken by Joan of Arc, 1429–31

1453 (end of war)
- English holdings
- French holdings
- Burgundian lands reconciled with France after 1435

■ **MAP 11.2 The Hundred Years' War, 1337–1453**

As rulers of Aquitaine and claimants to the throne of France, English kings contested the French monarchy for domination of France. Squeezed between England and Burgundy, the holdings of the French kings were vastly reduced after the battle of Poitiers in 1356.

■ **The Spoils of War**
This illustration from Jean Froissart's Chronicles *depicts soldiers pillaging a conquered city. During the Hundred Years' War, looting became the main source of income for mercenary troops and contributed to the general misery of late-medieval society. Food, furniture, even everyday household items were taken.* (Bibliothèque Nationale de France.)

Burgundy held a vast territory in the northeast that included the Low Countries. Burgundy was thus able to broker war or peace by shifting support first to the English and then to the French. But even with Burgundian support, the English could not establish firm control. In Normandy, a savage guerrilla war harassed the English army. Driven from their villages by pillaging and murdering soldiers, Norman peasants retreated into forests, formed armed bands, and attacked the English. The miseries of war inspired prophecies of miraculous salvation; among the predictions was that a virgin would deliver France from the English invaders.

At the court of the dauphin, in 1429, a sixteen-year-old peasant girl presented herself and her vision to save France. Born in a village in Lorraine, Joan of Arc, La Pucelle ("the Maid"), as she always referred to herself, grew up in a war-ravaged country that longed for divine deliverance. She had first presented herself as God's messenger to the local noble, who was sufficiently impressed to equip Joan with horse, armor, and a retinue to send her to the dauphin's court. Joan of Arc's extraordinary appearance inspired the beleaguered French to trust in divine providence. In 1429, she accompanied the French army that laid a prolonged but successful siege on Orléans, was wounded, and showed great courage in battle. Upon her urging, the dauphin traveled deep into hostile Burgundian territory to be anointed King Charles VII of France at Reims cathedral, thus strengthening his legitimacy by following the traditional ritual of coronation.

Although Joan's fortunes declined after Reims and she was burned as a heretic by the English in 1431, she had helped undermine the English position, which slowly crumbled thereafter. The duke of Burgundy recognized Charles VII as king of France, and Charles entered Paris in 1437. Skirmish by skirmish, the English were driven from French soil.

The Hundred Years' War profoundly altered the economic and political landscape of western Europe. It aggravated the demographic and economic crises of the fourteenth century by further ravaging the countryside. Constant insecurity caused by marauding bands of soldiers prevented the cultivation of fields even in times of truce. City and countryside united in 1358, unhappy with the heavy war taxes and the incompetence of the warrior nobility. The movement, called the Jacquerie, began when the townspeople of Paris, led by Étienne Marcel, the provost of the merchants there, sought to take over control of the city. His rebellion was put down and Marcel was killed, but meanwhile rebels in the countryside began their own revolt, de-

■ Joan the Warrior

Joan of Arc's career as a military leader was an extraordinary occurrence in fifteenth-century France. In this manuscript illumination, the charismatic Joan, in full armor, directs French soldiers as they besiege the English at Orléans. The victory she gained there amazed and emboldened the French people.

(Erich Lessing/Art Resource, NY.)

stroying manor houses and castles near Paris and massacring entire noble families in a savage class war. The chronicler Jean Froissart, sympathetic to the nobility, re-flected the views of the ruling class in describing the rebels as "small, dark, and very poorly armed." Repression by nobles was swift, as thousands of rebels died in battles or were executed.◆

In England, the war brought discontent to the rural and urban classes as well. The trigger for outright rebellion by the peasantry was the imposition of a poll tax passed by Parliament in 1377 to raise money for the war against France, a war that peasants believed benefited only the king and the nobility. Unlike tra-ditional subsidies to the king, the poll tax was levied on everyone. In May 1381, a revolt broke out to protest the taxes. Rebels in Essex and Kent joined bands in London to confront the king. The famous couplet of the radical preacher John Ball, who was executed after the revolt, expresses the rebels' egalitarian, anti-noble sentiment:

> *When Adam delved [dug] and Eve span [spun]*
> *Who was then the gentleman?*

Forced to address the rebels, young King Richard II (r. 1377–1399) agreed to abolish serfdom and impose a ceiling on land rent, but he immediately rescinded these concessions after the rebels' defeat.

Richard was not the only monarch to pay little attention to the pains of the war. In France, the ruler benefited from it: under Charles VII, a standing army was established to supplement the feudal noble levies, an army financed by increased taxation and expanded royal judicial claims. Steadily increasing in power and pre-tensions, in the 1470s the French monarchy dismantled and absorbed Burgundy, and in the 1490s it entered Italy with conquest in mind. By 1500, it was clear that the French monarchy was one of the leading powers of Europe.

Defeated in war, the English monarchy suffered more. From the 1460s to 1485, England was torn by civil war—the War of the Roses between the red rose of Lancaster and the rival white rose of York. A deposed king (Henry VI), a short reign (Edward IV), and the murder of two princes by their uncle (Richard III) followed in quick succession in a series of conflicts that decimated the leading noble fami-lies of England. When Henry Tudor succeeded to the throne as Henry VII in 1485, England was tired of civil war. Henry ended the fighting and united the houses of Lancaster and York. By the early sixteenth century, the English monarchy was poised to take advantage of the general prosperity and war-weariness to enhance its position and power.

◆ For a primary source that offers a view of France's ruling class different from Froissart's, see Document 34, Christine de Pisan, "Lament on the Evils of Civil War."

Ottoman Conquest and New Political Configurations in the East

The rise of the Ottoman Turks was the most astonishing fact of the late thirteenth century, when the Islamic Ottomans began a holy war against Byzantium. Under Osman I (r. 1280–1324), who gave the dynasty its name, and his son, the Ottomans became a formidable force in Anatolia and the Balkans, where political disunity opened the door for their advances (Map 11.3). By the end of the fourteenth century, they had reduced the Byzantine Empire to the city of Constantinople, Thessalonika, and a narrow strip of land in modern-day Greece.

Although the empire's fortunes were declining, Byzantium experienced a religious and cultural ferment as the elites compensated for their loss of power in a search for past glory. The majority asserted the superiority of the Greek Orthodox faith and opposed the reunion of the Roman and Greek churches, the political price for western European military aid. Many adhered to tradition, attacking any departures from ancient literary models and Byzantine institutions. A handful, such as the scholar George Gemistos (1353–1452), abandoned Christianity and embraced Platonic philosophy. The scholar Manuel Chrysoloras became professor of Greek in Florence in 1397, thus establishing the study of ancient Greece in western Europe, an important aspect of Renaissance culture.

Meanwhile, the Ottomans continued to expand. In 1364, they defeated a joint Hungarian-Serbian army at the Maritsa River, alerting Europe for the first time to the threat of an Islamic invasion. Pope Urban V called vainly for a crusade. In the Balkans, the Ottomans skillfully exploited Christian disunity, playing local interests against one another. An Ottoman army allied with the Bulgarians and some Serbian princes won the battle of Kosovo (1389), destroying the last organized Christian

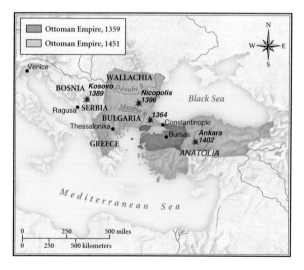

■ **MAP 11.3 Ottoman Expansion in the Fourteenth and Fifteenth Centuries**
The Balkans were the major theater of expansion for the Ottoman Empire, whose conquests also included Egypt and the North African coast. The Byzantine Empire was long reduced to the city of Constantinople and surrounded by the Ottomans before its final fall in 1453.

resistance south of the Danube. The Ottomans secured control of southeastern Europe after 1396, when at Nicopolis they crushed a crusading army summoned by Pope Boniface IX.

When Mehmed II (r. 1451–1481) ascended the throne, he proclaimed a holy war and laid siege to Constantinople in 1453. A city of 100,000, the Byzantine capital could muster only 6,000 defenders (including a small contingent of Genoese) against an Ottoman force estimated at between 200,000 and 400,000 men. The city's fortifications, many of which dated from Emperor Justinian's rule in the sixth century, were no match for fifteenth-century cannons. The defenders held out for fifty-three days. While the Christians confessed their sins and prayed for divine deliverance, in desperate anticipation of the Second Coming, the Muslim besiegers pressed forward, urged on by the certainty of rich spoils and Allah's promise of a final victory over the infidel Rome. Finally the defenders were overwhelmed, and the last Byzantine emperor, Constantine Palaeologus, died in battle. Some 60,000 residents were carried off in slavery, and the city was sacked. Mehmed entered Constantinople in triumph, rendered thanks to Allah in Justinian's Church of St. Sophia, which had been turned into a mosque, and was remembered as "the Conqueror."

At the same time, however, as we have seen, the Muslim ruler was ready to ask Italian court painter Matteo de Pasti to help create his Topkapi palace, intended to communicate Ottoman power. The Ottoman conquest was more than a continuation of the struggle between Christendom and Islam. The battle for territory transcended the boundaries of faith. Christian princes also served the Ottoman Empire as vassals to the sultan. The Janissaries, Christian slave children raised by the sultan as Muslims, constituted the fundamental backbone of the Ottoman army. They formed a service class, the *devshirme,* which was both dependent on and loyal to the ruler. At the sultan's court, Christian women were prominent in the harem; thus many Ottoman princes had Greek or Serbian mothers. In addition to the Janissaries, Christian princes and converts to Islam served in the emerging Ottoman administration. In areas conquered, existing religious and social structures remained intact when local people accepted Ottoman overlordship and paid taxes. Only in areas of persistent resistance did the Ottomans drive out or massacre the inhabitants, settling Turkish tribes in their place. A distinctive pattern of Balkan history was thus established at the beginning of the Ottoman conquest: the extremely diverse ethnic and religious communities were woven together into the fabric of an efficient central state.

The rise of strong, new monarchies—represented by France, England, and the Ottoman sultanate—contrasted sharply with the weakness of state authority in central and eastern Europe, where Hungary, Bohemia, and Poland were held together, like Burgundy, by personal dynastic authority alone (Map 11.4). Under Matthias Corvinus (r. 1456–1490), the Hungarian king who briefly united the Bohemian and Hungarian crowns, a central-eastern European empire seemed to be emerging. A patron of the arts and a humanist, Matthias created a great library in Hungary. He repeatedly defeated the encroaching Austrian Habsburgs and even occupied Vienna in 1485. However, his empire did not outlast his death in 1490. The powerful Hungarian magnates, who enjoyed the constitutional right to elect the king, ended it by refusing to acknowledge his son's claim to the throne.

In the mid-fourteenth century, two large monarchies—Poland and Lithuania—began to take shape in northeastern Europe. King Casimir III (r. 1333–1370) won recognition in most of Poland's regions. A problem that persisted throughout his reign, however, was conflict with the neighboring princes of Lithuania, Europe's last pagan rulers, who for centuries had fiercely resisted the Christianization demanded by the Teutonic Knights. After the Mongols conquered Russia, Lithuania extended its rule southward, offering western Russian princes protection against Mongol and Muscovite rule. By the late fourteenth century, a vast Lithuanian principality had arisen, embracing modern Lithuania, Belarus, and Ukraine.

Casimir III died in 1370 without a son; the failure of a new dynasty to take hold opened the way for the unification of Poland and Lithuania. In 1386, the Lithuanian prince Jogaila (Jagiellon) accepted Roman Catholicism, married the young queen of Poland, and assumed the Polish crown as Wladyslaw II. Under the Jagiellonian dynasty, Poland and Lithuania kept separate legal systems. Catholicism and Polish culture prevailed among the principality's upper class, while most native Lithuanian village folk remained pagan for several centuries. With only a few interruptions, the Polish-Lithuanian federation would last for five centuries.

North of the Black Sea and east of Poland-Lithuania, a different polity was taking shape. In the second half of the fifteenth century, the

■ MAP 11.4 Eastern Europe in the Fifteenth Century

The rise of Muscovy and the Ottomans shaped the map of eastern Europe. Some Christian monarchies, such as Serbia, lost their independence. Others, such as Hungary, held off the Ottomans until the early sixteenth century.

princes of Muscovy embarked on a spectacular path of success that would make their state the largest on earth. Subservient to the Mongols in the fourteenth century, the Muscovite princes began to assert their independence with the collapse of Mongol power. Ivan III (r. 1462–1505) was the first Muscovite prince to claim an imperial title, referring to himself as *tsar* (or *czar,* from the name *Caesar*). Expanding his power to Novgorod in 1471, Ivan then moved to the south and east, pushing back the Mongols to the Volga River. Unlike monarchies in western and central-eastern Europe, whose powers were bound by collective rights and laws, Ivan's Russian monarchy claimed absolute property rights over all lands and subjects.

The expansionist Muscovite state was shaped by two traditions: religion and service. After the fall of the Byzantine Empire, the tsar was the Russian Orthodox church's only defender of the faith against Islam and Catholicism. Orthodox propaganda thus legitimized the tsar's rule by proclaiming Moscow the "Third Rome" (the first two being Rome and Constantinople) and praising the tsar's autocratic power as essential to protect the faith. The Mongol system of service to rulers also deeply informed Muscovite statecraft. Ivan III and his descendants considered themselves heirs to the empire of the Mongols. In their conception of the state as private dominion, their emphasis on autocratic power, and their division of the populace into a landholding elite in service to the tsar and a vast majority of taxpaying subjects, the Muscovite princes created a state more in the despotic political tradition of the central Asian steppes and the Ottoman Empire than of western Europe.

Economic Contraction

The wars of the fourteenth and fifteenth centuries brought hard times to many members of the commercial classes. During the Hundred Years' War, the English king Edward III borrowed heavily from the largest Italian banking houses, the Bardi and Peruzzi of Florence. With many of their assets tied up in loans to the English monarchy, the Italian bankers had no choice but to extend new credits, hoping vainly to recover their initial investments. In the early 1340s, however, Edward defaulted, and the once-illustrious houses went bankrupt. Meanwhile, diminished production and trade eventually caused turmoil in northern Europe and a crisis for financiers in the Low Countries. Bruges, the financial center for northwestern Europe, saw its power fade during the fifteenth century when a succession of its money changers went bankrupt.

This breakdown in the most advanced economic sector reflected the general recession in the European economy. Merchants were less likely to take risks and more willing to invest their money in government bonds than in production and commerce. Fewer merchants traveled to Asia, partly because of the danger of attack by Ottoman Turks on the overland routes that had once been protected by the Mongols. Italians, while still exporting luxuries north and obtaining raw materials and silver in return, now tended to invest in the arts rather than in trade and industry. The Medici, who dominated Florence in the fifteenth century, are good examples. They stayed close to home, investing part of their banking profits in art and politics and relying on business agents to conduct their affairs in other European cities.

At the lower end of the economic ladder, this war-torn society rested on a broad base of underclass—poor peasants and laborers in the countryside, workers and servants in the cities. Lower still were the marginal elements of society, straddling the line between legality and criminality. Organized gangs prowled the larger cities, their members mostly artisans vacillating between work and crime. Paris, for example, teemed with thieves, thugs, beggars, prostitutes, and vagabonds. Some disguised themselves as clerics to escape the law, and others were bona fide clerics who turned to crime to make ends meet during an age of steadily declining clerical income. "Decent society" treated these marginal elements with suspicion and hatred.

Often the underclass served as soldiers as well. War was no longer mainly for knights; it absorbed young men from poor backgrounds. Initiated into a life of plunder and killing, soldiers adjusted poorly to civilian life after discharge; between wars, these men turned to crime, adding to the misery.

Women featured prominently in the underclass, reflecting the unequal distribution of power between the sexes. Urban domestic service was the major employment for girls from the countryside, who worked to save money for their dowries. In addition to the usual household chores, women also worked as wet nurses. Some women, unable to find other means of support, became prostitutes. In Mediterranean Europe, some 90 percent of slaves were women in domestic servitude. They came from Muslim or Greek Orthodox countries and usually served in upper-class households in the great commercial city republics of Venice, Florence, and Ragusa. Their actual numbers were small—several hundred in fourteenth-century Florence, for example—because only rich households could afford slaves.

The Crisis of the Papacy

By the second half of the fourteenth century, the Avignon papacy had taken on a definitive French character. All five popes elected between 1305 and 1378 were natives of southern France. Subjected to pressure from the French monarchy and turning increasingly secular in its opulence and splendor, the papacy was lambasted by the Italian poet Francesco Petrarch as being "in Babylonian Captivity," like the Jews of ancient Israel who were exiled by their Babylonian conquerors.

The popes did not see themselves as captives. Lawyers by training, they concentrated on consolidating the financial and legal powers of the church, mainly through appointments and taxes. Claiming the right to assign all benefices (the properties or income that supported clerical positions), the popes gradually secured authority over the clergy throughout western and central Europe. Under the skillful guidance of John XXII (r. 1316–1334), papal rights increased incrementally without causing much protest. By 1350, the popes had secured the right to grant all major benefices and many minor ones. To gain these lucrative positions, potential candidates often made gifts to the papal court. The imposition of papal taxes on all benefice holders originated in taxes to finance the crusades. Out of these precedents, the papacy instituted a regular system of papal taxation that produced the money it needed to consolidate papal government.

That government—the curia—consisted of the pope's personal household, the College of Cardinals, and the church's financial and judicial apparatuses. Combining elements of monarchy and oligarchy, the curia developed a bureaucracy that paralleled the organization of secular government. The pope's relatives often played a major role in his household; many popes came from extended noble lineages, and they often gave their family members preferential treatment.

After the pope, the cardinals as a collective body were the most elevated entity in the church. Like great nobles in royal courts, the cardinals, many of them nobles themselves, advised and aided the pope. They maintained their own households, employing scores of scribes, servants, and retainers. The papal army also expanded at the same time, as the popes sought to restore and control the Papal States in Italy.

This growing papal monarchy was sharply criticized by members of the Franciscan and Dominican orders, who denounced the papal pretension to worldly power and wealth. The scholastic William of Ockham, for example, believed that church power derived from the congregation of the faithful, both laity and clergy, not from the pope or church councils. Imprisoned by Pope John XXII for heresy, Ockham escaped in 1328 and found refuge with Emperor Louis of Bavaria.

Another antipapal refugee at the imperial court was Marsilius of Padua, a citizen of an Italian commune, a physician and lawyer by training, and rector of the University of Paris. Marsilius attacked the very basis of papal power in *The Defender of the Peace* (1324). The true church, Marsilius argued, was constituted by the people, who had the right to select the head of the church, either through the body of the faithful or through a "human legislator." Papal power, Marsilius asserted, was the result of historical usurpation, and its exercise represented tyranny. In 1327, John XXII, the living target of the treatise, decreed the work heretical.

Successes in Italy emboldened Gregory XI, elected pope in 1371, to return to Rome. When he died in 1378, sixteen cardinals—one Spanish, four Italian, and eleven French—met in Rome to elect the new pope. Although many in the curia were homesick for Avignon, the Roman people, determined to keep the papacy and its revenues in Rome, clamored for the election of a Roman. An unruly crowd rioted outside the conclave, drowning out the cardinals' discussions. Fearing for their lives, the cardinals elected the archbishop of Bari, an Italian, who took the title Urban VI. If the cardinals thought they had elected a weak man who would do their bidding and satisfy the Romans, they were wrong: Urban immediately tried to curb the cardinals' power. In response, thirteen cardinals elected another pope, Clement VII, and returned to Avignon.

Thus began the "Great Schism," which was perpetuated by political divisions in Europe (Map 11.5). Charles V of France, who did not want the papacy to return to Rome, immediately recognized Clement, his cousin, as did the rulers of Sicily, Scotland, Castile, Aragon, Navarre, Portugal, Ireland, and Savoy. An enemy of Charles V, Richard II of England, professed allegiance to Urban and was followed by the rulers of Flanders, Poland, Hungary, most of the Holy Roman Empire, and central and northern Italy. Faithful Christians were equally divided in their loyalties. Even the greatest mystic of the age—Catherine of Siena (1347–1380), who told of her mystical unions with God and spiritual ecstasies in more than 350 letters and was later can-

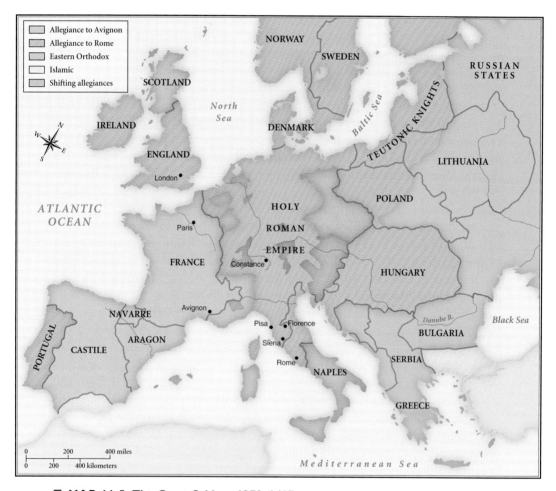

■ **MAP 11.5 The Great Schism, 1378–1417**
Allegiance to Roman and Avignon popes followed the political divisions among the European monarchs. The Great Schism weakened the Latin West during a period of Islamic expansion through the Ottoman Empire.

onized a saint—found herself forced to take sides. Catherine supported Urban. But another holy man, Vincent Ferrer (1350–1419), a popular Dominican preacher, supported Clement. All Christians theoretically found themselves deprived of the means of salvation, as bans from Rome and Avignon each placed part of Christian Europe under interdict, which deprived them of most sacraments and Christian burial.

Because neither pope would step down willingly, the leading intellectuals in the church tried to end the schism another way. Many of them became "conciliarists." According to canon law, only a pope could summon a general council of the church—a sort of parliament of all Christians. But given the state of confusion in Christendom, many intellectuals argued that the crisis justified calling a general council to represent the body of the faithful, over and against the head of the church. Jean Gerson, chancellor of the University of Paris, asserted that "the pope can be removed by a general council celebrated without his consent and against his will." He justified his claim by reasoning that "normally a council is not legally . . . celebrated without papal calling. . . . But, as in grammar and in morals, general rules have exceptions. . . . Because of these exceptions a superior law has been ordained to interpret the law."

The first attempt to resolve the question of church authority came in 1409, at the Council of Pisa, attended by cardinals who had defected from the two popes. The council asserted its supremacy by declaring both popes deposed and electing a new pontiff, Alexander V. When the popes at Rome and Avignon refused to yield to the authority of the council, Christian Europe found itself in the embarrassing position of choosing among three popes. Pressure to hold another council then came from central Europe, where a new heretical movement, ultimately known as Hussitism, undermined orthodoxy from Bohemia to central Germany. Threatened politically by challenges to church authority, Emperor Sigismund pressed Pope John XXIII, the successor to Alexander (who had died ten months after being elected), to convene a church council at Constance in 1414.

The cardinals, bishops, and theologians assembled in Constance felt compelled to combat heresy, heal the schism, and reform the church. They ordered Jan Hus, the Prague professor and inspiration behind the Hussite movement, burned at the stake in spite of an imperial safe conduct he had been promised, but this act failed to suppress dissent. They deposed John XXIII, the "Pisan pope," because of tyrannical behavior, condemning him as an antipope. The Roman pope, Gregory XII, accepted the council's authority and resigned in 1415 (having been elected in 1406). At its closing in 1417, the council also deposed Benedict XIII (Clement's successor), the "Spanish mule," who refused to abdicate the Avignon papacy and lived out his life in a fortress in Spain, still regarding himself as pope and surrounded by his own curia. The rest of Christendom, however, hailed Martin V, the council's appointment, as the new pope, thus ending the Great Schism. The council had taken a stand against heresy and had achieved unity under one pope. But the papacy's prestige had suffered a lasting blow.

Stamping Out Dissenters, Heretics, Jews, and Muslims

The stand against Hus was part of a wider movement. Everywhere church and state moved to stamp out groups that, in their view, did not fit within the established church. The church condemned the Free Spirits, for example. These groups, often associated with the Beguines (see page 415), were found mostly in northern Europe. They practiced an extreme form of mysticism, asserting that humans and God were of the same essence and that individual believers could attain salvation, even sanctity, without the church and its sacraments. In the 1360s, Emperor Charles IV and Pope Urban V extended the Inquisition to Germany in a move to crush this heresy. In the cities of the Rhineland, fifteen mass trials took place, most around the turn of the fifteenth century. By condemning the "heretics" and requiring beguinages to be under the control of the mendicant orders, the church contained potential dissent.

In England, intellectual dissent, social unrest, and nationalist sentiment combined to create a powerful anticlerical movement that the church hierarchy labeled Lollardy (from *lollar,* meaning "idler"). John Wycliffe (c. 1330–1384), who inspired the movement, was an Oxford professor who challenged the very foundations of the Roman church. His treatise *On the Church,* composed in 1378, advanced the view that the true church was a community of believers rather than a clerical hierarchy. In other writings, Wycliffe repudiated monasticism, excommunication, the Mass, and the priesthood, substituting reliance on Bible reading and individual conscience in place of the official church as the path to salvation. Responsibility for church reform, Wycliffe believed, rested with the king, whose authority he claimed exceeded that of the pope. In spite of persistent persecutions, Lollardy survived underground during the fifteenth century, to resurface during the convulsive religious conflict of the early sixteenth century known as the Reformation.

The most profound challenge to papal authority in the later Middle Ages came from Bohemia. Here the spiritual, intellectual, political, and economic criticisms of the papacy that sprang up in other countries fused in one explosive spark. Religious dissent quickly became the vehicle for a nationalist uprising and a social revolution.

Under Emperor Charles IV, the pace of economic development and social change in the Holy Roman Empire had quickened in the mid-fourteenth century. Prague, the capital, became one of Europe's great cities: the new silver mine at Kutná Hora boosted Prague's economic growth, and the first university in the empire was founded there in 1348. Prague was located in Bohemia, a part of the Holy Roman Empire settled by a Slavic people, the Czechs, since the early Middle Ages. Later, many German merchants and artisans migrated to Bohemian cities, and Czech peasants, uprooted from the land, flocked to the cities in search of employment. This diverse society became a potentially explosive mass when heightened expectations of commercial and intellectual growth collided with the grim realities of the plague and economic problems in the late fourteenth century. Tax protests, urban riots, and ethnic conflicts signaled growing unrest, but it was religious discontent that became the focus for popular revolt.

■ **Burning of a Heretic**

Execution by fire was the usual method of killing heretics. This illustration shows the burning of a Lollard, a follower of the teachings of Wycliffe, who opposed the established church. Although heretics were condemned by the church, their executioners were secular authorities, who are present here. (Hulton Getty/Liaison Agency.)

Critics of the clergy, often clergy themselves, decried the moral conduct of priests and prelates who held multiple benefices, led dissolute lives, and ignored their pastoral duties. How could the clergy, living in a state of mortal sin, legitimately perform the sacraments? critics asked. Advocating greater lay participation in the Mass and in the reading of Scripture, religious dissenters drew some of their ideas from the writings of Wycliffe. Among those influenced by Wycliffe's ideas were Jan Hus (d. 1415) and his follower Jerome of Prague (d. 1416), both Prague professors, ethnic Czechs, and leaders of a reform party in Bohemia. Although the reform party attracted adherents from all Czech-speaking social groups, the German minority, who dominated the university and urban elites in Prague, opposed it out of ethnic rivalry. The Bohemian nobility protected Hus; the common clergy rebelled against the bishops; and the artisans and workers in Prague were ready to back the reform party by force. These disparate social interests all focused on one symbolic but passionately felt religious demand: the ability to receive the Eucharist as both bread and wine at Mass. In traditional Roman liturgy, the chalice was reserved for the clergy; the Utraquists, as their opponents called them (from *utraque,* Latin for "both"), wanted to drink wine from the chalice as well, to achieve a measure of equality between laity and clergy.

When Hus was burned at the stake by the Council of Constance in 1415, his death caused a national uproar. The reform movement, which had thus far focused only on religious issues, burst forth as a national revolution. Sigismund's initial repression of the revolt in the provinces was brutal, and many dissenters were massacred. To organize their defense, Hussites gathered at a mountain in southern Bohemia, which they called Mount Tabor after the mountain in the New Testament where the transfiguration of Christ took place. Now called Taborites, they began to restructure their community according to biblical injunctions. Like the first Christian church, they initially practiced communal ownership of goods and thought of themselves as the only true Christians awaiting the return of Christ and the end of the world. As their influence spread, the Taborites compromised with the surrounding social order, collecting tithes from peasants and retaining magistrates in towns under their control. Taborite leaders were radical priests who ministered to the community in the Czech language, exercised moral and judicial leadership, and even led the people into battle. Resisting all attempts to crush them, the Czech revolutionaries eventually gained the right from the papacy to receive the Eucharist as both bread and wine, a practice that continued until the sixteenth century.

A still different group of heretics grew out of the anguish of the Black Death. Believing that the plague was God's way of chastising a sinful world, bands of men and women sought to save themselves by repenting their sins in a dramatic manner: wearing tattered clothes, they visited local churches and sang hymns while publicly whipping themselves until blood flowed. The flagellants, as they soon came to be called, cried out to God for mercy and called upon the congregation to repent their sins. But the clergy distrusted this lay movement that did not originate within the church hierarchy.

In some communities, the religious fervor aroused by the flagellants spawned violence against Jews. From 1348 to 1350, anti-Semitic persecutions, beginning in southern France and spreading through Savoy to the Holy Roman Empire, destroyed many Jewish communities in central and western Europe. Sometimes the clergy incited the attacks against the Jews, calling them Christ-killers, accusing them of poisoning wells and kidnapping and ritually slaughtering Christian children. In towns throughout Europe, economic resentment fueled anti-Semitism as those in debt turned on creditors, often Jews who had become rich from the commercial revolution of the thirteenth century.

Many anti-Semitic incidents were spontaneous, with mobs plundering Jewish quarters and killing anyone who refused baptism. But it is equally true that sometimes authorities orchestrated the violence. For example, the magistrates of Nuremberg obtained approval from Emperor Charles IV before organizing the 1349 persecution directed by the city government. Thousands of German Jews were slaughtered. Many fled to Poland, where the incidence of plague was low and where the authorities welcomed Jews as productive taxpayers. In western and central Europe, however, the persecutions destroyed the financial power of the Jews.

End of the Reconquista and Expulsion of the Jews in Spain, 1492

Like France and England, war wracked Spain as dynasties fought over the royal succession in the various kingdoms. But again, as in France and England, the end result was a strengthened monarchy. In 1469, Queen Isabella of Castile and King Ferdinand of Aragon married. Retaining their separate titles, the two monarchs ruled jointly over their dominions, each of which adhered to its traditional laws and privileges. Their union represented the first step toward the creation of a unified Spain out of two medieval kingdoms. Isabella and Ferdinand limited the privileges of the nobility and allied themselves with the cities, relying on the Hermandad (civic militia) to enforce justice and on lawyers to staff the royal council.

The united strength of Castile and Aragon brought the *reconquista* to a close with a final crusade against the Muslims. After more than a century of peace, war broke out in 1478 between Granada, the last Iberian Muslim state, and Catholic royal forces. Weakened by internal strife, Granada finally fell in 1492. Two years later, in recognition of the crusade, Pope Alexander VI bestowed the title "Catholic monarchs" on Isabella and Ferdinand, ringing in an era in which militant Catholicism became an instrument of state authority and shaped the national consciousness.

Unification of Spain, Late Fifteenth Century

In this climate, it no longer seemed possible for Iberian Muslims, Jews, and Christians to live side by side. The practice of Catholicism became a test of one's loyalty to the church and to the Spanish monarchy. In 1478, the king and queen introduced the Inquisition to Spain, primarily as a means to control the *conversos* (Jewish converts to Christianity), whose elevated positions in the economy and the government aroused widespread resentment from the so-called Old Christians. *Conversos* often were suspected of practicing Judaism, their ancestral religion, in secret while pretending to adhere to their new Christian faith. Appointed by the monarchs, the inquisitors presided over tribunals set up to investigate those suspected of religious deviancy. The accused, who were arrested on charges often based on anonymous denunciations and information gathered by the inquisitors, could defend themselves but not confront their accusers. The wide spectrum of punishments ranged from monetary fines to the *auto da fé* (a ritual of public confession) to burning at the stake. After the fall of Granada, many Muslims were forced to convert or resettle in Castile. At the same time, Ferdinand and Isabella ordered all Jews in their kingdoms to choose between exile and conversion. Many chose exile.

The expulsion of the Jews from Spain had far greater consequences than their earlier banishments from France and England. Spain had had the largest and most vibrant Jewish communities of Europe. On the eve of the expulsion, approximately 200,000 Jews and 300,000 *conversos* were living in Castile and Aragon. Faced with the choice to convert or leave, well over 100,000 Jews dispersed, some settling in North Africa, more in Italy, and many in the Ottoman Empire, Greek-speaking Thessalonika, and Palestine. Conversant in two or three languages, these Jews often served as intermediaries between the Christian West and Muslim East.

New Forms of Thought and Expression: The Renaissance

The Renaissance had its medieval roots in vernacular literature like Dante's *Divine Comedy* and the humanism of the Gothic sculptors who portrayed figures in the round, interacting with one another. But it grew far beyond those roots, to discover and embrace the classical past and to use classical themes to celebrate human glory. Fostered by the printing press, Renaissance writings spread far and wide to a literate middle class eager to absorb every sort of text. Meanwhile, Renaissance artists celebrated the newly powerful republics, principalities, and kingdoms of their age. Flush with power, these states intruded into the most intimate personal matters, such as sexuality, marriage, and childbirth.

Renaissance Humanism

From the epics and romances of the twelfth and thirteenth centuries, vernacular writings blossomed into a full-blown literature in the fourteenth. Poetry, stories, and chronicles composed in Italian, French, English, and other national languages helped articulate a new sense of aesthetics. The great writers of late medieval Europe were of urban middle-class origins, from families that had done well in government, church service, or commercial enterprises. Unlike the medieval troubadours, with their aristocratic backgrounds, the men and women who wrote vernacular literature in this age typically came from the cities, and their audience was the literate laity. Francesco Petrarch (1304–1374), the poet laureate of Italy's vernacular literature, and his younger contemporary and friend Giovanni Boccaccio (1313–1375) were both from the Florentine professional classes. Geoffrey Chaucer (c. 1342–1400), an important vernacular poet of medieval England, came from a family of wine merchants. Even writers who celebrated the life of the nobility were children of commoners. Though born in Valenciennes to a family of moneylenders and merchants, Jean Froissart (1333?–c. 1405), whose chronicle vividly describes the events of the Hundred Years' War, was an ardent admirer of chivalry. Christine de Pisan (1364–c. 1430), a poet and prose writer of great range, was the daughter of a Venetian municipal counselor.

Life in all its facets found expression in the new vernacular literature, as writers told of love, greed, and salvation. Boccaccio's *Decameron* popularized the short story, as the characters in this novella tell sensual and bizarre tales in the shadow of the Black Death. Members of different social orders parade themselves in Chaucer's *Canterbury Tales,* journeying together on a pilgrimage.

Noble patronage was crucial to the growth of vernacular literature, a fact reflected in the careers of the most famous writers. Perhaps closest to the model of an independent man of letters, Petrarch nonetheless relied on powerful patrons at various times. His early career began at the papal court in Avignon, where his father worked as a notary; during the 1350s, Petrarch enjoyed the protection and patronage of the Visconti duke of Milan. Boccaccio started out in the Neapolitan world of commerce. The court of King Robert of Naples initiated him into the realm of letters. Chaucer served in administrative posts and on many diplomatic missions, during which he met his two Italian counterparts. Noble patronage also shaped the literary creations of Froissart and Christine de Pisan. Christine would have been unable to produce most of her writings without the patronage of women in the royal household. She presented her most famous work, *The Book of the City of Ladies* (1405), a defense of women's reputation and virtue, to Isabella of Bavaria, the queen of France and wife of Charles VI.

Vernacular literature blossomed not at the expense of Latin but alongside a classical revival. In spite of the renown of their Italian writings, Petrarch and Boccaccio, for example, took great pride in their Latin works. In the second half of the fourteenth century, writers began to imitate the antiquated "classical" Latin of Roman literature. In the forefront of this literary and intellectual movement, Petrarch traveled to many monasteries in search of long-ignored Latin manuscripts. For writers like Petrarch, medieval church Latin was an artificial, awkward language, whereas classical Latin and, after its revival, Greek were the mother tongues of the ancients, even more authentic, vivid, and glorious than the poetry and prose written in Italian and other contemporary European languages. Classical allusions and literary influences abound in the works of Boccaccio, Chaucer, Christine de Pisan, and others. The new intellectual fascination with the ancient past also stimulated translations of classical works into the vernacular.

This attempt to emulate the virtues and learning of the ancients gave impetus to an intellectual movement: humanism. For humanists the study of history and literature was the chief means of identifying with the glories of the ancient world. By the early fifteenth century, the study of classical Latin had become fashionable among a small intellectual elite, first in Italy and gradually throughout Europe. Reacting against the painstaking logic and abstract language of the scholastic philosophy that predominated in the medieval period, the humanists of the Renaissance preferred eloquence and style in their discourse, imitating the writings of Cicero and other great Roman authors.

Gradually the imitation of ancient Roman rhetoric led to the absorption of ancient ideas. In the writings of Roman historians such as Livy and Tacitus, fifteenth-

■ **Poet and Queen**

Christine de Pisan, kneeling, presents a manuscript of her poems to Isabella of Bavaria, the queen of France. Isabella's royal status is indicated by the royal French emblem, the fleur-de-lis, which decorates the bedroom walls. The sumptuous interior (chairs, cushions, tapestry, paneled ceiling, glazed and shuttered windows) was typical of aristocratic domestic architecture. Even in the intimacy of her bedroom, Queen Isabella, like all royal personages, was constantly attended and almost never alone (notice her ladies-in-waiting).

(The British Library Picture Library, London.)

century Italian civic elites (many of them lawyers) found echoes of their own devout patriotism. Between 1400 and 1430 in Florence, a time of war and crisis, the study of the humanities evolved into a republican ideology that historians call "civic humanism." In the early fifteenth century, the Florentines waged a highly successful propaganda war on behalf of virtuous republican Florence against tyrannical Milan, invoking the memory of the overthrow of Etruscan tyrants by the first Romans. Thus, the study of ancient civilization was not only an antiquarian quest but a call to public service and political action.

The fall of Constantinople in 1453 sent Greek scholars to Italy for refuge, giving extra impetus to the revival of Greek learning in the West. Venice and Florence assumed leadership in this new field—the former by virtue of its commercial and political ties to the eastern Mediterranean, the latter thanks to the patronage of Cosimo de' Medici, who sponsored the Platonic Academy, a discussion group dedicated to the study of Plato and his followers under the intellectual leadership of Marsilio Ficino (1433–1499).

Most humanists did not consider the study of ancient cultures to be in conflict with their Christian faith. In "returning to the sources"—a famous slogan of the time—philosophers attempted to harmonize the disciplines of Christian faith and ancient learning. Ficino, the foremost Platonic scholar of the Renaissance, was deeply attracted to natural magic and was also a priest. He argued that the immortality of the soul, a Platonic idea, was perfectly compatible with Christian doctrine and that much of ancient wisdom actually foreshadowed later Christian teachings.◆

Through their activities as educators and civil servants, professional humanists gave new vigor to the humanist curriculum of grammar, rhetoric, poetry, history,

---

◆ For a primary source that expresses the ideals of Renaissance humanism, see Document 35, Giovanni Pico della Mirandola, *Oration on the Dignity of Man.*

and moral philosophy. By the end of the fifteenth century, European intellectuals considered a good command of classical Latin, with perhaps some knowledge of Greek, as one of the requirements of an educated person.

The invention of mechanical printing aided greatly in making the classical texts widely available. Printing from movable type—a revolutionary departure from the old practice of copying by hand—was invented in the 1440s by Johannes Gutenberg, a German goldsmith. Mass production of identical books and pamphlets made the world of letters more accessible to a literate audience.

The advent of mass printed books depended on paper production. The art of papermaking came to Europe from China via Arab intermediaries. By the fourteenth century, paper mills were operating in Italy, producing paper that was more fragile but much cheaper than parchment or vellum, the animal skins that Europeans had previously used for writing. To produce paper, old rags were soaked in a chemical solution, beaten by mallets into a pulp, washed with water, treated, and dried in sheets—a method that still produces good-quality paper today.

Even before the printing press, a brisk industry in manuscript books had been flourishing in Europe's university towns and major cities. Production was in the hands of stationers, who organized workshops known as *scriptoria,* where the manuscripts were copied, and acted as retail booksellers. Demand was high. The stationer for Cosimo de' Medici, for example, employed forty-five copyists to complete two hundred volumes in twenty-two months.

Nonetheless, bookmaking in *scriptoria* was slow and expensive, and the invention of movable type was an enormous technological breakthrough. It took bookmaking out of the hands of human copyists. Movable type consisted of reusable metal molds of letters, numbers, and various other characters. The typesetter arranged the characters by hand, page by page, to create a printable text. The surface of the type was inked, and sheets of paper pressed against the type picked up an impression of the text. Numerous copies could be made with only a small amount of human labor. In 1467, two German printers established the first press in Rome and produced twelve thousand volumes in five years, a feat that in the past would have required one thousand scribes working full-time.

After the 1440s, printing spread rapidly from Germany to other European countries. In Germany, Cologne, Strasbourg, Nuremberg, and Augsburg all had major presses; many Italian cities had established their own by 1480. In the 1490s, the German city of Frankfurt-am-Main became an international meeting place for printers and booksellers. The Frankfurt Book Fair, where printers from different nations exhibited their newest titles, represented a major international cultural event and remains an unbroken tradition to this day.

The invention of mechanical printing gave rise to a "communications revolution" as significant as the widespread use of the personal computer today. The multiplication of standardized texts altered the thinking habits of Europeans by freeing individuals from having to memorize everything they learned; it made possible the relatively speedy and inexpensive dissemination of knowledge; and it created a wider community of scholars, no longer dependent on personal patron-age or church sponsorship for texts. Printing facilitated the free expression and exchange of ideas, and its disruptive potential did not go unnoticed by political and ecclesiastical authorities. Emperors and bishops in Germany, the homeland of the printing industry, moved quickly to issue censorship regulations.

New Perspectives in Art and Music

New techniques in painting, architecture, and musical performance fostered origi-nal styles and subjects. Artists paid close attention to the human figure and strove to depict the world from nature rather than from pictorial models. Musicians enhanced polyphony with new harmonies and more versatile instruments.

As individual talent and genius were recognized by a society hungry for culture, artists themselves gained prestige. In exalting the status of the artist, Leonardo da Vinci (1452–1519), painter, architect, and inventor, described himself as a creative genius. He was not alone; Renaissance artists intended to convince society that their works were unique and their talents priceless. They exalted the artist above the "mere artisan," claiming to be independent of the blueprints of a patron. During the fifteenth century, as artists began to claim the respect and recognition of soci-ety, however, the reality was that most relied on wealthy patrons for support. And although they wished to create as their genius dictated, not all patrons of the arts allowed artists to work without restrictions. While the duke of Milan appreciated Leonardo's genius, the duke of Ferrara paid for his art by the square foot.

A successful artist who did fit the new vision of unfettered genius was the Florentine sculptor Donatello (1386–1466). Not only did Donatello's sculptures evoke classical Greek and Roman models, but the grace and movement of his work inspired Cosimo de' Medici, the ruler of Florence, to excavate antique works of art and put them on display. Donatello was one artist who enjoyed the long-term, high-status patronage of a prince. Others, like Andrea Mantegna (1431–1506), worked more precariously. Treated more as a skilled worker in service to the prince than as an independent artist, he was once even required to adorn his majestic Gonzaga tapestries with life sketches of farm animals.

The workshop—the normal place of production in Renaissance Italy and in northern European cities such as Nuremberg and Antwerp—afforded the artist greater autonomy. As heads of workshops, artists trained apprentices and negoti-ated contracts with clients. The most famous artists fetched good prices for their work. Famous artists developed followings, and wealthy consumers were willing to pay a premium for work done by a master instead of apprentices. Studies of art contracts show that in the course of the fifteenth century artists gained greater control over their work. Early in the century, clients routinely stipulated detailed conditions for works of art—specifying, for instance, gold paint or "ultramarine blue," which were among the most expensive pigments. Clients might also determine the arrangement of figures in a picture, leaving to the artist little more than the execution. After midcentury, such specific directions became less common. In 1487, for example, the Florentine painter Filippo Lippi (1457–1504), in his contract to paint frescoes in the Strozzi chapel, specified that the work should be "all from his own hand and particularly the figures." The shift underscores the increasing recognition of the unique skills of individual artists.

A market system for the visual arts emerged during the Renaissance, initially in the Low Countries. In the fifteenth century, most large-scale work was commissioned by specific patrons, but the art market, for which artists produced works without prior arrangement for sale, was to develop into the major force for artistic creativity, a force that prevails in contemporary society. The commercialization of art celebrated the new context of artistic creation itself: artists working in an open, competitive, urban civilization.

If the individual artist was a man of genius, what greater subject for the expression of beauty was there than the human body itself? Taking their cue from fourteenth-century painters such as Giotto (see page 425), Renaissance artists learned to depict ever more expressive human emotions and movements. The work of the short-lived but brilliant painter Masaccio (1401–1428) exemplifies this development. His painting *St. Peter Baptizing* shows the recipient of the baptism trembling in the cold water. In addition to rendering homage to classical and biblical

■ **Masaccio's *St. Peter Baptizing***
This detail from a cycle of frescos about the life of St. Peter painted by Masaccio in the church of Santa Maria del Carmine in Florence shows the artist's interest in the nude body. The man receiving baptism is portrayed in the round, light playing on his flesh and revealing its contours. This emphasis on human nakedness may have reflected an egalitarian strain in republican Florence. It also echoes what Masaccio found in ancient art and sculpture.
(Erich Lessing/Art Resource, NY.)

figures, Renaissance artists painted their contemporaries as well. For the first time after classical antiquity, sculptors again cast the human body in bronze, in life-size or bigger freestanding statues. Free from fabric and armor, the human body was idealized in the eighteen-foot marble sculpture *David*, the work of the great Michelangelo Buonarroti (1475–1564).

The increasing number of portraits in Renaissance painting illustrates the new, elevated view of human existence. Portraiture initially was limited to representations of pontiffs, monarchs, princes, and patricians, but soon portraits of middle-class people became more widespread. Painters from the Low Countries such as Jan van Eyck (1390?–1441) distinguished themselves in this genre; their portraits achieved a sense of detail and reality unsurpassed until the advent of photography.

All of this art was distinguished from its predecessors by its depiction of the world as the eye perceives it. The use of *visual perspective*—an illusory three-dimensional space on a two-dimensional surface and the ordered arrangement of painted objects from one viewpoint—became one of the distinctive features of Western art. Underlying the idea of perspective was a new Renaissance worldview: humans asserting themselves over nature in painting and design by controlling space. Optics became the organizing principle of the natural world in that it detected the "objective" order in nature. The Italian painters were keenly aware of their new technique, and they criticized the Byzantine and the northern Gothic stylists for "flat" depictions of the human body and the natural world. The highest accolade for a Renaissance artist was to be described as an "imitator of nature": this

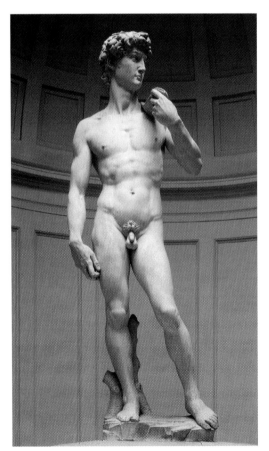

■ **Michelangelo's** *David*

Michelangelo realized a synthesis of the ancient nude statue and the biblical figure of David in this larger-than-life sculpture of the young David, his body poised for action against the giant Goliath. The figure's easy slouch recalls depictions of Greek athletes, but this sculpture was commissioned by the administrators of the cathedral at Florence and was placed in front of the Florentine town hall. Both church and state thus garnered prestige from the artist and his work.

(Nimatallah/Art Resource, NY.)

■ Mantegna's Frescoes in the Camera degli Sposi

For the "marital bedchamber" of the duke of Mantua, Mantegna painted scenes that integrated inside and out in a new way. To the right of the open doorway is the ducal family, portrayed as if outdoors, yet with their feet resting on the mantel of the fireplace. The painted curtain mimicked curtains that once decorated the interior of the room. To the left of the doorway is the duke greeting his son; behind them is a landscape. Thus Mantegna's paintings gave the illusion of the outside coming in, as if the walls were windows onto the world. (Scala/Art Resource, NY.)

epithet meant that the artist's teacher was nature, not design books or master painters. For the frescoes of the bridal chamber of the Gonzaga Palace (executed 1465–1474), Mantegna created an illusory extension of reality: the actual living space in the chamber "opened out" to the painted landscape on the walls.

Perhaps even more than visual artists, fifteenth-century architects embodied the Renaissance ideals of uniting artistic creativity and scientific knowledge. The Florentine architect Leon Battista Alberti (1404–1472) made such ideas explicit in *On Architecture* (1415). Alberti argued for large-scale urban planning, with monumental buildings set on open squares, harmonious and beautiful in their proportions. His ideas were put into action by Pope Sixtus IV (r. 1471–1484) and his successors in the urban renewal of Rome, and they served to transform the city into a geometrically constructed monument to architectural brilliance by recalling the grandeur of its ancient origins.

Musicians and composers, too, worked for wealthy patrons at court. Developments in polyphony were led by Guillaume Dufay (1400–1474), whose musical training began in the cathedral choir of his hometown, Cambrai, in the Low Countries. His successful career took him to all the cultural centers of the Renaissance, where nobles sponsored new compositions and maintained a corps of musicians for court and religious functions. In 1438, Dufay composed festive music to celebrate the completion of the cathedral dome in Florence designed by Filippo Brunelleschi (1377–1446) and modeled on Roman ruins. Dufay expressed the harmonic relationship among four voices in ratios that matched the mathematically precise dimensions of Brunelleschi's architecture. After a period of employment at the papal court, Dufay returned to his native north and composed music for the Burgundian and French courts.

Josquin des Prez (1440–1521), another Netherlander, wrote music in Milan, Ferrara, Florence, and Paris and at the papal court. Music was an integral part of courtly life: Lorenzo de' Medici sent Dufay a love poem to set to music, and the great composer maintained a lifelong relationship with the Medici family. Composers often adapted familiar folk melodies for sacred music, expressing religious feeling primarily through human voices instead of instruments. The tambourine and the lute were indispensable for dances, however, and small ensembles of wind and string instruments with contrasting sounds performed with singers in the fashionable courts of Europe. Also in use in the fifteenth century were new keyboard instruments—the harpsichord and clavichord—which could play several harmonic lines at once.

Republics and Principalities in Italy

In his book *The Prince,* the Florentine political theorist Niccolò Machiavelli (1469–1527) argued that the state was an artifice of human creation to be conquered, shaped, and administered by princes according to the principles of power politics. Whether a republic—which preserved the traditional institutions of the medieval commune by allowing a civic elite to control political and economic life—or a principality, ruled by one dynasty, each Italian Renaissance state was as centralized and controlling as the new monarchies of France and England.

Venice and Florence were republics. Venice, built on a lagoon, ruled an extensive colonial empire that extended from the Adriatic to the Aegean Sea. Venetian merchant ships sailed the Mediterranean, the Black Sea, and, increasingly, the Atlantic coast. Whether threatened by competing Italian states or by the Turks, Venice drew strength from its internal social cohesion. Under the rule of an oligarchy of aristocratic merchants, Venice enjoyed stability. Its maritime empire benefited citizens of all social classes, who joined efforts to defend the interests of the "Most Serene Republic," a contemporary name that reflected Venice's lack of social strife.

Compared with serene Venice, the republic of Florence was in constant agitation, as social classes and political factions engaged in ongoing conflict. By 1434, a single family had emerged dominant in this fractious city: the Medici. Cosimo de' Medici (1388–1464), head of the family, "disposed of his rivals, proceeded to administer the state at his pleasure and amassed wealth. . . . In Florence he built a palace fit for a king," as Pope Pius II put it. Head of one of the largest banks of

Europe, Cosimo de' Medici used his immense wealth to influence politics. Even though he did not hold any formal political office, he wielded influence in government through business associates and clients indebted to him for loans, political appointments, and other favors. Cosimo became the arbiter of war and peace, the regulator of law, more master than citizen. Yet the prosperity and security that Florence enjoyed made him popular as well. At his death, Cosimo was lauded as "father of his country."

Cosimo's grandson Lorenzo (called "the Magnificent"), who assumed power in 1467, bolstered the regime's legitimacy with his lavish patronage of the arts. But opponents were not lacking. In 1478, Lorenzo narrowly escaped an assassination attempt. Two years after Lorenzo's death in 1494, partisans who opposed the Medici drove them from Florence. The Medici returned to power in 1512, only to be driven out again in 1527. In 1530, the republic fell and the Medici once again seized control, declaring themselves dukes of Florence.

Milan had been a principality long before then. Since the fourteenth century, it had been a military state, relatively uninterested in supporting the arts but with first-class armaments and textile industries in the capital city and rich farmlands in Lombardy. Until 1447, the duchy was ruled by the Visconti dynasty, a group of powerful lords whose plans to unify all of northern and central Italy failed from the combined opposition of Venice, Florence, and other Italian powers. After a brief republican interlude (1447–1450) during which Milan fought against its neighbors, its ruling nobility appointed Francesco Sforza, who had married the illegitimate daughter of the last Visconti duke, to the post of general. Sforza promptly turned against his employers, claiming the duchy as his own. A bitter struggle between the nobility and the townspeople in Milan further undermined the republican cause, and in 1450 Sforza entered Milan in triumph.

The power of the Sforza dynasty reached its height during the 1490s. In 1493, Duke Ludovico married his niece Bianca Maria to Maximilian, the newly elected Holy Roman Emperor, promising an immense dowry in exchange for the emperor's legitimization of his rule. But the newfound Milanese glory was soon swept aside by France's invasion of Italy in 1494, and the duchy itself eventually came under Spanish rule.

In the violent arena of Italian politics, the papacy, an uneasy mixture of worldly splendor and religious authority, was a player like the other states. The popes' concern with politics stemmed from their desire to restore papal authority, greatly undermined by the Great Schism and the conciliar movement. To that end, the popes used both politics and culture. Politically, they curbed local power, expanded papal government, increased taxation, enlarged the papal army and navy, and cultivated diplomacy. Culturally, the popes renovated churches, created the Vatican Library, sponsored artists, and patronized writers to glorify their role and power. In undertaking these measures, the Renaissance papacy merely exemplified the larger trend toward the centralization of power evident everywhere else.

Concentrated power, competition between states, and the extension of warfare all raised the practice of diplomacy to nearly an art form. The first diplomatic handbook, composed in 1436, emphasized ceremonies, elegance, and eloquence. These masked the complex game of diplomatic intrigue and spying. In the fifteenth century, a resident ambassador was expected to keep a continuous stream of foreign political news flowing to the home government, not just to conduct temporary diplomatic missions, as earlier ambassadors had done. In some cases, the presence of semiofficial agents developed into full-fledged ambassadorships: the Venetian embassy to the sultan's court in Constantinople developed out of the merchant-consulate that had represented all Venetian merchants, and Medici Bank branch managers eventually acted as political agents for the Florentine republic.

Foremost in the development of diplomacy was Milan. Under the Visconti dukes, Milan sent ambassadors to Aragon, Burgundy, the Holy Roman Empire, and the Ottoman Empire. Under the Sforza dynasty, Milanese diplomacy continued to function as a cherished form of statecraft. For generations, Milanese diplomats at the French court sent home an incessant flow of information on the rivalry between France and Burgundy. Francesco Sforza, founder of the dynasty, also used his diplomatic corps to extend his political patronage. In letters of recommendation to the papacy, Francesco commented on the political desirability of potential ecclesiastical candidates by using code words, sometimes supplemented with instructions to his ambassador to indicate his true intent regardless of the coded letter of recommendation. Ciphers were used in more sensitive diplomatic reports to hide their real meaning from hostile powers.

The most outstanding achievement of Italy's Renaissance diplomacy was the negotiation of a general peace treaty that settled the decades of warfare engendered by Milanese expansion and civil war. The Treaty of Lodi (1454) established a complex balance of power among the major Italian states and maintained relative stability on the peninsula for half a century. Renaissance diplomacy eventually failed, however, when more powerful northern European neighbors invaded in 1494, bringing on the collapse of the whole Italian state system.

Intimate Matters

To deal with a mounting fiscal crisis, in 1427 the government of Florence ordered that a comprehensive tax record of households in the city and territory be compiled. Completed in 1430, this survey represented the most detailed population census then taken in European history. From the resulting mass of fiscal and demographic data, historians have been able to reconstruct a picture of Florentine society.

The state of Florence, roughly the size of Massachusetts, had a population of more than 260,000. Tuscany, the area in which the Florentine state was located, was one of the most urbanized regions of Europe. With 38,000 inhabitants, the capital city of Florence claimed 14 percent of the total population and an enormous 67 percent of the state's wealth. Straddling the Arno River, Florence was a beautiful, thriving city with a defined social hierarchy. In describing class divisions, the Florentines themselves referred to the "little people" and the "fat people." Some 60 percent of all households belonged to the "little people"—workers, artisans, small merchants. The "fat people" (roughly our middle class) made up 30 percent of the urban population and included the wealthier merchants, the leading artisans, notaries, doctors, and other professionals. At the very bottom of the hierarchy were slaves and servants, most of them women employed in domestic service. Whereas the small number of slaves were of Balkan origin, the much larger population of domestic servants came to the city from the surrounding countryside as contracted wage earners. At the top, a tiny elite of patricians, bankers, and wool merchants controlled the state with their enormous wealth. In fact, the richest 1 percent of urban households (approximately one hundred families) owned more than one-quarter of the city's wealth and one-sixth of Tuscany's total wealth. The patricians in particular owned almost all government bonds, a lucrative investment guaranteed by a state they dominated.

Surprisingly, men seem to have outnumbered women in the 1427 survey. For every 100 women there were 110 men, unlike most past and present populations, in which women are the majority. In addition to female infanticide, which was occasionally practiced, the survey itself reflected the society's bias against women: persistent underreporting on women probably explained the statistical abnormality; and married daughters, young girls, and elderly widows frequently disappeared from the memories of householders. Most people, men and women alike, lived in households with at least six inhabitants, although the form of family unit—nuclear or extended—varied, depending mainly on wealth. Poor people rarely were able to support extended families. Among urban patricians and landowning peasants, the extended family held sway. The number of children in a family, it seems, reflected class differences as well. Wealthier families had more children; childless couples existed almost exclusively among the poor, who were also more likely to abandon the infants they could not feed.

Wealth and class clearly determined family structure and the pattern of marriage and childbearing. In a letter to her eldest son, Filippo, dated 1447, Alessandra Strozzi announced the marriage of her daughter Caterina to the son of Parente Parenti. She described the young groom, Marco Parenti, as "a worthy and virtuous young man, and . . . the only son, and rich, 25 years old, and keeps a silk workshop; and they have a little political standing." The dowry was set at one thousand florins, a substantial sum—but for four to five hundred florins more, Alessandra admitted to Filippo, Caterina would have fetched a husband from a more prominent family.

The Strozzi belonged to one of Florence's most distinguished traditional families, but at the time of Caterina's betrothal the family had fallen into political disgrace. Alessandra's husband, an enemy of the Medici, was exiled in 1434; Filippo, a rich merchant in Naples, lived under the same political ban. Although Caterina was clearly marrying beneath her social station, the marriage represented an alliance in which money, political status, and family standing all balanced out. More an alliance between families than the consummation of love, an Italian Renaissance marriage was usually orchestrated by the male head of a household. In this case, Alessandra, as a widow, shared the matchmaking responsibility with her eldest son and other male relatives. Eighteen years later, when it came time to find a wife for Filippo, who had by then accumulated enough wealth to start his own household, Marco Parenti, his brother-in-law, would serve as matchmaker.◆

The upper-class Florentine family was patrilineal, tracing descent and determining inheritance through the male line. Because the distribution of wealth depended on this patriarchal system, women occupied an ambivalent position in the household. A daughter could claim inheritance only through her dowry, and she often disappeared from family records after her marriage. A wife seldom emerged from the shadow of her husband, and consequently the lives of many women have been lost to history.

Women's subordination in marriages often reflected the age differences between spouses. The Italian marriage pattern, in which young women married older men, contrasted sharply with the northern European model, in which partners were much closer in age. Significant age disparity also left many women widowed in their twenties and thirties, and remarriage often proved a hard choice. A widow's father and brothers frequently pressed her to remarry to form a new family alliance. A widow, however, could not bring her children into her new marriage because they belonged to her first husband's family. Faced with the choice between her children and her paternal family, not to mention the question of her own happiness, a widow could hope to gain greater autonomy only in her old age, when, like Alessandra, she might assume matchmaking responsibilities to advance her family's fortunes.

In northern Europe, however, women enjoyed a relatively more autonomous position. In England, the Low Countries, and Germany, for example, women played a significant role in the economy—not only in the peasant household, in which everyone worked, but especially in the town, serving as peddlers, weavers, seamstresses, shopkeepers, midwives, and brewers. In Cologne, for example, women could join one of several artisans' guilds, and in Munich they ranked among some of the richest brewers. Women in northern Europe shared inheritances with their brothers, retained control of their dowries, and had the right to represent themselves before the law. Italian men who traveled to the north were appalled at the differences in gender relations, criticizing English women as violent and brazen and disapproving of the mixing of the sexes in German public baths.

Child care and attitudes toward sexuality also reflected class differences in Renaissance life. Florentine middle- and upper-class fathers arranged business con-

---

◆ For more excerpts from Alessandra Strozzi's revealing correspondence, see Document 36, "Letters from a Widow and Matriarch of a Great Family."

tracts with wet nurses to breast-feed their infants; babies thus spent prolonged periods of time away from their families. Such elaborate child care was beyond the reach of the poor, who often abandoned their children to strangers or to public charity.

By the beginning of the fifteenth century, Florence's two hospitals were accepting large numbers of abandoned children in addition to the sick and infirm. In 1445, the government opened the Ospedale degli Innocenti to deal with the large number of abandoned children from poor families or from women who had given birth out of wedlock. Many of the latter were domestic slaves or servants impregnated by their masters; in 1445, one-third of the first hundred foundlings at the new hospital were children of the unequal liaisons between masters and women slaves. For some women, the foundling hospital provided an alternative to infanticide. Over two-thirds of abandoned infants were girls. Although Florence's government employed wet nurses to care for the foundlings, the large number of abandoned infants overtaxed the hospital's limited resources. The hospital's death rate for infants was much higher than the already high infant mortality rate of the time.

Illegitimacy in itself did not necessarily carry a social stigma in fifteenth-century Europe. Most upper-class men acknowledged and supported their illegitimate children as a sign of virility, and illegitimate children of noble lineage often rose to social and political prominence. Any social stigma was borne primarily by the woman, whose ability to marry became compromised. Shame and guilt drove some poor single mothers to kill their infants, a crime for which they paid with their own lives.

In addition to prosecuting infanticide, the public regulation of sexuality focused on prostitution and homosexuality. Intended "to eliminate a worse evil by a lesser one," a 1415 statute established government brothels in Florence. Concurrent with its higher tolerance of prostitution, the Renaissance state had a low tolerance of homosexuality. In 1432, the Florentine state appointed magistrates "to discover—whether by means of secret denunciation, accusations, notification, or any other method—those who commit the vice of sodomy, whether actively or passively." The government set fines for homosexual acts and carried out death sentences against pederasts (men who have sex with boys).

Fifteenth-century European magistrates took violence against women less seriously than illegal male sexual behavior, as the different punishments indicate. In Renaissance Venice, for example, the typical jail sentence for rape and attempted rape was only six months. Magistrates often treated noblemen with great leniency and handled rape cases according to class distinctions. For example, Agneta, a young girl living with a government official, was abducted and raped by two millers, who were sentenced to five years in prison; several servants who abducted and raped a slave woman were sentenced to three to four months in jail; and a nobleman who abducted and raped Anna, a slave woman, was freed. Whether in marriage, inheritance, illicit sex, or sexual crime, the Renaissance state regulated the behavior of men and women according to differing concepts of gender. The brilliant civilization of the Renaissance was experienced very differently by men and women.

On the Threshold of World History

The fifteenth century constituted the first time that Europe was a major player in world history. Before the maritime explorations of Portugal and Spain, Europe had remained at the periphery of world events. Fourteenth-century Mongols had been more interested in conquering China and Persia—lands with sophisticated cultures—than in invading Europe; Persian historians of the early fifteenth century dismissed Europeans as "barbaric Franks"; and China's Ming dynasty rulers, who sent maritime expeditions to Southeast Asia and East Africa around 1400, seemed unaware of the Europeans, even though Marco Polo and other Italian merchants had appeared at the court of the preceding Mongol Yuan dynasty. In the fifteenth century, Portuguese and Spanish vessels, followed a century later by English, French, and Dutch ships, sailed across the Atlantic, Indian, and Pacific Oceans, bringing with them people, merchandise, crops, and diseases in a global exchange that would shape the modern world. For the first time, the people of the Americas were brought into contact with a larger historical force that threatened to destroy not only their culture but their existence. European exploitation, conquest, and racism defined this historical era of transition from the medieval to the modern world, as Europeans left the Baltic and the Mediterranean for wider oceans.

The Divided Mediterranean

In the second half of the fifteenth century, the Mediterranean Sea, which had dominated medieval maritime trade, began to lose its preeminence to the Atlantic Ocean. To win control over the Mediterranean, the Ottomans embarked on an ambitious naval program to transform their empire into a major maritime power. War and piracy disrupted the flow of Christian trade: the Venetians mobilized all their resources to fight off Turkish advances, and the Genoese largely abandoned the eastern Mediterranean for trade opportunities presented by the Atlantic.

Mediterranean trade used ships made with relatively backward naval technology. The most common ship, the galley—a flat-bottom vessel propelled mainly by oarsmen with the help of a sail—dated from the time of ancient Rome. Most galleys could not withstand open-ocean voyages, although Florentine and Genoese galleys did make long journeys to Flanders and England, hugging the coast for protection. The galley's dependence on human labor was a more serious handicap. Because prisoners of war and convicted criminals toiled as oarsmen in both Christian and Muslim ships, victory in war or the enforcement of criminal penalties was crucial to a state's ability to float large numbers of galleys. Slaves, too, sometimes provided the necessary labor.

Portuguese Confrontations

The exploration of the Atlantic began with the Portuguese (Map 11.6). By 1415, they had captured Ceuta on the Moroccan coast, establishing a foothold in Africa. Thereafter, Portuguese voyages sailed farther still down the West African coast.

By midcentury, a chain of Portuguese forts reached Guinea, protecting the trade in gold and slaves. At home, the royal house of Portugal financed the fleets, with crucial roles played by Prince Peter, regent between 1440 and 1448; his more famous younger brother Prince Henry the Navigator; and King John II (r. 1481–1495). As a governor of the noble crusading Order of Christ, Henry financed many voyages out of the order's revenues. Private monies also helped, as leading Lisbon merchants participated in financing the gold and slave trades off the Guinea coast.

In 1455, Pope Nicholas V (r. 1447–1455) sanctioned Portuguese overseas expansion, commending King John II's crusading spirit and granting him and his successors the monopoly on trade with inhabitants of the newly "discovered" regions. In 1478–1488, Bartholomeu Dias took advantage of the prevailing winds in the South Atlantic to reach the Cape of Good Hope. A mere ten years later (1497–1499), under the captainship of Vasco da Gama, a Portuguese fleet rounded the cape and reached Calicut, India, center of the spice trade. In 1512, Ferdinand Magellan, a Portuguese sailor in Spanish service, led the first expedition to circumnavigate the globe. By 1517, a chain of Portuguese forts dotted the Indian Ocean.

In many ways a continuation of the struggle against Muslims on the Iberian peninsula, Portugal's maritime voyages displayed that country's mixed motives of piety, glory, and greed. The sailors dreamed of finding gold mines in West Africa and a mysterious Christian kingdom established by Prester John (actually the Coptic Christian kingdom of Abyssinia, or Ethiopia, in East Africa). The Portuguese hoped to reach the spice-producing lands of South and Southeast Asia by sea to bypass the Ottoman Turks, who controlled the traditional land routes between Europe and Asia.

The new voyages depended for their success on several technological breakthroughs. The lateen (triangular) sail permitted ships to tack against headwinds. Light caravels and heavy galleons, however different in size, were alike in using more than one mast and sail, harnessing wind—rather than human—power to move them. Better charts, maps, and instruments made long-distance voyages less risky.

After the voyages of Christopher Columbus, Portugal's interests clashed with Spain's. Mediated by Pope Alexander VI, the 1494 Treaty of Tordesillas reconciled Portugal and Spain by dividing the Atlantic world between the two royal houses. A demarcation 370 leagues west of the Cape Verdes Islands divided the Atlantic Ocean, reserving for Portugal the western coast of Africa and the route to India and giving Spain the oceans and lands to the west (see Map 11.6). Unwittingly, this agreement also allowed Portugal to claim Brazil in 1500, which Pedro Álvares Cabral (1467–1520) accidentally "discovered" on his voyage to India.

The Voyages of Columbus

Historians agree that Christopher Columbus (1451–1506) was born of Genoese parents; beyond that, we have little accurate information about this man who brought together the history of Europe and the Americas. In 1476, he arrived in Portugal,

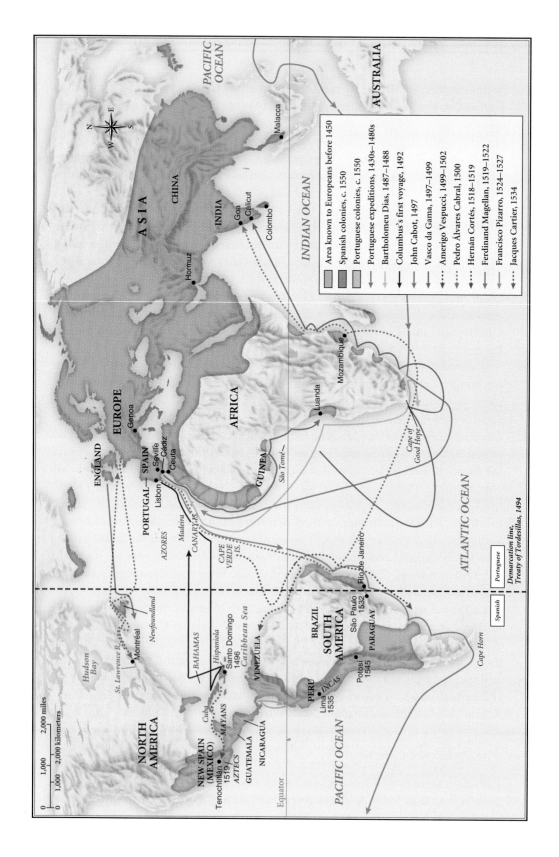

PACIFIC OCEAN

AUSTRALIA

Malacca

ASIA

CHINA

INDIA

Goa
Calicut
Colombo

INDIAN OCEAN

Hormuz

EUROPE

Genoa

ENGLAND

PORTUGAL — SPAIN

Lisbon
Seville
Cádiz
Ceuta

AZORES
Madeira
CANARY IS.
CAPE VERDE IS.

AFRICA

GUINEA

São Tomé

Luanda

Mozambique

Cape of
Good Hope

ATLANTIC OCEAN

NORTH
AMERICA

Hudson
Bay

St. Lawrence R.

Montréal

Newfoundland

NEW SPAIN
(MEXICO)
Tenochtitlán
1519
AZTECS
MAYANS
GUATEMALA
NICARAGUA

Cuba

BAHAMAS
Hispaniola
Santo Domingo
1496
Caribbean Sea
VENEZUELA

BRAZIL

São Paulo
1532

Rio de Janeiro

PARAGUAY

SOUTH
AMERICA

PERU
INCAS

Lima
1535

Potosí
1545

Cape Horn

Equator

PACIFIC OCEAN

Demarcation line,
Treaty of Tordesillas, 1494

Spanish   Portuguese

N
W   E
S

0   1,000   2,000 miles
0 1,000 2,000 kilometers

Area known to Europeans before 1450
Spanish colonies, c. 1550
Portuguese colonies, c. 1550
Portuguese expeditions, 1430s–1480s
Bartholomeu Dias, 1487–1488
Columbus's first voyage, 1492
John Cabot, 1497
Vasco da Gama, 1497–1499
Amerigo Vespucci, 1499–1502
Pedro Álvares Cabral, 1500
Hernán Cortés, 1518–1519
Ferdinand Magellan, 1519–1522
Francisco Pizarro, 1524–1527
Jacques Cartier, 1534

■ **MAP 11.6 Exploitation and Exploration in the Sixteenth Century**
At the end of the fifteenth century, Europeans began moving aggressively across the globe. Beginning with initial forays along the African coast, their voyages soon widened out to transatlantic crossings and, by 1522, the circumnavigation of the world. The web of arrows on this map suggests an earth bound together by many threads, and this is partly true, for never again would the two halves of the globe be isolated. At the same time, the threads pulled in one direction only—toward the Europeans. Africa was exploited for gold and slaves, while the discovery of precious metals fueled the explorations and settlements of Central and South America.

apparently a survivor in a naval battle between a Franco-Portuguese and a Genoese fleet; in 1479, he married a Portuguese noblewoman. He spent the next few years mostly in Portuguese service, gaining valuable experience in regular voyages down the west coast of Africa. In 1485, after the death of his wife, Columbus settled in Spain.

Fifteenth-century Europeans already knew that Asia lay beyond the vast Atlantic Ocean, and *The Travels of Marco Polo,* written more than a century earlier, still exerted a powerful hold on European images of the East. Columbus read it many times, along with other travel books, and proposed to sail west across the Atlantic to reach the lands of the khan, unaware that the Mongol Empire had already collapsed in eastern Asia. Vastly underestimating the distances, he dreamed of finding a new route to the East's gold and spices and partook of the larger European vision that had inspired the Portuguese voyages. (His critics had a much more accurate idea of the globe's size and of the difficulty of the venture.) But after the Portuguese and French monarchs rejected his proposal, Columbus found royal patronage with the recently proclaimed Catholic monarchs Isabella of Castile and Ferdinand of Aragon.

In August 1492, equipped with a modest fleet of three ships and about ninety men, Columbus set sail across the Atlantic. His contract stipulated that he would claim Castilian sovereignty over any new land and inhabitants and share any profits with the crown. Reaching what is today the Bahamas on October 12, Columbus mistook the islands to be part of the East Indies, not far from Japan and "the lands of the Great Khan." As the Castilians explored the Caribbean islands, they encountered communities of peaceful Indians, the Arawaks, who were awed by the Europeans' military technology, not to mention their appearance. Exchanging gifts of beads and broken glass for Arawak gold—an exchange that convinced Columbus of the trusting nature of the Indians—the crew established peaceful relationships with many communities. Yet in spite of many positive entries in the ship's log referring to Columbus's personal goodwill toward the Indians, the Europeans' objectives were clear: find gold, subjugate the Indians, and propagate Christianity.

Excited by the prospect of easy riches, many flocked to join Columbus's second voyage. When Columbus departed Cádiz in September 1493, he commanded seventeen ships that carried between 1,200 and 1,500 men, many believing all they had to do was "to load the gold into the ships." Failing to find the imaginary gold mines and spices, however, the colonial enterprise quickly switched its focus to finding slaves. Columbus and his crew first enslaved the Caribs, enemies of the Arawaks; in 1494, Columbus proposed a regular slave trade based in Hispaniola. The Spaniards exported enslaved Indians to Spain, and slave traders sold them in Seville. Soon the Spaniards began importing sugarcane from Madeira, forcing large numbers of Indians to work on plantations to produce enough sugar for export to Europe. Columbus himself was edged out of this new enterprise. When the Spanish monarchs realized the vast potential for material gain that lay in their new dominions, they asserted direct royal authority by sending officials and priests to the Americas, which were named after the Italian Amerigo Vespucci, who led a voyage across the Atlantic in 1499–1502.

Columbus's place in history embodies the fundamental transformations of his age. A Genoese in the service of Portuguese and Spanish employers, Columbus had a career illustrating the changing balance between the Mediterranean and the Atlantic. The voyages of 1492–1493 would eventually draw a triangle of exchange among Europe, the Americas, and Africa, an exchange gigantic in its historical impact and its human cost.

A New Era in Slavery

During the Middle Ages and Renaissance, female slaves served as domestic servants in wealthy Mediterranean homes, and male slaves toiled in the galleys of Ottoman and Christian fleets. Some were captured in war or by piracy; others—Africans— were sold by other Africans and Bedouin traders to Christian buyers. In western Asia, parents sold their children into servitude out of poverty. Many people in the Balkans became slaves when their land was devastated by Ottoman invasions. Slaves were Greek, Slav, European, African, and Turk.

The Portuguese maritime voyages changed this picture. From the fifteenth century, Africans increasingly filled the ranks of slaves. Exploiting warfare in West Africa, the Portuguese traded in gold and "pieces," as African slaves were called, a practice condemned at home by some conscientious clergy. Critical voices, however, could not deny the enormous profits that the slave trade brought to Portugal. Most slaves toiled in the sugar plantations of the Portuguese Atlantic islands and in Brazil. A fortunate few labored as domestic servants in Portugal, where African freedmen and slaves, some 35,000 in the early sixteenth century, constituted almost 3 percent of the population, a percentage that was much higher than in other European countries. In the Americas, slavery would truly flourish as an institution of exploitation.

Europeans in a New World

In 1500, on the eve of European invasion, the native peoples of the Americas were divided into many sedentary and nomadic societies. Among the settled peoples, the largest political and social organizations centered in the Mexican and Peruvian highlands. The Aztecs and the Incas ruled over subjugated Indian populations in their

■ **Dürer's Engraving of Katharina, an African Woman**
Like other artists in early-sixteenth-century Europe, Albrecht Dürer would have seen in person Africans who went to Portugal and Spain as students, servants, and slaves. Notice Katharina's noble expression and dignified attire. Before the rise of the slave trade in the seventeenth century, most Africans in Europe were household servants of the aristocracy. Considered symbols of prestige, such servants generally were not used for economic production.
(Foto Marburg/Art Resource, NY.)

respective empires. With an elaborate religious culture and a rigid social and political hierarchy, the Aztecs and Incas based their civilizations in large urban capitals.

The Spanish explorers organized their expeditions to the mainland from a base in the Caribbean (see Map 11.6). Two prominent leaders, Hernán Cortés (1485–1547) and Francisco Pizarro (c. 1475–1541), gathered men and arms and set off in search of gold. Catholic priests accompanied the fortune hunters to bring Christianity to allegedly uncivilized peoples and thus to justify brutal conquests. His small band swelled by peoples who had been subjugated by the Aztecs, Cortés captured the Aztec capital, Tenochtitlán, in 1519. To the south, Pizarro conquered the Andean highlands, exploiting a civil war between rival Incan kings.

By the mid-sixteenth century, the Spanish Empire stretched unbroken from Mexico to Chile. Not to be outdone by the Spaniards, other European powers joined the scramble for gold in the New World. In 1500, a Portuguese fleet led by Pedro Álvares Cabral landed at Brazil, but Portugal did not begin colonizing there until 1532, when it established a permanent fort on the coast. In North America, the French went in search of a "northwest passage" to China. By 1504, French fishermen had appeared in Newfoundland. Thirty years later, Jacques Cartier led three voyages that explored the St. Lawrence River as far as Montreal. An early attempt in 1541 to settle Canada failed because of the harsh winter and Indian hostility, and

IMPORTANT DATES			
1337–1453	Hundred Years' War	c. 1450–1500	Height of Florentine Renaissance
1347–1350	First outbreak of the Black Death in Europe; anti-Jewish persecutions in the empire	1453	Fall of Constantinople; end of Byzantine Empire
1358	Jacquerie uprising in France	1460s–1485	Wars of the Roses in England
1378	Beginning of the Great Schism; Ciompi rebellion in Florence; John Wycliffe's treatise *On the Church*	1462	Ivan III of Muscovy claims imperial title "tsar"
		1477	Death of Charles the Bold; end of Burgundy
1381	English peasant uprising	1478	Inquisition established in Spain
1389	Ottomans defeat Serbs at Kosovo	1492	Columbus's first voyage; Christians conquer Muslim Granada and expel Jews from Spain
1414–1417	Council of Constance ends the Great Schism	1499	Vasco da Gama reaches India
1415	Execution of Jan Hus; Portugal captures Ceuta, establishing foothold in Africa	1500	Portugal claims Brazil
1440s	Gutenberg introduces the printing press		

John Cabot's 1497 voyage to find a northern route to Asia also failed. More permanent settlements in Canada and the present-day United States would succeed only in the seventeenth century.

Conclusion

Confronted by war, plague, peasant uprisings, turbulence in the cities, anti-Jewish pogroms, and a disgraced papacy, Europe's ruling classes grasped the reins of power ever more tightly, creating more centralized and institutionalized states. Surrounding themselves with artists, musicians, and humanists, these new-style rulers supported the "Renaissance"—an attempt to resuscitate the classical past for the purposes of the present. The Renaissance, which emphasized human potential and achievement, was one of Europe's most brilliant periods in artistic activity, one that glorified both God and humanity. Overwhelming confidence spurred Renaissance artists to a new appreciation for the human body and a new visual perspective in art and to apply mathematics and science to architecture, music, and artistic composition.

This intense cultural production both resulted from and fueled the competition among the burgeoning Renaissance states and between Christian Europe and

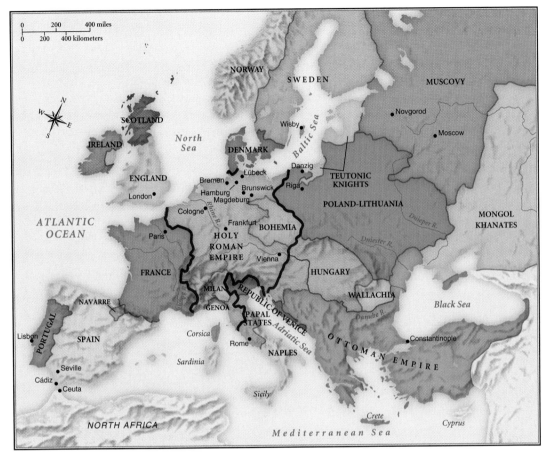

■ **MAPPING THE WEST** Renaissance Europe, c. 1500

By 1500, the shape of early modern Europe was largely set. It would remain stable until the eigh-teenth century, except for the disappearance of an independent Hungarian kingdom after 1529.

the Muslim Ottoman Empire. The competition also fostered an expansion of the frontiers of Europe first to Africa and then across the Atlantic Ocean to the Americas, ushering in the first period of global history. Few at the time would have guessed that Europe would soon enter yet another period of turmoil, one brought about not by demographic and economic collapse but by a profound crisis of conscience that the brilliance of Renaissance civilization had tended to obscure.

Suggested References for further reading and online research appear on page SR-17 at the back of the book.

www.bedfordstmartins.com/huntconcise   See the ONLINE STUDY GUIDE to assess your mastery of the material covered in this chapter.

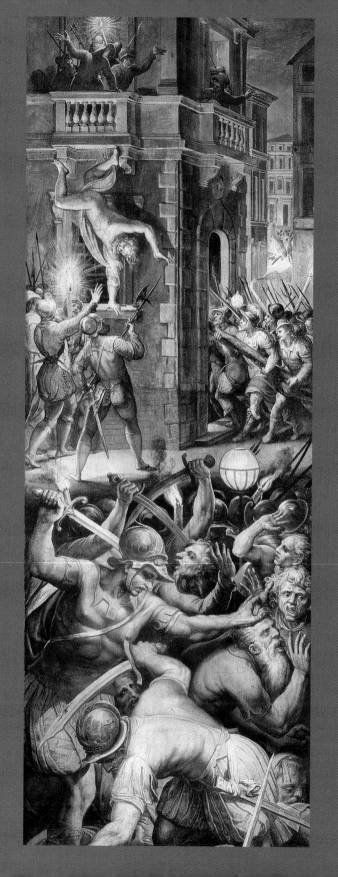

12

Struggles over Beliefs

1500–1648

H ILLE FEIKEN LEFT THE NORTHERN GERMAN TOWN of Münster on June 16, 1534, elegantly dressed, bedecked with jewels, and determined to kill. Münster, which religious radicals had declared a holy city, lay under siege by armies loyal to the local Catholic bishop—her intended victim. Hille crossed enemy lines and tried to persuade the commander of the besieging troops to take her to the bishop, promising to reveal a secret means of recapturing the city. When a defector from her camp recognized Hille and betrayed her, she was beheaded.

Hille Feiken belonged to the religious group known as Anabaptists, who wanted to form a holy community separate from the rest of society. Anabaptists organized in response to the Protestant Reformation, which was set in motion by the German friar Martin Luther in 1517 and quickly became a sweeping movement to uproot church abuses and restore early Christian teachings. Supporters of Luther were called "protestants," those who protested. Inspired by Luther and then by other reformers, ordinary men and women attempted to remake their heaven and earth. Their stories intertwined with bloody struggles among princes for domination in Europe, an age-old conflict now complicated by the clash of rival faiths.

Struggles over religious beliefs spread from the Holy Roman Empire northward into Scandinavia; westward into France, the Spanish-ruled Netherlands, and England; and eastward into Poland-Lithuania. These conflicts frequently erupted into armed confrontation, culminating in the Thirty Years' War of 1618–1648, which devastated much of central Europe. The orgy of mutual destruction in the Thirty Years' War left no winners in the religious struggle, and the cynical manipulation of religious issues by both Catholic and Protestant leaders showed that political interests eventually outweighed those of religion. The extreme violence of religious

■ **Massacre Motivated by Religion**
The Italian artist Giorgio Vasari (1511–1574) painted St. Bartholomew's Night: The Massacre of the Huguenots *for a public room in Pope Gregory XIII's residence. The pope and his artist intended to celebrate a Catholic victory over Protestant heresy.* (Scala/Art Resource.)

conflict pushed rulers and political thinkers to seek other, nonreligious grounds for governmental authority. Few would argue for genuine toleration of religious differences, but many began to insist that the interests of states had to take priority over the desire for religious conformity.

Although particularly dramatic and deadly, the church-state crisis was only one of a series of upheavals that shaped this era. After decades of rapid economic and population growth in the sixteenth century, a major economic downturn led to food shortages, famine, and disease in the first half of the seventeenth century. An upheaval in worldviews was also in the making, catalyzed by increasing knowledge of the new worlds discovered overseas and in the heavens. The development of new scientific methods of research would ultimately reshape Western attitudes toward religion and state power, as Europeans desperately sought alternatives to wars over religious beliefs.

The Protestant Reformation

Since the mid-fifteenth century, many clerics had tried to reform the church from within, criticizing clerical abuses and calling for moral renewal, but their efforts came up against the church's inertia and resistance. At the beginning of the sixteenth century, widespread popular piety and anticlericalism existed side by side, fomenting a volatile mixture of need and resentment. A young German friar, tormented by his own religious doubts, was to become the spokesman for a generation. From its origins as a theological dispute, Martin Luther's reform movement sparked explosive protests. By the time he died in 1546, half of western Europe had renounced allegiance to the Roman Catholic church. Christian unity fractured, opening the way not only to widespread turmoil but also to a host of new attitudes about the nature of religious and political authority.

Popular Piety and Christian Humanism

Numerous signs pointed to an intense spiritual anxiety among the laity. New shrines sprang up, reports of miracles multiplied, and prayer books printed in vernacular languages as well as Latin sold briskly. Expressions of piety could turn violent. In 1510, a priest in the German state of Brandenburg accused local Jews of stealing and stabbing the host, the consecrated bread that Catholics believed was the body of Christ. When, according to legend, the host bled, the Jews were killed. A shrine dedicated to the bleeding host attracted thousands of pilgrims.

Critics complained that the church gave external behavior more weight than spiritual intentions. In receiving the sacrament of penance—one of the central pillars of Christian morality and of the Roman church—sinners were expected to examine their consciences, sincerely confess their sins to a priest, and receive forgiveness. In practice, however, some priests abused their authority by demanding sexual or monetary favors in return for forgiveness. Priests also sold *indulgences,* which according to doctrine could alleviate suffering in purgatory after death. The faithful were supposed to earn indulgences by performing certain religious tasks— going on pilgrimage, attending mass, doing holy works. The sale of indulgences as a substitution for performing good works suggested that the church was more interested in making money than in saving souls.

Another way to diminish time in purgatory was to collect and venerate holy relics. A German prince, Frederick the Wise of Saxony, amassed the largest collection of relics outside of Italy. By 1518, his castle church contained 17,443 holy relics, including what were thought to be a piece of Moses' burning bush, parts of the holy cradle and Jesus' swaddling clothes, and thirty-five fragments of the True Cross. A diligent and pious person who rendered appropriate devotion to each of these relics could earn exactly 127,799 years and 116 days of remission from purgatory.

Dissatisfaction with the official church prompted some Christian intellectuals to link their scholarship to the cause of social reform and to dream of ideal societies based on peace and morality. The Dutch scholar Desiderius Erasmus (c. 1466–1536) and the English lawyer Thomas More (1478–1535) stood out as representatives of these Christian humanists, who, unlike Italian humanists, placed their primary emphasis on Christian piety. Each established close links to the powerful. Erasmus was on intimate terms with kings and popes, and his fame spread across all Europe. More became lord chancellor to England's king Henry VIII.

Erasmus advocated a simple piety devoid of greed and the lust for power, but he also promoted the new humanist learning. To this end he devoted years to translating a new Latin edition of the New Testament from the original Greek. He argued ironically in *The Praise of Folly* (1509) that the wise appeared foolish, because modesty, humility, and poverty had few adherents in this world. Although Erasmus mocked the clergy's corruption and Christian princes' bloody ambitions, he emphasized the role of education in reforming individuals and through them society as a whole. Even ordinary table manners drew his attention. In the *Colloquies* (1523), a compilation of Latin dialogues intended as language-learning exercises, he advised his cultivated readers not to pick their noses at meals, not to share half-eaten chicken legs, and not to speak while stuffing their mouths. Challenged by angry younger men and radical ideas once the Reformation took hold, Erasmus chose Christian unity over reform and schism. He died in the Swiss city of Basel, isolated from the Protestant community and condemned by many in the Catholic church, who found his writings too critical of the church's authority.

Erasmus's good friend Thomas More, to whom *The Praise of Folly* was dedicated,* met with even greater suffering for his beliefs. He would later pay with his

---

*The Latin title *Encomium Moriae* ("The Praise of Folly") was a pun on More's name and the Latin word for *folly.*

life for upholding conscience over political expediency. Inspired by the recent voyages of discovery, More's best-known work, *Utopia* (1516), describes an imaginary ideal place that offered a stark contrast to his own society. Because Utopians enjoyed public schools, communal kitchens, hospitals, and nurseries, they had no need for money. Greed and private property disappeared in this world. Dedicated to the pursuit of knowledge and natural religion, with equal distribution of goods and few laws, Utopia knew neither crime nor war (Utopia means both "no place" and "best place" in Greek). More believed that politics, property, and war fueled human misery, whereas for his Utopians, "fighting was a thing they absolutely loathe. They say it's a quite subhuman form of activity, although human beings are more addicted to it than any of the lower animals." Despite a few oddities—voluntary slavery, for instance, and strictly controlled travel—Utopia seemed a paradise compared with the increasing violence in a Europe divided by religion.

Martin Luther and the German Nation

Like Erasmus and More, Martin Luther (1483–1546) pursued a life of scholarship, but a personal crisis of faith led him to break with the Roman church and establish a competing one. The son of a miner, Luther abandoned his studies in the law to enter the Augustinian order. The choice of a monastic life did not resolve Luther's doubts about his own salvation. Appalled at his own sense of sinfulness and the weakness of human nature, he lived in terror of God's justice in spite of frequent confessions and penance. A pilgrimage to Rome only deepened his unease with the institutional church. Sent to study theology by a sympathetic superior, Luther gradually came to new insights through his study of Scripture. He later described his breakthrough experience:

> At last, by the mercy of God, meditating day and night, I gave heed to the context of the words [in Romans 1:17], namely, "In [the gospel] the righteousness of God is revealed, as it is written, 'He who through faith is righteous shall live.'" There I began to understand that the righteousness of God is that by which the righteous live by a gift of God, namely by faith.

Luther soon came into conflict with the church authorities. In 1516, the new archbishop ordered the sale of indulgences to help cover the cost of constructing St. Peter's Basilica in Rome and also to defray his expenses in pursuing his election. Such blatant profiteering outraged many, including Luther, who now served as professor of theology at the University of Wittenberg. In 1517, Luther composed ninety-five theses—propositions for an academic debate—that questioned indulgence peddling and the purchase of church offices. Once they became public, the theses unleashed a torrent of pent-up resentment and frustration among the laypeople. This apparently ordinary academic dispute soon engulfed the Holy Roman Empire in conflict.

■ Luther as Monk, Doctor, Man of the Bible, and Saint, 1521
This woodcut by an anonymous artist appeared in a volume that the Strasbourg printer Johann Schott published in 1521. In addition to being one of the major centers of printing, Strasbourg was also a stronghold of the reform movement. Notice the use of traditional symbols to signify Luther's holiness: the Bible in his hands, the halo, the Holy Spirit in the form of a dove, and his friar's robes. Although monasticism and the cult of saints came under severe criticism during the Reformation, the representation of Luther with traditional symbols of sanctity stressed his conservative values instead of his radical challenge to church authorities. (The Granger Collection.)

Initially, Luther presented himself as the pope's "loyal opposition," but in 1520, he composed three treatises that laid out his theological position, attacked the papacy in Rome as the embodiment of the Antichrist, and called upon the German princes to reform the church themselves. He insisted that faith alone, not good works or penance, could save sinners from damnation. Faith came from the believer's personal relationship with God, which he or she cultivated through individual study of Scripture. Ordinary laypeople thus made up "the priesthood of all believers," who had no need of a professional caste of clerics to show them the way to salvation. The attack on the church's authority could not have been more dramatic.

From Rome's perspective, the "Luther Affair," as church officials called it, was essentially a matter of clerical discipline. Rome ordered Luther to obey his superiors and keep quiet. But the church establishment had seriously misjudged the extent of Luther's influence. Luther's ideas, published in numerous German and Latin editions, spread rapidly throughout the Holy Roman Empire, unleashing forces that Luther himself could not control. Social, nationalist, and religious protests fused into an explosive mass very similar to the Czech revolution that Jan Hus had inspired a century earlier. Like Hus, Luther appeared before an emperor: in 1521, he defended his faith before Charles V (r. 1520–1558), the newly elected Holy Roman Emperor who at the age of nineteen was the ruler of the Low Countries, Spain,

Spain's Italian and New World dominions, and the Austrian Habsburg lands. At the Imperial Diet of Worms, the formal assembly presided over by this powerful ruler, Luther shocked Germans by declaring his admiration for the Czech heretic. But unlike Hus, Luther did not suffer martyrdom because he enjoyed the protection of Frederick the Wise, the elector of Saxony (one of the seven German princes entitled to elect the Holy Roman Emperor) and Luther's lord.

What began as an urban movement turned into a war in the countryside in 1525. Lutheran propaganda radiated outward from the German towns, where local officials had appointed clerics sympathetic to reform. Luther's anticlerical message struck home with merchants and artisans who resented the clergy's tax-exempt status, but peasants had even more reason for discontent because they paid taxes to both their lord and the church. The church was the largest landowner in the Holy Roman Empire: about one-seventh of the empire's territory consisted of ecclesiastical principalities in which bishops and abbots exercised both secular and churchly power. In the spring of 1525, many peasants in southern and central Germany rose in rebellion, sometimes inspired by wandering preachers. Some urban workers and artisans joined the peasant bands, plundering monasteries, refusing to pay church taxes, and demanding village autonomy, the abolition of serfdom, and the right to appoint their own pastors. In Thuringia, the rebels were led by an ex-priest, Thomas Müntzer (1468?–1525), who promised to chastise the wicked and thus clear the way for the Last Judgment.

The uprising of 1525, known as the Peasants' War, split the reform movement. In Thuringia, Catholics and reformers joined hands to crush Müntzer and his supporters. All over the empire, princes rallied their troops to defeat the peasants and hunt down their leaders. By the end of 1525, more than 100,000 rebels had been killed and others maimed, imprisoned, or exiled. Luther had tried to mediate, criticizing the princes for their brutality toward the peasants but also warning the rebels against mixing religion and social protest. Luther believed that rulers were ordained by God and thus must be obeyed even if they were tyrants. The Kingdom of God belonged not to this world but to the next. When the rebels ignored Luther's appeal and continued to follow radical preachers like Müntzer, Luther called on the princes to destroy "the devil's work" and slaughter the rebels. Fundamentally conservative in its political philosophy, the Lutheran church would henceforth depend on established political authority for its protection.

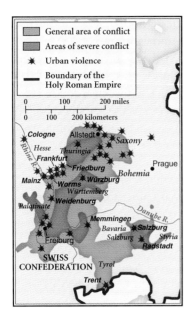

The Peasants' War of 1525

Emerging as the champions of an orderly religious reform, many German princes eventually confronted Emperor Charles V, who supported Rome. In 1529, Charles declared the Roman Catholic faith the empire's only legitimate religion. Proclaiming their allegiance to the reform cause, the Lutheran German princes protested and thus came to be called Protestants.

Huldrych Zwingli and John Calvin

While Luther provided the religious leadership for northern Germany, the south soon came under the influence of reformers based in Switzerland. In 1520, Huldrych Zwingli (1484–1531), the son of a Swiss village leader, broke with Rome and established his reform headquarters in German-speaking Zurich. In 1541, the Frenchman John Calvin (1509–1564) made French-speaking Geneva his center for reform campaigns in western Europe (see Map 12.1). Like Luther, Zwingli and Calvin began their careers as priests, but in contrast to their predecessor, they demanded an even more radical break with the Roman Catholic church.

Zwingli served as an army chaplain before declaring himself a reformer, and he brought to his version of church reform a stern disciplinarian's emphasis on a theocratic (church-directed) society in which religious values infused every aspect of politics and social life. Unlike Luther, who believed that his new church must accommodate to the established political powers and rely on their support, Zwingli refused to draw any distinction between the ideal citizen and the perfect Christian. Luther and Zwingli also differed in their views of the role of the Eucharist, or holy communion. Luther insisted that Christ was both truly and symbolically present in this central Christian sacrament; Zwingli, influenced by Erasmus, viewed the Eucharist as simply a ceremony symbolizing Christ's union with believers. In 1529, troubled by these disagreements, princes and magistrates who supported reform called a meeting at Marburg, in the center of the German lands. After several days of intense discussions, the north German and Swiss reformers managed to resolve many doctrinal differences, but Luther and Zwingli failed to agree on the meaning of the Eucharist.

In Zurich, Zwingli tolerated no dissent. When laypeople secretly set up their own new sect, called Anabaptists, Zwingli immediately attacked them. The Anabaptists believed that only adults had the free will to truly understand and accept baptism and therefore had to be rebaptized (*anabaptism* means "rebaptism"). How could a baby knowingly choose Christ? Rebaptism symbolized the Anabaptists' determination to withdraw from a social order corrupted, as they saw it, by power and evil. They therefore rejected the authority of courts and magistrates and refused to bear arms or swear oaths of allegiance. When persuasion failed to convince them, Zwingli urged Zurich magistrates to impose the death sentence.

Anabaptism spread quickly from Zurich to many cities in southern Germany, despite the Holy Roman Empire's general condemnation of the movement in 1529.

In 1534, one incendiary Anabaptist group, believing that the end of the world was imminent, seized control of the northwestern German town of Münster. Proclaiming themselves a community of saints and imitating the ancient Israelites, they were initially governed by twelve elders and later by Jan of Leiden, a Dutch Anabaptist tailor who claimed to be the prophesied leader—a second "King David." The Münster Anabaptists abolished private property and dissolved traditional marriages, allowing men, like Old Testament patriarchs, to have multiple wives, to the chagrin of many women. In 1535, besieged by a combined Protestant and Catholic army, many Münster Anabaptists died in battle or—like Hille Feiken—were executed. The remnants of the Anabaptist movement survived under the determined pacifist leadership of the Dutch reformer Menno Simons (1469–1561).

Yet another wave of reform surged forward under the leadership of John Calvin. As a young priest, Calvin believed it might be possible to reform the Roman Catholic church from within, but gradually he came to share Luther and Zwingli's conviction that only fundamental change could reestablish the true religion. While Calvin moved toward the Protestant position, his homeland of France experienced increasing turmoil over religion. On Sunday, October 18, 1534, in the so-called Affair of the Placards, Parisians found church doors posted with ribald broadsheets denouncing the Catholic Mass. Rumors of a Protestant conspiracy and massacre circulated, and magistrates swiftly organized repression of reform groups. The government arrested hundreds of French Protestants and executed scores of them, precipitating the flight into exile of many others, including Calvin.

Calvin did not intend to settle in Geneva, but when he stopped there, a local reformer threatened him with God's curse if he did not stay and help organize reform in the city. After intense conflict between the supporters of reform, many of whom were French refugees, and the opposition, led by the traditional elite families, the Calvinists triumphed in 1541. Geneva soon followed the precepts laid out in Calvin's great work, *The Institutes of the Christian Religion,* first published in 1536. Calvin took the reform doctrines to their logical conclusion. If God is almighty and humans cannot earn their salvation by good works, as all Protestants argued, then no Christian can be certain of salvation. Developing the doctrine of *predestination,* Calvin insisted that God had foreordained every man, woman, and child to salvation or damnation—even before the creation of the world. Only God knew who was among the "elect."

In practice, however, Calvinist doctrine demanded rigorous discipline: the knowledge that a small group of "elect" would be saved should guide the actions of the godly in an uncertain world. Fusing church and society into what followers named the "Reformed church," Geneva became a single theocratic community, in which dissent was not tolerated. The Genevan magistrates arrested the Spanish physician Michael Servetus when he passed through in 1553 because he had published books attacking Calvin and questioning the doctrine of the Trinity, the belief that God exists in three persons—the Father, Son (Christ), and Holy Spirit. Calvin urged the authorities to execute him, though he did not approve of their decision to burn him at the stake. Although critics cited Servetus's execution as an example of Calvinist despotism, Geneva quickly became the new center of the Reformation, the place where pastors trained for mission work and from which books propagating Calvinist doctrines were exported. The Calvinist movement spread to France, the Netherlands, England, Scotland, the German states, Poland, Hungary, and eventually New England, becoming the established form of the Reformation in many of these countries (Map 12.1).

The Progress of the Reformation	
1517	Martin Luther disseminates ninety-five theses attacking the sale of indulgences and other church practices
1520	Reformer Huldrych Zwingli breaks with Rome
1525	Radical reformer Thomas Müntzer killed in Peasants' War
1529	Lutheran German princes protest the condemnation of religious reform by Charles V; genesis of the term *Protestants*
1529	The English Parliament establishes King Henry VIII as head of the Anglican church, severing ties to Rome
1534–1535	Anabaptists control the city of Münster, Germany, in a failed experiment to create a holy community
1541	John Calvin and his followers take control in Geneva, making that city the center for Calvinist reforms

Reshaping Society through Religion

For all their differences over doctrine and church organization, the Protestant reformers shared a desire to instill greater discipline in Christian worship and in social behavior. As a consequence, they advocated changes in education, poor relief, and marriage to create a God-fearing, pious, and orderly Christian society. Some of these efforts grew out of developments that stretched back to the Middle Ages, but others, such as an emphasis on literacy and a new work ethic, appeared first in Protestant Europe.

Prior to the Reformation, the Latin Vulgate was the only Bible authorized by the church, though many vernacular translations of parts of the Bible circulated. In 1522, Martin Luther translated Erasmus's Greek New Testament into German, the first full translation in that language. Within twelve years, printers published more than 200,000 copies of it, an immense number for the time. In 1534, Luther completed a translation of the Old Testament. Peppered with witty phrases and colloquial expressions, Luther's Bible offered a treasure chest of the German language. In the same year that Luther's German New Testament appeared in print, the French humanist Jacques Lefèvre d'Étaples (c. 1455–1536) translated the Vulgate New Testament into French. Sponsored by the bishop of Meaux, who wanted to distribute free copies of the New Testament to the poor of the region, Lefèvre's translation represented an early attempt to reform the French church without breaking with Rome. By contrast, England's church hierarchy reacted swiftly

■ **MAP 12.1 Spread of Protestantism in the Sixteenth Century**
*The Protestant Reformation divided northern and southern Europe. From its heartland in the
Holy Roman Empire, the Reformation won the allegiance of Scandinavia, England, and Scotland
and made considerable inroads in the Low Countries, France, eastern Europe, the Swiss Confederation, and even parts of northern Italy. While the Mediterranean countries remained loyal to Rome,
a vast zone of confessional divisions and strife characterized the religious landscape of Europe from
Britain in the west to Poland in the east.*

against English-language Bibles, sensing in them the threat of heresy. Inspired by Luther's example during a visit to Wittenberg, the Englishman William Tyndale (1495–1536) translated the Bible into English. After he had his translation printed in Germany and the Low Countries, Tyndale smuggled copies into England. He paid for his boldness by being burned at the stake as a heretic. Because vernacular Bibles soon took pride of place in urban households as prized family heirlooms, especially in the German lands, Catholics could counter Protestant success only by printing their own translations.

Although the vernacular Bible occupied a central role in Protestantism, Bible reading did not become widespread until the 1600s. To increase literacy, educate children in the new religious principles, and replace the late medieval church schools, the Protestant reformers set up state school systems. Luther urged the German princes to use the proceeds of confiscated church properties to establish primary schools in every parish for children between six and twelve. The ordinance for a girls' school in Göttingen spelled out the emphasis on Christian discipline: "To fear God, they must learn their catechism, beautiful psalms, sayings, and other fine Christian and holy songs and little prayers." In addition to reading and writing, girls' schools included domestic skills in their curriculum. The Protestant churches developed a secondary system of humanist schools to train future pastors, scholars, and officials. These higher schools for boys, called *gymnasia* (from the Greek *gymnasion*), relied on the study of Greek and Latin classics and religious instruction to prepare students for university study.

To compete with the Protestant *gymnasia,* the new Catholic religious order, the Society of Jesus (known as the Jesuits), founded hundreds of colleges in Spain, Portugal, France, Italy, the German states, Hungary, Bohemia, and Poland. Among their alumni would be princes, philosophers, lawyers, churchmen, and officials— the elite of Catholic Europe. Except in the northern and central Italian cities, where most girls and boys received some education, Catholics nonetheless lagged behind Protestants in promoting primary education. The existence of competing Christian schools helped to perpetuate the religious divisions of Reformation Europe for many generations.

In their efforts to reshape society, Protestant reformers focused on poor relief as well as education. Although secular governments began to take over charity institutions from the church in both Protestant and Catholic regions, public poor relief quickly became more prevalent in Protestant areas. Among Protestants, private charity had ceased to be considered a good work necessary to earn salvation. In Protestant Nuremberg (1522) and Strasbourg (1523), for example, magistrates centralized poor relief with church funds; they appointed officials to head urban agencies that certified the genuine poor and distributed welfare funds to them. National measures soon followed. In 1531, Henry VIII asked justices of the peace (unpaid local magistrates) to license the poor in England and to differentiate between those capable of working and those who could not. In 1540, Charles V (who ruled Spain as Charles I) imposed a welfare tax in Catholic Spain to augment that country's inadequate system of private charity. Despite the efforts of Catholic cities and states to prohibit begging and institute public charity, the new work ethic acquired a distinctly Protestant cast. Protestants linked hard work and prosperity with piety and divine providence and considered laziness a sign of immorality—and frequently associated laziness with Catholics. Collective charity persisted in Catholic lands, supported by a theology of good works and by the elites' sense of social responsibility.

Like the reforms of education and poor relief, Protestant efforts to reshape marriage reflected their concern to discipline individual behavior and institute an orderly Christian society. Protestant magistrates established marital courts, promulgated new marriage laws, closed brothels, and inflicted harsher punishments for sexual deviance. Under canon law, the Catholic church recognized any promise made between two consenting adults (with the legal age of twelve for females, fourteen for males) as a valid marriage. In rural areas and among the urban poor, most couples simply lived together as common-law husband and wife, and some couples never even registered with the church. Sometimes young men promised marriage in a moment of passion only to renege later. Protestant governments declared a marriage illegitimate if the partners failed to register their marriage with a local official and a pastor. They usually also required parental consent, thus giving householders immense power in regulating marriage and the transmission of family property.

Enjoined to become obedient spouses and affectionate companions in Christ, women approached this new sexual regime with ambivalence. The new laws stipulated that women could seek divorce for desertion, impotence, and flagrant abuse, although in practice the marital courts encouraged reconciliation. These improvements came at a price, however: Protestant women were expected to be obedient wives, helpful companions, and loving mothers, but they could no longer join the convent and pursue their own religious paths outside the family. Luther's wife, Katharina von Bora, typified the new ideal Protestant woman. A former nun, she accepted her prescribed role in a patriarchal household: once married, Katharina ran the couple's household, feeding their children, relatives, and student boarders. Although she deferred to Luther—she addressed him as "Herr Doktor"—she nonetheless defended a woman's right as an equal in marriage. Other Protestant women spoke out even more decisively. Katharina Zell, wife of the reformer Matthew Zell, wrote hymns, fed the sick and imprisoned, and denounced the intolerance of the new Protestant clergy. Rebuking one for his persecution of dissenters, she wrote, "You young fellows tread on the graves of the first fathers of this church in Strasbourg and punish all who disagree with you, but faith cannot be forced." She also insisted that women should have a voice in religious affairs.◆

◆ For several primary sources that reveal the impact of the Reformation on women's lives, see Document 37, Argula von Grumbach and John Hooker, "Women's Actions in the Reformation."

■ **Twelve Characteristics of an Insanely Angry Wife**
This 1530 broadsheet depicts with a woodcut and accompanying text "the twelve properties of an insanely angry wife." The negative representation of female anger reflects the values dominant in Reformation society: a harmonious household ruled by a patriarch. (Schlossmuseum, Gotha.)

State Power and Religious Conflict, 1500–1618

Even as religious disputes heightened the potential for conflict within Europe, the European powers continued to fight their traditional dynastic wars and still faced the military threat posed by the Muslim Ottoman Turks in the east. But these wars did not long deflect attention from increasing divisions within European countries. Rulers viewed religious divisions as a dangerous challenge to the unity of their realms and the stability of their regimes; a subject could very well swear greater allegiance to God than to his lord. Yet rulers often proved powerless to stem the rising tide of religious strife. Lutheranism flourished in the northern German states and Scandinavia; Calvinism spread from its headquarters in the Swiss city of Geneva all the way to England and Poland-Lithuania. The rapid expansion of Lutheranism and Calvinism created deadly political conflicts between Protestants and Catholics.

Wars among Habsburgs, Valois, and Ottomans

While the Reformation was taking hold in the German states, the great powers of Spain and France fought each other for the domination of Europe (Map 12.2). French claims over Italian territories sparked conflict in 1494, but the ensuing

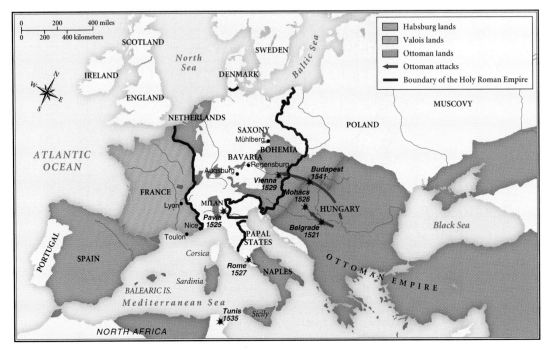

■ MAP 12.2 Habsburg-Valois-Ottoman Wars, 1494–1559

As the dominant European power, the Habsburg dynasty fought on two fronts: a religious war against the Islamic Ottoman Empire and a political war against the French Valois, who challenged Habsburg hegemony. The Mediterranean, the Balkans, and the Low Countries all became theaters of war.

Italian Wars soon involved most Christian monarchs and the Muslim Ottoman sultan as well. Despite some spectacular and bloody turns of fortune, no one power ultimately emerged victorious. In 1525, the troops of Emperor Charles V crushed the French army at Pavia, Italy, and captured the French king, Francis I (r. 1515–1547). Charles treated Francis as an honored guest but held him in Spain until he agreed to renounce his claims to Italy. Furious at this humiliation, Francis repudiated the agreement the moment he returned to France, reigniting the conflict. In 1527, Charles's troops invaded and then pillaged Rome to punish the pope for allying with the French. Among the imperial troops were German Protestant mercenaries, who delighted in tormenting the Catholic clergy. The sack of Rome shocked the Catholic church hierarchy and turned it toward reform.

Charles could not crush the French in one swift blow because he also had to counter the Muslim Ottomans in Hungary and along the Mediterranean coastline. The Ottoman Empire reached its height of power under Sultan Suleiman I, "the Magnificent" (r. 1520–1566). In 1526, a Turkish force destroyed the Hungarian army at Mohács. Three years later, the Ottoman army laid siege to Vienna; though unsuccessful, the siege set off alarms throughout Christian Europe. In 1535, Charles V tried to capture Tunis, the lair of North African pirates under Ottoman suzerainty. Desperate to overcome Charles's superior forces in Europe, Francis I eagerly forged an alliance with the Turkish sultan. The Turkish fleet besieged Nice, on the southern coast of France, to help the French wrest it from imperial occupiers. Francis even ordered all inhabitants of nearby Toulon to vacate their town so that he could turn it into a Muslim colony for eight months, complete with a mosque and slave market. Although the Turks eventually left Toulon, many Christians denounced the French alliance with the Turks against another Christian king. This brief Franco-Turkish alliance nonetheless showed that the age-old idea of Christian crusade against Islam had to make way for a new political strategy that considered religion as but one factor in power politics.

In 1559, the French king finally acknowledged defeat and signed the peace treaty of Cateau-Cambrésis. By then, years of conflict had drained the treasuries of all monarchs. Fueled by warfare, all armies grew in size, firepower became ever more deadly, and costs soared. For example, heavier artillery pieces meant that the rectangular walls of medieval cities had to be transformed into fortresses with jutting forts and gun emplacements. Charles V boasted the largest army in Europe—but he could not make ends meet with the proceeds from taxation, the sale of offices, and even outright confiscation.

■ The Battle at Mohács
This Ottoman painting shows the 1529 victory of the sultan's army over the Hungarians at Mohács. The battle resulted in the end of the Hungarian kingdom, which would be divided into three realms under Ottoman, Habsburg, and Transylvanian rule. Notice the prominence of artillery and the Ottoman fighting force (the Janissaries) with muskets. The Ottomans commanded a vast army with modern equipment, a key to their military prowess in the sixteenth century. (Topkapi Palace Museum.)

Like other rulers, Charles V looked to private bankers for funds. Charles relied on the Fugger bank, based in the southern German imperial city of Augsburg. Jakob Fugger (1459–1525), nicknamed "the Rich," had loaned money to Charles V's grandfather, Maximilian I, in exchange for mining and minting concessions as well as hefty interest payments. In 1519, Fugger assembled a consortium of German and Italian bankers to secure the election of Charles V as Holy Roman Emperor. The assets of the Fuggers more than doubled between 1527 and 1547; Charles V's debts nearly doubled, too. The French kings fared no better. On his death in 1547, Francis owed the bankers of Lyon nearly 7 million pounds—approximately the entire royal income for that year. As a result, the Valois and the Habsburgs had to pay 14 to 18 percent interest on their loans.

French Wars of Religion

During the 1540s and 1550s, one-third of the French nobles converted to Calvinism, usually influenced by noblewomen who protected pastors, provided money and advice, and helped found schools and establish relief for the poor. With this noble backing, the Reformed church organized openly and held synods (church meetings), especially in southern and western France. The Catholic Valois monarchy tried to maintain a balance of power between Catholics and Calvinists. Francis I and his successor, Henry II (r. 1547–1559), both succeeded to a degree. But when Henry was accidentally killed during a jousting tournament, the weakened monarchy could no longer hold together the fragile realm.

Henry's fifteen-year-old son Francis II died in 1560, and he was succeeded by his brother, ten-year-old Charles IX (r. 1560–1574). His mother, Catherine de Medicis (1519–1589), acted as regent. Catherine, an Italian and a Catholic, urged limited toleration for the Calvinists—called Huguenots in France—in an attempt to maintain political stability, but her influence was severely limited. As one ambassador commented, "It is sufficient to say that she is a woman, a foreigner, and a Florentine to boot, born of a simple house, altogether beneath the dignity of the Kingdom of France." She could not prevent the eruption of civil war between Catholics and Huguenots in 1562.

Although a Catholic herself, Catherine aimed to preserve the throne for her son by playing the Catholic and Huguenot factions off each

Protestant Churches in France, 1562

other. To this end, she arranged the marriage of the king's Catholic sister Marguerite de Valois to Henry of Navarre, head of the Bourbon family, which had converted to Calvinism. Just four days after the wedding in August 1572, assassins tried but failed to kill one of the Huguenot nobles allied with the Bourbons, Gaspard de Coligny. Panicked at the thought of Huguenot revenge and perhaps herself implicated in the botched plot, Catherine convinced her son to order the killing of leading Huguenots. On St. Bartholomew's Day, August 24, a bloodbath began, fueled by years of growing animosity between Catholics and Protestants. In three days, Catholic mobs murdered three thousand Huguenots in Paris. Ten thousand died in the provinces over the next six weeks. The pope joyfully ordered the church bells rung throughout Catholic Europe; Spain's Philip II wrote Catherine that it was "the best and most cheerful news which at present could come to me." Protestants and Catholics alike now saw the conflict as an international struggle for survival that required aid to coreligionists in other countries. In this way, the French Wars of Religion paved the way for wider international conflicts over religion in the future.

The religious division in France grew even more dangerous when Charles IX died and his brother Henry III (r. 1574–1589) became king. Like his brothers before him, Henry III failed to produce an heir. Next in line to succeed the throne was none other than the Calvinist Bourbon leader Henry of Navarre. Because Henry III saw an even greater threat to his authority in a newly formed Catholic League, which had requested Spain's help in rooting out Protestantism in France, he took action against the league. In 1588, he summoned two prominent league leaders to a meeting and had his men kill them. A few months later a fanatical monk stabbed Henry III to death, and Henry of Navarre became Henry IV (r. 1589–1610), despite Spain's attempt to block his way with military intervention.

The new king soon concluded that to establish control over the war-weary country he had to place the interests of the French state ahead of his Protestant faith. In 1593, Henry IV publicly embraced Catholicism, reputedly explaining his conversion with the phrase "Paris is worth a Mass." In 1598, he made peace with Spain and issued the Edict of Nantes, in which he granted the Huguenots a large measure of religious toleration.◆ The approximately 1.25 million Huguenots became a legally protected minority within an officially Catholic kingdom of some 20 million people. Protestants were free to worship in specified towns and were allowed their own troops, fortresses, and even courts. Few believed in religious toleration, but Henry IV followed the advice of those neutral Catholics and Calvinists called *politiques* who urged him to give priority to the development of a durable state. Although their opponents hated them for their compromising spirit, the *politiques* believed that religious disputes could be resolved only in the peace provided by strong government.

◆ For excerpts from Henry IV's proclamation, see Document 38, "Edict of Nantes."

The Edict of Nantes ended the French Wars of Religion, but Henry still needed to reestablish monarchical authority. He used court festivities and royal processions to rally subjects around him, and he developed a new class of royal officials to counterbalance the fractious nobility. In exchange for an annual payment, officials who had purchased their offices could pass them on to heirs or sell them to someone else. By buying offices that eventually ennobled their holders, rich middle-class merchants and lawyers could become part of a new social elite known as the "nobility of the robe" (named after the robes that magistrates wore, much like those judges wear today). New income raised by the increased sale of offices reduced the state debt and helped Henry build the base for a strong monarchy. His efforts did not, however, prevent his own assassination in 1610 after nineteen unsuccessful attempts.

Challenges to Habsburg Power and the Rise of the Dutch Republic

Charles V proved more successful at fending off the Turks and subduing the French than he did at resolving growing religious conflicts inside his empire. After an Imperial Diet at Regensburg in 1541 failed to patch up the theological differences between Protestants and Catholics, Charles secured papal support for a war against the Schmalkaldic League, a powerful alliance of Lutheran princes and cities. Charles's army occupied the German imperial cities in the south, restoring Catholic patricians and suppressing the Reformation wherever they triumphed. In 1547, Charles defeated the Schmalkaldic League armies at Mühlberg and captured the leading Lutheran princes. Jubilant, Charles proclaimed a decree, the "Interim," which restored Catholics' right to worship in Protestant lands while still permitting Lutherans to celebrate their own services. Riots broke out in many cities as resistance to the Interim spread. Charles's victory proved ephemeral, for after one of his former allies, Duke Maurice of Saxony, joined the other side, the princes revived the war in 1552 and chased a surprised, unprepared, and practically bankrupt emperor back to Italy.

Forced to negotiate, Charles V agreed to the Peace of Augsburg in 1555. The settlement recognized the Evangelical (Lutheran) church in the empire, accepted the secularization of church lands but "reserved" the existent ecclesiastical territories (mainly the bishoprics) for Catholics, and, most important, established the principle that all princes, whether Catholic or Lutheran, enjoyed the sole right to determine the religion of their lands and subjects. Significantly, the Peace excluded Calvinist, Anabaptist, and other dissenting groups from the settlement. The Peace of Augsburg preserved a fragile peace in central Europe until 1618, but the exclusion of Calvinists would plant the seeds for future conflict.

Exhausted by constant war and depressed by the disunity in Christian Europe, Charles V resigned his many thrones in 1555 and 1556, leaving his Netherlandish-Burgundian and Spanish dominions to his son, Philip II, and his Austrian lands to his brother, Ferdinand, who was also elected Holy Roman Emperor to succeed Charles. Retiring to a monastery in southern Spain, the once powerful Christian monarch spent his last years quietly seeking salvation. Although Philip II of Spain (r. 1556–1598) ruled over fewer territories than his father, his inheritance still left him the most powerful ruler in Europe (Map 12.3). In addition to the western Habsburg lands in Spain and the Netherlands, he had inherited all the Spanish colonies recently settled in the New World of the Americas. In 1580, when the king of Portugal died without a direct heir, Philip took over this neighboring realm with its rich empire in Africa, India, and the Americas. Gold and silver funneled from the colonies supported his campaigns against the Ottoman Turks and French and English Protestants.

A deeply devout Catholic, Philip II came to the Spanish throne at age twenty-eight determined to restore Catholic unity in Europe and lead the Christian defense against the Muslims. His brief marriage to Mary Tudor (Mary I of England) did not produce an heir, but it and his subsequent marriage to Elisabeth de Valois, the sister of Charles IX and Henry III of France, gave him reason enough to oppose the spread of Protestantism in England and France. In 1571, Philip joined with Venice and the papacy to defeat the Turks in a great sea battle off the Greek coast at Lepanto. But Philip could not rest on his laurels. Between 1568 and 1570, the Moriscos—Muslim converts to Christianity who remained secretly faithful to Islam—had revolted in the south of Spain, killing 90 priests and 1,500 Christians. The victory at Lepanto destroyed any prospect that the Turks might come to their aid, yet Philip nonetheless forced 50,000 Moriscos to leave their villages and resettle in other regions. In 1609, his successor, Philip

■ **Titian, *Gloria* (detail)**
All military glory and earthly power is doomed to fade away, as the Venetian painter Titian (1477–1576) vividly depicted in Gloria. *Among the multitude turning to the Trinity in the heavens is the Emperor Charles V, dressed in a white robe. Painted after his abdication in 1556,* Gloria *is a reminder to Charles of the transience of earthly glory, for white is both the color of newborn innocence and that of the burial shroud.*
(Institut Amatller d'Art Hispanic.)

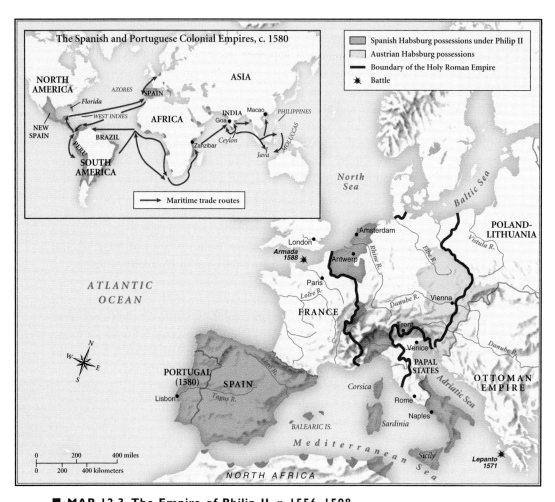

■ MAP 12.3 The Empire of Philip II, r. 1556–1598

Spanish king Philip II drew revenues from a truly worldwide empire. In 1580, he was the richest European ruler, but the demands of governing such far-flung territories eventually drained many of his resources.

III, ordered their expulsion, and by 1614 some 300,000 Moriscos had been forced to relocate to North Africa.

The Calvinists of the Netherlands were less easily intimidated than the Moriscos: they were far from Spain and accustomed to being left alone. In 1566, Calvinists in the Netherlands attacked Catholic churches, smashing stained-glass windows and statues of the Virgin Mary. Philip sent an army, which executed more than 1,100 people during the next six years. When resistance revived, the Spanish responded with more force, culminating in November 1576 when Philip's long-unpaid mercenary armies sacked Antwerp, then Europe's wealthiest commercial city.

In eleven days of horror known as the Spanish Fury, the Spanish soldiers slaughtered seven thousand people. Shocked into response, the ten largely Catholic southern provinces formally allied with the seven largely Protestant northern provinces and expelled the Spaniards. In 1579, however, the Catholic southern provinces returned to the Spanish fold. Despite the assassination in 1584 of William of Orange, the leader of the anti-Spanish forces, Spanish troops never regained control in the north.

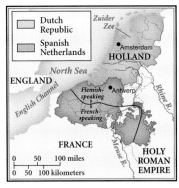

The Netherlands during the Revolt, c. 1580

Spain would not formally recognize the independence of the United Provinces until 1648, but by the end of the sixteenth century the Dutch Republic was a self-governing state sheltering a variety of religious groups. The princes of Orange (whose name came from family lands in southern France) resembled a ruling family in the Dutch Republic, but their powers paled next to those of local interests. Urban merchant and professional families known as "regents" controlled the towns and provinces. Each province (Holland was the most populous of the seven provinces) governed itself and sent delegates to the one common institution, the States General. Well situated for maritime commerce, the Dutch Republic developed a thriving economy based on shipping and shipbuilding. By 1670, the Dutch commercial fleet was larger than the English, French, Spanish, Portuguese, and Austrian fleets combined.

Since the Dutch traded with anyone anywhere, it is perhaps not surprising that Dutch society tolerated more religious diversity than the other European states. One-third of the Dutch population remained Catholic, and the secular authorities allowed Catholics to worship as they chose in private. Because Protestant sects could generally count on toleration from local regents, they remained peaceful. The Dutch Republic also had a relatively large Jewish population because many Jews had settled there after being driven out of Spain and Portugal; from 1597, Jews could worship openly in their synagogues. This openness to various religions helped make the Dutch Republic one of Europe's chief intellectual and scientific centers in the seventeenth and eighteenth centuries.

England Goes Protestant

Until 1527, England's king Henry VIII (r. 1509–1547) firmly opposed the Reformation, even receiving the title "Defender of the Faith" from Pope Leo X for a treatise Henry wrote against Luther. Henry's family problems changed his mind. Henry had married Catherine of Aragon (d. 1536), the daughter of Ferdinand and Isabella of Spain and the aunt of Charles V, and the marriage had produced a daughter, Princess Mary (known as Mary Tudor). Henry wanted a male heir to consolidate the rule of his Tudor dynasty, and he had fallen in love with Anne Boleyn, a lady-in-waiting at court and a strong supporter of the Reformation. In 1527, Henry asked the reigning pope, Clement VII, to declare his eighteen-year marriage to Catherine invalid on the grounds that she was the widow of his older brother, Arthur. Arthur and Catherine's marriage, which apparently was never consummated, had been annulled by Pope Julius II.

Around "the king's great matter" unfolded a struggle for political and religious control. When Henry failed to secure a papal dispensation for his divorce, he chose two Protestants as his new loyal servants: Thomas Cromwell (1485–1540) as chancellor and Thomas Cranmer (1489–1556) as archbishop of Canterbury. Under their leadership the English Parliament passed a number of acts between 1529 and 1536 that severed ties between the English church and Rome. The Act of Supremacy of 1529 established Henry as the head of the so-called Anglican church (the Church of England), invalidated the claims of Catherine and Princess Mary to the throne, recognized Henry's marriage to Anne Boleyn, and allowed the English crown to confiscate the properties of the monasteries.

By 1536, Henry had grown tired of Anne Boleyn, who had given birth to the future Queen Elizabeth I but had produced no sons. The king, who would go on to marry four other wives but father only one son, Edward (by his third wife, Jane Seymour), had Anne beheaded on the charge of adultery, an act that he defined as treason. Thomas More, once Henry's chancellor, had been executed in 1535 for treason—in his case, for refusing to recognize Henry as "the only supreme head on earth of the Church of England"—and Cromwell suffered the same fate in 1540 when he lost favor. After Henry's death in 1547, the Anglican church, nominally Protestant, still retained much traditional Catholic doctrine and ritual. But the principle of royal supremacy in religious matters would remain a lasting feature of Henry's reforms.

Under Edward VI (r. 1547–1553) and Mary Tudor (r. 1553–1558), official religious policies oscillated between Protestant reforms and Catholic restoration. The boy-king Edward welcomed prominent Protestant refugees from continental Europe. When Mary succeeded him, however, she restored Catholicism and executed three hundred Protestants. Hundreds more fled. Finally, after Anne Boleyn's daughter, Elizabeth, came to the throne in 1558, the Anglican cause again gained momentum. As Elizabeth I (r. 1558–1603) moved to solidify her personal power and the authority of the Anglican church, she had to squash uprisings by Catholics in the north and at least two serious plots against her life. She also had to hold off Calvinist Puritans who pushed for more reform and Spain's Philip II, who first wanted to be her husband then, failing that, planned to invade her country to restore Catholicism.

The Puritans were strict Calvinists who opposed all vestiges of Catholic ritual in the Church of England. After Elizabeth became queen, many Puritans returned from exile abroad, but Elizabeth resisted their demands for drastic changes in Anglican ritual and governance. She had assumed control as "supreme governor" of the Church of England, replacing the pope as the ultimate religious authority, and she appointed all bishops. The Church of England's Thirty-Nine Articles of Religion, issued in 1563, incorporated elements of Catholic ritual along with Calvinist doctrines. Puritan ministers angrily denounced the Church of England's "popish attire and foolish disguising, . . . tithings, holy days, and a thousand more abominations." Puritans tried to undercut the bishops' authority by placing control of church administration in the hands of a local presbytery made up of the minister and the elders of the congregation. Elizabeth rejected this Calvinist "presbyterianism." The Puritans nonetheless steadily gained influence. Known for their emphasis on strict moral lives, the Puritans tried to close the theaters and Sunday fairs and insisted that every father "make his house a little church" by teaching the children to read the Bible. At Puritan urging, a new translation of the Bible, known as the King James Bible after Elizabeth's successor, James I, was authorized in 1604. Believing themselves God's elect and England an "elect nation," the Puritans also urged Elizabeth to help Protestants in Europe.

Spain's Philip II had been married to Elizabeth's half-sister Mary Tudor and had enthusiastically seconded Mary's efforts to return England to Catholicism. When Mary died, Elizabeth rejected Philip's proposal of marriage and eventually provided funds and troops to the Dutch rebels. Philip II bided his time as long as she remained unmarried and her Catholic cousin Mary Stuart, better known as Mary, Queen of Scots, stood next in line to inherit the English throne. In 1568, Scottish Calvinists forced Mary to abdicate the throne of Scotland in favor of her year-old son James (eventually James I of England), who was then raised as a Protestant. The Scottish Calvinists feared Mary's connections to Catholic France; her mother was French and devoutly

■ **Glorifying the Ruler**
This exquisite miniature (c. 1560) attributed to Levina Teerlinc, a Flemish woman who painted for the English court, shows Queen Elizabeth I, dressed in purplish blue, participating in an Easter Week ceremony at which the monarch washed the feet of poor people before presenting them with money, food, and clothing. The ceremony was held to imitate Christ's washing of the feet of his disciples; it showed that the queen could exercise every one of the ruler's customary roles. (Private collection.)

Catholic, and Mary Stuart had earlier been married to France's Francis II (he died in 1560). After her abdication, Mary spent nearly twenty years under house arrest in England, fomenting plots against Elizabeth. In 1587, when Mary's letter offering her succession rights to Philip was discovered, Elizabeth overcame her reluctance to execute a fellow monarch and ordered Mary's beheading.

In response, Pope Sixtus V decided to subsidize a Catholic crusade under Philip's leadership against the heretical queen, "the English Jezebel." At the end of May 1588, Philip II sent his *armada* (Spanish for "fleet") of 130 ships from Lisbon toward the English Channel. The English scattered the Spanish Armada by sending blazing fire ships into its midst. A great gale then forced the Spanish to flee around Scotland. When the Armada limped home in September, half the ships had been lost and thousands of sailors were dead or starving. Protestants throughout Europe rejoiced. A Spanish monk lamented, "Almost the whole of Spain went into mourning."

By the time Philip II died in 1598, his great empire had begun to lose its luster. The costs of fighting the Dutch, the English, and the French mounted, and an overburdened peasantry could no longer pay the taxes required to meet rising expenses. In his novel *Don Quixote* (1605), the Spanish writer Miguel de Cervantes captured the sadness of Spain's loss of grandeur. Cervantes himself had been wounded at Lepanto, held captive in Algiers, and then served as a royal tax collector. His hero, a minor nobleman, wants to understand "this thing they call reason of state," but he reads so many romances and books of chivalry that he loses his wits and wanders the countryside hoping to re-create the heroic deeds of times past. He refuses to believe that these books are only fantasies: "Books which are printed under license from the king . . . can such be lies?" Don Quixote's futile adventures incarnated the thwarted ambitions of a declining military aristocracy.

England could never have defeated Spain in a head-to-head battle on land, but Elizabeth made the most of her limited means and consolidated the country's position as a Protestant power. In her early years, she held out the prospect of marriage to many political suitors but never married. She cajoled Parliament with references to her female weaknesses, but she showed steely-eyed determination in protecting the monarchy's interests. Her chosen successor, James I (r. 1603–1625), came to the throne as king of both Scotland and England. Elizabeth left James secure in a kingdom of growing weight in world politics.

Catholic Renewal and Missionary Zeal

Reacting to the waves of Protestant challenge, the Catholic church mobilized for defense in a movement that is sometimes called the Counter-Reformation. Pope Paul III (r. 1534–1549) convened a general church council to codify church doctrine, and he personally approved the founding of new religious orders to undertake aggressive missionary efforts. The Council of Trent (Trent sat on the border between the Holy Roman Empire and Italy) met intermittently between 1545 and

1563, when it concluded its work. Its decisions shaped the essential character of Catholicism until the 1960s. Emphatically rejecting the major Protestant positions, the council reasserted the supremacy of clerical authority over the laity and reaffirmed the doctrine known as *transubstantiation*—that in the sacrament of the Eucharist, the bread of communion actually becomes Christ's body. But the council also undertook reforms; it insisted that bishops reside in their dioceses and ordered every diocese to establish a seminary to train priests. It also stipulated that all weddings take place in churches and be registered by the parish clergy. It further declared that all marriages remain valid, explicitly rejecting the Protestant authorization of divorce. All hopes of reconciliation between Protestants and Catholics faded.

The Counter-Reformation found its shock troops in the Society of Jesus, the new Catholic religious order that would prove the most important of the sixteenth century. Its founder was Ignatius of Loyola (1491–1556), a Spanish nobleman and charismatic former military officer, who abandoned his quest for military glory in favor of serving the church. Ignatius soon attracted other young men to his side, and in 1540 the pope recognized his small band of "Jesuits." By the time of Ignatius's death, Europe had one thousand Jesuits. Together with other new religious orders, the Jesuits restored the confidence of the faithful in the dedication and power of the Catholic church.◆

Jesuit missionaries set sail throughout the globe in order to bring Roman Catholicism to Africans, Asians, and Native Americans. They saw their effort as proof of the truth of Roman Catholicism and the success of their missions as a sign of divine favor, both particularly important in the face of Protestant challenge. To ensure rapid Christianization, European missionaries focused initially on winning over local elites. A number of young African nobles went to Portugal to be trained in theology—among them Dom Henry, a son of King Afonso I of Kongo, a Portuguese ally. Catholic missionaries preached the Gospel to Confucian scholar-officials in China and to the samurai (the warrior aristocracy) in Japan. Measured in numbers alone, the missionary enterprise seemed highly successful: by the second half of the sixteenth century, vast multitudes of Native Americans had become Christians at least in name, and thirty years after Francis Xavier's 1549 landing in Japan the Jesuits could claim over 100,000 Japanese converts.

After an initial period of relatively little racial discrimination, the Catholic church in the Americas and Africa adopted strict rules based on color. For example, the first Mexican Ecclesiastical Provincial Council in 1555 declared that holy orders were not to be conferred on Indians, *mestizos* (people of mixed European-Indian parentage), and *mulattos* (people of mixed European-African heritage), groups deemed "inherently unworthy of the sacerdotal [priestly] office." Europeans

---

◆ For several letters that express Ignatius's convictions and goals, see Document 39, St. Ignatius of Loyola, "A New Kind of Catholicism."

■ The Portuguese in Japan

In this sixteenth-century Japanese black-lacquer screen painting of Portuguese missionaries, the Jesuits are dressed in black and the Franciscans in brown. At the lower right corner is a Portuguese nobleman depicted with exaggerated "Western" features. The Japanese considered themselves lighter in skin color than the Portuguese, whom they classified as "barbarians." In turn, the Portuguese classified Japanese (and Chinese) as "whites." The perception of ethnic differences in the sixteenth century depended less on skin color than on clothing, eating habits, and other cultural signals. Color classifications were unstable and changed over time: by the late seventeenth century, Europeans no longer regarded Asians as "white." (Laurie Platt Winfrey, Inc.)

reinforced their sense of racial superiority with their perception of the "treachery" that Native Americans and Africans exhibited whenever they resisted domination. Frustrated in his efforts to convert Brazilian Indians, a Jesuit missionary wrote to his superior in Rome in 1563 that "for this kind of people it is better to be preaching with the sword and rod of iron." The Dominican Bartolomé de Las Casas (1474–1566) criticized the treatment of the Indians in Spanish America, yet even he argued that Africans should be imported in order to relieve the indigenous peoples, who were being worked to death.

The Thirty Years' War and the Balance of Power, 1618–1648

In 1618, a new series of violent conflicts between Catholics and Protestants erupted in the Holy Roman Empire. The final and most deadly of the wars of religion, the Thirty Years' War eventually drew in most European states. By the end of the war in 1648, many central European lands lay in ruins and many rulers were bankrupt. Reformation and Counter-Reformation had shattered the Christian humanist dream of peace and unity. The Thirty Years' War brought the preceding religious conflicts to a head and by its very violence effectively removed religion from future European disputes. Although religion still divided people *within* various states, after 1648 religion no longer provided the rationale for wars *between* European states. Out of the carnage would emerge centralized and powerful states that made increasing demands on ordinary people.

Origins and Course of the War

The fighting that devastated central Europe had its origins in religious, political, and ethnic divisions within the Holy Roman Empire. The Austrian Habsburg emperor and four of the seven electors who chose him were Catholic; the other three electors were Protestants. The Peace of Augsburg of 1555 was supposed to maintain the balance between Catholics and Lutherans, but it had no mechanism for resolving conflicts. Tensions rose as the Jesuits won many Lutheran cities back to Catholicism and as Calvinism, unrecognized under the Peace, made inroads into Lutheran areas. By 1613, two of the three Protestant electors had become Calvinists. When the Catholic Habsburg heir Archduke Ferdinand was crowned king of Bohemia in 1617, he began to curtail the religious freedom previously granted to Protestants. Protestants wanted to build new churches; Ferdinand wanted to stop them. Tensions boiled over when two Catholic deputy-governors tried to dissolve the meetings of Protestants.

On May 23, 1618, a crowd of angry Protestants surged up the stairs of the royal castle in Prague, trapped the two Catholic deputies, dragged them screaming for mercy to the windows, and hurled them to the pavement below. One of the rebels jeered: "We will see if your [Virgin] Mary can help you!" But because they landed in a dung heap, the Catholic deputies survived. Although no one died, this "defenestration" (from the French for "window," *la fenêtre*) of Prague touched off a new cycle of conflict. The Czechs, the largest ethnic group in Bohemia, established a Protestant assembly to spearhead resistance. A year later, when Ferdinand was elected emperor (as Ferdinand II, r. 1619–1637), the rebellious Bohemians deposed him and chose in his place the young Calvinist Frederick V of the Palatinate (r. 1616–1623). A quick series of clashes ended in 1620 when the imperial armies defeated the outmanned Czechs at the Battle of White Mountain, near Prague (see Map 12.4). Like the martyrdom of the religious reformer Jan Hus in 1415, White

Mountain became an enduring symbol of the Czechs' desire for self-determination. They would not gain their independence until 1918.

White Mountain did not end the war. Private mercenary armies (armies for hire) began to form during the fighting, and the emperor had virtually no control over them. In 1625, a Czech Protestant, Albrecht von Wallenstein (1583–1634), offered to raise an army for the Catholic emperor and soon had in his employ 125,000 soldiers, who occupied and plundered much of Protestant Germany with the emperor's approval. In response, the Lutheran king of Denmark Christian IV (r. 1596–1648) invaded to protect the Protestants and to extend his own influence. Wallenstein's forces defeated him. Emboldened by his general's victories, Ferdinand issued the Edict of Restitution in 1629, which outlawed Calvinism in the empire and reclaimed Catholic church properties confiscated by the Lutherans.

With Protestant interests in serious jeopardy, Gustavus Adolphus (r. 1611–1632) of Sweden marched into Germany in 1630. A Lutheran by religion, he also hoped to gain control over trade in northern Europe, where he had already ejected the Poles from present-day Latvia and Estonia. Poland and Lithuania had joined in a commonwealth in 1569, and many Polish and Lithuanian nobles converted to Lutheranism or Calvinism, but this did not ensure common cause with Sweden. Gustavus's highly trained army of some 100,000 soldiers made Sweden, with a population of only one million, the supreme power of northern Europe, even more powerful than Russia, which had barely recovered from the "Time of Troubles" that followed on the rule of Tsar Ivan IV (r. 1533–1584). Ivan "the Terrible" initiated Russian expansion eastward into Siberia but his moves westward ran up against the Poles and the Swedes.

Although Gustavus had religious motives for intervention in German affairs, events soon showed that power politics trumped religious interests. The Catholic French government under the leadership of Louis XIII (r. 1610–1643) and his chief minister Cardinal Richelieu (1585–1642) offered to subsidize Gustavus—and the Lutheran ruler accepted. The French hoped to counter Spanish involvement in the war and win influence and perhaps territory in the Holy Roman Empire. Gustavus defeated the imperial army and occupied the Catholic parts of southern Germany before he was killed at the battle of Lützen in 1632 (see Map 12.4). Once again the tide turned, but this time it swept Wallenstein with it. Because Wallenstein was rumored to be negotiating with Protestant powers, Ferdinand dismissed his general and had his henchmen assassinate him.

France openly joined the fray in 1635 by declaring war on Spain and soon after forged an alliance with the Calvinist Dutch to aid them in their struggle for independence from Spain. The two Catholic powers, France and Spain, pummeled each other. The Swedes kept up their pressure in Germany, the Dutch attacked the Spanish fleet, and a series of internal revolts shook the cash-strapped Spanish crown. In 1640, peasants in the rich northeastern province of Catalonia rebelled, overrunning Barcelona and killing the viceroy; the Catalans resented government confiscation of their crops and demands that they house and feed soldiers on their way to the French frontier. The Portuguese revolted in 1640 and proclaimed independence like the Dutch. In 1643, the Spanish suffered their first major defeat at French hands. Although the Spanish were forced to concede independence to Portugal (part of Spain only since 1580), they eventually suppressed the Catalan revolt.

France, too, faced exhaustion after years of rising taxes and recurrent revolts. In 1642, Richelieu died. Louis XIII followed him a few months later and was succeeded by his five-year-old son Louis XIV. With the queen mother, Anne of Austria, serving as regent and depending on the Italian cardinal, Mazarin, for advice, French politics once again moved into a period of instability, rumor, and crisis. All sides were ready for peace.

The Effects of Constant Fighting

When peace negotiations began in the 1640s, they did not come a moment too soon for the ordinary people of Europe. Some towns faced up to ten or eleven prolonged sieges during the fighting. In 1648, as negotiations dragged on, a Swedish army sacked the rich cultural capital Prague, plundered its churches and castles, and effectively eliminated it as a center of culture and learning.

Even worse suffering took place in the countryside. One of the earliest German novels, *The Adventures of a Simpleton* (1669) by Hans Grimmelshausen, recounts the horror of the war in detail. In one scene, the boy Simplicius has to watch while unidentified enemy cavalrymen ransack the house; rape the maid, his mother, and his sister; and hold the feet of his father to the fire until he tells where he hid his gold and jewels. Peasants fled their villages, which were often burned down. War and intermittent outbreaks of plague cost some German towns one-third or more of their population. One-third of the inhabitants of Bohemia also perished.

Soldiers did not fare all that much better. Governments increasingly short of funds often failed to pay the troops, and frequent mutinies, looting, and pillaging resulted. Armies attracted all sorts of displaced people desperately in need of provisions. In the last year of the Thirty Years' War, the Imperial-Bavarian Army had 40,000 men entitled to draw rations—and more than 100,000 wives, prostitutes, servants, children, maids, and other camp followers forced to scrounge for their own food. The bureaucracies of early-seventeenth-century Europe simply could not cope with such demands: armies and their hangers-on had to live off the countryside. The result was scenes like those witnessed by Simplicius.

The Peace of Westphalia, 1648

The comprehensive settlement finally provided by the Peace of Westphalia—named after the German province where negotiations took place—would serve as a model for resolving conflict among warring European states. For the first time, a diplomatic

■ The Horrors of the Thirty Years' War

The French artist Jacques Collot produced this engraving of the Thirty Years' War as part of a series called The Miseries and Misfortunes of War *(1633). The actions depicted resemble those in Hans Grimmelshausen's novel* The Adventures of a Simpleton, *based on Grimmelshausen's personal experience of the Thirty Years' War.* (The Granger Collection.)

congress addressed international disputes, and the signatories to the treaties guaranteed the resulting settlement. A method still in use, the congress was the first to bring *all* parties together, rather than two or three at a time.

France and Sweden gained most from the Peace of Westphalia. Although France and Spain continued fighting until 1659, France acquired parts of Alsace and replaced Spain as the prevailing power on the European continent. Baltic conflicts would not be resolved until 1661, but Sweden took several northern territories from the Holy Roman Empire (Map 12.4).

The Habsburgs lost the most. The Spanish Habsburgs recognized Dutch independence after eighty years of war. The Swiss Confederation and the German princes demanded autonomy from the Austrian Habsburg rulers of the Holy Roman Empire. Each German prince gained the right to establish Lutheranism, Catholicism, or Calvinism in his state, a right denied to Calvinist rulers by the Peace of Augsburg in 1555. The independence ceded to German princes sustained political divisions that would remain until the nineteenth century and prepared the way for the emergence of a new power, the Hohenzollern Elector of Brandenburg, who increased his territories and developed a small but effective standing army. After losing considerable territory in the west, the Austrian Habsburgs turned eastward to concentrate on restoring Catholicism to Bohemia and wresting Hungary from the Turks.

The Peace of Westphalia permanently settled the distributions of the main religions in the Holy Roman Empire: Lutheranism would dominate in the north, Calvinism in the area of the Rhine River, and Catholicism in the south (see "Map-

■ MAP 12.4 The Thirty Years' War and the Peace of Westphalia, 1648

The Thirty Years' War involved many of the major continental European powers. The arrows marking invasion routes show that most of the fighting took place in central Europe in the lands of the Holy Roman Empire. The German states and Bohemia sustained the greatest damage during the fighting. None of the combatants emerged unscathed because even ultimate winners such as Sweden and France depleted their resources of men and money.

ping the West," page 524). Most of the territorial changes in Europe remained intact until the nineteenth century. In the future, warfare between European states would be undertaken for reasons of national security, commercial ambition, or dynastic pride rather than to enforce religious uniformity. As the *politiques* of the late sixteenth century had hoped, state interests now outweighed motivations of faith in political affairs.

Growth of State Authority

Warfare increased the reach of states: as the size of armies increased, governments needed more men, more money, and more supervisory officials. Most armies in the 1550s had fewer than 50,000 men, but Gustavus Adolphus had 100,000 men under arms in 1631. In France, the rate of land tax paid by peasants doubled in the eight years after France joined the Thirty Years' War. In addition to raising taxes, governments deliberately depreciated the value of the currency, which often resulted in inflation and soaring prices; sold new offices; and manipulated the embryonic stock and bond markets. When all else failed, they declared bankruptcy. The Spanish government, for example, did so three times in the first half of the seventeenth century.

As the demand for soldiers and for the money to supply them rose, the number of state employees multiplied, paperwork proliferated, and appointment to office began to depend on university education in the law. Monarchs relied on advisers who began to take on the role of modern prime ministers. Continuity in Swedish affairs, especially after the death of Gustavus Adolphus, largely depended on Axel Oxenstierna, who played a central part in Swedish governments between 1611 and 1654. As Louis XIII's chief minister, Richelieu arranged support for the Lutheran Gustavus even though Richelieu was a cardinal of the Catholic church. His priority was *raison d'état* ("reason of state")—that is, the state's interest above all else. Richelieu silenced Protestants within France because they had become too independent, and he crushed noble and popular resistance to Louis's policies. He set up *intendants*—delegates from the king's council dispatched to the provinces— to oversee police, army, and financial affairs.

To justify the growth of state authority and the expansion of government bureaucracies, rulers carefully cultivated their royal images. James I of England explicitly argued that he ruled by divine right and was accountable only to God: "kings are not only God's lieutenant on earth, but even by God himself they are called gods." But words rarely sufficed to make the point, and rulers used displays at court to overawe their subjects. Already in the 1530s, the French court of Francis I numbered 1,600 people. Included were officials to handle finances, guard duty, clothing, and food as well as physicians, librarians, musicians, dwarfs, animal trainers, and a multitude of hangers-on. When the court changed residence, which it did frequently, no fewer than eighteen thousand horses were required to transport the people, furniture, and documents—not to mention the dogs and falcons for the royal hunt. Hunting and mock battles honed the military skills of the male courtiers. Francis once staged a mock combat at court involving twelve hundred "warriors," and he led a party to lay siege to a model town during which several players were accidentally killed.

Just as soldiers had to learn new drills for combat, courtiers had to learn to follow precise rituals. Court etiquette or "courtesy" had first been elaborated in Italy and spread from there to France, Spain, and other countries. In his influential treatise, *The Courtier* (1528), the Italian diplomat Baldassare Castiglione (1478–1529) depicted the ideal courtier as a gentleman who speaks in a refined language and carries himself with nobility and dignity in the service of his prince and his lady. Spain's king Philip IV (r. 1621–1665) translated this notion of courtesy into detailed regulations that set the wages, duties, and ceremonial functions of every courtier. At his new palace near Madrid, the courtiers lived amid extensive parks and formal gardens, artificial ponds and grottoes, an iron aviary (which led some critics to call the whole thing a "chicken coop"), a wild animal cage, a courtyard for bullfights, and rooms filled with sculptures and paintings. State funerals, public festivities, and court display, like the acquisition of art and the building of sumptuous palaces, served to underline the power and glory of the ruler.

Economic Crisis and Realignment

The devastation caused by the Thirty Years' War deepened an economic crisis that was already under way. After a century of rising prices, caused partly by massive transfers of gold and silver from the New World and partly by population growth, in the early 1600s prices began to level off and even to drop, and in most places population growth slowed. With fewer goods being produced, international trade fell into recession. Agricultural yields also declined. Just when states attempted to field ever-expanding standing armies, peasants and townspeople alike were less able to pay the escalating taxes needed to finance the wars. Famine and disease trailed grimly behind economic crisis and war, in some areas causing large-scale uprisings and revolts. Behind the scenes, the economic balance of power gradually shifted as northwestern Europe began to dominate international trade and broke the stranglehold of Spain and Portugal in the New World.

From Growth to Recession

By 1500, the cycle of demographic collapse and economic depression triggered by the Black Death of 1348 had passed. Even though religious and political turbulence led to population decline in some cities, such as war-torn Antwerp, other places grew rapidly: parts of Spain doubled in population, and England's population grew by 70 percent. The supply of precious metals swelled, too. Improvements in mining techniques in central Europe raised the output of silver and copper mines, and in the 1540s new silver mines had been discovered in Mexico and Peru. Spanish gold imports peaked in the 1550s, silver in the 1590s. (See "Taking Measure," page 508.) This flood of precious metals combined with population growth to fuel an astounding inflation in food prices in western Europe—400 percent in the sixteenth century—and a more moderate rise in the cost of manufactured goods. Wages rose much more slowly, at about half the rate of the increase in food prices, putting those at the bottom of the social scale in jeopardy.

When recession struck again after 1600, all the economic indicators slumped. After 1625, silver imports to Spain declined, in part because so many of the Native Americans who worked in Spanish colonial mines died from disease and in part because the ready supply of precious metals was progressively exhausted. Textile

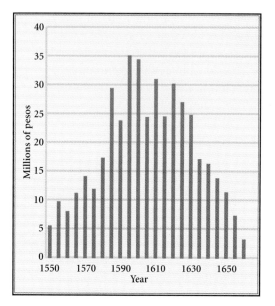

■ TAKING MEASURE The Rise and Fall of Silver Imports to Spain, 1550–1660

Gold and silver from the New World enabled the king of Spain to pursue aggressive policies in Europe and around the world. At what point did silver imports reach their highest level? Was the fall in silver imports precipitous or gradual? What can we conclude about the resources available to the Spanish king?

(From Earl J. Hamilton, *American Revolution and the Price Revolution in Spain, 1501–1650* [Cambridge: Harvard University Press, 1934].)

production fell in many countries and in some places nearly collapsed, largely because of decreased demand and a shrinking labor force. Even the relatively limited trade in African slaves stagnated, though its growth would resume after 1650 and skyrocket after 1700. African slaves were first transported to the new colony of Virginia in 1619, foreshadowing a major transformation of economic life in the New World colonies.

Demographic slowdown also signaled economic trouble. Overall, Europe's population may actually have declined, from 85 million in 1550 to 80 million in 1650. In the Mediterranean, growth apparently stopped in the 1570s. The most sudden reversal occurred in central Europe as a result of the Thirty Years' War: one-fourth of the inhabitants of the Holy Roman Empire perished in the 1630s and 1640s. The population continued to increase only in England and Wales, the Dutch Republic and the Spanish Netherlands, and Scandinavia.

Where the population stagnated or declined, agricultural prices dropped because of less demand, and farmers who produced for the market suffered. The price of grain fell most precipitously, causing many farmers to convert grain-growing land to pasture or vineyards. Interest in improvement of the land diminished. In some places, peasants abandoned their villages and left land to waste, as had happened during the plague epidemic of the late fourteenth century. The only country that emerged unscathed from this downturn was the Dutch Republic, principally because it had long excelled in agricultural innovation. Inhabiting Europe's most densely populated area, the Dutch developed systems of field drainage, crop rotation, and animal husbandry that provided high yields of grain for both people and animals. Their foreign trade, textile industry, crop production, and population all grew. After the Dutch, the English fared best; unlike the Spanish, the English never depended on New World gold and silver, and unlike most continental European countries, England escaped the direct impact of the Thirty Years' War.

Historians have long disagreed about the causes of the early-seventeenth-century recession. Some cite the inability of agriculture to support a growing population by the end of the sixteenth century; others blame the Thirty Years' War, the states' demands for more taxes, the irregularities in money supply resulting from rudimentary banking practices, or the waste caused by middle-class expenditures in the desire to emulate the nobility. To this list of causes, recent researchers have added climate change. Global cooling translated into advancing glaciers, falling temperatures, and great storms, like the one that blocked the escape of the Spanish Armada. Bad harvests, food shortages, and famine followed in short order.

Consequences of Economic Crisis

When grain harvests fell short, peasants immediately suffered because outside of England and the Dutch Republic, grain had replaced more expensive meat as the essential staple of most Europeans' diets. Peasants lived on bread, soup with a little fat or oil, peas or lentils, garden vegetables in season, and only occasionally a piece of meat or fish. Usually the adverse years differed from place to place, but from 1594 to 1597 most of Europe suffered from shortages that triggered revolts from Ireland to Muscovy. To head off social disorder, the English government drew up a new Poor Law in 1597 that required each community to support its poor. Many other governments also increased relief efforts.

Most people, however, did not respond to their dismal circumstances by rebelling or mounting insurrections. They simply left their huts and hovels and took to the road in search of food and charity. Overwhelmed officials recorded pitiful tales of suffering. Women and children died while waiting in line for food at convents or churches. Husbands left their wives and families to search for better conditions in other parishes or even other countries. Those left behind might be reduced to eating chestnuts, roots, bark, and grass. In eastern France in 1637, a witness reported, "The roads were paved with people. . . . Finally it came to cannibalism." Eventually compassion gave way to fear as these hungry vagabonds, who sometimes banded together to beg for bread, became more aggressive, occasionally threatening to burn a barn if they were not given food.

Successive bad harvests led to malnutrition, which weakened people and made them more susceptible to such epidemic diseases as the plague, typhoid fever, typhus, dysentery, smallpox, and influenza. Disease did not spare the rich, although many epidemics hit the poor hardest. The plague was feared most: in one year it could cause the death of up to half of a town's or village's population, and it struck with no discernible pattern. Nearly 5 percent of France's entire population died in the plague of 1628–1632.

Economic crisis heightened the contrast between prosperity and poverty. In England, the Dutch Republic, northern France, and northwestern Germany, the peasantry was disappearing: improvements gave some peasants the means to become farmers who rented substantial holdings, produced for the market, and in good times enjoyed relative comfort and higher status. Those who could not afford to plant new crops such as buckwheat or to use techniques that ensured higher yields became simple laborers with little or no land of their own. One-half to four-fifths of the peasants in Europe did not have enough land to support a family. They descended deeper into debt during difficult times and often lost their land to wealthier farmers or to city officials intent on developing rural estates. In the towns, widows who had been able to take over their late husbands' trade now found themselves excluded by the urban guilds or limited to short tenures.

Demographic historians have shown that European families reacted almost immediately to economic crisis. During bad harvests, they postponed marriages and had fewer children. When hard times passed, more people married and had more children. But even in the best of times, one-fifth to one-quarter of all children died in their first year, and half died before age twenty. Ten percent of women died in childbirth, and even in the richest homes, childbirth often occasioned an atmosphere of panic.

It might be assumed that families would have more children to compensate for high death rates, but from around 1600 to 1800, families in all ranks of society started to limit the number of children. Because methods of contraception were not widely known, they did this for the most part by marrying later; the average age at marriage during the seventeenth century rose from the early twenties to the late twenties. The average family had about four children. Poorer families seem to have had fewer children, wealthier ones more. Peasant couples, especially in eastern and southeastern Europe, had more children than urban couples because cultivation still required intensive manual labor.

The consequences of late marriage were profound. Young men and women were expected to put off marriage (*and* sexual intercourse) until their mid-to-late twenties—if they were among the lucky 50 percent who lived that long and not among the 10 percent who never married. Because both the Reformation and the Counter-Reformation stressed sexual fidelity and abstinence before marriage, the number of births out of wedlock was relatively small (2–5 percent of births); premarital intercourse was generally tolerated only after a couple had announced their engagement.

■ The Life of the Poor

This mid-seventeenth-century painting by the Dutch artist Adriaen Pietersz van de Venne depicts the poor peasant weighed down by his wife and child. An empty food bowl signifies their hunger. In retrospect, this painting seems unfair to the wife of the family; she is shown in clothes that are not nearly as tattered as her husband's and is portrayed entirely as a burden, rather than as a help in getting by in hard times. In reality, many poor men abandoned their homes in search of work, leaving their wives behind to cope with hungry children and what remained of the family farm.

(Allen Memorial Art Museum, Oberlin College, Oberlin, Ohio, Mrs. F. F. Prentiss Fund, 1960.)

The Economic Balance of Power

Just as the recession produced winners and losers among ordinary people, so, too, it created winners and losers among the competing states of Europe. The seventeenth-century downturn ended the dominance of Mediterranean economies, which had endured since the time of the Greeks and Romans, and ushered in the new powers of northwestern Europe with their growing Atlantic economies. With expanding populations and geographical positions that promoted Atlantic trade, England and the Dutch Republic vied with France to become the leading mercantile powers. Northern Italian industries were eclipsed; Spanish commerce with the New World dropped. Amsterdam replaced Seville, Venice, Genoa, and Antwerp as the center of European trade and commerce. The plague also had differing effects. Whereas central Europe and the Mediterranean countries took generations to recover from its ravages, northwestern Europe quickly replaced its lost population, no doubt because this area's people had suffered less from the effects of the Thirty Years' War and from the malnutrition related to the economic crisis.

All but the remnants of serfdom had disappeared in western Europe, but in eastern Europe nobles reinforced their dominance over peasants, and the burden of serfdom increased. The price rise of the sixteenth century had prompted Polish and eastern German nobles to expand their holdings and step up their production of grain for western markets. To raise production, they demanded more rent and dues from their peasants, who the government decreed had to stay in their villages. Although noble landlords lost income in the economic downturn of the first half of the seventeenth century, their peasants gained nothing. Those who were already dependent became serfs—completely tied to the land. In Muscovy, the complete enserfment of the peasantry would eventually be recognized in the Code of Laws in 1649. Although enserfment produced short-term profits for landlords, in the long run it retarded economic development in eastern Europe and kept most of the population in a stranglehold of illiteracy and hardship.

Competition for colonies overseas intensified because many European states, including Sweden and Denmark, considered it a branch of mercantilist policy. According to the doctrine of mercantilism, governments should sponsor policies to increase national wealth. To this end, they chartered private joint-stock companies to enrich investors by importing fish, furs, tobacco, and precious metals, if they could be found, and to develop new markets for European products. Because Spain and Portugal had divided among themselves the rich spoils of South America, other prospective colonizers had to carve niches in seemingly less hospitable places, especially North America and the Caribbean. Eventually the English, French, and Dutch would dominate commerce with these colonies (see Map 14.1, page 574).

In establishing permanent colonies, the Europeans created whole new communities across the Atlantic. Careful plans often fell afoul of the hazards of transatlantic shipping, however. Originally, the warm climate of Virginia made it an attractive destination for the Pilgrims, a small English sect that, unlike the Puritans, attempted to separate from the Church of England. But the *Mayflower,* which had sailed for Virginia with Pilgrim emigrants, landed far to the north in Massachusetts, where in 1620 the settlers founded New Plymouth Colony. As the religious situation for English Puritans worsened, wealthier people became willing to emigrate, and in 1629 a prominent group of Puritans incorporated themselves as the Massachusetts Bay Company. They founded a virtually self-governing colony headquartered in Boston.

Colonization gradually spread. Migrating settlers, including dissident Puritans, soon founded new settlements in Connecticut and Rhode Island. Catholic refugees from England established a much smaller colony in Maryland. By the 1640s, the British North American colonies had more than fifty thousand people—not including the Indians, whose numbers had been decimated in epidemics and wars—and the foundations of representative government in locally chosen colonial assemblies. By contrast, French Canada had only about three thousand European inhabitants by 1640. Because the French government refused to let Protestants emigrate from France and establish a foothold in the New World, it denied itself a ready population for the settling of permanent colonies abroad. Both England and France turned their attention to the Caribbean in the 1620s and 1630s when they occupied the islands of the West Indies after driving off the native Caribs. These islands would prove ideal for a plantation economy of tobacco and sugarcane.

A Clash of Worldviews

The countries that moved ahead economically in this period—England, the Dutch Republic, and to some extent France—turned out to be the most receptive to new secular worldviews. Although *secularization* did not entail a loss of religious faith, it did prompt a search for nonreligious explanations for political authority and natural phenomena. During the late sixteenth and early seventeenth centuries, art, political theory, and science all began to break some of their bonds with religion. A "scientific revolution" was in the making. Yet traditional attitudes such as belief in magic and witchcraft did not disappear. People of all classes accepted supernatural explanations for natural phenomena, a view only gradually and partially undermined by new ideas.

The Arts in an Age of Religious Conflict

A new form of artistic expression—professional theater—developed to express secular values in this age of conflict over religious beliefs. In previous centuries, traveling companies made their living by playing at major religious festivals and by repeating their performances in small towns and villages along the way. In London, Seville, and Madrid, the first professional acting companies performed before paying audiences in the 1570s. A huge outpouring of playwriting followed. The Spanish playwright Lope de Vega (1562–1635) alone wrote more than fifteen hundred plays. Between 1580 and 1640, three hundred English playwrights produced works for a hundred different acting companies. Theaters did a banner business despite Puritan opposition in England and Catholic objections in Spain. Shopkeepers, apprentices, lawyers, and court nobles crowded into open-air theaters to see everything from bawdy farces to profound tragedies.

The most enduring and influential playwright of the time was the Englishman William Shakespeare (1564–1616), son of a glovemaker, who wrote three dozen plays and acted in one of the chief troupes. Shakespeare never referred to religious disputes in his plays and did not set the action in contemporary England. Yet his works clearly reflected the political concerns of his age: the nature of power and the crisis of authority. Three of his greatest tragedies—*Hamlet* (1601), *King Lear* (1605), and *Macbeth* (1606)—show the uncertainty and even chaos that result when power is misappropriated or misused. In each play, family relationships are linked to questions about the legitimacy of government, just as they were for Elizabeth I herself. Hamlet's mother marries the man who murdered his royal father and usurped the crown; two of Lear's daughters betray him when he tries to divide his kingdom; Macbeth's wife persuades him to murder the king and seize the throne. One character in the final act describes the tragic story of Prince Hamlet as one "Of carnal, bloody, and unnatural acts;/Of accidental judgments, casual slaughters;/ Of deaths put on by cunning and forced cause." Like many real-life people, Shakespeare's tragic characters found little peace in the turmoil of their times.

Although many rulers commissioned paintings on secular subjects for their own uses, religion still played an important role in painting, especially in Catholic Europe. The popes competed with secular rulers to hire the most talented painters and sculptors. Pope Julius II, for example, engaged the Florentine Michelangelo Buonarroti (1475–1564) to paint the walls and ceiling of the Sistine Chapel and to prepare a tomb and sculpture for himself. Michelangelo's talents served to glorify a papacy under siege, just as other artists burnished the image of secular rulers.

In the late sixteenth century, the artistic style known as Mannerism departed abruptly from the Renaissance perspective of painters like Michelangelo. An almost

theatrical style, Mannerism allowed painters to distort perspective to convey a message or emphasize a theme. The most famous Mannerist painter, called El Greco because he was of Greek origin, trained in Venice and Rome before he moved to Spain in the 1570s. El Greco crowded figures or objects into every available space, used larger-than-life or elongated figures, and created new and often strange visual effects. The religious intensity of El Greco's pictures shows that faith still motivated many artists, as it did much political conflict.

■ **Mannerist Painting**

With its distortion of perspective, crowding of figures, and mysterious allusions, El Greco's painting The Dream of Philip II *(1577) is a typical Mannerist painting. Philip II can be seen in his usual black clothing with a lace ruffle as his only decoration.*

(© National Gallery, London.)

The most important new style was the baroque, which, like Mannerism, originated in the Italian states. Like many historical categories, *baroque* was not used as a label by people living at the time; in the eighteenth century, art critics coined the word to mean shockingly bizarre, confused, and extravagant, and until the late nineteenth century, art historians and collectors largely disdained the baroque. In place of the Renaissance emphasis on harmonious design, unity, and clarity, the baroque featured exaggerated lighting, intense emotions, release from restraint, and even a kind of artistic sensationalism.

Closely tied to the Counter-Reformation, the baroque melodramatically reaffirmed the emotional depths of the Catholic faith and glorified both church and monarchy. The style spread from Rome to other Italian states and then into central Europe. The Catholic Habsburg territories, including Spain and the Spanish Netherlands, embraced the style. The Spanish built baroque churches in their American colonies as part of their massive conversion campaign. Within Europe, Protestant countries largely resisted the baroque, as we can see by comparing Flemish painters from the Spanish Netherlands with Dutch artists. The first great baroque painter was an Italian-trained Fleming, Peter Paul Rubens (1577–1640). A devout Catholic, Rubens painted vivid, exuberant pictures on religious themes, packed with figures. His was an extension of the theatrical baroque style, conveying ideas through broad gestures and dramatic poses. The great Dutch Protestant painters of the next generation, such as Rembrandt van Rijn (1606–1669), sometimes used biblical subjects, but their pictures were more realistic and focused on everyday scenes. Many of them suggested the Protestant concern for an inner life and personal faith rather than the public expression of religiosity.

Differences in musical style also reflected religious divisions. The new Protestant churches developed their own distinct music, which differentiated their worship from the Catholic Mass and also marked them as Lutheran or Calvinist. Unlike Catholic services, for which professional musicians sang in Latin, Protestant services invited the entire congregation to sing, thereby encouraging participation. Martin Luther, an accomplished lute player, composed many hymns in German, including "Ein' feste Burg" ("A Mighty Fortress"). Protestants sang hymns before going into battle, and Protestant martyrs sang before their executions. Lutheran composers developed a new form, the strophic hymn, or chorale, a religious text set to a tune that is then enriched through harmony. Calvinist congregations, in keeping with their emphasis on simplicity and austerity, often sang in unison and avoided harmony.

A new secular musical form, the opera, grew up parallel to the baroque style in the visual arts. First influential in the Italian states, opera combined music, drama, dance, and scenery in a grand sensual display, often with themes chosen to please the ruler and the aristocracy. Operas could be based on typically baroque sacred subjects or on traditional stories. Like Shakespeare, opera composers often turned to familiar stories their audiences would recognize and readily follow. One of the

■ Baroque Painting

The Flemish baroque painter Peter Paul Rubens used monumental canvases to glorify the French queen Marie de Medici, wife of Henry IV and mother of Louis XIII. Between 1622 and 1625, Rubens painted twenty-four panels like this one to decorate Marie's residence in Paris (some were more than twenty feet wide). Baroque style is evident in its gigantic size, the imposing figures captured in rich colors, and the epic setting to exalt a secular ruler. In this scene, Henry is shown handing over government to his wife on behalf of his young son (Henry was assassinated in 1610).
(Giraudon/Art Resource, NY.)

most innovative composers of opera was Claudio Monteverdi (1567–1643), whose work contributed to the development of both opera and the orchestra. His earliest operatic production, *Orfeo* (1607), was the first to require an orchestra of about forty instruments and to include instrumental as well as vocal sections.

The Natural Laws of Politics

In reaction to the wars over religious beliefs, jurists and scholars not only began to defend the primacy of state interests over those of religious conformity but also insisted on secular explanations for politics. Machiavelli had pointed in this direction with his prescriptions for Renaissance princes in the early sixteenth century, but the intellectual movement gathered steam in the aftermath of the religious violence unleashed by the Reformation. Religious toleration could not take hold until government could be organized on some principle other than one king, one faith. The French *politiques* Michel de Montaigne and Jean Bodin and the Dutch jurist Hugo Grotius started the search for those principles.

Michel de Montaigne (1533–1592) was a French magistrate who resigned his office in the midst of the wars of religion to write about the need for tolerance and open-mindedness. Although himself a Catholic, Montaigne painted on the beams of his study the words "All that is certain is that nothing is certain." To capture this need for personal reflection in an age of religious turmoil, he invented the essay as a short and thoughtful form of expression. He revived the ancient doctrine of skepticism, which held that total certainty is never attainable—a doctrine, like toleration of religious differences, that was repugnant to Protestants and Catholics alike, both of whom were certain that their religion was the right one. Montaigne also questioned the common European habit of calling newly discovered peoples in the New World barbarous and savage: "Everyone gives the title of barbarism to everything that is not in use in his own country."

The French Catholic lawyer Jean Bodin (1530–1596) sought systematic secular answers to the problem of disorder in *The Six Books of the Republic* (1576). Comparing the different forms of government throughout history, he identified three basic types of sovereignty: monarchy, aristocracy, and democracy. Only strong monarchical power offered hope for maintaining order, he insisted. Bodin rejected any doctrine of the right to resist tyrannical authority: "I denied that it was the function of a good man or of a good citizen to offer violence to his prince for any reason, however great a tyrant he might be" (and, it might be added, whatever his ideas on religion). Bodin's ideas helped lay the foundation for absolutism, the idea that the monarch should be the sole and uncontested source of power. Nonetheless, the very discussion of types of governments in the abstract implied that they might be subject to choice rather than simply being God-given, as most rulers maintained.

During the Dutch revolt against Spain, the jurist Hugo Grotius (1583–1645) gave new meaning to the notion of "natural law"—laws of nature that give legitimacy to government and stand above the actions of any particular ruler or religious group. Grotius argued that natural law stood beyond the reach of either secular or divine authority; it would be valid even if God did not exist. Natural law should govern politics, by this account, not Scripture, religious authority, or tradition. Such ideas got Grotius into trouble with both Catholics and Protestants. When the Dutch Protestant government arrested him, his wife helped him escape prison by hiding him in a chest of books. Grotius was one of the first to argue that international conventions should govern the treatment of prisoners of war and the making of peace treaties.

At the same time that Grotius expanded the principles of natural law, many jurists worked on codifying the huge amount of legislation and jurisprudence devoted to legal forms of torture. Most states and the courts of the Catholic church used torture when the crime was very serious and the evidence seemed to point to a particular defendant but no definitive proof had been established. The judges ordered torture—hanging the accused by the hands with a rope thrown over a beam, pressing the legs in a leg screw, or just tying the hands very tightly—to extract a confession, which had to be given with a medical expert and notary present and had to be repeated without torture. Children, pregnant women, the elderly, aristocrats, kings, and even professors were exempt.

Grotius's conception of natural law directly challenged the use of torture. To be in accord with natural law, Grotius argued, governments had to defend natural rights, which he defined as life, body, freedom, and honor. Grotius's ideas would influence John Locke and the American revolutionaries of the eighteenth century: although Grotius did not encourage rebellion in the name of natural law or rights, he did hope that someday all governments would adhere to these principles and stop killing their own and one another's subjects in the name of religion. Natural law and natural rights would play an important role in the founding of constitutional governments from the 1640s forward and in the establishment of various charters of human rights in our own time.

Origins of the Scientific Revolution

Although the Catholic and Protestant churches encouraged the study of science and many prominent scientists were themselves clerics, the search for a secular, scientific method of determining the laws of nature eventually challenged the traditional accounts of natural phenomena. Christian doctrine had incorporated the scientific teachings of ancient philosophers, especially Ptolemy and Aristotle; now these came into question. A revolution in astronomy challenged the Ptolemaic view, endorsed by the Catholic church, which held that the sun revolved around the earth. Remarkable advances took place in medicine, too, which laid the foundations for modern anatomy and pharmacology. By the early seventeenth century, a new scientific method had been established based on a combination of experimental observation and mathematical deduction. Conflicts between the new science and religion followed almost immediately.

The "new science" began with the first subject ever studied by scientists, astronomy. The traditional account of the movement of the heavens derived from the second-century Greek astronomer Ptolemy, who put the earth at the center of the cosmos. Above the earth were fixed the moon, the stars, and the planets in concentric crystalline spheres; beyond these fixed spheres dwelt God and the angels. The planets revolved around the earth at the command of God. In this view, the sun revolved around the earth; the heavens were perfect and unchanging, and the earth was "corrupted." Ptolemy insisted that the planets revolved in perfectly circular orbits (because circles were more "perfect" than other figures). To account for the actual elliptical paths that could be observed and calculated, he posited orbits within orbits, or epicycles.

In 1543, the Polish clergyman Nicolaus Copernicus (1473–1543) attacked the Ptolemaic account in his treatise *On the Revolution of the Celestial Spheres*. He argued that the earth and planets revolved around the sun, a view known as *heliocentrism* (a sun-centered universe). Copernicus discovered that by placing the sun instead of the earth at the center of the system of spheres, he could eliminate many epicycles from the calculations. In other words, he claimed that the heliocentric view simplified the mathematics.

Copernicus's views began to attract widespread attention in the early seventeenth century, when astronomers systematically collected evidence that undermined the Ptolemaic view. A leader among them was the Danish astronomer Tycho Brahe (1546–1601), whose observations of a new star in 1572 and a comet in 1577 called into question the Aristotelian view that the universe was unchanging. Brahe still rejected heliocentrism, but the assistant he employed when he moved to Prague in 1599, Johannes Kepler (1571–1630), was converted to the Copernican view. Kepler continued Brahe's collection of planetary observations and used the evidence to develop his three laws of planetary motion, published between 1609 and 1619. Kepler's laws provided mathematical backing for heliocentrism and directly challenged the claim long held, even by Copernicus, that planetary motion was circular. Kepler's first law stated that the orbits of the planets are ellipses, with the sun always at one focus of the ellipse.

The Italian Galileo Galilei (1564–1642) provided more evidence to support the heliocentric view and also challenged the doctrine that the heavens were perfect and unchanging. In 1609, he developed an improved telescope and then observed the earth's moon, four satellites of Jupiter, the phases of Venus (a cycle of changing physical appearances), and sunspots. The moon, the planets, and the sun were no more perfect than the earth, he insisted, and the shadows he could see on the moon could only be the product of hills and valleys like those on earth. Galileo portrayed the earth as a moving part of a larger system, only one of many planets revolving around the sun, not as the fixed center of a single, closed universe. Because he recognized the utility of the new science for everyday projects and hoped to appeal to a lay audience of merchants and aristocrats, Galileo was the first scientist to publish his studies in the vernacular (Italian) rather than in Latin.◆

◆ For a primary source that focuses on the new science, see Document 40, Galileo Galilei, "Letter to the Grand Duchess Christina."

Since his discoveries challenged the Bible as well as the commonsensical view that the sun rises and sets while the earth stands still, Galileo's work alarmed the Catholic church. In 1616, the church forbade Galileo to teach that the earth moves and in 1633 accused him of not obeying the earlier order. Forced to appear before the Inquisition, he agreed to publicly recant his assertion that the earth moves to save himself from torture and death. Afterward he lived under house arrest and could publish his work only in the Dutch Republic, which had become a haven for iconoclastic scientists and thinkers.

Startling breakthroughs took place in medicine, too. Until the mid-sixteenth century, medical knowledge in Europe had been based on the writings of the second-century Greek physician Galen, a contemporary of Ptolemy. In the same year that Copernicus challenged the traditional account in astronomy (1543), the Flemish scientist Andreas Vesalius (1514–1564) did the same for anatomy. He published a new illustrated anatomical text, *On the Construction of the Human Body*, that revised Galen's work by drawing on public dissections in the medical faculties of European universities. Theophrastus Bombastus von Hohenheim, better known as Paracelsus (1493–1541), went even further than Vesalius. He burned Galen's text at the University of Basel, where he was a professor of medicine. Paracelsus experimented with new drugs, performed operations (at the time most academic physicians taught medical theory, not practice), and pursued his interests in magic, alchemy, and astrology. He helped establish the modern science of pharmacology.

The Englishman William Harvey (1578–1657) also used dissection to examine the circulation of blood within the body, demonstrating how the heart worked as a pump. The heart and its valves were "a piece of machinery," Harvey claimed. They obeyed mechanical laws just as the planets and earth revolved around the sun in a mechanical universe. Nature could be understood by experiment and rational deduction, not by following traditional authorities.

In the 1630s, the European intellectual elite began to accept the new scientific views. Ancient learning, the churches and their theologians, and even cherished popular beliefs seemed to be undermined by a new standard of truth—scientific method, which was based on systematic experiments and rational deduction. Two men were chiefly responsible for spreading the prestige of scientific method, the English politician Sir Francis Bacon (1561–1626) and the French mathematician and philosopher René Descartes (1596–1650). Respectively, they represented the two essential processes of scientific method: (1) inductive reasoning through observation and experimental research and (2) deductive reasoning from self-evident principles.

In *The Advancement of Learning* (1605), Bacon attacked reliance on ancient writers and optimistically predicted that scientific method would lead to social progress. The minds of the medieval scholars, he said, had been "shut up in the cells of a few authors (chiefly Aristotle, their dictator) as their persons were shut up in the cells of monasteries and colleges." Knowledge, in Bacon's view, must be empirically based—that is, gained by observation and experiment. Bacon ardently supported the scientific method over popular beliefs, which he rejected as "fables and popular errors." Claiming that God had called the Catholic church "to account for their degenerate manners and ceremonies," Bacon looked to the Protestant English state, which he served as lord chancellor, for leadership on the road to scientific advancement.

Although Descartes agreed with Bacon's denunciation of traditional learning, he saw that the attack on tradition might only replace the dogmatism of the churches with the skepticism of Montaigne—that nothing at all was certain. A Catholic who served in the Thirty Years' War, Descartes insisted that human reason could not only unravel the secrets of nature but also prove the existence of God. He aimed to establish the new science on more secure philosophical foundations, those of mathematics and logic. Not coincidentally, Descartes invented analytic geometry. In his *Discourse on Method* (1637), he argued that mathematical and mechanical principles provided the key to understanding all of nature, including the actions of people and states. All prior assumptions must be repudiated in favor of one elementary principle: "I think, therefore I am." Everything else could—and should—be doubted, but even doubt showed the certain existence of someone thinking. Begin with the simple and go on to the complex, he asserted, and believe only those ideas that present themselves "clearly and distinctly." Although Descartes hoped to secure the authority of both church and state, his reliance on human reason alone irritated authorities, and his books were banned in many places. He moved to the Dutch Republic to work in peace. Scientific research, like economic growth, became centered in the northern, Protestant countries, where it was less constrained by church control.

Magic and Witchcraft

Despite the new emphasis on clear reasoning, observation, and independence from past authorities, science had not yet become separate from magic. Paracelsus and other scholars studied alchemy alongside other scientific pursuits: magic and science were still closely linked. In a world in which most people believed in astrology, magical healing, prophecy, and ghosts, it is hardly surprising that many of Europe's learned people also firmly believed in witchcraft, the exercise of magical powers gained by a pact with the devil. The same Jean Bodin who argued against religious fanaticism insisted on death for witches—and for those magistrates who would not prosecute them. In France alone, 345 books and pamphlets on witchcraft appeared between 1550 and 1650. Trials of witches peaked in Europe between 1560 and 1640, the very time of the celebrated breakthroughs of the new science.

■ **Persecution of Witches**
This engraving from a pamphlet account of witch trials in England in 1589 shows three women hanged as accused witches. At their feet are frogs and toads, which were supposed to be the witches' "famil-iars," sent by the devil to help them ruin the lives of their neighbors by causing disease or untimely deaths among people and livestock. The ferret on the woman's lap was reported to be the devil himself in disguise.
(Lambeth Palace Library.)

Montaigne was one of the few to speak out against executing accused witches: "It is taking one's conjectures rather seriously to roast someone alive for them," he wrote in 1580.

Belief in witches was not new in the sixteenth century. Witches had long been thought capable of almost anything: passing through walls, flying through the air, destroying crops, and causing personal catastrophes from miscarriage to demonic possession. What was new was the official persecution, justified by the notion that witches were agents of Satan whom the righteous must oppose. In a time of economic crisis, plague, warfare, and the clash of religious differences, witchcraft trials provided an outlet for social stress and anxiety, legitimated by state power. At the same time, the trials seem to have been part of the religious-reform movement itself. Denunciation and persecution of witches coincided with the spread of reform, both Protestant and Catholic. The trials concentrated especially in the German lands of the Holy Roman Empire, the boiling cauldron of the Thirty Years' War.

The victims of the persecution were overwhelmingly female: women accounted for 80 percent of the accused witches in about 100,000 trials in Europe and North America during the sixteenth and seventeenth centuries. About one-third were sentenced to death. Before 1400, when witchcraft trials were rare, nearly half of those accused had been men. What explains the gender difference? Some historians argue that the trials expressed a fundamental hatred of women that came to a head dur-

IMPORTANT DATES

1517	Martin Luther criticizes sale of indulgences and other church practices; the Reformation begins	1598	French Wars of Religion end with Edict of Nantes
		1618	Thirty Years' War begins
1529	Henry VIII is declared head of the Anglican church	1619	First African slaves arrive in the colony of Virginia
1545–1563	Council of Trent	1629	English Puritans set up the Massachusetts Bay Company and begin to colonize New England
1555	Peace of Augsburg		
1571	Battle of Lepanto marks victory of West over Ottomans at sea	1633	Galileo Galilei is forced to recant his support of heliocentrism
1572	St. Bartholomew's Day massacre (August 24)	1648	Peace of Westphalia ends the Thirty Years' War
1588	Defeat of the Spanish Armada by England		

ing conflicts over the Reformation. Official descriptions of witchcraft oozed lurid details of sexual orgies, incest, homosexuality, and cannibalism, in which women acted as the devil's sexual slaves. Yet a social dimension also helps explain the prominence of women. The poorest and most socially marginal people in most communities were elderly spinsters and widows. Because they were thought likely to hanker after revenge on those more fortunate, they were singled out as witches. Another commonly accused woman was the midwife, who was a prime target for suspicion when a baby or mother died in childbirth.

Witchcraft trials declined when scientific thinking about causes and effects raised questions about the evidence used in court: how could judges or jurors be certain that someone was a witch? The tide turned everywhere at about the same time, as physicians, lawyers, judges, and even clergy came to suspect that accusations were based on popular superstition and peasant untrustworthiness. In 1682, a French royal decree treated witchcraft as fraud and imposture, meaning that the law did not recognize anyone as a witch. In 1693, the jurors who had convicted twenty witches in Salem, Massachusetts, recanted, claiming: "We confess that we ourselves were not capable to understand. . . . We justly fear that we were sadly deluded and mistaken." The Salem jurors had not stopped believing in witches; they had simply lost confidence in their ability to identify them. When physicians and judges had believed in witches and persecuted them officially, with torture, witches had gone to their deaths in record numbers. But when the same groups distanced themselves from popular beliefs, the trials and the executions stopped.

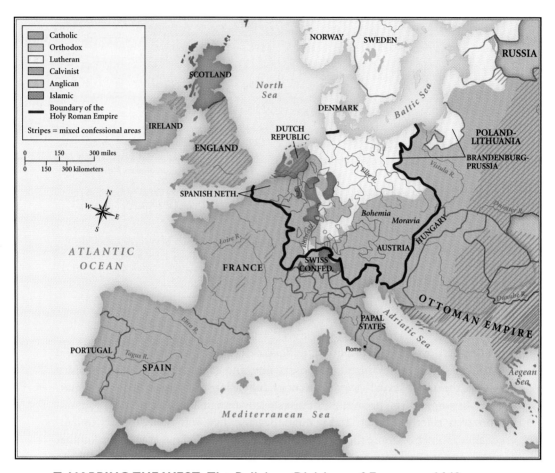

■ MAPPING THE WEST The Religious Divisions of Europe, c. 1648
The Peace of Westphalia recognized major religious divisions within Europe that have endured for the most part to the present day. Catholicism dominated in southern Europe, Lutheranism had its stronghold in northern Europe, and Calvinism flourished along the Rhine River. In southeastern Europe, the Islamic Ottoman Turks accommodated the Greek Orthodox Christians under their rule but bitterly fought the Catholic Austrian Habsburgs for control of Hungary.

Conclusion

The witchcraft persecutions reflected the traumas of these times of religious war and economic decline. Marauding armies combined with economic depression, disease, and the threat of starvation to shatter the lives of many ordinary Europeans, while religious conflicts shaped the destinies of every European power in this period. These conflicts began with the Protestant Reformation, which dispelled forever the Christian humanist dream of peace and unity, and came to a head from

1618 to 1648 in the Thirty Years' War, which cut a path of destruction through central Europe and involved most of the European powers. Shocked by the effects of religious violence, European rulers agreed to a peace that effectively removed disputes between Catholics and Protestants from the international arena.

The growing separation of political motives from religious ones did not mean that violence or conflict had ended, however. Struggles for religious uniformity within states would continue, though on a smaller scale. Bigger armies required more state involvement, and almost everywhere rulers emerged from these decades of conflict with expanded powers. The growth of state power directly changed the lives of ordinary people: more men went into the armies, and most families paid higher taxes. The constant extension of state power is one of the defining themes of modern history; religious warfare gave it a jump-start.

For all their increased power, rulers could not control economic, social, or intellectual trends, much as they often tried. The economic downturn of the seventeenth century produced unexpected consequences for European states even while it made life miserable for many ordinary people. Economic power and vibrancy shifted from the Mediterranean world to the northwest because the countries of northwestern Europe—England, France, and the Dutch Republic especially—suffered less from the fighting of the Thirty Years' War and recovered more quickly from the loss of population and production during bad times.

In the face of violence and uncertainty, some began to look for secular alternatives in art, politics, and science. Although it would be foolish to claim that everyone's mental universe changed because of the clash between religious and secular worldviews, a truly monumental shift in attitudes had begun. Secularization combined a growing interest in nonreligious forms of art, such as theater and opera, the search for nonreligious foundations of political authority, and the establishment of scientific method as the standard of truth. Proponents of these changes did not renounce their religious beliefs or even hold them less fervently, but they did insist that attention to state interests and scientific knowledge could serve as a brake on religious violence and popular superstitions. The search for order in the aftermath of religious warfare would continue in the decades to come.

Suggested References for further reading and online research appear on page SR-18 at the back of the book.

www.bedfordstmartins.com/huntconcise   See the ONLINE STUDY GUIDE to assess your mastery of the material covered in this chapter.

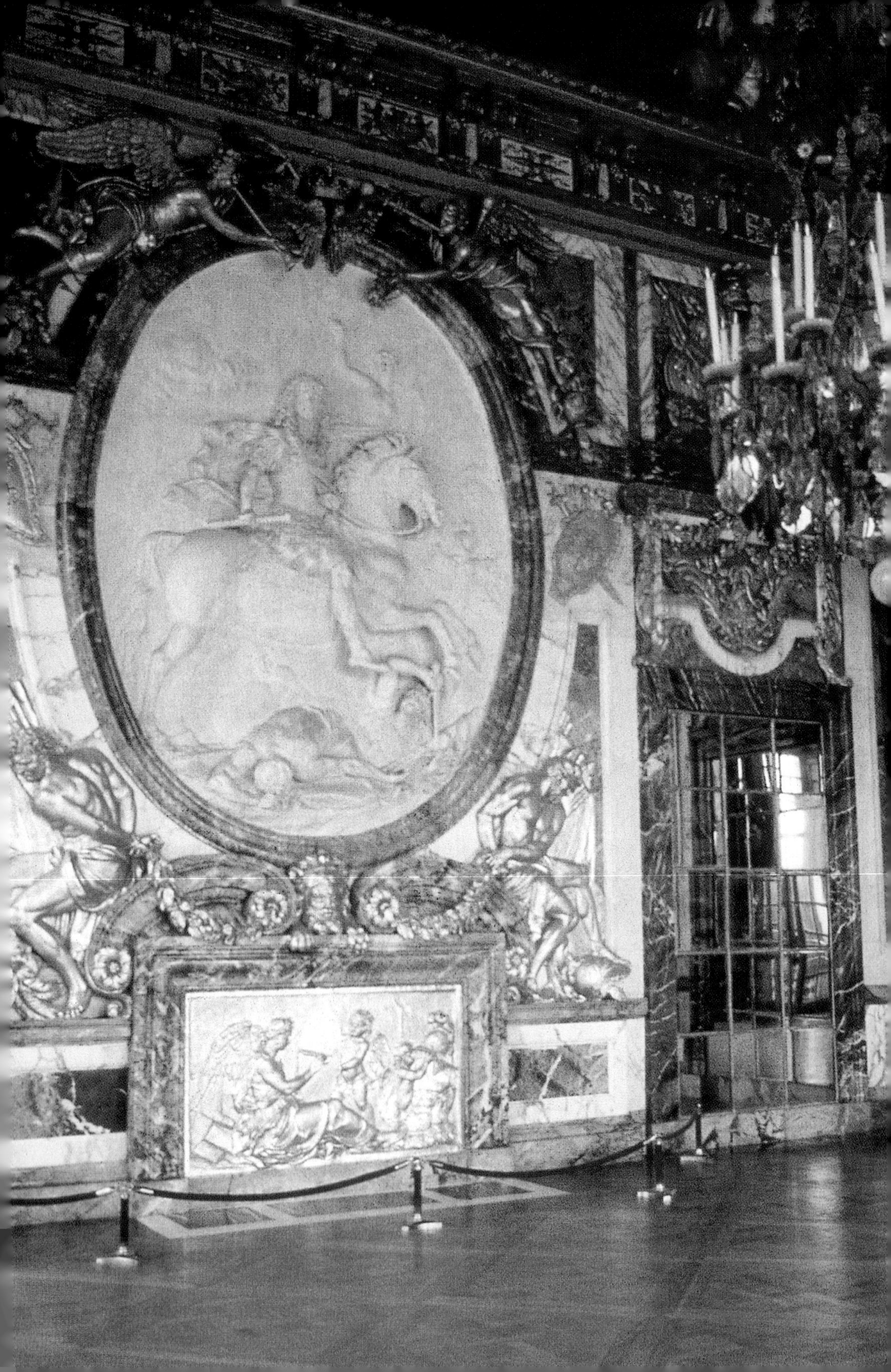

13

State Building and the Search for Order

1648–1690

I N ONE OF HER HUNDREDS OF LETTERS TO HER DAUGHTER, the French noblewoman Marie de Sévigné (1626–1696) told a disturbing story about a well-known cook. The cook got upset when he did not have enough roast for several unexpected guests at a dinner for King Louis XIV. Early the next morning, when the fish he had ordered did not arrive, the cook rushed up to his room, put his sword against the door, and, on the third try, ran it through his heart. The fish arrived soon after. The king regretted the trouble his visit had caused, but others soon filled in for the dead cook. That evening, Sévigné wrote, there was "a very good dinner, light refreshments later, and then supper, a walk, cards, hunting, everything scented with daffodils, everything magical."

It is difficult now for us to comprehend how anyone could care that much about a shipment of fish. The story nonetheless reveals an important aspect of state building in the seventeenth century: to extend state authority, which had been challenged during the wars over religion and threatened by economic recession, many rulers created an aura of overwhelming power and brilliance around themselves. Louis XIV, like many rulers, believed that he reigned by divine right. He served as God's lieutenant on earth and even claimed certain godlike qualities. The great gap between the ruler and ordinary subjects accounts for the extreme reaction of Louis's cook, and even leading nobles such as Sévigné came to see the king and his court as somehow "magical."

Louis XIV's model of state building was known as *absolutism*, a system of government in which the ruler claimed sole and uncontestable power. Although absolutism exerted great influence, especially in central and eastern Europe, it faced

■ **Louis XIV in Roman Splendor**
Images of Louis appear everywhere in his chateau at Versailles. This plaster relief by Antoine Coysevox in the Salon de la Guerre *(War Hall) represents Louis as Mars, the Roman god of war, riding roughshod over his enemies.* (Giraudon/Art Resource, NY.)

competition from *constitutionalism,* a system in which the ruler had to share power with parliaments made up of elected representatives. Constitutionalism led to weakness in Poland-Lithuania, but it provided a strong foundation for state power in England, the English North American colonies, and the Dutch Republic. Constitutionalism triumphed in England, however, only after one king had been executed as a traitor and another had been deposed.

These two methods of state building faced similar challenges in the mid-seventeenth century. Competition in the international arena required resources, and all states raised taxes, provoking popular protests and rebellions. The wars over religion that had culminated in the Thirty Years' War (1618–1648) left many economies in dire straits, and, even more significant, they created a need for new explanations of political authority. Monarchs still relied on religion to justify their divine right to rule, but they increasingly sought secular defenses of their powers, too.

The search for order took place not only at the level of states and rulers but also in intellectual, cultural, and social life. In science, the Englishman Isaac Newton explained the regular movement of the universe with the law of gravitation and thereby consolidated the scientific revolution. Artists sought means of glorifying power and expressing order and symmetry in new fashion. As states consolidated their power, elites endeavored to distinguish themselves more clearly from the lower orders. The upper classes emulated the manners developed at court and tried in every way to distance themselves from anything viewed as vulgar or lower class. Officials, clergy, and laypeople all worked to reform the poor, now seen as a major source of disorder. Whether absolutist or constitutionalist, seventeenth-century states all aimed to extend control over their subjects' lives.

Louis XIV: Model of Absolutism

French king Louis XIV (r. 1643–1715) personified the absolutist ruler who shared his power with no one. Louis personally made all important state decisions and left no room for dissent. In 1651, he reputedly told the Paris high court of justice, "*L'état, c'est moi*" ("I am the state"), emphasizing that state authority rested in him personally. Louis cleverly manipulated the affections and ambitions of his courtiers, chose as his ministers middle-class men who owed everything to him, built up Europe's largest army, and snuffed out every hint of religious or political opposition. Yet the absoluteness of his power should not be exaggerated. Like all rulers of his time, Louis depended on the cooperation of many others: local officials who enforced his decrees, peasants and artisans who joined his armies and paid his taxes, creditors who loaned crucial funds, and nobles who rather than stay home and cause trouble joined court festivities organized to glorify the king.

The Fronde, 1648–1653

Louis XIV built on a long French tradition of increasing centralization of state authority, but before he could extend it, he had to weather a series of revolts known as the *Fronde*. Derived from the French word for a child's slingshot, the term was used by critics to signify that the revolts were mere child's play. In fact, they posed an unprecedented threat to the French crown. Louis was only five when he came to the throne in 1643 upon the death of his father, Louis XIII. Louis XIV's mother, Anne of Austria, and her Italian-born adviser and rumored lover Cardinal Mazarin (1602–1661) ruled in the young monarch's name. To meet the financial pressure of fighting the Thirty Years' War, Mazarin sold new offices, raised taxes, and forced creditors to extend loans to the government. In 1648, a coalition of his opponents presented him with a charter of demands that, if granted, would have given the parlements (high courts) a form of constitutional power with the right to approve new taxes. Mazarin responded by arresting the coalition's leaders. He soon faced a series of revolts that at one time or another involved nearly every social group in France.

The Fronde posed an immediate menace to the young king. Fearing for his safety, his mother and members of his court took Louis and fled Paris. As civil war threatened, Mazarin and Anne agreed to compromise with the parlements. The nobles then tried to reassert their own claims to power by raising private armies. The middle and lower classes chafed at the constant tax increases and in some places organized revolts. Conflicts erupted throughout the kingdom, and rampaging soldiers devastated rural areas and disrupted commerce.

Neither the nobles nor the judges of the parlements really wanted to overthrow the king; they simply wanted a greater share in power. But Louis XIV never forgot the humiliation and uncertainty that marred his childhood. Years later he recalled an incident in which a band of Parisians invaded his bedchamber to determine whether he had fled the city, and he declared the event an affront not only to himself but also to the state. His own policies as ruler would be designed to prevent the repetition of any such revolts.

The Fronde, 1648–1653

Court Culture as a Form of State Power

When Cardinal Mazarin died in 1661, Louis XIV decided to rule without a first minister. He described the dangers of his situation in memoirs he wrote later for his son's instruction: "Everywhere was disorder. My Court as a whole was still very far removed from the sentiments in which I trust you will find it." Louis listed many other problems in the kingdom, but none occupied him more than his attempts to control France's leading nobles. Typically quarrelsome, the French nobles had long exercised local authority by maintaining their own fighting forces, meting out justice on their estates, arranging jobs for underlings, and resolving their own conflicts through dueling.

Louis set out to domesticate the warrior nobles by replacing violence with court ritual. Using a systematic policy of bestowing pensions, offices, honors, gifts, and the threat of disfavor or punishment, he made himself the center of French power and culture. The aristocracy vied for his favor, attended the ballets and theatricals he put on, and learned the rules of etiquette he supervised. Great nobles competed for the honor of holding his shirt when he dressed; foreign ambassadors squabbled for places near him; and royal mistresses basked in the glow of his personal favor. In a typically acerbic comment, Louis de Rouvroy, duke of Saint-Simon (1675–1755) complained, "There was nothing he [Louis XIV] liked so much as flattery . . . the coarser and clumsier it was, the more he relished it."◆ Madame de Lafayette described the effects on court life in her novel *The Princess of Clèves* (1678): "The Court gravitated around ambition. Nobody was tranquil or indifferent—everybody was busily trying to better his or her position by pleasing, by helping, or by hindering somebody else." Occasionally the results were tragic, as in the suicide of the cook recounted by Marie de Sévigné.

Louis XIV appreciated the political uses of every form of art. Mock battles, extravaganzas, theatrical performances, even the king's dinner—Louis's daily life was a public performance designed to enhance his prestige. Calling himself the Sun King, Louis adorned his court with statues of Apollo, Greek god of the sun, and emulated the style of ancient Roman emperors. Sculpture and paintings adorned his palace; commissioned histories vaunted his achievements; and coins and medals spread his likeness throughout the realm.

The king's officials treated the arts as a branch of government. Louis's ministers set up royal academies of dance, painting, architecture, and music and took control of the Académie française (French Academy), which to this day decides on correct usage of the French language. A royal furniture workshop at the Gobelins tapestry works on the outskirts of Paris turned out the delicate and ornate pieces whose style bore the king's name. Louis's government also regulated the number and locations of theaters and closely censored all forms of publication.

Music and theater enjoyed special prominence. Louis commissioned operas to celebrate royal marriages, baptisms, and military victories. The king himself danced in ballets if a role seemed especially important. Playwrights presented their new plays directly to the court. Pierre Corneille and Jean-Baptiste Racine wrote tragedies

---

◆ For a firsthand account of life in Louis XIV's court, see Document 41, Louis de Rouvroy, duke of Saint-Simon, "Memoirs."

set in Greece or Rome that celebrated the new aristocratic virtues that Louis aimed to inculcate: a reverence for order and self-control.

Louis glorified his image as well through massive public works projects. Military facilities, such as veterans' hospitals and new fortified towns on the frontiers, represented his military might. Urban improvements, such as the reconstruction of the Louvre palace in Paris, proved his wealth. But his most ambitious project was the construction of a new palace at Versailles, twelve miles from the turbulent capital. Building began in the 1660s, and by 1685, the frenzied effort engaged thirty-six thousand workers, not including the thousands of troops who diverted a local river to supply water for pools and fountains. Even the gardens designed by landscape architect André Le Nôtre reflected the spirit of Louis XIV's rule: their geometrical arrangements and clear lines showed that art and design could tame nature and that order and control defined the exercise of power. Versailles symbolized Louis's success in reining in the nobility and dominating Europe, and other monarchs eagerly mimicked French fashion and often conducted their business in French.

■ **Palace of Versailles**
In this defining statement of his ambitions, Louis XIV emphasized his ability to impose his personal will even on nature itself. The sheer size and precise geometrical design of the palace underlined the presence of an all-powerful personality—that of the Sun King. The palace became a national historical monument in 1837 and was used for many momentous historical occasions, including the signing of the peace treaty after World War I. (Giraudon/Art Resource, NY.)

By the time Louis actually moved from the Louvre to Versailles in 1682, he had reigned as monarch for thirty-nine years. Fifteen thousand people crowded into the palace's apartments, including all the highest military officers, the ministers of state, and the separate households of each member of the royal family. After the death of his queen in 1683, Louis secretly married his mistress, Françoise d'Aubigné, marquise de Maintenon, and conducted most state affairs from her apartments at the palace. De Maintenon's opponents at court complained that she controlled all the appointments, but her efforts focused on her own projects, including her favorite: the founding in 1686 of a royal school for girls from impoverished noble families. She also inspired one of Louis XIV's most critical decisions—to pursue his devotion to Catholicism.

Enforcing Religious Orthodoxy

Louis believed that he ruled by divine right. As Bishop Jacques-Benigne Bossuet (1627–1704) explained, "We have seen that kings take the place of God, who is the true father of the human species. We have also seen that the first idea of power which exists among men is that of the paternal power; and that kings are modeled on fathers." The king, like a father, should instruct his subjects in the true religion, or at least make sure that others did so.

Louis's campaign for religious conformity first focused on the Jansenists, Catholics whose doctrines and practices resembled some aspects of Protestantism. Following the posthumous publication of the book *Augustinus* (1640) by the Flemish theologian Cornelius Jansen (1585–1638), the Jansenists stressed the need for God's grace in achieving salvation. They emphasized the importance of original sin and insisted on an austere religious practice. Prominent among the Jansenists was Blaise Pascal (1623–1662), a mathematician of genius, who wrote his *Provincial Letters* (1656–1657) to defend Jansenism against charges of heresy. Many judges in the parlements likewise endorsed Jansenist doctrine.

Some questioned Louis's understanding of the finer points of doctrine: according to his German-born sister-in-law, Louis himself "has never read anything about religion, nor the Bible either, and just goes along believing whatever he is told." But Louis rejected any doctrine that gave priority to considerations of individual conscience over the demands of the official church hierarchy. He preferred teachings that stressed obedience to authority. Therefore, in 1660 he began enforcing various papal bulls (decrees) against Jansenism and closed down Jansenist theological centers. Jansenists were forced underground for the rest of his reign.

After many years of escalating pressure on the Calvinist Huguenots, Louis revoked the Edict of Nantes in 1685 and eliminated all of the Calvinists' rights. Louis considered the edict (1598), by which his grandfather Henry IV granted the Protestants religious freedom and civil rights, a temporary measure, and he fervently hoped to reconvert the Huguenots to Catholicism. He closed their churches and schools, banned all their public activities, and exiled those who refused to embrace the state religion. Thousands of Huguenots emigrated to England, Brandenburg-Prussia, or the Dutch Republic. Many now wrote for publications attacking Louis XIV's absolutism. Protestant European countries were shocked by this crackdown on religious dissent and would cite it when they went to war against Louis.

Extending State Authority at Home and Abroad

Louis XIV could not have enforced his religious policies without the services of a nationwide bureaucracy. *Bureaucracy*—a system of state officials carrying out orders according to a regular and routine line of authority—comes from *bureau*, the French word for "desk," which came to mean "office," in the sense of both a physical space and a position of authority. Louis extended the bureaucratic forms his predecessors had developed, especially the use of intendants, officials who held their positions directly from the king rather than owning their offices. Louis handpicked them to represent his will against entrenched local interests such as the parlements, provincial estates, and noble governors. The intendants reduced local powers over finances and insisted on more efficient tax collection. Despite the doubling of taxes in Louis's reign, the local rebellions that had so beset the crown from the 1620s to the 1640s subsided in the face of these better-organized state forces.

Louis's success in consolidating his authority depended on hard work, an eye for detail, and an ear to the ground. In his memoirs he explained his priorities:

> to be well-informed on an infinite number of matters about which we are supposed to know nothing; to elicit from our subjects what they hide from us with the greatest care; to discover the most remote opinions of our courtiers and the most hidden interests of those who come to us with quite contrary professions [claims].

To gather all this information, Louis relied on a series of talented ministers, usually of modest origins, who gained fame, fortune, and even noble status from serving the king. Most important among them was Jean-Baptiste Colbert (1619–1683), the son of a wool merchant turned royal official. Colbert had managed Mazarin's personal finances and worked his way up under Louis XIV to become controller-general, the head of royal finances, public works, and the navy. He founded a family dynasty that eventually produced five ministers of state, an archbishop, two bishops, and three generals.

Colbert used the bureaucracy to establish a new economic doctrine, *mercantilism*. According to mercantilist policy, governments must intervene to increase national wealth by whatever means possible. Such government intervention inevitably increased the role and eventually the number of bureaucrats needed. Under Colbert, the French government established overseas trading companies, granted manufacturing monopolies, and standardized production methods for textiles, paper, and soap. A government inspection system regulated the quality of finished goods and compelled all craftsmen to organize into guilds, in which masters could supervise the work of the journeymen and apprentices. To protect French production, Colbert rescinded many internal customs fees while enacting high foreign tariffs, which effectively cut imports of competing goods. To compete more effectively with England and the Dutch Republic, Colbert also subsidized shipbuilding, a policy that dramatically expanded the number of seaworthy vessels. Such mercantilist measures aimed to ensure France's prominence in world markets and to provide the resources needed to fight wars against the increasingly long list of enemies. Although later economists questioned the value of this state intervention in the economy, nearly every government in Europe embraced mercantilism.

Colbert's mercantilist projects extended to Canada, where in 1663 he took control of the trading company that had founded New France. He transplanted several thousand peasants from western France to the present-day province of Quebec, which France had claimed since 1608, and he sent fifteen hundred soldiers to fend off the Iroquois, who regularly raided French fur-trading convoys. Shows of French military force, including the burning of Indian villages and winter food supplies, forced the Iroquois to make peace, and from 1666 to 1680, French traders moved westward with minimal interference. In 1672, fur trader Louis Jolliet and Jesuit missionary Jacques Marquette reached the upper Mississippi River and traveled downstream as far as Arkansas. In 1684, French explorer Sieur de La Salle ventured all the way down to the Gulf of Mexico, claiming a vast territory for Louis XIV and calling it Louisiana after him. Louis and Colbert encouraged colonial settlement as part of their rivalry with the English and the Dutch in the New World.

Colonial settlement occupied only a small portion of Louis XIV's attention, however, for his main foreign policy goal was to extend French power in Europe. In pursuing this purpose, he inevitably came up against the Spanish and Austrian Habsburgs, whose lands encircled his. To expand French power, Louis needed the biggest possible army. The ministry of war centralized the organization of French troops. Barracks built in major towns received supplies from a central distribution system. The state began to provide uniforms for the soldiers and to offer veterans some hospital care. A militia draft instituted in 1688 supplemented the army in times of war and enrolled 100,000 men. Louis's wartime army could field a force as large as that of all his enemies combined.

Absolutist governments always tried to increase their territorial holdings, and as Louis extended his reach, he gained new enemies. In 1667–1668, in the first of his major wars after assuming personal control of French affairs, Louis defeated the Spanish armies but had to make peace when England, Sweden, and the Dutch Republic joined the war. In the Treaty of Aix-la-Chapelle in 1668, he gained control of towns on the border of the Spanish Netherlands. Pamphlets sponsored by the Habsburgs accused Louis of aiming for "universal monarchy," or domination of Europe.

In 1672, Louis XIV opened hostilities against the Dutch because they stood in the way of his acquisition of more territory in the Spanish Netherlands. He declared war again on Spain in 1673. By now the Dutch had allied themselves with their former Spanish masters to hold off the French. Louis also marched his troops into territories of the Holy Roman Empire, provoking many of the German princes to join with the emperor, the Spanish, and the Dutch in an alliance against Louis, now denounced as a "Christian Turk" for his imperialist ambitions. But the French armies more than held their own. Faced with bloody yet inconclusive results on the battle-field, the parties agreed to the Treaty of Nijmegen of 1678–1679, which ceded several Flemish towns and Franche-Comté to Louis (Map 13.1). These territorial additions were costly: French government deficits soared, and increases in taxes touched off the most serious antitax revolt of Louis's reign, in 1675.

■ **MAP 13.1 Louis XIV's Acquisitions, 1668–1697**

Every ruler in Europe hoped to extend his or her territorial control, and war was often the result. Louis XIV steadily encroached on the Spanish Netherlands to the north and the lands of the Holy Roman Empire to the east. Although coalitions of European powers reined in Louis's grander ambitions, he incorporated many neighboring territories into the French crown.

Louis had no intention of standing still. Heartened by the Habsburgs' seeming weakness, he pushed eastward, seizing the city of Strasbourg in 1681 and invading the province of Lorraine in 1684. In 1688, he attacked some of the small German cities of the Holy Roman Empire and was soon involved again in a long war against a Europe-wide coalition. Between 1689 and 1697, a coalition made up of England, Spain, Sweden, the Dutch Republic, the Austrian emperor, and various German princes fought Louis XIV to a stalemate. When hostilities ended in the Peace of Rijswijk in 1697, Louis returned many of his conquests made since 1678 with the exception of Strasbourg (see Map 13.1). Louis never lost his taste for war, but his allies learned how to set limits on his ambitions.

Louis was the last French ruler before Napoleon to accompany his troops to the battlefield. In later generations, as the military became more professional, French rulers left the fighting to their generals. Although Louis had managed to suppress the private armies of his noble courtiers, he constantly promoted his own military prowess in order to keep his noble officers under his sway. He had miniature battle scenes painted on his high heels and commissioned tapestries showing his military processions into cities, even those he did not take by force. He seized every occasion to assert his supremacy, insisting that other fleets salute his ships first.

War required money and men, which Louis obtained by expanding state control over finances, conscription into the army, and military supply. Thus absolutism and warfare fed each other, as the bureaucracy created new ways to raise and maintain an army and the army's success in war justified the expansion of state power. But constant warfare also eroded the state's resources. Further administrative and legal reform, the elimination of the buying and selling of offices, and the lowering of taxes—all were made impossible by the need for more money.

The playwright Corneille wrote, no doubt optimistically, "The people are very happy when they die for their kings." What is certain is that the wars touched many peasant and urban families. The people who lived on the routes leading to the battlefields had to house and feed soldiers; only nobles were exempt from this requirement. Everyone, moreover, paid the higher taxes that were necessary to support the army. By the end of Louis's reign, one in six Frenchmen had served in the military.

Absolutism in Central and Eastern Europe

Central and eastern European rulers saw in Louis XIV a powerful model of absolutist state building. Yet they did not blindly emulate the Sun King, in part because they confronted conditions peculiar to their regions. The ruler of Brandenburg-Prussia had to rebuild lands ravaged by the Thirty Years' War and unite far-flung territories. The Austrian Habsburgs needed to govern a mosaic of ethnic and religious groups while fighting off the Ottoman Turks. The Russian tsars wanted to extend their power over a far-flung but relatively impoverished empire. The great exception to absolutism in eastern Europe was Poland-Lithuania, where a long crisis virtually destroyed central authority and sucked much of eastern Europe into its turbulent wake.

Brandenburg-Prussia and Sweden: Militaristic Absolutism

Brandenburg-Prussia began as a puny state on the Elbe River, but it would have a remarkable future. In the nineteenth century, it would unify the disparate German states into modern-day Germany. The ruler of Brandenburg was an elector, one of the seven German princes entitled to select the Holy Roman Emperor. Since the sixteenth century, the ruler of Brandenburg had also controlled the duchy of East Prussia; after 1618, the state was called Brandenburg-Prussia. Despite meager resources, Frederick William of Hohenzollern, the Great Elector of Brandenburg-Prussia (r. 1640–1688), succeeded in welding his scattered lands into an absolutist state.

Pressured first by the necessities of fighting the Thirty Years' War and then by the demands of reconstruction, Frederick William determined to force his territories' estates (representative institutions) to grant him a dependable income. The Great Elector struck a deal with the Junkers (nobles) of each land: in exchange for allowing him to collect taxes, he gave them complete control over their enserfed peasants and exempted them from taxation. The tactic worked. By the end of his reign the estates met only on ceremonial occasions.

Supplied with a steady income, Frederick William could devote his attention to military and bureaucratic consolidation. Over forty years he expanded his army from eight thousand to thirty thousand men. (See "Taking Measure," below.) The

State	Soldiers	Population	Ratio of soldiers/ total population
France	300,000	20 million	1:66
Russia	220,000	14 million	1:64
Austria	100,000	8 million	1:80
Sweden	40,000	1 million	1:25
Brandenburg-Prussia	30,000	2 million	1:66
England	24,000	10 million	1:410

*Figures for the end of the seventeenth century, ranging from 1688 for Prussia to 1710 for France

■ **TAKING MEASURE The Seventeenth-Century Army**
The figures in this chart are only approximate but tell an important story. What conclusions can be drawn about the relative weight of the military in the different European states? Why did England have such a smaller army than the others? Is the absolute or the relative size of the military the more important indicator?

(From André Corvisier, *Armées et sociétés en Europe de 1494 à 1789* [Paris: Presses Universitaires de France, 1976], 126.)

army mirrored the rigid domination of nobles over peasants that characterized Brandenburg-Prussian society: peasants filled the ranks, and Junkers became officers. Nobles also took positions as bureaucratic officials, but military needs always had priority. The elector named special war commissars to take charge not only of military affairs but also of tax collection. To hasten military dispatches, he also established one of Europe's first state postal systems.

As a Calvinist ruler, Frederick William avoided the ostentation of the French court, even while following the absolutist model of centralizing state power. He boldly rebuffed Louis XIV by welcoming twenty thousand French Huguenot refugees after Louis's revocation of the Edict of Nantes. In pursuing foreign and domestic policies that promoted state power and prestige, Frederick William adroitly switched sides in Louis's wars and would stop at almost nothing to crush resistance at home. In 1701, his son Frederick I (r. 1688–1713) persuaded Holy Roman Emperor Leopold I to grant him the title "king in Prussia." Prussia had arrived as an important power (Map 13.2).

Across the Baltic, Sweden also stood out as an example of absolutist consolidation. In the Thirty Years' War, King Gustavus Adolphus's superb generalship and highly trained army had made Sweden the supreme power of northern Europe. The huge but sparsely populated state included not only most of present-day Sweden but also Finland, Estonia, half of Latvia, and much of the Baltic coastline of modern Poland and Germany. The Baltic, in short, was a Swedish lake. After Gustavus Adolphus died, his daughter Queen Christina (r. 1632–1654) conceded much authority to the estates. Absorbed by religion and philosophy, Christina eventually abdicated and converted to Catholicism. Her successors temporarily made Sweden an absolute monarchy.

In Sweden (as in neighboring Denmark-Norway), absolutism meant simply the estates standing aside while the king led the army in lucrative foreign campaigns. The aristocracy went along because it staffed the bureaucracy and reaped war profits. Intrigued by French culture, Sweden also gleamed with national pride. In 1668, the nobility demanded the introduction of a distinctive national costume: should Swedes, they asked, "who are so glorious and renowned a nation . . . let ourselves be led by the nose by a parcel of French dancing-masters"? Sweden spent the forty years after 1654 continuously warring with its neighbors. By the 1690s, war expenses began to outrun the small Swedish population's ability to pay, threatening the continuation of absolutism.

An Uneasy Balance: Austrian Habsburgs and Ottoman Turks

Holy Roman Emperor Leopold I (r. 1658–1705) ruled over a variety of territories of different ethnicities, languages, and religions, yet in ways similar to his French and Prussian counterparts, he gradually consolidated his power. Like all the Holy Roman emperors since 1438, Leopold was an Austrian Habsburg. He was simulta-

■ MAP 13.2 State Building in Central and Eastern Europe, 1648–1699

Brandenburg-Prussia emerged from relative obscurity after the Thirty Years' War to begin an aggressive program of expanding its military and its territorial base. The Austrian Habsburgs had long contested the Ottoman Turks for dominance of eastern Europe, and by 1699, they had pushed the Turks out of Hungary. Poland-Lithuania lost territory to Russia. Sweden still dominated the Baltic Sea.

neously duke of Upper and Lower Silesia, count of Tyrol, archduke of Upper and Lower Austria, king of Bohemia, king of Hungary and Croatia, and ruler of Styria and Moravia (see Map 13.2). Some of these territories were provinces in the Holy Roman Empire; others were simply ruled from Vienna as Habsburg family holdings.

Leopold needed to build up his armies and state authority in order to defend the Holy Roman Empire's international position, which had been weakened by the Thirty Years' War, and to push back the Ottoman Turks who steadily encroached from the southeast. The emperor and his closest officials took control over recruiting, provisioning, and strategic planning and worked to replace the mercenaries hired during the Thirty Years' War with a permanent standing army that promoted professional discipline. To pay for the army and to staff his growing bureaucracy, Leopold had to gain the support of local aristocrats and chip away at provincial institutions' powers. Intent on replacing Bohemian nobles who had supported the 1618 revolt against Austrian authority, the Habsburgs promoted a new nobility made up of Czechs, Germans, Italians, Spaniards, and even Irish, who used German as their common tongue, professed Catholicism, and loyally served the Austrian dynasty. Bohemia became a virtual Austrian colony. "You have utterly destroyed our home, our ancient kingdom, and have built us no new one in its place," lamented a Czech Jesuit in 1670, addressing Leopold. "Woe to you! . . . The nobles you have oppressed, great cities made small. Of smiling towns you have made straggling villages." Austrian censors prohibited publication of this protest for over a century.

In addition to holding Louis XIV in check on his western frontiers, Leopold confronted the ever-present challenge of the Ottoman Turks to his east. Hungary was the chief battle zone between Austria and the Turks for more than 150 years. In 1682, when war broke out again, Austria controlled the northwest section of Hungary; the Turks occupied the center; and in the east, the Turks demanded tribute from the Hungarian princes who ruled Transylvania. In 1683, the Turks pushed all the way to the gates of Vienna and laid siege to the Austrian

■ **The Siege of Vienna, 1683 (detail)**
In this stylized rendition by Frans Geffels, the Ottoman Turks bombard the city, which they have surrounded for two months, as cavalry forces commanded by Polish king Jan Sobieski arrive in the foreground to help lift the siege.
(Museen der Stadt, Wien.)

capital; after reaching this high-water mark, however, Turkish power ebbed. With the help of Polish cavalry, the Austrians finally broke the siege and turned the tide in a major counteroffensive. By the Treaty of Karlowitz of 1699, the Ottoman Turks surrendered almost all of Hungary to the Austrians.

Hungary's "liberation" from the Turks came at a high price. The fighting laid waste vast stretches of Hungary's central plain, and the population may have declined as much as 65 percent since 1600. To repopulate the land, the Austrians settled large communities of foreigners: Romanians, Croats, Serbs, and Germans. Magyar (Hungarian) speakers became a minority, and the seeds were sown for the poisonous nationality conflicts in nineteenth- and twentieth-century Hungary, Romania, and Yugoslavia.

Once the Turks had been beaten back, Austrian rule over Hungary tightened. In 1687, the Habsburg dynasty's hereditary right to the Hungarian crown was acknowledged by the Hungarian diet, a parliament revived by Leopold in 1681 to gain the support of Hungarian nobles. The diet was dominated by nobles who had amassed huge holdings in the liberated territories. They formed the core of a pro-Habsburg Hungarian aristocracy that would buttress the dynasty until it fell in 1918. As the Turks retreated from Hungary, Leopold systematically rebuilt churches, monasteries, roadside shrines, and monuments in the flamboyant Austrian baroque style.

The Ottoman Turks also pursued state consolidation but in a very different fashion from the Europeans. The Ottoman state centralized its authority through negotiation with and incorporation of bandit armies, which European rulers typically suppressed by armed force. In the seventeenth century, mutinous army officers often deposed the Ottoman ruler, or sultan, in a palace coup, but because the Ottoman state had learned to manage constant crises, the state itself survived and rarely faced popular revolts. Rather than remaining in their villages and resisting state authorities, Ottoman peasants often left to become bandits who periodically worked for the state as mercenaries. Leaders of bandit gangs entered into negotiation with the Ottoman sultan, sometimes providing thousands of bandit mercenaries to the sultan's armies and even taking major official positions. This constantly shifting social and political system explains how the coup-ridden Ottoman state could appear "weak" in Western eyes and still pose a massive military threat on Europe's southeastern borders. In the end, the Ottoman state lasted longer than Louis XIV's absolute monarchy.

Russia: Foundations of Bureaucratic Absolutism

Superficially, seventeenth-century Russia seemed a world apart from the Europe of Louis XIV. Straddling Europe and Asia, it stretched across Siberia to the Pacific Ocean. Western visitors either sneered or shuddered at the "barbarism" of Russian life, and Russians reciprocated by nursing deep suspicions of everything foreign. But under the surface, Russia was evolving along paths much like the rest of absolutist Europe; the tsars wanted to claim unlimited autocratic power, but they had to surmount internal disorder and come to an accommodation with noble landlords.

When Tsar Alexei (r. 1645–1676) tried to extend state authority by imposing new administrative structures and taxes in 1648, Moscow and other cities erupted in bloody rioting. The government immediately doused the fire. In 1649, Alexei convoked the Assembly of the Land (consisting of noble delegates from the provinces) to consult on a sweeping law code to organize Russian society in a strict social hierarchy that would last for nearly two centuries. The code of 1649 assigned all subjects to a hereditary class according to their current occupation or state needs. Slaves and free peasants were merged into a serf class. As serfs they could not change occupations or move; they were tightly tied to the soil and to their noble masters. To prevent tax evasion, the code also forbade townspeople to move from the community where they resided. Nobles owed absolute obedience to the tsar and were required to serve in the army, but in return no other group could own estates worked by serfs. Serfs became the chattel of their lord, who could sell them like horses or land. Their conditions of life differed little from those of the slaves on the plantations in the Americas.

Some peasants resisted enserfment. In 1667, Stenka Razin, a Cossack from the Don region in southern Russia, led a huge rebellion that promised liberation from "the traitors and bloodsuckers of the peasant communes"—the great noble landowners, local governors, and Moscow courtiers. Captured four years later by the tsar's army, Razin was dismembered, his head and limbs publicly displayed, and his body thrown to the dogs. Thousands of his followers also suffered grisly deaths, but his memory lived on in folk songs and legends.♦ Landlords successfully petitioned for the abolition of the statute of limitations on runaway serfs, the use of state agents in searching for runaways, and harsh penalties against those who harbored runaways. The increase in Russian state authority went hand in hand with the enforcement of serfdom.

To extend his power and emulate his western rivals, Tsar Alexei wanted a bigger army, exclusive control over state policy, and a greater say in religious matters. The size of the army increased dramatically from 35,000 in the 1630s to 220,000 by the end of the century. The Assembly of the Land, once an important source of noble consultation, never met again after 1653. Alexei also imposed firm control over the Russian Orthodox church. In 1666, a church council reaffirmed the tsar's role as God's direct representative on earth. The state-dominated church took action against a religious group called the Old Believers, who rejected church efforts to bring Russian worship in line with Byzantine tradition. Whole communities of Old

---

♦ For a contemporary account of the uprising, see Document 42, Ludwig Fabritius, "The Revolt of Stenka Razin."

■ Stenka Razin in Captivity
*After leading a revolt of thousands of serfs, peasants, and members of non-Russian tribes of
the middle and lower Volga region, Razin was captured by Russian forces and led off to
Moscow, as shown here, where he was executed in 1671. He has been the subject of songs,
legends, and poems ever since.* (Novosti Photo Library, London.)

Believers starved or burned themselves to death rather than submit. Religious
schism opened a gulf between the Russian people and the crown.

Nevertheless, modernizing trends prevailed. As the state bureaucracy expanded,
the government intervened more and more in daily life. Decrees regulated tobacco
smoking, card playing, and alcohol consumption and even dictated how people
should leash and fence their pet dogs. Western ideas began to seep into educated
circles in Moscow. Nobles and ordinary citizens commissioned portraits of themselves instead of only buying religious icons. Tsar Alexei set up the first Western-
style theater in the Kremlin, and his daughter Sophia translated French plays. The
most adventurous nobles began to wear German-style clothing. A long struggle over
Western influences had begun.

Poland-Lithuania Overwhelmed

Unlike the other eastern European powers, Poland-Lithuania did not follow the
absolutist model. Decades of war weakened the monarchy and made the great nobles
into practically autonomous warlords. They used the parliament and demands for
constitutionalism to stymie monarchical power. The result was a precipitous slide
into political disarray and weakness.

In 1648, Ukrainian Cossack warriors revolted against the king of Poland-Lithuania, inaugurating two decades of tumult known as the Deluge. Cossack bands had formed from runaway peasants and poor nobles in the no man's land of southern Russia and Ukraine. The Polish nobles who claimed this potentially rich land scorned the Cossacks as troublemakers, but to the Ukrainian peasant population they were liberators. In 1654, the Cossacks offered Ukraine to Russian rule, provoking a Russo-Polish war that ended in 1667 when the tsar annexed eastern Ukraine and Kiev (see Map 13.2). Neighboring powers tried to profit from the chaos in Poland-Lithuania; Sweden, Brandenburg-Prussia, and Transylvania sent armies to seize territory.

Many towns were destroyed in the fighting, and as much as a third of the Polish population perished. The once prosperous Jewish and Protestant minorities suffered greatly: some fifty-six thousand Jews were killed either by the Cossacks, Polish peasants, or Russian troops, and thousands more had to flee or convert to Christianity. One rabbi wrote, "We were slaughtered each day, in a more agonizing way than cattle: they are butchered quickly, while we were being executed slowly." Surviving Jews moved from towns to *shtetls* (Jewish villages), where they took up petty trading, moneylending, tax gathering, and tavern leasing—activities that fanned peasant anti-Semitism. Desperate for protection amid the war, most Protestants backed the violently anti-Catholic Swedes, and the victorious Catholic majority branded them as traitors. Some Protestant refugees fled to the Dutch Republic and England. In Poland-Lithuania—once an outpost of religious toleration—it came to be assumed that a good Pole was a Catholic.

The commonwealth revived briefly when a man of ability and ambition, Jan Sobieski (r. 1674–1696), was elected king. He gained a reputation throughout Europe when he led twenty-five thousand Polish cavalrymen into battle in the siege of Vienna in 1683. His cavalry helped rout the Turks and turned the tide against the Ottomans. Married to a politically shrewd French princess, Sobieski openly admired Louis XIV's France. Despite his efforts to rebuild the monarchy, he could not halt Poland-Lithuania's decline into powerlessness.

Elsewhere the ravages of war had created opportunities for kings to increase their power, but in Poland-Lithuania the great nobles gained all the advantage. They dominated the Sejm (parliament), and to maintain an equilibrium among themselves, they each wielded an absolute veto power. This "free veto" constitutional system soon deadlocked parliamentary government. The monarchy lost its room to maneuver, and with it much of its remaining power. An appalled Croat visitor in 1658 commented, "Among the Poles there is no order in the state. . . . Everybody who is stronger thinks to have the right to oppress the weaker, just as the wolves and bears are free to capture and kill cattle. . . . Such abominable depravity is called by the Poles 'aristocratic freedom.'" The Polish version of constitutionalism fatally weakened the state and made it prey to its neighbors.

Constitutionalism in England

In the second half of the seventeenth century, western and eastern Europe began to move in different directions. In general, the farther east one traveled, the more absolutist the style of government (with the exception of Poland-Lithuania) and the greater the gulf between landlord and peasant. In eastern Europe, nobles lorded over their serfs but owed almost slavish obedience in turn to their rulers. In western Europe, even in absolutist France, serfdom had almost entirely disappeared and nobles and rulers alike faced greater challenges to their control. The greatest challenges of all would come in England.

This outcome might seem surprising, for the English monarchs enjoyed many advantages compared with their continental rivals: they needed less money for their armies because they had stayed out of the Thirty Years' War, and their island kingdom was in theory easier to rule because they governed a population only one-fourth the size of France's and of relatively homogeneous ethnicity. Yet the English rulers failed in their efforts to install absolutist policies. The English revolutions of 1642–1660 and 1688–1689 overturned two kings, confirmed the constitutional powers of an elected parliament, and laid the foundation for the idea that government must guarantee certain rights under the law.

England Turned Upside Down, 1642–1660

Disputes about the right to levy taxes and the nature of authority in the Church of England had long troubled the relationship between the English crown and Parliament. For over a hundred years, wealthy English landowners had been accustomed to participating in government through Parliament and expected to be consulted on royal policy. Although England had no one constitutional document, a variety of laws, judicial decisions, charters and petitions granted by the king, and customary procedures all regulated relations between king and Parliament. When Charles I tried to assert his authority over Parliament, a civil war broke out. It set in motion an unpredictable chain of events, which included an extraordinary ferment of religious and political ideas. Some historians view the English civil war of 1642–1646 as the last great war of religion because it pitted Puritans against those trying to push the Anglican church toward Catholicism, but it should be considered the first modern revolution because it gave birth to democratic political and religious movements.

When Charles I (r. 1625–1649) succeeded his father, James I, he faced an increasingly aggressive Parliament that resisted new taxes and resented the king's efforts to extend his personal control. In 1628, Parliament forced Charles to agree to a Petition of Right by which he promised not to levy taxes without its consent. Charles hoped to avoid further interference with his plans by simply refusing to call

Parliament into session between 1629 and 1640. Without it, the king's ministers had to find every loophole possible to raise revenues. They tried to turn "ship money," a levy on seaports in times of emergency, into an annual tax collected everywhere in the country. The crown won the ensuing court case, but many subjects still refused to pay what they considered to be an illegal tax.

Religious tensions brought conflicts over the king's authority to a head. The Puritans had long agitated for the removal of any vestiges of Catholicism, but Charles, married to a French Catholic, moved in the opposite direction. With Charles's encouragement, the archbishop of Canterbury, William Laud (1573–1645), imposed increasingly elaborate ceremonies on the Anglican church. Angered by these moves toward "popery," the Puritans poured forth vituperative pamphlets and sermons. In response Laud hauled them before the feared Court of Star Chamber, which the king personally controlled. The court ordered harsh sentences for Laud's Puritan critics; they were whipped, pilloried, and branded, and even had their ears cut off and their noses split. When Laud tried to apply his policies to Scotland, however, they backfired completely: the stubborn Presbyterian Scots rioted against the imposition of the Anglican prayer book—the Book of Common Prayer—and in 1640 they invaded the north of England. To raise money to fight the war, Charles called Parliament into session and unwittingly opened the door to a constitutional and religious crisis.

The Parliament of 1640 did not intend revolution, but reformers in the House of Commons (the lower house of Parliament) wanted to undo what they saw as the royal tyranny of the 1630s. Parliament removed Laud from office, ordered the execution of an unpopular royal commander, abolished the Court of Star Chamber, repealed recently levied taxes, and provided for a parliamentary assembly at least once every three years, thus establishing a constitutional check on royal authority. Moderate reformers expected to stop there and resisted Puritan pressure to abolish bishops and eliminate the Anglican prayer book. But their hand was forced in January 1642, when Charles and his soldiers invaded Parliament and tried unsuccessfully to arrest those leaders who had moved to curb his power. Faced with mounting opposition within London, Charles quickly withdrew from the city and organized an army.

The ensuing civil war between king and Parliament lasted four years (1642–1646) and divided the country. The king's army of royalists, known as Cavaliers, enjoyed most support in northern and western England. The parliamentary forces, called Roundheads because they cut their hair short, had their stronghold in the southeast, including London. Although Puritans dominated on the parliamentary side, they were divided among themselves about the proper form of church government: the Presbyterians wanted a Calvinist church with some central authority, whereas the Independents favored entirely autonomous congregations free from other church government (hence the term *congregationalism*, often associated with the Independents). Putting aside their differences for the

sake of military unity, the Puritans united
under an obscure member of the House of Commons, the country gentleman Oliver Cromwell
(1599–1658), who sympathized with the Independents. After Cromwell skillfully reorganized
the parliamentary troops, his New Model Army
defeated the Cavaliers at the battle of Naseby in
1645. Charles surrendered in 1646.

Although the civil war between king and Parliament had ended in victory for Parliament, divisions within the Puritan ranks now came to the
fore: the Presbyterians dominated Parliament,
but the Independents controlled the army. The
disputes between elites drew lower-class groups
into the debate. When Parliament tried to disband the New Model Army in 1647, disgruntled
soldiers protested. Called Levellers because of
their insistence on leveling social differences, the

England during the Civil War

soldiers took on their officers in a series of debates about the nature of political authority. The Levellers demanded that Parliament meet annually, that members be
paid so as to allow common people to participate, and that all male heads of households be allowed to vote. Their ideal of political participation excluded servants,
the propertyless, and women but offered access to artisans, shopkeepers, and modest farmers. Cromwell and other army leaders rejected the Levellers' demands as
threatening to property owners. Cromwell insisted, "You have no other way to deal
with these men but to break them in pieces. . . . If you do not break them they will
break you."

Just as political differences between Presbyterians and Independents helped
spark new political movements, so, too, their conflicts over church organization fostered the emergence of new religious doctrines. The new sects had in common only
their emphasis on the "inner light" of individual religious inspiration and a disdain
for hierarchical authority. Their emphasis on equality before God and greater participation in church governance appealed to the middle and lower classes. The Bap-
tists, for example, insisted on adult baptism because they believed that Christians
should choose their own church and that every child should not automatically
become a member of the Church of England. The Quakers demonstrated their
beliefs in equality and the inner light by refusing to doff their hats to men in
authority. Manifesting their religious experience by trembling, or "quaking," the
Quakers believed that anyone—man or woman—inspired by a direct experience
of God could preach.

Parliamentary leaders feared that the new sects would overturn the whole social hierarchy. Rumors abounded, for example, of naked Quakers running through

the streets waiting "for a sign." Some sects did advocate sweeping change. The Diggers promoted rural communism—collective ownership of all property. Seekers and Ranters questioned just about everything. One notorious Ranter, John Robins, even claimed to be God. A few men advocated free love. These developments convinced the political elite that tolerating the new sects would lead to skepticism, anarchism, and debauchery.

In keeping with their notions of equality and individual inspiration, many of the new sects provided opportunities for women to become preachers and prophets. One Quaker prophet, Anna Trapnel, explained her vocation: "For in all that was said by me, I was nothing, the Lord put all in my mouth, and told me what I should say." Women presented petitions, participated prominently in street demonstrations, distributed tracts, and occasionally even dressed as men, wearing swords and joining armies. The duchess of Newcastle complained in 1650 that women were "affecting a Masculinacy . . . practicing the behaviour . . . of men." The outspoken women in new sects like the Quakers underscored the threat of a social order turning upside down.

At the heart of the continuing political struggle was the question of what to do with the king, who tried to negotiate with the Presbyterians in Parliament. In late 1648, Independents in the army purged the Presbyterians from Parliament, leaving a "rump" of about seventy members. This Rump Parliament then created a high court to try Charles I. The court found him guilty of attempting to establish "an unlimited and tyrannical power" and pronounced a death sentence. On January 30, 1649, Charles was beheaded before an enormous crowd, which reportedly groaned as one when the axe fell. Although many had objected to Charles's autocratic rule, few had wanted him killed. For royalists, Charles immediately became a martyr, and reports of miracles, such as the curing of blindness by the touch of a handkerchief soaked in his blood, soon circulated.

The Rump Parliament abolished the monarchy and the House of Lords (the upper house of Parliament) and set up a Puritan republic with Oliver Cromwell as chairman of the Council of State. Cromwell did not tolerate dissent from his policies. He saw the hand of God in events and himself as God's agent. Pamphleteers and songwriters ridiculed his red nose and accused him of wanting to be king, but few challenged his leadership. When his agents discovered plans for mutiny within the army, they executed the perpetrators; new decrees silenced the Levellers. Although Cromwell allowed the various Puritan sects to worship rather freely and permitted Jews with needed skills to return to England for the first time since the thirteenth century, Catholics could not worship publicly, nor could Anglicans use the Book of Common Prayer. The elites—many of whom were still Anglican—were troubled by Cromwell's religious policies but pleased to see some social order reestablished.

The new regime aimed to extend state power just as Charles I had before. Cromwell laid the foundation for a Great Britain made up of England, Wales, Ireland, and Scotland by reconquering Scotland and subduing Ireland. Anti-English

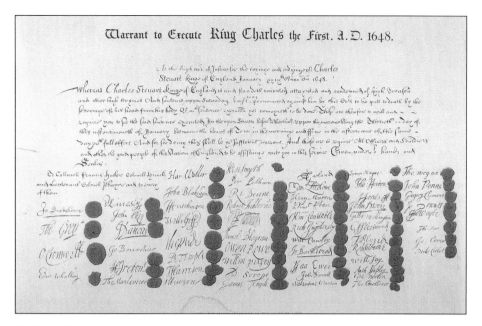

■ **Death Warrant of Charles I**
Parliament voted to try Charles I for treason, and the trial began in January 1649. A week later, the court found Charles to be a "tyrant, traitor, murderer, and public enemy" and ordered his execution. When the monarchy was restored in 1660, everyone who signed Charles I's death warrant was hunted down and executed. (Mary Evans Picture Library.)

rebels in Ireland had seized the occasion of troubles between king and Parliament to revolt in 1641. When Cromwell's position was secured in 1649, he went to Ireland with a large force and easily defeated the rebels, massacring whole garrisons and their priests. He encouraged expropriating the lands of the Irish "barbarous wretches," and Scottish immigrants resettled the northern county of Ulster. This seventeenth-century English conquest left a legacy of bitterness that the Irish even today call "the curse of Cromwell." In 1651, Parliament turned its attention overseas, putting mercantilist ideas into practice in the first Navigation Act, which allowed imports only if they were carried on English ships or came directly from the producers of goods. The Navigation Act was aimed at the Dutch, who dominated world trade; Cromwell tried to carry the policy further by waging naval war on the Dutch from 1652 to 1654.

At home, however, Cromwell faced growing resistance. His wars required a budget twice the size of Charles I's, and his increases in property taxes and customs duties alienated landowners and merchants. The conflict reached a crisis in 1653: Parliament considered disbanding the army, whereupon Cromwell abolished the Rump Parliament in a military coup and made himself Lord Protector. He now silenced his critics by banning newspapers and using networks of spies and mail readers to keep tabs on his enemies. Cromwell's death in 1658 revived the prospect

■ Oliver Cromwell
Shown here preparing for battle, Cromwell lived an austere life but believed fiercely in his own personal righteousness. As leader he tolerated no opposition. When he died, he was buried in Westminster Abbey, but in 1661 his body was exhumed and hanged in its shroud. His head was cut off and displayed outside Westminster Hall for nearly twenty years.
(Courtesy of the National Portrait Gallery, London.)

of civil war and political chaos. In 1660, a newly elected, staunchly Anglican Parliament invited Charles II, the son of the executed king, to return from exile.

The "Glorious Revolution" of 1688

The traditional monarchical form of government was reinstated in 1660, restoring the king to full partnership with Parliament. Charles II (r. 1660–1685) promised "a liberty to tender consciences" in an attempt to extend religious toleration, especially to Catholics, with whom he sympathized. Yet in the first years of his reign more than a thousand Puritan ministers lost their positions, and after 1664, attending a service other than one conforming with the Anglican prayer book was illegal. Natural disasters also marred the early years of Charles II's reign. The plague stalked London's rat-infested streets in May 1665 and claimed more than thirty thousand victims by September. Then in 1666, the Great Fire swept the city, causing cataclysmic destruction. The crown now had a city as well as a monarchy to rebuild.

The restoration of monarchy made some in Parliament fear that the English government would come to resemble French absolutism. This fear was not unfounded. In 1670, Charles II made a secret agreement, soon leaked, with Louis XIV in which he promised to announce his conversion to Catholicism in exchange for money for a war against the Dutch. Charles never proclaimed himself a Catholic, but in his Declaration of Indulgence (1673) he did suspend all laws against Catholics and Protestant dissenters. Parliament refused to continue funding the Dutch war unless Charles rescinded his Declaration of Indulgence. Asserting its authority further, Parliament passed the Test Act in 1673, requiring all government officials to profess

■ Great Fire of London, 1666

This painting shows the three-day fire at its height. The writer John Evelyn described the scene in his diary: "All the sky was of a fiery aspect, like the top of a burning oven, and the light seen above 40 miles round about for many nights. God grant mine eyes may never behold the like, who now saw above 10,000 houses all in one flame; the noise and cracking and thunder of people, the fall of towers, houses, and churches, was like an hideous storm." Everyone in London at the time felt overwhelmed by the catastrophe, and many attributed it to God's punishment for the upheavals of the 1640s and 1650s. (Museum of London Photographic Library.)

allegiance to the Church of England and in effect disavow Catholic doctrine. Then in 1678, Parliament precipitated the so-called Exclusion Crisis by explicitly denying the throne to a Roman Catholic. This action was aimed at the king's brother and heir, James, an open convert to Catholicism. Charles refused to allow it to become law.

The dynastic crisis over the succession of a Catholic gave rise to two distinct factions in Parliament: the Tories, who supported a strong, hereditary monarchy and the restored ceremony of the Anglican church, and the Whigs, who advocated parliamentary supremacy and toleration for Protestant dissenters such as Presbyterians. Both labels were originally derogatory: *Tory* meant an Irish Catholic bandit; *Whig* was the Irish Catholic designation for a Presbyterian Scot. The Tories favored James's succession despite his Catholicism, whereas the Whigs opposed a Catholic monarch. The loose moral atmosphere of Charles's court also offended some Whigs, who complained tongue in cheek that Charles was father of his country in much too literal a fashion (he had fathered more than one child by his mistresses but produced no legitimate heir).

Upon Charles's death, James succeeded to the throne as James II (r. 1685–1688). James pursued pro-Catholic and absolutist policies even more aggressively than his brother. When a male heir—who would take precedence over James's two adult Protestant daughters and be reared a Catholic—was born, Tories and Whigs banded together. They invited the Dutch ruler William, prince of Orange and the husband of James's older daughter, Mary, to invade England. James fled to France, and hardly any blood was shed. Parliament offered the throne jointly to William (r. 1689–1702) and Mary (r. 1689–1694) on the condition that they accept a bill of rights guaranteeing Parliament's full partnership in a constitutional government.

In the Bill of Rights (1689), William and Mary agreed not to raise a standing army or to levy taxes without Parliament's consent. They also agreed to call meetings of Parliament at least every three years, to guarantee free elections to parliamentary seats, and to abide by Parliament's decisions and not suspend duly passed laws. The agreement gave England's constitutional government a written, legal basis by formally recognizing Parliament as a self-contained, independent body that shared power with the rulers.♦ Victorious supporters of the coup declared it the "Glorious Revolution." Constitutionalism had triumphed over absolutism in England.

The propertied classes who controlled Parliament prevented any resurgence of the popular turmoil of the 1640s. The Toleration Act of 1689 granted all Protestants freedom of worship, though non-Anglicans were still excluded from the universities; Catholics got no rights but were more often left alone to worship privately. When the Catholics in Ireland rose to defend James II, William and Mary's troops brutally suppressed them. With the Whigs in power and the Tories in opposition, wealthy landowners now controlled political life throughout the realm. Differences between the factions had become minor; essentially, the Tories had less access to the king's patronage.

Constitutionalism in the Dutch Republic and the Overseas Colonies

When William and Mary came to the throne in England in 1689, the Dutch and the English put aside the rivalries that had brought them to war against each other in 1652–1654, 1665–1667, and 1672–1674. Under William, the Dutch Republic and England together led the coalition that blocked Louis XIV's efforts to dominate continental Europe. The two states had much in common: oriented toward commerce, especially overseas, they were the successful exceptions to absolutism in Europe. Also among the few outposts of constitutionalism in the seventeenth century were the British North American colonies, which developed representative government while the English were preoccupied with their revolutions at home. Constitution-

---

♦ For the complete text of the English Bill of Rights, see Document 43.

alism was not the only factor shaping this Atlantic world; as constitutionalism developed in the colonies, so, too, did the enslavement of black Africans as a new labor force.

The Dutch Republic

When the Dutch Republic gained formal independence from Spain in 1648, it had already established a decentralized, constitutional state. Rich merchants called *regents* effectively controlled the internal affairs of each province and through the Estates General (an assembly made up of deputies from each province) named the *stadholder*, the executive officer responsible for defense and for representing the state at all ceremonial occasions. They almost always chose one of the princes of the house of Orange, but the prince of Orange resembled a president more than a king.

The decentralized state encouraged and protected trade, and the Dutch Republic soon became Europe's financial capital. The Bank of Amsterdam offered interest rates less than half those available in England and France. Praised for their industriousness, thrift, and cleanliness—and maligned as greedy, dull "butter-boxes"—the Dutch dominated overseas commerce with their shipping (Map 13.3). They imported products from all over the world: spices, tea, and silk from Asia; sugar and tobacco from the Americas; wool from England and Spain; timber and furs from Scandinavia; grain from eastern Europe. A widely reprinted history of Amsterdam that appeared in 1662 described the city as "risen through the hand of God to the peak of prosperity and greatness. . . . The whole world stands amazed at its riches and from east and west, north and south they come to behold it."

The Dutch rapidly became the most prosperous and best-educated people in Europe. Middle-class people supported the visual arts, especially painting, to an unprecedented degree. Artists and engravers produced thousands of works, and Dutch artists were among the first to sell to a mass market. Whereas in other countries, kings, nobles, and churches bought art, Dutch buyers were merchants, artisans, and shopkeepers. Engravings, illustrated histories, and oil paintings, even those of the widely acclaimed Rembrandt van Rijn (1606–1669), were relatively inexpensive. The pictures reflected the Dutch interest in familiar daily details: children at play, winter landscapes, and ships in port.

The family household, not the royal court, determined the moral character of this intensely commercial society. Dutch society fostered public enterprise in men and work in the home for women, who were expected to filter out the greed and materialism of commercial society by maintaining domestic harmony and virtue. Relative prosperity decreased the need for married women to work, so Dutch society developed the clear contrast between middle-class male and female roles that would become prevalent elsewhere in Europe and in America more than a century later. As one contemporary Dutch writer explained, "The husband must be on the street to practice his trade; the wife must stay at home to be in the kitchen."

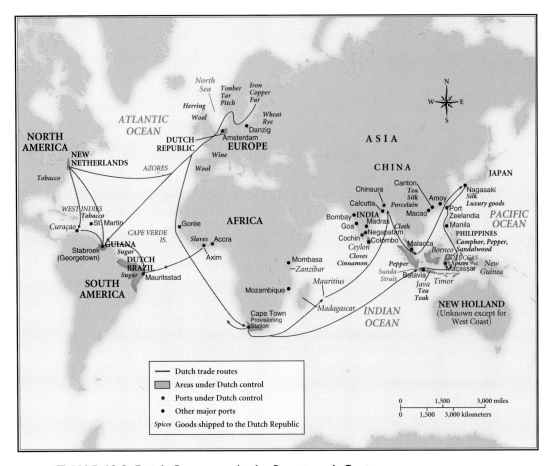

■ MAP 13.3 Dutch Commerce in the Seventeenth Century

Even before gaining formal independence from the Spanish in 1648, the Dutch had begun to compete with the Spanish and Portuguese all over the world. In 1602, a group of merchants established the Dutch East India Company, which soon offered investors an annual rate of return of 35 percent on the trade in spices with countries located on the Indian Ocean. Global commerce gave the Dutch the highest standard of living in Europe and soon attracted the envy of the French and the English.

Extraordinarily high levels of urbanization and literacy created a large reading public. Dutch presses printed books censored elsewhere (printers or authors censored in one province simply shifted operations to another), and the University of Leiden attracted students and professors from all over Europe. Dutch tolerance extended to the works of Benedict Spinoza (1633–1677), a Jewish philosopher and biblical scholar who was expelled by his synagogue for alleged atheism but was left alone by the Dutch authorities. Spinoza strove to reconcile religion with science and mathematics, but his work scandalized many Christians and Jews because he seemed to equate God and nature. Like nature, Spinoza's God followed unchangeable laws and could not be influenced by human actions, prayers, or faith.

■ A Typical Dutch Scene from Daily Life

Jan Steen painted The Baker Arent Oostward and His Wife *in 1658. Steen ran a brewery and tavern in addition to painting, and he was known for his interest in the details of daily life. Dutch artists popularized this kind of "genre" painting, which showed ordinary people at work and play.* (Rijksmuseum, Amsterdam.)

www.bedfordstmartins.com/huntconcise
See the ONLINE STUDY GUIDE for more help in analyzing this image.

Dutch learning, painting, and commerce all enjoyed wide renown in the seventeenth century, but this luster proved hard to maintain. The Dutch lived in a world of international rivalries in which strong central authority gave their enemies an advantage. Though inconclusive, the naval wars with England drained the state's revenues. Even more dangerous were the land wars with France, which continued into the eighteenth century. The Dutch survived these challenges but increasingly depended on alliances with other powers, such as England. By the end of the seventeenth century, the regent elite had become more exclusive, more preoccupied with ostentation, less tolerant of deviations from strict Calvinism, and more concerned with imitating French styles than with encouraging their own.

Freedom and Slavery in the New World

The French and English also increasingly overshadowed the Dutch in the New World colonies. While the Dutch concentrated on shipping, including the slave trade, the seventeenth-century French and English established settler colonies that would eventually provide fabulous revenues to the home countries. Many European governments encouraged private companies to vie for their share of the slave trade, and slavery began to take clear institutional form in the New World in this period. Even while slavery offered only a degrading form of despotism to black Africans, whites found in the colonies greater political and religious freedom than in Europe.

After the Spanish and Portuguese had shown that African slaves could be transported and forced to labor in South and Central America, the English and French endeavored to set up similar labor systems in their new Caribbean island colonies. White planters with large tracts of land bought African slaves to work fields of sugarcane, and as they gradually built up their holdings, the planters displaced most of the original white settlers, who moved to mainland North American colonies. After 1661, when Barbados instituted a slave code that stripped all Africans of rights under English law, slavery became codified as an inherited status that applied only to blacks. The result was a society of extremes: the very wealthy whites, about 7 percent of the population in Barbados; and the enslaved, powerless black majority. The English brought little of their religious or constitutional practices to the Caribbean. Other Caribbean colonies followed a similar pattern of development. Louis XIV promulgated a "black code" in 1685 to regulate the legal status of slaves in the French colonies. Although one of his aims was to prevent non-Catholics from owning slaves in the French colonies, the code had much the same effect as the English codes on the slaves themselves: they had no legal rights.

The highest church and government authorities in Catholic and Protestant countries alike condoned the gradually expanding slave trade; the governments of England, France, Spain, Portugal, the Dutch Republic, and Denmark all encouraged private companies to traffic in black Africans. The Dutch West India Company was the most successful of them. In 1600, about 9,500 Africans were exported from Africa to the New World every year; by 1700, this figure had increased nearly fourfold to 36,000 annually. Historians advance several different factors for the increase in the slave trade: some claim that improvements in muskets made European slavers more formidable; others cite the rising price for slaves, which made their sale more attractive for Africans; still others focus on factors internal to Africa, such as the increasing size of African armies and their use of muskets in fighting and capturing other Africans for sale as slaves. Whatever the reason, the way had been prepared for the development of an Atlantic economy based on slavery.

Virtually left to themselves during the upheavals in England, the fledgling English colonies in North America developed representative government on their own. Almost every colony had a governor and a two-house legislature. The colonial legislatures constantly sought to increase their power and resisted the efforts of Charles II and James II to reaffirm royal control. William and Mary reluctantly allowed emerging colonial elites more control over local affairs. The social and political elite among the settlers hoped to impose an English social hierarchy dominated by rich landowners. Ordinary immigrants to the colonies, however, took advantage of plentiful land to carve out their own farms using white servants and, later, in some colonies, African slaves.

For Native Americans, the expanding European presence meant something else altogether. They faced death through disease and warfare and the accelerating loss of their homelands. Unlike white settlers, Native Americans believed that land was a divine gift provided for their collective use and not subject to individual ownership. As a result, Europeans' claims that they owned exclusive land rights caused frequent skirmishes. In 1675–1676, for instance, three tribes allied under Metacomet (called King Philip by the English) threatened the survival of New England settlers, who savagely repulsed the attacks and sold their captives as slaves. Whites portrayed Native Americans as conspiring villains and sneaky heathens, akin to Africans in their savagery.

The Search for Order in Elite and Popular Culture

The early success of constitutionalism in England, the Dutch Republic, and the English North American colonies would help to shape a distinctive Atlantic world in the eighteenth century. Just how constitutionalism was linked to the growing commerce with the colonies remains open to dispute, however, because the constitutional governments, like the absolutist ones, avidly pursued profits in the burgeoning slave trade. Freedom did not mean liberty for everyone. One of the great debates of the time—and of much of the modern period that followed—concerned the meaning of freedom: for whom, under what conditions, with what justifiable limitations could freedom be claimed?

There was no freedom without order to sustain it, and most Europeans feared disorder above all else. Political theories, science, poetry, painting, and architecture all reflected in some measure the attempts to ground authority—to define the relation between freedom and order—in new ways. Authority concerned not just rulers and subjects but also the hierarchy of groups in society. As European states consolidated their powers, elites worked to distinguish themselves from the lower classes. They developed new codes of correct behavior for themselves and tried to teach order and discipline to their social inferiors.

Social Contract Theory: Hobbes and Locke

The turmoil of the times prompted a major rethinking of the foundations of all authority. Two figures stood out prominently amid the competing voices: Thomas Hobbes and John Locke. Their writings fundamentally shaped the modern subject of political science. Hobbes justified absolute authority; Locke provided the rationale for constitutionalism. Yet both argued that all authority came not from divine right but from a "social contract" between citizens.

Thomas Hobbes (1588–1679) was a royalist who sat out the English civil war of the 1640s in France, where he tutored the future king Charles II. Returning to England in 1651, he published his masterpiece, *Leviathan* (1651), in which he argued for unlimited authority in a ruler. Absolute authority could be vested in either a king or a parliament; it had to be absolute, he insisted, in order to overcome the defects of human nature. Believing that people are essentially self-centered and driven by the "right to self-preservation," Hobbes made his case by referring to science, not religion. To Hobbes, human life in a state of nature—that is, any situation without firm authority—was "solitary, poor, nasty, brutish, and short." He believed that the desire for power and natural greed would inevitably lead to unfettered competition. Only the assurance of social order could make people secure enough to act according to law; consequently, giving up personal liberty, he maintained, was the price of collective security. Rulers derived their power, he concluded, from a contract in which absolute authority protects people's rights.

Hobbes's notion of rule by an absolute authority left no room for political dissent or nonconformity, and it infuriated both royalists and supporters of Parliament. He enraged royalists by arguing that authority came not from divine right but from the social contract between citizens. Parliamentary supporters resisted Hobbes's claim that rulers must possess absolute authority to prevent the greater evil of anarchy; they believed that a constitution should guarantee shared power between king and parliament and protect individual rights under the law. Like Machiavelli before him, Hobbes became associated with a cynical, pessimistic view of human nature, and future political theorists often began their arguments by refuting Hobbes.

Rejecting both Hobbes and the more traditional royalist defenses of absolute authority, John Locke (1632–1704) used the notion of a social contract to provide a foundation for constitutionalism. Locke experienced political life firsthand as physician, secretary, and intellectual companion to the earl of Shaftesbury, a leading English Whig. In 1683, during the Exclusion Crisis, Locke fled with Shaftesbury to the Dutch Republic. There he continued work on his *Two Treatises of Government*, which, when published in 1690, served to justify the Glorious Revolution of 1688. Locke's position was thoroughly anti-absolutist. He denied the divine right of kings and ridiculed the common royalist idea that political power in the state mirrored the father's authority in the family. Like Hobbes, he posited a state of nature that applied to all people. Unlike Hobbes, however, he thought people were reasonable and the state of nature peaceful.

Locke insisted that government's only purpose was to protect life, liberty, and property, a notion that linked economic and political freedom. Ultimate authority rested in the will of a majority of men who owned property, and government should be limited to its basic purpose of protection. A ruler who failed to uphold his part of the social contract between the ruler and the populace could be justifiably resisted, an idea that would become crucial for the leaders of the American Revolution a century later. For England's landowners, however, Locke helped validate a revolution that consolidated their interests and ensured their privileges in the social hierarchy. Although he himself owned shares in the Royal African Company and justified slavery, Locke's writings were later used by abolitionists in their campaign against slavery.

Locke defended his optimistic view of human nature in the immensely influential *Essay Concerning Human Understanding* (1690). He denied the existence of any innate ideas and asserted instead that each human is born with a mind that is a *tabula rasa* (blank slate). Everything humans know, he claimed, comes from sensory experience, not from anything inherent in human nature. Locke's views promoted the belief that "all men are created equal," a belief that challenged absolutist forms of rule and ultimately raised questions about women's roles as well. Not surprisingly, Locke devoted considerable energy to rethinking educational practices; he believed that education crucially shaped the human personality by channeling all sensory experience.

Newton and the Consolidation of the Scientific Revolution

New breakthroughs in science lent support to Locke's optimistic view of human potential. Building on the work of Copernicus, Kepler, and Galileo (see Chapter 12), the English scientist Isaac Newton (1642–1727) finally synthesized astronomy and physics with his law of gravitation, further enhancing the prestige of the new science. A Cambridge University student at the time of Charles II's restoration, Newton was a pious Anglican who aimed to reconcile faith and science. By proving that the physical universe followed rational principles, Newton argued, scientists could prove the existence of God and so liberate humans from doubt and the fear of chaos. Newton applied mathematical principles to formulate three physical laws: (1) in the absence of force, motion continues in a straight line; (2) the rate of change in the motion of an object is a result of the forces acting on it; and (3) the action and reaction between two objects are equal and opposite. The basis of Newtonian physics thus required understanding mass, inertia, force, velocity, and acceleration—all key concepts in modern science.

Extending these principles to the entire universe in his masterwork, *Principia Mathematica* (1687), Newton united celestial and terrestrial mechanics—astronomy and physics—with his law of gravitation. This law held that every body in the universe exerts over every other body an attractive force directly proportional to the product of their masses and inversely proportional to the square of the distance between them. The law of gravitation explained Kepler's elliptical planetary orbits just as it accounted for the motion of ordinary objects on earth. Once set in motion, the universe operated like clockwork, with no need for God's continuing intervention. Gravity, though a mysterious force, could be expressed mathematically. In Newton's words, "From the same principles [of motion] I now demonstrate the frame of the System of the World." The English poet Alexander Pope later captured the intellectual world's appreciation of Newton's accomplishment:

> *Nature and Nature's laws lay hid in night*
> *God said, Let Newton be! and all was light.*

Newton's science was not just mathematical and deductive; he experimented with light and helped establish the science of optics. Even while making these fundamental contributions to scientific method, Newton carried out alchemical experiments in his rooms at Cambridge University and spent long hours trying to calculate the date of the beginning of the world and of the second coming of Jesus. Not all scientists accepted Newton's theories immediately, especially on the continent of Europe, but within a couple of generations his work was preeminent, partly because of experimental verification. His "frame of the System of the World" remained the basis of all physics until the advent of relativity theory and quantum mechanics in the early twentieth century.

Although not all Newton's peers immediately accepted the validity of his work, absolutist rulers quickly saw the potential of the new science for enhancing their prestige and glory. Frederick William, the Great Elector of Brandenburg-Prussia, for example, set up agricultural experiments in front of his Berlin palace, and various German princes supported the work of Gottfried Wilhelm Leibniz (1646–1716), one of the inventors of calculus. A lawyer, diplomat, and scholar who wrote about metaphysics, cosmology, and history, Leibniz helped establish scientific societies in the German states. Government involvement in science was greatest in France, where it became an arm of mercantilist policy; in 1666, Colbert founded the Royal Academy of Sciences, which supplied fifteen scientists with government stipends.

Constitutional states supported science less directly but nonetheless provided an intellectual environment that encouraged its spread. The English Royal Society, the counterpart to the Royal Academy of Sciences in France, grew out of informal meetings of scientists at London and Oxford rather than direct government involvement. It received a royal charter in 1662 but maintained complete independence. The society's secretary described its business to be "in the first place, to scrutinize the whole of Nature and to investigate its activity and powers by means of observations and experiments; and then in course of time to hammer out a more solid philosophy and more ample amenities of civilization." Whether the state was directly involved or not, thinkers of the day now tied science explicitly to social progress.

Because of their exclusion from most universities, women only rarely participated in the new scientific discoveries. In 1667, nonetheless, the English Royal Society invited Margaret Cavendish, a writer of poems, essays, letters, and philosophical treatises, to attend a meeting to watch the exhibition of experiments. She attacked the use of telescopes and microscopes because she detected in the new experimentalism a mechanistic view of the world that exalted masculine prowess and challenged the Christian belief in freedom of the will. She also urged the formal education of women, complaining that "we are kept like birds in cages to hop up and down in our houses." "Many of our Sex may have as much wit, and be capable of Learning as well as men," she insisted, "but since they want Instructions, it is not possible they should attain to it."

Freedom and Order in the Arts

Even though Newtonian science depicted an orderly universe, most artists and intellectuals had experienced enough of the upheavals of the seventeenth century to fear the prospect of chaos and disintegration. The French mathematician Blaise Pascal vividly captured their worries in his *Pensées* ("Thoughts") of 1660: "I look on all sides, and I see only darkness everywhere. Nature presents to me nothing which is not a matter of doubt and concern. . . . It is incomprehensible that God should exist, and incomprehensible that He should not exist." Poets, painters, and architects all tried to make sense of the individual's place within what Pascal called "the eternal silence of these infinite spaces."

The English Puritan poet John Milton (1608–1674) responded to the turmoil of the times by giving priority to individual liberty. In 1643, in the midst of the civil war between king and Parliament, he published writings in favor of divorce. When Parliament enacted a censorship law aimed at such literature, Milton countered in 1644 with one of the first defenses of freedom of the press, *Areopagitica* ("Tribunal of Opinion"). Forced into retirement after the restoration of the monarchy, Milton published in 1667 his epic poem *Paradise Lost*. He used Adam and Eve's Fall to meditate on human freedom and the tragedies of rebellion. Although Milton wanted to "justify the ways of God to man," his Satan, the proud angel who challenges God, is so compelling as to be heroic. In the end, Adam and Eve learn to accept moral responsibility. Individuals learn the limits to their freedom, yet personal liberty remains essential to their definition as human.

The dominant artistic styles of the time—the baroque and the classical—both submerged the individual in a grander design. The baroque style proved to be especially suitable for public displays of faith and power that overawed individual

■ **Gian Lorenzo Bernini, *Ecstasy of St. Teresa of Ávila* (c. 1650)**
In this baroque sculpture, Bernini captures the drama and sensationalism of a mystical religious faith. He based his figures on a vision of an angel reported by St. Teresa: "In his hands I saw a great golden spear, and at the iron tip there appeared to be a point of fire. This he plunged into my heart several times so that it penetrated my entrails. When he pulled it out I felt that he took them with it, and left me utterly consumed by the great love of God." (Scala/Art Resource, NY.)

beholders. The combination of religious and political purposes in baroque art is best exemplified in the architecture and sculpture of Gian Lorenzo Bernini (1598–1680), the papacy's official artist. His architectural masterpiece was the gigantic square facing St. Peter's Basilica in Rome (1656–1671). His use of freestanding colonnades and a huge open space is meant to impress the individual observer with the power of the popes and the Catholic religion. Bernini also sculpted tombs for the popes and a large statue of Constantine, the first Christian emperor of Rome— perfect examples of the marriage of power and religion. In 1665, Louis XIV hired Bernini to plan the rebuilding of the Louvre palace in Paris but then rejected his ideas as incompatible with French tastes.

Although France was a Catholic country, French painters, sculptors, and architects, like their patron Louis XIV, preferred the standards of classicism to those of the baroque. French artists developed classicism to be a national style, distinct from the baroque style that was closely associated with France's enemies, the Austrian and Spanish Habsburgs. As its name suggests, classicism reflected the ideals of the art of antiquity; geometric shapes, order, and harmony of lines took precedence over the sensuous, exuberant, and emotional forms of the baroque. Rather than being overshadowed by the sheer power of emotional display, in classicism the individual could be found at the intersection of converging, symmetrical, straight lines. These influences were apparent in the work of the leading French painters of the period, Nicolas Poussin (1594–1665) and Claude Lorrain (1600–1682), both of whom worked in Rome and tried to re-create classical Roman values in their mythological scenes and Roman landscapes.

Dutch painters found the baroque and classical styles less suited to their private market, where buyers sought smaller-scale works with ordinary subjects. Dutch artists came from common stock themselves—Rembrandt's father was a miller, and the father of his renowned contemporary, Jan Vermeer (1632–1675), was a silk worker. Their clients were people like themselves who purchased paintings much as they bought tables and chairs. Rembrandt occasionally worked on commission for the prince of Orange, but he often painted ordinary people, suffusing his canvases with a radiant, otherworldly light that made the plainest people and objects appear deeply spiritual. Vermeer's best-known paintings show women working at home, and, like Rembrandt, he made ordinary activities seem precious and beautiful. In Dutch art, ordinary individuals had religious and political significance.

Art might also serve the interests of science. One of the most skilled illustrators of insects and flowers was Maria Sibylla Merian (1646–1717), a German-born painter-scholar whose engravings were widely celebrated for their brilliant realism and microscopic clarity. Merian eventually separated from her husband and joined a sect called the Labadists (after their French founder, Jean de Labadie), who did not believe in formal marriage ties and established a colony in the northern Dutch province of Friesland. After moving there with her daughters, Merian went with missionaries from the sect to the Dutch colony of Surinam in South America and

■ European Fascination with Products of the New World

In this painting of a banana plant, Maria Sibylla Merian offers a scientific study of one of the many exotic plants and animals found by Europeans who traveled to the colonies overseas. Merian was fifty-one when she traveled to the Dutch South American colony of Surinam.

(Courtesy of Hunt Institute for Botanical Documentation, Carnegie Mellon University, Pittsburgh, PA.)

painted watercolors of the exotic flowers, birds, and insects she found in the jungle around the cocoa and sugarcane plantations. In the seventeenth century, many women became known for their still lifes and especially their paintings of flowers. Paintings by the Dutch artist Rachel Ruysch, for example, fetched higher prices than those received by Rembrandt.

Women and Manners

Poetry and painting imaginatively explored the place of the individual within a larger whole, but real-life individuals had to learn to navigate their own social worlds. Manners—the learning of individual self-discipline—were essential skills of social navigation, and women usually took the lead in teaching them. Under the tutelage of their mothers and wives, nobles learned to hide all that was crass and to maintain a fine sense of social distinction. In some ways, aristocratic men were expected to act more like women. Just as women had long been expected to please men, now aristocratic men had to please their monarch or patron by displaying proper manners and conversing with elegance and wit. Men as well as women had to master the art of pleasing—foreign languages (especially French), dance, a taste for fine music, and attention to dress.

As part of the evolution of new aristocratic ideals, nobles learned to disdain all that was lowly. The upper classes began to reject popular festivals and fairs in favor of private theaters, where seats were relatively expensive and behavior was formal. Clowns and buffoons now seemed vulgar; the last king of England to keep a court fool was Charles I. Chivalric romances that had entranced the nobility down to the time of Cervantes's *Don Quixote* (1605) now passed into popular literature.

The greatest French playwright of the seventeenth century, Molière (the pen name of Jean-Baptiste Poquelin, 1622–1673), wrote sparkling comedies of manners that revealed much about the new aristocratic behavior. Son of a tradesman, Molière left law school to form a theater company, which eventually gained the support of Louis XIV. His play *The Middle-Class Gentleman*, first performed at the royal court in 1670, revolves around the yearning of a rich, middle-class Frenchman, Monsieur Jourdain, to learn to act like a *gentilhomme* (meaning both "gentleman" and "nobleman" in French). The women in the family, including the servant girl Nicole, are reasonable, sincere, and keenly aware of what behavior is appropriate to their social station, whereas Jourdain stands for social ambition gone wild. The message for the court seemed to be a reassuring one: only true nobles by blood can hope to act like nobles. But the play also showed how the middle classes were learning to emulate the nobility; if one could learn to *act* nobly through self-discipline, could not anyone with some education and money pass himself off as noble?

As Molière's play demonstrated, new attention to manners trickled down from the court to the middle class. A French treatise on manners from 1672 explained:

> If everyone is eating from the same dish, you should take care not to put your hand into it before those of higher rank have done so. . . . Formerly one was permitted . . . to dip one's bread into the sauce, provided only that one had not already bitten it. Nowadays that would be a kind of rusticity. Formerly one was allowed to take from one's mouth what one could not eat and drop it on the floor, provided it was done skillfully. Now that would be very disgusting.

The key words *rusticity* and *disgusting* reveal the association of unacceptable social behavior with the peasantry, dirt, and repulsion. Ironically, however, once the elite had successfully distinguished itself from the lower classes through manners, scholars became more interested in studying popular expressions. They avidly collected proverbs, folktales, and songs—all of these now curiosities. In fact, many nobles at Louis XIV's court read fairy tales.

Courtly manners often permeated the upper reaches of society by means of the *salon,* an informal gathering held regularly in private homes and presided over by a socially eminent woman. In 1661, one French author claimed to have identified

■ Music and the Refinement of Manners

In Woman at the Clavecin, *the artist Emanuel de Witte celebrates the importance of music in the Dutch home. The woman herself remains a mystery, but the sumptuous setting of heavy draperies, mirrors, and chandeliers signals the association of keyboard music with refinement.*

(The Netherlands Institute of Cultural Heritage, Rijswijk, the Netherlands; Museum Boijmans–Van Beuningen, Rotterdam.)

251 Parisian women as hostesses of salons. Although the French government occasionally worried that these gatherings might be seditious, the three main topics of conversation were love, literature, and philosophy. Hostesses often worked hard to encourage the careers of budding authors. Before publishing a manuscript, many authors would read their compositions to a salon gathering. Corneille, Racine, and even Bishop Bossuet sought female approval for their writings.

Some women went beyond encouraging male authors and began to write on their own, but they faced many obstacles. Marie-Madeleine de La Vergne, known as Madame de Lafayette, wrote several short novels that were published anonymously because it was considered inappropriate for aristocratic women to appear in print. After the publication of *The Princess of Clèves* in 1678, she denied having written it. Hannah Wooley, the English author of many books on domestic conduct, published under the name of her first husband. Women were known for writing wonderful letters (Marie de Sévigné was a prime example), many of which circulated in handwritten form; hardly any appeared in print during their authors' lifetimes. In the 1650s, despite these limitations, French women began to turn out best-sellers in a new type of literature, the novel. Their success prompted the philosopher Pierre Bayle to remark in 1697 that "our best French novels for a long time have been written by women."

The new importance of women in the world of manners and letters did not sit well with everyone. Although the French writer François Poulain de la Barre (1647–1723), in a series of works published in the 1670s, used the new science to assert the equality of women's minds, most men resisted the idea. Clergy, lawyers, scholars, and playwrights attacked women's growing public influence. Women, they complained, were corrupting forces and needed restraint. Only marriage, "this salutary yoke," could control their passions and weaknesses. Women were accused of raising "the banner of prostitution in the salons, in the promenades, and in the streets." Molière wrote plays denouncing women's pretension to judge literary merit. English playwrights derided learned women by creating characters with names such as Lady Knowall, Lady Meanwell, and Mrs. Lovewit. A real-life target of the English playwrights was Aphra Behn (1640–1689), one of the first professional woman authors, who supported herself by journalism and wrote plays and poetry. Her short novel *Oroonoko* (1688) told the story of an African prince wrongly sold into slavery. The story was so successful that it was adapted by playwrights and performed repeatedly in England and France for the next hundred years. Behn responded to her critics by arguing that there was "no reason why women should not write as well as men."

Reforming Popular Culture

The illiterate peasants who made up most of Europe's population had little or no knowledge of the law of gravitation, upper-class manners, or novels, no matter who authored them. Their culture had three main elements: the knowledge needed to work at farming or in a trade; popular forms of entertainment such as village fairs and dances; and their religion, which shaped every aspect of life and death. What changed most noticeably in the seventeenth century was the social elites' attitude toward lower-class culture. The division between elite and popular culture widened as elites insisted on their difference from the lower orders and tried to instill new forms of discipline in their social inferiors.

In the seventeenth century, Protestant and Catholic churches alike pushed hard to change popular religious practices. Their campaigns against popular "paganism" began during the sixteenth-century Protestant Reformation and Catholic Counter-Reformation but reached much of rural Europe only in the seventeenth century. Puritans in England tried to root out maypole dances, Sunday village fairs, gambling, taverns, and bawdy ballads because they interfered with sober observance of the Sabbath. In Lutheran Norway, pastors denounced a widespread belief in the miracle-working powers of St. Olaf. *Superstition* previously meant "false religion" (Protestantism was a superstition for Catholics, Catholicism for Protestants). In the seventeenth century, it took on its modern meaning of irrational fears, beliefs, and

IMPORTANT DATES			
1642–1646	Civil war between King Charles I and Parliament in England	1678	Marie-Madeleine de La Vergne (Madame de Lafayette) anonymously publishes her novel *The Princess of Clèves*
1648	Peace of Westphalia ends Thirty Years' War; the Fronde revolt challenges royal authority in France; Ukrainian Cossack warriors rebel against the king of Poland-Lithuania	1683	Austrian Habsburgs break the Turkish siege of Vienna
1649	Execution of Charles I of England; new Russian legal code	1685	Louis XIV revokes toleration for French Protestants granted by the Edict of Nantes
1651	Thomas Hobbes publishes *Leviathan*	1687	Isaac Newton publishes *Principia Mathematica*
1660	Monarchy restored in England	1688	Parliament deposes James II and invites his daughter, Mary, and her husband, William of Orange, to take the throne
1661	Slave code set up in Barbados		
1667	Louis XIV begins the first of many wars that continue throughout his reign	1690	John Locke's *Two Treatises of Government* and *Essay Concerning Human Understanding*
1670	Molière's play *The Middle-Class Gentleman*		

practices, which anyone educated or refined would avoid. *Superstition* became synonymous with popular or ignorant beliefs.

The Catholic campaign against superstitious practices found a ready ally in Louis XIV. While he reformed the nobles at court through etiquette and manners, Catholic bishops in the French provinces trained parish priests to reform their flocks by using catechisms in local dialects and insisting that parishioners attend Mass. The church faced a formidable challenge. One bishop in France complained in 1671, "Can you believe that there are in this diocese entire villages where no one has even heard of Jesus Christ?" In some places, believers sacrificed animals to the Virgin, prayed to the new moon, and worshiped at the sources of streams as in pre-Christian times.

Like its Protestant counterpart, the Catholic campaign against ignorance and superstition helped extend state power. Clergy, officials, and local police worked together to limit carnival celebrations, to regulate pilgrimages to shrines, and to replace "indecent" images of saints with more restrained and decorous ones. In Catholicism, the cult of the Virgin Mary and devotions closely connected with Jesus, such as the Holy Sacrament and the Sacred Heart, took precedence over the celebration of more popular saints who seemed to have pagan origins or were credited with unverified miracles. Reformers everywhere tried to limit the number of feast days on the grounds that they encouraged lewd behavior.

■ **MAPPING THE WEST Europe at the End of the Seventeenth Century**

A map can be deceiving. Size does not always spell advantage. Poland-Lithuania looks like a large country, but it had been fatally weakened by internal conflicts and in the next century would disappear entirely. The Ottoman Empire still controlled an extensive territory, but outside of Anatolia, Ottoman rule depended on intermediaries. The Austrian Habsburgs had pushed the Turks out of Hungary and back into the Balkans. At the other end of the scale, the very small Dutch Republic had become very rich through international commerce.

www.bedfordstmartins.com/huntconcise   See the ONLINE STUDY GUIDE for more help in analyzing this map.

The campaign for more disciplined religious practices helped generate a new attitude toward the poor. Poverty previously had been closely linked with charity and virtue in Christianity: it was a Christian duty to give alms to the poor, and Jesus and many of the saints had purposely chosen lives of poverty. In the sixteenth and seventeenth centuries, the upper classes, the church, and the state increasingly regarded the poor as dangerous, deceitful, and lacking in character. "Criminal laziness is the source of all their vices," wrote a Jesuit expert on the poor. The courts had previously expelled beggars from cities; now local leaders, both Catholic and Protestant, tried to reform their character. Municipal magistrates collected taxes for poor relief, and local notables organized charities; together they transformed hospitals into houses of confinement for beggars. In Catholic France, upper-class women's religious associations, known as *confraternities,* set up asylums that confined prostitutes (by arrest if necessary) and rehabilitated them. Confraternities also founded hospices where orphans learned order and respect. Such groups advocated harsh discipline as the cure for poverty.

Although hard times had increased the numbers of poor people and the rates of violent crime as well, the most important changes were attitudinal. The elites wanted to separate the very poor from society either to change them or to keep them from contaminating others. Hospitals became holding pens for society's unwanted members, where the poor joined the disabled, the incurably diseased, and the insane. The founding of hospitals demonstrates the connection between these attitudes and state building. In 1676, Louis XIV ordered every French city to establish a hospital, and his government took charge of their finances. Other rulers soon followed the same path.

Conclusion

The search for order in the wake of religious warfare and political upheaval took place on various levels, from the reform of the disorderly poor to the establishment of more regular bureaucratic routines in government. The biggest factor shaping the search for order was the growth of state power. Whether absolutist or constitutionalist in form, seventeenth-century states all aimed to penetrate more deeply into the lives of their subjects. They wanted more men for their armed forces, higher taxes to support their projects, and more control over foreign trade, religious dissent, and society's unwanted.

Some tearing had begun to appear, however, in the seamless fabric of state power. In England, the Dutch Republic, and the English North American colonies, property owners successfully demanded constitutional guarantees of their right to participate in government. In the eighteenth century, moreover, new levels of economic growth and the appearance of new social groups would exert pressures on the European state system. The success of seventeenth-century rulers created the political and economic conditions in which their critics would flourish.

Suggested References for further reading and online research appear on page SR-20 at the back of the book.

www.bedfordstmartins.com/huntconcise   See the ONLINE STUDY GUIDE to assess your mastery of the material covered in this chapter.

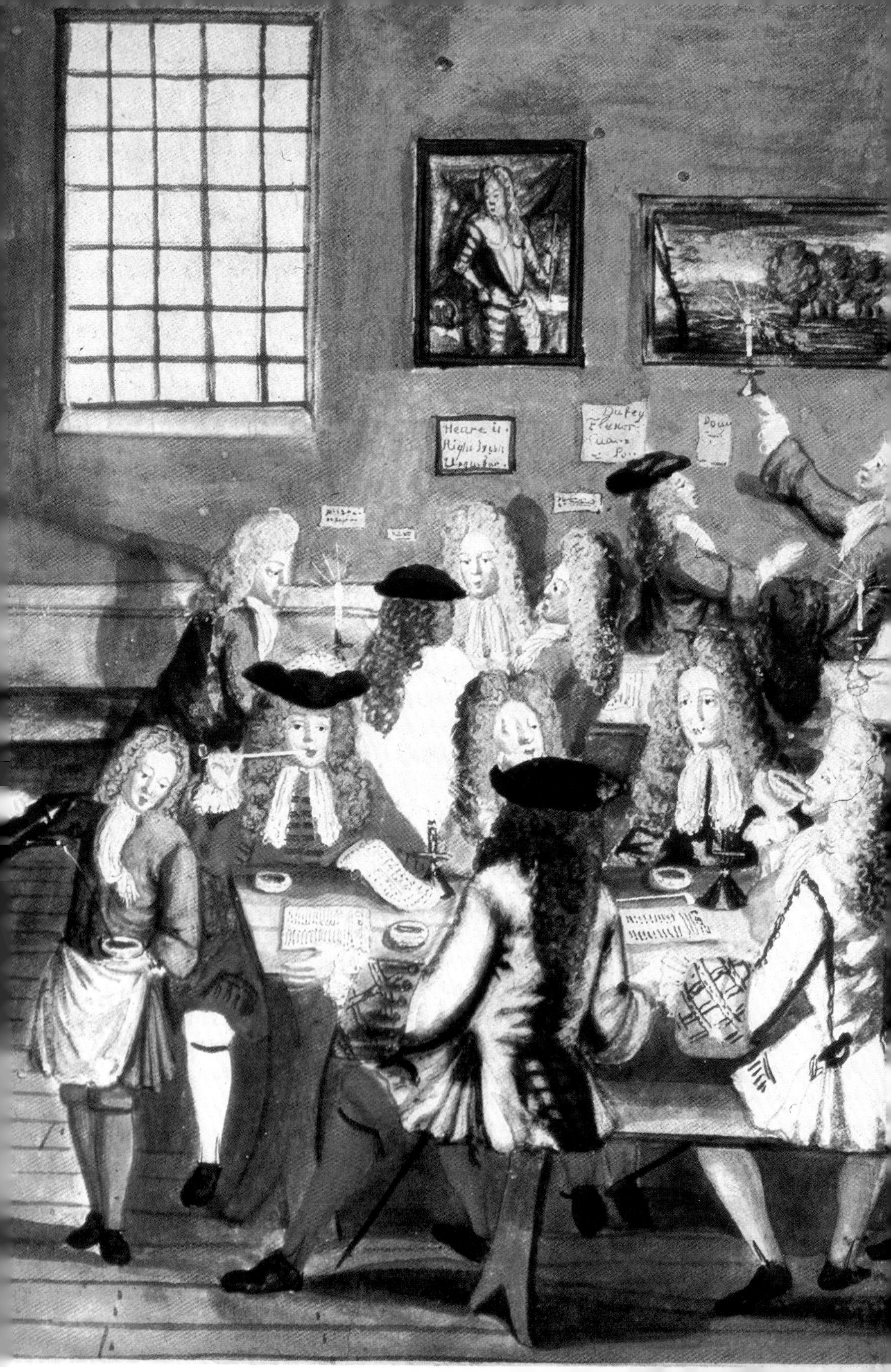
Heare is
Dufey

14

The Atlantic System and Its Consequences

1690–1740

JOHANN SEBASTIAN BACH (1685–1750), composer of mighty organ fugues and church cantatas, was not above amusing his Leipzig audiences, many of them university students. In 1732 he produced a cantata about a young woman in love— with coffee. Her old-fashioned father rages that he won't find her a husband unless she gives up the fad. She agrees, secretly vowing to admit no suitor who will not promise in the marriage contract to let her brew coffee whenever she wants. Bach offers this conclusion:

> The cat won't give up its mouse,
> Girls stay faithful coffee-sisters
> Mother loves her coffee habit,
> Grandma sips it gladly too—
> Why then shout at the daughters?

Bach's era might well be called the age of coffee. European travelers at the end of the sixteenth century had noticed Middle Eastern people drinking a "black drink," *kavah*. Few Europeans sampled it at first, and the Arab monopoly on its production kept prices high. This changed around 1700 when the Dutch East India Company introduced coffee plants to Java and other Indonesian islands. Coffee production then spread to the French Caribbean, where African slaves provided the plantation labor. In Europe, imported coffee spurred the development of a new kind of meet- ing place: the first coffeehouse opened in London in 1652, and the idea spread quickly

■ **London Coffeehouse**
This gouache (a variant on water-color painting) from about 1725 depicts a scene from a London coffeehouse located in the courtyard of the Royal Exchange (merchants' bank). Middle-class men (wearing wigs) read newspapers, drink coffee, smoke pipes, and discuss the news of the day. The coffeehouse draws them out of their homes into a new public space.
(British Museum, Bridgeman Art Library, NY.)

571

to other European cities. Coffeehouses became gathering places for men to drink, read newspapers, and talk politics. As a London newspaper commented in 1737, "There's scarce an Alley in City and Suburbs but has a Coffeehouse in it, which may be called the School of Public Spirit, where every Man over Daily and Weekly Journals, a Mug, or a Dram . . . devotes himself to that glorious one, his Country."

European consumption of coffee, tea, chocolate, and other novelties increased dramatically as European nations forged worldwide economic links. At the center of this new world economy was an "Atlantic system" that bound together western Europe, Africa, and the Americas. Europeans bought slaves in western Africa, transported and sold them in their colonies in North and South America and the Caribbean, bought the commodities such as coffee and sugar that were produced by the new colonial plantations, and then sold the goods in European ports for refining and reshipment. This Atlantic system first took clear shape in the early eighteenth century; it was the hub of European expansion all over the world.

Coffee drinking was one example among many of the new social and cultural patterns that took root between 1690 and 1740. Improvements in agricultural production at home reinforced the effects of trade overseas; Europeans now had more disposable income for "extras," and they spent their money not only in the new coffeehouses and cafés that sprang up all over Europe but also on newspapers, musical concerts, paintings, and novels. A new middle-class public began to make its presence felt in every domain of culture and social life.

Although the rise of the Atlantic system gave Europe new prominence in the global context, European rulers still focused most of their political, diplomatic, and military energies on their rivalries within Europe. A coalition of countries succeeded in containing French aggression, and a more balanced diplomatic system emerged. In eastern Europe, Prussia and Austria had to contend with the rising power of Russia under Peter the Great. In western Europe, both Spain and the Dutch Republic declined in influence but continued to vie with Britain and France for colonial spoils in the Atlantic. The more evenly matched competition among the great powers encouraged the development of diplomatic skills and drew attention to public health as a way of encouraging population growth.

In the aftermath of Louis XIV's revocation of the Edict of Nantes in 1685, a new intellectual movement known as the Enlightenment began to germinate. French Protestant refugees began to publish works critical of absolutism in politics and religion. Increased prosperity, the growth of a middle-class public, and the decline in warfare after Louis XIV's death in 1715 all fostered the development of this new critical spirit. Fed by the popularization of science and the growing interest in travel literature, the Enlightenment encouraged greater skepticism about religious and state authority. Eventually the movement would question almost every aspect of social and political life in Europe. The Enlightenment began in western Europe in those countries—Britain, France, and the Dutch Republic—most affected by the new Atlantic system. It, too, was a product of the age of coffee.

The Atlantic System and the World Economy

Although their ships had been circling the globe since the early 1500s, Europeans did not draw most of the world into their economic orbit until the 1700s. Western European trading nations sent ships loaded with goods to buy slaves from local rulers on the western coast of Africa; then transported the slaves to the colonies in North and South America and the Caribbean and sold them to the owners of plantations producing coffee, sugar, cotton, and tobacco; and bought the raw commodities produced in the colonies and shipped them back to Europe, where they were refined or processed and then sold to other parts of Europe and the world. The Atlantic system and the growth of international trade helped create a new consumer society.

Slavery and the Atlantic System

Spain and Portugal had dominated Atlantic trade in the sixteenth and seventeenth centuries, but in the eighteenth century European trade in the Atlantic rapidly expanded and became more systematically interconnected (Map 14.1, inset). By 1630, Portugal had already sent 60,000 African slaves to Brazil to work on the new plantations (large tracts of lands farmed by slave labor), which were producing some 15,000 tons of sugar a year. Realizing that plantations producing staples for Europeans could bring fabulous wealth, the European powers grew less interested in the dwindling trade in precious metals and more eager to colonize. Large-scale planters of sugar, tobacco, and coffee displaced small farmers who relied on one or two servants. Planters and their plantations won out because slave labor was cheap and therefore able to produce mass quantities of commodities at low prices.

State-chartered private companies from Portugal, France, Britain, the Dutch Republic, Prussia, and even Denmark exploited the 3,500-mile coastline of West Africa for slaves. Before 1675, most blacks taken from Africa had been sent to Brazil, but by 1700 half of the African slaves landed in the Caribbean (Figure 14.1). Thereafter, the plantation economy began to expand on the North American mainland. The numbers stagger the imagination. Before 1650, slave traders transported about 7,000 Africans each year across the Atlantic; this rate doubled between 1650 and 1675, nearly doubled again in the next twenty-five years, and kept going until the 1780s. In all, more than 11 million Africans, not counting those who died at sea or in Africa, were transported to the Americas before the slave trade began to wind down after 1850. Many traders gained spectacular wealth, but companies did not always make profits. The English Royal African Company, for example, delivered 100,000 slaves to the Caribbean, imported 30,000 tons of sugar to Britain, yet lost money after the few profitable years following its founding in 1672.

The balance of white and black populations in the New World colonies was determined by the staples produced. New England merchants and farmers bought few

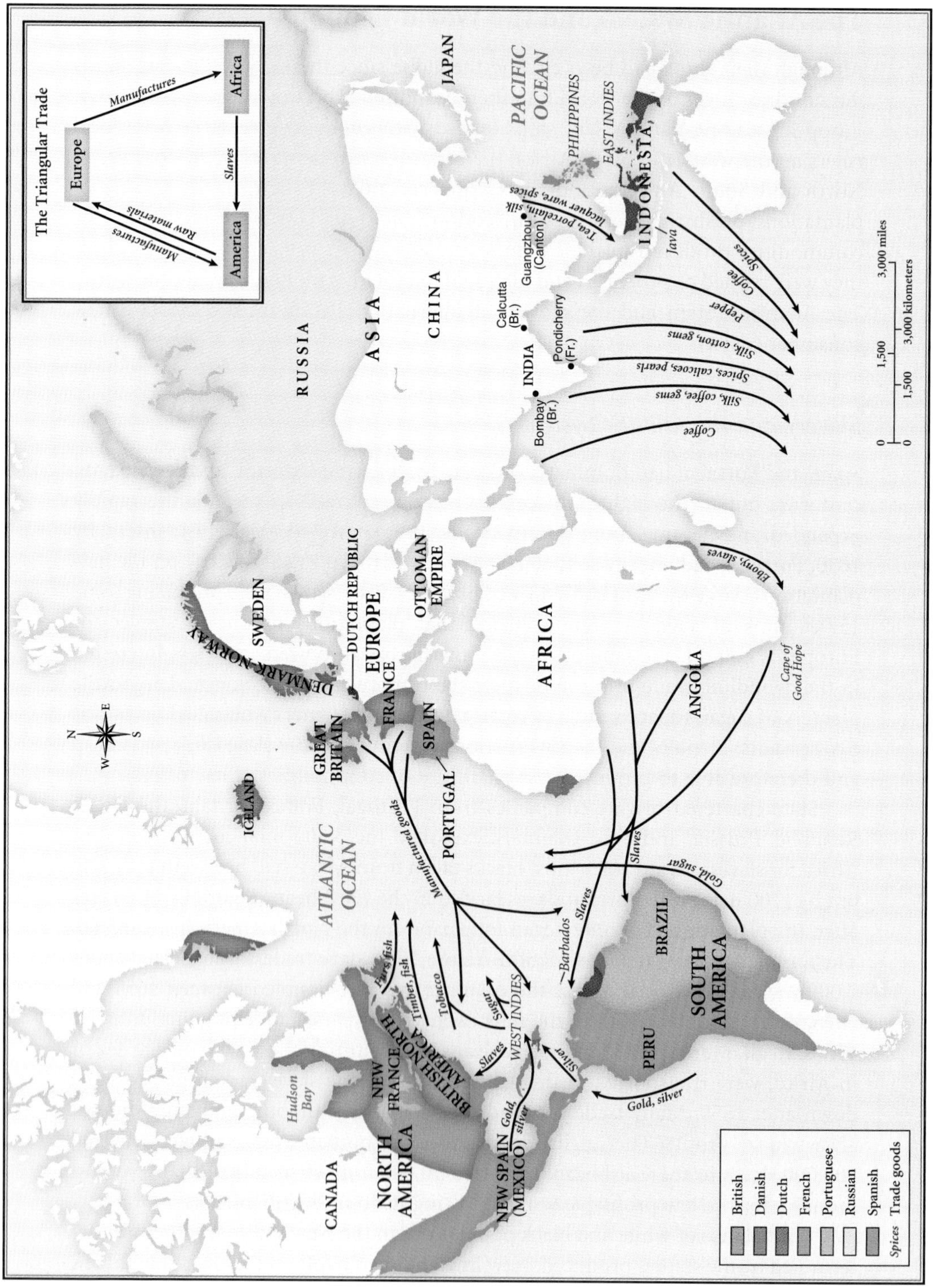
The Triangular Trade
Europe
Africa
America
Manufactures
Slaves
Raw materials
Manufactures
N
E
S
W
RUSSIA
ASIA
CHINA
JAPAN
PACIFIC OCEAN
PHILIPPINES
EAST INDIES
INDONESIA
Java
Guangzhou (Canton)
Calcutta (Br.)
Pondicherry (Fr.)
INDIA
Bombay (Br.)
Tea, porcelain, silk, lacquer ware, spices
Spices
Coffee
Pepper
Silk, cotton, gems
Spices, calicoes, pearls
Silk, coffee, gems
Coffee
0 1,500 3,000 miles
0 1,500 3,000 kilometers
SWEDEN
DENMARK-NORWAY
DUTCH REPUBLIC
EUROPE
OTTOMAN EMPIRE
AFRICA
Ebony, slaves
ANGOLA
Cape of Good Hope
GREAT BRITAIN
FRANCE
SPAIN
PORTUGAL
ICELAND
ATLANTIC OCEAN
Manufactured goods
Slaves
Gold, sugar
BRAZIL
SOUTH AMERICA
PERU
Gold, silver
Barbados
Slaves
Furs, fish
Timber, fish
Tobacco
Sugar
WEST INDIES
Slaves
Silver
NEW FRANCE
BRITISH NORTH AMERICA
Hudson Bay
CANADA
NORTH AMERICA
NEW SPAIN (MEXICO)
Gold, silver
British
Danish
Dutch
French
Portuguese
Russian
Spanish
Spices Trade goods

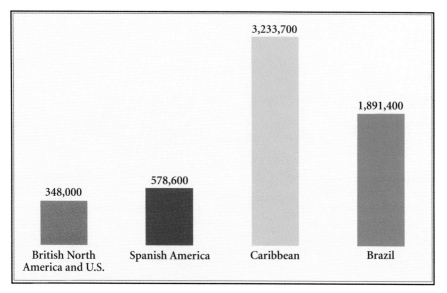

■ **FIGURE 14.1 African Slaves Imported into American Territories, 1701–1810**
During the eighteenth century, planters in the newly established Caribbean colonies imported millions of African slaves to work the new plantations. The vast majority of African slaves transported to the Americas ended up either in the Caribbean or in Brazil.
(Adapted from Philip D. Curtin, *The Atlantic Slave Trade: A Census* [Madison: University of Wisconsin Press, 1969].)

slaves because they did not own plantations. Blacks—both slave and free—made up only 3 percent of the population in eighteenth-century New England, compared with 60 percent in South Carolina. On the whole, the British North American colonies contained a higher proportion of African Americans from 1730 to 1765 than at any other time in American history. The imbalance of whites and blacks was even more extreme in the Caribbean; in the early 1700s, the British sugar islands had a population of about 150,000 people, only 30,000 of them Europeans. The remaining 80 percent were African slaves, as most indigenous people died fighting Europeans or the diseases brought by them.

Enslaved women and men suffered terribly. Most had been sold to European traders by Africans from the west coast who acquired them through warfare or kidnapping. The vast majority were between fourteen and thirty-five years old.

■ **MAP 14.1 European Trade Patterns, c. 1740**
By 1740, the European powers had colonized much of North and South America and incorporated their American colonies into a worldwide system of commerce centered on the slave trade and plantation production of staple crops. Europeans still sought spices and luxury goods in China and the East Indies, but outside of Java, few Europeans had settled permanently in these areas.

www.bedfordstmartins.com/huntconcise See the ONLINE STUDY GUIDE for more help in analyzing this map.

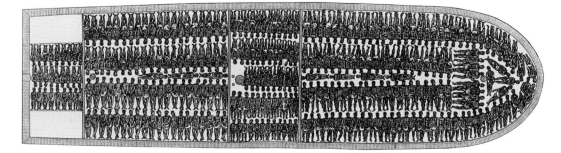

■ **Conditions on Slave Ships**

Although the viewer cannot tell whether the enslaved Africans are lying down or standing, this engraving, inspired by the campaign to abolish slavery, has a clear message: slaves endured desperately crowded conditions on the long voyage across the Atlantic. Many (like crew members, who also died in large numbers) fell victim to dysentery, yellow fever, measles, or smallpox; a few committed suicide by jumping overboard. (North Wind Picture Archive.)

Before they were crammed onto the ships for the three-month trip, their heads were shaved, they were stripped naked, and some were branded with red-hot irons. Men and women were separated. Men were shackled with leg irons. Sailors and officers raped the women whenever they wished and beat those who refused their advances. In the cramped and appalling conditions aboard ship, as many as one-fourth of the slaves died in transit.◆

Once they landed, slaves were forced into degrading and oppressive conditions. As soon as masters bought slaves, they gave them new names, often only first names, and in some colonies branded them as personal property. Slaves had no social identities of their own; they were expected to learn their master's language and to do any job assigned. Slaves worked fifteen- to seventeen-hour days and were fed only enough to keep them on their feet. Brazilian slaves consumed more calories than the poorest Brazilians do today, but that hardly made them well fed. The death rate among slaves was high, especially in Brazil, where quick shifts in the weather, lack of clothing, and squalid living conditions made them susceptible to a variety of deadly illnesses.

Not surprisingly, despite the threat of torture or death on recapture, slaves sometimes ran away. In Brazil, runaways hid in *quilombos* (hideouts) in the forests or backcountry. When it was discovered and destroyed in 1695, the *quilombo* of Palmares had thirty thousand fugitives who had formed their own social organization complete with elected kings and councils of elders. Outright revolt was uncommon, especially before the nineteenth century, but other forms of resistance included

◆ For a personal account of the eighteenth-century Atlantic slave trade, see Document 44, *The Interesting Narrative of the Life of Olaudah Equiano, Written by Himself.*

stealing food, breaking tools, and feigning illness or stupidity. Slaveholders' fears about conspiracy and revolt lurked beneath the surface of every slave-based society. In 1710, the royal governor of Virginia reminded the colonial legislature of the need for unceasing vigilance: "We are not to Depend on Either Their Stupidity, or that Babel of Languages among 'em; freedom Wears a Cap which Can Without a Tongue, Call Togather all Those who Long to Shake off the fetters of Slavery." Masters defended whipping and other forms of physical punishment as essential to maintaining discipline. Laws called for the castration of a slave who struck a white person.

Plantation owners often left their colonial possessions in the care of agents and collected the revenue to live as wealthy landowners back home, where they built opulent mansions and gained influence in local and national politics. William Beckford, for example, had been sent from Jamaica to school in England as a young boy. When he inherited sugar plantations and shipping companies from his father and older brother, he moved the headquarters of the family business to London in the 1730s to be close to the government and financial markets. His holdings formed the single most powerful economic interest in Jamaica, but he preferred to live in England, where he could collect art for his many luxurious homes, hold political office (he served as lord mayor of London and in Parliament), and even lend money to the government.

The slave trade permanently altered consumption patterns for ordinary people. Sugar had been prescribed as medicine before the end of the sixteenth century, but the development of plantations in Brazil and the Caribbean made it a standard food item. By 1700, the British sent home 50 million pounds of sugar a year, a figure that doubled by 1730. During the French Revolution of the 1790s, sugar shortages would become a cause for rioting in Paris. Equally pervasive was the spread of tobacco; by the 1720s, Britain imported two hundred shiploads of tobacco from Virginia and Maryland every year, and men of every country and class smoked pipes or took snuff.

The traffic in slaves disturbed many Europeans. As a government memorandum to the Spanish king explained in 1610: "Modern theologians in published books commonly report on, and condemn as unjust, the acts of enslavement which take place in provinces of this Royal Empire." Between 1667 and 1671, the French Dominican monk Father Du Tertre published three volumes in which he denounced the mistreatment of slaves in the French colonies.

In the 1700s, however, slaveholders began to justify their actions by demeaning the mental and spiritual qualities of the enslaved Africans. White Europeans and colonists sometimes described black slaves as animal-like, akin to apes. A leading New England Puritan asserted about the slaves: "Indeed their *Stupidity* is a *Discouragement.* It may seem, unto as little purpose, to *Teach,* as to *wash an Aethiopian* [Ethiopian]." One of the great paradoxes of this time was that talk of liberty and self-evident rights, especially prevalent in Britain and its North American colonies, coexisted with the belief that some people were meant to be slaves. Although Christians believed in principle in a kind of spiritual equality between blacks and whites, the churches often defended or at least did not oppose the inequities of slavery.

World Trade and Settlement

The Atlantic system helped extend European trade relations across the globe. The textiles that Atlantic shippers exchanged for slaves on the west coast of Africa, for example, were manufactured in India and exported by the British and the French East India Companies. As much as one-quarter of the British exports to Africa in the eighteenth century were actually re-exports from India. To expand its trade in the rest of the world, Europeans seized territories and tried to establish permanent settlements. The eighteenth-century extension of European power prepared the way for western global domination in the nineteenth and twentieth centuries.

In contrast to the sparsely inhabited trading outposts in Asia and Africa, the colonies in the Americas bulged with settlers. The British North American colonies, for example, contained about 1.5 million nonnative (that is, white settler and black slave) residents by 1750. While the Spanish competed with the Portuguese for control of South America, the French competed with the British for control of North America. Spanish and British settlers came to blows over the boundary between the British colonies and Florida, which was held by Spain.

Local economies shaped colonial social relations; men in French trapper communities in Canada, for example, had little in common with the men and women of the plantation societies in Barbados or Brazil. Racial attitudes also differed from place to place. The Spanish and Portuguese tolerated intermarriage with the native populations in both America and Asia. Sexual contact, both inside and outside marriage, fostered greater racial variety in the Spanish and Portuguese colonies than in the French or the English territories (though mixed-race people could be found everywhere). By 1800, *mestizos*, children of Spanish men and Indian women, accounted for more than a quarter of the population in the Spanish colonies, and many of them aspired to join the local elite. Greater racial diversity seems not to have improved the treatment of slaves, however, which was probably harshest in Portuguese Brazil.

Where intermarriage between colonizers and natives was common, conversion to Christianity proved most successful. Although the Indians maintained many of their native religious beliefs, the majority of Indians in the Spanish colonies had come to consider themselves devout Catholics by 1700. Indian carpenters and artisans in the villages produced innumerable altars, retables (painted panels), and sculpted images to adorn their local churches, and individual families put up domestic shrines. Yet the clergy remained overwhelmingly Spanish: the church hierarchy concluded that the Indians' humility and innocence made them unsuitable for the priesthood.

In the early years of American colonization, many more men than women emigrated from Europe. At the end of the seventeenth century, the sex imbalance began to decline but remained substantial; two and one-half times as many men as women were among the immigrants leaving Liverpool, England, between 1697 and 1707, for example. Women who emigrated as indentured servants ran great risks: if they did not die of disease during the voyage, they might end up giving birth to illegitimate children (the fate of at least one in five servant women) or being virtually sold into marriage.

The uncertainties of life in the American colonies provided new opportunities for European women and men willing to live outside the law, however. In the 1500s and 1600s, the English and Dutch governments had routinely authorized pirates to prey on the shipping of their rivals, the Spanish and Portuguese. Then, in the late 1600s, English, French, and Dutch bands made up of deserters and crews from wrecked vessels began to form their own associations of pirates, especially in the Caribbean. Called *buccaneers* from their custom of curing strips of beef, called *boucan* by the native Caribs of the islands, the pirates governed themselves and preyed on everyone's shipping without regard to national origin. After 1700, the colonial governments tried to stamp out piracy. As one British judge argued in 1705, "A pirate is in perpetual war with every individual and every state. . . . They are worse than ravenous beasts."

White settlements in Africa and Asia remained small and almost insignificant, except for their long-term potential. Europeans had little contact with East Africa and almost none with Africa's vast interior. A few Portuguese trading posts in Angola and Dutch farms on the Cape of Good Hope provided the only toeholds for future expansion. In China, the emperors had welcomed Catholic missionaries at court in the seventeenth century, but the priests' credibility diminished as they squabbled among themselves and associated with European merchants, whom the Chinese considered pirates. "The barbarians [Europeans] are like wild beasts," one Chinese official concluded. In 1720, only one thousand Europeans resided in Guangzhou (Canton), the sole place where foreigners could legally trade for spices, tea, and silk (see Map 14.1).

Europeans exercised more influence in Java in the East Indies and in India. Dutch coffee production in Java and nearby islands increased phenomenally in the early 1700s, and many Dutch settled there to oversee production and trade. In India, Dutch, English, French, Portuguese, and Danish companies competed for spices, cotton, and silk; by the 1740s the English and French had become the leading rivals in India, just as they were in North America. Both countries extended their power as India's Muslim rulers lost control to local Hindu princes, rebellious Sikhs, invading Persians, and their own provincial governors. A few thousand Europeans lived in India, though many thousand more soldiers were stationed there to protect them. The staple of trade with India in the early 1700s was calico—lightweight, brightly colored cotton cloth that caught on as a fashion in Europe.

■ **India Cottons and Trade with the East**
*This brightly colored cotton cloth was painted and embroidered in Madras in southern In-
dia in the late 1600s. The male figure with a mustache may be a European, but the female
figures are clearly Asian. Europeans—especially the British—discovered that they could
make big profits on the export of Indian cotton cloth to Europe. They also traded Indian
cottons in Africa for slaves and sold large quantities in the colonies.*
(Victoria and Albert Museum, London.)

Europeans who visited India were especially struck by what they viewed as
exotic religious practices. In a book published in 1696 of his travels to western India,
an Anglican minister described beggars of alms, "some of whom show their devotion
by a shameless appearance, and walking naked." Such writings increased European
interest in the outside world, but they also fed a European sense of superiority that
helped excuse violent forms of colonial domination.

The Birth of Consumer Society

Worldwide colonization produced new supplies of goods, from coffee to calico, and
population growth in Europe fueled demand for them. Beginning first in Britain,
then in France and the Italian states, and finally in eastern Europe, population
surged, growing by about 20 percent between 1700 and 1750. The gap between
a fast-growing northwest and a more stagnant south and central Europe now
diminished as regions that had lost population during the seventeenth-century

downturn recovered. Cities, in particular, grew. Between 1600 and 1750, London's population more than tripled, and Paris's more than doubled.

Although contemporaries could not have realized it then, this was the start of the modern "population explosion." It appears that a decline in the death rate, rather than a rise in the birthrate, explains the turnaround. Three main factors contributed to this decline in the death rate: better weather and hence more bountiful harvests, improved agricultural techniques, and the plague's disappearance after 1720.

By the early eighteenth century, the effects of economic expansion and population growth brought about a consumer revolution. The British East India Company began to import into Britain huge quantities of calicoes. British imports of tobacco doubled between 1672 and 1700; at Nantes, the center of the French sugar trade, imports quadrupled between 1698 and 1733. Tea, chocolate, and coffee became virtual necessities. In the 1670s, only a trickle of tea reached London, but by 1720 the East India Company sent 9 million pounds to England—a figure that rose to 37 million pounds by 1750. By 1700, England had two thousand coffeehouses; by 1740, every English country town had at least two. Paris got its first cafés at the end of the seventeenth century; Berlin opened its first coffeehouse in 1714; Bach's Leipzig boasted eight by 1725.

The birth of consumer society did not go unnoticed by eyewitnesses. In the English economic literature of the 1690s, writers began to express a new view of humans as consuming animals with boundless appetites. Such opinions gained a wide audience with the appearance of Bernard Mandeville's poem *Fable of the Bees* (1705), which argued that private vices might have public benefits. Mandeville insisted that pride, self-interest, and the desire for material goods (all Christian vices) in fact promoted economic prosperity: "every part was full of Vice, Yet the whole mass a Paradise." Many authors attacked the new doctrine of consumerism, and the French government banned the poem's publication. But Mandeville had captured the essence of the emerging market for consumption.

New Social and Cultural Patterns

The impact of the Atlantic system and world trade was most apparent in the cities, where people had more money for consumer goods. But rural changes also had significant long-term influence, as a revolution in agricultural techniques made it possible to feed more and more people with a smaller agricultural workforce. As population increased, more people moved to the cities, where they found themselves caught up in innovative urban customs such as attending musical concerts and reading novels. Along with a general increase in literacy, these activities helped create a public that responded to new writers and artists. Social and cultural changes were not uniform across Europe, however; as usual, people's experiences varied depending on whether they lived in wealth or poverty, in urban or rural areas, or in eastern or western Europe.

Agricultural Revolution

Although Britain, France, and the Dutch Republic shared the enthusiasm for consumer goods, Britain's domestic market grew most quickly. In Britain, as agricultural output increased 43 percent over the course of the 1700s, the population increased by 70 percent. The British imported grain to feed the growing population, but they also benefited from the development of techniques that together constituted an agricultural revolution. No new machinery propelled this revolution—just more aggressive attitudes toward investment and management. The Dutch and the Flemish had pioneered many of these techniques in the 1600s, but the British took them further.

Four major changes occurred in British agriculture that eventually spread to other countries. First, farmers increased the amount of land under cultivation by draining wetlands and by growing crops on previously uncultivated common lands (acreage maintained by the community for grazing). Second, farmers who could afford to do so consolidated smaller, scattered plots into larger, more efficient units. Third, livestock raising became more closely linked to crop growing, and the yields of each increased. (See "Taking Measure," below.) For centuries, most farmers had rotated their fields in and out of production to replenish the soil. Now farmers

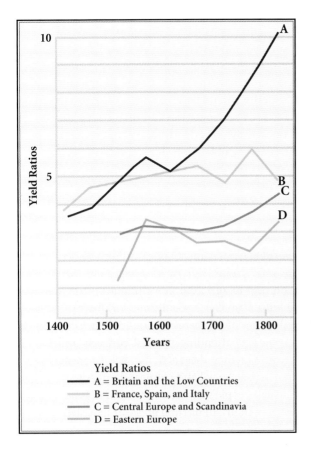

Yield Ratios

- A = Britain and the Low Countries
- B = France, Spain, and Italy
- C = Central Europe and Scandinavia
- D = Eastern Europe

■ **TAKING MEASURE**
Relationship of Crop Harvested to Seed Used, 1400–1800
The impact and even the timing of the agricultural revolution can be determined by this figure, based on yield ratios (the number of grains produced for each seed planted). Britain, the Dutch Republic, and the Austrian Netherlands all experienced huge increases in crop yields after 1700. Other European regions lagged behind right into the 1800s.

(From Peter J. Hugill, *World Trade since 1431: Geography, Technology, and Capitalism* [Baltimore: Johns Hopkins University Press, 1995], 56. Reprinted by permission of Johns Hopkins University Press.)

planted carefully chosen fodder crops such as clover and turnips that added nutrients to the soil, thereby eliminating the need to leave a field fallow (unplanted) every two or three years. With more fodder available, farmers could raise more livestock, which in turn produced more manure to fertilize grain fields. Fourth, selective breeding of animals combined with the increase in fodder to improve the quality and size of herds. New crops had only a slight impact; potatoes, for example, were introduced to Europe from South America in the 1500s, but because people feared they might cause leprosy, tuberculosis, or fevers, they were not grown in quantity until the late 1700s. By the 1730s and 1740s, agricultural output had increased dramatically, and prices for food had fallen because of these inter-connected innovations.

Changes in agricultural practices did not benefit all landowners equally. The biggest British landowners consolidated their holdings in the "enclosure movement." They put pressure on small farmers and villagers to sell their land or give up their common lands. The big landlords then fenced off ("enclosed") their property. Because enclosure eliminated community grazing rights, it frequently sparked a struggle between the big landlords and villagers, and in Britain it normally required an act of Parliament. Such acts became increasingly common in the second half of the eighteenth century, and by the century's end six million acres of common lands had been enclosed and developed. "Improvers" produced more food more efficiently and thus supported a growing population.

Contrary to the fears of contemporaries, small farmers and cottagers (those with little or no property) were not forced off the land all at once. But most villagers could not afford the litigation involved in resisting enclosure, and small landholders consequently had to sell out to landlords or farmers with larger plots. Landlords with large holdings leased their estates to tenant farmers at constantly increasing rents, and the tenant farmers in turn employed the cottagers as salaried agricultural workers. In this way the English peasantry largely disappeared, replaced by a more hierarchical society of big landlords, enterprising tenant farmers, and poor agricultural laborers.

The new agricultural techniques spread slowly from Britain and the Low Countries (the Dutch Republic and the Austrian Netherlands) to the rest of western Europe. Outside a few pockets in northern France and the western German states, however, subsistence agriculture (producing just enough to get by rather than surpluses for the market) continued to dominate farming in western Europe and Scandinavia. In southwestern Germany, for example, 80 percent of the peasants produced no surplus because their plots were too small. Unlike the populations of the highly urbanized Low Countries (where half the people lived in towns and cities), most Europeans, western and eastern, eked out their existence in the countryside.

In eastern Europe, the condition of peasants worsened in the areas where landlords tried hardest to improve their yields. To produce more for the Baltic grain market, aristocratic landholders in Prussia, Poland, and parts of Russia drained wetlands, cultivated moors, and built dikes. They also forced peasants off lands the

■ Treatment of Serfs in Russia

Visitors from western Europe often remarked on the cruel treatment of serfs in Russia. This drawing by one such visitor shows the punishment that could be inflicted by landowners. Serfs could be whipped for almost any reason, even for making a soup too salty or neglecting to bow when the lord's family passed by. Their condition actually deteriorated in the 1700s, as landowners began to sell serfs much like slaves. New decrees made it illegal for serfs to contract loans, enter into leases, or work for anyone other than their lord. Some landlords kept harems of serf girls. Although the Russian landlords' treatment of serfs was more brutal than the treatment they experienced in the German states and Poland, upper classes in every country regarded the serfs as dirty, deceitful, brutish, and superstitious.
(New York Public Library Slavonic Division.)

peasants worked for themselves, increased compulsory labor services (the critical element in serfdom), and began to manage their estates directly. Some eastern landowners grew fabulously wealthy. The Potocki family in the Polish Ukraine, for example, owned three million acres of land and had 130,000 serfs. In parts of Poland and Russia, the serfs hardly differed from slaves in status, and their "masters" ran their huge estates much like American plantations.

Social Life in the Cities

Because of emigration from the countryside, cities grew in population and consequently exercised more influence on culture and social life. Between 1650 and 1750, cities with at least ten thousand inhabitants increased in population by 44 percent. From the eighteenth century onward, urban growth would be continuous. Along with the general growth of cities, an important south-to-north shift occurred in the pattern of urbanization. Around 1500, half of the people in cities of at least ten thousand residents could be found in the Italian states, Spain, or Portugal; by 1700, the urbanization of northwestern and southern Europe was roughly equal. Eastern Europe, despite the huge cities of Istanbul and Moscow, was still less urban than western Europe. London was by far the most populous European city, with 675,000 inhabitants in 1750; Berlin had 90,000 people, Warsaw only 23,000.

Many landowners kept a residence in town, so the separation between rural and city life was not as extreme as might be imagined, at least not for the very rich.

At the top of the ladder in the big cities were the landed nobles. Some of them filled their lives only with conspicuous consumption of fine food, extravagant clothing, coaches, books, and opera; others held key political, administrative, or judicial offices. However they spent their time, these rich families employed thousands of artisans, shopkeepers, and domestic servants. Many English peers (highest-ranking nobles) had thirty or forty servants at each of their homes.

The middle classes of officials, merchants, professionals, and landowners occupied the next rung down on the social ladder. London's population, for example, included about twenty thousand middle-class families (constituting, at most, one-sixth of the city's population). In this period, the middle classes began to develop distinctive ways of life that set them apart from both the rich noble landowners and the lower classes. Unlike the rich nobles, the middle classes lived primarily in the cities and towns, even if they owned small country estates. They ate more moderately than nobles but much better than peasants or laborers. For breakfast, the British middle classes ate toast and rolls and, after 1700, drank tea. Dinner, served midday, consisted of roasted or boiled beef or mutton, poultry or pork, and vegetables. Supper was a light meal of bread and cheese with cake or pie. Beer was the main drink in London, and many families brewed their own. Even children drank beer because of the lack of fresh water.

In contrast to the gigantic and sprawling country seats of the richest English peers, middle-class houses in town had about seven rooms, including four or five bedrooms and one or two living rooms, still many more than the poor agricultural worker. New household items reflected society's increasing wealth and its exposure to colonial imports: by 1700, the middle classes of London typically had mirrors in every room, a coffeepot and coffee mill, numerous pictures and ornaments, a china collection, and several clocks. Life for the middle classes on the European continent was quite similar, though wine replaced beer in France.

Below the middle classes came the artisans and shopkeepers (most of whom were organized in professional guilds), then the journeymen, apprentices, servants, and laborers. At the bottom of the social scale were the unemployed poor, who survived by intermittent work and charity. Women married to artisans and shop-keepers often kept the accounts, supervised employees, and ran the household as well. Every home from the middle classes to the upper classes employed servants; artisans and shopkeepers frequently hired them, too. Women from poorer families usually worked as domestic servants until they married. Four out of five domestic servants in the city were female. In large cities such as London, the servant population grew faster than the population of the city as a whole.

Social status in the cities was readily visible. Wide, spacious streets graced rich districts; the houses had gardens and the air was relatively fresh. In poor districts, the streets were narrow, dirty, dark, humid, and smelly, and the houses were damp and crowded. The poorest people were homeless, sleeping under bridges or in abandoned homes. A Neapolitan prince described his homeless neighbors as "lying like filthy animals, with no distinction of age or sex." In some districts, rich and poor lived in the same buildings; the poor clambered up to shabby, cramped apartments on the top floors.

Like shelter, clothing was a reliable social indicator. The poorest workingwomen in Paris wore woolen skirts and blouses of dark colors over petticoats, bodice, and corset. They also donned caps of various sorts, cotton stockings, and shoes (probably their only pair). Workingmen dressed even more drably. Many occupations could be recognized by their dress: no one could confuse lawyers in their dark robes with masons or butchers in their special aprons, for example. People higher on the social ladder were more likely to sport a variety of fabrics, colors, and unusual designs in their clothing and to own many different outfits. Social status was not an abstract idea; it permeated every detail of daily life.

The Growing Public for Culture

The ability to read and write also reflected social differences. People in the upper classes were more literate than those in the lower classes; city people were more literate than peasants. Protestant countries appear to have been more successful at promoting education and literacy than Catholic countries, perhaps because of the Protestant emphasis on Bible reading. Widespread popular literacy was first achieved in the Protestant areas of Switzerland and in Presbyterian Scotland, and rates were also very high in the New England colonies and the Scandinavian countries. In France, literacy doubled in the eighteenth century thanks to the spread of parish schools, but still only one in two men and one in four women could read and write. Despite the efforts of some Protestant German states to encourage primary education, primary schooling remained woefully inadequate almost everywhere in Europe: few schools existed, teachers received low wages, and no country had yet established a national system of control or supervision.

Despite the deficiencies of primary education, a new literate public arose, especially among the middle classes of the cities. More books and periodicals were published than ever before. Britain and the Dutch Republic led the way in this powerful outpouring of printed words. The trend began in the 1690s and gradually accelerated. In 1695, the British government allowed the licensing system, through which it controlled publications, to lapse, and new newspapers and magazines appeared almost immediately. The first London daily newspaper came out in 1702, and in 1709 Joseph Addison and Richard Steele published the first literary magazine, *The Spectator*. They devoted their magazine to the cultural improvement of the increasingly influential middle class. By the 1720s, twenty-four provincial newspapers were published in England. In the London coffeehouses, an edition of a single newspaper might reach ten thousand male readers. Women did their reading at home. Newspapers on the continent lagged behind and often consisted mainly of advertising with little critical commentary. France, for example, had no daily paper until 1777.

The new literate public did not just read newspapers; its members now pursued an interest in painting, attended concerts, and besieged booksellers in search of popular novels. Because increased trade and prosperity put money into the hands of the growing middle classes, a new urban audience began to compete with the churches, rulers, and courtiers as chief patrons for new work. As the public for the arts expanded, printed commentary on them emerged, setting the stage for the appearance of political and social criticism. New artistic tastes thus had effects far beyond the realm of the arts.

Developments in painting reflected the tastes of the new public. The rococo style challenged the hold of the baroque and classical schools, especially in France. Like the baroque, the rococo emphasized irregularity and asymmetry, movement and curvature, but it did so on a much smaller, subtler scale. Many rococo paintings depicted scenes of intimate sensuality rather than the monumental, emotional grandeur favored by classical and baroque painters. Personal portraits and pastoral paintings took the place of heroic landscapes and large ceremonial canvases. Rococo paintings adorned homes as well as palaces and served as a form of interior decoration rather than as a statement of piety. Its decorative quality made rococo art an ideal complement to newly discovered materials such as stucco and porcelain, especially the porcelain vases now imported from China.

Rococo, like *baroque,* was an invented word (from the French word *rocaille,* meaning "shellwork") and originally a derogatory label, meaning "frivolous decoration." But the great French rococo painters, such as Antoine Watteau (1684–1721) and François Boucher (1703–1770), were much more than mere decorators. Although both emphasized the erotic in their depictions, Watteau captured the melancholy side of a passing

■ **Rococo Painting**
In this painting, the Venetian artist Rosalba Carriera (1675–1757) reveals Europeans' growing interest in the outside world and their misunderstanding of the actual experience of colonized peoples. Africa (the title of the work) is represented by a young black woman wearing a bejewelled turban and calmly holding a handful of writhing snakes; the scorpion that dangles from her necklace competes with an enormous pearl earring for the fascinated viewer's attention. Known for her use of pastels, Carriera journeyed in 1720 to Paris, where she became an associate of Antoine Watteau and helped inaugurate the rococo style in painting.
(Staatliche Kunstsammlungen Dresden, Gemaldegalerie Alte Meister.)

aristocratic style of life, and Boucher painted middle-class people at home during their daily activities. Both painters thereby contributed to the emergence of new sensibilities in art that increasingly attracted a middle-class public.

Music as well as art grew in popularity. The first public music concerts were performed in England in the 1670s, becoming much more regular and frequent in the 1690s. City concert halls typically seated about two hundred, but the relatively high price of tickets limited attendance to the better-off. Music clubs provided entertainment in smaller towns and villages. In continental Europe, Frankfurt organized the first regular public concerts in 1712; Hamburg and Paris began holding them within a few years. Opera continued to spread in the eighteenth century; Venice had sixteen public opera houses by 1700, and in 1732 Covent Garden opera house opened in London.

The growth of a public that appreciated and supported music had much the same effect as the extension of the reading public: like authors, composers could now begin to liberate themselves from court patronage and work for a paying audience. This development took time to solidify, however, and court or church patrons still commissioned much eighteenth-century music. Bach, a German Lutheran, wrote his *St. Matthew Passion* for Good Friday services in 1729 while he was organist and choirmaster for the leading church in Leipzig. He composed secular works (like the "Coffee Cantata") for the public and a variety of private patrons.

The composer George Frederick Handel (1685–1759) was among the first to grasp the new directions in music. He began his career playing second violin in the Hamburg opera orchestra and then moved to Britain in 1710, where he eventually turned to composing oratorios, a form he introduced in Britain. The oratorio combined the drama of opera with the majesty of religious and ceremonial music and featured the chorus over the soloists. Handel's most famous oratorio, *Messiah* (1741), reflected his personal, deeply felt piety but also his willingness to combine musical materials into a dramatic form that captured the enthusiasm of the new public. In 1740, a poem published in the *Gentleman's Magazine* exulted: "His art so modulates the sounds in all, / Our passions, as he pleases, rise and fall." Music had become an integral part of the new middle-class public's culture.

But nothing captured the imagination of the new public more than the novel, the literary genre whose very name underscored the eighteenth-century taste for novelty. Over three hundred French novels appeared between 1700 and 1730. During this unprecedented explosion, the novel took on its modern form and became more concerned with individual psychology and social description than with the picaresque adventures popular earlier (such as Cervantes's *Don Quixote*). The novel's popularity was closely tied to the expansion of the reading public, and novels were available in serial form in periodicals or from the many booksellers who popped up to serve the new market.

Women figured prominently in novels as characters, and women writers abounded. The English novel *Love in Excess* (1719) quickly reached a sixth printing, and its author, Eliza Haywood (1693?–1756), earned her living turning out a stream of novels with titles such as *Persecuted Virtue, Constancy Rewarded,* and *The History of Betsy Thoughtless*—all showing a concern for the proper place of women as models of virtue in a changing world. Haywood had first worked as an actress when her husband deserted her and her two children, but she soon turned to writing plays and novels. In the 1740s, she began publishing a magazine, *The Female Spectator,* which argued in favor of higher education for women.

Haywood's male counterpart was Daniel Defoe (1660?–1731), a merchant's son who had a diverse and colorful career as a manufacturer, political spy, novelist, and social commentator. Defoe's novel about a shipwrecked sailor, *Robinson Crusoe* (1719), portrayed the new values of the time: to survive, Crusoe had to meet every challenge with fearless entrepreneurial ingenuity. He had to be ready for the unexpected and be able to improvise in every situation. He was, in short, the model for the new man in an expanding economy. Crusoe's patronizing attitude toward the black man Friday now draws much critical attention, but his discovery of Friday shows how the fate of blacks and whites had become intertwined in the new colonial environment.

Religious Revivals

Despite the novel's growing popularity, religious books and pamphlets still sold in huge numbers, and most Europeans remained devout, even as their religions were changing. In this period, a Protestant revival known as Pietism rocked the complacency of the established churches in the German Lutheran states, the Dutch Republic, and Scandinavia. Pietists believed in a mystical religion of the heart; they wanted a more deeply emotional, even ecstatic religion. They urged intense Bible study, which in turn promoted popular education and contributed to the increase in literacy. Many Pietists attended catechism instruction every day and also went to morning and evening prayer meetings in addition to regular Sunday services.

Catholicism also had its versions of religious revival. A French woman, Jeanne Marie Guyon (1648–1717), attracted many noblewomen and a few leading clergymen to her own Catholic brand of Pietism, known as Quietism. Claiming miraculous visions and astounding prophecies, she urged a mystical union with God through prayer and simple devotion. Despite papal condemnation and intense controversy within Catholic circles in France, Guyon had followers all over Europe.

Even more influential were the Jansenists, who gained many new adherents to their austere form of Catholicism despite Louis XIV's harassment and repeated condemnation by the papacy. Under the pressure of religious and political persecution, Jansenism took a revivalist turn in the 1720s. At the funeral of a Jansenist priest in Paris in 1727, the crowd who flocked to the grave claimed to witness a series of miraculous healings. Within a few years, a cult formed around the priest's tomb, and clandestine Jansenist presses reported new miracles to the reading public. When the French government tried to suppress the cult, one enraged wit placed a sign at the tomb that read "By order of the king, God is forbidden to work miracles here." Some believers fell into frenzied convulsions, claiming to be inspired by the Holy Spirit through the intercession of the dead priest. After midcentury, Jansenism became even more politically active as its adherents joined in opposition to crown policies on religion.

Consolidation of the European State System

The spread of Pietism and Jansenism reflected the emergence of a middle-class public that now participated in every new development, including religion. The middle classes could pursue these interests because the European state system gradually stabilized. Warfare settled three main issues between 1690 and 1740: a coalition of powers held Louis XIV's France in check on the continent; Great Britain emerged from the wars against Louis as the preeminent maritime power; and Russia defeated Sweden in the contest for supremacy in the Baltic. After Louis XIV's death in 1715, Europe enjoyed the fruits of a more balanced diplomatic system, in which warfare became less frequent and less widespread. States could then spend their resources establishing and expanding control over their own populations, both at home and in their colonies.

The Limits of French Absolutism

Lying on his deathbed in 1715, the seventy-six-year-old Louis XIV watched helplessly as his accomplishments continued to unravel. Not only had his plans for territorial expansion been thwarted, but his incessant wars had exhausted the treasury, despite new taxes. In 1689, Louis's rival, William III, prince of Orange and king of England and Scotland (r. 1689–1702), had set out to forge a European alliance that eventually included Britain, the Dutch Republic, Sweden, Austria, and Spain. The allies fought Louis to a stalemate in the War of the League of Augsburg, sometimes called the Nine Years' War (1689–1697), and when hostilities resumed four years later, they finally put an end to Louis's expansionist ambitions.

The War of the Spanish Succession (1701–1713) broke out when the mentally and physically feeble Charles II (r. 1665–1700) of Spain died without a direct heir. The Spanish succession could not help but be a burning issue. Even though Spanish power had declined steadily since Spain's golden age in the sixteenth century, Spain still had extensive territories in Italy and the Netherlands and colonies overseas. Before Charles died, he named Louis XIV's second grandson, Philip, duke of Anjou, as his heir, but the Austrian emperor Leopold I refused to accept Charles's deathbed will. In the ensuing war, the French lost several major battles and had to accept disadvantageous terms in the Peace of Utrecht of 1713–1714 (Map 14.2). Although Philip was recognized as king of Spain, he had to renounce any future claim to the

English and French Claims after the Peace of Utrecht, 1714

Hudson Bay
Newfoundland
English claim
French claim
Nova Scotia
English claim

Territories gained after the Peace of Utrecht, 1714

- French Bourbon lands
- Spanish Bourbon lands
- Austrian Habsburg lands
- Prussian lands
- Great Britain
- To Great Britain
- To the Austrian Empire
- The Jacobite rising of 1715
- Main areas of fighting during the War of the Spanish Succession, 1701–1713
- Boundary of the Holy Roman Empire

■ MAP 14.2 Europe, c. 1715

Although Louis XIV succeeded in putting his grandson Philip on the Spanish throne, France emerged considerably weakened from the War of the Spanish Succession. France ceded large territories in Canada to Britain, which also gained key Mediterranean outposts from Spain as well as a monopoly on providing slaves to the Spanish colonies. Spanish losses were catastrophic: Philip had to renounce any future claim to the French crown and give up considerable territories in the Netherlands and Italy to the Austrians.

French crown, thus barring unification of the two kingdoms. Spain surrendered its territories in Italy and the Netherlands to the Austrians and Gibraltar to the British; France ceded possessions in North America (Newfoundland, the Hudson Bay area, and most of Nova Scotia) to Britain. France no longer threatened to dominate European power politics.

At home, Louis's policy of absolutism had fomented bitter hostility. Nobles fiercely resented his promotions of commoners to high office. The duke of Saint-Simon complained that "falseness, servility, admiring glances, combined with a dependent and cringing attitude, above all, an appearance of being nothing without him, were the only ways of pleasing him." On his deathbed, Louis XIV gave his blessing and some sound advice to his five-year-old great-grandson and successor, Louis XV (r. 1715–1774): "My child, you are about to become a great King. Do not imitate my love of building nor my liking for war."

After being named regent, the duke of Orléans (1674–1723), nephew of the dead king, revived some of the parlements' powers and tried to give leading nobles a greater say in political affairs. Financial problems plagued the Regency as they would beset all succeeding French regimes in the eighteenth century. In 1719, the regent appointed the Scottish adventurer and financier John Law to the top financial position of controller-general. Law founded a trading company for North America and a state bank that issued paper money and stock (without them, trade depended on the available supply of gold and silver). The bank was supposed to offer lower interest rates to the state, thus cutting the cost of financing the government's debts. The value of the stock rose rapidly in a frenzy of speculation, only to crash a few months later. With it vanished any hope of establishing a state bank or issuing paper money for nearly a century.

France finally achieved a measure of financial stability under the leadership of Cardinal Hercule de Fleury (1653–1743), the most powerful member of the government after the death of the regent. Fleury aimed to avoid adventure abroad and keep social peace at home; he balanced the budget and carried out a large project for road and canal construction. Colonial trade boomed. Peace and the acceptance of limits on territorial expansion inaugurated a century of French prosperity.

British Rise and Dutch Decline

The British and the Dutch had formed a coalition against Louis XIV under their joint ruler William III, who was simultaneously stadtholder of the Dutch Republic and, with his English wife, Mary (d. 1694), ruler of England, Wales, and Scotland. After William's death in 1702, the British and Dutch went their separate ways. Over the next decades, England incorporated Scotland and subjugated Ireland, becoming "Great Britain." At the same time Dutch imperial power declined, even though Dutch merchants still controlled a substantial portion of world trade. English relations with Scotland and Ireland were complicated by the problem of succession: William and Mary had no children. To ensure a Protestant succession, Parliament ruled that Mary's sister, Anne, would succeed William and Mary and that the Protestant House of Hanover in Germany would succeed Anne if she had no surviving heirs. Catholics were excluded. When Queen Anne (r. 1702–1714) died leaving no children, the elector of Hanover, a Protestant great-grandson of James I, consequently became King George I (r. 1714–1727). The House of Hanover—renamed the House of Windsor during World War I in response to anti-German sentiment—still occupies the British throne.

Support from the Scots and Irish for this solution did not come easily because many in Scotland and Ireland supported the claims to the throne of the deposed Catholic king, James II, and, after his death in 1701, his son James Edward. Out of fear of this "Jacobitism" (from the Latin *Jacobus* for "James"), Scottish Protestant leaders agreed to the Act of Union of 1707, which abolished the Scottish Parliament and affirmed the Scots' recognition of the Protestant Hanoverian succession. The Scots agreed to obey the Parliament of Great Britain, which would include Scottish members in the House of Commons and the House of Lords. A Jacobite rebellion in Scotland in 1715, aiming to restore the Stuart line, was suppressed. The threat of Jacobitism nonetheless continued into the 1740s (Map 14.2).

The Irish—90 percent of whom were Catholic—proved even more difficult to subdue. When James II had gone to Ireland in 1689 to raise a Catholic rebellion against the new monarchs of England, William III responded by taking command of the joint English and Dutch forces and defeating James's Irish supporters. James fled to France, and the Catholics in Ireland faced yet more confiscation and legal restrictions. By 1700, Irish Catholics, who in 1640 had owned 60 percent of the land in Ireland, owned just 14 percent. The Protestant-controlled Irish Parliament passed a series of laws limiting the rights of the Catholic majority: Catholics could not bear arms, send their children abroad for education, establish Catholic schools at home, or marry Protestants. Catholics could not sit in Parliament, nor could they vote for its members unless they took an oath renouncing Catholic doctrine. These and a host of other laws reduced Catholic Ireland to the status of a colony; one English official commented in 1745, "The poor people of Ireland are used worse than negroes." Most of the Irish were peasants who lived in primitive housing and subsisted on a meager diet that included no meat.

The Parliament of Great Britain was soon dominated by the Whigs. In Britain's constitutional system, the monarch ruled with Parliament. The crown chose the ministers, directed policy, and supervised administration, while Parliament raised revenue, passed laws, and represented the interests of the people to the crown. The powers of Parliament were reaffirmed by the Triennial Act in 1694, which provided that Parliaments meet at least once every three years (this was extended to seven years in 1716, after the Whigs had established their ascendancy). Only 200,000 propertied men could vote, out of a population of more than five million people, and not surprisingly, most members of Parliament came from the landed gentry. In fact, a few hundred families controlled all the important political offices.

■ **Sir Robert Walpole at a Cabinet Meeting**
Sir Robert Walpole and George II developed government by means of a cabinet, which consisted of Walpole as first lord of the treasury, the two secretaries of state, the lord chancellor, the chancellor of the exchequer, the lord privy seal, and the lord president of the council. Walpole's cabinet was the predecessor of modern cabinets in both Great Britain and the United States. Its similarities to modern forms should not be overstated, however. The entire staff of the two secretaries of state, who had charge of all foreign and domestic affairs other than taxation, numbered twenty-four in 1726. (The Fotomas Index, U.K.)

George I and George II (r. 1727–1760) relied on one man, Sir Robert Walpole (1676–1745), to help them manage their relations with Parliament. From his position as First Lord of the Treasury, Walpole made himself into first or "prime" minister, leading the House of Commons from 1721 to 1742. Although appointed initially by the king, Walpole established an enduring pattern of parliamentary government in which a prime minister from the leading party guided legislation through the House of Commons. Walpole also built a vast patronage machine that dispensed government jobs to win support for the crown's policies. Walpole's successors relied more and more on the patronage system and eventually alienated not only the Tories but also the middle classes in London and even the North American colonies.

The partisan division between the Whigs, who supported the Hanoverian succession and the rights of dissenting Protestants, and the Tories, who had backed the Stuart line and the Anglican church, did not hamper Great Britain's pursuit of economic, military, and colonial power. In this period, Great Britain became a great power on the world stage by virtue of its navy and its ability to finance major military involvement in the wars against Louis XIV. The founding in 1694 of the Bank of England—which, unlike the French bank, endured—enabled the government to raise money at low interest for foreign wars. By the 1740s, the government could borrow more than four times what it could in the 1690s.

By contrast, the Dutch Republic, one of the richest and most influential states of the seventeenth century, saw its power eclipsed in the eighteenth. When William of Orange (William III of England) died in 1702, he left no heirs, and for forty-five years the Dutch lived without a stadtholder. The merchant ruling class of some two thousand families dominated the Dutch Republic more than ever, but they presided over a country that counted for less in international power politics. In some areas, Dutch decline was only relative: the Dutch population was not growing as fast as populations elsewhere, for example, and the Dutch share of the Baltic trade decreased from 50 percent in 1720 to less than 30 percent by the 1770s. After 1720, the Baltic countries—Prussia, Russia, Denmark, and Sweden—began to ban imports of manufactured goods to protect their own industries, and Dutch trade in particular suffered. The output of Leiden textiles dropped to one-third of its 1700 level by 1740. Shipbuilding, paper manufacturing, tobacco processing, salt refining, and pottery production all dwindled as well. The biggest exception to the downward trend was trade with the New World, which increased with escalating demands for sugar and tobacco. The Dutch shifted their interest away from great-power rivalries toward those areas of international trade and finance where they could establish an enduring presence.

Russia's Emergence as a European Power

The commerce and shipbuilding of the Dutch and British so impressed Russian tsar Peter I (r. 1689–1725) that he traveled incognito to their shipyards in 1697 to learn their methods firsthand. Known to history as Peter the Great, he dragged Russia kicking and screaming all the way to great-power status. Although he came to the throne while still a minor (on the eve of his tenth birthday), grew up under the threat of a palace coup, and enjoyed little formal education, his accomplishments soon matched his seven-foot-tall stature. Peter transformed public life in Russia and established an absolutist state on the western model. His westernization efforts ignited an enduring controversy: did Peter set Russia on a course of inevitable westernization required to compete with the West, or did he forever and fatally disrupt Russia's natural evolution into a distinctive Slavic society?

Peter reorganized government and finance on western models and, like other absolute rulers, strengthened his army. With ruthless recruiting methods, which included branding a cross on every recruit's left hand to prevent desertion, he forged an army of 200,000 men and equipped it with modern weapons. He created schools for artillery, engineering, and military medicine and built the first navy in Russian history. Not surprisingly, taxes tripled.

The tsar allowed nothing to stand in his way. He did not hesitate to use torture and executed thousands. He allowed a special guards regiment unprecedented power to expedite cases against those suspected of rebellion, espionage, pretensions to the throne, or just "unseemly utterances" against him. Opposition to his policies reached into his own family: because his only son, Alexei, had allied himself with Peter's critics, he threw him into prison, where the young man mysteriously died.

To control the often restive nobility, Peter insisted that all noblemen engage in state service. A Table of Ranks (1722) classified them into military, administrative, and court categories, a codification of social and legal relationships in Russia that would last for nearly two centuries. All social and material advantages now depended on serving the crown. Because the nobles lacked a secure independent status, Peter could command them to a degree that was unimaginable in western Europe. State service was not only compulsory but also permanent. Moreover, the male children of those in service had to be registered by the age of ten and begin serving at fifteen. To increase his authority over the Russian Orthodox church, Peter allowed the office of patriarch (supreme head) to remain vacant, and in 1721 he replaced it with the Holy Synod, a bureaucracy of laymen under his supervision. To many Russians, Peter was the Antichrist incarnate.

With the goal of westernizing Russian culture, Peter set up the first greenhouses, laboratories, and technical schools and founded the Russian Academy of Sciences. He ordered translations of Western classics and hired a German theater company to perform the French plays of Molière. He replaced the traditional Russian calendar with the Western one,* introduced Arabic numerals, and brought out the first public newspaper. He ordered his officials and the nobles to shave their beards and dress in Western fashion, and he even issued precise regulations about the suitable style of jacket, boots, and cap (generally French or German). He published a book on manners for young noblemen and experimented with dentistry on his courtiers.

Peter built a new capital city, named St. Petersburg after him. It symbolized Russia's opening to the West. Construction began in 1703 in a Baltic province that had been recently conquered from Sweden. By the end of 1709, forty thousand recruits a year found themselves assigned to the work. Peter ordered skilled workers to move to the new city and commanded all landowners possessing more than forty serf households to build houses there. In the 1720s, a German minister described the city "as a wonder of the world, considering its magnificent palaces, . . . and the short time that was employed in the building of it." By 1710, the permanent population of St. Petersburg reached eight thousand. At Peter's death in 1725, it had forty thousand residents.

As a new city far from the Russian heartland around Moscow, St. Petersburg represented a decisive break with Russia's past. Peter widened that gap by every means possible. At his new capital, he tried to improve the traditionally denigrated, secluded status of women by ordering them to dress in European styles and appear publicly at his dinners for diplomatic representatives. Imitating French manners, he decreed that women attend his new social salons of officials, officers, and merchants for conversation and dancing. A foreigner headed every one of Peter's new technical and vocational schools, and for its first eight years the new Academy of

---

*Peter introduced the Julian calendar, then still used in Protestant but not Catholic countries. Later in the eighteenth century, Protestant Europe abandoned the Julian for the Gregorian calendar. Not until 1918 was the Julian calendar abolished in Russia, at which point it had fallen thirteen days behind Europe's Gregorian calendar.

■ Peter the Great Modernizes Russia

In this popular print, a barber forces a protesting noble to conform to Western fashions (the barber is sometimes erroneously identified as Peter himself). Peter ordered all nobles, merchants, and middle-class professionals to cut off their beards or pay a huge tax to keep them. An early biographer of Peter, the French writer Jean Rousset de Missy (1730), claimed that those who lost their beards saved them to put in their coffins, fearing that they would not enter heaven without them.
(Carole Frohlich Archive.)

Sciences included no Russians. Every ministry was assigned a foreign adviser. Upper-class Russians learned French or German, which they often spoke even at home. Such changes affected only the very top of Russian society, however; the mass of the population had no contact with the new ideas and ended up paying for the innovations either in ruinous new taxation or by building St. Petersburg, a project that cost the lives of thousands of workers. Serfs remained tied to the land, completely dominated by their noble lords.

Despite all his achievements, Peter could not ensure his succession. In the thirty-seven years after his death in 1725, Russia endured six different rulers: three women, a boy of twelve, an infant, and an imbecile. Recurrent palace coups weakened the monarchy and enabled the nobility to loosen Peter's rigid code of state service. In the process, the status of the serfs only worsened. They ceased to be counted as legal subjects; the criminal code of 1754 listed them as property. They not only were bought and sold like cattle but also had become legally indistinguishable from them. Westernization had not yet touched their lives.

The Balance of Power in the East

Peter the Great's success in building up state power changed the balance of power in eastern Europe. Overcoming initial military setbacks, Russia eventually defeated Sweden and took its place as the leading power in the Baltic region. Russia could then turn its attention to eastern Europe, where it competed with Austria and Prussia. Formerly mighty Poland-Lithuania became the playground for great-power rivalries.

Sweden had dominated the Baltic region since the Thirty Years' War and did not easily give up its preeminence. When Peter the Great joined an anti-Swedish coalition in 1700 with Denmark, Saxony, and Poland, Sweden's Charles XII (r. 1697–1718) stood up to the test. Still in his teens at the beginning of the Great Northern War, Charles first defeated Denmark, then destroyed the new Russian army, and quickly marched into Poland and Saxony. After defeating the Poles and occupying Saxony, Charles invaded Russia. Here Peter's rebuilt army finally defeated him at the battle of Poltava (1709).

The Russian victory resounded everywhere. The Russian ambassador to Vienna reported, "It is commonly said that the tsar will be formidable to all Europe, that he will be a kind of northern Turk." Prussia and other German states joined the anti-Swedish alliance, and when Charles XII died in battle in 1718, the Great Northern War finally came to an end. By the terms of the Treaty of Nystad (1721), Sweden ceded its eastern Baltic provinces—Livonia, Estonia, Ingria, and southern Karelia—to Russia. Sweden also lost territories on the north German coast to Prussia and the other allied German states (Map 14.3). An aristocratic reaction against Charles XII's incessant demands for war supplies swept away Sweden's absolutist regime, essentially removing Sweden from great-power competition.

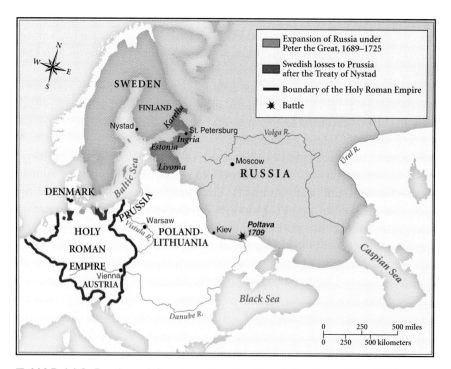

■ **MAP 14.3 Russia and Sweden after the Great Northern War, 1721**
After the Great Northern War, Russia supplanted Sweden as the major power in the north. Although Russia had a much larger population from which to draw its armies, Sweden made the most of its advantages and gave way only after a great military struggle.

Prussia had to make the most of every military opportunity, as it did in the Great Northern War, because it was much smaller in size and population than Russia, Austria, or France. King Frederick William I (r. 1713–1740) doubled the size of the Prussian army; though much smaller than the armies of his rivals, it was the best-trained and most up-to-date force in Europe. By 1740, Prussia had Europe's highest proportion of men at arms (1 of every 28 people, versus 1 in 157 in France and 1 in 64 in Russia) and the highest proportion of nobles in the military (1 in 7 noblemen, as compared with 1 in 33 in France and 1 in 50 in Russia).

The army so dominated life in Prussia that the country earned the label "a large army with a small state attached." So obsessed was Frederick William with his soldiers that the five-foot-five-inch-tall king formed a regiment of "giants," the Grenadiers, composed exclusively of men over six feet tall. Royal agents scoured Europe trying to find such men and sometimes kidnapped them right off the street. Frederick William, the "Sergeant King," was one of the first rulers to wear a military uniform as his everyday dress. He subordinated the entire domestic administration to the army's needs. He also installed a system for recruiting soldiers by local district quotas. He financed the army's growth by subjecting all the provinces to an excise tax on food, drink, and manufactured goods and by increasing rents on crown lands. Prussia was now poised to become one of the major players on the continent of Europe.

During the War of the Polish Succession (1733–1735), Prussia stood on the sidelines, content to watch the bigger powers fight each other. The war showed how the balance of power had changed since the heyday of Louis XIV: France had to maneuver within a complex great-power system that now included Russia, and Poland-Lithuania no longer controlled its own destiny. When the king of Poland-Lithuania died in 1733, France, Spain, and Sardinia went to war against Austria and Russia, each side supporting rival claimants to the Polish throne. After Russia drove the French candidate out of Poland-Lithuania, France agreed to accept the Austrian candidate; in exchange, Austria gave the province of Lorraine to the French candidate, the father-in-law of Louis XV, with the promise that the province would pass to France on his death. France and Britain went back to pursuing their colonial rivalries. Prussia and Russia concentrated on shoring up their influence within Poland-Lithuania.

Austria did not want to become mired in a long struggle in Poland-Lithuania because its armies still faced the Turks on its southeastern border. Even though the Austrians had forced the Turks to recognize their rule over all of Hungary and Transylvania in 1699 and occupied Belgrade in 1717, the Turks did not stop fighting. In the

Austrian Conquest of Hungary, 1657–1730

1730s, the Turks retook Belgrade, and Russia now claimed a role in the struggle against the Turks. Moreover, Hungary, though "liberated" from Turkish rule, proved less than enthusiastic about submitting to Austria. In 1703, the wealthiest Hungarian noble landlord, Ferenc Rákóczi (1676–1735), raised an army of seventy thousand men who fought for "God, Fatherland, and Liberty" until 1711. They forced the Austrians to recognize local Hungarian institutions, grant amnesty, and restore confiscated estates in exchange for confirming hereditary Austrian rule.

The Power of Diplomacy and the Importance of Numbers

No single power emerged from the wars of the first half of the eighteenth century clearly superior to the others, and the idea of maintaining a balance of power guided both military and diplomatic maneuvering. The Peace of Utrecht had explicitly declared that such a balance was crucial to maintaining peace in Europe, and in 1720 a British pamphleteer wrote, "There is not, I believe, any doctrine in the law of nations, of more certain truth . . . than this of the balance of power." It was the law of gravity of European politics. This system of equilibrium often rested on military force, such as the leagues formed against Louis XIV or the coalition against Sweden. All states counted on diplomacy, however, to resolve issues even after fighting had begun.

To meet the new demands placed on it, the diplomatic service, like the military and financial bureaucracies before it, had to develop regular procedures. The French set a pattern of diplomatic service that the other European states soon imitated. By 1685, France had embassies in all the important capitals. Nobles of ancient families served as ambassadors to Rome, Madrid, Vienna, and London, whereas royal officials were chosen for Switzerland, the Dutch Republic, and Venice. Most held their appointments for at least three or four years, and all went off with elaborate written instructions that included explicit statements of policy as well as full accounts of the political conditions of the country to which they were posted. The ambassador selected and paid for his own staff. This practice could make the journey to a new post very cumbersome, because the staff might be as large as eighty people, and they brought along all their own furniture, pictures, silverware, and tapestries. It took one French ambassador ten weeks to get from Paris to Stockholm.

By the early 1700s, French writings on diplomatic methods were read everywhere. François de Callières's manual *On the Manner of Negotiating with Sovereigns* (1716) insisted that sound diplomacy was based on the creation of confidence, rather than deception: "The secret of negotiation is to harmonize the real interests of the parties concerned." Callières believed that the diplomatic service had to be professional—that young attachés should be chosen for their skills, not their family connections. These sensible views did not prevent the development of a dual system of diplomacy, in which rulers issued secret instructions that often negated the official ones sent by their own foreign offices. Secret diplomacy had some advantages because it allowed rulers to break with past alliances, but it also led to confusion and, sometimes, scandal, for the rulers often employed unreliable adventurers as their confidential agents. Still, the diplomatic system in the early eighteenth century proved successful enough to ensure a continuation of the principles of the Peace of Westphalia (1648); in the midst of every crisis and war, the great powers would convene and hammer out a written agreement detailing the requirements for peace.

Adroit diplomacy could smooth the road toward peace, but success in war still depended on sheer numbers—of men and muskets. Because each state's strength depended largely on the size of its army, the growth and health of the population increasingly entered into government calculations. The publication in 1690 of the Englishman William Petty's *Political Arithmetick* quickened the interest of government officials everywhere. Petty offered statistical estimates of human capital—that is, of population and wages—to determine Britain's national wealth. In 1727, Frederick William I of Prussia founded two university chairs to encourage population studies, and textbooks and handbooks advocated state intervention to improve the population's health and welfare.

Public Hygiene and Health Care

Physicians used the new population statistics to explain the environmental causes of disease, another new preoccupation in this period. Petty devised a quantitative scale that distinguished healthy from unhealthy places largely on the basis of air quality, an early precursor of modern environmental studies. Cities were the unhealthiest places because excrement (animal and human) and garbage accumulated where people lived densely packed together. Paris seemed to a visitor "so detestable that it is impossible to remain there" because of the smell; even the façade of the Louvre palace in Paris was soiled by the contents of night commodes that servants routinely dumped out of windows every morning. Only the wealthy could escape walking in mucky streets, by hiring men to carry them in sedan chairs or to drive them in coaches.

After investigating specific cities, medical geographers urged government campaigns to improve public sanitation. Everywhere, environmentalists gathered and analyzed data on climate, disease, and population, searching for correlations to help direct policy. As a result of these efforts, local governments undertook such measures as draining low-lying areas, burying refuse, and cleaning wells, all of which eventually helped lower the death rates from epidemic diseases.

Hospitals and medical care underwent lasting transformations. Founded originally as charities concerned foremost with the moral worthiness of the poor, hospitals gradually evolved into medical institutions that defined patients by their diseases. The process of diagnosis changed as physicians began to use specialized Latin terms for illnesses. The gap between medical experts and their patients increased, as physicians now also relied on postmortem dissections in the hospital to gain better knowledge, a practice most patients' families resented. Press reports of body snatching and grave robbing by surgeons and their apprentices outraged the public well into the 1800s.

Despite the change in hospitals, individual health care remained something of a free-for-all in which physicians competed with bloodletters, itinerant venereal-disease doctors, bonesetters, druggists, midwives, and "cunning women," who specialized in home remedies. The medical profession, with nationwide organizations and licensing, had not yet emerged, and no clear line separated trained physicians from quacks. Physicians often followed popular prescriptions for illnesses because they had nothing better to offer. Patients were as likely to die of diseases caught in the hospital as to be cured there. Antiseptics were nearly unknown.

The various "medical" opinions about childbirth highlight the confusion people faced. Midwives delivered most babies, though they sometimes encountered criticism even from within their own ranks. One consulting midwife complained that ordinary midwives in Bristol, England, made women in labor drink a mixture of their husband's urine and leek juice. By the 1730s, female midwives faced competition from male midwives, who were known for using instruments such as forceps to pull the baby out of the birth canal. Women rarely sought a physician's help in giving birth, however; they preferred the advice and assistance of trusted local midwives. In any case, trained physicians were few in number and almost nonexistent outside cities.

Hardly any infectious diseases could be cured, though inoculation against smallpox spread from the Middle East to Europe in the early eighteenth century, thanks largely to the efforts of Lady Mary Wortley Montagu, who learned about the technique while living in Constantinople. After 1750, physicians developed successful procedures for wide-scale vaccination, although even then many people resisted the idea of inoculating themselves with a disease. Other diseases spread quickly in the unsanitary conditions of urban life. Ordinary people washed or changed clothes rarely, lived in overcrowded housing with poor ventilation, and got their water from contaminated sources, such as refuse-filled rivers.

Until the mid-1700s, most people considered bathing dangerous. Public bathhouses had disappeared from cities in the sixteenth and seventeenth centuries because they seemed a source of disorderly behavior and epidemic illness. In the eighteenth century, even private bathing came into disfavor because people feared the effects of contact with water. Fewer than one in ten newly built private mansions in Paris had baths. Bathing was hazardous, physicians insisted, because it opened the body to disease. One manners manual of 1736 admonished, "It is correct to clean the face every morning by using a white cloth to cleanse it. It is less good to wash with water, because it renders the face susceptible to cold in winter and sun in summer." The upper classes associated cleanliness not with baths but with frequently changed linens, powdered hair, and perfume, which was thought to strengthen the body and refresh the brain by counteracting corrupt and foul air.

The Birth of the Enlightenment

Economic expansion, the emergence of a new consumer society, and the stabilization of the European state system all generated optimism about the future. The intellectual corollary was the *Enlightenment*, a term used later in the eighteenth century to describe the loosely knit group of writers and scholars who believed that human beings could apply a critical, reasoning spirit to every problem they encountered in this world. The new secular, scientific, and critical attitude first emerged in the 1690s, scrutinizing everything from the absolutism of Louis XIV to the traditional role of women in society. After 1740, criticism took a more systematic turn as writers provided new theories for the organization of society and politics, but even by the 1720s and 1730s, established authorities realized they faced a new set of challenges.

Popularization of Science and Challenges to Religion

The writers of the Enlightenment glorified the geniuses of the new science and championed scientific method as the solution for all social problems. One of the most influential popularizations was the French writer Bernard de Fontenelle's *Conversations on the Plurality of Worlds* (1686). Presented as a dialogue between an aristocratic woman and a man of the world, the book made the Copernican, sun-centered view of the universe available to the literate public. By 1700, mathematics and science had become fashionable pastimes in high society, and the public flocked to lectures explaining scientific discoveries. Journals complained that scientific learning had become the passport to female affection: "There were two young ladies in Paris whose heads had been so turned by this branch of learning that one of them declined to listen to a proposal of marriage unless the candidate for her hand undertook to learn how to make telescopes." Such writings poked fun at women with intellectual interests, but they also demonstrated that women now participated in discussions of science.

Interest in science spread in literate circles because it offered a model for all forms of knowledge. As the prestige of science increased, some developed a skeptical attitude toward attempts to enforce religious conformity. A French Huguenot refugee from Louis XIV's persecutions, Pierre Bayle (1647–1706), launched an internationally influential campaign against religious intolerance from his safe haven in the Dutch Republic. His *News from the Republic of Letters* (first published in 1684) bitterly criticized the policies of Louis XIV and was quickly banned in Paris and condemned in Rome. After attacking Louis XIV's anti-Protestant policies, Bayle took a more general stand in favor of religious toleration. No state in Europe officially offered complete tolerance, though the Dutch Republic came closest with its tacit acceptance of Catholics, dissident Protestant groups, and open Jewish communities. In 1697, Bayle published the *Historical and Critical Dictionary*, which cited all the errors and delusions that he could find in past and present writers of all

▪ **A Budding Scientist**
In this engraving, Astrologia, *by the Dutch artist Jacob Gole (c. 1660–1723), an upper-class woman looks through a telescope to do her own astronomical investigations. Women were not allowed to attend university classes in any European country, yet the Italian Laura Bassi (1711–1778) still managed to become professor of physics at the University of Bologna. Because many astronomical observatories were set up in private homes rather than public buildings or universities, wives and daughters of scientists could make observations and even publish their own findings.*
(Bibliothèque Nationale de France.)

www.bedfordstmartins.com/huntconcise
See the ONLINE STUDY GUIDE for more help in analyzing this image.

religions. Even religion must meet the test of reasonableness: "Any particular dogma, whatever it may be, whether it is advanced on the authority of the Scriptures, or whatever else may be its origins, is to be regarded as false if it clashes with the clear and definite conclusions of the natural understanding [reason]."

Although Bayle claimed to be a believer himself, his insistence on rational investigation seemed to challenge the authority of faith. As one critic complained, "It is notorious that the works of M. Bayle have unsettled a large number of readers, and cast doubt on some of the most widely accepted principles of morality and religion." Bayle asserted, for example, that atheists might possess moral codes as effective as those of the devout. Bayle's *Dictionary* became a model of critical thought in the West.

Other scholars challenged the authority of the Bible by subjecting it to historical criticism. Discoveries in geology in the early eighteenth century showed that marine fossils dated immensely farther back than the biblical flood. Investigations of miracles, comets, and oracles, like the growing literature against belief in witchcraft, urged the use of reason to combat superstition and prejudice. Comets, for example, should not be considered evil omens just because such a belief had been passed on from earlier generations. Defenders of church and state published books warning of the dangers of the new skepticism. The spokesman for Louis XIV's absolutism, Bishop Bossuet, warned that "reason is the guide of their choice, but reason only brings them face to face with vague conjectures and baffling perplexities." Human beings, the traditionalists held, were simply incapable of subjecting everything to reason, especially in the realm of religion.

State authorities found religious skepticism particularly unsettling because it threatened to undermine state power, too. The extensive literature of criticism was not limited to France, but much of it was published in French, and the French government took the lead in suppressing the more outspoken works. Forbidden books were then often published in the Dutch Republic, Britain, or Switzerland and smuggled back across the border to a public whose appetite was only whetted by censorship.

The most influential writer of the early Enlightenment was a Frenchman born into the upper middle classes, François-Marie Arouet, known by his pen name, Voltaire (1694–1778). In his early years, Voltaire suffered arrest, imprisonment, and exile, but he eventually achieved wealth and acclaim. His tangles with church and state began in the early 1730s, when he published his *Letters Concerning the English Nation* (the English version appeared in 1733), in which he devoted several chapters to Newton and Locke and used the virtues of the British as a way to attack Catholic bigotry and government rigidity in France. Impressed by British toleration of religious dissent (at least among Protestants), Voltaire spent two years in exile in Britain when the French state responded to his book with yet another order for his arrest.

Voltaire also popularized Newton's scientific discoveries in his *Elements of the Philosophy of Newton* (1738). The French state and many European theologians considered Newtonianism threatening because it glorified the human mind and seemed to reduce God to an abstract, external, rationalistic force. So sensational was the success of Voltaire's book on Newton that a hostile Jesuit reported, "The great Newton, was, it is said, buried in the abyss, in the shop of the first publisher who dared to print him. . . . M. de Voltaire finally appeared, and at once Newton is understood or is in the process of being understood; all Paris resounds with Newton, all Paris stammers Newton, all Paris studies and learns Newton." The success was international, too. Before long, Voltaire was elected a fellow of the Royal Society in London and in Edinburgh, as well as to twenty other scientific academies. Voltaire's fame continued to grow, reaching truly astounding proportions in the 1750s and 1760s (see Chapter 15).

Travel Literature and the Challenge to Custom and Tradition

Just as scientific method could be used to question religious and even state authority, a more general skepticism also emerged from the expanding knowledge about the world outside of Europe. During the seventeenth and eighteenth centuries, accounts of travel to exotic places dramatically increased as travel writers used the contrast between their home societies and other cultures to criticize the customs of European society.

In their travels to the new colonies, visitors sought something resembling "the state of nature"—that is, ways of life that preceded sophisticated social and political organization—although they often misinterpreted different forms of society and politics as having no organization at all. Travelers to the Americas found "noble savages" (native peoples) who appeared to live in conditions of great freedom and equality; they were "naturally good" and "happy" without taxes, lawsuits, or much organized government. In China, in contrast, travelers found a people who enjoyed prosperity and an ancient civilization. Christian missionaries made little headway in China, and visitors had to admit that China's religious systems had flourished for four or five thousand years with no input from Europe or from Christianity. The basic lesson of travel literature in the 1700s, then, was that customs varied: justice, freedom, property, good government, religion, and morality all were relative to the place. One critic complained that travel encouraged free thinking and the destruction of religion: "Some complete their demoralization by extensive travel, and lose whatever shreds of religion remained to them. Every day they see a new religion, new customs, new rites."

Travel literature turned explicitly political in Montesquieu's *Persian Letters* (1721). Charles-Louis de Secondat, baron of Montesquieu (1689–1755), the son of an eminent judicial family, was a high-ranking judge in a French court. He published *Persian Letters* anonymously in the Dutch Republic, and the book went into ten printings in just one year—a best-seller for the times. Montesquieu tells the story of two Persians, Rica and Usbek, who leave their country "for love of knowledge" and travel to Europe. They visit France in the last years of Louis XIV's reign, writing of the king: "He has a minister who is only eighteen years old, and a mistress of eighty. . . . Although he avoids the bustle of towns, and is rarely seen in company, his one concern, from morning till night, is to get himself talked about." Other passages ridicule the pope. Beneath the satire, however, was a serious investigation into the foundation of good government and morality. Montesquieu chose Persians for his travelers because they came from what was widely considered the most despotic of all governments, in which rulers had life-and-death powers over their subjects. In the book, the Persians constantly compare France to Persia, suggesting that the French monarchy itself might verge on despotism.◆

The paradox of a judge publishing an anonymous work attacking the regime that employed him demonstrates the complications of the intellectual scene in this period. Montesquieu's anonymity did not last long, and soon Parisian society lionized him. In the late 1720s, he sold his judgeship and traveled extensively in Europe, including an eighteen-month stay in Britain. In 1748, he published a widely influential work on comparative government, *The Spirit of Laws*. The Vatican soon listed both *Persian Letters* and *The Spirit of Laws* in its index of forbidden books.

Raising the Woman Question

Many of the letters exchanged in *Persian Letters* focused on women, marriage, and the family because Montesquieu considered the position of women a sure indicator of the

---

◆ For an excerpt from Montesquieu's classic work, see Document 45, "Persian Letters: Letter 37."

IMPORTANT DATES			
1690s	Beginning of rapid development of plantations in Caribbean	1714	Elector of Hanover becomes King George I of England
1694	Bank of England established; Mary Astell's *A Serious Proposal to the Ladies* argues for the founding of a private women's college	1715	Death of Louis XIV
		1719	Daniel Defoe publishes *Robinson Crusoe*
1697	Pierre Bayle publishes *Historical and Critical Dictionary*, detailing errors of religious writers	1720	Last outbreak of bubonic plague in western Europe
		1721	Treaty of Nystad; Montesquieu publishes *Persian Letters* anonymously in the Dutch Republic
1699	Turks forced to recognize Habsburg rule over Hungary and Transylvania		
		1733	War of the Polish Succession; Voltaire's *Letters Concerning the English Nation* attacks French intolerance and narrow-mindedness
1703	Peter the Great of Russia begins construction of St. Petersburg, founds first Russian newspaper		
		1741	George Frederick Handel composes the *Messiah*
1713–1714	Peace of Utrecht		

nature of government and morality. Although he was not a feminist, his depiction of Roxana, the favorite wife in Usbek's harem, struck a chord with many women. Roxana revolts against the authority of Usbek's eunuchs and writes a final letter to her husband announcing her impending suicide: "I may have lived in servitude, but I have always been free, I have amended your laws according to the laws of nature, and my mind has always remained independent." Women writers used the same language of tyranny and freedom to argue for concrete changes in their status. Feminist ideas were not entirely new, but they were presented systematically for the first time and represented a fundamental challenge to the ways of traditional societies.

The most systematic of these women writers was the English author Mary Astell (1666–1731), the daughter of a businessman and herself a supporter of the Tory party and the Anglican religious establishment. In 1694, she published *A Serious Proposal to the Ladies,* in which she advocated founding a private women's college to remedy women's lack of education. Addressing women, she asked, "How can you be content to be in the World like Tulips in a Garden, to make a fine *shew* [show] and be good for nothing?" Astell argued for intellectual training based on Descartes's principles, in which reason, debate, and careful consideration of the issues took priority over custom or tradition. Her book was an immediate success: five printings appeared by 1701. In later works such as *Reflections upon Marriage* (1706), Astell criticized the relationship between the sexes within marriage: "If Absolute Sovereignty be not necessary in a State, how comes it to be so in a family? . . . *If all Men*

■ **MAPPING THE WEST** Europe in 1740

*By 1740, Europe had achieved a kind of diplomatic equilibrium in which no one power predomi-
nated. But the relative balance should not deflect attention from important underlying changes:
Spain, the Dutch Republic, Poland-Lithuania, and Sweden had all declined in power and influence
while Great Britain, Russia, Prussia, and Austria had solidified their positions, each in a different
way. France's ambitions had been thwarted, but the combination of a big army and rich overseas
possessions made France a major player for a long time to come.*

are born free, how is it that all Women are born slaves?"♦ Her critics accused her
of promoting subversive ideas and of contradicting the Scriptures.

Astell's work inspired other women to write in a similar vein. The anonymous
Essay in Defence of the Female Sex (1696) attacked "the Usurpation of Men; and the

---

♦ For an extended passage from Mary Astell's *Reflections upon Marriage,* see Document 46.

Tyranny of Custom," which prevented women from getting an education. In 1709, Elizabeth Elstob published a detailed account of the prominent role women played in promoting Christianity in English history. She criticized men who "would declare openly they hated any Woman who knew more than themselves."

Most male writers unequivocally stuck to the traditional view of women, which held that women were less capable of reasoning than men and therefore did not need systematic education. Such opinions often rested on biological suppositions. The long-dominant Aristotelian view of reproduction held that only the male seed carried spirit and individuality. At the beginning of the eighteenth century, however, scientists began to undermine this belief. More physicians and surgeons began to champion the doctrine of *ovism*—that the female egg was essential in making new humans. During the decades that followed, male Enlightenment writers would continue to debate women's nature and appropriate social roles.

Conclusion

Europeans crossed a major threshold in the first half of the eighteenth century. They moved silently but nonetheless momentously from an economy governed by scarcity and the threat of famine to one of ever increasing growth and the prospect of continuing improvement. Expansion of colonies overseas and economic development at home created greater wealth, longer life spans, and higher expectations for the future. In these better times for many, a spirit of optimism prevailed. People could now spend money on newspapers, novels, and travel literature as well as on coffee, tea, and cotton cloth. The growing literate public avidly followed the latest trends in religious debates, art, and music. Everyone did not share equally in the benefits: slaves toiled in abjection in the Americas; serfs in eastern Europe found themselves ever more closely bound to their noble lords; and rural folk almost everywhere tasted few fruits of consumer society.

Politics, too, changed as population and production increased and cities grew. Experts urged government intervention to improve public health, and states found it in their interest to settle many international disputes by diplomacy, which itself became more regular and routine. The consolidation of the European state system allowed a tide of criticism and new thinking about society to swell in Great Britain and France and begin to spill throughout Europe. Ultimately, the combination of the Atlantic system and the Enlightenment would give rise to a series of Atlantic revolutions.

Suggested References for further reading and online research appear on page SR-22 at the back of the book.

www.bedfordstmartins.com/huntconcise   See the ONLINE STUDY GUIDE to assess your mastery of the material covered in this chapter.

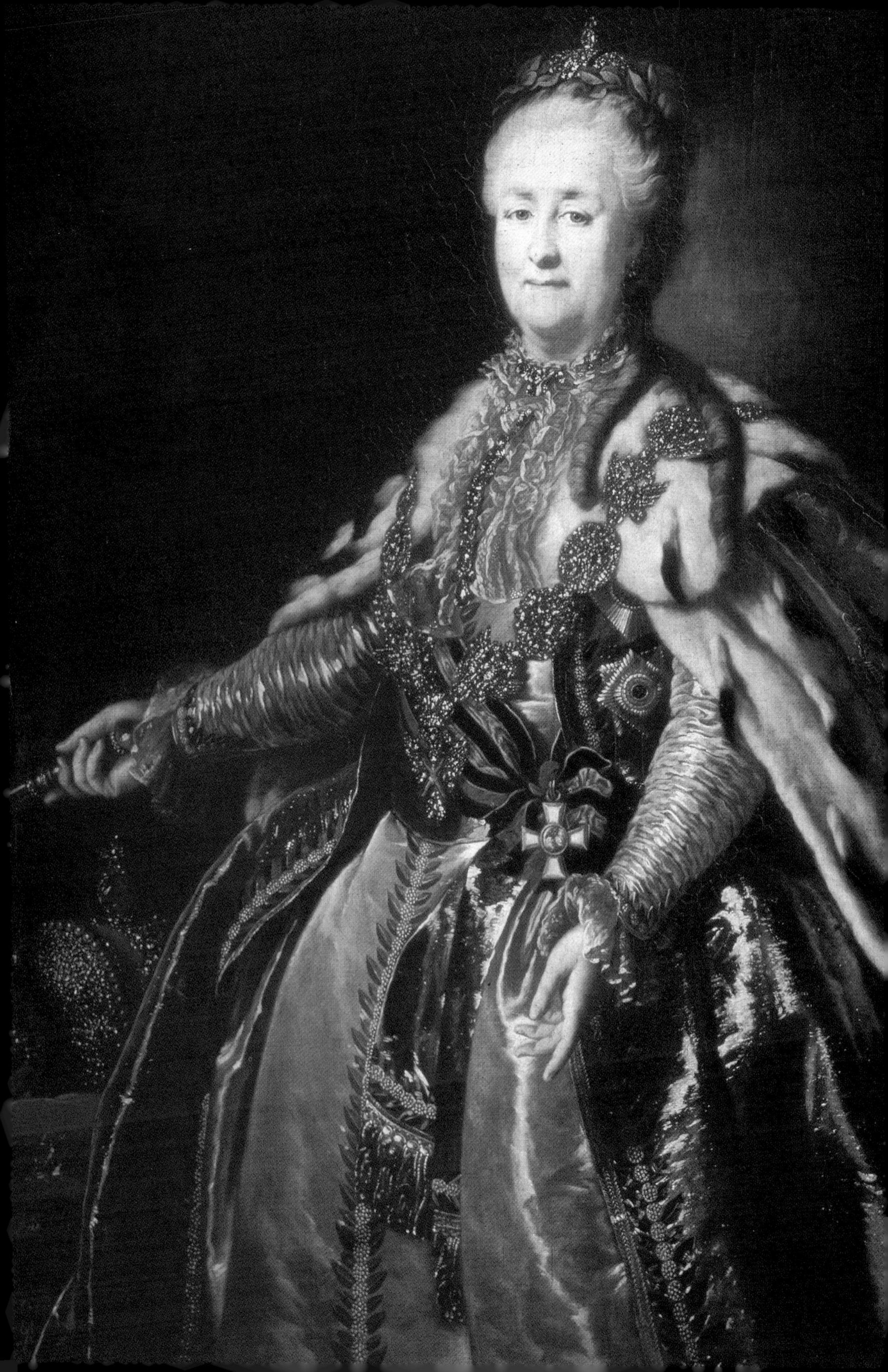

The Promise of Enlightenment

1740–1789

I N THE SUMMER OF 1766, Empress Catherine II ("the Great") of Russia wrote to Voltaire, one of the leaders of the Enlightenment:

> It is a way of immortalizing oneself to be the advocate of humanity, the defender of oppressed innocence. . . . You have entered into combat against the enemies of mankind: superstition, fanaticism, ignorance, quibbling, evil judges, and the powers that rest in their hands. Great virtues and qualities are needed to surmount these obstacles. You have shown that you have them: you have triumphed.

Over a fifteen-year period Catherine corresponded regularly with Voltaire, a writer who, at home in France, found himself in constant conflict with church and state authorities. Her admiring letter shows how influential Enlightenment ideals had become by the middle of the eighteenth century.

Catherine's letter aptly summed up Enlightenment ideals: progress for humanity could be achieved only by rooting out the wrongs left by superstition, religious fanaticism, ignorance, and outmoded forms of justice. Enlightenment writers used every means at their disposal—from encyclopedias to novels to personal interaction with rulers—to argue for reform. Everything had to be examined

■ **Catherine the Great**
At the time of this portrait (1793) by Johann Baptist Edler von Lampi, the Russian empress had ruled for thirty-one years and was only three years from her death. Born Sophia Augusta Frederika of Anhalt-Zerbst in 1729, she was the daughter of a minor German prince. When she married the future tsar Peter III in 1745, she promptly learned Russian and adopted Russian Orthodoxy. Peter, physically and mentally frail, proved no match for her, and she took his place on his death in 1762. The painter of this portrait was a native of northern Italy who had worked at the Austrian court in Vienna before being summoned to St. Petersburg. He painted many portraits of the Russian court and royal family between 1792 and 1797. (Art Resource, NY.)

in the clear light of reason, and anything that did not promote the improvement of humanity was to be jettisoned. As a result, Enlightenment writers attacked the legal use of torture to extract confessions, favored the spread of education to eliminate ignorance, supported religious toleration, and criticized censorship by state or church. The book trade and new places for urban socializing, such as coffeehouses and Masonic lodges (social clubs organized around the rituals of masons' guilds), spread these ideas within a new elite of middle- and upper-class men and women.

The lower classes had little contact with Enlightenment ideas. Their lives were shaped more profoundly by the continuing rise in population, the start of industrialization, and wars among the great powers. States had to balance conflicting social pressures: rulers pursued Enlightenment reforms that they believed might enhance state power, but they feared changes that might unleash popular discontent. For example, Catherine aimed to bring Western ideas, culture, and reforms to Russia, but when faced with a massive uprising of the serfs, she not only suppressed the revolt but also increased the nobles' powers over their serfs. All reform-minded rulers faced similar potential challenges to their authority.

Even though the movement for reform had its limits, governments now needed to respond to a new force: public opinion. Rulers wanted to portray themselves as modern, open to change, and responsive to the segment of the public that was reading newspapers and closely following political developments. Enlightenment writers appealed to public opinion, but they still looked to rulers to effect reform. Writers such as Voltaire expressed little interest in the future of peasants or lower classes; they favored neither revolution nor political upheaval. Yet their ideas paved the way for something much more radical and unexpected. The American Declaration of Independence in 1776 showed how Enlightenment ideals could be translated into democratic political practice. After 1789, democracy would come to Europe as well.

The Enlightenment at Its Height

The Enlightenment emerged as an intellectual movement before 1740 but reached its peak only in the second half of the eighteenth century. The writers of the Enlightenment called themselves *philosophes* (French for "philosophers"), but that term is somewhat misleading. Whereas philosophers concern themselves with abstract theories, the philosophes were public intellectuals dedicated to solving the real problems of the world. They wrote on subjects ranging from current affairs to art criticism, and they wrote in every conceivable format. The Swiss philosophe Jean-Jacques Rousseau, for example, wrote a political tract, a treatise on education, a constitution for Poland, an analysis of the effects of the theater on public morals, a best-selling novel, an opera, and a notorious autobiography. The philosophes wrote for a broad educated public of readers who snatched up every Enlightenment book they could find at their local booksellers', even when rulers or churches tried to forbid publication. Between 1740 and 1789, the Enlightenment acquired its name and, despite heated conflicts between the philosophes and state and religious authorities, gained support in the highest reaches of government.

The Men and Women of the Republic of Letters

Although *philosophe* is a French word, the Enlightenment was distinctly cosmo-politan; philosophes could be found from Philadelphia to Moscow. The philosophes considered themselves part of a grand "republic of letters" that transcended national political boundaries. They were not republicans in the usual sense, that is, people who supported representative government and opposed monarchy. What united them were the ideals of reason, reform, and freedom. In 1784, the German philoso-pher Immanuel Kant summed up the program of the Enlightenment in two Latin words: *sapere aude*, "dare to know"—have the courage to think for yourself.

The philosophes used reason to attack superstition, bigotry, and religious fanaticism, which they considered the chief obstacles to free thought and social reform. Voltaire took religious fanaticism as his chief target: "Once fanaticism has corrupted a mind, the malady is almost incurable. . . . The only remedy for this epi-demic malady is the philosophical spirit." Enlightenment writers did not necessarily oppose organized religion, but they strenuously objected to religious intolerance. They believed that the systematic application of reason could do what religious belief could not: improve the human condition by pointing to needed reforms. Rea-son meant critical, informed, scientific thinking about social issues and problems. Many Enlightenment writers collaborated on a new multivolume *Encyclopedia* that aimed to gather together knowledge about science, religion, industry, and society. The chief editor of the *Encyclopedia*, Denis Diderot (1713–1784), explained the goal: "All things must be examined, debated, investigated without exception and without regard for anyone's feelings."

The philosophes believed that the spread of knowledge would encourage reform in every aspect of life, from the grain trade to the penal system. Chief among their desired reforms was intellectual freedom, the freedom to use one's own reason and to publish the results. The philosophes wanted freedom of the press and freedom of religion, which they considered "natural rights" guaranteed by "natural law." In their view, progress depended on these freedoms. As Voltaire asserted, "I quite un-derstand that the fanatics of one sect slaughter the enthusiasts of another sect . . . [but] that Descartes should have been forced to flee to Holland to escape the fury of the ignorant . . . these things are a nation's eternal shame."

Most philosophes, like Voltaire, came from the upper classes, yet Rousseau's father was a modest watchmaker in Geneva, and Diderot was the son of a cutlery maker. Although it was a rare phenomenon, some women were philosophes, such as the French noblewoman Émilie du Châtelet (1706–1749), who wrote extensively about the mathematics and physics of Leibniz and Newton. (Her lover Voltaire

■ **Madame Geoffrin's Salon in 1755**
This 1812 painting by Anicet Charles Lemonnier claims to depict the best-known Parisian salon of the 1750s. Lemonnier was only twelve years old in 1755 and so could not have based his rendition on firsthand knowledge. Madame Geoffrin is the figure in blue on the right, facing the viewer. The bust is of Voltaire. Rousseau is the fifth person to the left of the bust (facing right) and behind him (facing left) is Raynal. (Giraudon/Art Resource, NY.)

learned much of his science from her.) Few of the leading writers held university positions, except those who were German or Scottish. Universities in France were dominated by the clergy and unreceptive to Enlightenment ideals.

Enlightenment ideas developed instead through personal contacts; through letters that were hand copied, circulated, and sometimes published; through informal readings of manuscripts; and through letters to the editor and book reviews in periodicals. Salons (*salon* is French for "living room") gave intellectual life an anchor outside the royal court and the church-controlled universities. Best known was the Parisian salon of Madame Marie-Thérèse Geoffrin (1699–1777), a wealthy middle-class widow who had been raised by her grandmother and married off at fourteen to a much older man. She brought together the most exciting thinkers and artists of the time; her social gatherings provided a forum for new ideas and an opportunity to establish new intellectual contacts. In the salon, the philosophes could discuss ideas they might hesitate to put into print and thus test public opinion and even push it in new directions. Madame Geoffrin corresponded extensively with influential people across Europe, including Catherine the Great. One Italian visitor commented, "There is no way to make Naples resemble Paris unless we find a woman to guide us, organize us, *Geoffrinize* us."◆

◆ For two primary sources that reveal Geoffrin's remarkable personality and influence, see Document 47, Marie-Thérèse Geoffrin and Monsieur d'Alembert, "The Salon of Madame Geoffrin."

Women's salons helped galvanize intellectual life and reform movements all over Europe. Wealthy Jewish women created nine of the fourteen salons in Berlin at the end of the eighteenth century, and in Warsaw, Princess Zofia Czartoryska gathered around her the reform leaders of Poland-Lithuania. Middle-class women in London used their salons to raise money to publish women's writings. Salons could be tied closely to the circles of power: in France, for example, Louis XV's mistress, Jeanne-Antoinette Poisson, first made her reputation as hostess of a salon frequented by Voltaire and Montesquieu. When she became Louis XV's mistress in 1745, she gained the title Marquise de Pompadour and turned her attention to influencing artistic styles by patronizing architects and painters.

Conflicts with Church and State

Madame Geoffrin did not approve of discussions that attacked the Catholic church, but elsewhere voices against organized religion could be heard. Criticisms of religion required daring because the church, whatever its denomination, wielded enormous power in society, and most influential people considered religion an essential foundation of good society and government. Defying such opinion, the Scottish philosopher David Hume (1711–1776) boldly argued in *The Natural History of Religion* (1755) that belief in God rested on superstition and fear rather than on reason.

Before the scientific revolution, nearly every European believed in God. After Newton, however, and despite Newton's own deep religiosity, people could conceive of the universe as an eternally existing, self-perpetuating machine in which God's intervention was unnecessary. In short, such people could become either *atheists*, who did not believe in any kind of God, or *deists*, who believed in God but gave him no active role in earthly affairs. For the first time, writers claimed the label *atheist* and disputed the common view that atheism led inevitably to immorality.

Deists continued to believe in a benevolent, all-knowing God who had designed the universe and set it in motion. But deists usually rejected the idea that God directly intercedes in the functioning of the universe, and they often criticized the churches for their dogmatic intolerance of dissenters. Voltaire was a deist, and in his popular *Philosophical Dictionary* (1764) he attacked most of the claims of organized Christianity, both Catholic and Protestant. Christianity, he argued, had been the prime source of fanaticism and brutality among humans. Throughout his life, Voltaire's motto was *Écrasez l'infâme*—"Crush the infamous thing" (the "thing" being bigotry and intolerance). French authorities publicly burned his *Philosophical Dictionary*.

Criticism of religious intolerance involved more than simply attacking the churches. Critics also had to confront the states to which churches were closely tied. In 1761, a judicial case in Toulouse provoked throughout France an outcry that Voltaire soon joined. When the son of a local Calvinist was found hanged (he probably committed suicide), authorities accused the father, Jean Calas, of murdering him to prevent his conversion to Catholicism. (Since Louis XIV's revocation of the Edict of Nantes in 1685, it had been illegal to practice Calvinism publicly in France.) The all-Catholic parlement of Toulouse tried to extract a confession using torture—breaking all Calas's bones—and then executed him when he still refused to confess. Voltaire launched a successful crusade to rehabilitate Jean Calas's good name and to restore the family's properties, which had been confiscated after his death. Voltaire's efforts eventually helped bring about the extension of civil rights to French Protestants and encouraged campaigns to abolish the legal use of torture.

Critics also assailed state and church support for European colonization and slavery. One of the most popular books of the time was the *Philosophical and Political History of European Colonies and Commerce in the Two Indies*, published in 1770 by Abbé Guillaume Raynal (1713–1796), a French Catholic clergyman. Raynal and his collaborators described in excruciating detail the destruction of native populations by Europeans and denounced the slave trade. Although Raynal was forced into exile and his work was banned by both the Catholic church and the French government, the Enlightenment belief in natural rights led many others to denounce slavery. An article in the new *Encyclopedia* proclaimed, "There is not a single one of these hapless souls . . . who does not have the right to be declared free . . . since neither his ruler nor his father nor anyone else had the right to dispose of his freedom." Some Enlightenment thinkers, however, took a more ambiguous or even negative view. Hume judged blacks to be "naturally inferior to the whites," concluding, "There never was a civilized nation of any other complexion than white."

Enlightenment critics of church and state advocated reform, not revolution. Although he lived near the French-Swiss border in case he had to flee arrest, Voltaire, for example, made a fortune from financial speculations, wrote a glowing history called *The Age of Louis XIV* (1751), and lived to be celebrated in his last years as a national hero even by many former foes. Other philosophes also lived respectably, believing that published criticism, rather than violent action, would bring about necessary reforms. As Diderot said, "We will speak against senseless laws until they are reformed; and, while we wait, we will abide by them." Those few who lived long enough to see the French Revolution in 1789 resisted its radical turn, for the philosophes generally regarded the lower classes—"the people"—as ignorant, violent, and prone to superstition, hence in need of leadership from above. They pinned their hopes on educated elites and enlightened rulers.

Despite the philosophes' preference for reform, in the long run their books often had a revolutionary impact. For example, Montesquieu's widely reprinted *Spirit of the Laws* (1748) warned against the dangers of despotism, opposed the divine right of kings, and favored constitutional government. In his somewhat rosy view, Great Britain was "the one nation in the world which has political liberty as the direct object of its constitution." His analysis of British constitutionalism inspired French critics of absolutism and would greatly influence the American revolutionaries.

The Individual and Society

The controversy created by the most notorious conflicts between the philosophes and the various churches and states of Europe drew attention away from a subtle but profound transformation in worldviews. In previous centuries, questions of theological doctrine and church organization had been the main focus of intellectual and even political interest. The Enlightenment writers shifted attention away from religious questions toward the secular study of society and the individual's role in it. Religion did not drop out of sight, but the philosophes tended to make religion a private affair of individual conscience, even while rulers and churches still considered religion very much a public concern.

The Enlightenment interest in secular society produced two major results: it advanced the secularization of European political life that had begun after the Wars of Religion of the sixteenth and seventeenth centuries, and it laid the foundations for the social sciences of the modern era. Not surprisingly, then, many historians and philosophers consider the Enlightenment to be the origin of "modernity," which they define as the belief that human reason, rather than theological doctrine, should set the patterns of social and political life. This belief in reason as the sole foundation for secular authority has often been contested, but it has also proved to be a powerful force for change.

Although most of the philosophes believed that human reason could understand and even remake society and politics, they disagreed about what that reason revealed. Among the many different approaches were two that proved enduringly influential, those of the Scottish philosopher Adam Smith and the Swiss writer Jean-Jacques Rousseau. Smith provided a theory of modern capitalist society and devoted much of his energy to defending free markets as offering the best way to maximize individual efforts. The modern discipline of economics took shape around the questions raised by Smith. Rousseau set out the principles of a more communitarian philosophy, one that emphasized the needs of the community over those of the individual. His work led both toward democracy and toward communism and continues to inspire heated debate in political science and sociology. A closer look at these two thinkers will demonstrate the breadth and depth of Enlightenment thought.

Adam Smith (1723–1790) optimistically believed that individual interests naturally harmonized with those of the whole society. To explain how this natural harmonization worked, he published *An Inquiry into the Nature and Causes of the Wealth of Nations* in 1776. Smith insisted that individual self-interest, even greed, was quite compatible with society's best interest: the laws of supply and demand served as an "invisible hand" ensuring that individual interests would be synchronized with those of the whole society. Market forces—"the propensity to truck, barter, and exchange one thing for another"—naturally brought individual and social interests in line.

Smith rejected the prevailing mercantilist views that the general welfare would be served by accumulating national wealth through agriculture or the hoarding of gold and silver. Instead, he argued that the division of labor in manufacturing would increase productivity and generate more wealth for society and well-being for the individual. To maximize the effects of market forces and the division of labor, Smith endorsed a concept called *laissez-faire* (that is, "to leave alone") to free the economy from government intervention and control. He insisted that governments eliminate all restrictions on the sale of land, remove restraints on the grain trade, and abandon duties on imports. He believed that free international trade would stimulate production everywhere and thus ensure the growth of national wealth. He argued:

> *The natural effort of every individual to better his own condition, when suffered to exert itself with freedom and security, is so powerful a principle, that it is alone, and without any assistance, not only capable of carrying the society to wealth and prosperity, but of surmounting a hundred impertinent obstructions with which the folly of human laws too often encumbers its operations.*

Governments should restrict themselves to providing "security"—that is, national defense, internal order and a secure framework for market activity, and public works.

Much more pessimistic about the relation between individual self-interest and the good of society was Jean-Jacques Rousseau (1712–1778). In Rousseau's view, society itself threatened natural rights or freedoms: "Man is born free, and everywhere he is in chains." Rousseau first gained fame by writing a prize-winning essay in 1749 in which he argued that the revival of science and the arts had corrupted social morals, not improved them. This startling conclusion seemed to oppose some of the Enlightenment's most cherished beliefs. Rather than improving society, he claimed, science and art raised artificial barriers between people and their natural state. Rousseau's works extolled the simplicity of rural life over urban society. Although he participated in the salons, Rousseau always felt ill at ease in high society, and he periodically withdrew to live in solitude far from Paris. Paradoxically, his "solitude" was often paid for by wealthy upper-class patrons, who lodged him on their estates, even as his writings decried the upper-class privilege that made his efforts possible.

Rousseau explored the tension between the individual and society in various ways, including his widely influential work on education, *Émile* (1762), in which a boy develops practical skills and independent thinking under the guidance of his tutor. In *The Social Contract* (1762), Rousseau proposed a political solution to the tension between the individual and society. Whereas earlier he had argued that society corrupted the individual by taking him out of nature, in this work Rousseau

■ **Rousseau's Worries**

Jean-Jacques Rousseau's novel The New Heloise *(1761) sold better than any other work in French in the second half of the eighteenth century. But Rousseau himself was deeply concerned about the effects of novel reading, especially on young women. The first of these illustrations for the novel (on the left) by Moreau the Younger, was rejected by Rousseau because the couple (Julie and Saint Preux) are shown in direct physical contact. He accepted the engraving on the right, by Gravelot, because it only hinted at passion.* (Bibliothèque Nationale.)

insisted that individual moral freedom could be achieved only by learning to sub-ject one's individual interests to "the general will"—that is, to the good of the com-munity. Individuals did this by entering into a social contract, not with their rulers but with one another. If everyone followed the general will, then all individuals would be equally free and equally moral because they lived under a law to which they had all consented.

These arguments threatened the legitimacy of eighteenth-century governments. Rousseau derived his social contract from human nature, not from history, tradi-tion, or the Bible. He implied that people would be most free and moral under a republican form of government with direct democracy, and his abstract model included no reference to differences in social status. He roundly condemned slav-ery: "To decide that the son of a slave is born a slave is to decide that he is not born a man." Not surprisingly, authorities in both Geneva and Paris banned *The Social*

Contract for undermining political authority. Rousseau's works would become a kind of political bible for the French revolutionaries of 1789, and his attacks on private property would inspire the communists of the nineteenth century such as Karl Marx. Rousseau's rather mystical concept of the general will remains controversial. The "greatest good of all," according to Rousseau, was liberty and equality, but he also insisted that the individual could be "forced to be free" by the terms of the social contract. He provided no legal protections for individual rights. In other words, Rousseau's particular version of democracy did not guarantee the individual freedoms so important to Adam Smith.

Spreading the Enlightenment

The Enlightenment flourished in places where an educated middle class provided an eager audience for ideas of constitutionalism and reform. Where constitutionalism and the guarantee of individual freedoms were most advanced, as in Great Britain and the Dutch Republic, the movement had less of an edge because there was, in a sense, less need for it. Scottish and English writers concentrated on economics, philosophy, and history rather than politics or social relations. Dutch printers made money publishing the books that were forbidden in France. In British North America, Enlightenment ideas helped stiffen growing colonial resistance to British rule after 1763. In places with small middle classes, such as Spain, the Italian states, and Russia, governments successfully suppressed writings they did not like. Italian philosophes, such as the Milanese penal reformer Cesare Beccaria (1738–1794), got moral support from their French counterparts in the face of stern censorship at home.

The hot spot of the Enlightenment was France. French writers published the most daring critiques of church and state and suffered the most intense harassment and persecution. Voltaire, Diderot, and Rousseau all faced arrest, exile, or even imprisonment. The Catholic church and royal authorities routinely forbade the publication of their books, and the police arrested publishers who ignored their warnings. Yet the French monarchy was far from the most autocratic in Europe, and Voltaire, Diderot, and Rousseau all ended their lives as cultural heroes. France seems to have been curiously caught in the middle during the Enlightenment: with fewer constitutional guarantees of individual freedom than Great Britain, it still enjoyed much higher levels of prosperity and cultural development than most other European countries. In short, French elites had reason to complain, the means to make their complaints known, and a government torn between the desires to censor dissident ideas and to appear open to modernity and progress. The government in France controlled publishing—all books had to get official permissions—but not as tightly as in Spain, where the Catholic Inquisition made up its own list of banned books, or in Russia, where Catherine the Great allowed no opposition.

By the 1760s, the French government regularly ignored the publication of many works once thought offensive or subversive. In addition, a growing flood of works printed abroad poured into France and circulated underground. In the Dutch Republic and Swiss cities, private companies made fortunes smuggling illegal books into France over mountain passes and back roads. Foreign printers provided secret catalogs of their offerings and sold their products through booksellers who were willing to market forbidden texts for a high price—among them, not only philosophical treatises of the Enlightenment but also pornographic works and pamphlets (some by Diderot) lampooning the Catholic clergy and leading members of the royal court. In the 1770s and 1780s, lurid descriptions of sexual promiscuity at the French court helped undermine the popularity of the throne.

Whereas the French philosophes often took a violently anticlerical and combative tone, their German counterparts avoided direct political confrontations with authorities. Gotthold Lessing (1729–1781) complained in 1769 that Prussia was still "the most slavish society in Europe" in its lack of freedom to criticize government policies. As a playwright, literary critic, and philosopher, Lessing promoted religious toleration for Jews and spiritual emancipation of Germans from foreign, especially French, models of culture, which still dominated. Lessing also introduced the German Jewish writer Moses Mendelssohn (1729–1786) into Berlin salon society. Mendelssohn labored to build bridges between German and Jewish culture by arguing that Judaism was a rational and undogmatic religion. He believed persecution and discrimination against the Jews would end as reason triumphed.

Reason was also the chief focus of the most influential German thinker of the Enlightenment, Immanuel Kant (1724–1804). A university professor who lectured on everything from economics to astronomy, Kant wrote one of the most important works in the history of Western philosophy, *The Critique of Pure Reason* (1781). He admired Adam Smith and especially Rousseau, whose portrait he displayed proudly in his lodgings. Just as Smith founded modern economics and Rousseau modern political theory, Kant in *Critique of Pure Reason* set the foundations for modern philosophy. In this complex book, Kant established the doctrine of *idealism*, the belief that true understanding can come only from examining the ways in which ideas are formed in the mind. Ideas are shaped, Kant argued, not just by sensory information (a position central to *empiricism*, a philosophy based on John Locke's writings) but also by the operation on that information of mental categories such as space and time. In Kant's philosophy, these "categories of understanding" were neither sensory nor supernatural; they were entirely ideal and abstract and located in the human mind. For Kant the supreme philosophical questions—Does God exist? Is personal immortality possible? Do humans have free will?—were unanswerable by reason alone. But like Rousseau, Kant insisted that people could achieve true moral freedom only by living in society and obeying its laws.

The Limits of Reason: Roots of Romanticism and Religious Revival

In reaction to what some saw as the Enlightenment's excessive reliance on the authority of human reason, a new artistic movement called *romanticism* took root. Although it would not fully flower until the early nineteenth century, romanticism traced its emphasis on individual genius, deep emotion, and the joys of nature to thinkers like Rousseau who had scolded the philosophes for ignoring those aspects of life that escaped and even conflicted with the power of reason. Rousseau's auto-biographical *Confessions*, published posthumously in 1782, caused an immediate sensation because it revealed so much about his inner emotional life, including his sexual longings and his almost paranoid distrust of other Enlightenment figures.

The appeal to feelings and emotions also increased interest in the occult. In the 1780s, a charismatic Austrian physician turned "experimenter," Franz Mesmer, awed crowds of aristocrats and middle-class admirers with his Paris demonstrations of "animal magnetism." He passed a weak electrical current through tubs filled with water or iron filings, around which groups of his disciples sat, holding hands; with this process of "mesmerism" he claimed to cure their ailments. (The word *mesmerize*, meaning "hypnotize" or "hold spellbound," is derived from Mesmer's name.)

A novel by the German writer Johann Wolfgang von Goethe (1749–1832) captured the early romantic spirit with its glorification of emotion. *The Sorrows of Young Werther* (1774) tells of a passionate youth who reveres nature and rural life and is unhappy in love. When the woman he loves marries someone else, he falls into deep melancholy and eventually kills himself. Reason cannot save him. The book spurred a veritable Werther craze: there were Werther costumes, Werther engravings and embroidery, Werther medallions, and a perfume called Eau de Werther. Tragically, there were even a few imitations of Werther's suicide. The young Napoleon Bonaparte, who was to build an empire for France, claimed to have read Goethe's novel seven times.

Religious revivals underlined the limits of reason in a different way. Much of the Protestant world experienced an "awakening" in the 1740s. In the German states, Pietist groups founded new communities; and in the British North American colonies, revivalist Protestant preachers drew thousands of fervent believers in a movement called the Great Awakening. In North America, bitter conflicts between revivalists and their opponents in the established churches prompted the leaders on both sides to set up new colleges to support their beliefs. These included Princeton, Columbia, Brown, and Dartmouth, all founded between 1746 and 1769.

Revivalism also stirred eastern European Jews at about the same time. Israel ben Eliezer (c. 1700–1760), later known as Ba'al Shem Tov (or the Besht, from the initials), laid the foundation for the Hasidic sect in the 1740s and 1750s. Teaching outside the synagogue system, Ba'al Shem Tov traveled the Polish countryside offering to cure men of their evil spirits. He invented a new form of popular prayer,

■ **A Hasid and His Wife**
The followers of Ba'al Shem Tov were known as Hasidim *("most pious Jews"). They insisted on wearing Polish peasant-style clothing even if they themselves were not peasants. The Hasidim stressed devotion to the* rebbe *("teacher and spiritual guide").*
(Encyclopedia of Jewish History.)

in which the believer aimed to annihilate his own personality in order to let the supernatural speak through him. His followers, the *Hasidim* (Hebrew for "most pious" Jews), often prayed at the top of their lungs, joyfully swaying and clapping their hands. They scorned the formality of the regular synagogues in favor of their own prayer houses, where they gathered in rustic clothing and broad fur hats to emphasize their piety and simplicity. Their practices soon spread all over Poland-Lithuania.

Most of the waves of Protestant revivalism ebbed after the 1750s, but in Great Britain the movement known as *Methodism* continued to grow through the end of the century. John Wesley (1703–1791), the Oxford-educated son of an Anglican cleric, founded Methodism, a term evoked by Wesley's insistence on strict self-discipline and a methodical approach to religious study and observance. In 1738, Wesley began preaching a new brand of Protestantism that emphasized an intense personal experience of salvation and a life of thrift, abstinence, and hard work. Traveling all over the British Isles, Wesley would mount a table or a box to speak to the ordinary people of the village or town. He slept in his followers' homes, ate their food, and treated their illnesses with various remedies, including small electric shocks for nervous diseases (Wesley eagerly followed Benjamin Franklin's experiments with electricity). In fifty years, Wesley preached forty thousand sermons, an average of fifteen a week. Not surprisingly, his preaching disturbed the Anglican authorities, who refused to let him preach in the churches. In response, Wesley began to ordain his own clergy. Nevertheless, during Wesley's lifetime the Methodist leadership remained politically conservative; Wesley himself denounced political agitation in the 1770s because, he said, it threatened to make Great Britain "a field of blood" ruled by "King Mob."

Society and Culture in an Age of Enlightenment

Religious revivals and the first stirrings of romanticism show that all intellectual currents did not flow in the same channel. Similarly, some social and cultural developments manifested the influence of Enlightenment ideas, but others did not. The traditional leaders of European societies—the nobles—responded to Enlightenment ideals in contradictory fashion: many simply reasserted their privileges and resisted the influence of the Enlightenment, but an important minority embraced change and actively participated in reform efforts. The expanding middle classes saw in the Enlightenment a chance to make their claim for joining society's governing elite. They bought Enlightenment books, joined Masonic lodges, and patronized new styles in art, music, and literature. The lower classes were more affected by economic growth. Continuing population increases contributed to a rise in prices for basic goods, but the industrialization of textile manufacturing, which began in this period, made cotton clothing more accessible to those at the bottom of the social scale.

The Nobility's Reassertion of Privilege

Nobles made up about 3 percent of the European population, but their numbers and way of life varied greatly from country to country. At least 10 percent of the population in Poland was noble and 7 to 8 percent in Spain, in contrast to only 2 percent in Russia and between 1 and 2 percent in the rest of western Europe. Many Polish and Spanish nobles lived in poverty; titles did not guarantee wealth. The wealthiest European nobles luxuriated in almost unimaginable opulence. Many of the English peers, for example, owned more than ten thousand acres of land (the average western European peasant owned about five acres), invested widely in government bonds and trading companies, kept several country residences with scores of servants as well as houses in London, and occasionally even had their own private orchestras as well as libraries of expensive books, greenhouses for exotic plants, kennels of pedigree dogs, and collections of antiques, firearms, and scientific instruments.

In the face of the commercialization of agriculture and inflation of prices, European aristocrats converted their remaining legal rights (called *seigneurial dues*, from the French *seigneur*, for "lord") into money payments and used them to support an increasingly expensive lifestyle. Peasants felt the squeeze as a result. French peasants, for instance, paid a wide range of dues to their landlords—including payments to grind grain at the lord's mill, bake bread in his oven, and press grapes at his winepress—and various inheritance taxes on the land. In addition, peasants had to work on the public roads without compensation for a specified number of days every year. They also paid taxes to the government on salt, an essential preservative, and on the value of their land; customs duties if they sold produce or wine in town; and the tithe on their grain (one-tenth of the crop) to the church.

In Britain, the landed gentry could not claim these same onerous dues from their tenants, but they tenaciously defended their exclusive right to hunt game. The game laws kept the poor from eating meat and helped protect the social status of the rich. The gentry enforced the game laws themselves by hiring gamekeepers who hunted down poachers and even set traps for them in the forests. According to the law, anyone who poached deer or rabbits while armed or disguised could be sentenced to death. After 1760, the number of arrests for breaking the game laws increased dramatically. In most other countries, too, hunting was the special right of the nobility and a cause of deep popular resentment.

Even though Enlightenment writers sharply criticized nobles' insistence on special privileges, most aristocrats maintained their marks of distinction. The male court nobility continued to sport swords, plumed hats, makeup, and powdered hair; middle-class men wore simpler and more somber clothing. Aristocrats had their own seats in church and their own quarters in the universities. Frederick II ("the Great") of Prussia (r. 1740–1786) made sure that nobles dominated both the army officer corps and the civil bureaucracy. Catherine II of Russia (r. 1762–1796) granted the nobility vast tracts of land, the exclusive right to own serfs, and exemption from personal taxes and corporal punishment. Her Charter of the Nobility of 1785 codified these privileges in exchange for the nobles' political subservience to the state. In many countries, including Spain and France, the law prohibited aristocrats from engaging directly in retail trade. In Austria, Spain, the Italian states, Poland-Lithuania, and Russia, most nobles consequently cared little about Enlightenment ideas; they did not read the books of the philosophes and feared reforms that might challenge their dominance of rural society.

In France, Britain, and the western German states, however, the nobility proved more open to the new ideas. Among those who personally corresponded with Rousseau, for example, half were nobles, as were 20 percent of the 160 contributors to the *Encyclopedia*. It had not escaped their notice that Rousseau had denounced inequality. In his view, it was "manifestly contrary to the law of nature . . . that a handful of people should gorge themselves with superfluities while the hungry multitude goes in want of necessities."

The Middle Class and the Making of a New Elite

The Enlightenment offered middle-class people an intellectual and cultural route to social improvement. The term *middle class* referred to the middle position on the social ladder; middle-class families did not have legal titles like the nobility above them but did not work with their hands like the peasants, artisans, or workers below them. Most middle-class people lived in towns or cities and earned their living in the professions—as doctors, lawyers, or lower-level officials—or through investment in land, trade, or manufacturing. In the eighteenth century, the ranks of the middle class—also known as the *bourgeoisie*, after *bourgeois*, the French word for "city dweller"—grew steadily in western Europe as a result of economic expansion. In France, for example, the overall population grew by about one-third in the 1700s, but the bourgeoisie nearly tripled in size. Although middle-class people had many reasons to resent the nobles, they also aspired to be like them.

Nobles and middle-class professionals mingled in Enlightenment salons and joined the new Masonic lodges and local learned societies. The members of Masonic lodges were known as *freemasons* because that was the term given to apprentice masons when they were deemed "free" to practice as masters of their guild. Although not explicitly political in aim, the lodges encouraged equality among members, and both aristocrats and middle-class men could join. Members wrote constitutions for their lodges and elected their own officers, thus promoting a direct experience of constitutional government.

Freemasonry arose in Great Britain and spread eastward: the first French and Italian lodges opened in 1726; Frederick II of Prussia founded a lodge in 1740; and after 1750, freemasonry spread in Poland, Russia, and British North America. In France, women set up their own Masonic lodges. Despite the papacy's condemnation of freemasonry in 1738 as subversive of religious and civil authority, lodges continued to multiply throughout the eighteenth century because they offered a place for socializing outside of the traditional channels and a way of declaring one's interest in the Enlightenment and reform. In short, freemasonry offered a kind of secular religion. After 1789 and the outbreak of the French Revolution, conservatives would blame the lodges for every kind of political upheaval, but in the 1700s many high-ranking nobles became active members and saw no conflict with their privileged status.

Shared tastes in travel, architecture, and the arts helped strengthen the links between nobles and members of the middle class. "Grand tours" of Europe often led upper-class youths to the recently discovered Greek and Roman ruins at Pompeii, Herculaneum, and Paestum in Italy. The excavations aroused enthusiasm for the neoclassical style in architecture and painting, which began pushing aside the rococo and the long dominant baroque. Urban residences, government buildings, furniture, fabrics, wallpaper, and even pottery soon reflected the neoclassical emphasis on purity and clarity of forms. The English potter Josiah Wedgwood (1730–1795) almost single-handedly created a mass market for domestic crockery by appealing to middle-class desires to emulate the rich and royal. His designs of special tea sets for the British queen, for Catherine the Great of Russia, and for leading aristocrats allowed him to advertise his wares as fashionable. By 1767, he claimed that his Queensware pottery had "spread over the whole Globe," and indeed by then his pottery was being marketed in France, Russia, Venice, the Ottoman Empire, and British North America.

■ Neoclassical Style
In this Georgian interior of Syon House on the outskirts of London, various neoclassical motifs are readily apparent: Greek columns, Greek-style statuary on top of the columns, and Roman-style mosaics in the floor. The Scottish architect Robert Adam created this room for the duke of Northumberland in the 1760s. Adam had spent four years in Italy and returned in 1758 to London to decorate homes in the "Adam style," meaning the neoclassical manner. (Fotomas Index, UK.)

This period also supported artistic styles other than neoclassicism. Frederick II of Prussia built himself a palace in the earlier rococo style, gave it a French name, *Sans-souci* ("worry-free"), and filled it with the works of French masters of the rococo. The new emphasis on emotion and family life was reflected in a growing taste for moralistic family scenes in painting. The paintings of Jean-Baptiste Greuze (1725–1805), much praised by Diderot, depicted ordinary families at moments of domestic crisis. Such subjects appealed in particular to the middle-class public, which now attended the official painting exhibitions in France that were held regularly every other year after 1737. Court painting nonetheless remained much in demand. Marie-Louise-Elizabeth Vigée-Lebrun (1755–1842), who painted portraits at the French court, reported that in the 1780s "it was difficult to get a place on my waiting list. . . . I was the fashion."

Although wealthy nobles still patronized Europe's leading musicians, music, too, began to reflect the broadening of the elite, and the spread of Enlightenment ideals as classical forms replaced the baroque style. Complex polyphony gave way to melody, which made music more accessible to the ordinary listener. Professional orchestras now played for large audiences of well-to-do listeners in sizable concert halls. The public concert gradually displaced the private recital, and a new attitude toward "the classics" developed: for the first time in the 1770s and 1780s, concert groups began to play older music rather than simply playing the latest commissioned works. This laid the foundation for what we still call *classical* music today, that is, a repertory of the greatest music of the eighteenth and early nineteenth centuries. Because composers now created works that would be performed over and over again as part of a classical repertory, rather than occasional pieces for the court or noble patrons, they deliberately attempted to write lasting works. As a result, the major composers began to produce fewer symphonies: the Austrian composer Franz Joseph Haydn (1732–1809) wrote more than one hundred symphonies, but his successor Ludwig van Beethoven (1770–1827) would create only nine.

The two supreme masters of the new musical style of the eighteenth century show that the transition from noble patronage to classical concerts was far from complete. The Austrians Haydn and Wolfgang Amadeus Mozart (1756–1791) both wrote for noble patrons, but by the early 1800s their compositions had been incorporated into the canon of concert classics all over Europe. Incredibly prolific, both excelled in combining lightness, clarity, and profound emotion. Both also wrote numerous Italian operas, a genre whose popularity continued to grow: in the 1780s, the Papal States alone boasted forty opera houses. Haydn spent most of his career working for a Hungarian noble family, the Eszterházys. Asked why he had written no string quintets (at which Mozart excelled), he responded simply: "No one has ordered any."

Interest in reading, like attending public concerts, took hold of the middle classes. Shaped by coffeehouses, Masonic lodges, and public concerts more than by formal schooling, the new reading public fed a frenzied increase in publication. By the end of the eighteenth century, six times as many books were being published in the German states, for instance, as at the beginning. One Parisian author commented that "people are certainly reading ten times as much in Paris as they did a hundred years ago." Provincial towns in Britain, France, the Dutch Republic, and the German states published their own newspapers; by 1780, thirty-seven English towns had local newspapers. Newspapers advertised arithmetic, dancing, and drawing lessons—and abortifacients and cures for venereal disease. Lending libraries multiplied, and, in England especially, even small villages housed secular book clubs. Women benefited as much as men from the spread of print. As one Englishman observed, "By far the greatest part of ladies now have a taste for books."

The novel had become a respectable and influential genre. Among the most widely read novels were those of the English printer and writer Samuel Richardson (1689–1761). In *Clarissa Harlowe* (1747–1748), a long novel in eight volumes, Richardson tells the story of a young woman from a heartless upper-class family who is torn between her family's choice of a repulsive suitor and her attraction to Lovelace, an aristocratic rake. Although she runs off with Lovelace to escape her family, she resists his advances; after being drugged and raped by Lovelace—despite the frantic pleas of readers of the first volumes to spare her—Clarissa dies of what can only be called a broken heart. One woman complained to Richardson, "I verily believe I have shed a pint of tears, and my heart is still bursting." Richardson claimed that he wrote *Clarissa* as a kind of manual of virtuous female conduct, yet critics nonetheless worried that novels undermined morals with their portrayals of low-life characters, the seductions of virtuous women, and other examples of immoral behavior.

Although he himself grew up reading novels with his father, Rousseau discouraged novel reading in *Émile*. Still, he helped change attitudes in the new elite toward children by offering an educational approach for gently drawing the best out of children rather than repressing their natural curiosity and love of learning. Paintings now showed individual children playing at their favorite activities rather than formally posed with their families. Books about and for children became popular. *The Newtonian System of the Universe Digested for Young Minds*, by "Tom Telescope," was published in Britain in 1761 and reprinted many times. Children's toys, jigsaw puzzles, and clothing designed for children all appeared for the first time in the 1700s. At the same time, however, the Enlightenment's emphasis on reason, self-control, and childhood innocence made parents increasingly anxious about their children's sexuality. Moralists and physicians wrote books about the evils of masturbation, "proving" that it led to physical and mental degeneration and even madness. One English writer linked masturbation to debility of body and of mind; infertility; epilepsy; loss of memory, sight, and hearing; distortions of the eyes, mouth, and face; a pale, sallow, and bluish complexion; wasting of the limbs; idiotism; and death itself. While the Enlightenment thus encouraged excessive concern about children being left to their own devices, it nevertheless taught the middle and upper classes to value their children and to expect their improvement through education.

Life on the Margins

Even more than worrying about their children, the upper and middle classes worried about the increasing numbers of poor people. Although booming foreign trade—French colonial trade, for example, increased tenfold in the 1700s—fueled a dramatic economic expansion, the results did not necessarily trickle all the way down the social scale. The population of Europe grew by nearly 30 percent, with especially striking gains in England, Ireland, Prussia, and Hungary. (See "Taking Measure," page 630.) Even though food production increased, shortages and crises still occurred periodically. Prices went up in many countries after the 1730s and continued to rise gradually until the early nineteenth century; wages in many trades rose as well, but less quickly than prices. Peasants who produced surpluses to sell in local markets and shopkeepers and artisans who could increase their sales to meet growing demand prospered. But those at the bottom of the social ladder—day laborers in the cities and peasants with small holdings—lived on the edge of dire poverty, and when they lost their land or work, they either migrated to the cities or wandered the roads in search of food and work. In France alone, 200,000 workers left their homes every year in search of seasonal employment elsewhere. At least 10 percent of Europe's urban population depended on some form of charity.

The growing numbers of poor people overwhelmed local governments and created fears about rising crime. In some countries, beggars and vagabonds had been locked up in workhouses since the mid-1600s. The expenses for running these

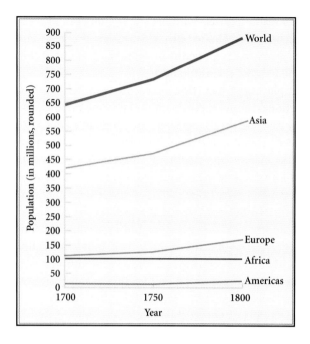

■ TAKING MEASURE
World Population Growth,
1700–1800
Asia had many more people than Europe, and both Asia and Europe were growing much more rapidly in the 1700s than Africa or the Americas. The population stagnation in Africa has been the subject of much scholarly controversy. What are the advantages of a growing population? What are the disadvantages?
(Adapted from Andre Gundar Frank, *Reorient: Global Economy in the Asian Age* [Berkeley: University of California Press, 1998].)

overcrowded institutions increased 60 percent in England between 1760 and 1785. After 1740, most German towns created workhouses that were part workshop, part hospital, and part prison. Such institutions also appeared for the first time in Boston, New York, and Philadelphia. To supplement the inadequate system of religious charity, offices for the poor, public workshops, and workhouse-hospitals, the French government created *dépôts de mendicité*, or beggar houses, in 1767. The government sent people to these new workhouses to labor in manufacturing, but most were too weak or sick to work, and 20 percent of them died within a few months of incarceration.

Those who were able to work or keep their land fared better: an increase in literacy, especially in the cities, allowed some lower-class people to participate in new tastes and ideas. One French observer insisted, "These days, you see a waiting-maid in her backroom, a lackey in an ante-room reading pamphlets. People can read in almost all classes of society."◆ In France, however, only 50 percent of men and 27 percent of women could read and write in the 1780s (although that was twice the rate of a century earlier). Literacy rates were higher in England and the Dutch Republic, much lower in eastern Europe. About one in four Parisians owned books, but the lower classes overwhelmingly read religious books, as they had in the past.

Whereas the new elite might attend salons, concerts, or art exhibitions, peasants enjoyed their traditional forms of popular entertainment, such as fairs and festi-

---

◆ For a primary source that shows the impact of Enlightenment ideas on one French artisan, see Document 48, Jacques-Louis Ménétra, *Journal of My Life.*

vals, and the urban lower classes relaxed in cabarets and taverns. Sometimes plea-sures were cruel. In Britain, bullbaiting, bearbaiting, dogfighting, and cockfighting were all common forms of entertainment that provided opportunities for orga-nized gambling. Even "gentle" sports frequented by the upper classes had their violent side, showing that the upper classes had not become so different as they sometimes thought. Cricket matches, whose rules were first laid down in 1744, were often accompanied by brawls among fans (not unlike soccer matches today, though on a much smaller scale). Many Englishmen enjoyed what one observer called a "battle royal with sticks, pebbles and hog's dung."

As population increased and villagers began to move to cities to better their prospects, sexual behavior changed, too. The rates of births out of wedlock soared, from less than 5 percent of all births in the seventeenth century to nearly 20 per-cent at the end of the eighteenth. Historians have disagreed about the causes and meaning of this change. Some detect in this pattern a sign of sexual liberation and the beginnings of a modern sexual revolution: as women moved out of the control of their families, they began to seek their own sexual fulfillment. Others view this change more bleakly, as a story of seduction and betrayal: family and community pressure had once forced a man to marry a woman pregnant with his child, but now a man could abandon a pregnant lover by simply moving away.

Increased mobility brought freedom for some women, but it also aggravated the vulnerability of those newly arrived in cities from the countryside. Desperation, not reason, often ruled their choices. Women who came to the city as domestic ser-vants had little recourse against masters or fellow servants who seduced or raped them. The result was a startling rise in abandoned babies. Most European cities established foundling hospitals in the 1700s, but infant and child mortality was 50 percent higher in such institutions than for children brought up at home. Some women tried herbs, laxatives, or crude surgical means of abortion; a few, usually servants who would lose their jobs if their employers discovered they had borne a child, resorted to infanticide. Reformers criticized the harshness of laws against infanticide, but they showed no mercy for "sodomites" (as male homosexuals were called), who in some places, in particular the Dutch Republic, were systematically persecuted and imprisoned or even executed. Male homosexuals attracted the attention of authorities because they had begun to develop networks and special meeting places. The stereotype of the effeminate, exclusively homosexual male seems to have appeared for the first time in the eighteenth century, perhaps as part of a growing emphasis on separate roles for men and women.

Roots of Industrialization

Although it was only starting to take hold, industrialization would eventually transform European society. The process began in England in the 1770s and 1780s and included four interlocking trends: (1) population increased dramatically, by more than 50 percent in England in the second half of the eighteenth century;

(2) manufacturers introduced steam-driven machinery to increase output; (3) they established factories to concentrate the labor of their workers; and (4) the production of cotton goods, which were lighter and more versatile than woolens, increased tenfold. Together these factors sparked the Industrial Revolution, which would change the face of Europe—indeed, of the entire world—in the nineteenth century.

Innovations in the technology of cotton production permitted manufacturers to make use of the growing supply of raw cotton shipped from the plantations of North America and the Caribbean. In 1733, the Englishman John Kay patented the flying shuttle, which weavers operated by pulling a cord that drove the shuttle to either side, enabling them to "throw" yarn across the loom rather than draw it back and forth by hand. When the flying shuttle came into widespread use in the 1760s, weavers began producing cloth more quickly than spinners could produce the thread. The shortage of spun thread propelled the invention of machines to speed the process of spinning: the spinning jenny and the water frame (a power-driven spinning machine) were introduced in the 1760s. In the following decades, water frames replaced thousands of women hand-spinning thread at home. In 1776, the Scottish engineer James Watt developed an improved steam engine, and, in the 1780s, Edmund Cartwright, an English clergyman and inventor, designed a mechanized loom, which when perfected could be run by a small boy and yield fifteen times the output of a skilled adult weaver working a handloom. By the end of the century, all the new power machinery was assembled in large factories that hired semiskilled men, women, and children to replace skilled weavers.

■ Handloom Weaving

This plate from the Encyclopedia *demonstrates handloom weaving of gold-threaded fabrics (tassels, trims, fringes, borders). Fancy threads could not be used on the early mechanical looms, which were suitable only for basic cotton thread. This kind of handloom weaving continued well into the 1800s.* (Stock Montage, Inc.)

Historians have no single explanation for why England led the Industrial Revolution. Some have emphasized England's large internal market, increasing population, supply of private investment capital from overseas trade and commercial profits, or natural resources such as coal and iron. Others have cited England's greater opportunities for social mobility, its relative political stability in the eighteenth century, or the pragmatism of the English and Scottish inventors who designed the necessary machinery. These early industrialists hardly had a monopoly on ingenuity, but they did come out of a tradition of independent capitalist enterprise. They also shared a culture of informal scientific education through learned societies and popular lectures (one of the prominent forms of the Enlightenment in Britain). For whatever reasons, the combination of improvements in agricultural production, growth in population and foreign trade, and willingness to invest in new machines and factories appeared first in this relatively small island.

Although the rest of Europe did not industrialize until the nineteenth century, textile manufacturing—long a linchpin in the European economy—expanded dramatically in the eighteenth century even without the introduction of new machines and factories. Textile production increased because of the spread of the "putting-out" or "domestic" system. Hundreds of thousands of families manufactured cloth in every country from Britain to Russia. Under the putting-out system, manufacturers supplied the families with raw materials, such as woolen or cotton fibers. Working at home in a dimly lit room, a whole family labored together. The mother and her children washed the fibers and carded and combed them. Then the mother and oldest daughters spun them into thread. The father, assisted by the children, wove the cloth. The cloth was then finished (bleached, dyed, smoothed, and so on) under the supervision of the manufacturer in a large workshop, located either in town or in the countryside. This system had existed in the textile industry for hundreds of years, but in the eighteenth century it expanded immensely, drawing in thousands of peasants in the countryside, and it included not only textiles but also the manufacture of such products as glassware, baskets, nails, and guns. The spread of the domestic system of manufacturing is sometimes called *proto-industrialization* to signify that the process helped pave the way for the full-scale Industrial Revolution.

All across Europe, thousands of people who worked in agriculture became part-time or full-time textile workers. Peasants turned to putting-out work because they did not have enough land to support their families. Men labored off-season and women often worked year-round to augment their meager incomes. At the same time, population growth and general economic improvement meant that demand for cloth increased because more people could afford it. Studies of wills left by working-class men and women in Paris at the end of the eighteenth century show that people owned more clothes of greater variety. Working-class men in Paris began to wear underclothes, something rare at the beginning of the century. Men and women now bought nightclothes; before, Europeans had slept naked except in cold weather. And white, red, blue, yellow, green, and even pastel shades of cotton now replaced the black, gray, or brown of traditional woolen dress.

State Power in an Era of Reform

All rulers recognized that manufacturing created new sources of wealth, but the start of industrialization had not yet altered the standard forms of competition between states: commerce and war. The diffusion of Enlightenment ideas of reform had a more immediate impact on the ways European monarchs exercised power than did industrialization. Historians label many of the sovereigns of this time "enlightened despots" or "enlightened absolutists," for they aimed to combine Enlightenment reforms with absolutist powers. Implementation of reforms, such as improvements in the peasantry's condition in Austria, freer markets for grain in France, extension of education in Russia, and new law codes in almost every country, were directly affected by the success or failure in the competition for trade and territory. French losses in the Seven Years' War, for example, prompted the French crown to introduce far-reaching reforms that provoked violent resistance and helped pave the way for the French Revolution of 1789. Reform proved to be a two-edged sword.

War and Diplomacy

Europeans no longer fought devastating wars over religion that killed hundreds of thousands of civilians; instead, professional armies and navies battled for control of overseas empires and for dominance on the European continent. Rulers continued to expand their armies: the Prussian army, for example, nearly tripled in size between 1740 and 1789. Widespread use of flintlock muskets required deployment in long lines, usually three men deep, with each line in turn loading and firing on command. Military strategy became cautious and calculating, but this did not prevent the outbreak of hostilities. The instability of the European balance of power resulted in two major wars, a diplomatic reversal of alliances, and the partition of Poland-Lithuania among Russia, Austria, and Prussia.

The War of the Austrian Succession (1740–1748) broke out when Holy Roman Emperor Charles VI died in 1740 without a male heir. Most European rulers recognized the emperor's chosen heiress, his daughter Maria Theresa, because Charles's Pragmatic Sanction of 1713 had given a woman the right to inherit the Habsburg crown lands. The new king of Prussia, Frederick II, who had just succeeded his father a few months earlier in 1740, saw his chance to grab territory and immediately invaded the rich Austrian province of Silesia. France joined Prussia in an attempt to further humiliate its traditional enemy Austria, and Great Britain allied with Austria to prevent the French from taking the Austrian Netherlands (Map 15.1). The war soon expanded to the overseas colonies of Great Britain and France as well. French and British colonials in North America fought each other all along their boundaries, enlisting Native American auxiliaries. Britain tried but failed to isolate the French Caribbean colonies during the war, and hostilities broke out in India, too.

■ **MAP 15.1 The War of the Austrian Succession, 1740–1748**

The accession of a twenty-three-year-old woman, Maria Theresa, to the Austrian throne gave the new king of Prussia, Frederick II, an opportunity to invade the province of Silesia. France joined on Prussia's side, Great Britain on Austria's. In 1745, the French defeated the British in the Austrian Netherlands and helped instigate a Jacobite uprising in Scotland. The rebellion failed, and British attacks on French overseas shipping forced the French to negotiate. The peace treaties guaranteed Frederick's conquest of Silesia, which soon became the wealthiest province of Prussia. France came to terms with Great Britain to protect its overseas possessions; Austria had to accept the peace settlement after a formal public protest.

www.bedfordstmartins.com/huntconcise   See the ONLINE STUDY GUIDE for more help in analyzing this map.

Maria Theresa (r. 1740–1780) survived only by conceding Silesia to Prussia in order to split the Prussians off from France. The Peace of Aix-la-Chapelle of 1748 recognized Maria Theresa as the heiress to the Austrian lands, and her husband, Francis I, became Holy Roman Emperor, thus reasserting the integrity of the Austrian Empire. The peace of 1748 failed to resolve the colonial conflicts between Britain and France, and fighting for domination continued unofficially.

In 1756, a major reversal of alliances—what historians call the "Diplomatic Revolution"—reshaped relations among the great powers. Prussia and Great Britain signed a defensive alliance, prompting Austria to overlook two centuries of hostility and ally with France. Russia and Sweden soon joined the Franco-Austrian alliance. When Frederick II invaded Saxony, an ally of Austria, with his bigger and better-disciplined army, the long-simmering hostilities between Great Britain and France over colonial boundaries flared into a general war that became known as the Seven Years' War (1756–1763).

Fighting soon raged around the world (Map 15.2). The French and British battled on land and sea in North America (where the conflict was called the French and Indian War), the West Indies, and India. The two coalitions also fought each other in central Europe. At first, in 1757, Frederick the Great surprised Europe with a spectacular victory at Rossbach in Saxony over a much larger Franco-Austrian army. But in time, Russian and Austrian armies encircled his troops. Frederick despaired: "I believe all is lost. I will not survive the ruin of my country." A fluke of history saved him. Empress Elizabeth of Russia (r. 1741–1762) died and was succeeded by the mentally unstable Peter III, a fanatical admirer of Frederick and things Prussian. Peter withdrew Russia from the war. (This was practically his only accomplishment as tsar. He was soon mysteriously murdered, probably at the instigation of his wife, Catherine the Great.) In a separate peace treaty, Frederick kept all his territory, including Silesia.

The Anglo-French overseas conflicts ended more decisively than the continental land wars. British naval superiority, fully achieved only in the 1750s, enabled Great Britain to rout the French in North America, India, and the West Indies. In the Treaty of Paris of 1763, France ceded Canada to Great Britain and agreed to remove its armies from India, in exchange for keeping its rich West Indian islands. Eagerness to avenge this defeat would motivate France to support the British North American colonists in their War of Independence just fifteen years later.

Although Prussia suffered great losses in the Seven Years' War—some 160,000 Prussian soldiers died either in action or of disease—the army helped vault Prussia to the rank of leading powers. In 1733, Frederick II's father, Frederick William I, had instituted the "canton system," which enrolled peasant youths in each canton (or district) in the army, gave them two or three months of training annually, and allowed them to return to their family farms the rest of the year. They remained "cantonists" (reservists) as long as they were able-bodied. In this fashion, the Prussian military steadily grew in size; by 1740, Prussia had the third or fourth largest army in Europe even though it was tenth in population and thirteenth in land area. Under Frederick II, Prussia's military expenditures rose to two-thirds of the state's revenue. Almost every nobleman served in the army, paying for his own support as an officer and buying a position as company commander. Once retired, the officers returned to their estates, coordinated the canton system, and served as

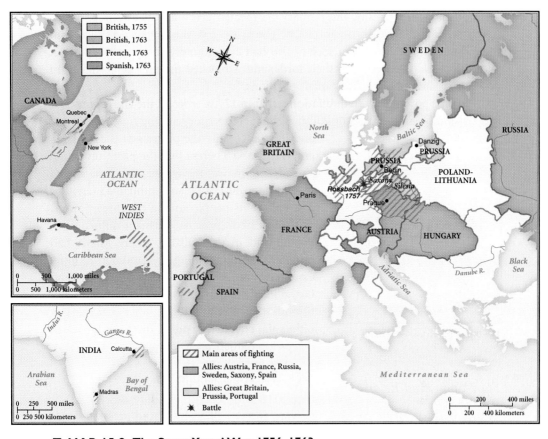

■ MAP 15.2 The Seven Years' War, 1756–1763

In what might justly be called the first worldwide war, the French and British fought each other on the European continent, in the West Indies, and in India. Their international struggle coincided with a realignment of forces within Europe caused by the desire of Austria, France, and Russia to check Prussian growth. Fearing, with reason, a joint Austrian-Russian attack, Frederick II of Prussia invaded Saxony in August 1756. Despite overwhelming odds, Frederick managed time and again to emerge victorious, until the Russians withdrew and the coalition against Prussia fell apart. The treaty between Austria and Prussia simply restored the status quo. The changes overseas were much more dramatic. Britain gained control over Canada and India but gave back to France the West Indian islands of Guadeloupe and Martinique. Britain was now the dominant power on the seas.

www.bedfordstmartins.com/huntconcise See the ONLINE STUDY GUIDE for more help in analyzing this map.

local officials. In this way, the military permeated every aspect of rural society, fusing army and agrarian organization. The army gave the state great power, but the militarization of Prussian society also had a profoundly conservative effect: it kept the peasants enserfed to their lords, and it blocked the middle classes from access to estates or high government positions.◆

Prussia's power grew so dramatically that in 1772 Frederick the Great proposed the division of large chunks of Polish-Lithuanian territory among Austria, Prussia, and Russia. Despite the protests of the Austrian empress Maria Theresa that the partition would spread "a stain over my whole reign," she agreed to split one-third of Poland-Lithuania's territory and half of its people among the three powers. Austria feared growing Russian influence in Poland and in the Balkans, where Russia had been successfully battling the Ottoman Empire. Conflicts between Catholics, Protestants, and Orthodox Christians in Poland were used to justify this cynical move. Russia took over most of Lithuania, effectively ending the large but weak Polish-Lithuanian commonwealth.

The First Partition of Poland, 1772

State-Sponsored Reform

In the aftermath of the Seven Years' War, all the belligerents faced pressing needs for more money to fund their growing armies, to organize navies to wage overseas conflicts, and to counter the impact of inflation. To make tax increases more palatable to public opinion, rulers appointed reform-minded ministers and gave them a mandate to modernize government. As one adviser to Joseph II put it, "A properly constituted state must be exactly analogous to a machine . . . and the ruler must be the foreman, the mainspring . . . which sets everything else in motion." Such reforms always threatened the interests of traditional groups, however, and the spread of Enlightenment ideas aroused sometimes unpredictable desires for more change.

Legal reform, both of the judicial system and of the often disorganized and irregular law codes, was central to the work of many reform-minded monarchs. Although Frederick II favored all things French in culture—he insisted on speaking French in his court and prided himself on his personal friendship with Voltaire—he made Prussian justice the envy of Europe. His institution of a uniform civil justice system created the most consistently administered laws and efficient

◆ For a primary source that outlines Frederick's political philosophy, see Document 49, Frederick II, "Political Testament."

■ Dividing Poland, 1772

In this contemporary depiction, Catherine the Great, Joseph II, and Frederick II point on the map to the portion of Poland-Lithuania each plans to take. The artist makes it clear that Poland's fate rested in the hands of neighboring rulers, not its own people. (Mansell/Time, Inc.)

judiciary of the time. Joseph II of Austria (r. 1780–1790) also ordered the compilation of a unified law code, a project that required many years for completion. Catherine II of Russia began such an undertaking even more ambitiously. In 1767, she called together a legislative commission of 564 deputies and asked them to consider a long document called the *Instruction*, which represented her hopes for legal reform based on the ideas of Montesquieu and the Italian writer Cesare Beccaria. Montesquieu had insisted that punishment should fit the crime; he criticized the use of torture and brutal corporal punishment. In his influential book *On Crimes and Punishments* (1764), Beccaria argued that laws should be printed for everyone to read and administered in rational procedures, that torture should be abolished as inhumane, and that the accused should be presumed innocent until proven guilty. Despite much discussion and hundreds of petitions and documents about local problems, little came of Catherine's commission because the monarch herself— despite her regard for Voltaire and his fellow philosophes—proved ultimately unwilling to see through far-reaching legal reform.

Rulers everywhere wanted more control over church affairs, and they used Enlightenment criticisms of the organized churches to get their way. In Catholic countries, many government officials resented the influence of the Jesuits, the major Catholic teaching order. The Jesuits trained the Catholic intellectual elite, ran a worldwide missionary network, enjoyed close ties to the papacy, and amassed great wealth. Critics mounted campaigns against the Jesuits in many countries, and by the early 1770s the Society of Jesus had been dissolved in Portugal, France, and Spain. In 1773, Pope Clement XIV (r. 1769–1774) agreed under pressure to disband the order, an edict that held until a reinvigorated papacy restored the society in 1814. Joseph II of Austria not only applauded the suppression of the Jesuits but also required Austrian bishops to swear fidelity and submission to him. Under Joseph, the Austrian state supervised seminaries, reorganized diocesan boundaries, abolished contemplative monastic orders, and confiscated their property to pay for education and poor relief.

Enlightened absolutists also tried to gain greater state authority over education, even while extending education to the lower classes. Joseph II launched the most ambitious educational reforms of the period. In 1774, once the Jesuits had been disbanded, a General School Ordinance in Austria ordered state subsidies for local schools, which the state would regulate. By 1789, one-quarter of the school-age children attended school. In Prussia, the school code of 1763 required all children between the ages of five and thirteen to attend school. Although not enforced uniformly, the Prussian law demonstrated Frederick II's belief that modernization depended on education. Catherine II of Russia also tried to expand elementary education—and the education of women in particular—and founded engineering schools.

No ruler pushed the principle of religious toleration as far as Joseph II of Austria, who became Holy Roman Emperor and co-regent with his mother, Maria Theresa, in 1765 and then ruled alone after 1780. In 1781, he granted freedom of religious worship to Protestants, Orthodox Christians, and Jews. For the first time these groups were allowed to own property, build schools, enter the professions, and hold political and military offices. The efforts of other rulers to extend religious toleration proved more limited. Louis XVI signed an edict in 1787 restoring French Protestants' civil rights—but still they could not hold political office. Great Britain continued to deny Catholics freedom of open worship and the right to sit in Parliament. Most European states limited the rights and opportunities available to Jews. In Russia, only wealthy Jews could hold municipal office, and in the Papal States, the pope encouraged forced baptism. The leading philosophes opposed persecution of the Jews in theory but often treated them with undisguised contempt. Diderot's comment was all too typical: the Jews, he said, bore "all the defects peculiar to an ignorant and superstitious nation."

Limits of Reform

When enlightened absolutist leaders introduced reforms, they often faced resistance from groups threatened by the proposed changes. The most contentious area of reform was agricultural policy. Whereas Frederick II and Catherine II reinforced the authority of nobles over their serfs, Joseph II tried to remove the burdens of serfdom in the Habsburg lands. In 1781, he abolished the personal aspects of serfdom: serfs could now move freely, enter trades, or marry without their lords' permission. Joseph abolished the tithe to the church, shifted more of the tax burden to the nobility, and converted peasants' labor services into cash payments.

The Austrian nobility furiously resisted these far-reaching reforms. When Joseph died in 1790, his brother Leopold II had to revoke most reforms to appease the nobles. On his deathbed, Joseph recognized the futility of many of his efforts; as his epitaph he suggested, "Here lies Joseph II, who was unfortunate in all his enterprises." Prussia's Frederick II, like Joseph, encouraged such agricultural innovations as planting potatoes and turnips (new crops that could help feed a growing population), experimenting with cattle breeding, draining swamplands, and clearing forests. But Prussia's noble landlords, the Junkers, continued to expand their estates at the expense of poorer peasants, and Frederick did nothing to ameliorate serfdom except on his own domains.

Reforming ministers also tried to stimulate agricultural improvement in France. Unlike most other western European countries, France still had about 100,000 serfs; though their burdens weighed less heavily than those in eastern Europe, serfdom did not entirely disappear until 1789. A group of economists called the *physiocrats* urged the French government to deregulate the grain trade and make the tax system more equitable to encourage agricultural productivity. In the interest of establishing a free market, they also insisted that urban guilds be abolished because they prevented free entry into the trades. Their proposed reforms applied the Enlightenment emphasis on individual liberties to the economy; Adam Smith took up many of the physiocrats' ideas in his writing in favor of free markets. The French government heeded some of this advice and gave up its system of price controls on grain in 1763, but it had to reverse this decision in 1770 when grain shortages caused a famine.

French reform efforts did not end there. To break the power of the parlements (the thirteen high courts of law that had led the way in opposing royal efforts to increase and equalize taxation), Louis XV appointed a reform-minded chancellor who in 1770 replaced the parlements with courts in which the judges no longer owned their offices and thus could not sell them or pass them on as an inheritance. Justice would then be more impartial. Nevertheless, the judges of the displaced parlements aroused widespread opposition to what they portrayed as tyrannical royal policy. The furor calmed down only when Louis XV died in 1774 and his successor, Louis XVI (r. 1774–1792), yielded to aristocratic demands and restored the old parlements. Louis XV died one of the most despised kings in French history, resented both for his high-handed reforms and for his private vices. Underground pamphlets lampooned him, describing his final mistress, Madame Du Barry, as a prostitute who pandered to the elderly king's well-known taste for young girls. This often pornographic literature linked despotism to the supposedly excessive influence of women at court.

Louis XVI tried to carry out part of the program suggested by the physiocrats, and he chose one of their disciples, Jacques Turgot (1727–1781), as his chief minister. Turgot pushed through several edicts that again freed the grain trade, suppressed many guilds, converted the peasants' forced labor on roads into a money tax payable by all landowners, and reduced court expenses. He also began making plans to introduce a system of elected local assemblies, which would have made government much more representative. Faced with broad-based resistance led by the parlements and his own courtiers, as well as with riots against rising grain prices, Louis XVI dismissed Turgot, and one of the last possibilities to overhaul France's monarchy collapsed.

The failure of reform in France paradoxically reflected the power of Enlightenment ideas; everyone now endorsed Enlightenment ideals but used them for different ends. The nobles in the parlements blocked the French monarchy's reform efforts using the very same Enlightenment language spoken by the crown's ministers. But unlike Austria, the other great power that faced persistent aristocratic resistance to reform, France had a large middle-class public that was increasingly frustrated by the failure to institute social change, a failure that ultimately helped undermine the monarchy itself. Where Frederick II, Catherine II, and even Joseph II used reform to bolster the efficiency of absolutist government, attempts at change in France backfired. French kings found that their ambitious programs for reform succeeded only in arousing unrealistic hopes.

Rebellions against State Power

Although traditional forms of popular discontent had not disappeared, Enlightenment ideals and reforms changed the rules of the game in politics. Governments had become accountable for their actions to a much wider range of people than ever before. In Britain and France, ordinary people rioted when they perceived government as failing to protect them against food shortages. The growth of informed public opinion had its most dramatic consequences in the North American colonies, where a struggle over the British Parliament's right to tax turned into a full-scale war for independence. The American War of Independence showed that once put into practice, Enlightenment ideals could have revolutionary implications.

Food Riots and Peasant Uprisings

Population growth, inflation, and the extension of the market system put added pressure on the already beleaguered poorest classes of people. Seventeenth-century peasants and townspeople had rioted to protest new taxes. In the last half of the eighteenth century, the food supply became the focus of political and social conflict. Poor people living in the villages and the towns believed it was the government's responsibility to ensure that they had enough food, and many governments did stockpile grain to make up for the occasional bad harvest. At the same time, in keeping with Adam Smith's and the French physiocrats' free market proposals, governments wanted to allow grain prices to rise with market demand, because higher profits would motivate producers to increase the supply of food.

Free trade in grain meant selling to the highest bidder even if that bidder was a foreign merchant. In the short run, in times of scarcity, big landowners and farmers could make huge profits by selling grain outside their hometowns or villages. This practice enraged poor farmers, agricultural workers, and city wage workers, who could not afford the higher prices. Lacking the political means to affect policy, they could enforce their desire for old-fashioned price regulation only by rioting. Most did not pillage or steal grain but rather forced the sale of grain or flour at a "just" price and blocked the shipment of grain out of their villages to other markets. Women often led these "popular price fixings," as they were called in France, in desperate attempts to protect the food supply for their children.

Such food riots occurred regularly in Britain and France in the last half of the eighteenth century. One of the most turbulent was the so-called Flour War in France in 1775. Turgot's deregulation of the grain trade in 1774 caused prices to rise in several provincial cities. Rioting spread from there to the Paris region, where villagers attacked grain convoys heading to the capital city. Local officials often ordered merchants and bakers to sell at the price the rioters demanded, only to find themselves arrested by the central government for overriding free trade. The government brought in troops to restore order and introduced the death penalty for rioting.

Frustrations with serfdom and hopes for a miraculous transformation provoked the Pugachev rebellion in Russia beginning in 1773. An army deserter from the southeast frontier region, Emelian Pugachev (1742–1775) claimed to be Tsar Peter III, the dead husband of Catherine II. Pugachev's appearance seemed to confirm peasant hopes for a "redeemer tsar" who would save the people from oppression. He rallied around him Cossacks like himself who resented the loss of their old tribal independence. Now increasingly enserfed or forced to pay taxes and endure army service, these nomadic bands joined with other serfs, rebellious mineworkers, and Muslim minorities. Catherine dispatched a large army to squelch the uprising, but Pugachev eluded them and the fighting spread. Nearly three million people eventually participated, making this the largest single rebellion in the history of tsarist Russia. When

The Pugachev Rebellion, 1773

■ Russian Peasants

This engraving from the 1700s shows Russian peasants in their one-room hut. Two or more married brothers, their wives, children, and parents would share the space with poultry and livestock. Cooking took place in one corner, which was always diagonally across from the icon corner (left), where socializing took place. The fathers and younger men slept on benches, the rest of the family in the loft (right). In the winter, everyone slept near the oven. (Fotomas Index, UK.)

Pugachev urged the peasants to attack the nobility and seize their estates, hundreds of noble families perished. Foreign newspapers called it "the revolution in southern Russia" and offered fantastic stories about Pugachev's life history. Finally, the army captured the rebel leader and brought him in an iron cage to Moscow, where he was tortured and executed. In the aftermath, Catherine tightened the nobles' control over their serfs and harshly punished those who dared to criticize serfdom.

Public Opinion and Political Opposition

Peasant uprisings might briefly shake even a powerful monarchy, but the rise of public opinion as a force independent of court society caused more enduring changes in European politics. Across much of Europe and in the North American colonies, demands for broader political participation reflected Enlightenment notions about individual rights. Aristocratic bodies such as the French parlements, which had no legislative role like that of the British Parliament, insisted that the monarch consult them on the nation's affairs, and the new educated elite wanted more influence, too. Newspapers began to cover daily political affairs, and the public learned the basics of political life, despite the strict limits on political participation in most countries.

Monarchs turned to public opinion to seek support against aristocratic groups that opposed reform. Gustavus III of Sweden (r. 1771–1792) called himself "the first citizen of a free people" and promised to deliver the country from "insufferable aristocratic despotism." Shortly after coming to the throne, Gustavus proclaimed a new constitution that divided power between the king and the legislature, abolished the use of torture in the judicial process, and assured some freedom of the press.

In France, both the parlements and the monarch appealed to the public through the printed word. The crown hired writers to make its case; the magistrates of the parlements wrote their own rejoinders. French-language newspapers published in the Dutch Republic provided many people in France with detailed accounts of political news and also gave voice to pro-parlement positions. One of the new French-language newspapers printed inside France, *Le Journal des Dames* ("The Ladies' Journal"), was published by women and mixed short stories and reviews of books and plays with demands for more women's rights.

The Wilkes affair in Great Britain showed that public opinion could be mobilized to challenge a government. In 1763, during the reign of George III (r. 1760–1820), John Wilkes, a member of Parliament, attacked the government in his newspaper, *North Briton*, and sued the crown when he was arrested. He won his release as well as damages. When he was reelected, Parliament denied him his seat, not once but three times.

The Wilkes episode soon escalated into a major campaign against the corruption and social exclusiveness of Parliament, complaints the Levellers had first raised during the English Revolution of the late 1640s. Newspapers, magazines, pamphlets, handbills, and cheap editions of Wilkes's collected works all helped promote his cause. Those who could not vote demonstrated for Wilkes. In one incident, eleven people died when soldiers broke up a huge gathering of his supporters. The slogan "Wilkes and Liberty" appeared on walls all over London. Middle-class voters formed a Society of Supporters of the Bill of Rights, which circulated petitions for Wilkes; they gained the support of about one-fourth of all the voters. The more determined Wilkesites proposed sweeping reforms of Parliament, including more frequent elections, more representation for the counties, elimination of "rotten boroughs" (election districts so small that they could be controlled by one big patron), and restrictions of pensions used by the crown to gain support. These demands would be at the heart of agitation for parliamentary reform in Britain for decades to come.

Popular demonstrations did not always support reforms. In 1780, the Gordon riots devastated London. They were named after the fanatical anti-Catholic crusader Lord George Gordon, who helped organize huge marches and petition campaigns against a bill the House of Commons passed to grant limited toleration to Catholics. The demonstrations culminated in a seven-day riot that left fifty buildings destroyed and three hundred people dead. Despite the continuing limitation on voting rights in Great Britain, British politicians were learning that they could ignore public opinion only at their peril.

Political opposition also took artistic forms, particularly in countries where governments restricted organized political activity. A striking example of a play with a political message was *The Marriage of Figaro* (1784) by Pierre-Augustin Caron de Beaumarchais (1732–1799), a watchmaker, a judge, a gunrunner in the American War of Independence, and a French spy in Britain. *The Marriage of Figaro* was first a hit at court, when Queen Marie-Antoinette had it read for her friends. But when her husband, Louis XVI, read it, he forbade its production on the grounds that "this man mocks at everything that should be respected in government." When finally performed publicly, the play caused a sensation. The chief character, Figaro, is a clever servant who gets the better of his noble employer. When speaking of the count, he cries, "What have you done to deserve so many rewards? You went to the trouble of being born, and nothing more." Two years later, Mozart based an equally famous but somewhat tamer opera on Beaumarchais's story.

Revolution in North America

Oppositional forms of public opinion came to a head in Great Britain's North American colonies, where the result was American independence and the establishment of a republican constitution that stood in stark contrast to most European regimes. The successful revolution was the only blow to Britain's increasing dominance in world affairs in the eighteenth century, and as such it was another aspect of the power rivalries existing at that time. Yet many Europeans saw the American War of Independence, or the American Revolution (1775–1783), as a triumph for Enlightenment ideas. As one German writer exclaimed in 1777, American victory would give "greater scope to the Enlightenment, new keenness to the thinking of peoples and new life to the spirit of liberty."

The American revolutionary leaders had been influenced by a common Atlantic civilization; they participated in the Enlightenment and shared political ideas with the opposition Whigs in Britain. Supporters demonstrated for Wilkes in South Carolina and Boston, and the South Carolina legislature donated a substantial sum to the Society of Supporters of the Bill of Rights. In the 1760s and 1770s, both British and American opposition leaders became convinced that the British government was growing increasingly corrupt and despotic. British radicals wanted to reform Parliament so the voices of a broader, more representative segment of the population would be heard. The colonies had no representatives in Parliament, and colonists claimed that "no taxation without representation" should be allowed. Indeed, they denied that Parliament had any jurisdiction over the colonies, insisting that the king govern them through colonial legislatures and recognize their traditional British liberties. The failure of the "Wilkes and Liberty" campaign to produce concrete results convinced many Americans that Parliament was hopelessly tainted and that they would have to stand up for their rights as British subjects.

The British colonies remained loyal to the crown until Parliament's encroachment on their autonomy and the elimination of the French threat at the end of the Seven Years' War transformed colonial attitudes. Unconsciously, perhaps, the colonies had begun to form a separate nation; their economies generally flourished in the eighteenth century, and between 1750 and 1776 their population almost doubled. With the British clamoring for lower taxes and the colonists paying only a fraction of the tax rate levied on the Britons at home, Parliament passed new taxes, including the Stamp Act in 1765, which required a special tax stamp on all legal

■ **Overthrowing British Authority**
The uncompromising attitude of the British government went a long way toward dissolving long-standing loyalties to the home country. During the American War of Independence, residents of New York City pulled down the statue of the hated George III. (Lafayette College Art Collection, Easton, PA.)

IMPORTANT DATES			
1740–1748	War of the Austrian Succession: France, Spain, and Prussia versus Austria and Great Britain	1776	American Declaration of Independence from Great Britain; James Watt improves the steam engine, making it suitable for new industrial projects; Adam Smith's The Wealth of Nations
1751–1772	Encyclopedia published in France		
1756–1763	Seven Years' War fought in Europe, India, and the American colonies	1781	Joseph II of Austria undertakes wide-reaching reform; Immanuel Kant's The Critique of Pure Reason
1762	Jean-Jacques Rousseau's The Social Contract and Émile		
1764	Voltaire's Philosophical Dictionary	1785	Catherine the Great's Charter of the Nobility grants nobles exclusive control over their serfs in exchange for subservience to the state
1770	Louis XV of France fails to break the power of the French law courts		
1772	First partition of Poland	1787	Delegates from the states draft a new United States Constitution
1773	Pugachev rebellion of Russian peasants		

documents and publications. After violent rioting in the colonies, the tax was repealed, but in 1773 a new Tea Act revived colonial resistance, which culminated in the so-called Boston Tea Party of 1773. Colonists dressed as Indians boarded British ships and dumped the imported tea (by this time an enormously popular beverage) into Boston's harbor. The British government tried to clamp down on the unrest, but British troops in the colonies soon found themselves fighting locally organized militias.

Political opposition in the American colonies turned belligerent when Britain threatened to use force to maintain control. In 1774, the First Continental Congress convened, composed of delegates from all the colonies, and unsuccessfully petitioned the crown for redress. The next year the Second Continental Congress organized an army with George Washington in command. After actual fighting had begun, in 1776, the congress proclaimed the Declaration of Independence. An eloquent statement of the American cause written by Thomas Jefferson, a delegate from Virginia, the Declaration of Independence was couched in the language of universal human rights, which enlightened Europeans could be expected to understand. George III denounced the American "traitors and rebels." But European newspapers enthusiastically reported on every American response to "the cruel acts of oppression they have been made to suffer." Two years after the Declaration was issued, France boosted the American cause by entering on the colonists' side in 1778. Spain, too, saw an opportunity to check the growing power of Britain, though without actually endorsing American independence out of fear of the response of its Latin American colonies. Spain declared war on Britain in 1779; in 1780, Great Britain declared war on the Dutch Republic in retaliation for Dutch support of the rebels. The worldwide conflict that resulted was more than Britain could handle. The American colonies achieved their independence in the peace treaty of 1783.

The newly independent states still faced the challenge of republican self-government. The Articles of Confederation, drawn up in 1777 as a provisional con-stitution, proved weak because they gave the central government few powers. In 1787, a constitutional convention met in Philadelphia to draft a new constitution. It established a two-house legislature, an indirectly elected president, and an in-dependent judiciary. The Constitution's preamble insisted explicitly, for the first time in history, that government derived its power solely from the people and did not depend on divine right or on the tradition of royalty or aristocracy. The new educated elite of the eighteenth century had now created government based on a "social contract" among male, property-owning, white citizens. It was by no means a complete democracy, and women and slaves were excluded from political par-ticipation. But the new government represented a radical departure from Euro-pean models. In 1791, a Bill of Rights was appended to the Constitution outlin-ing the essential rights (such as freedom of speech) that the government could never overturn. Although slavery continued in the American republic, the new em-phasis on rights helped fuel a movement for its abolition in both Britain and the United States.

Interest in the new republic was greatest in France. The United States Consti-tution and various state constitutions were published in French with commentary by leading thinkers. Even more important in the long run were the effects of the American war. Dutch losses to Great Britain aroused a widespread movement for political reform in the Dutch Republic, and debts incurred by France in support-ing the American colonies would soon force the French monarchy to the edge of bankruptcy and then to revolution. Ultimately, the entire European system of royal rule would be challenged.

Conclusion

The American Revolution was the most profound practical result of the general European movement known as the Enlightenment. When Thomas Jefferson looked back many years later on the Declaration of Independence, he said he hoped it would be "the signal of arousing men to burst the chains under which monkish ignorance and superstition had persuaded them to bind themselves." What began

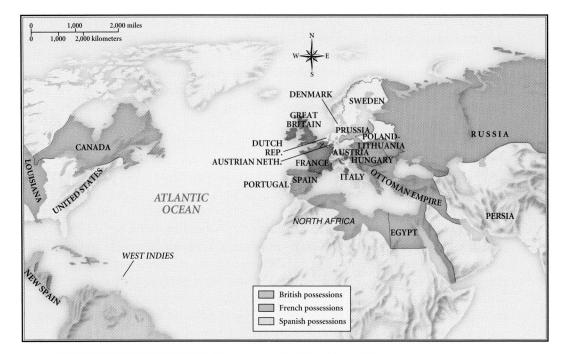

■ MAPPING THE WEST Europe and the World, c. 1780

Although Great Britain lost control over the British North American colonies, which became the new United States, European influence on the rest of the world grew dramatically in the eighteenth century. The slave trade linked European ports to African slave-trading outposts and to plantations in the Caribbean, South America, and North America. The European countries on the Atlantic Ocean benefited most from this trade. Yet almost all of Africa, China, Japan, and large parts of India still resisted European incursion, and the Ottoman Empire, with its massive territories, still towered over most European countries.

as a cosmopolitan movement of a few intellectuals in the first half of the eighteenth century reached a relatively wide audience among the educated elite of men and women. The spirit of reform swept from the salons and coffeehouses into the halls of government. Reasoned, scientific inquiry into the causes of social misery and laws defending individual rights and freedoms gained adherents everywhere.

For most Europeans, however, Enlightenment remained a promise rather than a reality. Rulers such as Catherine the Great had every intention of retaining their full, often unchecked, powers, even as they corresponded with leading philosophes, announced support for their causes, and entertained them at their courts. Moreover, would-be reformers often found themselves thwarted by the resistance of nobles, by the priorities rulers gave to waging wars, or by popular resistance to deregulation of trade that stripped away protection against the uncertainties of the market. Yet even the failure of reform contributed to the ferment in Europe after 1770. Peasant rebellions in eastern Europe, the "Wilkes and Liberty" campaign in Great Britain, the struggle over reform in France, and the revolution in America all occurred at about the same time, and their conjunction convinced many Europeans that the world was in fact changing. Just how much it had changed, and whether the change was for better or for worse, would become more evident in the next decades.

Suggested References for further reading and online research appear on page SR-23 at the back of the book.

www.bedfordstmartins.com/huntconcise   See the ONLINE STUDY GUIDE to assess your mastery of the material covered in this chapter.

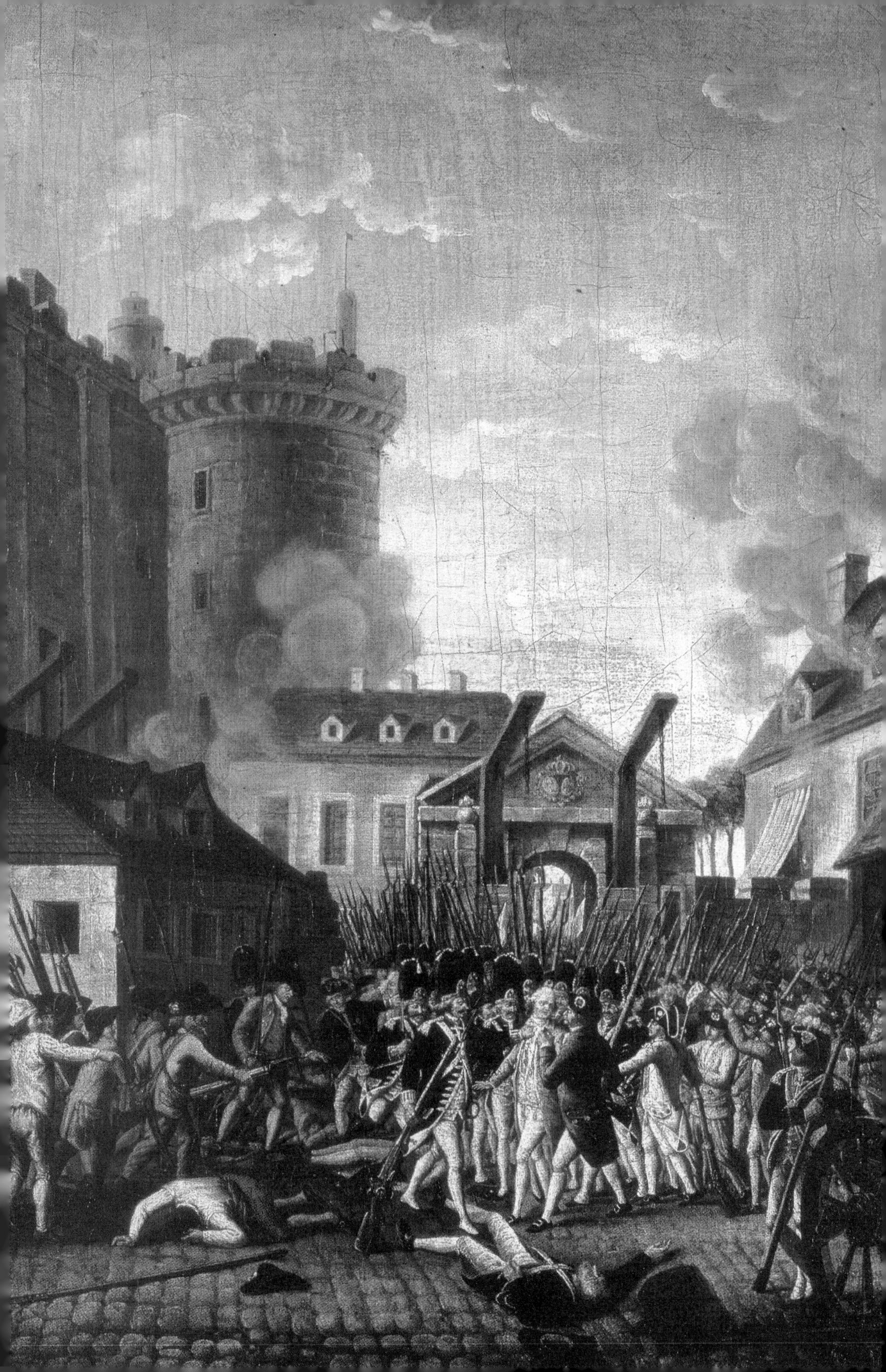

16

The French Revolution and Napoleon

1789–1815

O N OCTOBER 5, 1789, A CROWD OF SEVERAL THOUSAND WOMEN marched in a
drenching rain twelve miles from the center of Paris to Versailles. They demanded the king's help in securing more grain for the hungry and his reassurance
that he did not intend to resist the emerging revolutionary movement. Joined by
thousands of men who came from Paris to reinforce them, the next morning they
broke into the royal family's private apartments. To prevent further bloodshed—
two of the royal bodyguards had already been killed and their heads paraded on
pikes—the king agreed to move his family and his government back to Paris. A dramatic procession guarded by thousands of ordinary men and women made its slow
way back to Paris. The people's proud display of cannons and pikes underlined the
fundamental transformation that was occurring. Ordinary people had forced the
king of France to respond to their grievances. The French monarchy was in danger, and if such a powerful and long-lasting institution could come under fire, then
could any monarch of Europe rest easy?

Although even the keenest political observer did not predict its eruption in
1789, the French Revolution had its immediate origins in a constitutional crisis provoked by a growing government deficit, traceable to French involvement in the
American War of Independence. The constitutional crisis came to a head on July
14, 1789, when armed Parisians captured the Bastille, a royal fortress and symbol

■ **Fall of the Bastille**
*The Bastille appears in all its imposing grandeur. The event depicted here is the surrender of the
prison's governor, Bernard René de Launay. Because so many of the besieging citizens were killed
(only one defender died), popular anger ran high, and de Launay became a sacrificial victim. As a
hastily formed citizens' guard marched him off to city hall, crowds taunted and spat at him. When
he lashed out at one of the men nearest him, he was immediately stabbed and shot. A pastry cook
cut off the governor's head, which was promptly displayed as a trophy on a pike held high above
the crowd. Royal authority had been successfully challenged and even humiliated.*
(Château de Versailles, France/Bridgeman Art Library, NY.)

■ **Women's March to Versailles, October 5, 1789**
This anonymous engraving shows a crowd of armed women marching to Versailles to confront the king. The sight of armed women frightened many observers and demonstrated that the Revolution was not only men's affair. Notice the middle-class woman in a hat at the far left. She is obviously reluctant to join in but is being pulled along by the market women in their simple caps.
(Musée de la Ville de Paris/Musée Carnavalet, Paris/Giraudon/Art Resource, NY.)

of monarchical authority in the center of the capital. The fall of the Bastille, like the women's march to Versailles three months later, showed the determination of the common people to put their mark on events.

The French Revolution first grabbed the attention of the entire world because it seemed to promise universal human rights, constitutional government, and broad-based political participation. In the words of its most famous slogan, it pledged "Liberty, Equality, and Fraternity" for all. The revolutionaries used a blueprint based on the Enlightenment idea of reason to remake all of society and politics: they executed the king and queen, established a republic for the first time in French history, abolished nobility, and gave the vote to all adult men. Even as the Revolution promised democracy, however, it also inaugurated a cycle of violence and intimidation. When the revolutionaries encountered resistance to their programs, they set up a government of terror to compel obedience. Some historians therefore see in the French Revolution the origins of modern *totalitarianism*—that is, governments that try to control every aspect of life, including daily activities, while limiting all forms of political dissent.

The Revolution might have remained a strictly French affair if war had not involved the rest of Europe. After 1792, huge French republican armies, fueled by patriotic nationalism, marched across Europe, promising liberation from traditional monarchies but often delivering old-fashioned conquest and annexation. French victories spread revolutionary ideas far and wide, from the colonies in the Caribbean, where the first successful slave revolt established the republic of Haiti, to Poland and Egypt. The army's success ultimately undermined the republic and made possible the rise of Napoleon Bonaparte, a remarkable young general from Corsica, an island off Italy, who brought France more wars, more conquests, and a form of military dictatorship.

Bonaparte ended the French Revolution even while maintaining some of its most important innovations. He transformed France from a democratically elected republic to an empire with a new aristocracy based on military service. Although he tolerated no opposition at home, he prided himself on bringing French-style liberation to peoples elsewhere. Yet he also continued the revolutionary policy of conquest and annexation; by 1812, he ruled over an empire bigger than any Europe had seen since Roman times. Eventually, resistance to the French armies and the ever-mounting costs of military glory toppled Napoleon I, but not before he had established himself as an almost mythic figure. Reformer, revolutionary, dictator, and empire-builder: Napoleon played all the roles and has remained a figure of controversy right down to the present. The French Revolution produced many surprises; Napoleon Bonaparte was the most astonishing of them.

The Revolution of Rights and Reason

Between 1787 and 1789, revolts in the name of liberty broke out in the Dutch Republic, the Austrian Netherlands (present-day Belgium and Luxembourg), and Poland as well as in France. At the same time, the newly independent United States of America prepared a new federal constitution. Historians have sometimes referred to these revolts as the *Atlantic revolutions* because so many protest movements arose in countries on both shores of the North Atlantic in the late 1700s. These revolutions were the product of long-term prosperity and high expectations: Europeans in general were wealthier, healthier, more numerous, and better educated than they had ever been before; and the Dutch, Belgian, and French societies were among the wealthiest and best educated within Europe. Most scholars agree, however, that the French Revolution differed greatly from the others. Not only was France the richest, most powerful, and most populous state in western Europe, but its revolution was also more violent, longer lasting, and ultimately more influential.

Protesters in the Low Countries and Poland

Political protests in the Dutch Republic attracted European attention because Dutch banks still controlled a hefty portion of the world's capital at the end of the eighteenth century, even though the Dutch Republic's role in international politics had diminished. Government-sponsored Dutch banks owned 40 percent of the British national debt, and by 1796, they held the entire foreign debt of the United States. Relations with the British deteriorated during the American War of Independence, however, and by the middle of the 1780s, agitation in favor of the Americans had boiled over into an attack on the stadholder, the prince of Orange, who favored close ties with Great Britain and had kinglike powers.

Building on support among middle-class bankers, merchants, and writers who favored the American cause, the Dutch Patriots, as the protesters called themselves, soon gained a more popular audience by demanding political reforms and organizing armed citizen militias of men, called Free Corps. Parading under banners that read "Liberty or Death," they forced local officials to set up new elections to replace councils that had been packed with Orangist supporters through patronage or family connections. The future American president John Adams happened to be visiting Utrecht when such a revolt occurred. He wrote admiringly to Thomas Jefferson that "in no instance, of ancient or modern History, have the People ever asserted more unequivocally their own inherent and unalienable Sovereignty." In 1787, the Free Corps took on the troops of the prince of Orange and got the upper hand. In response, Frederick William II of Prussia, whose sister had married the stadholder, intervened with tacit British support. Thousands of Prussian troops soon occupied Utrecht and Amsterdam, and the House of Orange regained its former position.

Internal social divisions paved the way for successful outside intervention. Many of the Patriots from the richest merchant families feared the growing power of the Free Corps. The Free Corps wanted a more democratic form of government and encouraged the publication of pamphlets and cartoons attacking the prince and his wife, the rapid spread of clubs and societies made up of common people, and crowd-pleasing public ceremonies, such as parades and bonfires, which sometimes turned into riots. In the aftermath of the Prussian invasion in September 1787, the Orangists got their revenge: lower-class mobs pillaged the houses of prosperous Patriot leaders, forcing many to flee to the United States, France, or the Austrian Netherlands. Those Patriots who remained nursed their grievances until the French republican armies invaded in 1795.

The Austrian Netherlands experienced unrest, too. The Belgians of the ten provinces there might have remained tranquil if Austrian emperor Joseph II had not tried to introduce Enlightenment-inspired reforms. Joseph abolished torture, decreed toleration for Jews and Protestants (in this resolutely Catholic area), and suppressed monasteries. His reorganization of the administrative and judicial systems eliminated many offices that belonged to nobles and lawyers, sparking resistance among the upper classes in 1788. They claimed that they wanted only to defend historic local liberties against an overbearing government. Their resistance galvanized democrats, who wanted a more representative government and organized clubs to give voice to their demands. By late 1789, each province had separately declared its independence, and the Austrian administration had collapsed. Delegates from the various provinces declared themselves the United States of Belgium, a clear reference to the American precedent.

Once again, however, internal squabbling doomed the rebels. In the face of increasing democratic ferment, aristocratic leaders drew to their side the Catholic clergy and peasants, who had little sympathy for the democrats of the cities. Every Sunday in May and June 1790, thousands of peasant men and women, led by their priests, streamed into Brussels carrying crucifixes, nooses, and pitchforks to intimidate the democrats and defend the church. Faced with the choice between the Austrian emperor and "our current tyrants," the democrats chose to support the return of the Austrians under Emperor Leopold II (r. 1790–1792), who had succeeded his brother.

A reform party calling itself the Patriots also emerged in Poland, which had been shocked by the loss of a third of its territory in the First Partition of 1772. The Patriots sought to overhaul the weak commonwealth along modern western European lines and looked to King Stanislaw August Poniatowski (r. 1764–1795) to lead them. A nobleman who owed his crown to the dubious honor of being Catherine the Great's discarded lover but who was also a favorite correspondent of the Parisian salon hostess Madame Geoffrin, Poniatowski saw in moderate reform the only chance for his country to escape the consequences of a century's misgovernment and cultural decline. Ranged against the Patriots stood most of the aristocrats and the formidable Catherine the Great, determined to uphold imperial Russian influence.

Watchful but not displeased to see Russian influence waning in Poland, Austria and Prussia allowed the reform movement to proceed. In 1788, the Patriots got their golden chance. Bogged down in war with the Ottoman Turks, Catherine could not block the summoning of a reform-minded parliament, which with King Stanislaw's aid outmaneuvered the antireform aristocrats. Amid much oratory denouncing Russian overlordship, the parliament enacted the constitution of May 3, 1791, which established a hereditary monarchy with somewhat strengthened authority, at last freed the two-house legislature from the individual veto power of every aristocrat, granted townspeople limited political rights, and vaguely promised future Jewish emancipation. Abolishing serfdom was hardly mentioned. Modest though they were, the Polish reforms did not endure. Catherine II could not countenance the spread of revolution into eastern Europe and within a year engineered the downfall of the Patriots and further weakened the Polish state.

Origins of the French Revolution, 1787–1789

Many French enthusiastically greeted the American experiment in republican government and supported the Dutch, Belgian, and Polish patriots. But they did not expect the United States or the Dutch Republic to provide them a model. Montesquieu and Rousseau, the leading political theorists of the Enlightenment, taught that republics suited only small countries, not big ones like France. Moreover, the French monarchy on the surface seemed as strong as ever. After suffering humiliation at the hands of the British in the Seven Years' War (1756–1763), the French had regained international prestige by supporting the victorious Americans, and the monarchy had shown its eagerness to promote reforms. In 1787, for example, the French crown granted civil rights to Protestants. Yet by the late 1780s, the French monarchy faced a serious fiscal crisis caused by a mounting deficit. It soon provoked a constitutional crisis of epic proportions.

France's fiscal problems stemmed from its support of the Americans against the British in the American War of Independence. About half of the French national budget went to paying interest on the debt that had accumulated. In contrast to Great Britain, which had a national bank to help raise loans for the government, the French government lived off relatively short-term, high-interest loans from private sources including Swiss banks, government annuities, and advances from tax collectors. For years the French government had been trying unsuccessfully to modernize the tax system to make it more equitable. The peasants bore the greatest burden of taxes, whereas the nobles and clergy were largely exempt. Tax collection was also far from systematic: private contractors collected many taxes and pocketed a large share of the proceeds. With the growing support of public opinion, the bond and annuity holders from the middle and upper classes now demanded a clearer system of fiscal accountability.

Faced with a mounting deficit and growing criticism of Queen Marie-Antoinette's personal spending, Louis XVI (r. 1774–1792) tried every available avenue to raise funds. In 1787, he submitted proposals for reform to an Assembly of Notables, a group of handpicked nobles, clergymen, and officials. When it refused to cooperate, the king presented his proposals for a more uniform land tax to his old rival the parlement of Paris. When it too refused, he ordered the parlement judges into exile in the provinces. Overnight, the judges (members of the nobility because of the offices they held) became popular heroes for resisting the king's "tyranny"; in reality, however, the judges, like the notables, wanted reform only on their own terms. Louis finally gave in to demands that he call a meeting of the Estates General, which had last met 175 years before.

The calling of the Estates General electrified public opinion. Who would determine the fate of the nation? There were three estates, or orders, in the Estates General. The deputies in the First Estate represented some 100,000 clergy of the Catholic church, which owned about 10 percent of the land and collected its own taxes (the tithe) on peasants. The deputies of the Second Estate represented the nobility, about 400,000 men and women who owned about 25 percent of the land, enjoyed many tax exemptions, and collected seigneurial dues and rents from their peasant tenants. The deputies of the Third Estate represented everyone else, at least 95 percent of the nation. In 1614, at the last meeting of the Estates General, each order had voted separately, and either the clergy or the nobility could therefore veto

REVEIL DU TIERS ETAT.

Ma fainte, il etoit tems que je me réveillasse, car l'oppression de mes fers me donnoit le cochemar un peu trop fort

■ The Third Estate Awakens

This print, produced after the fall of the Bastille (notice the two heads raised on pikes out-side the prison), shows a clergyman (First Estate) and a nobleman (Second Estate) alarmed by the awakening of the commoners (Third Estate). The Third Estate breaks the chains of oppression and arms itself to battle for its rights. The message is that social conflicts lay be-hind the political struggles in the Estates General. (Musée Carnavalet/Photo Bulloz.)

www.bedfordstmartins.com/huntconcise   See the ONLINE STUDY GUIDE for more help in analyzing this image.

any decision of the Third Estate. Before the elections to the Estates General in 1789, the king agreed to double the number of deputies for the Third Estate (making them equal in number to the other two combined), but he left it to the Estates General to decide whether the estates would continue to vote separately by order rather than by individual head. Voting by order would conserve the traditional powers of the clergy and nobility; voting by head would give the Third Estate an advantage because many clergymen and even some nobles sympathized with the Third Estate.

As the state's censorship apparatus broke down, pamphleteers by the hundreds denounced the traditional privileges of the nobility and clergy and called for voting by head rather than by order. In the winter and spring of 1789, thousands of men (and a few women by proxy) held meetings to elect deputies and write down their grievances. The effect was immediate. Although educated men dominated the meetings at the regional level, the humblest peasants also voted in their villages and burst forth with complaints, especially about taxes. As one villager lamented, "The last crust of bread has been taken from us." The long series of meetings raised expectations that the Estates General would help the king to solve all the nation's ills.

These new hopes soared just at the moment France experienced an increasingly rare but always dangerous food shortage. (See "Taking Measure," below.) Bad weather damaged the harvest of 1788, causing bread prices to rise in many places in the spring and summer of 1789 and threatening starvation for the poorest people. A serious slump in textile production had been causing massive unemployment since 1786. Hundreds of thousands of textile workers were out of work and hungry, adding another volatile element to an already tense situation.

When some twelve hundred deputies journeyed to the king's palace of Versailles for the opening of the Estates General in May 1789, many readers avidly followed the developments in newspapers that sprouted overnight. Although most nobles insisted on voting by order, the deputies of the Third Estate refused to proceed on that basis. After six weeks of stalemate, on June 17, 1789, the deputies of the Third Estate took unilateral action and declared themselves and whoever would join them the "National Assembly," in which each deputy would vote as an individual. Two days later, the clergy voted by a narrow margin to join them. Barred from their meeting hall on June 20, the deputies met on a nearby tennis court and swore an oath not to disband until they had given France a constitution that reflected their newly declared authority. This "tennis court oath" expressed the determination of the Third Estate to carry through a constitutional revolution.

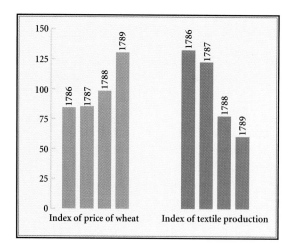

■ TAKING MEASURE
Wheat Prices and Textile Production in France, 1786–1789

This chart, comparing yearly averages against an index set at 100 (based on the average of all four years), shows the dramatic change over time in wheat prices and textile production.

The price of wheat steadily increased in the years just prior to the French Revolution, while the production of textiles dramatically declined. What would be the consequences of this movement in opposite directions? Which groups in the French population would be especially at risk?

(From Ernest Labrousse et al., *Historie économique et sociale de la France* [Paris: Presses Universitaires de France, 1970], 553.)

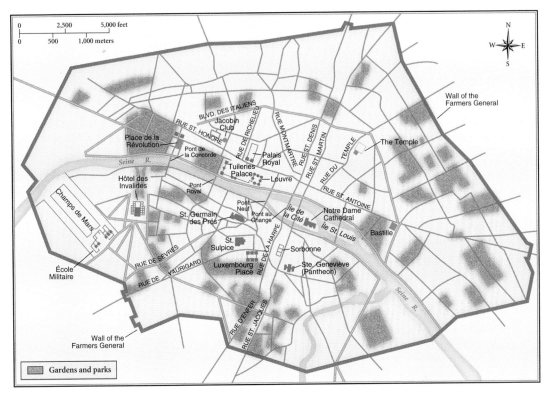

■ **MAP 16.1 Revolutionary Paris, 1789**

The French Revolution began with the fall of the Bastille on July 14, 1789. The huge fortified prison was located in a working-class neighborhood on the eastern side of the city. Before attacking the Bastille, crowds had torn down many of the customs booths located in the wall of the Farmers General (the private company in charge of tax collection) and had taken the weapons stored in the Hôtel des Invalides, a veterans' hospital on the western side of the city where the upper classes lived. In other words, the crowds had roamed throughout the city.

www.bedfordstmartins.com/huntconcise   See the ONLINE STUDY GUIDE for more help in analyzing this map.

At first Louis appeared to agree to the new representative assembly, but he also ordered thousands of soldiers to march to Paris. The deputies who supported the new National Assembly feared a plot by the king and high-ranking nobles to arrest them and disperse the assembly. "Everyone is convinced that the approach of the troops covers some violent design," one deputy wrote home. Their fears were confirmed when on July 11 the king fired Jacques Necker, the Swiss Protestant finance minister and the one high official regarded as sympathetic to the deputies' cause.

The popular reaction in Paris to Necker's dismissal and the threat of military force changed the course of the French Revolution. When the news spread, the common people in Paris began to arm themselves and attack places where either grain or arms were thought to be stored (Map 16.1). A deputy in Versailles reported home: "Today all of the evils overwhelm France, and we are between despotism, carnage, and famine." On July 14, 1789, an armed crowd marched on the Bastille, the fortified prison (see page 653) that symbolized royal authority. After a chaotic battle in which one hundred armed citizens died, the prison officials surrendered. The angry crowd shot and stabbed the governor of the prison and flaunted his head on a pike.

The fall of the Bastille (an event now commemorated as the French national holiday) set an important precedent. The common people showed themselves willing to intervene violently at a crucial political moment. All over France, food riots turned into local revolts. Local governments were forced out of power and replaced by committees of "patriots" loyal to the revolutionary cause. The patriots relied on newly formed National Guard units composed of civilians. One of their first duties was to calm the peasants in the countryside, who feared that the beggars and vagrants crowding the roads might be part of an aristocratic plot to starve the people by burning crops or barns. In some places, the Great Fear (the term used by historians to describe this rural panic) turned into peasant attacks on aristocrats or on seigneurial records of peasants' dues kept in the lord's château. The king's government began to crumble. One of Louis XVI's brothers and many other leading aristocrats fled into exile. In Paris, the marquis de Lafayette, a hero of the American War of Independence and a noble deputy in the National Assembly, became commander of the new National Guard. The Revolution thus had its first heroes, its first victims, and its first enemies.

From Monarchy to Republic

Until July 1789, the French Revolution followed a course much like that of the protest movements in the Low Countries. Unlike the Dutch and Belgian uprisings, however, the French Revolution did not come to a quick end. The French revolutionaries first tried to establish a constitutional monarchy based on the Enlightenment principles of human rights and rational government. This effort failed when the king attempted to raise a counterrevolutionary army. When war broke out in 1792, new tensions culminated in a second revolution on August 10, 1792, that deposed the king and established a republic in which all power rested in an elected legislature.

Before drafting a new constitution, the deputies of the National Assembly had to confront growing violence in the countryside, as peasants refused to pay seigneurial dues to their landlords and in some places took matters into their own hands and attacked lords' castles and records. In response to peasant unrest, on the night of August 4, 1789, noble deputies announced their willingness to give up their tax exemptions and seigneurial dues. By the end of the night, amid wild enthusiasm, dozens of deputies had come to the podium to relinquish the tax exemptions of their own professional groups, towns, or provinces. The National Assembly decreed the abolition of what it called "the feudal regime"—that is, it freed the few remaining serfs and eliminated all special privileges in matters of taxation, including all seigneurial dues on the land (a few days later, the deputies insisted on financial compensation for some of these dues, but most peasants refused to pay). Peasants had achieved their goals. The Assembly also mandated equality of opportunity in access to official posts. Talent, rather than birth, was to be the key to success. Enlightenment principles were beginning to become law.

Three weeks later, the deputies drew up a Declaration of the Rights of Man and of the Citizen as a preamble to the constitution. In words reminiscent of the American Declaration of Independence, whose author Thomas Jefferson was in Paris at the time, it proclaimed, "Men are born and remain free and equal in rights."◆ The Declaration granted freedom of religion, freedom of the press, equality of taxation, and equality before the law. By pronouncing all "men" free and equal, the Declaration immediately created new dilemmas. Did women have equal rights with men? What about free blacks in the colonies? How could slavery be justified if all men were born free? Did religious toleration of Protestants and Jews include equal political rights? Women never received the right to vote during the French Revolution, though Protestant and Jewish men did. Women were theoretically citizens under civil law but without the right to full political participation.

Some women did not accept their exclusion, viewing it as a betrayal of the promised new order. In addition to joining demonstrations, such as the march to Versailles in October 1789, women wrote petitions, published tracts, and organized political clubs to demand more participation. In her Declaration of the Rights of Women of 1791, Olympe de Gouges (1748–1793) played on the language of the official Declaration to make the point that women should also be included. In Article I, she announced, "Woman is born free and lives equal to man in her rights." Unresponsive to such calls for women's equality, the National Assembly gave voting rights only to white men who passed a test of wealth. The Constitution defined them as the "active citizens"; all others were "passive."

Despite these limitations, France became a constitutional monarchy in which the king served simply as the leading state functionary. A one-house legislature was responsible for making laws. The king could hold up enactment of laws but could not veto them absolutely. The deputies abolished all the old administrative divisions of the provinces and replaced them with a national system of eighty-three regional departments (*départements*) with identical administrative and legal structures (Map 16.2). All officials were elected; no offices could be bought and sold. The deputies also abolished the old taxes and replaced them with new ones that were supposed to be uniformly levied. The National Assembly had difficulty

◆ For the complete text of the Declaration of the Rights of Man and of the Citizen, see Document 50.

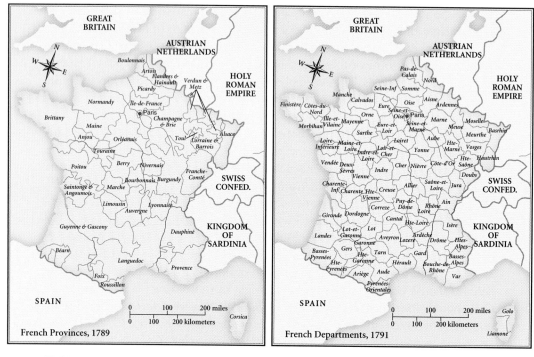

■ MAP 16.2 Redrawing the Map of France, 1789–1791

Before 1789, France was divided into provinces, each with its own administration. Some provinces had their own law codes. The new National Assembly determined to install uniform administrations and laws for the entire country. Discussion of the administrative reforms began in October 1789 and was completed on February 15, 1790, when the Assembly voted to divide the provinces into eighty-three departments with names based on their geographical characteristics: Basses-Pyrénées for the Pyrenees mountains, Haute-Marne for the Marne River, and so on. By eliminating the old names of provinces, with their historical associations, and supplanting them with geographical ones, the Assembly aimed to show that reason would now govern all French affairs.

collecting taxes, however, because many people had expected a substantial cut in the tax rate. The new administrative system survived, nonetheless, and the departments are still the basic units of the French state today.

When the deputies turned to reforming the Catholic church, they created enduring conflicts. Motivated partly by the ongoing financial crisis, the Assembly confiscated all the church's property and promised to pay clerical salaries in return. A Civil Constitution of the Clergy passed in July 1790 set pay scales for the clergy and provided that the voters elect their own parish priests and bishops just as they elected other officials. The impounded church property served as a guarantee for the new paper money, called *assignats*, issued by the government. The *assignats* soon became subject to inflation because the government began to sell the church lands to the highest bidders in state auctions. The sales increased the landholdings of wealthy city dwellers and prosperous peasants but cut the ground out from under the *assignats.*

Convinced that monastic life encouraged idleness and a decline in the nation's population, the deputies also outlawed any future monastic vows and encouraged monks and nuns to return to private life on state pensions. Many monks took the opportunity, but few nuns did. For nuns, the convent was all they knew. As the Carmelite nuns of Paris responded, "If there is true happiness on earth, we enjoy it in the shelter of the sanctuary."

Faced with resistance to these changes, in November 1790 the National Assembly required all clergy to swear an oath of loyalty to the Civil Constitution of the Clergy. Pope Pius VI in Rome condemned the constitution, and half of the French clergy refused to take the oath. The oath of allegiance permanently divided the Catholic population, which had to choose between loyalty to the old church and commitment to the Revolution with its "constitutional" church. The revolutionary government lost many supporters by passing laws against the clergy who refused the oath and by forcing them into exile, deporting them forcibly, or executing them as traitors. Riots and demonstrations led by women greeted many of the oath-taking priests who showed up to replace those who refused.

The reorganization of the Catholic church offended Louis XVI, who was reluctant to recognize the new limits on his powers. On June 20, 1791, the royal family escaped in disguise from the Tuileries palace in Paris and fled to the eastern border of France, where they hoped to gather support from Austrian emperor Leopold II, the brother of Marie-Antoinette. The plans went awry when a postmaster recognized the king from his portrait on the new French money, and the royal family was arrested at Varennes, forty miles from the Austrian border. The National Assembly tried to depict this incident as a kidnapping, but the "flight to Varennes" touched off demonstrations in Paris against the royal family, whom some now regarded as traitors. Cartoons circulated depicting the royal family as animals being returned "to the stable."

The Constitution finally completed in 1791 provided for the immediate election of a new Legislative Assembly. In a rare act of self-denial, the deputies of the National Assembly declared themselves ineligible for the new Assembly. Those who had experienced the Revolution firsthand departed from the scene, opening the door to men with little previous experience in national politics. The status of the king might have remained uncertain if war had not intervened, but by early 1792 everyone seemed intent on war with Austria. Louis and Marie-Antoinette hoped that war would lead to the definitive defeat of the Revolution, whereas the deputies who favored a republic believed that war would reveal the king's treachery and lead to his downfall. On April 21, 1792, Louis declared war on Austria. Prussia immediately entered on the Austrian side. Thousands of French aristocrats, including two-thirds of the army officer corps, had already emigrated, including both the king's brothers, and they were gathering along France's eastern border in expectation of joining Leopold's counterrevolutionary army.

When fighting broke out in 1792, all the powers expected a brief and relatively contained war. Instead, it would continue despite brief interruptions for the next twenty-three years. War had an immediate radicalizing effect on French politics. When the French armies proved woefully unprepared for battle, the authority of the Legislative Assembly came under fire. In June 1792, an angry crowd invaded the hall of the Assembly in Paris and threatened the royal family. In response, Lafayette left his command on the eastern front and came to Paris to insist on punishing the demonstrators. His appearance only fueled distrust of the army commanders, which increased to a fever pitch when the Prussians crossed the border and advanced on Paris. The Prussian commander, the duke of Brunswick, issued a manifesto—the Brunswick Manifesto—announcing that Paris would be totally destroyed if the royal family suffered any violence.

The ordinary people of Paris did not passively await their fate. Known as *sans-culottes* ("without breeches")—because men who worked with their hands wore long trousers rather than the knee breeches of the upper classes—they had followed every twist and turn in revolutionary fortunes. Political clubs had multiplied since the founding in 1789 of the first and most influential of them, the Jacobin Club, named after the former monastery in Paris where the club first met. Every local district in Paris had its club, where men and women listened to the news of the day and discussed their opinions. Faced with the threat of military retaliation and frustrated with the inaction of the Legislative Assembly, on August 10, 1792, the *sans-culottes* organized an insurrection and attacked the Tuileries palace, where the king resided. The Legislative Assembly ordered new elections, this time by universal male suffrage (no wealth qualifications as in the Constitution of 1791), for a National Convention that would write a new constitution.

When it met, the Convention abolished the monarchy and on September 22, 1792, established the first republic in French history. The republic would answer only to the people, not to any royal authority. Violence soon exploded again when early in September 1792 the Prussians approached Paris. Hastily gathered mobs stormed the overflowing prisons to seek out traitors who might help the enemy. In an atmosphere of near hysteria, eleven hundred inmates were killed, including many ordinary and completely innocent people. The princess of Lamballe, one of the queen's favorites, was hacked to pieces and her mutilated body displayed beneath the windows where the royal family was kept under guard. These "September massacres" showed the dark side of popular revolution, in which the common people demanded instant revenge on supposed enemies and conspirators.

The National Convention faced a dire situation. It needed to write a new constitution for the republic while fighting a war with external enemies and confronting increasing resistance at home. The Revolution had divided the population: for some it had not gone far enough toward providing food, land, and retribution against enemies; for others it had gone too far by dismantling the church and the monarchy. The French people had never known any government other than monarchy.

Only half the population could read and write at even a basic level. In this situation, symbolic actions became very important. Any public sign of monarchy was at risk, and revolutionaries soon pulled down statues of kings and burned reminders of the former regime.

The fate of Louis XVI and the future direction of the republic divided the deputies elected to the National Convention. Most of the deputies were middle-class lawyers and professionals who had developed their ardent republican beliefs in the national network of Jacobin Clubs. After the fall of the monarchy in August 1792, however, the Jacobins divided into two factions. The Girondins (named after a department in southwestern France, the Gironde, which provided some of its leading orators) met regularly at the salon of Jeanne Roland, the wife of a minister. They resented the growing power of Parisian militants and tried to appeal to the departments outside of Paris. The Mountain (so called because its deputies sat in the highest seats of the Convention), in contrast, was closely allied with the Paris militants.

The first showdown between the Girondins and the Mountain occurred during the trial of the king in December 1792. Although the Girondins agreed that the

■ The Guillotine

Before 1789, only nobles were decapitated if condemned to death; commoners were usually hanged. J. I. Guillotin, a professor of anatomy and a deputy for the Third Estate in the National Assembly, first proposed equalization of the death penalty. He also suggested that a mechanical device be constructed for decapitation, leading to the instrument's association with his name. The Assembly decreed decapitation as the death penalty in June 1791. Another physician, A. Louis, actually invented the guillotine. Its use began in April 1792 and did not end until 1981, when the French government abolished the death penalty. Although it was invented to make death equal and painless, the guillotine disturbed many observers; its mechanical operation and efficiency—the executioner merely pulled up the blade by a cord and then released it—seemed somehow inhuman. Nonetheless, the guillotine fascinated as much as it repelled. Reproduced in miniature, painted onto snuffboxes and china, worn as jewelry, and even serving as a toy, the guillotine became a part of popular culture, celebrated as the people's avenger by supporters of the Revolution and vilified as the preeminent symbol of the Terror by opponents. (Musée Carnavalet/Photo Bulloz.)

king was guilty of treason, many of them argued for clemency, exile, or a popular referendum on his fate. After a long and difficult debate, the Convention supported the Mountain and voted by a very narrow majority to execute the king. Louis XVI went to the guillotine on January 21, 1793, sharing the fate of Charles I of England in 1649. "We have just convinced ourselves that a king is only a man," wrote one newspaper, "and that no man is above the law."

Terror and Resistance

The execution of the king did not end the new regime's problems. The continuing war required even more men and money, and the introduction of a national draft provoked massive resistance in some parts of France. In response to growing pressures, the National Convention set up a highly centralized government designed to provide food, direct the war effort, and punish counterrevolutionaries. Thus began "the Terror," in which the guillotine became the most terrifying instrument of a government that suppressed almost every form of dissent. The leader of this government, Maximilien Robespierre, aimed to create a "Republic of Virtue," in which the government would teach, or force, citizens to become virtuous republicans through a massive program of political re-education. These policies only increased divisions, which ultimately led to Robespierre's fall from power and to a dismantling of government by terror.

Robespierre and the Committee of Public Safety

The conflict between the Girondins and the Mountain did not end with the execution of Louis XVI. Militants in Paris agitated for the removal of the deputies who had proposed a referendum on the king, and in retaliation the Girondins set up a special commission to investigate the situation in Paris, ordering the arrest of various local leaders. In response, Parisian militants organized an armed demonstration and invaded the National Convention on June 2, 1793, forcing the deputies to decree the arrest of their twenty-nine Girondin colleagues.

Setting the course for government and the war increasingly fell to the twelve-member Committee of Public Safety, set up by the Convention on April 6, 1793. When Robespierre (1758–1794) was elected to the committee three months later, he became in effect its guiding spirit and the chief spokesman of the Revolution. A lawyer from northern France known as "the incorruptible" for his stern honesty and fierce dedication to democratic ideals, Robespierre remains one of the most controversial figures in world history because of his association with the Terror. In September 1793, again in response to popular pressure, the deputies of the Convention voted to "put Terror on the agenda." Robespierre took the lead in implementing this decision. Although he originally opposed the death penalty and the war, he was convinced that the emergency situation of 1793 required severe measures, including death for those, such as the Girondins, who opposed the committee's policies.

Like many other educated eighteenth-century men, Robespierre read the classics of republicanism from the ancient Roman writers Tacitus and Plutarch to the Enlightenment thinkers Montesquieu and Rousseau. But he took them a step further. He spoke eloquently about "the theory of revolutionary government" as "the war of liberty against its enemies." He defended the people's right to democratic government, while in practice he supported many emergency measures that restricted their liberties. He personally favored a free market economy, as did almost all middle-class deputies, but in this time of crisis he was willing to enact price controls and requisitioning. The Convention had organized paramilitary bands called "revolutionary armies" to hunt down hoarders and political suspects, and on September 29, 1793, it established a General Maximum on the prices of thirty-nine essential commodities and on wages. In a speech to the Convention, Robespierre explained the necessity of a government by terror: "The first maxim of your policies must be to lead the people by reason and the people's enemies by terror . . . without virtue, terror is deadly; without terror, virtue is impotent." *Terror* was not an idle term; it seemed to imply that the goal of democracy justified what we now call totalitarian means—that is, the suppression of all dissent.

Through a series of desperate measures, the Committee of Public Safety set the machinery of the Terror in motion. It sent deputies out "on mission" to purge unreliable officials and organize the war effort. In the first universal draft of men in history, every unmarried man and childless widower between the ages of eighteen and twenty-five was declared eligible for conscription. Revolutionary tribunals set up in Paris and provincial centers tried political suspects. In October 1793, the Revolutionary Tribunal in Paris convicted Marie-Antoinette of treason and sent her to the guillotine. The Girondin leaders and Madame Roland were also guillotined, as was Olympe de Gouges. The government confiscated all the property of convicted traitors.

The Terror won its greatest success on the battlefield. As of April 1793, France faced war with Austria, Prussia, Great Britain, Spain, Sardinia, and the Dutch Republic—all fearful of the impact of revolutionary ideals on their own populations. To face this daunting coalition of forces, the French republic tapped a new and potent source of power, nationalist pride, in decrees mobilizing young and old alike: "The young men will go to battle; married men will forge arms and transport provisions; women will make tents and clothing and serve in hospitals; children will make bandages." Forges were set up in the parks and gardens of Paris to produce thousands of guns, and citizens everywhere helped collect saltpeter, a rock salt used to make gunpowder. By the end of 1793, the French nation in arms had stopped the advance of the allied powers, and in the summer of 1794 it invaded the Austrian Netherlands and crossed the Rhine River. The army was ready to carry the gospel of revolution and republicanism to the rest of Europe.

The Republic of Virtue, 1793–1794

The program of the Terror went beyond pragmatic measures to fight the war and internal enemies to include efforts to "republicanize everything"—in other words, to effect a cultural revolution. Refusing to tolerate opposition, the republic left no stone unturned in its endeavor to get its message across. Songs—especially the new national anthem, "La Marseillaise" (named after the soldiers from the city of Marseille who first sang it)—placards, posters, pamphlets, books, engravings, paintings, sculpture, even everyday crockery, chamberpots, and playing cards conveyed revolutionary slogans and symbols. Foremost among them was the figure of Liberty (an early version of the Statue of Liberty now in New York harbor), which appeared on coins and bills, letterheads and seals, and as statues in festivals. Hundreds of new plays were produced and old classics revised. To encourage the production of patriotic and republican works, the government sponsored state competitions for artists. Works of art were supposed to "awaken the public spirit and make clear how atrocious and ridiculous were the enemies of liberty and of the Republic."

At the center of this elaborate cultural campaign were the revolutionary festivals modeled on Rousseau's plans for a civic religion. The festivals first emerged in 1789 with the spontaneous planting of liberty trees in villages and towns. The Festival of Federation on July 14, 1790, marked the first anniversary of the fall of the Bastille. Under the Convention, the well-known painter Jacques-Louis David (1748–1825), who was a deputy and an associate of Robespierre, took over festival planning. David aimed to destroy the mystique of monarchy and to make the republic sacred. His Festival of Unity on August 10, 1793, for example, celebrated the first anniversary of the overthrow of the monarchy. In front of the statue of Liberty built for the occasion, a bonfire consumed the crowns and scepters of royalty while a cloud of three thousand white doves rose into the sky.

Some hoped the festival system would replace the Catholic church altogether. They initiated a campaign of de-Christianization that included closing churches (Protestant as well as Catholic), selling many church buildings to the highest bidder, and trying to force even those clergy who had taken the oath of loyalty to abandon their clerical vocations and marry. Great churches became storehouses for arms or grain, or their stones were sold off to contractors. The medieval statues of kings on the façade of Notre Dame cathedral were beheaded. Church bells were dismantled and church treasures melted down for government use.

In the ultimate step in de-Christianization, extremists tried to establish a Cult of Reason to supplant Christianity. In Paris in the autumn of 1793, a goddess of Liberty, played by an actress, presided over a Festival of Reason in Notre Dame cathedral. Local militants in other cities staged similar festivals, which alarmed deputies in the Convention, who were wary of turning rural, devout populations against the republic. The Committee of Public Safety halted the de-Christianization campaign, and Robespierre with David's help tried to institute an alternative, the Cult of the Supreme Being, in June 1794. Neither cult attracted many followers.

In principle, the best way to ensure the future of the republic was through the education of the young. The deputy Georges-Jacques Danton (1759–1794), Robespierre's main competitor as theorist of the Revolution, maintained that "after bread, the first need of the people is education." The Convention voted to make primary schooling free and compulsory for both boys and girls. It took control of education away from the Catholic church and tried to set up a system of state schools at the primary and secondary levels, but it lacked trained teachers to replace those the Catholic religious orders provided. As a result, opportunities for learning how to read and write may have diminished. In 1799, only one-fifth as many boys enrolled in the state secondary schools as had studied in church schools ten years earlier.

Although many of the ambitious republican programs failed, almost all aspects of daily life became politicized, even colors. The tricolor—the combination of red, white, and blue that was to become the flag of France—was devised in July 1789, and by 1793 everyone had to wear a cockade (a badge made of ribbons) with the colors. Using formal forms of speech—*vous* for "you"—or the title *Monsieur* or *Madame* might identify someone as an aristocrat; true patriots used the informal *tu* and *Citoyen* or *Citoyenne* ("Citizen") instead. Some people changed their names or gave their children new kinds of names. Biblical and saints' names, such as Jean,

■ The Revolutionary Tricolor
This painting by an anonymous artist probably shows a deputy wearing the uniform prescribed for those sent to supervise military operations. His dress prominently displays the revolutionary tricolor—red, white, and blue—both on his official sash and on the trim of his hat. Plumes had once been reserved for nobles; now nonnobles could wear them on their hats, but they still signaled dignity and importance. Dress became a contested issue during the Revolution, and successive governments considered prescribing some kind of uniform, at least for deputies in the legislature.

(Louvre/Reunion des Musées Nationaux.)

Pierre, Joseph, or Marie, gave way to names recalling heroes of the ancient Roman republic (Brutus, Gracchus, Cornelia), revolutionary heroes, or flowers and plants. Such changes symbolized adherence to the republic and to Enlightenment ideals rather than to Catholicism.

Even the measures of time and space were revolutionized. In October 1793, the Convention introduced a new calendar to replace the Christian one. Year I dated from the beginning of the republic on September 22, 1792. Twelve months of exactly thirty days each received new names derived from nature—for example, Pluviôse (roughly equivalent to February) recalled the rain (*la pluie*) of late winter. Instead of seven-day weeks, ten-day *décades* provided only one day of rest every ten days and pointedly eliminated the Sunday of the Christian calendar. The five days left at the end of the calendar year were devoted to special festivals called *sans-culottides*. The calendar remained in force for twelve years despite continuing resistance to it. More enduring was the new metric system based on units of ten that was invented to replace the hundreds of local variations in weights and measures. Other countries in Europe and throughout the world eventually adopted the metric system.

Successive revolutionary legislatures had also changed the rules of family life. The state took responsibility for all family matters away from the Catholic church: birth, death, and marriage registration now happened at city hall, not the parish church. Marriage became a civil contract and as such could be broken. The new divorce law of September 1792 was the most far-reaching in Europe: a couple could divorce by mutual consent or for reasons such as insanity, abandonment, battering, or criminal conviction. Thousands of men and women took advantage of the law to dissolve unhappy marriages, even though the pope had condemned the measure. (In 1816, the government revoked the right to divorce.) In one of its most influential actions, the National Convention passed a series of laws that created equal inheritance among all children in a family, including girls. A father's right to favor one child, especially the oldest male, was considered aristocratic and hence antirepublican.

Resisting the Revolution

By intruding into religion, culture, and daily life, the republic inevitably provoked resistance. Shouting curses against the republic, uprooting liberty trees, carrying statues of the Virgin Mary in procession, hiding a priest who would not take the oath, singing a royalist song—all these expressed dissent with the new symbols, rituals, and policies. Many women, in particular, suffered from the hard conditions of life that persisted in this time of war, and they had their own ways of voicing discontent. Long bread lines in the cities exhausted the patience of women, and police spies reported their constant grumbling, which occasionally turned into spontaneous demonstrations or riots over high prices or food shortages. Other forms of

■ **Anti-Robespierre Satire**
In The Purifying Pot of the Jacobins *(1793), the anonymous artist makes fun of the Jacobin
Club's penchant for constantly examining the political correctness of its members. The Robespierre-
like inquisitor uses a magnifying glass to check for loyalty, symbolized by the red cap of liberty
worn by militant revolutionaries, and carries a knife in his pocket. Those who failed the test suffered harsh, sometimes fatal consequences.* (Art Resource, NY.)

resistance were more individual. One young woman, Charlotte Corday, assassinated
the outspoken deputy Jean-Paul Marat in July 1793. Corday fervently supported the
Girondins, and she considered it her patriotic duty to kill the deputy who, in the
columns of his paper *The Friend of the People,* had constantly demanded more heads
and more blood. Marat was immediately eulogized as a great martyr: Corday went
to the guillotine vilified as a monster but confident that she had "avenged many innocent victims."

Organized resistance broke out in many parts of France. The arrest of the
Girondin deputies in June 1793 sparked in several departments insurrections that
if coordinated might have threatened the central government in Paris. But the army
promptly dispatched the rebels. After the government retook the city of Lyon, one
of the centers of the revolt, the deputy on mission ordered sixteen hundred houses
demolished. Special courts sentenced almost two thousand people to death. The
name of the city was changed to Ville Affranchie (Liberated Town).

In the Vendée region of western France, resistance turned into full-scale civil
war. Between March and December 1793, peasants, artisans, and weavers joined
under noble leadership to form a "Catholic and Royal Army." One rebel group

explained its motives: "They [the republicans] have killed our king, chased away our priests, sold the goods of our church, eaten everything we have and now they want to take our bodies [in the draft]." The uprising took two different forms: in the Vendée itself, a counterrevolutionary army organized to fight the republic; in nearby Brittany, resistance took the form of guerrilla bands, which united to attack a target and then quickly melted into the countryside. Great Britain provided money and underground contacts for these attacks.

For several months in 1793, the Vendée rebels stormed the largest towns in the region. Both sides committed atrocities. At the small town of Machecoul, for example, the rebels massacred five hundred republicans, including administrators and National Guard members; many were tied together, shoved into freshly dug graves, and shot. By the fall, however, republican soldiers had turned back the rebels. A republican general wrote to the Committee of Public Safety claiming, "There is no more Vendée, citizens, it has perished under our free sword along with its women and children. . . . Following the orders that you gave me I have crushed children under the feet of horses, massacred women who at least . . . will engender no more brigands." "Infernal columns" of republican troops marched through the region to restore control, military courts ordered thousands executed, and republican soldiers massacred thousands of others. In one especially gruesome incident, the deputy Jean-Baptiste Carrier supervised the drowning of some two thousand Vendée rebels, including a number of priests. Barges loaded with prisoners were floated into the Loire River near Nantes and then sunk. Controversy still rages about the rebellion's death toll. Estimates of rebel deaths alone range from about 20,000 to 250,000 and higher. Many thousands of republican soldiers and civilians also lost their lives. Even the low estimates reveal the carnage of this catastrophic confrontation between the republic and its opponents.

The Fall of Robespierre and the End of the Terror, 1794–1799

In an atmosphere of fear of conspiracy that these outbreaks fueled, Robespierre tried simultaneously to exert the Convention's control over popular political activities and to weed out opposition among the deputies. The Convention cracked down on popular clubs and societies in the fall of 1793. First to be suppressed were women's political clubs. Founded in early 1793, the Society of Revolutionary Republican Women played a very active part in *sans-culottes* politics. The society urged harsher measures against the republic's enemies and insisted that women have a voice in politics even if they did not have the vote. The Convention abolished women's political clubs in order to limit agitation in the streets. The deputies called on biological arguments about natural differences between the sexes to bolster their case. As one argued, "Women are ill suited for elevated thoughts and serious meditations."

■ A Women's Club

In this gouache by the Lesueur brothers, The Patriotic Women's Club, *the club president urges members to contribute funds for poor patriot families. Women's clubs focused on philanthropic work but also discussed revolutionary legislation and the debates in the National Assembly. The colorful but sober dress indicates that the women are middle class.*
(Musée de la Ville de Paris/Musée Carnavalet, Paris/Giraudon/Art Resource, NY.)

In the spring of 1794, the Committee of Public Safety moved against its critics among leaders in Paris and deputies in the Convention itself. First, a handful of men labeled "ultrarevolutionaries"—in fact a motley collection of local Parisian politicians—were arrested and executed. Next came the other side, the "indulgents," so called because they favored moderation of the Terror. Included among them was the deputy Danton himself, once a member of the Committee of Public Safety and a friend of Robespierre despite the striking contrast in their personalities. Danton was the Revolution's most flamboyant orator and, unlike Robespierre, was a high-living, high-spending, excitable politician. At every turning point in national politics, his booming voice had swayed opinion in the National Convention. Now, under government pressure, the Revolutionary Tribunal convicted him and his friends of treason and sentenced them to death.

With the arrest and execution of these leaders in Paris, the prophecies of doom for the Revolution seemed about to be realized. "The Revolution," as one of the Girondin victims of 1793 had remarked, "was devouring its own children." Even after the major threats to the committee's power had been eliminated, the Terror continued and even worsened. A law passed in June 1794 denied the accused the right of legal counsel, reduced the number of jurors necessary for conviction, and allowed only two judgments: acquittal or death. The category of political crimes expanded to include "slandering patriotism" and "seeking to inspire discouragement." Ordinary people risked the guillotine if they expressed any discontent. The rate of executions in Paris rose from five a day in the spring of 1794 to twenty-six a day in the summer. The political atmosphere darkened even though the military situation improved. At the end of June, French armies decisively defeated the main Austrian army and advanced through the Austrian Netherlands to Brussels and Antwerp. The emergency measures for fighting the war were working, yet Robespierre and his inner circle had made so many enemies that they could not afford to loosen the grip of the Terror.

The Terror hardly touched many parts of France, but overall, the experience was undeniably traumatic. Across the country, the official Terror cost the lives of at least 40,000 French people, most of them living in the regions of major insurrections or near the borders with foreign enemies, where suspicion of collaboration ran high. As many as 300,000 people—one out of every fifty French people—went to prison as suspects between March 1793 and August 1794. The toll for the aristocracy and the clergy was especially high. Many leading nobles perished under the guillotine, and thousands emigrated. Thirty thousand to forty thousand clergy who refused the oath emigrated, at least two thousand (including many nuns) were executed, and thousands were imprisoned. The clergy were singled out in particular in the civil war zones: 135 priests were massacred at Lyon in November 1793 and 83 shot in one day during the Vendée revolt. Yet many victims of the Terror were peasants or ordinary working people.

The final crisis of the Terror came in July 1794. Conflicts within the Committee of Public Safety and the National Convention left Robespierre isolated. On July 27, 1794 (the ninth of Thermidor, Year II, according to the revolutionary calendar), Robespierre appeared before the Convention with yet another list of deputies to be arrested. Many feared they would be named, and they shouted him down and ordered him arrested along with his followers on the committee, the president of the Revolutionary Tribunal in Paris, and the commander of the Parisian National Guard. An armed uprising led by the Paris city government failed to save Robespierre when most of the National Guard took the side of the Convention. Robespierre tried to kill himself with a pistol but only broke his jaw. The next day he and scores of followers went to the guillotine.

The men who led the attack on Robespierre in Thermidor (July 1794) did not intend to reverse all his policies, but that happened nonetheless because of a violent backlash known as the "Thermidorian Reaction." Newspapers attacked the Robespierrists as "tigers thirsting for human blood." The new government released hundreds of suspects and arranged a temporary truce in the Vendée. It purged Jacobins from local bodies and replaced them with their opponents. It arrested some of the most notorious "terrorists" in the National Convention, such as Carrier, and put them to death. Within the year, the new leaders abolished the Revolutionary

Tribunal and closed the Jacobin Club in Paris. Popular demonstrations met severe repression. In southeastern France, in particular, a "White Terror" replaced the Jacobins' "Red Terror." Former officials and local Jacobin leaders were harassed, beaten, and often murdered by paramilitary bands who had tacit support from the new authorities. Those who remained in the National Convention prepared yet another constitution in 1795, setting up a two-house legislature and an executive body—the Directory—headed by five directors.

The Rise of Napoleon Bonaparte

Between 1795 and 1799, the republic endured in France, but it directed a war effort abroad that would ultimately bring to power the man who would dismantle the republic itself. The story of the rise of Napoleon Bonaparte (1769–1821) is one of the most remarkable in Western history. It would have seemed astonishing in 1795 that the twenty-six-year-old son of a Corsican noble would within four years become the supreme ruler of France and one of the greatest military leaders in world history. In 1795, he was a penniless artillery officer, only recently released from prison as a presumed Robespierrist. Continuing warfare, the upheavals caused in the rest of Europe by the impact of the French Revolution, and political divisions within the revolutionary leadership gave Bonaparte the opportunity to change the course of history.

Revolution on the March

The powers allied against France had squandered their best chance to defeat France in 1793, when the French armies verged on chaos because of the emigration of noble army officers and the problems of integrating new draftees. At that moment, Prussia, Russia, and Austria were preoccupied once again with Poland. "I shall fight Jacobinism, and defeat it in Poland," vowed Catherine the Great in 1792. She abolished Poland's constitution of May 3, 1791, and joined with Prussia in gobbling up generous new slices of Polish territory in the Second Partition of 1793 (Map 16.3). When Tadeusz Kościuszko (1746–1817), an officer who had been a foreign volunteer in the War of American Independence, tried to lead a nationalist uprising, Catherine's army struck again. This time, Russia, Prussia, and Austria wiped Poland completely from the map in the Third Partition of 1795. "The Polish question" would plague international relations for more than a century as Polish rebels flocked to any international upheaval that might undo the partitions.

While Russia, Prussia, and Austria feasted on Poland, France regrouped. Because of the new national draft, the French had a huge and powerful fighting force of 700,000 men by the end of 1793. But the army faced many problems in the field. As many as a third of the recent draftees deserted before or during battle. Uniforms fashioned out of rough cloth constricted movements, tore easily, and retained the

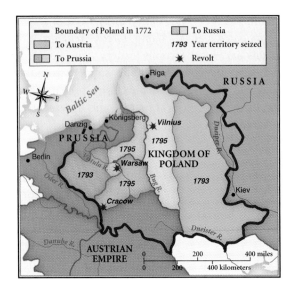

■ MAP 16.3 The Second and Third Partitions of Poland, 1793 and 1795

In 1793, after Russian armies invaded Poland, Russia and Prussia agreed to another partition of Polish territories. Prussia took over territory that included 1.1 million Poles while Russia gained 3 million new inhabitants. Austria gave up any claims to Poland in exchange for help from Russia and Prussia in acquiring Bavaria. When Kościuszko's nationalist uprising failed in 1794, Russia, Prussia, and Austria agreed to a final division. Prussia absorbed an additional 900,000 Polish subjects, including those in Warsaw; Austria incorporated 1 million Poles and the city of Cracow; Russia gained another 2 million Poles. The three powers determined never to use the term "Kingdom of Poland" again.

damp of muddy battlefields, exposing the soldiers to the elements and the spread of disease. At times, the soldiers were fed only moldy bread, and if their pay was late, they sometimes resorted to pillaging and looting. Generals might pay with their lives if they lost a key battle and their loyalty to the Revolution came under suspicion. France nevertheless had one overwhelming advantage: its soldiers, drawn largely from the peasantry and the lower classes of the cities, fought for a revolution that they and their brothers and sisters had helped make. The republic was their government, and the army was in large measure theirs, too; many officers had risen through the ranks by skill and talent rather than by inheriting or purchasing their positions. One young peasant boy wrote to his parents, "Either you will see me return bathed in glory, or you will have a son who is a worthy citizen of France who knows how to die for the defense of his country."

When French armies invaded the Austrian Netherlands and crossed the Rhine in the summer of 1794, they proclaimed a war of liberation. These promises profoundly divided European opinion. In 1789, many had greeted events with unabashed enthusiasm. The English Unitarian minister Richard Price had exulted, "Behold, the light . . . after setting AMERICA free, reflected to FRANCE, and there kindled into a blaze that lays despotism in ashes, and warms and illuminates EUROPE." Democrats and reformers from many countries flooded to Paris to witness events firsthand. Supporters of the French Revolution in Great Britain, like

■ The English Reaction to the French Revolution

In this caricature, James Gillray, a supporter of the Tories in Britain, satirizes the French version of liberty but also subtly mocks the British upper classes. He portrays French liberty as a creature (is it man or woman?) who has only onions to eat but still sings the praises of French freedom and plenty. The British figure is a fat magistrate who complains that high taxes will cause slavery and starvation, while he stuffs himself on the British national dish of roast beef. Gillray produced thousands of political caricatures. (British Museum.)

the earlier reformers of the 1760s and 1770s, joined constitutional and reform societies that sprang up in many cities. The most important of these societies, the London Corresponding Society, founded in 1792, corresponded with the Paris Jacobin Club and served as a center for reform agitation in England. Pro-French feeling ran even stronger in Ireland. Catholics and Presbyterians, both excluded from the vote, came together in 1791 in the Society of United Irishmen, which eventually pressed for secession from England.

European elites became alarmed when the French abolished monarchy and nobility and encouraged popular participation in politics. The British government, for example, quickly suppressed the corresponding societies and harassed their leaders, charging that their ideas and their contacts with the French were seditious. In the United States, opinion fiercely divided on the virtues of the French Revolution. In Sweden, King Gustavus III (r. 1771–1792) was assassinated by a nobleman who claimed that "the king has violated his oath . . . and declared himself an enemy of the realm." The king's son and heir, Gustavus IV (r. 1792–1809), was convinced that the French Jacobins had sanctioned his father's assassination. Although just across the border from France, Spain's royal government suppressed all news from France, fearing that it might ignite the spirit of revolt. This fear was not misplaced because even in Russia, for instance, 278 outbreaks of peasant unrest occurred between 1796 and 1798. One Russian landlord complained, "This is the self-same . . . spirit of in-subordination and independence, which has spread through all Europe."

Middle-class people near the northern and eastern borders of France reacted most positively to the French invasion. In the Austrian Netherlands, Mainz, Savoy, and Nice, French officers organized Jacobin Clubs that attracted middle-class lo-cals. The clubs petitioned for annexation to France, and French legislation was then introduced, including the abolition of seigneurial dues. Despite resistance, espe-cially in the Austrian Netherlands, these areas remained part of France until 1815, and the legal changes were permanent. Like Louis XIV a century before, most deputies in the National Convention considered the territories annexed in 1794 within France's "natural frontiers"—the Rhine, the Alps, and the Pyrenees.

The Directory government that came to power in 1795 was torn between de-fending the new frontiers and launching a more aggressive policy of creating semi-independent "sister" republics wherever the armies succeeded. Aggression won out. When Prussia declared neutrality in 1795, French armies swarmed into the Dutch Republic, abolished the stadtholderate, and—with the revolutionary penchant for renaming—created the new Batavian Republic, a satellite of France. The French set up a Cisalpine Republic when Bonaparte defeated the Austrian armies in northern Italy in 1797. After the French attacked the Swiss cantons in 1798, they set up the Helvetic Republic and curtailed many of the Catholic church's privileges. They con-quered the Papal States in 1798 and installed a Roman Republic; the pope fled to Siena.

As the French conquered more and more territory, "liberated" people in many places began to view them as an army of occupation. In the German Rhineland, for example, gangs of bandits preyed on the French and on Jews. One German traveler reported, "It is characteristic of the region in which the bandits are based that these two nations [the French and the Jews] are hated. So crimes against them are mo-tivated not just by a wish to rob them but also by a variety of fanaticism which is partly political and partly religious." Because the French offered the Jews religious toleration and civil and political rights wherever they conquered, anti-French groups sometimes attacked Jews.

Revolution in the Colonies

The revolution that produced so much upheaval in continental Europe had reper-cussions in France's Caribbean colonies. These colonies were crucial to the French economy. Twice the size in land area of the neighboring British colonies, they also produced nearly twice as much revenue in exports. The slave population had doubled in the French colonies in the twenty years before 1789. St. Domingue (present-day Haiti) was the most important French colony. Occupying the western half of the island of Hispaniola, it was inhabited by approximately 465,000 slaves, 30,000 whites, and 28,000 free people of color, whose primary job was to apprehend runaway slaves and ensure plantation security.

Despite the efforts of a Paris club called the Friends of Blacks, most French revolutionaries did not consider slavery a pressing problem. As one deputy explained, "This regime [in the colonies] is oppressive, but it gives a livelihood to several million Frenchmen. This regime is barbarous but a still greater barbarity will result if you interfere with it without the necessary knowledge."

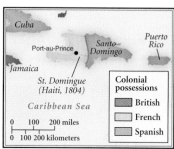

St. Domingue on the Eve of the Revolt, 1791

In August 1791, slaves in northern St. Domingue, inspired by the slogan "Listen to the voice of Liberty which speaks in the hearts of all," organized a large-scale revolt. To restore authority over the slaves, the Legislative Assembly in Paris granted civil and political rights to the free people of color. This action infuriated white planters and merchants, and in 1793 they signed an agreement with Great Britain, now France's enemy in war, declaring British sovereignty over St. Domingue. To complicate matters further, Spain, which controlled the rest of the island and had entered on Great Britain's side in the war with France, offered freedom to individual slave rebels who joined the Spanish armies as long as they agreed to maintain the slave regime for the other blacks.

The few thousand French republican troops on St. Domingue were outnumbered, and to prevent complete military disaster, the French commissioner freed all the slaves in his jurisdiction in August 1793 without permission from the government in Paris. In February 1794, the National Convention formally abolished slavery and granted full rights to all black men in France's colonies. These actions had the desired effect. One of the ablest black generals allied with the Spanish, the ex-slave François-Dominique Toussaint L'Ouverture (1743–1803), changed sides and committed his troops to the French. The French eventually appointed Toussaint governor of St. Domingue as a reward for his efforts.

The vicious fighting and flight of whites left the island's economy in ruins. In 1800, the plantations produced one-fifth of what they had in 1789. In the zones Toussaint controlled, army officers or government officials took over the great estates and kept all the freed people working in agriculture under military discipline. The former slaves were bound to their estates like serfs and were forced to work the plantations in exchange for an autonomous family life and the right to maintain personal garden plots.

Toussaint remained in charge until 1802, when Napoleon sent French armies to regain control of St. Domingue. They arrested Toussaint and transported him to

■ Toussaint L'Ouverture
The leader of the St. Domingue slave uprising appears in his general's uniform, sword in hand. This portrait appeared in one of the earliest histories of the revolt, Marcus Rainsford's Historical Account of the Black Empire of Hayti *(London, 1805). Toussaint, a former slave who educated himself, fascinated many of his contemporaries in Europe as well as the New World by turning a chaotic slave rebellion into an organized and ultimately successful independence movement.* (North Wind Picture Archives.)

France, where he died in prison. His arrest prompted the English romantic poet William Wordsworth (1770–1850) to write of him:

> *There's not a breathing of the common wind*
> *That will forget thee; thou hast great allies;*
> *Thy friends are exultations, agonies,*
> *And love, and man's unconquerable mind.*

Toussaint became a hero to abolitionists everywhere, a potent symbol of black struggles to win freedom.♦ Napoleon attempted to reimpose slavery, but the remaining black generals defeated his armies, which had been weakened by yellow fever, and in 1804 proclaimed the Republic of Haiti.

♦ For a set of primary sources that illuminate Toussaint's revolutionary principles and actions, see Document 51, Toussaint L'Ouverture, "Revolution in the Colonies."

The End of the French Republic

Toussaint had followed with interest Napoleon's rise to power in France; he once wrote to Bonaparte, "From the First of the Blacks to the First of the Whites." Like Toussaint, Napoleon Bonaparte made the most of the opportunities afforded by war. The Directory regime installed in 1795 had tenuously held on to power while trying to fend off challenges from the remaining Jacobins and the resurgent royalists. Bands of young men dressed in knee breeches and rich fabrics picked fights with known Jacobins and disrupted theater performances with loud antirevolutionary songs. All over France, people banded together and petitioned to reopen churches closed during the Terror. If necessary, they broke into a church to hold services with a priest who had been in hiding or with a lay schoolteacher who was willing to say Mass. Amid increasing political instability, generals in the field became practically independent, and the troops felt greater loyalty to their units and generals than to the republic. As one army captain wrote, "In a conquering people the military spirit must prevail over other social conditions." Military victories had made the army a parallel and rival force to the state.

Thanks to some early military successes and links to Parisian politicians, Bonaparte was named commander of the French army in Italy in 1796. His astounding success in the Italian campaigns of 1796–1797 launched his meteoric career. With an army of fewer than fifty thousand men, he defeated the Piedmontese and the Austrians. He negotiated with the Austrians himself, and in quick order he established client republics dependent on his own authority. He molded the army into his personal force by paying the soldiers in cash taken as tribute from the newly conquered territories. He mollified the Directory government by sending home wagonloads of Italian masterpieces of art, which were added to Parisian museum collections (most are still there) after being paraded in victory festivals.

In 1798, the Directory set aside its plans to invade England, gave Bonaparte command of the army raised for that purpose, and sent him across the Mediterranean Sea to Egypt, away from the Parisian centers of power. The French had encouraged the Irish to time a rebellion to coincide with their planned invasion, and when the French went elsewhere, the British mercilessly repressed the revolt. Thirty thousand people were killed. Twice as many regular British troops (seventy thousand) as fought in any of the major continental battles against Napoleon were required to put down the rebellion.

The Directory government hoped that French occupation of Egypt would strike a blow at British trade by cutting the route to India and thus compensate France for its losses there years before. Once the army disembarked in Egypt, however, the British admiral Horatio Nelson destroyed the French fleet while it was anchored in Aboukir Bay. In the face of determined resistance and an outbreak of the bubonic plague, Bonaparte's armies retreated from a further expedition in Syria. But the French occupation of Egypt lasted long enough for that largely Muslim country to experience the same kinds of Enlightenment-inspired legal reforms that had been introduced in Europe: the French abolished torture, introduced equality before the law, eliminated religious taxes, and proclaimed religious toleration.◆

Even the failures of the Egyptian campaign did not dull Bonaparte's luster. Bonaparte had taken France's leading scientists with him on the expedition, and his soldiers had discovered a slab of black basalt dating from 196 B.C. written in both hieroglyphic and Greek. Called the *Rosetta stone* after a nearby town, it enabled scholars to finally decipher the hieroglyphs used by the ancient Egyptians. When his army was pinned down after its initial successes, Napoleon slipped out of Egypt and made his way secretly across the Mediterranean to southern France.

In October 1799, Bonaparte arrived in Paris at just the right moment. The war in Europe was going badly. The departments of the former Austrian Netherlands had revolted against new conscription laws. Deserters swelled the ranks of the rebels in western France. A royalist army had tried to take the city of Toulouse in the southwest. And many government leaders wanted to revise the Constitution of 1795. Disillusioned members of the government saw in Bonaparte's return an occasion to overturn the Constitution of 1795.

On November 9, 1799 (18 Brumaire, Year VIII, by the revolutionary calendar), the conspirators persuaded the legislature to move out of Paris to avoid an imaginary Jacobin plot. But when Bonaparte stomped into the meeting hall the next day and demanded changes in the Constitution, he was greeted by cries of "Down with the dictator." His quick-thinking brother Lucien, president of the Council of Five Hundred (the lower house), saved Bonaparte's coup by summoning troops guarding the hall and claiming that the deputies had tried to assassinate the popular general. The soldiers ejected the deputies, and a hastily assembled rump legislature voted to abolish the Directory and establish a new three-man executive called the consulate.

Bonaparte became First Consul, a title revived from the ancient Roman republic. He promised to be a man above party and to restore order to the republic. A new constitution was submitted to the voters. Millions abstained from voting, and the government falsified the results to give an appearance of even greater support to the new regime. Inside France, political apathy had overtaken the original enthusiasm for revolutionary ideals. Bonaparte's coup d'état appeared to be just the latest in a long line of upheavals in revolutionary France. Within the year, however, he had effectively ended the French Revolution and set France on a new course toward an authoritarian state.

Napoleon had no long-range plans to establish himself as emperor and conquer most of Europe. The deputies of the legislature who engineered the coup d'état of November 1799 picked him as one of three provisional consuls only because he

---

◆ For a primary source that shows Napoleon's invasion from a native perspective, see Document 52, Abd al-Rahman al-Jabartî, "Napoleon in Egypt."

■ Napoleon as Military Hero

In this painting from 1800–1801, Napoleon Crossing the Alps at St. Bernard, *Jacques-Louis David reminds the French of Napoleon's heroic military exploits. Napoleon is a picture of calm and composure while his horse shows the fright and energy of the moment. David painted this propagandistic image shortly after one of his former students went to the guillotine on a trumped-up charge of plotting to assassinate the new French leader. The former organizer of republican festivals during the Terror had become a kind of court painter for the new regime.*

(© Photo RMN/Herve Lewandowski.)

was a famous general. Still, the constitution of 1799 made Bonaparte the First Consul with the right to pick the Council of State, which drew up all laws. He quickly exerted control by choosing men loyal to him. Government was no longer representative in any real sense: the new constitution eliminated direct elections for deputies and granted no independent powers to the three houses of the legislature. Bonaparte and his advisers chose the legislature's members out of a small pool of "notables." Almost all men over twenty-one could vote in the plebiscite (referendum) to approve the constitution, but their only option was to choose *Yes* or *No*.

Emperor Napoleon I, r. 1804–1814

Napoleon left an indelible stamp on French institutions and political life. He reconciled with the Catholic church and with exiled aristocrats willing to return to France. He sped up the centralization of political power and ensured order by suppressing political dissent. He supervised the unification of France's many law codes into one Napoleonic Code that has remained in force to this day. Yet his fame and much of his power rested on his military conquests. His military prowess brought him to the heights of power, but as a consequence, he could not survive defeat on the battlefield.

The Authoritarian State

Bonaparte's most urgent task was to reconcile to his regime Catholics who had been alienated by revolutionary policies. Though nominally Catholic, Napoleon held no deep religious convictions. "How can there be order in the state without religion?" he asked cynically. "When a man is dying of hunger beside another who is stuffing himself, he cannot accept this difference if there is not an authority who tells him: 'God wishes it so.'" In 1801, a concordat with Pope Pius VII (r. 1800–1823) ended a decade of church-state conflict. The pope validated all sales of church lands, and the government agreed to pay the salaries of bishops and priests who would swear loyalty to the state. Catholicism was officially recognized as the religion of "the great majority of French citizens." (The state also paid Protestant pastors' salaries.) The pope thus brought the huge French Catholic population back into the fold, and Napoleon gained the pope's support for his regime.

Napoleon continued the centralization of state power that had begun under the absolutist monarchy of Louis XIV and resumed under the Terror. As First Consul, he appointed prefects who directly supervised local affairs in every *département*, or region. He created the Bank of France to facilitate government borrowing and relied on gold and silver coinage rather than paper money. He also frequently made ends meet by exacting tribute from the territories he conquered.

Napoleon promised order and an end to the upheavals of ten years of revolutionary turmoil, but his regime severely limited political expression. He never relied on mass executions to achieve control, but he refused to allow those who opposed him to meet in clubs, influence elections, or publish newspapers. A decree reduced the number of newspapers in Paris from seventy-three to thirteen (and then finally to four), and the newspapers that remained became government mouthpieces. Government censors had to approve all operas and plays, and they banned "offensive" artistic works even more frequently than their royal predecessors. The minister of police, Joseph Fouché, a leading figure in the Terror of 1793–1794, could impose house arrest, arbitrary imprisonment, and surveillance of political dissidents. Political contest and debate shriveled to almost nothing. When a bomb attack on Napoleon's carriage failed in 1800, Fouché suppressed evidence of a royalist plot and instead arrested hundreds of former Jacobins. More than one hundred of them were deported and seven hundred imprisoned.

Napoleon's intention to eliminate the republic became clear in 1802. He named himself First Consul for life, and in 1804, with the pope's blessing, he crowned himself emperor. Plebiscites approved these decisions, but no alternatives were offered. Napoleon's charismatic personality dominated the new imperial regime. He worked hard at establishing his reputation as an efficient administrator with broad intellectual interests. He met frequently with scientists, jurists, and artists, and stories abounded of his unflagging energy. He worked constantly, whether on military campaigns or on state affairs, taking only a few minutes for each meal. "Authority," declared his adviser Sieyès, "must come from above and confidence from below."

As emperor, Napoleon cultivated personal symbolism to enhance his image as a hero. His face and name adorned coins, engravings, histories, paintings, and public monuments. His favorite painters embellished his legend by depicting him as a warrior-hero of mythic proportions. In his imperial court, Napoleon staged his entrances carefully to maximize his personal presence: his wife and courtiers were dressed in regal finery, and he was announced with great pomp—but he usually arrived dressed in a simple military uniform with no medals.

Believing that "what is big is always beautiful," Napoleon embarked on ostentatious building projects that would outshine even those of Louis XIV. Government-commissioned architects built the Arc de Triomphe, the Stock Exchange, fountains, and even slaughterhouses. Most of his new construction reflected his neoclassical taste for monumental buildings set in vast empty spaces. Old, winding streets with their cramped houses were demolished to make way for Napoleon's grand designs.

Napoleon did not rule alone. He relied on men who had served with him in the army. His chief of staff Alexandre Berthier, for example, became minister of war, and the chemist Claude Berthollet, who had organized the scientific part of the expedition to Egypt, became vice president of the Senate in 1804. Napoleon's bureaucracy was based on a patron-client relationship, with Napoleon as the ultimate patron. Some of Napoleon's closest associates married into his family.

Combining aristocratic and revolutionary values in a new social hierarchy that rewarded merit and talent, Napoleon used the Senate to dispense his patronage and personally chose as senators the nation's most illustrious generals, ministers, prefects, scientists, rich men, and former nobles. Intending to replace both the old nobility of birth and the republic's strict emphasis on equality, in 1802 he took a step toward creating a new nobility by founding a Legion of Honor. (Members of the legion received lifetime pensions along with their titles.) By 1814, the legion had thirty-two thousand members, 95 percent of them military men.

In 1808, Napoleon introduced a complete hierarchy of noble titles, ranging from princes down to barons and chevaliers. All Napoleonic nobles had served the state. Titles could be inherited but had to be supported by wealth—a man could not be a duke without a fortune of 200,000 francs, or a chevalier without 3,000 francs. To go along with their new titles, Napoleon gave his favorite generals huge fortunes, often in the form of estates in the conquered territories.

Napoleon's own family reaped the greatest benefits. He made his older brother, Joseph, ruler of the newly established kingdom of Naples in 1806, the same year he installed his younger brother Louis as king of Holland. He proclaimed his twenty-three-year-old stepson Eugène de Beauharnais viceroy of Italy in 1805 and established his sister Caroline and brother-in-law General Murat as king and queen of Naples in 1808, when he moved Joseph to the throne of Spain. Napoleon wanted to establish an imperial succession, but he lacked an heir. In thirteen years of marriage, his wife Josephine had borne no children, so in 1809 he divorced her and in 1810 married the eighteen-year-old Princess Marie-Louise of Austria. The next year she gave birth to a son to whom Napoleon immediately gave the title "king of Rome."

The New Paternalism

Because Napoleon shared the rewards of rule with his own family, it is perhaps not surprising that he brought a familial model of power to his empire, instilling his personal version of paternalism. The prime mover of this system was the new Civil Code. The revolutionary governments had tried to unify and standardize France's multiple legal codes; Napoleon finally succeeded because he personally presided over the commission that drafted the new code, completed in 1804. Called the Napoleonic Code as a way of further exalting his image, it defined and ensured property rights, guaranteed religious liberty, and established a uniform system of law that provided equal treatment for all adult males and affirmed the right of men to choose their professions.

The code sharply curtailed women's rights in almost every aspect of public and private life. One of the leading jurists remarked, "There have been many discussions on the equality and superiority of the sexes. Nothing is more useless than such disputes. . . . Women need protection because they are weaker; men are free because they are stronger." The law obligated a husband to support his wife, but he alone controlled any property held in common. A wife could not sue in court, sell or mortgage her own property, or contract a debt without her husband's consent.

The Civil Code modified even those few revolutionary laws that had been favorable to women, and in some instances it denied women rights they had exercised under the monarchy. Divorce was still possible, but a wife could petition for divorce only if her husband brought his mistress to live in the family home. In contrast, a wife convicted of adultery could be imprisoned for up to two years. The code's framers saw these discrepancies as a way to reinforce the family and make women responsible for private virtue, while leaving public decisions to men. The French code was imitated in many European and Latin American countries and in the French colony of Louisiana, where it had a similar negative effect on women's rights. Not until 1965 did French wives gain legal status equal to that of their husbands.

The Civil Code not only reasserted the old regime's patriarchal system of male domination over women but also insisted on a father's control over his children, which revolutionary legislation had limited. For example, children under age sixteen who refused to follow their fathers' commands could be sent to prison for up to a month with no hearing of any sort. At the same time, the code required fathers to provide for their children's welfare. Napoleon himself encouraged the foundation of private charities to help indigent mothers, and one of his decrees made it easier for women to abandon their children anonymously to a government foundling hospital. Napoleon hoped such measures would discourage abortion and infanticide, especially among the poorest classes in the fast-growing urban areas.

In periods of economic crisis, the government opened soup kitchens, but in time-honored fashion it also arrested beggars and sent them to newly established workhouses. For prostitutes, whose numbers had increased because of migration from the countryside to the cities and wartime upheavals, the Napoleonic state developed a novel paternalist approach. The authorities arrested prostitutes who worked on their own, but they tolerated brothels, which could be supervised by the police, and required the women working in them to have monthly medical examinations for venereal disease.

Napoleon took little interest in girls' education, believing that they should spend most of their time at home learning religion, manners, and such "female occupations" as sewing and music. For boys, by contrast, the government set up a new system of *lycées*, state-run secondary schools in which boys wore military uniforms and drumrolls signaled the beginning and end of classes. (Without the military trappings, the lycées are now coeducational and still the heart of the French educational system.)

The new paternalism extended to relations between employers and employees. The state required all workers to carry a work card attesting to their good conduct, and it prohibited all workers' organizations. The police considered workers without cards as vagrants or criminals and could send them to workhouses or prison. After 1806, arbitration boards settled labor disputes, but they took employers at their word while treating workers as minors, demanding that foremen and shop super-intendents represent them. Occasionally strikes broke out, led by secret, illegal jour-neymen's associations, yet many employers laid off employees when times were hard, deducted fines from their wages, and dismissed them without appeal for being absent or making errors. These limitations on workers' rights won Napoleon the support of French business.

Napoleon continued the central government's patronage of science and intel-lectual life but once again put his own distinctive paternalist stamp on these ac-tivities. He closely monitored the research institutes established during the Rev-olution, sometimes intervening personally to achieve political conformity. An impressive outpouring of new theoretical and practical scientific work rewarded the state's efforts. Experiments with balloons led to the discovery of laws about the ex-pansion of gases, and research on fossil shells prepared the way for new theories of evolutionary change later in the nineteenth century.

Napoleon aimed to modernize French society through science, but he could not tolerate criticism. He considered most writers useless or dangerous, "good for nothing under any government." Some of the most talented French writers of the time had to live in exile. The best-known expatriate was Germaine de Staël (1766–1817), known as Madame de Staël, the daughter of Louis XVI's chief min-ister Jacques Necker. When explaining his desire to banish her, Napoleon exclaimed, "She is a machine in motion who stirs up the salons." While exiled in the German states, Madame de Staël wrote a novel, *Corinne* (1807), whose heroine is a brilliant woman thwarted by a patriarchal system, and *On Germany* (1810), an account of the important new literary currents east of the Rhine. Her books were banned in France.

Although Napoleon restored the strong authority of state and religion in France, many royalists and Catholics still criticized him as an impious usurper. François-René de Chateaubriand (1768–1848) admired Napoleon as "the strong man who has saved us from the abyss," but he preferred monarchy. In his view, Napoleon had not properly understood the need to defend Christian values against the Enlight-enment's excessive reliance on reason. Chateaubriand wrote his *Genius of Chris-tianity* (1802) to draw attention to the power and mystery of faith. He warned, "It is to the vanity of knowledge that we owe almost all our misfortunes. . . . The learned ages have always been followed by ages of destruction."

"Europe Was at My Feet": Napoleon's Military Conquests

Building on innovations introduced by the republican governments before him, Napoleon revolutionized the art of war with tactics and strategy based on a highly mobile army. Napoleon attributed his military success "three-quarters to morale" and the rest to leadership and superiority of numbers at the point of attack. Con-

■ **Germaine de Staël**

One of the most fascinating intellectuals of her time, Anne-Louise Germaine de Staël seemed to irritate Napoleon more than any other person did. Daughter of Louis XVI's Swiss Protestant finance minister, Jacques Necker, and wife of a Swedish diplomat, Madame de Staël frequently criticized Napoleon's regime. She published best-selling novels and influential literary criticism, and whenever allowed to reside in Paris she encouraged the intellectual and political dissidents from Napoleon's regime.

(Photographie Bulloz.)

scription provided the large numbers: 1.3 million men of ages twenty to twenty-four were drafted between 1800 and 1812, another million in 1813–1814. Military service was both a patriotic duty and a means of social mobility. The men who rose through the ranks to become officers were young, ambitious, and accustomed to the new ways of war. Consequently, the French army had higher morale than the armies of other powers, most of which rejected conscription as too democratic and continued to restrict their officer corps to the nobility. Only in 1813–1814 did French morale plummet, as the military tide turned against Napoleon.

When Napoleon came to power in 1799, desertion was rampant, and the generals competed with one another for predominance. Napoleon united all the armies into one Grand Army under his personal command. By 1812, he commanded 700,000 troops. In any given battle, between 70,000 and 180,000 men, not all of them French, fought for France. Life on campaign was no picnic, yet Napoleon inspired almost fanatical loyalty. A brilliant strategist who carefully studied the demands of war, he outmaneuvered nearly all his opponents. He gathered the largest possible army for one great and decisive battle and then followed with a relentless pursuit to break enemy morale altogether. He fought alongside his soldiers in some sixty battles and had nineteen horses shot from under him. One opponent said that Napoleon's presence alone was worth 50,000 men.

One of Napoleon's greatest advantages was the lack of coordination among his enemies. Britain dominated the seas but did not want to field huge land armies. On the European continent, the French republic had already established satellite regimes in the Netherlands and Italy, which served as a buffer against the big powers to the east—Austria, Prussia, and Russia. By maneuvering diplomatically and militarily, Napoleon could usually take these on one by one. After reorganizing the French armies in 1799, for example, Napoleon won striking victories against the Austrians at Marengo and Hohenlinden in 1800, forcing them to agree to peace terms. Once the Austrians had withdrawn, Britain agreed to the Treaty of Amiens in 1802,

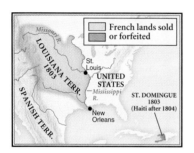

France's Retreat from America

effectively ending hostilities in Europe. Napoleon considered the peace with Great Britain merely a truce, however, and it lasted only until 1803. When the attempt to retake St. Domingue failed, Napoleon abandoned his plans to extend his empire to the Western Hemisphere. As part of his retreat, he sold the Louisiana Territory to the United States in 1803.

When war resumed in Europe, the British navy once more proved its superiority by defeating the French and their Spanish allies in a huge naval battle at Trafalgar in 1805. France lost many ships; the British lost no vessels, but their renowned admiral Lord Horatio Nelson died in the battle. On land, however, Napoleon remained invincible. In 1805, Austria took up arms again when Napoleon demanded that it declare neutrality in the conflict with Britain. Napoleon promptly captured 25,000 Austrian soldiers at Ulm in Bavaria in 1805. After marching on to Vienna, he again trounced the Austrians, who had been joined by their new ally, Russia. The battle of Austerlitz, often considered Napoleon's greatest victory, was fought on December 2, 1805, the first anniversary of his coronation.

After maintaining neutrality for a decade, Prussia declared war on France. In 1806, the French promptly destroyed the Prussian army at Jena and Auerstadt. In 1807, Napoleon defeated the Russians at Friedland. Personal negotiations between Napoleon and the young tsar Alexander I (r. 1801–1825) resulted in a humiliating settlement imposed on Prussia, which paid the price for temporary reconciliation between France and Russia. The Treaties of Tilsit turned Prussian lands west of the Elbe River into the kingdom of Westphalia under Napoleon's brother Jerome, and Prussia's Polish provinces became the duchy of Warsaw. Alexander recognized Napoleon's conquests in central and western Europe and promised to help him against the British in exchange for Napoleon's support against the Turks. Neither party kept the bargain. Napoleon once again had turned the divisions among his enemies in his favor.

Wherever the Grand Army conquered, Napoleon's influence soon followed. By annexing some territories and setting up others as satellite kingdoms with much-reduced autonomy, Napoleon attempted to colonize large parts of Europe. He brought the disparate German and Italian states together to rule them more effectively and to exploit their resources for his own ends. In 1806, he established the Confederation of the Rhine, which soon included almost all the German states except Austria and Prussia. The Holy Roman Emperor gave up his title, held since the thirteenth century, and became simply the emperor of Austria. Napoleon established three units in Italy: the territories directly annexed to France and the satellite kingdoms of Italy and Naples. Italy had not been so unified since the Roman Empire.

Consolidation of German and Italian States, 1812

Napoleon forced French-style reforms on both the annexed territories, which were ruled directly from France, and the satellite kingdoms, which were usually ruled by one or another of Napoleon's relatives but with a certain autonomy. Napoleon brought in French experts to work with handpicked locals to abolish serfdom, eliminate seigneurial dues, introduce the Napoleonic Code, suppress monasteries, subordinate church to state, and extend civil rights to Jews and other religious minorities. Reactions to these innovations were mixed. Napoleon's chosen rulers often made real improvements in roads, public works, law codes, and education. Yet tax increases and ever-rising conscription quotas also fomented discontent. The annexed territories and satellite kingdoms paid half the French war expenses. Napoleon's brother Louis would not allow conscription in his kingdom of the Netherlands because the Dutch had never had compulsory military service. In 1810, Napoleon annexed the satellite kingdom because his brother had become too sympathetic to Dutch interests.

Napoleon's victories forced defeated rulers to rethink their political and cultural assumptions. After suffering a crushing military defeat in 1806, Prussian king Frederick William III (r. 1797–1840) appointed a reform commission, and on its recommendation he abolished serfdom. Peasants gained their personal independence from their noble landlords, who could no longer sell them to pay gambling debts, for example, or refuse them permission to marry. Yet the lives of the former serfs remained bleak; they were left without land, and their landlords no longer had to care for them in hard times. The king's advisers also overhauled the army to make the high command more efficient and to open the way to the appointment of middle-class officers. Prussia instituted these reforms to try to compete with the French, not to promote democracy. As one reformer wrote to Frederick William, "We must do from above what the French have done from below."

Reform received lip service in Russia. Tsar Alexander I had gained his throne after an aristocratic coup deposed and killed his autocratic and capricious father, Paul (r. 1796–1801), and in the early years of his reign the remorseful young ruler created Western-style ministries, lifted restrictions on importing foreign books, and founded six new universities. There was even talk of drafting a constitution. But none of these efforts reached beneath the surface of Russian life, and by the second decade of his reign Alexander began to reject the Enlightenment spirit that his grandmother Catherine the Great had instilled in him.

Napoleon's Fall

Napoleon's empire ultimately failed because it was based on a contradiction: Napoleon tried to reduce almost all of Europe to the status of colonial dependents even though Europe had long consisted of independent states. His actions resulted instead in a great upsurge of the nationalist feeling that has dominated European politics to the present.

The one power always standing between Napoleon and total dominance of Europe was Great Britain. The British ruled the seas and financed anyone who would oppose Napoleon. In an effort to bankrupt this "nation of shopkeepers" by choking its trade, Napoleon inaugurated the Continental System in 1806. It prohibited all commerce between Great Britain and France, as well as between Great Britain and France's dependent states and allies. At first the system worked: British exports dropped 20 percent in 1807–1808, and industrial production declined 10 percent; unemployment and a strike of sixty thousand workers in northern England resulted. The British retaliated by confiscating merchandise on ships, even those of powers neutral in the wars, that sailed to or from ports from which the British were excluded by the Continental System.

In the midst of continuing wars, however, the system proved impossible to enforce, and widespread smuggling brought British goods into the European market. British industrial growth continued despite some setbacks. Calico-printing works, for example, quadrupled their production, and imports of raw cotton increased 40 percent. At the same time, French and other continental industries benefited from the temporary protection from British competition. By 1814, the Italian city of Bologna had five hundred factories and Modena four hundred. The French suffered their greatest commercial losses in the port cities, whose trade with the Caribbean colonies had been disrupted by war and Haitian independence.

Smuggling British goods was only one way of opposing the French. Almost everywhere in Europe, resistance began as local opposition to French demands for money or for draftees, but it eventually prompted that patriotic defense of the nation known as nationalism. In southern Italy, gangs of bandits harassed the French army and local officials; thirty-three thousand Italian bandits were arrested in 1809 alone. But resistance continued through a network of secret societies, called the *carbonari* ("charcoal-burners"), which got its name from the practice of marking each new member's forehead with a charcoal mark. Throughout the nineteenth century, the *carbonari* played a leading role in Italian nationalism. In the German states, intellectuals wrote passionate defenses of the virtues of the German nation and of the superiority of German literature. One of the greatest writers of the age, Friedrich Schiller (1759–1805), typified the turn in German sentiment against French revolutionary politics:

> *Freedom is only in the realm of dreams*
> *And the beautiful blooms only in song.*

The German states experienced a profound artistic and intellectual revival, which eventually connected with anti-French nationalism. This renaissance included a resurgence of intellectual life in the universities, a thriving press, and the multiplication of Masonic lodges and literary clubs.

No nations bucked under Napoleon's reins more than Spain and Portugal. In 1807, Napoleon sent 100,000 troops through Spain to invade Portugal, Great Britain's ally. The royal family fled to the Portuguese colony of Brazil, but fighting continued, aided by a British army. When Napoleon got his brother Joseph named king of Spain in place of the senile Charles IV (r. 1788–1808), the Spanish clergy and nobles raised bands of peasants to fight the French occupiers. Even Napoleon's taking personal command of French forces failed to quell the Spanish, who for six years fought a war of national independence that pinned down some 250,000 French soldiers. Germaine de Staël commented that Napoleon "never understood that a war might be a crusade. . . . He never reckoned with the one power that no arms could overcome—the enthusiasm of a whole people."

More than a new feeling of nationalism was aroused in Spain. Peasants hated French requisitioning of their food supplies and sought to defend their priests against French anticlericalism. Spanish nobles feared revolutionary reforms and were willing to defend the old monarchy in the person of the young Ferdinand VII, heir to Charles IV, even while Ferdinand himself was congratulating Napoleon on his victories. The Spanish Catholic church spread anti-French propaganda that equated Napoleon with heresy. As the former archbishop of Seville wrote to the archbishop of Granada in 1808, "You realize that we must not recognize as king a free-mason, heretic, Lutheran, as are all the Bonapartes and the French nation." In this tense atmosphere, the Spanish peasant rebels, assisted by the British, countered

■ **Napoleon's Mamelukes Massacre the Spanish**
In one of the paintings he produced to criticize Napoleon's occupation of Spain, Second of May
1808 at the Puerta del Sol *(1814), Francisco Goya depicts the brutal suppression of the Spanish
revolt in Madrid against Napoleon. Napoleon used Mamelukes, Egyptian soldiers descended from
freed Turkish slaves. For the Spanish Christians—and for European viewers of the painting—use
of these mercenaries made the event even more horrifying. Europeans considered Muslims, and
Turks in particular, as menacing because the Europeans had been fighting them for centuries.*
(Museo del Prado, Madrid.)

every French massacre with atrocities of their own. They tortured their French prisoners (boiling one general alive) and lynched collaborators.

Despite opposition, Napoleon ruled over an extensive empire by 1812 (see
"Mapping the West," page 700). He controlled more territory than any European
ruler had since Roman times. Only two major European states remained fully
independent—Great Britain and Russia—but once allied they would successfully
challenge his dominion and draw many other states to their side. Britain sent aid
to the Portuguese and Spanish rebels, while Russia once again prepared for war.
Tsar Alexander I made peace with the Ottoman Turks and allied himself with Great
Britain and Sweden. In 1812, Napoleon invaded Russia with 250,000 horses and
600,000 men, including contingents of Italians, Poles, Swiss, Dutch, and Germans.
This daring move proved to be his undoing.

Napoleon followed his usual strategy of trying to strike quickly, but the Russian generals avoided confrontation and retreated eastward, destroying anything that might be useful to the invaders. In September, on the road to Moscow, Napoleon finally engaged the main Russian force in the gigantic battle of Borodino. French casualties were 30,000 men, including 47 generals; the Russians lost 45,000. Once again the Russians retreated, leaving Moscow undefended. Napoleon entered the deserted city, but the victory turned hollow because the departing Russians had set the wooden city on fire. Within a week, three-fourths of it had burned to the ground. Still Alexander refused to negotiate, and French morale plunged with worsening problems of supply. Weeks of constant marching in the dirt and heat had worn down the foot soldiers, who were dying of disease or deserting in large numbers.

In October, Napoleon began his retreat; in November came the cold. Napoleon himself reported that on November 14 the temperature fell to 24 degrees Fahrenheit. A German soldier in the Grand Army described trying to cook fistfuls of raw bran with snow to make something like bread. For him the retreat was "the indescribable horror of all possible plagues." Within a week, the Grand Army lost 30,000 horses and had to abandon most of its artillery and food supplies. Russian forces harassed the retreating army, now more pathetic than grand. By December, only 100,000 troops remained, one-sixth the original number, and the retreat had turned into a rout: the Russians had captured 200,000 soldiers, including 48 generals and 3,000 other officers.

Napoleon had made a classic military mistake that would be repeated by Adolf Hitler in World War II: fighting a war on two distant fronts simultaneously. The Spanish war tied down 250,000 French troops and forced Napoleon to bully Prussia and Austria into supplying soldiers of dubious loyalty for the Moscow campaign. They deserted at the first opportunity. The fighting in Spain and Portugal also worsened the already substantial logistical and communications problems involved in marching to Moscow.

Napoleon's humiliation might have been temporary if the British and Russians had not successfully organized a coalition to complete the job. Napoleon still had resources at his command; by the spring of 1813 he had replenished his army with another 250,000 men. With British financial support, Russian, Austrian, Prussian, and Swedish armies met the French outside Leipzig in October 1813 and defeated Napoleon in the Battle of the Nations. One by one, Napoleon's German allies deserted him to join the German nationalist "war of liberation." The Confederation of the Rhine dissolved, and the Dutch revolted and restored the prince of Orange. Joseph Bonaparte fled Spain, and a combined Spanish-Portuguese army under British command invaded France. In only a few months, the allied powers crossed the Rhine and marched toward Paris. In March 1814, the French Senate deposed Napoleon, who abdicated when his remaining generals refused to fight. Napoleon

IMPORTANT DATES

1787	Prussian invasion stifles Dutch Patriot revolt	1795	Third (final) Partition of Poland
1788	Beginning of resistance of Austrian Netherlands against reforms of Joseph II; opening of reform parliament in Poland	1799	Napoleon Bonaparte comes to power in a coup
1789	French Revolution begins	1801	Napoleon signs a concordat with the pope
1791	Beginning of slave revolt in St. Domingue (Haiti)	1804	Napoleon crowns himself emperor of France and issues new Civil Code
1792	Beginning of war between France and the rest of Europe; second revolution of August 10 overthrows French monarchy	1805	British naval forces defeat the French at the battle of Trafalgar; Napoleon wins his greatest victory at the battle of Austerlitz
1793	Second Partition of Poland by Austria and Russia; Louis XVI of France executed for treason	1812	Napoleon invades Russia
1794	France annexes the Austrian Netherlands; abolition of slavery in French colonies; Robespierre's government by terror falls	1815	Napoleon defeated at Waterloo and exiled to island of St. Helena, where he dies in 1821

went into exile on the island of Elba off the Italian coast. His wife, Marie-Louise, refused to accompany him. The allies restored to the throne Louis XVIII (r. 1814–1824), the brother of Louis XVI (whose son was known as Louis XVII even though he died in prison in 1795 without ever ruling).

Napoleon had one last chance to regain power because Louis XVIII lacked a solid base of support. The new king tried to steer a middle course through a charter that established a British-style monarchy with a two-house legislature and guaranteed civil rights. But he was caught between returning émigré nobles who demanded a complete restoration of their lands and powers and those who had supported either the republic or Napoleon during the previous twenty-five years. Sensing an opportunity, Napoleon escaped from Elba in early 1815 and, landing in southern France, made swift and unimpeded progress to Paris. Although he had left in ignominy, now crowds cheered him and former soldiers volunteered to serve him. The period known as the "Hundred Days" (the length of time between his escape and his final defeat) had begun. Louis XVIII fled across the border, waiting for help from France's enemies.

Napoleon quickly moved his reconstituted army into present-day Belgium. At first it seemed that he might succeed in separately fighting the two armies arrayed against him—a Prussian army and a joint force of Belgian, Dutch, German, and British troops led by Sir Arthur Wellesley (1769–1852), duke of Wellington. But the Prussians evaded him and joined with Wellington at Waterloo. Completely routed, Napoleon had no choice but to abdicate again. This time the victorious allies banished him permanently to the remote island of St. Helena, far off the coast of West Africa, where he died in 1821 at the age of fifty-two.

Conclusion

The cost of Napoleon's rule was high: 750,000 French soldiers and 400,000 others from annexed and satellite states died fighting for the French between 1800 and 1815. The losses among those attempting to stop Napoleon were at least as high, but no military figure since Alexander the Great in the fourth century B.C. had made such an impact on world history. Napoleon's plans for a united Europe, his insistence on spreading the legal reforms of the French Revolution, his social welfare programs, and even his inadvertent awakening of national sentiment set the agenda for European history in the modern era.

The revolutionary cataclysm permanently altered the political landscape of Europe. The French executed their king as a traitor and set up Europe's first republic with universal male suffrage and a written guarantee of "the rights of man." Ordinary people marched in demonstrations, met in clubs, and in the case of men, voted in national elections for the first time. They got their first taste of democracy. But the ideals of universal education, religious toleration, and democratic participation could not prevent the institution of new forms of government terror to persecute, imprison, and kill dissidents. The French revolutionary experiment thus led to democracy *and* to a kind of totalitarianism. The French used the new spirit of national pride to inspire a huge citizen army, but the army conquered other peoples and gave a leading general the chance to take power for himself. Napoleon in turn created yet another new form of rule with a long history in the modern era: a police state in which the generals played a leading political role. Napoleon suppressed all other meaningful political participation and offered in its place law and order and modernization from above. Like many other authoritarian rulers after him, however, Napoleon could not maintain his position once he lost in battle.

As events unfolded between 1789 and 1815, the French Revolution became *the* model of modern revolution and in the process set the enduring patterns of all modern politics. Republicanism, democracy, terrorism, nationalism, and military dictatorship all took their modern forms during the French Revolution. Even the terms *left* and *right* got their political meaning in this period: "the left" was a

■ **MAPPING THE WEST** Europe under Napoleonic Domination, 1812

In 1812, Napoleon had at least nominal control of almost all of western Europe. Even before he made his fatal mistake of invading Russia, however, his authority had been undermined in Spain and seriously weakened in the Italian and German states. His efforts to extend French power sparked resistance almost everywhere. As Napoleon insisted on French domination, local people began to think of themselves as Italian, German, or Dutch. Thus Napoleon inadvertently laid the foundations for the nineteenth-century spread of nationalism.

reference to deputies who favored extensive change and sat together in seats to the speaker's left in 1789; deputies who preferred a more cautious and conservative stance sat as a group to the speaker's right. The breathtaking succession of regimes in France between 1789 and 1815 inevitably raised disturbing questions about the relationship between rapid political change and violence. Do all revolutions in the name of democracy inevitably degenerate into wars of conquest or terror? Is a regime democratic if it does not allow poor men, women, or blacks to vote? Is a militaristic, authoritarian style of government the only answer to divisive political conflicts in a time of war? The French Revolution and its aftermath—the era of Napoleon—raised these questions and many more.

Suggested References for further reading and online research appear on page SR-25 at the back of the book.

www.bedfordstmartins.com/huntconcise   See the ONLINE STUDY GUIDE to assess your mastery of the material covered in this chapter.

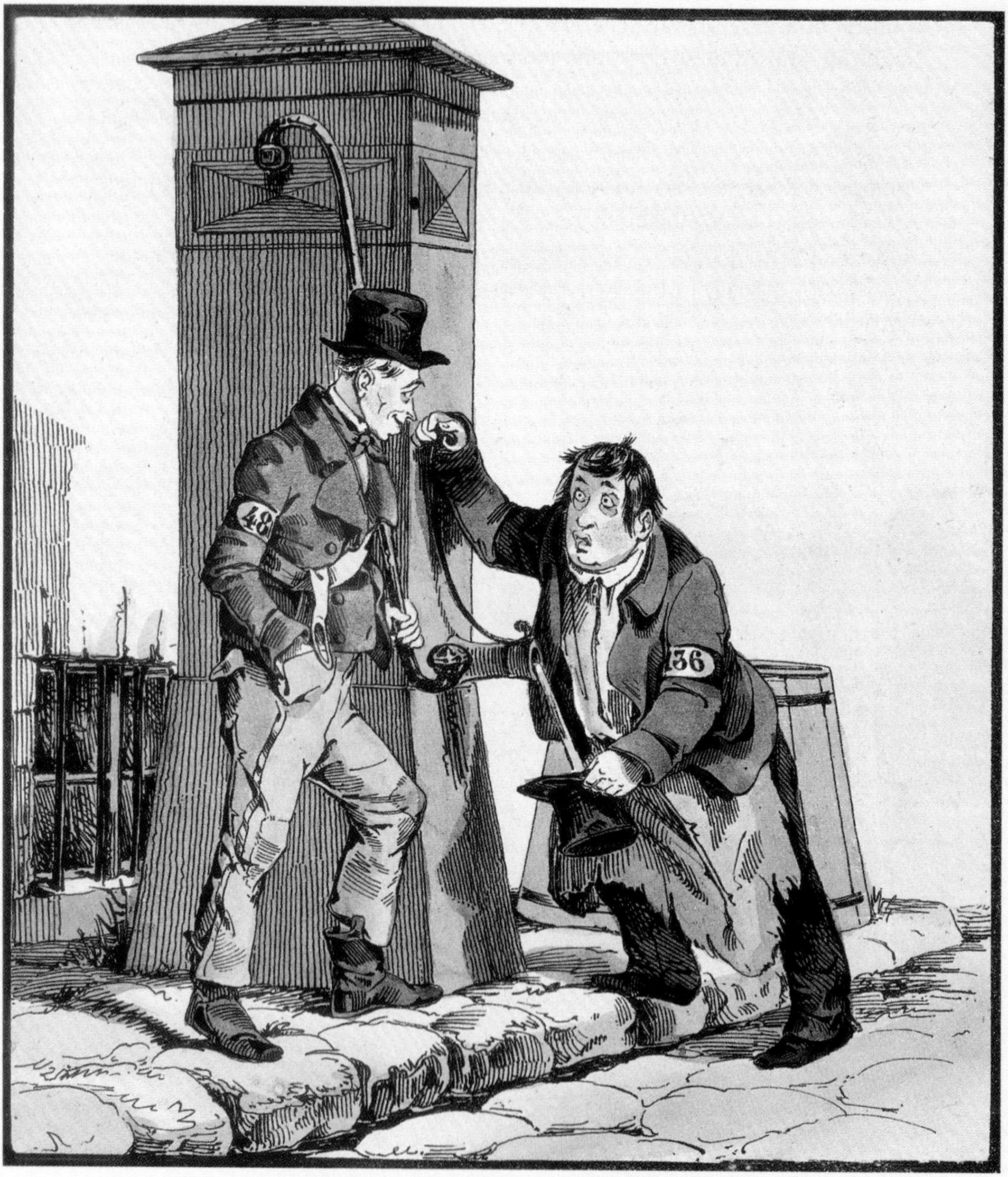
48
136

17

Industrialization and Social Ferment

1815–1850

A POPULAR GERMAN LITHOGRAPH published around 1830 shows two drunken workingmen standing in front of a water pump in Berlin. In the lithograph's caption, one says, "What'd you think, Schulze, what if that were Kümmel [the Berlin liqueur made with caraway]?" His comrade responds, "Yeah, that would be my first wish if I could wish three times." "So, and the second?" "That all [water] pumps were full of Kümmel."* The lithograph captures the new preoccupation with lower-class behavior in this time of social change and political upheaval. As industrialization spread across western Europe, peasants and workers streamed into the cities, creating unprecedented social problems. The population of Berlin, for example, more than doubled between 1819 and 1849, reaching 412,000. Already by 1840, more than half the residents of Berlin had been born outside the city. Many feared that the flood of newcomers would encourage the spread of disease, crime, and social unrest.

Although the people of Europe longed for peace and stability in the aftermath of the Napoleonic whirlwind, they lived in a world that was deeply unsettled

---

*Translation from Mary Lee Townsend, *Forbidden Laughter: Popular Humor and the Limits of Repression in Nineteenth-Century Prussia* (Ann Arbor: University of Michigan Press, 1992), 10.

■ **Drink and the Working Class**
In his lithograph Two Drunken Day Laborers *(c. 1830), the German artist Franz Burchard Dörbeck calls attention to the propensity of the working classes to drink. Lithography (from the Greek* lithos, "stone") *was invented by a German engraver in 1798, but its use spread across Europe only in the nineteenth century. The artist used a greasy crayon to trace an image on a flat stone. The grease attracted ink; the blank areas repelled it. The inked stone was embedded in a printing press that could produce thousands of identical images. By creating pictures of every class in society and their problems, and by publishing their images in daily and weekly newspapers, artists enlightened a mass audience about social and political problems created by industrial and urban growth.* (Stadtmuseum Berlin; photo: Hans-Joachim Bartsch, Berlin.)

703

by two parallel revolutions: the French Revolution and the Industrial Revolution. Even as restored monarchs tried to limit challenges to their rule, the French Revolution and its Napoleonic sequel created new expectations for constitutional government, democracy, and national self-determination. At the same time, the Industrial Revolution spread from Great Britain to continental Europe in the form of factories and railroads. Industrialization produced new social problems that reinforced demands for political change. Under the impact of the French and Industrial Revolutions, new ideologies emerged. Conservatism, nationalism, liberalism, socialism, and communism each offered their adherents a doctrine that explained social change and advocated a political program to confront it.

Social ferment bubbled up in a variety of forms. Painters, poets, and musicians advocated the new style of romanticism. While novelists depicted the social types created by economic change, middle-class men and women joined together in reform societies to urge specific programs for fighting prostitution, assisting poor mothers, encouraging temperance (abstention from alcohol), or abolishing slavery. Despite these efforts at reform, the most unfortunate sometimes pulled up stakes and emigrated to other places, such as the United States. Between 1815 and 1850, more than five million Europeans left their home countries for new lives overseas. For those who stayed behind, revolution remained an ever-present option. Political revolts shook Spain, Italy, Russia, Greece and almost all of Latin America in the 1820s. In 1830, a wave of liberal and nationalist revolutions washed over France, Belgium, Poland, and some of the Italian states. In 1848, yet another French Revolution sparked uprisings in much of Europe. Social ferment threatened to transform into cataclysmic upheaval.

The "Restoration" of Europe

When Napoleon went off to his permanent exile on St. Helena, those allied against him breathed a collective sigh of relief. Revolution, it seemed, had finally been defeated. Some of the returning rulers so detested French innovations that they tore French plants out of their gardens and threw French furniture out of their palaces. Even as Napoleon had made his last desperate bid for power in the Hundred Days between his escape from Elba and his final defeat, his enemies were meeting in the Congress of Vienna (1814–1815) to decide the fate of postrevolutionary Europe. Many of Europe's rulers hoped to nullify revolutionary and Napoleonic reforms and "restore" their old regimes; the Congress of Vienna settled the boundaries of European states, determining who would rule each nation. The congress also established a new framework for international relations based on periodic meetings—congresses—between the major powers. This congress system, or "concert of Europe," helped prevent another major war until the 1850s, and no conflict comparable to the Napoleonic wars would occur again until 1914.

The Congress of Vienna, 1814–1815

The Vienna settlement produced a new equilibrium that relied on cooperation among the major powers while guaranteeing the status of smaller states. In addition to determining the boundaries of France, the congress had to decide the fate of Napoleon's duchy of Warsaw, the German province of Saxony, the Netherlands, the states once part of the confederation of the Rhine, and various Italian territories. All had either changed hands or been created during the wars. These issues were resolved by face-to-face negotiations among representatives of the five major powers: Austria, Russia, Prussia, Britain, and France. With its aim to arrange a long-lasting, negotiated peace endorsed by all parties—both winners and losers—the Congress of Vienna provided a model for the twentieth-century League of Nations and United Nations.

Austria's chief negotiator, Prince Klemens von Metternich (1773–1859), took the lead in negotiations. A well-educated nobleman who spoke five languages, Metternich served as a minister in the Austrian cabinet from 1809 to 1848. Although his penchant for womanizing made him a security risk in the eyes of the British Foreign Office (he even had an affair with Napoleon's younger sister), he worked with the British prime minister Robert Castlereagh (1769–1822) to ensure a moderate

■ **The Congress of Vienna**

An unknown French engraver caricatured the efforts of the diplomats at the Congress of Vienna, complaining that they used the occasion to divide the spoils of European territory. At the far left stands Metternich preparing to take Venice and Lombardy (northern Italy).

(Historisches Museum der Stadt Wien.)

agreement that would check French aggression yet maintain France's great-power status. Metternich and Castlereagh believed that France must remain a major player so that no one European power might dominate the others. In this way, France could help Austria and Britain counter the ambitions of Prussia and Russia. When the French army failed to oppose Napoleon's return to power in the Hundred Days, the allies took away all territory conquered by France since 1790 and required France to pay an indemnity and support an army of occupation until it was paid.

The goal of the congress was to achieve postwar stability by establishing secure states with guaranteed borders (Map 17.1). Where possible, the congress simply re-

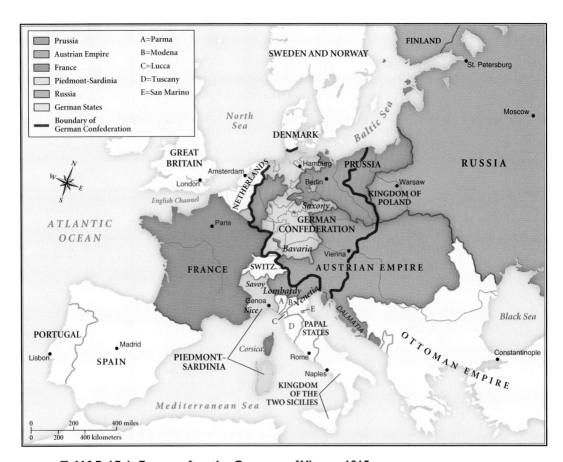

■ **MAP 17.1 Europe after the Congress of Vienna, 1815**

The diplomats meeting at the Congress of Vienna could not simply "restore" Europe to its prerevolutionary borders. Too much had changed since 1789. France was forced to return to its 1790 borders, and Spain and Portugal regained their former rulers. The Austrian Netherlands and the Dutch Republic were united in a new kingdom of the Netherlands, the German states were joined in a Germanic Confederation that built upon Napoleon's Confederation of the Rhine, and Napoleon's Grand Duchy of Warsaw became the kingdom of Poland with the tsar of Russia as king.

stored traditional rulers, as in Spain and the Italian states. The great powers decided to turn Napoleon's duchy of Warsaw into a new Polish kingdom but made the tsar of Russia its king. (Poland would not regain its independence until 1918.) The former Dutch Republic and the Austrian Netherlands, both annexed to France, now united as the new kingdom of the Netherlands under the restored stadholder. Prussia gained territory in Saxony and on the left bank of the Rhine to compensate for its losses in Poland. To make up for its losses in Poland and Saxony, Austria reclaimed the Italian provinces of Lombardy and Venetia and the Dalmatian coast. Austria now presided over the German Confederation, which replaced the defunct Holy Roman Empire and also included Prussia.

The lesser powers were not forgotten. The kingdom of Piedmont-Sardinia took Genoa, Nice, and part of Savoy. Sweden obtained Norway from Denmark but had to accept Russia's conquest of Finland. Finally, various international trade issues were also resolved. At the urging of Great Britain, the congress agreed to condemn in principle the slave trade, abolished by Great Britain in 1807. In reality, however, the slave trade continued in many places until the 1840s.

To impart spiritual substance to this very calculated settlement of political affairs, Tsar Alexander proposed a Holy Alliance that would ensure divine assistance in upholding religion, peace, and justice. Prussia and Austria signed the agreement, but Great Britain refused to accede to what Castlereagh called "a piece of sublime mysticism and nonsense." Pope Pius VII also refused on the grounds that the papacy needed no help in interpreting the Christian truth. Despite the reassertion of traditional religious principle, the congress had in fact given birth to a new diplomatic order: in the future, the legitimacy of states depended on the treaty system, not on divine right.

The Emergence of Conservatism

The French Revolution and Napoleonic domination of Europe had shown contemporaries that government could be changed overnight, that the old hierarchies could be overthrown in the name of reason, and that even Christianity could be written off or at least profoundly altered with the stroke of a pen. The potential for rapid change raised many questions about the proper sources of authority. Kings and churches could be restored and former revolutionaries locked up or silenced, but the old order no longer commanded automatic obedience. The old order was now merely *old,* no longer "natural" and "timeless." It had been ousted once and therefore might fall again. People insisted on having reasons to believe in their "restored" governments. The political doctrine that justified the restoration was *conservatism.*

Conservatives benefited from the disillusionment that permeated Europe after 1815. In the eyes of most Europeans, Napoleon had become a tyrant who ruled in his own interests. Conservatives believed it was crucial to analyze the roots of such tyranny so established authorities could use their knowledge of history to prevent its recurrence. They saw a logical progression in recent history: the Enlightenment based on reason led to the French Revolution, with its bloody guillotine and horrifying Terror, which in turn spawned the authoritarian and militaristic Napoleon. Conservative intellectuals therefore either rejected Enlightenment principles or at least subjected them to scrutiny and skepticism.

The most influential spokesman of conservatism was Edmund Burke (1729–1799), the British critic of the French Revolution. He argued that the revolutionaries erred in thinking they could construct an entirely new government based on reason. Government, Burke said, had to be rooted in long experience, which evolved over generations. All change must be gradual and must respect national and historical traditions.

Like Burke, later conservatives believed that religious and other major traditions were an essential foundation for any society. Conservatives blamed the French Revolution's attack on religion on the skepticism and anticlericalism of such Enlightenment thinkers as Voltaire, and they defended both hereditary monarchy and the authority of the church, whether Catholic or Protestant. The "rights of man," according to conservatives, could not stand alone as doctrine based simply on nature and reason. The community, too, had its rights, more important than those of any individual, and established institutions best represented those rights. The church, the state, and the family would provide an enduring social order for everyone. Faith, sentiment, history, and tradition must fill the vacuum left by the failures of reason and excessive belief in individual rights. Across Europe, these views were taken up and elaborated by government advisers, professors, and writers. Not surprisingly, they had their strongest appeal in ruling circles and guided the politics of men such as Metternich in Austria and Alexander I in Russia.

The restored monarchy in France provided a major test for conservatism because the returning Bourbons had to confront the legacy of twenty-five years of upheaval. Louis XVIII (r. 1814–1824) tried to ensure a measure of continuity by maintaining Napoleon's Civil Code. He also guaranteed the rights of ownership to church lands sold during the revolutionary period and created a parliament composed of a Chamber of Peers nominated by the king and a Chamber of Deputies elected by very restricted suffrage (fewer than 100,000 voters in a population of 30 million, or about 3 percent). In making these concessions, the king tried to follow a moderate course of compromise, but the Ultras (ultraroyalists) pushed for complete repudiation of the revolutionary past. When Louis returned to power after Napoleon's final defeat, armed royalist bands attacked and murdered hundreds of Bonapartists and former revolutionaries. In 1816, the Ultras insisted on abolishing divorce and set up special courts to punish opponents of the regime. When an assassin killed Louis XVIII's nephew in 1820, the Ultras demanded even more extreme measures.

The Revival of Religion

The experience of revolutionary upheaval and nearly constant warfare prompted many to renew their religious faith once peace returned. In France, the Catholic church sent missionaries to hold open-air "ceremonies of reparation" to express repentance for the outrages of revolution. In Rome, the papacy reestablished the Jesuit order, which had been disbanded during the Enlightenment. In the Italian states and Spain, governments used religious societies of laypeople to combat the influence of reformers and nationalists such as the Italian *carbonari*.

Revivalist movements, especially in Protestant countries, could on occasion challenge the status quo, not support it. In parts of the Protestant German states and Britain, religious revival had begun in the eighteenth century with the rise of Pietism and Methodism, movements that stressed individual religious experience rather than reason as the true path to moral and social reform. The English Methodists followed John Wesley (1703–1791), who preached an emotional, morally austere, and very personal "method" of gaining salvation. The Methodists, or Wesleyans, gradually separated from the Church of England and in the early decades of the nineteenth century attracted thousands of members in huge revival meetings that lasted for days. Shopkeepers, artisans, agricultural laborers, miners, and workers in cottage industry, both male and female, flocked to the new denomination. Even though Methodist statutes of 1792 had insisted that "none of us shall either in writing or in conversation speak lightly or irreverently of the government," Methodists fostered a sense of democratic community with their hostility to elaborate ritual and their encouragement of popular preaching. Methodist women traveled on horseback to preach in barns, town halls, and textile dye houses. Methodist Sunday schools that taught thousands of poor children to read and write eventually helped create greater demands for working-class political participation.

The religious revival was not limited to Europe. In the United States, the second "Great Awakening" began around 1790 with huge camp meetings that brought together thousands of people, many of them Methodist. (The original Great Awakening took place in the 1730s and 1740s, sparked by the preaching of George Whitefield, a young English evangelist and follower of John Wesley.) During this period, Protestant sects began systematic missionary activity in other parts of the world, with British and American missionary societies taking the lead in the 1790s and early 1800s. In the British colony of India, Protestant missionaries argued for the reform of Hindu customs. *Sati*—the burning of widows on the funeral pyres of their husbands—was abolished by the British administration of India in 1829. Missionary activity by Protestants and Catholics would become one of the arms of European imperialism and cultural influence in the nineteenth century.

Political Challenges to the Conservative Order

The conservative Vienna settlement disappointed all those who dreamed of constitutional freedoms and national independence, and within a few years, discontent rose to the surface. The Vienna powers joined together to confront these challenges, and they succeeded in areas where they were able to intervene militarily, most notably Spain and the Italian states. In Greece and Latin America, however, revolts for national independence succeeded. The Greeks eventually obtained European support because they wanted freedom from Europe's traditional enemy, the Ottoman Turks. The Latin Americans won their independence because Napoleon's occupation had undermined the authority of the Spanish and Portuguese rulers.

When Ferdinand VII regained the Spanish crown in 1814, he created opposition with extreme measures to restore the powers of the prerevolutionary nobility, church, and monarchy. He had foreign books and newspapers confiscated at the frontier and allowed the publication of only two newspapers. In 1820, disgruntled soldiers demanded that Ferdinand proclaim his adherence to the Constitution of 1812, which he had abolished in 1814. When the revolt spread, Ferdinand convened the *cortes* (parliament), which could agree on practically nothing. Ferdinand bided his time, and in 1823 a French army invaded with the consent of the other Vienna powers and restored him to power. His government then tortured and executed hundreds of rebels; thousands were imprisoned or forced into exile.

Hearing of the Spanish uprising, rebellious soldiers in the kingdom of Naples joined forces with the *carbonari* and demanded a constitution. When a new parliament met, it, too, broke down over internal disagreements. The promise of reform sparked rebellion in the northern Italian kingdom of Piedmont-Sardinia, where rebels urged Charles Albert, the young heir to the Piedmont throne, to fight the Austrians for Italian unification. He vacillated; but in 1821, after the rulers of Austria, Prussia, and Russia met and agreed on intervention, the Austrians defeated the rebels in Naples and Piedmont (see Map 17.1). Liberals were arrested in many Italian states, and the pope condemned the secret societies as "at heart only devouring wolves." Despite the opposition of Great Britain, which condemned the "indiscriminate" suppression of revolutionary movements, Metternich convinced the other powers to agree to his muffling of the Italian opposition to Austrian rule.

Aspirations for constitutional government surfaced in Russia when Alexander I died suddenly in 1825. On the December day that the troops assembled in St. Petersburg to take an oath of loyalty to Alexander's brother Nicholas as the new tsar, rebel officers insisted that the crown belonged to another brother, Constantine, who they hoped would be more favorable to constitutional reform. Constantine, though next in the line of succession after Alexander, had refused the crown. The soldiers nonetheless raised the cry "Long live Constantine, long live the Constitution." (Some troops apparently thought that "the Constitution" was Constantine's wife.) Soldiers loyal to Nicholas easily suppressed the Decembrists (so called after the month of their uprising), who were so outnumbered that they had no realistic chance to succeed. The subsequent trial, however, made the rebels into legendary heroes. For the next thirty years, Nicholas I (r. 1825–1855) used a new political police, the Third Section, to spy on potential opponents and stamp out rebelliousness.

The Ottoman Turks faced growing nationalist challenges in the Balkans, but the European powers feared that supporting them would encourage a rebellious spirit at home. The Serbs revolted against Turkish rule and won virtual independence by 1817. A Greek general in the Russian army, Prince Alexander Ypsilanti, tried to lead a revolt against the Turks in 1820 but failed when the tsar, urged on by Metternich, disavowed him. Metternich feared rebellion even by Christians against their Turkish rulers. A second revolt, this time by Greek peasants, sparked a wave of atrocities in 1821 and 1822. The Greeks killed every Turk who did not escape. In retaliation the Turks hanged the Greek patriarch (head of the Greek Orthodox church), and in the areas they still controlled they pillaged churches, massacred thousands of men, and sold the women into slavery.

Nationalistic Movements in the Balkans, 1815–1830

Western opinion turned against the Turks; Greece, after all, was the home of Western civilization. While the great powers negotiated, Greeks and pro-Greece committees around the world sent food and military supplies; a few enthusiastic European and American volunteers even joined the Greeks. The Greeks held on until the great powers were willing to intervene. In 1827, a combined force of British, French, and Russian ships destroyed the Turkish fleet at Navarino Bay; and in 1828, Russia declared war on the Turks and advanced close to Istanbul. The Treaty of Adrianople of 1829 gave Russia a protectorate over the Danubian principalities in the Balkans and provided for a conference among representatives of Britain, Russia, and France, all of whom had broken with Austria in support of the Greeks. In 1830, Greece was declared an independent kingdom under the guarantee of the three powers; in 1833, the son of King Ludwig of Bavaria became Otto I of Greece. Nationalism, with the support of European public opinion, had made its first breach in Metternich's system.

■ **Greek Independence**
From 1836 to 1839, the Greek painter Panagiotis Zographos worked with his two sons on a series of scenes depicting the Greek struggle for independence from the Turks. Response was so favorable that one Greek general ordered lithographic reproductions for popular distribution. In this way, nationalistic feeling could be encouraged even among people not directly touched by the struggle. Here Turkish sultan Mehmet the Conqueror, exulting over the fall of Constantinople in 1453, views a row of Greeks under the yoke, a sign of submission.
(Collection, Visual Connection.)

Across the Atlantic, national revolts also succeeded after a series of bloody wars of independence. Taking advantage of the upheavals in Spain and Portugal that began under Napoleon, restive colonists from Mexico to Argentina rebelled. Their leader was Simon Bolívar (1783–1830), son of a slave owner, who was educated in Europe on the works of Voltaire and Rousseau. Although Bolívar fancied himself a Latin American Napoleon, he had to acquiesce to the formation of a series of independent republics between 1821 and 1823, even in Bolivia, which is named after him. At the same time, Brazil (then still a monarchy) separated from Portugal (Map 17.2). The United States recognized the new states, and in 1823 President James Monroe (1758–1831) announced his Monroe Doctrine, closing the Americas to European intervention—a prohibition that depended on British naval power and British willingness to declare neutrality.

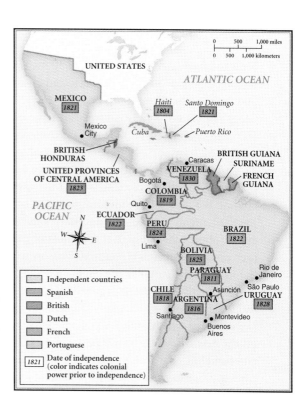

■ **MAP 17.2 Latin American Independence, 1804–1830**
The French lost their most important remaining American colony in 1804 when St. Domingue declared its independence as Haiti. But the impact of the French Revolution did not end there. Napoleon's occupation of Spain and Portugal seriously weakened the hold of those countries on their Latin American colonies. Despite the restoration of the Spanish and Portuguese rulers in 1814, most of their colonies successfully broke away in a wave of rebellions between 1811 and 1830. Meanwhile, a revolt in Spain in 1820–1823 led to a constitutional regime. The Spanish general sent to suppress the revolt in Mexico ended up joining the rebels' cause and helping them establish independence in 1821.

The Advance of Industrialization and Urbanization

French and English writers of the 1820s introduced the term *Industrial Revolution* to capture the drama of contemporary economic change and to draw a parallel with the French Revolution. But we should not take the comparison too literally. Unlike the French upheaval, the Industrial Revolution did not have definite dates that marked its beginning or ending. From their first appearance in Great Britain in the second half of the eighteenth century, steam-driven machinery, large factories, and a new working class spread slowly to the rest of Europe and eventually to the rest of the world. Still, historians have shown that industrialization and its corollary urbanization accelerated quite suddenly in the first half of the nineteenth century and touched off loud complaints about their effects. Contemporaries did not fully understand the link between industrial and urban growth, and even today, scholars debate the connection. Population growth did not just change life in the cities; it produced new tensions in the countryside, too.

The Rise of the Railroad

Steam-driven engines took on a dramatic new form in the 1820s when the English engineer George Stephenson perfected an engine to pull wagons along rail tracks. Suddenly, railroad building became a new industry. (See "Taking Measure," page 715.) The idea of a railroad was not new: iron tracks had been used since the seventeenth century to haul coal from mines in wagons pulled by horses. A railroad system of transport, however, developed only after Stephenson's invention of a steam-powered locomotive. In 1830, the Liverpool and Manchester Railway line opened to the cheers of crowds and the congratulations of government officials, including the duke of Wellington, the hero of Waterloo and now prime minister. In the excitement, some of the dignitaries gathered on a parallel track. When another engine approached at high speed, most of the gentlemen scattered to safety, but former cabinet minister William Huskisson fell and was hit. In a few hours he died, the first official casualty of the newfangled railroad.

Railroads were dramatic and expensive—the most striking symbol of the new industrial age. One German entrepreneur confidently predicted, "The locomotive is the hearse which will carry absolutism and feudalism to the graveyard." Placed on the new tracks, steam-driven carriages could transport people and goods to the cities and link coal and iron deposits to the new factories. In the 1840s alone, railroad track mileage more than doubled in Great Britain, and British investment in railways jumped tenfold. The British also began to build railroads in India. Canal building waned in the 1840s: the railroad had won out.

Britain's success with rail transportation led other countries to develop their own projects. Railroads grew spectacularly in the United States in the 1830s and 1840s. Belgium, newly independent in 1830, opened the first continental European railroad with state bonds backed by British capital in 1835. By 1850, France had 2,000 miles of railroad and the German states nearly twice as many; Great Britain had 6,000 miles and the United States 9,000 miles. In all, the world had 23,500 miles of track by midcentury.

Railroad building spurred both industrial development and state power (see "Mapping the West," page 752). Governments everywhere participated in the construction of railroads, which depended on private and state funds to pay for the massive amounts of iron, coal, heavy machinery, and human labor required to build and run them. One-third of all investment in the German states in the 1840s went into railroads. Demand for iron products accelerated industrial development. Until the 1840s, cotton had led industrial production; between 1816 and 1840, cotton output more than quadrupled in Great Britain. But from 1830 to 1850, Britain's output of iron and coal doubled. Similarly, Austrian output of iron doubled between the 1820s and the 1840s.

Steam-powered engines made Britain the world leader in manufacturing. By midcentury, more than half of Britain's national income came from manufacturing and trade. The number of steamboats in Great Britain increased from two in 1812 to six

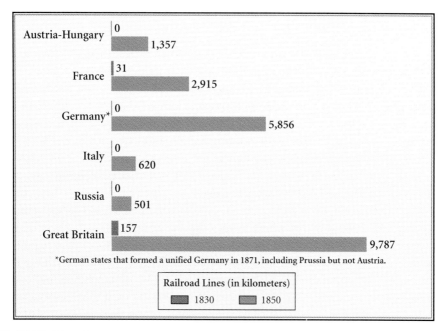

■ TAKING MEASURE Railroad Lines, 1830–1850

Great Britain quickly extended its lead in building railroads. The extension of commerce and, before long, the ability to wage war would depend on the development of effective rail networks. These statistics might be taken as predicting a realignment of power within Europe after 1850. What do the numbers say about the relative positions of Germany and Austria-Hungary and of Germany and France?

(From B. R. Mitchell, *European Historical Statistics, 1750–1970* [New York: Columbia University Press, 1975], F1.)

hundred in 1840. Between 1840 and 1850, steam-engine power doubled in Great Britain and increased even more rapidly elsewhere in Europe, as those adopting British inventions strove to catch up. The power applied in German manufacturing, for example, rose from 60,000 to 360,000 hp (units horsepower) during the 1840s but still amounted to only a little more than a quarter of the British figure.

Although Great Britain consciously strove to protect its industrial supremacy, thousands of British engineers defied laws against the export of machinery or the emigration of artisans. The best known of them, John Cockerill, set up a machine works in Belgium that was soon selling its products as far east as Poland and Russia. Cockerill claimed to know about every innovation within ten days of its appearance in Britain. Only slowly, thanks to such pirating of British methods and to new technical schools, did most continental European countries begin closing the gap. Belgium became the fastest-growing industrial power on the continent: between 1830 and 1844, the number of steam engines in Belgium quadrupled, and Belgians exported seven times as many steam engines as they imported. Even so, by 1850, continental Europe still lagged almost twenty years behind Great Britain in industrial development.

Formation of the Working Class

Steam-driven machines first brought workers together in factories in the textile industry. By 1830, more than one million people in Britain depended on the cotton industry for employment, and cotton cloth constituted 50 percent of the country's exports. The rapid expansion of the British textile industry had as its colonial corollary the destruction of the hand manufacture of textiles in India. The British put high import duties on Indian cloth entering Britain and kept such duties very low for British cloth entering India. The figures are dramatic: in 1813, the Indian city of Calcutta exported to England £2,000,000 of cotton cloth; by 1830, Calcutta was importing from England £2,000,000 of cotton cloth. When Britain abolished slavery in its Caribbean colonies in 1833, British manufacturers began to buy raw cotton in the southern United States, where slavery still flourished.

Factories drew workers from the urban population surge, which had begun in the eighteenth century and now accelerated. The reasons for urban growth are not entirely clear. The population of such new industrial cities as Manchester and Leeds increased 40 percent in the 1820s alone. Historians long thought that factory workers came from the countryside, pushed off the land by the field enclosures of the 1700s. But recent studies have shown that the number of agricultural laborers actually increased during industrialization in Britain, suggesting that a growing birthrate created a larger population and fed workers into the new factory system.

The new workers came from several sources: families of farmers who could not provide land for all their children, soldiers demobilized after the Napoleonic wars, artisans displaced by the new machinery, and children of the earliest workers who had moved to the factory towns. A system of employment that resembled family labor on farms or in cottage industry also developed in the new factories. Entire families came to toil for a single wage, although family members performed different tasks. Workdays of twelve to seventeen hours were typical, even for children, and the work was grueling. Community ties remained important as workers migrated from rural to urban areas to join friends and family from their original villages.

As urban factories grew, their workers gradually came to constitute a new socioeconomic class with a distinctive culture and traditions. Like *middle class*, the term *working class* came into use for the first time in the early nineteenth century. It referred to the laborers in the new factories. In the past, workers had labored in isolated trades: water and wood carrying, gardening, laundry, and building. In contrast, factories brought people together with machines, under close supervision by their employers. They soon developed a sense of common interests and organized societies for mutual help and political reform. From these would come the first labor unions.

Fearing their displacement by machines, bands of handloom weavers wrecked factory machinery and burned mills in the Midlands, Yorkshire, and Lancashire. To restore order and protect industry, the British government sent in an army of twelve thousand regular soldiers and made machine wrecking punishable by death. The rioters were called *Luddites* after the fictitious figure Ned Ludd, whose signature appeared on their manifestos. (The term is still used to describe those who resist new technology.)

Other British workers focused their organizing efforts on reforming Parliament, whose members were chosen in elections dominated by the landowning elite. One reformer complained that the members of the House of Commons were nothing but "toad-eaters, gamblers, public plunderers, and hirelings." Reform clubs held large open-air meetings, and ordinary people eagerly bought cheap newspapers that clamored for change. In August 1819, sixty thousand people attended an illegal meeting held in St. Peter's Fields in Manchester. When the local authorities sent the cavalry to arrest the speaker, panic resulted; eleven people were killed and many hundreds injured. Punsters called it the Battle of Peterloo or the Peterloo Massacre. An alarmed government passed the Six Acts, which forbade large political meetings and restricted press criticism, suppressing the reform movement for a decade.

Despite striking industrial growth, factory workers remained a minority everywhere. In the 1840s, factories in England employed only 5 percent of the workers; in France, 3 percent; in Prussia, 2 percent. Many peasants kept their options open by combining factory work with agricultural labor. They worked in agriculture during the spring and summer and in manufacturing in the fall and winter. Unstable industrial wages made such arrangements essential. Some new industries idled periodically: for example, iron forges stopped for several months when the water level in streams dropped, and blast furnaces shut down for repairs several weeks every year. In hard times, factory owners simply closed their doors until demand for their goods improved.

In addition, workers, both men and women, continued to toil at home in putting-out, or cottage, industries. In the 1840s, for example, two-thirds of the manufacturing workers in Prussia and Saxony labored at home for contractors or merchants who supplied raw materials and then sold the finished goods. Even without mechanization, some of the old forms of putting-out work changed, however. Tailoring, for example, had been the province of male artisans preparing entire garments in small shops but was now broken up into piecework that was farmed out to women working at home for much lower "piece rates."

Even though factories employed only a small percentage of the population, they attracted much attention because they created unheard-of riches and new forms of poverty all at once. "From this filthy sewer pure gold flows," wrote the French aristocrat Alexis de Tocqueville after visiting the new English industrial city of Manchester in the 1830s. "Here humanity attains its most complete development and its most brutish, here civilization works its miracles and civilized man is turned almost into a savage." Studies by physicians set the life expectancy of workers in Manchester at just seventeen years in 1840 (partly because of high rates of infant mortality), compared to the average in England of forty years. Visitors invariably complained about the smoke and soot. One American visitor to Britain in the late 1840s described how "in the manufacturing town, the fine soot or *blacks* darken the day, give white sheep the color of black sheep, discolor the human saliva, contaminate the air, poison many plants, and corrode monuments and buildings."

Authorities worried in particular about the effects on families. A doctor in the Prussian town of Breslau (population 111,000 in 1850), for example, reported that in working-class districts "several persons live in one room in a single bed, or perhaps a whole family, and use the room for all domestic duties, so that the air gets vitiated [polluted]. . . . Their diet consists largely of bread and potatoes." In Great Britain, the Factory Act of 1833 outlawed the employment of children under the age of nine in textile mills (except in the lace and silk industries) and limited the workdays of children ages nine to thirteen to nine hours a day and those ages thirteen to eighteen to twelve hours. Adults worked even longer hours. When investigating commissions showed that women and young children, sometimes under age six, were hauling coal trucks through low, cramped passageways in coal mines, the British Parliament passed a Mines Act in 1842 prohibiting the employment of women and girls underground. In 1847, the Central Short Time Committee, one of Britain's many social reform organizations, successfully pressured Parliament to limit the workday of women and children to ten hours. Countries in continental Europe followed the British lead, but since most did not insist on government inspection, enforcement was lax.

The advance of industrialization in eastern Europe was slow, in large part because serfdom still survived there, hindering labor mobility and tying up investment capital: as long as peasants were legally tied to the land as serfs, they could not migrate to the new factory towns, and landlords felt little incentive to invest their income in manufacturing. The problem was worst in Russia, where industrialization had hardly begun and would not take off until the end of the nineteenth century. Nevertheless, even in Russia signs of industrialization could be detected: raw cotton imports (a sign of a growing textile industry) increased sevenfold between 1831 and 1848, and the number of factories doubled along with the size of the industrial workforce.◆

Urbanization and Its Consequences

Industrial development spurred urban growth wherever factories were located in or near cities, yet cities grew even with little industry. Here, too, Great Britain led the way: half the population of England and Wales lived in towns by 1850, while

◆ For a primary source that illustrates the advance of industrialization in eastern Europe, see Document 53, "Factory Rules in Berlin."

in France and the German states the urban population was only about a quarter of the total. Both old and new cities teemed with growing population in the 1830s and 1840s. In the 1830s alone, London grew by 130,000 people; Paris expanded by 120,000 between 1841 and 1846, Vienna by 125,000 between 1827 and 1847, and Berlin by 180,000 between 1815 and 1848.

Massive rural emigration, rather than births to women already living in cities, accounted for this remarkable increase. Europe's population grew by nearly 100 percent between 1800 and 1850, yet agricultural yields increased only by 30 to 50 percent. City life and new factories beckoned those faced with hunger and poverty, including emigrants from other lands: thousands of Irish emigrated to English cities, Italians went to French cities, and Poles flocked to German cities. Since the construction of new housing could not keep up with population growth, overcrowding was inevitable. In Paris, 30,000 workers lived in lodging houses, eight or nine to a room, with no separation of the sexes. In 1847 in St. Giles, the Irish quarter of London, 461 people lived in just twelve houses. Men, women, and children huddled together on piles of filthy rotting straw or potato peels because they had no money for fuel to keep warm.

Severe crowding worsened already dire sanitation conditions. Residents dumped refuse into streets or courtyards, and human excrement collected in cesspools under apartment houses. At midcentury, London's approximately 250,000 cesspools were emptied only once or twice a year. Water was scarce and had to be fetched daily from nearby fountains. Despite the diversion of water from provincial rivers to Paris and a tripling of the number of public fountains, Parisians had enough water for only two baths annually per person (the upper classes enjoyed more baths; the lower classes, fewer). In London, private companies that supplied water turned on pumps in the poorer sections for only a few hours three days a week. In rapidly growing British industrial cities such as Manchester, one-third of the houses contained no latrines. Human waste ended up in the rivers that supplied drinking water. The horses that provided transportation inside the cities left droppings everywhere, and city dwellers often kept chickens, ducks, goats, pigs, geese, and even cattle, as well as dogs and cats, in their houses. The result was a "universal atmosphere of filth and stink."

Such conditions made cities prime breeding grounds for disease; those with 50,000 people or more had twice the death rates of rural areas. In 1830–1832 and again in 1847–1851, devastating outbreaks of cholera swept westward from Asia across Europe (touching the United States and South America as well in 1849–1850). Today we know that a waterborne bacterium causes the disease, but at the time no one understood the disease and everyone feared it. The usually fatal disease induced violent vomiting and diarrhea and left the skin blue, eyes sunken and dull, and hands and feet ice cold. While cholera particularly ravaged the crowded, filthy neighborhoods of rapidly growing cities, it also claimed many rural as well as some well-to-do victims. In Paris, 18,000 people died in the 1832 epidemic and 20,000 in that

FATHER THAMES INTRODUCING HIS OFFSPRING TO THE FAIR CITY OF LONDON.

■ **Lithograph of London**

This English lithograph draws attention to the connection between contaminated water supplies—in this case the Thames River in London—and epidemic disease. Notice that diphtheria, scrofula, and cholera are cited at the bottom of the print. The title, Father Thames Introducing His Offspring to the Fair City of London, *is particularly jarring. A monsterlike figure drags a dead body out of the slime and presents it to the fair maiden who represents London. The subtitle, "A Design for a Fresco in the New Houses of Parliament," challenges the political leadership to recognize the social problems festering nearby.* (Hulton Getty/Liaison Agency.)

www.bedfordstmartins.com/huntconcise   See the ONLINE STUDY GUIDE for more help in analyzing this image.

of 1849; in London, 7,000 died in each epidemic; in Russia, the epidemic was catastrophic, claiming 250,000 victims in 1831–1832 and a million in 1847–1851.

Rumors and panic followed in the epidemics' wakes. In Paris in April 1832, a crowd of workers attacked a central hospital, believing the doctors were poisoning the poor but using cholera as a hoax to cover up the conspiracy. Eastern European peasants burned estates and killed physicians and officials. Although devastating, cholera did not kill as many people as tuberculosis, Europe's number-one deadly disease. But tuberculosis took its victims one by one and therefore had less impact on social relations.

Raging epidemics spurred a growing concern for public health. When news of the cholera outbreak in eastern Europe reached Paris in 1831, the city set up commissions in each municipal district to collect information about lower-class housing and sanitation. In Great Britain, reports on sanitation conditions among the working class led to the passage of new public health laws.

But government intervention did little to ease the social tensions inspired by rapid urban growth. The middle and upper classes lived in large apartments or houses with more light, more air, and more water than lower-class dwellings. The lower classes lived nearby, however, sometimes in the cramped upper floors of the same apartment houses. Reformers believed that overcrowding among the poor led to sexual promiscuity and illegitimacy. They depicted the lower classes as dangerously lacking in sexual self-control. A physician visiting Lille, France, in 1835 wrote of "individuals of both sexes and of very different ages lying together, most of them without nightshirts and repulsively dirty. . . . The reader will complete the picture."

Officials collected statistics on illegitimacy that seemed to bear out these fears: one-quarter to one-half of the babies born in the big European cities in the 1830s and 1840s were illegitimate, and alarmed medical men wrote about thousands of infanticides. Between 1815 and the mid-1830s in France, 33,000 babies were abandoned at foundling hospitals every year; 27 percent of births in Paris in 1850 were illegitimate, compared with only 4 percent of rural births. Sexual disorder seemed to go hand in hand with drinking and crime. Beer halls and pubs dotted the urban landscape. One London street boasted twenty-three pubs in three hundred yards. Police officials estimated that London had 70,000 thieves and 80,000 prostitutes. In many cities, nearly half the urban population lived at the level of bare subsistence, and increasing numbers depended on public welfare, charity, or criminality to make ends meet. A Swiss pastor said of the workers, "Their hearts seethe with hatred of the well-to-do; their eyes lust for a share of the wealth about them; their mouths speak unblushingly of a coming day of retribution."

New Ideologies

A host of new political doctrines offered competing solutions to the new social tensions created by rapid urban growth and the spread of industry. Although traditional ways of life still prevailed in much of Europe, new modes of thinking about changes in the social and political order arose in the 1820s and 1830s. This was an era of "isms"—conservatism, liberalism, socialism, nationalism, and romanticism. The French Revolution had caused people to ask questions about the best possible form of government, and its effects had made clear that people acting together could change their political system. The events of the 1790s and the following decades, however, also produced enormous differences of opinion over what constituted the ideal government. Similarly, the Industrial Revolution posed fundamental questions about changes in society and social relations: How did the new social order differ from the earlier one, which was less urban and less driven by commercial concerns? Who should control this new order? Should governments try to moderate or accelerate the pace of change? Answers to these questions about the social and political order were called *ideologies*, a word coined during the French Revolution. An *ideology* is a coherent set of beliefs about the way a society's social and political order should be organized. New political and social movements organized around these ideologies.

Liberalism

As an ideology, liberalism traced its origins to the writings of John Locke in the seventeenth century and the Enlightenment philosophy of the eighteenth. The adherents of *liberalism* defined themselves in opposition to conservatives on one end of the political spectrum and revolutionaries on the other. Unlike conservatives, liberals supported the Enlightenment ideals of constitutional guarantees of personal liberty and free trade in economics, believing that greater liberty in politics and economic matters would promote social improvement and economic growth. For that reason, they also generally applauded the social and economic changes produced by the Industrial Revolution, while opposing the violence and excessive state power promoted by the French Revolution. The leaders of the rapidly expanding middle class composed of manufacturers, merchants, and professionals favored liberalism.

The foremost exponent of early-nineteenth-century liberalism was the English philosopher and jurist Jeremy Bentham (1748–1832). He called his brand of liberalism *utilitarianism* because he held that the best policy is the one that produces "the greatest good for the greatest number" and is thus the most useful, or utilitarian. Bentham's criticisms spared no institution; he railed against the injustices of the British parliamentary process, the abuses of the prisons and the penal code, and the educational system. In his zeal for social engineering, he proposed elaborate schemes for managing the poor and model prisons that would emphasize rehabilitation through close supervision rather than corporal punishment.

Bentham and many other liberals joined the abolitionist, antislavery movement that intensified between the 1790s and 1820s. Agitation by such groups as the London Society for Effecting the Abolition of the Slave Trade succeeded in gaining a first victory in 1807 when the British House of Lords voted to abolish the slave trade. The abolitionists' efforts finally bore fruit in 1833 when Britain abolished slavery in all its colonies.

British liberals pushed for two major reforms in addition to the abolition of slavery: expansion of the electorate to give representation to a broader segment of the middle class and repeal of the Corn Laws or tariffs on foreign grain. They gained their first goal in the Reform Bill of 1832. When the Tories in Parliament resisted the proposed extension of the right to vote, liberals and their supporters organized mass demonstrations. In this "state of diseased and feverish excitement" (according to its opponents), the Reform Bill passed after the king threatened to create enough new peers to obtain its passage in the House of Lords. Although the number of male voters increased by about 50 percent, only one in five Britons could now vote, and voting still depended on holding property. Nevertheless, the bill gave representation to new cities in the industrial north for the first time and set a precedent for further widening suffrage.◆

When landholders in the House of Commons thwarted efforts to lower grain tariffs, two Manchester cotton manufacturers set up an Anti–Corn Law League. The league denounced the landlords as "a bread-taxing oligarchy" and "blood-sucking vampires" and attracted working-class backing by promising lower food prices. The league established local branches, published newspapers and the journal *The Economist* (founded in 1843 and now one of the world's most influential periodicals), and campaigned in elections. They eventually won the support of the Tory prime minister Sir Robert Peel, whose government repealed the Corn Laws in 1846.

Liberalism had less appeal in continental Europe because industrial growth was slower and the middle classes smaller than in Britain. French liberals agitated for greater press freedoms and a broadening of the vote. Liberal reform movements also grew up in the pockets of industrialization in Prussia and the Austrian Empire. Some state bureaucrats, especially university-trained middle-class officials, favored economic liberalism. Hungarian count Stephen Széchenyi (1791–1860) personally campaigned for the introduction of British-style changes. He introduced British agricultural techniques on his own lands, helped start up steamboat traffic on the Danube, encouraged the importation of machinery and technicians for steam-driven textile factories, and pushed the construction of Hungary's first railway line, from Budapest to Vienna.

In the 1840s, however, Széchenyi's efforts paled before those of the flamboyant Magyar nationalist Lajos Kossuth (1802–1894). After spending four years in prison for sedition, Kossuth grabbed every opportunity to publicize American democracy and British political liberalism, all in a fervent nationalist spirit. In 1844, he founded the Protective Association, whose members bought only Hungarian products; to Kossuth, boycotting Austrian goods was crucial to ending "colonial dependence" on Austria. Born of a lesser landowning family without a noble title, Kossuth did not hesitate to attack "the cowardly selfishness of the landowner class."

Even in Russia, signs of liberal, even socialist, opposition appeared in the 1830s and 1840s. Small "circles" of young noblemen serving in the army or bureaucracy met in cities, especially Moscow, to discuss the latest Western ideas and to criticize the Russian state: "The world is undergoing a transformation, while we vegetate in

---

◆ For a primary source that argues for the bill and reveals liberal principles, see Document 54, T. B. Macaulay, "Speech on Parliamentary Reform."

our hovels of wood and clay," wrote one. Out of these groups came such future revolutionaries as Alexander Herzen (1812–1870), described by the police as "a daring
free-thinker, extremely dangerous to society." Tsar Nicholas I (r. 1825–1855) banned
Western liberal writings as well as all books about the United States. He sent nearly
ten thousand people a year into exile in Siberia as punishment for their political
activities.

Socialism and the Early Labor Movement

Socialism took up where liberalism left off: socialists believed that the liberties advocated by liberals benefited only the middle class, the owners of factories and businesses, not the workers. They sought to reorganize society totally rather than to reform it piecemeal through political measures. Many were utopians who believed
that ideal communities are based on cooperation rather than competition. Like
Thomas More, whose book *Utopia* (1516) gave the movement its name, the utopian
socialists believed that society would benefit all its members only if private property
ceased to exist.

Socialists criticized the new industrial order for dividing society into two classes:
the new middle class, or *capitalists*, who owned the wealth; and the working class,
their downtrodden and impoverished employees. Such divisions tore the social
fabric, and, as their name suggests, the socialists aimed to restore harmony and cooperation through social reorganization. Three early socialists helped instigate the
movement: Robert Owen, Claude Henri de Saint-Simon, and Charles Fourier.
Robert Owen (1771–1858) founded British socialism. A successful Welsh-born manufacturer, Owen bought a cotton mill in New Lanark, Scotland, in 1800 and began
to set up a model factory town, where workers labored only ten hours a day (instead of seventeen, as was common). He moved to the United States in the 1820s
to establish in Indiana a community he named New Harmony. The experiment
collapsed after three years, a victim of internal squabbling. Nonetheless, Owen's
experiments and writings inspired the movement for producer cooperatives
(businesses owned and controlled by their workers), consumer cooperatives (stores
in which consumers owned shares), and a national trade union.

Claude Henri de Saint-Simon (1760–1825) and Charles Fourier (1772–1837)
were Owen's contemporaries in France. Saint-Simon was a noble who had served
as an officer in the War of American Independence and lost a fortune speculating
in national property during the French Revolution. Fourier traveled as a salesman
for a Lyon cloth merchant. Both shared Owen's alarm about the effects of industrialization on social relations. Saint-Simon coined the terms *industrialism* and *industrialist* to define the new economic order and its chief animators. He believed
that work, the central element in the new society, should be controlled not by politicians but by scientists, engineers, artists, and industrialists. To correct the abuses of
the new industrial order, Fourier urged the establishment of communities that were

part garden city and part agricultural commune; all jobs would be rotated to max-imize happiness. The emancipation of women was essential to Fourier's vision of a harmonious community: "The extension of the privileges of women is the fundamental cause of all social progress."

Women participated actively in the socialist movements of the day, even though socialist men often shared the widespread prejudice against women's political ac-tivism. In Great Britain, many women joined the Owenites and helped form coop-erative societies and unions. They defended women's working-class organizations against the complaints of men in the new societies and trade unions. As one woman wrote, "Do not say the unions are only for men . . . 'tis a wrong impression, forced on our minds to keep us slaves!" As women became more active, Owenites agitated for women's rights, marriage reform, and popular education. In 1832, Saint-Simonian women founded a feminist newspaper in France, *The Free Woman*. Some followers of Saint-Simon's brand of socialism developed a quasi-religious cult with elaborate rituals and a "he-pope" and "she-pope," or ruling father and mother. They lived and worked together in cooperative arrangements and scandalized some by advocating free love.

The French activist Flora Tristan (1801–1844) devoted herself to reconciling the interests of male and female workers. She had seen the "frightful reality" of London's poverty and made a reputation reporting on British working conditions. Tristan published a stream of books and pamphlets urging male workers to address women's unequal status, arguing that "the emancipation of male workers is *impos-sible* so long as women remain in a degraded state." She advocated a Universal Union of Men and Women Workers.

Even though most male socialists ignored Tristan's plea for women's participa-tion, like her they also worked to found working-class associations. The French socialist Louis Blanc (1811–1882) explained the importance of working-class associations in *Organization of Labor* (1840), which deeply influenced the French labor movement. Similarly, Pierre-Joseph Proudhon (1809–1865) urged workers to form producers' associations so that the workers could control the work process and eliminate profits made by capitalists. His 1840 book *What Is Property?* argues that property is theft: labor alone is productive, and rent, interest, and profit are unjust.

After 1840, some socialists began to call themselves "communists," emphasiz-ing their desire to replace private property by communal, collective ownership. The Frenchman Étienne Cabet (1788–1856) first used the word *communist*. In 1840, he published *Travels in Icaria*, a novel describing a communist experiment in which a popularly elected dictatorship efficiently organized work, reduced the workday to seven hours, and made work tasks "short, easy, and attractive."

Out of the churning of socialist ideas of the 1840s emerged two men whose collaboration would change the definition of socialism and remake it into an ideology that would shake the world for the next 150 years. Karl Marx (1818–1883) and Friedrich Engels (1820–1895) were both sons of prosperous German-Jewish families that had converted to Christianity. Marx studied philosophy at the University of Berlin, edited a liberal newspaper until the Prussian government suppressed it, and then left for Paris, where he met Engels. While working in the offices of his wealthy family's cotton manufacturing interests in Manchester, England, Engels had been shocked into writing *The Condition of the Working Class in England in 1844* (1845), a sympathetic depiction of industrial workers' dismal lives. In Paris, where German and eastern European intellectuals could pursue their political interests more freely than at home, Marx and Engels organized a Communist League, in whose name they published the *Communist Manifesto* (1848). It eventually became the touchstone of Marxist and communist revolution all over the world.◆

Negligible as was Marx's and Engels's influence in the 1840s, they had already begun their lifework of scientifically understanding the "laws" of capitalism and fostering revolutionary organizations. Their principles and analysis of history were in place: communists, the *Manifesto* declared, must aim for "the downfall of the bourgeoisie [capitalist class] and the ascendancy of the proletariat [working class], the abolition of the old society based on class conflicts and the foundation of a new society without classes and without private property." Marx and Engels embraced industrialization because they believed it would eventually bring on the proletarian revolution and lead inevitably to the abolition of exploitation, private property, and class society.

Socialism accompanied, and in some places incited, an upsurge in working-class organization in western Europe. In 1824, the British government repealed laws prohibiting labor unions, though it maintained restrictions on strikes. Other European rulers forbade unions, though they tolerated cooperatives and societies for mutual aid. Working-class organization struck fear in the hearts of many in the upper classes. A British newspaper exclaimed in 1834, "The trade unions are, we have no doubt, the most dangerous institutions that were ever permitted to take root."

Many British workers joined in the Chartist movement, which aimed to transform Britain into a democracy. In 1838, political radicals drew up the People's Charter, which demanded universal manhood suffrage, vote by secret ballot, equal electoral districts, annual elections, and the elimination of property qualifications for and the payment of stipends to members of Parliament. Chartists denounced their opponents as seeking "to keep the people in social slavery and political degradation." Many women took part by founding female political unions, setting up Chartist Sunday schools, organizing boycotts of unsympathetic shopkeepers, and

---

◆ For an original source that reflects Marx and Engels's historical vision, see Document 55, Friedrich Engels, "Draft of a Communist Confession of Faith."

joining Chartist temperance associations. Nevertheless, the People's Charter refrained from calling for woman suffrage because the movement's leaders feared that doing so would alienate potential supporters.

The Chartists organized a massive campaign during 1838 and 1839, with large public meetings, fiery speeches, and torchlight parades. Presented with petitions for the People's Charter signed by more than a million people, the House of Commons refused to act. In response to this rebuff from middle-class liberals, the Chartists allied themselves in the 1840s with working-class strike movements in the manufacturing districts and associated with various European revolutionary movements. But at the same time, they—like their British and continental allies—distanced themselves from women workers. Chartists complained that working-women undermined men's manhood, taking men's jobs and turning the men into "women-men" or "eunuchs." Continuing agitation and organization prepared the way for a last wave of Chartist demonstrations in 1848.

Nationalism

Nationalists could be liberals, socialists, or even conservatives. *Nationalism* holds that all peoples derive their identities from their nations, which are defined by common language, shared cultural traditions, and sometimes religion. When such "nations" do not coincide with state boundaries, as they often did not in the nineteenth and twentieth centuries, nationalism can produce violence and warfare as different national groups compete for control over territory.

The French showed the power of national feeling in their revolutionary and Napoleonic wars, but they also provoked nationalism in the people they conquered. Once Napoleon and his satellite rulers departed, nationalist sentiment turned against other outside rulers—the Ottoman Turks in the Balkans, the Russians in Poland, and the Austrians in Italy. Intellectuals took the lead in demanding unity and freedom for their peoples. They collected folktales, poems, and histories and prepared grammars and dictionaries of their native languages (Map 17.3). Students, middle-class professionals, and army officers formed secret societies to promote national independence and constitutional reform.

Nationalist aspirations were especially explosive for the Austrian Empire, which included a variety of peoples united only by their enforced allegiance to the Habsburg emperor. The empire included three main national groups: the Germans, who made up one-fourth of the population; the Magyars of Hungary (which included Transylvania and Croatia); and the Slavs, who together formed the largest group in the population but were divided into different nationalities such as Poles, Czechs, Croats, and Serbs. The empire also included Italians in Lombardy and Venetia and Romanians in Transylvania. Efforts to govern such diverse peoples preoccupied Metternich, chief minister to the weak Habsburg emperor Francis I (r. 1792–1835). As a conservative, Metternich believed that the experience of the

■ MAP 17.3 Languages of Nineteenth-Century Europe
Even this detailed map of linguistic diversity understates the number of different languages and dialects spoken in Europe. In Italy, for example, few Italians spoke Italian as their first language. Instead, they spoke local dialects such as Piedmontese or Ligurian, and some might speak better French than Italian if they came from the regions bordering France. The map does underline the inherent contradictions of nationalism in eastern Europe, where many linguistic regions incorporated other languages and the result was constant conflict. But even in Spain, France, and Great Britain, linguistic diversity continued right up to the beginning of the 1900s.

French Revolution proved the superiority of monarchy and aristocracy as forms of government and society. His domestic policy aimed to restrain nationalist impulses, and with the help of a secret police set up on the Napoleonic model, he largely succeeded until the 1840s. He insisted, for example, that "the Lombards [northern Italians] must forget that they are Italians."

The new Germanic Confederation set up by the Congress of Vienna had a federal assembly, but it largely functioned as a tool of Metternich's policies. The only sign of resistance came from university students, who formed nationalist student societies, or *Burschenschaften*. In 1817, they held a mass rally at which they burned books they did not like, including Napoleon's Civil Code. One of their leaders, Friedrich Ludwig Jahn, spouted such xenophobic (antiforeign) slogans as "If you let your daughter learn French, you might just as well train her to become a whore." Metternich was convinced that the *Burschenschaften* in the German states and the *carbonari* in Italy were linked in an international conspiracy. In 1820, when a student assassinated the playwright August Kotzebue because he ridiculed the student movement, Metternich convinced the leaders of the biggest German states to pass the Karlsbad Decrees dissolving the student societies and more strictly censoring the press. No evidence for a conspiracy was found.

Tsar Alexander faced similar problems in Poland, his "congress kingdom" (so called because the Congress of Vienna had created it), which in 1815 was one of Europe's most liberal states. The tsar reigned in Poland as a limited monarch, having bestowed a constitution that provided for an elected parliament, a national army, and guarantees of free speech and a free press. But by 1818, Alexander had begun retracting his concessions. Polish students and military officers responded by forming secret nationalist societies to plot for change by illegal means. In 1830, they rebelled against Alexander's successor Nicholas I. In reprisal, the tsar abolished the Polish constitution and ordered thousands of Poles executed or banished.

Most of the ten thousand Poles who fled took up residence in western European capitals, especially Paris, where they campaigned for public support. Their intellectual leader was the poet Adam Mickiewicz (1798–1855), whose mystical writings portrayed the Polish exiles as martyrs of a crucified nation with an international Christian mission. Mickiewicz formed a Polish Legion to fight for national restoration, but rivalries and divisions prevented united action until 1846, when Polish exiles in Paris tried to launch a coordinated insurrection for Polish independence. Plans for an uprising in the Polish province of Galicia in the Austrian Empire collapsed, however, when peasants instead revolted against their noble Polish masters. Slaughtering some two thousand aristocrats, a desperate rural population served the Austrian government's end by defusing the nationalist challenge.

One of those most touched by Mickiewicz's vision was Giuseppe Mazzini (1805–1872), a fiery Italian nationalist and republican journalist. Exiled in 1831 for his opposition to Austrian rule in northern Italy, Mazzini founded Young Italy, a secret society that attracted thousands with its message that Italy would touch off a European-wide revolutionary movement. In the 1830s and 1840s, nationalism spread among the many different peoples of the Austrian Empire. During the revolutions of 1848, however, it would become evident that these different ethnic groups disliked each other as much as they disliked their Austrian masters.

In most of the German states, economic unification took a step forward with the foundation in 1834, under Prussian leadership, of the *Zollverein,* or "customs union." Economist Friedrich List argued that the elimination of tariffs within the borders of the union would promote industrialization and cooperation and enable the union to compete with the rest of Europe. German nationalists sought a government uniting German-speaking peoples, but they could not agree on its boundaries. Austria was not part of the Customs Union. Would the unified German state include both Prussia and the Austrian Empire? If it included Austria, what about the non-German territories of the Austrian Empire? And could the powerful and conservative kingdom of Prussia coexist in a unified German state with other, more liberal but smaller states? These questions would vex German history for decades to come.

In Russia, nationalism took the form of opposition to Western ideas. Russian nationalists, or "Slavophiles" (lovers of the Slavs), opposed the "Westernizers," who wanted Russia to follow Western models of industrial development and constitutional government. The Slavophiles favored maintaining rural traditions infused by the values of the Russian Orthodox church. Only a return to Russia's basic historical principles, they argued, could protect the country against the corrosion of rationalism and materialism. Slavophiles sometimes criticized the regime, however, because they believed the state exerted too much power over the church. The conflict between Slavophiles and Westernizers continues to shape Russian cultural and intellectual life to the present day.

The most significant nationalist movement in western Europe could be found in Ireland. The Irish had struggled for centuries against English occupation, but Irish nationalists developed strong organizations only in the 1840s. In 1842, a group of writers founded the Young Ireland movement that aimed to recover Irish history and preserve the Irish Gaelic language (spoken by at least one-third of the peasantry). Daniel O'Connell (1775–1847), a Catholic lawyer and landowner who sat in the British House of Commons, hoped to force the British Parliament to repeal the Act of Union of 1801, which had made Ireland part of Great Britain. In 1843, London newspapers reported "monster meetings" that drew crowds of as many as 300,000 people in support of repeal of the union. In response, the British government arrested O'Connell and convicted him of conspiracy. More radical leaders, who preached insurrection against the English, replaced him.

Romanticism

More an artistic movement than a true ideology, *romanticism* glorified nature, emotion, genius, and imagination. It proclaimed these as antidotes to the Enlightenment and to classicism in the arts, challenging the reliance on reason, symmetry, and cool geometric spaces. Classicism idealized models from Roman history; romanticism turned to folklore and medieval legends. Classicism celebrated orderly, crisp lines; romantics sought out all that was wild, fevered, and disorderly. Chief among the arts of romanticism were poetry, painting, and music, which captured the deep-seated emotion characteristic of romantic expression. George Gordon, Lord Byron (1788–1824), explained his aims in writing poetry:

> For what is Poesy but to create
> From overfeeling, Good and Ill, and aim
> At an external life beyond our fate,
> And be the new Prometheus of new man.

Prometheus was the mythological figure who brought fire from the Greek gods to human beings. Byron did not seek the new Prometheus among the men of industry; he sought him within his own "overfeeling," his own intense emotions.◆

Romantic poetry elevated the wonders of nature almost to the supernatural. Nature, wrote the English poet William Wordsworth (1770–1850), "to me was all in all." It allowed him to sing "the still, sad music of humanity." Like many poets of his time, Wordsworth greeted the French Revolution with joy; in his poem "French Revolution" (1809), he remembered his early enthusiasm: "Bliss was it in that dawn to be alive." But gradually he became disenchanted with the revolutionary experiment and celebrated British nationalism instead; in 1816, he published a poem to commemorate the "intrepid sons of Albion [England]" who died at the battle of Waterloo.

Their emphasis on authentic self-expression at times drew romantics to exotic, mystical, or even reckless experiences. Such transports drove one leading German poet to the madhouse and another to suicide. Some romantics depicted the artist as possessed by demons and obsessed with hallucinations. The aged German poet Johann Wolfgang von Goethe (1749–1832) denounced the extremes of romanticism, calling it "everything that is sick." In his epic poem *Faust* (1832), the retelling of a sixteenth-century legend, Faust offers his soul to the devil in return for a chance to taste all human experience—from passionate love to the heights of power—in his effort to reshape nature for humanity's benefit. Faust's striving leaves a wake of suffering and destruction. Goethe did not make the target of his warning explicit, but the French revolutionary legacy and industrialization both seemed to be releasing "faustian" energies that could be destructive.

Romanticism in painting also often expressed anxiety about the coming industrial order while idealizing nature. These concerns came together in an emphasis on natural landscape. The German romantic painter Caspar David Friedrich (1774–1840) depicted scenes—often in the mountains, far from any factory—that

◆ For a primary source that reveals the romantic vision, see Document 56, Victor Hugo, "Preface to *Cromwell.*"

■ **Caspar David Friedrich,**
Wanderer above the Sea of Fog
(1818)
Friedrich, a German romantic painter,
captured many of the themes most
dear to romanticism: melancholy, iso-
lation, and individual communion
with nature. He painted trees reaching
for the sky and mountains stretch-
ing into the distance. Nature to
him seemed awesome, powerful, and
overshadowing of human perspectives.
The French sculptor David d'Angers
said of Friedrich, "Here is a man
who has discovered the tragedy of
landscape."
(Co Elke Walford, Hamburg/Hamburger
Kunsthalle.)

captured the romantic fascination with the sublime power of nature. His melancholy individual figures look lost in the vastness of an overpowering nature.
Friedrich hated the new modern world and considered industrialization a disaster.
The English painter Joseph M. W. Turner (1775–1851) depicted his vision of nature
in mysterious, misty seascapes, anticipating later artists by blurring the outlines of
objects. The French painter Eugène Delacroix (1798–1863) chose contemporary as
well as medieval scenes of great turbulence to emphasize light and color and break
away from what he saw as "the servile copies repeated *ad nauseam* in academies of
art." Critics denounced the new techniques as "painting with a drunken broom." To
broaden his experience of light and color, Delacroix traveled in the 1830s to North
Africa and painted many exotic scenes in Morocco and Algeria.

   Architects of the period sought to recapture a preindustrial world. When the
British Houses of Parliament were rebuilt after they burned down in 1834, the architect Sir Charles Barry constructed them in a Gothic style reminiscent of the
Middle Ages. This medievalism was taken even further by A. W. N. Pugin, who
prepared the Gothic details for the Houses of Parliament. In his polemical book
Contrasts (1836), Pugin denounced modern conditions and compared them unfav-
orably with those in the 1400s. To underline his view, Pugin wore medieval clothes
at home.

The towering presence of the German composer Ludwig van Beethoven (1770–1827) in early-nineteenth-century music helped establish the direction for musical romanticism. His music, according to one leading German romantic, "sets in motion the lever of fear, of awe, of horror, of suffering, and awakens just that infinite longing which is the essence of Romanticism." Beethoven's symphonies conveyed the impression of growth, a metaphor for the organic process with an emphasis on the natural that was dear to the romantics. For example, his Sixth Symphony, the *Pastoral* (1808), used a variety of instruments to represent sounds heard in the country. Some of his work was explicitly political; his Ninth Symphony (1824) employed a chorus to sing the German poet Friedrich Schiller's verses in praise of universal human solidarity.

If any common political thread linked the romantics, it was support for nationalist aspirations, especially through the search for the historical origins of national identity. The Polish composer and pianist Frédéric Chopin (1810–1849) became a powerful champion for the cause of his native land with music that incorporated Polish folk rhythms and melodies. English poet Lord Byron died fighting for Greek independence. Romantic nationalism permeated *The Betrothed* (1825–1827), a novel by Alessandro Manzoni (1785–1873) that constituted a kind of bible for Italian nationalists. The career of the writer Sir Walter Scott (1771–1832) incorporated many of the strands of romanticism. He translated Goethe and published Scottish ballads that he heard as a child. After achieving immediate success with his poetry, he switched to historical novels, but he also wrote a nine-volume life of Napoleon and edited historical memoirs. His novels are almost all renditions of historical events, from *Rob Roy* (1817), with its account of Scottish resistance to the English in the early eighteenth century, to *Ivanhoe* (1819), with its tales of medieval England. The influence of Scott's historical novels was immense. One contemporary critic claimed that *Ivanhoe* was more historically true than any scholarly work: "There is more history in the novels of Walter Scott than in half of the historians."

Reform or Revolution?

Europeans faced a daunting set of challenges in the 1830s and 1840s: the settlement devised by the Congress of Vienna was cracking under the pressure of unsatisfied nationalist and democratic aspirations, and industrialization and urbanization had produced dangerous social tensions made vivid by an outpouring of government reports, medical accounts, and novelistic depictions. Reformers of various stripes organized to meet these challenges, as well as new problems appearing in overseas colonies. Their efforts failed to stem the tide of revolution, which rose again in 1830 and 1848 and threatened to wash away the conservative regimes of the Vienna settlement.

Depicting and Reforming the Social Order

Lithographs, poetry, painting, and even booklets of jokes helped drive home the need for social reform, but novels proved to be the art form best suited to portraying the new society created by industrialization and urbanization. Thanks to increased literacy, the spread of reading rooms and lending libraries, and serialization in newspapers and journals, novels reached a large reading public and helped shape public awareness. Unlike the fiction of the eighteenth century, which had focused on individual personalities, the great novels of the 1830s and 1840s specialized in the description of social life in all its varieties. Manufacturers, financiers, starving students, workers, bureaucrats, prostitutes, underworld figures, thieves, and aristocratic men and women filled the pages of works by popular writers such as Honoré de Balzac and Charles Dickens. Pushing himself to exhaustion and a premature death to get out of debt, the French writer Balzac (1799–1850) cranked out ninety-five novels and many short stories. He aimed to catalog the social types that could be found in French society. Many of his characters, like himself, were driven by the desire to climb higher in the social order.

The English author Charles Dickens (1812–1870) worked with a similar frenetic energy and for much the same reasons. When his father was imprisoned for debt in 1824, the young Dickens took a job in a shoe-polish factory. In 1836, he published a series of literary sketches of daily life and then produced a series of novels that appeared in monthly installments and attracted thousands of readers. In them he paid close attention to the distressing effects of industrialization and urbanization. In *The Old Curiosity Shop* (1841), for example, he depicts the Black Country, the manufacturing region west and northwest of Birmingham, as a "cheerless region," a "mournful place," in which tall chimneys "made foul the melancholy air." In addition to publishing such enduring favorites as *Oliver Twist* (1838) and *A Christmas Carol* (1843), he ran charitable organizations and pressed for social reforms. For Dickens, the ability to portray the problems of the poor went hand in hand with a personal commitment to reform.

Novels by women often revealed the bleaker side of women's situations. *Jane Eyre* (1847), a novel by the English writer Charlotte Brontë, describes the difficult life of an orphaned girl who becomes a governess, the only occupation open to most single middle-class women. Although in an economically weak position, Jane Eyre refuses to achieve respectability and security through marriage, the usual option for women. The French novelist George Sand (Amandine-Aurore Dupin, 1804–1876) took her social criticism a step further. She announced her independence in the 1830s by dressing like a man and smoking cigars. Like many other women writers of the time, she published her work under a male pseudonym while creating female characters who prevail in difficult circumstances through romantic love and moral idealism. Sand's novel *Indiana* (1832), about an unhappily married

■ **George Sand**
This lithograph (1842) by Alcide
Lorentz shows George Sand in one of
her notorious masculine costumes. Sand
published novels, plays, essays, travel
writing, and an autobiography. She
actively participated in the revolution of 1848
in France, writing pamphlets in support of the
new republic. Disillusioned by the rise to power of
Louis-Napoleon Bonaparte, she withdrew to her country
estate and devoted herself exclusively to her writing.
(The Granger Collection.)

woman, was read all over Europe. Her notoriety made the term *George-Sandism* a common expression of disdain for independent women.

Although women's professional opportunities were severely limited, they took a prominent role in charitable and reform work. Catholic religious orders, which by 1850 enrolled many more women than men, ran schools, hospitals, leper colonies, insane asylums, and old-age homes. New Catholic orders, especially for women, were established, and Catholic missionary activity overseas increased. Protestant women in Great Britain and the United States established Bible, missionary, and female reform societies by the hundreds. Many societies dedicated themselves to reforming prostitutes and castigating their male clients. As a pamphlet of the Boston Female Moral Reform Society explained, "Our mothers, our sisters, our daughters are sacrificed by the thousands every year on the altar of sin, and who are the agents in this work of destruction: Why, our fathers, our brothers, and our sons."

Religiously motivated reformers first had to overcome the perceived indifference of the working classes; less than 10 percent of the workers in the cities attended religious services. To combat such indifference, British religious groups launched the Sunday school movement, which reached its zenith in the 1840s. By 1851, more than half of all working-class children between five and fifteen were attending Sunday school, even though very few of their parents regularly went to religious services. The Sunday schools taught children how to read at a time when few working-class children could go to school during the week.

Catholics and Protestants alike promoted the temperance movement to fight the "pestilence of hard liquor." The first societies had appeared in the United States as early as 1813, and by 1835 the American Temperance Society claimed 1.5 million members. The London-based British and Foreign Temperance Society, established in 1831, matched its American counterpart in its opposition to all alcohol. Temperance advocates saw drunkenness as a sign of moral weakness and a threat to social order. Industrialists pointed to the loss of worker productivity, and efforts to promote temperance often reflected middle- and upper-class fears of the lower classes' lack of discipline. One German temperance advocate insisted, "One need not be a prophet to know that all efforts to combat the widespread and rapidly spreading pauperism will be unsuccessful as long as the common man fails to realize that the principal source of his degradation and misery is his fondness of drink." Yet temperance societies also attracted working-class people who shared the desire for respectability.

Social reformers saw education as one of the main prospects for uplifting the poor and the working class. In addition to setting up Sunday schools, British churches founded organizations such as the British and Foreign School Society. More secular in intent were the Mechanics Institutes, which provided education for workers in the big cities. In 1833, the French government passed an education law that required every town to maintain a primary school, pay a teacher, and provide free education to poor boys. As the law's author, François Guizot, argued, "Ignorance renders the masses turbulent and ferocious." Girls' schools were optional, although hundreds of women taught at the primary level, most of them in private, often religious schools. By the late 1830s, 60 percent of children attended primary school in France, still less than in Protestant Prussia, where 75 percent of children went to school. Popular education remained woefully undeveloped in most of eastern Europe. Peasants were specifically excluded from the few primary schools in Russia, where Tsar Nicholas I blamed the Decembrist uprising of 1825 on education.

Above all else, the elite sought to impose discipline and order on working people. Popular sports, especially blood sports such as cockfighting and bear-baiting, suggested a lack of control, and long-standing efforts in Great Britain to eliminate these recreations now gained momentum through organizations such as the Society for the Prevention of Cruelty to Animals. By the end of the 1830s, bullbaiting had been abandoned in Great Britain. "This useful animal," rejoiced one reformer in 1839, "is no longer tortured amidst the exulting yells of those who are a disgrace to our common form and nature." Other blood sports died out more slowly, and efforts in other countries generally lagged behind those of the British.

When private charities failed to meet the needs of the poor, governments often intervened. Great Britain sought to control the costs of public welfare by passing a

■ Bearbaiting

This colored engraving (1821) of Charley's Theater in London shows that bearbaiting did not attract only the lower classes, as reformers often implied. Top hats were most often worn by middle-class men, who seem to be enjoying the spectacle of dogs taunting the bear as much as the working-class men present. At this time, bearbaiting, like bullbaiting, began to come under fire as cruel to animals. (Mary Evans Picture Library.)

new poor law in 1834, called by its critics the "Starvation Act." The law required that all able-bodied persons receiving relief be placed in workhouses, with husbands separated from wives and parents from children. Workhouse life was designed to be as unpleasant as possible so that poor people would move on to regions of higher employment. British women from all social classes organized anti–poor law societies to protest the separation of mothers from their children in the workhouses.

Many women viewed charitable work as the extension of their domestic roles: they promoted virtuous behavior and morality and thus improved society. In one widely read advice book, Englishwoman Sarah Lewis suggested in 1839 that "women may be the prime agents in the regeneration of mankind." But women's social reform activities concealed a paradox. According to the set of beliefs that historians call the doctrine or ideology of domesticity, women should live their lives entirely within the domestic sphere; they should devote themselves to the home. The English poet Alfred, Lord Tennyson, captured this view in a popular poem published in 1847: "Man for the field and woman for the hearth; / Man for the sword and for the needle she. . . . All else confusion." Many believed that maintaining proper and distinct roles for men and women was critically important to maintaining social order in general.

Most women had little hope of economic independence. The notion of a separate, domestic sphere for women prevented them from pursuing higher education,

■ Life as a Married Couple
This lithograph by Honoré Daumier, titled All That One Would Want *(1846), shows a wife following meekly behind her husband. Daumier is criticizing the provision of Napoleon's Civil Code that required wives to go to live wherever their husbands chose. He published no fewer than four thousand prints and caricatures criticizing the social inequalities worsened by economic development. He satirized landlords, judges, lawyers, politicians, and even King Louis-Philippe himself. In the early 1830s, Daumier's political satires landed him in prison for six months. His work always took the side of the lowly and downcast and poked fun at the high and mighty.* (Jean-Loup Charmet.)

work in professional careers, or participation in politics through voting or holding office, all activities deemed appropriate only to men. Laws everywhere codified the subordination of women. Many countries followed the model of Napoleon's Civil Code, which classified married women as legal incompetents along with children, the insane, and criminals. In Great Britain, which had no national law code, the courts upheld the legality of a husband's complete control.

Distinctions between men and women were most noticeable in the privileged classes. Whereas boys attended secondary schools, most middle- and upper-class girls still received their education at home or in church schools, where they were taught to be religious, obedient, and accomplished in music and languages. As men began to wear practical clothing—long trousers and short jackets of solid, often dark colors, no makeup (previously common for aristocratic men), and simply cut hair—women continued to dress for decorative effect, now with tightly corseted waists that emphasized the differences between female and male bodies. Middle- and upper-class women had long hair that required hours of brushing and pinning up, and they wore long, cumbersome skirts. Advice books written by women detailed the tasks that such women undertook in the home: maintaining household accounts, supervising servants, and organizing social events.

Scientists reinforced stereotypes. Once considered sexually insatiable, women were now described as incapacitated by menstruation and largely uninterested in sex, an attitude that many equated with moral superiority. Thus was born the

"Victorian woman," a figment of the largely male medical imagination. Physicians and scholars considered women mentally inferior. In 1839, Auguste Comte, an influential early French sociologist, wrote, "As for any functions of government, the radical inaptitude of the female sex is there yet more marked . . . and limited to the guidance of the mere family."

Abuses and Reforms Overseas

Despite such attitudes, British women played a major role in the antislavery movement; as many as 350,000 women signed one major petition to Parliament demanding the abolition of slavery. Reformers gained one of their major objectives when Britain abolished slavery in its colonies in 1833. British missionary and evangelical groups condemned the conquest, enslavement, and exploitation of native African populations and successfully blocked British annexations in central and southern Africa in the 1830s. The new Latin American republics abolished slavery in the 1820s and 1830s after they defeated the Spanish with armies that included many slaves. In France, the government of Louis-Philippe (r. 1830–1848) took strong measures against clandestine slave traffic, virtually ending French participation during the 1830s. Slavery was abolished in the remaining French Caribbean colonies in 1848.

Slavery did not disappear immediately just because the major European powers had given it up. The transatlantic trade in slaves did not seriously diminish until 1850 (see Figure 14.1, page 575). Human bondage continued unabated in Brazil, Cuba (still a Spanish colony), and the United States. Some American reformers supported abolition, but it remained a minority movement. Like serfdom in Russia, slavery in the Americas involved a quagmire of economic, political, and moral problems that worsened over time.

As Europeans turned their interest away from the plantation colonies of the Caribbean toward colonies in Asia and Africa, they developed new forms of colonial rule. Colonialism became *imperialism*—a term first coined in the midnineteenth century. Colonialism most often led to the establishment of settler colonies, direct rule by Europeans, slave labor from Africa, and wholesale destruction of indigenous peoples. In contrast, imperialism usually meant more indirect forms of economic exploitation and political rule. Europeans still derived economic profit from their colonies, but now they also aimed to reform colonial peoples in their own image—when doing so did not conflict too much with their economic interests.

In the 1830s and 1840s, France and Britain continued to extend their influence across the globe. Using the pretext of an insult to its envoy, France invaded the north African country of Algeria in 1830 and after a long military campaign established political control over most of the region in the next two decades. By 1850, more than seventy thousand French, Italian, and Maltese colonists had settled there, often confiscating the lands of native peoples. The new French administration of the colony made efforts to balance native and settler interests, however, and eventually France would not only incorporate Algeria into France but also try to assimilate its native population to French culture. France also imposed a protectorate government over the South Pacific island of Tahiti.

Although the British granted Canada greater self-determination in 1839, they extended their dominion elsewhere by annexing Singapore (1819), an island off the Malay peninsula, and New Zealand (1840). They also increased their control in India through the administration of the East India Company, a private group of merchants chartered by the British crown. The British educated a native elite to take over much of the day-to-day business of administering the country and used native soldiers to augment their military control. By 1850, only one in six soldiers serving Britain in India was European.

The East India Company also tried to establish a regular trade with China in opium, a drug long known for its medicinal uses but increasingly bought in China as a recreational drug. The Chinese government did its best to keep the highly addictive drug away from its people, both by forbidding Western merchants to venture outside the southern city of Guangzhou (Canton) and by banning the export of precious metals and the import of opium. These measures failed. By smuggling opium grown in India into China and bribing local officials, British traders built up a flourishing market. When in 1839 the Chinese authorities expelled British merchants from southern China, Britain retaliated by bombarding Chinese coastal cities, beginning the First Opium War. In 1842, it dictated to a defeated China the Treaty of Nanking, by which the British forced the opening of four more Chinese ports to Europeans,

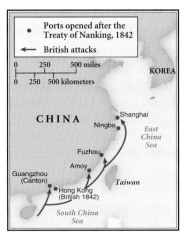

The First Opium War, 1839–1842

took sovereignty over the island of Hong Kong, received a substantial war indemnity, and were assured of a continuation of the opium trade. In this case, reform took a backseat to economic interest, despite the complaints of religious groups in Britain.

The Revolutions of 1830 and 1848

Imperialist ventures abroad continued even as the revolutionary legacy revived again in Europe, first in 1830 and then in a more widespread series of upheavals in 1848. Given its revolutionary past, it is not surprising that France took the lead. In 1830, a revolution overthrew the French king, Charles X (r. 1824–1830), the younger brother and successor to Louis XVIII. Charles X brought about his own downfall by pushing through a Law of Indemnity in 1825 to compensate nobles for the loss of their lands during the revolution of 1789. At the same time, he insisted on a Law of Sacrilege imposing the death penalty for such offenses as stealing religious objects from churches. He then dissolved the legislature, removed many wealthy and powerful voters from the rolls, and imposed strict censorship. Spontaneous demonstrations in Paris led to fighting on July 26, 1830. After three days of street battles in which 500 citizens and 150 soldiers died, a group of moderate liberal leaders, fearing the reestablishment of a republic, agreed to give the crown to Charles X's cousin Louis-Philippe, duke of Orléans.

Charles X went into exile in England, and the new king extended political liberties and voting rights. Although the number of voting men nearly doubled, it remained minuscule—approximately 170,000 in a country of 30 million, between 5 and 6 percent. Such reforms did little for the poor and working classes, who had manned the barricades in July. Dissatisfaction with the 1830 settlement boiled over in Lyon in 1831, when a silk-workers' strike over wages turned into a rebellion that died down only when the army arrived. Revolution had broken the hold of those who wanted to restore the pre-1789 monarchy and nobility, but it had gone no further this time than installing a more liberal, constitutional monarchy.

The success of the July Revolution in Paris ignited the Belgians, whose country had been annexed to the kingdom of the Netherlands in 1815. Differences in traditions, language, and religion separated the largely Catholic Belgians from the Dutch. King William of the Netherlands appealed to the great powers for help, but Great Britain and France opposed intervention and invited Russia, Austria, and Prussia to a conference that guaranteed Belgium independence in exchange for its neutrality in international affairs. Belgian neutrality would remain a cornerstone of European diplomacy for a century. After much maneuvering, the crown of the new kingdom of Belgium was offered to a German prince, Leopold of Saxe-Coburg, in 1831. Belgium, like France and Britain, now had a constitutional monarchy.

Political tensions boiled to the surface again in the late 1840s when crop failures across Europe threatened the food supply and food prices shot skyward. In the best of times, urban workers paid 50 to 80 percent of their income for a diet consisting largely of bread; now even bread was beyond their means. Overpopulation hastened famine in some places, especially Ireland, where an airborne blight destroyed the staple crop, potatoes, in 1846, 1848, and 1851. Out of a population of 8 million, as many as 1 million people died of starvation and disease. Corpses lay unburied on the sides of roads, and whole families were found dead in their cottages, half-eaten by dogs. Hundreds of thousands emigrated to England, the United States, and Canada.

High food prices also drove down the demand for manufactured goods, resulting in increased unemployment. Industrial workers' wages had been rising—in the German states, for example, wages rose an average of 5.5 percent in the 1830s

■ The Potato Blight and Irish Famine
Daniel McDonald's painting The Discovery of the Potato Blight *(1852) shows a family digging potatoes only to find the crop rotted from blight. Potato blight spelled disaster for thousands of families. The airborne blight spores landed on the potato plants and killed the leaves, which fell to the ground. Spores washed into the earth and infected the underground tubers. A crop could look normal yet be infected.*

and 10.5 percent in the 1840s—but the cost of living rose about 16 percent each decade, canceling out wage increases. Seasonal work and regular unemployment were already the norm when the crisis of the late 1840s intensified the uncertainties of urban life. "The most miserable class that ever sneaked its way into history" is how Friedrich Engels described underemployed and starving workers in 1847.

The specter of hunger tarnished the image of established rulers and amplified voices critical of them. Louis-Philippe's government had blocked all moves for electoral reform, and in February 1848, a banquet campaign sponsored by the political opposition turned into a revolution. At first the police and the army dispersed the demonstrators who took to the streets on February 22, 1848. The next day, however, forty or fifty people died when panicky soldiers opened fire on the crowd. On February 24, faced with fifteen hundred barricades and a furious populace, Louis-Philippe abdicated and fled to England. A hastily formed provisional government declared France a republic once again.

The new republican government issued liberal reforms—an end to the death penalty for political crimes, the abolition of slavery in the colonies, and freedom of the press—and agreed to introduce universal adult male suffrage despite misgivings about political participation by peasants and unemployed workers. To address the gnawing problem of unemployment, the government allowed Paris officials to organize a system of "national workshops" to provide those out of jobs with construction work. When women protested their exclusion, the city set up a few workshops for women workers, albeit with wages lower than men's. To meet a mounting deficit, the provisional government then levied a 45 percent surtax on property taxes, alienating peasants and landowners.

The establishment of the republic politicized many segments of the population. Scores of newspapers and political clubs revived grassroots democratic fervor; meeting in concert halls, theaters, and government auditoriums, clubs became a regular attraction for the citizenry. Women also formed clubs, published women's newspapers, and demanded representation in national politics. Street-corner activism alarmed middle-class liberals and conservatives. To maintain control, the republican government paid some unemployed youths to join a mobile guard with its own uniforms and barracks. Tension between the government and the workers in the national workshops rose; the communist Étienne Cabet led one demonstration of 150,000 workers. Class warfare loomed like a thunderstorm on the horizon.

Faced with rising radicalism in Paris and other big cities, the voters elected a largely conservative National Assembly in April 1848, which immediately appointed a five-man executive committee to run the government and deliberately excluded known supporters of workers' rights. Suspicious of all demands for rapid change, the deputies dismissed a petition to restore divorce and voted down women's suffrage, 899 to 1. When the numbers enrolled in the national workshops in Paris rocketed from a predicted 10,000 to 110,000, the government ordered the workshops closed to new workers, and on June 21 it directed that those already enrolled move to the provinces or join the army.

The workers of Paris responded to these measures on June 23 by taking to the streets in the tens of thousands. In the June Days, as the following week came to be called, the government summoned the army, the National Guard, and the newly recruited mobile guard to fight the workers. Provincial volunteers came to help put down the workers, who had been depicted to them as lazy ruffians intent on destroying order and property. One observer breathed a sigh of relief: "The Red Republic [red being associated with demands for socialism] is lost forever; all France has joined against it. The National Guard, citizens, and peasants from the remotest parts of the country have come pouring in." The republic's army crushed the workers; more than 10,000, most of them workers, were killed or injured, 12,000 were arrested, and 4,000 eventually were convicted and deported.

When the National Assembly adopted a new constitution calling for a presidential election in which all adult men could vote, the electorate chose Louis-Napoleon Bonaparte, nephew of the dead emperor. Bonaparte got more than

5.5 million votes out of some 7.4 million cast. He had lived most of his life outside of France, and the leaders of the republic expected him to follow their tune. In uncertain times, the Bonaparte name promised something to everyone. Even many workers supported him because he had no connection with the blood-drenched June Days.

In reality, Bonaparte's election spelled the end of the Second Republic, just as his uncle had dismantled the first one, established in 1792. In 1852, on the forty-eighth anniversary of Napoleon I's coronation as emperor, Louis-Napoleon declared himself Emperor Napoleon III (r. 1852–1870). (Napoleon I's son died and never became Napoleon II, but Napoleon III wanted to create a sense of legitimacy and so used the Roman numeral III.) Political division and class conflict had proved fatal to the Second Republic. Although the revolution of 1848 never had a period of terror like that in 1793–1794, it nonetheless ended in similar fashion, with an authoritarian government that tried to play monarchists and republicans off against each other.

The Parisian uprising soon sparked other revolts. Italian nationalists hoped to unite a diverse collection of territories. In January 1848, a revolt had already broken out in Palermo, Sicily, against the Bourbon ruler. When news came of the revolution in Paris, a huge nationalist demonstration in Milan quickly pitted Austrian forces against armed demonstrators. In Venice, an uprising drove out the Austrians. Peasants in the south of Italy occupied large landowners' estates, while across central Italy revolts mobilized the poor and unemployed against local rulers. But class tensions and regional differences stood in the way of national unity. Property owners, businessmen, and professionals wanted liberal reforms and national unification under a conservative regime; intellectuals, workers, and artisans dreamed of democracy and social reforms. Some nationalists

The Divisions of Italy, 1848

favored a loose federation; others wanted a monarchy under Charles Albert of Piedmont-Sardinia; still others urged rule by the pope. A few shared Mazzini's vision of a republic with a strong central government. Many leaders of national unification spoke Italian only as a second language; most Italians spoke regional dialects.

As king of the most powerful Italian state, Charles Albert played a central role. After some hesitation caused by fears of French intervention, he led a military campaign against Austria. It soon failed, partly because of dissension over goals and tactics among the nationalists. Although Austrian troops defeated Charles Albert in the north in the summer of 1848, democratic and nationalist forces prevailed at

Revolutions of 1848			
1848		**November**	Insurrection drives the pope out of Rome
January	Uprising in Palermo, Sicily	**December**	Francis Joseph becomes Austrian emperor; Louis-Napoleon elected president in France
February	Revolution in Paris; proclamation of republic		
March	Insurrections in Vienna, German cities, Milan, and Venice; autonomy movement in Hungary; Charles Albert of Piedmont-Sardinia declares war on Austrian Empire	**1849**	
		February	Rome declared a republic
		April	Frederick William of Prussia rejects crown of united Germany offered by Frankfurt parliament
May	Frankfurt parliament opens		
June	Austrian army crushes revolutionary movement in Prague; June Days end in defeat of workers in Paris	**July**	Roman republic overthrown by French intervention
		August	Russian and Austrian armies combine to defeat Hungarian forces
July	Austrians defeat Charles Albert and Italian forces		

first in the south. In the fall, the Romans drove the pope from the city and in February 1849 declared Rome a republic. For the next few months republican leaders, such as Mazzini and Giuseppe Garibaldi (1807–1882), congregated in Rome to organize the new republic. These efforts faltered in July when foreign powers intervened. The new president of republican France, Louis-Napoleon Bonaparte, sent an expeditionary force to secure the papal throne for Pius IX (r. 1846–1878). Mazzini and Garibaldi fled. Although revolution had been defeated in Italy, the memory of the Roman republic and the commitment to unification remained, and they would soon emerge again with new force.

News of the revolution in Paris also provoked popular demonstrations in the German states. "My heart beat with joy. The monarchy had fallen. Only a little blood had been shed for such a high stake, and the great watchwords Liberty, Equality, Fraternity were again inscribed on the banner of the movement." So responded one Frankfurt woman to Louis-Philippe's overthrow. The Prussian army's efforts to clear the square in front of Berlin's royal palace on March 18, 1848, provoked panic and street fighting around hastily assembled barricades. The next day the crowd paraded wagons loaded with dead bodies under

The German States, 1848

King Frederick William IV's window, forcing him to salute the victims killed by his own army. In a state of near collapse, the king promised to call an assembly to draft a constitution and adopted the German nationalist flag of black, red, and gold.

The goal of German unification soon took precedence over social reform or constitutional changes within the separate states. In March and April 1848, most of the German states agreed to elect delegates to a federal parliament at Frankfurt that would attempt to unite Germany. Local princes and even the more powerful kings of Prussia and Bavaria seemed to totter. In Bavaria, students marched to the "Marseillaise" and called for a republic. Yet the revolutionaries' weaknesses soon became apparent. The eight hundred delegates to the Frankfurt parliament had little practical political experience: "a group of old women," one socialist called them; a "Professors Parliament" was the common sneer. These delegates had no access to an army, and they dreaded the demands of the lower classes for social reforms. Unemployed artisans and workers smashed machines; peasants burned landlords' records and occasionally attacked Jewish moneylenders; women set up clubs and newspapers to demand their emancipation from "perfumed slavery."

The advantage lay with the princes, who retained legal authority and control over the armed forces. The most powerful German states, Prussia and Austria, expected to determine whether and how Germany should unite. While the Frankfurt parliament laboriously prepared a liberal constitution for a united Germany—one that denied self-determination to Czechs, Poles, and Danes within its proposed German borders—the Prussian king Frederick William IV (r. 1840–1860) recovered his confidence. First his army crushed the revolution in Berlin in the fall of 1848. Prussian troops then intervened to help other local rulers put down the last wave of democratic and nationalist insurrections in the spring. In April 1849, when the Frankfurt parliament finally concluded its work, offering the emperorship of a constitutional, federal Germany to the king of Prussia, Frederick William contemptuously refused this "crown from the gutter."

By the summer of 1848, the Austrian Empire, too, had reached the verge of complete collapse. Just as Italians were driving the Austrians out of their lands in northern Italy and Magyar nationalists were demanding political autonomy for Hungary, on March 13, 1848, in Vienna, a student-led demonstration for political reform turned into rioting, looting, and machine-breaking. Metternich resigned, escaping to England in disguise. Emperor Ferdinand promised a constitution, an elected parliament, and the end of censorship. Beleaguered authorities in Vienna could not refuse Magyar demands for home rule, and Széchenyi and Kossuth both became ministers in the new Hungarian government. The Magyars were the largest ethnic group in Hungary but still did not make up 50 percent of the population, which included Romanians, Slovaks, Croats, and Slovenes, who preferred Austrian rule to domination by local Magyars.

The ethnic divisions in Hungary foreshadowed the many political and social divisions that would doom the revolutionaries. Fears of peasant insurrection

■ **Revolution of 1848 in Eastern Europe**
This painting by an unknown artist shows Ana Ipatescu leading a group of Romanian revolution-aries in Transylvania in opposition to Russian rule. The Transylvanian provinces of Moldavia and Walachia had been under Russian domination since the 1770s and occupied directly since 1829. In April 1848, local landowners began to organize meetings. Paris-educated nationalists spearheaded the movement, which demanded the end of Russian control and various legal and political re-forms. By August the movement had split between those who wanted independence only and those who pushed for the end of serfdom and for universal manhood suffrage. In response, the Russians invaded Moldavia and the Turks moved into Walachia. By October, the uprising was over. Russia and Turkey agreed to control the provinces jointly. (The Art Archive.)

prompted the Magyar nationalists around Kossuth to abolish serfdom. This mea-sure alienated the largest noble landowners. In Prague, Czech nationalists convened a Slav congress as a counter to the Germans' Frankfurt parliament and called for a reorganization of the Austrian Empire that would recognize the rights of ethnic mi-norities. Such assertiveness by non-German peoples provoked German nationalists to protest on behalf of German-speaking people in areas with a Czech or Magyar majority.

The Austrian government slowly took advantage of these divisions. To quell peasant discontent and appease liberal reformers, it abolished all remaining peas-ant obligations to the nobility in March 1848. Rejoicing country folk soon lost interest in the revolution. Class conflicts flared in Vienna, where the middle classes had little sympathy for the starving artisans and workers. The new Hungarian government alienated the other nationalities when it imposed the Magyar language on them. Similar divisions sapped national unity in the Polish and Czech lands of the empire.

Military force finally broke up the revolutionary movements. The first blow fell in Prague in June 1848; General Prince Alfred von Windischgrätz, the military governor, bombarded the city into submission when a demonstration led to violence (including the shooting death of his wife, watching from a window). After another uprising in Vienna a few months later, Windischgrätz marched 70,000 soldiers into the capital and set up direct military rule. In December, the Austrian monarchy came back to life when the eighteen-year-old Francis Joseph (r. 1848–1916), unencumbered by promises extracted by the revolutionaries from his now-feeble uncle Ferdinand, assumed the imperial crown after intervention by leading court officials. In the spring of 1849, General Count Joseph Radetsky defeated the last Italian challenges to Austrian power in northern Italy, and his army moved east, joining with Croats and Serbs to take on the Hungarian rebels. In August, the Austrian army teamed up with Tsar Nicholas I, who marched into Hungary with more than 300,000 Russian troops. Hungary was put under brutal martial law. Széchenyi went mad, and Kossuth found refuge in the United States. Social conflicts and ethnic divisions weakened the revolutionary movements from the inside and gave the Austrian government the opening it needed to restore its position.

Aftermath to 1848

The revolutionaries of 1848 failed to achieve most of their goals, but their efforts left a profound mark on the political and social landscape. Between 1848 and 1851, the French served a kind of republican apprenticeship that prepared the population for another, more lasting republic after 1870. No French government could henceforth rule without extensive popular consultation. In Italy, the failure of unification did not stop the spread of nationalist ideas and the rooting of demands for democratic participation. In the German states, the revolutionaries of 1848 turned nationalism from an academic idea into a popular movement. The very idea of a Frankfurt parliament and the insistence on brandishing a German national flag at demonstrations showed that German nationalism had become a practical reality. The initiation of artisans, workers, and journeymen into democratic clubs increased political awareness in the lower classes and helped prepare them for broader political participation. Almost all the German states had a constitution and a parliament after 1850. The spectacular failures of 1848 thus hid some important successes.

The absence of revolution in 1848 was just as significant as its presence. No revolution occurred in Great Britain, the Netherlands, or Belgium, three places where industrialization and urbanization had developed most rapidly. In Great

Britain, the prospects for revolution actually seemed quite good: the Chartist movement took inspiration from the European revolutions in 1848 and mounted several gigantic demonstrations to force Parliament into granting all adult males the vote. But Parliament refused and no uprising occurred, in part because the government had already proved its responsiveness. The middle classes in Britain had been co-opted into the established order by the Reform Bill of 1832, and the working classes had won parliamentary regulation of children's and women's work.

The other notable exception to revolution among the great powers was Russia, where Tsar Nicholas I maintained a tight grip through police surveillance and censorship. The Russian schools, limited to the upper classes, taught Nicholas's three most cherished principles: autocracy (the unlimited power of the tsar), orthodoxy (obedience to the church in religion and morality), and nationality (devotion to Russian traditions). These provided no space for political dissent. Social conditions also fostered political passivity: serfdom continued in force, and the slow rate of industrial and urban growth created little discontent.

For all the differences between countries, some developments touched them all. European states continued to expand their bureaucracies. For example, in 1750 the Russian government employed approximately 10,500 functionaries; a century later it needed almost 114,000. In Great Britain, a swelling army of civil servants produced parliamentary studies on industrialization, foreign trade, and colonial profits, while new agencies such as the British urban police forces (10,000 strong in the 1840s) intruded increasingly in ordinary people's lives. States wanted to take children out of the fields and factories where they worked with their families and educate them. In some German cities, the police reported people who cleared snow off their roofs after the permitted hour or smoked in the street. A few governments even prescribed the length of sermons.

Although much had changed, the aristocracy remained the dominant power almost everywhere. As army officers, aristocrats put down revolutionary forces. As landlords, they continued to dominate the rural scene and control parliamentary bodies. They also held many official positions in the state bureaucracies. One Italian princess explained, "There are doubtless men capable of leading the nation . . . but their names are unknown to the people, whereas those of noble families . . . are in every memory." Aristocrats kept their authority by adapting to change: they entered the bureaucracy and professions, turned their estates into moneymaking enterprises, and learned how to invest shrewdly.

The reassertion of conservative rule hardened gender definitions. Women everywhere had participated in the revolutions, especially in the Italian states, where they joined armies in the tens of thousands and applied household skills toward making bandages, clothing, and food. Schoolgirls in Prague had thrown desks and chairs out of windows and helped build students' barricades. Many women in Paris had supported the new republic and seized the occasion of greater political openness to demand women's rights, only to experience isolation as their claims were

IMPORTANT DATES			
1814–1815	Congress of Vienna	1833	Factory Act regulates work of children in Great Britain; abolition of slavery in the British Empire
1820	Revolt of liberal army officers against the Spanish crown; Karlsbad Decrees abolish German student societies and tighten press censorship	1834	German customs union (Zollverein) established under Prussian leadership
1824	Ludwig van Beethoven, Ninth Symphony	1839	Beginning of Opium War between Britain and China
1825	Russian army officers demand constitutional reform in the Decembrist uprising	1846	Famine strikes Ireland; Corn Laws repealed in England; peasant insurrection in Austrian province of Galicia
1830	Manchester and Liverpool Railway opens in England; Greece gains independence from Ottoman Turks; France invades and begins conquest of Algeria; rebels overthrow Charles X of France and install Louis-Philippe; beginning of cholera epidemic in Europe	1847	Charlotte Brontë, Jane Eyre
		1848	Last great wave of Chartist demonstration in Britain; Karl Marx and Friedrich Engels, The Communist Manifesto; revolutions of 1848 throughout Europe; abolition of slavery in French colonies; end of serfdom in Austrian Empire
1832	British Parliament passes Reform Bill; Johann Wolfgang von Goethe, Faust	1851	Crystal Palace exhibition in London

denied by most republican men. Men in the revolutions of 1848 almost always defined universal suffrage as a male right. When workingmen gained the vote and women did not, the notion of separate spheres penetrated even into working-class life: political participation became one more way to distinguish masculinity from femininity. As conservatives returned to power, all signs of women's political activism disappeared. The French feminist movement, the most advanced in Europe, fell apart after the June Days when the increasingly conservative republican government forbade women to form political clubs and arrested and imprisoned two of the most outspoken women leaders for their socialist activities.

In May 1851, Europe's most important female monarch presided over a mid-century celebration of peace and industrial growth that helped dampen the still-smoldering fires of revolutionary passion. Queen Victoria (r. 1837–1901), who herself promoted the notion of domesticity as women's sphere, opened the international Exhibition of the Works of Industry of All Nations in London on May 1.

■ **The Crystal Palace**
This color lithograph (1851) by George Baxter provides a good view of the exterior of the main building for the Exhibition of the Works of Industry of All Nations in London. Sir Joseph Paxton (1801–1865) designed the gigantic building. It stood 1,848 feet long by 456 feet wide by 135 feet high; 772,784 square feet of ground-floor area covered no less than 18 acres.
(© The Bridgeman Art Library International Ltd.)

A monument of modern iron and glass architecture had been constructed to house the display; the building was more than a third of a mile long and so tall that it was erected over the trees of its Hyde Park site. Soon people referred to it as the "Crystal Palace"; its nine hundred tons of glass created an aura of fantasy, and the abundant goods from all nations inspired satisfaction and pride. One German visitor described it as "this miracle which has so suddenly appeared to dazzle the inhabitants of our globe." In the place of revolutionary fervor, the Crystal Palace offered a government-sponsored spectacle of what industry, hard work, and technological imagination could produce.

Conclusion

Many of the six million people who visited the Crystal Palace display had not forgotten the threat of disease, fears of overpopulation, popular resentments, and political upheavals that had been so prominent in the 1830s and 1840s. Even though industrial growth brought railroads, cheaper clothing, and access to exhibitions like the Crystal Palace, it also produced urban overcrowding and miserable working

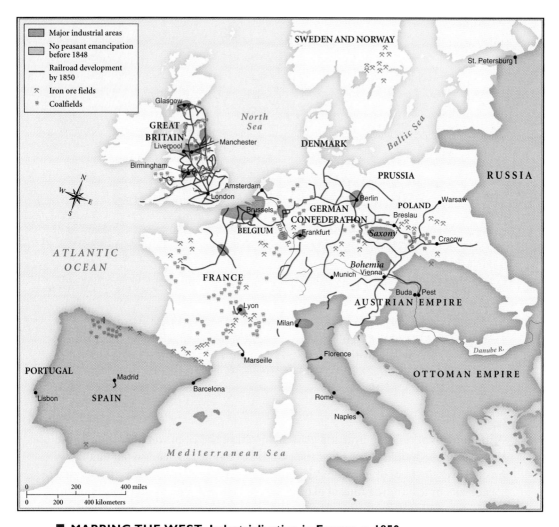

■ **MAPPING THE WEST** **Industrialization in Europe, c. 1850**
Industrialization first spread across northern Europe in a band that included Great Britain, north-
ern France, Belgium, the northern German states, the region around Milan in northern Italy, and
Bohemia. Much of Scandinavia and southern and eastern Europe did not participate in this first
phase of industrial development. Although railroads were not the only factor in promoting indus-
trialization, the map makes clear the interrelationship between railroad building and the
development of new industrial sites of coal mining and textile production.

conditions. The Crystal Palace presented the rosy view, but the housing shortages,
inadequacy of water supplies, and recurrent epidemic diseases had not disappeared.
Social reform organizations still drew attention to prostitution, child abandonment,
alcohol abuse, and other problems associated with burgeoning cities.

Although the revolutions of 1848 brought to the surface the profound tensions within a European society in transition toward industrialization and modernization, they did not definitively resolve those tensions. Industrialization and urbanization continued, workers developed more extensive organizations, and liberals, conservatives, and socialists fought over the pace of reform. The revolutions made their most striking impact negatively rather than positively: confronted with the menace of revolution, elites sought alternatives that would be less threatening to the established order and still permit some change. This search for alternatives became immediately evident in the question of national unification in Germany and Italy. National unification would hereafter depend on what the Prussian leader Otto von Bismarck would call "blood and iron," not speeches and parliamentary resolutions.

Suggested References for further reading and online research appear on page SR-26 at the back of the book.

www.bedfordstmartins.com/huntconcise   See the ONLINE STUDY GUIDE to assess your mastery of the material covered in this chapter.

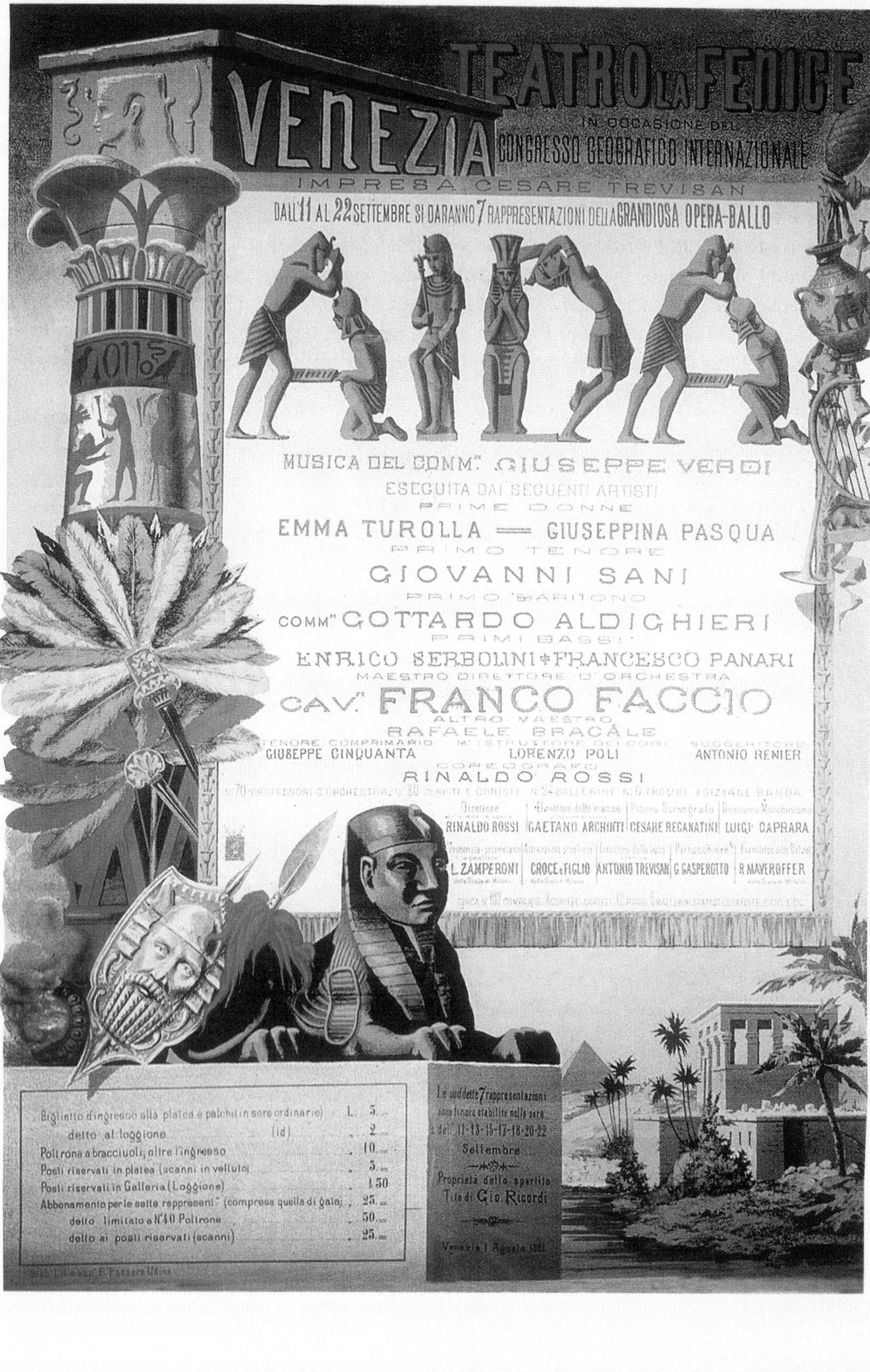
VENEZIA
TEATRO LA FENICE
IN OCCASIONE DEL
CONGRESSO GEOGRAFICO INTERNAZIONALE
IMPRESA CESARE TREVISAN
DALL'11 AL 22 SETTEMBRE SI DARANNO 7 RAPPRESENTAZIONI DELLA GRANDIOSA OPERA-BALLO
AIDA
MUSICA DEL COMM.RE GIUSEPPE VERDI
ESEGUITA DAI SEGUENTI ARTISTI
PRIME DONNE
EMMA TUROLLA — GIUSEPPINA PASQUA
PRIMO TENORE
GIOVANNI SANI
PRIMO BARITONO
COMM.RE GOTTARDO ALDIGHIERI
PRIMI BASSI
ENRICO SERBOLINI • FRANCESCO PANARI
MAESTRO DIRETTORE D'ORCHESTRA
CAV.RE FRANCO FACCIO
ALTRO MAESTRO
RAFAELE BRACÀLE
TENORE COMPRIMARIO
GIUSEPPE CINQUANTA
M.O ISTRUTTORE DEI CORI
LORENZO POLI
SUGGERITORE
ANTONIO RENIER
COREOGRAFO
RINALDO ROSSI
N. 70 PROFESSORI D'ORCHESTRA, N. 80 CORISTI E CORISTE N. 24 BALLERINE N. 6 TROMBE EGIZIANE BANDA
Direttore
RINALDO ROSSI
Direttore delle masse
GAETANO ARCHINTI
Pittore Scenografo
CESARE RECANATINI
Direttore del Macchinismo
LUIGI CAPRARA
Vestiarista
L. ZAMPERONI
della Scala di Milano
Attrezzista
CROCE e FIGLIO
della Scala di Milano
Fornitore della luce
elettrica
ANTONIO TREVISAN
Parrucchiere
G. GASPEROTTO
Fornitrice delle Calzat.
R. MAVEROFFER
della Scala di Milano
CIRCA N. 100 COMPARSE, 8 CORIFEI, CORIFEE, 12 PASSI, 6 BALLERINI, STATISTI, STATISTE, ECC. ECC.
Biglietto d'ingresso alla platea e palchi (in sere ordinarie) L. 5.—
detto al loggione (id) 2.—
Poltrona a bracciuoli, oltre l'ingresso 10.—
Posti riservati in platea (scanni in velluto) 5.—
Posti riservati in Galleria (Loggione) 1.50
Abbonamento per le sette rappresent.ni (compresa quella di gala) 25.—
detto limitato a N. 40 Poltrone 50.—
detto ai posti riservati (scanni) 25.—
Le suddette 7 rappresentazioni sono fissate stabilite nelle sere del 11-13-15-17-18-20-22 Settembre
Proprietà dello spartito Tito di Gio. Ricordi
Venezia 1 Agosto 1881

18

Constructing the Nation-State

c. 1850–1880

I N 1859, THE NAME VERDI SUDDENLY APPEARED scrawled on walls across the disunited cities of the Italian peninsula. The graffiti seemed to celebrate the composer Giuseppe Verdi, whose operas thrilled crowds of Europeans. Verdi was a particular hero among Italians, however, for his stories of downtrodden groups struggling against tyrannical government seemed to refer specifically to their plight. As his operatic choruses thundered out calls to rebellion in the name of the nation, Italian audiences were sure that Verdi meant for them to throw off Austrian and papal rule and unite in a new version of the ancient Roman Empire. Yet the graffiti was doubly political, a call to arms in the days before mass media. For VERDI also formed an acronym for *Vittorio Emmanuele Re* ("king") *d'Italia*, and in 1859 it summoned Italians to unite immediately under Victor Emmanuel II, king of Sardinia and Piedmont—the one leader with a nationalist, modernizing profile. The graffiti did its work, for the very next year Italy united as a result of warfare, popular uprisings, and hard bargaining by political realists.

In the wake of the failed revolutions of 1848, European statesmen and the politically conscious public increasingly rejected the politics of idealism in favor of *Realpolitik*—a politics of tough-minded realism aimed at strengthening the state and tightening social order. Claiming to distrust the romanticism and high-minded ideologies of the revolutionaries and hoping to control nationalism, Realpolitikers believed in playing power politics, strengthening the national economy, and using violence to attain their goals. Two particularly skilled practitioners of Realpolitik, the Italian Camillo di Cavour and the Prussian Otto von Bismarck, succeeded in

■ *Aïda* **Poster**

Aïda, Giuseppe Verdi's opera of human passion and state power, became a staple of Western culture. As the opera played across Europe, it brought Europeans into a common cultural orbit. Written to celebrate the opening of the Suez Canal, Aïda *also celebrated Europe's better access to Asian resources provided by the new waterway. As the poster shows, the opera ushered in another wave of Egyptomania—the craze for Egyptian styles and objects.* (Madeline Grimoldi.)

unifying Italy and Germany, respectively, not by consensus but by war and diplomacy. Most leading figures of these decades, enmeshed like Verdi's operatic heroes in violent political maneuverings, advanced state power by harnessing the forces of nationalism and liberalism that had led to earlier romantic revolts.

Many ingredients went into making modern nation-states and empires during these momentous decades. Continued economic development was crucial, and entrepreneurs produced a host of new inventions, new procedures, and new ways of doing business. A growing sense of national identity and common purpose was forged by both culture and government policy. As productivity and wealth increased, governments took vigorous steps to improve the urban environment, monitor public health, and promote national sentiment. State support for cultural developments ranging from public schools to opera productions helped establish a common fund of knowledge and even shared political beliefs. Authoritarian leaders such as Bismarck and the new French emperor Napoleon III believed that a better quality of life would not only calm revolutionary impulses and build state power but also keep political liberals at bay.

Culture also built a sense of belonging. Reading novels, attending art exhibitions, keeping up-to-date at the newly fashionable world's fairs, and attending theater and opera created a greater sense of being French or German or British but also of being European. Cultural works increasingly rejected romanticism, featuring instead realistic aspects of ordinary people's lives. Artists painted nudes in shockingly blunt ways, eliminating romantic hues and poses. Verdi's celebrated opera *La Traviata* showed a frolicking courtesan menacing a middle-class family. The Russian author Leo Tolstoy depicted the bleak life of soldiers in the Crimean War that erupted in 1853 between the Russian and Ottoman Empires, while his countryman Fyodor Dostoevsky wrote of criminals and murders in urban neighborhoods.

Realpolitik cared less for the costs than for the outcomes of state building. Advancing state power entailed intensifying colonization and stamping out resistance to global expansion. At home it uprooted neighborhoods in favor of constructing public buildings, roads, and parks. The process of nation building was often brutal, bringing war, arrests, protests, and outright civil war—all of these the centerpieces of Verdi's operas as well. As the wars of German unification drew to a close in 1871, an uprising of Parisians threw the new terms of national and industrial growth into question as citizens challenged the central government's intrusion into everyday life and its failure to count the costs. For the most part, the powerful Western state did not take shape automatically during these years. Instead, its growth occasioned warfare, dislocation, new inroads on the lives of people around the world, shrewd policy, and heated debate. Realpolitik produced all of these, as well as a general climate of modern opinion that valued realism and hard facts.

The End of the Concert of Europe

The revolutions of 1848 had weakened the concert of Europe, driving out its architect Metternich and allowing the forces of nationalism to flourish. It became more difficult for countries to control their competing ambitions and act together. In addition, the dreaded resurgence of Bonapartism in the person of Napoleon III (Louis-Napoleon, the nephew of Napoleon I) added to the volatility in international politics as France sought to reassert itself. One of Napoleon's targets was Russia, formerly a mainstay of the concert of Europe. From Russia's pursuit of further expansion, France helped engineer the Crimean War of 1853–1856. Taking a huge toll in human life, the war weakened Russia and Austria and made way for a massive shift in the distribution of European power.

Napoleon III and the Quest for French Glory

Louis-Napoleon Bonaparte encouraged the resurgence of French grandeur and the cult of his famous uncle as part of nation building. "There are certain men who are born to serve as a means for the march of the human race," he wrote. "I consider myself to be one of these." In deft political coups Louis-Napoleon converted himself from president of the Second Republic to emperor. Repressing opposition in towns and cities, he declared himself Emperor Napoleon III (r. 1852–1870) and proclaimed the Second Empire on December 2, 1852, anniversary of Napoleon I's own ascension to power.

Napoleon III acted as Europe's schoolmaster, showing its leaders how to combine economic liberalism and nationalism with authoritarian rule. Cafés where men might discuss politics were closed, and a rubber-stamp legislature (the *Corps législatif*) reduced representative government to a façade. Imperial style replaced republican rituals. Napoleon's opulent court dazzled the public, and the emperor cultivated a masculine image of strength and majesty by wearing military uniforms (like his namesake) and by conspicuously maintaining mistresses. Napoleon's wife, Empress Eugénie, however, followed middle-class conventions such as separate spheres for men and women by serving as a devoted mother to her only son and supporting many volunteer charities. The authoritarian, apparently old-fashioned order imposed by Napoleon satisfied the many peasants who opposed urban radicals as they went to the polls.

Yet Napoleon III was simultaneously a modernizer, and he promoted a strong economy, public works programs, and jobs, which lured the middle and working classes away from radical politics. International trade fairs, artistic expositions, and the magnificent rebuilding of Paris helped sustain French prosperity as Europe recovered from the hard times of the late 1840s. Empress Eugénie wore lavish gowns, encouraging French silk production and keeping Paris at the center of the lucrative

■ **Napoleon III and Eugénie Receive the Siamese Ambassadors**
At a splendid gathering of their court, Emperor Napoleon III, Empress Eugénie, and their son and heir greet ambassadors from Siam, whose exoticism and servility before the French imperial family are the centerpiece of this depiction. Amid the grandeur of the Napoleonic dynasty, the West towers above the East. (Giraudon/Art Resource, NY.)

fashion trade. The regime also reached a free-trade agreement with Britain and backed an innovative investment bank—the Crédit Mobilier. Such new institutions led the way in financing railroad expansion, and railway mileage increased fivefold during Napoleon III's reign. During the economic downturn of the late 1850s, he wooed support by allowing for working-class organizations and introducing democratic features into his governing methods. Although some historians have judged Napoleon III to be enigmatic and shifty because of these abrupt changes, his maneuvers were pragmatic responses to the fluid conditions.

On the international scene, Napoleon III's main goals were to overcome the containment of France imposed by the Congress of Vienna, realign continental politics to benefit France, and acquire international glory like a true Bonaparte. To realign European politics, Napoleon pitted France first against Russia in the Crimean War, then against Austria in the War of Italian Unification, and finally against Prussia in the Franco-Prussian War of 1870. Beyond Europe, Napoleon's army continued to enforce French rule in Algeria and Southeast Asia and tried to install Habsburg emperor Francis Joseph's brother Maximilian as ruler of Mexico and ultimately of all Central America—an assault that ended in 1867 with Maximilian's execution. Napoleon's foreign policy transformed relations among the great powers by causing a breakdown in the international system of peaceful diplomacy established at the Congress of Vienna. While his encouragement of projects like the Suez Canal to connect the Mediterranean and the Red Seas proved visionary, this push for worldwide influence eventually destroyed him: the French overthrew him after Prussia easily defeated his army in 1870.

The Crimean War, 1853–1856: Turning Point in European Affairs

Napoleon first flexed his diplomatic muscle in the Crimean War (1853–1856), which began as a conflict between the Russian and Ottoman Empires but ended as a war with long-lasting consequences for much of Europe. While professing to uphold the concert of Europe, Russia continued to build state power by making further inroads into Asia and the Middle East. In particular, Tsar Nicholas I wanted to absorb much of the Ottoman Empire, fast becoming known as "the sick man of Europe" because of its disintegrating authority. Napoleon III maneuvered Tsar Nicholas to be more aggressive, and amid this increasing belligerence war erupted in October 1853 between the two eastern empires (Map 18.1).

Behind the widening war lay the question of Europe's balance of power. To protect its Mediterranean routes to East Asia, Britain prodded the Ottomans to stand up to Russia. The Austrian government still resented its dependence on Russia in putting down Hungarian revolutionaries in 1849 and felt threatened by continuing Russian expansion into the Balkans. This anxiety helped Napoleon III gain a promise of Austrian neutrality during the war, thus fracturing the conservative Russian-Austrian coalition that had quashed French ambitions since 1815. In the fall of 1853, the Russians blasted the wooden Turkish ships to bits at the Ottoman port of Sinope on the Black Sea; in 1854, France and Great Britain, enemies in war for more than a century, declared war on Russia to defend the Ottoman Empire's sovereignty and territories.

■ MAP 18.1 The Crimean War, 1853–1856

The most destructive war in Europe between the Napoleonic Wars and World War I, this conflict drew attention to the conflicting ambitions around territories of the declining Ottoman Empire. Importantly for state building in these decades, it fractured the alliance of conservative forces from the Congress of Vienna, allowing Italy and Germany to come into being as unified states and permitting Napoleon III to pursue his ambitions for France.

www.bedfordstmartins.com/huntconcise
See the ONLINE STUDY GUIDE for more help in analyzing this map.

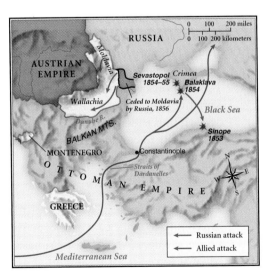

Faced with attacking the massive Russian Empire, the allies settled for limited military goals focused on capturing the Russian naval base at Sevastopol on the Black Sea in the Crimea. Even so, the Crimean War was spectacularly bloody. British and French troops landed in the Crimea in September 1854 and waged a long siege of the fortified city, which fell after a year of savage and costly combat. Generals on both sides demonstrated their incompetence, and governments failed to provide combatants with even minimal supplies, sanitation, or medical care. The war claimed a massive toll. Three-quarters of a million men died, more than two-thirds from disease and starvation.

In the midst of this unfolding catastrophe, Alexander II (r. 1855–1881) ascended the Russian throne after the death of his father, Nicholas I, in 1855. With casualties mounting, the new tsar sued for peace. As a result of the Peace of Paris, signed in March 1856, Russia lost the right to base its navy in the Straits of Dardanelles and the Black Sea, which were declared neutral waters. Moldavia and Walachia (which soon merged to form Romania) became autonomous Turkish provinces under the victors' protection.

Some historians have called the Crimean War one of the most senseless conflicts in modern history because competing claims in southeastern Europe could have been settled by diplomacy had it not been for Napoleon III's driving ambition. Yet the war was full of consequence. New technologies were introduced into warfare: the railroad, shell-firing cannon, breech-loading rifles, steam-powered ships, and the telegraph. The relationship of the home front to the battlefront was beginning to change with the use of the telegraph and increased press coverage. Home audiences received news from the Crimean front lines more rapidly and in more detail than ever before. However, reports of incompetence, poor sanitation, and the huge death toll outraged the public. One admirable figure rose above the carnage—Florence Nightingale. She seized the moment to escape the confines of middle-class domesticity by organizing a battlefield nursing service to care for the British sick and wounded. Through her tough-minded organization of nursing units, she improved the sanitary conditions of the troops both during and after the war and pioneered nursing as a profession. Finally, the war accomplished Napoleon III's goal of severing the alliance between the Habsburgs and Russia, the two conservative powers on which the Congress of Vienna peace settlement had rested since 1815. It thus ended Austria's and Russia's grip on European affairs and undermined their ability to contain the forces of liberalism and nationalism.

Spirit of Reform in Russia

Defeat in the Crimean War not only thwarted Russia's territorial ambition but also forced Russia on the path of reform. Hundreds of peasant insurrections had erupted during the decade before the Crimean War. Serf defiance ranged from malingering while at forced labor to boycotting vodka to protest its heavy taxation. "Our own and neighboring households were gripped with fear," one aristocrat reported, because everyone expected "a serf rising at any minute." Although economic development spread in parts of eastern Europe, the Russian economy stagnated compared with western Europe. Old-fashioned farming techniques led to depleted soil and food shortages, and the nobility was often contemptuous of ordinary people's suffering. Nonetheless, through sympathetic portrayals of serfs and frank depiction of brutal masters, such as in novelist Ivan Turgenev's *A Hunter's Sketches* (1852), a spirit of reform grew. A Russian translation of Harriet Beecher Stowe's antislavery novel *Uncle Tom's Cabin* (1852) also appeared in the 1850s and struck a responsive chord. When Russia lost the Crimean War, the educated public, including some government officials, found the poor performance of serf-conscripted armies a disgrace and the system of serf labor an intolerable liability.

Confronted with the need for change, Alexander proved more flexible than his father Nicholas I. Well educated and more widely traveled, he ushered in what came to be known as the age of Great Reforms, granting Russians new rights from above as a way of ensuring that violent action from below would not force change. The most dramatic reform was the emancipation of the serfs—almost 50 million people—beginning in 1861.◆ By the terms of emancipation, communities of former serfs, headed by male village elders, received grants of land. The community itself, called a *mir*, had full power to allocate this land among individuals and to direct their economic activity. Thus, although emancipation partially laid the groundwork for a modern labor force in Russia, communal landowning and decision making prevented unlimited mobility and the development of a pool of free labor. The condition attached to these so-called land grants was that peasants were not *given* land along with their personal freedom: they were forced to "redeem" the land they farmed by paying the government through long-term loans, which in turn compensated the original landowners. With much land and the best of it going to the nobility, most peasants ended up owning less land than they had tilled as serfs. These conditions, especially the huge burden of debt and communal regulations, blunted Russian agricultural development for decades. But idealistic reformers believed the emancipation of the serfs, once treated by the nobility practically as livestock, produced miraculous results. As one of them put it, "The people are without any exaggeration transfigured from head to foot. . . . The look, the walk, the speech, everything is changed."

Local administration, the judiciary, and the military were also reformed. The government compensated the nobility for loss of peasant services and set up *zemstvos*—regional councils through which aristocrats could direct neglected local matters such as education, public health, and welfare. Aristocratic dominance

---

◆ For the text of his emancipation proposal, see Document 57, Alexander II, "Address in the State Council."

■ Emancipation of the Russian Serfs
The Crimean War came as a harsh warning that the Russian Empire sorely needed social reform in an age of growing state power. The plight of tens of millions of serfs was often dire compared to the condition of western Europeans, and the emancipation of 1861 was seen as key to stabilizing both state and society. (Hulton Getty/Liaison Agency.)

assured that *zemstvos* would remain a conservative structure, but they became a countervailing political force to the distant central government, especially as some nobles profited from the relaxation of censorship and of restrictions on travel to see how the rest of Europe was governed. Simultaneously, judicial reform gave all Russians, even former serfs, access to modern civil courts, rather than leaving them at the mercy of a landowner's version of justice or secret, blatantly preferential practices. The Western principle of equality of all persons before the law, regardless of social rank, was introduced in Russia for the first time. Military reform followed in 1874 when the government ended the twenty-five-year period of conscription, substituting a six-year term and attention to education, efficiency, and humane treatment of recruits to make the Russian army more competitive with those in western Europe.

Alexander's reforms assisted modernizing and market-oriented landowners just as enclosures and emancipation had done much earlier in western Europe. At the same time, the changes diminished the personal prerogatives of the nobility, leaving their authority weakened and sparking intergenerational conflict. "An epidemic seemed to seize upon [noble] children . . . an epidemic of fleeing from the parental roof," one observer noted. Rejecting aristocratic leisure, youthful rebels from the upper class valued practical activity and sometimes identified with peasants and workers. Some formed communes where they hoped to do humble manual labor; others turned to higher education, especially the sciences. Rebellious daughters of the nobility flouted parental expectations by cropping their hair short, wearing black, and escaping from home through phony marriages so they could study in European universities. This repudiation of traditional society led Turgenev to label radical youth as *nihilists* (from the Latin for "nothing"), a term that meant a lack of belief in any values whatsoever.

The atmosphere of reform also produced resistance among Russian-dominated nationalities, including an uprising by aristocratic and upper-class nationalist Poles in 1863. By 1864, Alexander II's army regained control of the Russian section of Poland, having used reforms to buy peasant support in defeating the rebels. In the Caucasus and elsewhere, Alexander responded to nationalist unrest with repression and programs of intensive Russification—a tactic meant to reduce the threat of future rebellion by national minorities within the empire by forcing them to adopt Russian language and culture. In this era of the Great Reforms, the tsarist regime only partially succeeded in developing the administrative, economic, and civic institutions of the nation-state elsewhere.

War and Nation Building

With the concert of Europe a thing of the past, politicians in the German and Italian states used the opportunity to unify their countries quickly and violently through warfare. When disunity threatened, the United States also waged a bloody civil war to ensure its borders. Historians sometimes treat the rise of powerful nation-states such as Italy, Germany, and the United States as part of an inevitable process, but millions of individuals in these states and elsewhere maintained a local or some other complex sense of identity in the midst of national unification.

Cavour, Garibaldi, and the Process of Italian Unification

Despite the failure of the revolutions of 1848 in the Italian states, the issue of *Risorgimento* (literally meaning "rebirth" but associated with the movement for Italian unification) continued to percolate, aided by the disintegration of diplomatic stability across Europe. This time the clear leader of Risorgimento would be the kingdom of Piedmont-Sardinia, in the economically modernizing north of Italy. The kingdom rallied to the operas of Verdi, but it was fortified with railroads, a modern army, and the support of France against the Austrian Empire, which still dominated the peninsula.

The architect of the new Italy was the pragmatic Camillo di Cavour (1810–1861), prime minister of the kingdom of Piedmont-Sardinia from 1852 until his death. A rebel in his youth, the young Cavour had conducted agricultural experiments on his aristocratic father's land. He organized steamship companies, played the stock market, and inhaled the heady air of modernization during his travels to Paris and London. Cavour thus made economic development rather than democratic uprising the means to achieve a united Italy. As prime minister to the capricious and scheming king, Victor Emmanuel II (r. 1861–1878), he capitalized on favorable conditions to develop a healthy Piedmontese economy, a modern army, and a liberal political climate as the foundation for Piedmont's control of the unification process (Map 18.2).

■ **MAP 18.2 Unification of Italy, 1859–1870**

The many states of the Italian peninsula had different languages, ways of life, and economic inter-
ests. In the north, the Kingdom of Sardinia, which included the commercially advanced state of
Piedmont, had much to gain from a unified market and a more extensive pool of labor. Although
King Victor Emmanuel's and Garibaldi's armies unified these states into a single country, it would
take decades to construct a culturally, socially, and economically connected nation.

To unify Italy, however, Piedmont would have to confront Austria, which governed the provinces of Lombardy and Venetia and exerted strong influence over most
of the peninsula. Cavour turned for help to Napoleon III, who at a meeting in the
summer of 1858 promised French assistance in exchange for the city of Nice and the
region of Savoy. Napoleon III expected that France rather than Austria would influence the peninsula thereafter. Sure of French help, Cavour provoked the Austrians
to invade northern Italy in April 1859, and using the newly built Piedmontese rail-

road to move troops, the French and Piedmontese armies achieved rapid victories at Solferino and Magenta. The cause of Piedmont now became the cause of nationalist Italians everywhere, even those who had supported romantic republicanism in 1848. Political liberals in Tuscany and other central Italian states rose up on the side of Piedmont. Suddenly fearing Piedmontese force, Napoleon independently signed a peace treaty with Habsburg emperor Francis Joseph. Its terms gave Lombardy but not Venetia to Piedmont, and the rest of Italy remained disunited.

Napoleon's plans for controlled liberation of Lombardy and Venetia and a partitioned Italy were derailed as support for Piedmont continued to swell inside Italy and as a financially strapped Austria stood by helplessly. Ousting their rulers, citizens of Parma, Modena, Tuscany, and the Papal States (except Rome, which French troops had occupied) elected to join Piedmont. In May 1860, Giuseppe Garibaldi (1807–1882), a committed republican, inspired guerrilla fighter, and veteran of the revolutions of 1848, set sail from Genoa with a thousand red-shirted volunteers (many of them teenage boys) to liberate Sicily, where peasant revolts against landlords and the corrupt government were under way. In the autumn of 1860, the forces of King Victor Emmanuel of Piedmont-Sardinia and Garibaldi finally met in Naples. Although some of his supporters still clamored for social reform and a republic, Garibaldi threw his support to the king. In 1861, the kingdom of Italy was proclaimed with Victor Emmanuel as king.

Exhausted by a decade of overwork, Cavour died within months of leading the unification, leaving lesser men to organize the new Italy. Consensus among Italy's elected political leaders was often elusive once the war was over, and admirers of Cavour, such as Verdi (who had been made senator), fled the heated political scene. The wealthy commercial north and impoverished agricultural south remained at odds, as they do even today. Italian borders did not yet seem final because Venetia and Rome remained outside them,

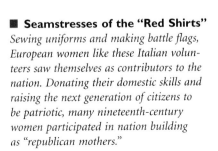

■ **Seamstresses of the "Red Shirts"**
Sewing uniforms and making battle flags, European women like these Italian volunteers saw themselves as contributors to the nation. Donating their domestic skills and raising the next generation of citizens to be patriotic, many nineteenth-century women participated in nation building as "republican mothers."

under Austrian and French control, respectively. But the legend of an Italian struggle for freedom symbolized by the figure of Garibaldi and his Red Shirts sentimentalized the economic and military Realpolitik that had made unification possible.

Bismarck and the Realpolitik of German Unification

The most momentous act of nation building for the future of Europe and of the world was the creation of a united Germany in 1871. This, too, was the work of Realpolitik, undertaken once the concert of Europe was smashed and the champions of the status quo were defeated. Employing the old military order to wage war, yet with the support of economic modernizers who saw profits in one huge national market, the Prussian state brought a vast array of cities and kingdoms under its control within a single decade. From then on, Germany prospered, continuing to consolidate its economic and political might.

The architect of a unified Germany was Otto von Bismarck (1815–1898), the Prussian minister-president. Bismarck came from a traditional *Junker* (Prussian landed nobility) family on his father's side; his mother's family included high-ranking bureaucrats and literati of the middle class. At university, the young Bismarck had gambled and womanized, interested only in a course on the economic foundations of politics. After failing in the civil service, he worked to modernize operations on his landholdings while leading an otherwise loutish life, but his marriage to a pious Lutheran woman gave him new purpose. In the 1850s, his diplomatic service to the Prussian state made him increasingly angry at Habsburg domination of German affairs and the roadblock it created to the full flowering of Prussia.

In 1862, William I (king of Prussia, r. 1861–1888; German emperor, r. 1871–1888) appointed Bismarck prime minister in hopes that he would quash the growing power of the liberals in the Prussian parliament. The liberals, representing the prosperous professional and business classes, had gained parliamentary strength at the expense of conservative landowners during the decades of industrial expansion. Indeed, the liberals' wealth was crucial to the Prussian state's ability to augment its power. Desiring Prussia to be like western Europe, Prussian liberals advocated the extension of political rights and increased civilian control of the military. William I, along with members of the traditional Prussian elite such as Bismarck, rejected the western European model. Bismarck simply rammed through programs to build the army and thwart civilian control. "Germany looks not to Prussia's liberalism, but to its power," he preached. "The great questions of the day will not be settled by speeches and majority decisions—that was the great mistake of 1848 and 1849—but by blood and iron."

After his triumph over the parliament, Bismarck led Prussia into a series of wars, against Denmark in 1864, against Austria in 1866, and, finally, against France in 1870. Using war as a political tactic, he kept the disunited German states from choosing Austrian leadership and instead united them around Prussia. Bismarck drew Austria into a joint war with Prussia against a rebellious Denmark in 1864 over Denmark's proposed incorporation of the provinces of Schleswig and Holstein, with their partially German population. Their joint victory resulted in an agreement that Prussia would administer Schleswig, and Austria, Holstein. Such an arrangement stretched Austria's geographic interests far from its central European base.

Austria proved weaker than Prussia, as the Habsburgs dealt with lagging economic development, a swelling national debt, and the restless national minorities within its borders. Bismarck encouraged Habsburg pretensions to its former grandeur and influence and simultaneously fomented disputes over the administration of Schleswig and Holstein, goading Austria into declaring war on Prussia itself. In the summer of 1866, Austria went to war with the support of most small states in the German Confederation. Within seven weeks, the modernized Prussian army, using railroads and breech-loading rifles against the outdated Austrian military, had won decisively. Victory allowed Bismarck to drive Austria from the German Confederation, create a North German Confederation led by Prussia, and coordinate economic and political programs (Map 18.3).

To bring the remaining German states into the rapidly developing nation, Bismarck next moved to entrap France in a war with Prussia. During the Austro-Prussian War, Bismarck had suggested to Napoleon III that his neutrality would bring France territory, thus heating up nationalist sentiments in both France and Germany. The atmosphere became even more charged when Spain proposed a minor Prussian prince to fill its vacant throne. This candidacy threatened the French with Prussian rulers on two of their borders and inflated Prussian pride. Bismarck used the occasion to stir up nationalist journalism in both countries by editing a diplomatic communication (the Ems telegram) to make it look as if the king of Prussia had insulted France. Release of the revised version to journalists inflamed the French public into demanding war. The parliament gladly declared it on July 19, 1870, setting in motion the alliances Prussia had created with the other German states. The Prussians captured Napoleon III with his army on September 2, 1870, and the Second Empire fell two days later. With Prussian forces still besieging Paris, in January 1871 in the Hall of Mirrors at Versailles, King William of Prussia was proclaimed the *kaiser* of a new, imperial Germany. The terms of the peace signed in May 1871 required France to cede the rich industrial provinces of Alsace and Lorraine to Germany and to pay a multi-billion-franc indemnity. Without French protection for the papacy, Rome became part of Italy. Germany was now poised to dominate continental politics.

Prussian military might served as the foundation for German state building, and a complex constitution ensured the continued political dominance of the aristocracy and monarchy. The kaiser, who remained Prussia's king, controlled the military and appointed Bismarck to the powerful position of imperial chancellor. The German states balanced monarchical authority somewhat through the *Bundesrat*, a body composed of representatives from each state. The *Reichstag,* an assembly

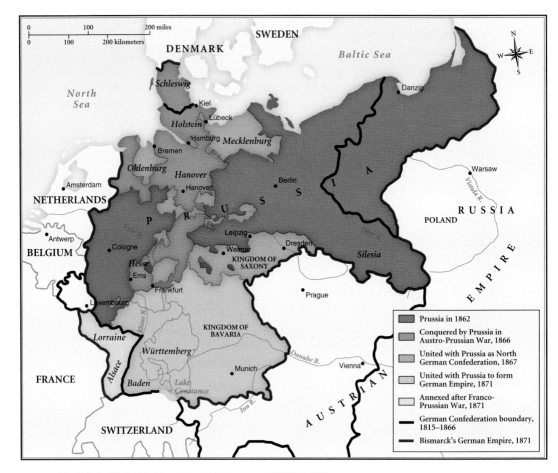

■ MAP 18.3 Unification of Germany, 1862–1871

In a complex series of diplomatic maneuvers, Bismarck welded disunited kingdoms and small states into a major continental power independent of the other dominant German dynasty, the Habsburg monarchy. Prussia's use of force unified Germany politically, and almost immediately that unity unleashed the new nation's economic potential. An aristocratic and agrarian elite remained firmly in power, but a rapidly growing working class would soon become a political force to be reckoned with.

elected by universal male suffrage, ratified all budgets. In framing this constitutional settlement, Bismarck accorded rights such as suffrage in the belief that the masses would uphold autocracy out of their fear of "the domination of finance capital"— shorthand for "liberal power." He balanced this move, however, with an electoral system in which votes from the upper classes counted more than votes from the lower classes. He had little to fear from liberals, who, dizzy with German military success, came to support the blend of economic progress, constitutionalism, and militaristic nationalism that Bismarck represented.

■ Emperor William I of Germany, 1871

The defeat of France in the Franco-Prussian War of 1870–1871 ended with the proclamation of the king of Prussia as emperor of a unified Germany. Otto von Bismarck, who had orchestrated the wars of unification, appropriately appears in this artistic rendering as the central figure attired in heroic white. The event in the French palace of Versailles symbolized the militaristic and antagonistic side of state building, especially the Franco-German rivalry that would disastrously motivate European politics in the future. (AKG London.)

Francis Joseph and the Creation of the Austro-Hungarian Monarchy

There was no blueprint for nation building. Just as the Crimean War left Russia searching for solutions to its social and political problems, so the confrontation with Cavour and Bismarck left the Habsburg Empire at bay. At first, the Habsburg Empire emerged from the revolutions of 1848 and 1849 renewed by the ascension of Francis Joseph (r. 1848–1916), who favored absolutist rule. A tireless worker, Francis Joseph enhanced his authority through stiff, formal court ceremonies, playing to the popular fascination with the trappings of power. Although the emperor stubbornly resisted change, official standards of honesty and efficiency improved, and the government promoted local education. The German language was used by the administration and taught by the schools, but the government respected the rights of national minorities—Czechs and Poles, for instance—to receive education and to communicate with officials in their native tongues. Above all, the government abolished most internal customs barriers, freed trade with Germany, fostered a boom in private railway construction, and attracted foreign capital. The capital city of Vienna underwent extensive rebuilding, and people found jobs as industrialization progressed.

In a fast-paced age, the absolutist emperor could not match Bismarck in advancing modernization and the power of the state. Prosperous liberals resented the swarm of police informers, the nearly free hand of the Catholic church in education and in civil institutions such as marriage, and their own lack of representation in such important policy matters as taxation and finance. Funds for modernizing the military dried up. After Prussia's victory over Francis Joseph's scaled-back armies in 1866, the most disaffected but wealthy part of the empire, Hungary, became the key to stability, even to the empire's existence. The leaders of the Hungarian agrarian elites forced the emperor to accept a "dual monarchy"—that is, Magyar home rule over the Hungarian kingdom. This agreement restored the Hungarian parliament and gave it control of internal policy (including the right to decide how to treat Hungary's national minorities). Although the Habsburg emperor Francis Joseph was crowned king of Hungary and Austro-Hungarian foreign policy was coordinated from Vienna, the Hungarians mostly ruled themselves after 1867 and hammered out common policies such as tariffs in acrimonious negotiations with Vienna.

The Austro-Hungarian Monarchy, 1867

The dual monarchy of Austria-Hungary, or Austro-Hungarian monarchy as the new arrangement was also called, was designed specifically to address Hungarian demands, but in so doing it strengthened the voices of Czechs, Slovaks, and at least half a dozen additional national groups in the Habsburg Empire wanting the same kind of self-rule. Czechs who helped the empire advance industrially failed to gain Hungarian-style liberties, and for some of the dissatisfied ethnic groups, Pan-Slavism—that is, the transnational loyalty of all ethnic Slavs—became a rallying cry as the various Slav peoples saw themselves as linked through a common heritage. Instead of looking toward Vienna, they turned to the largest Slavic country—Russia—as a focal point for potential national unity. As the nation-state grew in strength, transnational movements like Pan-Slavism would emerge to provide alternative allegiances for those not recognized as equal citizens in their home countries.

Political Stability through Gradual Reform in Great Britain

In contrast to the turmoil in continental Europe, Britain appeared the epitome of liberal progress. By the 1850s, the monarchy symbolized domestic tranquility and propriety. Unlike their predecessors, Queen Victoria (r. 1837–1901) and her hus-

■ **Queen Victoria and Prince Albert**

In the mid-nineteenth century, rulers started using the new photographic technology to portray themselves as respectable and distinguished figures. Queen Victoria and her husband were expert publicists, often posing as an ordinary middle-class couple and the epitome of domestic order in marked contrast to their often dissolute royal predecessors. Photos of them were sold or given away on small cards called cartes de visites, *which many leaders used to spread their fame.*

(The Royal Archives © Her Majesty Queen Elizabeth II.)

band, Prince Albert, were considered models of morality, British stability, and middle-class virtues. Britain's parliamentary system incorporated new ideas and steadily brought more men into the political process. Economic prosperity further fortified peaceful political reform except for Ireland's continued suffering and thwarted demands for justice. Smooth governmental decision making was fostered by an ever-changing and focused party system: the Tory party evolved into the Conservatives, many of whose policies favored the aristocracy. Nonetheless, the Conservatives still went along with the developing liberal consensus around economic development and representative government. The Whigs changed names, too, and became the Liberals. In 1867, the Conservatives, led by Benjamin Disraeli, passed the Second Reform Bill, which made a million more men eligible to vote.

Political parties supported reforms because pressure groups now influenced the party system. The Law Amendment Society and the Social Science Association, for example, lobbied for laws to improve social conditions, and women's groups advocated the Matrimonial Causes Act of 1857, which facilitated divorce, and the Married Women's Property Act of 1870, which allowed married women to own property and keep the wages they earned. Dissension over new policies was papered over by plush ceremonies that united critics and activists and, more important, different social classes. Whereas previous monarchs' sexual infidelities had incited mobs to riot, the monarchy of Queen Victoria and Prince Albert, with its newly devised celebrations of royal marriages, anniversaries, and births, drew respectful crowds. Promoting the monarchy in this way was so successful that the term *Victorian* came to symbolize almost the entire century and could refer to anything from manners to political institutions. Yet Britain's politicians were as devoted to Realpolitik as were those in Germany, Italy, or France, especially using violence to expand their overseas empire. The violence was far beyond the view of most British people, however, allowing them to imagine their nation as peaceful, advanced, and united.

Civil War and Nation Building in the United States and Canada

In North America, increasing nationalism and powerful economic growth characterized the nation-building experience. The United States entered a midcentury period of upheaval with a more democratic political culture than existed in Europe. Almost universal white male suffrage, a rambunctiously independent press, and mass political parties endorsed the accepted view that sovereignty derived from the people.

The United States continued to expand its territory to the west (Map 18.4). In 1848, victory in a war with Mexico almost doubled the size of the country: Texas was officially annexed, and large portions of California and the American Southwest extended the borders of the United States into former Mexican land. Politicians and ordinary citizens alike favored banning the native Indian peoples from these western lands. Complicating matters, however, was the question of whether the U.S. West would be settled by free white farmers or whether southern slaveholders could bring in their slaves.

The issue polarized the country. In the North, the new Republican party emerged to demand "free soil, free labor, free men," although few Republicans endorsed the abolitionist demand to end slavery. With the 1860 election of Republican Abraham Lincoln to the presidency, most of the slaveholding states of the South seceded to form the Confederate States of America. Between 1861 and 1865, the United States was torn apart by civil war between North and South.

Under Lincoln's leadership, the North fought to restore the Union. Lincoln did not initially aim to abolish slavery, but in January 1863 his Emancipation Proclamation came into force as a wartime measure, officially freeing all slaves in the Confederate states and turning the war into a fight not only for the Union but also for liberation from slavery. After the summer of 1863, the superior industrial strength and military might of the North overpowered and physically destroyed much of the South. By April 1865, the North had prevailed even though a Confederate sympathizer had assassinated Lincoln. Distancing the United States still further from the colonial plantation model, constitutional amendments ended slavery and promised free African American men full political rights.

■ **MAP 18.4 United States Expansion, 1850–1870**

*Like Russia, the United States expanded into adjacent regions to create a continental nation-state,
conquering indigenous peoples and taking over their territories. The United States' treatment of
those whose lands it took was different from Russia's, however. Native American peoples were
herded into small confined spaces called reservations so that settlers could acquire thousands of
square miles for farming and other enterprises. Gradually some Native Americans acquired the
right to vote, and the U.S. government granted full citizenship for all in 1925.*

Northerners hailed their victory as the triumph of American values, but racism
remained entrenched throughout the United States. By 1871, northern interest in
promoting African American political rights was waning, and southern whites began regaining control of state politics, often by organized violence and intimidation. The end of northern occupation of the South in 1877 put on hold for nearly
a century the promise of rights for blacks.

The North's triumph had profound effects elsewhere in North America. It allowed the reunited United States to contribute to Napoleon III's defeat in Mexico
in 1867. The United States also demanded the annexation of Canada in retribution
for Britain's partiality to the Confederacy because of British dependence on cotton.
To head off this threat, the British government allowed Canadians to form a united,
self-governing dominion. According dominion status answered Canadian appeals
for home rule and lessened domestic opposition to Britain's control of Canada.

Industry and Nation Building

Behind the growing power of European states lay the often dramatic development of economic and technological power. Industry turned out a cornucopia of products that improved people's material well-being. Paris, Vienna, and other cities experienced a frenzy of building, and the wages of many workers increased. Unpredictable downturns in business, however, threatened both entrepreneurs and the working class. Businesspeople sought remedies in further innovation, in new managerial techniques, and in revolutionizing marketing, most visibly in the development of the department store. Governments played their part by changing business law and supporting the drive for global profits. The steady advance of industry and the rise of a consumer economy further transformed the work lives of millions of people.

Industrial Innovation

Industrial, technological, and commercial innovation transformed nineteenth-century Europe. New products ranging from the bicycle, typewriter, and telephone to the internal combustion engine provided dizzying proof of industrial progress. Many independent tinkerers and inventor-manufacturers created new products, and sophisticated engineers—for example, Karl Benz of Germany and Armand Peugeot of France—invented revolutionary technologies such as the gasoline engine. Electricity began to provide the power to light everything from private drawing rooms to government office buildings. To fuel industrial growth, the leading industrial nations mined and produced massive quantities of coal, iron, and steel during the 1870s and 1880s. Production of iron increased from 11 million to 23 million tons. Steel output in the industrial nations grew just as impressively, increasing from 500,000 to 11 million tons in the 1870s and 1880s. Manufacturers used the metal to build the more than 100,000 locomotives that pulled trains during these years—trains that transported two billion people annually.

Historians used to contrast a "second" Industrial Revolution, with its concentration on heavy industrial products, to the "first" Industrial Revolution of the eighteenth and early nineteenth centuries, in which innovations in textile making and the use of steam energy predominated. But many historians now believe this distinction applies mainly to Britain. In countries where industrialization came later, the two stages occurred simultaneously. Numerous textile mills were installed on the European continent later than in Britain, for instance, at the same time as blast furnaces were constructed. Industrialization led to the decline of cottage production in traditional crafts like weaving. But home industry—or *outwork*—persisted in garment making, metalwork, and "finishing trades" such as porcelain painting and button polishing. The coexistence of home and factory enterprise continued through all the changes in manufacturing, to the present day.

Industrial innovations also transformed agriculture. Chemical fertilizers boosted crop yields, and reapers and threshers mechanized harvesting. In the 1870s, Sweden produced a cream separator, a first step toward mechanizing dairy farming. Wire fencing and barbed wire replaced wooden fencing and stone walls, both of which were labor-intensive to create. Refrigeration, developed during this period, allowed fruits, vegetables, and meat to be transported without spoiling, thus diversifying and increasing the urban food supply. Tin from colonial trade facilitated large-scale commercial canning, which made many foods available year-round to people in the cities.

During these decades, Britain's rate of industrial growth slowed as its entrepreneurs remained wedded to older, successful technologies. Two countries began surpassing Britain in research, technical education, innovation, and rate of growth: Germany and the United States. Profiting from the acquisition of resource-rich Alsace and Lorraine, German businesses invested in research and began to mass-produce goods that other countries had originally manufactured. Germany also spent as much money on education as on its military in the 1870s and 1880s. This investment resulted in highly skilled engineers and technical workers whose productivity enabled Germany's electrical and chemical engineering capabilities to soar. The United States began an intensive exploitation of its vast natural resources, including coal, ores, gold, and oil. Whereas German accomplishments rested more on state promotion of industrial efforts, U.S. growth often involved innovative entrepreneurs, such as Andrew Carnegie in iron and steel and John D. Rockefeller in oil.

Most other countries trailed the three leaders in the pervasiveness of industry. French industry grew steadily, but French businesses remained smaller than businesses in Germany and the United States. Although France had some huge mining, textile, and metallurgical establishments, many French businessmen retired early to imitate the still-enviable aristocratic way of life. Industrial development in Spain, Austria-Hungary, and Italy was primarily a local phenomenon. Austria-Hungary had densely industrialized areas around Vienna and in Styria and Bohemia, but the rest of the country remained tied to traditional, unmechanized agriculture. Italy's economy continued to industrialize in the north while remaining rural and agricultural in the south. The Italian government spent more on building Rome into a grand capital than it invested in economic growth. A mere 1.4 percent of Italy's 1872 budget went to education and science, compared with 10.8 percent in Germany. The commercial use of electricity helped Scandinavians, who were poor in coal and ore, to industrialize in the last third of the nineteenth century. Sweden and Norway became leaders in the use of hydroelectric power and the development of electrical products. Russia's road to industrialization was torturous, slowed partly by its relatively small urban labor force. Many Russian peasants who may have wished to take advantage of the opportunities of industrialization were tied to the *mir*, or landed community, by the terms of the serf emancipation. By the end of the century, however, the burgeoning of the railroads combined with growth in metallurgical and mining operations lifted Russia toward industrial development.

Facing Economic Crisis

Although innovations and business expansion often conveyed a sense of optimism, economic health was far from steady. Sharp downturns occurred in the business cycle throughout these decades, and within two years of the end of the Franco-Prussian War, prosperity abruptly gave way to a severe economic depression in many industrial countries. The crisis of 1873 was followed by almost three decades of economic fluctuations, most alarmingly a series of sharp downturns whose severity varied from country to country. People of all classes lost their jobs or businesses and faced consequences ranging from long stretches of unemployment to bankruptcy. Economists of the day were stunned by the relentlessness and pervasiveness of the slump. Because economic ties bound industrialized western Europe to international markets, recession affected the economies of such diverse regions as Australia, South Africa, California, Newfoundland, and the West Indies.

By the 1870s, industrial and financial setbacks—not agricultural ones, as in the past—were sending businesses into long-term tailspins in a climate of innovation and fundamentally new economic problems. First, the start-up costs of new enterprises skyrocketed. Textile mills had required relatively modest amounts of capital in comparison with factories producing steel and iron. Industrialization had become what modern economists call *capital-intensive* rather than *labor-intensive:* industrial growth required the purchase of expensive machinery, not merely the hiring of more workers. Second, the distribution and consumption of goods were inadequate to sustain industrial growth, in part because businessmen kept wages so low despite rising productivity that workers could afford little besides food. Industrialists had made their fortunes by emphasizing production, not consumption. The series of slumps refocused entrepreneurial policy on finding ways to enhance sales and distribution and to control markets and prices.

New laws and institutions helped raise capital. Development of the limited-liability corporation protected businesspeople from personal responsibility for the firm's debt and thus encouraged their investment. Before limited liability, business owners drew the necessary capital primarily from their own family assets, and financial backers were individually responsible for a firm's financial difficulties. In one case in England, a former partner who failed to have his name removed from a legal document after leaving the business remained responsible to creditors when the company went bankrupt. He lost everything he owned except a watch and the equivalent of $100. Public financing in stocks also helped raise vast amounts of new capital. Early stock exchanges had dealt mainly in government bonds and in government-sponsored enterprises such as railroads. By the end of the century, stock markets traded heavily in industrial corporate stock, thus raising money from a larger pool of private capital than before.

In another adaptive move, firms in the same industry banded together in cartels and trusts to control prices and competition. Cartels flourished particularly in

German chemical, iron, coal, and electric industries. For example, the Rhenish-Westphalian Coal Syndicate, founded in 1893, eventually dominated more than 95 percent of coal production in Germany. Although business owners continued to advocate free trade, cartels broke with free-trade practices by restricting output and setting prices. Smaller businesses trying to compete and consumers had no effective means of resisting these new business techniques. Trusts appeared first in the United States. In 1882, John D. Rockefeller created the Standard Oil Trust by acquiring stock from many different oil companies and placing it under the direction of trustees. The trustees then controlled so much of the companies' stock that they could set prices for the entire industry and even dictate to the railroads the rates for transporting the oil.

Like the practices of cartels and trusts, government imposition of tariffs expressed declining faith in classical liberal economics. Much of Europe had adopted free trade after midcentury, but during the recessions of the 1870s, huge trade deficits—caused when imports exceed exports—had soured many Europeans on the concept. A country with a trade deficit had less capital available to invest internally; fewer jobs were created, and the chances of social unrest increased. Farmers in many European countries were hurt when improvements in transportation made it possible to import perishable food, such as cheaper grain from the United States and Ukraine. With broad popular support, governments approved tariffs throughout these decades to prevent competition from foreign goods.

Revolution in Business Practices

Industrialists tried to minimize the damage of economic downturns by revolutionizing the everyday conduct of their businesses in offices. A generation earlier, a factory owner was directly involved in every aspect of his business and often learned to run the firm through trial and error. In the late 1800s, industrialists began to hire managers to run their increasingly complex day-to-day operations. Managers who specialized in sales and distribution, finance, and the purchase of raw materials made decisions and oversaw the implementation of their policies. Simultaneously the emergence of a "white-collar" service sector of office workers meant the employment of secretaries, file clerks, and typists to guide the flow of business information. Banks that accepted savings from the general public and that invested those funds heavily in business needed tellers and clerks; railroads, insurance companies, and government-run telegraph and telephone companies all needed armies of white-collar employees.

Workers with mathematical skills and literacy acquired in the new public primary schools staffed this service sector, which provided clean work for educated, middle-class women. Whether to help pay the growing cost of raising and educating children or to support themselves, unmarried and a greater number of married women of the respectable middle class took jobs despite the dominant ideology of

■ **Crespin and Dufayel Department Store**
*The department store marked the definitive transition of European society from one of subsistence
and scarcity to one of relative abundance. Centralizing the sale of all varieties of goods, department stores displayed more consumer items than any single person could possibly use. This particular Parisian department store is relatively subdued in its displays, but others ran sales and so
seductively arranged goods that Europe's uninitiated consumers were often tempted into irrational
purchasing.* (Jean-Loup Charmet.)

domesticity. Employers, as one put it, found in the new women workers a "quick-
ness of eye and ear, and the delicacy of touch" essential to office work. By hiring
women for newly created clerical jobs, business and government contributed to a
dual labor market in which certain categories of jobs were predominantly male and
others were overwhelmingly female. White-collar work gradually became ghettoized
around cheap female labor. In the absence of competition, businesses in the service sector saved significantly by paying women chronically low wages—much less
than they would have had to pay men for the same work.

Finally, the rise of consumer capitalism transformed the scale of consumption
the way industrial capitalism had transformed the scale of production. The principal
institution of this change was the department store. Founded after midcentury in
the largest cities, department stores gathered such an impressive variety of goods
in one place that consumers popularly called them "marble palaces" or "the eighth
wonder of the world." Created by daring entrepreneurs, department stores eventually replaced the single-item stores that people entered knowing clearly what they
wanted to purchase. Instead, these modern palaces sought to stimulate consumer
whims and desires with lavish displays spilling over railings and counters in glori-

ous disarray. Shoppers no longer bargained rationally over prices; now they reacted to sales, a new marketing technique that could incite a buying frenzy. Because most men lacked the time for shopping expeditions, department stores appealed mostly to women, who came out of their domestic sphere into a new public role. Attractive salesgirls, another variety of service workers, were hired to inspire customers to buy. Glossy mail-order catalogs brought to rural households both necessities and exotic items from the faraway dream world of the city.

Establishing Social Order

This age of nation building and economic expansion disturbed everyday life, often bringing chaos and sometimes dramatic public protest. Thus government officials developed mechanisms to forge internal social unity and order, hoping to offset the violence and economic change by which the nation-state was expanding. Confronted with growing populations and crowded cities, governments throughout Europe intervened to preserve social peace by attending to public health and safety. Many liberal theorists advocated a laissez-faire government that left social and economic life largely to private enterprise. Nevertheless, confident in the benefits of European institutions in general, bureaucrats and reformers paid more attention to citizens' lives and, with the help of missionaries and explorers, spread European influence to the farthest reaches of the globe.

Bringing Order to the Cities

European cities became the backdrop for displays of state power and national solidarity; thus efforts to improve sanitation and control disease redounded to the state's credit. Governments focused their refurbishing efforts on their capital cities, although many noncapital cities acquired handsome parks, widened streets, and erected stately museums and massive city halls. In 1857, Francis Joseph ordered the destruction of the old Viennese city walls and their replacement with concentric boulevards lined with major public buildings such as an opera house and government offices. Opera houses and government buildings were tangible displays of national wealth and power, and the broad boulevards allowed crowds to observe royal pageantry. These wide roads were also easier for troops to navigate than the twisted, narrow medieval streets that in 1848 had concealed insurrectionists in cities such as Vienna and Paris—an advantage that convinced some otherwise reluctant officials to approve the expense. Impressive parks and public gardens showed the state's control of nature while they helped order people's leisure time.

One effect of refurbished cities was to highlight class differences. Construction first required destruction; buildings and entire neighborhoods of housing for the poor disappeared, and thousands of city dwellers were dislocated. The boulevards often served as boundaries marking rich and poor sections of the city. In Paris, the process of urban change was called *Haussmannization,* named for the prefect Georges-Eugène Haussmann, who implemented a grand design that included eighty-five miles of new city streets, many lined with showy dwellings for the wealthy. Tens of thousands of poor people lost their homes when old buildings were torn down. Improved architectural taste including "Victorian" ornamentation, many believed, would blot out the ugliness of commerce and industry. Moreover, the size and spaciousness of the many new banks and insurance companies built in London "help[ed] the impression of stability," as an architect put it, and this would foster social order.

Amid signs of economic prosperity, the devastation caused by repeated epidemics of diseases such as cholera debilitated city dwellers and gave the strong impression of social decay. Poor sanitation allowed typhoid bacteria to spread through sewage and into water supplies, infecting rich and poor alike. In 1861, Britain's Prince Albert reputedly died of typhus, commonly known as a "filth disease." Unregulated urban slaughterhouses and tanneries; heaps of animal excrement in chicken coops, pigsties, and stables; human waste alongside buildings; open cesspools; and garbage everywhere facilitated the spread of disease. The stench, diseases, and "morbid air" of cities indicated such a degree of failure, disorder, and danger that sanitation became a government priority.

Scientific research, increasingly undertaken in public universities and hospitals, provided the means to promote public health and control disease. France's Louis Pasteur, whose three young daughters had died of typhus, advanced the germ theory of disease. Seeking a method to prevent wine from spoiling, Pasteur began his work in the mid-1850s by studying fermentation. He found that the growth of living organisms caused fermentation, and he suggested that certain organisms—bacteria and parasites—might be responsible for human and animal diseases. Pasteur further demonstrated that heating foods such as wine and milk to a certain temperature, a process soon known as *pasteurization,* killed these organisms and made food safe. In the mid-1860s, English surgeon Joseph Lister applied the germ theory in medicine. He connected Pasteur's theory of bacteria to infection and developed antiseptics for treating wounds and preventing puerperal fever, a condition that was caused by the dirty hands of physicians and midwives and that killed innumerable women after childbirth.

Governments undertook projects to improve sewer and other sanitary systems, and citizens prized such urban improvements, often attributing them to national superiority. In Paris, huge underground collectors provided a watertight terminus for accumulated sewage. In addition, Haussmann piped in water from uncontaminated sources in the countryside to provide each household with a secure supply. Such ventures were imitated throughout Europe: the Russian Empire's port city Riga (now in Latvia), for example, organized its first water company in 1863. Improved sanitation testified to progress and a more active role for the state. Shopkeepers agitated for paved streets to end the difficulties of transporting goods along

■ **Vienna Opera House**
The era of nation building saw the construction of architectural monuments in the center of capital cities to display cultural power and to bring music, art, and science to the people. Vienna's center was rebuilt around imposing façades like that of the Imperial Opera House, which opened in 1869. (Hulton Getty/Liaison Agency.)

muddy or flooded roadways. When public toilets for men became a feature of modern cities, women petitioned governments for similar facilities. On the lookout for disease and sanitary dangers, the average person became more aware of smells and the foul air that had been an accepted part of daily life for thousands of years. To show that they were becoming more "civilized," the middle and lower-middle classes bathed more regularly. Middle-class concerns for refinement and health mirrored the quest of governments for order.

Expanding the Reach of Bureaucracy

Central to enacting new programs to build social order and enhance the nation was an expansion of state bureaucracies. The nation-state required citizens to follow a growing catalog of regulations as government authority reached further into the realm of everyday life. The regular censuses that Britain, France, and the United States had begun early in the nineteenth century became routine in most other countries as well. Censuses provided the state with personal details of citizens' lives such as age, occupation, marital status, residential patterns, and fertility. Governments used these data for a variety of endeavors, ranging from setting quotas for military conscription to predicting needs for new prisons. Reformers like Florence Nightingale, who gathered medical and other statistics to support sanitary reform, believed that such quantitative information made government less susceptible to corruption, special deals, and inefficiency. In 1860, Sweden introduced taxation based on income, which opened an area of private life—one's earnings from work or investment—to government scrutiny.

To bring about their vision of social order, most governments, including those of Britain, Italy, Austria, and France, also expanded their regulation and investigation of prostitution. Venereal disease, especially syphilis, was a scourge that, like typhus, infected individuals and whole families. Officials blamed prostitutes, not their clients, for its spread. The police picked up suspect women and turned them over to public health doctors, who examined them for syphilis. If necessary, they were incarcerated for mandatory treatment. As states began monitoring prostitution and other social matters like public health and housing, they had to add departments and agencies. In 1867, Hungary's bureaucracy handled fewer than 250,000 individual cases, ranging from health to poverty issues; twenty years later it handled more than a million. Eager to acquire these jobs, the middle classes lobbied to eliminate the aristocrats' stranglehold on the top positions and to end the practice of dispensing civil service jobs as rewards for political loyalty. In Britain, a civil service law passed in 1870 required competitive examinations to ensure competency in government posts—an idea in the air since the West had become familiar with the Chinese examination system in the sixteenth and seventeenth centuries.

Schooling and Professionalizing Society

As governments imposed new standards of competency, they became more knowledge based and professional. Growing numbers of middle-class doctors, lawyers, managers, professors, and successful journalists found their positions enhanced by the prestige of science, information, and regulation. Governments began to allow professional people to influence policy and to determine rules specifying who would and would not be admitted to "the professions." Such legislation had both positive and negative effects: groups could set their own standards, but some otherwise qualified people were prohibited from working because they lacked the established credentials. The German medical profession, for example, was granted authority to control licensing, which led to more rigorous university training for future doctors but also pushed midwives out of medicine and caused the arrest of healers not trained in medical school. Science, too, became the province of the trained specialist rather than the amateur genius. Scientists were likely to be employed by universities and institutes, funded by the government, and provided with equipment and assistants. Like other members of the middle class, professors of science were intensely patriotic, often interpreting their work as part of an international struggle for prestige and excellence.

Bureaucrats and professionals called for radical changes in the scope, curriculum, and personnel of schools—from kindergarten to university—to make the general population more fit for citizenship and useful in fostering economic progress. Ongoing expansion of the electorate along with lower-class activism prompted one British aristocrat to exclaim, "We must now educate our masters!" The growth of commerce and the state was partly behind a craze for learning, which made traveling lecturers, public forums, reading groups, and debating societies popular among the middle and working classes. Governments also introduced compulsory schooling to reduce illiteracy (more than 65 percent in Italy and Spain in the 1870s and even higher in eastern than in western Europe; see "Taking Measure," below). Even a few hours of lessons each day were said to teach important social habits and the responsibilities of citizenship, along with practical knowledge.

Accomplishing this goal was not easy. Initially, various religious denominations had supervised schools and charged tuition, making primary education an option chosen only by prosperous or religious parents. After the 1850s, many leaders felt that liberal rationalism should supplant religiosity as a guiding principle. In 1861, an English commission on education concluded that, instead of the Bible, "the knowledge most important to a labouring man is that of the causes which regulate the amount of his wages, the hours of his work, the regularity of his employment, and the prices of what he consumes." Supplanting religion was one challenge and enforcing school attendance another. Although the Netherlands, Sweden, and Switzerland had functioning primary-school systems before midcentury, rural

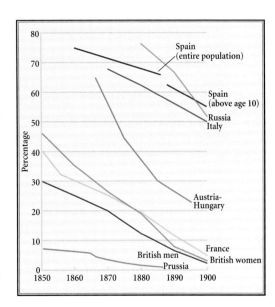

■ TAKING MEASURE Decline of Illiteracy, 1850–1900

The development of mass politics and the consolidation of the nation-state depended on building a cohesive group of citizens concerned with the progress of the nation. Increasing literacy was thus a national undertaking but one with national variations ranging from the low levels of illiteracy in Prussia to the high levels in Austria-Hungary and Russia. Even in regions of high illiteracy, however, governments successfully got people reading.

(Theodore Hamerow, *The Birth of New Europe: State and Society in the Nineteenth Century* [Chapel Hill: University of North Carolina Press, 1983], 169.)

parents depended on their children to perform farm chores and believed that boys and girls would gain useful knowledge in the fields or the household. Urban home-makers needed their children to help with domestic tasks such as fetching water, disposing of waste, tending the younger children, and scavenging for household necessities such as stale bread from bakers or soup from local missions. Secondary and university education was even more of a luxury, and Russia and some other countries saw modern subjects such as science and technology as potentially subversive.

Nonetheless, primary-school systems grew, women's education developed, and the secondary school became more systematized, reflecting the demands of both an industrial society and a bureaucratic state. In Prussia, secondary schools (*Gymnasia*) offered a liberal arts curriculum that trained students for a variety of careers. In the 1860s, however, new *Realschulen*, less prestigious at the time, em-phasized math, science, and modern languages for those who would not attain a Gymnasium degree or go on to attend the university. Reformers pushed for more advanced and more complex courses for young women. In France and Russia, for example, government leaders themselves saw that "public education has had in view only half the population—the male sex," as the Russian minister of education wrote to Tsar Alexander II in 1856. Both Napoleon III and Alexander II sponsored secondary- and university-level courses for women as part of their programs to control the modernization of society. Reformers from across the political spec-trum concurred that women who knew some science, history, and literature would rear their children better and prove more interesting wives. Even so, higher educa-tion for women remained a hotly contested issue because religion, sewing, deport-ment, and writing appeared more than adequate.

Education, however, opened professional doors to young women, who in the 1860s began to attend universities in Zurich and Paris, where medical training was open to them. Despite criticism that they would undermine the system of sepa-rate spheres, women doctors thought their practice of medicine would protect fe-male patients' modesty and bring feminine values to health care. In Britain, the founders of two women's colleges, Girton (1869) and Newnham (1871) at Cam-bridge University, believed that exacting standards in women's higher education would provide an example of a modern curriculum, reward merit, and thus raise the low standards of scholarship prevalent in the men's colleges of Cambridge and Oxford.

The expanding need for instructed citizens offered opportunities for large num-bers of women to enter teaching, a field once dominated by men. Hundreds of women founded nurseries, kindergartens, and primary schools based on the En-lightenment idea that developmental processes start at an early age. In Italy, women founded schools as a way to expand knowledge and teach civics lessons, thus providing a service to the fledgling state. Yet the idea of women teaching also aroused intense opposition: "I shudder at philosophic women," wrote one critic of female kindergarten teachers. Seen as radical because it enticed middle-class women out of the home, the cause of early childhood education, or the "kindergarten movement," was as controversial as most other educational reforms.

Spreading Western Order beyond the West

In an age of nation building and industrial development, colonies took on new importance, adding a political dimension to the economic role that global trade already played in national prosperity. After midcentury, Great Britain, France, and Russia revised their colonial policies by instituting direct rule, expanding colonial bureaucracies, and in many cases providing a wider array of social and cultural services such as schools. For instance, in the 1850s and 1860s provincial governors and local officials promoted the extension of Russian borders to gain control over nomadic tribes in central and eastern Asia. As in areas like Poland and the Ukraine, they instituted educational and religious policies that they felt essential to social order.

Great Britain, the era's mightiest colonial power, made a dramatic change of course toward direct political rule during these decades. Before the 1850s, British liberals desired commercial gain from colonies, but believing in laissez-faire, they kept political involvement in colonial affairs minimal. In India, for example, an East India trading company ruled on Britain's behalf, and many regional rulers awarded the company commercial advantages. Since the eighteenth century, the East India Company had expanded its dominion over various kingdoms on the Indian subcontinent whenever a regional throne fell vacant and had built railroads throughout the countryside. Gradually the British bureaucratic and economic presence expanded, allowing some Indian merchants to grow wealthy and send their children to British schools. Other local men enlisted in the British-run Indian army, despite resistance to British institutions.

In 1857, Indian troops, both Muslim and Hindu, violently rebelled against this expanded presence and its disregard for local beliefs. Ignoring the Hindu ban on beef and the Muslim prohibition on pork, the British had forced Indian soldiers to use cartridges greased with cow and pig fat. The infuriated soldiers stormed and conquered Delhi and declared the independence of the Indian nation—an uprising that became known as the Sepoy Mutiny. Simultaneously the Rani Lakshmibai, widow of the ruler of the state of Jhansi in central India, led a separate military revolt when the East India Company tried to take over her lands after her husband died. Brutally

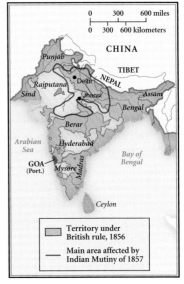

Indian Resistance, 1857

put down by the British, the Sepoy Mutiny and the Jhansi revolt gave birth to Indian nationalism. They also persuaded the British government to issue the Government of India Act of 1858, by which Britain took direct control of India.◆ In
1876, the British Parliament declared Queen Victoria the empress of India.

A system of rule emerged in which close to half a million Indians governed a
region the British called *India* under the supervision of a few thousand British men.
Indians also collected taxes and distributed patronage. Colonial rule meant both
blatant domination and more subtle intervention in everyday life. British policy
forced the end to indigenous production of finished goods such as cotton textiles
that would compete with Britain's own manufactures. Instead, the British wanted
cheaper raw materials such as wheat, cotton, and jute to supply their industries. En-
claves of British civil servants enforced segregation and an inferior status on all
classes of Indians. Simultaneously, however, ordinary Indians benefited in some
places from improved sanitation and medicine. After the British attack on their
practices, some upper-class Indians rejected Indian customs such as infanticide,
child marriage, and *sati*—a widow's self-immolation on her husband's funeral pyre.
British notions of a scientific society also proved attractive to some, and the unity
that British rule brought to what were once small localities and princedoms with
separate allegiances promoted nationalism.

French political expansion was similarly a matter of push, pull, and paradox.
The French government pushed to establish its dominion over Cochin China (modern southern Vietnam) in the 1860s. But missionaries in the area, ambitious French
naval officers stationed in Asia, and even some local peoples pulled the French government to make successive attacks in the region. Like the British, the French
brought improvements, such as the Mekong Delta project that increased the amount
of cultivated land and spurred rapid growth of the food supply. Sanitation and public health programs proved a mixed blessing because they led to population growth
that strained other resources. Furthermore, landowners and French imperialists siphoned off most of the profits from economic improvement. The French also
undertook a cultural mission to transform cities, such as Saigon, with tree-lined
boulevards and other signs of Western urban life. French literature, theater, and art
diverted not only colonial officials but also upper-class Indochinese.

Strategic commercial and military advantages remained an important motivation for some European overseas ventures in this age of Realpolitik. The Crimean
War had shown the great powers that the Mediterranean basin was pivotal and thus
needed to be tamed. Napoleon III, remembering his uncle's campaign in Egypt,
took an interest in building the Suez Canal, which would connect the Mediterranean
with the Red Sea and the Indian Ocean and thus dramatically shorten the route to

---

◆ For an autobiographical account of Indian life in the British colony, see Document 58, Krupa Sattianadan,
"Saguna: A Story of Native Christian Life."

Asia. The canal was completed in 1869, and as canal fever spread, Verdi composed the opera *Aïda* (set in ancient Egypt) in celebration.

Great Britain and France were especially eager to do business with Egypt, where the combined value of imports and exports had jumped from 3.5 million Egyptian pounds in 1838 to 21 million in 1880 (and would grow to 60 million in 1913). European capital investment in the region also rose, first in ventures such as the Suez Canal in the 1860s and then in the laying of thousands of miles of railroad track and the creation of telegraph systems. Improvement-minded rulers in Asia and Africa paid dearly in 12 percent interest rates for modernization. The completion of harbors, dams, canals, and railroads increased the Middle East's desirability as a market for European exports and as an intermediate stop on the way to trade with Asia. Having invested in the Suez Canal and in other commercial development, the British and French soon took over the Egyptian treasury to secure their own financial investments, and after invading Egypt in 1882, the British effectively took over the government. Despite heated parliamentary opposition at home, Britain reshaped the Egyptian economy from a system based on multiple crops that maintained the country's self-sufficiency to one that emphasized the production of a few crops—mainly cotton, raw silk, wheat, and rice—that were especially useful to European manufacturing. Colonial powers, local landowners, and moneylenders profited from these agricultural changes, while the bulk of the rural population barely eked out an existence.

The rest of the Mediterranean and the Ottoman Empire felt the heightened presence of the European powers. Driving into the North African hinterland, the French army occupied all of Algeria by 1870, and the number of European immigrants reached one-quarter million by then. There was also a pull: French rule in Algeria as elsewhere was aided by the attraction of European goods, technology, and institutions to the local peoples. Merchants and local leaders cooperated in building railroads, sought bank loans and trade from the French, and sent their children to European-style schools. Many local peoples, however, resisted the invasions and died from European-spread diseases. By 1872, the native population in Algeria had declined by more than 20 percent from five years earlier. As a further guarantee of their Mediterranean claims, the French occupied neighboring Tunisia in 1881. Elsewhere, businessmen from Britain, France, and Germany flooded Asia Minor with cheap goods, driving artisans from their trades and into low-paid work building railroads or processing tobacco. Instead of basing wage rates on gender (as they did at home), Europeans used ethnicity and religion, paying Muslims less than Christians, and Arabs less than other ethnic groups. Such practices, as well as contact with European technology and nationalism, planted the seeds for anticolonial movements.

The vastness of China allowed it to escape complete takeover, but traders and Christian missionaries from European countries, carrying their message of Christian salvation, made inroads for the Western powers. Directing the Christian message to a population that had almost doubled during the preceding century and now numbered about 430 million, missionaries spread Christianity among people already disturbed by demographic growth, defeat in the Opium War, and economic pressures from European trade. These contacts with the West had helped generate the mass movement known as the Taiping (Heavenly Kingdom). Its millions wanted an end to the ruling Qing dynasty, the elimination of foreigners, more equal treatment of women, and land reform. By the mid-1850s, the Taiping controlled half of China. The Qing regime, its dynasty threatened, promised the British and French greater influence in exchange for aid. The result was a bloody civil war that lasted until 1864 with some 30 million to 60 million Chinese killed (compared with 600,000 dead in the United States' Civil War). When peace finally came, Western governments controlled much of the Chinese customs service and had almost unlimited access to the country.

Japan alone was able to escape European domination. Through Dutch traders at Nagasaki, the Japanese had become keenly aware of industrial, military, and commercial innovations of European society. By 1854, when Americans claimed to be opening Japan to trade, contacts with Europe had already given the Japanese a healthy appetite for Western goods and knowledge and an interest in superior Western weaponry. Trade agreements with the United States and European nations followed. In 1867, the ruling Tokugawa shogun (the dominant military leader) abdicated under pressure from reformers, who subsequently restored the emperor to full power. The goal of the Meiji Restoration (1868) was to establish Japan as a modern, technologically powerful state free from Western control. The word *Meiji*, chosen by the new emperor to name his reign, meant "enlightened rule," and the regime professed to combine "Western science and Eastern values" as a way of "making new"—hence, a combination of *restoration* and innovation.

The Culture of Social Order

The complex reactions of artists and writers to the rising nation-state and its expanding reach ushered in an age of realism in the arts in the 1850s to 1870s. After 1848, many artists and writers expressed profound grievances, notably about political repression, economic growth, and the effect of enfranchising working-class men. To many artists, daily life, infused with commercial values and organized by government officials, seemed tawdry and hardly bearable. Unlike the romantics of the first half of the century, artists of the second half often had difficulty depicting heroic ideals. "How tired I am of the ignoble workman, the inept bourgeois, the stupid peasant, and the odious priest," wrote the French novelist Gustave Flaubert, frustrated by his inability to romanticize these figures as previous generations had done. Such disenchantment promoted the literary and artistic style called *realism*. In contrast, intellectuals proposed theories called *positivism* and *Darwinism*, which appraised social change and even political upheaval as part of human progress.

Realism, positivism, and Darwinism shared a claim to look at society with an objective eye and to depict social order starkly.

The Arts Confront Social Reality

The quest for national power enlisted culture in its cause. The reading public devoured biographies of political leaders, past and present, and credited heroes with creating the triumphant nation-state. As literacy spread, readers of all classes responded to the mid-nineteenth-century novel and to an increasing number of artistic, scientific, and natural history exhibitions. Whether reading the same novels or attending musical events together, citizens were schooled in a common artistic style called *realism*.

A well-financed press and commercially minded publishers produced an age of best-sellers out of the craving for realism. The novels of Charles Dickens appeared in serial form in magazines and periodicals, and each installment attracted eager buyers for the latest plot twist. His characters came from contemporary English society and included starving orphans, grasping lawyers, heartless bankers, and ruthless opportunists. *Bleak House* (1852) used dark humor to portray the judicial bureaucracy's intrusion into private life; *Hard Times* (1854) depicted the grinding poverty and ill health of workers. The novelist George Eliot (the pseudonym of Mary Ann Evans) examined contemporary moral values and deeply probed private, "real-life" dilemmas in works such as *The Mill on the Floss* (1860) and *Middlemarch* (1871–1872). Depicting rural society—high and low—Eliot allowed Britons to see one another's predicaments, wherever they lived. She knew the pain of ordinary life from her own experience: she was a social outcast because she lived with a married man. Despite her fame, she was not received in polite society. These popular novels showed a hard reality and thus helped form a shared culture among people in distant parts of a nation much as state institutions did.

French writers also scorned dreams of political utopias and ideals of transcendent beauty. In *Madame Bovary* (1857), Gustave Flaubert told the story of a bored doctor's wife who, full of romantic longings and eager for distraction, has one love affair after another and becomes so hopelessly indebted that she commits suicide. Serialized in a Paris journal, *Madame Bovary* scandalized French society for its frank picture of women's sexuality. The poet Charles-Pierre Baudelaire, called "Satanic" by his critics, wrote explicitly about sex; in *Les Fleurs du mal* ("Flowers of Evil," 1857), he expressed sexual passion, described drug- and wine-induced fantasies, and spun out visions condemned as perverse. French authorities fought this violation of social convention, successfully prosecuting Flaubert and Baudelaire on obscenity charges. The issue was social and artistic order: "Art without rules is no longer art," the prosecutor maintained.

During the era of the Great Reforms, Russian writers debated whether western European values were insidiously transforming Russian culture. Rather than dividing the nation, this discussion about Russian culture united people around a national issue. From one viewpoint, Ivan Turgenev created a powerful novel of Russian life, *Fathers and Sons* (1862), a story of nihilistic children rejecting the older, romantic generation's spiritual values and espousing science instead. Popular in the West, Turgenev aroused anger in Russian readers for the way he criticized both romantics and the new generation of hardheaded "materialists." From another point of view, Fyodor Dostoevsky in *The Possessed* (1871–1872) and other works showed the dark, ridiculous, and neurotic side of nihilists, thus holding up Turgenev as a soft-headed romantic. Dostoevsky's highly intelligent characters in *Notes from the Underground* (1864) and *Crime and Punishment* (1866) are often personally tormented and condemned to lead absurd, even criminal lives. He used these antiheroes to emphasize spirituality and traditional Russian values, but with a "realistic" spin by planting such values in ordinary people.

Unlike writers, visual artists across Europe depended on government commissions and government-sponsored exhibitions and drew a more limited set of buyers. Prince Albert of England was an active patron of the arts, purchasing works for official collections and for himself until his death in 1861. Having artwork chosen for display at government-sponsored exhibitions (called *salons* in Paris, the center of the art world) was the best way for an artist to gain prominence and earn a living. Officially appointed juries selected works of art to be exhibited and then chose prizewinners from among them. Hundreds of thousands of people from all classes attended these exhibitions.

After 1848, artists began rejecting romantic conventions idealizing ordinary folk and grand historic events. Instead, Gustave Courbet, for example, portrayed weary laborers at backbreaking work because he believed an artist should "never permit sentiment to overthrow logic." The city, artists found, had become a visual spectacle, a place of great destruction but also of wide new boulevards where urban residents performed as part of the cityscape. Artists' canvases showed the renovated city as a stage for individual ambition and display. *Universal Exhibition* (1867) by Édouard Manet used the World's Fair of 1867 as the background; figures from all social classes in the foreground were separated from one another by the planned urban spaces as they promenaded, gazing at the Paris scene and watching one another to learn the new social rules of modern life. Manet also broke with romantic conventions of the nude. His *Olympia* (1865) depicted a white courtesan lying on her bed, attended by a black woman. This disregard for the classical traditions of showing women in mythical or idealized settings was too much for the critics: "A sort of female gorilla," one wrote of *Olympia*. "Her greenish, bloodshot eyes appear to be provoking the public," wrote another. Shocking at first, graphic portrayals that shattered comforting illusions became a feature of modern art.

Artistic realism faced a challenge from photography—a challenge that found its response in the 1860s to 1890s in a new style called *impressionism*. Manet coined the term to reflect the artist's attempt to capture a single moment by focusing on

■ **Gustave Courbet,**
Wrestlers (1850)
Courbet painted his dirty, grunting
wrestlers in the realist style, which
rejected the hazy romanticism of
revolutionary Europe. These mus-
cular men summed up the resort
to physical struggle during these
state-building decades and con-
veyed the art world's recognition
that Realpolitik had taken over
the governance of society.
(Museum of Fine Arts, Budapest/The
Bridgeman Art Library, NY.)

the ever-changing light and color found in everyday vision. Using splotches and dots, impressionists moved away from the precise realism of earlier painters: Claude Monet, for example, was fascinated by the way light transformed an object, and he often portrayed the same place—a bridge or a railroad station—at different times of day. Dutch-born Vincent Van Gogh used vibrant colors in great swirls to capture sunflowers, corn stacks, and the starry evening sky. Such distortions of reality made the impressionists' visual style seem outrageous to those accustomed to realism, but others enthusiastically greeted impressionism's luminous quality as more real than realism. Industry contributed to the new style, as factories produced a range of pigments that allowed artists to use a wider, more intense spectrum of colors.

In both composition and style, impressionists borrowed heavily from Asian art and architecture, knowledge of which rapidly infiltrated Europe as the West extended its reach. The concept of the fleetingness of situations came from a centuries-old and well-developed Japanese concept—*mono no aware* (serenity before and sensitivity to the fleetingness of life). The color, line, and delicacy of Japanese art (which many impressionists collected) is evident, for example, in Monet's later paintings of water lilies, his studies of wisteria, and even his re-creation of a Japanese garden at his home in France as the subject for artistic study. Similarly, the American expatriate Mary Cassatt used the two-dimensionality of Japanese art in her *In the Loge* (1879) and other paintings. Other artists, such as Edgar Degas, imitated Asian art's use of wandering and conflicting lines to orchestrate space on a canvas, and Van Gogh filled the background of portraits with copies of intensely colored Japanese prints.

As art departed from photographic realism, it nonetheless kept commenting on the changing economic scene, especially the fact that a growing segment of service workers did less physical work and had more energy for leisure. The works of French painter Georges Seurat, for example, depicted the newly created parks with their walking paths and Sunday bicyclists; white-collar workers carrying books or newspapers paraded in their store-bought clothing. Degas focused on portraying women—from ballet dancers to laundry women—in various states of exertion and fatigue. Van Gogh, avoiding the intense colors he typically used for the countryside, depicted the bleak outskirts of cities, where industries were often located and where the desperately poor lived.

Unlike most of the visual arts, opera was commercially profitable, accessible to most classes of society, and thus effective artistically for reaching the nineteenth-century public. Verdi used musical theater to contrast noble ideals with the corrosive effects of power, love of country with the inevitable call for sacrifice and death, and the lure of passion with the need for social order. The German composer Richard Wagner, the most flamboyant and musically innovative composer of this era, hoped to revolutionize opera by fusing music and drama to arouse the audience's fear, awe, and engagement. A gigantic cycle of four operas, *The Ring of the Nibelungen* (1854–1874), reshaped ancient German myths into a modern, nightmarish allegory of a world doomed by its obsessive pursuit of money and power and redeemable only through unselfish love. Another of his operas, *The Master Singer of Nürnberg* (1867), was a nationalistic tribute to German culture, and like the arts elsewhere, helped unite isolated individuals into a public with a shared, if debated, cultural experience.

Religion and Secular Order

Organized religion formed one bulwark of traditional social and political order after the revolutions of 1848, but the expansion of state power set the stage for clashes over influence. Should religion have the same hold on government and public life as in the past, thus competing with the national loyalty? The views were mixed and would remain so. In the 1850s, many politicians supported religious institutions and attended public church rituals because they were another source of order. Simultaneously, some nation builders, intellectuals, and economic liberals rejected the competing worldviews and competition for jurisdiction of established churches, particularly Roman Catholicism. Bismarck was one of these. Believing that the church impeded the growth of nationalist sentiment, in 1872 he mounted a full-blown *Kulturkampf* (culture war) against Catholic influence. The government expelled the Jesuits in 1872, increased state power over the clergy in Prussia in 1873, and introduced obligatory civil marriage in 1875. Bismarck, however, overestimated his ability to manipulate politics, for both conservatives and Catholics objected to religious repression in the name of state building.

The Catholic church felt assaulted on two fronts: by the growth of rationalism, which supplanted religious faith for many people, and by state building in Italy and Germany, which competed for people's traditional loyalty. In addition, nation build-ing had resulted in the extension of liberal rights to Jews, whom many Christians considered enemies. Provocatively attacking reform and changing values, Pope Pius IX (r. 1846–1878) issued *The Syllabus of Errors* (1864), which put the church and the pope at odds "with progress, with liberalism, and with modern civilization." In 1870, the First Vatican Council approved the dogma of papal infallibility. This teaching proclaimed that the pope spoke divinely revealed truth on issues of moral-ity and faith. Eight years later, a new pontiff, Leo XIII (r. 1878–1903), began the process of reconciliation with modern politics by encouraging up-to-date scholar-ship in Catholic institutes and universities and by accepting aspects of democracy. Leo's ideas marked a dramatic turn, ending the Kulturkampf and fortifying belea-guered Catholics across Europe.

Religious doctrine continued to have powerful popular appeal, but the place of organized religion in society was changing. Church attendance declined among workers and artisans, but many people in the upper and middle classes and most of the peasantry remained faithful. The Orthodox church of Russia and eastern Europe with its Pan-Slavic appeal fostered nationalism among oppressed Serbs and became a rallying point. Women's spirituality intensified, and Roman Catholic and Russian Orthodox religious orders of women increased in size and number. Men, by contrast, were falling away from religious devotion. In 1858, an outburst of popular religious fervor, especially among women, followed a young peasant girl's visions of the Virgin Mary at Lourdes in southern France. Bernadette Soubirous said that Mary told her to drink from the ground, at which point a spring appeared. Crowds besieged the area to be cured of ailments by the waters of Lourdes. In 1867, less than ten years later, a railroad track was laid to Lourdes to enable millions of pilgrims to visit the shrine on church-organized trips. The Catholic church thus showed that it was not passé and was willing to use modern means, such as rail-roads, medical verification of miraculous cures, and journalism, to make Lourdes itself the center of a brisk commercial as well as religious culture.

Almost contemporaneously with Bernadette's vision, the English naturalist Charles Darwin published *On the Origin of Species* (1859), a challenge to the Judeo-Christian worldview that humanity was a unique creation of God. Darwin argued that life had taken shape over countless millions of years before humans existed and that human life was the result of this slow development, or evolution. As a young scientist on an expedition to South America, Darwin theorized that because of evo-lution, species of animals varied from one tropical island to another even though climate and other natural conditions were roughly the same: new biological forms arise from older ones as the most fit forms survive and reproduce. Instead of the Enlightenment vision of nature and society as harmonious, Darwin saw the constant turmoil of all species, including humans, struggling to survive. In this fight, only the hardiest prevail and in the selection of sexual partners pass their natural strength to the next generation. In a perpetual challenge to meet the forces of nature, Darwin suggested, some species die out and those with better-adapted characteristics survive in a new environment.

Darwin's theories angered adherents of traditional Christianity because the idea of evolution undercut the story of creation described in Genesis. According to the biblical account, God miraculously brought the universe and all life into being in six days. According to Darwin, life developed from lower forms through a primal battle for survival and through the sexual selection of mates—processes that Darwin called *natural selection.* An eminently respectable Victorian gentleman, Darwin announced that the Bible gave a "manifestly false history of the world."

Darwin's theories also undermined certain liberal, secular beliefs. Enlightenment principles, for example, glorified nature as tranquil and noble and viewed human nature as essentially rational. The theory of natural selection—survival of the fittest—suggested a different kind of human society, one based in a hostile environment where combative individuals and groups constantly fight one another.◆

Darwin's findings and other innovative biological research influenced contemporary beliefs about society. In the 1860s, working in obscurity on pea plants in his monastery garden, Gregor Mendel discovered the principles of heredity from which the science of genetics later developed. Investigation into the female reproductive cycle led German scientists to discover the principle of spontaneous ovulation—the automatic release of the egg by the ovary whether sexual intercourse took place or not. This discovery caused theorists to conclude that men had aggressive and strong sexual drives because reproduction depended on their sexual arousal. In contrast, the spontaneous and cyclical release of the egg independent of arousal indicated that women were passive and lacked sexual feeling.

Darwin added to the social commentary. The legal, political, and economic privilege of white European men in the nineteenth century, he maintained, naturally derived from their being more highly evolved than white women or people of color. Despite his belief in a common ancestor for people of all races, Darwin held that people of color, or "lower races," were far behind whites in intelligence and civilization. As for women, "the chief distinction in the intellectual powers of the two sexes," Darwin declared, "is shewn by man's attaining to a higher eminence in whatever he takes up." A school of Social Darwinism, derived from this Darwinist

---

◆ For an excerpt from Charles Darwin's *The Descent of Man,* see Document 59.

thought, arose to lobby for public policy based on a vulgarized version of evolution and natural selection.

From Natural Science to Social Science

Darwin's thought accelerated the search for alternatives to the religious understanding of social order as being divinely ordained. Simultaneously the theories of the French social philosopher Auguste Comte, whose ideas formed the basis of a "positive science" of society and politics, also inspired a host of reform organizations. *Positivism* claimed that careful study of facts would generate accurate, or "positive," laws of society. Comte's *System of Positive Politics, or Treatise on Sociology* (1851) proposed that social scientists construct knowledge of the political order as they would construct understanding of the natural world—by means of informed investigation. This idea inspired people to believe they could solve the problems spawned by economic and social change. Comte also promoted women's participation in reform because he deemed "womanly" compassion and love and scientific public policy to be equally fundamental to social harmony. Positivism led not only to women's increased social and political activism but to the growth of the social sciences.

■ **Darwin Ridiculed, c. 1860**
Charles Darwin's theories claimed that humans evolved from animal species and rejected the long-standing explanation of a divine human origin. His scientific ideas so diverged from people's beliefs that cartoonists lampooned both the respectable Darwin and his theory. Despite the controversy, evolution withstood the test of further scientific study.
(Hulton Getty/Liaison Agency.)

www.bedfordstmartins.com/huntconcise
See the ONLINE STUDY GUIDE for more help in analyzing this image.

For a time, the influential English philosopher John Stuart Mill became an enthusiast of Comte, whose theories led Mill to espouse widespread reform and mass education and to support the complete enfranchisement of women. Mill's political treatise *On Liberty* (1859) couched his aspiration for general social improvement in a concern that superior people not be brought down or confined by the will of the masses. Influenced by his wife, Harriet Taylor Mill, he notoriously advocated the extension of rights to women and introduced a woman suffrage bill into the House of Commons after her death. The bill's defeat prompted Mill to publish *The Subjection of Women* (1869), a work recapitulating his studies with his wife. Translated into many languages and influential in eastern Europe, Scandinavia, and the Western Hemisphere, *The Subjection of Women* presented the family as maintaining an older kind of politics devoid of modern concepts of rights and freedom. Mill also proposed that women's voluntary obedience and love in marriage made each woman deceptively appear "not a forced slave, but a willing one." Critiquing the century's basic beliefs about men's and women's roles, *The Subjection of Women* became a respected guide for a growing women's movement committed to expanding liberal rights.

The more progressive side of Mill's social thought was soon lost in the flood of Social Darwinist theories. Even before *Origin of Species,* Herbert Spencer's *Social Statics* (1851) advocated the study of society but also promoted laissez-faire and unadulterated competition, claiming that the "unfit" should be allowed to perish in the name of progress. Spencer's opposition to public education, social reform, and any other attempt to soften the harshness of the struggle for existence struck a receptive chord among the middle and upper classes and contributed to the surge of Social Darwinism in the next decades. The influence of Darwinism and Mill's liberalism, like that of the arts, religion, and science, would serve to shape the public, setting the subjects and terms of social and political thought. In an age of nation building, culture often enhanced the political call for realistic, hardheaded thinking about social order.

Contesting the Order of the Nation-State

By the end of the 1860s, the unchecked growth of the state and the ongoing process of economic change had led to palpable tensions in European society. New theories of work life and politics appeared—most notably those of economist and philosopher Karl Marx (1818–1883), who advocated socialism. Protests abounded over the terms of work and especially against the upheavals in everyday life caused by the expanding power of the state as it ripped apart cities for improvements and sent workers scurrying for new places to live. In France, anger at defeat in the Franco-Prussian War and at economic hardship made these tensions erupt into a bitter though brief civil war. In the spring of 1871, the people of Paris—blaming the centralized state for the French surrender to the Germans—declared Paris a *commune*, a community of equals without bureaucrats and pompous politicians. Marx's books analyzing the growth of capitalism and national politics—as well as analysis of the Paris Commune—provided workers with a popular and politically galvanizing account of events. From the 1870s on, these two phenomena—the writings of Karl Marx and the fury of working people—renewed fear among the middle classes that both nation-state and industrial society might be violently destroyed.

Changes in Worklife and the Rise of Marxism

Changes in technology and management practices eliminated outmoded jobs and often made the work of those who survived job cuts more difficult. Workers complained that new machinery sped up the pace of work to an unrealistic level. For example, new furnaces at a foundry in suburban Paris required workers to turn out 50 percent more metal per day than they had produced using the old furnaces. Stepped-up productivity demanded much more physical exertion to tend and repair machines, often at a faster pace, but workers did not receive additional pay for their extra efforts. Workers also grumbled about the proliferation of managers; many believed that foremen, engineers, and other supervisors interfered with their work. For women, supervision sometimes brought on-the-job harassment, as in the case of female workers in a German food-canning plant who kept their jobs only in return for granting sexual favors to the male manager.

As new machines replaced old, managers established formal skill levels, from the most knowledgeable machinist to the untrained carrier of supplies. On the one hand, the introduction of machinery "deskilled" some jobs—traditional craft ability was not a prerequisite for operating many new machines. Employers could increasingly use untrained workers, often women, and pay them less than they paid skilled workers. On the other hand, inventions always demanded new skills, especially for those who had to understand work processes or repair machinery. Employers began to use the concept of skill (based in the old craft traditions) to segment the labor force, but sometimes the designations were arbitrary. Already prevalent in such trades as garment making, the trend toward breaking down and separating work processes into discrete tasks continued. For example, builders employed excavators, scaffolders, and haulers to do the "dirty work," hiring fewer highly paid carpenters. Those filling unskilled jobs could not count on regular employment and spent much of their time searching out temporary jobs. On the other end of the scale, foremen were no longer the most skilled workers but instead were supervisors chosen, as one worker complained, for the "pushing powers . . . of driving fellow men."

Many in the urban labor force continued to do outwork at home. Every branch of industry—from metallurgy to toy manufacturing to food processing—employed women at home, and their work was essential to the family economy. They painted

tin soldiers, wrapped chocolate, made cheese boxes, decorated porcelain, and polished metal. Factory owners liked to employ outworkers because low piece rates
made them desperate for work under any conditions and they were willing to work
extremely long days. A German seamstress at her new sewing machine reported that
she "pedaled at a stretch from six o'clock in the morning until midnight. . . . At four
o'clock I got up and did the housework and prepared meals." Owners could lay off
women at home during slack times and rehire them whenever needed with little
fear of organized protest. Although joblessness and destitution always threatened,
some city workers prospered in comparison to those left behind in rural areas, despite the decline of traditional artisanal work.

By and large, the urban working class was better informed, more visible, and
more connected to the progress of industry and the nation-state. After a period of
repression in the 1850s, workers' organizations slowly reemerged as a political force
in the West, many of them influenced either by the ideas of former printer Pierre-
Joseph Proudhon (1809–1865) or by anarchist thought. In the 1840s, Proudhon had
coined the explosive phrase "Property is theft," suggesting that ownership robbed
propertyless people of their rightful share of the earth's benefits. He opposed the
centralized state and proposed that society be organized instead around natural
groupings of men (but not women, who should work in seclusion at home for their
husbands' comfort) in artisans' workshops. These workshops and a central bank
crediting each worker for his labor would replace government and would lead to a
mutualist social organization. Anarchism maintained that the existence of the state
was the root of social injustice. According to Russian nobleman and anarchist leader
Mikhail Bakunin (1814–1876), the slightest infringement on freedom, especially by
the central state and its laws, was unacceptable. The political theory of *anarchism*
thus advocated the destruction of all state power.

As workers' movements revived, Marx constantly battled mutualism and anarchism. These doctrines, he insisted, were emotional and wrongheaded, lacking the
sound, scientific basis of his own theory, subsequently called *Marxism.* Marx's analysis, expounded most notably in *Das Kapital* ("Capital"), adopted the liberal idea,
dating back to John Locke in the seventeenth century, that human existence was
defined by the requirement to work as a way of fulfilling basic needs such as food,
clothing, and shelter. Published between 1867 and 1894, *Das Kapital* was based on
mathematical calculations of production and profit that would justify Realpolitik
for the working classes. Marx held that the fundamental organization of any society, including its politics and culture, derived from the relationships arising from
work or production. This idea, known as *materialism,* meant that the foundation
of a society rested on class relationships—such as those between serf and medieval
lord, slave and master, or worker and capitalist. Marx called the class relationships
that developed around work the *mode of production*—for instance, feudalism, slavery, or capitalism. Rejecting the liberal focus on individual rights, he emphasized
the unequal class relations caused by feudal lords, slaveholders, and the capitalists

or bourgeoisie—that is, those who took control of the "means of production" in the form of the capital, land, tools, or factories necessary to fulfill basic human needs. Workers' awareness of their oppression would produce class consciousness among those in the same predicament and ultimately lead them to revolt against their exploiters. Capitalism would be overthrown by these workers—the *proletariat*—and an era of socialism would ensue. Tough-minded theories that social conflict was necessary for progress were common to Marx and Darwin.

The Paris Commune versus the French State

The conditions of working-class life remained harsh, and a wave of strikes erupted in the late 1860s. In France alone, 40,000 workers participated in strikes in 1869, followed by more than 85,000 in 1870. The strikers included artisans and industrial workers who felt overworked and underpaid because of the continuing pace and expense of technological innovation. In the 1870s, three decades of economic boom and bust would open to aggravate the situation. More often than not, the strikes focused on economic issues. But at times, such as in the Paris Commune, protesters questioned the system as a whole.

The bloody and bitter struggle over the Paris Commune developed using mutualist and socialist political ideas that churned to the surface in Paris as the Franco-Prussian War ended. The Haussmannization of Paris, which had displaced workers from their homes in the heart of the city, embittered many Parisians against the state. As the Prussians pressed on to Paris in 1870, the besieged Parisians demanded new republican liberties, new systems of work, and a more balanced distribution of power between the central government and localities. By the winter of 1870–1871, the Parisian population was suffering from the harsh weather and a Prussian siege that deprived them of sufficient food to feed more than 2 million people. As Parisians demanded to elect their own local officials to handle the emergency, the temporary republican government replacing the fallen Napoleon III sent the army into Paris in mid-March. For Parisians, this decision revealed the utter despotism of the centralized government, and they declared themselves a self-governing commune on March 28, 1871. Other French municipalities would do the same in an attempt to form a decentralized state of independent, confederated units.

In the Paris Commune's two months of existence, its forty-member council, its National Guard, and its many other improvised offices found themselves at cross-purposes. Trying to maintain "communal" instead of "national" values, Parisians quickly developed a wide array of political clubs, local ceremonies, and self-managed, cooperative workshops. Women workers, for example, banded together to make National Guard uniforms on a cooperative rather than a profit-making basis. Beyond liberal political equality, the Commune proposed to liberate the worker and ensure "the absolute equality of women laborers." Thus a *commune* in contrast to a *republic* was meant to entail a social revolution. But Communards often disagreed on what specific route to take to change society: mutualism, anti-clericalism, feminism, international socialism, and anarchism were but a few of the proposed avenues to social justice.

In the meantime, the provisional government at Versailles struck back to reinstitute national order. It quickly stamped out similar uprisings in other French cities. On May 21, the army entered Paris. In a week of fighting, both Communards and the army set the city ablaze (the Communards did so to slow the progress of government troops). Both sides executed hostages, and in the wake of victory the army shot tens of thousands of citizens found on the streets. Just to be in the city meant treason: Parisian insurgents, one citizen commented, "deserved no better judge than a soldier's bullet." The Communards had fatally promoted a kind of antistate in an age of growing national power. Soon a different interpretation of the Commune emerged: it was the work of the *pétroleuse*, or "woman incendiary"—a case of women run mad, crowding the streets in frenzy and fury. Within a year, writers were blaming the burning of Paris on women—"shameless slatterns, half-naked women, who kindled courage and breathed life into arson." Revolutionary men often became heroes in the history books, but women in political situations were characterized as "sinister females, sweating, their clothing undone, [who] passed from man to man."

Defeat in the Franco-Prussian War, the Commune, and the civil war were all horrendous blows from which the French state struggled to recover. Key to restoring order in France after 1870 were instilling family virtues, fortifying religion, and claiming that the Commune had resulted from the collapsed boundaries between the male political sphere and the female domestic sphere. Karl Marx

■ **Woman Incendiary**
The Paris Commune galvanized women activists, many of whom hoped to reform social conditions. After the fall of the Commune, women Communards were denigrated as half-clothed degenerates as a way of underscoring the disorderliness of the Commune's resistance to the state.
(Jean-Loup Charmet.)

IMPORTANT DATES			
1850s–1860s	Positivism and Darwinism become popular in social and political thought	1868	The Meiji Restoration begins in Japan
1850s–1870s	Realism in the arts	1869–1871	Women's colleges founded at Cambridge University
1852	The Second Empire begins in France	1870	Bismarck manipulates the Ems telegram and sparks the Franco-Prussian War
1854–1856	Britain and France clash with Russia in the Crimean War	1871	Franco-Prussian War ends; German Empire proclaimed at Versailles; Parisians form Commune in March to oppose the central government; the French army crushes the Commune in May
1857	Sepoy Mutiny in India		
1860s–1890s	Impressionism flourishes in the arts; absorption of Asian influences		
1861	Victor Emmanuel declared king of a unified Italy; abolition of serfdom in Russia	1872	Bismarck begins the Kulturkampf against Catholic influence
1861–1865	Civil War in the United States	1873	Extended economic recession begins; the impact is global
1867	Second Reform Bill, increasing the ranks of male voters, passed by English Parliament; Austro-Hungarian monarchy established	1876	Queen Victoria declared empress of India

disagreed: he analyzed the Commune as a class struggle of workers attacking bourgeois interests, which were embodied in the centralized state. Executions and deportations by the thousands nearly shut down the French labor movement and kept fear of workers smoldering across Europe.

Conclusion

Throughout modern history, the development of nation-states and the economic prosperity on which they depended has been neither inevitable nor uniform nor peaceful. This was especially true in the nineteenth century, when ambitious politicians, resilient monarchs, and determined bureaucrats transformed very different countries into various kinds of states by a variety of methods and policies. Nation building was most dramatic in Germany and Italy, where states unified through military force and where people of many political tendencies ultimately agreed that national unity trumped most other causes. Compelled by military defeat to shake off centuries of tradition, the Austrian and Russian monarchs instituted reforms as

■ MAPPING THE WEST Europe and the Mediterranean, c. 1880

European nation-states consolidated their power by building unified state structures and by developing the means to foster social and cultural integration of the diverse peoples within their borders. They also were rapidly expanding outside their boundaries, extending the economic and political reach of the nation-state. North Africa and the Middle East—parts of the declining Ottoman Empire—had particular appeal for their resources and for their potential for further European settlement. They were one gateway to the rest of the world.

a way of keeping their systems viable. In eastern Europe, the middle class was far less powerful than in western Europe, and reform came from above to preserve autocratic power rather than from popular agitation to democratize it.

After decades of romantic fervor, hardheaded realism in politics and the industrial economy became a much-touted norm, often with unexpected consequences. Darwin and Marx breathed the air of realism, and their theories were disturbing to those who maintained an Enlightenment faith in social and political harmony. Realist novels and art jarred polite society; like the operas of Verdi, they also portrayed dilemmas of the times. The internal policies of the growing state apparatus that were meant to bring order often brought disorder. When the ordinary people of the Paris Commune rose up to protest the loss of French power and prestige but also to defy the trend toward economic modernity and state building, their actions raised difficult questions. How far should the power of the state extend in both domestic and international affairs? Would nationalism be a force for war or for peace? As these issues ripened, the next decades would see continued economic advance, growing competition for global power, and unprecedented changes that ultimately would lead to war.

Suggested References for further reading and online research appear on page SR-28 at the back of the book.

www.bedfordstmartins.com/huntconcise   See the ONLINE STUDY GUIDE to assess your mastery of the material covered in this chapter.

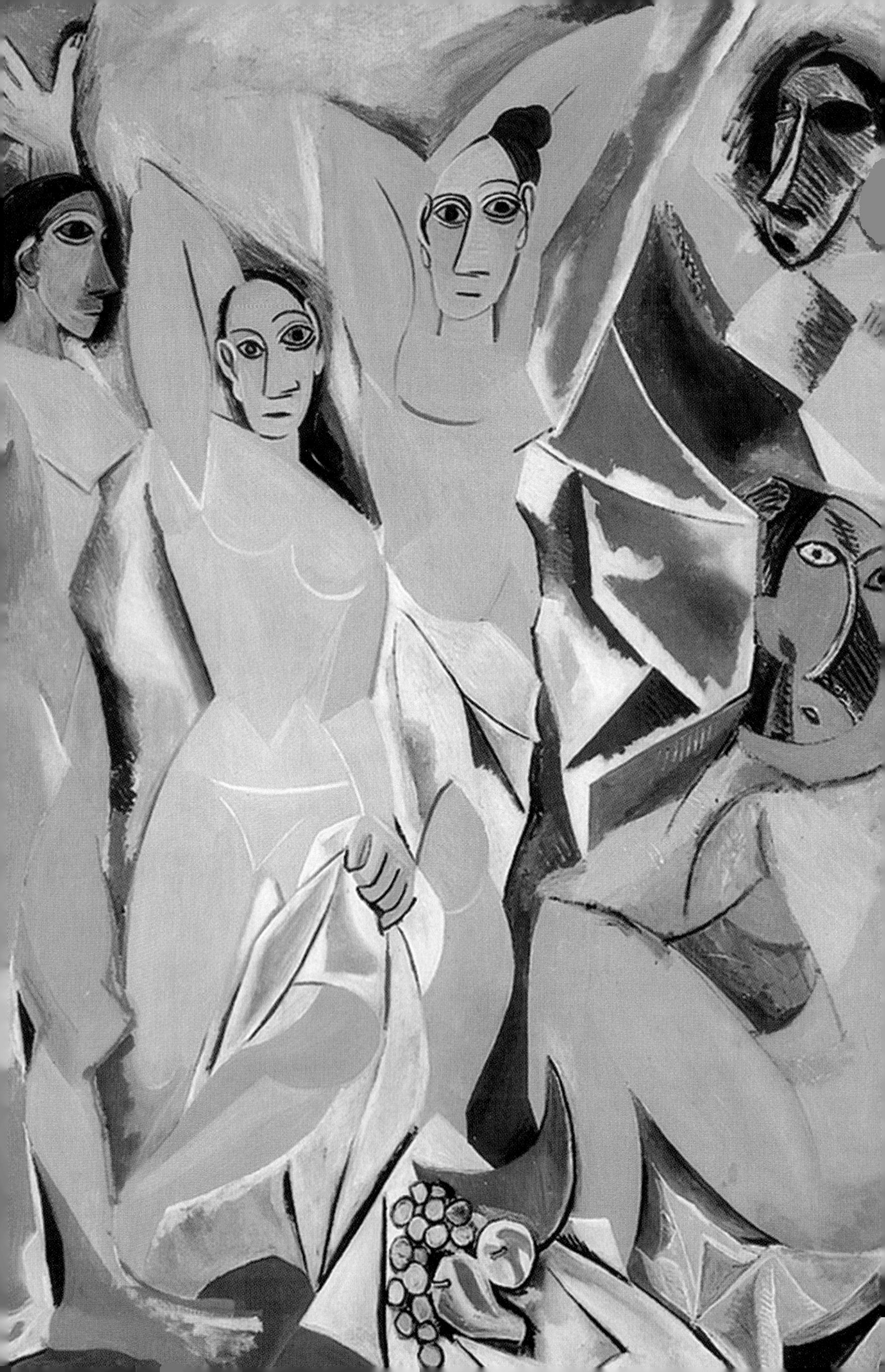

19

Empire, Modernity, and the Road to War

c. 1880–1914

IN THE FIRST DECADE OF THE TWENTIETH CENTURY, a wealthy young Russian man traveled from one country to another to find relief from neurasthenia, a common malady in those days. Its symptoms included fatigue, lack of interest in life, depression, and sometimes physical sickness. In 1910, the young man encountered Sigmund Freud, a Viennese physician whose unconventional treatment—eventually called *psychoanalysis*—took the form of conversations about the patient's dreams, sexual experiences, and everyday life. Over the course of four years, Freud uncovered his patient's deeply rooted fear of castration disguised as a phobia for wolves—thus the name Wolf-Man by which the young man is known to us. Often building his theories from information about colonized peoples and cultures, Freud worked his cure, as the Wolf-Man himself put it, "by bringing repressed ideas into consciousness." Freud's theories laid the groundwork for an understanding of the human psyche that has endured, with modifications and some controversy, to our own time.

The Wolf-Man is evocative of the age. Born into a family that owned vast estates, he reflected the growing prosperity of Europeans, albeit on a grander scale

■ **Pablo Picasso, *Les Demoiselles d'Avignon* (1907)**
The work of Spanish artist Pablo Picasso has become emblematic of modernity. Drawing on images from around the colonized world, modernist painters drew special inspiration from the art of Africa by imitating the clean lines and elongated limbs of its wooden statuary. In Les Demoiselles d'Avignon *("The Young Ladies of Avignon"), Picasso also borrowed the facial structure of African masks for his depiction of a group of prostitutes. ("Avignon" does not refer to the French town but to Avignon Street in a notorious section of Barcelona.) In addition to such imperial borrowings, modernists broke with harmonious melodies in music and pleasing depictions of the natural world. To many in polite society, modernism was jolting and shocking, an unwelcome reflection of growing violence among nations, the oppression of empire, and escalating militarism.*
(Picasso, Pablo. *Les Demoiselles d'Avignon.* Paris [June–July 1907]. Oil on canvas, 8′ × 7′8″. The Museum of Modern Art, New York. Acquired through the Lillie P. Bliss Bequest. Photograph © The Museum of Modern Art, New York © 2001 Estate of Pablo Picasso/Artists Rights Society, NY.)

805

than most. Countless individuals seemed, like him, anguished and mentally disturbed. Suicide was not uncommon. The Wolf-Man's own sister and father died from intentional drug overdoses. Throughout European society people engaged in agonized questioning about family life, gender relationships, empire, religion, and the consequences of technology and progress. Conflict rattled Europe and the rest of the world as an array of powers, including Japan, fought their way into even more territories and took political control. Every sign of imperial wealth brought on an apparently irrational sense of Europe's decline. The British writer H. G. Wells saw in this era "humanity upon the wane . . . the sunset of mankind."

Governments expanded the male electorate during this period in the hope of making politics more harmonious and manageable. Ethnic chauvinism, anti-Semitism, and militant nationalism, however, increased the violence of political rhetoric. Women suffragists along with politically disadvantaged groups such as the Slavs and Irish demanded full rights, but the liberal ethos of tolerance was swept away by a wave of political assassinations and public brutality. As the race for worldwide empire continued—most notably in an intense contest among the European powers for control of Africa and its vast natural wealth—colonized peoples developed a variety of liberation movements, many of them matching the progressive values but also the violence of the colonizing powers. While the great powers fought to dominate people around the world, the competition for empire fueled an arms race that threatened to turn Europe, the "most civilized" continent in the world according to its leaders, into a savage battleground.

Those were just some of the conflicts associated with *modernity*—a term often used to describe the accelerated pace of life, the rise of mass politics, and the decline of a rural social order that were so visible in the West from the late nineteenth century on. *Modernity* also refers to the response of artists and intellectuals to this rapid change. The celebrated "modern" art, music, science, and philosophy of this period still resonate for their brilliant, innovative qualities. Yet these same innovations were often considered offensive at the time: cries of outrage at the new music echoed in concert halls, and educated people were shocked at Freud's ideas that sexual drives motivate even the smallest children. Every advance in science and the arts had consequences that undermined middle-class faith in artistic and scientific progress.

When the heir to the Austro-Hungarian throne was assassinated in June 1914, few gave any thought to the global significance of the event, least of all Wolf-Man, whose treatment with Freud was just ending and who viewed that fateful day of June 28 simply as the day he "could now leave Vienna a healthy man." Yet the assassination was the catalyst for an eruption of political and societal discord that had been simmering for several decades, as the nations of Europe lurched from one diplomatic crisis to another. The consequences of the resulting war—World War I—like the insights of Freud, would shape modern life.

The Challenge of Empire

The quest for empire remained intense and became increasingly paradoxical. In a climate of ongoing boom and bust, colonies provided crucial markets for some businesses. Late in the century, for example, French colonies bought 65 percent of France's exports of soap, and imperialism provided huge numbers of jobs to people in European port cities. Yet Europeans did not benefit uniformly from the search for new markets, which often proved more costly than profitable. Whether they benefited or not, taxpayers in all parts of a nation paid for colonial armies, increasingly costly weaponry, and colonial administrators. As politicians debated the economic value of colonies, imperialism intensified distrust in international politics though empire-building was meant to ensure great-power status. Countries vied with one another for a share of world influence. In securing India's borders, for example, the British faced Russian expansion in Afghanistan and along the borders of China. Bringing conflict around the world, imperial competition made areas of Europe, such as the Balkans, more volatile than ever as states sought status and national security in the control of disputed territory.

Motives for imperialism were equally paradoxical. Goals such as fostering national might, boosting national loyalty, and the centuries-old effort to Christianize peoples often proved unattainable or difficult to measure. Governments worried that imperialism—because of its expense and the constant possibility of war— might weaken rather than strengthen them. The French statesman Jules Ferry (1832–1893) argued that France "must keep its role as the soldier of civilization." But it was unclear whether imperialists should emphasize soldiering—that is, conquest and conflict—or the more encompassing goal of exporting culture and religion.◆ Hoping to Christianize colonized peoples, European missionaries ventured to newly secured areas of Africa and Asia. A woman missionary working among the Tibetans reflected a common view when she remarked that the native peoples were "going down, down into hell, and there is no one but me . . . to witness for Jesus amongst them." Europeans were confident of their religious and cultural superiority. In the judgment of many, Asians and Africans—variously characterized as lying, lazy, self-indulgent, or irrational—were a class beneath Europeans. One English official pontificated that "accuracy is abhorrent to the Oriental mind." Viewing other races as "degenerate" prompted missionaries and other "civilizers" to turn a blind eye toward the most brutal military measures against the growing local resistance to imperialism.

◆ For a source that reveals Europeans' passionate debate over imperialism, see Document 60, Jules Ferry, "Speech before the French National Assembly."

Scramble for Africa

After the British takeover of the Egyptian government in the 1880s, European in-fluence turned into direct control as one sub-Saharan African territory after an-other fell to European military force (Map 19.1). The centuries-old slave trade had drastically diminished by this time, and Europeans' principal objective was ex-panding trade in Africa's raw materials, such as palm oil, cotton, diamonds, cocoa, and rubber. Additionally, with its industrial and naval supremacy and its empire in India, Britain hoped to keep the southern and eastern coasts of Africa secure for stopover ports on the route to Asia. The British, French, Belgians, Portuguese, Italians, and Germans jockeyed to dominate peoples, land, and resources—"the magnificent cake of Africa," as King Leopold II of Belgium (r. 1865–1909) put it. Driven by insatiable greed, Leopold claimed the Congo region of central Africa, thereby initiating competition with France for that territory and inflicting on lo-cal African peoples unparalleled acts of cruelty. German chancellor Otto von Bis-marck, who saw colonies mostly as political bargaining chips, sent out explorers in 1884 and established German control over Cameroon and a section of East Africa. Faced with competition, the British poured millions of pounds into pre-serving their position by dominating the continent "from Cairo to Cape Town," as the slogan went, and the French cemented their hold on large portions of western Africa.

Technological development of powerful guns, railroads, steamships, and med-icines were central to the expansion of Western domination. The gunboats that forced the Chinese to open their borders to opium played a part in forcing African ethnic groups to give up their independence. Quinine and guns were also an im-portant factor in African conquest. Before the development of medicinal quinine in the 1840s and 1850s, the deadly tropical disease malaria had threatened to dec-imate any European party embarking on exploration or military conquest, giving Africa the nickname "White Man's Grave." The use of quinine, extracted from cin-chona bark from the Andes, to treat malaria sent death rates among missionaries, adventurers, traders, and bureaucrats plummeting. While quinine saved white lives, technology to take lives was also advancing. Improvements to the breech-loading rifle and the development of the machine gun, or "repeater," between 1862 and the 1880s dramatically increased firepower. Europeans carried on a brisk trade selling inferior guns to Africans on the coast, but peoples of the interior used bows and

■ **MAP 19.1 Africa, c. 1890**

The scramble for Africa entailed a real reversal of European trading practices, which until approxi-mately 1880 generally were limited to the coastline. The effort to conquer, economically penetrate, and rule the interior would result in a map of the continent (see Map 19.2) that made sense only to the imperial powers, for it divided ethnic groups and created colonial entities that had nothing to do with Africans' sense of geography, patterns of settlement, or political organization.

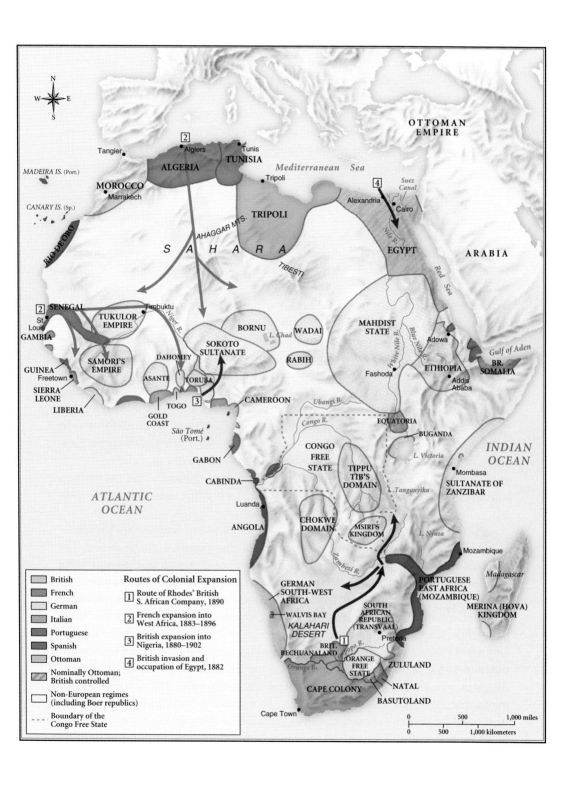

N
W   E
S

Tangier
Algiers •Tunis
• TUNISIA
ALGERIA
*Tripoli
MOROCCO
•Marrakech
MADEIRA IS. (Port.)
CANARY IS. (Sp.)
RIO DE ORO

Mediterranean   Sea

OTTOMAN
EMPIRE

Suez
Canal
Alexandria
•Cairo

AHAGGAR MTS.
S A H A R A
TIBESTI

TRIPOLI

EGYPT

ARABIA

SENEGAL
St.
Louis
GAMBIA
Timbuktu
TUKULOR
EMPIRE
Niger R.
BORNU
L. Chad
WADAI
SOKOTO
SULTANATE
RABIH
MAHDIST
STATE

White Nile R.
Blue Nile R.
Adowa
Fashoda
ETHIOPIA
Addis
Ababa

Red Sea

Gulf of Aden
BR.
SOMALIA

GUINEA
Freetown
SIERRA
LEONE
LIBERIA
SAMORI'S
EMPIRE
DAHOMEY
ASANTE
YORUBA
TOGO
GOLD
COAST
São Tomé
(Port.)
CAMEROON

GABON
CABINDA

Ubangi R.
Congo R.
EQUATORIA
BUGANDA
L. Victoria

INDIAN
OCEAN

ATLANTIC
OCEAN

Luanda•
ANGOLA

CONGO
FREE
STATE
TIPPU
TIB'S
DOMAIN
CHOKWE
DOMAIN
MSIRI'S
KINGDOM

L. Tanganyika
Mombasa•
SULTANATE OF
ZANZIBAR
L. Nyasa
•Mozambique

Zambezi R.

GERMAN
SOUTH-WEST
AFRICA
•WALVIS BAY
KALAHARI
DESERT
SOUTH
AFRICAN
REPUBLIC
(TRANSVAAL)
•Pretoria
PORTUGUESE
EAST AFRICA
(MOZAMBIQUE)
MERINA (HOVA)
KINGDOM
Madagascar

BRIT.
BECHUANALAND
Limpopo R.
ORANGE
FREE
STATE
Orange R.
ZULULAND
CAPE COLONY
NATAL
BASUTOLAND
Cape Town•

Routes of Colonial Expansion

British
French
German
Italian
Portuguese
Spanish
Ottoman
Nominally Ottoman;
British controlled
Non-European regimes
(including Boer republics)
Boundary of the
Congo Free State

1 Route of Rhodes' British
S. African Company, 1890
2 French expansion into
West Africa, 1883–1896
3 British expansion into
Nigeria, 1880–1902
4 British invasion and
occupation of Egypt, 1882

0   500   1,000 miles
0   500   1,000 kilometers

arrows. Muslim slave traders and European Christians alike crushed African resistance with blazing gunfire: "The whites did not seize their enemy as we do by the body, but thundered from afar," claimed one local African resister. "Death raged everywhere—like the death vomited forth from the tempest."

Nowhere did this destructive capacity have greater effect than in southern Africa, where farmers of European descent and prospectors, rather than military personnel, battled African peoples for control of the frontier regions of Transvaal, Natal, the Orange Free State, and the Cape Colony. Although the Dutch originally settled the area in the seventeenth century, the British had gained control by 1815. Thereafter, descendants of the Dutch, called *Boers* (Dutch for "farmers"), were joined by British immigrants in their fight to wrest farmland and mineral resources from natives. British businessman and politician Cecil Rhodes (1853–1902), sent to South Africa for his health just as diamonds were being discovered in 1870, cornered the diamond market and claimed a huge amount of African territory with the help of official charters from the British government, all before he turned forty. Pushing hundreds of miles into the interior of southern Africa (a region soon to be named Rhodesia after him), Rhodes moved into gold mining, too. His ambition for Britain and for himself was boundless: "I contend that we are the finest race in the world," he explained, "and that the more of the world we inhabit the better it is." Europeans credited China and India with a scientific and artistic heritage, but Africans were seen as valuable only for manual labor despite their many accomplishments such as dyeing, road building, and architecture. By confiscating Africans' land, Europeans forced native peoples to work for them to earn a living and to pay the taxes they imposed. Subsistence agriculture, often performed by women and slaves, thus declined in favor of mining and farming cash crops. Standards of living dropped for Africans who lost their lands without realizing the Europeans were claiming permanent ownership. Systems of family and community unity provided support networks for Africans during this upheaval in everyday life.

Almost immediately, the scramble for Africa escalated tensions in Europe itself, prompting Bismarck to call a conference of European nations at Berlin. The fourteen nations at the conference, held in a series of meetings in 1884 and 1885, decided that their settlements along the African coast guaranteed their rights to internal territory. This agreement led to the strictly linear dissection of the continent; geographers and diplomats cut across indigenous boundaries of African culture and ethnic life (Map 19.2). The Berlin conference also banned the sale of alcohol and controlled the sale of arms to native peoples. The purpose of the meeting was supposed to be the reduction of bloodshed and the tempering of European ambitions in Africa, but European leaders were intent on maintaining and expanding their power, and rapacious individuals like King Leopold continued to plunder the continent and terrorize its people. The news from Berlin whetted the popular appetite for more imperialist ventures and increased competition among a greater number of nations for colonies.

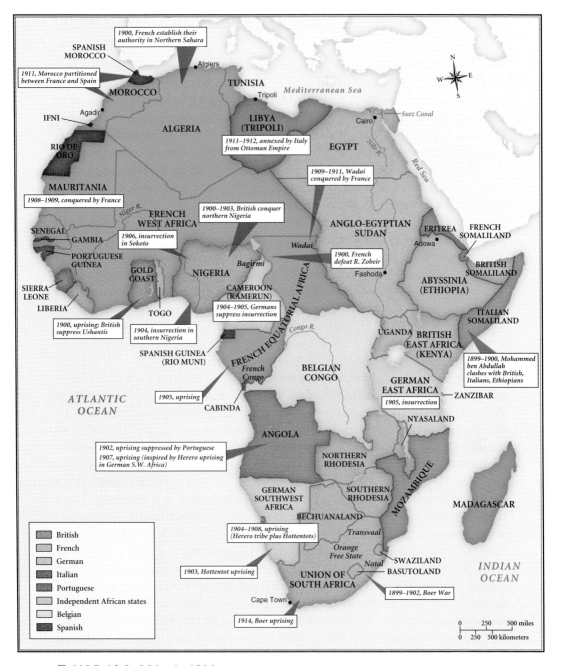

MAP 19.2 Africa in 1914

Uprisings intensified in Africa in the early twentieth century as Europeans tried both to consolidate their rule through bureaucratization and military action and to extract more wealth from the Africans. While the Europeans were putting down rebellions against their rule, a pan-African movement arose, attempting to unite Africans as one people. As in Asia and the Middle East, the more the colonial powers tried to impose their will, the greater the political forces—including the force of political ideas—that took shape against them.

www.bedfordstmartins.com/huntconcise See the ONLINE STUDY GUIDE for more help in analyzing this map.

811

Skirmishes with the French in Africa and the Boer War turned this mood sour for the British. Accustomed to crushing resistance to their imperial ambitions, the British experienced a bloody defeat in 1896, when Cecil Rhodes, prime minister of the Cape Colony in southern Africa, directed his right-hand man, Dr. Leander Jameson, to lead a raid into the neighboring territory of the Transvaal. The foray was intended to stir up trouble between the Boers and the more recent immigrants from Britain and elsewhere who had come to southern Africa in search of gold and other riches. Rhodes hoped the raid would justify a British takeover of the Transvaal and the Orange Free State, which the Boers independently controlled. The Boers, however, easily routed the raiders, striking a blow at British imperial pride. The British did not accept defeat: for the next three years they fought the Boer War directly against the Transvaal and the Orange Free State. Britain finally annexed the area after defeating the Boers in 1902, but the cost of war—in money, destruction, and loss of life—horrified many Britons and caused them to see imperialism as a burden.

Imperial Newcomers

Europeans' confident approach to imperialism was also eroded by the rise of Japan as a power. Led by the Satcho Hito clan, whose accession to power in 1868 ushered in the Meiji Restoration, Japan escaped the "new" European imperialism by its rapid transformation into a modern industrial nation with its own imperial agenda. "All classes high and low shall unite in vigorously promoting the economy and welfare of the nation," ran one of the first pronouncements of the new regime. The Japanese had long acquired knowledge from other countries and embraced it. In the 1870s, Japanese government officials traveled to Europe and the United States to study technological and industrial developments. Western dress became the rule at the imperial court, and when fire destroyed Tokyo in 1872 a European directed the rebuilding in Western architectural style. The new central government, led by some of the old *samurai*, or warrior elite, crushed massive rebellions by any who resisted modernization. It also merged older samurai traditions, such as spiritual discipline and the drive to excel, with a large, technologically modern military and sponsorship of trade. The state stimulated economic development by building railroads and shipyards, establishing financial institutions, and encouraging daring innovators like Iwasaki Yataro, founder of the Mitsubishi firm, to develop heavy industries such as mining and shipping. In Japan, unlike the rest of Asia, the adaptation of Western-style enterprises became a patriotic goal.

Like its Western models, Japan started intervening in nationalist and imperialist struggles elsewhere in Asia. This interference ultimately provoked war with its traditionally more powerful neighbors China and Russia. The Japanese had started building an empire by invading the Chinese island of Formosa (present-day Taiwan) in 1874 and in 1894 by sparking the brief Sino-Japanese War, which in 1895 ended

■ **Modernization in Japan**

Japan modernized with breathtaking speed. As this view of a railroad station indicates, Japan borrowed from the West but did not abandon its own culture. In this woodcut by Ando Hiroshige II—son of an artist imitated by many in the West—many of the Japanese wear Western-style clothes and others continue to wear traditional styles. Notice, too, the native cherry trees and the portrayal of traditional modes of transportation. The train schedule appears across the top.
(Laurie Platt Winfrey Inc.)

China's domination of Korea. Japan's growing imperial ambitions soon clashed with those of the great powers. Russian expansion to the east and south in Asia, the building of the Trans-Siberian Railroad through Manchuria, and sponsorship of anti-Japanese groups in Korea so angered the Japanese that they attacked tsarist forces at Port Arthur in 1904 (Map 19.3). The conservative Russian military proved inept in the ensuing year-long Russo-Japanese War: in an astonishing display of poor leadership, Russia's Baltic Fleet sailed halfway around the globe only to be completely destroyed in the battle of Tsushima Straits (1905). Opening an era of Japanese domination in East Asian politics, the victory was the first by a non-European nation over a European great power in the modern age. As one English general ominously observed of the Russian defeat: "I have today seen the most stupendous spectacle it is possible for the mortal brain to conceive—Asia advancing, Europe falling back." Japan went on to annex Korea in 1910 and to eye other areas in which to challenge the West.

There were other troublesome newcomers to the imperial table. Almost simultaneously, Spain lost Cuba, Puerto Rico, and the Philippines as a result of its defeat in the Spanish-American War of 1898. Urged on the United States by the expansionist-minded Theodore Roosevelt (1858–1919), then assistant secretary

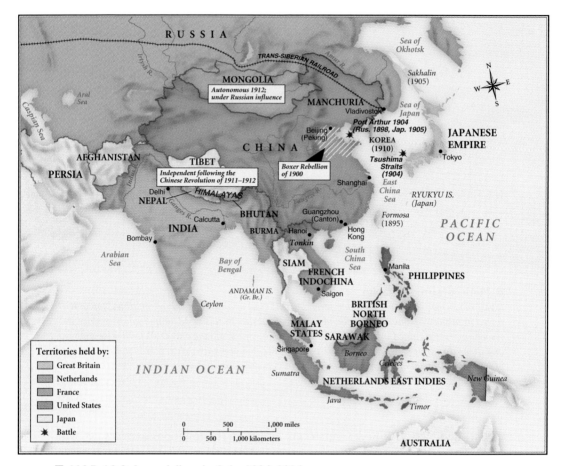

■ **MAP 19.3 Imperialism in Asia, 1894–1914**
Most of the modernizing states converged on Asia. The established imperialists came to blows in East Asia as they struggled for influence in China and encountered a formidable new rival—Japan. Simultaneously, liberation movements like that of the Boxers in China were taking shape, committed to throwing off restraints imposed by foreign powers. In 1911, Sun Yat-Sen overthrew the Qing dynasty and started the country along a different course.

of the navy, and the inflammatory daily press, this war revealed the fragility of established European empires and the unpredictability of imperial fortunes. Even the triumphant United States, encouraged by the British poet Rudyard Kipling (1865–1936) to "take up the white man's burden" by bringing the benefits of Western civilization to those liberated from Spain, had to wage a bloody war against the Filipinos, who wanted independence, not another imperial ruler. Reports of American brutality in the Philippines further disillusioned the European public, who liked to imagine native peoples joyously welcoming the bearers of civilization.

Emerging powers had an emotional stake in gaining colonies. In the early twentieth century, Italian public figures aimed to restore Italy to its ancient position of world domination by conquering Africa. After its disastrous war against Ethiopia in 1896, Italy won a costly victory over Turkey in Libya. But these wars roused Italian hopes for national grandeur only to dash them. Germany likewise demanded an end to the virtual British-French monopoly of colonial power. Foremost among the new competitors for empire, German bankers and businessmen were ensconced throughout Asia, the Middle East, and Latin America. Colonial skirmishes Germany had once ignored became matters of utmost concern. Germany, too, instead of winning unalloyed glory, met humiliation and constant problems, especially in its dealings with Britain and France. As Italy and Germany aggressively pursued new territory, the rules set for imperialism at the Berlin conference a generation earlier gave way to increasingly heated rivalry and nationalist fury.

Growing Resistance to Colonial Domination

The Japanese military victory over two important dynasties—the Qing in China and the Romanov in Russia—within a single decade had repercussions in the colonies. Uprisings began in China after its 1895 defeat by Japan forced the ruling Qing to grant more economic concessions to Western powers. Humiliated by these events, peasants organized into secret societies to restore Chinese integrity. One organization, based on beliefs in the spiritual values of boxing, was the Society of the Righteous and Harmonious Fists (or Boxers), whose members maintained that ritual boxing would protect them from a variety of evils, including bullets. Encouraged by the Qing ruler and desperate because of worsening economic conditions, the Boxers rebelled in 1900, massacring the missionaries and Chinese Christians to whom they attributed China's troubles.◆ The colonial powers put down the Boxer Rebellion and forced the Chinese to pay a huge indemnity, to destroy many of their defensive fortifications, and to allow more extensive foreign military occupation. The Boxer Rebellion thoroughly discredited the Qing dynasty; in 1911 a successful group of revolutionaries overthrew the dynasty and the next year declared China a republic. Their leader, Sun Yat-Sen (1866–1925), who had been educated in Hawaii and Japan, combined Western concepts with traditional Chinese values, including revival of the Chinese tradition of correctness in behavior between governors and the governed and modern economic reform. Sun's stirring leadership and the changes brought about by China's revolution seriously threatened Western channels of trade and domination.

In 1885, the Indian elite founded the Indian National Congress, which challenged Britain's right to rule, but the Japanese victory over Russia stimulated

---

◆ For a statement of beliefs distributed by the Boxers at the height of their rebellion, see Document 61, the I-ho-ch'uan (Boxers), "The Boxers Demand Death for All 'Foreign Devils.'"

Indian politicians to take a more radical course. An anti-British Hindu leader, B. G. Tilak (1856–1920), preached noncooperation: "We shall not give them assistance to collect revenue and keep peace. We shall not assist them in fighting beyond the frontiers or outside India with Indian blood and money." Tilak promoted Hindu customs, asserted Hindus' distinctiveness from British ways, and inspired violent rebellion in his followers. This brand of nationalism broke with that based on assimilating to British culture and promoting gradual change. Trying to repress Tilak, the British sponsored the Muslim League, a rival nationalist group favored for its restraint and its potential to divide Muslim nationalists from Hindus in the Congress. Facing political activism on many fronts, however, Britain made two concessions: voting rights based on property ownership and Indian representation in ruling councils. Because the independence movement had not fully reached the masses, these small concessions allowed the British to maintain power by appeasing influential dissidents among the upper and middle classes. But Britain's hold on India was weakening.

Revolutionary nationalism also was sapping the Ottoman Empire, which for centuries had controlled much of the Mediterranean. In the nineteenth century, several rebellions had plagued Ottoman rule, and more erupted early in the twentieth century because of growing resistance to the empire and to European

■ **Boxer Rebellion**

The Boxers sought to fortify the Chinese government against the many powers threatening its survival. They used brightly colored placards to spread information about their mission and its importance and to build support. The placards also depicted battles with imperialist forces and showed Boxer triumphs over foreign missionaries and other menacing groups.

(Photo courtesy Thames and Hudson, Ltd., London.)

influence. Sultan Abdul Hamid II (r. 1876–1909) tried to revitalize the multiethnic empire by using Islam to counteract the rising nationalism of the Serbs, Bulgarians, and Macedonians. Instead, he unwittingly provoked the burgeoning of Turkish nationalism in Constantinople itself. Turkish nationalists rejected the sultan's pan-Islamic solution and built their movement on the uniqueness of their culture, history, and language, changing the word *Turk* from one of derision to one of pride and purging their language of words from Arabic and Persian. The events of 1904–1905 electrified these nationalists with the vision of a modern Turkey becoming "the Japan of the Middle East," as they called it. In 1908, a group called the Young Turks took control of the government in Constantinople. Their triumph motivated others in the Middle East and the Balkans to demand an end to Ottoman domination in their regions as well. But the Young Turks, often aided by European powers with financial and political interests in the region, brutally tried to repress the uprisings in Egypt, Syria, and the Balkans that their own success had encouraged.

Modern Life in an Age of Empire

Advancing empire not only made the world an interconnected marketplace but transformed everyday culture and society. Success in manufacturing and foreign ventures created millionaires, and consumers in the West could purchase goods that poured in from around the world. Many Europeans grew healthier, partly because of improved diet and partly because of the efforts of reformers who sponsored government programs aimed at promoting the fitness necessary for citizens of imperial powers. Opportunities for mobility arose as Europeans opened up the globe. Working people's experience of the internationalizing force of imperialism was different from that of the middle class: increasingly from the mid-nineteenth century on, millions facing political or economic insecurity migrated to the United States, Canada, Australia, Argentina, Brazil, and Siberia and, as frequently, from country to city and back.

Growing European power was nonetheless accompanied by hazards to social norms and stability. Prosperity for global and industrial entrepreneurs contributed to social mixing, challenging the position of established groups such as the landed nobility. Even as Western ideals of a comfortable family life flourished because of Europe's improved standard of living, these norms were challenged: a falling birthrate, a rising divorce rate, and growing activism for marriage reform provoked intense debate by the turn of the century. Homosexuality became acknowledged as a way of life and the topic of politics. Middle-class women took jobs and became active in public to such an extent that some feared the disappearance of distinct gender roles. Discussions of gender roles and private life contributed to rising social tensions while they also fueled the optimism of reformers that Western society was making constant progress.

Life in the "Best Circles"

Profits from empire and industrial expansion swelled the ranks of the upper class, or "best circles," so called at the time because of their members' wealth, education, and social status. Many people in the best circles came from the aristocracy, which retained much of its power and was still widely emulated. Increasingly, however, aristocrats had to socialize with new millionaires from the bourgeoisie. In fact, the very distinction between aristocrat and bourgeois became blurred, as monarchs gratefully bestowed aristocratic titles on millionaire industrialists and business-people. Moreover, down-at-the-heels aristocrats were only too willing to offer their children in marriage to families from the newly rich. Such arrangements brought much-needed infusions of funds to old, established families and the cachet of an aristocratic title to upstart families. Thus Jeanette Jerome, daughter of a wealthy New York financier, married England's Lord Randolph Churchill (their son Winston later became England's prime minister). Even millionaires without official connections to the aristocracy discarded the modest ways of a century earlier to build palatial country homes and villas, engage in conspicuous displays of wealth, and wall themselves off from the poor in suburbs or new sections of town. To justify their success, the wealthy often appealed to Social Darwinist principles, which assured them that their accumulation of money demonstrated the natural superiority of the rich.

Upper-class men bonded around hunting, their favorite leisure activity, which was reshaped by imperial contact. For centuries, fox and bird hunting had been aristocratic pastimes in parts of Europe; now, big-game hunting in Asia and Africa became the rage. European hunters forced native Africans, who traditionally depended on hunting for income or food and for group unity, to work as guides, porters, and domestics on hunts. By mastering foreign games like polo (an Asian sport) or activities like big-game hunting, Europeans demonstrated that they could conquer not only territory but less tangible things like culture. Collectors on the hunts brought exotic specimens back to Europe for zoological exhibits, natural history museums, and traveling displays, all of which flourished during this period.

Members of the upper class did their best to exclude others by controlling their children's social lives, especially by monitoring girls' sexual activity and relationships with the lower classes. Upper-class men had liaisons with lower-class women—a double standard judged promiscuity normal for men and immoral for women—but few thought of marrying them. Parents still arranged many marriages directly, and visiting days brought eligible young people together to help ensure correct matrimonial decisions.

Ritualistic visits filled the everyday lives of upper-class women. Instead of working for pay, upper-class women devoted themselves to having children, directing staffs of servants, and maintaining standards of etiquette and social conduct. Furnishings in fashionable homes displayed imperial motifs in these decades:

■ Lord and Lady Curzon on a Tiger Shoot

Big-game hunting became the imperial sport of choice, and real adventurers came to see fox hunting and other traditional pastimes of the elites as effeminate if not decadent. European hunters took the sport over from local Africans and Asians who previously had depended on the hunt for their livelihood. Now these Africans and Asians served the European amateurs, many of whom were in wretched physical shape. Some women enjoyed hunting, too. As a gesture of chivalry, men would let a woman deliver the coup de grâce, *or death shot, if a tiger materialized during a hunt.*
(India Office Library/British Library.)

Persian-inspired designs in textiles, Oriental carpets, wicker furniture, and Chinese porcelains. With the importation of azaleas, rhododendrons, and other plants from around the world, private gardens replaced parks and lawns and became another responsibility. Being an active consumer of fashionable clothing was also a time-consuming female activity. In contrast to men's plain garments, upper-class women's clothing was elaborate, ornate, and dramatic, featuring constricting corsets, long voluminous skirts, bustles, and low-cut necklines for evening wear. Women took their roles seriously by keeping detailed accounts of their expenditures and monitoring their children's religious and intellectual development. In addition, they tried to offset the drabness of industrial life with the rigorous practice of art and music. One Hungarian observer wrote, "The piano mania has become almost an epidemic in Budapest as well as Vienna." Some upper-class women were also quite active outside the home, engaging in religious and philanthropic activities to aid lower-class women and children.

Although middle-class professionals could sometimes mingle with people at the apex of society, especially in charity work, their lives remained more modest. They employed at least one servant, which created the illusion of leisure for busy middle-class women performing the onerous duties of maintaining a home. Professional men working at home did so from the best-appointed room. Middle-class domesticity substituted cleanliness and polish for upper-class conspicuous consumption. The soap and tea used in middle-class homes were becoming signs— along with hard work—of a sense of racial superiority over the colonized peoples who actually produced those goods.

The "Best Circles" Transformed

Despite the well-being of the middle and upper classes, urgent concerns over population, marriage, and sexuality clogged the agendas of politicians and reformers from the 1880s on. (See "Taking Measure," below.) The staggering population increases of the eighteenth century had continued through the nineteenth. At the turn of the twentieth century, cities looked chaotic, as population soared and changed the urban landscape. Germany increased in size from 41 million people in 1871 to

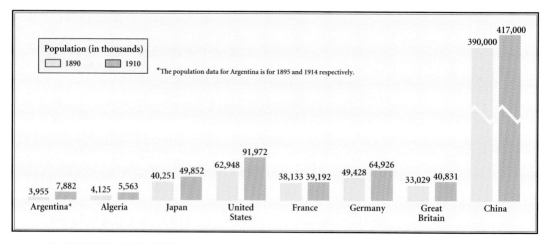

■ **TAKING MEASURE** Population Growth Worldwide, 1890–1910
Countries in the West were undergoing a demographic revolution in these decades as birthrates declined sharply. Nevertheless, population in many countries soared because of improved health, and nations such as Argentina and the United States received vast numbers of immigrants. Exceptions were China and other regions suffering the effects of imperialism, and France, where growth stagnated because the French had drastically curtailed reproduction early in the nineteenth century.
(B. R. Mitchell, *International Historical Statistics: Africa, Asia, and Oceania, 1750–1993*, 3d ed. [London: Macmillan Reference, 1998], 3, 56, 57; Mitchell, *International Historical Statistics: The Americas, 1750–1993*, 4th ed. [London: Macmillan Reference, 1998], 6, 24; Mitchell, *International Historical Statistics: Europe, 1750–1993*, 4th ed. [London: Macmillan Reference, 1998], 4, 8.)

64 million in 1910; tiny Denmark, from 1.7 million in 1870 to 2.7 million in 1911. Such growth resulted from improvements in sanitation and public health that extended longevity and reduced infant mortality. To cope with their burgeoning populations, Berlin, Budapest, and Moscow were torn apart and rebuilt, following the lead of Vienna and Paris. The German government pulled down eighteenth-century Berlin and reconstructed the city with new roadways and mass-transport systems that helped push the capital city's population to over 4 million. Rebuilding for population growth was not confined to the capitals of the most powerful states: Balkan cities such as Sofia, Belgrade, and Bucharest gained tree-lined boulevards, public buildings, and improved sanitation.

While the absolute size of the population was rising in much of the West, the birthrate (measured in births per thousand people) was falling because of urbanization and industrialization. The birthrate had been decreasing in France since the eighteenth century; other European countries began experiencing the decline late in the nineteenth century. The Swedish rate dropped from 35 births per thousand people in 1859 to 24 per thousand in 1911; even populous Germany went from 40 births per thousand in 1875 to 27 per thousand in 1913. In an age of agricultural industrialization, farm families needed fewer hands, and individual couples increasingly practiced birth control to limit family size. Abstinence was a common method, but the spread of new birth-control practices that would encompass most of the globe by the end of the twentieth century mainly accounted for modern Europe's ebbing birthrate. In cities, pamphlets and advice books for those with enough money and education spread information about coitus interruptus—the withdrawal method of preventing pregnancy. Technology also played a role in curtailing reproduction: condoms, improved after the vulcanization of rubber in the 1840s, proved fairly reliable in preventing conception. In the 1880s, Aletta Jacobs (1851–1929), a Dutch physician, opened the first birth-control clinic, which specialized in promoting the new, German-invented diaphragm. Abortions were also legion.

The wider use of birth control stirred controversy. Critics accused middle-class women, whose fertility was falling most rapidly, of holding a "birth strike." Anglican bishops, meeting early in the twentieth century, deplored family limitation, especially by artificial means, as "demoralizing to character and hostile to national welfare." Politicians worried about a crisis in masculinity that would undermine military strength. In the United States, Theodore Roosevelt, now president, blamed middle-class women's selfishness for the population decline, calling it "one of the most unpleasant and unwholesome features of modern life." The "quality" of those being born worried activists and politicians: if the "best" classes had fewer children, they asked, what would society look like when peopled mostly by the "worst" classes? The decline in fertility, one German nationalist warned, would make the country a "conglomerate of alien peoples, above all Slavs and probably East European Jews as well." The Social Darwinist focus on national peril in a menacing world merged the

■ A Large German Family

Improved medicine, hygiene, and diet at the turn of the century helped more people survive infancy and childhood. Thus in many cases family size grew larger, as this photo from a working-class apartment suggests. Even opponents of birth control were appalled that lower-class families were becoming larger than families in the "best circles," where limitation of childbirth was increasingly practiced. (AKG London.)

debate on gender and family issues with anxieties over class and race, inflaming the political climate.

Reformers focused on improving both the conditions within marriage and the quality of children born. The fear that one's nation or "race" was being polluted by the presence of "aliens," the mentally ill, and the severely disabled gave rise to *eugenics*, a pseudoscience popular among wealthy, educated Europeans at the turn of the century. As a famed Italian criminologist put it, such classes were not people but "orangutans." Eugenicists favored increased fertility for "the fittest" and limitations on the fertility of "degenerates," leading even to their sterilization or elimination. Women of the better classes, reformers felt, would be more inclined to reproduce if the shackles in the traditional system of marriage were removed and wives gained the legal right to their wages and to their own property. Sweden, which made men's and women's control over property equal in marriage, allowed women to work without their husbands' permission. Other countries, among them France (1884), legalized divorce and made it less complicated, and thus less costly, to obtain. Reformers had good reason to believe that these legal changes would result in an upswing of the birthrate. Given the existing constraints of motherhood—no financial resources to leave the home, no legal rights to their own children, little recourse in the event of an abusive or miserable marriage—women were reluctant to have more than two or three, if any, children. Divorce would allow unhappy couples to separate and undertake a new, more loving, and thus more fertile marriage. By the early twentieth century, several countries had passed legislation that provided government subsidies to needy mothers.

The conditions of marriage, motherhood, and other aspects of women's lives varied throughout Europe: women could get university degrees in Austrian universities long before they could at Oxford or Cambridge. A greater number of legal reforms occurred in western Europe, however. In much of rural eastern Europe, the father's power over the extended family remained almost dictatorial. According to a survey of family life in eastern Europe in the early 1900s, fathers married off their children so young that 25 percent of women in their early forties had been pregnant more than ten times. Yet reform of everyday customs occurred, as community control gave way to individual practice in places, even though the pace of such change was slower than it was in western Europe. For instance, in some Balkan villages, a kind of extended-family system called the *zadruga* survived from earlier times: all the nuclear families shared a common great house, but now individual couples developed a degree of privacy by building one-room sleeping dwellings surrounding the great house. Among the middle and upper classes of eastern Europe, many grown children were coming to believe they had a right to select a marriage partner, not just to accept the spouse their parents chose for them for economic or social reasons.

The spread of empire and rapid social change set the stage for even bolder behaviors among some middle-class women. Adventurous women traveled the globe to promote Christianity, make money, or obtain knowledge of other cultures. The increasing availability of white-collar jobs for the educated meant that more European women could afford to adopt an independent way of life. So-called new women dressed more practically, wearing fewer petticoats and looser corsets, biked and hiked through city streets and down country lanes, lived apart from the family in women's clubs or apartments, and supported themselves. Italian educator Maria Montessori, for example, went to medical school and secretly gave birth to an illegitimate child. Artists such as the German painter Gabriele Münter lived openly with their lovers. The growing number of women living on their own and freely moving in public challenged accepted views of women's economic dependence and relative seclusion in the traditional middle-class family. The "new woman," German philosopher Friedrich Nietzsche wrote, had led to the "uglification of Europe."

Not just gendered behavior but sexual identity fueled discussion. Among books in the new field of "sexology," which studied sex scientifically from a clinical and medical point of view, *Sexual Inversion* (1894) by Havelock Ellis was

■ **Sydney Grundy, *The New Woman* (1900)**

By the opening of the twentieth century, the "new woman" had become a much-discussed phenomenon. Artists painted portraits of this independent creature, while playwrights such as Henrik Ibsen and novelists such as Nobel Prize winner Sigrid Undset depicted her ambition to throw off the wifely role—or at least to shape that role more to her own personality. The new woman was also well educated: she had been to university, or wrote as a journalist, or entered professions such as law and medicine.
(Jean-Loup Charmet.)

popular. Ellis, a British medical doctor, postulated a new personality type—the homosexual—identifiable by such traits as effeminate behavior and a penchant for the arts in males and physical passion for members of their own sex in both males and females. Homosexuals joined the discussion, calling for recognition that they composed a legitimate and natural "third sex" and were not just people behaving sinfully. The press provoked debate on the other side: in the spring of 1895, reporters covered the trial of Irish playwright Oscar Wilde, who was sentenced to two years in prison for indecency—a charge that referred to his sexual affairs with young men. After Wilde's conviction, one newspaper rejoiced, "Open the windows! Let in the fresh air!" Between 1907 and 1909, German newspapers also publicized the courts-martial of men in Kaiser William II's closest circle who were condemned for homosexuality and transvestitism. Amid growing concern over population and family values, the public received assurances from the government itself that William's own family life "provides the entire country with a fine model." Sexuality thus took on patriotic overtones: the accused homosexual elite in Germany were said by journalists to be out to "emasculate our courageous master race." Although these cases paved the way for growing sexual openness in the next generations, sexual issues would simultaneously become regular weapons in politics.

Working People's Strategies

For centuries, working people had migrated from countryside to city and from country to country to make a living. By the end of the nineteenth century, empire and economic change were spurring millions more to migrate. Older port cities of Europe, such as Riga, Marseille, and Hamburg, offered jobs in industry and global trade; new colonies provided land, posts for soldiers and administrators, and the possibility of unheard-of wealth in diamonds, gold, and other natural resources.

Some Europeans moved far beyond their national borders. In parts of Europe, the land simply could not produce enough to support a rapidly expanding population: Sicilians by the hundreds of thousands left the eroded soil of their island to find work in the industrial cities of northern Europe or the United States. The British Isles, especially Ireland, yielded one-third of all European emigrants between 1840 and 1920, first because of the potato famine and then because of uncertain farm tenancy and periodic economic crisis. Between 1886 and 1900, half a million Swedes out of a population of 4.75 million quit their country (Figure 19.1). Millions of rural Jews, especially in eastern Europe, left their villages for economic reasons. Russian Jews fled in the face of vicious anti-Semitism. Russian mobs attacked Jewish communities, destroying homes and businesses and even murdering some Jews.

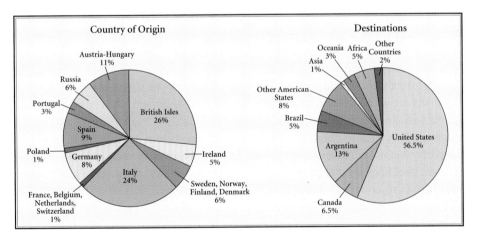

■ **FIGURE 19.1 European Emigration, 1881–1910**
The suffering caused by economic change and by political persecution motivated people from almost every European country to leave their homes for greater security elsewhere. North America attracted nearly two-thirds of these migrants, many of whom followed reports of vast quantities of available land in Canada and the United States. Both countries were known for following the rule of law and for economic opportunity in urban as well as rural areas.
(Data adapted from Walter F. Willcox, ed., *International Migrations.* Volume I: Statistics [New York: Gordon and Breach Science Publishers, rep. 1969], 242–47.)

Commercial and imperial prosperity determined destinations. As news of op-portunity reached Europe, most migrants went to North and South America, Australia, and New Zealand. The railroad and steamship made journeys across and then out of Europe more affordable, more comfortable, and faster, even though most migrants sailed in steerage, with few amenities. Once established elsewhere, migrants frequently sent money back home and thus remained part of the family economy. Nationalist commentators in Slovakia, Poland, Hungary, and other parts of eastern and central Europe bemoaned the loss of ethnic vigor, but peasants them-selves welcomed the arrival of "magic dollars" from their kin. Migrants appreciated the chance to begin anew without the deprivation and social constrictions of the old world. One settler in the United States was relieved to escape the meager peas-ant meal of rye bread and herring: "God save us from . . . all that is Swedish," he wrote home sourly.

Migration out of Europe often meant the end of the old ways of life. Men and women seeking employment had to learn new languages and civic practices and compete for jobs in unfamiliar, growing cities, where they formed the cheapest pool of labor, often in factories or sweatshops. Women who stayed at home working, however, tended to associate with others like themselves, preserving traditional ways. More insulated at home, they might never learn the new language or put away their peasant dresses. Their husbands and children were more likely than they to put the past behind them as they faced the challenges of the factories and schools of the new world.

Internal migration from rural areas to European cities—more common than international migration—accelerated urbanization. The most urbanized countries were Great Britain and Belgium, followed by Germany, France, and the Netherlands. In Russia, only 7 percent of the population lived in cities of 10,000 or more; in Portugal the figure was 12 percent. Cities of more than 100,000 grew the most, but every urban area attracted migrants seeking employment. Nevertheless, more people lived in rural areas with under 2,000 people than lived in towns and cities, and migration back to rural areas occurred at harvest time. Temporary migrants to the cities worked as masons, drivers of horse-drawn cabs, or factory hands to sup-plement declining income from agriculture. In the winter, those remaining on the land turned to cottage industry, making bricks, pottery, sieves, shawls, lace, locks, and samovars. To maintain their status as independent artisans, handweavers sent their wives and daughters to towns to work in factories.

Toward National Fitness: Reforming the Working Class, Expanding Sports and Leisure

Two phenomena softened the upheavals of migration and the stresses of economic modernization. One was the rise of middle- and upper-class reform organizations and charities to improve urban conditions. The other was the emergence of com-petitive sports and the growing interest in healthy recreation. Influenced by Social

Darwinist thought, which associated moral behavior and physical fitness with national strength, governments generally endorsed both phenomena.

Settlement houses, clinics, and maternal and child wellness societies seemed to spring up overnight in cities. Young men and women, often from universities, flocked to staff these new organizations. Reformers eagerly took up residence in settlement houses in poor neighborhoods to study and help the people. Believing in the scientific approach to solving social problems, they sought the causes of social ills and their solutions. One group devoted to this enterprise was the Fabian Society in London, a small organization established in 1884. Committed to a socialism based on reform and state planning rather than revolution, the Fabians helped found the Labour Party in 1893 as a way of making social improvement a political issue. Religious fervor often added a moral component to reform efforts: some Protestants and Catholics countered growing secularization through increased missionary efforts abroad and among the urban poor at home. In the 1890s, Pope Leo XIII called for a more active ministry among the working classes. In response, the church in Hungary, for example, channeled some of its efforts away from its traditional constituency in villages and toward ministering to workers in cities.

Impelled as well by a Social Darwinist fear that Europeans would lack the fitness to survive in a competitive world, philanthropists and government agencies intervened more and more in the lives of working-class families. They sponsored health clinics and milk centers to provide good medical care and food for children, and they instructed mothers in child-care techniques, including breast-feeding—an important way, reformers maintained, to promote infant health. Some schools distributed free lunches, medicine, and clothing. Some professionals began to make birth-control information available in the belief that small families were more likely to survive the rigors of urban life. But some reformers believed that the sexual exploitation of women would increase if the likelihood of pregnancy were overcome so easily. On the downside, government officials and private reformers deemed themselves the overseers of working-class families and entered apartments without being invited. Such intrusions pressured poor, overworked mothers to conform to standards for their children—such as finding them respectable shoes and other clothing—that they often could not afford.

The fear that women were not producing healthy enough children and were stealing jobs from men led reformers to push for protective legislation. Such legislation barred women across Europe from night work and from pottery and other "dangerous" trades, allegedly for health reasons even though medical statistics demonstrated that women became sick on the job less often than men. The new laws assigning some jobs to women and others to men did not prevent women from earning their livelihood, but they made the task harder by limiting women's access to well-paying jobs.

Also serving to enhance national fitness, as well as providing some release from the stresses of daily life, were competitive sports and healthy leisure-time activities. As nations competed for territory and economic markets, male athletes banded

■ **Anglo-Indian Polo Team**
*Team sports underwent rapid development during the imperial years, as spectators rooted for the
success of their football team in the same spirit they rooted for their armies abroad. Some educators believed that team sports formed the male character so that men could be more effective soldiers against peoples of other races. Thus this mixed team of polo players was uncharacteristic. In
cricket, soccer, and other sports, city challenged city, nation challenged nation, and race often challenged race.* (Hulton Getty Collection/Liaison Agency.)

together to organize team sports that eventually replaced village games. Soccer,
rugby, and cricket drew mass followings and helped to integrate migrants as well as
people from the lower and upper classes into a common national culture. Large audiences drawn from all classes backed their favorite teams, and competitive sports
began to be seen as valuable promoters of national strength and spirit. Newspapers
reported the results of all sorts of contests, including the Tour de France bicycle race,
sponsored by tire makers who wanted to prove the superiority of their products.

Team sports further differentiated male and female spheres and thus promoted
social order based on distinctions between the sexes. Some team sports for women
emerged—soccer, field hockey, and rowing—but women generally were encouraged to engage in individual sports. "Riding improves the temper, the spirits and
the appetite," wrote one sportswoman. "Black shadows and morbid fancies disappear from the mental horizon." Rejecting the idea of women's natural frailty, reformers introduced exercise and gymnastics into schools for girls, often with the
idea that they would strengthen young women for motherhood and thus help build
the nation-state. So-called Swedish exercises for young women spread through
respectable homes across Europe, while more cosmopolitan women practiced
yoga.

The middle classes believed their leisure pursuits should not only be fun but also hone mental and physical skills. Thus mountain climbing became a popular middle-class hobby. Working-class people adopted middle-class habits by joining clubs for bicycling, touring, and hiking. Laborers and their families also sought the benefits of fresh air and exercise by visiting the beach, taking the train into the countryside, and enjoying day trips on river steamships. Clubs that sponsored trips often had names such as "The Patriots" or "The Nationals," again associating physical fitness with national strength. The new emphasis on healthy recreation gave individuals a greater sense of individual freedom and power and thereby fostered a sense of citizenship based less on constitutions and rights than on an individual nation's exercise of raw power. A farmer's son in the 1890s boasted that with a bicycle "I was king of the road, since I was faster than a horse."

Sciences of the Modern Self

Scientists and Social Darwinists found cause for alarm not only in the condition of the working class but also in modern society's complaints about fatigue and irritability. Such illnesses originated in the "nerves," they reasoned, which were overstimulated by the pace and demands of urban living. A rash of books in the 1890s expounded on the subject of nervous illness. The most widely translated of them, *Degeneration*, written by Hungarian-born physician Max Nordau (1849–1923), blamed overstimulation for both individual and national deterioration. According to Nordau, increasingly bizarre modern art, male lethargy, and female hysteria were all symptoms of overstimulation and signs of a general downturn in the human species. The Social Darwinist prescription for curing such mental decline was imperial adventure, renewed virility, and increased childbearing.

Some researchers attempted to quantify and classify mental characteristics. Scientific study of the origins of criminal traits created the field of criminology. The French psychologist Alfred Binet (1857–1911) designed intelligence tests that he claimed could measure the capacity of the human mind more accurately than schoolteachers could. In Russia, physiologist Ivan Pavlov (1849–1936) proposed that conditioning mental reflexes—that is, causing a subject to associate a desired response with a previously unrelated stimulus—could modify behavior. His experiments, especially his success in changing the behavior of a dog, formed the basis of modern psychology.

Sigmund Freud (1856–1939) devised an approach to modern anxieties that, he claimed, avoided traditional moral evaluations of human behavior. He became convinced that the human psyche was far from rational. Dreams, he explained in *The Interpretation of Dreams* (1900), reveal a repressed part of personality—the "unconscious"—where all sorts of desires are more or less hidden. Freud also believed that the human psyche is made up of three competing parts: the *ego*, the part that is most in touch with external reality; the *id* (or libido), the part that governs instinctive drives and sexual energies; and the *superego,* the part that serves as the force of conscience. Like Darwin's ideas, Freud's notions challenged the widespread liberal beliefs in a unified, rational self that acts in its own interest and, by implication, in the certainty of progress.◆

Freud shocked many of his contemporaries by insisting that all children have sexual drives from the moment of birth. He also believed that many of these sexual impulses have to be repressed for the individual to attain maturity and for society to remain civilized. Attaining one's adult sexual identity is always a painful process because it depends on repressing infantile urges, which include bisexuality and incest. Thus the Wolf-Man's nightmare of white wolves outside his window symbolized his unresolved sexual feelings for members of his family. Freud claimed that certain aspects of gender roles—such as motherhood—are normal and that throughout their lives women in general achieve far less than men do. At the same time, he believed that adult gender identity results not from anatomy alone (motherhood is not the only way to be female) but from inescapable mental processing of life experiences as well. He thus made gender more complicated than simple biology would suggest. Finally, Freud's psychoanalytic theory maintained that girls and women have powerful sexual feelings, an assertion that broke with ideas of women's passionlessness.

The influence of psychoanalysis became pervasive in the twentieth century, offering paradoxes and representing another turn toward global thinking. Two mainstays of psychoanalysis—free association of ideas and interpretation of dreams—derived from African and Asian influences on Freud's thought: the "talking cure," as it was quickly labeled, gave rise to a general acceptance of talking out one's problems. As psychoanalysis became a respected means of recovering mental health, terms such as *neurosis, unconscious,* and *libido* came into widespread use and could apply to anyone, not just the mentally ill. By way of paradox, psychoanalysis reflected the many contradictions at work in turn-of-the-century Europe. For example, Freud attributed girls' complaints about unwanted sexual advances or abuse to fantasies caused by "penis envy." This idea led members of the new profession of social work to believe that most claims of such abuse were not true. So on the one hand, Freud was a meticulous scientist, examining symptoms, urging attention to the most minute evidence from everyday life, and demanding that sexual life be regarded with a rational rather than a religious eye. But on the other hand, he was a pessimistic visionary who abandoned the optimism of the Enlightenment and pre-Darwinian science and instead theorized that humans are motivated by irrational drives toward death and destruction and that these drives shape society's collective mentality. Freud would later interpret the devastation of World War I as bearing out his bleak conclusions.

◆ For an excerpt from Freud's best-known work, see Document 62, Sigmund Freud, *The Interpretation of Dreams.*

■ **Freud's Office**
Sigmund Freud's therapy room, where his patients experienced the "talking cure," was filled with imperial trophies such as Oriental rugs and African art objects. Freud himself was fascinated by cures brought about through shamanism, trances, and other practices of non-Western medicine as well as through drug-induced mental states. In 1938, Freud fled to England to escape the Nazis. This photo shows his office in London. (Mary Evans Picture Library/Sigmund Freud copyrights.)

Modernity and the Revolt in Ideas

Although the intellectuals and artists who participated in the turmoil and triumph of turn-of-the-century society did not know it at the time, their rejection of accepted beliefs and artistic forms announced a new era. Scientific theories that time is relative and that energy and mass are interchangeable rocked established truths about time, space, matter, and energy. Philosophers emphasized the role of the irrational and accidental in everyday life. Art and music became unrecognizable. Artists and musicians who deliberately produced shocking, lurid works were, like Freud, heavily influenced by advances in science, critical thinking, and empire. Amid contradictions such as the blending of the scientific and the irrational, "West" and "non-West," intellectuals and artists helped launch the disorienting revolution in ideas and creative expression that we now identify collectively as *modernism.*

The Challenge to Positivism

Late in the nineteenth century, at the height of empire-building and reform efforts, many philosophers and social thinkers rejected the century-old belief that scientific methods would lead to the discovery of enduring social laws. This belief, called *positivism,* had emphasized the permanent nature of fundamental laws and had motivated reformers' attempts to perfect legislation based on studies of society. Challenging positivism, the philosophers Wilhelm Dilthey (1833–1911) in Germany and John Dewey (1859–1952) in the United States declared that because human experience is ever changing, theories and standards cannot be constant or enduring. Just as scientific theory was modified over time, so must social theories and practice react pragmatically to the immediate conditions at hand. In the same vein, German political theorist Max Weber (1864–1920) maintained that the sheer numbers involved in policymaking would often make decisive action by bureaucrats impossible—especially in times of crisis, when a charismatic leader might usurp power because of his ability to make flexible and instinctive decisions. Thus the development of impartial forms of government such as bureaucracy carried the potential for undermining the rule of law. Turn-of-the-century thinkers called *relativists* and *pragmatists* influenced thinking about society throughout the twentieth century.

The most radical scholar was the German philosopher Friedrich Nietzsche (1844–1900), who early in his career developed the challenging distinction between the "Apollonian," or rational, side of human existence and the "Dionysian" side, with its expression of more primal urges. Nietzsche believed that people generally cling to rational, Apollonian explanations of life because Dionysian ideas about nature, death, and love such as those found in Greek tragedy are too disturbing. He maintained that all assertions of scientific fact and theory are mere illusions, that knowledge of nature has to be expressed in mathematical, linguistic, or artistic representation. Truth, Nietzsche insisted, thus exists only in the representation itself, for humans can never experience unfiltered knowledge of nature or reality. This aspect of Nietzsche's philosophy would lead to the late-twentieth-century school of thought called *postmodernism.*

Much of Nietzsche's writing took the form of aphorisms—short, disconnected statements of truth or opinion—a form that broke with the logical rigor of traditional Western philosophy. Nietzsche used aphorisms to convey the impression that his ideas were a single individual's unique perspective, not universal truths that thinkers since the Enlightenment had claimed were attainable. Influenced by a range of Asian philosophies, Nietzsche was convinced that late-nineteenth-century Europe was witnessing the decline of dogmatic truth, most notably in religion—hence his announcement that "God is dead, we have killed him." Far from arousing dread, the death of God, according to Nietzsche, would give birth to a joyful quest for new "poetries of life" to replace worn-out religious and middle-class rules. Not the rule-bound bourgeois but the untethered "superman" was Nietzsche's highly influential model. On his death, however, Nietzsche's sister edited his diatribes against middle-class values into attacks on Jews. She revised his complicated concepts about each individual's "will to power" and the "superman" so as to appeal to nationalists and to justify violent anti-Semitism and competition for empire.

Revolutionizing Science

While philosophers questioned the ability of science to provide timeless truths, scientific inquiry itself flourished, and the scientific method gained authority in history, psychology, and other fields beyond the traditional sciences. Many people still held positivist assumptions. Technological breakthroughs and improvements in hygiene earned science public prestige. Around the turn of the century, however, discoveries by pioneering researchers shook the foundations of traditional scientific certainty and challenged accepted knowledge about the nature of the universe.

In 1896, Antoine Becquerel (1852–1908) discovered radioactivity and suggested the mutability of elements by the rearrangement of their atoms. French chemist Marie Curie (1867–1934) and her husband, Pierre Curie (1859–1906), isolated the elements polonium and radium, which are more radioactive than the uranium Becquerel used. From these and other discoveries, scientists concluded that atoms are composed of subatomic particles moving about a core. Instead of being solid, as scientists had believed since ancient times, atoms are largely empty space and act not as a concrete substance but as an intangible electromagnetic field. German physicist Max Planck (1858–1947) announced his influential quantum theorem in 1900; it demonstrated that energy is emitted in irregular packets, not in a steady stream.

Scientists had already demonstrated that light has a uniform velocity regardless of the direction it travels from the earth and that the speed of light is unrelated to the motion of the earth. Thus older theories of light on which scientists had relied were no longer tenable. It was in this unsettled situation that physicist Albert Einstein (1879–1955) published his special theory of relativity. On his own, working in a Swiss patent office, he proclaimed in his 1905 paper that space and time are not absolute categories but instead vary according to the vantage point of the observer. Only the speed of light is constant. That same year, he also suggested that the solution to problems in Planck's quantum theorem lay in considering light both as little packets *and* as waves. These theories continued to undercut Newtonian physics as well as commonsense understanding.

Einstein later proposed yet another blurring of two distinct physical properties, mass and energy. He expressed this equivalence in the formulation $E = mc^2$, or energy equals mass times the square of the speed of light. In 1916, his general theory of relativity connected the force, or gravity, of an object with its mass and postulated a fourth mathematical dimension to the universe. Much more lay ahead, once Einstein's theories of energy were developed: television, nuclear power, and, within forty years, nuclear bombs.

The revolutionary findings of Planck, Einstein, and others were not accepted immediately because power and time-honored beliefs were at stake. Einstein like Planck struggled against mainstream science and its professional institutions. Marie Curie faced such resistance that even after she became the first person ever to

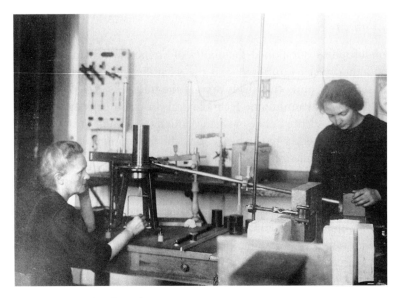

■ **Marie Curie and Her Daughter**
Recipient of two Nobel Prizes, Marie Curie came from Poland to western Europe to study science. Curie's extraordinary career made her the epitome of the new womanhood; her daughter Irene Joliot-Curie followed her into the field and also won a Nobel Prize. Both women died of leukemia caused by their exposure to radioactive materials. Today a reconstruction of the Curie laboratory as a museum contains a display indicating the intense radioactivity remaining in the scientific instruments they used a century ago. (ACJC—Archives Curie et Joliot-Curie.)

receive a second Nobel Prize (1911), the prestigious French Academy of Science turned down her candidacy for membership that year. Traditionalists, however, eventually gave way, and Max Planck institutes were established in German cities, streets across Europe were named after Marie Curie, and Einstein's name became synonymous with genius. These scientists achieved what historians call a *paradigm shift*—that is, in the face of staunch resistance they transformed the foundations of science and came themselves to supersede other names.

Modern Art

Conflicts between traditional values and new ideas also raged in the arts, as artists distanced themselves from classical Western realism and from the conventions of polite society. Modernism in the arts not only fractured traditional standards but ushered in competing artistic styles and disagreement about art's relationship to society. Some modern artists tried both to challenge and to comfort urbanites caught up in the rush of modern life. Abandoning the soft colors of impressionism as too subtle for a dynamic industrial society, a group of Parisian artists exhibiting in 1905 combined blues, greens, reds, and oranges so intensively that they were called *fauves*, or "wild beasts." A leader of the short-lived fauvism, Henri Matisse (1869–1954) soon struck out in a new direction, targeting the expanding class of white-collar workers. Matisse dreamed of "an art . . . for every mental worker, be he businessman or writer, like an appeasing influence, like a mental soother, something like a good armchair in which to rest from physical fatigue."

In the work of the French artist Paul Cézanne (1839–1906), one of the most powerful and enduring trends in modern art took shape. Emphasizing structure, Cézanne used rectangular daubs of paint to capture a geometric vision of dishes, fruit, drapery, and the human body. Accentuating the lines and planes found in nature, Cézanne's art, like science, was removed from the realm of ordinary perception. Following in Cézanne's footsteps, Spanish artist Pablo Picasso (1881–1973) initiated *cubism*, a style whose radical emphasis on planes and surfaces portrayed people as bizarre, inhuman, almost unrecognizable forms. Picasso's painting *Les Demoiselles d'Avignon* (1907) depicted the bodies of the *demoiselles*, or young ladies (prostitutes in this case), as fragmented and angular, with their heads modeled on African masks (see page 805). Continuing along the path of impressionism and fauvism, Picasso's work showed the profound influences of African, Asian, and South American arts, but his interpretation of these influences was less decorative and more brutal than those by Matisse, for example. Like explorers, botanists, and foreign journalists, he was bringing knowledge of the empire into the imperial homeland, this time in a distinctly disturbing form.

Across Europe, political critique also shaped art. "Show the people how hideous is their actual life, and place your hands on the causes of its ugliness" was the anarchist challenge at the time. Picasso, who had spent his youth in the heart of working-class Barcelona, a hotbed of anarchist thought, aimed to replace middle-class sentimentality in art with truth about industrial society. In 1912, Picasso and the French painter Georges Braque (1882–1963) devised a new kind of collage that incorporated bits of newspaper, string, and other artifacts. The effect was a canvas that appeared to be cluttered with refuse. The newspaper clippings Picasso included described battles and murders, suggesting the shallowness of Western pretensions to high civilization. In eastern and central Europe, artists criticized the growing nationalism that determined official purchases of sculpture and painting: "The whole empire is littered with monuments to soldiers and monuments to Kaiser William of the same conventional type," one German artist complained. Such groups as the Berlin Secession and the Vienna Workshop were at the forefront of depicting psychological complexity in experimental form.

Scandinavian and eastern European artists produced anguished works. Like the vision of Freud, their style of portraying inner reality—called *expressionism*—broke with middle-class optimism. Norwegian painter Edvard Munch (1863–1944) aimed "to make the emotional mood ring out again as happens on a gramophone." His painting *The Scream* (1895) used twisting lines and a depiction of tortured skeletal human form to convey the horror of modern life that many artists perceived. The German avant-garde artist Gabriele Münter (1877–1962) and Russian painter Wassily Kandinsky (1866–1944) opened their "Blue Rider" exhibit in Munich featuring "expressive" work that made use of geometric forms and striking colors. Artists of the Blue Rider group imitated the paintings of children and the mentally ill to achieve their depiction of psychological reality. Kandinsky, who employed these forms and colors to express an inner, spiritual truth, is often credited with producing the first fully abstract paintings. The expressionism of Austrian painter Oskar Kokoschka (1886–1980) was even more intense, displaying ecstasy, horror, and hallucinations. As a result, his work—like that of other expressionists and cubists before World War I—was a commercial failure in an increasingly complex marketplace that featured not only museum curators but professional dealers and art "experts." Trade in art became professionalized, as had medicine and government work before it, even as modern artists sought to shatter traditional norms.

Only one innovative style emerged an immediate commercial success: *art nouveau* ("new style") won approval from government, critics, and the masses. Creating everything from dishes and advertising posters to streetlamps and even entire buildings in this new style, designers manufactured beautiful things for the general public. As one French official said about the first version of art nouveau coins issued in 1895, "Soon even the most humble among us will be able to have a masterpiece in his pocket." Adapted from Asian design, the organic and natural elements of art nouveau were meant to offset the fragmentation of factory and office work with images depicting the unified forms of nature. The impersonality of machines was replaced by intertwined vines and flowers and the softly curving bodies of female nudes that would psychologically soothe the individual viewer—an idea that directly contrasted with Picasso's artistic vision. Gustav Klimt (1862–1918), son of a Czech goldsmith, flourished in Viennese high society because his paintings captured the psychological essence of dreamy, sensuous women, their bodies Eastern-inspired mosaics liberally dotted with gold. Art nouveau was the notable exception to the public outcries over innovations in the visual arts.

Musical Iconoclasm

"Astonish me!" was the motto of modern dance and music, both of which shocked audiences in the concert halls of Europe. American dancer Isadora Duncan (1877–1927) took Europe by storm at the turn of the century when, draped in a flowing garment, she danced barefoot in the first performance of modern dance. Drawing on sophisticated Japanese practices, hers was nonetheless called a primitive style that "lifted from their seats people who had never left theater seats before except to get up and go home." Similarly, experimentation with forms of bodily expression animated the Russian Ballet's performance in 1913 of *Rite of Spring* by Igor Stravinsky (1882–1971), the tale of an orgiastic dance to the death performed

■ **Léon Bakst, *Nijinsky in "L'Après-Midi d'un Faune"*** ("Nijinsky in 'The Afternoon of a Faun,'" 1912)

Theater sets, costume designs, and performance itself resonated with the experimental climate of early-twentieth-century Europe. Léon Bakst, a Russian painter and set designer, used art nouveau style to capture the faunlike character of ballet star Vaslav Nijinsky. Yet on the eve of World War I, Nijinsky was part of a revolution in ballet that introduced jerky, awkward, pounding movements to indicate the primal nature of dance. (Wadsworth Atheneum, Hartford. The Ella Gallup Sumner and Mary Catlin Sumner Collection Fund.)

to ensure fertile soil and a bountiful harvest. The choreography of its star, Vaslav Nijinsky (1890–1950), created a scandal. Nijinsky and the troupe struck awkward poses and danced to rhythms intended to sound primitive. At the work's premiere in Paris, one journalist reported that "the audience began shouting its indignation.... Fighting actually broke out among some of the spectators." Such controversy made *Rite of Spring* a box-office hit, although its choreographer was called a "lunatic" and the music itself "the most discordant composition ever written."

Music had been making this turn for several decades. Having heard Asian musicians at international expositions, French composers such as Claude Debussy (1862–1918) transformed their style to reflect non-European musical patterns and themes. The twentieth century opened with *Scheherazade* by Frenchman Maurice Ravel (1875–1937) and *Madame Butterfly* by the Italian composer Giacomo Puccini (1858–1924), both with non-Western subject matter. Using non-Western tonalities, sound became jarring to many listeners. Austrian composer Richard Strauss (1864–1949) upset convention by using several keys simultaneously in his compositions. Like the fragmented representation of reality in cubism, atonality or several tonalities at once distorted familiar harmonic patterns for the audience. Strauss's operas *Salome* (1905) and *Elektra* (1909) reflected modern fascination with violence and obsessive passion. A newspaper critic claimed that Strauss's dissonant works "spit and scratch and claw each other like enraged panthers." The Hungarian pianist Béla Bartók (1881–1945) incorporated folk melodies into his compositions in order to elevate Hungarian ethnicity above the Habsburg Empire's multinationalism. His music disturbed some audiences because of its nationalism and others because of its dissonance.

The early orchestral work of Austrian composer Arnold Schoenberg (1874–1951), who also wrote cabaret music to earn a living, shocked even Strauss. In *Theory of Harmony* (1911), Schoenberg proposed eliminating tonality altogether; a decade later he devised a new twelve-tone scale. "I am aware of having broken through all the barriers of a dated aesthetic ideal," Schoenberg wrote of his music. But new aesthetic models distanced artists like Schoenberg from their audiences, separating high from low culture even more and ending the support of many in the upper classes, who found this music not only incomprehensible but unpleasant. The artistic elite and the social elite parted ranks. "Anarchist! Nihilist!" shouted Schoenberg's audiences, showing their contempt for modernism and bringing the language of politics into the arts.

Politics in a New Key

The political atmosphere grew charged alongside the modernist disturbances in intellectual life, even though the advance of liberal opinions opened the door to expanded political representation and growing tolerance. Networks of communication, especially the development of journalism, enhanced the trend toward universal male suffrage in Europe, leading to the creation of mass politics. Working-class people seemed to come into their own: even high-ranking politicians such as William Gladstone, the prime minister of Great Britain, had to campaign by railroad to win their support. Simultaneously, however, political activists were no longer satisfied with the liberal rights sought by reformers a century earlier. Militant nationalists, anti-Semites, socialists, suffragists, and others demanded changes that challenged liberal values. Traditional elites, resentful of the rising middle classes and urban peoples, aimed to stem constitutional processes and the development of modern life. Mass politics soon threatened social unity, especially in central and eastern Europe, where governments often answered reformers' demands with refusal and repression.

Mass Politics and the Growing Power of Labor

Mass politics was a combination of the right to vote accorded to men across Europe before World War I and the rise of popular activism, especially among working people. In the fall of 1879, William Gladstone (1809–1898), leader of the British Liberals, whose party was then out of power, waged an experimental electoral campaign across the country. Speaking before thousands of workingmen and -women, he urged greater self-determination in India and Africa and advocated a way of life based on "honest, manful, humble effort" in the middle-class tradition of "hard work." Newspapers around the country highlighted his trip, further fueling public interest in politics. Gladstone's Liberals won the election, and he became prime minister—testimonial to the trend toward expanded participation in political life. The Reform Act of 1884 doubled the British electorate, to around 4.5 million men, enfranchising many urban workers and artisans and thus diminishing traditional aristocratic influence in the countryside. This move reflected the universal manhood suffrage already granted in France and in Germany; the rest of Europe would follow suit before World War I.

Journalism helped elite politicians forge a broad national community of up-to-date citizens by providing ready access to information (and misinformation) about politics and world events. The invention of mechanical typesetting and the production of newsprint from wood pulp lowered the costs of printing; the telephone allowed reporters to communicate news to their papers almost instantly. Once philosophical and literary in content, daily newspapers now emphasized the sensational, using banner headlines and gruesome or lurid details—particularly about murders, sexual scandals, and sagas of the empire—to sell papers as well as political points of view. In the hustle and bustle of industrial society, one editor wrote, "you must strike your reader right between the eyes." Elites grumbled that the sensational press was another sign of social decay. But for up-and-coming people from the working and middle classes it provided an entrée into politics and an avenue to success. As London, Paris, Vienna, Berlin, and St. Petersburg became centers not only of politics but of news, a number of European politicians got their start working for daily newspapers.

Working-class solidarity in neighborhoods, shop-floor activism, the development of labor unions, and the rise of worker or socialist parties formed the other side of mass politics. Community bonds forged by homemakers and neighborhood groups were a necessary precondition for collective worker action. School officials or police looking for truant children and delinquents met a phalanx of housewives ready to hide the children or to lie for their neighbors. When landlords evicted tenants, women would gather in the streets and return household goods as fast as they were removed from the rooms of ousted families. Meeting on doorsteps or at fountains, laundries, pawnshops, and markets, women initiated rural newcomers into urban ways and developed class unity. Conditions of economic life also led workers to organize formal unions, which attracted the allegiance of millions. Unions demanded a say in working conditions and aimed, as one union's rule book put it, "to ensure that wages . . . always follow the rises in the price of basic commodities." Despite worker turbulence of the Paris Commune, strong unions even appealed to some industrialists because a union could make strikes more predictable (or even prevent them), present demands more coherently, and provide a liaison for labor-management relations.

From the 1880s on, the pace of collective action for more pay, lower prices, and better working conditions accelerated. In 1888, for example, hundreds of young women who made matches, the so-called London matchgirls, struck to end the fining system, under which they could be penalized an entire day's wage for being a minute or two late to work. This system, the matchgirls maintained, helped companies reap profits of more than 20 percent. Newspapers and philanthropists picked up the strikers' story, helping them win their case. Soon after, London dockworkers and gasworkers protested their precarious working conditions. Across Europe, the number of strikes and demonstrations rose from 188 in 1888 to 289 in 1890. Housewives, who often demonstrated in support of strikers, carried out their own protests against high food prices. In keeping with centuries of women's protest, they confiscated merchants' goods and sold them at what they considered a just price. "There should no longer be either rich or poor," argued organized Italian peasant women. "All should have bread for themselves and for their children. We should all be equal." Fearing threats to industrial and agricultural productivity, governments increasingly responded with force, even though most strikes were about the conditions of everyday life for workers and not about political revolution.

From unions soon evolved working-class political parties. Craft-based unions of skilled artisans, such as carpenters and printers, were the most active and cohesive, but from the mid-1880s on, a *new unionism* attracted transport workers, miners, matchgirls, and dockworkers. These new unions were nationwide groups with salaried managers who could plan massive general strikes across the trades, focusing on such common goals as the eight-hour workday, and thus paralyze an entire nation. Large unions of the industrialized countries of western Europe, like cartels and trusts, increasingly influenced business practices. They were joined by working-class parties: the Labour Party in England, the Socialist Party in France, and the Social Democratic Parties of Sweden, Hungary, Austria, and Germany—most of them inspired by Marxist theories. Germany was home to the largest socialist party in Europe after 1890.

Workingwomen joined these parties, but in much smaller numbers than men. Not able to vote in national elections and usually responsible for housework in addition to their paying jobs, women had little time for party meetings. Furthermore, their low wages hardly allowed them to survive, much less to pay party or union dues. Many workingmen opposed their presence, fearing women would dilute the union's masculine camaraderie. Contact with women would mean "suffocation," one Russian workingman believed, and end male union members' sense of being "comrades in the revolutionary cause." The shortage of women's voices in unions and political parties paralleled women's exclusion from government; it helped make the middle-class belief in separate spheres part of a working-class ideology that glorified the heroic struggles of a male proletariat against capitalism. Marxist leaders continued to maintain that injustice to women was caused by capitalism and would disappear in socialist society. As a result, although the new political organizations encouraged women's support, they downplayed women's concerns about lower wages and sexual coercion.

Socialist parties attracted workingmen because they promised the triumph of new male voters who could become a powerful collective force in national elections. Those who accepted Marx's assertion that "workingmen have no country," however, wanted an international movement that could address workers' common interests. In 1889, some four hundred socialists from across Europe (joined by many on-lookers and unofficial participants) met in Paris to form the Second International, a federation of working-class organizations and political parties replacing the First International, founded by Marx before the Paris Commune. Growing strength, especially electoral victories, raised issues for socialists. Some felt uncomfortable sitting with the upper classes in parliaments. Others worried that their participation in cabinets would produce reform but compromise their ultimate goal of revolution. Often these deputies refused seats in the government. Between 1900 and 1904, the Second International wrestled with the issue of reformism—that is, whether socialists should employ evolutionary tactics rather than pushing for a violent revolution to overthrow governments.

European leaders watched with dismay the rise of working-class political power late in the century. Some trade union members, known as *syndicalists*, along with anarchists kept Europe in a panic with their terrorist acts. Anarchism flourished in the less industrial parts of Europe—Russia, Italy, and Spain, where many rural people looked to the possibility of life without the domination of large landowners and government. Many advocated extreme tactics, including physical violence and even murder. "We want to overthrow the government . . . with violence since it is by the use of violence that they force us to obey," wrote one Italian anarchist. In the 1880s, anarchists bombed stock exchanges, parliaments, and businesses and by the 1890s were assassinating heads of state: Spanish premier Antonio Canovas del Castillo in 1897, Empress Elizabeth of Austria-Hungary in 1898, King Umberto of Italy in 1900, and President William McKinley of the United States in 1901, to name a few famous victims. Syndicalists advocated the use of direct action, such as general strikes and sabotage, to bring industry and government under the control of labor unions by paralyzing the economy.

But much worker organization was also sociable, intertwining community solidarity with activities of everyday life. The gymnastic and choral societies that had once united Europeans in nationalistic fervor now served working-class goals. Songs emphasized worker freedom, progress, and eventual victory. Socialist gymnastics, bicycling, and marching societies rejected competition and prizes as middle-class preoccupations, but they valued physical fitness for helping workers in the "struggle for existence"—a reflection of Darwinian thinking about "survival of the fittest." Workers also held festivals and gigantic parades, most notably on May 1, proclaimed by the Second International as a labor holiday. Like religious processions of an earlier time, parades were rituals that fostered unity. European governments at the time could not discriminate among the various worker organizations and frequently prohibited such public gatherings, fearing they were tools for agitators.

Another group of working-class parties operated in exile. The Russian government, for instance, outlawed political parties until 1905 and persecuted activists. The foremost Russian activist, V. I. Lenin (1870–1924), migrated to western Europe after his release from confinement in Siberia and earned his reputation among Russian Marxists there with his hard-hitting journalism and political intrigue. Lenin advanced the theory that a highly disciplined socialist elite would lead a lightly industrialized Russia immediately into socialism. Outmaneuvering the Mensheviks, who dominated Russian Marxism, Lenin's Bolsheviks, so named after the Russian word for "majority" (which they had briefly formed), constantly struggled to suppress other groups. Neither of these factions, however, had as large a constituency within Russia as the Socialist Revolutionaries, whose objective was to politicize peasants rather than industrial workers as the prelude to a populist revolution. All these groups prepared for the revolutionary moment through study, propaganda efforts, and organizing—not through the electoral politics successfully employed elsewhere in Europe. Whether operating in representative or authoritarian countries, working-class organizations caused the upper and middle classes grave anxiety. Despite growing acceptance of representative institutions and despite the spread of education, many in the "best circles" still believed that they alone should hold political power.

Rights for Women and the Battle for Suffrage

Singly or in groups, women continued to agitate against their exclusion from benefits of liberalism such as parliamentary representation. They usually could not vote, exercise free speech, or own property if married. Laws in France, Austria, and Germany curtailed women's political activism, including their attendance at political meetings. Influenced by the cultural ideal of *Bildung*—the belief that education can strengthen character and that individual development has public importance—German women sought better education for themselves and more opportunity to teach, instead of agitating for political reform. In several countries, women continued to monitor the regulation of prostitution. Their goal was to prevent prostitutes from being imprisoned on suspicion of having syphilis when men with syphilis faced no such incarceration. Other women took up pacifism as their special cause. Many of them were inspired by Bertha von Süttner's popular book, *Lay Down Your Arms* (1889), which emphasized the terror inflicted on women and families by the ravages of war. (Later von Süttner would influence Alfred Nobel to institute a peace prize and then win the prize herself in 1903.)

By the 1890s, however, many activists had concluded that only the right to vote would correct the problems caused by male privilege, which they were combating in piecemeal fashion. Thus, major suffrage organizations with millions of activists, paid officials, and permanent offices emerged out of the earlier reform groups and women's clubs. Using skills gained from their charity work and from this organizing, British suffrage leader Millicent Garrett Fawcett (1847–1929) and other women pressured members of Parliament for the vote, recruited members, and participated in national and international congresses on behalf of suffrage. Similarly, American Susan B. Anthony (1820–1906) traveled throughout the United States, organized suffrage societies, edited a newspaper, raised money for the movement, and founded the International Woman Suffrage Association in 1904. The leadership argued that men had promised to protect disfranchised women but that this system of male chivalry had led to exploitation and abuse. Power and privilege—no matter how couched in expressions of goodwill—worked to the detriment of those without them. "So long as the subjection of women endures, and is confirmed by law and custom, . . . women will be victimized," a leading suffragist claimed. Other activists believed that women had the attributes needed to counterbalance masculine qualities in the running of society. The characteristics that came from mothering should shape a country's destiny as much as qualities that stemmed from work in industry and trade, they asserted.

Women's rights activists were predominantly, though not exclusively, from the middle class. Enjoying conveniences like freestanding stoves, running water, and household help, they had more time than workingwomen to be activists, and a higher level of education allowed them to read the works of feminist theorists such as Harriet Taylor and John Stuart Mill. Many were influenced by such works as Norwegian playwright Henrik Ibsen's *A Doll's House* (1879), whose heroine Nora leaves a loveless and oppressive marriage. Olive Schreiner's *The Story of an African Farm* (1889) was equally influential. Her heroine rejects the role of submissive wife and describes the British Empire as a "dirty little world, full of confusion." Some working-class women also participated, although many distrusted the middle class and saw suffrage for women as less important than economic concerns. Textile workers in Manchester, England, for example, put together a vigorous suffrage movement connecting the vote to improved working conditions. Socialists and suffragists, however, usually differed over issues of class and gender.

In 1906 in Finland, suffragists achieved their first major victory when the Finnish parliament granted women the vote. But the failure of parliaments elsewhere in Europe to enact similar legislation provoked some suffragists to violence. Part of the British suffragist movement adopted a militant political style. Emmeline Pankhurst (1858–1928) and her daughters had founded the Women's Social and Political Union (WSPU) in 1903 in the belief that women would accomplish nothing unless they threatened men's property. In 1907, WSPU members began to stage parades in English cities, and in 1909 they began a campaign of violence, blowing up railroad stations, slashing works of art, and chaining themselves to the gates of Parliament. Easily disguising themselves as ordinary shoppers, they carried little hammers in their muffs to smash the plate-glass windows of department stores and

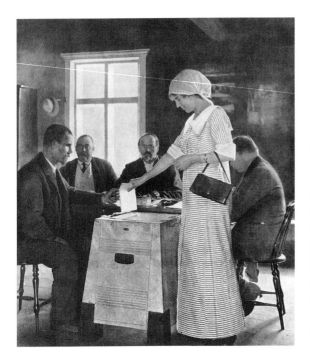

■ **Woman Suffrage in Finland**
In 1906, Finnish women became the first women in Europe to receive the vote in national elections when the socialist party—usually opposed to feminism as a middle-class rather than a working-class project—supported woman suffrage. The Finnish vote elated activists in the West, now linked by many international organizations and ties, because it showed that more than a century of lobbying for reform could lead to gains.
(Mary Evans Picture Library.)

shops. Parades and demonstrations made suffrage a public spectacle, provoking violent attacks on the marchers by outraged men. Arrested for disturbing the peace, the marchers went on hunger strikes in prison. Like striking workers, these women were willing to use confrontational tactics to obtain rights. As politicians continued to deny women the vote, militant suffragists added to the tensions of conflict-ridden urban life.◆

Liberalism Modified

Governments in western Europe, where liberal institutions seemed well entrenched, sought to control the conflicts of the late nineteenth century with pragmatic policies that often (and paradoxically) struck at liberalism's very foundations. Some ended laissez-faire in trade by instituting protective tariffs; some politicians and reformers decided that government needed to intervene in more than economic matters and expand social welfare legislation. In 1905, the British Liberal Party won a solid majority in the House of Commons and seemed determined to enact social legislation to gain working-class support. "We are keenly in sympathy with the

◆ For a primary source that explains the goals and defends the strategies of militant suffragists, see Document 63, Emmeline Pankhurst, "Speech from the Dock."

representatives of Labour," one Liberal politician announced. "We have too few of them in the House of Commons." The British government initiated a system of relief for the unemployed in the National Insurance Act of 1911, provided new taxes on the wealthy to fund the system, and eliminated the veto power of the House of Lords.

A modified liberalism advanced in Britain on social issues, but the Irish question tested British commitment to such values as self-determination and individual rights. British political reforms armed disaffected Irish tenant farmers with the secret ballot, making them less like colonized peoples than before. The political climate in Ireland was explosive mainly because of the repressive tactics of absentee landlords, many of them English and Protestant. These landlords evicted unsuccessful and prosperous tenants alike so they could raise the rents of newcomers. But Irish tenants elected a solid bloc of nationalist representatives to the British Parliament. The Irish members of Parliament, voting as a group, had sufficient strength to defeat legislation proposed by either the Conservatives or the Liberals. Irish leader Charles Parnell (1846–1891) demanded support for home rule—allowing Ireland to have its own parliament—in return for Irish votes. The House of Lords vetoed the bills.

Parnell's leadership ended because of scandal in his personal life, but in the 1890s, new groups formed to foster Irish culture. In 1901, the circle around the modernist poet William Butler Yeats (1865–1939) and the charismatic patriot and actress Maud Gonne (1865–1953) founded the Irish National Theater. Gonne took Irish politics into everyday life by opposing British efforts to woo the young. Every time an English monarch visited Ireland, he or she held special receptions for children. Gonne and other Irish volunteers sponsored competing events, handing out candies and other treats for patriotic youngsters. Speaking Gaelic instead of English, singing Gaelic songs, using Catholicism as a rallying point, and generally reconstructing an "Irish way of life," the promoters of Irish culture threw into question the educated class's preference for everything English. This cultural agenda took political shape with the founding in 1905 of Sinn Fein ("Ourselves Alone"), a group that strove for complete Irish independence. In 1913, Parliament approved home rule for Ireland, but the outbreak of World War I prevented the legislation from taking effect and cut short dreams of independence.

Liberal Italian nation-builders, left with a towering debt from unification and with massive pockets of discontent, drifted more rapidly from liberalism's moorings. With little money being spent on education and sanitary improvements, the average Italian feared the devastating effects of national taxes and the military draft on the family economy. Corruption plagued Italy's constitutional monarchy, which had developed neither the secure parliamentary system of England nor the authoritarian monarchy of Germany to guide its growth. To forge a national consensus in the 1890s, prime ministers used patriotic rhetoric, bribes to gain support from the press, and imperial adventure, culminating in a second thwarted attempt to conquer Ethiopia in 1896. Riots and strikes, followed by armed government re-pression, erupted, until Giovanni Giolitti, who served as prime minister for three terms between 1903 and 1914, adopted a policy known as *trasformismo* (from the word for "transform"), by which he used bribes, public works programs, and other benefits to localities to influence their deputies in parliament. Political opponents called Giolitti the "Minister of the Underworld" and accused him of preferring to buy the votes of local bosses instead of spending money to develop the Italian econ-omy. He hoped to appease unrest in the industrializing cities of Turin and Milan and in the depressed agrarian south by instituting social welfare programs and, in 1912, nearly complete manhood suffrage.

Anti-Semitism, Nationalism, and Zionism in Mass Politics

In the two decades leading up to World War I, anti-Semitism and nationalism suggested pat answers to complex questions. Leaders invoked these concepts to maintain interest-group support, to direct hostility away from themselves, and to win elections. The public responded vehemently, coming to see Jews as villains re-sponsible for the perils of modern society and the nation-state as the hero in the struggle to survive. In both republics and monarchies, anti-Semitism and nation-alism played key roles in mass politics by providing a focus for the creation of a radical right increasingly committed to combating the radical left of social democ-racy. Adopting the imperiled nation as its theme and using the Social Darwinist category of race to identify threats to the nation, the right fundamentally changed the older notion of nationalism based on liberal ideas of rights. Liberals had hoped that voting by the masses would make politics more harmonious as parliamentary debate and compromise smoothed out class differences. But anti-Semites and nationalists, scorning tolerant liberal values as effete, often preferred fights in the street to consensus-building in parliaments.

The most notorious instance of anti-Semitism occurred in France, where the political compromise that had created the Third Republic after the French defeat in the Franco-Prussian War produced institutional fragility. An alliance of busi-nessmen, shopkeepers, professionals, and rural property owners backed republican government, but destabilizing economic downturns, widespread corruption, at-tempted coups, and the politics of anti-Semitism threatened political chaos at every turn. The press attributed failures of almost any kind to Jews, and despite an ex-cellent system of primary education promoting literacy and rational thinking, the public was quick to agree. The clergy and monarchists also contributed to the be-lief that the republic was backed by a conspiracy of Jews.

Amid rising anti-Semitism, a French army captain, Alfred Dreyfus (1859–1935), was charged with spying for Germany in 1894. A Jew, Dreyfus had attended the elite École Polytechnique in Paris and become an officer in the French military, whose upper echelons were traditionally aristocratic, Catholic, and monarchist. Dreyfus's conviction and harsh exile to Devil's Island failed to stop the espionage, but the republican government adamantly upheld his guilt. Then several newspapers received proof that the army had used perjured testimony and fabricated documents to convict Dreyfus. In 1898, the celebrated French novelist Émile Zola published "J'accuse" ("I accuse") on the front page of a Paris daily. Zola cited a list of military lies and cover-ups perpetrated by highly placed government officials to create an illusion of Dreyfus's guilt. The article was explosive because it named names and endorsed a liberal government based on truth and tolerance. "I have but one passion, that of Enlightenment," wrote Zola. "J'accuse" led to public riots, quarrels among families and friends, and denunciations of the army, eroding public confidence in the republic and in French institutions. The government finally pardoned Dreyfus in 1899, ousted from office the aristocratic and Catholic officers held responsible, and ended religious teaching orders to ensure a public school system that was secular and that taught liberal values of toler-

ance. Nonetheless, the Dreyfus Affair made anti-Semitism a standard tool of politics by producing hate-filled slogans that would shape the mainstream of politics.

　　The ruling elites in Germany also used anti-Semitism as a political weapon to garner support from those who feared the consequences of Germany's sudden and overwhelming industrialization. Bismarck had pursued a culture war against Catholics and then in 1882–1884

■ Public Opinion in the Dreyfus Affair: "Ah! The Dirty Beast!"

The French army used forged documents and perjured testimony to convict Captain Alfred Dreyfus of espionage. In a climate of escalating anti-Semitism, the conviction of a Jew struck many in the public as yet another narrow escape for the country. Only intense detective work by pro-Dreyfus activists and lobbying by Dreyfus's family convinced republican leaders that the system of equal rights was imperiled not by Dreyfus but by the bigotry of the army and those right-wing politicians who had trumped up the case against him.

(Photothèque des Musées de la Ville de Paris.)

turned his attention to wooing the working classes with an array of social programs such as accident and disability insurance. Outlawing the Social Democrats, he next used high tariffs to forge a conservative alliance of agricultural and industrial magnates. The agrarian elites, unlike French conservatives, still controlled the highest reaches of government and influenced the kaiser's policy. But the basis of their power was rapidly eroding, as agriculture, from which they drew their fortunes and social prestige, declined as a percentage of Germany's gross national product. As new opportunities lured rural people away from the land and as industrialists grew wealthier than they, the agrarian elites came to loathe industry and the working class. As a Berlin newspaper noted, "The agrarians' hate for cities . . . blinds them to the simplest needs and the most natural demands of the urban population."

Conservatives and a growing radical right claimed that Jews, who made up less than 1 percent of the German population, were responsible for the disruption of traditional society and charged them with being the main beneficiaries of economic change. In the 1890s, nationalist and anti-Semitic pressure groups flourished, spewing diatribes against Jews and "new women" but also against Social Democrats, whom they branded as internationalist, socially destructive, and unpatriotic. In the 1890s, the new Agrarian League played to the fears of small farmers by accusing Jews of causing agricultural booms and busts. Other parties directed hate-filled speeches against an array of groups. Expressions of extremist hatred and violent feelings of nationalism rather than rational programs to meet problems of economic change became regular features of campaigns.

People in Austria-Hungary—the Dual Monarchy—also expressed their political and economic discontent in militantly nationalistic and anti-Semitic terms, but nationalism there felt the presence of many competing ethnic groups. From 1879 to 1893, Austrian prime minister Count Edouard von Taaffe favored Catholics and the Slavic parties in order to break the growing power of liberals. But every favor to one group brought protest from the others. Foremost among the nationalists were the Hungarians, who wanted autonomy for themselves while forcibly imposing Hungarian language and culture on all other ethnic groups in Hungary. The demands for greater Hungarian influence (or *Magyarization,* from Magyars, the principal ethnic group) stemmed from Budapest's importance as a thriving industrial city and the massive export of Hungarian grain from the vast estates of the Hungarian nobility, which balanced the monarchy's foreign trade deficit. Political chaos ensued from Magyar domination, as

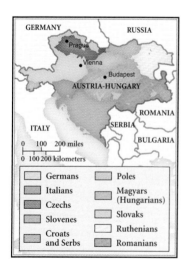

Principal Ethnic Groups in Austria-Hungary, c. 1900

Slovaks, Romanians, and Ruthenians protested horrendous labor conditions and tens of thousands of others demanded the vote. In the face of this resistance, Hungarians intensified Magyarization, even decreeing that all tombstones be engraved in Magyar.

Hungarian policies changed the course of Habsburg politics by arousing other nationalists to intensify their demands for rights. Croats, Serbs, and other Slavic groups in the south organized and called for equality with the Hungarians. The central government gave more privileges to the Czechs and allowed them to increase the proportion of Czech officials in the government simply because growing industrial prosperity in their region gave them more influence. But every step toward recognition of Czech ethnicity provoked outrage from the traditionally dominant ethnic Germans, causing more tensions in the empire. When in 1897 Austria-Hungary decreed that government officials in the Czech region of the empire would have to know Czech as well as German, the Germans rioted.

Tensions mounted as politicians in Vienna linked the growing power of Hungarian and Czech politicians to Jews. A prime instigator of this "politics of the irrational"—as historians often label this ultranationalist and anti-Semitic phenomenon—was Karl Lueger (1844–1910), whose newly formed Christian Social Party attracted members from among the aristocracy, Catholics, artisans, shopkeepers, and white-collar workers. Lueger used hatred to appeal to those groups for whom modern life meant a loss of privilege and security. In 1895, he was elected mayor of Vienna after using rough language and verbal abuse against Jews and ethnic groups in his campaign. Lueger's ethnic nationalism and anti-Semitism destabilized the multinational coexistence on which Austria-Hungary was based. By the turn of the century, Jewishness became a symbol that politicians often harped on in their election campaigns, calling Jews the "sucking vampire" of modernity and blaming them for the tumult of migration, social dislocation, and just about anything else that other people did not like. Politics became a thing not of parliaments but of the streets, inflaming the atmosphere with racism.

The prevailing view in the West that a Jewish identity was inferior to a Christian one provoked varying responses from Jews themselves. Jews in western Europe had responded to the spread of legal tolerance by adopting liberal political and cultural values, intermarrying with Christians, and in some cases converting to Christianity—a practice known as assimilation. Many Jews also favored the German Empire because classical German culture seemed more appealing than the Catholic ritual promoted by Austria-Hungary. By contrast, Jews in Russia and Romania were increasingly singled out for persecution, legally disadvantaged, and forced to live in ghettos. If Jews wanted refuge, the cities of central and eastern Europe provided the best opportunity to succeed. They often adopted the cosmopolitan culture of Vienna or Magyar ways in Budapest. Despite escalating anti-Semitism, the celebrated composer Gustav Mahler, the budding writer Franz Kafka, and the pioneer of psychoanalysis Sigmund Freud were shaped in the crucible of Habsburg society. By

1900, Jews were both prominent in cultural and economic affairs in cities across the continent and discriminated against, even victimized, elsewhere.

Most Jews, however, were not so accomplished or prosperous as these cultural giants, and pogroms and economic change brought their escalating migration to the United States and other countries. Amid this vast migration and continued persecution, a spirit of Jewish nationalism arose, as Jews began organizing resistance to pogroms and anti-Semitic politics, and intellectuals drew upon Jewish folklore, philology, and history to establish a national identity. In the 1880s, the Ukrainian physician Leon Pinsker, seeing the Jews' lack of national territory as fundamental to the persecution heaped on them, advocated the migration of Jews to Palestine. Strongly influenced by Pinsker, Theodor Herzl (1860–1904) called not simply for migration but for the creation of a Jewish nation-state. A Hungarian-born Jew, Herzl experienced anti-Semitism firsthand as a Viennese journalist and writer in Paris during the Dreyfus Affair. With the support of poorer eastern European Jews, he succeeded in calling the first International Zionist Congress (1897), which endorsed settlement in Palestine and helped gain financial backing from the Rothschild banking family. By 1914, some 85,000 Jews had resettled in Palestine.

Tempests in the Russian Empire

Nonetheless, European domestic politics remained explosive and nowhere more so than in Russia, where anti-Semitism escalated and internal affairs were in disarray. Russia was almost the only European country without a constitutional government, and reform-minded Russian youth increasingly turned to revolutionary, even terrorist groups for solutions to political and social problems. Writers fueled an intense debate over Russia's future. Novelist Leo Tolstoy, author of the epic *War and Peace* (1869), opposed the revolutionaries' desire to overturn the social order and believed that Russia above all required spiritual regeneration. In his novel *Anna Karenina* (1877), Tolstoy tells the story of an impassioned, adulterous love affair but also weaves in the spiritual quest of Levin, a former "progressive" landowner who, like Tolstoy himself, eventually rejects modernization and idealizes the peasantry's tradition of stoic endurance. Radicals, however, sought to change Russia by violent action rather than by spiritual uplift, and in 1881, one of them killed Tsar Alexander II in a bomb attack. His death failed to provoke the peasant uprising the terrorists expected because peasants thought the assassination of the "tsar liberator" was directed against them.

Alexander III (r. 1881–1894), rejecting the liberal reforms that his father had proposed on the eve of his assassination, unleashed a new wave of oppression against religious and ethnic minorities and gave the police almost unchecked power. Intensified Russification aggravated old grievances among oppressed nationalities such as the Poles; it also turned the once-loyal German middle and upper classes of the Baltic provinces against Russian rule, with serious long-term consequences. But the major victims were the five million Russian Jews, confined to the eighteenth-century Pale of Settlement (the name for the restricted territory in which they were permitted to live), against whom local officials instigated new pogroms. Distinctive language, dress, and isolation in ghettos made Jews easy targets in an age when the Russian government was enforcing cultural uniformity and national identity. Government officials also encouraged people to blame Jews for escalating taxes and living costs—though the true cause was the policy of raising taxes to force the peasantry to pay for industrialization and reform.

When Alexander III's son Nicholas II took the throne in 1894, the empire was trapped in the contradictions of European modernity. Taught as a child to hate Jews, Nicholas II (r. 1894–1917) stepped up the persecutions, and in his reign many high officials eagerly endorsed anti-Semitism to gain his favor. Pogroms became a regular feature of the Easter holiday in Russia, and Nicholas increasingly limited where Jews could live and how they could earn a living. He supported even more severe Russification and further restrictions on the empire's many minorities such as the Poles, Ukrainians, and Tatars—giving the impression that Russia enjoyed a uniform national culture. Simultaneously, Russians settled much of Siberia, and the government sponsored industrialization, especially the growth of transport and industry. Industrialization, however, produced onerous taxes and urban unrest as Marxist and union activists incited workers to demand better conditions. In 1903, skilled workers led strikes in Baku, where Armenians and Tatars united in a demonstration that showed how urbanization and Russification could actually facilitate political action that challenged the autocratic regime.

In the context of Russia's trouncing in the Russo-Japanese War, the situation exploded into revolution. One Sunday in January 1905, a crowd gathered outside the tsar's Winter Palace in St. Petersburg to try to make Nicholas aware of brutal working conditions. Instead of allowing the demonstration to pass, troops guarding the palace shot into the crowd, killing hundreds and wounding thousands. News of "Bloody Sunday" prompted turmoil across Russia, as workers struck over wages, hours, and factory conditions and demanded political representation in the government. They rejected the leadership of both Social Democrats and Social Revolutionaries and instead organized their own councils, called *soviets*. In February, Grand Duke Sergei, the tsar's uncle, was assassinated; in June, sailors on the battleship *Potemkin* mutinied; in October, a massive railroad strike brought rail transportation to a halt and the Baltic states and Transcaucasia rebelled; and in November, uprisings broke out in Moscow. Professionals and the upper classes joined the assault on autocracy, demanding a

The Russian Revolution of 1905

constitutional monarchy and a representative legislature. They believed the reliance on censorship and the secret police that was characteristic of Romanov rule had relegated Russia to the ranks of the most backward states.

Impelled by the continuing violence, the tsar created a representative body— the Duma. Although very few could vote for representatives to the Duma, its mere existence, coupled with the right of public political debate, liberalized government and allowed people to present their grievances to a responsive body. Political parties took shape, and the Revolution of 1905 drew to an end. But people soon wondered whether anything had really changed. From 1907 to 1917, the Duma convened, but twice when the tsar disliked its recommendations, he sent the delegates home and forced new elections. Prime Minister Pyotr Stolypin (1863–1911), a successful administrator and landowner, was determined to eliminate one source of discontent by ending the *mir* system of communal farming, canceling the peasants' burden of redemption payments, and making loans available to peasants for the purchase of land. Although these reforms did not eradicate rural poverty, they did allow people to move to the cities in search of jobs, and they created a larger group of independent peasants. However, Stolypin took stern steps against political groups, urged more pogroms, and stepped up Russification. The industrial proletariat also grew, and another round of strikes broke out, culminating in a general strike in St. Petersburg in 1914. Despite the creation of the Duma and other reforms, the imperial government and the conservative nobility had no solution to the ongoing social turmoil and felt little inclination to share power. Their ineffectual response to the Revolution of 1905 would foster an even greater revolution in 1917, while ongoing domestic conflicts opened one of the roads to war.

Roads to World War I

Unsettled internal politics made the international scene increasingly dangerous, while imperial rivalries intensified antagonisms among European states. After centuries of global expansion, imperial adventure soured for Britain and France as the twentieth century opened, and being an imperial power proved difficult for such newcomers as Italy and Germany. As a result of imperial competition, one British economist wrote in 1902, "Diplomatic strains are of almost monthly occurrence between the Powers." Western nationalism in its many varieties swelled. In the spring of 1914, U.S. president Woodrow Wilson sent his trusted adviser Colonel Edward House abroad to assess the tensions among the European powers. "It is militarism run stark mad," House reported. Government spending on what people called the "arms race" stimulated European economies; but arms were not stockpiled only for economic growth. Europe was jittery, as it waged a growing number of wars to keep colonial peoples in line. In German East Africa, for example, colonial forces countered native resistance in 1905 with a scorched-earth policy, which eventually killed more than 100,000 Africans (see Map 19.2). The French closed the University of

Hanoi, executed Indochinese intellectuals, and deported thousands of suspected nationalists to maintain a tenuous grip on Indochina (see Map 19.3). A French general stationed there noted "the growing hatred that our subjects show toward us more and more." By 1914, the air was even more charged, with militant nationalism in the Balkan states and conflicts in domestic politics also setting the stage for war. Although historians have long debated whether World War I could have been avoided, they have had to content themselves with tracing the steps Europeans took along the road toward mass destruction.

Competing Alliances and Clashing Ambitions

As the twentieth century opened, an alliance system first established by Bismarck to ensure the peaceful consolidation of the new German Empire and to maintain European stability was changing rapidly. Anxious about the Balkans and Russian leadership of the Slavs, Austria-Hungary had entered a defensive alliance with Germany in 1879. The Dual Alliance, as it was called, offered protection against Russia, which appeared to threaten Hungarian control of its Slavic peasantry. In 1882, Italy joined this partnership (henceforth called the Triple Alliance), largely because of Italy's imperial rivalries with France, but Bismarck also signed the Reinsurance Treaty (1887) with Russia to stifle Habsburg illusions about having a free hand against rivals for Slavic loyalty. Bismarck intended these alliances to show that Germany was now a "satisfied" nation and one that hoped to prevent further destabilizing wars.

Bismarck's delicate alliance started unraveling, however, when a blustering but deeply insecure young kaiser, William II, mounted the German throne in 1888. Advisers flattered the twenty-nine-year-old into thinking that his own personal talent made Bismarck a hindrance, even a rival. William II (r. 1888–1918) dismissed Bismarck in 1890 and, because he ardently supported German nationalism and thus the alliance with a supposedly kindred Austria-Hungary, let the alliance with Russia lapse, driving the Russians to ally with the French. Next, Germany under William II became "dissatisfied" with its international status and inflamed rather than calmed the diplomatic atmosphere. Convinced of British hostility toward France and emboldened by Germany's growing industrial might, the kaiser used the opportunity presented by the defeat of France's ally Russia in the Russo-Japanese War to contest French claims in Morocco, brashly landing his own ship in Morocco in 1905 to challenge personally French predominance. To resolve what became known as the First Moroccan Crisis, an international conference met in Spain in 1906. Instead of awarding Germany new territory, the powers supported French rule. The French and British military, faced with German aggression in Morocco, drew closer together. When the French finally took over Morocco in 1911, Germany triggered the Second Moroccan Crisis by sending a gunboat to the port of Agadir and demanding concessions from the French (see Map 19.2). This time no power—not even

Austria-Hungary—backed the German move or acknowledged this dominant country's economic might.

William's brazen diplomatic demands were predicated on imperial rivalry between France and Britain, which seemed to preclude an alliance between these traditional enemies. Constant rivals in Africa, Britain and France had edged to the brink of war in 1898 at Fashoda in the Sudan (see Map 19.2). The French government, however, backed away, and both nations were frightened into getting along for mutual self-interest. To prevent another Fashoda, they entered into secret agreements, the first of which (1904) guaranteed British claims in Egypt and French claims in Morocco. This agreement marked the beginning of the British-French alliance called the *Entente Cordiale*. After the Moroccan incident, the British and French made binding military provisions for the deployment of their forces in case of war, strengthening the Entente Cordiale. Thus two opposing alliance systems were now in place.

Smarting from its setbacks on the world stage, Germany refocused on its role in continental Europe. German statesmen began envisioning the creation of a *Mitteleuropa* that included central Europe, the Balkans, and Turkey under their sway. Russia, however, saw itself as the protector of Slavs in the region and wanted to replace the Ottomans as the dominant Balkan power, especially after Japan had crushed its hopes for expansion to the east. In 1877–1878, in the Russo-Turkish War, Russia had helped Bulgaria, Bosnia-Herzegovina, Serbia, and Montenegro in their revolts against the declining Ottoman Empire. Although Bulgarian independence was rolled back by the great powers, Serbia and Montenegro became fully independent. Austria's swift annexation of Bosnia-Herzegovina during the Young Turk revolt in 1908 enraged not only the Russians but the Serbs as well, because these southern Slavs wanted Bosnia as part of an enlarged Serbia. The Balkans thus whetted many appetites, and the region was ripe for war (Map 19.4).

Even without the greedy eyes cast on the Balkans by outside powers, the situation would have been extremely complex given the tensions created by political modernity and the lure of national independence. By the early twentieth century, the Balkan states, composed of several ethnicities as well as Orthodox Christians, Roman Catholics, and Muslims, sought more Ottoman and Habsburg territory that included their own ethnic group—a complicated desire given the mixed ethnicities of every region. In the First Balkan War, in 1912, Serbia, Bulgaria, Greece, and Montenegro joined forces to gain Macedonia and Albania from the Ottomans. The victors divided up their booty but soon turned against one another. Serbia, Greece, and Montenegro contested Bulgarian gains in the Second Balkan War in 1913. Much to Austrian dismay, these allies won a quick victory, though Austria-Hungary managed in the peace terms to prevent Serbia from annexing parts of Albania. Grievances between the Serbs and the Habsburgs, who feared that any disturbance in the Balkan balance of power would encourage ethnic rebellion at home, now seemed irreconcilable, and angry Serbs looked to Russia for help.

■ MAP 19.4 The Balkans, 1908–1914

Balkan peoples—mixed in religion, ethnicity, and political views—were successful in developing and asserting their desire for independence, especially in the First Balkan War, which claimed territory from the Ottoman Empire. Their increased autonomy sparked rivalries among them and continued to attract attention from the great powers. Three empires in particular—the Russian, Ottoman, and Austro-Hungarian—simultaneously sought greater influence for themselves in the region, which became a powder keg of competing ambitions.

The Race to Arms

In the nineteenth century, global rivalries and aspirations for national greatness made constant readiness for war seem increasingly necessary. On the seas and in foreign lands, the colonial powers battled to establish control, and they developed railroad, telegraph, and telephone networks everywhere to link their conquests and to move troops as well as commerce. Governments began to conscript ordinary citizens for periods of two to six years into large standing armies, in contrast to smaller eighteenth-century forces that had served the more limited military goals of the time. By 1914, escalating tensions in Europe boosted the annual intake of conscripts: Germany, France, and Russia called up 250,000 or more troops each year; Austria-Hungary and Italy, about 100,000. Per capita expenditures on the military rose in all the major powers between 1890 and 1914; the proportion of national budgets devoted to defense in 1910 was lowest in Austria-Hungary at 10 percent and highest in Germany at 45 percent.

The modernization of weaponry also transformed warfare. Swedish arms manufacturer Alfred Nobel (1833–1896) patented dynamite and developed a kind of gunpowder that improved the accuracy of guns and produced a less cloudy battlefield environment by reducing smoke from the process of firing. The industrial revolution in chemicals affected long-range artillery, which by 1914 could fire on targets as far as six miles away. Greater accuracy and heavy firepower made military offensives more difficult to win than in the past because neither side could overcome such weaponry. Military leaders devised strategies to protect their armies from overwhelming firepower. In the Russo-Japanese War, Chinese defenders dug trenches and strung barbed wire in an attempt to hold on to Port Arthur. In that conflict and in the Boer War, new weapons were used, including howitzers, Mauser rifles, and Hotchkiss machine guns. Munitions factories across Europe manufactured ever-growing quantities of these weapons.

Naval construction also played a major role in nationalist politics. To defend against more powerful, accurate weaponry, ships were made of metal rather than wood after the mid-nineteenth century. In 1905, the English launched the HMS *Dreadnought*, a warship with unprecedented firepower and the centerpiece of a program to update the British navy by constructing at least seven battleships per year. Germany followed British naval building step by step and made itself a force to be feared not just on land but also at sea. Grand Admiral Alfred von Tirpitz (1849–1930) encouraged the insecure William II to see the navy as the essential ingredient needed to make Germany a world power and oversaw an immense buildup of the fleet. Tirpitz admired the American naval theorist Alfred Thayer Mahan (1840–1914) and planned to build bases as far away as the Pacific, following Mahan's conclusion that command of the seas had historically been the key factor in determining international power. The German drive to build battleships further motivated Britain to ally with France in the Entente Cordiale. Britain raised its naval spending from $50 million per year in the 1870s to $130 million in 1900; Germany, from $8.75 million to $37.5 million; France, from $37 million to $62.5 million. The Germans announced the fleet buildup as "a peaceful policy," but, like the British buildup, it led only to a hostile international climate and intense competition in weapons manufacture.

Military policy was made with the use of public relations campaigns and an eye on internal politics. When critics of the arms race suggested a temporary "naval holiday" to stop British and German shipbuilding, British officials opposed the moratorium by warning that it "would throw innumerable men on the pavement." Colonial leagues, nationalist organizations, and other patriotic groups lobbied for military spending, while enthusiasts in government publicized large navies as beneficial to international trade and domestic industry. To enlarge the German fleet, Tirpitz made sure the German press connected the buildup to the cause of national power and pride. The press accused Social Democrats, who wanted an equitable tax system more proportionate to wealth, of being unpatriotic. The Conservative Party in Great Britain, eager for more battleships, made popular the slogan "We want eight and we won't wait." The remarks of one military leader typified the sentiments of the time, even among the public at large. When asked in 1912 about his predictions for war and peace, he responded enthusiastically, "We shall have war. I will make it. I will win it."

1914: War Erupts

June 28, 1914, began as an ordinary day for Austria's Archduke Francis Ferdinand and his wife, Sophie, as they ended a state visit to Sarajevo in Bosnia. Wearing full military regalia, the archduke was riding in a motorcade to bid farewell to various officials when a group of young Serb nationalists threw bombs in an unsuccessful assassination attempt. The full danger did not register, and after a stop the archduke and his wife set out again. In the crowd was another nationalist, Gavrilo Princip, who for several weeks had traveled clandestinely to reach this destination, dreaming of reuniting his homeland of Bosnia-Herzegovina with Serbia and smuggling weapons with him to accomplish his end. The unprotected and unsuspecting couple became Princip's victims, as he shot both dead.

■ **Archduke Francis Ferdinand and His Wife in Sarajevo, June 1914**
Archduke Francis Ferdinand, heir to the Austro-Hungarian monarchy, was a thorn in the side of many politicians because he did not want to favor Hungarian interests over other ethnic interests in his kingdom. His own family life was also unusual for royalty in those days: his wife, Sophie, and he had married for love and did not like to be apart. They were traveling together to Bosnia in 1914. The double assassination was the immediate prelude to the outbreak of World War I. (Mary Evans Picture Library.)

Some in the Habsburg government saw an opportunity to put down the Serbians once and for all. Evidence showed that Princip had received arms and information from Serbian officials who directed a terrorist organization from within the government. Endorsing a quick defeat of Serbia, German statesmen and military leaders urged the Austrians to be unyielding and reiterated promises of support in case of war. The Austrians sent an ultimatum to the Serbian government, demanding public disavowals of terrorism, suppression of terrorist groups, and the participation of Austrian officials in an investigation of the crime. The ultimatum was severe. "You are setting Europe ablaze," the Russian foreign minister remarked of the humiliating demands made upon a sovereign state. Yet the Serbs were conciliatory, accepting all the terms except one—the presence of Austrian officials in the investigation. Kaiser William was pleased: "A great moral success for Vienna! All reason for war is gone." His relief proved unfounded. Confident of German backing, Austria-Hungary used the Serbs' resistance to that one demand as the pretext for declaring war against Serbia on July 28.

Complex and ineffectual maneuvering now consumed statesmen, some of whom tried very hard to avoid war. The tsar and the kaiser sent pleading letters to one another not to start a European war. The British foreign secretary proposed an all-European conference, but to no avail. Germany displayed firm support for Austria in hopes of convincing the French and British to shy away from the war. The failure of either France or Britain to fight, German officials believed, would keep Russia from mobilizing. At the same time, German military leaders had become fixed on fighting a short, preemptive war that would provide territorial gains leading toward the goal of a *Mitteleuropa*. Furthermore, martial law would justify the arrest of the leadership of the German Social Democratic Party, which posed a threat to conservative rule.

The European press caught the war fever of the expansionist, imperialist, and other pro-war organizations, even as many governments were torn over what to do. Likewise, military leaders, especially in Germany and Austria-Hungary, promoted mobilization rather than diplomacy in the last days of July. The Austrians declared war and then ordered mobilization on July 31 without fear of a Russian attack. They did so in full confidence of German military aid, because as early as 1909 the German chief of staff Helmuth von Moltke had promised that his government would defend Austria-Hungary, believing Russia would not dare intervene. But Nicholas II ordered the Russian army to mobilize in defense of Russia's Slavic allies, the Serbs. Encouraging the Austrians to attack Serbia, the German general staff mobilized on August 1.

German strategy was based on the Schlieffen Plan, named after its author, Alfred von Schlieffen, a former chief of the general staff. The plan outlined a way to combat antagonists on two fronts by concentrating on one foe at a time. First would come a rapid and concentrated German blow to the west against Russia's

IMPORTANT DATES

1870s–1914	Vast emigration from Europe continues; the new imperialism	1903	Emmeline Pankhurst founds the Women's Social and Political Union to fight for woman suffrage in Great Britain
1882	Triple Alliance formed among Germany, Austria-Hungary, and Italy	1904–1905	Japan defeats Russia in the Russo-Japanese War
1882–1884	Bismarck sponsors social welfare legislation in Germany	1905	Revolution erupts in Russia; violence forces Nicholas II to establish an elected body, the Duma; Albert Einstein publishes his special theory of relativity
1884	Reform Act doubles the size of the male electorate in Britain		
1884–1885	European nations carve up Africa at the Berlin conference	1906	Women receive the vote in Finland
1889	Socialists meet in Paris and establish the Second International	1907	Pablo Picasso launches cubism with his painting Les Demoiselles d'Avignon and other works
1894–1899	Dreyfus Affair lays bare anti-Semitism in France		
1899–1902	Boer War fought between Dutch descendants and the British in South African states	1908	Young Turks revolt against rule by the sultan in the Ottoman Empire
1900	Sigmund Freud publishes The Interpretation of Dreams	1911–1912	Revolutionaries overthrow the Qing dynasty and declare China a republic
1901	Irish National Theater established by Maud Gonne and William Butler Yeats	1914	Assassination of the Austrian archduke Francis Ferdinand and his wife by a Serbian nationalist precipitates World War I

ally France, which would lead to France's defeat in six weeks; accompanying that strike would be a light holding action to the east. With France beaten, German armies in the west would then be deployed against Russia, which, German war planners believed, would be slow to mobilize. The attack on France was to proceed through Belgium, whose neutrality was guaranteed by the European powers. Events did not occur as the Germans hoped. The Belgian government rejected an ultimatum to allow the uncontested passage of the German army through the country, and Germany's subsequent violation of Belgium's neutrality brought Britain into the war on the side of Russia and France, which already was mobilizing in support of its ally Russia.

■ MAPPING THE WEST Europe at the Outbreak of World War I, August 1914

All the powers expected a great, swift victory when war broke out. Sharing borders, many saw a chance to increase their territories; and as rivals for trade and empire, they were almost all convinced that war would bring them many advantages. But if the European powers appeared well prepared and invincible at the start of the war, relatively few would survive the conflict intact.

Conclusion

Rulers soon forgot their last-minute hesitation in the general celebration that erupted with the war. "Old heroes have reemerged from the books of legends," wrote a Viennese actor after watching the troops march off. "A mighty wonder has taken place, we have become *young*." Both sides exulted, believing in certain victory and a resolution to tensions ranging from the rise of the working class to political problems caused by global imperial competition.

Imperialism and the arms race had stimulated militant nationalism and brought many Europeans to favor war over peace. The crisis of modernity had helped blaze the path to war. Facing continuing violence in politics, incomprehensibility in the arts, and problems in the industrial order, Europeans had come to believe that war would set events back on course and save them from the perils of modernity. "Like men longing for a thunderstorm to relieve them of the summer's sultriness," wrote one Austrian official, "so the generation of 1914 believed in the relief that war might bring." Such a possibility caused Europeans to rejoice. But instead of bringing the refreshment of summer rain, war opened an era of political turmoil, widespread suffering, massive human slaughter, and even greater doses of modernity.

Suggested References for further reading and online research appear on page SR-30 at the back of the book.

www.bedfordstmartins.com/huntconcise   See the ONLINE STUDY GUIDE to assess your mastery of the material covered in this chapter.

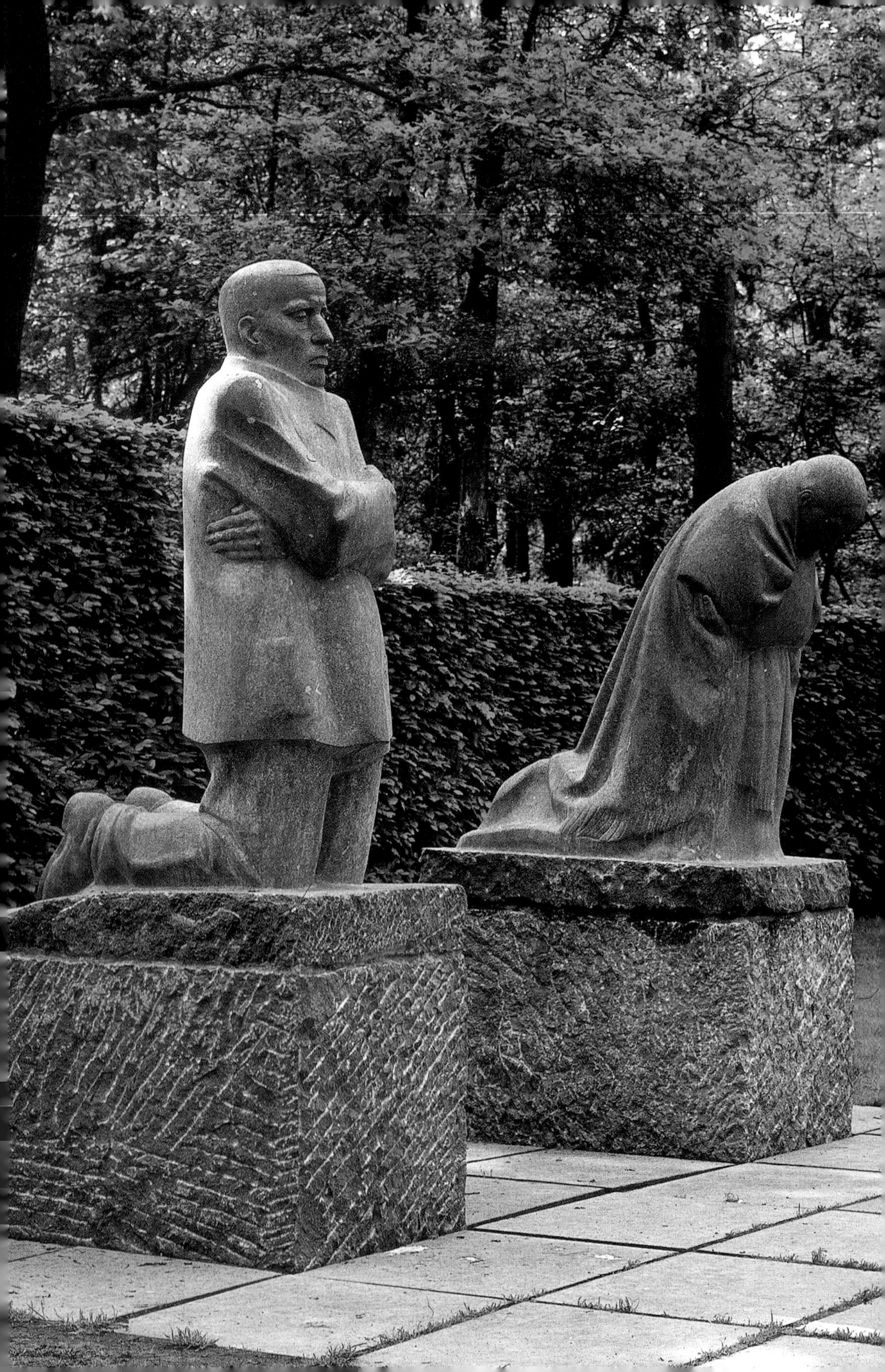

CHAPTER

20

War, Revolution, and Reconstruction

1914–1929

J ULES AMAR FOUND HIS TRUE VOCATION in World War I. A French expert on making industrial work more efficient, Amar switched focus after 1914 as hundreds
of thousands of men returned from the battlefront missing body parts. Plastic surgery developed rapidly, as did the construction of masks and other devices to hide
deformities. Amar, who designed artificial limbs and appendages in these traumatic years, sought to devise prostheses that would allow the wounded soldier to
return to normal life by "mak[ing] up for a function lost, or greatly reduced." So
the arms that he designed used hooks, magnets, and other mechanisms with which
the veteran could hold a cigarette, play a violin, and most important work with
tools such as typewriters. Mangled by the weapons of modern technological warfare, the survivors of World War I would be made whole, it was thought, by technology such as Amar's.

Amar dealt with the human tragedy of the "Great War," so named by contemporaries because of its staggering human toll—forty million wounded or killed in
battle. The Great War was also what historians call a "total war," meaning one built
on full mobilization of soldiers, civilians, and the technological capacities of the
most highly industrialized nations. The Great War did not settle problems or restore social order as the European powers hoped it would. Instead, the war produced political cataclysm, overturning the Russian, German, Ottoman, and Austro-
Hungarian Empires. The crushing burden of war on the European powers

■ **Grieving Parents**
*Before World War I, the German artist Kaethe Köllwitz gained her artistic reputation with wood-
cuts of handloom weavers whose livelihoods were threatened by industrialization. From 1914 on,
she depicted the suffering and death that swirled around her and never with more sober force than
in these two monuments to her son Peter, who had died on the western front in the first months of
battle. Today one can still travel to his burial place in Vladslo, Belgium, to see this father and
mother mourning their loss, like millions across Europe in those heartbreaking days.*
(The John Parker Picture Library.)

accelerated the rise of the United States, while service in the war intensified the demands of colonized peoples for autonomy.

For all the vast changes that the Great War ushered in, it also hastened transformations under way before it started. Nineteenth-century optimism, already on the decline, gave way to postwar cynicism. Many Westerners turned their backs on politics and attacked life with frenzied gaiety in the Roaring Twenties, snapping up new consumer goods, drinking in entertainment provided by films and radio, and enjoying personal freedoms that Victorianism had forbidden. Others found reason for hope in the new political systems the war made possible: Soviet communism and Italian fascism. Modern communication technologies such as radio gave politicians the means to promote a mass politics that ironically was often antidemocratic, militaristic, and eventually totalitarian.

Seen as a solution to the conflicts of modernity, a war that was long anticipated and even welcomed in some quarters destabilized Europe and the rest of the world far into the next decades. From statesmen to ordinary citizens, many Europeans like Amar would devote their peacetime efforts to making war-ravaged society function normally, while others saw that task as utterly futile, given the globally transformative force of the Great War.

The Great War, 1914–1918

When war erupted in August 1914, the ground had been prepared with long-standing alliances, the development of strategies for war, and the buildup of military technologies such as heavy artillery, machine guns, and the airplane. Seeing precedents in Prussia's rapid victories in the 1860s and 1870 and the swift blows that Japan dealt Russia in 1904–1905, most people felt that the conflict would be short and decisive. But the unforeseen happened: the war lasted for more than four years, and it was a total war, mobilizing entire societies and producing the unprecedented horror that made it "great."

Blueprints for War

World War I pitted two sets of opponents formed roughly out of the alliances developed during the previous fifty years. On one side stood the Central Powers (Austria-Hungary and Germany), which had evolved from Bismarck's Triple Alliance. On the other side stood the Allies (France, Great Britain, and Russia), which had emerged as a bloc from the Entente Cordiale between France and Great Britain and the 1890s treaties between France and Russia. In 1915, Italy, originally part of the Triple Alliance, joined the Allies in hopes of postwar gain. The two sides expanded globally almost from the start: in late August 1914, Japan, eager to extend its empire into China, went over to the Allies; in the fall the Ottoman Empire united with the Central Powers against its traditional enemy, Russia (see Map 20.1).

The same ferocious hunger for power, prestige, and prosperity that had inspired imperialism motivated the antagonists. Germany aspired to a far-flung empire to be gained by annexing Russian territory and incorporating parts of Belgium, France, and Luxembourg. Some German leaders wanted to annex Austria-Hungary as well. Austria-Hungary hoped to retain its great-power status in the face of competing nationalisms within its borders. Among the Allies, Russia wanted to reassert its status as a great power and as the protector of the Slavs by adding a reunified Poland to the Russian Empire and by taking formal leadership of other Slavic peoples. France, too, craved territory, especially the return of Alsace and Lorraine, taken after the Franco-Prussian War, to secure its boundaries with Germany. Britain sought to cement its hold on Egypt and the Suez Canal, as well as to secure the rest of the British world empire. By the Treaty of London (1915), France and Britain promised Italy territory in Africa, Asia Minor, the Balkans, and elsewhere in return for joining the Allies.

The colonial powers enlisted or conscripted tens of thousands of colonized men into their military forces. Britain deployed Indian regiments in western Europe in the first days of the war and enlisted Arabs against the Turks. France relied heavily on Senegalese and North African recruits, promising them French citizenship for their service. Germany used colonial soldiers in Europe and later in Africa and Asia.

From the start, machine guns and rifles, airplanes, battleships, submarines, and motorized transport—cars and railroads—were at the disposal of the armies. As the war proceeded, chlorine gas, tanks, bombs, and other new technologies would develop. The war itself became a lethal testing ground, as both new and old weapons were used, often ineffectively. Despite the availability of the new, more lethal technology, an old-fashioned vision of warfare made many officers unwilling to abandon sabers, lances, bayonets, and cavalry charges. Officers on both sides believed in a "cult of the offensive": they were sure that spirited attacks and high troop morale would be decisive. They were mistaken. In the face of massive firepower, the "cult of the offensive" would cost millions of lives.

Battlefronts

The first months of the war crushed hopes for a quick victory. All the major armies mobilized rapidly. Guided by the Schlieffen Plan (see page 858), the Germans quickly reached Luxembourg and Belgium and expected unchallenged passage through them and into France. Tricked by German diversionary tactics, the main body of French troops attacked the Germans in Alsace and Lorraine instead of meeting the invasion from the north. The Schlieffen Plan disintegrated when the Belgians unexpectedly resisted, slowing the German advance and allowing British and French troops to reach the northern front. In September, British and French armies engaged the Germans along the Marne River in France. Neither side could defeat the other, and the number of casualties was shocking: in the first three months of

■ The Toll of Trench Warfare

On both sides, the war took an enormous toll in male lives, leaving politicians and citizens alike concerned about society's future. Depictions of bodies shattered by heavy firepower, however, rarely reached the home front, so the illusions that the war was about individual prowess and that individual soldiers had a fighting chance of survival remained intact. Troops from the colonies were often depicted as bringing an innate savagery to the battlefront, although these soldiers had even less chance of surviving because usually they were placed in the front lines.

(Left: Imperial War Museum, London; right: Robert Hunt Library.)

war, more than 1.5 million men fell on the western front alone. Firepower turned what was supposed to be an offensive war of movement into a stationary, defensive impasse along a line stretching from the North Sea through Belgium and northern France to Switzerland. Deep within parallel trenches dug along this western front, soldiers lived a nightmarish existence (Map 20.1).◆

On the eastern front, the "Russian steam-roller"—so named because of the number of men mobilized, some twelve million in all—drove far more quickly than expected into East Prussia. The Russians believed that no army could withstand their massive numbers, no matter how ill equipped and poorly trained Russian forces were. The Germans, however, crushed the tsar's army in East Prussia and turned south to Galicia. Victory boosted German morale and made heroes of the military leaders Paul von Hindenburg (1847–1934) and Erich Ludendorff (1865–1937). But despite heartening victories, by year's end German triumphs in the east had failed to knock out the Russians and also had undermined the

◆ For German and British accounts of the experience of the battlefront, see Document 64, Fritz Franke and Siegfried Sassoon, "Two Soldiers' Views of the Horrors of War."

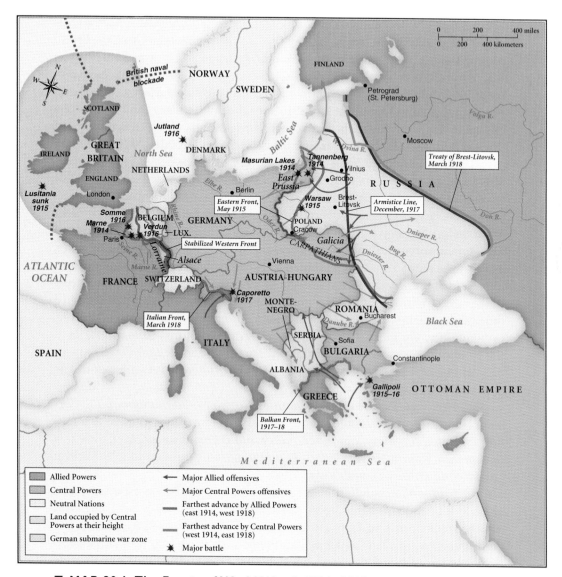

■ MAP 20.1 The Fronts of World War I, 1914–1918

Fighting on all fronts destroyed portions of Europe's hard-won industrial and agricultural capacity. Because the western front remained relatively stationary, the devastation of land and resources in northern and eastern France was especially intense. Men engaged in trench warfare developed an intense camaraderie based on their mutual suffering and deprivation.

Schlieffen Plan, which called for only a light holding action in the east until the western front had been won.

War at sea proved equally indecisive. Confident in Britain's superior naval power, the Allies blockaded ports to prevent supplies from reaching Germany and Austria-Hungary. William II and his advisers planned a massive submarine, or

U-boat (*Unterseeboot*, "underwater boat"), campaign against Allied and neutral shipping around Britain and France. In May 1915, German submarines sank the British
passenger ship *Lusitania* and killed 1,198 people, including 124 Americans. Despite
U.S. outrage, Woodrow Wilson (1856–1924; president 1913–1921) maintained a policy of U.S. neutrality; Germany, unwilling to provoke Wilson further, called off unrestricted submarine warfare. In May 1916, the navies of Germany and Britain finally
clashed in the North Sea at the inconclusive battle of Jutland, which demonstrated
that the German fleet could not master British seapower (see Map 20.1).

Ideas of a negotiated peace were discarded: "No peace before England is defeated and destroyed," the kaiser railed against his cousin King George V. "Only
amidst the ruins of London will I forgive Georgy." French leadership called for a
"war to the death." General staffs continued to prepare fierce attacks several times
a year. Indecisive campaigns opened with heavy artillery pounding enemy trenches
and gun emplacements. Troops then scrambled "over the top" of their trenches,
usually to be mowed down by machine-gun fire from defenders secure in their own
trenches. On the western front, throughout 1915 the French assaulted the enemy
in the north to drive the Germans from industrial regions, but they accomplished
little, and casualties of 100,000 and more during a single campaign became
commonplace. On the eastern front, Russian armies captured parts of Galicia in
the spring of 1915 and lumbered toward Hungary. The Central Powers struck
back in Poland later that year, bringing the front closer to Petrograd (formerly
St. Petersburg), the Russian capital.

The next year was even more disastrous. To cripple French morale, the Germans launched massive assaults on the fortress at Verdun, firing as many as a million shells in a single day. Combined French and German losses totaled close to a
million men. Nonetheless, the French held. Hoping to relieve their allies, the British
unleashed an artillery pounding of German trenches in the Somme River region in
June 1916. In several months of battle at the Somme, 1.25 million men were killed
or wounded, but the final result was stalemate. By the end of 1916, the French had
absorbed more than 3.5 million casualties. To help the Allies engaged at Verdun and
the Somme, the Russians struck again, driving once more into the Carpathians,
recouping territory, and menacing the Habsburg Empire. Only the German army
stopped the Russian advance.

Had military leaders thoroughly dominated the scene, historians judge, all
armies would have been demolished in nonstop offensives by the end of 1915. Yet
ordinary soldiers in this war were not automatons in the face of what seemed to
them suicidal orders. For long periods of time, some battalions experienced hardly
any casualties. These low rates stemmed from agreements among troops to avoid
battles. Enemies facing each other across the "no man's land" separating the trenches
frequently ate their meals in peace even though the trenches were within hand
grenade reach. Throughout the war, soldiers on opposing sides fraternized. During
pauses in the fighting, they played an occasional game of soccer, shouted to each

other across the battlefield, exchanged mementos, and made gestures of agreement not to fight. One British veteran of the trenches explained to a new recruit that the Germans "don't want to fight any more than we do, so there's a kind of understanding between us. Don't fire at us and we'll not fire at you." Burying enemy dead in common graves with their own fallen comrades, many ordinary soldiers came to feel more warmly toward enemies who shared the trench experience than toward uncomprehending civilians back home.

Newly forged bonds of male camaraderie alleviated some of the misery of trench life and aided survival. The sharing of the danger of death and the deprivations of front-line experience weakened traditional class distinctions. Some upper-class officers and working-class draftees became friends in that "wholly masculine way of life uncomplicated by women," as one soldier put it. Soldiers picked lice from one another's bodies and clothes, revered section leaders who tended their blistered feet, and came to love one another, sometimes even passionately. Positive memories of this front-line sense of community survived the war and influenced postwar politics.

Troops of colonized soldiers from Asia and Africa had different experiences, especially because they were often put in the very front ranks where the risks were greatest. European observers noted that these soldiers suffered particularly from the rigors of a totally unfamiliar climate and strange food as well as from the ruin inflicted by Western war technology. Yet, like class divisions, racial barriers sometimes fell—for instance, whenever a European understood enough to alleviate the distress that cold inflicted. The perspectives of colonial troops changed, too, as they saw their "masters" completely undone and "uncivilized." When fighting did break out, trenches became a veritable hell of shelling and sniping, flying body parts, rotting cadavers, and blinding gas. Some soldiers were reduced to hysteria or were shell-shocked by the violence of battle. Alienation and cynicism helped others to cope: "It might be me tomorrow," a young British soldier wrote his mother in 1916. "Who cares?" Soldiers who had gone to war to escape ordinary life in industrial society learned, as one German put it, "that in the modern war . . . the triumph of the machine over the individual is carried to its most extreme form." They took this hard-won knowledge into battle, pulling their comrades back when an offensive seemed lost or too costly.

The Home Front

World War I was taking place off the battlefield, too. Even before the war reached the stage of catastrophic impasse, it was "total." Total war meant the indispensable involvement of civilians in war-related industry: manufacturing shells and machine guns, poisonous gases, bombs and airplanes, and eventually tanks. The increased production of coffins, canes, wheelchairs, and the artificial limbs devised by the likes of Jules Amar was also a wartime necessity. Civilians had to work overtime for, believe in, and sacrifice for victory. To keep the war machine operating smoothly, governments oversaw factories, transportation systems, and resources ranging from food to coal to textiles. Before the war, such tight government control would have outraged many liberals, but now it was accepted as a necessary condition for victory.

At first, political parties put aside their differences. Many socialists and working-class people who had criticized the military buildup announced their support for the war. For decades, socialist parties had preached that "the worker has no country" and that nationalism was mere ideology meant to keep workers disunited and subject to the will of their employers. In August 1914, however, the socialist rank and file, along with most of the party leaders, became as patriotic as the rest of society. Feminists divided over whether to maintain their traditional condemnation of militarism or to support the war. Although many feminists actively opposed the conflict, Emmeline Pankhurst and her daughter Christabel were among those who became militant nationalists, even changing the name of their suffrage paper to *Britannia*. Parties representing the middle classes shelved their distrust of the socialists and working classes. In the name of victory, national leaders wanted to end political division of all kinds: "I no longer recognize [political] parties," William II declared on August 4, 1914. "I recognize only Germans."

Governments mobilized the home front with varying degrees of success. All countries were caught without ready replacements for their heavy losses of weapons and military equipment and soon also felt the shortage of food and labor. War ministries set up boards to allocate labor on the home front and the

■ **War Propaganda, 1915**
"Never Forget!" screams the headline of this propaganda poster depicting an assaulted woman in despair. Intended to incite sentiment against the Germans, the poster suggests what German passage through neutral Belgium came to be called—"the rape of Belgium." Propaganda offices for the Allies sent out reports of women attacked and children massacred as the German armies moved through Belgian territories.
(Mary Evans Picture Library.)

battlefront and give industrialists financial incentives to encourage productivity. Emergency measures in several countries allowed the drafting of both men and women for military or industrial service, further blurring distinctions between military and civilian life. In Russia, however, the bureaucracy only reluctantly and ineffectively cooperated with industrialists and other groups that could aid the war effort. Desperate for factory workers, the Germans forced Belgian citizens to move to Germany, housing them in prison camps. In the face of rationing, municipal governments set up canteens and day-care centers. Rural Russia, Austria-Hungary, Bulgaria, and Serbia, where youths, women, and old men struggled to sustain farms, had no such relief programs.

Governments throughout Europe passed sedition laws that made it a crime to criticize official policies. To ensure civilian acceptance of longer working hours and shortages of consumer goods, governments created propaganda agencies to tout the war as a patriotic mission to resist villainous enemies. British propagandists fabricated atrocities that the German "Huns" supposedly committed against Belgians, and German propaganda warned that French African troops would rape German women if Germany was defeated. In Russia, Nicholas II changed the German-sounding name of St. Petersburg to the Russian Petrograd in 1914.

Playing on fears and arousing hatred, propaganda rendered a compromise peace unlikely. Nonetheless, some individuals sought to shatter the nationalist consensus supporting the war. In 1915, activists in the international women's movement met in The Hague, site of late-nineteenth-century peace conferences, in their own effort to end the war. "We can no longer endure . . . brute force as the only solution of international disputes," declared Dutch physician Aletta Jacobs. Despite their lack of success, many spent the remainder of the war urging statesmen to work out a peace settlement. In Austria-Hungary, nationalist groups agitating for ethnic self-determination hampered the empire's war effort. The Czechs undertook a vigorous anti-Habsburg campaign at home, while exiled politicians in Paris established the Czechoslovak National Council to lobby Western governments for recognition of Czech rights. In the Balkans, Croats, Slovenes, and Serbs formed a committee to plan a South Slav state carved from Habsburg possessions and other Balkan territory. The Allies encouraged such independence movements as part of their strategy to defeat the Habsburgs.

The war upset the social order as well as the political one. In the war's early days, many women had lost their jobs when luxury shops, textile factories, and other nonessential establishments closed. With men at the front, many women headed households with little support and few opportunities to work. But governments and businesses soon recognized the amount of labor it would take to wage technological war. As more and more men left for the trenches, women who had lost their jobs in nonessential businesses as well as many low-paid domestic workers took over higher-paying jobs in formerly restricted munitions and metallurgical

■ **German Welder Being Trained**
As men were siphoned off to the battle-front in World War I, women took their places in factories and transportation and service industries—working over-time to supply the insatiable needs of modern, technological warfare. Women thus gained higher pay and learned new productive skills such as welding. A new working-class woman emerged from the experience of war.
(Ullstein Bilderdienst.)

industries. In Warsaw, they drove trucks, and in London, they worked as streetcar conductors. Some young women nursed the wounded near the front lines.◆

Women's assumption of men's jobs looked to many like the reversal of tra-ditional gender roles. From the start, a steady flood of wounded and weakened men returned home to women who had adapted resourcefully and taken full charge. Workingmen commonly protested that women, in the words of one metalworker, were "sending men to the slaughter." Men feared that when the war was over women would remain in the workforce, robbing them of their role as breadwinner. Many people, even some women, objected to women's loss of fem-ininity. "The feminine in me decreased more and more, and I did not know whether to be sad or glad about this," wrote one Russian nurse about learning to wear rough male clothing near the battlefield. Others criticized young female munitions workers for squandering their pay on ribbons and jewelry and echoed other prewar gender tensions.

◆ For an interview with a French female factory worker, see Document 65, L. Doriat, "Women on the Home Front."

Although many soldiers from different social backgrounds felt bonds of solidarity in the trenches, wartime conditions increasingly pitted civilians against one another or against the government. Workers toiled longer hours eating less, while many in the upper classes bought abundant food and fashionable clothing on the black market (outside the official system of rationing). Governments allowed many businesses high rates of profit, a step that resulted in a surge in the cost of living and thus contributed to social strife. Shortages of staples like bread, sugar, and meat grew worse as the brutal "turnip winter" of 1916–1917—when turnips were often the only available food—progressed. A German roof workers' association pleaded for relief: "We can no longer go on. Our children are starving." Civilians in occupied areas and in the colonies suffered the most oppressive working conditions. The combatants deported or conscripted able-bodied people in territories they occupied. The French forcibly transported some 100,000 Vietnamese to work in France for the war effort. Africans also faced grueling forced labor along with skyrocketing taxes and prices. All such actions, like increasing class divisions, led to further politicization.

1917–1918: Protest, Revolution, and War's End

By 1917, the situation was becoming desperate, and discontent on the home front started shaping the course of the war. Neither patriotic slogans before the war nor propaganda during it had prepared people for wartime suffering. Cities across Europe experienced civilian revolt; soldiers mutinied, and nationalist struggles continued to plague Britain and Austria-Hungary. Soon revolution was sweeping Europe, toppling the Russian dynasty for good.

War Protest

On February 1, 1917, the German government, hard-pressed by public clamor over mounting casualties and by the military's growing control over decision making, resumed unrestricted submarine warfare. The military made the irresistible promise to end the war in six months by cutting off imported food and military supplies to Britain and thus forcing the island nation to surrender before the United States could come to its rescue. The British responded by mining harbors and the seas and by developing the convoy system of shipping, in which a hundred or more warships and freighters traveling the seas together could drive off the submarines. The Germans' submarine gamble failed to thwart the British. Moreover, unrestricted submarine warfare brought the United States into the war in April 1917, after German U-boats had sunk several American ships.

Political opposition increased in Europe, and deteriorating living conditions sparked outright revolt by civilians. "We are living on a volcano," warned an Italian politician in the spring of 1917. High prices and food shortages plagued everyday life. Food shortages in the cities of Italy, Russia, Germany, and Austria provoked riots by women who were unable to feed their families. As inflation mounted, tenants conducted rent strikes, factory hands and white-collar workers alike walked off the job, and female workers protested the skyrocketing cost of living and their fatigue from overwork. Amid protest, the new emperor of Austria-Hungary secretly asked the Allies for a negotiated peace to avoid a total collapse of his empire. In the summer of 1917, the German Reichstag made peace overtures. Woodrow Wilson further weakened civilian resolve in Germany and Austria-Hungary in January 1918 by issuing his Fourteen Points, a blueprint for a new international order that held out the promise of a nonvindictive peace settlement to war-weary citizens of the Central Powers. The Allies, too, faced dissent. In the spring of 1917, French soldiers mutinied against further bloody and fruitless offensives. In Russia, wartime protest turned into outright revolution.

Revolution and Civil War in Russia

Of all the warring nations, Russia sustained the greatest number of casualties—7.5 million by 1917. Slaughter on the eastern front drove hundreds of thousands of peasants into the Russian interior, bringing hunger, homelessness, and disease. In March 1917, crowds of workingwomen swarmed the streets of Petrograd demanding relief from harsh conditions, and soon factory workers and other civilians joined them. Russia's comparative economic underdevelopment made the demands of the war impossible to meet. Instead of remaining loyal to the tsar, many in the army were embittered by the massive casualties caused by their inferior weapons and their leaders' foolhardy tactics.

  Since the Revolution of 1905, the masses had become politicized and increasingly willing to protest the government's incompetence, in particular Nicholas II's ineptitude. Unlike other heads of state, Nicholas failed to unify the bureaucracy and his peoples in a concerted wartime effort. Grigori Rasputin, a combination of holy man and charlatan, held Nicholas and his wife, Alexandra, in his thrall by claiming to control the hemophilia of their son and heir. Rasputin's disastrous influence on state matters led educated and influential leaders to withdraw their support. When riots erupted in March 1917, Nicholas abdicated, and the three-hundred-year-old Romanov dynasty came to an end.

  Politicians from the old Duma formed a new ruling entity called the Provisional Government. At first, hopes were high that under the Provisional Government, as one revolutionary poet put it, "our false, filthy, boring, hideous life should become a just, pure, merry, and beautiful life." Composed essentially of moderates, the Provisional Government had to pursue the war successfully, manage internal affairs better, and set government on a firm constitutional footing to establish its credibility. However, it did not rule alone, for the Russian Revolution felt the tug of many different political forces. Spontaneously elected soviets—councils of workers and soldiers—competed with the government for political support. Born during the Revolution of 1905, the soviets campaigned to end the deference society usually paid the wealthy and officers, urged respect for workers and the poor, and temporarily gave an air of celebration and carnival to this political cataclysm. The peasantry, another force competing for power, began to confiscate gentry estates and withhold produce from the market because of the lack of consumer goods for which to exchange food. Urban food shortages intensified.

In hopes of further destabilizing Russia, in April 1917 the Germans provided safe rail transportation for Lenin and other prominent Bolsheviks to return from exile through German territory. Lenin had devoted his entire existence to bringing about socialism through the force of his small band of Bolsheviks, and as a political exile he had no parliamentary experience. Upon his return to Petrograd, Lenin issued the April Theses, a radical document that called for Russia to withdraw from

■ **Lenin Addressing the Second All-Russian Congress of Soviets**
In the spring of 1917, the German government craftily let Lenin and other Bolsheviks travel from their exile in Switzerland back to the scene of the unfolding revolution in Russia. A committed revolutionary instead of a political reformer, Lenin used oratory and skillful maneuvering to convince many in the soviets to follow him in overthrowing the Provisional Government, taking Russia out of the war, and implementing his brand of communism. (Novosti, London.)

the war, for the soviets to seize power on behalf of workers and poor peasants, and for all private land to be nationalized. The Bolsheviks aimed to supplant the Provisional Government with the slogans "All power to the soviets" and "Peace, land, and bread."

Time was running out for the Provisional Government, which saw a battlefield victory as the only way to ensure its position. On July 1, the Russian army attacked the Austrians in Galicia but was defeated once again (see Map 20.1). The new prime minister, the Socialist Revolutionary Aleksandr Kerensky (1881–1970), used commanding oratory to arouse patriotism but lacked the political skills to fashion an effective wartime government. In November 1917, the Bolshevik leadership, urged on by Lenin, seized power on behalf of a congress of soviets while simultaneously asserting its own right to form a government. When elections for a constituent assembly in January 1918 failed to give the Bolsheviks a plurality, the party used troops to disrupt the assembly and took over the government by force. They seized town and city administrations, closing down the *zemstvos* (local councils) and other institutions in the countryside where opposition support was keen. In the winter of 1918–1919, the Bolshevik government, observing Marxist doctrine, abolished private property and nationalized factories in order to restore production, which had fallen off precipitously. The Provisional Government had allowed both men and women to vote in 1917; Russia was thus the first great power to legalize universal suffrage—a hollow privilege once the Bolsheviks limited electoral slates to candidates from the Communist Party.

The Bolsheviks asked Germany for peace and agreed to the Treaty of Brest-Litovsk (March 1918), which placed vast regions of the old Russian Empire under German occupation (Map 20.2). The treaty partially realized the German ideal of a central European region, or *Mitteleuropa,* under German control. Because the loss of millions of square miles put Petrograd at risk, the Bolsheviks relocated the capital to Moscow and formally adopted the name *Communists* (taken from Marx's writings) to distinguish themselves from the socialists and social democrats who had voted for the disastrous war in the first place. Lenin agreed to the catastrophic terms of the treaty not only because he had promised to bring peace to Russia but also because he believed that the rest of Europe would soon rebel against war and overthrow the capitalist order.

Resistance to Bolshevik policies mushroomed into a civil war in which the pro-Bolsheviks (or "Reds") faced an array of antirevolutionary forces (the "Whites"). On the White side, the tsarist military leadership, composed of many landlords and supporters of aristocratic rule, fielded whatever troops it could muster. Dispossessed businessmen and the liberal intelligentsia soon lent their support. Many non-Russian nationality groups, formerly incorporated into the empire through force, Russification, and other bureaucratic efforts, fought the Bolsheviks because they saw their chance for independence. Before World War I ended, Russia's former allies, notably the United States, Britain, France, and Japan, landed troops in the coun-

■ MAP 20.2 The Russian Civil War, 1917–1922

Nationalists, aristocrats, middle-class citizens, and property-owning peasants tried to combine their interests to defeat the Bolsheviks, but they failed to create an effective political consensus. The result was more suffering for ordinary people, whose produce was confiscated to fight the civil war. The Western powers and Japan also sent in troops to put down this revolution that so threatened the economic and political order.

try both to block the Germans and to stop Bolshevism. To compete effectively with the Bolsheviks, the counterrevolutionary groups desperately needed a strong leader and unified goals. Instead, the groups competed with one another: the pro-tsarist forces, for example, alienated those aspiring to nation-state status, such as the Ukrainians, Estonians, and Lithuanians. Ultimately, without a common purpose or unified command, the opponents of revolution could not win.

The civil war shaped communism. Leon Trotsky (1879–1940), Bolshevik commissar of war, built the highly disciplined Red Army by ending democratic procedures, such as the election of officers, that had originally attracted soldiers to Bolshevism. Lenin and Trotsky introduced the policy of war communism, whereby urban workers and troops moved through the countryside, brutally confiscating grain from the peasantry to feed the army and workforce. The Cheka (secret police) set up detention camps for political opponents and black marketeers and shot many of them without trial. The expansion of the size and strength of the Cheka and the Red Army—the latter would eventually number five million men—accompanied the expansion of the bureaucracy, making government more authoritarian and undermining the promise of Marxism that revolution would bring a "withering away" of the state.

As the Bolsheviks clamped down on opposition during the bloody civil war, they organized their supporters to foster revolutionary Marxism across Europe. In March 1919, they founded the Third International, also known as the Comintern (Communist International) for the explicit purpose of replacing the old International with a centralized organization dedicated to preaching communism. By mid-1921, the Cheka had shored up Bolshevism in Russia, and the Red Army had secured the Crimea, the Caucasus, and the Muslim borderlands. When the Japanese withdrew from Siberia in 1922, the civil war ended in central and east Asia. The Bolsheviks were now in charge of a state as multinational as the old Russian Empire had been (see Map 20.2).

The Russian Revolution led by the Bolsheviks promised bold experiments in social and political leadership. The revolution turned out the inept Romanovs and the privileged aristocracy, but the civil war turned Russia into a battlefield stalked by disease, hunger, and death. Moreover, the brutal way in which the Bolsheviks came to power—by crushing their opponents—ushered in a political style and direction far different from earlier socialist hopes.

Ending the War: 1918

Having pulled Russia out of World War I, the Bolsheviks left the rest of Europe's leaders confronting a new balance of forces. Facing war protest as well, these leaders also were left fearing that communism might lie in their future.

In the spring of 1918, the Central Powers made one final attempt to smash through the Allied lines, but the offensive ground to a bloody halt within weeks. By then, the British and French had started making limited but effective use of tanks supported by airplanes. Although the first tanks were cumbersome, their ability to withstand machine-gun fire made offensive attacks possible. In the summer of 1918, the Allies, now fortified by the Americans, pushed back the Germans all along the western front and headed toward Germany. The German armies, suffering more than two million casualties between spring and summer, rapidly disintegrated.

By October 1918, the desperate German command helped create a civilian government, hoodwinking inexperienced politicians to take responsibility for the defeat and to sue for peace. Deflecting blame from the military, generals proclaimed themselves still fully capable of winning the war. Weak-willed civilians, they claimed, had dealt the military a "stab in the back" that forced a surrender. Amid this blatant political deceit, naval officers called for a final sea battle, sparking mutiny against what the sailors saw as a suicide mission. The sailors' revolt spread to the workers, who demonstrated in Berlin, Munich, and other major German cities. The uprisings pro-

voked Social Democratic politicians to declare a German republic in an effort to prevent revolution. On November 9, 1918, Kaiser William II fled as Germans declared
a republic and the Central Powers collapsed on all fronts. Since the previous winter,
Austria-Hungary had kept many combat divisions at home simply to maintain civil
order. At the end of October, Czechs and Slovaks had declared an independent state,
and the Croatian parliament simultaneously announced Croatia's independence.

Finally, on November 11, 1918, at 5:00 A.M., an armistice was signed. The guns
fell silent on the western front six hours later. In the course of four years, European
civilization had been sorely tested, if not shattered. Conservative figures put the
battlefield toll at a minimum of ten million deaths and thirty million wounded,
incapacitated, or eventually to die of their wounds. In every European combatant
country, industrial and agricultural production had plummeted, and much of
the reduced output had been put to military use. Asia, Africa, and the Americas,
which depended on European trade, also felt the painful impact of Europe's declining production. From 1918 to 1919, the weakened global population suffered an
influenza epidemic that left at least twenty million more dead.

Moral questioning accompanied the suffering. Soldiers returning home in 1918
and 1919 flooded the book market with their memoirs, trying to give meaning to
their experiences. Whereas many had begun by emphasizing heroism and glory,
others were cynical and bitter by war's end. They insisted the fighting had been
meaningless. Total war had drained society of resources and population and had
inadvertently sown the seeds of future catastrophes.

The Search for Peace in an
Era of Revolution

Amid the quest for peace, revolutionary fervor swept the continent of Europe, especially in the former empires of Germany and Austria-Hungary. Until 1921, the
triumph of socialism seemed plausible, as many of the newly independent peoples
of eastern and central Europe fervently supported socialist principles. The revolutionary mood captured workers and peasants in Germany, too. In contrast, many
liberal and right-wing opponents hoped for a political order based on military authority of the kind they had relied on during the war. Faced with a volatile mix of
revolution and counterrevolution, diplomats from around the world arrived in Paris
in January 1919 to negotiate the terms of peace, often without recognizing the mag-
nitude of the changes brought about by war.

Europe in Turmoil

Urban people and returning soldiers ignited the protest that swept Europe in 1918
and 1919. In January 1919, the red flag of socialist revolution flew from city hall in
Glasgow, Scotland, while in cities of the collapsing Austro-Hungarian Empire workers set up councils to direct factory production and to influence politics. Many

soldiers did not disband at the armistice but formed volunteer armies, making Europe ripe not for parliamentary politics but for revolution by force.

Germany was politically unstable, partly because of the shock of defeat. Independent socialist groups and workers' councils vied with the dominant Social Democrats for control of the government, and workers and veterans took to the streets to demand food and back pay. Whereas in 1848 revolutionaries had marched to city hall or the king's residence, these protesters took over newspapers and telegraph offices, thus controlling the flow of information. Some were inspired by one of the most radical socialist factions, the Spartacists, led by cofounders Karl Liebknecht (1871–1919) and Rosa Luxemburg (1870–1919). Unlike Lenin, the two Spartacist leaders favored political uprisings that would give workers political experience and thus eliminate the need for an all-knowing party leadership. They argued for *direct* worker control of institutions, but they shared Lenin's dislike for parliamentary politics.

Social Democratic leader Friedrich Ebert (1871–1925), who headed the new government, shunned revolution and supported the creation of a parliamentary republic. Splitting with his former socialist allies, he called on the German army and the Freikorps—a roving paramilitary band of students, demobilized soldiers, and others—to suppress the workers' councils and demonstrators. He thus gave official credence to the idea that political differences could be settled with violence. "The enthusiasm is marvelous," wrote one young soldier. "No mercy's shown. We shoot even the wounded.... We were much more humane against the French in the field." Protest continued even as a constituent assembly meeting in the city of Weimar in February 1919 approved a constitution and founded a parliamentary republic. This time the right rebelled, for the military leadership dreamed of a restored monarchy: "As I love Germany, so I hate the Republic," wrote one officer. Facing a military coup by Freikorps officers, Ebert called for a general strike that abruptly averted a takeover by showing the lack of popular support for a military regime. In so doing, the Weimar Republic had set the dangerous precedent of relying on street violence, paramilitary groups, and protests to solve political problems.

Revolutionary activism surged and was smashed. Late in the winter of 1919, leftists proclaimed soviet republics—governments led by workers' councils—in Bavaria and Hungary. These soon fell before the assault of the volunteer armies and troops. The Bolsheviks tried to establish a Marxist regime in Poland in the belief that its people wanted a workers' revolution. Instead, the Poles resisted and drove the Red Army back in 1920, while the Allied powers rushed supplies and advisers to Warsaw (see Map 20.2). Though this and other revolts failed, they provided further proof that total war had loosened political and social order.

The Paris Peace Conference, 1919–1920

As political turmoil engulfed peoples from Berlin to Moscow, the Paris peace conference opened in January 1919. Visions of communism spreading westward haunted the assembled statesmen, but the desperation of millions of war-ravaged citizens, the status of Germany, and the reconstruction of a secure Europe topped their agenda. Leaders such as French premier Georges Clemenceau needed to satisfy their angry citizens, who demanded revenge or, at the very least, compensation for their suffering. France had lost 1.3 million people—almost an entire generation; and more than a million buildings, six thousand bridges, and thousands of miles of railroad lines and roads had been destroyed while the war was fought on French soil. Great Britain's representative, Prime Minister David Lloyd George, caught the mood of the British public by campaigning in 1918 with such slogans as "Hang the kaiser." Italians arrived on the scene demanding the territory promised to them in the 1915 Treaty of London. Meanwhile, U.S. president Woodrow Wilson, head of the new world power that had helped achieve the Allied victory, had his own agenda. His Fourteen Points, on which the truce had been based, was steeped in the language of freedom and called for open diplomacy, arms reduction, an "open-minded" settlement of colonial issues, and the self-determination of peoples.

The Fourteen Points did not represent the mood of the victors, however. Allied propaganda had made the Germans seem like inhuman monsters, and many citizens demanded a harsh peace. Moreover, some military experts feared that Germany was using the armistice only to regroup for more warfare. Indeed, Germans widely refused to admit that their army had lost the war. Eager for army support, Ebert had given returning soldiers a rousing welcome: "As you return unconquered from the field of battle, I salute you." Thus, conservative leaders among Wilson's former allies campaigned to make him look naive and deluded. "Wilson bores me with his Fourteen Points," Clemenceau complained. "Why, the good Lord himself has only ten."

Nevertheless, Wilson's Fourteen Points appealed to European moderates and persuaded Germans that the settlement would not be vindictive. His commitment to *settlement* as opposed to *surrender* contained tough-minded stipulations, for Wilson wisely recognized that Germany was still the strongest state in Europe. He merely pushed for a treaty that balanced the strengths and interests of various European powers. Economists and other specialists accompanying Wilson to Paris agreed that, harshly dealt with and humiliated, Germany might soon become vengeful and chaotic.

After six months, the statesmen and their teams of experts produced the Peace of Paris (1919–1920), composed of a cluster of individual treaties. These treaties shocked the countries that had to accept them, and in retrospect historians see how they destabilized eastern and east-central Europe (Map 20.3). The treaties separated Austria from Hungary, reduced Hungary by almost two-thirds of its inhabitants and three-quarters of its territory, broke up the Ottoman Empire, and treated Germany severely. They replaced the Habsburg Empire with a group of small, internally divided, and relatively weak states: Czechoslovakia, Poland, and the Kingdom of the Serbs, Croats, and Slovenes, soon renamed Yugoslavia. After a century and a half of partition, Poland was reconstructed from parts of Russia, Germany, and Austria-Hungary; one-third of its population was ethnically non-Polish. The statesmen in Paris also created a Polish Corridor that connected Poland to the Baltic

■ **MAP 20.3 Europe and the Middle East after the Peace Settlements of 1919–1920**

The political landscape of central, east, and east-central Europe changed dramatically as a result of the Russian Revolution and the Peace of Paris. The Ottoman, German, Russian, and Austro-Hungarian Empires were either broken up altogether into multiple small states or territorially reduced in size. The settlement left resentments among Germans and Hungarians and created a group of weak, struggling nations in the heartland of Europe. The victorious powers took over much of the oil-rich Middle East.

www.bedfordstmartins.com/huntconcise   See the ONLINE STUDY GUIDE for more help in analyzing this map.

Sea and separated East Prussia from the rest of Germany. Austria and Hungary were both left reeling at their loss of territory and resources. Many of the new states became rivals and were for the most part politically and economically weak.

The Treaty of Versailles with Germany was the centerpiece of the Peace of Paris, however. France recovered Alsace and Lorraine, and the victors would temporarily occupy the left, or western, bank of the Rhine and the coal-bearing Saar basin. Wilson accepted his allies' expectations that Germany would pay substantial reparations for civilian damage during the war. The specific amount was set in 1921 at the crushing sum of 132 billion gold marks. Germany also had to reduce its army, almost eliminate its navy, stop manufacturing offensive weapons, and deliver a large amount of free coal each year to Belgium and France. Furthermore, it was forbidden to have an air force and had to give up its colonies. The average German saw in these terms an unmerited humiliation that was compounded by Article 231 of the treaty, which described Germany's "responsibility" for damage "imposed . . . by the aggression of Germany and her allies." The outraged German people interpreted this as a "war guilt" clause, which allowed the victors to collect reparations from economically viable Germany rather than from decimated Austria. War guilt made Germany an outcast in the community of nations.

Besides redrawing the map of Europe, the Peace of Paris set up an organization called the League of Nations, whose responsibility for maintaining peace—a principle called *collective security*—was to replace the divisive secrecy of prewar power politics. As part of Wilson's vision, the league would guide the world toward disarmament, arbitrate its members' disputes, and monitor labor conditions around the world. Returning to prewar isolationism, the United States Senate, in a humiliating defeat for the president, failed to ratify the peace settlement and refused to join the league. Moreover, both Germany and Russia initially were excluded from the league and were thus blocked from acting in legal concert with other nations.

The covenant, or charter, of the League of Nations organized the administration of the colonies and territories of Germany and the Ottoman Empire—such as Togo, Cameroon, Syria, and Palestine—through a system of mandates (see "Mapping the West," page 905). The European powers exercised political control over mandated territory, but local leaders retained limited authority. The league covenant justified the mandate system as providing governance by "advanced nations" over territories "not yet able to stand by themselves under the strenuous conditions of the modern world." However, colonized and other people of color who had served on the battlefield began to challenge the claims of their European masters. They had seen how savage and degraded these people who claimed to be racially superior, politically more advanced, and leaders of global culture could be. "Never again will the darker people of the world occupy just the place they had before," the African American leader W. E. B. Du Bois predicted in 1918. The mandate system continued the practice of apportioning the globe among European powers, but like the Peace of Paris it aroused anger and resistance.

Economic and Diplomatic
Consequences of the Peace

The financial and political settlement in the Peace of Paris had repercussions in the 1920s and beyond. Western leaders worried deeply about two intertwined issues in the aftermath of the war. The first was economic recovery. France, the hardest hit by wartime destruction and billions of dollars in debt to the United States, estimated that Germany owed it at least $200 billion. The British, by contrast, worried about maintaining their empire and restoring trade with Germany, not about exacting huge reparations. Nevertheless, both France and Britain depended on some monetary redress to pay their war debts to the United States because Europe's share of world trade had plunged during the war.

Germany claimed that the demand for reparations strained its government, already beset by political upheaval. But hardship was not the result of the Peace of Paris alone. The kaiser had refused to raise taxes, especially on the rich, to pay for the war, so the new German republic had to pay reparations and to manage the staggering war debt. As an experiment in democracy, the Weimar Republic needed to woo the citizenry, not alienate it by hiking taxes. In 1921, when Germans refused to present a realistic payment scheme, the French occupied several cities in the Ruhr until a settlement was reached.

Embroiled with powers to the west, the German government deftly sought economic and diplomatic relations in eastern Europe. It reached an agreement to foster economic ties with Russia, desperate for western trade, in the Treaty of Rapallo (1922). Its relations with powers to the west, however, continued to deteriorate. In 1923, after Germany defaulted on coal deliveries, the French and Belgians sent troops into the Ruhr basin, planning to use its abundant resources to recoup their wartime expenditures. Urged on by the government, Ruhr citizens fought back, shutting down industry by staying home from work. The German government printed trillions of marks to support the workers and to pay its own war debts with practically worthless currency. Soon Germany was in the midst of a staggering inflation that demoralized its citizens and gravely threatened the international economy: at one point a single U.S. dollar cost 4.42 trillion marks, and wheelbarrows of money were required to buy a turnip. The spirit of the League of Nations demanded a resolution to this economic chaos through negotiations. The Dawes Plan (1924) and eventually the Young Plan (1929) reduced payments to the victors and restored the value of German currency. Nonetheless, the inflation had wreaked enduring psychological havoc, wiped out people's savings, and ruined those living on fixed incomes.

A second burning issue in addition to economic recovery involved ensuring that peace would last. Statesmen recognized that peace demanded disarmament, a return of Germany to the fold, and security for the new countries of eastern Europe. It took hard diplomatic bargaining outside the league to produce two plans in Germany's favor. At the Washington Conference in 1921, the United States, Great Britain, Japan, France, and Italy agreed to reduce their number of battleships and to stop constructing new ones for ten years. Four years later, in 1925, the league sponsored a meeting of the great powers, including Germany, at Locarno, Switzerland. The Treaty of Locarno provided Germany with a seat in the League of Nations as of 1926. In return, Germany agreed not to violate the borders of France and Belgium and to keep the nearby Rhineland demilitarized (unfortified by troops).

To the east, the door seemed open to a German attempt to regain territory lost to Poland, to form a merger with Austria, or to launch aggression against the states spun off from Austria-Hungary (see Map 20.3). To meet the threat, Czechoslovakia, Yugoslavia, and Romania formed the "Little Entente" in 1920–1921. This was a collective security agreement to protect themselves from their two powerful neighbors, Germany and Russia, and to guard against Hungarian expansionism. Then, between 1924 and 1927, France allied itself with the Little Entente and with Poland. The major European powers, Japan, and the United States also signed the Kellogg-Briand Pact (1928), which formally rejected international violence. The nations failed, however, to commit themselves to concrete action to prevent its outbreak.

The publicity and planning that yielded the international agreements during the 1920s sharply contrasted with old-style diplomacy, which was conducted in secret and subject to little public scrutiny or democratic influence. The development of a system of collective security and the new openness suggested a diplomatic revolution that would promote peace in international relations. Despite this promise, openness allowed diplomats of the era to feed the press reports calculated to arouse the masses. For example, much of the German populace was lashed into a nationalist frenzy by the press and opposing parties whenever Germany's diplomats, who were successfully working to undo the Treaty of Versailles, seemed to compromise. Although international meetings such as the one at Locarno appeared to promote the goal of collective security, they also exposed the diplomatic process to the nationalist press and to demagogues who could rekindle political hatreds.

A Decade of Recovery: Europe in the 1920s

The 1920s was devoted to coming to terms with the cultural and political legacy of the war. The wartime spirit endured in words and phrases from the battlefield that punctuated everyday speech. Before the war, the word *lousy* had meant "lice-infested," but English-speaking soldiers returning from the trenches now applied it to anything bad. Raincoats became *trenchcoats*, and terms like *bombarded* and *rank and file* entered peacetime usage. Maimed, disfigured veterans were present everywhere. Some used prostheses designed by Jules Amar; others without limbs were sometimes carried in baskets—hence the expression *basket case*. They overflowed hospitals and mental institutions, and family life centered on their care. Total war had generally strengthened military values, authoritarian government, and a

■ Otto Dix, *The Sleepwalkers* (1928)

Artists in the defeated countries were especially attuned to the tragic absurdity of the war. The German ex-soldier Otto Dix sketched smashed faces and corpses in varying states of decay, depicting people who survived as grotesque or be-numbed "sleepwalkers" who picked their way through the postwar wreckage. The simple horror of death and disfigurement made painted whores of those seeking a return to ordinary life.

("The Sleepwalkers" by Otto Dix from *The Nature of War* by John Keegan and Joseph Darra-cott [Holt, Rinehart and Winston, 1981]. Private Collection, Essen.)

controlled economy. A key question facing society was how to restore civilian government. Although contemporaries referred to the 1920s as the "Roaring Twenties" and the "Jazz Age," the sense of cultural release masked the serious problem of restoring social stability and implementing democracy. Four autocratic governments—in Germany, Austria-Hungary, Russia, and the Ottoman Empire—had collapsed as a result of the war, but how newly empowered citizens would act politically remained a burning question.

Changes in the Political Landscape across Europe

The threat of revolution coexisted with a sense of democratic rebirth because of the collapse of autocratic government and the extension of suffrage to women, widely granted at the war's end. Woman suffrage resulted in part from decades of activism; more immediately, many governments gave women the vote to reward them for their war efforts and to make revolution less tempting. In the first postwar elections, women were voted into parliaments, and the impression grew that they had also made extraordinary gains in the workplace. French men pointedly denied women the vote, insisting they would use their vote to bring

Women Gain Suffrage in the West	
1906	Finland
1913	Norway
1915	Denmark, Iceland
1917	Netherlands, Russia
1918	Czechoslovakia, Great Britain (limited suffrage)
1919	Germany
1920	Austria, United States
1921	Poland
1925	Hungary (limited suffrage)
1945	Italy, France
1971	Switzerland

back the rule of kings and priests. (Only at the end of World War II would France and Italy extend suffrage to women.) Governments continued building the welfare state by expanding payments to families with children and insurance programs for workers. New government benefits attested to a spreading belief that more evenly distributed wealth—sometimes referred to as *economic democracy*—was important to social stability in postwar society.

The slow trend toward economic democracy was not easy to maintain, however, because the cycles of boom and bust that had characterized the late nineteenth century reemerged. A short postwar boom prompted by rebuilding war-torn areas and filling consumer needs unsatisfied during the war was followed by an economic downturn that was most severe between 1920 and 1922. Skyrocketing unemployment led some to question the effectiveness of their governments and the fairness of society. By the mid-1920s, many of the economic opportunities for women had disappeared, and they made up a smaller percentage of the workforce than in 1913.

Hard times especially corroded the new republics of eastern Europe, which were unprepared for independence in the sophisticated world market. None but Czechoslovakia had a mature industrial sector, and agricultural techniques were often primitive. The development of Poland exemplified the postwar political landscape in eastern Europe. Nationalism was increasingly defined in ethnic terms, and the reunified Poland consisted of one-third Ukrainians, Belorussians, Germans, and other ethnic minorities—many of whom had grievances against the dominant Poles. Moreover, varying religious,

National Minorities in Postwar Poland

dynastic, and cultural traditions divided the Poles, who for 150 years had been split among Austria, Germany, and Russia. Polish reunification occurred without a common currency, political structure, or language—even the railroad tracks were not a standard size.

With practically no economic or other support from the Allies, a constitutional government nonetheless took shape in this new Poland. Under a constitution that professed equal rights for all ethnicities and religions, the new democratic government, run by the Sejm (parliament), tried to legislate the redistribution of large estates to the peasantry, but declining crop prices and overpopulation made life in the countryside difficult. Urban workers were better off than the peasantry (two-thirds of the population lived by subsistence farming) but worse off than laborers across Europe. The economic downturn brought strikes and violence in 1922–1923, and the inability of coalition parliaments to effect economic prosperity led to a coup in 1926 by strongman Jozef Pilsudski. Economic hardship and strong-arm solutions went hand in hand in east-central Europe.

Germany was a different case. The industrially sophisticated Weimar Republic confronted daunting challenges to making Germany democratic, even after putting down the postwar revolution. Although the German economy picked up and Germany became a center of experimentation in the arts, political life remained precarious because so many people felt nostalgia for imperial glory and loathed the Versailles treaty's restrictions. On the surface, Weimar's political system—a bicameral parliament and a chancellor responsible to the lower house—appeared similar to the parliamentary system in Britain and France, but extremist politicians heaped daily abuse on parliamentary politics. Anyone who cooperated with the parliamentary system, wrote the wealthy newspaper and film magnate Alfred Hugenberg, "is a moral cripple." Right-wing parties favored violence rather than consensus building, and nationalist thugs murdered democratic leaders and Jews.

Support for the far right came from wealthy landowners and businessmen, white-collar workers whose standard of living had dropped during the war, and members of the lower-middle and middle classes hurt by inflation. Bands of disaffected youth and veterans proliferated, among them a group called Brown Shirts led by ex-soldier and political newcomer Adolf Hitler (1889–1945). In the wake of the Ruhr occupation of 1923, Ludendorff and Hitler launched a coup d'état from a beer hall in Munich. Government troops suppressed the Beer Hall Putsch, but Hitler spent less than a year in jail and Ludendorff was acquitted. For conservative judges as for former aristocrats and most of the prewar bureaucrats who remained in government, such men were national heroes.

In France and Britain, parties of the right had less effect than elsewhere because parliamentary institutions were better established and the upper classes were not plotting to restore an authoritarian monarchy. In France, politicians from the conservative right and moderate left successively formed coalitions and rallied general support to rebuild war-torn regions and to force Germany to pay for the reconstruction. Hoping to stimulate population growth after the devastating loss of life, the French parliament made distributing birth-control information illegal and abortion a severely punished crime.

Britain encountered postwar boom and bust and continuing strife in Ireland. Ramsay MacDonald, elected the first Labour prime minister in 1924, represented the newly formed political ambitions of the working masses. Like other postwar British leaders, he had to swallow the paradoxical fact that although Britain had the largest world empire, many of its industries were obsolete or in poor condition. A showdown came in the ailing coal industry, where prices fell and wages plummeted once the Ruhr mines reopened to offer tough competition to British mines. On May 3, 1926, workers launched a nine-day general strike against wage cuts and danger-ous conditions in the mines. The strike provoked unprecedented middle-class re-sistance. University students, homemakers, and businessmen shut down the strike by driving trains, working on docks, and replacing workers in other jobs. Thus cit-izens from many walks of life revived the wartime spirit to defend the declining economy.

In Ireland, the British government met bloody confrontation over the contin-uing failure to implement home rule. Irish republicans had attacked government buildings in Dublin on Easter Monday 1916 in an effort to wrest Irish independence from Brit-ain. The ill-prepared Easter Uprising was easily defeated, and many participants were executed. The severe punishment only intensified demands for home rule, and in January 1919, republican leaders announced Ireland's independence from Britain and created a separate parliament. The British government refused to recognize the par-liament and sent in the Black and Tans, a volun-teer army of demobilized soldiers so called for the color of their uniforms. Terror reigned in Ire-land, as both the pro-independence forces and the Black and Tans waged guerrilla warfare, tak-ing hostages, blowing up buildings, and even shooting into crowds at soccer matches. By 1921,

The Irish Free State and
Ulster, 1921

public outrage forced the British to negotiate a treaty. It reversed the Irish declara-tion of independence and made the Irish Free State a self-governing dominion owing allegiance to the British crown. Northern Ireland, a group of six northern counties containing a majority of Protestants, gained a separate status: it was self-governing but still had representation in the British Parliament. Incomplete in-dependence and the rights of religious minorities remained contentious issues.

European powers encountered rebellion in overseas empires as well. Colonized peoples who had fought in the war expected more rights and even independence. Indeed, European politicians and military recruiters had actually promised the vote and many other reforms in exchange for support. But colonists' political activism, now enhanced by increasing education, trade, and experience with the West, mostly met a brutal response. Fearful of losing India, British forces massacred protesters at Amritsar in 1919 and put down revolts against the mandate system in Egypt and Iran in the early 1920s. The Dutch jailed political leaders in Indonesia; the French punished Indochinese nationalists. For many Western governments, maintaining empires abroad was crucial to ensuring democracy at home, for any hint of declining national prestige fed antidemocratic forces.

Reconstructing the Economy

New worldwide economic competition was as big a challenge to recovery as were global political struggles. During the war, the European economy had lost many of its international markets to India, Canada, Australia, Japan, and the United States. Nonetheless, the war had forced European manufacturing to become more efficient and had expanded the demand for automotive and air transport, electrical products, and synthetic goods. The prewar pattern of mergers and cartels continued after 1918, giving rise to gigantic food-processing firms such as Nestlé in Switzerland and petroleum enterprises such as Royal Dutch Shell. Owners of these large manufacturing conglomerates wielded more financial and political power than entire small countries. By the late 1920s, Europe had overcome the wild economic swings of the immediate postwar years and was enjoying renewed economic prosperity.

Despite this growth, the United States had become the trendsetter in economic modernization. Many European businessmen made pilgrimages to Henry Ford's Detroit assembly line, which by 1929 produced a Ford automobile every ten seconds. Ford touted this miracle of productivity as resulting in a lower cost of living and increased purchasing power for workers. Indeed, whereas French, German, and British citizens in total had under two million cars, some seventeen million cars were on U.S. streets in 1925.

Scientific management, sometimes called the science of work, also aimed to raise productivity. American efficiency expert Frederick Taylor (1856–1915) developed methods to streamline workers' tasks and motions for maximum productivity. European industrialists adopted Taylor's methods during the war and after, but they were also influenced by European psychologists who emphasized the mental aspects of productivity and the need for a balance of work and leisure activities, such as moviegoing and sports, for both workers and managers. In theory, increased productivity not only would produce prosperity for all but also would bind workers and management together, avoiding Russian-style worker revolution. In practice, streamlining did help reduce working hours in many industries, a result that encouraged union leaders to embrace modernization and the "cult of efficiency." For many workers, however, the emphasis on efficiency seemed inhuman; in some workplaces, the restrictions on time and motion were so severe that workers were allowed to use the bathroom only on a fixed schedule. "When I left the factory, it followed me," wrote one worker. "In my dreams I was a machine."

The managerial sector in industry had expanded during the war and continued to do so thereafter. Workers' initiative became devalued; managers alone were considered to be creative and innovative. Managers reorganized work procedures and classified workers' skills. They categorized as "female jobs" work that required less skill and therefore deserved lower wages, thus adapting the old segmentation of the labor market to the new working conditions. Because male workers' jobs were increasingly threatened by labor-saving machinery, unions usually agreed to hold down women's wages to keep women from competing with men for scarce high-paying jobs. Like the managerial sector, union bureaucracy had ballooned during World War I to help monitor labor's part in the war. Union bureaucrats became specialists: negotiators, membership organizers, educators and propagandists, and political liaisons. Playing a key role in politics, unions could mobilize masses of people, as they demonstrated when they blocked coups against the Weimar government in the 1920s and organized the 1926 general strike in Great Britain.

Restoring Society

With combined joy and trepidation, postwar society met the returning millions of brutalized, incapacitated, and shell-shocked veterans. Many veterans harbored hostility toward civilians, who had rebelled against wartime conditions, these soldiers charged, instead of patriotically enduring them. The places the veterans returned to differed from the homes they had left. Veterans often had no jobs. Some soldiers found that their wives and sweethearts had abandoned them—a wrenching betrayal of those who had risked their lives to protect the homeland.

The war had blurred class distinctions, giving rise to expectations that life would be fairer. The massive battlefield casualties had fostered social mobility, making it possible for commoners to move into the ranks of officers, positions often monopolized by the prewar aristocracy. Members of all classes had rubbed shoulders in the trenches. The identical, evenly spaced crosses in military cemeteries implied that all the dead were equal, as did the mass "brothers' graves" at the battlefront, in which rich and poor lay side by side in a single burial pit. On the home front, middle-class daughters worked outside the home, and their mothers did their own housework because their former servants could earn more money working in factories. Women of all classes had cut their hair, wore sleeker clothes, smoked, and had money of their own.

United by patriotism when the war erupted, civilians, especially women, sometimes felt estranged from these returning warriors, who had inflicted so much death and had lived daily with filth, rats, and decaying animal and human flesh. Civilian anxieties were often valid. Tens of thousands of German, central European, and Italian soldiers refused to disband; a few British veterans even vandalized university classrooms and assaulted women streetcar conductors and factory workers. Women who had served at the front could empathize with the soldiers' woes. But many suffragists in England, for instance, who had fought for an end to separate spheres before the war, now embraced gender segregation, so fearful were they of returning veterans.

Fearing the spread of Bolshevism, governments tried to make civilian life as comfortable as possible to reintegrate men into society and prevent revolution. Politicians believed in the stabilizing power of traditional family values and supported social programs such as pensions, benefits for out-of-work men, and housing for veterans to alleviate their pent-up anger. The new housing—"homes for heroes," politicians called the program—was a vast improvement over nineteenth-century working-class tenements. In Vienna, Frankfurt, Berlin, and Stockholm, modern housing projects provided common laundries, day-care centers, and rooms for group socializing. They featured gardens, terraces, and balconies to provide a soothing, country ambiance that offset the hectic nature of industrial life. Inside they boasted modern kitchens, indoor plumbing, central heating, and electricity. Imitating the clean lines of East Asian and African dwellings to create a sense of modernity, domestic architects avoided ornate moldings, plasterwork, and curlicues—now seen as "old-fashioned." Some architects, such as the Swiss-born French architect Le Corbusier (1887–1965), favored "high-rise" apartments that

■ Le Corbusier's Paris of the Future
While the war profoundly disillusioned many in the West, peace aroused utopian hopes for a better future. For modern architects like Swiss-born Le Corbusier (1887–1965), the "future city" and the "radiant city" would organize space, and thus life, for ordinary people. Horizontal windows, roof gardens, and very plain façades were hallmarks of this new design—a radical break with ornate prewar styles in building. (Fondation Le Corbusier/A.D.A.G.P.)

adapted the principles of New York's skyscrapers to the domestic environment and satisfied the criterion of urban planning that called for an efficient use of space.

Despite government efforts to restore traditional family values, war had dissolved many middle-class conventions, among them attempts to keep unmarried young men and women apart. Freer relationships and more open discussions of sex characterized the 1920s. Middle-class youth of both sexes visited jazz clubs and attended movies together. Revealing bathing suits, short skirts, and body-hugging clothing emphasized women's sexuality, seeming to invite men and women to join together and replenish the postwar population. Still, the context for sexuality remained marriage. In 1918, British scientist Marie Stopes published the best-seller *Married Love,* and in 1927, the wildly successful *Ideal Marriage: Its Physiology and Technique* by Dutch author Theodor van de Velde appeared. Both described sex in rhapsodic terms and offered precise information about birth control and sexual physiology. Changing ideas about sex were not limited to the middle and upper classes. One Viennese reformer described working-class marriage as "an erotic-comradely relationship of equals" rather than the economic partnership of past centuries. The flapper, a sexually liberated workingwoman, vied with the dedicated housewife to represent the ordinary woman in the public's eyes. Meanwhile, such writers as the Englishman D. H. Lawrence and the American Ernest Hemingway glorified men's sexual vigor in, respectively, *Women in Love* (1920) and *The Sun Also Rises* (1926). Mass culture's focus on heterosexuality encouraged the return to traditional social norms after the gender disorder that troubled the prewar and war years.

As images of men and women changed, people paid more attention to bodily improvement. The increasing use of toothbrushes and toothpaste, safety and electric razors, and deodorants reflected new standards of personal hygiene and grooming. For Western women, a multi-billion-dollar cosmetics industry sprang up almost overnight. Women went to beauty parlors regularly to have their short hair cut, set, dyed, conditioned, straightened, or curled. They also tweezed their eyebrows, applied makeup, and even submitted to cosmetic surgery. Ordinary women painted their faces as formerly only prostitutes had done and competed in beauty contests that judged physical appearance. Instead of wanting to look plump and prosperous, people aimed to become thin and tan. The proliferation of boxers, hikers, gymnasts, and tap dancers spurred people to exercise and to participate in amateur sports. Modern industry encouraged consumers' new focus on personal health, which coincided with the need for a physically fit workforce.

The strong economic upturn encouraged people to buy more and more consumer goods. Thanks to the gradual postwar increase in real wages, middle- and upper-class families snapped up sleek modern furniture, washing machines, and vacuum cleaners. Other modern conveniences such as electric irons and gas stoves appeared in better-off working-class households. Installment buying, popularized from the 1920s on, helped people finance these purchases. Housework became more mechanized, and family intimacy increasingly depended on machines of mass communication such as radios and phonographs, and on automobiles. These new products that transformed private life also brought unforeseen changes in the public world of culture and mass politics.

Mass Culture and the Rise of Modern Dictators

Wartime propaganda had aimed to unite all classes against a common enemy. In the 1920s, the merging of diverse groups into a homogeneous Western culture, increasingly seen as a "mass culture," continued. The homogenizing instruments—primarily radio, film, and newspapers—expanded their influence in the 1920s. Some intellectuals urged elites to form an experimental avant-garde and distance themselves from "the drab mass of society." Others wanted to use modern media and art to reach out to and even control the masses. The mass media had the potential for creating an informed citizenry and thus enhancing democracy. Paradoxically, in the troubled postwar climate, they also provided the tools for dictatorship. They made it possible for authoritarian rulers—Benito Mussolini, Joseph Stalin, and Adolf Hitler—to control the masses in unprecedented ways.

Culture for the Masses

An array of media had received a big boost from the war. Bulletins from the battlefront had whetted the public's craving for news and real-life stories, and sales of nonfiction books soared. After years of deprivation, people felt driven to achieve material success, and they devoured books that advised how to do so. Henry Ford's biography, a story of social mobility and technological accomplishment, became a best-seller in Germany. With postwar readers avidly pursuing practical knowledge, institutes and night schools became popular, and school systems promoted reading in geography, science, and history. Photographs, the radio, and movies also contributed to the formation of national culture.

In the 1920s, filmmaking changed from an experimental medium to a thriving international business, in which large corporations set up theater chains and marketed films worldwide. The war years, when the U.S. film industry began to outstrip the European, gave rise to specialization: directors, producers, marketers, photographers, film editors, and many others subdivided the process. A "star" system turned film personalities into celebrities, promoted by professional publicity and living like royalty. Films of literary classics and political events developed people's sense of a common heritage. Thus the British government sponsored documentaries that articulated national goals, and Bolshevik leaders backed the innovative work of director Sergei Eisenstein (1898–1948), whose films *Potemkin* (1925) and *Ten Days That Shook the World* (1927–1928) presented a Bolshevik view of history to Russian and international audiences.

Films incorporated familiar elements from other cultural forms to cement viewer loyalty. The piano accompaniment that went along with the action of silent films derived from music halls; comic characters, farcical plots, and slapstick humor were borrowed from street or burlesque shows and from trends in postwar living. The popular comedies of the 1920s poked fun at men's and women's feckless attempts to achieve emotional intimacy or featured the flapper and made her more visible to the masses. Lavish movie houses attracted some 100 million weekly viewers, most of them women. As the popularity of films and books crossed national borders, cosmopolitanism and culture for an international audience flourished.

Cinematic portrayals also played to postwar fantasies and fears. In Germany, where filmmakers used expressionist sets and costumes to make films frightening, the influential hit *The Cabinet of Doctor Caligari* (1919) depicted events in an insane asylum as horrifying symbols of state power. Popular detective and cowboy films portrayed heroes who could restore wholeness to the disordered world of murder, crime, and injustice. Depictions of the plight of gangsters appealed to veterans, whose combat experiences had raised questions about the value of life in the modern world. Charlie Chaplin (1889–1977), an English comedian, actor, and producer, created the character of the "Little Tramp," who won international popularity as the defeated hero, the anonymous modern man, trying to preserve his dignity in a mechanized world.

Film remained experimental well into the 1920s, but radio was even more so. Developed from Guglielmo Marconi's wireless technology introduced at the turn of the century, radio broadcasts in the first half of the 1920s were heard by mass audiences in public halls (much like movie theaters) and featured orchestras and song followed by audience discussion. The radio quickly became an affordable consumer item, and public concerts and lectures could then penetrate the individual's private living space. (See "Taking Measure," page 896.) Specialized programming for men (such as sports reporting) and for women (such as advice on home management) soon followed. By the 1930s, radio allowed politicians to reach the masses wherever they might be—even alone at home.

Cultural Debates over the Future

Cultural leaders in the 1920s had different visions of the future. Some were obsessed by the negative implications of the horrendous experience of war. Others—like modernists before the war—held high hopes for creating a fresh future that would bear little relation to the past.

The vision of those haunted by the war was bleak or violent. This outlook was especially a theme in German art. Kaethe Köllwitz (1867–1945), whose son died in the war, portrayed in her woodcuts bereaved parents, starving children, and other heartwrenching, antiwar images (see page 863). Other artists used satire, irony, and

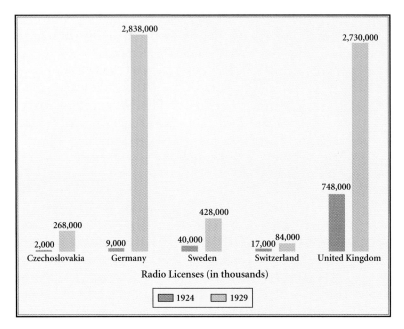

■ TAKING MEASURE The Growth of Radio, 1924–1929
The spread of radio technology, like the earlier development of printing, advanced the cultural and political unity of nation-states. The most rapid diffusion of radios occurred in the most industrially and commercially developed societies. At first, governments both programmed and taxed radios. Because of this centralized control and the paperwork it created, historians can compare the country-by-country use of radio in Europe and in much of the rest of the world.

flippancy to express postwar rage and revulsion at civilization's apparent failure. George Grosz (1893–1959), stunned by the carnage like so many other German veterans, joined Dada, an artistic and literary movement that had emerged during the war. Dadaists produced works marked by nonsense, incongruity, and shrieking expressions of alienation. Grosz's paintings and cartoons of maimed soldiers and brutally murdered women reflected his psychic wounds and his self-proclaimed desire "to bellow back." In the postwar years, the modernist desire to shock audiences intensified. Avant-garde portrayals of seediness and perversion in everyday life flourished in cabarets and theaters in the 1920s and reinforced veterans' visions of civilian decadence.

The art world itself became a battlefield, especially in defeated Germany, where art mirrored the Weimar Republic's contentious politics. Popular writers such as Ernst Jünger glorified life in the trenches and called for the militarization of society to restore order. Erich Maria Remarque cried out for an end to war in his controversial novel *All Quiet on the Western Front* (1928). This international best-seller depicted the life shared by enemies on the battlefield, thus aiming to dampen the national hatred stoked by wartime propaganda.

Poets reflected on postwar conditions in more general terms, using styles that rejected the comforting rhymes or accessible metaphors of earlier verse. T. S. Eliot, an American-born poet who for a time worked as a banker in Britain, portrayed postwar life as petty and futile in "The Waste Land" (1922) and "The Hollow Men" (1925). The Irish nationalist poet William Butler Yeats joined Eliot in mourning the replacement of traditional society, with its moral conviction and religious values, by a new, superficial generation gaily dancing to jazz and engaging in promiscuous sex and vacuous conversation. Yeats's "Sailing to Byzantium" (1928) starts:

> *That is no country for old men. The young*
> *In one another's arms, birds in the trees*
> *—Those dying generations*

Both poets had an uneasy relationship with the modern world and at times advocated authoritarianism rather than democracy.

The postwar arts produced many a utopian fantasy turned upside down; *dystopias* of life in postrevolutionary, traumatized Europe proliferated. In expressionist and bizarre stories, Franz Kafka, an employee of a large insurance company in Prague, showed the world as a vast, impersonal machine. His novels *The Trial* (1925) and *The Castle* (1926) evoked the hopelessness of individuals confronting a relentless, machinelike society in which they are minor cogs; his portrayal of postwar civilian life seemed to capture the helplessness that soldiers had felt at the front. As the old social order collapsed under the weight of political and technological innovation, other writers depicted the complex, sometimes nightmarish inner life of individuals. French author Marcel Proust, in his multivolume novel *Remembrance of Things Past* (1913–1927), explored the workings of memory, the passage of time, and sexual modernity through the life of his narrator. At the beginning of the first volume, the narrator is obsessed with his mother's absence as he tries to fall asleep at night. He witnesses progressively disturbing obsessions, such as violent sexuality and personal betrayals of love. The haunted inner life analyzed by Freud was infiltrating fiction: for Proust redemption lay in producing beauty from the raw material of life, not in promoting outmoded conventions of decency and morality.

The Irish writer James Joyce and the English writer Virginia Woolf shared Proust's vision of an interior self built on memories and sensations. Joyce in *Ulysses* (1922) and Woolf in *Mrs. Dalloway* (1925) illuminated the fast-moving inner lives of their characters in the course of a single day. In one of *Ulysses'* most celebrated passages, a long interior monologue traces a woman's lifetime of erotic and emotional sensations. Woolf believed that the war dissolved the solid society from which absorbing stories and fascinating characters were once fashioned. Her characters experience fragmented conversations, momentary sensations, and incomplete relationships.

The other view of the future focused not on the interior life of traumatized society but on the promise of technology. Avant-garde artists before the war had celebrated the new, the futuristic, the utopian. After the war, like Jules Amar crafting prostheses for shattered limbs, they were optimistic that technology could make an entire society whole. The aim of art, observed one of them, "is not to decorate

■ **Virginia Woolf**
Along with Marcel Proust and James Joyce, Virginia Woolf represented the peak of literary modernism with its emphasis on interior states of mind and disjointed, dreamlike slices of reality. Woolf's novels and essays also captured the unappreciated centrality of women, who provided an array of personal services to their more highly valued husbands. Woolf boldly announced that for a woman to be as creative as a man, she needed to be partially relieved of the burdens of family and to have "a room of [her] own."
(Gisele Freund/Photo Researchers, Inc.)

our life but to organize it." German architects and artists influenced by the Bauhaus school of design (after the idea of a craft association, or *Bauhütte*) created streamlined office buildings and designed functional furniture, utensils, and decorative objects, many of them inspired by forms from "untainted" East Asia and Africa. Russian artists, temporarily entranced by the Communist experiment, optimistically wrote novels about cement factories and created ballets about steel—an element common to artificial limbs and to advanced, utopian design.

Artists fascinated by technology and machinery were drawn to the most modern of all countries: the United States. Hollywood films, glossy advertisements, and the bustling metropolis of New York tempted careworn Europeans. They were especially attracted to jazz, the improvisational music emanating from Harlem. African American jazz musicians showed a resiliency of spirit, and performers such as Josephine Baker (1906–1976) and Louis Armstrong (1900–1971) became international sensations when they toured Europe's capital cities. Like jazz, the skyscrapers rising in New York provided Europeans with a potent example of avant-garde expression that rejected a terrifying past and boldly embraced the future.

The Communist Utopia

Communism also promised a shining future and a modern, technological culture. But the Bolsheviks encountered powerful obstacles to consolidating their rule. In the early 1920s, peasant bands called Green Armies revolted against the policy of war communism that permitted the government to seize agricultural produce. Industrial production stood at only 13 percent of prewar levels; the civil war had produced still more casualties; shortages of housing affected everyone; and millions of refugees clogged the cities and roamed the countryside. In the early spring of 1921, workers in Petrograd and sailors at the nearby naval base at Kronstadt revolted. They protested their short rations and the privileged standard of living that Bolshevik supervisors enjoyed, and they called for "soviets without Communists"— that is, a return to the early Bolshevik promise of a worker state.

The government had many of the rebels shot, but the Kronstadt revolt pushed Lenin to institute reform. His New Economic Policy (NEP) returned parts of the economy to the free market. This temporary compromise with capitalist methods allowed peasants to sell their grain freely and to profit from free trade in consumer goods. The state still controlled large industries and banking, but the NEP encouraged people to produce, sell, and even, in the words of one leading Communist, "get rich." Consumer goods and more food to eat soon became available. Some peasants and merchants did indeed get rich, but many more remained impoverished. The rise of "NEPmen," who bought and furnished splendid homes and who cared only about conspicuous consumption, belied the Bolshevik goal of a classless utopia.

Protest erupted within Communist ranks. At the 1921 party congress, a group called the Worker Opposition objected to the party's usurpation of economic control from worker organizations and pointed out that the NEP was an agrarian program, not a proletarian one. In response to such charges of growing bureaucratization, Lenin suppressed the Worker Opposition faction and set up procedures for purging dissidents. Bolshevik leaders also tightened their grip on politics by making the Communist revolution a cultural reality that would inform people's daily lives and reshape their thoughts. Party leaders invaded the countryside to set up classes in a variety of political and social subjects, and volunteers harangued the public about the importance of literacy—only 40 percent on the eve of World War I. To facilitate social equality between men and women, which was part of the Marxist vision of the future, the state made birth control, abortion, and divorce readily available. The commissar for public welfare, Aleksandra Kollontai (1872–1952), promoted birth-control education and the establishment of day care for children of working parents.

The bureaucracy swelled to bring modern culture to every corner of life. *Hygiene* and *efficiency* became watchwords, as they were in the rest of Europe. Such agencies as the Zhenotdel (Women's Bureau) sought to teach women about their rights under communism and about modern sanitary practices. Efficiency experts aimed to replace tsarist backwardness with technological modernity based on American techniques. The short-lived government agency Proletkult tried to develop proletarian culture through such undertakings as workers' universities, a workers' encyclopedia, a workers' theater, and workers' publishing. Russian artists experimented with blending high art and technology in mass culture, and composers punctuated their music with the sound of train or factory whistles. The poet Vladimir Mayakovsky edited a journal advocating utilitarian art, wrote verse praising his Communist passport and essays promoting toothbrushing, and staged uproarious farces for ordinary citizens.

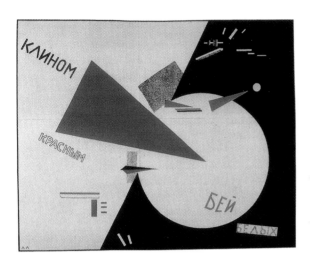

■ **El Lissitzky, *Beat the Whites with the Red Wedge* (1919)**
Russian artist El Lissitzky traveled Europe to bring news of Soviet experimentation. In particular, the Soviets were taken with the new physics, and their works of art surrounded the viewer with geometric forms. But abstract art was also political: in this 1919 painting, the "red" wedge uses the force of physical principles to defeat the objectively greater counterrevolutionary power of the "whites."
(David King Collection.)

As with war communism, many resisted the reshaping of culture to "modern" or "Western" standards. Bolsheviks threatened everyday customs and the distribution of power within the family. As Zhenotdel workers moved into the countryside, for example, they attempted to teach women to behave as men's equals. Peasant families were still strongly patriarchal, however, and Zhenotdel activists threatened gender relations. In Islamic regions incorporated from the old Russian Empire into the new Communist one, Bolsheviks urged Muslim women to remove their veils and change their way of life, but fervent Muslims often attacked both Zhenotdel workers and women who followed their advice.

In the spring of 1922, Lenin suffered a debilitating stroke, and in January 1924, amid ongoing cultural experimentation, factional fighting, and repression, the architect of the Bolshevik Revolution died. The party congress declared the day of his death a permanent holiday, changed the name of Petrograd to Leningrad, and elevated the deceased leader into a secular god. After Lenin's death, no one was allowed to criticize anything associated with his name, a situation that paved the way for abuses of power by later Communist leaders.

Joseph Stalin (1879–1953), who held the powerful position of general secretary of the Communist Party, led the deification of Lenin. Organizing the Lenin cult and dealing with thousands of local party officials gave Stalin the opportunity to dispense an enormous amount of patronage, and his welding in 1924 of Russian and non-Russian regions into the Union of Soviet Socialist Republics gave him a claim to executive accomplishment. Wary of Stalin's growing influence and ruthlessness, Lenin in his last will and testament had asked that "the comrades find a way to remove Stalin." Stalin, however, discredited Leon Trotsky, his chief rival, and prevented Lenin's will from being publicized. Bringing in several hundred thousand new party members who owed their positions in government and industry to him, Stalin by 1928–1929 was advancing toward complete dictatorship in the USSR.

Fascism on the March in Italy

Political chaos and postwar discontent brought Benito Mussolini (1883–1945) to power in Italy. Like the Bolsheviks, he promised an efficient utopia. Italian ire was first aroused when the Allies at Paris refused to honor the territorial promises of the Treaty of London. Domestic unrest swelled when peasants and workers protested their economic plight, made worse by the slump of the early 1920s. Since the late nineteenth century, many Europeans had come to blame parliaments for their ills. So Italians were responsive when Mussolini, a socialist journalist who turned to the radical right, built a personal army (the Black Shirts) of veterans and the unemployed to overturn parliamentary government. In 1922, his supporters, known as Fascists, started a march on Rome, forcing King Victor Emmanuel III (r. 1900–1946) to make the dynamic Mussolini prime minister.

The Fascist movement flourished in the soil of poverty, social unrest, and wounded national pride. It attracted to its bands of Black Shirts many young men who felt cheated of glory by the Allies and veterans who missed the vigor of military life. The *fasces*, an ancient Roman symbol depicting a bundle of sticks wrapped around an ax with the blade exposed, served as the movement's emblem; to Mussolini's supporters it represented both unity and force. Unlike Marxism, fascism scoffed at coherent ideology: "Fascism is not a church," Mussolini announced upon taking power in 1922. "It is more like a training ground." Fascism was thus defined by its political grounding in an instinctual male violence and its opposition to the "antinationalist" socialist movement and parliamentary rule.◆

Mussolini consolidated his power by making criticism of the state a criminal offense and by violently steamrolling parliamentary opposition. Fascist bands demolished socialist newspaper offices, attacked striking workers, used their favorite tactic of forcing castor oil (which causes diarrhea) down the throats of socialists, and even murdered certain powerful opponents. Yet this brutality and the sight of the Black Shirts marching through the streets like disciplined soldiers signaled to many Italians that their country was ordered and modern. Large landowners and businessmen approved Fascist attacks on strikers and financially supported the movement. Their generous funding allowed Mussolini to build a large staff by hiring the unemployed and thus fostering the belief that Fascists could spark the economy when no one else could.

In addition to violence, Mussolini used mass propaganda and the media to foster support for a kind of military campaign to remake Italy. Peasant men huddled around radios to hear him call for a "battle of wheat" to enhance farm productivity. Peasant women, responding to his praise of maternal duty, adored him for appearing to value womanhood. In the cities, the government launched avant-garde architecture projects, designed new statues and public adornments, and used public

---

◆ For a primary source that details Mussolini's political theory, see Document 66, Benito Mussolini, "The Doctrine of Fascism."

■ Mussolini and the Black Shirts

For movements like fascism, the best society was one controlled by militarized politics that killed its critics and political opponents. Fascism saw parliamentary democracies as effeminate and doomed in the modern world, which would need dictators and obedient warriors to make it strong, efficient, and machinelike. Thus, in the name of promoting state power, Mussolini gained adherents both within and outside of Italy. (Farabolafoto.)

relations promoters to advertise its achievements. Mussolini claimed that he made the trains run on time, and this one triumph of modern technology fanned people's hopes that he could restore order out of wartime and postwar chaos.

Mussolini added a strong dose of traditional values and prejudices to his modern order. Although he was an atheist, he recognized the importance of Catholicism to most Italians. In 1929, the Lateran Agreement between the Italian government and the church made the Vatican a state under papal sovereignty. The government recognized the church's right to determine marriage and family doctrine and endorsed its role in education. In return, the church ended its criticism of Fascist tactics. Mussolini also introduced a "corporate" state that denied individual political rights in favor of duty to the state. Corporatist decrees in 1926 organized employers, workers, and professionals into groups or corporations that would settle grievances and determine conditions of work. These decrees outlawed

IMPORTANT DATES			
1914, August	World War I begins	**1919**	Constitution for German republic drawn up at Weimar
1914–1925	Suffrage for women expands	**1919–1920**	Paris Peace Conference redraws the map of Europe
1916	Irish nationalists stage Easter Uprising against British rule	**1922**	By Anglo-Irish treaty of 1921, Ireland is split in two: the inde-
1917, March	Revolution in Russia overturns tsarist autocracy		pendent Irish Free State in the south and British-affiliated
1917, April	The United States enters World War I		Ulster in the north; Fascists march on Rome; Mussolini becomes Italy's prime minister;
1917, November	Bolshevik Revolution in Russia		T. S. Eliot publishes "The Waste Land"; James Joyce publishes
1918, March	Russia signs Treaty of Brest-Litovsk and withdraws from the war	**1924**	*Ulysses* Lenin dies; Stalin and Trotsky contend for power
1918, November	Revolutionary turmoil throughout Germany; the kaiser abdicates; armistice ends fighting of World War I	**1924–1929**	Period of general economic prosperity and stability
1918–1922	Civil war in Russia	**1929, October**	Stock market crash in United States

independent labor unions and peasant groups, effectively ending societal and work-place activism. Mussolini drew more applause from business leaders when he an-nounced cuts in women's wages; and then late in the 1920s he won the approval of civil servants, lawyers, and professors by banning women from those professions. Mussolini did not want women out of the workforce altogether but aimed to con-fine them to low-paying jobs as part of his scheme for reinvigorating men.

Mussolini's admirers were numerous across the West and included Adolf Hitler, who throughout the 1920s had been building a paramilitary group of storm troop-ers and a political organization called the National Socialist German Workers' Party, or Nazis. During his brief stint in jail for the Beer Hall Putsch in 1923, Hitler wrote *Mein Kampf* ("My Struggle," 1925), which articulated both a vicious anti-Semitism and a political psychology for manipulating the masses. Hitler was fascinated by the dramatic success of the Fascists' march on Rome, by Mussolini's legal accession to power, and by his ability to thwart socialists and trade unionists. However, the austere conditions that had allowed Mussolini to rise to power in 1922 no longer existed in Germany. Although Hitler was welding the Nazi Party into a strong po-litical instrument, the Weimar parliamentary government was actually working as the decade wore on.

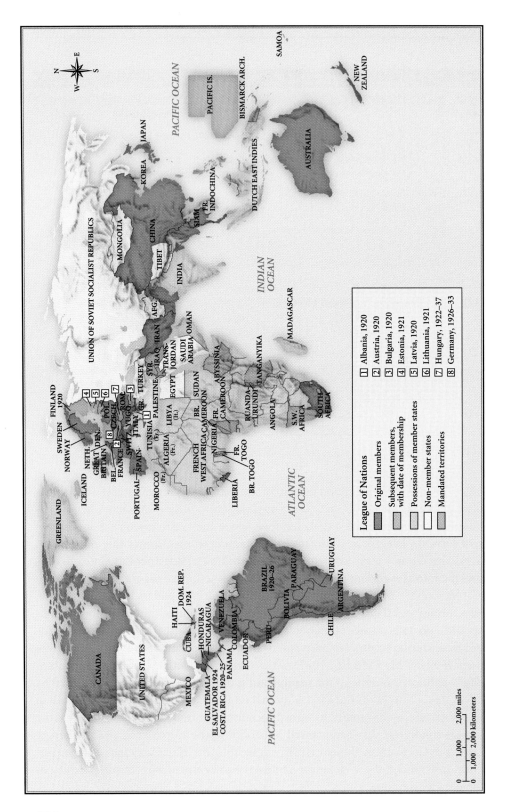

League of Nations

- ☐ Original members
- ☐ Subsequent members, with date of membership
- ☐ Possessions of member states
- ☐ Non-member states
- ☐ Mandated territories

1 Albania, 1920
2 Austria, 1920
3 Bulgaria, 1920
4 Estonia, 1921
5 Latvia, 1920
6 Lithuania, 1921
7 Hungary, 1922–37
8 Germany, 1926–33

■ **MAPPING THE WEST Europe and the World in 1929**
The map reflects the partitions and nations that came into being as a result of war and revolution, while it obscures the increasing movement toward throwing off colonial rule. The year 1929 was the true high point of empire: the desire for empire would diminish after 1929 except in Italy, which still craved colonies, and in Japan, which continued searching for land and resources to fuel its rapid growth.

Conclusion

The year 1929 was to prove just as fateful as 1914 had been. In 1914, an orgy of death had begun, leading to tens of millions of casualties, the destruction of major dynasties, and the collapse of aristocratic classes. For four years, war promoted the free play of military technology, virulent nationalism, and the control of everyday life by bureaucracy. While dynasties collapsed, the centralization of power increased the scope of the nation-state. The Peace of Paris in 1919 left Germans bitterly resentful, and in eastern and central Europe it created new states built on principles of nationalist ethnic unity—a settlement that, given the intense intermingling of ethnicities, religions, and languages in the area, failed to guarantee a peaceful future.

War furthered the development of mass society. It leveled social classes on the battlefield and in the graveyard, standardized political thinking through wartime propaganda, and extended many political rights to women for their war effort. Peacetime turned improved techniques of wartime production toward churning out consumer goods and technological innovations like air transport, cinema, and radio transmission for greater numbers of people. Modernity in the arts intensified after the war, probing the nightmarish battering endured by all segments of the population.

By the end of the 1920s, the legacy of war had so militarized politics that strongmen had come to power in Hungary, Poland, Romania, the Soviet Union, and Italy, and Adolf Hitler was waiting in the wings in Germany. Many Westerners were impressed by the tough, modern efficiency of the Fascists and Communists, who made parliaments and citizen rule seem out-of-date, even effeminate. Fascist and Communist commitment to violence, compared to that in the war, seemed so tame. When the U.S. stock market crashed in 1929 and economic disaster circled the globe, authoritarian solutions and militarism continued to look appealing. What followed was a series of catastrophes even more devastating than World War I.

Suggested References for further reading and online research appear on page SR-32 at the back of the book.

www.bedfordstmartins.com/huntconcise   See the ONLINE STUDY GUIDE to assess your mastery of the material covered in this chapter.

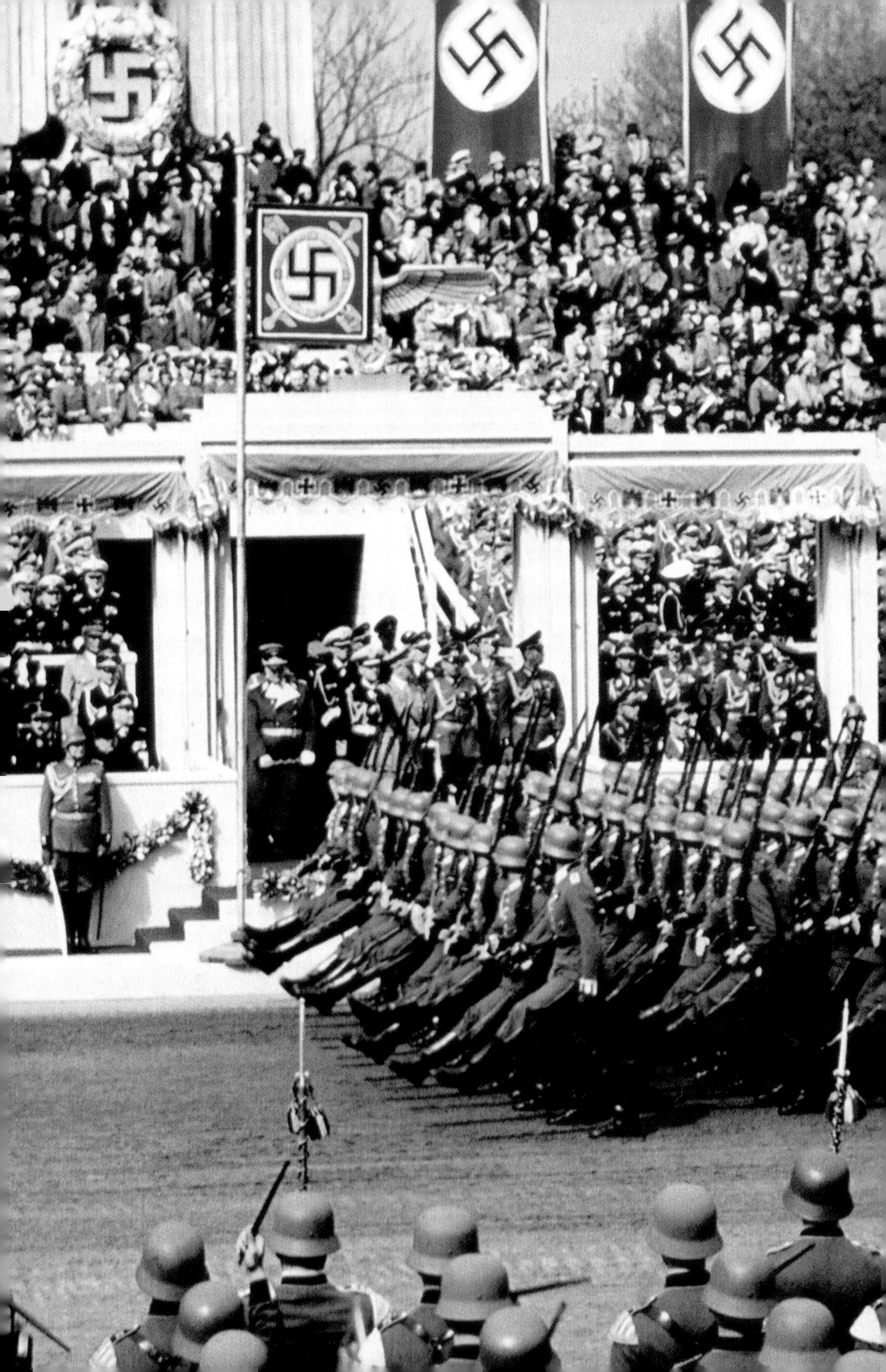

An Age of Catastrophes
1929–1945

WHEN ETTY HILLESUM MOVED TO AMSTERDAM in the early 1930s to attend law school, an economic depression gripped the world. A resourceful young Dutch woman, Hillesum pieced together a living as a housekeeper and part-time language teacher. The pressures and pleasures of everyday life blinded her, however, to Adolf Hitler's spectacular rise to power in Germany on a platform demonizing her fellow Jews for the economic slump. World War II ruptured her world. The German conquest of the Netherlands in 1940 led to persecution of Dutch Jews and brought Hillesum to the shattering realization, noted in her diary: "What they are after is our total destruction." The Nazis started relocating Jews to camps in Germany and Poland. Hillesum went to work for Amsterdam's Jewish Council, which was compelled by the Nazis to organize the transportation of Jews to the east. Changing from self-absorbed student to heroine, she did what she could to help other Jews and minutely recorded the deportation. "I wish I could live for a long time so that one day I may know how to explain it." When she was taken prisoner, she smuggled out letters describing the brutal treatment in the transit camps. Etty Hillesum never fulfilled her ambition to become a professional writer: she died in the Auschwitz death camp in November 1943.

The U.S. stock market crash of 1929 opened a horrific era in world history. During the Great Depression of the 1930s, suffering was global, intensifying social grievances throughout the world. In Europe, many people turned to military-style

■ **Nazis on Parade**
By the time Hitler came to power in 1933, Germany was mired in economic depression. Hated by Communists, Nazis, and conservatives alike, the German republic had few supporters. To Germans still reeling from their defeat in World War I, the Nazis looked as though they would restore national power by defeating enemies both within and beyond Germany's borders. Hitler took his cue from Mussolini by promising an end to democracy and tolerance. (Hugo Jaeger/LIFE/Time Pix.)

www.bedfordstmartins.com/huntconcise See the ONLINE STUDY GUIDE for more help in analyzing this image.

strongmen for answers. Adolf Hitler roused the German masses to rededicate themselves to national greatness. Authoritarian, militaristic, and fascist regimes spread to Portugal, Spain, Poland, Hungary, Japan, China, and elsewhere, trampling on representative institutions. Joseph Stalin oversaw the Soviet Union's rapid industrialization and justified the killing of millions of citizens as being necessary for Soviet growth.

The international scene became doubly menacing because elected leaders in the democracies reacted cautiously to the depression and to fascist aggression. In an age of new mass media, civilian leaders appeared weak and fearful of conflict, while dictators in uniform looked bold and decisive. The German invasion of Poland in 1939 finally roused the democracies, and World War II erupted in Europe. By the end of 1941, the war had spread to the rest of the world with the United States, Great Britain, and the Soviet Union allied in combat against Germany, Italy, and Japan. Tens of millions would perish in this war because technology and ideology had become more deadly than they had been just two decades earlier. Half the dead were civilians, among them Etty Hillesum, whose only "crime" was being a Jew.

The Great Depression

The depression triggered by the U.S. stock market crash of 1929 threw millions out of work and brought suffering to rural and urban folk alike. The whole world felt the depression's impact as commerce and investment in industry fell off, social life and gender roles were upset, and the birthrate plummeted. From peasants in Asia to industrial workers in Germany and the United States, the lives of large segments of the global population were ravaged.

Economic Disaster

In the 1920s, U.S. corporations and banks as well as millions of individual Americans had optimistically invested their money in the stock market or, more often, borrowed money to invest. Taking advantage of easy credit, they bought shares in popular new companies, confident that these investments would yield endless profits. Then, in an attempt to stabilize the market, the Federal Reserve Bank—the nation's central bank, which controlled financial policy—tightened the availability of credit. Brokers demanded that their clients immediately repay the money they had borrowed to buy stock. When millions of shares of stock were sold to pay brokerage bills, the market collapsed. Between early October and mid-November 1929, the value of businesses listed on the U.S. stock market dropped from $87 billion to $30 billion.

The crash spawned a global depression because the United States, a leading international creditor, had financed the relative economic growth of the previous five years. Suddenly strapped for credit, U.S. financiers cut back on loans and called

ILLUSTRAZIONE DEL POPOLO

■ Italian Newspaper Depicts Crash on Wall Street
The collapse of the U.S. stock market was felt around the world, from Italian cities to the Asian countryside. Credit, the lifeblood of business, dried up. Governments greatly increased import tariffs to protect their nations' industries, thereby curtailing trade. At first, they also cut back on aid to unemployed people, reducing consumer purchasing, worsening financial hardship, and inflicting psychological pain. (Mary Evans Picture Library.)

in debts, undermining banks and industry at home and abroad. The recent U.S. lead in industrial production and the rise of Japanese manufacturing compounded the collapse in Europe. A decline in consumer buying and overproduction further eroded the European economy, from the aging industries of Britain to the fledgling factories of eastern Europe.

The Great Depression left no sector of the world economy unscathed, and government actions worsened the economic catastrophe. To spur their economies, governments used standard tools such as budget cuts and high tariffs against foreign goods, but these policies further dampened trade and spending in the great industrial powers. (See "Taking Measure," page 910.) Great Britain, with its textile, steel, and coal industries near ruin because of out-of-date technology and foreign competition, had close to 3 million unemployed in 1932. By 1933, almost 6 million German workers, about one-third of the workforce, were unemployed, and many Germans were underemployed. France had a more self-sufficient economy, but big businesses such as the innovative Citroën car manufacturer began to fail, and by the mid-1930s more than 800,000 French people had lost their jobs.

In the agricultural sector, prices had been declining for several years because of abundant harvests and technological innovation. The onset of economic

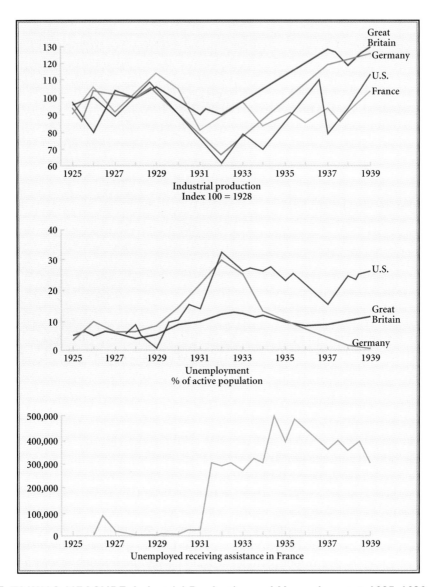

■ **TAKING MEASURE** Industrial Production and Unemployment, 1925–1939

The depression had many dimensions, both measurable and psychological. A calamitous fall in production in the most advanced industrial countries—Germany and the United States—was accompanied by rising unemployment. Whatever the resistance to providing government assistance, the trend toward the welfare state continued, moving from veterans' and old-age pensions to unemployment compensation, as the case of France demonstrates. Although less-industrialized countries around the world experienced smaller cuts in production, for them even the smallest decline was a setback on the road to modernizing their economies.

(Data adapted from V. R. Berghahn, *Modern Germany: Society, Economy, and Politics in the Twentieth Century*, 2d ed. [New York: Cambridge University Press, 1987], 284, and *Atlas Historique, histoire de l'humanité de la préhistoire à nos jours* [Paris: Hachette, 1987].)

depression forced creditors to foreclose on farms and confiscate equipment. Millions of small farmers had no money to buy the chemical fertilizers and motorized machinery they needed to remain competitive; they, too, went under. In eastern and southern Europe, peasants who had pressed for the redistribution of land after World War I could not afford to operate their newly acquired farms. In Poland, many of the 700,000 new landowners fell into debt trying to make their farms viable. Eastern European governments often ignored the farmers' plight—a situation that increased tensions in rural society.

Social Effects of the Crash

Life during the Great Depression was not uniformly bleak. Despite the slump, modernization proceeded. Bordering English slums, one traveler in the mid-1930s noticed, were "filling stations and factories that look like exhibition buildings, giant cinemas and dance halls and cafés, bungalows with tiny garages, cocktail bars, Woolworth's [and] swimming pools." Municipal and national governments continued road construction and sanitation projects. Running water, electricity, and sewage pipes were installed in many homes for the first time. New factories manufactured synthetic fabrics, electrical products such as stoves, and automobiles—all of them in demand. With government assistance, industry developed in eastern Europe. In Romania, for example, industrial production increased by 55 percent between 1929 and 1939.

Throughout the 1930s, the majority of Europeans and Americans had jobs, and people with steady employment benefited from a drastic drop in prices. Despite the depression, many service workers, managers, and business leaders enjoyed considerable prosperity. People with jobs, however, worried about becoming unemployed and having to scrape, like thousands of others, for a bare existence. In towns with heavy industry, sometimes more than half the population was out of work. In England in the mid-1930s, close to 20 percent of the population lacked adequate food, clothing, or housing. In a 1932 school assignment, a German youth wrote: "My father has been out of work for two and a half years. He thinks that I'll never find a job." Thus, despite the prosperity of many people, a dark cloud of fear and resentment settled over Western society.

The economic catastrophe upset social life and strained gender relations. Women often found low-paying jobs doing laundry and cleaning houses. Unemployed men sometimes stayed home all day, increasing the tension in small, overcrowded apartments. Men who stayed home sometimes took over the housekeeping chores but often felt that this "women's work" demeaned their masculinity. As many women became breadwinners, men could be seen standing on street corners begging—a rearrangement of gender expectations that fueled discontent. Young men in cities faced severe unemployment. Some loitered in parks, intruding in areas usually frequented by mothers and their children and old people. As the percentage of farmworkers in the western European population decreased, rural men also faced the erosion of patriarchal authority, once central in overseeing farm labor and allocating property among inheritors. Demagogues everywhere berated parliamentary politicians for their failure to stop the collapse of traditional values. The climate was thus primed for Nazi and fascist politicians who promised to restore prosperity and male dignity.

Politicians of all stripes forecast national collapse as declining birthrates (after a brief postwar upturn) combined with the economic decline. In difficult economic times, people chose to have fewer children. There were other reasons, too, for falling birthrates. Mandatory education and more years of required schooling, enforced more strictly after World War I, resulted in greater expenses for parents. Working-class children no longer earned wages to supplement the family income; instead, they cost the family money while they went to school. As family-planning centers opened, knowledge of birth control spread to the working and lower-middle classes, who continued the half-century-long trend of cutting family size.

Many politicians used the population "crisis" to gain votes by igniting racism: "superior" peoples were selfishly failing to breed, they charged, and "inferior" peoples were poised to take their place. This racism took a violent form in eastern Europe, where the rural population was growing because of increased life expectancy despite an overall drop in the birthrate. The population increase compounded the burdens of eastern European farm families, who faced an unprecedented struggle for survival. Throughout eastern Europe, peasant political parties blamed Jewish bankers for farm foreclosures and Jewish civil servants (of whom there were actually very few) for new taxes and inadequate relief programs. Thus population issues along with economic misery fueled ethnic hatred and anti-Semitism.

Global Dimensions of the Crash

The effects of the depression extended beyond the West, further accelerating the pace of change and spread of discontent in the European colonial empires. World War I and postwar investment had generated economic development, a rising population, and explosive urban growth in Asia, Africa, and Latin America. Between 1920 and 1940, Shanghai ballooned from 1.7 million to 3.75 million residents, Calcutta from 1.8 million to 3.4 million. The depression, however, cut the demand for copper, tin, and other raw materials and for the finished products made in urban factories beyond the West. It drove down the price of foodstuffs such as rice and coffee, and this proved disastrous to people who had been forced to grow a single cash crop. However, the economic picture was uneven in the colonies as well as in Europe. Established industrial sectors of the Indian economy, for instance, gained strength. In textiles, India achieved virtual independence from British cloth.

Economic distress added to smoldering grievances. Millions of African and Asian colonial troops fought for Britain and France in World War I, but after the war these countries gave little back to their colonial populations. In fact, the League of Nations charter pointedly omitted any reference to the principle of racial equality demanded by people of color at the Paris Peace Conference. Their resolve fortified by these slights and by the model of Japan's and their own growing industrial competence, colonial peoples focused on winning independence.

In the 1930s, upper-class Indians who had organized to gain rights from Britain in the late nineteenth century were joined by millions of working people, including hundreds of thousands of returning soldiers. The charismatic Mohandas K. Gandhi (1869–1948) emerged as the leader for Indian independence. Of privileged birth and trained in England as a Western-style lawyer, Gandhi embraced Hindu self-denial, rejecting the elaborate trappings of British life in favor of simple clothing made of thread he had spun. His followers called him "Mahatma," a Hindu term meaning "great-souled." Gandhi advocated *civil disobedience*—the deliberate but peaceful breaking of the law. He claimed that his tactics were modeled on British suffragists' tactics and on the teachings of Jesus, Buddha, and other spiritual leaders. Boycotting British-made goods and disobeying

■ **An Historic Act of Civil Disobedience**
Mohandas Gandhi used nonviolent resistance to challenge British rule. Because of the British government's monopoly on salt, Indians were prohibited from gathering this natural product and every Indian family had to pay a tax on salt. In 1930, Gandhi led his supporters on a 200-mile march to India's salt flats to protest the hated salt tax and to extract salt from seawater. Gandhi was arrested and jailed, but his followers continued their march to the sea.
(© Bettmann/Corbis.)

British laws, he aimed to end the Indians' traditional deference toward the British. British officials jailed Gandhi repeatedly and tried to split the independence movement by encouraging the rival Muslim League and fomenting Hindu-Muslim antagonism.

In the Middle East, Westernizer Mustafa Kemal (1881–1938), known as Atatürk ("first among Turks"), led the Turks to found the independent republic of Turkey in 1923 and to craft a capitalist economy. In an effort to nationalize and modernize Turkish culture, Kemal moved the national capital from Constantinople to Ankara in 1923, changed the ancient Greek *Constantinople* to the Turkish *Istanbul* in 1930, mandated Western dress for men and women, introduced the Latin alphabet, and abolished polygamy. In 1936, women received the vote and became eligible to serve in the Turkish parliament. Also in the Middle East, Persia loosened the European grip on its economy, forced the negotiation of oil contracts, updated its government, and in 1935 changed its name to Iran. In 1936, Britain agreed to end its military occupation of Egypt (though not the Suez Canal), fulfilling the promise of self-rule granted in 1922.

France made fewer concessions to colonized peoples. The French were obsessed by rising trade barriers in Europe and by their own population decline. Their trade with their colonies increased as their trade with Europe lagged, and the demographic surge in Asia and Africa bolstered French optimism. One French official remarked: "One hundred and ten million strong, France can stand up to Germany." Western-educated native leaders, however, contested their people's subjection. In 1930, the French government crushed a peasant uprising that Ho Chi Minh, founder of the Indochinese Communist Party, led.

Preoccupied with their empires, Britain and France let totalitarian forces spread unchecked throughout Europe during the crisis-ridden 1930s.

Totalitarian Triumph

Representative government collapsed in many countries under the sheer weight of social and economic crisis. After 1929, Italy's Benito Mussolini, the Soviet Union's Joseph Stalin, and Germany's Adolf Hitler were able to mobilize vast support for their violent regimes. Overlooking the brutal side of modern dictatorship, many people admired Mussolini and Hitler for the discipline they brought to social and economic life. In an age of crisis, utopian hopes led many to support political violence. Unity and obedience—not freedom and civil rights—were seen as keys to rebirth. The common use of violence has led scholars to apply the term *totalitarianism* to the Fascist, Nazi, and Communist regimes of the 1930s. The term refers to highly centralized systems of government that attempt to control society and ensure conformity through a single party and police terror. Forged in the crucible of war and its aftermath, totalitarian regimes broke with liberal principles and eventually waged war on their own citizens.

The Rise of Stalinism

In the 1930s, Joseph Stalin led the astonishing transformation of the USSR from a rural society into a formidable industrial power. Having taken firm control against Lenin's express wishes, Stalin ended the New Economic Policy (NEP), Lenin's temporary compromise between Marxism and capitalism, with the first of several five-year plans presented in 1929. Outlining a program for massive increases in the output of coal, iron ore, steel, and industrial goods, Stalin warned that without an end to Soviet backwardness "the advanced countries . . . will crush us." He thus established central economic planning—a policy used on both sides in World War I and increasingly favored by economists and industrialists around the world. Between 1928 and 1940, the number of Soviet workers in industry, construction, and transport grew from 4.6 million to 12.6 million. From 1927 to 1937, production in metallurgy and machinery rose 1,400 percent. Stalin's first five-year plan helped make the USSR a leading industrial nation.

Central planning led to the creation of a new elite of bureaucrats and industrial officials. Mostly party officials and technical experts, these managers dominated Soviet workers by limiting their ability to change jobs or move from place to place. Nonetheless, skilled workers as well as bureaucrats benefited substantially from the redistribution of privileges that accompanied industrialism and central planning. Compared with people working the land, both managers and workers in industry had better housing and higher wages, and Communist officials enjoyed additional perquisites such as country homes and luxurious vacations.

Unskilled workers faced a grim plight, often with real dedication. Newcomers from the countryside were herded into barracklike dwellings, even tents, and subjected to dangerous factory conditions. Many took pride in the skills they acquired: "We mastered this profession—completely new to us—with great pleasure," a female lathe operator recalled. More often, however, workers lacked the technical education and even the tools necessary to accomplish goals prescribed by the five-year plan. Because fulfilling the plan had top priority as a measure of progress toward the Communist utopia, official lying about productivity became ingrained in the economic system. Acceptance of grim conditions and fierce determination turned the Soviet Union from an illiterate peasant society into an advanced industrial economy in a single decade. Intense suffering was tolerated because Soviet workers believed in the ethos of "constant struggle, struggle, and struggle" to achieve a Communist society, in the words of one worker: "Man himself is being rebuilt."

In country and city alike, work was politicized. Stalin demanded more grain from peasants (who had prospered under NEP), both to feed the urban workforce and to export as a way to finance industrialization. Peasants resisted government demands by cutting production or withholding produce from the market. Faced with such recalcitrance, Stalin announced a new revolutionary challenge: "liquidation of the kulaks." The name *kulak* ("fist") was a derogatory term for prosperous peasants, but Stalin applied it to anyone who opposed his plans to end independent farming. In the winter of 1929–1930, party workers scoured villages for produce and forced villagers to identify the kulaks in their midst. Propaganda units instilled hatred for anyone connected with kulaks. One Russian remembered believing they were "bloodsuckers, cattle, swine, loathsome, repulsive: they had no souls; they stank." As "enemies of the state," whole families and even entire villages were robbed of their possessions, left to starve, or even murdered outright. Confiscated kulak land formed the basis of the *kolkhoz*, or collective farm, where peasants were to create a Communist agricultural system using cooperative farming and modern machinery.

Once work life was politicized, economic failure took on political meaning and ushered in violent purges. The inexperience of factory workers, farmers, and party officials with advanced industrialization often meant an inability to meet quotas. In the face of the murder of farmers and the experiment with collectivization, Soviet citizens starved as the grain harvest declined from 83 million tons in 1930 to 67 million in 1934. Stalin blamed failure on "wreckers," saboteurs of communism. To rid society of these villains, he instituted *purges*—state violence in the form of widespread arrests, imprisonment in labor camps, and executions. The purges touched nearly all segments of society, but "bourgeois" engineers were the first group condemned for causing low productivity. Trials of prominent figures followed. In 1934, Sergei Kirov, the popular first secretary of the Leningrad Communist Party, was murdered. Stalin used Kirov's death (which he may have instigated) as the pretext to try former Bolshevik leaders. Between 1936 and 1938, a series of "show trials" for alleged conspiracy to overthrow Soviet rule again targeted prominent Bolsheviks. Tortured and coerced to confess in court, most of those found guilty were shot.

The spirit of purge swept society. One woman poet described the scene: "Great concert and lecture halls were turned into public confessionals. . . . People did penance for [everything]. . . . Beating their breasts, the 'guilty' would lament that they had 'shown political short-sightedness' and 'lack of vigilance' . . . and were full of 'rotten liberalism.' " In 1937 and 1938, military leaders were arrested and executed without public trials; in some ranks every officer was killed. From industry and education to the party and the army, not even the Soviet power structure escaped the great purges. Simultaneously, the government developed a system of prison camps stretching several thousand miles from Moscow to Siberia. Called the *Gulag*—an acronym for the administrative arm of the camps—the system held millions of prisoners under lethal conditions. A million people died annually as a result of the harsh conditions. Insufficient food and housing, twelve- to sixteen-hour workdays at mining and other crushing labor, and regular beatings and murder of prisoners rounded out Gulag life, which became another aspect of Soviet violence.

Some historians have seen the purges as a clear-headed attempt by Stalin to eliminate barriers to total control; others, as the machinations of a psychopath. More recently, historians have judged the purges as resulting from power struggles among party officials and fueled by those looking for a quick route to the top. Still other interpretations see many of the denunciations and confessions as sincere expressions of workers' commitment to rooting out enemies of their proletarian utopia. Despite this historical controversy, there is no question about the outcome: ongoing arrests, incarcerations, and executions removed rivals to Stalin's power.

The 1930s also marked a sharp reversal of revolutionary experimentation in social life. Sexual freedom was forced into retreat. Much like the rest of Europe, the Soviet Union experienced a rapid decline in its birthrate in the 1930s. This drop, combined with the need to replace the millions of people lost since 1914, motivated Stalin to end the reproductive freedom of the early revolutionary years. Birth-control information and abortions became difficult to obtain. Lavish wedding ceremonies came back into fashion; divorce became difficult to obtain; and the state criminalized homosexuality. Whereas Bolsheviks had once derided the family as a "bourgeois" institution, propaganda now referred to the family unit as a "school for socialism." Nevertheless, women made gains. More and more women in rural areas learned to read and had access to health-care facilities. As the purges continued, positions in the lower ranks of the party opened to women, and women increasingly were accepted into the professions. The stress on women, particularly those in the industrial workforce, increased, however. In addition to working long hours in factories, they also waited in long lines to obtain scarce consumer goods, and they performed all household and child-care tasks under harsh conditions.

Cultural life was similarly paradoxical under Stalin. Stalinism brought avant-garde experimentation to an end, but modernist artists and intellectuals continued to promote their ability to mobilize the masses through appeals to the unconscious and the emotions in their works. Stalin endorsed this role, calling artists and writers "engineers of the soul," but he controlled their work through the Union of Soviet Writers. The union assigned housing, office space, supplies, equipment, and secretarial help and even determined the types of books authors could write. In return, the "comrade artist" adhered to the official style of "socialist realism," derived from the 1920s focus on the common worker as a type of social hero. Some artists, such as the poet Anna Akhmatova (1889–1966), refused to accept this system.

> Stars of death stood above us, and Russia,
> In her innocence, twisted in pain
> Under blood-spattered boots . . .

wrote Akhmatova in those years. Many others, including the composer Sergei Prokofiev (1891–1953), found ways to accommodate their talents to the state's demands. Prokofiev composed scores for the delightful *Peter and the Wolf* and for Sergei Eisenstein's 1938 film *Alexander Nevsky*, a work that transparently compared Stalin to the towering medieval rulers of the Russian people. Aided by adaptable artists, workers, and bureaucrats, Stalin stood triumphant as the 1930s drew to a close.

■ **N. J. Altman,** *Anna Akhmatova*
(1914)
*This modernist painting portrays the poet
when she was a centerpiece of literary salon life in Russia and the subject of several
avant-garde portraits. In the 1930s and
1940s, Akhmatova gave poetic voice to
Soviet suffering, recording in her verse
ordinary people's endurance of purges,
deprivation, and warfare. As she encouraged people to resist the Nazis during
World War II, Stalin allowed her to revive
Rus-sian patriotism instead of socialist
internationalism.*
(State Russian Museum, St. Petersburg/The
Bridgeman Art Library.)

Hitler's Rise to Power

Hitler ended German democracy. Since the early 1920s, he had been trying to rouse
the German people to crush the fragile Weimar Republic. In his coup attempt, in
his influential book *Mein Kampf* ("My Struggle," 1925), and in his leadership of the
Nazi Party, he drummed a message of anti-Semitism and the rebirth of the German
"race." When the Great Depression struck Germany, his party began to outstrip its
rivals in elections thanks in part to massive support from businessmen such as film
and press mogul Alfred Hugenberg. Hugenberg's newspapers relentlessly slammed
the Weimar government, blaming it for the disastrous economy and inflaming
wounded German pride over the defeat in World War I. Parliamentary government
practically ground to a halt in the face of economic crisis. The Reichstag failed to
approve emergency plans to improve the economy, and Hitler's followers made parliamentary government look even more inept by rampaging through the streets and
attacking Jews, Communists, and Social Democrats. By targeting all these as a
single, monolithic group of "Bolshevik" enemies, the Nazis won wide approval.

　　As a result of the depression, media publicity, and its own street tactics, Hitler's
National Socialist German Workers' Party (NSDAP)—the Nazi Party—which had
received little more than 2 percent of the vote in 1928, won almost 20 percent in
the Reichstag elections of 1930 and more than doubled its representation in 1932.

Many of Hitler's supporters, like Stalin's, were young and idealistic. In 1930, 70 percent of Nazi Party members were under forty, a stark contrast to the image of Weimar politicians as aged and ineffectual. Although businessmen provided substantial sums of money, Germans of every class supported the Nazis. The largest number of supporters came from the industrial working class, which had the most voters, but white-collar workers and members of the lower middle class joined the party in percentages out of proportion with their numbers in the population.

Hitler's modern propaganda techniques also served him well. His propaganda chief, Joseph Goebbels, released thousands of recordings of Hitler's speeches while circulating Nazi mementos widely among the citizenry.◆ Teenagers painted their fingernails with swastikas, a symbol used by the Nazis, and soldiers flashed metal match covers with Nazi insignia. Nazi rallies were masterpieces of political display. Hitler mesmerized the crowds as their *Führer*, or leader—a strong, superior being. Frenzied and inspirational, he seemed neither a calculating politician nor a rational bureaucrat but "the creative element," as one poet put it. In actuality, however, Hitler viewed the masses as tools. In *Mein Kampf* he explained his philosophy of how to deal with them:

> The receptivity of the great masses is very limited, their intelligence is small. In consequence of these facts, all effective propaganda must be limited to a very few points and must harp on those in slogans until the last member of the public understands what you want him to understand.

With Hitler, as with Stalin, mass politics reached terrifying and cynical proportions.

Nazi success along with Communist electoral strength in the 1932 Reichstag elections made the leader of one of those parties the logical choice as chancellor. Germany's conservative elites—from the military, industry, and the state bureaucracy—loathed the Communists and favored Hitler as a common type they thought they could easily manipulate. In January 1933, he was invited to become chancellor.

The Nazification of German Politics

Hitler took office amid jubilation in Berlin. Tens of thousands of storm troopers (SA or *Sturmabteilung*) holding blazing torches paraded through the streets. Millions of Germans celebrated Hitler's ascent to power. One recalled: "My father went down to the cellar and brought up our best bottles of wine. . . . And my mother wept for joy."

Within a month of Hitler's taking power, the elements of Nazi political domination were in place. In February 1933, the Reichstag building was gutted by fire. Hitler blamed the Communists and used the fire as the excuse for suspending civil rights, imposing censorship of the press, and prohibiting meetings of the opposition.

◆ For a primary source that reveals Hitler's remarkable talent to shape public opinion, see Document 67, Joseph Goebbels, "Nazi Propaganda Pamphlet."

■ Toys Depicting Nazis

As a totalitarian ideology, Nazism permeated everyday life. Nazi insignia decorated clothing, dishes, cigarette lighters, and even toys. Men and women became husbands and wives in accordance with Nazi rules and sent their children to Nazi clubs and organizations. Nazi songs, Nazi parades and festivals, and Nazi radio filled leisure hours. (Imperial War Museum, London.)

He had always claimed that *all* political parties except the NSDAP were his enemies. "Our opponents complain that we National Socialists, and I in particular, are intolerant and intractable," he declared. "They are right, we are intolerant! I have set myself one task, namely to sweep those parties out of Germany."

Storm troopers' political violence became a way of life. At the end of March, intimidated Reichstag delegates let pass the Enabling Act, which suspended the constitution for four years and allowed Nazi laws to take effect without parliamentary approval. Solid middle-class Germans approved the Enabling Act as a way to advance the creation of a *Volksgemeinschaft* ("people's community") of like-minded, racially pure Germans—"Aryans" in Nazi terminology. Heinrich Himmler headed the elite SS (*Schutzstaffel*) organization that protected Hitler, and he commanded the government's political police system. The Gestapo, an internal security police force organized by Hermann Goering, also enforced complete obedience to Nazism. These organizations had vast powers to arrest, execute, or imprison people in concentration camps, the first of which opened at Dachau near Munich in March 1933. The Nazis filled it and later camps with socialists, homosexuals, Jews, and others said to interfere with the *Volksgemeinschaft*. As one Nazi leader proclaimed:

> [*National socialism*] *does not believe that one soul is equal to another, one man equal to another. It does not believe in rights as such. It aims to create the German man of strength, its task is to protect the German people, and all . . . must be subordinate to this goal.*

Hitler deliberately blurred authority in the government and party so that confusion and bitter competition reigned. He thus prevented the emergence of coalitions against him and allowed himself to arbitrate the confusion, often with violence. When Ernst Roehm, leader of the SA and Hitler's long-time collaborator, called for a "second revolution" to end the corrupt influence of the old business and military elites on the Nazi leadership, Hitler ordered Roehm's assassination. The bloody "Night of the Long Knives" (June 30, 1934), during which hundreds of SA leaders and innocent civilians were killed, enhanced Hitler's support among conservatives. Nazism's terroristic politics remained as the foundation of Hitler's "Third Reich"—a German empire succeeding the empires of Charlemagne and William II.

New economic and social programs, especially those that put people back to work, also bolstered Hitler's regime. Economic revival built popular support, strengthened military industries, and provided the basis for German expansion. The Nazi government pursued *pump priming*—that is, stimulating the economy through government spending on tanks and airplanes and the Autobahn highway system. From farms to factories, the government demanded high productivity, and unemployment declined from a peak of almost 6 million in 1932 to 1.6 million by 1936. When labor shortages began to appear in some areas, the government conscripted single women into service as farmworkers and domestics. The Nazi Party closed down labor unions. Government bureaucrats classified jobs, determined work procedures, and set pay levels, rating women's jobs lower than men's regardless of the level of expertise required. Imitating Stalin, Hitler announced a four-year plan in 1936 with the secret aim of preparing Germany for war by 1940, and he instituted central planning. His programs produced large deficits, which the spoils of future conquests were supposed to eliminate.

Hitler exercised unprecedented power over the workings of everyday life, especially gender roles. In June 1933, a bill took effect that encouraged "Aryans" (individuals whom the Nazis defined as racially pure Germans) to marry and have children. The bill provided for loans to "Aryan" newlyweds, but only to those couples in which the wife left the workforce. The loans were forgiven on the birth of a couple's fourth child. Nazi marriage programs enforced a nineteenth-century ideal of femininity; women were supposed to be subordinate so men would feel tough and industrious despite military defeat and economic depression.

Nazism impoverished ordinary life. Although 70 percent of households had "people's radios" by 1938, the programming that was broadcast was severely censored. Books like Remarque's *All Quiet on the Western Front* were banned, and in May 1933 a huge book-burning ceremony rid libraries of works by Jews, socialists, homosexuals, and modernist writers out of favor with the Nazis. Modern art in museums and in private collections was destroyed or confiscated, and laws took jobs from Jews and women and bestowed them on Nazi Party members. In the Hitler Youth organization, which boys and girls over age ten had to join, children learned to report to Nazi authorities any adults they suspected of disloyalty to the regime, even their own parents. Germans boasted that they could leave their bicycles outdoors at night without fear of robbery, but their world was filled with inform-ers—some 100,000 of them on the Nazi payroll. In general, the improved economy led many to believe that Hitler was working an economic miracle while restoring pride in Germany and the harmonious community of an imaginary past. For hun-dreds of thousands if not millions of Germans, however, Nazi rule in the 1930s brought anything but community.

Nazi Racism

The Nazis defined Jews as an inferior "race" dangerous to the superior "Aryan" or Germanic "race" and responsible for most of Germany's problems, including the defeat in World War I and the intensity of the depression. Hitler attacked many eth-nic and social groups, but he propelled the nineteenth-century politics of anti-Semitism to new and frightening heights. In the rhetoric of Nazism, Jews were "ver-min," "abscesses," "parasites," and "Bolsheviks," whom the Germans would have to eliminate to create a true *Volksgemeinschaft*. By defining the Jews as evil financiers and businessmen and as working-class Bolsheviks, Hitler fashioned an enemy for many segments of the German population to hate.

Nazi policy was called "racial," and it led to laws against "non-Aryans"—a group that, like "Aryans," was never defined. Racial classifications were made to appear scientific, however, by lists of physical and other characteristics that the Nazis claimed determined a person's "race." In 1935, the government enacted the Nuremberg Laws, legislation that specifically deprived Jews of citizenship, defined Jewishness according to a person's ancestry, ended special consideration for Jewish war veterans, and prohibited marriage between Jews and other Germans. Women whom the Nazis defined as "Aryan" faced increasing difficulty obtaining abortions or birth-control information, but both were readily available to the outcast groups, including Jews, gypsies, Slavs, and people with mental or physical disabilities. In the name of improving the "Aryan" race, German doctors helped organize the T4 proj-ect, which used carbon monoxide poisoning and other means to kill large numbers of people—200,000 with disabilities and the elderly—late in the 1930s, preparing the way for the even larger mass exterminations that would occur later.

Jews were forced into slave labor, evicted from their apartments, and prevented from buying most clothing and food. In 1938, a Jewish teenager, reacting to the ha-rassment of his parents, killed a German official. In retaliation, Nazis attacked some two hundred synagogues, smashed the windows of Jewish-owned stores, ransacked apartments of known or suspected Jews, and threw more than twenty thousand Jews into prisons and camps. The night of November 9–10 became known as *Kristallnacht*, the "Night of Broken Glass." Faced with relentless persecution, which some historians have called a "social death," by the outbreak of World War II in 1939 more than half of Germany's 500,000 Jews had emigrated. The confiscation of the emigrants' property enriched their neighbors and individual Nazis; the pay-ment of enormous emigration fees helped finance Germany's revival.

Democracies on the Defensive

Nazism, communism, and fascism offered bold new approaches to modern politics and new kinds of economic and social policies. Their leaders' energetic, military style of mobilizing the masses made the representative governments and democratic values of the United States, France, and Great Britain seem to be the effeminate, decadent systems of declining peoples. During the 1930s, democracies were on the defensive in a variety of arenas—economic, political, and cultural.

Confronting the Economic Crisis

As the depression wore on, some governments undertook notable experiments to solve social and economic crises and still maintain democratic politics. In the early days of the slump, U.S. president Herbert Hoover (1874–1964) opposed direct federal help to the unemployed and in the summer of 1932 even ordered the army to use tanks to break up a march of unemployed World War I veterans in Washington, D.C. With unemployment close to fifteen million, Franklin Delano Roosevelt, the wealthy, patrician governor of New York, defeated Hoover in the fall presidential election, promising innovation. Roosevelt (1882–1945) pushed through a torrent of legislation, known as the "New Deal," some of it inspired by the central control of the economy achieved during World War I: relief for businesses, price supports for hard-pressed farmers, and public works programs for unemployed youth. The Social Security Act of 1935 set up a fund to which employers and employees contributed. It provided retirement benefits for workers, unemployment insurance, and payments to dependent mothers, their children, and people with disabling physical conditions.

Roosevelt's New Deal advanced the trend toward the *welfare state*—a society in which the government guarantees a certain level of economic well-being for individuals and businesses—not only in the United States but elsewhere across the West. The New Deal angered businesspeople and the wealthy, who considered it "socialist." But even as the depression remained severe, Roosevelt (quickly nicknamed FDR) maintained widespread support. Like other successful politicians of the 1930s and thereafter, he made expert use of the mass media, especially in his "fireside chats" broadcast by radio to the American people. In sharp contrast to Mussolini and Hitler, however, Roosevelt aimed in his public statements to sustain—not to denounce—faith in democratic rights and popular government. Eager to separate themselves from Hoover's position, First Lady Eleanor Roosevelt (1884–1962) rushed to greet the next group of veterans marching on Washington and the president received a delegation of veterans at the White House. The Roosevelts insisted that justice and human rights must not be surrendered in difficult times. "We Americans of today . . . are characters in the living book of democracy," FDR told a group of teenagers in 1939. "But we are also its author." Lynchings, racial violence, and harsh discrimination continued to cause enormous suffering in the

■ **Fireside Chat with FDR**
President Franklin Delano Roosevelt was a master of words, uttering many memorable phrases
that inspired Americans during the depression and World War II. Here he addresses the nation on
August 23, 1938, over a radio hookup while Eleanor Roosevelt and his mother, Sarah, observe.
Although Roosevelt was disabled by polio, wore leg braces, and could not walk unassisted, the press
never showed or mentioned Roosevelt's impairment, even on the rare occasions when he used
crutches or a wheelchair in public. (© Hulton Getty/Liaison Agency.)

United States during the Roosevelt administration, nor did the economy fully
recover. But the president's media success and bold programs kept the masses committed to a democratic future.

Sweden also developed a coherent program for solving economic and population problems that reconceived the government's role in promoting social welfare
and economic democracy. Sweden industrialized later than western Europe and the
United States but had a tradition of community responsibility for working through
social and economic difficulties. Sweden succeeded in turning its economy around
in the 1930s and instituted central planning of the economy and social welfare programs. It also devalued the currency to make Swedish exports more attractive on
the international market. Thanks to pump-priming programs, Swedish productivity rose 20 percent between 1929 and 1935, a time when other democracies were
still experiencing decline.

Sweden addressed the population problem with government programs but
without racist and antidemocratic coercion. Alva Myrdal (1902–1986), a leading

member of Sweden's parliament, believed fertility rates reflected economic conditions and individuals' sense of their personal well-being. Acting on her advice to promote "voluntary parenthood," the government of Sweden started a loan program for married couples in 1937 and introduced prenatal care, free childbirth in a hospital, a food relief program, and subsidized housing for large families. By the end of the decade, almost 50 percent of all Swedish mothers were receiving government aid. Long a concern of feminists and other social reformers in Sweden, care of families became integral to the tasks of the modern state, which now saw itself as responsible for citizen welfare in hard times.

Because the United States, the most powerful democracy, had withdrawn from world leadership by refusing to participate in the League of Nations, Britain and France had greater responsibility for international peace and well-being than their postwar resources could sustain. When the Great Depression hit, Britain was already mired in economic difficulties. Faced with falling government revenues, Prime Minister Ramsay MacDonald, though leader of the Labour Party, reduced payments to the unemployed, and Parliament effectively denied unemployment insurance to women even though they had contributed to the unemployment fund. To protect jobs, the government imposed huge protective tariffs that actually discouraged a revival of international trade and did not relieve British misery. Only in 1933, with the economy continuing to worsen, did the government begin to take effective steps with massive programs of slum clearance, new housing construction, and health insurance for the needy.

Depression struck later in France, but the country endured a decade of public strife in the 1930s due to severe postwar demoralization, stagnant population growth, and wage cuts. Deputies with opposing views on the economic crisis frequently came to blows in the Chamber of Deputies, and governments were voted in and out with dizzying rapidity. Parisians took to the streets to protest the government's belt-tightening policies, and right-wing paramilitary groups mushroomed, attracting the unemployed, students, and veterans to the cause of ending representative government. In February 1934, the paramilitary groups joined Communists and other outraged citizens in riots around the parliament building. "Let's string up the deputies," chanted the crowd. "And if we can't string them up, let's beat in their faces, let's reduce them to a pulp." Hundreds of demonstrators were wounded and killed, but the antirepublican right lacked both substantial support outside Paris and a leader like Hitler or Mussolini capable of unifying its various groups.

Shocked into action by the force of fascism, French liberals, socialists, and Communists established an antifascist coalition known as the Popular Front. Until that time, such a merging of groups had been impossible in democratic countries because of Stalin's strict opposition to Communist collaboration with liberals and socialists, who disavowed Communist-style revolutions. As fascism spread throughout Europe, however, Stalin reversed course and allowed Communists to join such efforts. For just over a year in 1936–1937 and again very briefly in 1938, the French

Popular Front formed a government, with the socialist leader Léon Blum (1872–1950) as premier.

Like the American New Dealers and the Swedish Social Democrats, the French Popular Front instituted long-overdue reforms. Blum extended family subsidies and welfare benefits, and he appointed women to his government (though women in France still were not allowed to vote). In June 1936, the government guaranteed workers two-week paid vacations, a forty-hour workweek, and the right to collective bargaining. Working people would long remember Blum as the man who improved their living standards and provided them with benefits and vacations.

During its brief life, the French Popular Front offered the masses a youthful but democratic political culture. "In 1936 everyone was twenty years old," one man recalled, evoking the atmosphere of idealism. Local cultural centers sprang up, and to express their opposition to fascism, citizens celebrated Bastille Day and other democratic holidays with new enthusiasm. But despite this support from workers, the Popular Front governments were politically weak. Fearing for their investments, bankers and industrialists greeted Blum's appointment by sending their capital out of the country, leaving France financially strapped. "Better Hitler than Blum" was the slogan of the upper classes. Blum's government fell when it also lost the left by refusing material support in the fight against fascism in Spain. As in Britain, memories of World War I caused leaders to block crucial support to foreign democratic forces, such as the republicans in Spain, and to keep domestic military budgets small. The collapse of the antifascist Popular Front in late June 1937 showed the difficulties that pluralistic and democratic societies faced in crisis-ridden times.

Fledgling democracies in central Europe, hit hard by the depression, also fought the twin struggle for economic survival and representative government, but less successfully. In 1932, Engelbert Dollfuss (1892–1934) came to power in Austria, dismissing the parliament and ruling briefly as a dictator. Despite his authoritarian stance, Dollfuss would not submit to the Nazis, who assassinated him in 1934. In Hungary, where outrage over the Peace of Paris remained intense, a crippled economy resulted in right-wing general Gyula Gömbös (1886–1936) taking over in 1932. Gömbös reoriented his country's foreign policy toward Mussolini and Hitler. He stirred up anti-Semitism and ethnic hatreds and left considerable pro-Nazi feeling after his death in 1936. In democratic Czechoslovakia, the Slovaks, who were both poorer and less educated than the urbanized Czechs, built a strong Slovak Fascist Party. In Poland, Romania, Yugoslavia, and Bulgaria, ethnic tensions simmered, and the appeal of fascism grew as the Great Depression lingered.

Cultural Visions in Hard Times

Just as culture had been mobilized during World War I, cultural leaders now mobilized to meet the crisis of economic hard times and political menace. Some empathized with the situations of factory workers, homemakers, and shopgirls struggling to support themselves or their families; others, with the ever-growing numbers of the unemployed and destitute. In 1931, French director René Clair's film *À nous la liberté* ("Give Us Liberty") related prison life to work on a factory assembly line. In 1936, Charlie Chaplin's film *Modern Times* showed the Little Tramp again, this time as a factory worker so molded by his monotonous job that he assumes that anything he can see, even a coworker's body, needs mechanical adjustment. This sympathetic and humorous representation of the modern factory and hard times made Chaplin a hit even in the Soviet Union.

Media sympathy poured out to victims of the crisis. Women were portrayed alternately as the cause of and as the cure for society's problems. *The Blue Angel* (1930), a German film starring Marlene Dietrich, showed how a vital, modern woman could destroy men—and civilization; it depicted a woman's power to dominate over the ineffectuality of an impractical professor. In contrast, heroines in comedies and musicals behaved bravely, pulling their men out of the depths of despair and setting things right. For example, in *Keep Smiling* (1938) and other films, the British comedienne Gracie Fields portrayed spunky working-class women who remained cheerful despite hard times.

Techniques of modern art, such as montage, which overlaid two or more photos or parts of photos, were used to grab visual and psychic attention in the cultural battles of the 1930s. Some intellectuals turned away from experimentation with nonrepresentational forms as they drove home their antifascist, pacifist, or pro-

■ **Paul Klee, *Dancing with Fear* (1938)**
Swiss-German artist Paul Klee (1879–1940) explored modern art's ability to evoke universal truths behind surface reality. Delightful shapes and colors often marked his work, although he was always concerned with how technology would affect people's values. As the danger of Nazism's triumph mounted, Klee grew depressed and produced dark visions of fear and death.
("Tanze vor Angst," 1938, 90 [G 10] by Paul Klee. Paul-Klee-Stiftung, Kunstmuseum Bern, photo: Peter Lauri. © ARS, New York.)

worker beliefs. Popular Front writers created realistic studies of human misery and the threat of war that haunted life in the 1930s. The British writer George Orwell described his experiences among the poor of Paris and London, wrote investigative pieces about the unemployed in the north of England, and published an account of atrocities committed by both sides during the Spanish Civil War (1936–1939). Politicized, art reaffirmed Western values such as rationalism, rights, and concern for the poor. German writer Thomas Mann, a Christian, went into exile when Hitler came to power and began a series of novels based on the Old Testament hero Joseph to convey the struggle between humanist values and barbarism. The fourth volume, *Joseph the Provider* (1944), eulogized Joseph's welfare state, in which the granaries were full and the rich paid taxes so the poor might live decent lives. In *Three Guineas* (1938), one of her last works, the English writer Virginia Woolf rejected experimental form for a direct attack on militarism, poverty, and the oppression of women, claiming they were interconnected parts of a single, devastating ethos undermining Europe in the 1930s.

While writers rekindled moral concerns, scientists in research institutes and universities continued to point out limits to human understanding—limits that seemed at odds with the megalomaniacal pronouncements of dictators. Astronomer Edwin Hubble in California determined in the early 1930s that the universe was an expanding entity. Czech mathematician Kurt Gödel maintained that any mathematical system contains some propositions that are undecidable. The German physicist Werner Heisenberg developed the "uncertainty," or "indeterminacy," principle in physics. Scientific observation of atomic behavior, according to this theory, actually disturbs the atom and thereby makes precise formulations impossible. Even scientists, Heisenberg asserted, had to settle for statistical probability.

Religious leaders helped foster a spirit of resistance to dictatorship among religious people. The Swiss theologian Karl Barth encouraged rebellion against the Nazis, teaching that the faithful had to take seriously scriptural justifications of resistance to oppression. Pope Pius XI in his 1931 social encyclical (a letter addressed to the world on social issues), condemned the failure of modern societies to provide their citizens with a decent life and supported government intervention to create better moral and material conditions. The encyclical, *Quadragesimo Anno*, seemed to some an endorsement of the heavy-handed intervention of the fascists, but German Catholics frequently opposed Hitler, and religious commitment inspired many other individuals to oppose the rising tide of fascism.

The Road to World War II

In the wake of economic catastrophe, Hitler, Mussolini, and Japan's military leaders marched the world toward another catastrophic war. Each of these leaders believed that his nation was destined to rule a far larger territory. At first, many ordinary citizens and statesmen in Britain and France hoped that sanctions imposed by the League of Nations would work to contain aggression. Others, believing that the powers had rushed into World War I, counseled the appeasement of Mussolini and Hitler. The widespread desire for peace in the 1930s sprang from fresh and painful memories: the destruction of World War I and the economic turmoil of the Great Depression. But it left many people blind to Japanese actions in China, Hitler's expansionist goals, and the fascist attack on the Spanish republic. So brutal were the interwar years that some historians claim that along with World War I and World War II, they make up a "Thirty Years' War" of the twentieth century.

Japan, Germany, and Italy Strike

Japan's military leaders chafed to control more of Asia and saw China, the Soviet Union, and the other Western powers as obstacles to the empire's prosperity and the fulfillment of its destiny. Renewed military vigor was seen as key to pulling agriculture and small business from the depths of economic depression. The Japanese army took the lead. In September 1931, a train in the Chinese province of Manchuria blew up. Japanese officers used the explosion, which they had set, as an excuse to invade Manchuria, set up a puppet government, and push farther into China. The Japanese public agreed with journalistic calls for aggressive expansion to restore Japan's economy and boost the nation's prestige, and businessmen wanted new markets and resources for their burgeoning but wounded industries. Advocating Asian conquest as part of Japan's "divine mission," the military extended its influence in the government. By 1936–1937, Japan was spending 47 percent of its budget on arms.

The situation in East Asia had international repercussions. Japanese aggression compounded the effect of the growing international market in Japanese goods. The League of Nations condemned the invasion but imposed no sanctions that would have put economic teeth into its condemnation. Nevertheless, the rebuff outraged the Japanese public and goaded the government to ally with Hitler and Mussolini. In 1937, Japan attacked China again, justifying its offensive as a first step toward liberating the region

The Road to World War II	
1929	Global depression begins with U.S. stock market crash
1931	Japan invades Manchuria
1933	Hitler comes to power in Germany
1935	Italy invades Ethiopia
1936	Civil war breaks out in Spain; Hitler remilitarizes the Rhineland
1937	Japan invades China
1938	Germany annexes Austria; European leaders meet in Munich to negotiate with Hitler
1939	Germany seizes Czechoslovakia; Hitler and Stalin sign nonaggression pact; Germany invades Poland; Britain and France declare war on Germany

from Western imperialism. Hundreds of thousands of Chinese were massacred in the "Rape of Nanjing"—an atrocity so named because of the brutality toward girls and women and the grim acts of torture perpetrated by the Japanese. President Roosevelt immediately announced an embargo on the U.S. export of airplane parts to Japan and later enforced stringent economic sanctions on the crucial raw materials that drove Japanese industry. But the Western powers, including the Soviet Union, did not effectively resist Japan's territorial expansion in Asia and the Pacific.

Like Japanese leaders, Mussolini and Hitler called their countries "have-nots." Mussolini threatened "permanent conflict" to expand Italy's borders, and Hitler's agenda included breaking free from the Versailles treaty's military restrictions and providing the "Aryans" with *Lebensraum* (living space) in which to thrive. Nazi plans called for territory to be seized from the "inferior" Slavic peoples and Bolsheviks, who would serve as slaves to the "Aryans" or would be moved to Siberia. Both dictators portrayed themselves as peace-loving men who resorted to extreme measures only to benefit their countries and humanity. Their anticommunism appealed to statesmen across Europe.

In the autumn of 1933, Hitler announced Germany's withdrawal from the League of Nations. In 1935, Hitler loudly rejected the clauses of the Treaty of Versailles that limited German military strength; he reintroduced military conscription and publicly started rearming, although Germany had been rearming in secret for years. Mussolini also chose 1935 to invade Ethiopia, one of the very few African states not overwhelmed by European imperialism. The attack was intended to demonstrate his regime's youth and vigor and to raise Italy's standing among the colonial powers. "The Roman legionnaires are again on the march," one soldier exulted. Although the poorly equipped Ethiopians resisted, their capital, Addis Ababa, fell in the spring of 1936. The League of Nations voted sanctions against Italy, but Britain and France opposed an embargo with teeth in it— one on oil—and thus kept the sanctions from being effective while also suggesting a lack of resolve to fight aggression.

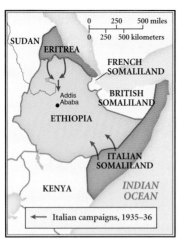

The Ethiopian War, 1935–1936

Profiting from the diversion of Italy's attack on Ethiopia, in March 1936 Hitler had defiantly sent his troops into what was supposed to be a permanently demilitarized zone in the Rhineland. The inhabitants greeted the Germans with wild enthusiasm. The French, whose security was most endangered by this action, protested to the League of Nations instead of countering with an invasion of their own as they had done in the Ruhr in 1923. The British accepted the fait accompli. The two dictators thus appeared as powerful military heroes forging, in Mussolini's muscular phrase, a "Rome-Berlin Axis." Next to them, the politicians of France and Great Britain looked timid.

The Spanish Civil War, 1936–1939

In what seemed like an exception to the trend toward authoritarian government, Spanish republicans overthrew their king in 1931. Nonetheless, large landowners and the Catholic clergy, who had the impoverished peasantry at their mercy, continued to dominate without modernizing the rural economy. The republicans hoped to modernize Spain by promoting industry and efficient, independent farming, but the government they established failed to enact land redistribution, which might have ensured popular loyalty and diminished the power of landowners and the church. This failure was all the more damaging because the antimonarchist forces included a mutually hostile array of liberals, anarchists, Communists, and other splinter groups constantly vying for power and harassing one another. In contrast, wealthy right-wing forces from the large landowners and clergy acted in concert.

In 1936, pro-republican forces temporarily banded together in a Popular Front coalition to win elections and prevent the republic from collapsing under the weight of internal squabbling and growing monarchist opposition. With the Popular Front victory, euphoria swept Spain as coveted municipal jobs were doled out and unemployment abated. The right recovered and revolted under the leadership of General Francisco Franco (1892–1975), who had the support of a host of right-wing groups, including the fascist Falange Party. The military uprising led to the Spanish Civil War (Map 21.1), which pitted the republicans, or Loyalists, against the fascist Falangists and the powerful forces of the authoritarian right.

The struggle became a rehearsal for World War II when Hitler and Mussolini sent military personnel in support of the right and Franco to test new weapons and

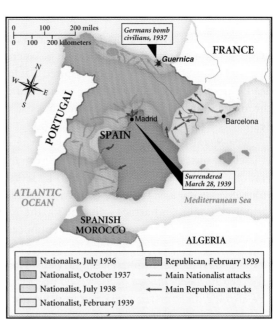

■ **MAP 21.1 The Spanish Civil War, 1936–1939**
Pro-republican and antirepublican forces fought one another to determine whether Spain would be a democracy or an authoritarian state. Germany and Italy sent military assistance, notably airplanes to experiment with bombing civilians, while volunteers from around the world arrived to fight for the losing cause of the republic. Defeating these ill-organized groups, General Francisco Franco instituted a pro-fascist government that sent many to jail and into exile.

■ The Spanish Republic Appeals for Aid

The government of the Spanish republic sent out modern advertising and propaganda to attract support from the remaining democracies—especially Great Britain and France. Antiwar sentiment remained high among the British and French, however. Thus, despite the horrifying and deliberate bombing of civilians by Franco's German allies, aid for the republic failed to arrive.
(Imperial War Museum, London.)

to practice new tactics, particularly the terror bombing of civilians. In 1937, low-flying German planes attacked the town of Guernica, mowing down civilians in the streets. This gratuitous slaughter inspired Pablo Picasso's memorial mural to the dead, *Guernica* (1937), in which the intense suffering is starkly displayed in monochromatic grays and whites to capture a sense of moral decay as well as physical death.

The Spanish Republic appealed everywhere for assistance but received little official response except for brief support from the Soviet Union. While Britain and France again showed their war-wariness by refusing to provide aid, a few thousand volunteers from a variety of countries—students, journalists, writers (George Orwell was one), and artists—fought for the republic. As these volunteers put it, "Spain was the place to stop fascism." Republican ranks again splintered into competing groups of liberals, Trotskyites, anarchists, and Communists. In this bitter contest, both sides committed widespread atrocities against civilians. The aid Franco received ultimately proved decisive, and his troops defeated the republicans in 1939. The ensuing dictatorship remained in place until 1975.

Hitler's Conquest of Central Europe, 1938–1939

The fall of central Europe that ultimately led to World War II began with Hitler's annexation of Austria in 1938 (Map 21.2). Many Austrians actually wished for such a merger, or *Anschluss*, after the Paris peace settlement stripped them of their empire. So Hitler's troops entered Austria as easily as tourists, and Austrian enthusiasm made the Anschluss appear to support the Wilsonian idea of "self-determination." The annexation began the unification of "Aryan peoples" into one greater German nation, and it marked the first step in Hitler's planned takeover of the resources of central and eastern Europe. Austria was declared a German province, the Ostmark, and Hitler's thugs ruled once-cosmopolitan Vienna. An observer later commented on the scene: "University professors were obliged to scrub the streets with their naked hands, pious white-bearded Jews were dragged into the synagogue by hooting youths and forced to do knee-exercises and to shout 'Heil Hitler' in chorus."

With Austria firmly in his grasp, Hitler turned to Czechoslovakia and its rich resources. Overpowering this democracy did not appear as simple a task as seizing Austria. Czechoslovakia had a large army and formidable border defenses and armament factories, and most Czech citizens were prepared to fight for their country. However, Hitler gambled correctly that the other Western powers would not interfere, especially as the Nazi propaganda machine poured tremendous abuse on Czechoslovakia for allegedly "persecuting" the German minority. By October 1, 1938, he warned, Czechoslovakia would have to grant autonomy (amounting to Nazi rule) to the German-populated border region, the Sudetenland, or face German invasion.

As the October deadline approached, the British prime minister Neville Chamberlain (1869–1940), Mussolini, and the French premier Edouard Daladier (1884–1970) met with Hitler in Munich and agreed not to oppose Germany's claim to the Sudetenland. The strategy of preventing a war by making concessions for legitimate grievances (in this case, the alleged affront to Germans in the Peace of Paris) was called *appeasement*. At the time, it was widely seen as a positive act, and the agreement between Germany and Great Britain—the Munich Pact—prompted Chamberlain to announce that he had secured "peace in our time."◆ Stalin, excluded from the Munich conference, learned from the deliberations that the democracies were not going to fight to protect eastern Europe.

Having portrayed himself as a man of peace, Hitler waited until March 1939 to invade Czechoslovakia. Britain and France responded by promising military support to Poland, Romania, Greece, and Turkey in case of Nazi invasion. In May 1939, Hitler and Mussolini countered this agreement by signing a pledge of offensive and defensive support called the Pact of Steel.

◆ For the speech in which Chamberlain defined and defended the policy of appeasement, see Document 68, Neville Chamberlain, "Speech on the Munich Crisis."

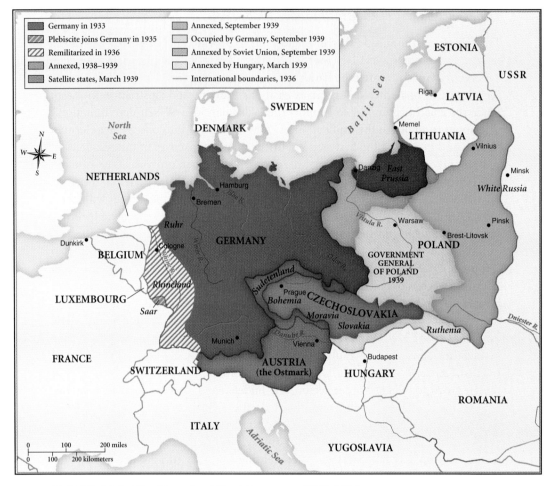

■ MAP 21.2 The Growth of Nazi Germany, 1933–1939

German expansion was rapid and surprising, as Hitler's forces and Nazi diplomacy brought about the annexation of the new states of central and eastern Europe. Though committed to defending the sovereignty of these states through the League of Nations, French and British diplomats were more interested in satisfying Hitler because they believed that doing so would prevent his claiming even more of Europe. They were mistaken, and Hitler proceeded to acquire the human and material resources of adjacent countries to support the Third Reich.

www.bedfordstmartins.com/huntconcise   See the ONLINE STUDY GUIDE for more help in analyzing this map.

Historians have sharply criticized the Munich Pact because it bought Hitler time to build his army and seemed to give him the green light for further aggression. Some historians believe that a confrontation might have stopped Hitler and that even if war had resulted, the democracies would have triumphed. According to proponents of this view, each military move by Germany, Italy, and Japan should have been met with stiff opposition, and the Soviet Union should have been made a partner to this resistance. Others counter that appeasement provided France and Britain precious time to beef up their own armies, which the Munich crisis prompted them to do, and to prepare their citizens for another war.

On August 23, 1939, to the astonishment of public opinion in the West, Germany and the USSR signed a nonaggression agreement. Despite Hitler's ambition to wipe the Bolsheviks off the face of the earth, Stalin needed time to reconstitute his military because he had destroyed his officer corps in the purges. The Nazi-Soviet Pact provided that if one country became embroiled in war, the other country would remain neutral. Moreover, the two dictators secretly agreed to divide Poland and the Baltic states—Latvia, Estonia, and Lithuania—at some future date. The Nazi-Soviet Pact ensured that if war came, the democracies would be fighting a Germany with no fear of attack on its eastern borders. Believing that Great Britain and perhaps even France would not fight because his aggression had met no resistance so far, Hitler now aimed his forces at Poland.

World War II, 1939–1945

The global catastrophe that quickly came to be called the Second World War opened when Hitler launched an all-out attack on Poland on September 1, 1939. In contrast to 1914, no jubilation in Berlin accompanied the invasion. Two days later, when Britain and France declared war, the mood in other capitals was similarly grim. Japan, Italy, and the United States did not join the battle immediately; their later participation spread the fighting throughout the world. By the time World War II ended in 1945, many Europeans were starving, much of the European continent lay in ruins, and unparalleled atrocities and genocide had killed 6 million Jews and countless others.

The German Onslaught

German ground forces quickly defeated the ill-equipped Polish troops by launching an overpowering *Blitzkrieg* ("lightning war"). The Germans concentrated airplanes, tanks, and motorized infantry to encircle Polish defenders and capture the capital, Warsaw, with overwhelming speed. Allowing the German army to conserve supplies, Blitzkrieg lulled Germans at home into believing that the human costs of gaining Lebensraum for the full flowering of the "Aryan race" would be low. On September 17, 1939, Soviet forces invaded Poland from the east. By the end of the month, the Polish army was in shambles, and the victors had divided Poland according to the Nazi-Soviet Pact. Hitler sold the war within the Third Reich as one of self-defense, especially from what Nazi propagandists called the "warlike menace" of world Jewry.

Hitler ordered an attack on France for November 1939, but his generals, who feared that Germany was ill prepared for total war, were able to postpone the offensive until the spring of 1940. In April 1940, the Blitzkrieg crushed Denmark and Norway; the battles of Belgium, the Netherlands, and France followed in May and June. On June 5, Mussolini, eyeing future spoils for Italy, invaded France from the southeast, as the French defense rapidly collapsed. Nor could the British army, allied with the French, withstand the German onslaught. Trapped on the beaches of Dunkirk in northern France, 370,000 British and French soldiers were rescued in a heroic effort by an improvised fleet of naval ships, fishing boats, and pleasure craft. The dejected French government surrendered on June 22, 1940, leaving Germany to rule the northern half of France, including Paris. In the south, known as Vichy France after the spa town where the government sat, Germany allowed the reactionary and aged World War I hero Henri Philippe Pétain to govern. Stalin used the diversion in western Europe to annex the Baltic states.

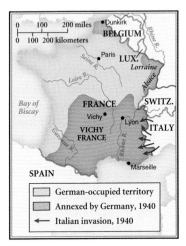

The Division of France, 1940

Britain now stood alone. Blaming Germany's rapid victories on Chamberlain's policy of appeasement, the British swept him out of office and installed as prime minister Winston Churchill (1874–1965), an early advocate of resistance to Hitler. After Hitler ordered the bombardment of Britain in the summer of 1940, Churchill rallied the nation by radio—now in more than nine million British homes—to protect the ideals of liberty with their "blood, toil, tears, and sweat." In the battle of Britain, or Blitz as the British called it, the German air force (*Luftwaffe*) bombed public buildings and monuments, harbors and weapons depots, and industry. Using the wealth of their colonies, the British poured resources into anti-aircraft weapons, a highly successful code-detecting group called Ultra, and development of Britain's advantage in radar. At year's end, the British air industry was outproducing the Germans by 50 percent.

By the fall of 1940, German air losses forced Hitler to abandon his plan for a naval invasion of Britain. Forcing Hungary, Romania, and Bulgaria to join the Axis, Hitler gained access to more food and oil. He then made his fateful decision to attack what he called the "center of judeobolshevism"—the Soviet Union. In June 1941, the German army crossed the Soviet border, as Hitler promised to "raze Moscow and Leningrad to the ground." Deployed along a 2,000-mile front, three million German and other Axis troops quickly penetrated Soviet lines. Stalin disappeared for several days but then rallied to direct the defense. By July, the German army had rolled to within 200 miles of Moscow and eventually reached its suburbs. Using a strategy of rapid encirclement, German troops killed, captured, and wounded more than half the 4.5 million Soviet soldiers defending the borders. Then Hitler blundered. Considering himself a military genius and the Slavic people inferior, he proposed attacking Leningrad, the Baltic states, and the Ukraine simultaneously, ignoring his generals' recommendation to concentrate on Moscow. Carrying out Hitler's cumbersome strategy cost the German forces precious time. Driven by Stalin, local party members, and rising patriotic resolve, the Soviet people fought back. The onset of winter turned Nazi soldiers to frostbitten wretches because Hitler had feared that equipping his army for the harsh Russian winter would suggest to the German people that a prolonged campaign lay in store. His ill-supplied armies succumbed to the weather and disease.

War Expands: The Pacific and Beyond

As the German army stalled in the Soviet Union, a dramatic attack ignited war in the Pacific. On December 7, 1941, Japanese planes bombed American naval and air bases at Pearl Harbor in Hawaii and then decimated a fleet of U.S. airplanes in the Philippines. President Roosevelt summoned Congress to declare war on Japan. The outbreak of war in Europe had intensified U.S.-Japanese competition, as Japan had taken control of parts of the British Empire, bullied the Dutch in Indonesia, and invaded Indochina to procure raw materials for its industrial and military expansion. The militarist Japanese government decided to settle matters with the West once and for all. By spring 1942, the Japanese had conquered Guam, the Philippines, Malaya, Burma, Indonesia, Singapore, and much of the southwestern Pacific.

On December 11, 1941, Hitler declared war on the United States—an appropriate enemy, he proclaimed, as it was "half Judaized and the other half Negrified." Mussolini followed suit. The United States was not prepared for a prolonged struggle. Isolationist sentiment remained strong. U.S. armed forces numbered only 1.6 million, and no plan existed for producing the necessary guns, tanks, and airplanes. Also working against war-preparedness was U.S. ambivalence toward the Soviet Union even in the face of Hitler's attack, and Stalin himself reciprocated the mistrust. Nevertheless, Hitler's four enemies came together in the Grand Alliance of Great Britain, the Free French (an exile government led by General Charles de Gaulle and based in London), the Soviet Union, and the United States. Given the urgency of war and the partners' competing interests, the Grand Alliance and a larger coalition with twenty other countries—known collectively as the Allies—had much internal strife to overcome in their struggle against the Axis—Germany, Italy, and Japan.

The Holocaust

As the German army swept through eastern Europe, it slaughtered Jews, Communists, Slavs, and others whom the Nazis deemed "racial inferiors" and enemies. In Poland, the SS murdered hundreds of thousands of Polish citizens or relocated them to forced labor camps. Across Europe, the German army rounded up civilians to work on farms and in labor camps throughout the Reich—all to power the voracious Nazi war machine. Herded into urban ghettos and living on minimal rations, eastern European Jews became special targets of SS violence. Around captured Soviet towns, Jews were usually shot in pits, some of which they had been forced to dig themselves. After shedding their clothes and putting them in orderly piles for later Nazi use, ten thousand or more at a time were killed, often with the help of anti-Semitic villagers. However, the "Final Solution"—the Nazis' diabolical plan to exterminate all of Europe's Jews—was not yet fully under way.

In addition to the massacres, a bureaucratically organized and efficient technological system for rounding up Jews and transporting them to extermination sites had taken shape by the fall of 1941. On the eve of war in 1939, Hitler had predicted "the destruction of the Jewish race in Europe." Although no clear order written by Hitler exists, he discussed the Final Solution's progress, issued oral directives for it, and from the beginning made lethal anti-Semitism a basis for Nazism. Modern social and legal science and technology, managed by efficient scientists, doctors, lawyers, and government workers, also made the Holocaust work. Six camps in Poland were developed specifically for the purposes of mass murder, although some, like Auschwitz-Birkenau, served as both extermination and labor camps. Using techniques developed in the T4 project in the late 1930s, the camp at Chelmno first gassed Christian Poles and Soviet prisoners of war. Specially designed crematoria for the mass burning of corpses started functioning in 1943. By then, Auschwitz had the capacity to burn 1.7 million bodies per year. About 60 percent of new arrivals—particularly children, women, and old people—were selected directly for murder in the gas chambers. The other 40 percent labored until they were utterly used up; then they, too, were sent to their deaths.

Extermination camps received their victims from across the European continent. In the ghettos in various European cities, councils of Jewish leaders, such as the council in Amsterdam where Etty Hillesum worked, were ordered to identify those to be "resettled in the east." For weakened, poorly armed ghetto inhabitants, open resistance meant certain death. When Polish Jews rose up against their Nazi captors in Warsaw in 1943, they were mercilessly butchered. The Nazis took pains to cloak their true purposes in the extermination camps. Bands played when trainloads of victims arrived; some were given postcards with reassuring messages to mail home. Those not chosen for immediate murder had their heads shaved, were showered and disinfected, and were then given prison garments. So began life in "a living hell," as one survivor wrote.◆

Overworked inmates usually took in less than five hundred calories per day, leaving them vulnerable to typhus and other diseases that swept through the camps. The brutality of mentally disturbed and criminal prison guards and of inhumane medical experiments failed to crush everyone's spirit: women observed religious

---

◆ For more survivor accounts, see Document 69, Sam Bankhalter and Hinda Kibort, "Memories of the Holocaust."

■ Persecution of Warsaw Jews

Hitler was determined to exterminate Jews, Slavs, gypsies, homosexuals, and others he deemed "undesirable," and he often enlisted community leaders to cooperate in deportation and even executions. In the 1930s, people fled Germany and then countries the Nazis conquered. In the city of Warsaw, where Jews were crowded into ghettos and deprived of food and fuel, a Jewish uprising brought massive retaliation. (© Bettmann/Corbis.)

holidays, celebrated birthdays, and re-created other sustaining aspects of domestic life. Prisoners forged new friendships that helped in the struggle for survival. Thanks to those sharing a bread ration and doing him favors, wrote the Auschwitz survivor Primo Levi, "I managed not to forget that I myself was a man." By the end of the war in 1945, six million Jews, the vast majority from eastern Europe, along with an estimated five million to six million gypsies, homosexuals, Slavs, and others were murdered.

Societies at War

Even more than World War I, World War II depended on industrial productivity geared totally toward war and mass murder. The Axis countries remained at a disadvantage throughout the war despite their vast conquests. Although the war accelerated economic production some 300 percent between 1940 and 1944 in all belligerent countries, the Allies produced more than three times the Axis output in 1943. Even with its territory occupied and many of its cities besieged, the Soviet Union increased its production of weapons. Both Japan and Germany made the most of their lower capacity, most notably in the strategy of Blitzkrieg. Hitler had to avoid imposing wartime austerity because he had come to power promising to end economic suffering, not increase it. The use of millions of slave laborers and assets from occupied areas helped, but both Japan and Germany underestimated the resources and morale of their enemies.

Allied governments were overwhelmingly successful in generating civilian participation, especially among women. In the Axis countries, where government policy particularly exalted motherhood, women avoided paid work even though they were desperately needed in offices and factories. In contrast, women constituted more than half the Soviet workforce by war's end. They dug massive antitank trenches around Moscow and other threatened cities, and 800,000 volunteered for the military, even serving as pilots. As the Germans invaded, Soviet citizens moved entire factories eastward.

Governments used propaganda to mobilize loyalty; even more than in World War I, propaganda saturated society in movie theaters and on the radio. Accustomed to listening to politicians on the air, people were glued to their radios for war news. Films depicted aviation heroes and infantrymen as well as the workingwomen and wives left behind. Government agencies monitored filmmaking and allocated supplies to approved films. In the United States, military leaders loaned authentic props only if they could censor the scripts.

Just as governments sought to mobilize culture between 1939 and 1945, they organized many aspects of everyday life. Bureaucrats regulated the production and distribution of food, clothing, and household products, all of which were rationed and generally of low quality. They gave hints for preparing meals without meat, sugar, fat, and other staples and exhorted women and children to embrace deprivation so their fighting men would survive. Governments hired economists, statisticians, and other specialists to influence civilian thought and behavior. With governments standardizing such items as food, clothing, and entertainment, World War II furthered the development of mass society.

On both sides, propaganda and government policies promoted racial thinking. Since the early 1930s, the German government had drawn ugly caricatures of Jews, Slavs, and gypsies. Similarly, Allied propaganda during the war depicted Germans as sadists and perverts and the "Japs" as uncivilized, insectlike fanatics. The U.S. government forced citizens of Japanese origin into internment camps. In the Soviet Union, Muslims and minority ethnic groups were uprooted and relocated as potential Nazi collaborators. Simultaneously, colonized peoples were drawn into the war through conscription into the armies and forced labor. Some two million Indian men served the Allied cause, as did several hundred thousand Africans. As the Japanese swept through the Pacific and parts of East Asia, they, too, conscripted men into their army. Both sides bombarded colonized societies with propaganda, as radio stations and newspapers proliferated during the war. This propaganda, in the context of forced labor, politicized colonized peoples to seek postwar liberation.

From Resistance to Allied Victory

Professional armies ultimately defeated the Axis powers, but civilian resistance in Nazi-occupied areas also contributed to the Allied triumph. General Charles de Gaulle (1890–1970) directed the Free French government and its forces from England; some 20 percent of these French troops were colonized Asians and Africans. Other French resisters fought in Communist-dominated groups, some of whom gathered information to aid a planned Allied landing on the French coast. Rural partisans plotted assassinations of German officers and civilian collaborators and bombed bridges, rail lines, and military facilities in German-occupied areas. The spirit of resistance produced heroes such as Swedish diplomat Raoul Wallenberg (1912–1947?), whose dealings with Nazi officials saved thousands of Hungarian Jews.

Ordinary people fought back through everyday activities. Homemakers circulated newsletters urging demonstrations at prisons where civilians were detained and in marketplaces where food was rationed. In central Europe, hikers smuggled Jews and others through dangerous mountain passes. Danish villagers created vast escape networks. Resisters played on stereotypes of femininity: women often carried weapons to assassination sites in the correct belief that the Nazis were not likely to suspect or search them; they also seduced and murdered enemy officers. Other actions subtly undermined the demands of fascist leaders. Couples in Germany and Italy limited family size in defiance of pro-birth policies. German teenagers danced the forbidden American jitterbug, thus defying the Nazis and forcing the police to monitor their groups. Resistance underscored the importance of the liberal ideal of individual political action and courage.

Amid civilian resistance, Allied forces started tightening a noose around the Axis in mid-1942 (Map 21.3). A major turning point came in August when the German army began a siege on Stalingrad, a city whose capture would give access to Soviet oil and cut access to the Soviet Union's interior. Months of ferocious fighting ended when the Soviet army captured the ninety thousand German survivors in February 1943. Allied victories in North Africa in 1942 were followed in July 1943 by an Allied landing in Sicily. However, the Germans came to their ally's aid and fought bitterly for the peninsula of Italy until April 1945, when Allied forces finally triumphed. After Italy's liberation, partisans shot Mussolini and his mistress and hanged their dead bodies for public display.

The victory at Stalingrad marked the beginning of the costly Soviet drive westward—during which the Soviets bore the brunt of the Nazi war machine. As Stalin pressed for the opening of a western front, Roosevelt, Churchill, and Stalin met at Teheran, Iran, in November and December 1943 to coordinate their efforts. On June 6, 1944, the combined Allied forces under the command of U.S. General Dwight Eisenhower landed on the heavily fortified beaches of Normandy, France, and then fought their way through the German-held territory of western France. In late July, Allied forces broke through German defenses and a month later helped

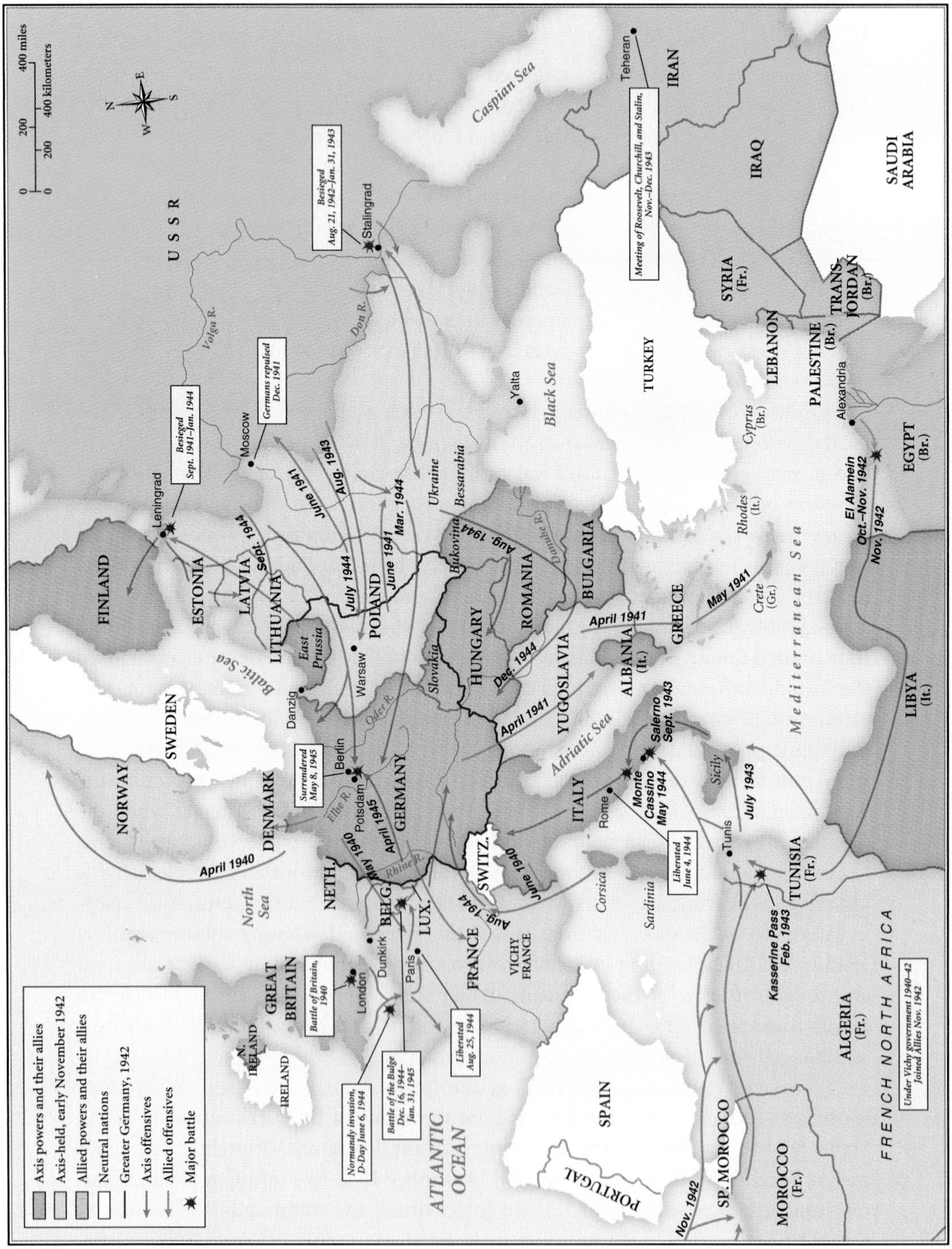

Axis powers and their allies
Axis-held, early November 1942
Allied powers and their allies
Neutral nations
Greater Germany, 1942
Axis offensives
Allied offensives
Major battle
0 200 400 miles
0 200 400 kilometers
N
E
S
W
USSR
Leningrad
Besieged Sept. 1941–Jan. 1944
Moscow
Germans repulsed Dec. 1941
Stalingrad
Besieged Aug. 21, 1942–Jan. 31, 1943
Volga R.
Don R.
Caspian Sea
Teheran
Meeting of Roosevelt, Churchill, and Stalin, Nov.–Dec. 1943
IRAN
IRAQ
SAUDI ARABIA
SYRIA (Fr.)
TRANS-JORDAN (Br.)
LEBANON
PALESTINE (Br.)
TURKEY
Black Sea
Yalta
Cyprus (Br.)
Alexandria
EGYPT (Br.)
El Alamein Oct.–Nov. 1942
Nov. 1942
LIBYA (It.)
Mediterranean Sea
Rhodes (It.)
Crete (Gr.)
May 1941
GREECE
April 1941
ALBANIA (It.)
BULGARIA
ROMANIA
Danube R.
Aug. 1944
Bessarabia
Bukovina
Ukraine
Mar. 1944
Aug. 1943
June 1941
July 1944
POLAND
Warsaw
HUNGARY
Dec. 1944
Slovakia
YUGOSLAVIA
Adriatic Sea
April 1941
FINLAND
ESTONIA
LATVIA
Sept. 1944
LITHUANIA
East Prussia
Baltic Sea
Danzig
SWEDEN
NORWAY
DENMARK
April 1940
North Sea
Oder R.
Berlin
Surrendered May 8, 1945
Potsdam
Elbe R.
April 1945
GERMANY
May 1940
NETH.
BELG.
LUX.
Rhine R.
SWITZ.
June 1940
Aug. 1944
ITALY
Rome
Monte Cassino May 1944
Salerno Sept. 1943
Liberated June 4, 1944
Corsica
Sardinia
Sicily
July 1943
Tunis
TUNISIA (Fr.)
Kasserine Pass Feb. 1943
FRANCE
VICHY FRANCE
Paris
Liberated Aug. 25, 1944
Dunkirk
London
Battle of Britain, 1940
GREAT BRITAIN
N. IRELAND
IRELAND
Normandy invasion, D-Day June 6, 1944
Battle of the Bulge Dec. 16, 1944–Jan. 31, 1945
ATLANTIC OCEAN
SPAIN
PORTUGAL
SP. MOROCCO
MOROCCO (Fr.)
Nov. 1942
ALGERIA (Fr.)
FRENCH NORTH AFRICA
Under Vichy government 1940–42 Joined Allies Nov. 1942

■ **Battle of Leningrad**
In the face of Nazi invasion, Soviet citizens reacted heroically, moving entire factories to the interior of the country and building fortifications. Nowhere was their resolve so tested as in Leningrad (now St. Petersburg). For more than two years, the German army besieged the city, causing the deaths of hundreds of thousands. Before the Allied landing at Normandy in 1944, the people of the USSR bore the brunt of Nazi military might in Hitler's attempt to defeat what he called "judeo-bolshevism." (Sovfoto.)

liberate Paris, where rebellion had erupted against the Nazis. British, Canadian, U.S., and other Allied forces then fought their way eastward to join the Soviets in squeezing the Third Reich to its final defeat.

In July 1944, a group of German military officers, fearing their country's military humiliation, attempted to assassinate, but only wounded, Hitler. As the Allies advanced, Hitler maintained that Germans were proving themselves unworthy of his greatness and deserved to perish in a cataclysmic conflagration. He refused all negotiations that might have spared Germans further death and destruction. Soviet

■ **MAP 21.3 World War II in Europe and North Africa**
The Axis and Allied powers waged war in Africa and Europe, inflicting massive loss of life and destruction of property on civilians, armies, and all the infrastructure—including factories, equipment, and agriculture—needed to wage total war. The war swept the European continent as well as areas in Africa colonized by or allied with the major powers. Ultimately, the Allies crushed the Axis by moving from east, west, and south to inflict a total defeat.

armies took Poland, and then, facing more than twice as many troops as on the western front, Stalin's forces withstood a fierce German defense in Hungary during the winter of 1944–1945. Hitler's refusal to surrender resulted in massive bombing of Germany. As the Soviet army took Berlin, Hitler committed suicide with his wife, Eva Braun. Although many German soldiers remained committed to the Third Reich, Germany finally surrendered on May 8, 1945.

After the German surrender, the Allies were able to focus solely on the war in the Pacific (Map 21.4). In 1940 and 1941, Japan had ousted the Europeans from many of their colonial holdings in Asia. In 1942, the Allies turned the tide, despite their diminished forces, destroying some of Japan's formidable naval power in battles at Midway Island and Guadalcanal. Unlike the United States, Japan lacked the capacity to recoup losses of ships or manpower. The Allies stormed one Pacific island after another, gaining bases from which to cut off the import of supplies and to launch bombers toward Japan itself. Despite these losses and the firebombing of Tokyo, the Japanese ruled out surrender and resorted instead to *kamikaze* tactics, in which pilots deliberately crashed their planes into American ships, killing themselves in the process.

Meanwhile, a U.S.-based international team of more than 100,000 scientists, technicians, and other workers had developed the atomic bomb. The Japanese practice of dying almost to the man rather than surrender caused Allied military planners to calculate that defeating Japan with conventional weapons might cost hundreds of thousands of Allied lives and take many more months. Thus, on August 6 and 9, 1945, the U.S. government unleashed its new atomic weapons on Hiroshima and Nagasaki, respectively, instantly killing 140,000 people and causing tens of thousands of later deaths from burns, wounds, and other afflictions. Hardliners in the Japanese military wanted to continue the war, but on August 14, 1945, Japan surrendered.

An Uneasy Postwar Settlement

The shape of the postwar settlement was a major Allied concern throughout the war. The aftermath of World War II, however, was unlike the aftermath of World War I. There was neither a celebrated peace conference nor a definitive, formal agreement among all the Allies about the final resolution of the war. The victorious Allies distrusted one another in varying degrees, and the United States and the Soviet Union were poised on the brink of another war.

Wartime agreements among members of the Grand Alliance about the future reflected ongoing differences that roused intense postwar debate. In 1941, Roosevelt and Churchill had forged the Atlantic Charter, which condemned aggression, reaffirmed the ideal of collective security, and endorsed the right of all peoples to choose their governments. Not only had the Allies come to focus on these points, but so had colonized peoples to whom, Churchill had said, the charter was not meant to

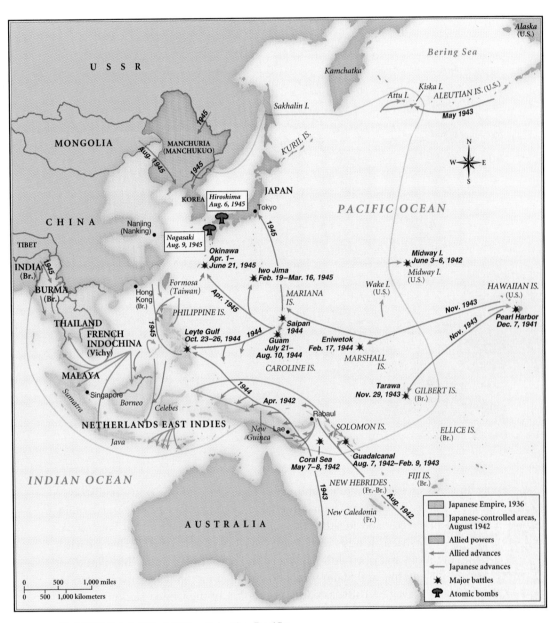

■ MAP 21.4 World War II in the Pacific

As in Europe, the early days of World War II gave the advantage to the Axis, as Japan took the offensive in conquering islands in the Pacific and territories in Asia—many of them colonies of the European states. Britain countered by mobilizing a vast Indian army. After the disastrous losses at Pearl Harbor and in the Philippines, the United States gradually gained the upper hand by costly assaults, island by island. The Japanese strategy of fighting to the last person instead of surrendering when a loss was in sight was one factor in the decision to drop the atomic bomb in August 1945.

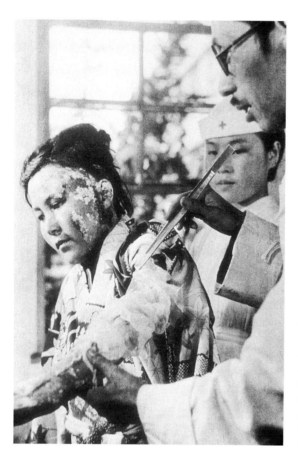

■ **Hiroshima Victim**
In early August 1945, the United States dropped atomic bombs on Hiroshima and Nagasaki, Japan, killing tens of thousands outright and leaving tens of thousands more to die of their wounds. A few days later, Japan surrendered. Controversy still swirls around the decision to drop the bomb. People who see it as a racist act point out that no atomic weapons were dropped on Germany. People who see it as a justified act of warfare point out that Japan's no-surrender policy increased the likelihood of countless more casualties. (Gamma Liaison.)

apply. In October 1944, Churchill and Stalin had agreed on the postwar distribution of territories. The Soviet Union would control Romania and Bulgaria, Britain would control Greece, and together they would oversee Hungary and Yugoslavia. These agreements were at odds with Roosevelt's preference for collective security, self-determination, and open doors in trade. In February 1945, the "Big Three"— as Roosevelt, Churchill, and Stalin were known—had met in the Crimean town of Yalta. There Roosevelt had advocated the formation of the United Nations organization to replace the League of Nations as a global peace mechanism, and he had supported future Soviet influence in Korea, Manchuria, and the Sakhalin and Kurile Islands. At their last meeting, at Potsdam, Germany, in the summer of 1945, the Allied leaders had agreed to give the Soviets control of eastern Poland, to cede a large stretch of eastern Germany to Poland, and to adopt a temporary four-way occupation of Germany that would include France as one of the supervising powers. But as victory unfolded, the Allies scrambled to outmaneuver one another.

IMPORTANT DATES			
1929	U.S. stock market crashes; global depression begins; Soviet leadership initiates war against the kulaks	1938	Virginia Woolf publishes *Three Guineas*
1930	Nationalist ruler Mustafa Kemal changes the name of Turkey's capital from Constantinople to Istanbul; French crush peasant uprising led by Ho Chi Minh, founder of the Indochinese Communist Party; Marlene Dietrich stars in *The Blue Angel*	1939	Germany invades Poland; World War II begins; Spanish Civil War ends
		1940	France falls to the German army
		1940–1941	British air force fends off German attacks in the battle of Britain
1930s	Movement for Indian independence; Sweden constructs welfare state	1941	Germany invades USSR; Japan attacks Pearl Harbor; United States enters the war
		1941–1945	The Holocaust
1933	Hitler comes to power in Germany	1944	Allied forces land at Normandy, France
1936	Show trials start in the USSR; Stalin purges top Communist Party officials and military leaders; Spanish Civil War begins	1945	Germany surrenders; United States drops atomic bombs on Hiroshima and Nagasaki; World War II ends

The Great Depression had inflicted global suffering. The Second World War left fifty million to sixty million people dead, an equal number of refugees without homes, and probably the most tragic moral legacy in human history. Peacemaking proved a long and bitter process that did not end in 1945. Forced into armies or into labor camps for war production, colonial peoples in Asia and Africa were in full rebellion or close to it. For the second time in three decades, they had seen Europeans killing one another, slaughtered by the very technology that Europeans had insisted made European civilization superior to theirs. Deference to Europe was virtually finished; independence was only a matter of time.

Western values at home were imperiled as well. Rational, democratic Europe had succumbed to permanent wartime values. It was this debased Europe that George Orwell captured in his novel *1984* (1949). Poor food and worn clothing, grimy streets and dwellings, people prematurely aged and careworn—all characterized London of the 1940s and Orwell's fictional state, Oceania. Orwell had worked for Britain's wartime Ministry of Information (called the Ministry of Truth in the novel) churning out propaganda and doctored news for wartime audiences. Propagandists had chosen their words carefully. Information and truth hardly mattered: *disengagement* replaced *retreat*, *battle fatigue* substituted for *insanity*, and *liberating*

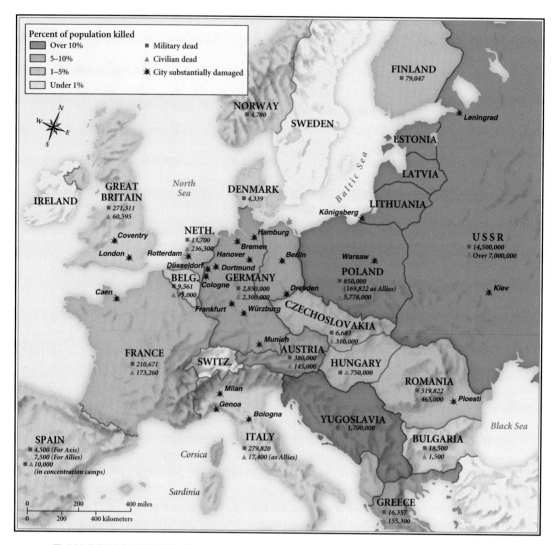

Percent of population killed

■ Over 10%	■ Military dead
■ 5–10%	▲ Civilian dead
■ 1–5%	✳ City substantially damaged
□ Under 1%	

FINLAND ■ 79,047

NORWAY ■ 4,780

SWEDEN

Leningrad

ESTONIA

Baltic Sea

LATVIA

GREAT BRITAIN ■ 271,311 ▲ 60,595

North Sea

DENMARK ■ 4,339

IRELAND

LITHUANIA

Königsberg

USSR ■ 14,500,000 ▲ Over 7,000,000

NETH. ■ 13,700 ▲ 236,300

Coventry

Hamburg

Bremen

London ✳ Rotterdam ✳ Hanover ✳ Berlin

Warsaw ✳

Düsseldorf ✳ Dortmund

BELG. ■ 9,561 Cologne ▲ 75,000

GERMANY ■ 2,850,000 ▲ 2,300,000

Dresden ✳

POLAND ■ 850,000 (169,822 as Allies) ▲ 5,778,000

Kiev ✳

Caen ✳

Frankfurt ✳ Würzburg ✳

CZECHOSLOVAKIA ■ 6,683 ▲ 310,000

FRANCE ■ 210,671 ▲ 173,260

Munich ✳

AUSTRIA ■ 380,000 ▲ 145,000

SWITZ.

HUNGARY ■ 750,000

ROMANIA ■ 519,822 ▲ 465,000 Ploesti ✳

Milan ✳

Genoa ✳

Bologna ✳

YUGOSLAVIA ▲ 1,700,000

Black Sea

SPAIN ■ 4,500 (For Axis) 7,500 (For Allies) ■ ▲ 10,000 (in concentration camps)

Corsica

ITALY ■ 279,820 ▲ 17,400 (as Allies)

BULGARIA ■ 18,500 ▲ 1,500

Sardinia

GREECE ■ 16,357 ▲ 155,300

0   200   400 miles
0   200   400 kilometers

■ MAPPING THE WEST   Europe at War's End, 1945

All of Europe was severely shocked during the age of catastrophe, but wartime damage left scars that would last for decades. Major German cities were bombed to bits. The Soviet Union suffered an unimaginable toll of perhaps 25 million deaths due to the war alone. Everything from politics to family life needed rebuilding. The chaos fueled postwar tensions stemming both from the quest to punish those held responsible for such suffering and from the Allied powers' manipulation of recovery assistance to gain political advantage in the cold war.

(From *The Hammond Atlas of the Twentieth Century* [London: Times Books, 1996], 102.)

a country could mean invading it and slaughtering its civilians. Millions rejoiced at the demise of Nazi evil in 1945, but Orwell saw as part of the war's legacy the end of prosperity, the deadening of creativity, and the intrusion of big government into everyday life. For Orwell, bureaucratic intrusion would intensify from the perpetuation of conflict, and fresh conflict was indeed brewing even before the war ended. As Allied powers competed for territory, a new struggle—known as the *cold war*—was beginning.

Conclusion

The Great Depression produced social dislocation and fear—conditions in which dictators were able to thrive because of their promises to restore national greatness and economic prosperity. Enticed by the mass media, people turned from representative institutions toward dynamic, if brutal, leaders. Memories of World War I permitted Hitler and Mussolini to menace Europe unimpeded throughout the 1930s. When a coalition formed to stop them, it was an uneasy one among the imperial powers France and Britain, the Stalinist Soviet Union, and the industrial giant the United States.

The brutal war—waged against civilians as well as armies—taught these powers different lessons and raised different expectations. The United States, Britain, and France emerged from the conflict convinced that at least some citizen well-being would be necessary to prevent a recurrence of fascism. Soviet citizens hoped that their lives would become easier and less restricted. The devastation of the USSR's population and resources, however, made Stalin increasingly obsessed with national security and reparations. Britain and France confronted the final eclipse of their imperial might, underscoring Orwell's insight that the war had transformed society irrevocably. The militarization of society and the deliberate murder of millions of innocent citizens like Etty Hillesum left a permanent blight on the European legacy. Nonetheless, competing visions of how to deal with Germany and eastern Europe and vast arsenals of sophisticated weaponry led the former Allies to threaten one another—and the world—with yet another war.

Suggested References for further reading and online research appear on page SR-34 at the back of the book.

www.bedfordstmartins.com/huntconcise   See the ONLINE STUDY GUIDE to assess your mastery of the material covered in this chapter.

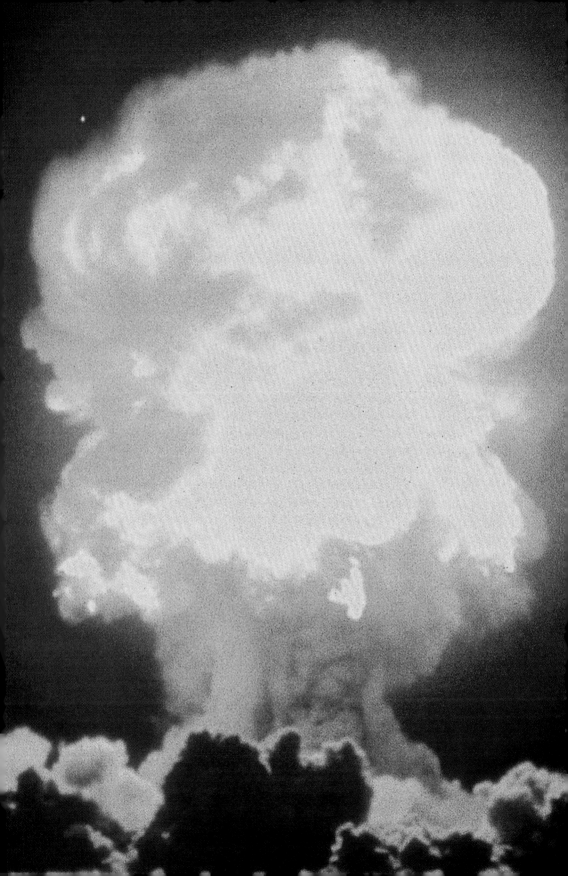

22

The Atomic Age

c. 1945–1960

I N LATE AUGUST 1949, THE SOVIET UNION DETONATED its first atomic bomb. Two days after President Harry S. Truman announced the news of this test, Billy Graham, a young Baptist minister, based his sermon at a revival meeting on the fearsome event. Graham warned that U.S. officials believed "we have only five to ten years and our civilization will be ended." He announced that Russia had aimed bombs to strike New York, Chicago, and Los Angeles, where the revival was taking place. "Time is desperately short. . . . Prepare to meet thy God," he warned. People flocked to hear Graham, launching the evangelist's astonishing career of spiritual and political influence in the United States and around the globe.

Graham's message—"We don't know how soon, but we do know this, that right now the grace of God can still save a poor lost sinner"—captured the extremes of postwar sentiment in an atomic age. On the one hand, the postwar situation was tragic. Fifty million people had died globally; Europe and Japan were prostrate and their peoples starving; evidence of genocide and other inhumanity was everywhere; the menace of nuclear annihilation loomed. It was to this menace that Graham referred. The old international order was gone, replaced by the rivalry of the United States and the Soviet Union for control of a devastated Europe, whose political and economic systems had collapsed. The nuclear arsenals of these two "superpowers"— a term coined in 1947—grew massively in the 1950s, but they were enemies who did not fight outright. Thus their terrifying rivalry was called the *cold war*. The cold war divided the West and caused acute anxiety, even for someone like Graham from the victorious and wealthy United States.

■ **The Atomic Age**
The dropping of atomic bombs on Hiroshima and Nagasaki in 1945 was followed by several decades of increasingly powerful detonations for testing purposes. The Soviet Union used underground testing, while the United States carried out atmospheric tests in the Pacific region. Protests against testing arose in the 1950s, many of them citing the hazards of radioactivity and the growing threat of nuclear annihilation. Simultaneously, nuclear power was converted to peacetime use, notably serving both as a source of energy and as a therapy for cancer. (Mark Meyer/Liaison Agency.)

On the other hand, the defeat of Nazism inspired an upsurge of hope, a revival of religious feeling like Graham's, and a new commitment to humanitarian goals. Heroic effort had defeated fascism, and that defeat raised hopes that a new age would begin. Atomic science promised advances in medicine, and nuclear energy was trumpeted as a replacement for coal and oil. The creation of the United Nations heralded an era of international cooperation. Around the globe, colonial peoples won independence from European masters, while in the United States the civil rights movement gained new momentum. The welfare state expanded, and by the end of the 1950s economic rebirth, stimulated in part by the cold war, had made much of Europe more prosperous than ever before. An "economic miracle" had occurred.

Extremes of hope and fear infused the atomic age, as society, culture, and the international order were transformed. Gone was the definition of a West comprising Europe and its cultural offshoots, such as the United States, and an East comprising Asian countries, such as India, China, and Japan. During the cold war, *West* came to stand for the United States and its client countries in western Europe, while *East* meant the Soviet Union and its tightly controlled bloc in eastern Europe. Still another terminology arose in the 1950s. The *first world* was the capitalist bloc of countries; the *second world*, the socialist bloc; and the *third world*, the countries emerging from imperial domination. As the world's people redefined themselves politically and culturally, the superpowers took the world to the brink of nuclear disaster when the United States discovered Soviet missile sites on the island of Cuba. From the dropping of the atomic bomb on Japan in 1945 to the Cuban missile crisis of 1962, Graham's dread that "we are moving madly toward destruction" gripped much of the world.

World Politics Transformed

The turmoil of wartime ended the global leadership of Europe. Many countries lay in ruins by the summer of 1945, and conditions would deteriorate before they got better. Bombed and bankrupt, victorious Britain could not feed its people. In contrast, the United States, whose territory was virtually untouched in the war, emerged as the world's sole economic giant, and the Soviet Union, despite suffering immense destruction, retained formidable military might. Having occupied Europe as part of the victorious alliance against Nazism and fascism, the two superpowers used Germany—at the heart of the continent and its politics—to divide Europe in two. By the late 1940s, the USSR imposed Communist rule throughout most of eastern Europe and in the 1950s quashed rebellions against its dominance. Western Europeans found themselves at least partially constricted by the very U.S. economic power that helped them rebuild, as the United States maintained air bases and nuclear weapon sites on their soil. The age of bipolar world politics had begun, with Europe as its testing ground.

Europe Prostrate

In contrast to World War I, when devastation was limited to the front lines around the trenches, armies in World War II had fought a war of movement that leveled thousands of square miles of territory. Across the continent, whole cities were clogged with rubble; homeless survivors wandered the streets. In Sicily and on the Rhine River, almost no bridge remained standing; in the Soviet Union, seventy thousand villages and more than a thousand cities lay in shambles. Everywhere people were suffering. In the Netherlands, the severity of Nazi occupation now brought the Dutch population close to death, relieved only by a U.S. airlift of food. In Britain, basic commodities were difficult to obtain, and many died in the bitterly cold winter of 1946–1947 because of a shortage of fuel. Italian bakers sold bread by the slice. When Allied troops passed through German towns, the famished inhabitants lined the roads in hopes that someone would toss them something to eat. "To see the children fighting for food," one British soldier noted, "was like watching animals being fed in a zoo." There were no uprisings as after World War I. Until the late 1940s, people were exhausted by the struggle for bare survival.

The tens of millions of refugees suffered the most. Many had been inmates of prisons and death camps; others, especially ethnic Germans, had fled westward to escape the victorious but destructive Red Army as it pushed toward Berlin. Native Germans in the Western-occupied zones viewed refugees as competitors for food and work. Many refugees ultimately found homes in countries that experienced little or no war damage, such as Denmark, Sweden, Canada, and Australia. Following the exodus of refugees from the east, western Europe became one of the world's most densely populated regions (Map 22.1).

The USSR drove many people from eastern Europe, yet it lobbied hard for the repatriation of several million Soviet prisoners of war and forced laborers—the first signal of Stalin's determination to revive Communist orthodoxy, which had weakened during the war. The Allies transported the majority of the Russian refugees back to the Soviet Union, where exile or execution for being "contaminated" by Western ideas awaited. As stories of executions filtered out, the Allies slowed the process, leaving hundreds of thousands of Soviets to join the ocean of refugees in western Europe.

Survivors of the concentration camps also discovered that their suffering had not ended with Germany's defeat. Many returned diseased and disoriented, while others often had no home to return to, for property had been confiscated and entire communities destroyed. Moreover, anti-Semitism had become official policy under the Nazis. In the summer of 1946, a vicious crowd in Kielce, Poland, rioted against returning Jewish survivors, killing at least 40 of the 250. Elsewhere in eastern Europe, such violence was common. Meanwhile, some officials across Europe even denied that unprecedented atrocities had been committed and wanted to refuse Jews any help. The U.S. government, fearing anti-Semitic backlash, let only about 12,000 Jews

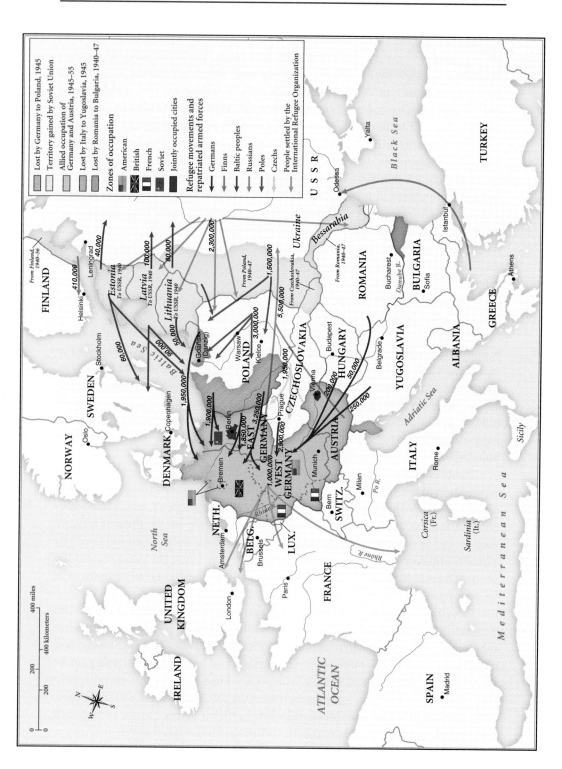

Lost by Germany to Poland, 1945
Territory gained by Soviet Union
Allied occupation of
Germany and Austria, 1945–55
Lost by Italy to Yugoslavia, 1945
Lost by Romania to Bulgaria, 1940–47
Zones of occupation
    American
    British
    French
    Soviet
    Jointly occupied cities
Refugee movements and
repatriated armed forces
    Germans
    Finns
    Baltic peoples
    Russians
    Poles
    Czechs
    People settled by the
    International Refugee Organization

■ MAP 22.1 The Impact of World War II on Europe

European governments, many of them struggling to provide food and other necessities for their populations, found themselves responsible for hundreds of thousands, if not millions, of new refugees. Simultaneously, millions of prisoners of war, servicemen, and slave laborers were returned to the Soviet Union, many of them by force. This situation unfolded amid political instability and even violence.

into the country. Many survivors crammed into the port cities of Italy and other Mediterranean countries, eventually to escape Europe for Palestine, where Zionists had been settling for half a century. As they had in the 1930s, the British balked at this vast migration to the Middle East, for they saw their interests threatened by likely Arab-Jewish conflict over control of the region. Unwilling or unable to help Hitler's most abused victims, many European countries had simply lost the capacity for moral and economic leadership.

New Superpowers: The United States and the Soviet Union

Only two powerful countries were left in 1945: the United States and the Soviet Union. The United States was now the richest country in the world. Its industrial output had increased a remarkable 15 percent annually between 1940 and 1944, a rate of growth that was reflected in workers' wages. By 1947, the United States controlled almost two-thirds of the world's gold bullion and more than half of its commercial shipping, up from almost one-fifth of the total in the 1930s. With continued spending on industrial and military research, a confident mood swept the United States at the end of the war. Casting aside the post–World War I policy of nonintervention, Americans embraced their position as global leaders. Many had learned about the world while tracking the war's progress; hundreds of thousands of soldiers, government officials, and relief workers had direct experience of Europe, Africa, and Asia. Although some feared a postwar depression and many shared Billy Graham's worries about nuclear annihilation, a wave of suburban housing development and consumer spending kept the economy buoyant. Temporarily reversing the trend toward a lower birthrate, a "baby boom" exploded from the late 1940s through the early 1960s in response to economic abundance.

The Soviets also emerged from the war with a well-justified sense of accomplishment. Withstanding horrendous losses, they had resisted the most massive onslaught ever launched against a modern nation. Instead of the international isolation dealt Russia after World War I, Soviet leadership expected equality in decision making with the United States, and indeed many Europeans and Americans had great respect for the Soviet contribution to Hitler's defeat. Ordinary Soviet citizens believed that a victory that had cost the USSR as many as 25 million lives would bring improvement in everyday conditions and a continuation of the war's relatively relaxed politics. "Life will become pleasant," one writer prophesied. "There will be much coming and going, and a lot of contacts with the West." The Stalinist goals of industrialization and defense against Nazism had been won, and thus many Soviets expected an end to decades of hardship.

Stalin took a different view and moved ruthlessly to reassert control. In 1946, his new five-year plan set increased production goals and mandated more stringent collectivization of agriculture. Stalin cut back the army by two-thirds to beef up the labor force and also turned his attention to the low birthrate, a result of wartime male casualties and women's long, arduous working days, which discouraged them from adding child care to their already heavy responsibilities. He introduced an intense propaganda campaign emphasizing that workingwomen should hold down jobs and also fulfill their "true nature" by producing many children.

Origins of the Cold War

In the immediate postwar years, the United States and the Soviet Union engaged in a cold war that would afflict the world for more than four decades. Because no peace treaty officially ended the conflict with Germany as a written record of contest and compromise or of things gone wrong (as in the Peace of Paris), the origins of the cold war remain a matter of debate. Some historians point to consistent U.S., British, and French hostility that began with the Bolshevik Revolution and continued through the war. Others stress Stalin's aggressive policies, notably the Nazi-Soviet alliance in 1939 and his quick claims on the Baltic states and Polish territory when World War II broke out.

During the war, suspicion ran deep. Stalin felt that Churchill and Roosevelt were deliberately letting the USSR bear the brunt of Hitler's onslaught on Europe as part of their anti-Communist policy. Some Americans believed that dropping the atomic bomb on Japan would also frighten the Soviets from land grabs, and the new U.S. president, Harry Truman, was far tougher than Roosevelt toward the Soviet Union. Given what Stalin interpreted as a menace from the West and his own country's exhausted condition, he saw the USSR as needing not just a temporary military occupation but a permanent "buffer zone" of European states loyal to the USSR as a safeguard. Across the Atlantic, Truman saw the initial Soviet occupation of eastern Europe as heralding an era of Communist expansion. By 1946, members of the U.S. State Department were describing Stalin as prepared to continue the centuries-old Russian thirst for "world domination."

The cold war thus became a series of moves and countermoves in the shared occupation of the rich European heartland by two very different countries—the United States and the Soviet Union. In line with its geopolitical needs, the USSR proceeded to repress democratic, coalition governments of liberals, socialists, Communists, and peasant parties in central and eastern Europe between 1945 and 1948. It imposed Communist rule almost immediately in Bulgaria and Romania.

The Cold War, to 1962			
1945–1949	USSR establishes satellite states in eastern Europe	**1950–1954**	U.S. senator Joseph McCarthy leads hunt for American Communists
1947	Truman Doctrine announces U.S. commitment to contain communism; U.S. Marshall Plan provides massive aid to rebuild Europe	**1953**	Stalin dies
		1955	USSR and Eastern bloc countries form military alliance, the Warsaw Pact
1948–1949	Soviet troops blockade Berlin; United States airlifts provisions to Berliners	**1956**	Khrushchev denounces Stalin in "secret speech" to Communist Party Congress; Hungarians revolt unsuccessfully against Soviet domination
1949	Western democracies form North Atlantic Treaty Organization (NATO); Soviet bloc establishes Council for Mutual Economic Assistance (COMECON); USSR tests its first nuclear weapon	**1959**	Fidel Castro comes to power in Cuba
		1961	Berlin Wall erected
		1962	Cuban missile crisis
1950–1953	Korean War		

In Romania, Stalin cited citizen violence in 1945 as the excuse to demand an ouster of all non-Communists from the civil service and cabinet. In Poland, the Communists fixed the election results of 1945 and 1946 to create the illusion of approval for communism. Nevertheless, the Communists had to share power between 1945 and 1947 in partnership with the popular Peasant Party of Stanisław Mikołajczyk, which had a large constituency of rural workers and peasant landowners.

The United States put its new interventionist spirit to work. It acknowledged Soviet influence in areas the Soviet Union occupied but worried that Communist power would spread to western Europe. The difficult conditions of postwar life made Communist programs promising better conditions increasingly attractive to workers, while Communist leadership in the resistance gave the party a powerful allure. U.S. and British concern mounted when Communist insurgents threatened to overrun the right-wing monarchy the British had installed in Greece in 1944. In March 1947, Truman reacted to the Communist threat by announcing what quickly became known as the *Truman Doctrine*, the countering of political crises with economic and military aid. The president requested $400 million in military aid for Greece and for Turkey, where the Communists were also pressuring. Fearing that Americans would balk at backing Greece, U.S. congressmen would agree to the program only if Truman would "scare hell out of the country," as one put it. Truman thus publicized a massive aid program as necessary to fortify the world against a tide of global Soviet conquest. The show of American support convinced the Communists to back off, and in 1949 the Greek rebels declared a cease-fire.

"The seeds of totalitarian regimes are nurtured by misery and want," the president warned in the same speech that introduced the Truman Doctrine.♦ His linkage of poverty to the rise of dictatorship led to the *Marshall Plan*, a program of massive U.S. economic aid to Europe named after Secretary of State George C. Marshall. The Marshall Plan claimed that it was not directed "against any country or doctrine but against hunger, poverty, desperation, and chaos." Stalin, however, saw it as a U.S. political ploy that caught him without similar economic aid to offer to his client countries in eastern Europe. By the early 1950s, the United States had sent Europe more than $12 billion in food, equipment, and services.

The Soviet Union reacted by suppressing the remaining coalition governments, notably in Hungary and Poland, and assuming political control in central and eastern Europe. Czechoslovakia, which by eastern European standards had prospered under a Communist-led coalition, welcomed the Marshall Plan as the beginning of East-West rapprochement. This illusion ended, however, during a purge of non-Communist officials that began in the autumn of 1947. By June 1948, the socialist president, Edouard Beneš, had resigned and been replaced by a Communist figurehead. Nonetheless, the populace remained so passive that Communist leaders called the takeover "like cutting butter with a knife." The Soviet Union had successfully created a buffer of satellite states in eastern Europe directed by "people's governments."

Yugoslavia after the Revolution, 1948

The only exception to the Soviet sweep in eastern Europe came in Yugoslavia, under the Communist ruler Tito (Josip Broz). During the war, Tito led the powerful anti-Nazi Yugoslav "partisans." After the war, he drew on support from Serbs, Croats, and Muslims to mount a Communist, but not a Soviet, revolution. Eager for Yugoslavia to develop industrially rather than simply serve Soviet needs, he remarked: "We study and take as an example the Soviet system, but we are developing socialism in our country in somewhat different forms." Stalin was furious, for commitment to communism meant obedience to him. Nonetheless, Yugoslavia emerged from its Communist revolution as a culturally diverse federation of six republics and two independent provinces within Serbia. Holding these groups together until his death in 1980, Tito's forceful personality and strong organization also held the Soviets at bay.

♦ For a primary source that elucidates U.S. cold war tactics and the fears and perceptions underlying them, see Document 70, National Security Council, "Paper Number 68."

The Division of Germany

The cold war became most menacing in the superpowers' struggle for control of Germany. The terms of the agreements reached at Yalta provided for Germany's occupation by troops divided among four zones, each of which was controlled by one of the four principal victors in World War II—the United States, the Soviet Union, Britain, and France (Map 22.2). However, the superpowers disagreed on fundamental matters in German history. Many in the United States had come to believe that there was something inherently wrong with the character of Germans, who had provoked two world wars and the Holocaust. After the war, the U.S. oc- cupation forces undertook a reprogramming of German cultural attitudes by con- trolling the press and censoring the content of all media in the U.S. zone to ensure that they did not express fascist or authoritarian values. In contrast, Stalin believed that Nazism was merely another form of advanced capitalism, and he therefore confiscated and redistributed the estates of wealthy Germans.

A second disagreement over Germany's economic potential led to the partition of Germany. According to the American vision of economic coordination, surplus produce from the Soviet-occupied areas would feed urban populations in the Western-controlled zones; in turn, industrial goods would be sent to the USSR. The Soviets upset this plan and, following the Grand Alliance agreement that the USSR receive reparations from German resources, immediately sent equipment and dis- mantled industries to the Soviet Union. They transported skilled workers, engi- neers, and scientists to the USSR to work as virtual slave laborers. Meanwhile, the three Western Allies agreed to merge their zones into a West German state. Instead of continuing to curtail German power as wartime agreements called for, the United

■ **MAP 22.2 Divided Germany and the Berlin Airlift, 1946–1949**
Berlin, controlled by the United States, Great Britain, France, and the Soviet Union, was deep in the Soviet zone of occupation and became a major point of contention among the former allies. When the USSR blockaded the western half of the city, the United States re- sponded with a massive airlift. To stop movement between the two zones, the USSR built a wall in 1961 and used troops to patrol it.

States embarked on an economic buildup under the Marshall Plan to make the Western zone a buffer against the Soviets. By 1948, notions of a permanently weakened Germany had come to an end.

Stalin struck back at the Marshall Plan on July 24, 1948, when Soviet troops blockaded Germany's capital, Berlin. Like Germany as a whole, the city had been divided into four occupation zones, even though it was located more than one hundred miles deep into the Soviet zone and was thus cut off from Western territory (see Map 22.2). Expecting the West to capitulate, the Soviets declared Berlin part of their zone of occupation and refused to allow vehicles to travel through the entire Soviet zone, including Berlin. Instead, the United States responded decisively, flying in millions of tons of provisions to the stricken city. During the winter of 1948–1949, the Berlin airlift—Operation Vittles, as U.S. pilots called it—even funneled coal to the city to warm some two million isolated Berliners. Cold war culture increasingly centered on heroic deeds enacted in Berlin long after the end of the blockade in May 1949, as the divided city became the symbol of the cold war.

The division of Germany and the new bipolarity led to the formation of competing military alliances. The United States, Canada, and their European allies in western Europe and Scandinavia formed the North Atlantic Treaty Organization, or NATO, in 1949. NATO provided a unified military force for the member countries. In 1955, after the United States forced France and Britain to invite West Germany to join NATO, the Soviet Union retaliated by establishing with its satellite countries the military organization commonly called the Warsaw Pact, which included Albania, Bulgaria, Czechoslovakia, East Germany, Hungary, Poland, and Romania. These two massive regional alliances formed the military muscle for the new cold war politics and definitively replaced the individual might of the European powers (Map 22.3).

■ **MAP 22.3 European NATO Members and the Warsaw Pact in the 1950s**

The two superpowers intensified their rivalry by creating large military alliances: NATO, formed in 1949, and the Warsaw Pact, formed in 1955 after NATO invited West German membership. The United States and Canada also were NATO members. International politics revolved around these two alliances, which faced off in the heart of Europe. Military planners on both sides devised war games to plan strategies for fighting a massive war in central Europe over control of Germany.

www.bedfordstmartins.com/huntconcise   See the ONLINE STUDY GUIDE for more help in analyzing this map.

The Political and Economic Recovery of Europe

The ideological clash between East and West served as a background to a remarkable recovery that took place between 1945 and 1960. The first order of business on the political front was a highly charged eradication of the Nazi past. Simultaneously, western Europe revived its democratic political structures, its individualistic culture, and its productive capabilities. Eastern Europe restlessly endured a far less prosperous and far more repressive existence under Stalinism, although the conditions of everyday life improved as peasant societies were forced to modernize. By 1960, people across the continent had escaped the poverty of the depression and war to enjoy a higher standard of living—an "economic miracle" it was even called—than ever before in human history. As governments took increasing responsibility for the health and well-being of citizens, the atomic age also became the age of the welfare state.

Dealing with the Nazi Past

In May 1945, Europeans lived under a complex system of political jurisdiction: local resistance leaders, Allied armies of occupation, international relief workers, and the remnants of bureaucracies often worked at odds to restore society. Amid confusion, starvation, and a thriving black market, the goals of feeding civilians, dealing with the tens of millions of refugees, purging Nazis, and setting up new governments all competed for attention. Occupying armies that covered much of the continent were often a law unto themselves: the Soviets were especially feared for inflicting rape and robbery. Distributing food and clothing, other armed forces tried to instill order. The desire for revenge against Nazis hardened with the discovery of the death camps' skeletal survivors and the remains of the millions murdered there. Swift vigilante justice by civilians released pent-up rage and aimed to punish collaborators for their complicity in the Holocaust and other occupation crimes. Villagers often shaved the heads of women suspected of associating with Germans and made them parade naked through the local streets. Members of the resistance summarily executed tens of thousands of Nazi officers and collaborators on the spot. These became the founding acts of a reborn European political community.

Allied representatives undertook a more systematic "denazification," including official investigations of suspected local collaborators. The trials conducted at Nuremberg, Germany, by the victorious Allies in the fall of 1945 used the Nazis' own documents to provide a horrifying panorama of crimes by Nazi leaders. Although international law lacked a precedent for defining genocide as a crime, the judges at Nuremberg found sufficient cause to sentence half of the twenty-four defendants to death, among them Hitler's closest associates, and the remainder to prison terms. The Nuremberg trials introduced current notions of prosecution for crimes against humanity and an international politics based on demands for human rights.

■ **The Punishment of Collaborators**
Women who had romantic involvements with Germans were called "horizontal" collaborators to suggest that they were traitorous prostitutes. With heads shaved and often stripped of their clothing, they were forced to parade through cities and towns enduring verbal and other abuse. The public shaming of these women, a vivid part of the memory of the war, served as the background for the film Hiroshima Mon Amour, *which gripped audiences late in the 1950s.*
(Robert Capra/Magnum Photos Inc.)

Allied prosecution of Nazi and fascist leadership never succeeded completely because some of the leaders most responsible for war crimes disappeared. Many Germans were skeptical about denazification. As women in Germany endured starvation and savage rape and, in addition, performed the arduous labor of clearing rubble, the belief took hold that Germans were the main victims of the war. German civilians also interpreted the trials of Nazis as the characteristic retribution of victors rather than the well-deserved punishment of the guilty. Allied officials themselves, eager to restore government services and pursue the cold war, often relied on the expertise of high-ranking fascists and Nazis. The Nazi past haunts European debates, cultural life, and politics to this day, yet political expediency led Westerners at the time to forgive some Nazis quite easily.

Rebirth of the West

Against all political and economic odds, western Europe revived. Reform-minded civilian governments reflected the coalitions that had opposed the Axis. They conspicuously emphasized democracy to show their rejection of the totalitarian regimes that had earlier attracted so many Europeans—with such dire consequences. Re-building devastated towns and cities spurred industrial recovery, while bold projects for economic cooperation like the European Common Market and the conversion of wartime technological know-how to peacetime use produced a brisk trade in consumer goods and services in western Europe by the late 1950s.

Resistance leaders had the first claim on office in postfascist western Europe. In France, the leader of the Free French, General Charles de Gaulle, governed briefly as chief of state; he quit over limitations on the president's power that were reminiscent of the Third Republic. The French approved a constitution in 1946 that established the Fourth Republic and finally granted the vote to French women. Meanwhile, Italy replaced its constitutional monarchy with a full parliamentary system that also allowed women the vote for the first time. As in France, a resistance-based socialist government initially governed. Then late in 1945, this was replaced by a coalition headed by the conservative Christian Democrats, descended from the traditional Catholic centrist parties of the prewar period.

It was the Communist Party, however, that seemed to attract the most vocal loyalty of a consistently large segment of the western European population. Symbol of the common man, the ordinary Soviet soldier was a hero to many western Europeans outside occupied Germany, as were the resistance leaders—most of them Communist until late in the war when the impending Nazi collapse lured mainline politicians to join the anti-Nazi bandwagon. People still remembered the common man's plight in the depression of the 1930s. Thus, in Britain, despite the successes of Winston Churchill's Conservative Party leadership, the Labour government of Clement Attlee appeared more socialist by fulfilling promises that it would share prosperity equitably among the classes through expanded social welfare programs and the nationalization of key industries.

In West Germany, however, communism had no appeal. In 1949, centrist politicians helped create a new state, the German Federal Republic, whose constitution aimed to prevent the emergence of a dictator and to guarantee individual rights. West Germany's first chancellor was the seventy-three-year-old Catholic anti-Communist Konrad Adenauer, who allied himself with the economist Ludwig Erhard. Committed to the free market, Erhard had stabilized the postwar German currency so that commerce could resume. The economist and the politician successfully guided Germany away from both fascism and communism and restored the representative government that Hitler had overthrown.

Paradoxically, given U.S. leadership in the fight against fascism, postwar politics in the United States most imperiled individual freedom and democracy. The 1949 explosion of the Soviet atomic bomb and the successful Communist revolution in China brought to the fore Joseph McCarthy, a U.S. senator facing a reelection struggle in 1950. McCarthy warned of a great conspiracy to overthrow the United States. As during the Soviet purges, people were called before congressional panels to confess, testify against friends, think about whether they had ever had Communist thoughts or sympathies. The atmosphere was electric with fear because only five years before, the mass media had run glowing stories about Stalin and the Soviet system. By 1952, more than six million people had been investigated or imprisoned or had lost their jobs. McCarthy had books like Thomas Paine's *Common Sense*, written in the eighteenth century to support the American Revolution, removed from government shelves, and he personally oversaw book burnings. Although the Senate finally voted to censure McCarthy in the winter of 1954, the assault on freedom had been devastating and anticommunism dominated political life.

Given the incredible devastation, the economic rebirth of western Europe was even more surprising than the revival of democracy. In the first weeks and months after the war, the job of rebuilding often involved menial physical labor that mobilized entire populations. With so many men dead, wounded, or detained as prisoners of war, German housewives, called "women of the ruins," earned their living clearing rubble by hand. Initially governments diverted labor and capital into rebuilding infrastructure—transportation, communications, industrial capacity. However, the scarcity of goods sparked unrest and made communism attractive politically because it proclaimed less interest in the revival of big business than in the ordinary person's standard of living. But as the Marshall Plan sustained the initial recovery with American dollars, food and consumer goods became more plentiful, and demand for automobiles, washing machines, and vacuum cleaners boosted economies. The growth in production of all kinds wiped out most unemployment. Labor-short northern Europe even arranged for "guest" workers to migrate from Sicily and other impoverished regions to help rebuild cities. The outbreak of war in Korea in 1950 further encouraged the astonishing rates of economic growth. (See "Taking Measure," page 965.)

The postwar recovery also featured the adaptation of wartime technology to consumer industry and the continuation of military spending. Civilian travel expanded as nations organized their own air systems based on improved airplane technology. Developed to relieve wartime shortages, synthetic goods such as nylon now became part of peacetime civilian life. Factories churned out a vast assortment of plastic products, ranging from pipes to household goods and rainwear. In the climate of cold war, governments ordered bombs, fighter planes, tanks, and missiles; and they also continued to sponsor military research. The cold war ultimately prevented a repeat of the 1920s, when reduced military spending threw people out of jobs and thus fed the growth of fascism.

International cooperation and planning that led to the creation of the Common Market and ultimately the European Union of the 1990s provided a final ingredient in recovery. The Marshall Plan demanded as the condition for assistance that recipients undertake far-reaching economic cooperation. In 1951, Italy, France, Germany, Belgium, Luxembourg, and the Netherlands formed the European Coal and Steel Community (ECSC). This organization managed coal and steel production and prices and, most important, arranged for West German output to benefit western Europe. According to the ECSC's principal architect, Robert Schuman, the

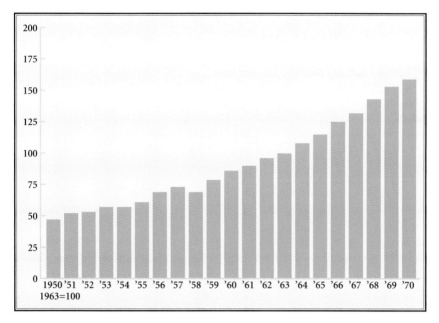

■ TAKING MEASURE World Manufacturing Output, 1950–1970

During the "long boom" from the 1950s to the early 1970s, the world experienced increased indus-
trial output, better agricultural production, and rising consumerism. This era of prosperity resulted
not only from the demand generated by the need to rebuild Europe but also from the adaptation of
war technology to peacetime uses. The General Agreement on Trade and Tariffs (GATT) was also
implemented after the war, lowering tariffs and thus advancing trade.
(*Hammond Atlas of the Twentieth Century* [London: Times Books, 1987], 127.)

economic unity created by the organization would make another war "materially
impossible." Simply put, the bonds of common productivity and trade would keep
France and Germany from another cataclysmic war.

In 1957, "the Six," as the ECSC members were called, took another major step
toward regional prosperity when they signed the Treaty of Rome. The treaty provided for a trading partnership called the European Economic Community (EEC),
known popularly as the Common Market. The EEC reduced tariffs among the six
partners and worked to develop common trade policies. According to one of its
founders, the EEC aimed to "prevent the race of nationalism, which is the true curse
of the modern world." Increased cooperation produced great economic rewards for
the six members. Britain pointedly refused to join the partnership; membership
would have required that it surrender certain imperial trading rights. Since 1945,
British statesmen had shunned the developing continental trading bloc because, as
one of them put it, participation would make it "just another European country."
As a result, Britain continued its relative decline. By contrast, the Italian economy,
which had also lagged behind that of France and Germany, boomed. The future lay
with the soaring prosperity of a new western Europe joined in the Common Market.

Behind the move to the Common Market stood the use of economic planning and coordination by specialists during wartime. Called *technocrats* after 1945, specialists were to base decisions on expertise rather than on personal interest; those working for the Common Market were to disregard the self-interest of any one nation and thus reduce the potential for irrationality and violence in politics, both domestic and international. However, some critics insisted, some even today, that expert planning diminished democracy by putting massive control in the hands of bureaucracy, not legislatures.

The Welfare State: Common Ground East and West

On both sides of the cold war, governments intervened forcefully to ameliorate social conditions. This policy of intervention became known as the *welfare state*, indicating that states were no longer interested solely in maintaining order and augmenting their power. Because the European population had declined during the war, almost all countries now desperately supported reproduction with direct financial aid. Imitating the sweeping Swedish programs of the 1930s, nations expanded or created family allowances, health-care and medical benefits, and programs for pregnant women and new mothers. The French gave larger allowances for each birth after the first; for many French families this allowance provided as much as a third of the household income.

Britain's maternity benefits and child allowances, announced in a wartime report, favored women who did not work outside the home and provided little coverage of any kind to workingwomen. The West German government passed strict legislation that discouraged employers from hiring women. In fact, West Germans bragged about removing women from the workforce, claiming it distinguished democratic practices from Communist ones that were said to demand women's work outside the home. One result of the cutback in pensions and benefits to married women was their high rate of poverty in old age.

In eastern Europe and the Soviet Union, where wartime loss of life had been enormous, women worked nearly full-time and usually outnumbered men in the workforce. Child-care programs, family allowances, and maternity benefits were designed to encourage pregnancies by such women. The scarcity of consumer goods, the housing shortages, and the lack of household conveniences in the Eastern bloc, however, discouraged workingwomen from having large families. Because women had sole responsibility for onerous domestic duties on top of their paying jobs, their already heavy workload increased with the birth of each additional child.

Across Europe, welfare-state programs aimed to improve people's health. State-funded medical insurance, subsidized medical care, or nationalized health-care systems covered health-care needs in industrial nations except in the United States. The combination of better material conditions and state provision of health care dramatically extended life expectancy and lowered rates of infant mortality. Contributing to the overall progress, the number of medical doctors and dentists more than doubled between the end of World War I and 1950, and vaccines greatly reduced the death toll from such diseases as tuberculosis, diphtheria, measles, and polio. In England, schoolchildren on average stood an inch taller than children of the same age a decade earlier. As people lived longer, governments began to establish programs for the elderly. All in all, per capita expenditures on civilian well-being shot up after the war. Belgium, for example, which had spent $12 per capita in 1930, led western European countries with $148 per capita in 1956; Britain, which had led in 1930 with welfare expenditures of $59, now lagged behind with $93 because of its near-bankrupt condition.

State initiatives in other areas played a role in the higher standard of living. A growing network of government-built atomic power plants brought more thorough electrification of eastern Europe and the Soviet Union. Governments legislated better conditions and more leisure time for workers. Beginning in 1955, Italian workers received twenty-eight paid holidays annually; in Sweden workers received twenty-nine vacation days, and the number grew in the 1960s. Planning also helped provide a more varied diet and more abundant food, with meat, fish, eggs, cheese, milk, and fresh fruit supplementing the traditional grain-based foods. Housing shortages posed a daunting challenge after three decades of economic depression and destructive war. Postwar Europeans often lived with three generations sharing one or two rooms. Eastern Europeans faced the worst conditions, whereas Germans and Greeks fared better because only 20 to 25 percent of their prewar housing had been lost. To rebuild, governments sponsored a postwar housing boom. New cities formed around the edges of major urban areas in both East and West. Many buildings went up slapdash, and restored towns took on an undistinguished look and a constantly deteriorating condition. Westerners labeled many Eastern bloc apartments "environmentally horrible." Housing shortages persisted, but the modernized appearance of many European cities suggested that the century's two cataclysmic wars had swept away much of the old Europe.

Recovery in the East

To create a Soviet bloc according to Stalin's prewar vision of industrialization, Communists revived the crushing methods that had served before to transform peasant economies. In eastern Europe, Stalin enforced collectivized agriculture and badly needed industrialization through the nationalization of private property. In Hungary, for example, Communists seized and reapportioned all estates over twelve hundred acres. Having gained support of the poorer peasants through this redistribution, Communists later pushed them into cooperative farming. The process of collectivization was brutal and slow everywhere, and rural people looked back on the 1950s as "dreadful." But others felt that ultimately their lives and their children's

■ Postwar Housing in Poland
Wartime devastation worsened the shortage of housing that had begun with the diversion of re-sources to fight World War I and had increased during the depression of the 1930s, when housing construction almost halted. In the post–World War II years, shortages were so grave that slapdash, cheap buildings with far less than one room per person went up from England to eastern Europe and the Soviet Union. Not until the 1960s did the Soviets begin building anywhere near the million or more housing units needed each year. (Sovfoto.)

lives had improved. "Before we peasants were dirty and poor, we worked like dogs. . . . Was that a good life? No sir, it wasn't. . . . I was a miserable sharecropper and my son is an engineer," said one Romanian peasant.

An admirer of American industrial know-how, Stalin prodded all the socialist economies in his bloc to match U.S. productivity. The Soviet Union formed regional organizations, instituting the Council for Mutual Economic Assistance (COMECON) in 1949 to coordinate economic relations among the satellite countries and Moscow. Modernization of production in the Eastern bloc opened new technical and bureaucratic careers, and modernizers in the satellite states touted the virtues of steel plants and modern transport. The terms of the COMECON relationship thwarted development of the satellite states, for the USSR was allowed to buy goods from its clients at bargain prices and sell to them at exorbitant ones. Nonetheless, these formerly peasant states became oriented toward technology and bureaucratically directed industrial economies. People moved to cities where they received better education, health care, and, ultimately, jobs, albeit at the price of repression. The Catholic clergy, which often protested the imposition of communism, was crushed. Old agrarian elites, professionals, intellectuals, and other members of the middle class were discriminated against, imprisoned, or executed. Prisoners in East German camps did hard labor in uranium and other dangerous mines.

Science and culture were the building blocks of Stalinism in the satellite countries as well as in the USSR. State-instituted programs aimed to build loyalty to the modernizing regime: citizens found themselves obliged to attend adult education classes, women's groups, and public ceremonies. An intense program of Russification and de-Christianization forced students in eastern Europe to read histories of the war that ignored native resistance and gave the Red Army sole credit for fighting the Nazis. Stalinists replaced national symbols with Soviet ones. For example, the Hungarians had to accept a new flag with a Soviet red star beaming rays onto a hammer and sickle; Hungary's national colors were reduced to a small band on the flag. Utter historical distortion, revivified anti-Semitism, and rigid censorship resulted in what one staunchly socialist writer characterized as "a dreary torrent of colorless, mediocre literature." In the USSR itself, Stalin also instituted new purges to ensure obedience and conformity. Marshall Zhukov, a popular leader of the armed forces, was shipped to a distant command, while Anna Akhmatova, the great poet whose popular writing had emphasized perseverance and individual heroism

■ **Re-Creating Hungarian Youth**

People across Europe focused on the well-being of young people after World War II, and regimes in the Soviet sphere took steps to provide education in Communist ways. Youth groups like those in the early Stalinist USSR served this end, and vivid posters in the Soviet realist style carried inspirational messages. "Forward for the Congress of the Young Fighters of Peace and Socialism," exhorts this poster informing Hungarian youth about a conference to be held in June 1950.
(Magyar Nemzeti Múzeum, Budapest [Hungarian National Museum].)

ELŐRE A BÉKE ÉS A SZOCIALIZMUS
IFJÚ HARCOSAINAK KONGRESSZUSAÉRT
1950. JUNIUS 17-18

during the war, died confined to a crowded hospital room because she refused to glorify Stalin in her postwar poetry.

In March 1953, Stalin died. As people openly mourned this man they considered their savior from backwardness and Nazism, troubles already loomed in the empire he ruled so tyrannically. Political prisoners in the labor camps who had started rioting late in the 1940s now pressed their demands for reform. Consumer goods were much scarcer than in the West because of the government's high military spending and the enormous cost of recovery. Amid deprivation and discontent, Soviet officials enjoyed country homes, luxury goods, and plentiful food, but many of them had come to distrust Stalinism and were ready for some changes. A power struggle ensued within the Communist leadership, and protests took place throughout the Soviet bloc. In response, the government freed some prisoners of the Gulag labor camp and beefed up production of consumer goods—a policy called "goulash communism" because in part it resulted in more food for ordinary people.

The old ways could not hold. In 1955, Nikita Khrushchev, an illiterate coal miner before the revolution, outmaneuvered other rivals to emerge the undisputed leader of the Soviet Union, but he did so without the usual executions. The next year he attacked Stalinism. At a party congress, Khrushchev denounced the "cult of personality" Stalin had built about himself and announced that Stalinism did not equal socialism. The "secret speech"—it was not published in the USSR but became widely known—sent tremors through Communist parties around the world. In this climate of uncertainty, protest erupted once more in early summer 1956, when discontented Polish railroad workers struck for better wages. Popular support for their cause ushered in a more liberal Communist program. Inspired by the Polish example, Hungarians rebelled against forced collectivization in October 1956—"the golden October," they would call their uprising. As in Poland, economic issues, especially announcements of reduced wages, sparked some of the first outbreaks of violence, but the protest soon targeted the entire Communist system. Tens of thousands of protesters filled the streets of Budapest and succeeded in returning a popular hero, Imre Nagy, to power. When Nagy announced that Hungary might leave the Warsaw Pact, Soviet troops moved in, killing tens of thousands and causing hundreds of thousands more to flee to the West. Nagy was hanged. The U.S. refusal to intervene showed that, despite a rhetoric of "liberation," it would not risk World War III by militarily challenging the Soviet sphere of influence.

The failure of eastern European uprisings overshadowed significant changes—called a climate of "thaw"—in Soviet policy. In the process of defeating his rivals, Khrushchev ended the Stalinist purges and reformed the courts (which came to function according to procedures, not like the stage for show trials of the past). The gates of the Gulag opened, and the secret police lost many of its arbitrary powers. A new sense of security acquired from increased productivity, military buildup, and stunning successes in aerospace development were also part of the thaw. In 1957, the Soviets successfully launched the first artificial earth satellite, *Sputnik*, and in 1961 they put the first cosmonaut, Yuri Gagarin, in orbit around the earth. The Soviets' edge in space technology shocked the Western bloc and motivated the creation of the U.S. National Aeronautics and Space Administration (NASA).

Soviet successes indicated that the USSR was on the way to achieving Stalin's goal of modernization. Nevertheless, Khrushchev continued to fear and bully dissidents. For example, he forced Boris Pasternak to refuse the 1958 Nobel Prize in literature because his novel *Doctor Zhivago* (1957) cast doubt on the glory of the revolution and affirmed the value of the individual. Yet under the thaw, Khrushchev himself made several trips to the West and was more widely seen by the public than Stalin had been. More confident and more affluent, the Soviets took steps to reduce their diplomacy's paranoid style and concentrated their efforts on spreading socialism in the emerging nations of Asia, Africa, and Latin America.

Decolonization in a Cold War Climate

World War II dealt the final blow to the ability of European powers to maintain their vast empires. The Western powers attempted to stamp out nationalist groups that had strengthened during the war and to reimpose their control—with fatal results. As before, colonized peoples had been on the front lines defending the West; and as before, they had witnessed the full barbarism of Western warfare. Excluded from victory parades and other ceremonies so the powers could maintain the illusion of Western supremacy, adult men in the colonies still did not receive the political rights promised them. Instead, people in Asia, Africa, and the Middle East, often led by individuals steeped in Western values and experienced in war, embraced the cause of independence and often clashed with the West in bloody warfare.

The path to achieving independence was paved with difficulties. In Africa, a continent whose peoples spoke more than five thousand languages, the European conquerors' creation of convenient administrative units such as "Nigeria" and "Rhodesia" had obliterated living arrangements that had relied on ethnic ties and local cultures. In addition, religion played a divisive role in independence movements. In India, Hindus and Muslims battled one another even though they shared the goal of eliminating the British. In the Middle East and North Africa, pan-Arab and pan-Islamic movements might seem to have been unifying forces. Yet many Muslims were not Arab, not all Arabs were Muslim, and Islam itself encompassed many competing beliefs and sects. Differences among religious beliefs, ethnic groups, and cultural practices—many of them invented or promoted by the colonizers to divide and rule—overlapped and undermined political unity. Despite these complications, peoples in what was coming to be called the third world succeeded in throwing off the imperial yoke while they offered a new battlefield for cold war competition between the United States and the Soviet Union.

The End of Empire in Asia

At the end of World War II, leaders in Asia began to mobilize the mass discontent that had intensified during the war and, often facing stiff resistance from white settlers, were able to drive out foreign rulers. Declining from an imperial power to a small island nation, Britain was the biggest loser. In 1947, it parted with India, the "jewel" of its empire. The British had promised in the 1930s to grant India its independence, but they postponed it when war broke out. Some two million Indian men were mobilized, anchoring the war in the Middle East and Asia. Local industry became an important wartime supplier, and Indian business leaders bought out British entrepreneurs short of cash. During this period of economic prosperity for some people, however, food shortages drove many others to overcrowded cities, and political fissures between Hindus and Muslims, long encouraged by the British, widened.

The British faced the inevitable after the war and decreed that two countries should emerge from the old colony, so great was the mistrust between the parties of the Indian National Congress and Muslim League. Thus, in 1947, India was created for Hindus and Pakistan for Muslims. Yet during the independence year, political tensions exploded among opposing members of the two religions. Hundreds of thousands were massacred in the great shift of populations between the two nations. In 1948, a radical Hindu assassinated Gandhi, who though a Hindu himself had continued to champion religious reconciliation. Confronting nationalist movements elsewhere, Britain retained control of Hong Kong; but before two decades of the postwar era had passed, almost half a billion Asians had gained their freedom from the rule of fifty million British (see "Mapping the West," page 989).

In 1949, a Communist takeover in China brought in a government led by Mao Zedong that was no longer the plaything of the traditional colonial powers. Mao Zedong (1893–1976) led his army of Communists to victory over Jiang Jieshi's unpopular, corrupt Nationalist government, which the United States had bankrolled. Chinese communism in the new People's Republic of China emphasized above all the welfare of the peasantry rather than the industrial proletariat and was thus distinct from Marxism and Stalinism. Mao instituted social reforms such as civil equality for women but at the same time copied Soviet collectivization, rapid industrialization, and brutal repression of the privileged classes. Although China began to distance itself from the USSR in the mid-1950s, the Western bloc saw only monolithic red from Leningrad to Beijing.

The United States and the Soviet Union were deeply interested in East Asia, the United States because of the region's economic importance and the USSR because of its shared borders. Thus the Communist Chinese victory spurred both superpowers to increase their involvement in Asian politics. They faced off indirectly in Korea, which had been split at the thirty-eighth parallel after World War II. In 1950, the North Koreans, supported by the Soviet Union, invaded the U.S.-backed South.

The United States maneuvered the UN Security Council into approving a "police action" against the North, and its forces quickly drove well into North Korean territory, where they were met by the Chinese rather than the Soviet army. After two and a half years of stalemate, the opposing sides finally agreed to a settlement in 1953: Korea would remain split at its prewar border, the thirty-eighth parallel.

The United States lost more than 50,000 men in the Korean War and increased its military spending from $10.9 billion in 1948 to almost $60 billion in 1953 to hold the line on Communist expansion. Communist potential in decolonizing areas led the American secretary of state, John Foster Dulles, to characterize Asian countries as a row of dominoes: "You knock over the first one and what will happen is that it will go over [to communism] very quickly." The expansion of the cold war to Asia prompted the creation of an Asian counterpart to NATO.

The Korean War, 1950–1953

Established in 1954, the Southeast Asia Treaty Organization (SEATO) included Pakistan, Thailand, the Philippines, Britain, Australia, New Zealand, France, and the United States. One side effect was the rapid reindustrialization of Japan to provide the United States with supplies.

The cold war spread to Indochina, where nationalists had been struggling against the postwar revival of French imperialism. Their leader, the European-educated Ho Chi Minh, preached both nationalism and socialism and built a powerful organization, the Viet Minh, to fight colonial rule.◆ He advocated the redistribution of land held by big landowners, especially in the rich agricultural area in southern Indochina where some six thousand owners possessed more than 60 percent of the land. Viet Minh peasant guerrillas ultimately forced the technologically advanced French army to withdraw from the country after the bloody battle of Dien Bien Phu in 1954. Later that year the Geneva Convention carved out an independent Laos and divided Vietnam into North and South, each free from French control. The Viet Minh was ordered to retreat to an area north of the seventeenth parallel. But the superpowers' intervention undermined the peace treaty while risking the nuclear brink and subjecting native peoples to the force of their military

---

◆ For a primary source that reveals the goals and motives of the Viet Minh, see Document 71, Ho Chi Minh, "Declaration of Independence of the Republic of Vietnam."

Indochina, 1954

might. In fighting to prevent national liberation in the name of fighting communism, the United States in particular was acquiring a reputation as an "imperialist" power of the old school, nowhere more so than in Vietnam.

The Struggle for Identity in the Middle East

The power of oil and the ability of small countries to see the opportunity for maneuvering between antagonists in the cold war gave new impetus to independence struggles in the Middle East. As in the rest of the world after the war, Middle Eastern peoples renewed their commitment to independence and resisted attempts by the major powers to regain imperial control. Weakened by the war, British oil companies wanted to tighten their grip on profits, as the value of oil soared. The cold war gave Middle Eastern leaders an opening to bargain with the superpowers, playing them off one against another, especially over resources to reestablish war-torn economies. The legacy of the Holocaust, however, complicated the political scene as the Western powers' commitment to secure a Jewish homeland in the Middle East further stirred up Arab determination to regain control of the region.

When World War II broke out, 600,000 Jewish settlers and twice as many Arabs lived, in intermittent conflict, in British-controlled Palestine. In 1947, an exhausted Britain ceded the area to the United Nations to work out a settlement between the Jews and the Arabs. In the aftermath of the Holocaust, the UN voted to partition Palestine into an Arab region and a Jewish one (Map 22.4). Conflicting claims, however, led to war, and Jewish military forces prevailed. On May 14, 1948, the state of Israel came into being. "The dream had come true," Golda Meir, the future president of Israel, remembered, but "too late to save those who had perished in the Holocaust." Israel opened its gates to immigrants, driving its ambitions against those of its Arab neighbors.

One of those neighbors, Egypt, had gained its independence from Britain at the end of the war. Britain, however, retained its control of Middle Eastern oil and its dominance of Asian shipping through the Suez Canal, which was owned by a British-run company. In 1952, Colonel Gamal Abdel Nasser became Egypt's president on a platform of economic modernization and true national independence. A prime goal was reclaiming the Suez Canal, "where 120,000 of our sons had lost their

■ MAP 22.4 The Partition of Palestine and the Creation of Israel, 1947–1948

The creation of the Jewish state of Israel in 1948 against a backdrop of ongoing wars among Jews and indigenous Arab peoples made the Middle East a powder keg. The struggle for resources and for securing the borders of viable nation-states was at the heart of these bitter contests, threatening to pull the superpowers into a third world war.

lives in digging it [by force]," he stated. In July 1956, Nasser nationalized the canal. Britain, supported by Israel and France, attacked Egypt, bringing the Suez crisis to a head while the Hungarian revolt was in full swing. The British branded Nasser another Hitler, but American opposition made the British back down. Nasser's triumph inspired confidence that the Middle East could confront the West and win.

New Nations in Africa

In sub-Saharan Africa, nationalist leaders roused their people to challenge Europeans' increasing demand for resources and labor, which resulted in poverty for African peoples. "The European Merchant is my shepherd, and I am in want," went one African version of the Twenty-third Psalm. Disrupted in their traditional agricultural patterns, many Africans flocked to shantytowns in cities during the war, where they kept themselves alive through scavenging, craft work, and menial labor for whites. At war's end, Kwame Nkrumah led the diverse inhabitants of the British-controlled West African Gold Coast in Gandhian-style passive resistance. After years of arresting and jailing the protesters, the British withdrew, allowing the state of Ghana to come into being in 1957. Nigeria, the most populous African region, became independent in 1960 after the leaders of its many regional groups and political organizations reached agreement on a federal-style government. In these and other African states where the population was mostly black, independence came less violently than in mixed-race territory (Map 22.5).

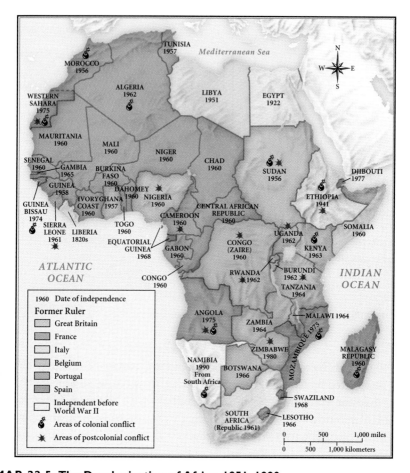

■ MAP 22.5 The Decolonization of Africa, 1951–1990
*The liberation of Africa from European rule was an uneven process, sometimes occurring peace-
fully and at other times demanding armed struggle to drive out European settlers, governments,
and armies. After liberation, the difficult process of nation building—forming governments, educating children, providing social services—began. Creating national unity also proved challenging,
except in places where the struggle against colonialism had already brought people together.*

The eastern coast and southern and central areas of Africa had numerous
European settlers who violently resisted independence movements. In British East
Africa, where white settlers ruled in splendor and where blacks lacked both land
and economic opportunity, violence erupted in the 1950s. African men formed rebel
groups named the Land Freedom Army but known as "Mau Mau." With women
serving as provisioners, messengers, and weapon stealers, Mau Mau bands, composed mostly of war veterans from the Kikuyu ethnic group, tried to recover land

from whites. In 1964, after the British had slaughtered some ten to fifteen thousand Kikuyus, Kenya gained formal independence.

France—though eager to regain its great-power status after its humiliating defeat and occupation in World War II—easily granted certain demands for independence, such as those of Tunisia, Morocco, and West Africa, where there were fewer settlers, more limited economic stakes, and less military involvement. Elsewhere, French struggles against independence movements were prolonged and bloody. The ultimate test of the French empire came in Algeria. When Algerian nationalists rebelled against the restoration of French rule in the final days of World War II, the French army massacred tens of thousands of protesters. The liberation movement resurfaced with ferocious intensity as the Front for National Liberation in 1954. In response, the French dug in, sending in more than 400,000 troops. Neither side fought according to the rules of warfare: the French tortured natives, while Algerian women, shielded by gender stereotypes, planted bombs in European cafés and carried weapons to assassination sites.

Shedding its colonies at a rapid rate, France drew the line at Algeria. "The loss of Algeria," warned one statesman, "would be an unprecedented national disaster."

■ **Jomo Kenyatta, First President of the New Kenyan Nation**
Educated in England, Kenyatta wrote Facing Mount Kenya, *a work that explained Kikuyu life as a distinct culture to Westerners. After a costly struggle during which he was imprisoned by the British, Kenyatta became president (1964–1978) of the new republic of Kenya. He stifled political debate by outlawing opposition parties. His one-party government brought social calm, which made Kenya a good place for Western investment.*
(© Bettmann/CORBIS.)

Although many agreed, the Algerian War also threatened social stability as protests in Paris greeted reports of the army's barbarous practices. The French military and settlers in Algeria met the antiwar movement with terrorism against citizens in France. They threatened coups, set off bombs, and assassinated politicians in the name of Algérie Française (French Algeria).

France's Fourth Republic collapsed over Algeria, and in 1958, Charles de Gaulle came back to power. In return for leading France out of its Algerian quagmire, de Gaulle demanded the creation of a new republican government—the Fifth Republic—one with a strong president who could choose the prime minister and exercise emergency power. As his plans actually to decolonize Algeria unfolded, terrorism against him escalated. But by 1962, de Gaulle had negotiated independence with the Algerian nationalists. Hundreds of thousands of *pieds noirs* ("black feet"), as the French condescendingly called Europeans in Algeria, as well as their Arab supporters fled to France. The Dutch and Belgian empires also disintegrated. Violent resistance to the reimposition of colonial rule led to the establishment of the large independent states of Indonesia and Zaire.

As independent nations emerged from colonialism and as continental Europe received immigrants from former colonies, structures arose to promote international security and worldwide deliberations that included voices from the new states. The United Nations convened for the first time in 1945, and one notable change ensured it a greater chance of success than the League of Nations: both the United States and the Soviet Union were active members from the outset. The charter of the UN outlined a collective global authority that would adjudicate conflicts and provide military protection if any members were threatened by aggression. In 1955, Achmed Sukarno, who succeeded in wrenching Indonesian independence from the Dutch, sponsored the Bandung Convention of nonaligned nations to set a common policy for achieving modernization and facing the major powers. Both the UN and the meetings of emerging nations began shifting global issues away from those of the Western powers. Human rights and economic inequities among developing countries and the West nudged their way into public consciousness.

Cultural Life on the Brink of Nuclear War

Both the Holocaust and the cold war shaped postwar leisure and political culture, as the responsibility for Nazism, the cause of ethnic and racial justice, and the merits of the two superpowers set people against one another. Yet this was a time of intense self-scrutiny as Europeans debated decolonization and the Americanization that seemed to accompany the influx of U.S. dollars, consumer goods, and cultural media. While Europeans examined their past and grew prosperous, the cold war menaced. In October 1962, the world held its breath while the leaders of the Soviet Union and the United States provoked the real possibility of nuclear conflagration over the issue of missiles on the island of Cuba.

Restoring "Western" Values

After the depravity and inhumanity of Nazism, cultural currents in Europe and the United States reemphasized universal values and spiritual renewal. Some, like Billy Graham, saw the churches as central to the restoration of values through an active commitment to "re-Christianizing" Europe and the United States. Their success was only partial, however, as the trend toward a more secular culture continued. Thus, in the early postwar years people in the U.S. bloc emphasized the triumph of a Western heritage, a Western civilization, and Western values over fascism, and they characterized the war as one "to defend civilization [from] a conspiracy against man." This definition of *West* often emphasized the heritage of Greece and Rome and the rise of national governments in England, France, and western Europe as they encountered "barbaric" forces, be they nomadic tribes, Nazi armies, Communist agents, or national liberation movements in Asia and Africa. University courses in Western civilization flourished after the war to reaffirm those values. At the same time, the postwar renewal of humanitarianism pushed issues of cultural pluralism and human rights to the forefront of culture.

Memoirs of the death camps and tales of the resistance became compelling reading material. Rescued from the Third Reich in 1940, Nelly Sachs won the Nobel Prize in literature in 1966 for her poetry about the Holocaust. Anne Frank's *Diary of a Young Girl* (1947), the poignant record of a teenager hidden with her family in the back of an Amsterdam warehouse, was emblematic of the survival of Western values in the face of Nazi persecution. Confronted with the small miseries of daily life and the grand evils of Nazism, Anne never stopped believing that "people are really good at heart."

Histories of the resistance also tapped into the public's need for inspiration after an orgy of savagery. Governments erected permanent plaques at spots where resisters had been killed; their biographies filled magazines and bookstalls; organizations of resisters commemorated their role in winning the war. Although resistance efforts were publicized, discussion of collaboration threatened to open old wounds. French filmmakers, for instance, avoided the subject for decades after the war. Many a politician with a Nazi past moved into the new cultural mainstream even as the stories of resistance took on mythical qualities.

By the end of the 1940s, existential philosophy became the rage among the cultural elites and students and in universities. It explored the meaning (or lack of meaning) of human existence in a world where evil flourished. Two of its leaders, Albert Camus and Jean-Paul Sartre, had written for the resistance during the war, although Nazi censors had also allowed the production of Sartre's plays. Existentialists confronted the question of what "being" was about, given what they perceived as the absence of God and the breakdown of morality. Their answer was that "being," or existing, was not the automatic process either of God's creation or of birth into the natural world. One was not born with spiritual goodness in the image

■ **Zbigniew Cybulski, the Polish James Dean**
Zbigniew Cybulski depicted a tortured young resistance fighter in Andrzej Wajda's film Ashes and Diamonds *(1958). On the last day of World War II, Cybulski's character is supposed to assassinate a Communist resistance leader, and his ambivalence about this act plays out amid the chaos in Poland at war's end. Like existentialist philosophers and other cinema directors at the time, Wajda captured the debate over human values and the interest in young heroes of the postwar era.* (Photofest.)

of a creator; instead, through action and choice, one created an "authentic" existence. Camus's novels, such as *The Stranger* (1942) and *The Plague* (1947), dissected the evils of a corrupt political order and pondered human responsibility in such situations. Sartre's writings emphasized political activism and resistance under totalitarianism. Despite the fact that they had never confronted the enormous problems of making choices while living under fascism, young people in the 1950s found existentialism compelling and made it the most fashionable philosophy of the day.

In 1949, Simone de Beauvoir, Sartre's lifetime companion, published the twentieth century's most important work on the condition of women, *The Second Sex*. Beauvoir believed that most women had failed to take the kind of action necessary to lead authentic lives. Instead, they lived in the world of "necessity," devoting themselves exclusively to reproduction and motherhood. Failing to create an authentic self through considered action and accomplishment, they had become its opposite—an object or "Other." Moreover, instead of struggling to define themselves and assert their freedom, women passively accepted their own "Otherness" and lived as defined by men. Beauvoir's book was a smash hit, in large part because people thought Sartre had written it.◆ Both were celebrities, for the media spread the new commitment to humane values just as it had spread support for Nazism or for its wartime enemies.

While Europeans debated decolonization among peoples of color in Africa and Asia, intellectuals spawned new theories of what liberation would mean for people of color. The first half of the century had witnessed the rise of pan-Africanism, but it was in the 1950s and 1960s that the immensely influential writing of Frantz Fanon, a black psychiatrist from the French colony of Martinique, began analyzing liberation movements. He called the mental functioning of the colonized person "traumatized" by the violence and the brutal imposition of a culture other than one's own as the only standard of value. Ruled by guns, the colonized person knew only violence and would thus naturally decolonize by means of violence. Translated into many languages, Fanon's *Black Skin, White Masks* (1952) and *The Wretched of the Earth* (1961) posed the question of how to "decolonize" one's mind.

Simultaneous with decolonization, in the 1950s the commitment to the civil rights cause embodied in such long-standing organizations as the National Association for the Advancement of Colored People (NAACP, founded 1909) intensified. In principle, African Americans had fought in the war to defeat the Nazi idea of white racial superiority and now hoped to advance that ideal in the United States. In 1954, the U.S. Supreme Court declared segregated education unconstitutional in *Brown v. Board of Education*, a case initiated by the NAACP. On December 1, 1955, in Montgomery, Alabama, Rosa Parks, a part-time secretary for the local branch of the NAACP, boarded a bus and took the first available seat in the so-called white section at the front of the bus. When a white man found himself without a seat, the driver screamed at Parks, "Nigger, move back." Sitting in the front violated southern laws, which encompassed a host of inequitable, even brutal policies toward African Americans. Parks confronted that system through the studied practice of civil disobedience, and her action led to a boycott of public transportation that pushed the civil rights movement into the African American community as a whole.

The culture of rights and human values generated further organizing. A variety of civil rights groups boycotted discriminatory businesses, "sat in" at segregated facilities, and registered black voters disfranchised by local regulations. Many talented leaders emerged, foremost among them Martin Luther King Jr., a minister from Georgia whose oratorical power galvanized activists to Gandhian nonviolent resistance despite brutal white retaliation. For a few years, the postwar culture of nonviolence would shape the civil rights movement. Soon, however, the voices of

---

◆ For an excerpt, see Document 72, Simone de Beauvoir, *The Second Sex.*

thinkers like Fanon would merge with those of the civil rights movement to revolutionize thinking about race and rights.

Rising Consumerism and Shifting Gender Norms

Government spending on reconstruction, productivity, and welfare helped prevent the kind of social, political, and economic upheaval that had followed World War I. Nor did the same tensions prevail among men and women. A rising birthrate, bustling youth culture, and upsurge in consumerism edged out wartime behavior. Because of the decisive result of World War II, men returned from World War II much less frustrated than they had been in the 1920s. Nonetheless, the war affected men's roles and sense of themselves. Young men who had missed World War II adopted the rough, violent style of soldiers, and roaming gangs posed as tough military types. While Soviet youth admired aviator aces, elsewhere groups such as the "teddy boys" in England (named after their Edwardian style of dressing) and the gamberros in Spain took their cues from new forms of pop culture in music and film.

The leader of rock-and-roll style and substance was the American singer Elvis Presley. Sporting slicked-back hair and an aviator-style jacket, Presley bucked his hips and sang sexual lyrics to screaming and devoted fans. In a German nightclub late in the 1950s, members of a group of Elvis fans called the Quarrymen per-formed, fighting and yelling at one another as part of their show. They would soon become known as the Beatles. Young American film stars, like James Dean in *Rebel without a Cause* and Marlon Brando in *The Wild One,* created the beginnings of a conspicuous postwar youth culture.

The rebellious and rough masculine style appeared also in literature such as James Watson's autobiography explaining how he and Francis Crick had discovered the structure of the gene. Portraying himself as a fanatic bad boy in his 1968 book *The Double Helix,* Watson described how he had rifled people's desk drawers (among other dishonest acts) to become a scientific hero. In the revival of West German lit-erature, Heinrich Böll published *The Clown* (1963), a novel whose young hero takes to performing as a clown and begging in a railroad station. Böll protested that West Germany's postwar goal of respectability had allowed the resurgence of precisely those groups of people who had produced Nazism. Across the Atlantic, the Ameri-can "Beat" poets, who looked dirty, bearded, and sometimes crazy, like prisoners or labor-camp survivors, critiqued traditional ideals of the upright and rational male achiever.

Both elite and popular culture revealed that two horrendous world wars had weakened the Enlightenment view of men as rational, responsible breadwinners. The 1953 inaugural issue of the American magazine *Playboy* ushered in a widely imitated depiction of a changed male identity. *Playboy* differed from typical porno-graphic magazines: along with pictures of nude women, it featured serious articles, especially on the topic of masculinity. This segment of the media presented modern man as sexually aggressive and independent of dull domestic life—just as he had been in the war. Breadwinning for a family only destroyed a man's freedom and sense of self. The notion of men's liberty had come to include not just political and economic rights but freedom of sexual expression.

In contrast, Western society promoted a postwar model for women that differed from their wartime experience as essential workers and heads of families in the absence of their men. Instead, postwar women were made to symbolize the return to normalcy—a domestic, nonworking norm. Late in the 1940s, the fashion house of Christian Dior launched a clothing style called the "new look." It featured a pinched waist, tightly fitting bodices, and full skirts. This restoration of the nineteenth-century female silhouette invited a renewal of clear gender roles. Women's magazines publicized the "new look" and urged a return to domesticity and thus normalcy. Even in the hard-pressed Soviet Union, recipes for homemade face creams passed from woman to woman, and beauty parlors did a brisk business. New

■ **The "New Look"**
Immediately after the war, the French fashion industry swung into action to devise styles for the return to normal life in the West. Cinched or corseted waists and ample skirts brought to mind the nineteenth century rather than the depression and war years, when some women had started regularly wearing trousers. The elegant middle-class Western lifestyle implied by the "new look" contrasted sharply with the conditions facing most women in the Soviet Union, who had to work to rebuild their devastated country. (Liaison Agency.)

household products such as refrigerators and washing machines raised standards for women's accomplishment in the home by giving them the means to be "perfect" housewives.

However, "new look" propaganda did not mesh with reality. Dressmaking fabric was still being rationed in the late 1940s; even in the next decade women could not get enough of it to make voluminous skirts. In Europe, where people had barely enough to eat, the underwear needed for "new look" contours simply did not exist. Consumers had access only to standardized undergarments available with ration tickets. European women continued to work outside the home after the war; indeed, mature women and mothers were working more than ever before—especially in the Soviet bloc. The female workforce was going through a profound revolution as it gradually became less youthful and more populated by wives and mothers who would work outside the home all their lives despite being bombarded with images of nineteenth-century middle-class femininity.

The advertising business presided over the creation of cultural messages as well as over the rise of a new consumerism that accompanied recovery. Guided by marketing experts, western Europeans were imitating Americans by driving some forty million motorized vehicles, including motorbikes, cars, buses, and trucks. The demand for cars made the automobile industry a leading economic sector. The number of radios in homes grew steadily—for example, by 10 percent a year in Italy between 1945 and 1950—and the 1950s marked a high tide of radio influence. The development of television in the 1920s and 1930s was interrupted by the war, but peacetime saw its rapid spread in the United States, which had twenty million sets by 1953. Only in the 1960s did television become an important consumer item for most Europeans, however. In the 1950s, radio was still king.

The Culture of Cold War

Radio was at the center of the cold war. As superpower rivalry heated up, radio's propaganda function remained at the fore. During the late 1940s and early 1950s, the Voice of America, with its main studio in Washington, D.C., broadcast in thirty-eight languages from one hundred transmitters and provided an alternative source of news for people in eastern Europe. The Soviet counterpart broadcast in Russian around the clock but initially spent much of its wattage jamming U.S. programming. Russian programs stressed a uniform Communist culture and values; the United States, by contrast, emphasized diverse programming and promoted debate about current affairs.

Its issues and events conveyed by radio and other media, the cold war acquired a far-reaching emotional impact. The public heard reports about nuclear buildups or tests of emergency power facilities that sent them scurrying for cover; in school, children rehearsed for nuclear war, and families built bomb shelters in their backyards. Books like George Orwell's *1984* (1949) were claimed by ideologues on both sides as vindicating their beliefs. Ray Bradbury's popular *Fahrenheit 451* (1953), whose title indicated the temperature at which books would burn, condemned cold war curtailment of intellectual freedom. In the USSR, official writers churned out spy stories, and espionage novels topped best-seller lists in the West. *Casino Royale* (1953) by the British author Ian Fleming introduced James Bond, who survived tests of wit and physical prowess at the hands of Communist and other political villains. Soviet pilots would not take off for flights when the work of Yulian Simyonov, the Russian counterpart of Ian Fleming, was playing on radio or television. Reports of Soviets and Americans—fictional or real—facing one another down became part of everyday life.

Culture as a whole came under the cold war banner, as people debated the "Americanization" they saw taking place in Europe. While many Europeans were proponents of American business practices, the Communist Party in France led a successful campaign to ban Coca-Cola for a time in the 1950s. Both sides tried to win the war by pouring vast sums of money into high culture, though the United States did it by secretly channeling government money into foundations to award fellowships to artists and writers or promote favorable journalism around the world. As leadership of the art world passed to the United States, art became part of the cold war. *Abstract expressionism*, practiced by American artists such as Jackson Pollock, produced abstract works by dripping, spattering, and pouring paint. In contrast, abstract works such as those of Pablo Picasso still had elements of realism. Abstract expressionists spoke of the importance of the artist's self-discovery, spiritual growth, and sensations in the process of painting. "If I stretch my arms next to the rest of myself and wonder where my fingers are, that is all the space I need as a painter," commented Dutch-born Willem de Kooning on his relationship with his canvas. Said to exemplify Western "freedom," such painters were given shows in Europe and awarded commissions at the secret direction of the U.S. Central Intelligence Agency (CIA).

The USSR openly promoted an official Communist culture. When a show of abstract art opened in the Soviet Union, Khrushchev yelled that it was "dog shit." Pro-Soviet critics in western Europe saw U.S.-style abstract art as "an infantile sickness" and supported socialist realist art with "human content," showing the condition of the workers and the oppressed races in the United States. In Italy, the *neorealist* technique was developed by filmmakers such as Roberto Rossellini in *Open City* (1945) and Vittorio De Sica in *The Bicycle Thief* (1948). Such works challenged Hollywood-style sets and costumes by using ordinary characters living in devastated, impoverished cities. By depicting stark conditions, neorealist directors conveyed their distance both from middle-class prosperity and from fascist bombast. "We are in rags? Let's show everyone our rags," said one Italian director. Seen or unseen, the cold war entered the most unsuspected aspects of cultural life.

■ **Mark Rothko, *Light Red over Black* (1957)**
Lithuanian-born Mark Rothko spread large, luminous fields of color across his canvases in an attempt to capture universal spiritual values. Usually his paintings contained only two or three of these fields, prompting the viewer to experience long periods of contemplation. Rothko belonged to a school of artists who aimed in the 1950s to reach enduring truths with such primal or "primitive" forms.
(Tate Gallery, London/Art Resource, NY.)

Kennedy, Khrushchev, and the Atomic Brink

It was in this pervasive climate of cold war that John F. Kennedy became U.S. president in 1960. Kennedy represented American affluence and youth but also the nation's commitment to cold war. Kennedy's media advisers and ghostwriters recognized how perfect a match their articulate, good-looking president was to the power of television. A war hero and early fan of the fictional cold war spy James Bond, Kennedy intensified the arms race and escalated the cold war. In 1959, a revolution in Cuba had brought to power Fidel Castro, who allied his government with the Soviet Union. In the spring of 1961, Kennedy, assured by the CIA of success, launched an invasion of Cuba at the Bay of Pigs to overthrow Castro. The invasion failed miserably and humiliated the United States. A few months later, Kennedy had a chilling meeting with Khrushchev in Vienna, at which the Soviet leader brandished the specter of nuclear holocaust over the continuing U.S. presence in Berlin.

In the summer of 1961, East German workers, supervised by police and the army, stacked bales of barbed wire across miles of the city's east-west border to begin construction of the Berlin Wall. The divided city had served as an escape route by which some three million people had fled to the West. Kennedy responded

IMPORTANT DATES			
1945	Cold war begins	1955	Soviet Union establishes the Warsaw Pact
1947	India and Pakistan win independence from Britain; U.S. President Harry Truman announces the "Truman Doctrine"	1956	Egyptian leader General Abdel Nasser nationalizes the Suez Canal; uprising in Hungary against USSR
1948	State of Israel established	1957	Boris Pasternak publishes *Doctor Zhivago*; USSR launches *Sputnik*; European Economic Community formed
1949	Mao Zedong leads Communist revolution in China; Western allies establish NATO; Simone de Beauvoir publishes *The Second Sex*		
		1958	Fifth Republic begins in France
1950	Korean War begins	1961	East German workers begin to construct the Berlin Wall
1952	Samuel Beckett publishes *Waiting for Godot*	1962	United States and USSR face off in the Cuban missile crisis
1953	Stalin dies; Korean War ends; first issue of *Playboy*		
1954	*Brown v. Board of Education* prohibits segregated schools in the United States; Vietnamese forces defeat the French at Dien Bien Phu		

at home with a call for more weapons and an enhanced civil defense program. In October 1962, matters came to a head when the CIA reported the installation of Soviet medium-range missiles in Cuba. Kennedy now responded forcefully, calling for a blockade of ships headed for Cuba and threatening nuclear war if the missiles were not removed. For several days, the world stood on the brink of nuclear disaster. Then, between October 25 and 27, Khrushchev and Kennedy negotiated an end to the crisis. Kennedy spent the remainder of his short life working to improve nuclear diplomacy; Khrushchev did the same. The two leaders, who had looked deeply into the nuclear future, clearly feared what they saw.

Conclusion

World War II began the atomic age and transformed international power politics. Two superpowers, the Soviet Union and the United States, each controlling atomic arsenals, replaced the former European leadership and engaged in a menacing cold war. The cold war saturated everyday life, giving birth to cold war religion in the

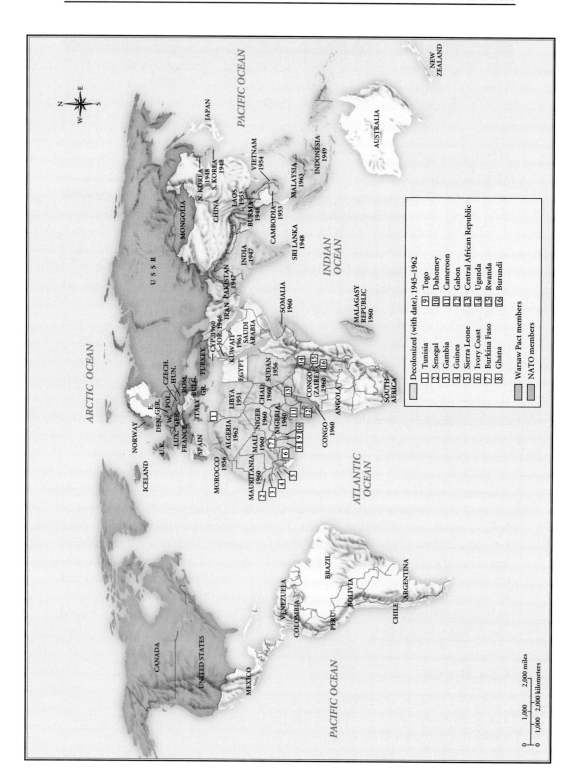

PACIFIC OCEAN

NEW ZEALAND

AUSTRALIA

JAPAN

N. KOREA 1948
S. KOREA 1948
VIETNAM 1954
INDONESIA 1949
MALAYSIA 1963

MONGOLIA

CHINA

LAOS 1953
BURMA 1948
CAMBODIA 1953

INDIA 1947
PAKISTAN 1947

SRI LANKA 1948

INDIAN OCEAN

USSR

SOMALIA 1960

MALAGASY REPUBLIC 1960

ARCTIC OCEAN

IRAN
JOR. 1946
CYP. 1960
KUWAIT 1961
SAUDI ARABIA
EGYPT 1956
SUDAN 1956

TURKEY
GR.
BULG.
ROM.
HUN.
CZECH.
POL.
W. GER.
E. GER.
DEN.

NORWAY

ICELAND

U.K.
LUX.
FRANCE
SPAIN
ITALY

LIBYA 1951
CHAD 1960
NIGER 1960

MOROCCO 1956

ALGERIA 1962

MAURITANIA 1960

MALI 1960

NIGERIA

CONGO (ZAIRE) 1960
CONGO 1960
ANGOLA

SOUTH AFRICA

14
15
16
13
11
12

8 9 10
7
6
5
4
2
1
3

ATLANTIC OCEAN

Decolonized (with date), 1945–1962

1	Tunisia	9	Togo
2	Senegal	10	Dahomey
3	Gambia	11	Cameroon
4	Guinea	12	Gabon
5	Sierra Leone	13	Central African Republic
6	Ivory Coast	14	Uganda
7	Burkina Faso	15	Rwanda
8	Ghana	16	Burundi

Warsaw Pact members

NATO members

CANADA

UNITED STATES

MEXICO

VENEZUELA
COLOMBIA
PERU
BOLIVIA
BRAZIL
CHILE
ARGENTINA

PACIFIC OCEAN

0   1,000   2,000 miles
0   1,000   2,000 kilometers

■ **MAPPING THE WEST** The Cold War World, c. 1960

Superpower rivalry resulted in the division of much of the industrial world into cold war alliances. The United States and the Soviet Union also vied for the allegiance of the newly decolonized countries of Asia and Africa by providing military, economic, and technological assistance. Wars such as those in Vietnam and Korea were also products of the cold war.

preachings of the Reverend Billy Graham and to a secular culture of bomb shelters, spies, and witch-hunts. The postwar reconstruction of Europe created a cold war division into an Eastern bloc dominated by the Soviets and a freer West mostly allied with the United States.

Yet both halves of Europe recovered almost miraculously. Eastern Europe, where wartime devastation was greatest, experienced less prosperity, while in western Europe wartime technology served as the basis for new consumer goods and improved health. Western Europe formed a successful Common Market that would become the foundation for the trend toward European unity. Yet as a result of the war, Germany recovered as two countries, not one, and the former European powers shed their colonies. Newly independent nations emerged in Asia and Africa, opening the possibility for a more equitable distribution of global power.

As the West as a whole grew in prosperity, its cultural life focused on eradicating the evils of Nazism and on surviving the atomic rivalry of the superpowers. In the midst of consumerism and a heated cold war culture, many came to wonder whether cold war was really worth the threat of nuclear annihilation.

Suggested References for further reading and online research appear on page SR-36 at the back of the book.

www.bedfordstmartins.com/huntconcise   See the ONLINE STUDY GUIDE to assess your mastery of the material covered in this chapter.

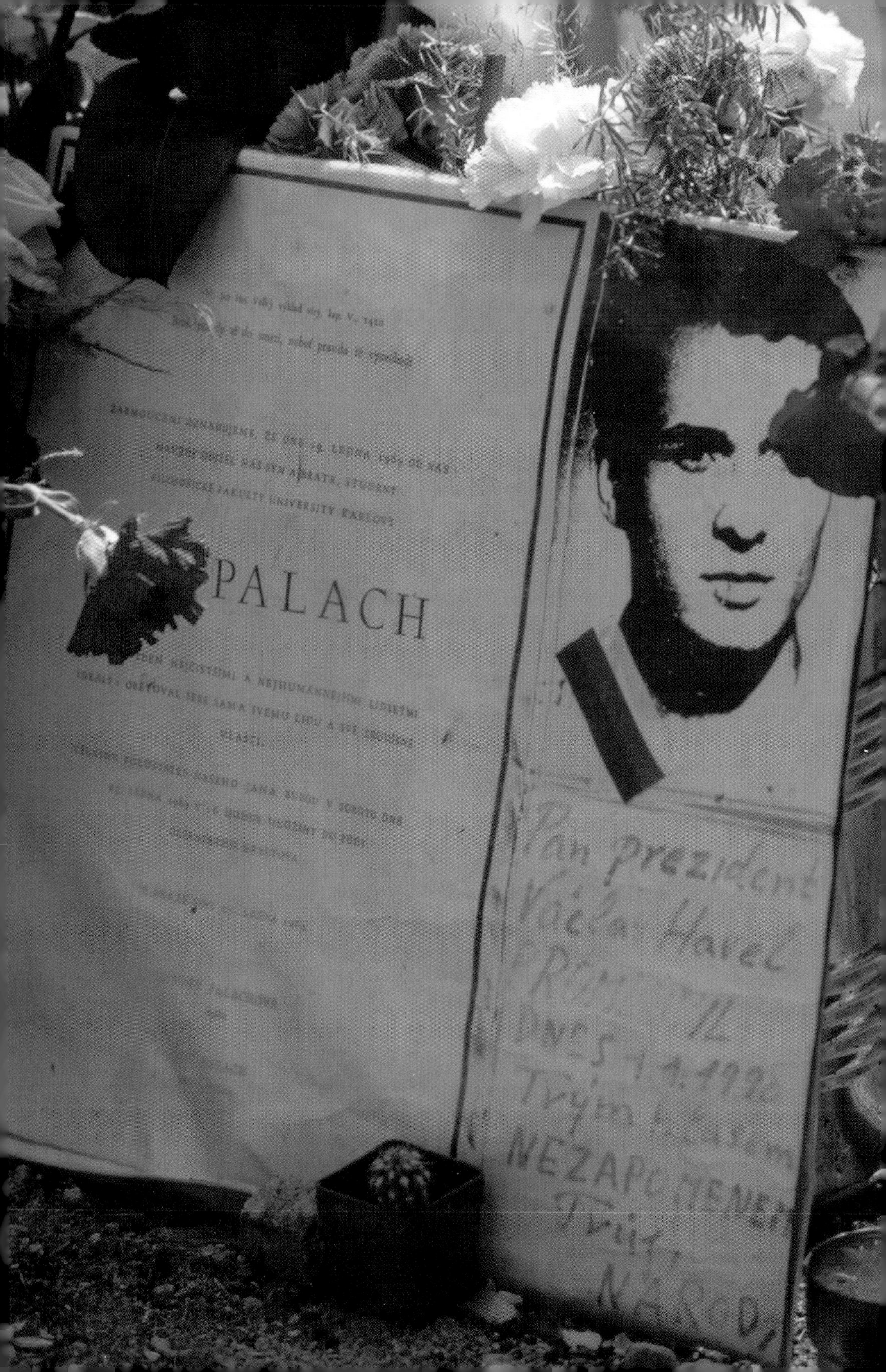
PALACH
Pan prezident

Challenges to the Postindustrial West

1960–1980

IN JANUARY 1969, JAN PALACH, a twenty-one-year-old philosophy student, drove to a main square in Prague, doused his body with gasoline, and set himself ablaze. In his coat—deliberately put to one side—was a paper demanding an end to Soviet-style repression in Czechoslovakia. It promised more such suicides unless the government lifted state censorship. The manifesto was signed: "Torch No. 1." Across a stunned nation, black flags were flown, close to a million people flocked to Palach's funeral, and shrines to his memory seemed to spring up overnight. For the next few months, as repression continued, more Czech youth followed Palach's grim example and became torches for freedom.

In an age of conspicuous technological growth, Jan Palach's self-immolation was a primal and horrifying scene. It was part of a massive uprising of youth, women, minorities, and many others in the 1960s and 1970s against repression, war, inequality, and technology itself. From Czechoslovakia to the United States and around the world, protests arose against the way in which industrial nations in general and the superpowers in particular were directing society. Political repression outraged these activists, and they objected to the human consequences of technology's dizzying pace. Technological advances, reformers believed, had given enormous power to a handful of financiers, managers, and bureaucrats—the new (but unelected) leaders of "postindustrial society." The term *postindustrial* indicated the emergence of the service sector—including finance, engineering, and health care—as the dominant force in the economy in the West, replacing heavy industry. Many of the protesters were being educated to enter this service elite. As critics, however,

■ **Shrine to Jan Palach**

Jan Palach was a martyr to the cause of an independent Czechoslovakia free to pursue a non-Soviet destiny. His self-immolation for that cause roused the nation. Makeshift shrines that sprang up throughout the 1970s and 1980s served as rallying points that ultimately contributed to the overthrow of Communist rule. (© Mark Garanger/Corbis.)

they saw mindless bondage resulting from work in which the majority of people merely watched over an ever-growing number of machines.

While reformers questioned the values of technological society, whole nations challenged the superpowers' monopoly of international power. An agonizing war in Vietnam sapped the resources of the United States, and China confronted the Soviet Union with increasing confidence. The oil-producing states of the Middle East formed a cartel and reduced the flow of oil to the leading industrial nations in the 1970s. The resulting price increases helped bring on a recession in the West. Other third-world countries resorted to terrorism to achieve their ends, and all the wealth and military might of the superpowers could not guarantee that they would emerge victorious in this age of increasingly global competition. Nor during these decades could the superpowers prevent the erosion of their legitimacy—an erosion often brought on by the individual acts of citizens like the human torches.

The Technology Revolution

Three decades after World War II, continuing technological advances steadily boosted prosperity and changed daily life in industrial countries. In Europe and the United States, people awoke to instantaneous radio and television news, worked with computers, and used revolutionary contraceptives to control reproduction. Satellites orbiting the earth reported weather conditions, relayed telephone signals, and collected military intelligence. Household gadgets from electric popcorn poppers and portable radios to automatic garage door openers made life more pleasant. The reliance on machines led one scientist and philosopher, Donna Haraway, to insist that people were no longer self-sufficient individuals but rather *cyborgs*, humans who needed machines to sustain ordinary life processes. However, as with the invention of textile machinery and the railroads in the eighteenth and nineteenth centuries, the full range of social implications—positive and negative—would not take shape all at once.

The Information Age: Television and Computers

Information technology catalyzed social change in these postindustrial decades just as innovations in textile making and the spread of railroads had in the nineteenth century. Its ability to convey knowledge, culture, and politics globally appeared even more revolutionary. In the first half of the twentieth century, mass journalism, film, and radio had begun to forge a more homogeneous society based on shared information and images; in the last third of the century, television, computers, and telecommunications made information more accessible and, some critics said, culture more standardized.

Americans embraced television in the 1950s; after the postwar recovery, it was Europe's turn. Between the mid-1950s and the mid-1970s, Europeans rapidly adopted television as a major entertainment and communications medium. In 1954, 1 percent of French households had television; by 1974, almost 80 percent did. With the average viewer tuning in about four and a half hours a day, the audience for newspapers and theater declined. "We devote more . . . hours per year to television than [to] any other single artifact," one sociologist commented in 1969. As with radio, European governments funded television broadcasting with tax dollars and controlled TV programming to avoid what they perceived as the substandard fare offered by American commercial TV; instead, they featured drama, ballet, concerts, variety shows, and news. In Europe at least, the welfare state assumed a new obligation—to fill citizens' leisure time—and gained more power to shape daily life.

With the emergence of communications satellites and video recorders in the 1960s, state-sponsored television encountered competition. Satellite technology allowed for the transmission of sports broadcasts and other programming to a worldwide audience. Feature films on videotape became readily available to television stations (though not yet to individuals) and competed with made-for-television movies and other programs. The competition increased in 1969 when Sony Corporation introduced the first affordable color videocassette recorder to the consumer market. What statesmen and intellectuals considered the junk programming of the United States—soap operas, game shows, sitcoms—arrived dubbed in the native language, amusing a vast audience with the joys, sorrows, tensions, and aspirations of daily life. Critics charged that both state-sponsored and commercial television avoided extremes to keep sponsors happy, instead spoon-feeding audiences only "official" or "moderate" opinions.

■ **Venice Skyline**
Television swept Europe in the 1960s and 1970s, increasingly uniting people by means of the daily news, theater, films, and game shows. Satellite transmission allowed programming to cross national boundaries, further linking the peoples and cultures of the Common Market. In divided Germany, the exchange of programming bridged even the Berlin Wall and was an early contributor to the erosion of cold war divisions.
(Tom Bross/Stock Boston.)

They complained that, although TV provided more information than had ever been available before, the resulting shared culture represented the lowest common denominator.

East and west, television exercised a powerful political and cultural influence. Even in one rural area of the Soviet Union, over 70 percent of the inhabitants watched television regularly in the late 1970s; the rest continued to prefer radio. Educational programming united the far-flung population of the USSR by broadcasting shows designed to advance Soviet culture. At the same time, with travel impossible or forbidden to many, shows about foreign lands were among the most popular—as were postcards from these lands, which became household decorations. Heads of state could usually preempt regular programming. In the 1960s, French president Charles de Gaulle addressed his fellow citizens frequently, employing the grandiose gestures of an imperial ruler to stir patriotism. As electoral success in Western Europe increasingly depended on cultivating a successful media image, political staffs came to rely on media experts as much as they did policy experts.

Just as revolutionary, the computer reshaped work in science, defense, and ultimately industry. Computers had evolved dramatically since the first electronic computer, Colossus, which the British used in 1943 to decode Nazi military and diplomatic messages. Awesome in its day, Colossus was primitive by later standards—gigantic, slow, able only to decode, and noisy. With growing use in civilian industry and business after the war, computing machines shrank from the size of a gymnasium in the 1940s to the size of an attaché case in the mid-1980s. They also became far less expensive and fantastically more powerful than Colossus, thanks to the development of sophisticated digital electronic circuitry implanted on tiny silicon chips, which replaced the clumsy vacuum tubes used in 1940s and 1950s computers. Within a few decades the computer could perform hundreds of millions of operations per second, and the price of the integrated circuit at the heart of computer technology would fall to less than a dollar, allowing businesses and households access to computing ability at a reasonable cost.

Computers changed the pace and patterns of work not only by speeding up and easing tasks but also by performing many operations that workers had once done themselves. Garment workers, for example, no longer painstakingly figured out how to arrange patterns on cloth for maximum efficiency and economy. A computer specified instructions for the optimal positioning of pattern pieces, and trained workers, usually women, followed the machine's directions. By the end of the 1970s, the miniaturization of the computer had made possible a renewal of the eighteenth-century-style "cottage industry." As in earlier times, people could work in the physical isolation of their homes but be connected to a central mainframe.

Did computers transform society for the better? Whereas the Industrial Revolution had seen physical power replaced by machine capabilities, the information

revolution witnessed brainpower augmented by computer technology. Many believed computers would profoundly expand mental life, providing, in the words of
one scientist, "boundless opportunities . . . to resolve the puzzles of cosmology, of
life, and of the society of man." Others maintained that computers programmed
people, reducing human capacity for inventiveness, problem solving, and initiative.
As the 1970s closed, such predictions were still untested as this information
revolution moved toward a more dramatic unfolding in the 1980s and 1990s.

The Space Age: Science and Satellites

When the Soviets launched the satellite *Sputnik* in 1957, they ignited competition
with the United States that was quickly labeled the "space race." U.S. president John
F. Kennedy became determined to beat the Soviets in space by putting a man on
the moon by the end of the 1960s. Throughout the decade, increasingly complex
space flights tested humans' ability to survive the process of space exploration, including weightlessness. Astronauts walked in space, endured weeks (and, later,
months) in orbit, docked with other craft, fixed satellites, and carried out experiments for the military and private industry. Meanwhile, a series of unmanned rock-
ets filled the earth's gravitational sphere with weather, television, intelligence, and
other communications satellites. In July 1969, a worldwide television audience
watched as U.S. astronauts Neil Armstrong and Edwin "Buzz" Aldrin walked on the
moon's surface—the climactic moment in the space race.◆

The space race also drove Western cultural developments. Astronauts and cos-
monauts were perhaps the era's most admired figures: Yuri Gagarin, Neil Armstrong,
and Valentina Tereshkova—the first woman in space—topped the list. A new fantasy world developed. Children's toys and games increasingly had space-related
themes. Films such as *2001: A Space Odyssey* portrayed space explorers answering
questions about life that were formerly the domain of church leaders. Likewise, in
the internationally popular television series *Star Trek*, members of the starship *Enterprise*'s diverse crew wrestled with the problems of maintaining humane values
against less-developed, often menacing civilizations. In the Eastern bloc, Polish author Stanislaw Lem's novel *Solaris* (1971) similarly portrayed space-age individuals
engaged in personal quests and likewise drew readers and ultimately viewers into a
futuristic fantasy.

This space age grew out of cold war concerns, but it also offered the possibility
of more global political cooperation: the diffusion of rocket technology, for example,
resulted from international efforts. From the 1960s on, U.S. spaceflights often involved
the participation of other countries such as Great Britain and the Netherlands.

◆ For two sources that capture the mood of the astronauts and their audience, see Document 73, The *New
York Times* and Neil Armstrong and Edwin Aldrin, "The First Men Walk on the Moon."

■ **Valentina Tereshkova, Russian Cosmonaut**
People sent into space were considered heroes personifying modern values of courage, strength, and well-honed skills. Insofar as the space age was part of the cold war race for superpower superiority, the USSR held the lead during the first decade. The Soviets trained both women and men, and the 1963 flight of Valentina Tereshkova—the first woman in space—supported Soviet claims of gender equality in contrast to the U.S. program. (Archive Photos.)

In 1965, an international consortium headed by the United States launched the first commercial communications satellite, *Intelsat I,* and by the 1970s more than four hundred stations worldwide and some 150 countries worked together to maintain global satellite communications.

Lunar landings and experiments in space advanced pure science despite space-race hype. Astronomers, for example, previously dependent on remote sensing for their work, used mineral samples from the moon to calculate the age of the solar system more precisely. Unmanned spacecraft provided data on cosmic radiation, magnetic fields, and infrared sources. Although the media touted the human conquerors of space, breakthroughs in space exploration and astronomy were dependent on a range of technology including the radiotelescope, which depicted space by receiving, measuring, and calculating nonvisible rays. These findings reinforced the "big bang" theory of the origins of the universe, first posited in the 1930s by American astronomer Edwin Hubble and given crucial support in the 1950s by the discovery of a low level of radiation permeating the universe in all directions. Based on the work of Albert Einstein and Max Planck, the "big bang" theory explains the development of the universe from a condition of extremely high density and temperature some ten billion years ago. Nuclei emerged when these conditions dissipated in a rapid expansion of space—the so-called big bang.

Revolutions in Biology, Reproductive Technologies, and Sexual Behavior

Sophisticated technologies extended to the life sciences, bringing dramatic new health benefits and ultimately changing reproduction itself. In 1952, scientists Francis Crick, an Englishman, and James Watson, an American, discovered the configuration of DNA, the material in a cell's chromosomes that carries hereditary information. Apparently solving the mystery of the gene and thus of biological inheritance, they showed how the "double helix" of the DNA molecule splits in cellular reproduction to form the basis of each new cell. This genetic material, biologists concluded, provides a chemical pattern for an individual organism's life. Beginning in the 1960s, genetics and the new field of molecular biology progressed rapidly. Growing understanding of nucleic acids and proteins advanced knowledge of viruses and bacteria that effectively ended the ravages of polio, tetanus, syphilis, tuberculosis, and such dangerous childhood diseases as mumps and measles in the West.

In the wake of this biological revolution came questions about the ethics of humans' tampering with the natural processes of life. For example, understanding how DNA works allowed scientists to bypass natural animal reproduction by means of a process called *cloning*—obtaining the cells of an organism and dividing or reproducing them (making an exact copy) in a laboratory. Ethicists and politicians questioned whether scientists *should* interfere with so basic and essential a process as reproduction. Similarly, the possibility of genetically altering species and even creating new ones (for instance, to control agricultural pests) led to concern about how such actions would affect the balance of nature. In a related medical field, Dr. Christiaan Barnard of South Africa performed the first successful human heart transplant in 1967, and U.S. doctors later developed an artificial heart. These medical miracles, however, prompted questions and even protests. For example, given the shortage of reusable organs, what criteria should doctors use to select recipients? Commentators also debated whether the enormous cost of new medical technology to save a few people would be better spent on helping the many who lacked even basic medical and health care.

Technology also influenced the most intimate areas of human relations— sexuality and procreation. In traditional societies, community and family norms dictated marital arrangements and sexual practices, in large part because too many or too few children threatened the crucial balance between population size and agricultural productivity. As Western societies industrialized and urbanized, however, not only did these considerations become less urgent but the growing availability of reliable birth-control devices permitted young people to begin sexual relations earlier, with less risk of pregnancy. In the 1960s, these trends accelerated, as the birth-control pill, first produced in the United States and tested on women in developing areas, came on the Western market. By 1970, its use was spreading around the world. Millions sought out voluntary surgical sterilization through tubal ligations and vasectomies. New techniques brought abortion, traditionally performed by amateurs, into the hands of medical professionals, making it a safe procedure for the first time.

Childbirth and conception itself were similarly transformed. Whereas only a small minority of Western births took place in hospitals in 1920, more than 90 percent did by 1970. Obstetricians now performed much of the work midwives had once done. As pregnancy and birth became a medical process, innovative new procedures and equipment made it possible to monitor women and fetuses throughout pregnancy, labor, and delivery. The number of medical interventions rose: cesarean births increased 400 percent in the United States in the 1960s and 1970s, and the number of prenatal visits per patient in Czechoslovakia, for example, rose 300 percent between 1957 and 1976. In 1978, the first "test-tube baby," Louise Brown, was born to an English couple. She had been conceived when her mother's eggs were fertilized with her father's sperm in a laboratory dish and then implanted in her mother's uterus—a complex process called *in vitro fertilization.* If a woman could not carry a child to term, a laboratory-fertilized embryo could be implanted in the uterus of a surrogate, or substitute, mother. Researchers even began working on an artificial womb to allow for reproduction entirely outside the body—from storage bank to artificial embryonic environment.

A host of controversies—and some tragedies—accompanied these breakthroughs. In the early 1960s, a West German drug firm, without prior testing, distributed the tranquilizer thalidomide, claiming that it safely prevented miscarriages. Pregnant women used the drug widely, with unforeseen results: thousands of children were born with physical and mental disabilities. The Catholic church firmly opposed all mechanical and chemical means of birth control as a sinful intervention in a sacred process. Many Catholics and others maintained that life begins at conception, and they branded abortion as murder. In vitro fertilization also stirred disapproval, appearing to some as "playing God" with human life.

Often publicizing these controversies, the expanding media helped democratize knowledge of birth-control procedures after World War II and made public discussions of sexual matters explicit, technical, and widespread. Popular use of birth control allowed Western society to be saturated with highly sexualized music, literature, and journalism without a corresponding rise in the birthrate—evidence of the increasing separation of sexuality from reproduction. Abundant statistical surveys showed that regular sexual activity began at an ever-younger age, and people talked more openly about sex—another component of cultural change. Finally, in a climate of increased publicity to sexuality, more open homosexual behavior became apparent, along with continued efforts to decriminalize it across the West. The Western media announced the arrival of a "sexual revolution." From the late nineteenth century to the 1960s, however, sexual revolution had been trumpeted with each advance in birth-control technology, showing once again the social and political impact of technological transformation.

■ Children Disabled by Thalidomide

In the last third of the century, the increasingly destructive side effects of some powerful medicines became apparent. Women who had taken the tranquilizer thalidomide during their pregnancies gave birth to children with severe disabilities. In the race to profit from scientific and technological developments, companies sometimes ignored the consequences for human beings.

(Deutsche Press Agentur/Archive Photos.)

Postindustrial Society and Culture

Reshaped by soaring investments in science and the spread of technology, Western countries in the 1960s started on what social scientists labeled a *postindustrial* course. Instead of being centered on manufacturing and heavy industry, post-industrial society emphasized the distribution of such services as health care and education. The service sector was the leading force in the economy, and this meant that intellectual work, not industrial or manufacturing work, had become primary. Moreover, all parts of society and industry interlocked, forming a system constantly in need of complex analysis. These characteristics of postindustrial society would carry over from the 1960s and 1970s into the next century.

Multinational Corporations

One of the major innovations of the postindustrial era was the rise of multinational corporations. These companies produced for a global market and conducted business worldwide, but unlike older kinds of international firms, they established major factories in countries other than their home base. For example, of the five hundred largest businesses in the United States in 1970, more than one hundred did over a quarter of their business abroad. IBM, for example, operated in more than one hundred countries. Although U.S.-based corporations led the way, Volkswagen, Shell, Nestlé, Sony, and other European and Japanese multinationals also had a broad global scope.

Some multinational corporations had bigger revenues than entire nations. They appeared to burst the bounds of the nation-state as they set up shop in whatever part of the world offered cheap labor. Their interests differed starkly from those of ordinary people with a local or national outlook. In the first years after the war, multinationals preferred European employees, who constituted a highly educated labor pool, had a strong consumer tradition, and eagerly sought secure work. Then, beginning in the 1960s, multinationals moved more of their operations to the emerging economies of formerly colonized states as labor costs, taxes, and regulations increased at home. Although multinational corporations provided jobs in developing areas, profits usually enriched foreign stockholders and thus looked like imperialism reborn.

Many European firms believed that they could stay competitive only by expanding or forming mergers or becoming partners with government in doing business. In France, for example, a massive glass conglomerate merged with a metallurgical company to form a new group specializing in all phases of construction—a wise move given the postwar building boom. European firms increased their investment in research and used international cooperation to produce major new products. This new emphasis on research was a crucial ingredient in postindustrial society. Ventures like the British-French Concorde supersonic aircraft, which, beginning with its first flight in 1976, flew from London to New York in under four hours, and the Airbus, a more practical series of passenger jets inaugurated in 1972 by a consortium of European firms, attested to the strong relationship among government, business, and science (Map 23.1). European firms now commanded large enough research budgets to compete successfully with U.S.-based multinational giants. Whereas U.S. production had surpassed the combined output of West Germany, Great Britain, France, Italy, and Japan in the immediate postwar years, by the mid-1970s the situation was reversed.

The New Worker

In its formative stage, industrial production had depended on workers who often labored to exhaustion and lived in a state of poverty that sometimes led to violence. This scenario changed fundamentally in postwar Europe with the reduction of the blue-collar workforce—a new development resulting from resource depletion in coal mines, the substitution of oil for coal and of plastics for steel, the growth of off-shore manufacturing, and the automation of industrial processes. Within firms,

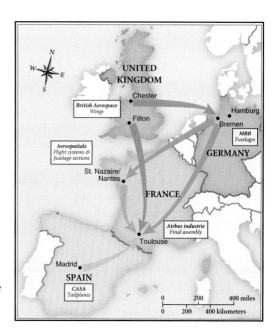

■ MAP 23.1 The Airbus Production System

The international consortium Airbus played an important role in the economic and industrial integration of Europe. It also advanced the revitalization of the individual national economies by establishing new manufacturing centers away from capital cities and by modernizing older ones. Its formation presaged the international mergers and cooperative production that would characterize the late twentieth and early twenty-first centuries. Today Airbus is a global enterprise with parts and service centers around the world, including the United States, China, and India.

the relationship of workers to bosses shifted, as managers started grouping workers into teams that set their own production quotas, organized and assigned tasks, and competed with other teams to see who could produce more. As blue-collar positions disappeared and workers gained responsibilities that had once been managerial prerogatives, union membership declined.

In both U.S.-led and Soviet-bloc countries, a new working class consisting of white-collar service personnel emerged. Its rise undermined old social distinctions based on the way one worked: those who performed service work or had managerial functions were not necessarily better paid than blue-collar workers. The ranks of service workers swelled with researchers, health-care and medical workers, technicians, planners, and government functionaries. Employment in traditional parts of the service sector—banks, insurance companies, and other financial institutions—also surged because of the vast sums of money needed to finance technology and research. Entire categories of employees, such as flight attendants, devoted much of their skill to the psychological well-being of customers. The consumer economy provided more jobs in restaurants and personal health, fitness, and grooming, and in hotels and tourism. By 1969, the percentage of service-sector employees had passed that of manufacturing workers in several industrial countries: 61.1 percent versus 33.7 percent in the United States and 48.8 percent versus 41.1 percent in Sweden. (See "Taking Measure," page 1002.)

Postindustrial work life had some different ingredients in the Soviet bloc. Late in the 1960s, Communist leaders announced a program of "advanced socialism"—

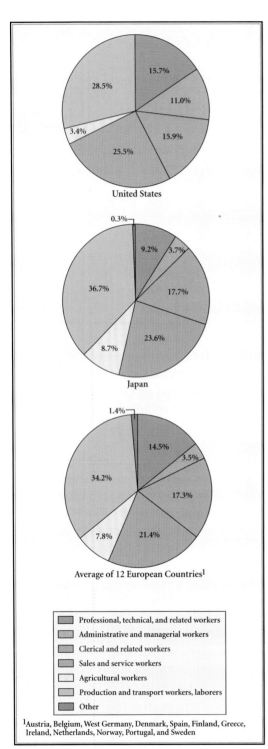

United States

Japan

Average of 12 European Countries[1]

- Professional, technical, and related workers
- Administrative and managerial workers
- Clerical and related workers
- Sales and service workers
- Agricultural workers
- Production and transport workers, laborers
- Other

[1]Austria, Belgium, West Germany, Denmark, Spain, Finland, Greece, Ireland, Netherlands, Norway, Portugal, and Sweden

■ TAKING MEASURE Postindustrial Occupational Structure, 1984

Striking changes occurred in the composition of the workforce in the postwar period. Agriculture continued to decline in importance as a source of jobs, and by the 1980s the percentage of agricultural workers in the most advanced industrial countries had fallen below 10 percent. The most striking development was the expansion of the service sector, which came to employ more than half of all workers. In the United States, the agricultural and industrial sectors, which had dominated a century earlier, now offered less than a third of all jobs.

(*Yearbook of Labour Statistics* [Geneva: International Labour Office, 1992], Table 2.7.)

more social leveling, greater equality of salaries, and nearly complete absence of private production. The percentage of farmers remained higher in the Soviet bloc than in Western Europe. Despite the stated goals of "advanced socialism," a huge difference between professional occupations and those involving physical work remained in socialist countries, where less mobility existed between the two classifications than in Western nations. Much as in the U.S.-led bloc, however, gender helped to shape the workforce into two groups: generally, men earned higher pay for better jobs, and women were relegated to lower paying lesser jobs. Somewhere between 80 and 95 percent of women worked in socialist countries, but they generally held the most menial and worst-paying jobs.

As the postwar boom accelerated, West Germany and other Western nations absorbed immigrant, or "guest," laborers. Coming from Turkey, Greece, southern Italy, Portugal, and North

Africa, these workers collected garbage, built roads, held factory jobs, and cleaned homes. In an environment where desirable work usually required mental operations performed in clean settings, these jobs appeared especially lowly. Males predominated among migrant workers. Female migrants who worked performed similar chores for less pay. Migrants' menial work often was "off the books," so they were cut off from social security and other employee benefits.

Farm life was updated, even bureaucratized. By the 1970s, one could travel for miles in Europe without seeing a farmhouse. Small landowners sold family plots to farmers engaged in *agribusiness*. Governments, farmers' cooperatives, and planning agencies took over decision making from the individual farmer; they set production quotas and handled an array of marketing transactions. In the 1960s, agricultural output rose an average of 3 percent per year in Greece and Spain and 2.5 percent in the Netherlands, France, and Great Britain. Genetic research and the skyrocketing use of machinery contributed to growth. Between 1965 and 1979, the number of tractors in Germany more than tripled from 384,000 to 1,340,000. But bureaucracy played its part, too. For example, in the 1970s a French farmer, Fernande Pelletier, made a living on her hundred-acre farm in southwestern France in the new setting of international agribusiness. Advised by a government expert, Pelletier produced whatever foods might sell competitively in the Common Market—from lamb and veal to foie gras and walnuts—and joined with other farmers in her region to buy heavy machinery and to sell her products. Agricultural solvency required as much managerial and intellectual effort as did success in the industrial sector.

The Boom in Education and Research

Education and research were key to running postindustrial society and offered the means by which nations could maintain their economic and military might. In the West, common sense, hard work, and creative intuition had launched the earliest successes of the Industrial Revolution. By the late twentieth century, success in business or government demanded humanistic or technological expertise and evergrowing staffs of researchers. As one French official put it, "the accumulation of knowledge, not of wealth, . . . makes the difference" in the quest for power.

Investment in research was essential to military and industrial leadership. The United States funneled more than 20 percent of its gross national product into research in the 1960s, in the process siphoning off many of Europe's leading intellectuals and technicians in a so-called brain drain. Complex systems—for example, nuclear power generation with its many components, from scientific conceptualization to plant construction to the publicly supervised disposal of radioactive waste—required intricate professional oversight. Scientists and bureaucrats frequently made more crucial decisions than did elected politicians in the realm of space programs, weapons development, and economic policy. Soviet-bloc nations proved less adept at linking their considerable achievements in science to actual applications because of bureaucratic red tape. In the 1960s, some 40 percent of Soviet-bloc scientific findings became obsolete before the government approved them for application to technology.

The new criteria for success fostered unprecedented growth in education, especially in universities, scientific institutes, and other postsecondary institutions. The number of university students in Sweden rose by about 580 percent and in West Germany by 250 percent between 1950 and 1969. Great Britain established a new network of polytechnic universities to encourage the technical research that elite universities often scorned. France set up administrative schools for future high-level bureaucrats. By the late 1970s, the Soviet Union had built its scientific establishment so rapidly that the number of its advanced researchers in the natural sciences and engineering surpassed that of the United States. Meanwhile, institutions of higher learning added courses in business and management, information technology, and systems analysis.

In principle, education made the avenues to success more democratic by basing them on talent instead of wealth. In fact, societal leveling did not occur in most Western European universities, and instruction often remained rigid and old-fashioned. Although eighteenth-century Europeans had pioneered educational reform, students in the 1960s reported that teachers lectured even young children, who spoke in class only to echo the teacher or to recite homework memorized the night before. At the university level, as one angry student put it, the professor was "a petty, threatened god" who puffed himself up "on the passivity and dependence of students." Such judgments would provoke young people to rebel late in the 1960s against the traditional authority of teachers, officials, and parents.

A Redefined Family and a Generation Gap

Just as education changed dramatically to meet the needs of postindustrial society, the contours of the family and the nature of parent-child relationships shifted from what they had been a century earlier: family roles were transformed, and the relationship between parents and children—long thought to be natural and unchangeable—looked alarmingly different. Even though television and media commentators often delivered messages about what the family should be, technology, consumer goods, and a constant flow of guest laborers and migrants from the former colonies made for enormous variety in what households actually were. Households were now headed by a single parent, by remarried parents merging two sets of unrelated children, by unmarried couples cohabitating, or by traditionally married parents who had fewer children. Households of same-sex partners also became more common. At the end of the 1970s, the marriage rate had fallen 30 percent in the West from its 1960s level. Despite a rising divorce rate, the average marriage lasted one-third longer than it had a century earlier because of increased longevity.

After almost two decades of baby boom, the birthrate dropped significantly. On average, a Belgian woman, for example, bore 2.6 children in 1960 but only 1.8 by the end of the 1970s. Although the birthrate fell, the percentage of children born outside of marriage soared.

Daily life within the family changed. Technological consumer items saturated domestic space, as radio and television often formed the basis of the household's common social life. Machines such as dishwashers, washing machines, and clothes dryers became more affordable and more widespread, reducing (in theory) the time women had to devote to household work and raising standards of cleanliness. More middle-class women worked outside the home during these years to pay for the prolonged economic dependence of children. To advance in a knowledge-based society, postwar youth did not enter the labor force in their teens but instead attended school and required their parents' support. Whereas the early modern family organized labor, taught craft skills, and monitored reproductive behavior, the modern family seemed to have a primarily psychological or postin-dustrial mission. Parents were to provide emotional nurture while their children learned intellectual skills in school. They could also count on psychologists, social workers, and other social service experts to provide counseling and assistance. Television programs portrayed a variety of family experiences on soap operas and sit-coms and gave viewers an opportunity to see how other families dealt with the tensions of modern life.

Most notably, postindustrial society transformed teenagers' lives. A century earlier, teens had been full-time wage earners; now most were students, finan-cially dependent on their parents into their twenties. Amid the new tensions caused by this prolonged childhood, youth simultaneously gained new roles as consumers. Advertisers and industrialists saw the baby boomers as a multi-billion-dollar market and wooed them with consumer items associated with rock music—records, portable radios, stereos. Replacing romantic ballads, rock music celebrated youthful rebellion against adult culture in biting, critical, and often ex-plicitly sexual lyrics. Sex roles for the young did not change, however. Despite the popularity of a few individual women rockers, promoters focused on men, whom they depicted as surrounded by worshiping female "groupies." The new models for youth were themselves the products of advanced technology and savvy mar-keting for mass consumption. The Beatles were a little-known English bar band in 1962 when they hired a new manager, Brian Epstein. Epstein remade their im-age and their music, booking them in major theaters throughout Europe and the United States; by the mid-1960s, public appearances of the Beatles summoned thousands of fans whose hysteria intensified during the group's performances. The mixture of high-tech music, pop-star marketing, and the youthful hysteria of fans contributed to a sense that there was a unique youth culture and a grow-ing "generation gap."

▪ Rolling Stones Tour Europe

The Rolling Stones took the youth revolution in music to a new level of raw energy and social critique. Much like the modernist avant-garde early in the twentieth century, they were dissonant and shocking. Unlike modernists, however, the Stones were commercially successful, all of them becoming multimillionaires, international celebrities, and role models to youth around the world.
(Dominique Berretty.)

Art, Ideas, and Religion in a Technocratic Society

Cultural trends evolved with technology itself. Like modernists in the past, a new generation of artists addressed growing consumerism and technology with their art. Even as colonies continued officially to rip away from the old imperial powers, their influence on the Western mind remained powerful, leading musicians, scholars, and religious leaders to turn in their direction. At the same time, many of these intellectuals enjoyed increasing international recognition and—like the multinationals they often criticized—global markets.

The "pop art" movement, spearheaded by Richard Hamilton (b. 1922) of Britain and Robert Rauschenberg (b. 1925) of the United States, expanded artistic boundaries as it mocked mass culture. Pop art featured images from everyday life and employed the glossy techniques and products of what these artists called "admass," or mass advertising, society. "There's no reason," they maintained of modern society's commercialism, "not to consider the world as one gigantic painting." Rauschenberg made collages from comic strips, magazine clippings, and fabric to fulfill his vision that "a picture is more like the real world when it's made out of the real world." By the early 1960s, the movement had become a financial success, attracting such maverick American artists as Jasper Johns (b. 1930) and Andy Warhol (1927?–1987), who advanced the parody of modern commercialism. Warhol showed, for example, how the female body, the classic form that attracted nineteenth-century male art buyers, was used to sell everything mass culture had to offer in the 1960s and 1970s. Swedish-born artist Claes Oldenburg (b. 1929) depicted the grotesque aspects of ordinary consumer products in *Giant Hamburger with Pickle Attached* (1962) and *Lipstick Ascending on Caterpillar Tractor* (1967). "High" art picked up "low" objects such as scraps of metal, cigarette butts, dirt, and even excrement: the Swiss sculptor Jean Tinguely (1925–1991) used rusted parts of old machines to make moving fountains. His partner Niki de Saint Phalle (b. 1930) then constructed huge, exuberant figures—many of them inspired by the folk traditions of the Caribbean and Africa—to decorate them. These colorful fountains adorned main squares in Stockholm, Montreal, Paris, and other cities.

■ **Niki de Saint Phalle, *Fontaine Stravinsky* (1983)**
Niki de Saint Phalle's exuberant and playful art, seen in the fountains of Paris and cities around the world, captured the accessibility of pop art. Her other work drew inspiration from Caribbean and African styles and celebrated women of decolonizing countries. Living during the rebirth of activism, de Saint Phalle lined up suspended bags of paint and machine-gunned them to create a spattered canvas—her answer to the alleged "macho" style of abstract expressionists like Jackson Pollock. (Barbara Alper/Stock Boston.)

The American composer John Cage (1912–1992) had been working to the same ends when he added sounds produced by such everyday items as combs, pieces of wood, and radio noise into his musical scores. Buddhist influence led Cage also to incorporate silence in music and to compose by randomly tossing coins and then choosing notes by the corresponding numbers in the ancient Chinese *I Ching* ("Book of Changes")—moves that continued the trend away from classical melody that had begun with modernism. Other composers, called *minimalists*, simplified music by featuring repetition and sustained notes as well as by rejecting the "masterpiece" tradition of lush classical compositions. Some stressed modern technology; they introduced tape recordings into vocal pieces and used computers and synthesizers both to compose and to perform their works. German composer Karlheinz Stockhausen (b. 1928) incorporated electronic music into classical composition in 1953, as did Cage soon after. Influenced by his own travels, Stockhausen continued the modern style of fully exploring non-Western tonalities in such 1970s pieces as *Ceylon*. While this music echoed the electronic and increasingly interconnected state of human society, its appeal remained limited and concert audiences diminished. At the same time, improved recording technology and mass marketing brought music of all varieties to a wider home audience than ever before.

The Information Age influenced social science as much as it did art and music. The social sciences reached the peak of their prestige during these decades, often because of their increasing use of statistical models and predictions. Sociologists and psychologists produced empirical studies that purported to demonstrate rules for understanding individual, group, and societal behavior. Simultaneously, the social sciences undermined some of the foundations for the belief that individuals had true freedom and for the assertion that Western civilization was more sophisticated or just than non-Western societies. French anthropologist Claude Lévi-Strauss (b. 1908) developed a theory called *structuralism*. The theory insisted that all societies function within controlling structures—kinship and exchange, for example—that operate according to coercive rules similar to those of language. Structuralism challenged existentialism's tenet that humans could create a free existence, and it shook the social sciences' faith in the triumph of rationality. In the 1960s and 1970s, the findings of the social sciences generally paralleled concerns that technology was creating a society of automatons and that complex managerial systems would eradicate individualism and human freedom.

Debates about free will coincided with new Christian preachings about the changing times. Responding to what he saw as a crisis in faith caused by affluence and secularism, Pope John XXIII (r. 1958–1963) in 1962 convened the Second Vatican Council, known as Vatican II.◆ The council modernized the liturgy, democratized many church procedures, and at the last session in 1965 renounced church

---

◆ For the text of Pope John XXIII's proclamation, see Document 74, "Vatican II."

doctrine that condemned the Jewish people as guilty of killing Jesus. The Catholic church thus opened itself to some new influences. Although Pope John's successor, Paul VI (r. 1963–1978), kept Catholic opposition to artificial birth control alive, he also became the first pontiff to visit Africa, Asia, and South America, and encouraged Catholicism in the Soviet bloc, strengthening religion as a primary focal point for anticommunism there.

Simultaneously, a Protestant revival occurred in the United States, and growing numbers of people joined sects that stressed the literal truth of the Scripture. In Western Europe, however, Christian churchgoing remained at a low ebb. In the 1970s, for example, only 10 percent of the British population went to religious services—about the same number that attended live soccer matches. The composition of the Western religious public was also metamorphosing as migrants from the former colonies increased the strength of non-Christian religions such as Islam and Hinduism.

Contesting the Cold War Order in the 1960s

Affluence, scientific sophistication, and military might elevated the United States and the Soviet Union to the peak of their power early in the 1960s. By 1965, however, the six nations of the Common Market had replaced the United States as the leader in worldwide trade and often acted in their own self-interest across the U.S.-Soviet divide. Communist China, along with countries in Eastern Europe, contested Soviet leadership, and many decolonizing regions refused to become pliable allies to the superpowers. The struggle for Indochinese independence had never ended, and by the mid-1960s a devastating war in Vietnam was under way. But in some respects the most serious challenge to the cold war order came from the rising discontent of citizens like Jan Palach. In the 1960s, they rose up in protest against the consequences of technological development, the lack of fundamental rights, and the prospect of nuclear holocaust latent in the cold war.

Cracks in the Cold War Consensus

In the summer of 1963, less than a year after the shock of the Cuban missile crisis, the United States and the Soviet Union signed a test-ban treaty outlawing the testing of nuclear weapons in the atmosphere and in the seas. The agreement suggested that the superpowers would reduce international tensions to focus on domestic politics. The new Soviet middle class of bureaucrats and managers demanded a better standard of living and a reduction in cold war animosity. In Western European countries, voters elected politicians who promoted an increasing array of social programs designed to ensure economic democracy. A significant minority shifted their votes away from the conservative Christian Democratic coalitions to Socialist, Labor, and Social Democratic parties in hopes of placing more attention on ordinary people's needs during rapid change than on the cold war.

Germany and France took different roads to skirting the cold war. In Germany, Social Democratic politicians had enough influence to shift money from defense spending to domestic programs. Willy Brandt, the Socialist mayor of West Berlin, became foreign minister in 1966 and pursued an end to frigid relations with Communist East Germany. This policy, known as *Ostpolitik,* unsettled cold war thinking. It gave West German business leaders what they wanted: "the depoliticization of Germany's foreign trade," as one industrialist put it, and an unlocking of Soviet-bloc consumerism. To break the cold war stranglehold, French president Charles de Gaulle poured more money into French nuclear development, withdrew French forces from NATO, and signed trade treaties with the Soviet bloc. However, he also protected France's good relations with Germany to prevent further encroachments from the Soviet bloc. At home, de Gaulle's government mandated the cleaning of all Parisian buildings and sponsored the construction of modern housing. With his haughty and stubborn pursuit of French grandeur, de Gaulle offered the European public an alternative to superpower toadying.

Brandt's Ostpolitik and de Gaulle's assertiveness had their echoes in the Soviet bloc. Pushing de-Stalinization, Khrushchev took the dangerous course of trying to reduce Communist officialdom's privileges, and he sanctioned the publication of dissident Aleksandr Solzhenitsyn's *One Day in the Life of Ivan Denisovitch* (1962), which revealed firsthand the terrible conditions in the labor camps. Khrushchev's blunders—notably his humiliation in the Cuban missile crisis, his ineffectual schemes to improve Soviet agriculture, and his inability to patch the rift with China—led to his ouster in 1964. Nevertheless, the new leadership of Leonid Brezhnev and Alexei Kosygin continued attempts at reform, encouraging plant managers to turn a profit and allowing the production of televisions, household appliances, and cheap housing to alleviate the discontent of a better-educated citizenry. The government also loosened restrictions to allow cultural and scientific meetings with Westerners, another move that relaxed the cold war atmosphere in the mid-1960s. The Soviet satellites in Eastern Europe grasped the economic opportunity presented by Moscow's relaxed posture. Poland allowed private farmers greater freedom to make money, and Hungarian leader János Kádár introduced elements of a market system into the national economy.

In the arts, Soviet-bloc writers continued for a time to thaw the frozen monolith of socialist realism. Ukrainian poet Yevgeny Yevtushenko exposed Soviet complicity in the Holocaust in *Babi Yar* (1961), a passionate protest against the slaughter of tens of thousands of Jews near Kiev during World War II. Challenging the celebratory nature of socialist art, East Berlin writer Christa Wolf showed a couple tragically divided by the Berlin Wall in her novel *Divided Heaven* (1965). But repression returned later in the 1960s. The Soviet government took to bulldozing outdoor art shows, forcing visual artists to hold exhibitions in secret in their apartments and

■ **Hagop Hagopian, *No to the Neutron Bomb!* (1977)**
In an era of ongoing cold war, culture continued to be on the front line, with the Soviets persecuting those who produced abstract or critical art. Artists were adept, however, at incorporating Soviet icons in work critical of the regime. They might, for instance, depict Lenin's portrait but with citizens turning their back on it instead of being inspired by it. Or, as in this painting, they bravely critiqued the course of the arms race.
(The Jane Voorhees Zimmerli Art Museum. Rutgers, The State University of New Jersey. The Norton and Nancy Dodge Collection of Nonconformist Art from the Soviet Union. Photo: Jack Abraham.)

even to turn their living spaces into a new kind of art known as "installations"—the arrangement of everyday objects in large spaces. Dissident artists depicted Soviet citizens as worn and tired in grays and other monochromatic color schemes instead of the brightly attired and heroic figures of socialist realism. Dissident writers relied on the underground *samizdat* system of distribution: uncensored publications were reproduced by hand and carefully passed from reader to reader.

Even in the United States, other issues challenged the cold war for front-page attention. The assassination of President John F. Kennedy in November 1963 shocked the nation and the world. Only momentarily did it quiet escalating demands for civil rights for African Americans and other minorities. White segregationists reacted with extraordinary violence to sit-ins at lunch counters, efforts to register black voters, and freedom marches. This violent racism was a weak link in the American claim to moral superiority in the cold war. In response to the murders and destruction, Kennedy had introduced civil rights legislation and forced the desegregation of schools and universities. In a massive rally in Washington, D.C., in August 1963, hundreds of thousands of marchers assembled around the Lincoln Memorial, where they heard the electrifying words of African American minister Martin Luther King Jr.:

> *I have a dream that . . . all of God's children, black men and white men, Jews and Gentiles, Protestants and Catholics, will be able to join hands and sing in the words of the old Negro spiritual, "Free at last! Free at last! Thank God Almighty, we are free at last!"*

Lyndon B. Johnson (1908–1973), Kennedy's successor, steered the Civil Rights Act through Congress in 1964. This legislation forbade segregation in public facilities and created the Equal Employment Opportunity Commission (EEOC) to fight job discrimination based on "race, color, national origin, religion, and sex." Southern conservatives had tacked on the provision against sex discrimination in the vain hope that it would doom the bill. Modeling himself on his hero Franklin Roosevelt, Johnson envisioned a "Great Society," in which new government programs would improve the chances of the forty million Americans living in poverty. He sponsored myriad reform projects, among them Project Head Start for disadvantaged preschool children and the Job Corps for training youth. Black novelist Ralph Ellison called Johnson "the greatest American president for the poor and the Negroes."

Vietnam and Turmoil in Asia

During the 1960s, third-world nations increasingly distanced themselves from the superpowers. Many were still tied by technical systems such as radio and telephone networks and by trade to their former rulers; where the cold war was concerned, however, they sought to be nonaligned. Communist China's independent way was the biggest surprise to both the Soviet Union and the United States. Mao Zedong, ever hostile to Western capitalism, also detested Soviet leadership and its stagnating bureaucracy. In 1966, Mao unleashed the Cultural Revolution, a movement to remake individual personality according to his own vision of an ever-evolving socialism. As economic goals lost their importance, China's youth were empowered to haul away people of every class for "reeducation"—which translated to personal humiliation and millions of deaths.

Both superpowers had interests in East and Southeast Asia, but they often failed to see the complex changes under way in the region. American policymakers, for example, did not detect the growing dispute between the two Communist giants because they had an inflexible vision of monolithic communism. While China plunged into Mao's bloody cultural and economic experiments, the peoples of Southeast Asia were coming to grips with decades of demographic upheaval. Despite war and nationalist revolution, the region's population more than tripled between 1920 and 1970, reaching 370 million by the end of the 1970s. Like the 85 percent of third-world leaders who rose from the military, most East and Southeast Asian rulers were dictators, lacking the expertise to make their countries economically sound in the face of soaring population.

Superpower intervention in this unstable part of the world was loaded with risk, and nowhere was this truer than in the U.S. intervention in Vietnam (Map 23.2). After the Geneva settlement in 1954, the United States escalated its commitment to the corrupt and incompetent leaders in non-Communist South Vietnam. North Vietnam, China, and the Soviet Union backed the rebel Vietcong, as the South Vietnamese Communists came to be called. The strength of the Vietcong seemed to grow daily, and by 1966, the United States had more than a half-million soldiers in South Vietnam. Before the war ended in 1975, the United States would drop more bombs on North Vietnam than the Allies had launched on both Germany and Japan during World War II. Television reports carried the optimistic predictions of Johnson's advisers of imminent victory despite mounting U.S. casualties. But after decades of anticolonial struggle, the insurgents rejected a negotiated peace. North Vietnam's leaders calculated that the United States would give in first as the American public recoiled from the horrors of televised slaughter, including scenes of children burned alive by U.S. chemical weapons. Confronting growing antiwar sentiment and increasing military costs, President Johnson announced in March 1968 that he would not run for president again. The U.S. superpower was tarnished, irreparably it seemed at the time; so, too, was the Soviet Union.

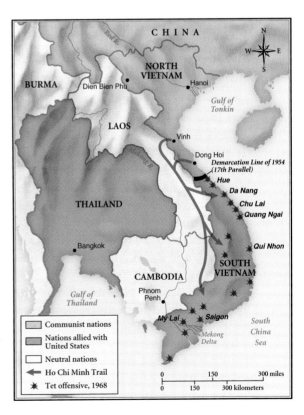

■ **MAP 23.2 The Vietnam War, 1954–1975**

The local peoples of Southeast Asia had long resisted incursions by their neighbors. Since the end of the nineteenth century, they also had resisted French rule, never more fiercely than in the war that liberated them after World War II. Though poorly equipped in comparison with the French, the Vietnamese triumphed in the battle of Dien Bien Phu in 1954. Then the Americans became involved, trying to halt what they saw as the tide of Communist influence behind the Vietnamese liberation movement. The ensuing war in Vietnam in the 1960s and 1970s spread into neighboring countries, making the region the scene of vast destruction.

The Explosion of Civic Activism: Civil Rights, Student Protests, and the Women's Movement

In the midst of cold war, technological transformation, and bloody conflict, a new social activism emerged in the West. Students, blacks and other racial minorities, Soviet-bloc citizens, women, environmentalists, and homosexuals sometimes brought their societies to the brink of revolution in their fiery protests.

The U.S. civil rights movement expanded its bold activism. In 1965, César Chávez led Mexican American migrant workers in the California grape agribusiness to strike for better wages and working conditions. Deeply religious and ascetic, Chávez helped Hispanic Americans define their identity and struggle against deportation, inferior schooling, and discrimination. Meanwhile, the African American civil rights movement took a dramatic turn as urban riots erupted across the United States in the summer of 1965. Frustrated and angry, activists transformed their struggle into a militant celebration of their race under the banner "Black is beautiful." The issue they faced was one they felt they had in common with decolonizing people: how to shape an identity different from that of white oppressors. Some urged a push for "black power" to reclaim rights instead of begging for them nonviolently. Turning from the nonviolence of Martin Luther King Jr., formerly pacifist black leaders turned their rhetoric to violence: "Burn, baby, burn" chanted rioters who destroyed the grim inner cities around them.

As a result of the new turn in black activism, white American university students who had participated in the early stages of the civil rights movement found themselves excluded from leadership positions. Many soon joined the swelling protest against technological change, consumerism, and the Vietnam War. European youth caught the fever. In the mid-1960s, university students in Rome occupied an administration building after right-wing opponents assassinated one of their number during a protest against the 200-to-1 student-teacher ratio. Prague students held carnival-like processions, commemorated the tenth anniversary of the 1956 Hungarian uprisings, and took to chanting "The only good Communist is a dead one." The "situationists" in France called on students to wake up from the slumbering pace of mass society and student life by jolting individuals to action with shocking graffiti and street theater.

Students attacked the traditional university curriculum and flaunted their own countercultural values. They questioned how studying Plato or Dante would help them after graduation. "How to Train Stuffed Geese" was French students' satirical version of teaching methods inflicted on them. "No professors over forty" and "Don't trust anyone over thirty" were powerful slogans of the day. Long hair, communal living, and a repudiation of personal hygiene announced students' rejection of middle-class values, as did their denunciation of sexual chastity. With the widespread use of the pill, abstinence became unnecessary as a method of birth control, and students made the sexual revolution explicit and public with open promiscuity. Marijuana use became common among student protesters, and amphetamines and barbiturates became part of the drug culture, which had its own rituals, songs, and gathering places. Scorned by students, businesses nonetheless made billions of dollars selling blue jeans, dolls dressed as "hippies," natural foods, and drugs, as well as packaging and managing the stars of the counterculture.

Women's activism erupted across the political spectrum. Those in the civil rights and student movements soon realized that protest organizations devalued women just as society at large did. Male activists adopted the leather-jacketed machismo style of their film and rock heroes, but women in the movements were often judged by the status of their male-protester lovers. "A woman was [expected] to 'inspire' her man," African American activist Angela Davis complained, noting that women aiming for equality were often accused of "want[ing] to rob [male protesters] of their manhood." A speaker in Frankfurt, West Germany, interrupted a student meeting, demanding "that our problems be discussed substantively. It is no longer enough that women are occasionally allowed to say a few words." More politically conventional middle-class women eagerly responded to the international best-seller *The Feminine Mystique* (1963) by American journalist Betty Friedan. Pointing to the stagnating talents of many housewives, Friedan helped organize the National Organization for Women (NOW) in 1966 "to bring women into full participation in the mainstream of American society now." Working for reproductive rights, women in France helped end the ban on birth control in 1965. In Sweden, they lobbied to make tasks both at home and in the workplace less gender-segregated.

■ **Gay Activists in London**
The reformist spirit of the 1960s and 1970s changed the focus of homosexuals' activism. Instead of concentrating mostly on legal protection from criminal prosecution, gays and lesbians began affirming a special and positive identity. As other groups who had endured discrimination began making similar affirmations, "identity politics" was born. Critics charged that traditional universal values were sufficient and that homosexuals and others constituted "special-interest" groups. Gays, women, and ethnic or racial minorities countercharged that the universal values first put forth in the Enlightenment seemed to apply only to a privileged few.
(© Hulton Getty/Liaison Agency.)

Women also took to the streets on behalf of such issues as abortion rights and the decriminalization of gay and lesbian sexuality. Many flouted social conventions in their attire, language, and attitudes. Renouncing brassieres, high-heeled shoes, cosmetics, and other adornments, they spoke openly about taboo subjects such as their sexual feelings and even announced that they had resorted to illegal abortions. This brand of feminist activity was meant to shock polite society—and it did. At a Miss America contest in 1968, women protesters crowned a sheep the new beauty queen. West German women students tossed tomatoes at male protest leaders in defiance of standards for ladylike behavior. Many women of color, however, broke with feminist solidarity and spoke out against the "double jeopardy" of being "black and female."

1968: Year of Crisis

The West seethed with protest and calls for reform, which erupted in 1968. In January, on the first day of Tet, the Vietnamese New Year, the Vietcong and the North Vietnamese attacked more than one hundred South Vietnamese towns and American bases, inflicting heavy casualties. The Tet offensive, as it came to be called, caused many Americans to conclude that the war might be unwinnable and gave the antiwar movement crucial momentum. Then, on April 4, 1968, Martin Luther King Jr. was assassinated by a white racist, and more than a hundred cities in the United States erupted in violence as African Americans vented their anguish and rage. On campuses, strident confrontation over the intertwined issues of war, technology, racism, and sexism closed down classes. At the same time, student dissent was escalating in France where in January, students had gone on strike, shockingly invading administration offices to protest their inferior education and status. When later students at the prestigious Sorbonne in Paris took to the streets, police assaulted them. The Parisian middle classes reacted with unexpected sympathy to the student uprising because of their own resentment of bureaucracy. They were also horrified at seeing the elite and brutal police force, the CRS, beating middle-class students and passersby who expressed their support. French workers joined in: some nine million went on strike, occupying factories and calling not only for higher wages but also for "participation" in everyday decision making. To some, the revolt of youth and workers looked as if it might spiral into another French revolution. The normally decisive president Charles de Gaulle seemed paralyzed at first, but he soon sent tanks into Paris. Although demonstrations continued throughout June, the student movement in France at least had been closed down.◆

◆ For a set of firsthand accounts of the wave of rebellion that swept college campuses throughout Europe and the United States in 1968, see Document 75, "Student Voices of Protest."

In Prague, the 1968 revolt began within the Czechoslovak Communist Party itself. In the autumn of 1967 at a party congress, Alexander Dubček, head of the Slovak branch of the party, had called for more social and political openness. Attacked
as an inferior Slovak by the leadership, Dubček nonetheless struck a chord among
frustrated party officials, technocrats, and intellectuals; Czechoslovaks began to
dream of creating a new society—one based on "socialism with a human face."
Party officials elevated Dubček to the top position, where he quickly changed the
Communist style of government, ending censorship, instituting the secret ballot for
party elections, and allowing competing political groups to form. The "Prague
Spring" had begun—"an orgy of free expression," one Czech journalist called it.
People bought uncensored publications, packed uncensored theater productions,
and engaged in almost nonstop political debate.

The Polish, East German, and Soviet regimes threatened the reform government daily. When Dubček failed to attend a meeting of Warsaw Pact leaders, Soviet

■ **Prague Spring**
When the Soviets and other Warsaw Pact members cracked down on the Czech dissidents, they
met determined citizen resistance. People refused aid of any kind to the invaders. Indeed, despite
dejection at the repression of Dubček's government, protest was ongoing until the final fall of
Communist rule two decades later. (Prache-Levin/Sygma.)

threats became intense. Finally in August 1968, Soviet tanks rolled into Prague in a massive show of antirevolutionary force. Citizens tried to halt the return to Communist orthodoxy by using free expression as sabotage. They painted graffiti on tanks and confused invading troops by removing street signs. Illegal radio stations broadcast testimonials of resistance, and merchants refused to sell food or other commodities to Soviet troops. As the Soviets gradually removed reformers from power, Jan Palach and other university students immolated themselves, and protest of one type or another never stopped. In November 1968, the Soviets announced the Brezhnev Doctrine: reform movements, a "common problem" of all socialist countries, would face swift repression.

Protest in 1968 challenged the political direction of Western societies, including superpower dominance. Whether burning draft cards in the United States or scribbling graffiti on public buildings in Europe, activists made all government open to question and would continue to do so into the 1970s. Yet change did not necessarily occur in the way reformers had hoped. Governments turned to conservative solutions, while some disappointed reformers considered more violent measures.

The Erosion of Superpower Mastery in the 1970s

The 1970s brought an era of *détente*—a lessening of cold war tensions—as the United States pulled out of the Vietnam War and as the superpowers negotiated to limit the nuclear arms race. Despite this relaxation in the cold war, the superpowers appeared to lose their dominance. By the early 1970s, student protest evolved into ongoing reform movements, while other groups, such as those favoring Basque independence in Spain and Catholic rights in Northern Ireland, took violent action. This violence affected the superpowers as it threw their allies off balance. Although the United States and the Soviet Union still controlled the balance of power, their grip was also loosening because of their own internal corruption, the challenge of terrorism, and competition from the oil-producing states, Japan, and the Common Market.

The Superpowers Tested

As the 1970s opened, both superpowers faced daunting internal and external challenges to their dominance, but the United States was the most visibly shaken. Elected in 1968 to replace Johnson, the conservative Richard Nixon promised to bring peace to Southeast Asia. In 1970, however, he ordered U.S. troops to invade Cambodia, the site of North Vietnamese bases (see Map 23.2). Campuses erupted again in protest, and on May 4 the National Guard killed four students and wounded eleven others at a demonstration at Kent State University in Ohio. Nixon called the victims "bums," and a growing reaction against the counterculture made many Americans agree with him that the guardsmen "should have fired sooner and longer." Mired in turmoil, the United States and North Vietnam agreed to peace in January 1973 but continued to support the hostilities. In 1975, South Vietnam collapsed under a determined North Vietnamese offensive, and Vietnam was forcibly reunified. The United States reeled from the conflict, suffering loss of young lives, turbulence at home, vast military costs, and a weakening of its reputation around the world.

Simultaneously, the United States pulled off a foreign policy triumph when Henry Kissinger, Nixon's secretary of state and a believer—like Bismarck—in Realpolitik, decided to take advantage of the ongoing conflict between China and the USSR. In 1972, Kissinger's efforts to bring the United States and China closer resulted in Nixon's visiting the *other* Communist power. Within China, the meeting helped stop the brutality and excesses of the Cultural Revolution and helped advance the careers of Chinese pragmatists interested in technology, trade, and relations with the West. Fearful of the Chinese diplomatic advantage, the Soviets made their own overtures to the U.S.-led bloc. In 1972, the superpowers signed the Strategic Arms Limitation Treaty (SALT I), which set a cap on the number of antimissile defenses each country could have. In 1975, in the Helsinki accords on human rights, the Western bloc officially acknowledged Soviet territorial gains in World War II in exchange for the Soviet bloc's guarantee of basic human rights.

Despite these successes, the enigmatic Nixon focused on reelection at any price. His reelection committee paid several men—caught in the act and arrested—to wiretap the telephones at Democratic Party headquarters in Washington's Watergate office building. Not only did the presidential office work against free elections, but after his landslide victory in 1972 Nixon himself attempted to cover up the truth about the Watergate break-in. Between 1968 and 1972, Nixon had forged a powerful conservative consensus; in the summer of 1974, however, the Watergate scandal forced Nixon to resign in disgrace—the first U.S. president ever to do so.

The Soviet leadership also met mounting criticism as it intensified repression. By the early 1970s, the hard-liner Brezhnev had eclipsed Kosygin's influence in the Soviet Union and freely clamped down on critics. After the events in Czechoslovakia in 1968, the Soviet dissident movement was at a low ebb. "The shock of our tanks crushing the Prague Spring . . . convinced us that the Soviet colossus was invincible," explained one pessimistic liberal. Other voices persisted, however. In 1974, Brezhnev expelled Solzhenitsyn from the USSR after the publication of the first volume of *Gulag Archipelago* (1973–1976) in the U.S.-led bloc. Composed from myriad biographies, firsthand reports, and other sources of information about prison camp life, Solzhenitsyn's story of the Gulag (the Soviet system of internment and forced-labor camps) documented the brutal conditions Soviet prisoners endured under Stalin and his successors.

The Kremlin persecuted many ordinary people who did not have Solzhenitsyn's international reputation. Soviet psychologists, complying with the government, certified the "mental illness" of people who did not play by the rules; thus dissidents wound up as prisoners in mental institutions. The crudest Soviet persecutions, however, involved anti-Semitism: Jews were subject to educational restrictions (especially in university admissions), severe job discrimination, and constant assault on their religious practice. A commonplace accusation by Soviet officials was that Jews were "unreliable, they think only of emigrating. . . . It's madness to give them an education, because it's state money wasted." Ironically, even dissidents blamed Jews for the Bolshevik Revolution and for the terror of Stalinist collectivization. As attacks intensified in the 1970s, Soviet Jews sought to emigrate to Israel or the United States, often unsuccessfully.

Dissent persisted in satellite states, and repression prompted some people to flee. In an open letter to the Czechoslovak Communist Party leadership, playwright Václav Havel accused Marxist-Leninist rule of making people materialistic, not socialist, and indifferent to civic life. In 1977, Havel, along with a group of fellow intellectuals and workers, signed Charter 77, a public protest against the Communist regime. The police imprisoned and tormented many of the charter's signatories, including Havel. By this time, the brain drain of Eastern European intellectuals had become significant. The modernist composer Gyorgy Ligeti had left Hungary in 1956, after which his work was celebrated in concert halls and in films such as *2001: A Space Odyssey* (1968). From exile in Paris, Czech writer Milan Kundera enthralled audiences with *The Book of Laughter and Forgetting* (1978) and other novels that chronicled the lives of tortured characters caught in the grim realities of Communist institutions. The presence of these exiles and escapees in the United States and Western European capitals helped erode any lingering support for communism.

The West, the World, and the Politics of Energy

While the superpowers wrestled with internal political embarrassments and the intricacies of nuclear diplomacy, other nations were developing new economic muscle. Since 1960, the six Common Market countries, led by West Germany, had surpassed the United States in percentage of gross world product. This achievement made the Common Market a countervailing economic power to the Soviet Union and the United States. A partial slowdown in the mid-1960s brought rising unemployment, the use of pump-priming techniques to stimulate industrial investment, and layoffs of foreign "guest" laborers and married women in favor of native-born men. Offsetting the slowdown, the opening of Eastern European markets helped bolster Western European prosperity; by the end of the decade, Western European exports to the Soviet bloc totaled some $45 billion annually, producing a burden of debt that Communist countries could ill afford. In 1973, Britain joined the Common Market, followed by Ireland and Denmark (see "Mapping the West," page 1027). The market's exports now amounted to almost three times those of the United States.

The United States faced still other challenges to its power to dominate the international economy, from Japan as well as from the effects of its own policies. Rising purchases of military and imported goods brought inflation and made the United States a debtor nation. Dollars flooded the international currency markets. In 1971, the Bretton Woods currency system, created during World War II to maintain stable international markets, collapsed. As Common Market countries united to prevent financial chaos, they forced the United States to relinquish its single-handed direction of Western economic strategy. Thanks to massive U.S. expenditures in the Korean and Vietnam Wars, Japan emerged as a manufacturing and exporting giant. Even without oil and other key natural resources, Japan experienced an astonishing 11 percent rate of economic growth in the 1960s and had become the world's largest shipbuilder by the 1970s.

Not only Japan but the Middle East's oil-producing nations also dealt Western dominance a critical blow. Tensions between Israel and the Arab world provided the catalyst. On June 5, 1967, Israeli forces, responding to Palestinian guerrilla attacks, seized Gaza and the Sinai peninsula from Egypt, the Golan Heights from Syria, and the West Bank from Jordan. Although Israel won a stunning victory in this Six-Day War, the Arab humiliation led the Arab states to try to forge a common political and economic strategy. In 1973, Egypt and Syria attacked Israel on Yom Kippur, the most holy day in the Jewish calendar, but Israel, with material assistance from the United States, stopped the assault. Having failed militarily, the Arab nations turned decisively to economic clout. The Organization of Petroleum Exporting Countries (OPEC), a relatively loose consortium before the Yom Kippur War, quadrupled the price of its oil and imposed an embargo, cutting off all exports of oil to the United States in retaliation for its support of Israel. For the first time since imperialism's heyday, the *producers* of raw materials—not the industrial powers—controlled the flow of commodities and set prices to their own advantage. The West became mired in an oil crisis.

Israel after the Six-Day War, 1967

Throughout the 1970s, oil-dependent Westerners watched in astonishment as OPEC upset the balance of economic power. Instead of being controlled by the Western powers, the oil-producing nations helped provoke an economic recession by restricting the flow of oil and charging more for it (Figure 23.1). These actions caused unemployment to rise by more than 50 percent in Europe and the United

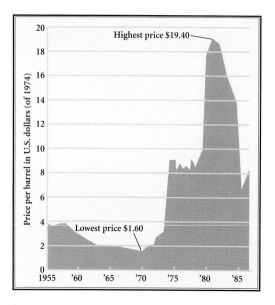

■ **FIGURE 23.1 Fluctuating Oil Prices, 1955–1985**

Colonization allowed the Western imperial powers to obtain raw materials at advantageous prices. Even with decolonization, European and American firms often had such deep roots in newly independent economies that they were able to set the terms for trade. The OPEC oil embargo and price hikes of the 1970s were signs of change, which included decolonized countries' exercise of control over their own resources. OPEC's action not only led to a decade of painful economic downturn but also encouraged some European governments to improve public transportation and to impose policies designed to make individual consumers reduce their dependence on oil.

States and the inflation rate to soar because of energy prices. By the end of 1973, the inflation rate jumped to over 8 percent in West Germany, 12 percent in France, and 20 percent in Portugal. Eastern-bloc countries, dependent on Soviet oil, fared little better. Skyrocketing interest rates in the U.S.-led bloc discouraged both industrial investment and consumer buying. With prices, unemployment, and interest rates soaring—the unusual combination of economic conditions was dubbed *stagflation*—Westerners were forced to realize that both energy resources and economic growth had limits.

Political Alternatives in Hard Times: Environmentalism, Feminism, and Terrorism

The unprecedented economic situation and the changing global balance of power inspired new waves of citizen activism ranging from reform to the most violent terrorism. On the reform end, a sense of limits to global resources encouraged the formation of environmental political parties. An escapee from Nazi Germany, E. F. "Fritz" Schumacher, produced one of the bibles of the environmental movement, *Small Is Beautiful* (1973), which spelled out how technology and industrialization threatened the earth and its inhabitants. Environmentalists like Schumacher and the American Rachel Carson, author of *Silent Spring* (1962), advocated the immediate rescue of rivers, forests, and the soil from the ravages of factories and chemical farming. These attitudes challenged almost two centuries of faith in industrial growth and in the infinite ability of humanity to extract progress from the natural world.

Initially the environmental movement had its greatest political effect in West Germany. As student protest subsided in the 1970s, environmentalism united members of older and younger generations around the 1960s political tactic called *citizen initiatives*, in which groups of people blocked everything from public transportation fare increases to plans for urban growth. Taking their cue from Chancellor Willy Brandt's Ostpolitik, citizen initiative groups targeted nuclear power and nuclear installations and attracted tens of thousands to demonstrations in the 1970s. Then, in 1979, the Green Party was founded in West Germany, and across Europe Green Party candidates forced other politicians to voice concern for the environment. In the Soviet bloc, Communist commitment to industrial development blinded governments to environmental destruction and to the effects of pollution on people; citizen protest continued to focus on basic needs and individual freedom.

Feminist activism made real gains in the 1970s. Environmental parties attracted many women angered by the birth of "thalidomide babies" and concerned about the chemical contamination of their families' food. Men could escape to the moon or into their careers, a West German ecologist maintained, but not women, "who must give birth to children, willingly or unwillingly, in this polluted world of ours." Other women's activism had notable successes in the 1970s. In Catholic Italy, feminists won the right to divorce, to gain access to birth-control information, and to obtain legal abortions. The demand for these rights as well as for equal pay, job opportunities, and protection from rape, incest, and battering framed the major legal struggles of thousands of women's groups in the 1970s.

Activism ranged from individual to international efforts. In the U.S.-led bloc, personal change also became a goal for women. Consciousness-raising sessions in which groups of women shared individual experiences with marriage, with children, and in the workforce alleviated some of the isolation women felt at home. Soviet-bloc women, who often formed the majority of the workforce and shouldered responsibility for all domestic work, received inspiration from feminist stories spread through the *samizdat* network. At the other extreme were international meetings begun in 1977, when fifteen thousand activist women from around the globe poured into Houston, Texas, to mark the International Year of Women. The meeting brought together Westerners interested in political and economic rights and cultural equality and third-world women who called for an end to violence, starvation, and disease. The utter poverty afflicting women in less-developed countries called into question the commonality on which Western feminist politics was based. The issue of sexual orientation also challenged many mainstream activists in Houston, as lesbians exposed the greater privileges heterosexual women enjoyed. Organization, raised consciousness, and some economic gains backed women's entry into local and national government from the 1970s on.

Terrorist bands took a radically different path, responding to the conservative political climate and worsening economic conditions with kidnappings, bank robberies, bombings, and assassinations. Disaffected and well-to-do youth, steeped in the most extreme theories of society's decay, often joined these groups. Eager to bring down the Social Democratic coalition that led West Germany throughout the 1970s,

**Nationalist Movements
of the 1970s**

the Baader-Meinhof gang assassinated prominent businessmen as well as judges and other public officials. Practiced in assassinations of public figures and random shootings of pedestrians, Italy's Red Brigades kidnapped and then murdered the head of the dominant Christian Democrats in 1978. Advocates of independence for the Basque nation in northern Spain assassinated Spanish politicians and police.

In Britain, nationalist and religious violence in the 1970s pitted the Catholics in Northern Ireland against the dominant Protestants. Catholics experienced job discrimination and a lack of civil rights. Demonstrators urged union with the Irish Republic, and with protest escalating, the British government sent in troops. On January 30, 1972, which became known as "Bloody Sunday," British troops fired at demonstrators and killed thirteen, setting off a cycle of violence that left five hundred dead within the year. Protestants fearful of losing their dominant position combated a reinvigorated Irish Republican Army (IRA), which carried out bombings and assassinations to achieve the union of the two Irelands in order to end the oppression of Catholics.

Terrorists failed in their goal of overturning the existing democracies, and, sorely tried as it was, parliamentary government scored some important successes in the 1970s. The Iberian peninsula, suffering under dictatorship since the 1930s, regained its freedom and set out on a course of greater prosperity. The death of Spain's Francisco Franco ended more than three decades of dictatorial rule. Franco's handpicked successor, King Juan Carlos (b. 1938), surprisingly steered his nation to Western-style constitutional monarchy, facing down threatened military coups. Portugal and Greece also ousted right-wing dictators, thus paving the way for their integration into Western Europe and for substantial economic growth.

Yet the dominance of the West was deteriorating. In 1976, Jimmy Carter, a wealthy farmer and governor of Georgia, narrowly won the U.S. presidential election (the first after the Watergate scandal) by selling himself as an outsider to Washington corruption. Carter could do little to return the economy to its pre-Vietnam and pre–oil embargo prosperity or stem global terrorism. His administration faced an insurmountable crisis late in the 1970s when students, clerics, shopkeepers, and unemployed men in Iran began a religious agitation that brought to power Ayatollah Ruhollah Khomeini, a fundamentalist Muslim leader. From exile in Paris, Khomeini had rallied the impoverished people and discontented Shi'ite Muslims

■ **Soldiers and Civilians in Northern Ireland**
Separatist, civil rights, and terrorist movements made everyday life unpredictably dangerous in the
last third of the century as activists increasingly directed their violence against ordinary people.
The world wars had often targeted civilians, and those leading internal struggles did so even when
the declared wars were over. In Belfast, Northern Ireland, British troops fought to put down the
Irish Republican Army and restore unity. Civilians were often drawn into the conflict. Only late in
the 1990s did both sides call a halt to the killing and agree to negotiate.
(Brian Aris/Camera Press London.)

of Iran with audiotaped messages calling for a transformation of the region into a
truly Islamic society and the renunciation of Western ways advocated by the deposed shah. In the autumn of 1979, revolutionary supporters of Khomeini took
hostages at the American embassy in Teheran and would not release them. The
paralysis of the United States in the face of Islamic militancy along with soaring inflation following another round of OPEC price hikes suggested that the 1980s and
1990s might cripple the West even more.

Conclusion

The 1960s and 1970s left the West with a sense of emergency. In these decades, an
unprecedented level of technological development transformed businesses, the nature of warfare, the exploration of space, and the functioning of government. It also
had an enormous impact on everyday life. Work changed as society reached a stage
called *postindustrial*, in which the service sector predominated. New patterns of

IMPORTANT DATES

c. 1960	"Pop art" movement begins to win mainstream support	**1968**	"Prague Spring" reform movement in Czechoslovakia against communism; student uprisings throughout Europe and the United States
1962–1965	Vatican II reforms Catholic ritual and dogma		
1963	U.S. civil rights leader Martin Luther King Jr. leads March on Washington; U.S. president John F. Kennedy assassinated; Betty Friedan publishes *The Feminine Mystique*	**1969**	U.S. astronauts walk on the moon's surface
		1972	SALT I treaty between the United States and Soviet Union
		1973	North Vietnam and the United States sign treaty ending war in Vietnam; OPEC raises price of oil and imposes oil embargo on the West
1964	Nikita Khrushchev ousted in the USSR, replaced by Leonid Brezhnev and Alexei Kosygin		
1965	International consortium led by the United States launches *Intelsat I*, the first commercial communications satellite; Christa Wolf publishes *Divided Heaven*	**1973–1976**	Aleksandr Solzhenitsyn publishes *Gulag Archipelago*
		1974	Watergate scandal forces resignation of U.S. president Richard Nixon
1966	Willy Brandt becomes West German foreign minister and develops Ostpolitik, a policy designed to bridge tensions between the two Germanys	**1977**	Feminists gather in Houston to mark the first International Year of Women
1967	South Africa's Dr. Christiaan Barnard performs first successful human heart transplant; Israel expands its territory in the Six-Day War	**1978**	Birth of the first "test-tube baby"
		1979	Environmentalists found the Green Party in West Germany; Iranians take U.S. hostages in Teheran

family life, new relationships among the generations, and revised standards for sexual behavior also characterized these years. Optimism about the potential of humans to perpetuate progress and affluence abounded. Yet technological change produced stubborn problems: concentrations of bureaucratic and industrial power, social inequality, environmental degradation, even uncertainty about humankind's future.

A surge of rebellion among youth, ethnic and racial minorities, and women condemned these conditions along with the threats posed by the continued cold war. By the end of the 1970s, war in Vietnam, protests throughout the Soviet bloc, the power of oil-producing states, and the growing political force of Islam had weakened superpower preeminence. The U.S.-led bloc also confronted terrorism, and the Soviet Union, long able to repress dissent in a growing economy, was put-

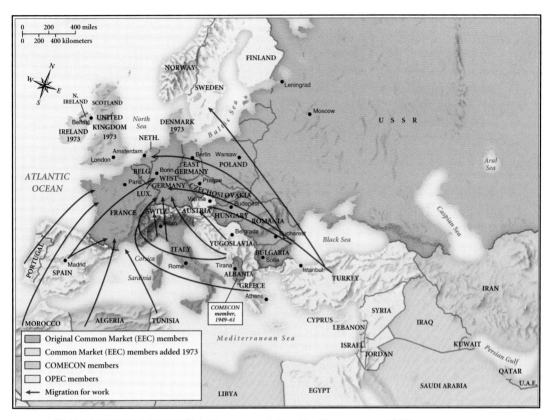

■ **MAPPING THE WEST** Europe and the Mediterranean, 1980

Despite the continuation of the cold war and the division of Europe into two antagonistic blocs, the superpowers' grip diminished during the 1960s and 1970s. Within the Soviet bloc, several governments introduced features of a market economy, and communications technology brought news of life in the U.S.-led bloc. U.S. allies protested American policies in Vietnam, and anti-American elements were very much in evidence in the uprisings of 1968. Mediterranean countries played their role in the West's transformation during these decades, not only during the oil embargo but in sending tens of thousands of migrants to work in labor-short Europe and often to settle there permanently.

ting more resources into military buildup than it could ultimately support. While the superpowers faltered, society approached the global age—one prepared by the array of technology of the 1960s and 1970s.

Suggested References for further reading and online research appear on page SR-37 at the back of the book.

www.bedfordstmartins.com/huntconcise   See the ONLINE STUDY GUIDE to assess your mastery of the material covered in this chapter.

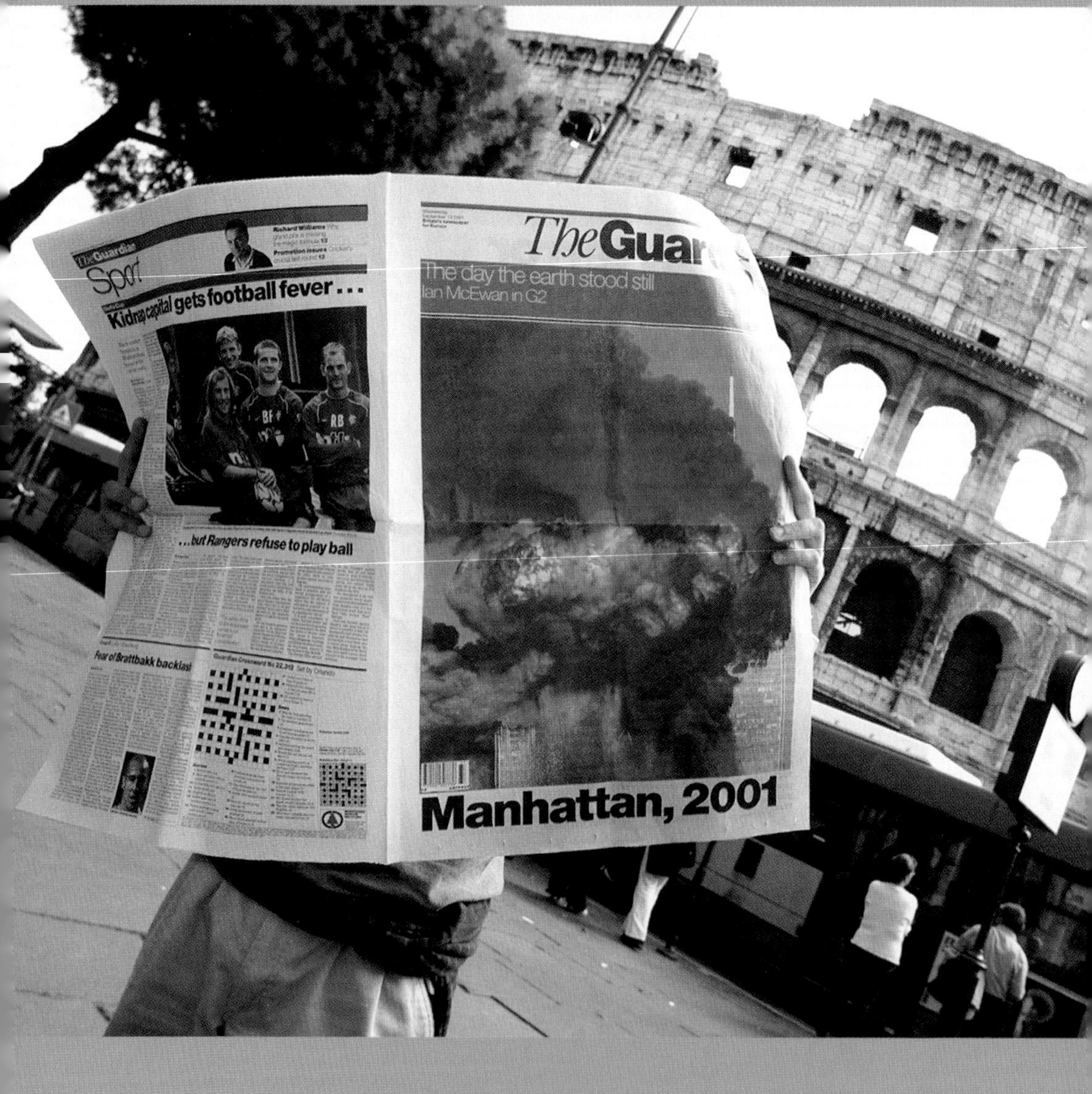
TheGuardian
Sport
Richard Williams
Promotion issues
Kidnap capital gets football fever . . .
. . . but Rangers refuse to play ball
Fear of Brattbakk backlash
TheGuar
The day the earth stood still
Ian McEwan in G2
Manhattan, 2001

24

The New Globalism: Opportunities and Dilemmas

1980 to the Present

I NSTEAD OF MAKING UP PATRIOTIC "LETTERS TO THE EDITOR" as was the custom under communism, in the mid-1980s the Soviet magazine *Ogonyok* ("Small Fires") began printing actual reports from readers. A woman identifying herself as a "mother of two" protested that the cost-cutting policy of reusing syringes in hospitals was spreading AIDS. "Why should little kids have to pay for the criminal actions of our Ministry of Health?" she asked. Other readers complained of corrupt factory managers, of "the radioactive sausages" foisted on the public after the disastrous explosion at the Chernobyl nuclear power plant, and of endless lines at nearly empty grocery stores. Sales of *Ogonyok* soared from a few hundred thousand copies to four million, and the experiment in printing real letters flooded the offices with hundreds of thousands of pieces of mail. The *Ogonyok* example was not unique: all across the Soviet bloc people were exploring political participation and resistance. They wrote, picketed, and protested; in so doing, they created an unprecedented public activism that, with incredibly little bloodshed, toppled the Soviet empire in 1989 and ended the cold war.

The collapse of communism in Europe had some unexpected negative repercussions, including the eruption of ethnic violence in the region, the deterioration of everyday life, and the decline of public services. The last result was part of a general trend in the West, as advanced industrial economies questioned the century-long trend toward the welfare state. Government support for citizens' health,

■ **Europeans React to 9/11 Terror**
On September 11, 2001, terrorists killed thousands of people from dozens of countries in airplane attacks on the World Trade Center in New York. Globally, people expressed their shock and sorrow in vigils, and like this British tourist in Rome, they remained glued to the latest news. Terrorism, which had plagued Europeans for several decades, easily traveled the world in these days of more open borders, economic globalization, and cultural exchange, finally reaching the sole superpower left after the collapse of the Soviet Union. Led by the United States, an international coalition took shape to attempt to eliminate this destructive by-product of a shrinking globe. (© Corbis.)

housing, and social security diminished, although governments increased subsidies and incentives for businesses facing global competition from the rising economic power of Japan, China, and other Asian countries. International business mergers accelerated from the 1990s on, and the Internet connected enterprises around the world in a matter of seconds, providing a force for international unity that offset competition.

The end of the cold war thus hastened the arrival of the "global age"—marked by the national and international migration of millions of people; the further expansion of markets; the lively cultural exchange of popular music, books, films, and television entertainment; and worldwide awareness of AIDS, environmental degradation, genocide, and terrorism. The end of superpower rivalry eased the way for this global exchange. It also resulted in the unprecedented dominance of the United States in world affairs. Nevertheless, new forces arose to compete with the West, in particular the economic power of the "Asian tigers" and the cultural might of Islam. As the twentieth century drew to a close, many observers equated globalism first and foremost with the revolutionary power of the Internet. Whatever the meaning of these many new phenomena, there was no question that people living in the twenty-first century would face extraordinary opportunities and dilemmas that had worldwide resonance.

Global Challenges

The end of the cold war ushered in many challenges. First, the health of the world's peoples and of the environment encountered a three-pronged attack from nuclear disaster, acid rain, and surging population. Second, economic prosperity and physical safety continued to elude great masses of people, especially in the southern half of the globe. Third, more states than ever before exercised economic and political power, especially through multinational organizations such as the World Bank and the World Trade Organization, but at the same time allegiance to nonstate and transnational ideas such as Islamic fundamentalism and ethnic autonomy called into question not only national borders but the concept of the nation-state itself.

Pollution and Population

Whereas industrialization and population growth had once seemed positive developments, people became aware of their downside. Despite the spread of ecological awareness, technological development continued to threaten the environment. The dangers were laid bare in 1986 when an explosion in the reactor at the nuclear power plant at Chernobyl, in the Soviet Union north of Kiev, blew the roof off the containment building and spewed radioactive dust into the atmosphere. The reactor, like most in the USSR, had minimal safety features. Many plant workers died within the year from the effects of radiation; others perished more slowly. Levels of

radioactivity rose hundreds of miles in all directions, contaminated meat and produce across Europe had to be destroyed, and by the 1990s cancer rates in the region were soaring, particularly among children.

Other environmental problems also had devastating global effects. Pollutants
from automobile exhausts and the burning of high-sulfur coal mixed with atmospheric moisture to produce acid rain, a poisonous brew that contaminates drinking water and destroys vegetation when it falls to earth as rain or snow. In Eastern
Europe, the unchecked use of high-sulfur coal produced acid rain that ravaged
forests and air pollution that inflicted ailments such as chronic bronchial disease
on children. In South America, rain forests were cut down at an alarming rate to
open land for cattle grazing or for cultivation of cash crops. Clearing the forests
threatened both the global oxygen supply and the biological diversity of the entire
planet.

By the late 1980s, scientists determined that the use of chlorofluorocarbons
(CFCs), chemicals used in aerosols and refrigerants, had blown a hole in the earth's
atmospheric ozone layer. Part of the blanket of gases surrounding the earth, ozone
prevents harmful ultraviolet rays from reaching the planet. Simultaneously, emissions from automobiles and industry were adding to the density of gases in the
thermal blanket. The result was *global warming*, an increase in the temperature of
the earth's atmosphere. Changes in temperature and dramatic weather cycles of
drought or drenching rain indicated that a *greenhouse effect* might be permanently
warming the earth.

The global public stepped up pressure on governments to check pollution. The
affluent West possessed the resources to begin to undo some of the damage accompanying industrialization. Automobile manufacturers in Western Europe and
the United States began building cars with lower carbon monoxide emissions, and
industrialists scaled back on factory pollution of air and waterways. Consumers began recycling newspaper, glass, aluminum cans, and plastic containers. Municipal
governments in Europe turned some streets into automobile-free pedestrian zones,
established "green" areas, and even banned cars altogether when ozone levels reached
a danger point. European countries and Japan led the world in providing efficient
public transportation, thus reducing the number of polluting automobiles on the
streets.

Nations with less-developed economies struggled with the pressing issue of
surging population. By 1995, Europe was actually experiencing negative growth
(more deaths than births), and the less industrially developed countries accounted
for 98 percent of all population growth—in part because of the spread of Western
medicine. By late 1999, the globe's population had reached 6 billion, and a doubling was forecast for 2045. (See "Taking Measure," page 1032.) In nonindustrial
countries, life expectancy rose by an average of sixteen years between 1950 and 1980.
By this measure of social health, the superpowers did not fare particularly well. Life
expectancy in the Soviet Union fell steadily in the 1970s to 1990s, from a peak of

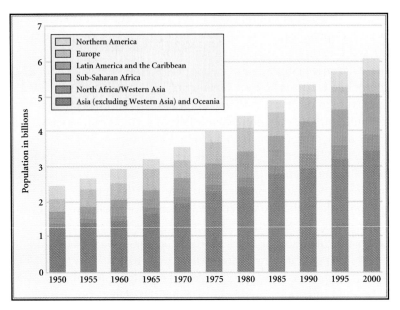

■ TAKING MEASURE World Population Growth, 1950–2000
In the twenty-first century, a major question is whether the global environment can sustain billions of people indefinitely. In the early modern period, local communities lived in accordance with unwritten rules that worked to balance population size with the productive capacities of individual farming regions. Centuries later, the need for balance had reached global proportions. As fertility dropped around the planet because of contraception, population continued to grow because of improved health. The political, social, and environmental results remain unclear.

seventy years in the mid-1970s to fifty-three for Russian men in 1995. By 1995, the United States had fallen from the top twenty in longevity for both women and men. Meanwhile, fertility rates, which had been dropping in the West for decades, were also declining in the less-developed world by 1995, as some 58 percent of couples were estimated to use birth control. Demographers hoped the slowdown in population increase signaled an alternative to ongoing, calamitous growth. Nonetheless, migration and urbanization worsened the problems of nations lacking the resources to care for their swelling numbers.

Despite the spread of Western medicine in the form of vaccines and drugs for diseases such as malaria and smallpox into the less-developed world, half of all Africans did not have access to safe drinking water. Drought and poverty, along with the maneuvers of politicians in some cases, spread famine in regions such as Sudan. Critics said these conditions were the result of a growing divide not between East and West but among countries of the wealthy North and the far poorer South. Medical practice in the industrialized nations focused on high-tech solutions to health problems. Specialists performed heart bypass surgery, transplanted organs, and treated cancer with radiation and chemotherapy. Preventive care for the masses received less attention. Instead, a disproportionate amount of expensive and high-tech hospital services went to the upper classes, especially men. At the other end of the scale, the unemployed suffered more chronic illnesses than people who were better off, but they received less care. The distribution of health services became a hotly debated issue in the general argument of whether technological solutions could remedy global problems.

North versus South?

During the 1980s and 1990s, world leaders tried to address the growing economic schism between the earth's northern and southern regions. Southern peoples—except for Australians and New Zealanders—suffered lower living standards and greater health problems than northerners. Recently emerging from colonial rule and economic exploitation by the North, citizens of the South could not yet count on their new governments to provide welfare services or public education. International organizations such as the World Bank and the International Monetary Fund provided loans for economic development, but the conditions tied to those loans, such as cutting government spending, led to the criticism that underprivileged southerners would gain no real benefit if education and health care had to be cut. Some twenty-first-century leaders advocated that wealthy countries simply acknowledge centuries of imperial pillage and give the South the money it needs.

Southern regions encountered various barriers to economic development. In Latin America, some nations grappled with government corruption, multi-billion-dollar debt, widespread crime, and grinding poverty. Mexico and some other countries, however, began to strengthen their economies by marketing their oil and other natural resources more effectively. Sub-Saharan Africa suffered from drought, famine, disease, and civil war. In Rwanda, for example, military rule, ideological factionalism, and ethnic antagonism produced a lethal mixture of conflict and genocide in the 1990s. Millions perished; others were left starving and homeless. Although African countries began turning away from military dictatorship and toward parliamentary government, global economic advance was uneven in Africa, and the scourge of AIDS made matters worse.

Emerging economies in the Southern Hemisphere as a whole, however, continued to increase their share of gross domestic product during the 1980s and 1990s, and some achieved political gains as well. In South Africa, black peoples began winning the struggle for political rights. In 1990, the moderate government of F. W. de Klerk released the African political leader Nelson Mandela (b. 1918), imprisoned for almost three decades because of his antiapartheid activism. De Klerk's government followed Mandela's release with the gradual end of segregation in parks and on beaches and in 1993 agreed to a democratic constitution that granted the vote to the nonwhite majority while guaranteeing the civil liberties of whites and other minorities. The next year, Mandela became South Africa's president in a landslide electoral victory,

formalizing the institution of a multiracial democracy attractive to international business. In India, Rajiv Gandhi (1944–1991), the grandson of India's first prime minister, Jawaharlal Nehru, worked for education, women's rights, and an end to bitter local rivalries. His assassination in 1991 by Tamil nationalists raised questions about
whether India would have the strong leadership necessary to attract investment and
continue modernization. The answer was soon obvious as India forged ahead in communications and other high-tech industries.

Islam Confronts the West

The Iran hostage crisis, which began in 1979, showed religion, nationalism, and the
power of oil uniting to make the Middle East an arbiter of international order. The
region's charismatic leaders—in the 1980s, Iran's Ayatollah Khomeini, Libya's
Muammar Qaddafi, and Iraq's Saddam Hussein; in the 1990s, Osama bin Laden—
variously promoted a pan-Arab or pan-Islamic world order that gathered increasing support. Khomeini's program of "Neither East, nor West, only the Islamic
Republic" had wide appeal. Turning from the Westernization encouraged by the
shah, his regime required women to cover their bodies almost totally in special
clothing, restricted their access to divorce, and eliminated a range of other rights.
Islamic revolutionaries believed these restrictions would restore the pride and Islamic identity that imperialism had stripped from Middle Eastern men. Khomeini
won widespread support among Shi'ite Muslims. Even though Shi'ites constituted
the majority in many Middle Eastern countries, they had long been ruled by Sunni
Muslims. The tables turned in Iran when Khomeini proclaimed the ascendancy of
the Shi'ite clergy in revolutionary Iran's Islamic society.

   Power in the Middle East remained fragmented, however, and Islam did not
achieve its unifying goals (Map 24.1). Instead, war plagued the region. The refusal
of the Iranian Shi'ites to release the hostages seized in 1979 at the U.S. embassy contributed to the collapse of the Carter presidency and the election of Ronald Reagan
in 1980 (the hostages were freed soon after his inauguration in January 1981). Meanwhile, in September 1980, Iraq's president, Saddam Hussein, launched an attack on
Iran. He feared that Iraq's Shi'ite minority might rebel against his Sunni regime,
and he sought to deflect their aggression into a patriotic crusade against the non-
Arab Iranians. The Iraqi leader also coveted oil-rich territory in Iran. Eight years of
combat, however, led only to stalemate and massive loss of life on both sides.

   The Soviet Union became entangled with Islamic forces in Afghanistan when
it supported a coup by a Communist faction against Afghanistan's Communist
government in 1979. The factionalism provided an opening for stiff resistance by
Afghanis who saw their traditional way of life being threatened by communism's
modernizing thrust. By 1980, tens of thousands of Soviet troops were fighting in
Afghanistan, using the USSR's most advanced missiles and artillery in an ultimately
unsuccessful effort to overcome Muslim leaders. After the withdrawal of Soviet

■ Muslims at Prayer in Marseille, France

As migration increased during the 1980s and 1990s, Europe became more ethnically and racially diverse than it had been for centuries. In most European countries, immigrants eventually could become citizens. Switzerland and Germany used the criterion of common ancestry to determine who would have political and civil rights. Cultural exchange and interaction accelerated during these decades, and debates over cultural values and cultural identity multiplied.

(Steve McCurry/Magnum Photos, Inc.)

forces in 1989 and the collapse of the USSR in 1992, power in Afghanistan remained contested until the late 1990s, when the Islamic fundamentalist Taliban party succeeded in imposing a strict regime.

As the Soviet bloc fell apart in 1989–1992, Saddam Hussein was the first to test the post–cold war waters. At the end of the Iran-Iraq war in 1988, Iraq staggered under a heavy debt and a lowered standard of living. Hussein viewed the annexation of neighboring Kuwait, whose 600,000 citizens enjoyed the world's highest per capita income, as a solution to Iraq's troubles. In 1990, Iraqi forces invaded the oil-rich country. Much to Hussein's surprise, the deployment of Iraqi troops on the Saudi Arabian border galvanized a UN coalition (joined by the USSR) to stop the Iraqi invasion. A multinational force led by the United States pummeled the Iraqi army. Iraq's defeat in 1991 heightened pressure on Middle Eastern leaders to negotiate peaceful solutions to their disputes.

Nevertheless, some leaders willingly resorted to violence and international terrorism to advance their causes. Hopes for peace among Palestinians and Israelis

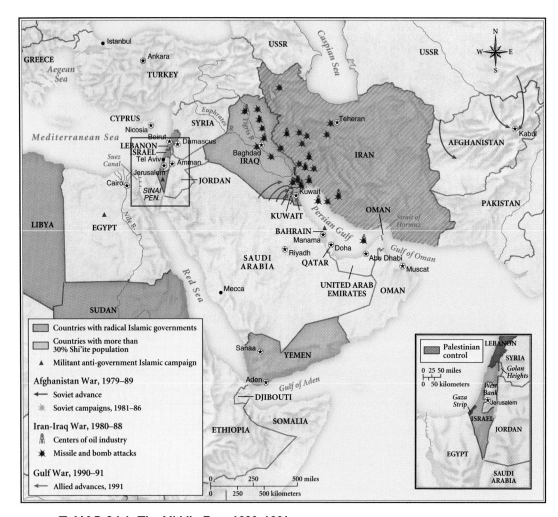

■ MAP 24.1 The Middle East, 1980–1991

Tensions among states in the Middle East, especially the ongoing conflict between Palestinians and Israelis, increased in the 1980s. As Islam took center stage in politics, Middle Eastern populations divided over such issues as the extent of religious determination of state policies, the role of religion in everyday life, and access to human rights including freedom of speech and of movement. Conflicts erupted around some of these questions because, as elsewhere, politicians exploited people's fears and emotions in their pursuit of power. In the 1990s, the increasing demands of globalization pulled some citizens in the direction of secularization, high-tech international partnerships, and a reduction in the costly politics of violence. In 2001, however, violence escalated among Arabs and Israelis, bringing the region to the breaking point.

dimmed after 2000, as peace talks broke down and armed clashes escalated. An unprecedented act of terrorism against the United States occurred on September 11, 2001, when militants from Arab countries hijacked planes and flew them into the Twin Towers of the World Trade Center in New York City and the Pentagon on the outskirts of Washington, D.C. Inspired by the radical leader Osama bin Laden, who sought to end the presence of U.S. armed forces in Saudi Arabia and other areas important to Islam, the hijackers had trained in bin Laden's terrorist camps in Afghanistan and learned to pilot planes in the United States. The loss of more than three thousand lives—not only Americans but people from dozens of other countries—led to a "war against terrorism." The administration of U.S. president George W. Bush forged a multinational coalition with the vital cooperation of dissidents within Afghanistan and predominantly Islamic countries such as Pakistan. The coalition enjoyed quick successes against the terrorists in Afghanistan and brought to an end the harsh Taliban rule, but it became clear that terrorist cells existed throughout the world and that terrorism would pose one of the most frightening global challenges of the twenty-first century.

The Rise of the Pacific Economy

From the last third of the twentieth century and into the twenty-first, an incredible global diffusion of industry and technology took place, especially in Asia. Just as economic change in the early modern period had redirected European affairs from the Mediterranean to the Atlantic, so explosive productivity from Japan to Singapore in the 1980s began to transfer economic power from the Atlantic region to the Pacific. In 1982, the Asian Pacific nations accounted for 16.4 percent of global gross domestic product, a figure that had doubled since the 1960s. More surprising, by the mid-1990s China was achieving economic growth rates of 8 percent and more, and Japan had developed the second largest national economy after the United States.

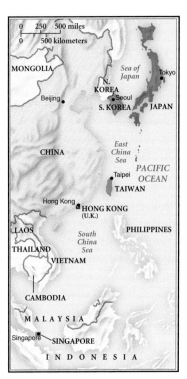

South Korea, Taiwan, Singapore, Hong Kong, and China were popularly called the "Asian tigers" because of the ferocity of their growth. Japan, however, led the charge. Investment in high-tech consumer industries drove the Japanese economy. In 1982, Japan had 32,000 industrial robots in operation, Western Europe had 9,000, and the United States had 7,000. In 1989, the Japanese government and private businesses in Japan invested $549 billion to modernize Japan's industrial capacity—a full $36 billion more than U.S. public and private investment combined. Such spending paid off handsomely: buyers around the world snapped up automobiles, televisions, videocassette recorders, and

"Tigers" of the Pacific Rim, c. 1985

computers from Japanese or other Asian Pacific companies. By the end of the 1980s, Japan was home to the world's eight largest banks and to a brokerage house that was twenty times larger than its nearest American competitor. As the United States poured vast sums into its cold war military budget, Asian Pacific investors purchased U.S. government bonds, thus financing America's ballooning national debt. Forty years after its defeat in World War II, Japan was bankrolling its former conqueror.

Despite rising national prosperity in Asia, many individual Asian workers, particularly outside of Japan, saw only modest gains. Women in South Korea and Taiwan labored in sweatshops to produce clothing for J. C. Penney, Calvin Klein, and other U.S.-based companies. Using the lure of a low-paid, docile female workforce, Asian governments were able to attract foreign electronics and other industries. Educational standards rose, however, and these women gained access to birth control and medical care. Despite the persistent grip of authoritarian governments, some of the "Asian tigers" ranked high in human development by UN standards.

In Japan, too, results were mixed: workers were expected to subordinate their personal interests to those of the business firm, just as Japanese businesses followed the dictates of the national government. The rewards for this discipline were great, and for a time Japanese ideas about business and management were touted as offering a model that the West should follow. Then dissatisfaction with Japan's patriarchal political elite developed. In 1989, Japanese women led the way in voting out of office a prime minister who kept a mistress. Women also entered the parliament and cabinet, long a bastion of elderly men. In 2002, the women of Japan threatened the downfall of another prime minister, who had dismissed a woman minister of foreign affairs. Government attempts to maintain cultural homogeneity brought charges of racism from abroad, as hundreds of thousands of non-Japanese who illegally entered Japan to perform the menial labor shunned by native workers experienced considerable discrimination. Critics began to express concern about environmental deterioration, the quality of life in Japan's overcrowded cities, and the growing menace of domestic terrorism.

In the 1990s and early twenty-first century, mounting economic difficulties plagued Japan and the other "Asian tigers." Financial scandals and widespread corruption, which the government refused to address, destabilized the Japanese economy. The stock market plunged, as did the value of the yen. Domestic consumers cut back, and some investors sent their money abroad for higher returns. From 1997 on, Japan's depressed economy menaced the region and the world. A severe business crisis struck the Pacific Rim as currency speculation and irresponsible and corrupt financial practices—"crony capitalism"—brought down the Thai currency in 1997 and then toppled politicians and industrial leaders in Indonesia, South Korea, and elsewhere in the region; by 2001 recession had spread to Europe and the United States. Many Asian leaders, notably the Japanese, seemed reluctant to take corrective action despite the growing realization that in the "global age" worldwide industrial and financial health was affected by economic conditions everywhere.

The Welfare State in Question

As the 1980s opened, stagflation and the realignment of global economic power forced non-Communist governments in the West to put their economic houses in order. The unprecedented mix of the energy crisis, soaring unemployment, and double-digit inflation sparked the election of conservative politicians, who maintained that decades of supporting a welfare state were at the heart of economic problems. Across the West, tough times intensified feelings that the unemployed and new migrants were responsible for the downturn. Nineteenth-century emphases on competitiveness, individualism, and revival of privilege for the "best circles" replaced the twentieth-century trend toward advancing economic democracy to combat totalitarianism.

Thatcher Reshapes Political Culture

More than anyone else, Margaret Thatcher (b. 1925), the outspoken leader of Britain's Conservative Party from 1979 to 1990, reshaped the West's political and economic ideas. Coming to power amid continuing economic decline, revolt in Northern Ireland, and labor unrest, the combative prime minister eschewed the politics of consensus building. Believing that only a resurgence of private enterprise could revive the sluggish British economy, she lashed out at union leaders, Labour politicians, and people who received welfare-state benefits as enemies of British prosperity. Her anti-welfare-state policies struck a revolutionary chord. She called herself "a nineteenth-century liberal," referring to the economic individualism

■ **Margaret Thatcher**
As British prime minister for more than a decade, Margaret Thatcher profoundly influenced European history by cutting back the welfare state. Thatcher believed, and convinced others, that the welfare state did not advance society and made citizens lazy by rewarding those who were not contributing to the nation. Her tenure in office encouraged other politicians from Ronald Reagan to Helmut Kohl to execute similar cuts in programs. More than any other head of state, she set the general course in domestic policy for the late twentieth century.
(Stuart Franklin/Sygma.)

of that age. In her view, business leaders and entrepreneurs were the key members of society. Although immigrants often worked for the lowest wages and contributed to profits, she characterized as inferior the unemployed and immigrants from Britain's former colonies, saying that neither group contributed to national wealth. Under Thatcher, even workers blamed labor leaders or newcomers for Britain's trauma.

The policies of "Thatcherism" were based on *monetarist* or *supply-side* theories associated most prominently with U.S. economist Milton Friedman. Monetarists contend that inflation results when government pumps money into the economy at a rate higher than a nation's economic growth rate. They advocate a tight rein on the money supply to keep prices from rising rapidly. Supply-side economists maintain that the economy as a whole flourishes when business prosperity "trickles down" throughout the society. To implement such theories, the British government cut income taxes on the wealthy to spur new investment and pushed up sales taxes to compensate for the lost revenue. The result was an increased burden on working people, who bore the brunt of the sales tax. Thatcher also vigorously pruned government intervention in the economy: she sold publicly owned businesses and utilities such as British Airways; refused to prop up "outmoded" industries such as coal mining; and slashed education and health programs. These economic policies came to be known as *neo-liberalism.*

In the first three years of Thatcher's government, the British economy responded poorly to her shock treatment. The quality of universities, public transportation, highways, and hospitals deteriorated, and leading scholars and scientists left Britain in a renewal of the brain drain. In addition, social unity fragmented— in 1981, blacks and Asians rioted in major cities—and Thatcher's popularity sagged. A turning point came in March 1982, when Argentina invaded the British Falkland Islands in the South Atlantic. Thatcher invoked patriotism to unify the nation and refused to surrender the distant islands without a fight. The gamble paid off, as the prime minister's public support soared. When inflation eventually dissipated, historians and economists debated whether the change resulted from Thatcher's policies or from the lack of spending power that burdened the poor and unemployed. In any case, Thatcher's program became the standard. Britain had been one of the pioneers of the welfare state, and now it pioneered in changing course. By the twenty-first century even the Labour government of Tony Blair (b. 1953) had adopted a neo-liberal program.

The Reagan Revolution and Its Aftermath

Moved by the same social and political vision as Thatcher, Ronald Reagan (b. 1911; president, 1981–1989) worked a similar revolution. The former actor was at his best in carefully planned television appearances. During these, Reagan vowed to promote the values of the "moral majority," which included commitment to Bible-based religion, dedication to work, sexual restraint, and unquestioned patriotism. Chastising so-called spendthrift and immoral "liberals," he introduced "Reaganomics"—a program of whopping income tax cuts combined with massive reductions in federal spending for student loans, school lunch programs, and mass transit. Like Thatcher, Reagan believed that tax cuts would lead to investment and reinvigorate the economy; federal outlays for welfare programs, which he felt only encouraged sloth, would generally be unnecessary thereafter.

In foreign policy, Reagan spent most of his time in office preoccupied with the Communist threat. The long-time cold warrior labeled the Soviet Union an "evil empire" and demanded huge military budgets to counter the Soviet arms buildup of the 1970s. Reagan announced the Strategic Defense Initiative, known popularly as "Star Wars," a costly plan to put lasers in space to defend the United States against a nuclear attack.

The combination of tax cuts and military expansion had pushed the federal budget deficit to $200 billion by 1986. Critics held Reaganomics accountable for the escalating violence and drug use in schools across the country and the growing numbers of homeless Americans sleeping on the streets. Although Reagan's administration spent less of the gross national product on the military than Eisenhower's had (7.5 percent as opposed to 10 percent), it did so at a time when the United States faced stiff competition from such global powers as Japan and West Germany.

The election of Democrat Bill Clinton (b. 1946) as U.S. president in 1992 did not fundamentally change the move away from the welfare state and toward neoliberalism. As in Britain, an ethic of *workfare* (a term suggesting that people receiving government benefits should work for them) continued in the United States, and the goal of competitiveness in an increasingly global economy justified crumbling urban schools and the statistical decline in real wages for the lower and middle segments of society. In fact, the U.S. economy as a whole soared in the 1990s, lifting people in the professions and top management to ever greater wealth. Seen from this vantage point, the cuts in social programs were a real success. Other people attributed rising wealth to technology's boosting productivity and streamlining business processes.

Alternatives to Thatcherism

Other Western European leaders found retrenchment of the welfare state in the face of stagflation necessary, but did so without Thatcher's politically divisive rhetoric. West German leader Helmut Kohl (b. 1930), who took power in 1982, reduced welfare spending, froze government wages, and cut corporate taxes. By 1984, the inflation rate was only 2 percent, and West Germany had acquired a 10 percent share of world trade. Unlike Thatcher, Kohl did not fan class and racial hatreds. The politics of divisiveness was particularly unwise in Germany, where terrorism on the left and on the right continued to flourish. Moreover, the legacy of Nazism loomed menacingly. "Let's gas 'em," said unemployed German youth of immigrant Turkish workers. The revival of Nazi rhetoric appalled many in Germany's middle class rather than gaining their support. This divisiveness would become even more menacing a few years later when Germany faced the economic problems posed by the reunification of the country.

France took a different political path, though by 1981 stagflation had put more than 1.5 million people out of work and reduced the economic growth rate to an anemic 1.2 percent. The French elected a socialist president, François Mitterrand (1916–1996), who nationalized banks and certain industries and stimulated the economy by wage increases and social spending—the opposite of Thatcherism. Museums, libraries, and other new public buildings arose; new subway lines opened; and public transportation improved. Financial leaders reacted by sending capital abroad, and in Mitterrand's second term, conservatives captured the majority of seats in the assembly, which entitled them to choose the prime minister. When the conservative prime minister Jacques Chirac succeeded Mitterrand as president, neo-liberal policies came into their own as a respected way of ensuring prosperity. Even the selection of socialist prime minister Lionel Jospin in 1997 did not turn back the clock: by 2002, under Jospin there had been greater privatization of publicly owned companies and the consequent accomplishment of more business mergers than ever before. Repercussions similar to those elsewhere in Europe emerged, as the politically racist National Front leader Jean-Marie Le Pen won 17 percent of the vote in the first round of balloting in the 2002 presidential elections. Le Pen promised to deport African and Muslim immigrants and cut France's ties with nonwhite nations.

Meanwhile, a cluster of smaller states without heavy defense commitments enjoyed increasing prosperity, though many slashed away at welfare programs. In Spain, tourist dollars helped rebuild the southern cities of Granada and Córdoba, and the country joined the Common Market in 1986. In Ireland, a surge of investment in education for high-tech jobs combined with low wages to bring much new business to the country in the 1990s. Prosperity and the increasingly unacceptable death toll led to a political rapprochement between Ireland and Northern Ireland in 1999. Austria prospered, too, in part by reducing government pensions and aid to business. Austrian chancellor Franz Vranitsky summed up the changed focus of government in the 1980s and 1990s: "In Austria, the shelter that the state has given to almost everyone—employee as well as entrepreneur—has led . . . a lot of people [to] think not only what they can do to solve a problem but what the state can do. . . . This needs to change." The century-long growth of the welfare state seemed to be over by the 1990s, but the future mission of government was unclear.

Almost alone, Sweden maintained a full array of social programs for everyone. The government also offered each immigrant a choice of subsidized housing in neighborhoods inhabited primarily by Swedes or primarily by people from the immigrant's native land. Such programs were expensive: the tax rate on income over

$46,000 was 80 percent. Despite a highly productive workforce, Sweden dropped from fourth to fourteenth place among nations in per capita income by 1998. Although the Swedes reduced their costly dependence on foreign oil by cutting consumption in half between 1976 and 1986, their welfare state came to seem extreme to many citizens. As in politics elsewhere, immigrants were cast as the major threat to the country: "How long will it be before our Swedish children will have to turn their faces toward Mecca?" ran one politician's campaign speech in 1993.

The Collapse of Soviet Communism

The most consequential event of the 1980s and 1990s was the breakup of the Soviet bloc in 1989 followed by the collapse of the USSR itself in the 1990s. Emblematic of other trends, the end of bipolarity hastened globalization, while socialist collapse undermined the largest single system providing government benefits to citizens. But what most struck people at the time was the suddenness of it all, for throughout the 1980s U.S.-bloc analysts erroneously reported that the Soviet empire was in robust health. Yet protest by workers, artists, and others had never really stopped across the Soviet realm despite repression of the Prague Spring. CIA reports to the contrary, the Soviet economy was not robust but deteriorating, even with steps toward economic reform in Poland and Hungary. Communications, international trade, and democratic movements were pulling apart a vast region that communism had structured for almost half a century. Ironically, the triumph of democracy in the former Soviet empire opened an era of painful adjustment, uncertainty, and violence for hundreds of millions of people.

Rebellion in Poland, Reform in the Soviet Union

Dissent against Soviet rule reached crisis stage in the summer of 1980, when Poles reacted furiously to government-increased food prices by going on strike. As the protest spread, workers at the Gdańsk shipyards, led by electrician Lech Walesa, created an independent labor movement called Solidarity. The organization soon embraced much of the adult population, including a million members of the Communist Party. The Catholic church, long in the forefront of opposition to socialist secularization, and intellectuals supported Solidarity workers as they occupied factories in protest against inflation, the scarcity of food, and other deteriorating conditions of everyday life. Solidarity members waved Polish flags and paraded giant portraits of the Virgin Mary and Pope John Paul II (b. 1920)—a Polish native.

Having achieved mass support at home and worldwide sympathy through media coverage, Solidarity leaders insisted that the government recognize the organization as an independent union—a radical demand under communism. As food became scarce and prices rose, tens of thousands of women marched in the streets crying, "We're hungry!" The Communist Party teetered toward collapse until the police and the army, with Soviet support, imposed a military government and in the winter of 1981 outlawed Solidarity. Reporters and dissidents, using global communications, kept Solidarity alive as a force both inside and outside of Poland. Stern and puritanical, General Wojciech Jaruzelski took over as the head of Poland's new regime in 1981, but the general could not push repression too far: he needed new loans from the U.S.-led bloc to keep the sinking Polish economy afloat. Instability in Poland set the stage for communism's downfall.

The rise of Solidarity exposed the economic woes of people living in the Soviet bloc. Years of stagnant and then negative growth led to a deteriorating standard of living. After working a full day, Soviet homemakers stood in long lines to obtain basic commodities; housing and food shortages necessitated a three-generation household in which grandparents took over tedious homemaking tasks from their working children and grandchildren. "There is no special skill to this," a seventy-three-year-old grandmother and former garbage collector remarked: "You just stand in line and wait." Even so, they often went away empty-handed, as basic household supplies like soap disappeared instantly from stores. One cheap and readily available product—vodka—often formed the center of people's social lives. Alcoholism reached crisis levels, diminishing productivity and tremendously straining the nation's morale.

Economic stagnation had many other ramifications. Ordinary people decided not to have children, and fertility fell below replacement levels throughout the Soviet bloc, except in Muslim areas of Soviet Central Asia. The country was forced to import massive amounts of grain because 20 to 30 percent of the grain produced in the USSR rotted before it could be harvested or shipped to market, so great was the inefficiency of the state-directed economy. Industrial pollution, spewed out by enterprises interested only in meeting production quotas, reached scandalous dimensions. A massive and privileged party bureaucracy hobbled industrial innovation and failed to achieve socialism's professed goal of a decent standard of living for working people. To match American military growth, the Soviet Union diverted 15 to 20 percent of its gross national product (more than double the U.S. proportion) to armaments. As this combustible mix of problems heated up, a new generation was coming of age that had no memory of World War II or Stalin's purges. One Russian observer found members of the younger generation "cynical but less afraid." "They believe in nothing," a mother said of Soviet youth in 1984.

In 1985, a new leader, Mikhail Gorbachev (b. 1931), opened an era of unexpected change. The son of peasants, Gorbachev had risen through the party ranks as an agricultural specialist and had traveled abroad to gain a firsthand glimpse of life in the West. He quickly proposed several unusual programs. The first, *perestroika* ("restructuring"), aimed to reinvigorate the Soviet economy by improving productivity, increasing the rate of capital investment, encouraging the use of up-to-date technology, and gradually introducing such market features as prices and profits. The second, a policy called *glasnost* (usually translated as "openness" or

■ The Gorbachevs and Reagans at the Reagans' Ranch

Ronald Reagan raised the temperature of the cold war with a massive arms buildup in the 1980s that caused the U.S. budget deficit to soar. When Mikhail Gorbachev came to power in the USSR, he changed course, encouraging freer speech, seeking innovation in the economy, and reducing cold war tensions. The two leaders' regular meetings helped slow the arms race.

(Ruelas, L.A. Daily News/Sygma.)

"publicity"), called for disseminating "wide, prompt, and frank information" and allowing Soviet citizens new measures of free speech.♦ When officials complained that glasnost threatened their status, Gorbachev replaced more than a third of the party's leadership in the first months of his administration. The pressing need for glasnost became most evident after the Chernobyl catastrophe in 1986, when bureaucratic cover-ups delayed the spread of information about the accident, with lethal consequences for people living near the plant.

After Chernobyl, even the Communist Party and Marxism-Leninism were opened to public criticism and contestation. Party meetings suddenly witnessed complaints about the highest leaders and their policies. Television shows such as *The Fifth Wheel* adopted the outspoken methods of American investigative reporting; one program showed an interview with an executioner of political prisoners and exposed the plight of Leningrad's homeless children. Political factions arose

---

♦ For a pair of newspaper articles that illustrate Gorbachev's revolutionary policies, see Document 76, "Glasnost and the Soviet Press."

across the political spectrum. In the fall of 1987, one of Gorbachev's erstwhile allies, Boris Yeltsin, quit the governing Politburo after denouncing perestroika as inadequate for real reform. Yeltsin's political daring, which in the past would have consigned him to oblivion (or Siberia), inspired others to organize in opposition to the crumbling ruling orthodoxy. By the spring of 1989, in remarkably free balloting, not a single Communist was chosen for office in Moscow's local elections.

Glasnost and perestroika dramatically affected superpower relations as well. Recognizing how severely the cold war arms race was draining Soviet resources, Gorbachev almost immediately began scaling back missile production. His unilateral actions gradually won over Ronald Reagan. Beginning in 1985, the two leaders initiated a personal relationship and began defusing the cold war. "I bet the hard-liners in both our countries are bleeding when we shake hands," said the jovial Reagan at the conclusion of one meeting. In early 1989, Gorbachev at last withdrew Soviet forces from the debilitating war in Afghanistan, and by the end of the year the United States started to cut back its own vast military buildup.

The Revolutions of 1989

Tremors shook the Communist world in the spring of 1989. Inspired by Gorbachev's visit to China's capital, Beijing, thousands of students massed in Tiananmen Square to demand democracy. They used telex machines and electronic mail to rush their messages to the international community, and they effectively conveyed their goals through the cameras that Western television trained on them. China's aged Communist leaders, while pushing economic modernization and even allowing market operations, refused to consider the introduction of democracy. As workers began joining the Democracy forces, the government crushed the movement and executed as many as a thousand rebels.

Despite the setback to the forces of democracy in China, the spirit of revolt advanced in Eastern Europe in 1989 and brought decades of Communist rule to an end. Indeed, the year 1989 has been designated the twentieth century's *annus mirabilis* ("year of miracles") because of the sudden and unexpected disintegration of Communist power throughout the region (Map 24.2). Events in Poland took a dramatic turn first. In June, the Polish government, weakened by its own bungling of the economy and lacking Soviet support for further repression, held free parliamentary elections. Solidarity candidates drove out the Communists, and by early 1990 Walesa became president, hastening Poland's rocky transition to a market economy.

As it became evident that the Soviet Union would not intervene in Poland, the fall of communism repeated itself in country after country. In Hungary, which had experimented with "market socialism" since the 1960s, popular demands for liberalization led the parliament to dismiss the Communist Party as the official ruling institution. In Czechoslovakia, which after 1968 had been firmly restored to Soviet-style rule, people watched the progress of glasnost expectantly. Although they could

■ **MAP 24.2 The Collapse of Communism in Europe, 1989–1991**
In one form or another, resistance to communism had been continuous since the 1940s; thus, the 1989 overthrow of Communist governments in the USSR satellite countries in Eastern Europe occurred with surprising rapidity. In 1991, Communist Yugoslavia began to break up into individual states composed of competing ethnicities and religions. Then the USSR itself fell apart, as the Baltic states seceded, followed by the official dissolution of the rest of the USSR on January 1, 1992.

see Gorbachev on television calling for free speech, he never mentioned reform in Czechoslovakia. Demonstrators protested in the streets for democracy, but the government cracked down by turning the police on them. The turning point came in November 1989 when Alexander Dubček, leader of the Prague Spring of 1968, addressed crowds in Prague's Wenceslas Square with a call for the ouster of Stalinists from the government. Almost immediately, the Communist leadership resigned. Capping the country's "velvet revolution," as it became known because of its lack of bloodshed, the formerly Communist-dominated parliament elevated dissident playwright Václav Havel to the presidency.

The most potent symbol of a divided Europe—the Berlin Wall—stood in the midst of divided Germany. East Germans had attempted to escape over the wall for decades, despite their country's reputation as having the most dynamic economy in the socialist world. In the summer of 1989, crowds of East Germans flooded the borders of the crumbling Soviet bloc, and hundreds of thousands of urban protesters at home rallied throughout the fall against the regime. On November 9, an ambiguous statement from the East German government encouraged guards to allow free passage across the wall. Protest turned to festive holiday: West Berliners handed out bananas, a consumer good that had been in short supply in the Eastern zone, and that fruit became the unofficial symbol of reunion. Almost immediately, Berliners released years of frustration at their division by assaulting the wall with sledgehammers and bringing home chunks as souvenirs. The government finished its complete destruction in the fall of 1990.◆

Almost as soon as the Berlin Wall tumbled, the world's attention fastened on the political drama in Romania. Since the mid-1960s, Nicolae Ceauşescu had ruled as the harshest dictator in Communist Europe since Stalin. In the name of modernization, he destroyed whole villages; to build up the population, he outlawed contraceptives and abortion, a restriction that led to the abandonment of tens of thousands of children. Most Romanians lived in utter poverty as Ceauşescu channeled almost all the country's resources into building himself an enormous palace in Bucharest. Yet, in early December 1989, an opposition movement rose up. Most of the army turned against the government and crushed the forces loyal to Ceauşescu. On Christmas Day, viewers watched on television as the dictator and his wife were tried by a military court and then executed.

■ **Destroying the Berlin Wall**
The most disturbing symbol of the cold war, the Berlin Wall came down in 1989 as dramatically as it had gone up in 1961. The next decade saw not only the reunification of Germany but the massive rebuilding of Berlin as the nation's capital.
(© Reuters Newmedia Inc./Corbis.)

◆ For an interview with one of the grassroots organizers against Soviet control, see Document 77, Cornelia Matzke, "Revolution in East Germany: An Activist's Perspective."

The collapse of communism in Europe paved the way for the reunification of Germany. Chancellor Helmut Kohl of West Germany based the campaign for re-unification on the promise of a more comfortable way of life. A shrewd politician, Kohl acted on what he called his "grass-roots instinct that the East Germans wanted their microwaves now, and not in three years." Full political union took place on October 3, 1990, far earlier than anyone had expected at the end of 1989. The re-alities of unification, however, did not live up to the dream. East German industry passed into the hands of West German managers, whose efficiencies in downsizing the workforce caused unemployment to soar, especially among women and youth. Many social services, such as day-care centers that allowed women to work to sup-port their families, closed down. Social tensions flared, leading to violent attacks or hateful rhetoric against immigrants. Amid these stresses, the economy declined late in the 1990s relative to other countries in Europe, and its health became a major issue in the 2002 elections. Throughout the former Soviet bloc, the transition to democracy and free markets gave rise simultaneously to economic upheaval, expressions of wide-ranging discontent, and hope for a better future.

The Breakup of Yugoslavia and the Soviet Union

After a few euphoric months, the problems of post-Communist life intensified, as first Yugoslavia and then the Soviet Union itself fell apart. The Soviet empire, like the Russian empire from which it grew, had held together more than one hundred ethnic groups, and the five republics of Soviet Central Asia were home to fifty mil-lion Muslims. Similarly in Yugoslavia, Communist rulers had enforced unity among religious and ethnic groups, but in 1990 the Serb Communist Slobodan Milosevic won the presidency of his republic and began to assert Serb ascendancy. In the spring of 1991, Slovenia and Croatia seceded, but the Croats soon lost almost a quarter of their territory to the Serb-dominated Yugoslav army (Map 24.3). An even more devastating civil war engulfed Bosnia-Herzegovina, where the republic's Mus-lim majority tried to create a multiethnic state. Many Bosnian Serb men formed a guerrilla army, backed by the covert support of Milosevic's government, and gained the upper hand; the Muslim Bosnians were prevented by a UN arms embargo from equipping their forces adequately to resist. Late in the 1990s, the Serb forces started attacking people of Albanian ethnicity living in the Yugoslav province of Kosovo. From 1997 to 1999, hundreds of thousands of Albanian Kosovars fled their homes as Serb militias and the Yugoslav army began attacking the civilian population. NATO pilots bombed the region in an attempt to drive back the army and Serb militias. Amid incredible violence and suffering, UN peacekeeping forces stepped in to enforce an interethnic truce.

During the 1990s, civilians died by the tens of thousands as Yugoslav republics broke away and as Serbs pursued a policy they called "ethnic cleansing"—that is, genocide—against the other nationalities. They raped women to leave them

■ MAP 24.3 The Former Yugoslavia, c. 2000

After a decade of destructive civil war, UN forces and UN-brokered agreements attempted to protect civilians in the former Yugoslavia from the brutal consequences of post-Communist rule. Ambitious politicians, most notably Slobodan Milosevic, used the twentieth-century Western strategy of fostering ethnic and religious hatred as a powerful tool to build support for themselves while making those favoring peace look softhearted and unfit to rule.

pregnant with Serb babies. Men and boys were often taken away and massacred. Military units destroyed libraries and museums, architectural treasures like the Mostar Bridge, and cities rich with medieval history such as Dubrovnik. Ethnic cleansing thus entailed destroying actual people as well as all traces of their complex cultural past. Many in the West explained violence in the Balkans as part of "age-old" blood feuds manifesting the backwardness of an almost "Asian" society. Others saw ethnic rivals' use of genocide to achieve national power as a thoroughly modern phenomenon of the West in the twentieth century. Driven from office, Milosevic was handed over in 2001 to an international tribunal to be tried for crimes against humanity.

■ **Yugoslavia in 1990, before Destruction of the Mostar Bridge (top)
and after (bottom)**
*In modern history, the construction of a nation-state has depended on the growth of institutions,
such as armies and bureaucracies, and the promotion of a common national culture. In an effort
to dominate Bosnia and Croatia, Serbs destroyed non-Serb architecture, books, and such ancient
symbols as the Mostar Bridge.* (Top: Sygma. Bottom: Stephane Cardinale/Sygma.)

In the USSR, Gorbachev announced late in 1990 that there was "no alternative
to the transition to the market," but his plan was too little, too late and satisfied no
one. Perestroika failed to improve the Soviet economy: people confronted soaring
prices, unemployment, and even greater scarcity of goods than they had endured
in the past. The Russian parliament's election of Boris Yeltsin as president of the
Russian Republic over a Communist candidate provoked a coup attempt in August
1991 by antireform hard-liners that included the powerful head of the Soviet secret police, or KGB. While they held Gorbachev, who held the title of President of
the Congress of People's Deputies, under house arrest, Yeltsin, standing atop a tank

outside the Russian Republic's parliament building, called for mass resistance. Hundreds of thousands of residents of Moscow and Leningrad filled the streets, and units of the army defected to protect Yeltsin's headquarters. People used fax machines and computers to coordinate internal resistance and send messages to the rest of the world. The coup was in complete disarray in the face of citizen determination not to allow a return of Stalinism or any form of Soviet orthodoxy.

The Soviet Union disintegrated. People tore down statues of Soviet heroes; Yeltsin outlawed the party newspaper, *Pravda*, and sealed the KGB files. The Soviet parliament suspended operations of the Communist Party itself. One republic after another followed the lead of the Baltic states, which declared their independence in September 1991. Ethnic conflict erupted. In the Soviet republic of Tajikistan, native Tajiks rioted against Armenians living there; in Azerbaijan, Azeris and Armenians clashed over contested territory; and in the Baltic states, anti-Semitism revived as a political tool. The USSR finally dissolved on January 1, 1992. Twelve of the fifteen former Soviet republics banded together as the Commonwealth of Independent States (Map 24.4).

Politics and the conditions of everyday life continued to deteriorate. The coup and drive for dissolution of the USSR so tainted Gorbachev's regime that he ceded power to Yeltsin. But increasingly plagued by corruption, the Russian economy plunged into an ever-deepening crisis. Yeltsin's political allies bought up national resources, stripped them of their value, and sent billions of dollars out of the country. Ethnic and religious battles continued, and the military attacked Muslim dissenters in the province of Chechnya, leaving massive casualties on both sides. In Russia, the political right appealed to nationalist sentiments and won increasing support. As members of the so-called Russian mafia interfered in the economy and assassinated legitimate entrepreneurs and anyone who criticized them, Western powers reduced their aid to rebuild Russian infrastructure. People took drastic steps to stay alive. Hotel lobbies became clogged with women turning to prostitution because they were the first people fired as industry privatized and service jobs were cut back. Ordinary citizens stood on the sidewalks of major cities selling their household possessions. A low point was reached in August 1998 with the crash of the Soviet stock market and the devaluation of the ruble. Investors around the world lost amounts equivalent to millions of dollars.

There were, of course, many pluses to the end of communism. People were able to travel freely, and the media were more open than ever before in Russian history. Some people, many of them young and highly educated, profited from contacts with technology and business. However, their frequent emigration to more prosperous parts of the world further depleted Russia's human resources. "I knew in my heart that it would collapse," said one ex-dissident, commenting sadly on the exodus of youth from his country, "but it never crossed my mind that the future would look like this."

■ **MAP 24.4 Countries of the Former Soviet Union, c. 2000**

Following an agreement of December 1991, twelve of the republics of the former Soviet Union formed the Commonwealth of Independent States (CIS). Dominated by Russia and with Ukraine often disputing this domination, the CIS worked to bring about common economic and military policies. As nation-states dissolved rapidly in the late twentieth century, regional alliances and coordination were necessary to meet the political and economic challenges of the global age.

In May 2000, Vladimir Putin, former head of the security services (the successor organization to the KGB), became president of Russia. Putin argued that the free market and democracy would have to fit with Russian "realities," notably the tradition of a paternalistic state. Attacking corruption and building a string of alliances in the West, Putin seemed to offer a steadier hand, especially over the massive Soviet-era arsenal of nuclear weapons and in the escalating fight against terrorists—many of them operating on Russia's doorstep in Afghanistan, Tajikistan, and Uzbekistan.

Global Culture and Western Civilization at the Dawn of a New Millennium

As the final years of the twentieth century unfolded, thinkers began to debate the future. On the one side was a view that the end of the cold war meant "an end of history" because the great ideological struggles were over and Western values had triumphed. Attached to this view was a related one: the rest of the world was absorbing Western cultural values rapidly as it developed technologically and adopted more and more features of representative government and human rights. An opposing view predicted a "clash of civilizations" in which the increasing incompatibility of religions and cultures would lead to global strife. According to this scenario, Islam, as it gathered more than one billion followers, would confront Western values rather than absorb them, and citizens of the growing number of small states populated by different ethnic and racial groups would simply refuse to live under a common national umbrella.

The actual movement of peoples and cultures in the late twentieth century suggests that neither view holds. International migration, the movement of disease, the information revolution, and the global sharing of culture have produced neither a successful Western homogenization nor a convincing argument for the cultural purity of any group: "Civilizations," as Nobel Prize winner Amartya Sen wrote after the terrorist attacks of September 11, 2001, "are hard to partition . . . given the diversities within each society as well as the linkages among different countries and cultures." In the 1980s and 1990s, Western society changed as rapidly as it had changed hundreds of years earlier when it came into intense contact with the rest of the globe. Moreover, national boundaries in the traditional European center of the West were weakening politically and economically with the growing strength of the European Union and the simultaneous splintering of large nations into small states based on claims to ethnic uniqueness. Culture ignored national boundaries as East, West, North, and South became saturated with one another's cultural products. Some observers even labeled the new millennium an era of "denationalization." But there is no denying that even while the West absorbed peoples and cultures, it continued to exercise not only economic but also cultural influence over the rest of the globe. Long acknowledged, this power was also debated and contested.

Redefining the West: The Impact of Global Migration

The movement of people globally was massive in the last third of the twentieth century and into the twenty-first. Uneven economic development, political persecution, and warfare (which has claimed as many as 100 million victims worldwide since 1945) sent tens of millions in search of safety and opportunity. In the 1970s alone, more than 4.7 million people moved to the United States. By 1982, France had about 4.5 million foreign residents, and by 2001 six million Muslims. Other parts of the world were as full of people on the move as the West. The oil-producing nations of the Middle East employed millions of foreign workers, who generally constituted one-third of the labor force. Singapore and Nigeria were home to millions of foreign-born inhabitants. Ongoing violence in Africa sent Rwandans, Zairians, and others to South Africa as its government became dominated by blacks. War in Afghanistan made Iran one of the most popular asylums, with close to 2 million refugees in 1995.

Migrants often earned desperately needed income for family members who remained in the native country, and in some cases they propped up the economies of entire nations. In the southern African country of Lesotho, where the soil had been ruined by overuse during colonial rule, between 40 and 50 percent of national income came from migrant workers, particularly from those who toiled in the mines of South Africa. In countries as different as Yugoslavia, Egypt, Spain, and Pakistan, money sent home from abroad constituted up to 60 percent of national income. In places where immigration was restricted, millions of people nevertheless successfully crossed borders: from Mexico and China to the United States, over unguarded African frontiers, between European states. Unprotected by law, such migrants risked exploitation and abuse of their human rights. Those at greatest risk were Eastern European and Asian prostitutes, many of whom were coerced into international sex rings that controlled their passports, wages, and lives. Foreign workers were a convenient scapegoat for native peoples suffering from economic woes such as unemployment caused by downsizing. Political parties with racist programs came to life in Europe, where unemployment was in double digits at various times in the 1980s and 1990s.

Among migrants to the West, women had little to say in decisions about leaving home; a patriarchal head of the household generally made such choices. Once abroad, migrant women suffered the most from unstable working conditions and usually obtained more menial, lower-paying jobs than migrant men or native Europeans. They also were more likely than men to be refused political asylum. Rape and other violence against them, even during civil war, were classified as part of everyday life, not politics. The offspring of immigrants also had a difficult time adjusting to their new surroundings. Young people generally struggled for jobs, and unemployment hit them especially hard because "whites" and "real" citizens received preference. They also struggled with questions of identity, often feeling torn between two cultures. Young black immigrants in particular began to forge an international or transnational identity, one that combined elements of African, Caribbean, American, and European cultures. As tens of millions of people migrated in the 1980s and 1990s, belief in a national identity based on a single, unique culture began losing ground.

Uncertain Borders of the Nation-State

The Western nation-state had been an increasingly powerful source of identity for five hundred years, never more so than in the twentieth century. By the twenty-first century, however, the nature of European national borders was changing through the force of mass migration, international cooperation, technology, and transnational allegiances. Regional alliances like NATO and the Warsaw Pact had appeared to override national interests, but nothing compared with the turn-of-the-millennium merging of individual nation-states into the European Union (Map 24.5). In 1992, the twelve countries of the EC ended national distinctions in the spheres of business activity, border controls, and transportation. Citizens of EC member countries carried a common burgundy-colored passport, and governments, whether municipal or national, had to treat all member nations' firms the same. In 1994, by the terms of the Maastricht Treaty, the EC became the European Union, and on January 1, 2002, citizens of twelve EU countries (Britain, Denmark, and Sweden declined to participate) shed their national currencies for the euro (the European Currency Unit or ECU). Using the euro for the first time, an Irish architect enthused, gave "a sense of Europe coming together as one." Common policies governed everything from the number of American soap operas aired on television to pollution controls on automobiles.◆

Some national leaders had opposed tighter integration as an infringement on national sovereignty. In the 1980s, Margaret Thatcher, Britain's then prime minister, warned that terrorists would pass freely across borders, objected to the use of a common currency, and criticized moves toward closer pan-European unity, but her forceful opposition seemed so out of step with the times that her own party forced her resignation in 1991. Despite warnings of an emerging "Eurospeak" and a dull standardization of culture, countries continued to join the original twelve. Sweden, Finland, and Austria joined the EU in 1995; Turkey and Cyprus were officially scheduled for entry. Most former Communist-run nations also sought inclusion. As union tightened, a highly advanced industrial megastate complete with its own bureaucracy overlaid the traditionally distinct individual nations of the Western heartland.

◆ For a source that encapsulates proponents' arguments for a truly unified Europe, see Document 78, François Mitterrand, "Speech to the European Parliament."

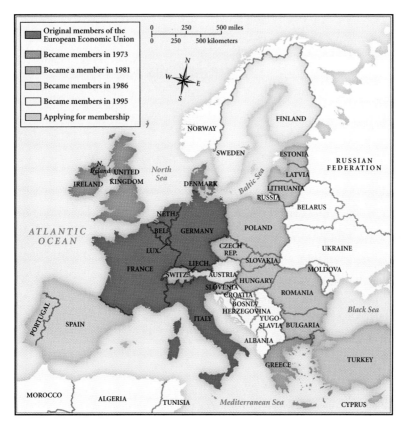

■ **MAP 24.5 The European Union in 2000**
The European Union appeared to increase the economic health of its members despite the rocky valuation of the common currency—the euro. The EU decidedly helped end the traditional warfare member nations had waged against one another for centuries, and common passports, common business laws, and borders open to member countries facilitated trade and the migration of workers. Many critics feared the further loss of cultural distinctiveness among peoples in an age of mass communications if the economic union turned into a political one. Other skeptics predicted "Americanization" if political cooperation among European countries was lacking.

Rapid technological change in electronic communications also made traditional national borders appear easily permeable, if not obsolete. In 1969, the U.S. Department of Defense developed a computer network to carry communications in case of nuclear war. This system and others like it in universities, government, and business grew into an unregulated system of more than ten thousand networks globally. These came to be known as the *Internet*—shorthand for *internetworking*. By 1995, users in more than 137 countries were connected to the Internet, creating new "communities" based on business needs, shared cultural interests, or other factors that transcended common citizenship in a particular nation-state.

■ Euro Currency
People in twelve countries of the European Union confronted a common currency—the euro—on January 1, 2002. These residents at a German senior citizens' home learn to recognize the different denominations and value of the new currency. The shift from a national to an international currency concerned many citizens, but most quickly realized that a common currency would inhibit great fluctuation in prices from country to country while also allowing shoppers to cross borders freely and compare costs. A less tangible benefit was the common European identity that the euro promoted. (© AFP/Corbis.)

Communicating over the Internet allowed users often to escape censorship and other forms of state regulation. A global marketplace emerged, offering goods and services ranging from advanced weaponry to organ transplants. While enthusiasts claimed that electronic communication could promote world democracy, critics charged that communications technology favored elites and disadvantaged those without computer skills. Yet these skills advanced so quickly that in 2001 Estonia, Hungary, and the Czech Republic as well as Morocco, India, and the Philippines were successfully luring businesses to employ their citizens as help-desk and call-center service workers. The Internet allowed the service industry to globalize (see "Mapping the West," page 1066).

Internet and other communications technology promoted business mergers and the rise of "global cities" in the 1990s. Access to almost up-to-the-minute information on inventory, wages, costs, and transportation worldwide allowed businesses to move in and out of countries rapidly in response to changes in economic and political conditions. As a result, workers in one country were pitted against workers in a similar job category on the other side of the globe. Global corporations neither inspired nor displayed national loyalty. Moreover, high technology consigned people without modern skills to minimum-wage jobs as clerks and fast-food attendants. "Global cities," such as New York, Hong Kong, Tokyo, and London, swelled in the 1990s; their postmodernist architecture soared to new heights. In these cities, high-level information specialists—lawyers, accountants, financiers, and a variety of analysts—formed a decision-making loop in the technological network. Their financial power changed the complexion of most cities, making them unaffordable to low-level information managers and service workers.

Disease also operated on a global terrain. In the early 1980s, the spread of a global epidemic disease, acquired immune deficiency syndrome (AIDS), challenged Western values and Western technological expertise. An incurable, virulent killer

■ **Hong Kong Skyline**
The 1980s saw Hong Kong, Singapore, China, and other Pacific economies soar and develop the most modern technological capabilities. Skylines changed, reshaped by mountainous glass and steel skyscrapers, and cities like Hong Kong came to symbolize everything postmodern. No longer could the East be used as an exotic foil to help those in the West lay claim to a superior civilization.
(Jane Tyska/Stock Boston.)

that shuts down the body's immune system, AIDS initially afflicted heterosexuals in central Africa; the disease later turned up in Haitian immigrants to the United States and in homosexual men worldwide. At the turn of the twenty-first century, no cure had been discovered, though protease-inhibiting drugs helped alleviate the symptoms. The mounting death toll prompted some to liken AIDS to the bubonic plague that had decimated Europe in the fourteenth century and it reinforced negative stereotypes about some of the most vulnerable victims. As millions contracted the disease in Africa, treatment was not forthcoming there because the ill were too poor to pay for the necessary drugs. The Ebola virus and dozens of other diseases also smoldered, deadly and incurable.

The Global Diffusion of Culture

Culture has long transcended political boundaries; archaeologists point to cultural diffusion as a constant feature of human history. In the ancient world, the Romans studied the work of Greek philosophers. In the eighteenth and nineteenth centuries, Western scholars immersed themselves in Asian languages. In the postwar period, new forms of transportation and communication vastly accelerated cultural exchange. Tourism, for instance, became the largest single industry in Britain and in many other Western countries by the early 1990s. Throngs of visitors from Japan and elsewhere testified to the powerful hold of the West on the world's imagination. The Chinese students demonstrating in Tiananmen Square had rallied around their own representation of the Statue of Liberty (which itself was a gift from France to the United States). In Japan, businesspeople wore Western-style clothing, and sports fans watched soccer, baseball, and other Western sports and used English sports terminology.

Remarkable innovations in communications have also integrated cultures and made the earth seem a much smaller place with a distinctly Western flavor. Videotapes and satellite-beamed telecasts carry American television shows to Hong Kong and Japanese movies to Europe and North America. American rock music sells briskly in Russia and elsewhere in the former Soviet bloc. When more than 100,000 Czechoslovakian rock fans, including President Václav Havel, attended a Rolling Stones concert in Prague in 1990, it was clear that despite a half-century of supposedly insular Communist culture, Czechs and Slovaks had been tuned in to the larger world. Sports stars like the Brazilian soccer player Pelé and the American basketball hero Michael Jordan became better known to countless people than their own national leaders. In today's world, millions of people anywhere on the planet might be spectators at a "live" event, whether a World Cup competition or an Academy Awards broadcast from Hollywood.

The political power of the United States and the Western presence in the global economy have given Western culture an edge. U.S. success in "marketing" culture, along with the legacy of British imperialism, has helped to make English the dominant international language. Many English words—for example, *stop, shopping, parking, okay, weekend,* and *rock*—have infiltrated dozens of non-English vocabularies. English is the official language of the European Union and of the new Central European University in Budapest. Unofficially, it is the language of travel. In the 1960s, French president de Gaulle, fearing corruption of the French language, banned new words such as *computer* in government documents; but such a directive could not stop the influx of English into scientific, technical, diplomatic, and daily life. Germany, the Netherlands, and other European countries with polyglot traditions rapidly assimilated new words.

As it had been doing for centuries, the West continued to devour material from elsewhere—Hong Kong films, African textiles, Indian music, Latin American pop culture. Publishers successfully marketed written works by major non-Western artists and intellectuals, and Hollywood made many of their novels into internationally distributed films. Some of this literature won both popular and critical acclaim and exerted a strong influence on European and North American writers. The lush, exotic fantasies of Colombian-born Nobel Prize winner Gabriel García Márquez, for example, attracted a vast Western readership. His novels, including *One Hundred Years of Solitude* (1967) and *Love in the Time of Cholera* (1988), portray people of titanic ambitions and passions who endure war and all manner of personal trials. Another Nobel Prize recipient who won high regard in the West was Egyptian writer Naguib Mahfouz. Having immersed himself in his youth in great Western literature, Mahfouz authored more than forty books. His celebrated *Cairo Trilogy,* written in the 1950s, describes a middle-class family—from its practice of Islam and seclusion of women to the business and cultural life of men in the family. British colonialism forms the trilogy's backdrop; it impassions the protagonists and shapes their lives and destinies. In the eyes of many Arab observers, Mahfouz was a "safe" choice for the Nobel Prize, not only because he produced a literature about the history of colonialism but also because he had adopted a European style. "He borrowed the novel from Europe; he imitated it," charged one fellow Egyptian writer. "It's not an Egyptian art form. Europeans . . . like it very much because it is their own form." The globally read Egyptian Nawal el-Saadawi was also accused of producing exotic accounts of women's oppression to appeal to Western feminists. Thus, although non-Western literature reshaped Western taste, it sometimes provoked charges of inauthenticity in its authors' homelands.

Immigrants to Europe described how the experience of Western culture felt to the refugee. The popular writer Buchi Emecheta in her novel *In the Ditch* (1972) and her autobiography *Head above Water* (1986) explored her experiences as a newcomer to Britain. Her *Joys of Motherhood* (1979) was an imaginary foray back in time to probe the nature of mothering under colonial rule in her native Lagos in West Africa. While critiquing colonialism and the welfare state from a non-Western perspective, Emecheta, like many writers and politicians from less-developed countries, felt the lure of Western education and Western values. International conflict around artistic expression became dangerous. Salman Rushdie (b. 1947), also an immigrant to Great Britain (from India), produced the novel *The Satanic Verses* (1988), which ignited outrage among Muslims around the world because it appeared to blaspheme the prophet Muhammad. From Iran, the Ayatollah Khomeini promised both a monetary reward and salvation in the afterlife to anyone who would assassinate the writer. In a display of Western cultural unity, international leaders took bold steps to protect Rushdie until the threat was lifted a decade later.

The mainstream became fraught with conflict as groups outside the accepted circles engaged in artistic production. From within the West, novelist Toni Morrison, who in 1993 became the first African American woman to win the Nobel Prize for literature, described the nightmares, daily experiences, and dreams of the descendants of men and women who had been brought as slaves to the United States. But many parents objected to the inclusion of Morrison's work in high school and college curricula. Critics charged that, unlike Shakespeare's universal Western truth, the writing of African Americans, Native Americans, and women represented only a partial vision, not great literature. Eastern-bloc writers who found success in the West were also criticized. Milan Kundera left Czechoslovakia in 1975 after Communist police harassed him for his rebellious writing. Settling in Paris, Kundera produced *The Book of Laughter and Forgetting* (1979) and *The Unbearable Lightness of Being* (1984). In these works, he dwelt on the importance of remembering the oppressive climate of the Eastern bloc instead of following a natural tendency to forget or to search for material ease. He and other dissident writers who were often wildly successful in the United States and Western Europe met with suspicion and criticism from their colleagues who

■ **Toni Morrison Receiving the Nobel Prize**
The first African American woman to receive the Nobel Prize for literature, Toni Morrison used her literary talents to depict the condition of blacks under slavery and after emancipation. Morrison also published cogent essays on social, racial, and gender issues in the United States.
(Pressens Bild/Gamma Liaison.)

remained behind. In the land of prosperous book contracts, charged one Polish critic, writing was not literature but merely a "line of business."

Some writers and artists chose not to leave the Communist world, and they survived by creating acceptable art, even if the government did not embrace it wholeheartedly. East German writer Christa Wolf explored subjects, such as individuality, personal guilt, and the search for self-identity, that went against the grain of East Germany's Communist ideology. In such works as *The Quest for Christa T.* (1970), she touched on themes that appealed deeply to Westerners in the 1970s and 1980s. Others in the Communist world mixed global cultures no matter how dangerous or unpopular. The acclaimed composer Sofia Gubaidulina (b. 1931)—a Tatar, granddaughter of a teacher of Islam, and herself a Christian strongly influenced by Asian mysticism—created music with electronic guitars, tam-tams, and accordion along with screams and whispers. Her music was tonal and atonal, like the chant of monks and like Wagner—a collage of sound and music from everywhere. Her music, however, lacked the harshness of modernists from the middle of the century and represented a turn toward accessibility in classical music.

Some called such hyper-mixing of influences *postmodernism*, and one definition of *postmodernism* referred to multiplicity without a central unifying theme or privileged canon. Striking examples of postmodern art abounded in Western society, including the AT&T building in New York City, the work of architect Philip Johnson. The structure itself, designed in the late 1970s, looked sleek and modern, but its entryway was a Roman arch, and its cloud-piercing top suggested the eighteenth-century Chippendale style. The blueprints of Johnson and other postmodernists recalled the human past and drew from cultural styles that spanned millennia and continents without valuing one style above others. The Guggenheim Museum in Bilbao, Spain, opened in 1997 and designed by the American architect Frank Gehry, was similarly bizarre by classical or even modern standards as it represented forms, materials, and perspectives that by rules of earlier decades did not belong together. These were aesthetic examples of the postmodern, which also gave rise to films and novels without the unity of a single narrative or plot.

Other intellectuals defined *postmodernism* in political terms as an outgrowth of the demise of the eighteenth-century ideals of human rights, individualism, personal freedom, and their guarantor—the Western nation-state. A structure like the Bilbao Guggenheim was just an international tourist attraction that had no Spanish roots or purpose; consumption, global technology, mass communications, and international migration made citizenship, nationalism, and rights irrelevant to its meaning. It was a rootless structure, unlike the Louvre in Paris or the Prado in Madrid. Moreover, the end of formal imperialism meant an end to the white privilege behind modern civil rights as defined in the eighteenth century. The 1982 American film *Blade Runner*, for example, depicted a dangerous, densely packed, multiethnic Los Angeles patrolled by police with high-tech gear—a metropolis with no place for national or personal identity or human rights. For postmodernists of

■ **Christo and Jeanne-Claude,** *Umbrellas* **(1984–1991)**

Attuned to global differences and similarities in landscape, environment, and ways of life, the artists Christo and Jeanne-Claude created an art that enhanced people's sensual experience of the everyday world. Their installation of umbrellas in California (top) and Japan (bottom) featured colors that complemented distinctive rural terrain, just as their wrapping of the Reichstag in Berlin (1971–1995) had enhanced urban architecture. As global citizens, they recycle the vast quantities of materials once their works are dismantled, and they pay for their projects themselves.

(Top: Christo and Jeanne-Claude: *The Umbrellas, Japan-USA*, 1984–1991. California site. Photo: Wolfgang Volz. © Christo 1991. Bottom: Christo and Jeanne-Claude: *The Umbrellas, Japan-USA*, 1984–1991. Ibaraki, Japan site. Photo: Wolfgang Volz. © Christo 1991.)

1064

IMPORTANT DATES			
1979	Islamic revolution in Iran; Prime Minister Margaret Thatcher begins dismantling the welfare state in Britain and introduces neo-liberalism	1990–1991	War in the Persian Gulf
		1991	Civil war erupts in the former Yugoslavia
1980	An independent trade union, Solidarity, organizes resistance to Polish communism	1992	Soviet Union is dissolved
		1993	Toni Morrison becomes the first African American woman to win the Nobel Prize for literature
Early 1980s	AIDS epidemic strikes the West; rise of the Pacific economy	1994	Postapartheid elections held in South Africa
1981	Ronald Reagan becomes U.S. president	1997	Collapse of Thai currency and upset of the "Asian tigers"
1985	Mikhail Gorbachev comes to power in the USSR	1999	World population reaches six billion
1986	Explosion at Soviet nuclear power plant at Chernobyl; Spain joins the Common Market	2000	Vladimir Putin becomes president of Russia
1989	Chinese students revolt in Tiananmen Square and government suppresses them; fall of the Berlin Wall	2001	Terrorist attack on the United States and declaration of a "war against terrorism"
		2002	Euro currency goes into circulation in the European Union
1990s	Internet revolution		

a political bent, computers had replaced the autonomous, free self and bureaucracy had rendered representative government obsolete.

A third definition of *postmodernism* investigated the "unfreedom" or irrationality that shaped human life. French psychoanalyst Jacques Lacan (1901–1981), who deeply influenced Western literary criticism in the 1980s and 1990s, maintained that people operate in an unfree, predetermined world of language with its own patriarchal laws. In becoming social, communicating beings, we must bow to these laws already implanted in us at birth. Another prominent French thinker, Michel Foucault (1926–1984), professed to deplore the easy acceptance of such liberal ideas as the autonomous self, the progressive march of history, and the advance of freedom. The sexual revolution, he insisted, was not liberating at all; rather, sexuality was merely a way in which humans exercised power over one another and through which society, by allowing sexual expression, actually controlled individuals. Freedom, in the opinion of these postmodern intellectuals, had lost credibility: even in the most intimate part of human experience, individuals were locked in a grid of social and individual constraints. For some people struggling with the legacy of colonialism, racism, and sexism, the message that the image of the rational and superior West was illusory actually provided hope.

Conclusion: The Making of the West Continues

Although some postmodernists proclaimed an end to centuries of faith in progress, they themselves worked within the modern Western tradition of constant criticism and reevaluation. Moreover, said their critics, the daunting problems of contemporary life—population explosion, resource depletion, North-South inequities, global pollution, ethnic hatred, and global terrorism—demanded the exercise of humanistic values and the renewal of a rational commitment to progress now more than ever. Postmodernists and other philosophers countered with the question of "unintended consequences"—that is, the question of whether one could begin to know the consequences of an act. Who would have predicted, for example, the human misery resulting from the fall of the Soviet empire?

The years since 1980 proved both sides correct. The collapse of communism signaled the eclipse of an ideology that was perhaps noble in intent but deadly in practice. Events in South Africa and Northern Ireland, for example, indicated that certain long-feuding groups were wearying of conflict and groping for peace, even as other peoples took up arms against their neighbors. Yet the unintended consequences of communism's fall were bloodshed, sickness, and hardship, and the global age ushered in by the Soviet collapse brought "denationalization" to many regions of the world. Instead of being advocates for peace, prosperous militants from Saudi Arabia, Egypt, Indonesia, and the Philippines have unleashed unprecedented terrorism on the world, while many in Africa and Asia also face disease and the dramatic social and economic change associated with the global age.

Western traditions of democracy, human rights, and economic equality have much to offer. Given that these were usually intended only for certain people, global debates about their value abound. The nation-state, which protected those values for privileged Westerners, is another legacy that must be rethought in an age of transnationalism, when more people than ever are demanding the dignity of citizenship without its being pegged to a single ethnicity. At the same time, the West faces questions of its own cultural identity—an identity made from the far-flung cultural, natural, and human resources of Asia, Africa, and the Western Hemisphere.

■ **MAPPING THE WEST The World at the Start of the New Millennium**
By the twenty-first century, the Internet had transformed communications and economic organization into an interconnected global network. People in the so-called North had greater access to this network in 1999 and for the most part enjoyed greater wealth than people in the South. Despite globalization, historians still find local and national conditions of political, social, and economic life important in telling the full story of peoples and cultures.
(From **www.mids.org** [Austin: Matrix Information and Directory Services, Inc.].)

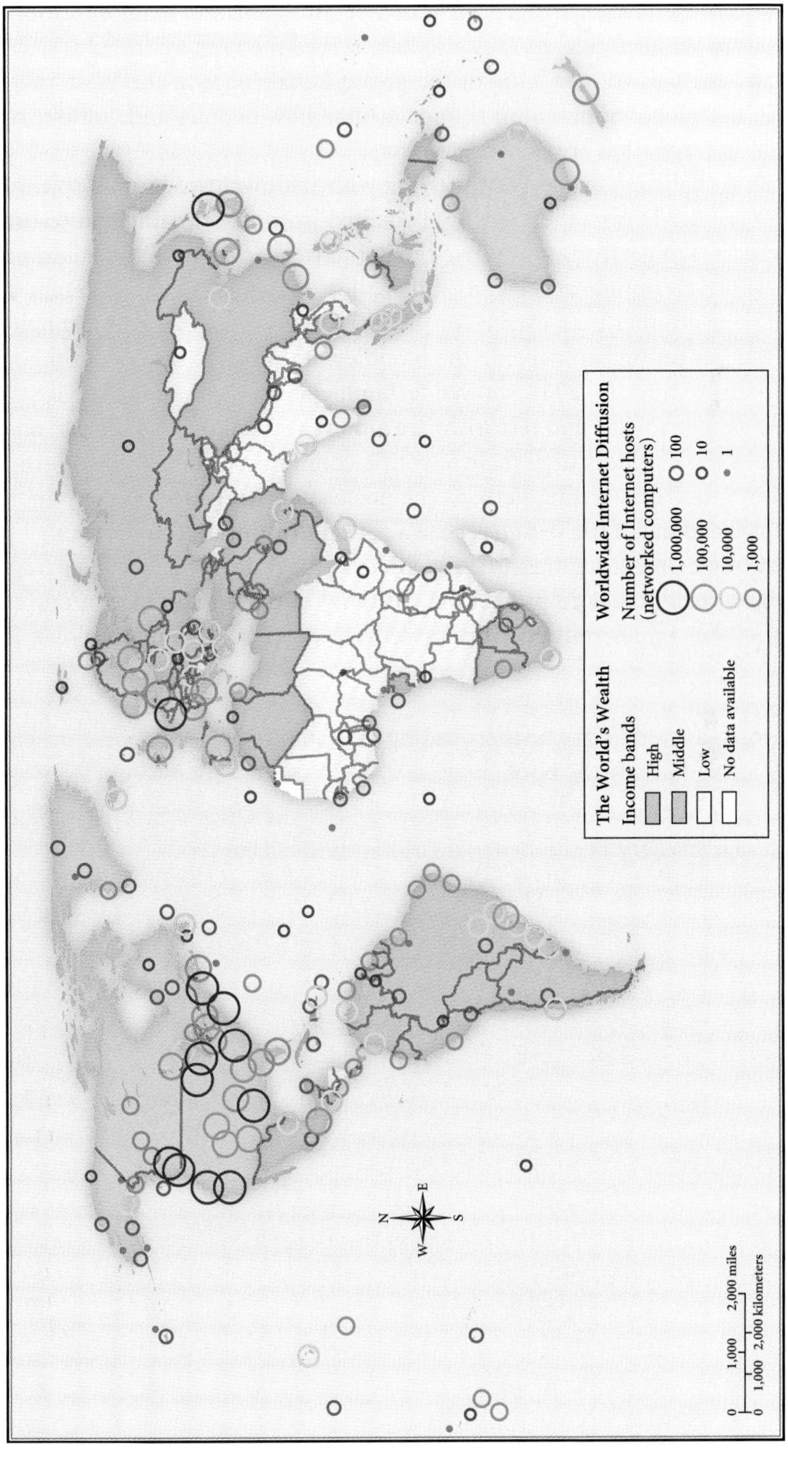
The World's Wealth
Income bands
High
Middle
Low
No data available
Worldwide Internet Diffusion
Number of Internet hosts (networked computers)
1,000,000
100,000
10,000
1,000
100
10
1
N
E
S
W
0 1,000 2,000 miles
0 1,000 2,000 kilometers

Non-Westerners have challenged, criticized, refashioned, and made enormous contributions to Western culture; they also have served the West's citizens as slaves, servants, and menial workers. One of the greatest challenges to the West and to the world in this global millennium is to determine how peoples and cultures can live together on terms that are fair for everyone.

A final challenge to the West is living with the inventive human spirit. In the past five hundred years, the West has benefited from its scientific and technological advances. Longevity and improved material well-being have spread around the world, while communication and information technology have brought people closer to one another than ever before. At the same time, the use of technology allowed the last century to become the bloodiest in human history, and the searing events of September 11, 2001, showed technology once again in the service of mass murder. War, genocide, and terrorism are among technology's hallmarks, and even now the world's leaders urge their scientific communities to search for ever more destructive weapons, posing perhaps the greatest challenge to the West and to the world. The making of the West has been a constantly inventive undertaking but also an often tragic one. What mixture of peoples and cultures will face the paradoxical challenge of technology to protect the creativity of the human race in our current century? What opportunities will they seize to forge our common global future?

Suggested References for further reading and online research appear on page SR-39 at the back of the book.

www.bedfordstmartins.com/huntconcise   See the ONLINE STUDY GUIDE to assess your mastery of the material covered in this chapter.

Suggested References

CHAPTER II
Crisis and Renaissance, 1340–1500

A Multitude of Crises

The plague has always been a subject of great interest to historians (Horrox), and the work of Jordan shows that its ravages were clearly linked to the earlier Great Famine. Froissart thought that the Hundred Years' War was a chivalric venture, but Allmand shows how it helped create two modern states.

Allmand, Christopher. *The Hundred Years' War: England and France at War, c. 1300–1450*. 1988.

The Black Death. Ed. and trans. Rosemary Horrox. 1994.

*Froissart, Jean, *Chronicles*. Trans. Geoffrey Brereton. 1968.

Inalcik, Halil. *The Ottoman Empire: The Classical Age, 1300–1600*. Trans. Norman Itzkowitz and Colin Imber. 1973.

Jordan, William Chester. *The Great Famine: Northern Europe in the Early Fourteenth Century*. 1996

Nirenberg, David. *Communities of Violence: Persecution of Minorities in the Middle Ages*. 1996.

---

*Primary sources are indicated with an asterisk.

Oatley, Francis. *The Western Church in the Later Middle Ages.* 1979.

Plague and public health in Renaissance Europe: http://jefferson.village.virginia.edu/osheim/intro.html

New Forms of Thought and Expression: The Renaissance

The old association between the Renaissance and the history of Florence is slowly giving way to a wider view (see Kirkpatrick, Welch, and the anthology edited by Elmer). In addition to the study of great artists and writers, recent scholars (such as Jardine) have turned their attention to the ways in which a market for cultural goods such as books and manuscripts was created by savvy, prestige-seeking consumers.

Blockmans, Wim, and Walter Prevenier. *The Promised Lands: The Low Countries under Burgundian Rule, 1369–1530.* Trans. Elizabeth Fackelman. Ed. Edward Peters. 1999.

Eisenstein, Elizabeth L. *The Printing Press as an Agent of Change: Communications and Cultural Transformations in Early-Modern Europe.* 1980.

Herlihy, David, and Christiane Klapisch-Zuber. *Tuscans and Their Families: A Study of the Florentine Catasto of 1427.* 1978.

Jardine, Lisa. *Worldly Goods.* 1996.

Kirkpatrick, Robin. *The European Renaissance, 1400–1600.* 2002.

Renaissance art links: http://www.lincolnu.edu/~kluebber/euroart.htm

*The Renaissance in Europe: An Anthology. Eds. Peter Elmer, Nicholas Webb, and Roberta Wood. 2000.

Welch, Evelyn. *Art in Renaissance Italy, 1350–1500.* 1997.

On the Threshold of World History

The traditional view of "Europe discovering the world" has been replaced by a more nuanced and complex discussion that includes non-European views and uses Asian, African, and Mesoamerican sources.

Epstein, Steven A. *Speaking of Slavery: Color, Ethnicity, and Human Bondage in Italy.* 2001.

*The Log of Christopher Columbus. Ed. Robert H. Fuson. 1987.

Russell-Wood, A. J. R. *A World on the Move: The Portuguese in Africa, Asia, and America, 1415–1808.* 1992.

Subrahmanyam, Sanjay. *The Career and Legend of Vasco da Gama.* 1997.

CHAPTER 12

Struggles over Beliefs, 1500–1648

The Protestant Reformation

While continuing to refine our understanding of the leading Protestant reformers, recent scholars have also offered new interpretations that take into consideration the popular impact of the reformers' teachings.

Bainton, Roland. *Women of the Reformation in Germany and Italy.* 1971.

Blickle, Peter. *The Revolution of 1525.* 1981.

Bouwsma, William J. *John Calvin: A Sixteenth-Century Portrait.* 1988.

Brady, Thomas A. *Turning Swiss: Cities and Empire, 1450–1550.* 1985.

Carney, Jo Eldridge, ed. *Renaissance and Reformation,1500–1620: A Biographical Dictionary.* 2001.

*Essential Works of Erasmus. Ed. W. T. Jackson. 1965.

**Hillerbrand, Hans J., ed. *The Protestant Reformation.* 1969.

Hsia, R. Po-chia. *The World of the Catholic Renewal.* 1997.

Luther's writings in English: http://history.hanover.edu/early/luther.htm

Oberman, Heiko A. *Luther: Man between God and Devil.* 1990.

Scribner, R. W. *For the Sake of Simple Folk: Popular Propaganda for the German Reformation.* 1981.

State Power and Religious Conflict, 1500–1618

The personalities of rulers such as Charles V, Philip II, and Elizabeth I remain central to the religious and political conflicts of this period. Recent scholarship also highlights more structural factors, especially in the French Wars of Religion and the rise of the Dutch Republic.

Cameron, Euan, ed. *Early Modern Europe: An Oxford History.* 1999.

*Guicciardini, Francesco. *The History of Italy.* Trans. Sidney Alexander. 1969.

Holt, Mack P. *The French Wars of Religion, 1562–1629.* 1995.

Israel, Jonathan. *The Dutch Republic: Its Rise, Greatness, and Fall, 1477–1806.* 1995.

Kamen, Henry. *Philip of Spain.* 1997.

Mattingly, Garrett. *The Defeat of the Spanish Armada.* 2d ed. 1988.

Richardson, Glenn. *Renaissance Monarchy: The Reigns of Henry VIII, Francis I, and Charles V.* 2002.

Strong, Roy. *The Cult of Elizabeth: Elizabethan Portraiture and Pageantry.* 1977.

The Thirty Years' War and the Balance of Power, 1618–1648

As ethnic conflicts erupt again in Eastern Europe, historians have traced their roots back to the intertwined religious, ethnic, and dynastic struggles of the Thirty Years' War.

Asch, Ronald G. *The Thirty Years War: The Holy Roman Empire and Europe, 1618–48.* 1997.

Lee, Stephen J. *The Thirty Years War.* 1991.

Parker, Geoffrey. *The Military Revolution: Military Innovation and the Rise of the West, 1500–1800.* 1988.

———, ed. *The Thirty Years' War.* 2d ed. 1997.

*Rabb, Theodore K., ed. *The Thirty Years' War.* 2d ed. 1972.

Economic Crisis and Realignment

Painstaking archival research has enabled historians to reconstruct the demographic, economic, and social history of this period. Recently, attention has focused more specifically on women, the family, and the early history of slavery.

Ashton, Trevor H., ed. *Crisis in Europe.* 1965.

Braudel, Fernand. *The Mediterranean and the Mediterranean World in the Age of Philip the Second.* 2 vols. Trans. Siân Reynolds. 1972–1973.

De Vries, Jan. *The Economy of Europe in an Age of Crisis, 1600–1750.* 1982.

Parry, J. H. *The Age of Reconnaissance.* 1981.

Wiesner, Merry E. *Women and Gender in Early Modern Europe.* 1993.

A Clash of Worldviews

The transformation of intellectual and cultural life has long fascinated scholars. Recent works have developed a new kind of study called "microhistory," focused on one person (like Ginzburg's Italian miller) or a series of individual stories (as in Roper's analysis of witchcraft in the German states).

Baroque architecture: http://www.lib.virginia.edu:80/dic/colls/arh102/index.html

*Drake, Stillman, ed. *Discoveries and Opinions of Galileo*. 1957.

The Galileo Project: http://riceinfo.rice.edu/Galileo

Ginzburg, Carlo. *The Cheese and the Worms: The Cosmos of a Sixteenth-Century Miller*. Trans. John and Anne Tedeschi. 1992.

Jacob, James. *The Scientific Revolution*. 1998.

Roper, Lyndal. *Oedipus and the Devil: Witchcraft, Sexuality, and Religion in Early Modern Europe*. 1994.

Skinner, Quentin. *The Foundations of Modern Political Thought*. Vol. 2, *The Age of Reformation*. 1978.

Thomas, Keith. *Religion and the Decline of Magic*. 1971.

Zagorin, Perez. *Francis Bacon*. 1998.

CHAPTER 13
State Building and the Search for Order, 1648–1690

Louis XIV: Model of Absolutism

Recent studies have examined Louis XIV's uses of art and imagery for political purposes and have also rightly insisted that absolutism could never be entirely absolute because the king depended on collaboration and cooperation to enforce his policies. Some of the best sources for Louis XIV's reign are the letters written by important noblewomen. The Web site of the Château of Versailles includes views of rooms in the castle.

Beik, William. *Absolutism and Society in Seventeenth-Century France: State Power and Provincial Aristocracy in Languedoc*. 1985.

*———. *Louis XIV and Absolutism: A Brief Study with Documents*. 1999.

Burke, Peter. *The Fabrication of Louis XIV*. 1992.

Collins, James B. *The State in Early Modern France*. 1995.

*Forster, Elborg, trans. *A Woman's Life in the Court of the Sun King: Elisabeth Charlotte, Duchesse d'Orléans*. 1984.

Ranum, Oreste. *The Fronde: A French Revolution, 1648–1652*. 1993.

*Sévigné, Madame de. *Selected Letters*. Trans. Leonard Tancock. 1982.

Versailles: http://www.chateauversailles.fr

Absolutism in Central and Eastern Europe

Too often central and eastern European forms of state development have been characterized as backward in comparison with those of western Europe. Now historians emphasize the patterns of ruler-elite cooperation shared with western Europe, but they also underscore the weight of serfdom in eastern economies and political systems.

Barkey, Karen. *The Ottoman Route to State Centralization*. 1994.

Dukes, Paul. *The Making of Russian Absolutism, 1613–1801*. 1990.

Friedrich, Karin. *The Other Prussia: Royal Prussia, Poland and Liberty, 1569–1772*. 2000.

Kivelson, Valerie A. *Autocracy in the Provinces: The Muscovite Gentry and Political Culture in the Seventeenth Century*. 1996.

Vierhaus, Rudolf. *Germany in the Age of Absolutism.* Trans. Jonathan B. Knudsen. 1988.

Wilson, Peter H. *German Armies: War and German Politics, 1648–1806.* 1998.

Constitutionalism in England

Although recent interpretations of the English revolutions emphasize the limits on radical change, Hill's portrayal of the radical ferment of ideas remains fundamental.

Carlin, Norah. *The Causes of the English Civil War.* 1999.

Cust, Richard, and Ann Hughes, eds. *The English Civil War.* 1997.

*Graham, Elspeth, et al., eds. *Her Own Life: Autobiographical Writings by Seventeenth-Century English Women.* 1989.

*Haller, William, and Godfrey Davies, eds. *The Leveller Tracts, 1647–1653.* 1944.

Hill, Christopher. *The World Turned Upside Down: Radical Ideas during the English Revolution.* 1972.

Israel, Jonathan, ed. *The Anglo-Dutch Moment: Essays on the Glorious Revolution and Its World Impact.* 1991.

Mack, Phyllis. *Visionary Women: Ecstatic Prophecy in Seventeenth-Century England.* 1992.

Manning, Brian. *Aristocrats, Plebeians, and Revolution in England, 1640–1660.* 1996.

Constitutionalism in the Dutch Republic and the Overseas Colonies

Studies of the Dutch Republic emphasize the importance of trade and consumerism. Recent work on the colonies has begun to explore the intersecting experiences of settlers, Native Americans, and African slaves.

*Campbell, P. F., ed. *Some Early Barbadian History.* 1993.

Delâge, Denys. *Bitter Feast: Amerindians and Europeans in Northeastern North America, 1600–64.* Trans. Jane Brierley. 1993.

*Foster, William C., ed. *The La Salle Expedition to Texas: The Journal of Henri Joutel, 1684–1687.* Trans. Johanna S. Warren. 1998.

Israel, Jonathan. *Dutch Primacy in World Trade, 1585–1740.* 1989.

Merrell, James Hart. *Into the American Woods: Negotiators on the Pennsylvania Frontier.* 1999.

Price, J. L. *The Dutch Republic in the Seventeenth Century.* 1998.

Schama, Simon. *The Embarrassment of Riches: An Interpretation of Dutch Culture in the Golden Age.* 1988.

Thornton, John. *Africa and Africans in the Making of the Atlantic World, 1400–1800.* 1992.

The Search for Order in Elite and Popular Culture

Historians do not always agree about the meaning of popular culture: was it something widely shared by all social classes, or was it a set of activities increasingly identified with the lower classes, as Burke argues? The central Web site for Dutch museums allows the visitor to tour rooms and see paintings in scores of Dutch museums, many of which have important holdings of paintings by Rembrandt and Vermeer.

Burke, Peter. *Popular Culture in Early Modern Europe.* 1978.

Davis, Natalie Zemon. *Women on the Margins: Three Seventeenth-Century Lives.* 1995.

DeJean, Joan E. *Tender Geographies: Women and the Origins of the Novel in France.* 1991.

Dobbs, Betty Jo Teeter, and Margaret C. Jacob. *Newton and the Culture of Newtonianism.* 1994.

Dutch museums: http://www.hollandmuseums.nl

Elias, Norbert. *The Civilizing Process: The Development of Manners.* Trans. by Edmund Jephcott. 1978.

*Fitzmaurice, James, ed. *Margaret Cavendish: Sociable Letters.* 1997.

Todd, Janet M. *The Secret Life of Aphra Behn.* 1997.

CHAPTER 14
The Atlantic System and Its Consequences, 1690–1740

The Atlantic System and the World Economy

It is easier to find sources on individual parts of the system than on the workings of the interlocking trade as a whole, but work has been rapidly increasing in this area. Dunn's book nonetheless remains one of the classic studies of how the plantation system took root. Eze's reader should be used with caution, as it sometimes distorts the overall record with its selections.

Blackburn, Robin. *The Making of New World Slavery: From the Baroque to the Modern, 1492–1800.* 1997.

Dunn, Richard S. *Sugar and Slaves: The Rise of the Planter Class in the English West Indies, 1624–1713.* 1972.

*Eze, Emmanuel Chukwudi, ed. *Race and the Enlightenment: A Reader.* 1997.

Jordan, Winthrop D. *The White Man's Burden: Historical Origins of Racism in the United States.* 1974.

Mintz, Sidney W. *Sweetness and Power: The Place of Sugar in Modern History.* 1985.

Morgan, Philip D. *Slave Counterpoint: Black Culture in the Eighteenth-Century Chesapeake and Low Country.* 1998.

Northrup, David. *Africa's Discovery of Europe.* 2002.

Slave movement during the eighteenth and nineteenth centuries:
  http://dpls.dacc.wisc.edu/slavedata/

Smith, Alan K. *Creating a World Economy: Merchant Capital, Colonialism, and World Trade, 1400–1825.* 1991.

New Social and Cultural Patterns

Many of the novels of the period provide fascinating insights into the development of new social attitudes and customs. In particular, see Daniel Defoe's *Robinson Crusoe* (1719) and *Moll Flanders* (1722); the many novels of Eliza Heywood; and Antoine François Prévost's *Manon Lescaut* (1731), a French psychological novel about a nobleman's fatal love for an unfaithful woman, which became the basis for an opera in the nineteenth century.

Artwork of Boucher, Chardin, and Watteau:
  http://mistral.culture.fr/lumiere/documents/peintres.html

De Vries, Jan. *European Urbanization, 1500–1800.* 1984.

Earle, Peter. *The Making of the English Middle Class: Business, Society, and Family Life in London, 1660–1730.* 1989.

Handel's Messiah: The New Interactive Edition (CD-ROM). 1997.

Raynor, Henry. *A Social History of Music, from the Middle Ages to Beethoven.* 1972.

Roche, Daniel. *The People of Paris: An Essay in Popular Culture in the Eighteenth Century.* Trans. Marie Evans. 1987.

Consolidation of the European State System

Studies of rulers and states can be supplemented by work on "political arithmetic" and public health.

Aspromourgos, Tony. *On the Origins of Classical Economics: Distribution and Value from William Petty to Adam Smith.* 1996.

Black, Jeremy, ed. *Britain in the Age of Walpole.* 1984.

Brewer, John. *The Sinews of Power: War, Money, and the English State, 1688–1783.* 1990.

Brockliss, Laurence, and Colin Jones. *The Medical World of Early Modern France.* 1997.

Campbell, Peter R. *Power and Politics in Old Regime France, 1720–1745.* 1996.

Frey, Linda, and Marsha Frey. *Societies in Upheaval: Insurrections in France, Hungary, and Spain in the Early Eighteenth Century.* 1987.

Hughes, Lindsey. *Russia in the Age of Peter the Great.* 1998.

Lawrence, Susan C. *Charitable Knowledge: Hospital Pupils and Practitioners in Eighteenth-Century London.* 1996.

Raeff, Marc. *Understanding Imperial Russia: State and Society in the Old Regime.* Trans. Arthur Goldhammer. 1984.

The Birth of the Enlightenment

The definitive study of the early Enlightenment is the book by Hazard, but many others have contributed biographies of individual figures or, more recently, studies of women writers.

Besterman, Theodore. *Voltaire.* 1969.

Grendy, Isobel. *Lady Mary Wortley Montagu.* 1999.

Hazard, Paul. *The European Mind: The Critical Years, 1680–1715.* 1990.

*Hill, Bridget, ed. *The First English Feminist: Reflections upon Marriage and Other Writings by Mary Astell.* 1986.

*Jacob, Margaret C. *The Enlightenment: A Brief History with Selected Readings.* 2000.

Rothkrug, Lionel. *The Opposition to Louis XIV: The Political and Social Origins of the French Enlightenment.* 1966.

Smith, Hilda L. *Reason's Disciples: Seventeenth-Century English Feminists.* 1982.

CHAPTER 15

The Promise of Enlightenment, 1740–1789

The Enlightenment at Its Height

The interpretive study by Gay remains useful even though it is over thirty years old. Starobinski's intellectual biography of Rousseau shows the unities in the life and work of this enduringly controversial figure. Much more emphasis has been placed in recent studies on the role of women; on this point see Goodman and Landes. Equiano, an ex-slave, offers one of the earliest firsthand views of the experience of slavery. Voltaire's *Candide* is an accessible introduction to the thought of the philosophes.

*Equiano, Olaudah. *The Interesting Narrative and Other Writings.* Ed. Vincent Carretta. 1995.

Gay, Peter. *The Enlightenment: An Interpretation.* 2 vols. 1966, 1969.

Goodman, Dena. *The Republic of Letters: A Cultural History of the French Enlightenment.* 1994.

Griswold, Charles. *Adam Smith and the Virtues of Enlightenment.* 1999.

Jacob, Margaret C. *Living the Enlightenment: Freemasonry and Politics in Eighteenth-Century Europe.* 1991.

Landes, Joan B. *Women and the Public Sphere in the Age of the French Revolution.* 1988.

McMahon, Darrin M. *Enemies of the Enlightenment: The French Counter-Enlightenment and the Making of Modernity.* 2001.

Starobinski, Jean. *Jean-Jacques Rousseau: Transparency and Obstruction.* Trans. Arthur Goldhammer. 1988.

*Voltaire. *Candide.* Ed. and trans. Daniel Gordon. 1999.

Voltaire Foundation: http://www.voltaire.ox.ac.uk

Society and Culture in an Age of Enlightenment

Recent work has drawn attention to the lives of ordinary people. The personal journal of the French glass-worker Ménétra is a rarity: it offers extensive documentation of the inner life of an ordinary person during the Enlightenment. Ménétra claimed to have met Rousseau. Even if not true, the claim shows that Rousseau's fame was not limited to the upper classes.

Darnton, Robert. *The Great Cat Massacre and Other Episodes in French Cultural History.* 1984.

Gullickson, Gay L. *Spinners and Weavers of Auffay: Rural Industry and the Sexual Division of Labor in a French Village, 1750–1850.* 1986.

Hull, Isabel V. *Sexuality, State, and Civil Society in Germany, 1700–1815.* 1996.

Jarrett, Derek. *England in the Age of Hogarth.* 1986.

McManners, John. *Death and the Enlightenment.* 1981.

*Ménétra, Jacques Louis. *Journal of My Life.* Trans. Arthur Goldhammer. Introd. Daniel Roche. 1986.

Mozart Project: http://www.mozartproject.org/

Stone, Lawrence. *The Family, Sex, and Marriage in England, 1500–1800.* Abridged ed. 1979.

Trumbach, Randolph. *Sex and the Gender Revolution.* 1998.

State Power in an Era of Reform

Biographies and general histories of this period tend to overemphasize the individual decisions of rulers. Although these are incontestably important, side-by-side reading of Büsch, Frederick II's writings on war, and Showalter's book on the wars themselves offers a broader view that puts Frederick II's policies into the context of military growth and its impact on society.

Blanning, T. C. W. *Joseph II.* 1994.

Büsch, Otto. *Military System and Social Life in Old Regime Prussia, 1713–1807: The Beginnings of the Social Militarization of Prusso-German Society.* Trans. John G. Gagliardo. 1997.

Cronin, Vincent. *Catherine, Empress of All the Russias.* 1996.

*Frederick II, King of Prussia. *Frederick the Great on the Art of War.* Ed. and trans. Jay Luvaas. 1999.

Showalter, Dennis E. *The Wars of Frederick the Great.* 1996.

Szabo, Franz A. J. *Kaunitz and Enlightened Absolutism, 1753–1780.* 1994.

Venturi, Franco. *The End of the Old Regime in Europe, 1768–1776: The First Crisis.* Trans. R. Burr Litchfield. 1989.

Rebellions against State Power

Exciting work has focused on specific instances of riot and rebellion. One of the most interesting studies is Thompson's work on the British repression of poaching and its significance for British social and political history. Palmer's overview remains valuable, especially for its comparative aspects.

Alexander, John T. *Autocratic Politics in a National Crisis: The Imperial Russian Government and Pugachev's Revolt, 1773–1775*. 1969.

Palmer, R. R. *The Age of Democratic Revolution: A Political History of Europe and America, 1760–1800*. Vol. 1, *The Challenge*. 1959.

*Rakove, Jack N. *Declaring Rights: A Brief History with Documents*. 1998.

Thomas, P. D. G. *John Wilkes: A Friend to Liberty*. 1996.

Thompson, E. P. *Whigs and Hunters: The Origin of the Black Act*. 1975.

Wood, Gordon S. *The Radicalism of the American Revolution*. 1992.

CHAPTER 16
The French Revolution and Napoleon, 1789–1815

The Revolution of Rights and Reason

In the 1950s and 1960s, historians debated vehemently about whether the French Revolution should be considered part of a more general phenomenon of Atlantic revolutions, as Palmer argues. The most influential book on the meaning of the French Revolution is still the classic study of Tocqueville, who insisted that the Revolution continued the process of state centralization undertaken by the monarchy. Among the most important additions to the debate have been new works on women, Jews, Protestants, and slaves.

*Baker, Keith Michael, ed. *The Old Regime and the French Revolution*. University of Chicago Readings in Western Civilization, vol. 7. 1987.

Chartier, Roger. *The Cultural Origins of the French Revolution*. Trans. Lydia G. Cochrane. 1991.

*Hunt, Lynn, ed. *The French Revolution and Human Rights: A Brief Documentary History*. 1996.

Lefebvre, Georges. *The Coming of the French Revolution*. Trans. with a new preface, R. R. Palmer. 1989.

*Levy, Darline Gay, Harriet Branson Applewhite, and Mary Durham Johnson, eds. *Women in Revolutionary Paris, 1789–1795*. 1979.

Palmer, R. R. *The Age of the Democratic Revolution: A Political History of Europe and America, 1760–1800*. Vol. 2, *The Struggle*. 1964.

Polasky, Janet L. *Revolution in Brussels, 1787–1793*. 1987.

Tocqueville, Alexis de. *The Old Regime and the French Revolution*. Trans. Stuart Gilbert. 1955. Originally published 1856.

Terror and Resistance

The most controversial episode in the French Revolution has not surprisingly provoked conflicting interpretations. Soboul offers the Marxist interpretation, which Furet specifically opposes. Very recently, interest has shifted from these broader interpretive issues back to the principal actors themselves: Robespierre, the Jacobins, and women's clubs have all attracted scholarly attention.

Desan, Suzanne. *Reclaiming the Sacred: Lay Religion and Popular Politics in Revolutionary France*. 1990.

Furet, François. *Interpreting the French Revolution*. Trans. Elborg Forster. 1981.

Godineau, Dominique. *The Women of Paris and Their French Revolution*. Trans. Katherine Streip. 1998.

Haydon, Colin, and William Doyle, eds. *Robespierre*. 1999.

Hunt, Lynn. *Politics, Culture, and Class in the French Revolution*. 1984.

Soboul, Albert. *The Sans-Culottes: The Popular Movement and Revolutionary Government, 1793–1794*. Trans. Remy Inglis Hall. 1980.

Sutherland, D. M. G. *France, 1789–1815: Revolution and Counterrevolution*. 1986.

The Rise of Napoleon Bonaparte

In the past, controversy about the Revolution in France raged while its influence on other places was relatively neglected. This imbalance is now being redressed in studies of the colonies and the impact of the revolutionary wars on areas from Egypt to Ireland. Recent work pays close attention to the social background of soldiers as well as their experiences in warfare.

Beaucour, Fernand Emile, Yves Laissus, and Chantal Orgogozo. *The Discovery of Egypt.* Trans. Bambi Ballard. 1990.

Blanning, T. C. W. *The French Revolutionary Wars, 1787–1802.* 1996.

Censer, Jack R., and Lynn Hunt. *Liberty, Equality, Fraternity: Exploring the French Revolution* (includes a CD-ROM of images and music). 2001.

Elliot, Marianne. *Partners in Revolution: The United Irishmen and France.* 1982.

Forrest, Alan I. *The Soldiers of the French Revolution.* 1990.

James, C. L. R. *Black Jacobins: Toussaint L'Ouverture and the San Domingo Revolution.* 2d ed. 1989.

Emperor Napoleon I, r. 1804–1814

Much has been written about Napoleon as a military leader, but only recently has his regime within France attracted interest. Historians now emphasize the mixed quality of Napoleon's rule. He carried forward some revolutionary innovations and halted others.

Alexander, R. S. *Napoleon.* 2001.

*Arnold, Eric A., Jr., ed. *A Documentary Survey of Napoleonic France.* 1994.

*Brunn, Geoffrey, ed. *Napoleon and His Empire.* 1972.

Crook, Malcolm. *Napoleon Comes to Power: Democracy and Dictatorship in Revolutionary France, 1795–1804.* 1998.

Ellis, Geoffrey James. *Napoleon.* 1996.

Gates, David. *The Napoleonic Wars, 1803–1815.* 1997.

Kafker, Frank A., and James M. Laux. *Napoleon and His Times: Selected Interpretations.* 1989.

Lyons, Martyn. *Napoleon Bonaparte and the Legacy of the French Revolution.* 1994.

Napoleon Foundation: http://www.napoleon.org

Simms, Brendan. *The Impact of Napoleon: Prussian High Politics, Foreign Policy, and the Crisis of the Executive, 1797–1806.* 1997.

Wilson-Smith, Timothy. *Napoleon and His Artists.* 1996.

CHAPTER 17
Industrialization and Social Ferment, 1815–1850

The "Restoration" of Europe

New visions of diplomacy are emerging in recent scholarship, but internal affairs are relatively understudied. As a consequence, Artz's book is still a good introduction.

Artz, Frederick B. *Reaction and Revolution, 1814–1832.* 1934.

Colley, Linda. *Britons: Forging the Nation, 1707–1837.* 1992.

Di Scala, Spencer. *Italy: From Revolution to Republic, 1700 to the Present.* 2d ed. 1998.

Johnson, Paul. *The Birth of the Modern: World Society, 1815–1830.* 1991.

Laven, David, and Lucy Riall, eds. *Napoleon's Legacy: Problems of Government in Restoration Europe.* 2000.

Schroeder, Paul W. *The Transformation of European Politics, 1763–1848.* 1994.

Seward, Desmond. *Metternich: The First European.* 1991.

The Advance of Industrialization and Urbanization

Because the analysis of industrialization occupied a central role in Marxism, the spread of industrialization has elicited much more historical interest than the process of urbanization. Some of the best recent work on urbanization, such as Kudlick's book on cholera, combines an interest in urban history with an interest in the history of public health. The *Spartacus Internet Encyclopedia* has an excellent section on the textile industry and its transformation.

Engerman, Stanley. "Reflections on 'The Standard of Living Debate.'" In John A. James and Mark Thomas, eds., *Capitalism in Context: Essays on Economic Development and Cultural Change in Honor of R. M. Hartwell.* 1994.

Hobsbawm, E. J. *The Age of Revolution, 1789–1848.* 1996.

Kudlick, Catherine J. *Cholera in Post-Revolutionary Paris: A Cultural History.* 1996.

Mokyr, Joel, ed. *The British Industrial Revolution: An Economic Perspective.* 2d ed. 1999.

More, Charles. *Understanding the Industrial Revolution.* 2000.

Pinkney, David H. *Decisive Years in France, 1840–1847.* 1986.

*Pollard, S., and C. Holmes, eds. *Documents of European Economic History.* Vol. 1, *The Process of Industrialization, 1750–1870.* 1968.

Spartacus Internet Encyclopedia, British History 1700–1950:
http://www.spartacus.schoolnet.co.uk/Britain.html

Thompson, Victoria Elizabeth. *The Virtuous Marketplace: Women and Men, Money and Politics in Paris, 1830–1870.* 2000.

New Ideologies

Ideologies are too often studied in an exclusively national context, so broader generalizations are difficult. The works by Clark and Taylor show how gender entered into working-class organization and socialist ideology.

Beecher, Jonathan. *Charles Fourier: The Visionary and His World.* 1986.

Berlin, Sir Isaiah. *The Roots of Romanticism.* 1999.

Clark, Anna. *The Struggle for the Breeches: Gender and the Making of the British Working Class.* 1995.

*Hugo, Howard E., ed. *The Romantic Reader.* 1957.

Kramer, Lloyd S. *Nationalism: Political Cultures in Europe and America, 1775–1865.* 1998.

*Marx, Karl, and Frederick Engels. *The Communist Manifesto: With Related Documents,* ed. John E. Toews. 1999.

Romantic chronology: http://english.ucsb.edu:591/rchrono/

Sewell, William H., Jr. *Work and Revolution in France: The Language of Labor from the Old Regime to 1848.* 1980.

Taylor, Barbara. *Eve and the New Jerusalem: Socialism and Feminism in the Nineteenth Century.* 1983.

Thompson, E. P. *The Making of the English Working Class.* 1964.

Wright, Beth S. *Painting and History during the French Restoration: Abandoned by the Past.* 1997.

Reform or Revolution?

Interest in the revolutions of 1848 has revived of late, perhaps because the recent upsurge of ethnic violence in the Balkans has prompted scholars to look again at this critical period. Not to be overlooked is the excellent treatment of the Irish famine by O'Grada. The Web site Gallica, produced by the National Library of France, offers a wealth of imagery and information on French cultural history.

Davidoff, Leonore, and Catherine Hall. *Family Fortunes: Men and Women of the English Middle Class, 1780–1850.* 1987.

The Dickens Project: http://humwww.ucsc.edu/dickens/index.html

Evans, R. J. W., and Hartmut Pogge von Strandmann, eds. *The Revolutions in Europe, 1848–1849: From Reform to Reaction.* 2000.

Gallica: Images and Texts from Nineteenth-Century French-Speaking Culture: http://gallica.bnf.fr/

Lincoln, W. Bruce. *Nicholas I: Emperor and Autocrat of All the Russias.* 1978.

O'Grada, Cormac. *The Great Irish Famine.* 1989.

Roberts, James S. *Drink, Temperance, and the Working Class in Nineteenth-Century Germany.* 1984.

Rodner, William S. *J. M. W. Turner: Romantic Painter of the Industrial Revolution.* 1997.

Sperber, Jonathan. *The European Revolutions, 1848–1851.* 1994.

Townsend, Mary Lee. *Forbidden Laughter: Popular Humor and the Limits of Repression in Nineteenth-Century Prussia.* 1992.

*Walker, Mack, ed. *Metternich's Europe.* 1968.

CHAPTER 18
Constructing the Nation-State, c. 1850–1880

The End of the Concert of Europe

The inglorious Crimean War has often been left behind in historiography despite its impact on European politics. Much of the best new literature focuses not only on political changes but on the war's social impact in Russia. Engel and the Kingston-Mann and Mixter anthology give searching looks at Russian peasant life in this age of transition.

Edgerton, Robert B. *Death or Glory: The Legacy of the Crimean War.* 1999.

Engel, Barbara Alpern. *Between the Fields and the City: Women, Work, and Family in Russia, 1861–1914.* 1994.

Hazareesingh, Sudhir. *From Subject to Citizen: The Second Empire and the Emergence of Modern French Democracy.* 1998.

Kingston-Mann, Esther, and Timothy Mixter, eds. *Peasant Economy, Culture, and Politics of European Russia, 1800–1921.* 1991.

*Seacole, Mary. *Wonderful Adventures of Mrs. Seacole in Many Lands.* 1857.

Wortman, Richard S. *Scenarios of Power: Myth and Ceremony in Russian Monarchy.* 2000.

War and Nation Building

Nation building has produced a varied literature ranging from biographies to studies of ceremonials and the presentation of royalty as celebrities and unifying figures. Two Web sites show the complexities of this process. Brown University's Victorian Web demonstrates the connections among royalty, politicians, religion, and culture. Bucknell University's Russian Studies site opens to the strains of the Russian national anthem, composed in the reign of Nicholas I to foster reverence for the dynasty and homeland.

Blackbourn, David. *Fontana History of Germany, 1780–1918: The Long Nineteenth Century.* 1997.

Breuilly, John. *The Formation of the First German Nation-State, 1800–1871.* 1996.

DiScala, Spencer. *Italy: From Revolution to Republic, 1700 to the Present.* 1995.

Homans, Margaret. *Royal Representations: Queen Victoria and British Culture, 1837–1876.* 1998.

Russian studies: http://www.departments.bucknell.edu/Russian/

Smith, Paul. *Disraeli: A Brief Life.* 1996.

The Victorian Web: http://landow.stg.brown.edu/victorian/victov.html

Industry and Nation Building

Industry advanced on every front, from the development of new products and procedures to the reorganization of work life and consumption. Trebilcock's classic work on the creation of an economic infrastructure contrasts with more recent studies (such as Rappaport's) on the impact of consumers and taste in driving economic change.

Coffin, Judith. *The Politics of Women's Work: The Paris Garment Trades, 1750–1915.* 1996.

Crossick, Geoffrey, and Serge Jaumin, eds. *Cathedrals of Consumption: The European Department Store, 1850–1939.* 1999.

Franzoi, Barbara. *At the Very Least She Pays the Rent: Women and German Industrialization.* 1985.

Good, David. *The Economic Rise of the Habsburg Empire.* 1984.

Marks, Steven G. *Road to Power: The Trans-Siberian Railroad and the Colonization of Asian Russia, 1850–1917.* 1991.

Rappaport, Erika. *Shopping for Pleasure: Women in the Making of London's West End.* 2000.

Trebilcock, Clive. *The Industrialization of the Continental Powers.* 1981.

Establishing Social Order

Nation building entailed state-sponsored activities stretching from promoting education to rebuilding cities. New histories show the process of creating a sense of nationality through government management of people's environment, so that citizenship became part of seemingly nonpolitical life.

Eley, Geoff, and Ronald Grigor Suny, eds. *Becoming National: A Reader.* 1996.

Hamm, Michael F. *Kiev: A Portrait, 1800–1917.* 1993.

Johanson, Christine. *Women's Struggle for Higher Education in Russia, 1855–1900.* 1987.

Jordan, David. *Transforming Paris: The Life and Labor of Baron Haussmann.* 1995.

Lebra-Chapman, Joyce. *The Rani of Jhansi: A Study in Female Heroism in India.* 1986.

Rotenberg, Robert. *Landscape and Power in Vienna.* 1995.

Slezkine, Yuri. *Arctic Mirrors: Russia and the Small Peoples of the North.* 1994.

Wohl, Anthony. *Endangered Lives: Public Health in Victorian Britain.* 1983.

The Culture of Social Order

Like the biographies of politicians, the lives of artists and intellectuals have proved crucial to understanding this period of realism and Realpolitik. They show artists, intellectuals, and scientists addressing the central issues of their day amid dramatic social change.

Bordenheimer, Rosemarie. *The Real Life of Mary Ann Evans: George Eliot, Her Letters and Fiction.* 1994.

*Darwin, Charles. *Autobiography.* 1969.

Gieson, Gerald L. *The Private Science of Louis Pasteur.* 1996.

Kaufman, Suzanne. "Lourdes, Popular Religion, and Tourism." In Shelley Baranowski and Ellen Furlough, eds. *Being Elsewhere: Tourism, Consumer Culture, and Identity in Modern Europe and North America.* 2000.

Mayr, Ernst. *One Long Argument: Charles Darwin and the Genesis of Modern Evolutionary Thought.* 1991.

*Turgenev, Ivan. *A Hunter's Sketches.* 1852.

Contesting the Order of the Nation-State

The teachings of Karl Marx and the story of the Paris Commune haunted Europeans at the time and have since fascinated historians. The following works capture the fear of the working classes that shaped middle-class thought in the nineteenth century, and they show the energy that working- and middle-class people alike put into politics and into developing political theories, especially in this period of political transformation.

Gullickson, Gay. *Unruly Women of Paris: Images of the Commune.* 1996.

McClellan, David. *Karl Marx: His Life and Thought.* 1978.

Nord, Philip. *The Republican Moment: Struggles for Democracy in Nineteenth-Century France.* 1995.

CHAPTER 19
Empire, Modernity, and the Road to War, c. 1880–1914

The Challenge of Empire

New studies of imperialism show not only increasing conquest and the creation of an international economy but also the social and cultural impulses behind it. The University of Pennsylvania's African studies Web site offers an exciting look at African history, politics, and culture—some of it from this era. Depictions of African art and architecture, such as works confiscated for Western museums, are especially vivid. In the midst of raucous political and social debate, the European powers faced growing resistance to their domination and increasingly serious setbacks. Many historians now judge Europe to have played a less commanding role in the rest of the world than the leading empires claimed.

African Studies Center: http://www.sas.upenn.edu/African_Studies/AS.html

Baumgart, Winfried. *Imperialism: The Idea and Reality of British and French Colonial Expansion.* 1989.

Cohen, Paul A. *History in Three Keys: The Boxers as Event, Experience, and Myth.* 1997.

Crosby, Alfred W. *Ecological Imperialism: The Biological Expansions of Europe, 900–1900.* 1993.

Ferro, Marc. *Colonization: A Global History.* 1997.

Gouda, Frances. *Dutch Culture Overseas: Colonial Practice in the Netherlands Indies, 1900–1942.* 1995.

Hane, Mikiso. *Modern Japan: A Historical Survey.* 1992.

Headrick, Daniel R. *The Tools of Empire: Technology and European Imperialism in the Nineteenth Century.* 1981.

Japanese history: http://www.csuohio.edu/history/japan/ index.html

Kansu, Aykut. *The Revolution of 1908 in Turkey.* 1997.

Meyers, Ramon H., and Mark R. Peattie, eds. *The Japanese Colonial Empire, 1895–1945.* 1984.

*Pruitt, Ida. *A Daughter of Han: The Autobiography of a Chinese Working Woman.* 1945.

Rotberg, R. I. *The Founder: Cecil Rhodes and the Pursuit of Power.* 1988.

Sinha, Mrinalini. *Colonial Masculinity: The "Manly Englishman" and the "Effeminate Bengali" in the Late Nineteenth Century.* 1995.

Wesseling, H. L. *Divide and Rule: The Partition of Africa, 1880–1914.* 1996.

Modern Life in an Age of Empire

Historians are engaged in serious study of the transformations of everyday life that industrial and imperial advance had brought about by the early twentieth century. In particular, personal and domestic life, as seen in the works of Hull, Walkowitz, and Duberman et al., have taken on greater importance as components of social movements and political developments.

Accampo, Elinor A., Rachel G. Fuchs, and Mary Lynn Stewart, eds. *Gender and the Politics of Social Reform in France, 1870–1914.* 1995.

Blakely, Allison. *Blacks in the Dutch World: The Evolution of Racial Imagery in Modern Society.* 1993.

*Bonnell, Victoria, ed. *The Russian Worker.* 1983.

Duberman, Martin, Martha Vicinus, and George Chauncey, Jr. *Hidden from History: Reclaiming the Gay and Lesbian Past.* 1989.

Engelstein, Laura. *The Keys to Happiness: Sex and the Search for Modernity in Fin-de-Siècle Russia.* 1992.

Gillis, John. *A World of Their Own Making: Myth, Ritual, and the Quest for Family Values.* 1996.

Hull, Isabell. *The Entourage of Kaiser Wilhelm II, 1888–1918.* 1982.

MacKenzie, John. *The Empire of Nature: Hunting, Conservation, and British Imperialism.* 1988.

Maynes, Mary Jo. *Taking the Hard Road: Life Course in French and German Workers' Autobiographies in the Era of Industrialization.* 1995.

Moch, Leslie Page. *Moving Europeans: Migration in Western Europe since 1650.* 1993.

Walkowitz, Judith. *City of Dreadful Delight: Narratives of the Sexual Danger in Late-Victorian London.* 1993.

Worobec, Christine D. *Peasant Russia: Family and Community in the Post-Emancipation Period.* 1991.

Modernity and the Revolt in Ideas

Some of the most controversial historiography sees the road to World War I as paved with cultural conflict. Many of the studies here suggest that new forms of art, music, dance, and philosophy were as central to the challenges Europe faced as were ethnic, economic, and international turmoil.

Eksteins, Modris. *Rites of Spring: The Great War and the Birth of the Modern Age.* 1989.

Everdell, William R. *The First Moderns: Profiles in the Origins of Twentieth-Century Thought.* 1997.

Jensen, Robert. *Marketing Modernism in Fin-de-Siècle Europe.* 1994.

Kern, Steven. *The Culture of Space and Time, 1880–1918.* 1983.

*Mann, Thomas. *Buddenbrooks.* 1901.

Nehamas, Alexander. *Nietzsche: Life as Literature.* 1985.

Nineteenth- and twentieth-century philosophy: http://www.epistemelinks.com/index.asp

Silverman, Debora L. *Van Gogh and Gauguin: The Search for Sacred Art.* 2000.

Politics in a New Key

Historians are uncovering the dramatic changes in political life and assessing the consequences of the rise of mass politics across Europe, including the development of suffragist movements. Some studies cited here investigate a second major political phenomenon: the formation of a politics of hatred and the rise of aggressive, warlike nationalism to replace nationalism based on rights and constitutional values.

Burns, Michael. *Dreyfus: A Family Affair.* 1992.

Chickering, Roger. *We Men Who Feel Most German: A Cultural Study of the Pan-German League, 1886–1914.* 1984.

Dennis, David B. *Beethoven in German Politics, 1870–1989.* 1996.

Kent, Susan. *Gender and Power in Britain, 1640–1990.* 1999.

Kornberg, Jacques. *Theodor Herzl: From Assimilation to Zionism.* 1993.

MacKenzie, David. *Violent Solutions: Revolutions, Nationalism, and Secret Societies in Europe to 1918.* 1996.

Schorske, Carl E. *Fin-de-Siècle Vienna: Politics and Culture.* 1981.

Scott, Joan. *Only Paradoxes to Offer: French Feminism and the Rights of Man.* 1996.

Weeks, Theodore R. *Nation and State in Late Imperial Russia: Nationalism and Russification on the Western Frontier.* 1996.

Roads to World War I

The question of why World War I broke out remains widely debated. There are always newcomers to the discussion devoted to assessing the responsibility for the war's beginning, but while these historians fix on a single country, other historians like to look at the full range of diplomatic, military, social, and economic conditions.

Ascher, Abraham. *The Revolution of 1905: Authority Restored.* 1992.

Berghahn, Volker. *Germany and the Approach of War.* 1993.

Cecil, Lamar. *Wilhelm II, Prince and Emperor, 1859–1900.* 1989.

Fenyvesi, Charles. *When the World Was Whole.* 1990.

Ferguson, Niall. *The Pity of War: Explaining World War I.* 1999.

Hoensch, Jorg K. *A History of Modern Hungary, 1867–1986.* 1988.

Lambi, Ivo. *The Navy and German Power Politics.* 1984.

Manning, Roberta. *The Crisis of the Old Order in Russia.* 1982.

Tech, Mikulás, and Roy Porter, eds. *The National Question in Europe in Historical Context.* 1993.

Williamson, Samuel. *Austria-Hungary and the Origins of the First World War.* 1991.

CHAPTER 20

War, Revolution, and Reconstruction, 1914–1929

The Great War, 1914–1918

The most recent histories of the Great War consider its military, technological, psychic, social, and economic aspects. This vision of the war as a phenomenon occurring beyond the battlefield as well as on it characterizes the newest scholarship.

Bourke, Joanna. *Dismembering the Male: Men's Bodies, Britain, and the Great War.* 1996.

*Brittain, Vera. *Testament of Youth.* 1933.

Downs, Laura Lee. *Manufacturing Inequality: Gender Division in the French and British Metalworking Industries, 1914–1939.* 1995.

Echenberg, Myron. *Colonial Conscripts: The "Tirailleurs Sénégalais" in French West Africa, 1857–1960.* 1990.

Ellis, John. *A Social History of the Machine-Gun.* 1986.

*Hasek, Jaroslav. *The Good Soldier Schweik.* 1920.

Leed, Eric J. *No Man's Land: Combat and Identity in World War I.* 1979.

Panchasi, Roxanne. "Reconstructions: Prosthetics and the Rehabilitation of the Male Body in World War I." *Differences.* 1995.

Roshwald, Aviel, and Richard Stites, eds. *European Culture in the Great War: The Arts, Entertainment, and Propaganda, 1914–1918.* 1999.

Schmitt, Bernadotte E., and Harold C. Vederler. *The World in the Crucible, 1914–1919.* 1984.

Winter, Jay, and Jean-Louis Robert, eds. *Capital Cities at War: Paris, London, Berlin, 1914–1919.* 1997.

World War I Documents Archive: http://www.lib.byu.edu/%7Erdh/wwi/

1917–1918: Protest, Revolution, and War's End

Histories of the war's end account for the cataclysmic setting: deprivation, ongoing mass slaughter, and the eruption of revolution. Peacemaking also occurred and that, too, was complex. In all, the violence of the postwar scene has made historians call into question the idea that wars end with an armistice.

Lewis, David Levering. *W. E. B. Du Bois.* 2 vols. 1993–2000.

Neuberger, Joan. *Hooliganism: Crime, Culture, and Power in St. Petersburg.* 1994.

Pipes, Richard. *A Concise History of the Russian Revolution.* 1995.

Schwabe, Klaus. *Woodrow Wilson, Revolutionary Germany, and Peacemaking, 1918–1919: Missionary Diplomacy and the Realities of Power.* 1985.

Smith, Leonard. *Between Mutiny and Obedience: The Case of the French Fifth Infantry Division during World War I.* 1994.

Stites, Richard. *Revolutionary Dreams: Utopian Vision and Experimental Life in the Russian Revolution.* 1989.

Wohl, Robert. *A Passion for Wings: Aviation and the Western Imagination.* 1994.

A Decade of Recovery: Europe in the 1920s

Two themes shape the history of the 1920s: recovery from the trauma of war and revolution and ongoing modernization of work and social life. The great technological innovations of the prewar period, such as films and airplanes, receive sophisticated treatment by historians for their impact on people's imagination. The radio is another phenomenon just beginning to find its historians.

Grossman, Atina. *Reforming Sex: The German Movement for Birth Control and Abortion Reform, 1920–1930.* 1995.

Kah, Douglas, and Gregory Whitehead. *Wireless Imagination: Sound, Radio, and the Avant-Garde.* 1992.

Kent, Susan. *Making Peace: The Reconstruction of Gender in Postwar Britain.* 1994.

Miller, Michael. *Shanghai on the Metro: Spies, Intrigue, and the French between the Wars.* 1994.

Nolan, Mary. *Visions of Modernity: American Business and the Modernization of Germany.* 1994.

Rabinbach, Anson. *The Human Motor: Energy, Fatigue, and the Origins of Modernity.* 1990.

Roberts, Mary Louise. *Civilization without Sexes: Reconstructing Gender in Postwar France, 1917–1927.* 1994.

Schwartz, Vanessa, and Leo Charney, eds. *Cinema and the Invention of Modern Life.* 1995.

Mass Culture and the Rise of Modern Dictators

Mass communications advances in cinema and radio provided new tools for the rule of modern dictators who arose from the shambles of war and revolution. Many of the most interesting recent studies look at the cultural components of the consolidation of dictatorial power, while not forgetting the violence that was a particular feature of authoritarian rule in the postwar twentieth century.

Berghaus, Gunter. *Futurism and Politics: Between Anarchist Rebellion and Fascist Reaction, 1909–1944.* 1996.

De Grazia, Victoria. *How Fascism Ruled Women.* 1994.

Harsch, Donna. *German Social Democracy and the Rise of Nazism.* 1994.

*Kollontai, Alexsandra. *Love of Worker Bees.* 1923.

Lyttleton, Adrian. *The Seizure of Power: Fascism in Italy, 1919–1929.* 1987.

Schnapp, Jeffrey. *Staging Fascism: 18BL and the Theater of Masses for Masses.* 1996.

Tumarkin, Nina. *Lenin Lives! The Lenin Cult in Soviet Russia.* 1997.

CHAPTER 21
An Age of Catastrophes, 1929–1945

The Great Depression

Historians look to the depression as a complex event with economic, social, and cultural consequences, but in addition they see its impact as yet another indication of the tightening of global economic connections. To follow some of the political implications for European empires, see in particular Columbia University's South Asia Web site, which explores Gandhi's economic resistance to British colonialism.

Brown, Ian. *The Economies of Africa and Asia in the Inter-war Depression.* 1989.

Evans, Richard J., and Dick Geary. *The German Unemployed: Experiences and Consequences of Mass Unemployment from the Weimar Republic to the Third Reich.* 1987.

James, Harold. *The German Slump: Politics and Economics, 1924–1936.* 1986.

Johnson, H. Clark. *Gold, France, and the Great Depression, 1919–1932.* 1997.

Roszkowski, Wojciech. *Landowners in Poland, 1918–1939.* 1991.

Rothermund, Dietmar. *The Global Impact of the Great Depression, 1929–1939.* 1996.

South Asia and Gandhi: http://www.columbia.edu/cu/libraries/indiv/area/sarai

Totalitarian Triumph

The vicious dictators Stalin, Hitler, and Mussolini are among the most popular subjects for historians and readers alike. Recent historical works have moved beyond this fascination to study their mobilization of art and the media and to consider people's reactions to totalitarian regimes. Historians are especially intrigued with the mixture of modernism and traditionalism or even antimodernism in the dictators' programs and policies.

Ades, Dawn, et al. *Art and Power: Europe under the Dictators, 1930–1945.* 1995.

Berezin, Mabel. *Making the Fascist Self: The Political Culture of Interwar Italy.* 1997.

Burleigh, Michael. *The Third Reich: A New History.* 2000.

Engel, Barbara Alpern, and Anastasia Posadskaya-Vanderbeck, eds. *A Revolution of Their Own: Voices of Women in Soviet History.* 1998.

Fest, Joachim. *Hitler.* 1974.

Fitzpatrick, Sheila. *Stalin's Peasants.* 1994.

Fritzsche, Peter. *Germans into Nazis.* 1998.

Groys, Boris. *The Total Art of Stalinism: Avant-Garde, Aesthetic Dictatorship, and Beyond.* 1992.

Kaplan, Marion. *Between Dignity and Despair: Jewish Life in Nazi Germany.* 1998.

Koonz, Claudia. *Mothers in the Fatherland: Women, the Family, and Nazi Politics.* 1987.

Kotkin, Stephen. *Magnetic Mountain: Stalinism as Civilization.* 1995.
Petrone, Karen. *Life Has Become More Joyous, Comrades. Celebrations in the Time of Stalin.* 2000.

Democracies on the Defensive

The democracies attacked the depression from a variety of perspectives ranging from state policy to film and the arts, yet another indication of how complex politics can be. Further departures from liberal policies, whether in trade or in the development of the activist welfare state, also have attracted historical study.

Kalvemark, Ann-Sofie. *More Children or Better Quality? Aspects of Swedish Population Policy.* 1980.
Kennedy, David M. *Freedom from Fear: The American People in Depression and War, 1929–1945.* 1999.
Lavin, Maud, et al. *Montage and Modern Life, 1919–1942.* 1992.
Rearick, Charles. *The French in Love and War: Popular Culture in the Era of the World Wars.* 1997.
Richards, Jeffrey, ed. *The Unknown 1930s: An Alternative History of the British Cinema, 1929–39.* 1998.

The Road to World War II

The road to war encircled the globe, involving countries seemingly peripheral to the struggles among the antagonists. The perennial question for many historians is whether Hitler could have been stopped, but with globalization there is new attention to the beginnings of war beyond the West as a prelude to decolonization.

Crozier, Andrew. *The Causes of the Second World War.* 1997.
Iriye, Akira. *The Origins of the Second World War in Asia and the Pacific.* 1987.
Knight, Patricia. *The Spanish Civil War.* 1991.
*Mangini González, Shirley. *Memories of Resistance: Women's Voices from the Spanish Civil War.* 1995.
Watt, D. Cameron. *How War Came: The Immediate Causes of the Second World War.* 1989.

World War II, 1939–1945

In a vast literature, historians have charted the war's innumerable and global horrors. The Holocaust, industrial killing, and the nature of racial thinking have drawn particular attention. The United States Memorial Holocaust Museum provides online exhibits giving the history of the Holocaust in different locations. While looking at the social aspects of war, historians have intently debated the development of the cold war within the "hot" war.

Browning, Christopher. *The Path to Genocide: Essays on Launching the Final Solution.* 1992.
*Dawidowicz, Lucy S., ed. *A Holocaust Reader.* 1976.
Dower, John W. *War without Mercy: Race and Power in the Pacific War.* 1986.
Fussell, Paul. *Wartime: Understanding and Behavior in the Second World War.* 1989.
Holocaust Museum: http://usholocaustmuseum.org
Lewis, Peter. *A People's War.* 1986.
Ofer, Dalia, and Lenore J. Weitzman, eds. *Women in the Holocaust.* 1998.
O'Neill, William L. *A Democracy at War: America's Fight at Home and Abroad in World War II.* 1993.
Rhodes, Richard. *The Making of the Atomic Bomb.* 1986.
*Vassiltchikov, Marie. *Berlin Diaries, 1940–1945.* 1988.
Weinberg, Gerhard. *A World at Arms: A Global History of World War II.* 1994.

CHAPTER 22
The Atomic Age, c. 1945–1960

World Politics Transformed

In the past decade, the opening of Soviet archives and closer research in American records have allowed for more-informed views of the diplomacy and politics of the cold war in Europe and around the world. Although few defend Stalin, we now benefit from balanced assessments of superpower rivalry. Two Web sites contain biographies of the main players, time lines, and miscellaneous details of cold war events.

Cold war: http://history.acusd.edu/gen/20th/coldwarO.html
Cold war: http://library.thinkquest.org/10826.mainpage.htm
Cronin, James. *The World the Cold War Made: Order, Chaos, and the Return of History.* 1996.
Eisenberg, Carolyn Woods. *Drawing the Line: The American Decision to Divide Germany, 1944–1949.* 1996.
Gaddis, John. *We Now Know: Rethinking Cold War History.* 1997.
Hogan, Michael J. *A Cross of Iron: Harry S Truman and the Origins of the National Security State, 1945–1954.* 1998.
*Pasternak, Boris. *Doctor Zhivago.* 1958.
Vadney, T. E. *The World Since 1945.* 1992.
Zubkova, Elena. *Russia after the War: Hopes, Illusions, and Disappointments, 1945–1957.* 1998.
Zubok, Vladislav, and Constantine Pleshakov. *Inside the Kremlin's Cold War: From Stalin to Khrushchev.* 1996.

The Political and Economic Recovery of Europe

Though painstaking and complex, recovery in its material and political forms yielded a distinctly new Europe whose characteristics historians are still uncovering. Because of the opening of the archives, historical attention has focused on charting Soviet occupation, recovery, and Communist takeover.

Herf, Jeffrey. *Divided Memory: The Nazi Past in the Two Germanies.* 1997.
Kenney, Padraic. *Rebuilding Poland: Workers and Communists, 1945–1950.* 1997.
Marrus, Michael. *The Unwanted: European Refugees in the Twentieth Century.* 1985.
Medvedev, Roy. *Khrushchev.* 1983.
Moeller, Robert, ed. *West Germany under Construction: Politics, Society, and Culture in the Adenauer Era.* 1997.
Naimark, Norman M. *The Russians in Germany: A History of the Russian Zone of Occupation, 1945–1949.* 1995.
Pinder, John. *European Community: The Building of a Union.* 1991.

Decolonization in a Cold War Climate

Novelists, philosophers, and historians debate the impact and issues of decolonization. Powerful evocations of the brutality of the process appear most often in novels such as *Cracking India,* recently made into the film *Earth.*

Brown, L. Carl. *International Politics and the Middle East.* 1984.
Dunbabin, J. P. D. *The Post-Imperial Age: The Great Powers and the Wider World.* 1994.
*Fanon, Frantz. *The Wretched of the Earth.* 1961.
Flaghan, Simha. *The Birth of Israel: Myths and Realities.* 1987.
Hargreaves, J. D. *Decolonization in Africa.* 1996.

McIntyre, W. David. *British Decolonization, 1946–1997: When, Why, and How Did the British Empire Fall?* 1999.

*Sidhwa, Bapsi. *Cracking India: A Novel.* 1992.

Cultural Life on the Brink of Nuclear War

Cold war culture, including the growth of consumerism, make the 1950s a fertile field for research, especially as new sources become available. Saunders and other historians have focused on governments' direction of high culture to the point that some artists and writers were made "stars" because of government intervention.

*Beauvoir, Simone de. *The Mandarins.* 1956.

Boyer, Paul. *By the Bomb's Early Light: American Thought and Culture at the Dawn of the Atomic Age.* 1985.

Cohen-Solal, Annie. *Sartre.* 1987.

Heineman, Elizabeth D. *What Difference Does a Husband Make? Women and Marital Status in Nazi and Postwar Germany.* 1999.

Kuisel, Richard. *Seducing the French: The Dilemma of Americanization.* 1993.

Lapidus, Gail. *Women in Soviet Society: Equality, Development, and Social Change.* 1978.

Marcus, Milicent. *Italian Film in the Light of Neorealism.* 1986.

Marling, Karal Ann. *As Seen on TV: The Visual Culture of Everyday Life in the 1950s.* 1994.

McDowell, Colin. *Forties Fashion and the New Look.* 1997.

Poiger, Uta. *Jazz, Rock, and Rebels: Cold War Politics and American Culture in a Divided Germany.* 2000.

Saunders, Frances Stonor. *Who Paid the Piper?* 1999.

Swann, Abram de. *In Care of the State: Health Care, Education, and Welfare in Europe and the United States in the Modern Era.* 1988.

CHAPTER 23
Challenges to the Postindustrial West, 1960–1980

The Technology Revolution

Wartime technological development came to have profound consequences for the peacetime lives of individuals and for society. The following works describe the new technologies and analyze their importance. Authors are divided on whether the new developments should be feared or embraced.

Hecht, Gabrielle. *The Radiance of France: Nuclear Power and National Identity after World War II.* 1998.

Kimbrell, Andrew. *The Human Body Shop: The Cloning, Engineering, and Marketing of Life.* 1997.

Mazlich, Bruce. *The Fourth Discontinuity: The Co-Evolution of Humans and Machines.* 1994.

*Rhodes, Richard, ed. *Visions of Technology: A Century of Vital Debate about Machines, Systems, and the Human World.* 1999.

Singer, Edward Nathan. *The Twentieth Century Revolution in Technology.* 1998.

*Stanworth, Michelle, ed. *Reproductive Technologies: Gender, Motherhood, and Medicine.* 1987.

Postindustrial Society and Culture

Changes in the way people worked became striking in the 1960s, causing social observers to analyze the meaning of the transformation. Many critics agree that technology's creation of a postindustrial workplace changed not only the way people worked but also how they lived in families and interacted with peers.

Bennett, Tony, ed. *Rock and Popular Music: Politics, Policies, Institutions.* 1993.

Evans, Christopher. *The Micro Millennium.* 1979.

Hochschild, Arlie. *The Time Bind: When Work Becomes Home and Home Becomes Work.* 1997.

Proctor, Robert. *Cancer Wars: The Politics behind What We Know and Don't Know about Causes and Trends.* 1994.

Sampson, Anthony. *The New Europeans.* 1968.

Sinfield, Alan. *Literature, Politics, and Culture in Post-War Britain.* 1989.

Contesting the Cold War Order in the 1960s

Historians look to domestic politics, international events, social change, and cultural life to capture the texture of this tumultuous decade. But the momentous changes on so many fronts still need synthetic treatment. A Martin Luther King Web site introduces visitors to the biography, speeches, sermons, and major life events of the slain civil rights leader.

Caute, David. *Sixty-Eight.* 1988.

*Dubček, Alexander. *Hope Dies Last: The Autobiography of Alexander Dubček.* 1993.

Fineberg, Jonathan. *Art since 1940: Strategies of Being.* 1995.

Fink, Carole, et al. *1968: The World Transformed.* 1998.

*Guy-Sheftall, Beverly, ed. *Words of Fire: An Anthology of African-American Feminist Thought.* 1995.

Katsiaficas, George. *The Subversion of Politics: European Autonomous Social Movements and the Decolonization of Everyday Life.* 1997.

*Lévi-Strauss, Claude. *Tristes Tropiques.* 1961.

The Martin Luther King Jr. Papers Project at Stanford University:
http://www.stanford.edu/group/King

Tarrow, Sidney. *Democracy and Disorder: Protest Politics in Italy, 1965–1975.* 1989.

The Erosion of Superpower Mastery in the 1970s

As the superpowers continued their standoff, historians found that myriad global changes affected their status. Some of the most compelling reading is found in personal testimonies such as Chang's account of Maoism and the Cultural Revolution, while the dissident art of the Soviet Union is striking for its deft and moving critique of life under communism. Many interesting Web sites explore the development of green parties over the past three decades, the most inclusive being that of the global organization with links to green parties of all continents and countries.

Battah, Abdalla M., and Yehuda Lukachs, eds. *The Arab-Israeli Conflict: Two Decades of Change.* 1988.

*Chang, Jung. *Wild Swans: Three Daughters of China.* 1991.

Green parties worldwide: http://www.greens.org

Huelsberg, Werner. *The German Greens: A Social and Political Profile.* 1988.

Koshar, Rudy. *Germany's Transient Pasts: Preservation and National Memory in the Twentieth Century.* 1998.

Laqueur, Walter. *The Age of Terrorism.* 1987.

Olson, James S., and Randy Roberts. *Where the Domino Fell: America and Vietnam, 1945–1990.* 1996.

Rosenfeld, Alla, and Norton T. Dodge. *From Gulag to Glasnost: Nonconformist Art from the Soviet Union.* 1995.

Smith, Dennis B. *Japan since 1945: The Rise of an Economic Superpower.* 1995.

*Solzhenitsyn, Aleksandr Isaevich. *The Gulag Archipelago.* 1973–1976.

Swain, Geoffrey, and Nigel Swain. *Eastern Europe since 1945.* 1993.

CHAPTER 24

The New Globalism: Opportunities and Dilemmas, 1980 to the Present

Global Challenges

Historians see the challenges since the 1980s as enormously diverse, ranging from conditions in the environment to issues of leadership in international affairs to the safety of the world's citizens in a global age. However, as Rives and Yousefi show, challenges such as the globalization of work have benefits as well as costs.

Appleyard, Reginald. *International Migration: Challenges for the Nineties.* 1991.

Feshbach, Murray. *Ecological Disaster: Cleaning Up the Hidden Legacy of the Soviet Regime.* 1995.

Keylor, William R. *The Twentieth-Century World: An International History.* 1992.

*Khadduri, Majid, and Edmund Ghareeb. *War in the Gulf, 1990–1991.* 1997.

Moin, Baqr. *Khomeini: Life of the Ayatollah.* 1999.

Rives, Janet, and Mahmood Yousefi. *Economic Dimensions of Gender Inequality: A Global Perspective.* 1997.

UN population data: http://www.unfpa.org/swp/swpmain.htm

The Welfare State in Question

The transformation of the welfare state involved powerful political personalities and raised fundamental issues about the nature of citizenship. Much cutting-edge history concerns an analysis of citizens' relationships to their states and their relationships to one another in an age of global migration and dramatic economic change. The work of Gilroy in particular has brought these questions to the fore.

Ash, Timothy Garton. *In Europe's Name: Germany and the Divided Continent.* 1993.

Caciagli, Mario, and David I. Kertzer, eds. *Italian Politics: The Stalled Transition.* 1996.

Gilroy, Paul. *"There Ain't No Black in the Union Jack": The Cultural Politics of Race and Nation.* 1987.

Sassen, Saskia. *Globalization and Its Discontents: Essays on the New Mobility of People and Money.* 1998.

Schaller, Michael. *Reckoning with Reagan: America and Its President in the 1980s.* 1992.

Thompson, Juliet S., and Wayne C. Thompson. *Margaret Thatcher: Prime Minister Indomitable.* 1994.

The Collapse of Soviet Communism

Historians will be telling and retelling this story, for the full consequences of communism's collapse are still unfolding. As new archives open, scholars, such as Kligman, focus on recounting some of the most horrendous aspects of Communist rule. Others, like Wachtel, explain the post-Communist situation in terms of very long-standing trends such as the obstacles to creating cultural unity among peoples of the former Yugoslavia.

Funk, Nanette, and Magda Mueller. *Gender Politics and Post-Communism: Reflections from Eastern Europe and the Former Soviet Union.* 1993.

Glenny, Misha. *The Fall of Yugoslavia: The Third Balkan War.* 1996.

*Gorbachev, Mikhail. *Memoirs.* 1996.

Jarausch, Konrad. *The Rush to German Unity.* 1994.

Kazanov, Anatoly M. *After the USSR: Ethnicity, Nationalism, and Politics in the Commonwealth of Independent States.* 1995.

Kligman, Gail. *The Politics of Duplicity: Controlling Reproduction in Ceaușescu's Romania.* 1998.

Sternhal, Suzanne. *Gorbachev's Reforms: De-Stalinization through Demilitarization.* 1997.

Strayer, Robert. *Why Did the Soviet Union Collapse?* 1998.

Wachtel, Andrew B. *Making a Nation, Breaking a Nation: Literature and Cultural Politics in Yugoslavia.* 1998.

Weigel, George. *Witness to Hope: The Biography of Pope John Paul II.* 1999.

Global Culture and Western Civilization at the Dawn of a New Millennium

The fate of cultural identity in an age of globalization engages a wide range of investigation and theorizing. From the nation-state to our individual relationships, as Applegate and Turkle, among others, suggest, long-standing identities are open to rethinking.

Agre, Philip. *Computation and Human Experience.* 1997.

Applegate, Celia. "A Europe of Regions: Reflections on the Historiography of Sub-National Places in Modern Times." *American Historical Review* 104 (1999): 1157–82.

Bales, Kevin. *Disposable People: New Slavery in the Global Economy.* 1999.

Dery, Mark. *Escape Velocity: Cyberculture at the End of the Century.* 1996.

*Emecheta, Buchi. *The Joys of Motherhood.* 1979.

Geddes, Andrew. *Immigration and European Integration.* 2000.

Huntington, Samuel P. *The Clash of Civilizations and the Remaking of the World Order.* 1996.

Iriye, Akira. *Cultural Internationalism and World Order.* 1997.

*Morrison, Toni. *Paradise.* 1998.

Piening, Christopher. *Global Europe: The European Union in World Affairs.* 1997.

Public Broadcasting Service: http://www.pbs.org

Rashid, Ahmed. *Jihad: The Rise of Militant Islam in Central Asia.* 2002.

Redmond, John, and Glenda S. Rosenthal. *The Expanding European Union: Past, Present, Future.* 1998.

Turkle, Sherry. *Life on the Screen: Identity in the Age of the Internet.* 1995.

Index

A note about the index:

Names of individuals appear in boldface; biographical dates are included for major historical figures.

Letters in parentheses following pages refer to:
(i)   illustrations, including photographs and artifacts
(f)   figures, including charts and graphs
(m)   maps

continued

continued

continued

William I (Netherlands; r. 1815–1840), 741
William II (Germany; r. 1888–1918), 853–854,
    856, 858, 867–868, 870, 879
William III (prince of Orange, king of England
    and Scotland; r. 1689–1702), 552, 556,
    590, 592–593
Wilson, Woodrow (1856–1924), 852, 868, 874
  Paris peace conference and, 881, 883
Windischgrätz, Prince Alfred von (VIN dish
    GRETZ), 748
Windsor, House of, 593
Witches and witchcraft, 521–523, 522 (i)
Wladyslaw II (Poland; r. 1386–1434), 442
Wolf, Christa (b. 1929), 1010, 1063
Wolf-Man, 805–806, 830
Women. See also Divorce; Family; Feminism;
    Gender differences; Marriage; Prostitution;
    Sex and sexuality
  in the 1920s, 891–893, 895, 899–901, 903
  in the 1930s, 911, 914, 917, 921, 922, 925, 927, 940
  activism (1960s), 1015
  in American colonies, 579
  Asian, 1038
  Christianity and, 609
  domesticity ideology and, 737–738, 750, 760,
    778, 820, 983
  education of, nineteenth-century, 784
  in the eighteenth century, 631
    novels, 588–589, 628
  in England (Great Britain), 464, 548, 560, 585,
    718, 771
    social reform and charitable work, 737
  the Enlightenment and, 603, 604 (i), 606–609,
    613, 615, 626, 628
  in Florence (fifteenth century), 463–465
  in France, 613, 626, 743
    Civil Code (Napoleonic Code), 688–689
    French Revolution, 653, 654 (i), 663, 672,
      674, 675 (i)
    seventeenth-century, 564–566, 569
  Jewish, 615
  in late nineteenth and early twentieth centuries
    in labor force, 840
    reformers and, 822–824, 824 (i)
    sports and leisure, 826–829
    suffrage (voting rights), 842–844, 844 (i)
    unions and working-class political parties,
      840–841
    upper-class women, 818–819
  in the Middle Ages
    fourteenth and fifteenth centuries, 435, 444
  in Nazi Germany, 921
  in the nineteenth century
    Great Britain, 718, 737, 771

  John Stuart Mill's views on, 796
  in labor force, 777–778, 797–798
  nation building and, 765 (i)
  Paris Commune (1871), 800, 800 (i)
  positivism and, 795
  reform movements and, 736–739
  religion and, 793
  after revolutions of 1848, 749–750
  as teachers, 784–785
  in northern Europe (fifteenth century), 464
  Protestant Reformation and, 486, 487 (i)
  reform movements and, 735
  reproductive technologies and, 997–998
  in Russia and the Soviet Union, 899, 900
  in the seventeenth century, 553, 560
    artists, 562–563
    authors, 565–566
    manners, 563–566
    salons, 564–565
  socialist movements and, 725
  in the Soviet Union, 917
  suffrage (voting rights), 842, 844, 844 (i),
    886–887, 887 (m)
  welfare state and (1945–1960), 966
  witches (witchcraft) and, 522–523
  World War I and, 870, 871–872, 872 (i)
  after World War II, 980, 983–984
  World War II and, 940, 941
Women's Social and Political Union (WSPU), 843
Woolen industry, 434–435
Wooley, Hannah, 565
Woolf, Virginia (1882–1941), 897, 898 (i), 928
Wordsworth, William (1770–1850), 682, 731
Worker Opposition (Soviet Union), 899
Workers (working class). See also Labor unions;
    Unemployment
  in the 1920s, 890–891
  Asian (1980s to the present), 1038
  in the eighteenth century, 633
  in France, 689–690
    Popular Front, 926
    revolution of 1848, 743
  in late nineteenth and early twentieth centuries
    mass politics, 838–842
    migrations (1881–1910), 825–826
  in the nineteenth century, 703 (i), 741–742
    changes in worklife, 797–799
    formation of the working class, 716–718
    Marxism and, 797–799
    religiously motivated reformers, 735–736
  in postindustrial society, 1000–1003, 1002 (f)
  in the Soviet Union, 915
  women, 840
    nineteenth-century, 777–778, 797–798

Elevation

Feet	Meters
Over 13,120	Over 4,001
6,561–13,120	2,001–4,000
1,641–6,560	501–2,000
661–1640	201–500
0–660	0–200
Below sea level	Below sea level

⊛ National capital

• Major city

N
W   E
S

0   150   300 miles
0   150   300 kilometers

Trondheim

NORWAY

Bergen

SWEDEN

Oslo

Stockholm

Göteborg

North Sea

Aarhus

DENMARK
Copenhagen

Balti

Gdan

Berlin

POLAN

NORTHERN
IRELAND
SCOTLAND
Glasgow   Edinburgh

Belfast

IRELAND   Dublin

UNITED

Liverpool

KINGDOM

Birmingham

WALES   ENGLAND

Cork

Thames R.

London

NETHERLANDS
Amsterdam

Elbe R.

Prague
CZECH REP.

Brno

Antwerp   Rotterdam
Brussels

BELGIUM

GERMANY

Frankfurt

Rhine R.

English Channel

ATLANTIC
OCEAN

Paris

Seine R.

Luxembourg

LUXEMBOURG

Loire R.

FRANCE

Bay of
Biscay

Lyon

Bern
SWITZERLAND

Zürich
Vaduz
LIECHTENSTEIN

Munich

Danube R.

Bratislava
Vienna

AUSTRIA

Innsbruck

Graz

Milan

SLOVENIA
Ljubljana
Zagre

CROATIA

Po R.

San
Marino

BOSNIA ANI
HERZEGOVIN

SAN
MARINO

Sarajev

Split

APENNINES

Adriatic Sea

Oporto

PYRENEES

ANDORRA
Andorra
la Vella   Marseille

MONACO

PORTUGAL

Madrid

SPAIN

Lisbon

Seville

Barcelona

Corsica

BALEARIC IS.

Sardinia

Rome   ITALY

Naples

Tyrrhenian
Sea

Gibraltar
(Br.)

Rabat

Algiers

Tunis

Palermo

Sicily

Ionia
Sea

Valletta

MALTA

MOROCCO

TUNISIA

ALGERIA

Tripoli

LIBYA

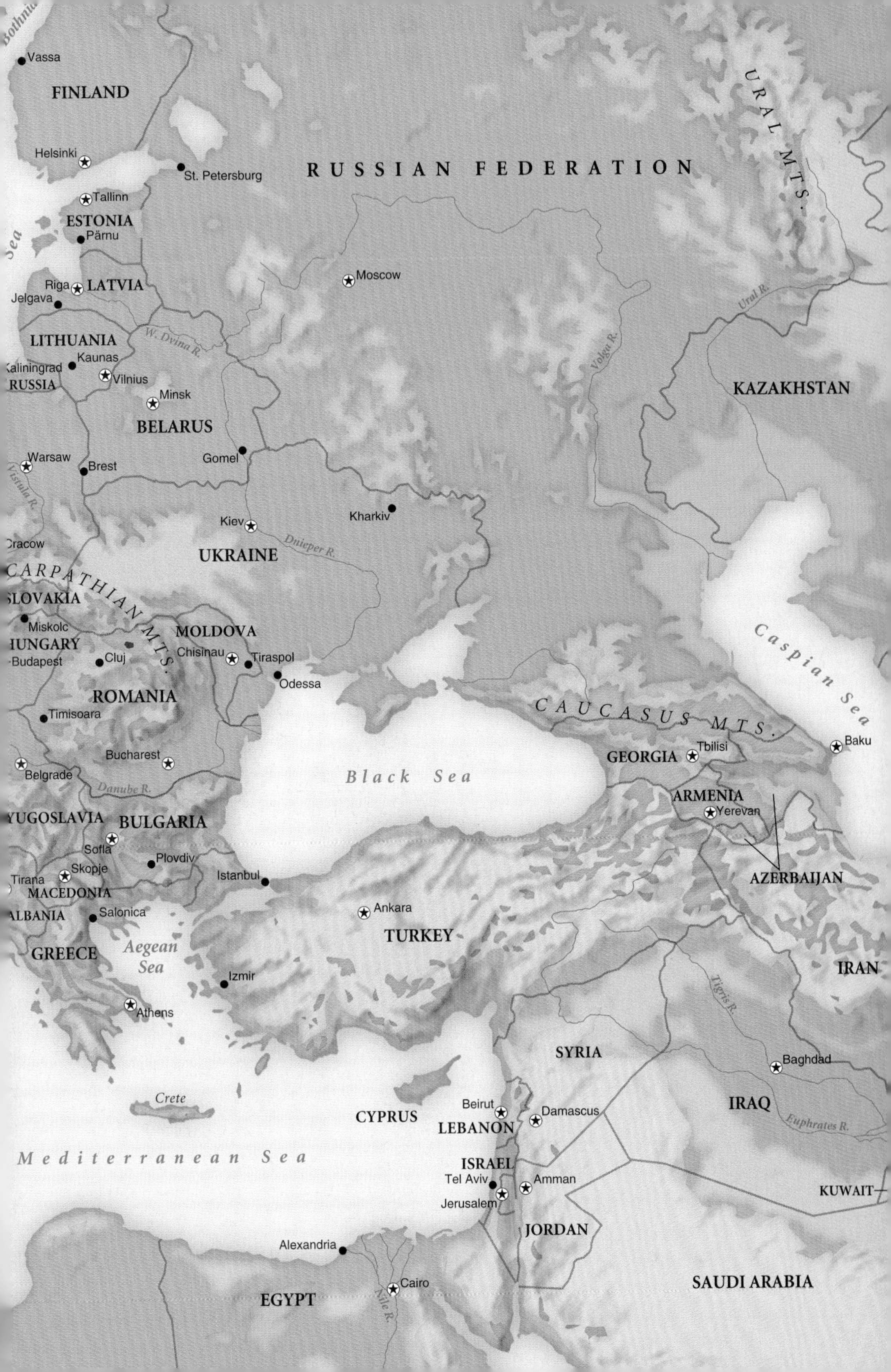

Bothnia
Vassa
FINLAND
Helsinki
St. Petersburg
RUSSIAN FEDERATION
URAL MTS.
Tallinn
ESTONIA
Pärnu
Sea
Riga
LATVIA
Jelgava
Moscow
Ural R.
LITHUANIA
W. Dvina R.
Volga R.
Kaunas
Kaliningrad
RUSSIA
Vilnius
Minsk
KAZAKHSTAN
BELARUS
Warsaw
Gomel
Brest
Vistula R.
Kharkiv
Kiev
Cracow
Dnieper R.
UKRAINE
CARPATHIAN MTS.
SLOVAKIA
Miskolc
MOLDOVA
HUNGARY
Caspian Sea
Budapest
Cluj
Chisinau
Tiraspol
Odessa
ROMANIA
Timisoara
CAUCASUS MTS.
Baku
Tbilisi
Bucharest
GEORGIA
Belgrade
Black Sea
Danube R.
ARMENIA
Yerevan
YUGOSLAVIA
BULGARIA
Sofia
Plovdiv
Skopje
Istanbul
Tirana
AZERBAIJAN
MACEDONIA
Ankara
ALBANIA
Salonica
TURKEY
GREECE
Aegean Sea
IRAN
Izmir
Tigris R.
Athens
SYRIA
Baghdad
Crete
Beirut
IRAQ
Damascus
CYPRUS
LEBANON
Euphrates R.
Mediterranean Sea
ISRAEL
Tel Aviv
Amman
KUWAIT
Jerusalem
JORDAN
Alexandria
Cairo
SAUDI ARABIA
EGYPT
Nile R.

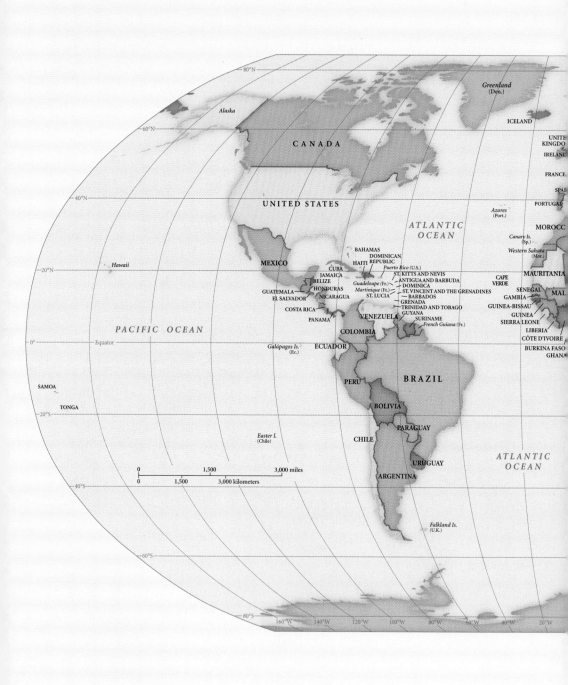

80°N

Greenland
(Den.)

ICELAND

Alaska

60°N

UNITE
KINGDO

CANADA

IRELAN

FRANCE

40°N

SPAI

UNITED STATES

PORTUGAL

Azores
(Port.)

MOROCC

ATLANTIC
OCEAN

Canary Is.
(Sp.)

Hawaii

Western Sahara
(Mor.)

20°N

BAHAMAS

MEXICO

DOMINICAN
REPUBLIC

CUBA

HAITI

Puerto Rico (U.S.)

CAPE
VERDE

MAURITANIA

JAMAICA

ST. KITTS AND NEVIS

BELIZE

ANTIGUA AND BARBUDA

SENEGAL

Guadeloupe (Fr.)

MAL

GUATEMALA

HONDURAS

DOMINICA

EL SALVADOR

Martinique (Fr.)

ST. VINCENT AND THE GRENADINES

GAMBIA

NICARAGUA

ST. LUCIA

BARBADOS

GUINEA-BISSAU

GRENADA

GUINEA

COSTA RICA

TRINIDAD AND TOBAGO

SIERRA LEONE

PANAMA

VENEZUELA

GUYANA

LIBERIA

PACIFIC OCEAN

SURINAME

CÔTE D'IVOIRE

COLOMBIA

French Guiana (Fr.)

BURKINA FASO

0°

Equator

GHANA

Galápagos Is.
(Ec.)

ECUADOR

SAMOA

BRAZIL

PERU

TONGA

20°S

BOLIVIA

PARAGUAY

Easter I.
(Chile)

CHILE

0	1,500	3,000 miles
0	1,500	3,000 kilometers

URUGUAY

ATLANTIC
OCEAN

ARGENTINA

40°S

Falkland Is.
(U.K.)

60°S

80°S

160°W   140°W   120°W   100°W   80°W   60°W   40°W   20°W

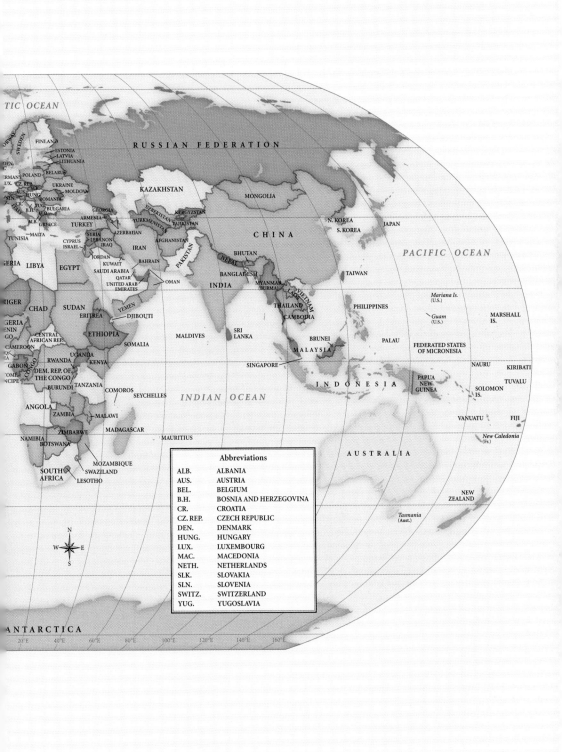

TIC OCEAN

NORWAY
SWEDEN
FINLAND
ESTONIA
LATVIA
LITHUANIA
DEN.
GERMANY POLAND
BELARUS
LUX. CZ. REP.
UKRAINE
AUS.
HUNG.
MOLDOVA
SLN.
ROMANIA
ITALY
B.H.
BULGARIA
ALB.
GREECE
TURKEY

RUSSIAN FEDERATION

KAZAKHSTAN

MONGOLIA

N. KOREA
S. KOREA

JAPAN

PACIFIC OCEAN

TUNISIA
MALTA
CYPRUS
SYRIA LEBANON
ISRAEL
IRAQ
JORDAN
KUWAIT

GERIA
LIBYA
EGYPT

GEORGIA
ARMENIA
AZERBAIJAN
TURKMENISTAN

UZBEKISTAN KYRGYZSTAN
TAJIKISTAN

AFGHANISTAN

IRAN

PAKISTAN

NEPAL
BHUTAN

CHINA

TAIWAN

NIGER
CHAD
SUDAN

SAUDI ARABIA
QATAR
BAHRAIN
UNITED ARAB
EMIRATES
OMAN

YEMEN
ERITREA
DJIBOUTI

BANGLADESH

INDIA

MYANMAR
(BURMA)
THAILAND
LAOS
VIETNAM

CAMBODIA

PHILIPPINES

Mariana Is.
(U.S.)

Guam
(U.S.)

MARSHALL
IS.

GERIA
BENIN
GO
CAMEROON
A
GABON
OME
NCIPE
CENTRAL
AFRICAN REP.
CONGO
DEM. REP. OF
THE CONGO
RWANDA
UGANDA
KENYA
BURUNDI
TANZANIA

ETHIOPIA

SOMALIA

MALDIVES

SRI
LANKA

BRUNEI

MALAYSIA

SINGAPORE

PALAU

FEDERATED STATES
OF MICRONESIA

NAURU

KIRIBATI

TUVALU

ANGOLA
ZAMBIA
MALAWI
ZIMBABWE
MADAGASCAR

COMOROS
SEYCHELLES

INDIAN OCEAN

INDONESIA

PAPUA
NEW
GUINEA

SOLOMON
IS.

NAMIBIA
BOTSWANA

MAURITIUS

VANUATU

FIJI

New Caledonia
(Fr.)

SOUTH
AFRICA
SWAZILAND
LESOTHO
MOZAMBIQUE

N
W E
S

AUSTRALIA

NEW
ZEALAND

Tasmania
(Aust.)

Abbreviations	
ALB.	ALBANIA
AUS.	AUSTRIA
BEL.	BELGIUM
B.H.	BOSNIA AND HERZEGOVINA
CR.	CROATIA
CZ. REP.	CZECH REPUBLIC
DEN.	DENMARK
HUNG.	HUNGARY
LUX.	LUXEMBOURG
MAC.	MACEDONIA
NETH.	NETHERLANDS
SLK.	SLOVAKIA
SLN.	SLOVENIA
SWITZ.	SWITZERLAND
YUG.	YUGOSLAVIA

ANTARCTICA

20°E   40°E   60°E   80°E   100°E   120°E   140°E   160°E

Sources of
THE MAKING OF THE WEST

PEOPLES AND CULTURES

A CONCISE HISTORY

Volume II: Since 1340

Sources of
THE MAKING OF THE WEST

PEOPLES AND CULTURES

A CONCISE HISTORY

Volume II: Since 1340

Katharine J. Lualdi

University of Southern Maine

BEDFORD / ST. MARTIN'S   Boston   ◆   New York

For Bedford/St. Martin's

Publisher for History: Patricia A. Rossi
Executive Editor for History: Elizabeth M. Welch
Production Editor: Lori Chong Roncka
Production Supervisor: Maria R. Gonzalez
Marketing Manager: Jenna Bookin Barry
Editorial Assistant: Brianna Germain
Production Assistants: Thomas P. Crehan, Courtney Jossart, Kendra LeFleur
Copyeditor: Patricia Herbst
Text Design: Wanda Kossak
Cover Design: Donna Dennison
Cover Art: Charles J. Staniland, *The Emigrant Ship*, c. 1880. Bradford Art Galleries and
    Museums, West Yorkshire, UK/The Bridgeman Art Library International Ltd.
Composition: TechBooks
Printing and Binding: R.R. Donnelley & Sons Company

President: Joan E. Feinberg
Director of Marketing: Karen Melton
Director of Editing, Design, and Production: Marcia Cohen
Managing Editor: Elizabeth M. Schaaf

Copyright © 2003 by Bedford/St. Martin's

All rights reserved. No part of this book may be reproduced, stored in a retrieval system, or transmitted in any form or by any means, electronic, mechanical, photocopying, recording, or otherwise, except as may be expressly permitted by the applicable copyright statutes or in writing by the Publisher.

Manufactured in the United States of America.

7 6 5 4 3 2
f e d c b a

For information, write: Bedford/St. Martin's, 75 Arlington Street, Boston, MA 02116
(617-399-4000)

ISBN: 0–312–40718–1 (Vol. I)
       0–312–40719–X (Vol. II)

Acknowledgments

Chapter 11

The Black Death (14th Century). Translated and edited by Rosemary Horrox. Copyright © 1994. Reprinted with the permission of Manchester University Press.

Christine de Pisan. *Laments on the Evils of the Civil War* (1410). From *The Epistle of the Prison of Human Life with an Epistle to the Queen of France and Lament on the Evils of the Civil War,* edited and translated by Josette A. Wisman. Copyright © 1984. Reprinted with the permission of Garland Publishing.

Acknowledgments and copyrights are continued at the back of the book on pages 134–36, which constitute an extension of the copyright page. It is a violation of the law to reproduce these selections by any means whatsoever without the written permission of the copyright holder.

Preface for Instructors

Sources of THE MAKING OF THE WEST: A CONCISE HISTORY is a collection of firsthand accounts intended to provide depth and breadth to the discussion of important events, ideas, and experiences discussed in *The Making of the West: Peoples and Cultures, A Concise History*, the text for which it was specifically compiled. Organized chapter by chapter to parallel the textbook, these sources offer teachers varied opportunities to ignite a dialogue in the classroom between the past and present.

Together, these documents yield a rich array for such a dialogue within the strong, succinct framework of *The Making of the West: A Concise History*. For example, when the textbook discusses the European slave trade, students can experience it for themselves in the source collection through the eyes of Olaudah Equiano, the African slave who survived to tell his story (Document 44). Information and ideas thus come alive with the emotions, opinions, and observations of contemporaries, revealing to students the relationship between narrative history and original sources and showing them that history is not a fixed set of immutable facts but rather an ongoing process of evaluation and interpretation. *Sources of* THE MAKING OF THE WEST: A CONCISE HISTORY provides the raw materials for this process.

Inspired by and tailored to *The Making of the West*, the criteria governing the selection of documents naturally reflect historians' changing understanding of Western civilization. Although traditional political sources are included, these views are broadened by less conventional documents illuminating not only social and cultural life but also Europe's increasing interconnectedness with the larger world. Women's voices received special attention in the selection process because of their crucial and often underappreciated role in shaping the course of Western history from both within and outside the corridors of power. The documents were also selected based on their accessibility and appeal to students. For this reason, I edited each primary source to speak to specific themes without impairing its overall sense and tone.

To assist students with their journey into the past, I prepared with equal care the wide range of learning aids that appear in the sourcebook. Each chapter opens with a short introduction that situates the documents within the broader historical context and addresses their relationship to one another. An explanatory headnote accompanies each document to provide fundamental background information on the author and the source while highlighting its significance. Discussion questions are also included to help students examine the key points and issues in greater depth and to suggest topics for discussion or writing assignment. Although these editorial features intentionally strengthen the coherency of each chapter as a unit, they also allow instructors to choose documents and questions that best suit their specific teaching goals and methods.

Acknowledgments

I owe many people thanks for helping to bring this project to fruition. First among them are the authors of *The Making of the West: A Concise History*, Lynn Hunt, Thomas R. Martin, Barbara H. Rosenwein, R. Po-chia Hsia, and Bonnie G. Smith, who provided invaluable suggestions, advice, and insight. I would also like to thank Larissa Juliet Taylor, Julia O'Brien, Megan Armstrong, and David K. Smith for their help and encouragement, as well as my development editor, Molly Kalkstein, for her careful eye and enthusiasm. Those at Bedford/St. Martin's also helped make this book possible: in particular, my thanks to Joan E. Feinberg, President; Charles H. Christensen, former President; Patricia A. Rossi, Publisher for History; Elizabeth M. Welch, Executive Editor for History; John Amburg, Assistant Managing Editor; Maria R. Gonzalez, Production Supervisor; and Lori Chong Roncka, Production Editor.

I also owe a debt of gratitude to the staff of the University of Maine library system who patiently endured my seemingly endless requests for books and articles. Without them, compiling this collection would not have been possible.

Last and above all, I thank my husband, John, for his sense of humor and understanding as I lost myself in books and Post-it notes.

Introduction for Students

Your textbook, *The Making of the West: Peoples and Cultures, A Concise History,* provides an essential chronological and thematic framework for understanding the development of the West as a cultural and geographic entity. Yet the process of historical inquiry extends beyond the text into the thoughts, words, and experiences of people living at the time. Firsthand accounts—that is, primary sources—expose the world that their writers inhabited, revealing the ideas, emotions, and beliefs of contemporary historical actors. Primary-source collections like this one allow you to observe, analyze, and interpret the past as it unfolds before you; unlike other sourcebooks, however, this reader's thorough integration with your textbook reveals the relationship between historical narrative and the original sources that inform it.

As the main title of your textbook, *The Making of the West,* suggests, history is not a static collection of names, facts, and dates. Rather, it is an ongoing attempt to make sense of the past and its relationship to the present, usually through the lens of primary sources. *Sources of* THE MAKING OF THE WEST: A CONCISE HISTORY provides this lens for you, with firsthand accounts representing a wide range of the documents historians use—from Egyptian chronicles and Greek poems to English feminist tracts and German political memoirs. When combined, the documents reflect historians' appreciation of the need to examine Western civilization from a variety of conceptual angles (political, social, cultural, economic) and geographic viewpoints. The composite picture that emerges as a result reveals a variety of historical experiences shaping each era from both within and outside Europe. Furthermore, the documents demonstrate that the most historically significant of these experiences are not always those of people in formal positions of power. Women, minorities, and everyday folk likewise influenced profoundly the course of Western history.

The sources in this reader were selected with an eye to their ability not only to capture the multifaceted dimensions of the past but also to ignite your historical imagination. Each document is a unique product of human endeavor and as such is often colored by the author's personal concerns, biases, and objectives. Among the most exciting challenges facing you is to sift through such nuances for what they reveal about the source and its links to the broader historical context.

Understanding how each document is connected to its author and to larger historical issues is key to the study of history. To this end, as you read each document, you should keep a series of questions at the front of your mind, just like a reporter investigating a breaking news story: Who wrote the document, when, for whom, why, and where? Each of these questions represents a crucial piece of the puzzle of the past and

is an essential means of meeting every historian's basic goal, to chart change and continuity over time.

A Nazi propaganda pamphlet written in 1930 (Document 67) offers an instructive
example. The author of the pamphlet, Joseph Goebbels, was the propaganda chief of
Adolf Hitler, the leader of the Nazi party. Similar political goals and beliefs bound both
men, including virulent anti-Semitism. At the time Goebbels wrote the document, Germany was mired in economic recession. Capitalizing on the downhearted mood of the
day with promises of a better life, he successfully used pamphlets such as this one to
broaden the Nazis' popular support on the eve of Hitler's rise to power. All of these factors—Goebbels's position within the Nazi party, what he was writing, for whom, when,
and why—shaped the document's content, and thus should inform your interpretation
of what it suggests about the Nazis and Germany in this period. By contrast, the recollections of Jews who were the victims of this propaganda (Document 69) offer a far
different view of the Nazis and the human impact of their regime. This difference can
be attributed not only to the nature of the sources themselves but also to the opposing
perspectives they represent.

Mining documents for their multiple layers of meaning thus requires a careful bal-
ancing act, first between fact and interpretation, and second between the content of the
document and the larger historical backdrop. To aid you with this process, *Sources of
THE MAKING OF THE WEST: A CONCISE HISTORY* was compiled to use directly alongside
your textbook. Each chapter in the collection contains three or four documents illus-
trative of the central ideas, issues, and events discussed in the corresponding textbook
chapter, where cross-references link the narrative to the readings. In addition, *Sources
of THE MAKING OF THE WEST: A CONCISE HISTORY* includes a variety of useful learning
aids that supplement the materials offered in the textbook. An introduction linking the
documents to the historical period in which they were written opens each chapter, and
each document has an explanatory headnote that provides essential information about
the author and the source and why the document is historically significant. Finally, three
or four questions conclude each document to help you probe beneath the surface to
understand what each document communicates and to see the similarities and differences among them.

The documents included in *Sources of THE MAKING OF THE WEST: A CONCISE HIS-
TORY* invite you to become an active participant in discovering how history was actually lived over time by an array of different people in an array of different places. They
are meant to offer snapshots of the past that, when viewed and interpreted together
within the broader historical context found in the textbook, will help you paint a colorful and interconnected picture of the historical development of Western civilization—
while learning that history, unlike a picture, is never finished.

Contents

Sources of

THE MAKING OF THE WEST

PEOPLES AND CULTURES

A CONCISE HISTORY

Volume II: Since 1340

CHAPTER II
Crisis and Renaissance, 1340–1500

Pestilence, warfare, a church in crisis, rebellions, pogroms, famines, and floods—to people living in the fourteenth century, it must have appeared that the end of the world was at hand. Fourteenth-century men and women came up with explanations, yet with the historian's luxury of retrospect, we can see the interconnectedness of events—what French historians call a conjuncture. Overpopulation, soil depletion, and warfare had reduced the average life span even before plague struck. During the Black Death, scapegoats were often sought, even though many saw the plague as divine punishment. The documents in this chapter evince both a grim side to the Renaissance, particularly the horror of war and danger of politics, and man's potential to overcome his condition.

33. *The Black Death*   (Fourteenth Century)

Few events have had such a shattering impact on every aspect of society as the plague, which reached Europe in 1347. The Black Death decimated a society already weakened by a demographic crisis, famines, and climatic disasters. It is estimated that one-third of Europe's population died in the first wave of plague, which was followed by repeated outbreaks. Some cities may have lost over half their people in 1347–1348 alone. The devastation was social, psychological, economic, political, and even artistic, yet many historians believe that it led to significant changes and even improvements in Western life. This set of documents describes the arrival of the plague in various places and responses to it, including searches for its cause and for people on whom to fix blame.

FROM GABRIELE DE' MUSSIS (D. 1356), A LAWYER IN PIACENZA

In 1346, in the countries of the East, countless numbers of Tartars and Saracens were struck down by a mysterious illness which brought sudden death. . . . An eastern settlement under the rule of the Tartars called Tana, which lay to the north of Constantinople and was much frequented by Italian merchants, was totally abandoned after an incident there which led to its being besieged and attacked by hordes of Tartars who gathered in a short space of time. The Christian merchants, who had been driven out by force, were so terrified of the power of the Tartars that, to save themselves and their belongings, they fled in an armed ship to Caffa, a settlement in the same part of the world which had been founded long ago by the Genoese.

Oh God! See how the heathen Tartar races, pouring together from all sides, suddenly invested the city of Caffa and besieged the trapped Christians there for almost three years. There, hemmed in by an immense army, they could hardly draw breath, although food could be shipped

From *The Black Death*, ed. and trans. Rosemary Horrox (Manchester: Manchester University Press, 1994), 16–21, 23, 207, 208, 219–22.

in, which offered them some hope. But behold, the whole army was affected by a disease which overran the Tartars and killed thousands upon thousands every day. It was as though arrows were raining down from heaven to strike and crush the Tartars' arrogance. All medical advice and attention was useless; the Tartars died as soon as the signs of disease appeared on their bodies: swellings in the armpit or groin caused by coagulating humours, followed by a putrid fever.

The dying Tartars, stunned and stupefied by the immensity of the disaster brought about by the disease, and realising that they had no hope of escape, lost interest in the siege. But they ordered corpses to be placed in catapults and lobbed into the city in the hope that the intolerable stench would kill everyone inside. What seemed like mountains of dead were thrown into the city, and the Christians could not hide or flee or escape from them, although they dumped as many of the bodies as they could in the sea. And soon the rotting corpses tainted the air and poisoned the water supply, and the stench was so overwhelming that hardly one in several thousand was in a position to flee the remains of the Tartar army. Moreover, one infected man could carry the poison to others, and infect people and places with the disease by look alone. No one knew, or could discover, a means of defence.

Thus almost everyone who had been in the East, or in the regions to the south and north, fell victim to sudden death after contracting this pestilential disease, as if struck by a lethal arrow which raised a tumour on their bodies. The scale of the mortality and the form which it took persuaded those who lived, weeping and lamenting, through the bitter events of 1346 to 1348— the Chinese, Indians, Persians, Medes, Kurds, Armenians, Cilicians, Georgians, Mesopotamians, Nubians, Ethiopians, Turks, Egyptians, Arabs, Saracens, and Greeks (for almost all the East has been affected) that the last judgement had come. . . .

As it happened, among those who escaped from Caffa by boat were a few sailors who had been infected with the poisonous disease. Some boats were bound for Genoa, others went to Venice and to other Christian areas. When the sailors reached these places and mixed with the people there, it was as if they had brought evil spirits with them: every city, every settlement, every place was poisoned by the contagious pestilence. . . .

Scarcely one in seven of the Genoese survived. In Venice, where an inquiry was held into the mortality, it was found that more than 70 percent of the people had died, and that within a short period 20 out of 24 excellent physicians had died. The rest of Italy, Sicily, and Apulia and the neighbouring regions maintain that they have been virtually emptied of inhabitants.' The people of Florence, Pisa, and Lucca, finding themselves bereft of their fellow residents, emphasize their losses. The Roman Curia at Avignon, the provinces on both sides of the Rhône, Spain, France, and the Empire cry up their griefs and disasters—all of which makes it extraordinarily difficult for me to give an accurate picture.

By contrast, what befell the Saracens can be established from trustworthy accounts. In the city of Babylon alone (the heart of the Sultan's power), 480,000 of his subjects are said to have been carried off by the disease in less than three months in 1348—and this is known from the Sultan's register which records the names of the dead, because he receives a gold bezant for each person buried. . . .

I am overwhelmed, I can't go on. Everywhere one turns there is death and bitterness to be described. The hand of the Almighty strikes repeatedly, to greater and greater effect. The terrible judgement gains power as time goes by.

FROM HERMAN GIGAS, A FRANCISCAN FRIAR IN GERMANY, WHOSE ACCOUNT GOES UNTIL 1349

In 1347 there was such a great pestilence and mortality throughout almost the whole world that in the opinion of well-informed men scarcely a tenth of mankind survived. The victims did not linger long, but died on the second or third day. . . . Some say that it was brought about by the corruption of the air; others that the Jews planned to wipe out all the Christians with poison and had poisoned wells and springs everywhere. And many Jews confessed as much under torture: that they had bred spiders and toads in pots and pans, and had obtained poison from overseas; and that not every Jew knew about this, only the more powerful ones, so that it would not be betrayed. . . . [M]en say that bags full of poison were found in many wells and springs.

FROM HEINRICH TRUCHESS, A FORMER PAPAL CHAPLAIN AND CANON OF CONSTANCE

The persecution of the Jews began in November 1348, and the first outbreak in Germany was at Sölden, where all the Jews were burnt on the strength of a rumour that they had poisoned wells and rivers, as was afterwards confirmed by their own confessions and also by the confessions of Christians whom they had corrupted. . . . Within the revolution of one year, that is from All Saints [1 November] 1348 until Michaelmas [29 September] 1349 all the Jews between Cologne and Austria were burnt and killed for this crime, young men and maidens and the old along with the rest. And blessed be God who confounded the ungodly who were plotting the extinction of his church.

FROM THE COUNCILLORS OF COLOGNE TO CONRAD VON WINTERTHUR TO THE BÜRGERMEISTER AND COUNCILLORS OF STRASSBURG ON 12 JANUARY 1349

Very dear friends, all sorts of rumours are now flying about against Judaism and the Jews prompted by this unexpected and unparalleled mortality of Christians, which, alas, has raged in various parts of the world and is still woefully active in several places. Throughout our city, as in yours, many-winged Fame clamours that this mortality was initially caused, and is still being spread, by the poisonings of springs and wells, and that the Jews must have dropped poisonous substances into them. When it came to our knowledge that serious charges had been made against the Jews in several small towns and villages on the basis of this mortality, we sent numerous letters to you and to other cities and towns to uncover the truth behind these rumours, and set a thorough investigation in train. . . .

  If a massacre of the Jews were to be allowed in the major cities (something which we are determined to prevent in our city, if we can, as long as the Jews are found to be innocent of these or similar actions) it could lead to the sort of outrages and disturbances which would whip up a popular revolt among the common people—and such revolts have in the past brought cities to misery and desolation. In any case we are still of the opinion that this mortality and its attendant circumstances are caused by divine vengeance and nothing else. Accordingly we intend to forbid any harassment of the Jews in our city because of these flying rumours, but to defend them faithfully and keep them safe, as our predecessors did—and we are convinced that you ought to do the same.

PAPAL BULL SICUT JUDEIS OF CLEMENT VI ISSUED IN JULY 1348

Recently, however, it has been brought to our attention by public fame—or more accurately, infamy—that numerous Christians are blaming the plague with which God, provoked by their sins, has afflicted the Christian people, on poisonings carried out by the Jews at the instigation of the devil, and that out of their own hot-headedness they have impiously slain many Jews, making no exception for age or sex; and that the Jews have been falsely accused of such outrageous behaviour. . . . [I]t cannot be true that the Jews, by such a heinous crime, are the cause or occasion of the plague, because throughout many parts of the world the same plague, by the hidden judgment of God, has afflicted and afflicts the Jews themselves and many other races who have never lived alongside them.

We order you by apostolic writing that each of you upon whom this charge has been laid, should straitly command those subject to you, both clerical and lay . . . not to dare (on their own authority or out of hot-headedness) to capture, strike, wound or kill any Jews or expel them from their service on these grounds; and you should demand obedience under pain of excommunication.

■ Discussion Questions

1. Examine the documents and try to determine their historical accuracy from internal evidence alone. What gives you clues about an author's objectivity (or lack thereof)?
2. What explanations are offered for the onset of plague? What (if any) is the understanding of the disease process?
3. Look at the account by Mussis and the bull of Pope Clement VI. What do they have in common? How did different groups of people react to the plague?
4. Why would some Christian authorities (the city councillors or the pope mentioned in these documents) attempt to protect the Jews? Why was such protection of no avail in many places? Why did some Jews confess? Discuss the attempt of societies (in some cases) to find scapegoats.

34. Christine de Pisan, *Lament on the Evils of the Civil War* (1410)

Christine de Pisan (1364–c. 1430) is considered by some to be the first feminist. Born in Italy, she was raised in Paris after her father, a scholar and physician who gave her a superb education, was called to the court of Charles V. After his death, and then that of her husband in 1389, Christine turned to writing to support her children. She became the first professional female writer in Europe. Patronized by kings, queens, and dukes, Christine wrote numerous works of prose and poetry, in-cluding The Book of the City of Ladies, *a defense of women. The epistle quoted here was written in 1410, when France was at a low point in the Hundred Years' War. In this letter she urges the lead-ers of society to look at what their disunity has done to France and its people, and she urges them to come together instead of fighting one another.*

Alone, and suppressing with great difficulty the tears which blur my sight and pour down my face like a fountain, so much that I am surprised to have the time to write this weary lament, whose writing the pity for the coming disaster makes me erase with bitter tears, and I say in pain: Oh, how can it be that the human heart, as strange as Fortune is, can make man revert to the nature of a voracious and cruel beast? Where is the reason that gives him the name of a rational animal? How can Fortune have the power to transform a man so much, that he is changed into a serpent, the enemy of mankind? Oh, alas, here is the reason why, noble French princes. With deference to you, where is now the sweet natural blood among you which has been for a long time the true summit of kindness in the world? . . .

For God's sake! For God's sake! High Princes, let these facts open your eyes and may you see as already accomplished what the preparations for taking arms will do in their end; thus you will see ruined cities, towns and castles destroyed, and fortresses razed to the ground. And where?

From Christine de Pisan, *The Epistle of the Prison of Human Life with an Epistle to the Queen of France and Lament on the Evils of the Civil War,* ed. and trans. Josette A. Wisman (New York: Garland Publishing, 1984), 85, 87, 89, 91, 93, 95.

In the very heart of France! The noble knights and youth of France, all of one nature, one single soul and body, which used to defend the crown and the public good, are now gathered in a shameful battle one against another, father against son, brother against brother, relatives against one another, with deadly swords, covering the pitiful fields with blood, dead bodies, and limbs. Oh, dishonorable victory may be to the one who has it! What glory will Fame give to it? . . .

Oh you, knight who comes from such a battle, tell me, I pray you, what honor did you win there? . . . And what will follow, in God's name? Famine, because of the wasting and ruining of things that will ensue, and the lack of cultivation, from which will spring revolts by the people who have been too often robbed, deprived and oppressed, their food taken away and stolen here and there by soldiers, subversion in the towns because of outrageous taxes. . . . So cry, cry, beat your hands and cry—as once the sad Argia did in such a case, along with the ladies of Argos— you ladies, damsels, and women of the kingdom of France! Because the swords that will make you widows and deprive you of your children and kin have already been sharpened! . . .

Oh, crowned Queen of France, are you still sleeping? Who prevents you from restraining now this side of your kin and putting an end to this deadly enterprise? Do you not see the heritage of your noble children at stake? . . .

Come, all you wise men of this realm, come with your queen! What use are you if not for the royal council? Everyone should offer his hand. You used to concern yourselves even with small matters. How shall France be proud of so many wise men, if now they cannot see to her safety, and the fount of the clergy keep her from perishing? Where then are your plans and wise thoughts? . . . For you resemble Nineveh, which God condemned to perish, and which received his wrath because of the great sins which were many there, and because of this, the situation is very doubtful, unless the sentence is not revoked by the intercession of devout prayers.

People, be firm! And you, pious woman, cry mercy for this grievous storm! Ah, France, France, once a glorious kingdom! . . .

Oh, Duke of Berry, Noble Prince, excellent father and scion of royal children, son of a King of France, brother and uncle, father of all the antiquity of the lily! How is it possible that your tender heart can bear to see you, on a given day, assembled in deadly battle array to bear painful arms against your nephews? . . .

So, come, come, Noble Duke of Berry, Prince of High Excellence, and follow the divine law which orders peace! Take a strong hold of the bridle, and stop this dishonorable army, at least until you have talked to the parties. So come to Paris, to your father's city where you were born and which cries to you with tears and sighs, asking and begging for you to come. Come quickly to comfort this suffering city. . . . [A]lthough it is now discussed in various tongues on each side that hopes for victory in the battle and they all say: "We will win and work for it"—they are bragging foolishly. For it must not be ignored that the outcome of all battles is strange and unknown. For although man proposed it, Fortune disposes it. . . . Was the victory of the King of Athens, mortally wounded in battle, of any worth to him? Is a multitude of men an advantage in such a case? Was Xerxes not defeated, although he had so many men that all vales and hills were covered with them? Are a good reason and a just quarrel of any value? If it were so, the king Saint Louis, who obtained so many beautiful victories, would not have been defeated at Tunis by the infidels. . . . And above all, although war and battles are in all cases very dangerous and difficult to avoid, no doubt that among such close kin, tied by nature in one bond of love, they are perverse. . . . I believe the cost would be less, and that this army, by a common will and true unity, should be directed against those who are our natural enemies, and that the good and faithful French should take care of these people, and not kill one another. . . . Ah, Very Reverend Prince, Noble Duke of Berry, do hear this. . . . May the Blessed Holy Spirit, Author of all peace, give you the heart and the courage to achieve such a thing! Amen. And may he greet me, a poor voice crying in this kingdom, wanting peace and welfare for all, your servant Christine, moved by a very fair mind, the gift to see that day!

■ Discussion Questions

1. What, in Christine's view, are the costs of war, in human and dynastic terms?
2. How important is it that Christine refers in several instances to "the French" and "France"? To whom does Christine direct her admonitions? Why?
3. What kind of allusions does Christine use to convince her readers that they should not continue a civil war that is keeping them from fighting the "common enemy"? What does this tell you about her education?
4. Do you think this "poor voice crying in the kingdom" can be seen as a precursor to Joan of Arc? Why or why not?

35. Giovanni Pico della Mirandola, *Oration on the Dignity of Man* (1496)

The work of Giovanni Pico della Mirandola (1463–1494), a Neo-platonic thinker and Dominican friar, celebrates man's potential. The Oration on the Dignity of Man *was the preface to nine hundred theses written by Pico in his early twenties, for a public disputation that never in fact took place. Steeped in the Aristotelian and Platonic traditions, Pico knew Latin, Arabic, Greek, Hebrew, and Aramaic. He was deeply interested in Hebrew mysticism, pre-Socratic thought, and occult knowledge attributed at the time to Hermes Trismegistus. Not surprisingly, some of Pico's ideas were deemed heretical by a papal commission. Thereafter, he lived under the protection of Lorenzo de' Medici until he died at the age of thirty-one. The* Oration *explores the concept of free will—the human ability to choose, for good or ill.*

I have read in the ancient annals of the Arabians, most reverend Fathers, that when asked what on the world's stage could be considered most admirable, Abdala the Saracen answered that there is nothing more admirable to be seen than man. In agreement with this opinion is the saying of Hermes Trismegistus: "What a great miracle, O Asclepius, is man!"

When I had thought over the meaning of these maxims, the many reasons for the excellence of man advanced by many men failed to satisfy me. . . .

At last, it seems to me that I have understood why man is the most fortunate living thing worthy of all admiration and precisely what rank is his lot in the universal chain of being, a rank to be envied not only by the brutes but even by the stars and by minds beyond this world. It is a matter past faith and extraordinary! . . .

God the Father, the supreme Architect, had already built this cosmic home which we behold, this most majestic temple of divinity, in accordance with the laws of a mysterious wisdom. He had adorned the region above the heavens with intelligences, had quickened the celestial spheres with eternal souls and had filled the vile and filthy parts of the lower world with a multitude of animals of every kind. But when the work was completed, the Maker kept wishing that there were someone who could examine the plan of so great an enterprise, who could love its beauty, who could admire its vastness. On that account, when everything was completed, as Moses and Timaeus both testify, He finally took thought of creating man. However, not a single archetype remained from which he might fashion this new creature, not a single treasure remained which he might bestow upon this new son, and not a single seat remained in the whole world in

From *The Italian Renaissance Reader,* ed. Julia Conaway Bondanella and Mark Musa (New York: Meridian, 1987), 180–83.

which the contemplator of the universe might sit. All now was complete; all things had been as-signed to the highest, the middle, and the lowest orders. But it was not in the nature of the Fa-ther's power to fail in this final creative effort, as though exhausted; nor was it in the nature of His wisdom to waver in such a crucial matter through lack of counsel; and it was not in the na-ture of His Beneficent Love that he who was destined to praise God's divine generosity in regard to others should be forced to condemn it in regard to himself. At last, the Supreme Artisan or-dained that the creature to whom He could give nothing properly his own should share in what-ever He had assigned individually to the other creatures. He therefore accepted man as a work of indeterminate nature, and placing him in the center of the world, addressed him thus:

"O Adam, we have given you neither a place nor a form nor any ability exclusively your own, so that according to your wishes and your judgment, you may have and possess whatever place, form, or abilities you desire. The nature of all other beings is limited and constrained in accor-dance with the laws prescribed by us. Constrained by no limits, in accordance with your own free will, in whose hands we have placed you, you shall independently determine the bounds of your own nature. We have placed you at the world's center, from where you may more easily observe whatever is in the world. We have made you neither celestial nor terrestrial, neither mortal nor immortal, so that with honor and freedom of choice, as though the maker and molder of your-self, you may fashion yourself in whatever form you prefer. You shall have the power to degen-erate into the inferior forms of life which are brutish; you shall have the power, through your soul's judgment, to rise to the superior orders which are divine." . . .

In man alone, at the moment of his creation, the Father placed the seeds of all kinds and the germs of every way of life. Whatever seeds each man cultivates will mature and bear their own fruit in him; if vegetative, he will be like a plant; if sensitive, he will become a brute; if rational, he will become a celestial being; if intellectual, he will be an angel and the son of God. . . .

Who would not admire this our chameleon? Or who could admire any other being more greatly than man? Asclepius the Athenian justly says that man was symbolized in the mysteries by the figure of Proteus because of his ability to change his character and transform his nature. This is the origin of those metamorphoses or transformations celebrated among the Hebrews and the Pythagoreans. For the occult theology of the Hebrews sometimes transforms the holy Enoch into an angel of divinity and sometimes transforms other people into other divinities. The Pythagoreans transform impious men into beasts and, if Empedocles is to be believed, even into plants. Echoing this, Mohammed often had this saying on his lips: "He who deviates from divine law becomes a beast," and he was right in saying so. For it is not the bark that makes the beast of burden but its irrational and sensitive soul; neither is it the spherical form which makes the heavens, but their undeviating order; nor is it the freedom from a body which makes the angel but its spiritual intelligence. . . .

Are there any who will not admire man? In the sacred Mosaic and Christian writings, man, not without reason, is sometimes described by the name of "all flesh" and sometimes by that of "every creature," since man molds, fashions, and transforms himself according to the form of all flesh and the character of every creature. For this reason, the Persian Evantes, in describing Chaldean theology, writes that man does not have an inborn and fixed image of himself but many which are external and foreign to him; whence comes the Chaldean saying: "Man is a being of varied, manifold, and inconstant nature."

But why do we reiterate all these things? To the end that from the moment we are born we are born into the condition of being able to become whatever we choose.

■ Discussion Questions

1. Examine the words Pico uses to describe God and how God went about the process of cre-ation. Why might these ideas have been considered dangerous?

2. What, according to Pico, are man's abilities? Why were these abilities and possibilities given to human beings?
3. What kinds of sources does Pico use to support his ideas? What is their importance as part of his philosophy?
4. What makes this document a "statement" of Renaissance thought?

36. Alessandra Strozzi, *Letters from a Widow and Matriarch of a Great Family*   (1450–1465)

Women in medieval and Renaissance Europe were usually under legal guardianship—typically that of a father or husband. Women of the lower classes may have enjoyed a semblance of freedom in work and marriage early in their lives. In contrast, their upper-class counterparts gained their greatest prestige and power through widowhood. Alessandra (1407–1471) married Matteo Strozzi, a wealthy merchant whose business had branches throughout Europe. When Matteo died of the effects of the plague while exiled for being in opposition to Cosimo de' Medici (1389–1464), Alessandra's financial situation became difficult, for she had sons and daughters to marry and a great household to maintain. She engaged in lengthy correspondence with her sons about political, marital, and economic conditions that affected the family. In these excerpts from letters to her son Filippo, we can glimpse the "other" side of the Renaissance—exile; political danger if one did not agree with the ruling faction; marriages that were contracted solely for reasons of politics, honor, and clientage; and slavery.

To Filippo, 1450

Really, as long as there are young girls in the house, you do nothing but work for them, so when she leaves I will have no one to attend to but you three. And when I get the house in a little better shape I would love it if you would think about coming home. You would have no cause to be ashamed with what there is now, and you could do honor to any friend who dropped in to see you at home. But two or three years from now it will all be much better. And I would love to get you a wife; you're of an age now to know how to manage the help and to give me some comfort and consolation. I have none. . . .

You know that some time ago I bought Cateruccia, our slave, and for several years now, though I haven't laid a hand on her, she has behaved so badly toward me and the children that you wouldn't believe it if you hadn't seen it. Our Lorenzo could tell you all about it. . . . I've always suffered it because I can't chastise her, and besides I thought you would come once a month so that we could come to a decision together or she could be brought to better obedience. For several months now she has been saying and is still saying that she doesn't want to stay here, and she is so moody that no one can do a thing with her. If it weren't for love of Lesandra, I would have told you to sell her, but because of her malicious tongue, I want to see Lesandra safely out of the house first. But I don't know if I can hold out that long: mark my words, I'm going to get her out of my sight because I don't want this constant battle. She pays no more attention to me than if I were the slave and she were the mistress, and she threatens us all so that Lesandra and I are both afraid of her.

From *University of Chicago Readings in Western Civilization, 5: The Renaissance,* ed. Eric Cochrane and Julius Kirshner (Chicago: University of Chicago Press, 1986), 109, 113–17.

TO FILIPPO, 1459

It grieves me, my son, that I'm not near you to take some of these troublesome things off your hands. You should have told me the first day Matteo fell sick so I could have jumped on a horse and been there in just a few days. But I know that you didn't do it for fear I would get sick or would be put to trouble. . . . I have been told that in the honors you arranged for the burial of my son you did honor to yourself as well as to him. You did all the better to pay him such honor there, since here they don't usually do anything for those who are in your condition [that is, in exile]. Thus I am pleased that you did so. Here these two girls, who are unconsolable over the death of their brother, and I have gone into mourning, and because I had not yet gotten the woolen cloth to make a mantle for myself, I have gotten it now and I will pay for it.

TO FILIPPO, 1465

I told you in my other [letter] what happened about 60 [the daughter of Francesco Tanagli], and there's nothing new there. And you have been advised that there is no talk of 59 [a woman who belonged to the Adimari family] until we have placed the older girl. 13 [Marco Parenti] believes we should do nothing further until we can see our way clearly concerning these two and see what way they will go. Considering their age, this shouldn't take too long. It's true that my wish would be to see both of you with a companion, as I have told you many times before. That way when I die I would think you ready to take the step all mothers want—seeing their sons married—so your children could enjoy what you have acquired with enormous effort and stress over the long years. To that end, I have done my very best to keep up the little I have had, foregoing the things that I might have done for my soul's sake and for that of our ancestors. But for the hope I have that you will take a wife (in the aim of having children), I am happy to have done so. So what I would like would be what I told you. Since then I have heard what Lorenzo's wants are and how he was willing to take her to keep me happy, but that he would be just as glad to wait two years before binding himself to the lady. I have thought a good deal about the matter, and it seems to me that since nothing really advantageous to us is available, and since we have time to wait these two years, it would be a good idea to leave it at that unless something unexpected turns up. Otherwise, it doesn't seem to me something that requires immediate thought, particularly considering the stormy times we live in these days, when so many young men on this earth are happy to inhabit it without taking a wife. The world is in a sorry state, and never has so much expense been loaded on the backs of women as now. No dowry is so big that when the girl goes out she doesn't have the whole of it on her back, between silks and jewels. . . . If 60 works out well, we could sound out the possibility of the other girl for him. There's good forage there if they were to give her, and at any [other] time it would have been a commendable move. As things are going now, it seems to me better to wait and see a while for him. . . . This way something may come of it, and they will not offer a wife without money, as people are doing now, since it seems superfluous to those who are giving 50 to give her a dowry. 13 wrote you that 60's father touched on the matter with him in the way I wrote you about. He says that you should leave it to us to see to it and work it out. For my part, I've done my diligent best, and I can't think what more I could have done—for your consolation than my own. . . .

Niccolò has gone out of office, and although he did some good things, they weren't the ones I would have wanted. Little honor has been paid to him or to the other outgoing magistrates, either when they were in office, or now that they have stepped down. Our scrutineer was quite upset about it, as were we, but I feel that what was done will collapse, and it is thought they will start fresh. This Signoria has spent days in deliberation, and no one can find out anything about them. They have threatened to denounce whoever reveals anything as a rebel, so things are being done in total secrecy. I have heard that 58 [the Medici] is everything and 54 [the Pitti] doesn't stand a chance. For the moment, it looks to me as if they will get back to 56 [the Pucci] in the runoffs, if things continue to go as now. May God, who can do all, set this city right, for it is in a bad way. Niccolò went in proudly and then lost heart—as 14's [Soderini] brother said, "He went in a lion and he will go out a lamb," and that's just what happened to him. When he saw the votes were going against him, he began to humble himself. Now, since he left office, he goes about accompanied by five or six armed men for fear. . . . It would have been better for him if [he had never been elected], for he would never have made so many enemies. . . .

[T]hink about having Niccolò Strozzi touch on the matter with Giovanfrancesco for 45 [Lorenzo], if you think it appropriate. Although I doubt that she would deign [to marry] so low, still, it sometimes happens that you look in places that in other times you wouldn't have dreamed of, by the force of events—deaths or other misfortunes. So think about it.

■ Discussion Questions

1. What is Alessandra's role as matriarch of her family? What else can you tell about women during the Renaissance?
2. What is Alessandra's view of the politics of the city in her day? Why would Alessandra use numbers to designate people?
3. What is Alessandra's relation to her slave? How does the existence of slavery affect your view of Florence's vaunted "liberty for all"?
4. How were marriages formed among the middle and upper classes? What was required before one could marry?

CHAPTER 12
Struggles over Beliefs, 1500–1648

For kings, nobles, and ordinary folk alike, the sixteenth through mid-seventeenth centuries was a time of turmoil and change, as the following documents illustrate. These conflicts began with the Protestant Reformation, which shattered the Christian humanist ideal of peace and unity, and came to a head in the Thirty Years' War (1618–1648), which devastated central Europe and left many rulers bankrupt. The religious wars that galvanized much of Europe in this period were fueled by both ecclesiastical and lay leaders' attempts to maintain the commonly held idea that political and social stability depended on religious conformity. With the escalation of violence, however, some people argued successfully that peace would come only if state interests took precedence over religious ones. Europeans' views of the earth and the heavens also expanded because of the rise of new scientific methods and overseas exploration.

37. Argula von Grumbach and John Hooker,
Women's Actions in the Reformation (1520s–1530s)

Throughout the Middle Ages, laywomen were actively involved in their religion, through attendance at Mass, sermons, and pilgrimages, and their "greater piety" (than that of men) was remarked on by many churchmen. This trend continued in the early decades of the Reformation but assumed new forms, providing a particular window of opportunity for women to defend their faith when challenged through speech, print, or action. The first document is from the writings of Argula von Grumbach (1492–c. 1554), a Bavarian noblewoman who was by 1522 a follower of Martin Luther (1483–1546), whose challenges and writings initiated the Protestant Reformation. Called a silly bag, a shameless whore, and a female desperado, among other epithets, von Grumbach wrote prose and poetry beginning in 1523 in defense of Luther and Philipp Melanchthon (1497–1560), Luther's coworker and follower, and against the arrest of a Lutheran student at Ingolstadt. She also responded in kind to the sarcasm of another student. Tens of thousands of copies of her writings were in circulation within a few years. The second document is by the Englishman John Hooker, who was Exeter's city chamberlain during the dissolution of the monasteries, when the city's Catholic women took matters into their own hands on the arrival of Thomas Cromwell's visitors in 1535 or 1536.

From *http://home.infi.net/`ddisse/grumbach.html*; Argula von Grumbach, ". . . A Hundred Women Would Emerge to Write"; and Joyce Youings, *The Dissolution of the Monasteries* (London: Allen & Unwin; New York: Barnes & Noble, 1971), 164–65.

ARGULA VON GRUMBACH

To the Scholars of Ingolstadt

I find there is a text in Matthew 10 which runs: "Whosoever confesses me before another I too will confess before my heavenly Father." . . . Words like these, coming from the very mouth of God, are always before my eyes. For they exclude neither woman or man.

And this is why I am compelled as a Christian to write to you.

To Bavarian Princes

My heart goes out to our princes, whom you have seduced and betrayed so deplorably. For I realize that they are ill informed about divine Scripture. If they could spare the time from other business, I believe they, too, would discover the truth that no one has a right to exercise sovereignty over the word of God. . . . My heart goes out to them; for they have no one with enough integrity to tell them what is going on. And I realize very well that it is for their wealth, torn from them every day, that they are loved rather than for themselves. I am prepared to write to them in this vein, since, because of other business, they have no leisure to sit down and read for themselves.

To the Ingolstadt Scholars

I beseech you for the sake of God, and exhort you by God's judgment and righteousness, to tell me in writing which of the articles written by Martin or Melanchthon you consider heretical. In German not a single one seem heretical to me. And the fact is that a great deal has been published in German, and I've read it all. . . . I beseech and request a reply from you if you consider I am in error, though I am not aware of it. For Jerome was not ashamed of writing a great deal to women, to Blessilla, for example, to Paula, Eustochium, and so on. Yes, and Christ himself, he who is the only teacher of us all, was not ashamed to preach to Mary Magdalene, and to the young woman at the well.

I do not flinch from appearing before you, from listening to you, from discussing with you. For by the grace of God I, too, can ask questions, hear answers, and read in German. . . . I have no Latin, but you have German, being born and brought up in this tongue. What I have written to you is no woman's chit-chat, but the word of God, and as a member of the Christian Church, against which the gates of Hell cannot prevail.

In Response to a Verse Attack by an Ingolstadt Student

Now Judith when this she heard,
To the priests went straight away,
Gave them instruction manifold
How God their fathers led of old,
When, as now, in tribulation;
Gave ample scriptural demonstration.
She also took the rulers on:
Boldly said: "What have you done
To leave the people in such pain?"
Soon caused their hearts to lift again.

. . .

God therefore made her hand so strong
That Holofernes was undone.
She then lopped off his very head.
Who'd ever have believed this deed?
That him they called a mighty god
Should thus become a laughing stock.

. . .

More of the same in Judges is found,
You can read of there [*sic*], if you care.
There was a seer, Deborah by name,
Who was sent by God, much the same,
To lead the people of Israel
To judge and govern them as well.
Had you been living at that time,
Wise man, no doubt you'd have tried
To stop God carrying out his plan
By acting through a poor woman.
You'd surely could never have endured
God's victory through woman assured.

                    . . .

If you argue I'm too ignorant
Then share with me your wisdom grand!
But a spindle is all you offer,
In every teaching it's what you proffer.
But this fine Master of the Sentence
Would teach me my domestic duties!
These duties I carry out day by day
How could I ever forget them, pray?
Though Christ tells me—I hear his voice—
To hear his words is the very best choice.

JOHN HOOKER: POPULAR REACTIONS AT EXETER

The commissioners came to this city in the summertime to execute their commission, and beginning first with the priory of St. Nicholas, after that they [had] viewed the same they went thence to dinner and commanded [a man] in the time of their absence to pull down the rood loft in the church. In the meanwhile, and before they did return, certain women and wives in the city, namely Joan Reeve, Elizabeth Glandfield, Agnes Collaton, Alice Miller, Joan Reed and others, minding to stop the suppressing of that house, came in all haste to the said church, some with spikes, some with shovels, some with pikes, and some with such tools as they could get and, the church door being fast, they broke it open. And finding there the man pulling down the rood loft they all sought, [by] all the means they could, to take him and hurled stones unto him, in so much that for his safety he was driven to take to the tower for his refuge. And yet they pursued him so eagerly that he was enforced to leap out at a window and so to save himself, and very hardly he escaped the breaking of his neck, but yet he broke one of his ribs. John Blakealler, one of the aldermen of the city, being advertised thereof, he with all speed got him to the said monastery, he thinking what with fair words and what with foul words to have stayed and pacified the women. But how so ever he talked with them they were plain with him and the aforesaid Elizabeth Glandfield gave him a blow and set him packing. The Mayor [William Hurst], having understanding hereof and being very loathe the visitors should be advertised of any such disorders and troubles, he came down with his officers, before whose coming they [the women] had made fast the church doors and had bestowed themselves in places meet as they thought to stand to their defences. Notwithstanding, the Mayor broke in upon them and with much ado he apprehended and took them all and sent them to ward. The visitors being then made acquainted herewith, they gave thanks to the Mayor for his care and diligence . . . and so they proceeded to the suppressing of the house, and before their departure they intreated the Mayor for releasing of the women.

■ Discussion Questions

1. What can you tell of Argula von Grumbach's background and learning from her writings alone?
2. What main points does Argula von Grumbach make against the princes and, primarily, the Ingolstadt scholars?
3. Why did the Catholic women of Exeter attack the commissioners sent out to dissolve the monastery? Are you surprised by their behavior?
4. Despite their many differences, do you see anything in common between Argula von Grumbach and the women of Exeter?

38. Henry IV, *Edict of Nantes* (1598)

Henry IV's promulgation of the Edict of Nantes in 1598 marked the end of the French Wars of Religion by recognizing French Protestants as a legally protected religious minority. Drawing largely on earlier edicts of pacification, the Edict of Nantes comprised ninety-two general articles, fifty-six secret articles, and two royal warrants. The two series of articles represented the edict proper and were registered by the highest courts of law in the realm (parlements). The following excerpts from the general articles reveal the triumph of political concerns over religious conformity on the one hand, and the limitations of religious tolerance in early modern France on the other.

Henry, By the Grace of God, King of *France*, and *Navarre*, To all Present, and to Come, greeteth. Among the infinite Mercies that God hath pleased to bestow upon us, that most Signal and Remarkable is, his having given us Power and Strength not to yield to the dreadful Troubles, Confusions, and Disorders, which were found at our coming to this Kingdom, divided into so many Parties and Factions, that the most Legitimate was almost the least, enabling us with Constancy in such manner to oppose the Storm, as in the end to surmount it, reducing this Estate to Peace and Rest. . . . For the general difference among our good Subjects, and the particular evils of the soundest parts of the State, we judged might be easily cured, after the Principal cause (the continuation of the Civil Wars) was taken away, in which we have, by the blessing of God, well and happily succeeded, all Hostility and Wars through the Kingdom being now ceased, and we hope he will also prosper us in our other affairs, which remain to be composed, and that by this means we shall arrive at the establishment of a good Peace, with tranquility and rest. . . . Amongst our said affairs . . . one of the principal hath been, the many complaints we received from divers of our Provinces and Catholick Cities, for that the exercise of the Catholick Religion was not universally re-established, as is provided by Edicts or Statutes heretofore made for the Pacification of the Troubles arising from Religion; as also the Supplications and Remonstrances which have been made to us by our Subjects of the reformed Religion, as well upon the execution of what hath been granted by the said former Laws, as that they desire to have some addition for the exercise of their Religion, the liberty of their Consciences and the security of their Persons and Fortunes; presuming to have just reasons for desiring some enlargement of Articles, as not being without great apprehensions, because their Ruine hath been the principal pretext and original foundation of the late Wars, Troubles, and Commotions. Now not to burden us with too much

English text of "The Edict" as in Edmund Everard, *The Great Pressures and Grievances of the Protestants in France*, London, 1681. Appendix 4 in Roland Mousnier, *The Assassination of Henry IV*, trans. Joan Spencer (London: Faber and Faber, 1973), 316–47.

business at once, as also that the fury of War was not compatible with the establishment of Laws, how good soever they might be, we have hitherto deferred from time to time giving remedy herein. But now that it hath pleased God to give us a beginning of enjoying some Rest, we think we cannot imploy our self better, than to apply to that which may tend to the glory and service of his holy name, and to provide that he may be adored and prayed unto by all our Subjects: and if it hath not yet pleased him to permit it to be in one and the same form of Religion, that it may at the least be with one and the same intention, and with such rules that may prevent amongst them all troubles and tumults. . . . For this cause, we have upon the whole judged it necessary to give to all our said Subjects one general Law, Clear, Pure, and Absolute, by which they shall be regulated in all differences which have heretofore risen among them, or may hereafter rise, where-with the one and other may be contented, being framed according as the time requires: and having had no other regard in this deliberation than solely the Zeal we have to the service of God, praying that he would henceforward render to all our subjects a durable and Established peace. . . . We have by this Edict or Statute perpetuall and irrevocable said, declared, and ordained, saying, declaring, and ordaining;

That the memory of all things passed on the one part and the other, since the beginning of the month of *March*, 1585. untill our coming to the Crown, and also during the other precedent troubles, and the occasion of the same, shall remain extinguished and suppressed, as things that had never been. . . .

We prohibit to all our Subjects of what State and Condition soever they be, to renew the memory thereof, to attaque, resent, injure, or provoke one the other by reproaches for what is past, under any pretext or cause whatsoever, by disputing, contesting, quarrelling, reviling, or offending by factious words; but to contain themselves, and live peaceably together as Brethren, Friends, and fellow-Citizens, upon penalty for acting to the contrary, to be punished for breakers of Peace, and disturbers of the publick quiet.

We ordain, that the Catholick Religion shall be restored and re-established in all places, and quarters of this Kingdom and Countrey under our obedience, and where the exercise of the same hath been intermitted, to be there again, peaceably and freely exercised without any trouble or impediment. . . .

And not to leave any occasion of trouble and difference among our Subjects, we have permitted and do permit to those of the Reformed Religion, to live and dwell in all the Cities and places of this our Kingdom and Countreys under our obedience, without being inquired after, vexed, molested, or compelled to do any thing in Religion, contrary to their Conscience. . . .

We permit also to those of the said Religion to hold, and continue the Exercise of the same in all the Cities and Places under our obedience, where it hath by them been Established and made publick by many and divers times, in the Year 1586, and in 1597, until the end of the Month of *August*. . . .

In like manner the said Exercise may be Established, and re-established in all the Cities and Places where it hath been established, or ought to be by the Statute of Pacification, made in the Year 1577. . . .

As also not to exercise the said Religion in our Court, nor in our Territories and Countries beyond the Mountains, nor in our City of *Paris*, nor within five Leagues of the said City. . . .

We prohibit all Preachers, Readers, and others who speak in public, to use any words, discourse, or propositions tending to excite the People to Sedition; and we enjoin them to contain and comport themselves modestly, and to say nothing which shall not be for the instruction and edification of the Auditors, and maintaining the peace and tranquillity established by us in our said Kingdom. . . .

They shall also be obliged to keep and observe the Festivals of the Catholick Church, and shall not on the same dayes work, sell, or keep open shop, nor likewise the Artisans shall not work out of their shops, in their chambers or houses privately on the said Festivals, and other dayes forbidden, of any trade, the noise whereof may be heard without by those that pass by, or by the Neighbours. . . .

We ordain, that there shall not be made any difference or distinction upon the account of the said Religion, in receiving Scholars to be instructed in the Universities, Colledges, or Schools, nor of the sick or poor into Hospitals, sick houses or publick Almshouses. . . .

We Will and Ordain, that all those of the Reformed Religion, and others who have followed their party, of what State, Quality or Condition soever they be, shall be obliged and constrained by all due and reasonable wayes, and under the penalties contained in the said Edict or Statute relating thereunto, to pay tythes to the Curates, and other Ecclesiasticks, and to all others to whom they shall appertain. . . .

To the end to re-unite so much the better the minds and good will of our Subjects, as is our intention, and to take away all complaints for the future; We declare all those who make or shall make profession of the said Reformed Religion, to be capable of holding and exercising all Estates, Dignities, Offices, and publick charges whatsoever. . . .

We declare all Sentences, Judgments, Procedures, Seisures, Sales, and Decrees made and given against those of the Reformed Religion, as well living as dead, from the death of the deceased King *Henry* the Second our most honoured Lord and Father in Law, upon the occasion of the said Religion, Tumults and Troubles since happening, as also the execution of the same Judgments and Decrees, from henceforward cancelled, revoked, and annulled. . . .

Those also of the said Religion shall depart and desist henceforward from all Practices, Negotiations, and Intelligences, as well within as without our Kingdom; and the said Assemblies and Councels established within the Provinces, shall readily separate, and also all the Leagues and Associations made or to be made under what pretext soever, to the prejudice of our present Edict, shall be cancelled and annulled, . . . prohibiting most expresly to all our Subjects to make henceforwards any Assesments or Leavy's of Money, Fortifications, Enrolments of men, Congregations and Assemblies of other than such as are permitted by our present Edict, and without Arms. . . .

We give in command to the People of our said Courts of Parliaments, Chambers of our Courts, and Courts of our Aids, Bayliffs, Chief-Justices, Provosts and other our Justices and Officers to whom it appertains, and to their Leivetenants, that they cause to be read, published, and Registred this present Edict and Ordinance in their Courts and Jurisdictions, and the same keep punctually, and the contents of the same to cause to be injoyned and used fully and peaceably to all those to whom it shall belong, ceasing and making to cease all troubles and obstructions to the contrary, for such is our pleasure: and in witness hereof we have signed these presents with our own hand; and to the end to make it a thing firm and stable for ever, we have caused to put and indorse our Seal to the same. Given at *Nantes* in the Month of *April* in the year of Grace 1598. and of our Reign the ninth.

Signed

HENRY

■ Discussion Questions

1. What are the edict's principal objectives?
2. In what ways does the edict balance the demands of French Catholics and Protestants?
3. What limits does the edict place on Protestants' religious rights?
4. Did Henry IV regard this edict as a permanent solution to the religious divisions in the realm?

39. Saint Ignatius of Loyola, *A New Kind of Catholicism*   (1546, 1549, 1553)

The interests of Ignatius of Loyola (1491–1556), born of a Spanish noble family, centered more on chivalry and national glory than religion before his serious injury in battle. While recovering, he experienced a conversion when he began reading the only books available to him, The Golden Legend *(about saints' lives) and the* Life of Christ. *Entering a monastery, he started work on* The Spiritual Exercises, *a manual of discernment for the pilgrim journeying to God. After studying at the University of Paris, Ignatius, Francis Xavier (1506–1552), and other friends made vows of chastity and poverty, determining to travel to Jerusalem. When this became impossible, they went to Italy. The Society of Jesus (the Jesuits), founded by Ignatius and his early companions, was officially recognized by Pope Paul III in 1540 as a new order directly under the papacy. Its spirituality would be expressed most prominently in teaching and missionary work. The letters of Ignatius evince a new form of Catholic spiritual expression that was active and apostolic in its orientation. It was less a "response" to Protestantism than a model for Catholic life and work. Along with the works of other early Jesuits, it embodied a new spirit that so many had sought but not found in the late medieval church.*

Conduct at Trent: On Helping Others, 1546

Our main aim [to God's greater glory] during this undertaking at Trent is to put into practice (as a group that lives together in one appropriate place) preaching, confessions and readings, teaching children, giving good example, visiting the poor in the hospitals, exhorting those around us, each of us according to the different talents he may happen to have, urging on as many as possible to greater piety and prayer. . . .

In their preaching they should not refer to points of conflict between Protestants and Catholics, but simply exhort all to upright conduct and to ecclesiastical practice, urging everyone to full self-knowledge and to greater knowledge and love of their Creator and Lord, with frequent allusions to the Council. At the end of each session, they should (as has been mentioned) lead prayers for the Council.

They should do the same with readings as with sermons, trying their best to influence people with greater love of their Creator and Lord as they explain the meaning of what is read; similarly, they should lead their hearers to pray for the Council. . . .

They should spend some time, as convenient, in the elementary teaching of youngsters, depending on the means and disposition of all involved, and with more or less explanation according to the capacity of the pupils. . . . Let them visit the almshouses once or twice a day, at times that are convenient for the patients' health, hearing confessions and consoling the poor, if possible taking them something, and urging them to the sort of prayers mentioned above for confession. If there are three of ours in Trent, each should visit the poor at least once every four days.

When they are urging people in their dealings with them to go to confession and communion, to say mass frequently, to undertake the Spiritual Exercises and other good works, they should also be urging them to pray for the Council.

From *Saint Ignatius of Loyola, Personal Writings: Reminiscences, Spiritual Diary, Select Letters, Including the Text of The Spiritual Exercises,* ed. and trans. Joseph A. Munitiz and Philip Endean (New York: Penguin Books, 1996), 165, 166, 230, 233–34, 257, 259, 262–63.

It was said that there are advantages in being slow to speak and measured in one's statements when doctrinal definitions are involved. The opposite is true when one is urging people to look to their spiritual progress. Then one should be eloquent and ready to talk, full of sympathy and affection.

SPREADING GOD'S WORD IN A GERMAN UNIVERSITY, 1549

The aim that they should have above all before their eyes is that intended by the Supreme Pontiff who has sent them: to help the University of Ingolstadt, and as far as is possible the whole of Germany, in all that concerns purity of faith, obedience to the Church, and firmness and soundness of doctrine and upright living. . . .

They must be very competent in them, and teach solid doctrine without many technical terms (which are unpopular), especially if these are hard to understand. The lectures should be learned yet clear, sustained in argument yet not long-winded, and delivered with attention to style. . . . Besides these academic lectures, it seems opportune on feast days to hold sermons on Bible readings, more calculated to move hearts and form consciences than to produce learned minds. . . . They should make efforts to attract their students into a friendship of spiritual quality, and if possible towards confession and making the Spiritual Exercises, even in the full form, if they seem suitable to join the Society. . . .

On occasion they should give time to works of mercy of a more visible character, such as in hospitals and prisons and helping other kinds of poor; such works arouse a "sweet fragrance" in the Lord. Opportunity may also arise to act as peacemakers in quarrels and to teach basic Christian doctrine to the uneducated. Taking account of local conditions and the persons concerned, prudence will dictate whether they should act themselves or through others.

They should make efforts to make friends with the leaders of their opponents, as also with those who are most influential among the heretics or those who are suspected of it yet seem not absolutely immovable. They must try to bring them back from their error by sensitive skill and signs of love. . . . All must try to have at their finger-tips the main points concerning dogmas of faith that are subjects of controversy with heretics, especially at the time and place when they are present, and with those persons with whom they are dealing. Thus they will be able, whenever opportunity arises, to put forward and defend the Catholic truth, to refute errors and to strengthen the doubtful and wavering, whether by lectures and sermons or in the confessional and in conversations. . . .

It will be helpful to lead people, as far as possible, to open themselves to God's grace, exhorting them to a desire for salvation, to prayer, to alms, and to everything that conduces to receiving grace or increasing it. . . .

Let [the duke] understand also what glory it will mean for him if he is the first to introduce into Germany seminaries in the form of such colleges, to foster sound doctrine and religion.

THE FINAL WORD ON OBEDIENCE, 1553, TO THE BROTHERS IN PORTUGAL

To form an idea of the exceptional intrinsic value of this obedience in the eyes of God Our Lord, one should weigh both the worth of the noble sacrifice offered, involving the highest human power, and the completeness of the self-offering undertaken, as one strips oneself of self, becoming a "living victim" pleasing to the Divine Majesty. Another indication is the intensity of the difficulty experienced as one conquers self for love of God, opposing the natural human inclination felt by us all to follow our own opinions. . . .

Let us be unpretentious and let us be gentle! God Our Lord will grant the grace to enable you, gently and lovingly, to maintain constantly the offering you have made to Him. . . .

All that has been said does not exclude your bringing before your superiors a contrary opinion that may have occurred to you, once you have prayed about the matter and you feel that it would be proper and in accord with your respect for God to do so. . . . Such is the model on which divine Providence "gently disposes all things," so that the lower via the middle, and the middle via the higher, are led to their final ends. . . . The same can be seen upon the earth with respect to all secular constitutions that are duly established, and with respect to the ecclesiastical hierarchy, which is subordinated to you in virtue of holy obedience to select among the many routes open to you that which will bring you back to Portugal as soon and as safely as possible. So I order you in the name of Christ Our Lord to do this, even if it will be so as to return soon to India. . . . Firstly, you are well aware how important for the upkeep and advancement of Christianity in those lands, as also in Guinea and Brazil, is the good order that the King of Portugal can grant from his kingdom. When a prince of such Christian desires and holy intentions as is the King of Portugal receives information from someone of your experience about the state of affairs in those parts, you can imagine what influence this will have on him to do much more in the service of God Our Lord and for the good of those countries that you will describe to him. . . .

You are also aware how important it is for the good of the Indies that the persons sent there should be suitable for the aim that one is pursuing in those and in other lands. . . . Quite apart from all these reasons, which apply to furthering the good of India, it seems to me that you would fire the King's enthusiasm for the Ethiopian project, which has been planned for so many years without anything effective having been seen. Similarly, with regard to the Congo and Brazil, you could give no small help from Portugal, which you cannot do from India as there are not the same commercial relations. If people in India consider that your presence is important given your post, you can continue to act as superior no less from Portugal than from Japan or China, and probably much better. Just as you have gone away on other occasions for longer periods, do the same now.

▪ Discussion Questions

1. What does the Catholic life mean to Ignatius? What is innovative in his program for Catholic reform?
2. What advice does Ignatius give about dealing with the problem of heresy?
3. What role does Ignatius envision Jesuits playing throughout Europe and the rest of the world?
4. How does Ignatius think political leaders can be enlisted to support the aims of the reform movement?

40. Galileo Galilei, *Letter to the Grand Duchess Christina*   (1615)

Italian-born and educated, Galileo Galilei (1564–1642) was among the most illustrious proponents of the new science in the seventeenth century. Early in his studies, he embraced Copernicus's theory that the sun, not the Earth, was at the center of the universe. Having improved on the newly invented telescope in 1609, he was able to substantiate the heliocentric view through his observations of the moon and other planets. Because Galileo's work challenged traditional scientific views, it sparked considerable controversy. In the letter excerpted here, written in 1615 to the Grand Duchess Christina of Tuscany, an important Catholic patron of learning, Galileo defends the validity of his findings while striving to separate matters of religious faith from the study of natural phenomena.

Stillman Drake, trans., *Discoveries and Opinions of Galileo* (New York: Doubleday, 1957), 175–86.

GALILEO GALILEI TO THE MOST SERENE GRAND DUCHESS MOTHER

Some years ago, as Your Serene Highness well knows, I discovered in the heavens many things that had not been seen before our own age. The novelty of these things, as well as some consequences which followed from them in contradiction to the physical notions commonly held among academic philosophers, stirred up against me no small number of professors—as if I had placed these things in the sky with my own hands in order to upset nature and overturn the sciences. . . .

Well, the passage of time has revealed to everyone the truths that I previously set forth. . . . But some, besides allegiance to their original error, possess I know not what fanciful interest in remaining hostile not so much toward the things in question as toward their discoverer. No longer being able to deny them, these men now take refuge in obstinate silence, but being more than ever exasperated by that which has pacified and quieted other men, they divert their thoughts to other fancies and seek new ways to damage me. . . .

Persisting in their original resolve to destroy me and everything mine by any means they can think of, these men are aware of my views in astronomy and philosophy. They know that as to the arrangement of the parts of the universe, I hold the sun to be situated motionless in the center of the revolution of the celestial orbs while the earth rotates on its axis and revolves about the sun. . . .

Now as to the false aspersions which they so unjustly seek to cast upon me, I have thought it necessary to justify myself in the eyes of all men, whose judgment in matters of religion and of reputation I must hold in great esteem. I shall therefore discourse of the particulars which these men produce to make this opinion detested and to have it condemned not merely as false but as heretical. To this end they make a shield of their hypocritical zeal for religion. They go about invoking the Bible, which they would have minister to their deceitful purposes. Contrary to the sense of the Bible and the intention of the holy Fathers, if I am not mistaken, they would extend such authorities until even in purely physical matters—where faith is not involved—they would have us altogether abandon reason and the evidence of our senses in favor of some biblical passage, though under the surface meaning of its words this passage may contain a different sense. . . .

The reason produced for condemning the opinion that the earth moves and the sun stands still is that in many places in the Bible one may read that the sun moves and the earth stands still. Since the Bible cannot err, it follows as a necessary consequence that anyone takes an erroneous and heretical position who maintains that the sun is inherently motionless and the earth movable.

With regard to this argument, I think in the first place that it is very pious to say and prudent to affirm that the holy Bible can never speak untruth—whenever its true meaning is understood. But I believe nobody will deny that it is often very abstruse, and may say things which are quite different from what its bare words signify. Hence in expounding the Bible if one were always to confine oneself to the unadorned grammatical meaning, one might fall into error. Not only contradictions and propositions far from true might thus be made to appear in the Bible, but even grave heresies and follies. Thus it would be necessary to assign to God feet, hands, and eyes, as well as corporeal and human affections, such as anger, repentance, hatred, and sometimes even the forgetting of things past and ignorance of those to come. These propositions uttered by the Holy Ghost were set down in that manner by the sacred scribes in order to accommodate them to the capacities of the common people, who are rude and unlearned. For the sake of those who deserve to be separated from the herd, it is necessary that wise expositors should produce the true senses of such passages, together with the special reasons for which they were set down in these words. This doctrine is so widespread and so definite with all theologians that it would be superfluous to adduce evidence for it.

Hence I think that I may reasonably conclude that whenever the Bible has occasion to speak of any physical conclusion (especially those which are very abstruse and hard to understand), the rule has been observed of avoiding confusion in the minds of the common people which would render them contumacious toward the higher mysteries. Now the Bible, merely to condescend to popular capacity, has not hesitated to obscure some very important pronouncements, attributing to God himself some qualities extremely remote from (and even contrary to) His essence. Who, then, would positively declare that this principle has been set aside, and the Bible has confined itself rigorously to the bare and restricted sense of its words, when speaking but casually of the earth, of water, of the sun, or of any other created thing? Especially in view of the fact that these things in no way concern the primary purpose of the sacred writings, which is the service of God and the salvation of souls—matters infinitely beyond the comprehension of the common people.

This being granted, I think that in discussions of physical problems we ought to begin not from the authority of scriptural passages, but from sense-experiences and necessary demonstrations; for the holy Bible and the phenomena of nature proceed alike from the divine Word, the former as the dictate of the Holy Ghost and the latter as the observant executrix of God's commands. It is necessary for the Bible, in order to be accommodated to the understanding of every man, to speak many things which appear to differ from the absolute truth so far as the bare meaning of the words is concerned. But Nature, on the other hand, is inexorable and immutable; she never transgresses the laws imposed upon her, or cares a whit whether her abstruse reasons and methods of operations are understandable to men. For that reason it appears that nothing physical which sense-experience sets before our eyes, or which necessary demonstrations prove to us, ought to be called in question (much less condemned) upon the testimony of biblical passages which may have some different meaning beneath their words. For the Bible is not chained in every expression to conditions as strict as those which govern all physical effects; nor is God any less excellently revealed in Nature's actions than in the sacred statements of the Bible. . . .

From this I do not mean to infer that we need not have an extraordinary esteem for the passages of holy Scripture. On the contrary, having arrived at any certainties in physics, we ought to utilize these as the most appropriate aids in the true exposition of the Bible and in the investigation of those meanings which are necessarily contained therein, for these must be concordant with demonstrated truths. I should judge that the authority of the Bible was designed to persuade men of those articles and propositions which, surpassing all human reasoning, could not be made credible by science, or by any other means than through the very mouth of the Holy Spirit.

Yet even in those propositions which are not matters of faith, this authority ought to be preferred over that of all human writings which are supported only by bare assertions or probable arguments, and not set forth in a demonstrative way. This I hold to be necessary and proper to the same extent that divine wisdom surpasses all human judgment and conjecture.

But I do not feel obliged to believe that that same God who has endowed us with senses, reason, and intellect has intended to forgo their use and by some other means to give us knowledge which we can attain by them. He would not require us to deny sense and reason in physical matters which are set before our eyes and minds by direct experience or necessary demonstrations. This must be especially true in those sciences of which but the faintest trace (and that consisting of conclusions) is to be found in the Bible. Of astronomy, for instance, so little is found that none of the planets except Venus are so much as mentioned, and this only once or twice under the name of "Lucifer." If the sacred scribes had had any intention of teaching people certain arrangements and motions of the heavenly bodies, or had they wished us to derive such knowledge from the Bible, then in my opinion they would not have spoken of these matters so sparingly in comparison with the infinite number of admirable conclusions which are demonstrated in that science. . . .

From these things it follows as a necessary consequence that, since the Holy Ghost did not intend to teach us whether heaven moves or stands still, whether its shape is spherical or like a discus or extended in a plane, nor whether the earth is located at its center or off to one side, then so much the less was it intended to settle for us any other conclusion of the same kind. And the motion or rest of the earth and the sun is so closely linked with the things just named, that without a determination of the one, neither side can be taken in the other matters. Now if the Holy Spirit has purposely neglected to teach us propositions of this sort as irrelevant to the highest goal (that is, to our salvation), how can anyone affirm that it is obligatory to take sides on them, and that one belief is required by faith, while the other side is erroneous? Can an opinion be heretical and yet have no concern with the salvation of souls? Can the Holy Ghost be asserted not to have intended teaching us something that does concern our salvation? I would say here something that was heard from an ecclesiastic of the most eminent degree: "That the intention of the Holy Ghost is to teach us how one goes to heaven, not how heaven goes." . . .

From this it is seen that the interpretation which we impose upon passages of Scripture would be false whenever it disagreed with demonstrated truths. And therefore we should seek the incontrovertible sense of the Bible with the assistance of demonstrated truth, and not in any way try to force the hand of Nature or deny experiences and rigorous proofs in accordance with the mere sound of words that may appeal to our frailty. . . .

To that end they would forbid him the use of reason, divine gift of Providence, and would abuse the just authority of holy Scripture—which, in the general opinion of theologians, can never oppose manifest experiences and necessary demonstrations when rightly understood and applied. If I am correct, it will stand them in no stead to go running to the Bible to cover up their inability to understand (let alone resolve) their opponents' arguments.

■ Discussion Questions

1. What is Galileo's goal in writing this letter to the Grand Duchess?
2. What is the basis of the attacks by Galileo's critics?
3. According to Galileo, what role should the Bible play in scientific inquiry?
4. Historians have credited Galileo for helping to popularize the principles and methods of the new science. How does this document support this view?

CHAPTER 13

State Building and the Search for Order, 1648–1690

The wars over religion not only left bitter memories in late-seventeenth-century Europe but also ruined economies and weakened governments. Politically, the quest for order fueled the development of two rival systems of state building: absolutism and constitutionalism, with France (first document) and England (third document), respectively, taking the lead. Despite their differences, rulers in both systems centralized their power and expanded their bureaucracies, casting an increasingly wide net over their subjects' lives. The second document indicates that not everyone submitted willingly to the expansion of state power, but such resistance was typically fruitless.

41. Louis de Rouvroy, Duke of Saint-Simon, *Memoirs* (1694–1723)

A nobleman and godson of Louis XIV, Louis de Rouvroy, duke of Saint-Simon (1675–1755), was raised at the royal palace of Versailles. He began recording his life and impressions of the court at the age of nineteen and continued for almost three decades. The result was his multivolume Memoirs, *which paint an intimate portrait of the Sun King and the workings of the absolutist state. Saint-Simon was not an entirely objective observer. Never achieving great success within the court, he often viewed it through the lens of his own resentment. This excerpt provides insight into the reasons behind Louis XIV's move to Versailles and his method of rule there.*

Let me touch now upon some other incidents in his career, and upon some points in his character.

He early showed a disinclination for Paris. The troubles that had taken place there during the minority made him regard the place as dangerous; he wished, too, to render himself venerable by hiding himself from the eyes of the multitude; all these considerations fixed him at St. Germains soon after the death of the Queen, his mother. It was to that place he began to attract the world by fêtes and gallantries, and by making it felt that he wished to be often seen.

His love for Madame de la Vallière, which was at first kept secret, occasioned frequent excursions to Versailles, then a little card castle, which had been built by Louis XIII.—annoyed, and his suite still more so, at being frequently obliged to sleep in a wretched inn there, after he had been out hunting in the forest of Saint Leger. That monarch rarely slept at Versailles more than one night, and then from necessity; the King, his son, slept there, so that he might be more in

Bayle St. John, trans., *The Memoirs of the Duke of Saint Simon,* vol. II (Philadelphia: Gebbie and Co., 1890), 363–69.

private with his mistress; pleasures unknown to the hero and just man, worthy son of Saint Louis, who built the little château.

These excursions of Louis XIV. by degrees gave birth to those immense buildings he erected at Versailles; and their convenience for a numerous court, so different from the apartments at St. Germains, led him to take up his abode there entirely shortly after the death of the Queen. He built an infinite number of apartments, which were asked for by those who wished to pay their court to him; whereas at St. Germains nearly everybody was obliged to lodge in the town, and the few who found accommodation at the château were strangely inconvenienced.

The frequent fêtes, the private promenades at Versailles, the journeys, were means on which the King seized in order to distinguish or mortify the courtiers, and thus render them more assiduous in pleasing him. He felt that of real favours he had not enough to bestow; in order to keep up the spirit of devotion, he therefore unceasingly invented all sorts of ideal ones, little preferences and petty distinctions, which answered his purpose as well.

He was exceedingly jealous of the attention paid him. Not only did he notice the presence of the most distinguished courtiers, but those of inferior degree also. He looked to the right and to the left, not only upon rising but upon going to bed, at his meals, in passing through his apartments, or his gardens of Versailles, where alone the courtiers were allowed to follow him; he saw and noticed everybody; not one escaped him, not even those who hoped to remain unnoticed. He marked well all absentees from the court, found out the reason of their absence, and never lost an opportunity of acting towards them as the occasion might seem to justify. With some of the courtiers (the most distinguished), it was a demerit not to make the court their ordinary abode; with others 'twas a fault to come but rarely; for those who never or scarcely ever came it was certain disgrace. When their names were in any way mentioned, "I do not know them," the King would reply haughtily. Those who presented themselves but seldom were thus characterised: "They are people I never see"; these decrees were irrevocable. He could not bear people who liked Paris.

Louis XIV. took great pains to be well informed of all that passed everywhere; in the public places, in the private houses, in society and familiar intercourse. His spies and telltales were infinite. He had them of all species; many who were ignorant that their information reached him; others who knew it; others who wrote to him direct, sending their letters through channels he indicated; and all these letters were seen by him alone, and always before everything else; others who sometimes spoke to him secretly in his cabinet, entering by the back stairs. These unknown means ruined an infinite number of people of all classes who never could discover the cause; often ruined them very unjustly; for the King, once prejudiced, never altered his opinion, or so rarely, that nothing was more rare. He had, too, another fault, very dangerous for others and often for himself, since it deprived him of good subjects. He had an excellent memory; in this way, that if he saw a man who, twenty years before, perhaps, had in some manner offended him, he did not forget the man, though he might forget the offence. This was enough, however, to exclude the person from all favour. The representations of a minister, of a general, of his confessor even, could not move the King. He would not yield.

The most cruel means by which the King was informed of what was passing—for many years before anybody knew it—was that of opening letters. The promptitude and dexterity with which they were opened passes understanding. He saw extracts from all the letters in which there were passages that the chiefs of the post-office, and then the minister who governed it, thought ought to go before him; entire letters, too, were sent to him, when their contents seemed to justify the sending. Thus the chiefs of the post, nay, the principal clerks were in a position to suppose what they pleased and against whom they pleased. A word of contempt against the King or the government, a joke, a detached phrase, was enough. It is incredible how many people, justly or unjustly, were more or less ruined, always without resource, without trial, and without knowing why. The secret was impenetrable; for nothing ever cost the King less than profound silence and dissimulation. . . .

He liked splendour, magnificence, and profusion in everything: you pleased him if you shone through the brilliancy of your houses, your clothes, your table, your equipages. Thus a taste for extravagance and luxury was disseminated through all classes of society; causing infinite harm, and leading to general confusion of rank and to ruin.

▪ Discussion Questions

1. How did Louis XIV use court etiquette as a form of power?
2. Why did nobles reside at Versailles? What benefits did they gain?
3. What is Saint-Simon's attitude toward Louis XIV's style of governing?
4. In what ways did court life embody the principles of absolutism?

42. Ludwig Fabritius, *The Revolt of Stenka Razin* (1670)

Despite its geographical and cultural isolation from the rest of Europe, Russia followed France's lead down the path of absolutism. In the process, Tsar Alexei (r. 1645–1676) legally combined millions of slaves and free peasants into a single serf class bound to the land and to their aristocratic masters. Not everyone passively accepted this fate, however. In 1667, a Cossack named Stenka Razin led a revolt against serfdom that gained considerable support among people whose social and economic status was threatened by the tsar's policies, including soldiers of peasant stock. Razin's ultimate defeat at the hands of the tsar elucidates the close ties between the Russian government's enhanced power and the enforcement of serfdom. Ludwig Fabritius, a Dutch soldier who lived in Russia from 1660 to 1677 while employed as a military expert in the Russian army, wrote this account of one stage of the revolt.

Then Stenka with his company started off upstream, rowing as far as Tsaritsyn, whence it took him only one day's journey to Panshin, a small town situated on the Don. Here he began straightaway quietly gathering the common people around him, giving them money, and promises of great riches if they would be loyal to him and help to exterminate the treacherous boyars.[1]

This lasted the whole winter, until by about spring he had assembled 4,000 to 5,000 men. With these he came to Tsaritsyn and demanded the immediate surrender of the fortress; the rabble soon achieved their purpose, and although the governor tried to take refuge in a tower, he soon had to give himself up as he was deserted by one and all. Stenka immediately had the wretched governor hanged; and all the goods they found belonging to the Tsar and his officers as well as to the merchants were confiscated and distributed among the rabble.

Stenka now began once more to make preparations. Since the plains are not cultivated, the people have to bring their corn from Nizhniy-Novgorod and Kazan down the Volga in big boats known as *nasady*, and everything destined for Astrakhan has first to pass Tsaritsyn. Stenka Razin duly noted this, and occupied the whole of the Volga, so that nothing could get through to Astrakhan. Here he captured a few hundred merchants with their valuable goods, taking possession of all kinds of fine linen, silks, striped silk material, sables, soft leather, ducats, talers, and many thousands of rubles in Russian money and merchandise of every description. . . .

---

[1]**boyars:** Noblemen.

Anthony Glenn Cross, ed. *Russia under Western Eyes, 1517–1825* (London: Elek Books, 1971), 120–23.

In the meantime four regiments of *streltsy*[2] were dispatched from Moscow to subdue these brigands. They arrived with their big boats and as they were not used to the water, were easily beaten. Here Stenka Razin gained possession of a large amount of ammunition and artillery-pieces and everything else he required. While the above-mentioned *streltsy* were sent from Moscow, about 5,000 men were ordered up from Astrakhan by water and by land to capture Stenka Razin. As soon as he had finished with the former, he took up a good position, and, being in possession of reliable information regarding our forces, he left Tsaritsyn and came to meet us half way at Chernyy Yar, confronting us before we had suspected his presence or received any information about him. We stopped at Chernyy Yar for a few days and sent out scouts by water and by land, but were unable to obtain any definite information. On 10 July [*sic*: June] a council of war was held at which it was decided to advance and seek out Stenka. The next morning, at 8 o'clock, our look-outs on the water came hurriedly and raised the alarm as the Cossacks were following at their heels. We got out of our boats and took up battle positions. General Knyaz Semen Ivanovich Lvov went through the ranks and reminded all the men to do their duty and to remember the oath they had taken to His Majesty the Tsar, to fight like honest soldiers against these irresponsible rebels, whereupon they all unanimously shouted: "Yes, we will give our lives for His Majesty the Tsar, and will fight to the last drop of our blood."

In the meantime Stenka prepared for battle and deployed on a wide front; to all those who had no rifle he gave a long pole, burnt a little at one end, and with a rag or small hook attached. They presented a strange sight on the plain from afar, and the common soldiers imagined that, since there were so many flags and standards, there must be a host of people. They [the common soldiers] held a consultation and at once decided that this was the chance for which they had been waiting so long, and with all their flags and drums they ran over to the enemy. They began kissing and embracing one another and swore with life and limb to stand together and to exterminate the treacherous boyars, to throw off the yoke of slavery, and to become free men.

The general looked at the officers and the officers at the general, and no one knew what to do; one said this, and another that, until finally it was decided that they and the general should get into the boats and withdraw to Astrakhan. But the rascally *streltsy* of Chernyy Yar stood on the walls and towers, turning their weapons on us and opened fire; some of them ran out of the fortress and cut us off from the boats, so that we had no means of escape. In the meantime those curs of ours who had gone over to the Cossacks came up from behind. We numbered about eighty men, officers, noblemen, and clerks. Murder at once began. Then, however, Stenka Razin ordered that no more officers were to be killed, saying that there must be a few good men among them who should be pardoned, whilst those others who had not lived in amity with their men should be condemned to well-deserved punishment by the Ataman and his *Krug*. [A *Krug* is a meeting convened by the order of the Ataman, at which the Cossacks stand in a circle with the standard in the centre; the Ataman then takes his place beside his best officers, to whom he divulges his wishes, ordering them to make these known to the common brothers and to hear their opinion on the matter.] . . .

A *Krug* was accordingly called and Stenka asked through his chiefs how the general and his officers had treated the soldiers under their command. Thereupon the unscrupulous curs, *streltsy* as well as soldiers, unanimously called out that there was not one of them who deserved to remain alive, and they all asked that their father Stepan Timofeyevich Razin should order them to be cut down. This was granted with the exception of General Knyaz Semen Ivanovich Lvov, whose life was specially spared by Stenka himself. The officers were now brought in order of rank out of the tower, into which they had been thrown bound hand and foot the previous day, their ropes were cut and they were led outside the gate. When all the bloodthirsty curs had lined up, each

---

[2] **streltsy:** Sharpshooters.

was eager to deal his former superior the first blow, one with the sword, another with the lance, another with the scimitar, and others again with martels, so that as soon as an officer was pushed into the ring, the curs immediately killed him with their many wounds; indeed, some were cut to pieces and straightaway thrown into the Volga. My stepfather, Paul Rudolf Beem, and Lt. Col. Wundrum and many other officers, senior and junior, were cut down before my eyes.

My own time had not yet come: this I could tell by the wonderful way in which God rescued me, for as I—half-dead—now awaited the final blow, my [former] orderly, a young soldier, came and took me by my bound arms and tried to take me down the hill. As I was already half-dead, I did not move and did not know what to do, but he came back and took me by the arms and led me, bound as I was, through the throng of curs, down the hill into the boat and immediately cut my arms free, saying that I should rest in peace here and that he would be responsible for me and do his best to save my life. . . . Then my guardian angel told me not to leave the boat, and left me. He returned in the evening and brought me a piece of bread which I enjoyed since I had had nothing to eat for two days.

The following day all our possessions were looted and gathered together under the main flag, so that both our bloodthirsty curs and the Cossacks got their share.

■ Discussion Questions

1. What motivated Razin and his followers to take action?
2. Why were Razin and his forces able to defeat the tsar's soldiers?
3. What does this account suggest about the role of the military in the growth of the Russian government's authority?
4. With whom do you think Fabritius's sympathies lie, and why?

43. British Parliament, *The English Bill of Rights* (1689)

Louis XIV had many admirers in Europe, including King James II of England. Unlike Louis, however, James faced a major challenge to his power: Parliament. The king and Parliament had been at odds for decades over the nature of royal authority, and James's absolutist policies proved too much for Parliament to bear. As a result, in 1688 Parliament ousted the king and offered the throne to Prince William of Orange and his wife, Mary, the eldest of James's adult daughters. In exchange, William and Mary agreed to accept the Bill of Rights, which legally defined the role of Parliament as the monarchy's partner in government. The bill marked the victory of constitutionalism over absolutism in England and formed the cornerstone of the idea that government should ensure certain rights by law to protect citizens from the dangers of arbitrary power.

Whereas the said late King James II having abdicated the government, and the throne being thereby vacant, his Highness the prince of Orange (whom it hath pleased Almighty God to make the glorious instrument of delivering this kingdom from popery and arbitrary power) did (by the advice of the lords spiritual and temporal, and diverse principal persons of the Commons) cause letters to be written to the lords spiritual and temporal, being Protestants, and other letters to the several counties, cities, universities, boroughs, and Cinque Ports, for the choosing of such persons to represent them, as were of right to be sent to parliament, to meet and sit at Westminster upon the two and twentieth day of January, in this year 1689, in order to such an

Great Britain, *The Statutes,* rev. ed. (London: Eyre and Spottiswoode, 1871), vol. II, 10–12.

establishment as that their religion, laws, and liberties might not again be in danger of being subverted; upon which letters elections have been accordingly made.

And thereupon the said lords spiritual and temporal and Commons, pursuant to their respective letters and elections, being now assembled in a full and free representation of this nation, taking into their most serious consideration the best means for attaining the ends aforesaid, do in the first place (as their ancestors in like case have usually done), for the vindication and assertion of their ancient rights and liberties, declare:

1. That the pretended power of suspending laws, or the execution of laws, by regal authority, without consent of parliament is illegal.

2. That the pretended power of dispensing with the laws, or the execution of law by regal authority, as it hath been assumed and exercises of late, is illegal.

3. That the commission for erecting the late court of commissioners for ecclesiastical causes, and all other commissions and courts of like nature, are illegal and pernicious.

4. That levying money for or to the use of the crown by pretense of prerogative, without grant of parliament, for longer time or in other manner than the same is or shall be granted, is illegal.

5. That it is the right of the subjects to petition the king, and all commitments and prosecutions for such petitioning are illegal.

6. That the raising or keeping a standing army within the kingdom in time of peace, unless it be with consent of parliament, is against law.

7. That the subjects which are Protestants may have arms for their defense suitable to their conditions, and as allowed by law.

8. That election of members of parliament ought to be free.

9. That the freedom of speech, and debates or proceedings in parliament, ought not to be impeached or questioned in any court or place out of parliament.

10. That excessive bail ought not to be required, nor excessive fines imposed, nor cruel and unusual punishments inflicted.

11. That jurors ought to be duly impaneled and returned, and jurors which pass upon men in trials for high treason ought to be freeholders.

12. That all grants and promises of fines and forfeitures of particular persons before conviction are illegal and void.

13. And that for redress of all grievances, and for the amending, strengthening, and preserving of the laws, parliament ought to be held frequently.

And they do claim, demand, and insist upon all and singular the premises, as their undoubted rights and liberties: and that no declarations, judgments, doings, or proceedings, to the prejudice of the people in any of the said premises, ought in any wise to be drawn hereafter into consequence or example.

To which demand of their rights they are particularly encouraged by the declaration of his Highness the prince of Orange, as being the only means for obtaining a full redress and remedy therein.

Having therefore an entire confidence that his said Highness the prince of Orange will perfect the deliverance so far advanced by him, and will still preserve them from the violation of their rights, which they have here asserted, and from all other attempt upon their religion, rights, and liberties:

The said lords spiritual and temporal, and commons, assembled at Westminster, do resolve that William and Mary, prince and princess of Orange, be, and be declared, king and queen of England, France, and Ireland, the dominions thereunto belonging, to hold the crown and royal dignity of the said kingdoms and dominions to them the said prince and princess during their lives. . . .

Upon which their said Majesties did accept the crown and royal dignity of the kingdoms of England, France, and Ireland, and the dominions thereunto belonging, according to the resolution and desire of the said lords and commons contained in the said declaration.

■ Discussion Questions

1. In what ways does the Bill of Rights limit the powers of the crown?
2. What role does the Bill of Rights grant Parliament in government?
3. How does the Bill of Rights give weight to the attitude of members of Parliament who thought that they had "made" the king and queen, William and Mary?

CHAPTER 14

The Atlantic System and Its Consequences, 1690–1740

The growth of European domestic economies and overseas colonization in the eighteenth century infused Europe with money, new products, and a new sense of optimism. Yet, as the first document illustrates, the good times came at a horrible price for the millions of African slaves who formed the economic backbone of the colonial system. Changes were afoot on the political front, too, with the stabilization of the European state system. Consequently, states such as Russia shone more brightly over the political landscape while others lost their luster. The second and third documents reveal that intellectual circles were also ablaze with change as scholars and writers cast political, social, and religious issues in a new, critical light. Even women's traditional place in society was for the first time systematically called into question.

44. Olaudah Equiano, *The Interesting Narrative of the Life of Olaudah Equiano, Written by Himself* (1789)

The autobiography of Olaudah Equiano (c. 1745–1797) puts a human face on the eighteenth-century Atlantic slave trade and its tragic consequences. While historians debate whether he was born in what is now Nigeria or in the colonies, Equiano was captured by local raiders and sold into slavery in his early teens. He gained his freedom in 1766 and soon thereafter became a vocal supporter of the English abolitionist movement. Having learned English as a young man, he published his autobiography in 1789, a best-seller in its day, with numerous editions published in Britain and America. In this excerpt, Equiano recounts his experience on the slave ship that took him away from his homeland, his freedom, and his very identity. Millions of others shared this same fate.

The first object which saluted my eyes when I arrived on the coast was the sea, and a slave ship which was then riding at anchor and waiting for its cargo. These filled me with astonishment, which was soon converted into terror when I was carried on board. I was immediately handled and tossed up to see if I were sound by some of the crew, and I was now persuaded that I had gotten into a world of bad spirits and that they were going to kill me. Their complexions too differing so much from ours, their long hair and the language they spoke (which was very different from any I had ever heard) united to confirm me in this belief. Indeed such were the horrors of

---

Abridged and edited by Paul Edwards, *Equiano's Travels: His Autobiography* (London: Heinemann, 1967), 25–32.

my views and fears at the moment that, if ten thousand worlds had been my own, I would have freely parted with them all to have exchanged my condition with that of the meanest slave in my own country. When I looked round the ship too and saw a large furnace or copper boiling and a multitude of black people of every description chained together, every one of their countenances expressing dejection and sorrow, I no longer doubted of my fate; and quite overpowered with horror and anguish, I fell motionless on the deck and fainted. When I recovered a little I found some black people about me, who I believed were some of those who had brought me on board and had been receiving their pay; they talked to me in order to cheer me, but all in vain. I asked them if we were not to be eaten by those white men with horrible looks, red faces, and loose hair. They told me I was not, and one of the crew brought me a small portion of spirituous liquor in a wine glass, but being afraid of him I would not take it out of his hand. One of the blacks therefore took it from him and gave it to me, and I took a little down my palate, which instead of reviving me, as they thought it would, threw me into the greatest consternation at the strange feeling it produced, having never tasted such any liquor before. Soon after this the blacks who brought me on board went off, and left me abandoned to despair.

I now saw myself deprived of all chance of returning to my native country or even the least glimpse of hope of gaining the shore, which I now considered as friendly; and I even wished for my former slavery in preference to my present situation, which was filled with horrors of every kind, still heightened by my ignorance of what I was to undergo. I was not long suffered to indulge my grief; I was soon put down under the decks, and there I received such a salutation in my nostrils as I had never experienced in my life: so that with the loathsomeness of the stench and crying together, I became so sick and low that I was not able to eat, nor had I the least desire to taste anything. I now wished for the last friend, death, to relieve me; but soon, to my grief, two of the white men offered me eatables, and on my refusing to eat, one of them held me fast by the hands and laid me across I think the windlass, and tied my feet while the other flogged me severely. I had never experienced anything of this kind before, and although, not being used to the water, I naturally feared that element the first time I saw it, yet nevertheless could I have got over the nettings I would have jumped over the side, but I could not; and besides, the crew used to watch us very closely who were not chained down to the decks, lest we should leap into the water: and I have seen some of these poor African prisoners most severely cut for attempting to do so, and hourly whipped for not eating. This indeed was often the case with myself. In a little time after, amongst the poor chained men I found some of my own nation, which in a small degree gave ease to my mind. I inquired of these what was to be done with us; they gave me to understand we were to be carried to these white people's country to work for them. I then was a little revived, and thought if it were no worse than working, my situation was not so desperate: but still I feared I should be put to death, the white people looked and acted, as I thought, in so savage a manner; for I had never seen among my people such instances of brutal cruelty, and this not only shewn towards us blacks but also to some of the whites themselves. One white man in particular I saw, when we were permitted to be on deck, flogged so unmercifully with a large rope near the foremast that he died in consequence of it; and they tossed him over the side as they would have done a brute. This made me fear these people the more, and I expected nothing less than to be treated in the same manner. . . . At last, when the ship we were in had got in all her cargo, they made ready with many fearful noises, and we were all put under deck so that we could not see how they managed the vessel. But this disappointment was the last of my sorrow. The stench of the hold while we were on the coast was so intolerably loathsome that it was dangerous to remain there for any time, and some of us had been permitted to stay on the deck for the fresh air; but now that the whole ship's cargo were confined together it became absolutely pestilential. The closeness of the place and the heat of the climate, added to the number in the ship, which was so crowded that each had scarcely room to turn himself, almost suffocated us. This produced copious perspirations, so that the air soon became unfit for respiration from a variety of loathsome smells, and brought on a sickness among the slaves, of which many died, thus falling victims to the improvident avarice, as I may call it, of their purchasers. This wretched situation was again aggravated by the galling of the chains, now become insupportable, and the filth of the necessary tubs, into which the children often fell and were almost suffocated. The shrieks of the women and the groans of the dying rendered the whole a scene of horror almost inconceivable. Happily perhaps for myself I was soon reduced so low here that it was thought necessary to keep me almost always on deck, and from my extreme youth I was not put in fetters. In this situation I expected every hour to share the fate of my companions, some of whom were almost daily brought upon deck at the point of death, which I began to hope would soon put an end to my miseries. . . . At last we came in sight of the island of Barbados, at which the whites on board gave a great shout and made many signs of joy to us. We did not know what to think of this, but as the vessel drew nearer we plainly saw the harbour and other ships of different kinds and sizes, and we soon anchored amongst them off Bridgetown. Many merchants and planters now came on board, though it was in the evening. They put us in separate parcels and examined us attentively. They also made us jump, and pointed to the land, signifying we were to go there. . . . We were not many days in the merchant's custody before we were sold after their usual manner, which is this: On a signal given, (as the beat of a drum) the buyers rush at once into the yard where the slaves are confined, and make choice of that parcel they like best. The noise and clamour with which this is attended and the eagerness visible in the countenances of the buyers serve not a little to increase the apprehensions of the terrified Africans, who may well be supposed to consider them as the ministers of that destruction to which they think themselves devoted. In this manner, without scruple, are relations and friends separated, most of them never to see each other again. I remember in the vessel in which I was brought over, in the men's apartment there were several brothers who, in the sale, were sold in different lots; and it was very moving on this occasion to see and hear their cries at parting. O, ye nominal Christians! might not an African ask you, Learned you this from your God who says unto you, Do unto all men as you would men should do unto you?

■ Discussion Questions

1. What are Equiano's impressions of the white men on the ship and their treatment of the slaves?
2. How does this treatment reflect the slave traders' primary concerns?
3. What message do you think Equiano sought to convey to his readers?
4. To whom do you think Equiano's book especially appealed?

45. Montesquieu, *Persian Letters: Letter 37*   (1721)

As Europe's economy expanded, so did its intellectual horizons with the birth of the Enlightenment in the 1690s. Charles-Louis de Secondat, baron of Montesquieu (1689–1755), was an especially important literary figure on this front. In 1721, he published Persian Letters, *in which he uses fictional characters to explore an array of topics with the critical, reasoning spirit characteristic of the period. Letter 37 points to one of his and other Enlightenment writers' main targets: Louis XIV and his absolutist state. Along with its criticism of the king's vanity, ostentation, and life at court, the letter implicitly passes even more serious judgment on the aging ruler in noting his esteem for "oriental policies." Montesquieu condemns these same policies elsewhere in the letters as inhumane and unjust.*

Charles-Louis de Secondat, baron of Montesquieu, *Persian Letters*, vol. I, trans. John Davidson (London: Privately printed, 1892), 85–86.

USBEK TO IBBEN, AT SMYRNA

The King of France is old.[1] We have no examples in our histories of such a long reign as his. It is said that he possesses in a very high degree the faculty of making himself obeyed: he governs with equal ability his family, his court, and his kingdom: he has often been heard to say, that, of all existing governments, that of the Turks, or that of our august Sultan, pleased him best: such is his high opinion of Oriental statecraft.[2]

I have studied his character, and I have found certain contradictions which I cannot reconcile. For example, he has a minister who is only eighteen years old,[3] and a mistress who is fourscore;[4] he loves his religion, and yet he cannot abide those who assert that it ought to be strictly observed;[5] although he flies from the noise of cities, and is inclined to be reticent, from morning till night he is engaged in getting himself talked about; he is fond of trophies and victories, but he has as great a dread of seeing a good general at the head of his own troops, as at the head of an army of his enemies. It has never I believe happened to anyone but himself, to be burdened with more wealth than even a prince could hope for, and yet at the same time steeped in such poverty as a private person could ill brook.

He delights to reward those who serve him; but he pays as liberally the assiduous indolence of his courtiers, as the labours in the field of his captains; often the man who undresses him, or who hands him his serviette at table, is preferred before him who has taken cities and gained battles; he does not believe that the greatness of a monarch is compatible with restriction in the distribution of favours; and, without examining into the merit of a man, he will heap benefits upon him, believing that his selection makes the recipient worthy; accordingly, he has been known to bestow a small pension upon a man who had run off two leagues from the enemy, and a good government on another who had gone four.

Above all, he is magnificent in his buildings; there are more statues in his palace gardens[6] than there are citizens in a large town. His bodyguard is as strong as that of the prince before whom all the thrones of the earth tremble;[7] his armies are as numerous, his resources as great, and his finances as inexhaustible.

Paris, the 7th of the moon of Maharram, 1713.

■ Discussion Questions

1. What contradictions does Usbek see in Louis's character, and what do they reveal about his method of rule?
2. In what ways does this letter reflect Montesquieu's general interest in the foundation of good government?
3. Having read this letter, why do you think that scholars regard Montesquieu as a herald of the Enlightenment?

---

[1] Louis XIV. was then seventy-five years old, and had reigned for seventy. [All notes are Davidson's.]

[2] When Louis XIV. was in his sixteenth year, some courtiers discussed in his presence the absolute power of the Sultans, who dispose as they like of the goods and the lives of their subjects. "That is something like being a king," said the young monarch. Marshal d'Estrées, alarmed at the tendency revealed in that remark, rejoined, "But, sire, several of these emperors have been strangled even in my time."

[3] Barbezieux, son of Louvois, Louis's youngest minister, held office at twenty-three, not eighteen; and he was dead in 1713.

[4] Madame de Maintenon.   [5] The Jansenists.

[6] At Versailles.   [7] The shah of Persia.

46. Mary Astell, *Reflections upon Marriage*   (1706)

Like Montesquieu, English author Mary Astell (1666–1731) helped to usher in the Enlightenment by surveying society with a critical eye. First published anonymously in 1700, Reflections upon Marriage *is one of her best-known books; it shows her keen interest in the institution of marriage, education, and relations between the sexes. Only the third edition (1706) divulged her gender, but still not her name. As this excerpt reveals, Astell held a dim view of women's inequality in general and of their submissive role in marriage in particular. She argues that one should abhor the use of arbitrary power within the state, and so, too, within the family. Among the book's principal goals was to present spinsterhood as a viable alternative to marriage. Perhaps not surprisingly, Astell herself never married.*

These Reflections being made in the Country, where the Book that occasion'd them came but late to Hand, the *Reader* is desir'd to excuse their Unseasonableness as well as other Faults; and to believe that they have no other Design than to Correct some Abuses, which are not the less because Power and Prescription seem to Authorize them. If any are so needlessly curious as to enquire from what Hand they come, they may please to know, that it is not good Manners to ask, since the Title-Page does not tell them: We are all of us sufficiently Vain, and without doubt the Celebrated Name of *Author*, which most are so fond of, had not been avoided but for very good Reasons: To name but one; *Who will care to pull upon themselves an Hornet's nest?* 'Tis a very great Fault to regard rather who it is that Speaks, than what is Spoken; and either to submit to Authority, when we should only yield to Reason; or if Reason press too hard, to think to ward it off by Personal Objections and Reflections. Bold Truths may pass while the Speaker is Incognito, but are not endur'd when he is known; few Minds being strong enough to bear what Contradicts their Principles and Practices without Recriminating when they can. And tho' to tell the Truth be the most Friendly Office, yet whosoever is so hardy as to venture at it, shall be counted an Enemy for so doing.

Thus far the old Advertisement, when the Reflections first appear'd, A.D. 1700.

But the *Reflector*, who hopes *Reflector* is not bad English, now Governor is happily of the feminine Gender, had as good or better have said nothing; For People by being forbid, are only excited to a more curious Enquiry. A certain Ingenuous Gentleman (as she is inform'd) had the Good-Nature to own these Reflections, so far as to affirm that he had the Original M.S. in his Closet, a Proof she is not able to produce;[1] and so to make himself responsible for all their Faults, for which she returns him all due Acknowledgment. However, the Generality being of Opinion, that a Man would have had more Prudence and Manners than to have Publish'd such unseasonable Truths, or to have betray'd the *Arcana Imperii* of his Sex, she humbly confesses, that the Contrivance and Execution of this Design, which is unfortunately accus'd of being so destructive to the government, of the Men I mean, is entirely her own. She neither advis'd with Friends, nor turn'd over Antient or Modern Authors, nor prudently submitted to the Correction of such as are, or such as *think* they are good Judges, but with an *English* Spirit and Genius, set out upon the Forlorn Hope, meaning no hurt to any body, nor designing any thing but the Publick Good, and to retrieve, if possible, the Native Liberty, the Rights and Privileges of the Subject.

---

[1] Alas, Mary Astell never revealed the identity of this "Ingenuous Gentleman." [All notes are Hill's.]

Bridget Hill, ed., *The First English Feminist:* Reflections upon Marriage *and Other Writings by Mary Astell* (New York: St. Martin's Press, 1986), 69–76.

Far be it from her to stir up Sedition of any sort, none can abhor it more; and she heartily wishes that our Masters wou'd pay their Civil and Ecclesiastical Governors the same Submission, which they themselves extract from their Domestic Subjects. Nor can she imagine how she any way undermines the Masculine Empire, or blows the Trumpet of Rebellion to the Moiety of Mankind. Is it by exhorting Women, not to expect to have their own Will in any thing, but to be entirely Submissive, when once they have made choice of a Lord and Master, tho' he happen not to be so Wise, so Kind, or even so Just a Governor as was expected? She did not indeed advise them to think his Folly Wisdom, nor his Brutality that Love and Worship he promised in his Matrimonial Oath, for this required a Flight of Wit and Sense much above her poor Ability, and proper only to Masculine Understandings. However she did not in any manner prompt them to Resist, or to Abdicate the Perjur'd Spouse, tho' the Laws of GOD and the Land make special Provision for it, in a case wherein, as is to be fear'd, few Men can truly plead Not Guilty.

Tis true, thro' Want of Learning, and of that Superior Genius which Men as Men lay claim to, she was ignorant of the *Natural Inferiority* of our Sex, which our Masters lay down as a Self-Evident and Fundamental Truth.[2] She saw nothing in the Reason of Things, to make this either a Principle or a Conclusion, but much to the contrary; it being Sedition at least, if not Treason to assert it in this Reign. For if by the Natural Superiority of their Sex, they mean that every Man is by Nature superior to every Woman, which is the obvious meaning, and that which must be stuck to if they would speak Sense, it wou'd be a Sin in *any* Woman to have Dominion over *any* Man, and the greatest Queen ought not to command but to obey her Footman, because no Municipal Laws can supersede or change the Law of Nature; so that if the dominion of the Men be such, the *Salique Law*, as unjust as *English Men* have ever thought it, ought to take place over all the Earth, and the most glorious Reigns in the *English, Danish, Castilian*, and other Annals, were wicked Violations of the Law of Nature!

If they mean that *some* Men are superior to *some* Women, this is no great Discovery; had they turn'd the Tables they might have seen that *some* Women are Superior to *some* Men. Or had they been pleased to remember their Oaths of Allegiance and Supremacy, they might have known that *One* Woman is superior to *All* the Men in these Nations, or else they have sworn to very little purpose. And it must not be suppos'd, that their Reason and Religion wou'd suffer them to take Oaths, contrary to the Law of Nature and Reason of things.

By all which it appears, that our Reflector's Ignorance is very pitiable, it may be her Misfortune but not her Crime, especially since she is willing to be better inform'd, and hopes she shall never be so obstinate as to shut her Eyes against the Light of Truth, which is not to be charg'd with Novelty, how late soever we may be bless'd with the Discovery. Nor can Error, be it as Ancient as it may, ever plead Prescription against Truth. And since the only way to remove all Doubts, to answer all Objections, and to give the Mind entire Satisfaction, is not by *Affirming*, but by *Proving*, so that every one may see with their *own* Eyes, and Judge according to the best of their *own* Understandings, She hopes it is no Presumption to insist on this Natural Right of Judging for her self, and the rather, because by quitting it, we give up all the Means of Rational Conviction. Allow us then as many Glasses as you please to help our Sight, and as many good Arguments as you can afford to Convince our Understandings: But don't exact of us we beseech you, to affirm that we see such things as are only the Discovery of Men who have quicker Senses; or that we understand and Know what we have by Hearsay only, for to be so excessively Complaisant, is neither to see nor to understand.

---

[2]Possibly a reference to William Nichols, D.D., *The Duty of Inferiours Towards their Superiours in Five Practical Discourses,* 1701, in which he argued that man possesses "a higher state of natural perfection and dignity, and thereupon puts in a just claim of superiority, which everything which is of more worth has a right to, over that which has less" (pp. 87–88).

That the Custom of the World has put Women, generally speaking, into a State of Subjection, is not deny'd; but the Right can no more be prov'd from the Fact, than the Predominancy of Vice can justifie it. A certain great Man has endeavour'd to prove by Reasons not contemptible, that in the Original State of things the Woman was the Superior, and that her Subjection to the Man is an Effect of the Fall, and the Punishment of her Sin. And that Ingenious Theorist Mr. *Whiston*[3] asserts, That before the Fall there was a greater equality between the two Sexes. However this be 'tis certainly no Arrogance in a Woman to conclude, that she was made for the Service of GOD, and that this is her End. Because GOD made all Things for Himself, and a Rational Mind is too noble a Being to be Made for the Sake and Service of any Creature. The Service she at any time becomes oblig'd to pay to a Man, is only a Business by the Bye. Just as it may be any Man's Business and Duty to keep Hogs; he was not Made for this, but if he hires himself out to such an Employment, he ought conscientiously to perform it. Nor can anything be concluded to the contrary from St. *Paul's* Argument, *I Cor. II.* For he argues only for Decency and Order, according to the present Custom and State of things. Taking his Words strictly and literally, they prove too much, in that *Praying and Prophecying in the Church* are allow'd the Women, provided they do it with their Head Cover'd, as well as the Men; and no inequality can be inferr'd from hence, their Reverence to the Sacred Oracles who engage them in such Disputes. And therefore the blame be theirs, who have unnecessarily introduc'd them in the present Subject, and who by saying that the *Reflections* were not agreeable to Scripture, oblige the Reflector to shew that those who affirm it must either mistake her Meaning, or the Sense of Holy Scripture, or both, if they think what they say, and do not find fault merely because they resolve to do so. For had she ever writ any thing contrary to those sacred Truths, she wou'd be the first in pronouncing its Condemnation.

But what says the Holy Scripture? It speaks of Women as in a State of Subjection, and so it does of the *Jews* and *Christians* when under the Dominion of the *Chaldeans* and *Romans*, requiring of the one as well as of the other a quiet submission to them under whose Power they liv'd. But will any one say that these had a *Natural Superiority* and Right to Dominion? that they had a superior Understanding, or any Pre-eminence, except what their greater Strength acquir'd? Or that the other were subjected to their Adversaries for any other Reason but the Punishment of their sins, and in order to their Reformation? Or for the Exercise of their Vertue, and because the Order of the World and the Good of Society requir'd it?

If Mankind had never sinn'd, Reason wou'd always have been obey'd, there wou'd have been no struggle for Dominion, and Brutal Power wou'd not have prevail'd. But in the laps'd State of Mankind, and now that Men will not be guided by their Reason but by their Appetites, and do not what they *ought* but what they *can*, the Reason, or that which stands for it, the Will and Pleasure of the Governor is to be the Reason of those who will not be guided by their own, and must take place for Order's sake, altho' it shou'd not be conformable to right Reason. Nor can there be any Society great or little, from Empires down to private Families, with a last Resort, to determine the Affairs of that Society by an irresistible Sentence. Now unless this Supremacy be fix'd somewhere, there will be a perpetual Contention about it, such is the love of Dominion, and let the Reason of things be what it may, those who have least Force, or Cunning to supply it, will have the Disadvantage. So that since Women are acknowledg'd to have least Bodily strength, their being commanded to obey is in pure kindness to them and for their Quiet and Security, as well as for the Exercise of their Vertue. But does it follow that Domestic Governors have more Sense than their Subjects, any more than that other Governors have? We do not find that any Man

---

[3]William Whiston (1667–1752), divine, mathematician, and Newtonian. Author of many works including *A New Theory of the Earth* (1696). He succeeded Newton as the Lucasian Professor and did much to popularize Newton's ideas. In 1710 he was deprived of his chair for casting doubt on the doctrine of the Trinity.

thinks the worse of his own Understanding because another has superior Power; or concludes himself less capable of a Post of Honour and Authority, because he is not Prefer'd to it. How much time wou'd lie on Men's hands, how empty wou'd the Places of Concourse be, and how silent most Companies, did Men forbear to Censure their Governors, that is in effect to think themselves Wiser. Indeed Government wou'd be much more desirable than it is, did it invest the Possessor with a superior Understanding as well as Power. And if mere Power gives a Right to Rule, there can be no such thing as Usurpation; but a Highway-Man so long as he has strength to force, has also a Right to require our Obedience.

Again, if Absolute Sovereignty be not necessary in a State, how comes it to be so in a family? or if in a Family why not in a State; since no Reason can be alledg'd for the one that will not hold more strongly for the other? If the Authority of the Husband so far as it extends, is sacred and inalienable, why not of the Prince? The Domestic Sovereign is without Dispute Elected, and the Stipulations and Contract are mutual, is it not then partial in Men to the last degree, to contend for, and practise that Arbitrary Dominion in their Families, which they abhor and exclaim against in the State? For if Arbitrary Power is evil in itself, and an improper Method of Governing Rational and Free Agents, it ought not to be Practis'd any where; Nor is it less, but rather more mischievous in Families than in Kingdoms, by how much 100000 Tyrants are worse than one. What tho' a Husband can't deprive a Wife of Life without being responsible to the Law, he may however do what is much more grievous to a generous Mind, render Life miserable, for which she has no Redress, scarce Pity which is afforded to every other Complainant. It being thought a Wife's Duty to suffer everything without Complaint. *If all Men are born free,* how is it that all Women are born slaves? as they must be if the being subjected to the *inconstant, uncertain, unknown, arbitrary Will of Men,* be the *perfect Condition of Slavery?* and if the Essence of Freedom consists, as our Masters say it does, in having a *standing Rule to live by?* And why is Slavery so much condemn'd and strove against in one Case, and so highly applauded, and held so necessary and so sacred in another?

■ **Discussion Questions**

1. According to Mary Astell, what is women's customary status in society, and why?
2. What evidence does Astell present to challenge this status?
3. What does the language Astell uses reveal about her style of thinking and basic intellectual beliefs?
4. Why do you think scholars characterize *Reflections upon Marriage* as a "feminist" work?

CHAPTER 15

The Promise of Enlightenment, 1740–1789

In these documents, we hear some of the voices of the Enlightenment, an intellectual and cultural movement in the eighteenth century that captured the minds of middle- and upper-class people across Europe and British North America. Enlightenment writers were united by their belief that reason provided the key to humanity's advancement as the basis of truth, liberty, and justice. They cultivated and spread their ideals through letters, published works, and personal exchanges, particularly at gatherings known as *salons*, which were organized by upper-class women. By midcentury, people as diverse as a French artisan and the king of Prussia began to echo the Enlightenment principle that progress depended on the destruction of all barriers to reason, including religious intolerance.

47. Marie-Thérèse Geoffrin and Monsieur d'Alembert, *The Salon of Madame Geoffrin* (1765)

Beginning as an intellectual movement against absolutism, the Enlightenment became a formidable force of change by the mid-eighteenth century. The role of salons was crucial in this regard. By bringing innovative intellectuals, writers, and artists together in private homes on a regular basis, salons provided an arena for the discussion and dissemination of Enlightenment ideas. Madame Marie-Thérèse Geoffrin (1699–1777) presided over the most influential salon in Paris at the time, as described in the memoirs of a beneficiary of her patronage, Jean d'Alembert (1717–1783). In addition to nurturing the intellectual scene in Paris, Madame Geoffrin also cultivated it abroad by corresponding with important European leaders, including King Stanislaw of Poland, to whom she wrote the following letter in 1765. Together, these two documents elucidate the life of a woman who was actively engaged in Enlightenment thinking.

[MONSIEUR D'ALEMBERT RECALLS MADAME GEOFFRIN'S SALON]

Much has been said respecting Madame Geoffrin's goodness, to what a point it was active, restless, obstinate. But it has not been added, and which reflects the greatest honour upon her, that, as she advanced in years, this habit constantly increased. For the misfortune of society, it too often happens that age and experience produce a directly contrary effect, even in very virtuous characters, if virtue be not in them a powerful sentiment indeed, and of no common stamp. The more disposed they have been at first to feel kindness towards their fellow creatures, the more,

Correspondance inédite du roi Stanislaw-Auguste Poniatowski et de Madame Geoffrin, ed. Charles de Nouy (Geneva: Satine, 1970; reprint of 1875 edition); trans. by Lynn Hunt as published in *Connecting with the Past*, 164–68.

finding daily their ingratitude, do they repent of having served them, and even consider it almost as a reproach to themselves to have loved them. Madame Geoffrin had learnt, from a more reflected study of mankind, from taking a view of them more *enlightened* by reason and justice, that they are more weak and vain than wicked; that we ought to compassionate their weakness, and bear with their vanity, that they may bear with ours. . . .

The passion of *giving*, which was an absolute necessity to her, seemed born with her, and tormented her, if I may say so, even from her earliest years. While yet a child, if she saw from the window any poor creature asking alms, she would throw whatever she could lay her hands upon to them; her bread, her linen, and even her clothes. She was often scolded for this *intemperance* of charity, sometimes even punished, but nothing could alter the disposition, she would do the same the very next day. . . .

Always occupied with those whom she loved, always anxious about them, she even anticipated every thing which might interrupt their happiness. A young man,[1] for whom she interested herself very much, who had till that moment been wholly absorbed in his studies, was suddenly seized with an unfortunate passion, which rendered study, and even life itself insupportable to him. She succeeded in curing him. Some time after she observed that the same young man, mentioned to her, with great interest, an amiable woman with whom he had recently become acquainted. Madame Geoffrin, who knew the lady, went to her. "I am come," she said, "to intreat a favour of you. Do not evince too much friendship for **** or too much desire to see him, he will be soon in love with you, he will be unhappy, and I shall be no less so to see him suffer; nay, you yourself will be a sufferer, from consciousness, of the sufferings you occasion him." This woman, who was truly amiable, promised what Madame Geoffrin desired, and kept her word.

As she had always among the circle of her society persons of the highest rank and birth, as she appeared even to seek an acquaintance with them, it was supposed that this flattered her vanity. But here a very erroneous opinion was formed of her; she was in no respect the dupe of such prejudices, but she thought that by managing the humours of these people, she could render them useful to her friends. "You think," said she, to one of the latter, for whom she had a particular regard, "that it is for my own sake I frequent ministers and great people. Undeceive yourself,—it is for the sake of you, and those like you who may have occasion for them. . . ."

MADAME GEOFFRIN WRITES TO THE KING OF POLAND

I am sending to you a banker named Claudel who is returning to Warsaw. He will have with him a printed memoir on a new kind of mill. The more I have learned about it, the more I see that this machine is very well-known. Your Majesty is best advised to invite a miller to come from France; he will know how to set it up and show how to use it, and use of it can spread from there.

Prince Sulkowski [a Polish nobleman] met Mr. Hennin at my salon. Mr. Hennin had been for a long time in Warsaw, and they talked together about Poland. I see with pain that it has a very bad government [Stanislaw was elected king only in 1764]; it seems almost impossible to make it better. . . .

I sent you the catalogue of the diamonds of Madame de Pompadour [King Louis XV's mistress had died recently and her diamonds were auctioned off]. . . .

Do not forget, my dear son, to send the memoir on commerce to Mr. Riancourt when he returns. . . .

I cannot report any news yet on your project for paintings; I am very sad about the death of poor Carle Vanloo [a leading French painter who died in July 1765]. It was a horrible loss for the arts.

---

[1] This young man was Monsieur d'Alembert himself.

■ **Discussion Questions**

1. Given these documents, how would you describe Madame Geoffrin's personality? In what ways was she "enlightened"?
2. What impressions do the documents give of her salon and how it functioned?
3. What does Madame Geoffrin's letter to the king of Poland suggest about the range of her interests? How was this typical of Enlightenment thinkers?

48. Jacques-Louis Ménétra, *Journal of My Life* (1764–1802)

The philosophes *directed their message to the educated elite, but Jacques-Louis Ménétra's* Journal of My Life *suggests that some people from the lower classes heard it, too. Born in Paris in 1738, Ménétra learned to read and write in local parish schools. Following his father's example, he became a master glazier. He began the* Journal *in 1764 and organized it principally around his recollections of his journeyman's "tour de France" from 1757 to 1764. Here he reveals not only his quick wit and sense of adventure but also his affinity for the intellectual spirit of criticism that characterized the Enlightenment. Alongside the tales of his amusements, Ménétra commented on many of the fundamental issues of the day, including the question of religious tolerance. The excerpt is printed as it was originally written, without punctuation.*

I went to Paris to see Denongrais   Madame la Police had been interfering with business   she made up her mind to sell her property and to retire with her cuckold of a husband to her native village for she'd put by quite a bit in the course of her work   I was all for it   She said to me I see clearly from what you've just said that you never loved me   She was right   for never had a woman touched my heart except for sensual pleasure and nothing else   I promised her to come say my farewells and they've yet to be said

   Since it was the good season we went to Champigny and went with some friends of mine to what are called *guinguettes* [open-air cafés with music and dancing—Trans.]   Sundays and holidays we went to dance in front of the castle and other days usually with the people from the *guinguette* we played tennis or went visiting the local festivals   One holiday in a village one league from Montigny people were playing tennis on the square when Du Tillet showed up accompanied by the lord the magistrate or sheriff and the priest   I heard somebody say   That's the Parisian over there   I wondered what this was all about   It's because they know you're good at tennis said my friend   they're going to propose a match   In fact six young men came and politely gave each of us a racket   My friend said no since he didn't know how to play but he said   But as for my friend he'll give you a good show   I declined   They insisted   the lord the sheriff and the priest joined in   I played   applause   hands were heard to clap   They took us to the castle (and) gave us refreshment

   I was greatly applauded   I promised again that the fellows from Montigny and I would be waiting for them next Sunday   People came from all around   I was all over the court and we had a good time   we won and whatever else they were well entertained   My friend went all out because M Trudaine had wanted to see me play and when I passed in front of him he and the people around him said to me Courage   So I answered that that was one thing I wasn't lacking

---

Jacques-Louis Ménétra, *Journal of My Life*, intro. Daniel Roche, trans. Arthur Goldhammer (New York: Columbia University Press, 1986), 129–30.

One day I followed the game warden   Since I had no rifle I let him run all over the fields and went to a village where I had seen the curate pay his respects to M Trudaine   who recognized me   and said I was pretty nimble at tennis and took me to his presbytery for a drink

After some idle talk we finally got onto the subject of religion   We talked about the mysteries of the sacraments. . . . I spoke passionately about the sufferings that had been inflicted on men who worshipped the same God except for a few matters of opinion   And (I said that) the Roman religion should be tolerant if it followed the maxims of its lawgiver   that because of its mysteries it was absurd and that all mysteries were in my opinion nothing but lies   And that so long as they sold indulgences and gave remission for sins in exchange for money   fear of hell which was like purgatory just an invention of the first impostors   that Jesus had never spoken of purgatory   And that all those sacraments were nothing but pure inventions to make money and impress the vulgar   And that he himself who was a very intelligent man was not capable of making his God   chewing him and then swallowing him   That we mistreated those peoples who did not share our belief (and who) according to the Church should have been damned because all the priests went around saying   Outside the Church there is no salvation   And that we accused those who worship idols of being idolators when we prostrate ourselves before statues   We even worship a piece of dough which we eat in the firm belief that it is God   And those idolators only worship all those things to keep from being hurt by them and other things in the hope of getting some good out of them while we on the other hand we were real man-eaters   After praying to him and worshipping him in order to satisfy him we've got to eat him too

He answered me with objections as many others had answered me   His one and only response was to say to me   All these mysteries must be believed because the Church believes them   he said to me   My friend you are enlightened   It is necessary that for the sake of government nations live always in ignorance and credulity   I answered him So be it. . . .

■ Discussion Questions

1. Why is Ménétra so critical of the Catholic church?
2. How do his criticisms echo those of the great Enlightenment thinkers?
3. What does the priest mean when he describes Ménétra as enlightened?
4. How would you characterize Ménétra's style of writing?

49. Frederick II, *Political Testament*   (1752)

The Enlightenment's triumph is perhaps best reflected in the politics of the second half of the eighteenth century. Rather than working to suppress the philosophes' *calls for change, rulers across continental Europe now embraced them as a means of enhancing their power and prestige. They did so at their own discretion, however, and often with an iron hand, as the case of Frederick II of Prussia (r. 1740–1786) vividly reveals. A devotee of the Enlightenment as well as an exemplary soldier and statesman, Frederick transformed Prussia into a leading European state during his reign. In his Political Testament of 1752, he outlines his political philosophy, which blended Enlightenment ideals with an uncompromising view of his own power.*

George L. Mosse, Rondo E. Cameron, Henry Bertram Hill, and Michael B. Petrovich, eds., *Europe in Review* (Chicago: Rand McNally and Company, 1957), 111–12.

One must attempt, above all, to know the special genius of the people which one wants to govern in order to know if one must treat them leniently or severely, if they are inclined to revolt . . . to intrigue. . . .

[The Prussian nobility] has sacrificed its life and goods for the service of the state, its loyalty and merit have earned it the protection of all its rulers, and it is one of the duties [of the ruler] to aid those [noble] families which have become impoverished in order to keep them in possession of their lands: for they are to be regarded as the pedestals and the pillars of the state. In such a state no factions or rebellions need be feared . . . it is one goal of the policy of this state to preserve the nobility.

A well conducted government must have an underlying concept so well integrated that it could be likened to a system of philosophy. All actions taken must be well reasoned, and all financial, political and military matters must flow towards one goal: which is the strengthening of the state and the furthering of its power. However, such a system can flow but from a single brain, and this must be that of the sovereign. Laziness, hedonism and imbecility, these are the causes which restrain princes in working at the noble task of bringing happiness to their subjects . . . a sovereign is not elevated to his high position, supreme power has not been confined to him in order that he may live in lazy luxury, enriching himself by the labor of the people, being happy while everyone else suffers. The sovereign is the first servant of the state. He is well paid in order that he may sustain the dignity of his office, but one demands that he work efficiently for the good of the state, and that he, at the very least, pay personal attention to the most important problems. . . .

You can see, without doubt, how important it is that the King of Prussia govern personally. Just as it would have been impossible for Newton to arrive at his system of attractions if he had worked in harness with Leibnitz and Descartes, so a system of politics cannot be arrived at and continued if it has not sprung from a single brain. . . . All parts of the government are inexorably linked with each other. Finance, politics and military affairs are inseparable; it does not suffice that one be well administered; they must all be . . . a Prince who governs personally, who has formed his [own] political system, will not be handicapped when occasions arise where he has to act swiftly: for he can guide all matters towards the end which he has set for himself. . . .

Catholics, Lutherans, Reformed, Jews and other Christian sects live in this state, and live together in peace: if the sovereign, actuated by a mistaken zeal, declares himself for one religion or another, parties will spring up, heated disputes ensue, little by little persecutions will commence and, in the end, the religion persecuted will leave the fatherland and millions of subjects will enrich our neighbors by their skill and industry.

It is of no concern in politics whether the ruler has a religion or whether he has none. All religions, if one examines them, are founded on superstitious systems, more or less absurd. It is impossible for a man of good sense, who dissects their contents, not to see their error; but these prejudices, these errors and mysteries were made for men, and one must know enough to respect the public and not to outrage its faith, whatever religion be involved.

■ Discussion Questions

1. Given this excerpt, in what ways does the term *enlightened despot* apply to Frederick II? How is he enlightened? How is he despotic?
2. What reasons does Frederick advance in favor of religious tolerance?
3. According to Frederick, what should the one goal of government be?

CHAPTER 16

The French Revolution and Napoleon, 1789–1815

When the Estates General convened at Versailles in May 1789, no one could have foreseen what lay ahead: ten years of upheaval that established the model of modern revolution and set the course of modern politics. At each stage—from the politically charged months preceding the convocation of the Estates General to the formation of a republic and a government of terror designed to destroy enemies of the Revolution from both within and without—the revolutionaries remained committed to the Enlightenment principle of using reason to reshape society and government (Document 50). Nonetheless, they were not always in control of events either in France or beyond, as peasants, working-class city folk, and even slaves from the French colony of St. Domingue (modern-day Haiti) rose up with their own demands, taking the Revolution in ever more radical directions (Document 51).

    Napoleon Bonaparte (1769–1821) ended the French Revolution even while maintaining some of its most important innovations. He transformed France from a democratically elected republic to an empire with a new aristocracy based on military service. Although he tolerated no opposition at home, he prided himself on bringing French-style liberation to peoples elsewhere. At the same time, he continued the revolutionary policy of conquest and annexation to forge the biggest empire Europe had experienced since Roman times. The third document describes a key stage in this transformation, Napoleon's invasion of Egypt in 1798. Although the campaign ultimately failed, it foreshadowed Napoleon's subsequent efforts to colonize large parts of Europe along similar lines.

50. National Assembly, *The Declaration of the Rights of Man and of the Citizen* (1789)

Promulgated by the fledgling National Assembly in August 1789, the Declaration gave the Revolution a clear sense of purpose and direction after the dizzying series of events of that summer. In it, the delegates set forth the guiding principles of the new government, echoing many of the ideals of influential eighteenth-century thinkers. The document also marked the definitive end of the old regime by presenting the protection of individual rights, not royal prerogative, as the cornerstone of political authority. The deputies did not regard the Declaration as an end in and of itself, however, but

James Harvey Robinson, *Readings in European History,* vol. 2 (Boston: Ginn and Company, 1906), 409–11.

rather as a preliminary step toward their primary goal: to write a constitution that would transform France into an enlightened constitutional monarchy. This goal was met with the Constitution of 1791, to which the Declaration was attached.

The representatives of the French people, organized as a National Assembly, believing that the ignorance, neglect, or contempt of the rights of man are the sole cause of public calamities and of the corruption of governments, have determined to set forth in a solemn declaration the natural, inalienable, and sacred rights of man, in order that this declaration, being constantly before all the members of the social body, shall remind them continually of their rights and duties; in order that the acts of the legislative power, as well as those of the executive power, may be compared at any moment with the objects and purposes of all political institutions and may thus be more respected; and, lastly, in order that the grievances of the citizens, based hereafter upon simple and incontestable principles, shall tend to the maintenance of the constitution and redound to the happiness of all. Therefore the National Assembly recognizes and proclaims, in the presence and under the auspices of the Supreme Being, the following rights of man and of the citizen:

Article 1. Men are born and remain free and equal in rights. Social distinctions may be founded only upon the general good.

2. The aim of all political association is the preservation of the natural and imprescriptible rights of man. These rights are liberty, property, security, and resistance to oppression.

3. The principle of all sovereignty resides essentially in the nation. No body nor individual may exercise any authority which does not proceed directly from the nation.

4. Liberty consists in the freedom to do everything which injures no one else; hence the exercise of the natural rights of each man has no limits except those which assure to the other members of the society the enjoyment of the same rights. These limits can only be determined by law.

5. Law can only prohibit such actions as are hurtful to society. Nothing may be prevented which is not forbidden by law, and no one may be forced to do anything not provided for by law.

6. Law is the expression of the general will. Every citizen has a right to participate personally, or through his representative, in its formation. It must be the same for all, whether it protects or punishes. All citizens, being equal in the eyes of the law, are equally eligible to all dignities and to all public positions and occupations, according to their abilities, and without distinction except that of their virtues and talents.

7. No person shall be accused, arrested, or imprisoned except in the cases and according to the forms prescribed by law. Any one soliciting, transmitting, executing, or causing to be executed, any arbitrary order, shall be punished. But any citizen summoned or arrested in virtue of the law shall submit without delay, as resistance constitutes an offense.

8. The law shall provide for such punishments only as are strictly and obviously necessary, and no one shall suffer punishment except it be legally inflicted in virtue of a law passed and promulgated before the commission of the offense.

9. As all persons are held innocent until they shall have been declared guilty, if arrest shall be deemed indispensable, all harshness not essential to the securing of the prisoner's person shall be severely repressed by law.

10. No one shall be disquieted on account of his opinions, including his religious views, provided their manifestation does not disturb the public order established by law.

11. The free communication of ideas and opinions is one of the most precious of the rights of man. Every citizen may, accordingly, speak, write, and print with freedom, but shall be responsible for such abuses of this freedom as shall be defined by law.

12. The security of the rights of man and of the citizen requires public military forces. These forces are, therefore, established for the good of all and not for the personal advantage of those to whom they shall be intrusted.

13. A common contribution is essential for the maintenance of the public forces and for the cost of administration. This should be equitably distributed among all the citizens in proportion to their means.

14. All the citizens have a right to decide, either personally or by their representatives, as to the necessity of the public contribution; to grant this freely; to know to what uses it is put; and to fix the proportion, the mode of assessment and of collection and the duration of the taxes.

15. Society has the right to require of every public agent an account of his administration.

16. A society in which the observance of the law is not assured, nor the separation of powers defined, has no constitution at all.

17. Since property is an inviolable and sacred right, no one shall be deprived thereof except where public necessity, legally determined, shall clearly demand it, and then only on condition that the owner shall have been previously and equitably indemnified.

■ Discussion Questions

1. In delineating the rights of the individual, how did the National Assembly respond to Enlightenment writers' calls for reforms?
2. According to the Declaration, what are the fundamental roles of government and the individual citizen?
3. How does the Declaration define political sovereignty, and how is this definition related to the deputies' collective sense of identity and purpose?

51. François-Dominique Toussaint L'Ouverture, *Revolution in the Colonies* (1794–1795)

In declaring that all men are born free and equal, the National Convention unleashed a debate with momentous consequences. Did blacks fall within the category of "all men"? This question proved explosive in the French colony of St. Domingue. News of the Revolution's progress traveled quickly to the island, prompting slaves in the north to launch an insurrection against their white masters in August 1791. Their revolt sparked more than a decade of war. The former slave François Dominique Toussaint L'Ouverture (1743–1803) became the most prominent black leader of the revolution. Allied first in 1793 with Spain, which controlled much of the island, he and his troops switched sides to join the French the following year, for reasons he explained in the letter excerpted here to the chief French commander in northern St. Domingue. The letter is followed by extracts from two proclamations made by Toussaint to local dissenters in 1795 that further illuminate his revolutionary principles and actions.

TOUSSAINT L'OUVERTURE TO GENERAL ETIENNE LAVEAUX, MAY 1794

It is very true, general, that I was led into error by the enemies of the Republic [of France] and of mankind, but who is the man who can hope to avoid all the traps of the wicked? Indeed, I fell

Gérard M. Laurent, *Toussaint L'Ouverture à travers sa correspondance (1794–1798)* (Madrid, 1953), 103–04, 169–72. Translated by Katharine J. Lualdi.

into their nets, but not without reason . . . the Spanish offered me their protection, and freedom for all those who fought for the kings' cause;[1] and having always fought to possess this same freedom, I clung to their offer, seeing myself abandoned by the French, my brothers.[2] But an experience a little later opened my eyes to these treacherous protectors; and being aware of their deceit and villainy, I saw clearly that their intentions were to make us cut each other's throats in order to reduce our numbers and oppress those remaining in chains and cause them to sink back into their former slavery. No, they never would reach their base goal! And in our turn we will avenge ourselves of these wretched beings in every respect. Thus let us unite forever and, forgetting the past, henceforth concern ourselves only with crushing our enemies. . . .

TOUSSAINT L'OUVERTURE TO THE FRENCH CITIZENS ENCAMPED IN MOTET, MARCH 1795

Frenchmen, the alarm rings, wake up, return from the deadly errors where you have been thrown; the opportunity for it is offered to you for the last time. The chains of the despot of England were not made for you; recover your dignity as French citizens, recover your national character. The heroic trumpet must have instructed you about the great feats of your country, which is cloaked in glory before the eyes of the universe. I was sent by Laveaux . . . to bring you words of peace. If, cured by time and experience, you return under the benevolent laws of the Republic, say the word, and nothing will be neglected to spare you from the deplorable fate which awaits you if you persist in your dreadful rebellion.

I exhort you to return to the nation. . . . Like all republicans, I am motivated by an ardent desire to find only brothers and friends wherever I have the troops under my command march. Humanity is one of the sacred duties that will make us surpass all other peoples. It is also among our principles to rescue our brothers from their error and to hold out a helping hand to them. . . .

After this outpouring of my heart for you, I can call upon you, in the name of the Republic, to join me within an hour. Once this hour is up, I will deploy force against you and I will conquer you.

TOUSSAINT L'OUVERTURE TO THE PEOPLE OF VERRETTES, MARCH 1795

Brothers and sisters,

The moment has arrived when the thick veil that was blocking the light must fall. One must no longer forget the decrees of the National Convention. Its principles, its love of liberty, are unchanging, and henceforth, there can be no hope of this sacred edifice crumbling. . . .

I have learned with infinite joy about the return of some citizens of Verrettes to the bosom of the Republic; they will find the happiness that eluded them at the instigation of the soldiers of tyranny and royalty.

---

[1]The royalist governments of both Britain and Spain participated in the war. Spain already controlled the eastern half of the island of Hispaniola, and jumped at the opportunity to expand its holdings once the slave revolts had begun. To this end, they joined forces with Britain, which had been at war with France since February 1793, to destroy France's hold on St. Domingue.
[2]In 1793, Toussaint wrote to Laveaux, offering to join the French in exchange for a full amnesty for black rebels and freedom for all slaves. Laveaux rejected the offer, and Toussaint continued fighting for royalist Spain. By spring 1794, the situation had changed radically. Not only had British and Spanish forces gained control of most of the island, making Laveaux desperate for Toussaint's support, but the National Convention had also sanctioned the abolition of slavery.

. . . To give them help, console them regarding past faults and prompt them to abjure the errors in which they were insidiously nourished, is an absolute duty and the sacred maxim of the French for all republicans.

This is why not only by virtue of the powers entrusted by General Laveaux, but also animated by the feelings of humanity and brotherhood with which I am filled, I must remind the citizens of Verrettes of their errors; but as much as they are detrimental to the interests of the Republic, as much I feel that their return, if sincere, can be advantageous to the growth of our success. . . .

The French are brothers; the English, the Spanish, and royalists are ferocious beasts who caress them only in order to suck their blood, that of their wives, and of their children at leisure, until satiation.

Citizens, I am not searching here to make a show of your faults. . . . You have returned to the bosom of the Republic, and well! Since then the past is forgotten; your duty is now to unite all of your physical and moral means to revive your parish and let the principles of sacred liberty germinate.

■ Discussion Questions

1. What links can you find between the ideals of the French Revolution and those of Toussaint as expressed in the preceding documents?
2. What was Toussaint's ultimate goal as a leader in the Revolution, whether fighting for the Spanish or the French?
3. What do these documents reveal about his strategies for achieving this goal?

52. Abd al-Rahman al-Jabartî, *Napoleon in Egypt*   (1798)

While the Directory government that came to power in 1795 worked to establish order in France, Napoleon continued the Revolution's policy of conquest and annexation abroad, first in Italy (1796–1797) and then in Egypt (1798–1801). At the time, Egypt was France's most important trading partner outside of the Caribbean; it was also a key base for challenging British interests in Asia. Egyptian historian Abd al-Rahman al-Jabartî's (1753–c. 1826) account of the first six months of the French invasion allows us to see Napoleon from a native's perspective. In this excerpt, Jabartî views Napoleon's actions skeptically through the lens of his own culture. His skepticism proved well founded, for Napoleon failed to colonize Egypt. Even so, he retained his reputation as a great military leader, preparing the way for his mastery of France and much of Europe through a similar blend of authoritarian policies and revolutionary principles as that used in Egypt.

On Monday news arrived that the French had reached Damanhūr and Rosetta, bringing about the flight of their inhabitants to Fuwwa and its surroundings. Contained in this news was mention of the French sending notices throughout the country demanding impost for the upkeep of the military. Furthermore they printed a large proclamation in Arabic, calling on the people to obey them and to raise their "Bandiera." In this proclamation were inducements, warnings, all

Shmuel Moreh, trans. *Napoleon in Egypt: al-Jabartî's Chronicle of the French Occupation, 1798* (Princeton: Markus Wiener, 1993), 24–33.

manner of wiliness and stipulations. Some copies were sent from the provinces to Cairo and its text is:

In the name of God, the Merciful, the Compassionate. There is no god but God. He has no son, nor has He an associate in His Dominion.

On behalf of the French Republic which is based upon the foundation of liberty and equality, General Bonaparte, Commander-in-Chief of the French armies makes known to all the Egyptian people that for a long time the Sanjaqs[1] who lorded it over Egypt have treated the French community basely and contemptuously and have persecuted its merchants with all manner of extortion and violence. Therefore the hour of punishment has now come.

Unfortunately this group of Mamlūks,[2] imported from the mountains of Circassia and Georgia have acted corruptly for ages in the fairest land that is to be found upon the face of the globe. However, the Lord of the Universe, the Almighty, has decreed the end of their power.

O ye Egyptians, they may say to you that I have not made an expedition hither for any other object than that of abolishing your religion; but this is a pure falsehood and you must not give credit to it, but tell the slanderers that I have not come to you except for the purpose of restoring your rights from the hands of the oppressors and that I more than the Mamlūks, serve God. . . .

And tell them also that all people are equal in the eyes of God and the only circumstances which distinguish one from the other are reason, virtue, and knowledge. But amongst the Mamlūks, what is there of reason, virtue, and knowledge, which would distinguish them from others and qualify them alone to possess everything which sweetens life in this world? Wherever fertile land is found it is appropriated to the Mamlūks; and the handsomest female slaves, and the best horses, and the most desirable dwelling-places, all these belong to them exclusively. If the land of Egypt is a fief of the Mamlūks, let them then produce the title-deed, which God conferred upon them. But the Lord of the Universe is compassionate and equitable toward mankind, and with the help of the Exalted, from this day forward no Egyptian shall be excluded from admission to eminent positions nor from acquiring high ranks, therefore the intelligent and virtuous and learned ('ulamā') amongst them, will regulate their affairs, and thus the state of the whole population will be rightly adjusted. . . .

Blessing on blessing to the Egyptians who will act in concert with us, without any delay, for their condition shall be rightly adjusted, and their rank raised. Blessing also, upon those who will abide in their habitations, not siding with either of the two hostile parties, yet when they know us better, they will hasten to us with all their hearts. But woe upon woe to those who will unite with the Mamlūks and assist them in the war against us, for they will not find the way of escape, and no trace of them shall remain. . . .

Here is an explanation of the incoherent words and vulgar constructions which he put into this miserable letter.

His statement "In the name of God, the Merciful, the Compassionate. There is no god but God. He has no son, nor has He an associate in His Dominion." In mentioning these three sentences there is an indication that the French agree with the three religions, but at the same time they do not agree with them, not with any religion. They are consistent with the Muslims in stating the formula "In the name of God," in denying that He has a son or an associate. They dis-

---

[1]**Sanjaqs:** Provincial governors in the Ottoman Empire.
[2]**Mamlūks:** Descendants of medieval slave-soldiers who enjoyed considerable political power until the French invasion.

agree with the Muslims in not mentioning the two Articles of Faith, in rejecting the mission of Muhammad, and the legal words and deeds which are necessarily recognized by religion. They agree with the Christians in most of their words and deeds, but disagree with them by not mentioning the Trinity, and denying the mission and furthermore in rejecting their beliefs, killing the priests and destroying the churches. Then, their statement "On behalf of the French Republic, etc.," that is, this proclamation is sent from their Republic, that means their body politic, because they have no chief or sultan with whom they all agree, like others, whose function is to speak on their behalf. For when they rebelled against their sultan six years ago and killed him, the people agreed unanimously that there was not to be a single ruler but that their state, territories, laws, and administration of their affairs, should be in the hands of the intelligent and wise men among them. They appointed persons chosen by them and made them heads of the army, and below them generals and commanders of thousands, two hundreds, and tens, administrators and advisers, on condition that they were all to be equal and none superior to any other in view of the equality of creation and nature. They made this the foundation and basis of their system. This is the meaning of their statement "based upon the foundation of liberty and equality." . . . They follow this rule: great and small, high and low, male and female are all equal. Sometimes they break this rule according to their whims and inclinations or reasoning. Their women do not veil themselves and have no modesty; they do not care whether they uncover their private parts. Whenever a Frenchman has to perform an act of nature he does so wherever he happens to be, even in full view of people, and he goes away as he is, without washing his private parts after defecation. If he is a man of taste and refinement he wipes himself with whatever he finds, even with a paper with writing on it, otherwise he remains as he is. They have intercourse with any woman who pleases them and vice versa. Sometimes one of their women goes into a barber's shop, and invites him to shave her pubic hair. If he wishes he can take his fee in kind. It is their custom to shave both their moustaches and beard. Some of them leave the hair of their cheeks only. . . .

His saying *qad hattama* etc. (has decreed) shows that they are appointing themselves controllers of God's secrets, but there is no disgrace worse than disbelief. . . .

His statement *wa-qūlū li 'l-muftariyīn* (but tell the slanderers) is the plural of *muftari* (slanderer) which means liar, and how worthy of this description they are. The proof of that is his saying "I have not come to you except for the purpose of restoring your rights from the hands of the oppressors," which is the first lie he uttered and a falsehood which he invented. Then he proceeds to something even worse than that, may God cast him into perdition, with his words: "I more than the Mamlūks serve God. . . ." There is no doubt that this is a derangement of his mind, and an excess of foolishness. . . .

His saying [all people] are equal in the eyes of God the Almighty, this is a lie and stupidity. How can this be when God has made some superior to others as is testified by the dwellers in the Heavens and on the Earth? . . .

May God hurry misfortune and punishment upon them, may He strike their tongues with dumbness, may He scatter their hosts, and disperse them, confound their intelligence, and cause their breath to cease. He has the power to do that, and it is up to Him to answer.

■ Discussion Questions

1. What strategy did Napoleon use in his proclamation to garner the support of the Egyptian people?
2. What does this strategy suggest about his personal ambitions and method of rule?
3. Why is Jabartî critical of Napoleon's intentions as stated in his proclamation?
4. What do Jabartî's criticisms suggest about the differences between French and Egyptian culture?

CHAPTER 17
Industrialization and Social Ferment, 1815–1850

The nineteenth century was a time of momentous economic and social change as factories sprang up across much of Europe and railroad tracks crisscrossed the landscape. Although Britain initially led the way in industrial growth, continental Europe soon began to catch up. For the middle classes, industrialization opened the door to new riches, comforts, and prestige. By contrast, for the men, women, and children who labored in the new factories, it often meant a life of urban drudgery and extreme poverty. The first document here reveals the grueling regime of factory work, while the second and third illuminate the great political ideologies that industrialization fostered: liberalism and communism. The final document shows the cultural response to the changing European landscape, romanticism, which strove to strip away artifice and expose truth as embodied in nature and daily life.

53. *Factory Rules in Berlin* (1844)

Industrialization did not simply create new social classes, new jobs, and new problems; it also created new work habits regimented by the pace of machines and the time clock. It fell upon the factory owners and managers to instill these habits in their workforce to ensure efficient and consistent levels of production. This was no easy task, as most people, whether former peasants or skilled workers, were accustomed to controlling their own time. The list of rules distributed to the employees of the Foundry and Engineering Works of the Royal Overseas Trading Company in Berlin provides a telling example of one approach to this challenge. This document also illustrates the spread of industrialization eastward across continental Europe.

In every large works, and in the co-ordination of any large number of workmen, good order and harmony must be looked upon as the fundamentals of success, and therefore the following rules shall be strictly observed.

Every man employed in the concern named below shall receive a copy of these rules, so that no one can plead ignorance. Its acceptance shall be deemed to mean consent to submit to its regulations.

(1) The normal working day begins at all seasons at 6 a.m. precisely and ends, after the usual break of half an hour for breakfast, a hour for dinner and half an hour for tea, at 7 p.m., and it shall be strictly observed.

Sidney Pollard and C. Holmes, *Documents of European Economic History,* vol. I, *The Process of Industrialization, 1750–1870* (New York: St. Martin's Press, 1968), 534–36.

Five minutes before the beginning of the stated hours of work until their actual commencement, a bell shall ring and indicate that every worker employed in the concern has to proceed to his place of work, in order to start as soon as the bell stops.

The doorkeeper shall lock the door punctually at 6 a.m., 8.30 a.m., 1 p.m. and 4.30 p.m.

Workers arriving 2 minutes late shall lose half an hour's wages; whoever is more than 2 minutes late may not start work until after the next break, or at least shall lose his wages until then. Any disputes about the correct time shall be settled by the clock mounted above the gatekeeper's lodge.

These rules are valid both for time- and for piece-workers, and in cases of breaches of these rules, workmen shall be fined in proportion to their earnings. The deductions from the wage shall be entered in the wage-book of the gatekeeper whose duty they are; they shall be unconditionally accepted as it will not be possible to enter into any discussions about them.

(2) When the bell is rung to denote the end of the working day, every workman, both on piece- and on day-wage, shall leave his workshop and the yard, but is not allowed to make preparations for his departure before the bell rings. Every breach of this rule shall lead to a fine of five silver groschen to the sick fund. Only those who have obtained special permission by the overseer may stay on in the workshop in order to work.—If a workman has worked beyond the closing bell, he must give his name to the gatekeeper on leaving, on pain of losing his payment for the overtime.

(3) No workman, whether employed by time or piece, may leave before the end of the working day, without having first received permission from the overseer and having given his name to the gatekeeper. Omission of these two actions shall lead to a fine of ten silver groschen payable to the sick fund.

(4) Repeated irregular arrival at work shall lead to dismissal. This shall also apply to those who are found idling by an official or overseer, and refuse to obey their order to resume work.

(5) Entry to the firm's property by any but the designated gateway, and exit by any prohibited route, e.g. by climbing fences or walls, or by crossing the Spree, shall be punished by a fine of fifteen silver groschen to the sick fund for the first offences, and dismissal for the second.

(6) No worker may leave his place of work otherwise than for reasons connected with his work.

(7) All conversation with fellow-workers is prohibited; if any worker requires information about his work, he must turn to the overseer, or to the particular fellow-worker designated for the purpose.

(8) Smoking in the workshops or in the yard is prohibited during working hours; anyone caught smoking shall be fined five silver groschen for the sick fund for every such offence.

(9) Every worker is responsible for cleaning up his space in the workshop, and if in doubt, he is to turn to his overseer.—All tools must always be kept in good condition, and must be cleaned after use. This applies particularly to the turner, regarding his lathe.

(10) Natural functions must be performed at the appropriate places, and whoever is found soiling walls, fences, squares, etc., and similarly, whoever is found washing his face and hands in the workshop and not in the places assigned for the purpose, shall be fined five silver groschen for the sick fund.

(11) On completion of his piece of work, every workman must hand it over at once to his foreman or superior, in order to receive a fresh piece of work. Pattern makers must on no account hand over their patterns to the foundry without express order of their supervisors. No workman may take over work from his fellow-workman without instruction to that effect by the foreman.

(12) It goes without saying that all overseers and officials of the firm shall be obeyed without question, and shall be treated with due deference. Disobedience will be punished by dismissal.

(13) Immediate dismissal shall also be the fate of anyone found drunk in any of the workshops.

(14) Untrue allegations against superiors or officials of the concern shall lead to stern reprimand, and may lead to dismissal. The same punishment shall be meted out to those who knowingly allow errors to slip through when supervising or stocktaking.

(15) Every workman is obliged to report to his superiors any acts of dishonesty or embezzlement on the part of his fellow workmen. If he omits to do so, and it is shown after subsequent discovery of a misdemeanour that he knew about it at the time, he shall be liable to be taken to court as an accessory after the fact and the wage due to him shall be retained as punishment. Conversely, anyone denouncing a theft in such a way as to allow conviction of the thief shall receive a reward of two Thaler, and, if necessary, his name shall be kept confidential.—Further, the gatekeeper and the watchman, as well as every official, are entitled to search the baskets, parcels, aprons etc. of the women and children who are taking dinners into the works, on their departure, as well as search any worker suspected of stealing any article whatever. . . .

(18) Advances shall be granted only to the older workers, and even to them only in exceptional circumstances. As long as he is working by the piece, the workman is entitled merely to his fixed weekly wage as subsistence pay; the extra earnings shall be paid out only on completion of the whole piece contract. If a workman leaves before his piece contract is completed, either of his own free will, or on being dismissed as punishment, or because of illness, the partly completed work shall be valued by the general manager with the help of two overseers, and he will be paid accordingly. There is no appeal against the decision of these experts.

(19) A free copy of these rules is handed to every workman, but whoever loses it and requires a new one, or cannot produce it on leaving, shall be fined 2½ silver groschen, payable to the sick fund.

■ Discussion Questions

1. As delineated here, what new modes of discipline did factory work require, and why?
2. What was the principal method used to encourage compliance to these rules?
3. Given this document, how would you describe a typical workday in this factory?

54. T. B. Macaulay, *Speech on Parliamentary Reform*   (1831)

Upon Napoleon's defeat in 1815, the allied powers worked to erase the imprint that the French Revolution and Napoleon's conquests had left on European society and politics. They faced many obstacles, however, including the new ideology of liberalism. Unlike their political rivals, liberals heralded individual rights and the need for broader political representation, two hallmarks of the French Revolution. Even so, they shared conservatives' fear of popular unrest. British politician Thomas B. Macaulay (1800–1859) sought to capitalize on this common ground in a speech he delivered to Parliament in support of a bill for electoral reform at the very moment when mass unrest gripped Europe. His words struck a chord, for the bill passed a year later, expanding the British electorate to more than 800,000. Although this represented a tiny fraction of the country's growing population, which reached more than 20 million by 1850, it marked a triumph over exclusive aristocratic politics and opened the door to yet more sweeping changes.

T. B. Macaulay, *Miscellanies,* vol. I (Boston: Houghton Mifflin, 1901), 1–19.

It is a circumstance, Sir, of happy augury for the motion before the House, that almost all those who have opposed it have declared themselves hostile on principle to parliamentary reform. . . . For what I feared was, not the opposition of those who are averse to all reform, but the disunion of reformers. I knew that, during three months, every reformer had been employed in conjecturing what the plan of the government would be. I knew that every reformer had imagined in his own mind a scheme. . . . I felt therefore great apprehension that one person would be dissatisfied with one part of the bill, that another person would be dissatisfied with another part, and that thus our whole strength would be wasted in internal dissensions. That apprehension is now at an end. I have seen with delight the perfect concord which prevails among all who deserve the name of reformers in this House. . . . I will not, Sir, at present express any opinion as to the details of the bill; but, having during the last twenty-four hours given the most diligent consideration to its general principles, I have no hesitation in pronouncing it a wise, noble, and comprehensive measure, skilfully framed for the healing of great distempers, for the securing at once of the public liberties and of the public repose, and for the reconciling and knitting together of all the orders of the state.

The honorable Baronet who has just sat down[1] has told us, that the Ministers have attempted to unite two inconsistent principles in one abortive measure. Those were his very words. He thinks, if I understand him rightly, that we ought either to leave the representative system such as it is, or to make it perfectly symmetrical. I think, Sir, that the Ministers would have acted unwisely if they had taken either course. Their principle is plain, rational, and consistent. It is this, to admit the middle class to a large and direct share in the representation, without any violent shock to the institutions of our country. . . . The government has, in my opinion, done all that was necessary for the removal of a great practical evil, and no more than was necessary.

I consider this, Sir, as a practical question. I rest my opinion on no general theory of government. I distrust all general theories of government. I will not positively say, that there is any form of polity which may not, in some conceivable circumstances, be the best possible. I believe that there are societies in which every man may safely be admitted to vote. Gentlemen may cheer, but such is my opinion. I say, Sir, that there are countries in which the condition of the laboring classes is such that they may safely be entrusted with the right of electing Members of the Legislature. If the laborers of England were in that state in which I, from my soul, wish to see them, if employment were always plentiful, wages always high, food always cheap, if a large family were considered not as an encumbrance but as a blessing, the principal objection to Universal Suffrage would, I think, be removed. Universal Suffrage exists in the United States without producing any very frightful consequences; and I do not believe that the people of those States, or of any part of the world, are in any good quality naturally superior to our own countrymen. But, unhappily, the laboring classes in England, and in all old countries, are occasionally in a state of great distress. Some of the causes of this distress are, I fear, beyond the control of the government. We know what effect distress produces, even on people more intelligent than the great body of the laboring classes can possibly be. . . . It is therefore no reflection on the poorer class of Englishmen, who are not, and who cannot in the nature of things be, highly educated, to say that distress produces on them its natural effects, those effects which it would produce on the Americans, or on any other people, that it blinds their judgment, that it inflames their passions, that it makes them prone to believe those who flatter them, and to distrust those who would serve them. For the sake, therefore, of the whole society, for the sake of the laboring classes themselves, I hold it to be clearly expedient that, in a country like this one, the right of suffrage should depend on a pecuniary qualification.

---

[1]Sir John Walsh.

But, Sir, every argument which would induce me to oppose Universal Suffrage induces me to support the plan which is now before us. I am opposed to Universal Suffrage, because I think that it would produce a destructive revolution. I support this plan, because I am sure that it is our best security against a revolution. . . . I do in my conscience believe that, unless the plan proposed, or some similar plan, be speedily adopted, great and terrible calamities will befall us. Entertaining this opinion, I think myself bound to state it, not as a threat, but as a reason. I support this bill because it will improve our institutions; but I support it also because it tends to preserve them. That we may exclude those whom it is necessary to exclude, we must admit those whom it may be safe to admit. At present we oppose the schemes of revolutionists with only one half, with only one quarter of our proper force. We say, and we say justly, that it is not by mere numbers, but by property and intelligence, that the nation ought to be governed. Yet, saying this, we exclude from all share in the government great masses of property and intelligence, great numbers of those who are most interested in preserving tranquility, and who know best how to preserve it. We do more. We drive over to the side of revolution those whom we shut out from power. Is this a time when the cause of law and order can spare one of its natural allies? . . .

If it be said that there is an evil in change as change, I answer that there is also an evil in discontent as discontent. This, indeed, is the strongest part of our case. It is said that the system works well. I deny it. I deny that a system works well, which the people regard with aversion. We may say here, that it is a good system and a perfect system. But if any man were to say so to any six hundred and fifty-eight respectable farmers or shopkeepers, chosen by lot in any part of England, he would be hooted down, and laughed to scorn. Are these the feelings with which any part of the government ought to be regarded? Above all, are these the feelings with which the popular branch of the legislature ought to be regarded? It is almost as essential to the utility of a House of Commons, that it should possess the confidence of the people, as that it should deserve that confidence. Unfortunately, that which is in theory the popular part of our government is in practice the unpopular part. Who wishes to dethrone the King? Who wishes to turn the Lords out of their House? Here and there a crazy radical, whom the boys in the street point at as he walks along. Who wishes to alter the constitution of this House? The whole people. It is natural that it should be so. . . .

Now, . . . if I were convinced that the great body of the middle class in England look with aversion on monarchy and aristocracy, I should be forced, much against my will, to come to this conclusion, that monarchical and aristocratical institutions are unsuited to my country. Monarchy and aristocracy, valuable and useful as I think them, are still valuable and useful as means, and not as ends. The end of government is the happiness of the people, and I do not conceive that, in a country like this, the happiness of the people can be promoted by a form of government in which the middle classes place no confidence, and which exists only because the middle classes have no organ by which to make their sentiments known. But, Sir, I am fully convinced that the middle classes sincerely wish to uphold the Royal prerogatives and the constitutional rights of the Peers. . . .

Now therefore while everything at home and abroad forebodes ruin to those who persist in a hopeless struggle against the spirit of the age, now, while the crash of the proudest throne of the Continent is still resounding in our ears, now, while the roof of a British palace affords an ignominious shelter to the exiled heir of forty kings, now, while we see on every side ancient institutions subverted, and great societies dissolved, now, while the heart of England is still sound, now, while old feelings and old associations retain a power and a charm which may too soon pass away, now, in this your accepted time, now, in this your day of salvation, take counsel, not of prejudice, not of party spirit, not of the ignominious pride of a fatal consistency, but of history, of reason, of the ages which are past, of the signs of this most portentous time. Pronounce in a manner worthy of the expectation with which this great debate has been anticipated, and of the long remembrance which it will leave behind. Renew the youth of the state. Save property, divided against itself. Save the multitude, endangered by its own ungovernable passions. Save the aristocracy, endangered by its own unpopular power. Save the greatest, and fairest, and most highly civilized community that ever existed, from calamities which may in a few days sweep away all the rich heritage of so many ages of wisdom and glory. The danger is terrible. The time is short. If this bill should be rejected, I pray to God that none of those who concur in rejecting it may ever remember their votes with unavailing remorse, amidst the wreck of laws, the confusion of ranks, the spoliation of property, and the dissolution of social order.

■ Discussion Questions

1. What, according to Macaulay, is the main goal of the reform bill?
2. Why is he against universal manhood suffrage?
3. What strategy does Macaulay use to sway opponents of the bill to support it?
4. In what ways does Macaulay's speech reflect liberal principles?

55. Friedrich Engels, *Draft of a Communist Confession of Faith*   (1847)

When Friedrich Engels (1820–1895) composed this draft of a communist "confession of faith" in 1847, the Industrial Revolution was in full swing in Great Britain and rapidly gaining ground in continental Europe. Engels observed the impact of this process on the working class with a critical eye. Two years earlier, he had joined forces with another critic of industrialization, Karl Marx (1818–1883), and together they launched an ideological revolution with the publication of the Communist Manifesto in 1848. There they set forth a new understanding of industrial society and its problems and proposed a new set of solutions centered on the abolition of capitalist, "private" property. Engels's "confession of faith" illuminates key landmarks on his and Marx's intellectual journey, for it was among the materials Marx used to compose the Manifesto. *The confession was debated and approved in 1847 at the first congress of the Communist League. The first six questions reveal Engels's debt to the utopian principle of the community of property. The rest reflect his and Marx's distinct historical vision.*

DRAFT OF A COMMUNIST CONFESSION OF FAITH
JUNE 9, 1847

QUESTION 1:   *Are you a Communist?*
ANSWER: Yes.
QUESTION 2:   *What is the aim of the Communists?*
ANSWER: To organise society in such a way that every member of it can develop and use all his capabilities and powers in complete freedom and without thereby infringing the basic conditions of this society.
QUESTION 3:   *How do you wish to achieve this aim?*
ANSWER: By the elimination of private property and its replacement by community of property.
QUESTION 4:   *On what do you base your community of property?*

John E. Toews, ed., *The Communist Manifesto with Related Documents* (Boston: Bedford/St. Martin's, 1999), 99–104.

Answer: Firstly, on the mass of productive forces and means of subsistence resulting from the development of industry, agriculture, trade and colonisation, and on the possibility inherent in machinery, chemical and other resources of their infinite extension.

Secondly, on the fact that in the consciousness or feeling of every individual there exist certain irrefutable basic principles which, being the result of the whole of historical development, require no proof.

Question 5:   *What are such principles?*

Answer: For example, every individual strives to be happy. The happiness of the individual is inseparable from the happiness of all, etc.

Question 6:   *How do you wish to prepare the way for your community of property?*

Answer: By enlightening and uniting the proletariat.

Question 7:   *What is the proletariat?*

Answer: The proletariat is that class of society which lives exclusively by its labour and not on the profit from any kind of capital; that class whose weal and woe, whose life and death, therefore, depend on the alternation of times of good and bad business; in a word, on the fluctuations of competition.

Question 8:   *Then there have not always been proletarians?*

Answer: No. There have always been poor and working classes; and those who worked were almost always the poor. But there have not always been proletarians, just as competition has not always been free.

Question 9:   *How did the proletariat arise?*

Answer: The proletariat came into being as a result of the introduction of the machines which have been invented since the middle of the last century and the most important of which are: the steam-engine, the spinning machine, and the power loom. These machines, which were very expensive and could therefore only be purchased by rich people, supplanted the workers of the time, because by the use of machinery it was possible to produce commodities more quickly and cheaply than could the workers with their imperfect spinning wheels and handlooms. The machines thus delivered industry entirely into the hands of the big capitalists and rendered the workers' scanty property which consisted mainly of their tools, looms, etc., quite worthless, so that the capitalist was left with everything, the worker with nothing. In this way the factory system was introduced. Once the capitalists saw how advantageous this was for them, they sought to extend it to more and more branches of labour. They divided work more and more between the workers so that workers who formerly had made a whole article now produced only a part of it. Labour simplified in this way produced goods more quickly and therefore more cheaply and only now was it found in almost every branch of labour that here also machines could be used. As soon as any branch of labour went over to factory production it ended up, just as in the case of spinning and weaving, in the hands of the big capitalists, and the workers were deprived of the last remnants of their independence. We have gradually arrived at the position where almost *all* branches of labour are run on a factory basis. This has increasingly brought about the ruin of the previously existing middle class, especially of the small master craftsmen, completely transformed the previous position of the workers, and two new classes which are gradually swallowing up all other classes have come into being, namely:

I.   The class of the big capitalists, who in all advanced countries are in almost exclusive possession of the means of subsistence and those means (machines, factories, workshops, etc.) by which these means of subsistence are produced. This is the *bourgeois* class, or the *bourgeoisie.*

II.   The class of the completely propertyless, who are compelled to sell their labour to the first class, the bourgeois, simply to obtain from them in return their means of subsistence. Since the parties to this trading in labour are not *equal*, but the bourgeois have the advantage, the propertyless must submit to the bad conditions laid down by the bourgeois. This class, dependent on the bourgeois, is called the class of the *proletarians* or the *proletariat.*

QUESTION 10:   *In what way does the proletarian differ from the slave?*

ANSWER: The slave is sold once and for all, the proletarian has to sell himself by the day and by the hour. The slave is the property of one master and for that very reason has a guaranteed subsistence, however wretched it may be. The proletarian is, so to speak, the slave of the entire bourgeois *class,* not of one master, and therefore has no guaranteed subsistence, since nobody buys his labour if he does not need it. The slave is accounted a *thing* and not a member of civil society. The proletarian is recognised as a *person,* as a member of civil society. The slave *may,* therefore, have a better subsistence than the proletarian but the latter stands at a higher stage of development. The slave frees himself by *becoming a proletarian,* abolishing from the totality of property relationships *only* the relationship of *slavery.* The proletarian can free himself only by abolishing *property in general.*

QUESTION 11:   *In what way does the proletarian differ from the serf?*

ANSWER: The serf has the piece of land, that is, of an instrument of production, in return for handing over a greater or lesser portion of the yield. The proletarian works with instruments of production which belong to someone else who, in return for his labour, hands over to him a portion, determined by competition, of the products. In the case of the serf, the share of the labourer is determined by his own labour, that is, by himself. In the case of the proletarian it is determined by competition, therefore in the first place by the bourgeois. The serf has guaranteed subsistence, the proletarian has not. The serf frees himself by driving out his feudal lord and becoming a property owner himself, thus entering into competition and joining for the time being the possessing class, the privileged class. The proletarian frees himself by doing away with property, competition, and all class differences.

QUESTION 12:   *In what way does the proletarian differ from the handicraftsman?*

ANSWER: As opposed to the proletarian, the so-called handicraftsman, who still existed nearly everywhere during the last century and still exists here and there, is at most a *temporary* proletarian. His aim is to acquire capital himself and so to exploit other workers. He can often achieve this aim where the craft guilds still exist or where freedom to follow a trade has not yet led to the organisation of handwork on a factory basis and to intense competition. But as soon as the factory system is introduced into handwork and competition is in full swing, this prospect is eliminated and the handicraftsman becomes more and more a proletarian. The handicraftsman therefore frees himself *either* by becoming a bourgeois or in general passing over into the middle class, *or,* by becoming a proletarian as a result of competition (as now happens in most cases) and joining the movement of the proletariat—i.e., the more or less conscious communist movement.

QUESTION 13:   *Then you do not believe that community of property has been possible at any time?*

ANSWER: No. Communism has only arisen since machinery and other inventions made it possible to hold out the prospect of an all-sided development, a happy existence, for all members of society. Communism is the theory of a liberation which was not possible for the slaves, the serfs, or the handicraftsmen, but only for the proletarians and hence it belongs of necessity to the nineteenth century and was not possible in any earlier period.

QUESTION 14:   *Let us go back to the sixth question. As you wish to prepare for community of property by the enlightening and uniting of the proletariat, then you reject revolution?*

ANSWER: We are convinced not only of the uselessness but even of the harmfulness of all conspiracies. We are also aware that revolutions are not made deliberately and arbitrarily but that everywhere and at all times they are the necessary consequence of circumstances which are not in any way whatever dependent either on the will or on the leadership of individual parties or of whole classes. But we also see that the development of the proletariat in almost all countries of the world is forcibly repressed by the possessing classes and that thus a revolution is being forcibly worked for by the opponents of communism. If, in the end, the oppressed proletariat is thus driven into a revolution, then we will defend the cause of the proletariat just as well by our deeds as now by our words.

QUESTION 15:   *Do you intend to replace the existing social order by community of property at one stroke?*

ANSWER: We have no such intention. The development of the masses cannot be ordered by decree. It is determined by the development of the conditions in which these masses live, and therefore proceeds gradually.

QUESTION 16:   *How do you think the transition from the present situation to community of property is to be effected?*

ANSWER: The first, fundamental condition for the introduction of community of property is the political liberation of the proletariat through a democratic constitution.

QUESTION 17:   *What will be your first measure once you have established democracy?*

ANSWER: Guaranteeing the subsistence of the proletariat.

QUESTION 18:   *How will you do this?*

ANSWER: I. By limiting private property in such a way that it gradually prepares the way for its transformation into social property, e.g., by progressive taxation, limitation of the right of inheritance in favour of the state, etc., etc.

II. By employing workers in national workshops and factories and on national estates.

III. By educating all children at the expense of the state.

QUESTION 19:   *How will you arrange this kind of education during the period of transition?*

ANSWER: All children will be educated in state establishments from the time when they can do without the first maternal care.

QUESTION 20:   *Will not the introduction of community of property be accompanied by the proclamation of the community of women?*

ANSWER: By no means. We will only interfere in the personal relationship between men and women or with the family in general to the extent that the maintenance of the existing institution would disturb the new social order. Besides, we are well aware that the family relationship has been modified in the course of history by the property relationships and by periods of development, and that consequently the ending of private property will also have a most important influence on it.

QUESTION 21:   *Will nationalities continue to exist under communism?*

ANSWER: The nationalities of the peoples who join together according to the principle of community will be just as much compelled by this union to merge with one another and thereby supersede themselves as the various differences between estates and classes disappear through the superseding of their basis—private property.

QUESTION 22:   *Do Communists reject the existing religions?*

ANSWER: All religions which have existed hitherto were expressions of historical stages of development of individual peoples or groups of peoples. But communism is that stage of historical development which makes all existing religions superfluous and supersedes them.

■ Discussion Questions

1. According to the confession, what were the central goals of the communists, and how did they aim to achieve them?
2. How does Engels define the proletariat, and what sets it apart from other types of workers?
3. How does the confession explicitly link communist ideology to industrialization? What place did revolution have in this ideology?

56. Victor Hugo, *Preface to* Cromwell   (1827)

The economic and political changes sweeping across Europe in the first half of the nineteenth century found cultural expression in the reigning artistic movement of the period: romanticism. As a whole, the movement shunned the rules and models of the past and embraced freedom, creative genius, and originality instead. Victor Marie, Count Hugo (1802–1885), was among the most celebrated Romantic French poets and novelists of his day. In this excerpt from the preface to one of his early works, the play Cromwell, *published in 1827, he paints a colorful picture of his artistic ideals. His passionate vision helped shape the explosion of culture after 1830 when painters, poets, playwrights, and authors turned not only to nature for inspiration but also to the gritty realities of everyday life in an increasingly industrial and urban society.*

Let us then speak boldly. The time for it has come, and it would be strange if, in this age, liberty, like the light, should penetrate everywhere except to the one place where freedom is most natural—the domain of thought. Let us take the hammer to theories and poetic systems. Let us throw down the old plastering that conceals the façade of art. There are neither rules nor models; or, rather, there are no other rules than the general laws of nature, which soar above the whole field of art, and the special rules which result from the conditions appropriate to the subject of each composition. The former are of the essence, eternal, and do not change; the latter are variable, external, and are used but once. The former are the framework that supports the house; the latter the scaffolding which is used in building it, and which is made anew for each building. In a word, the former are the flesh and bones, the latter the clothing, of the drama. But these rules are not written in the treatises on poetry. Richelet has no idea of their existence. Genius, which divines rather than learns, devises for each work the general rules from the general plan of things, the special rules from the separate *ensemble* of the subject treated; not after the manner of the chemist, who lights the fire under his furnace, heats his crucible, analyzes and destroys; but after the manner of the bee, which flies on its golden wings, lights on each flower and extracts its honey, leaving it as brilliant and fragrant as before.

The poet—let us insist on this point—should take counsel therefore only of nature, truth and inspiration, which is itself both truth and nature. *"Quando he,"* says Lope de Vega:

Quando he de escrivir una comedia,
Encierro los preceptos con seis llaves.[1]

To secure these precepts "six keys" are none too many, in very truth. Let the poet beware especially of copying anything whatsoever—Shakespeare no more than Molière, Schiller no more than Corneille. If genuine talent could abdicate its own nature in this matter, and thus lay aside its original personality, to transform itself into another, it would lose everything by playing this role of its own double. It is as if a god should turn valet. We must draw our inspiration from the original sources. . . .

Let there be no misunderstanding: if some of our poets have succeeded in being great, even when copying, it is because, while forming themselves on the antique model, they have often listened to the voice of nature and to their own genius—it is because they have been themselves in some one respect. Their branches became entangled in those of the near-by tree, but their roots were buried deep in the soil of art. They were the ivy, not the mistletoe. Then came imitators of

[1]When I have to write a comedy, / I enclose the precepts with six keys.
The Dramatic Works of Victor Hugo, vol. III (New York: The Athenaeum Society, 1909), 3–54.

the second rank, who, having neither roots in the earth, nor genius in their souls, had to confine themselves to imitation. As Charles Nodier says: "After the school of Athens, the school of Alexandria." Then there was a deluge of mediocrity; then there came a swarm of those treatises on poetry, so annoying to true talent, so convenient for mediocrity. We were told that everything was done, and God was forbidden to create more Molières or Corneilles. Memory was put in place of imagination. Imagination itself was subjected to hard-and-fast rules, and aphorisms were made about it: "To imagine," says La Harpe, with his naive assurance, "is in substance to remember, that is all."

But nature! Nature and truth!—And here, in order to prove that, far from demolishing art, the new ideas aim only to reconstruct it more firmly and on a better foundation, let us try to point out the impassable limit which in our opinion, separates reality according to art from reality according to nature. It is careless to confuse them as some ill-informed partisans of *romanticism* do. Truth in art cannot possibly be, as several writers have claimed, *absolute* reality. Art cannot produce the thing itself. Let us imagine, for example, one of those unreflecting promoters of absolute nature, of nature viewed apart from art, at the performance of a romantic play, say *Le Cid*. "What's that?" he will ask at the first word. "The Cid speaks in verse? It isn't *natural* to speak in verse."—"How would you have him speak, pray?"—"In prose." Very good. A moment later, "How's this!" he will continue, if he is consistent; "the Cid is speaking French!"—"Well?"— "Nature demands that he speak his own language; he can't speak anything but Spanish."

We shall fail entirely to understand but again—very good. You imagine that this is all? By no means: before the tenth sentence in Castilian, he is certain to rise and ask if the Cid who is speaking is the real Cid, in flesh and blood. By what right does the actor, whose name is Pierre or Jacques, take the name of the Cid? That is *false*. There is no reason why he should not go on to demand that the sun should be substituted for the footlights, *real* trees and *real* houses for those deceitful wings. For, once started on that road, logic has you by the collar, and you cannot stop.

We must admit therefore, or confess ourselves ridiculous, that the domains of art and of nature are entirely distinct. Nature and art are two things—were it not so, one or the other would not exist. Art, in addition to its idealistic side, has a terrestrial, material side. Let it do what it will, it is shut in between grammar and prosody, between Vaugelas and Richelet. For its most capricious creations, it has formulae, methods of execution, a complete apparatus to set in motion. For genius there are delicate instruments, for mediocrity, tools.

It seems to us that someone has already said that the drama is a mirror wherein nature is reflected. But if it be an ordinary mirror, a smooth and polished surface, it will give only a dull image of objects, with no relief—faithful, but colourless; everyone knows that colour and light are lost in a simple reflection. The drama, therefore, must be a concentrating mirror, which, instead of weakening, concentrates and condenses the coloured rays, which make a mere gleam a light, and of a light a flame. Then only is the drama acknowledged by art.

The stage is an optical point. Everything that exists in the world—in history, in life, in man— should be and can be reflected therein, but under the magic wand of art. Art turns the leaves of the ages, of nature, studies chronicles, strives to reproduce actual facts (especially in respect to manners and peculiarities, which are much less exposed to doubt and contradiction than are concrete facts), restores what the chroniclers have lopped off, harmonises what they have collected, divines and supplies their omissions, fills their gaps with imaginary scenes which have the colour of the time, groups what they have left scattered about, sets in motion anew the threads of Providence which work the human marionettes, clothes the whole with a form at once poetical and natural, and imparts to it that vitality of truth and brilliancy which gives birth to illusion, that prestige of reality which arouses the enthusiasm of the spectator, and of the poet first of all, for the poet is sincere. Thus the aim of art is almost divine: to bring to life again if it is writing history, to create if it is writing poetry. . . .

It will readily be imagined that, for a work of this kind, if the poet must *choose* (and he must), he should choose, not the *beautiful*, but the *characteristic*. Not that it is advisable to "make local colour," as they say to-day; that is, to add as an afterthought a few discordant touches here and there to a work that is at best utterly conventional and false. The local colour should not be on the surface of the drama, but in its substance, in the very heart of the work, whence it spreads of itself, naturally, evenly, and, so to speak, into every corner of the drama, as the sap ascends from the root to the tree's topmost leaf. The drama should be thoroughly impregnated with this colour of the time, which should be, in some sort, in the air, so that one detects it only on entering the theatre, and that on going forth one finds one's self in a different period and atmosphere. It requires some study, some labour, to attain this end; so much the better. It is well that the avenues of art should be obstructed by those brambles from which everybody recoils except those of powerful will. Besides, it is this very study, fostered by an ardent inspiration, which will ensure the drama against a vice that kills it—the *commonplace*. To be commonplace is the failing of short-sighted, short-breathed poets. In this tableau of the stage, each figure must be held down to its most prominent, most individual, most precisely defined characteristic. Even the vulgar and the trivial should have an accent of their own. Like God, the true poet is present in every part of his work at once. Genius resembles the die which stamps the king's effigy on copper and golden coins alike. . . .

■ Discussion Questions

1. According to Hugo, why should artists turn to nature for guidance and inspiration?
2. As described here, what is the relationship between art and reality?
3. Why does Hugo think that it is especially important for poets to include "local color" in their works?
4. What links do you see between Hugo's ideas and the broader political and social context?

CHAPTER 18

Constructing the Nation-State, c. 1850–1880

The second half of the nineteenth century marked the dawning of a new age in European politics and culture. After the failed revolutions of 1848–1849, politicians, artists, intellectuals, and the general public cast aside the promises of idealists and claimed to see society as it really was: combative, competitive, and inherently disordered. The first document elucidates how European leaders sought to master this unruly scene and strengthen state power from above. The making of the modern nation-state also assumed global proportions as governments expanded their empires abroad. The second document illuminates the human scope of such efforts by the greatest colonial power of the day, Great Britain. The biological research of Charles Darwin reflected the scientific dimensions of the new age, as the final document reveals. To some observers, his work suggested that just as in politics, only the hardiest survived in the natural world. The social applications of Darwin's theories supported industrial Europe's march toward world dominance.

57. Alexander II, *Address in the State Council* (1861)

Russia's defeat in the Crimean War (1853–1856) revealed its inability to compete in the rapidly changing industrial world. Among its greatest liabilities was the institution of serfdom, which, by binding the peasant population to the land, inhibited the growth of a modern labor force while fostering widespread discontent. To combat these problems, Alexander II chose a momentous solution: the emancipation of the serfs. After years of discussion and debate, drafts of the reform were presented at a meeting of the State Council on January 28, 1861. The tsar began the meeting with the following speech, in which he underscores the importance of emancipation to Russia's future. His audience clearly shared his sense of urgency, for the general statute on the emancipation of the serfs was approved less than a month later.

The matter of the liberation of the serfs, which has been submitted for the consideration of the State Council, I consider to be a vital question for Russia, upon which will depend the development of her strength and power. I am sure that all of you, gentlemen, are just as convinced as I am of the benefits and necessity of this measure. I have another conviction, which is that this matter cannot be postponed; therefore I demand that the State Council finish with it in the first half of February so that it can be announced before the start of work in the fields; . . . I repeat— and this is my absolute will—that this matter should be finished right away.

A Source Book for Russian History, vol. III (New Haven: University Press, Yale, 1972), 599–600.

For four years now it has dragged on and has been arousing various fears and anticipations among both the estate owners and the peasants. Any further delay could be disastrous to the state. I cannot help being surprised and happy, and I am sure all of you are happy, at the trust and calm shown by our good people in this matter. Although the apprehensions of the nobility are to a certain extent understandable, for the closest and material interests of each are involved, notwithstanding all this, I have not forgotten and shall never forget that the approach to the matter was made on the initiative of the nobility itself, and I am happy to be able to be a witness to this before posterity. In my private conversations with the guberniia marshals of the nobility, and during my travels about Russia, when receiving the nobility, I did not conceal the trend of my thoughts and opinions on the question that occupies us all and said everywhere that this transformation cannot take place without certain sacrifices on their part and that all my efforts consist in making these sacrifices as little weighty and burdensome as possible for the nobility. I hope, gentlemen, that on inspection of the drafts presented to the State Council, you will assure yourselves that all that can be done for the protection of the interests of the nobility has been done; if on the other hand you find it necessary in any way to alter or to add to the presented work, then I am ready to receive your comments; but I ask you only not to forget that the basis of the whole work must be the improvement of the life of the peasants—an improvement not in words alone or on paper but in actual fact.

Before proceeding to a detailed examination of this draft itself, I would like to trace briefly the historical background of this affair. You are acquainted with the origin of serfdom. Formerly it did not exist among us; this law was established by autocratic power and only autocratic power can abolish it, and that is my sincere will.

My predecessors felt all the evils of serfdom and continually endeavored, if not to destroy it completely, to work toward the gradual limitation of the arbitrary power of the estate owners.

. . . My late father [Nicholas I] was continuously occupied with the thought of freeing the serfs. Sympathizing completely with this thought, already in 1856, before the coronation, while in Moscow I called the attention of the leaders of the nobility of the Moscow guberniia to the necessity for them to occupy themselves with improving the life of the serfs, adding that serfdom could not continue forever and that it would therefore be better if the transformation took place from above rather than from below. . . .

The Editorial Commissions worked for a year and seven months and, notwithstanding all the reproaches, perhaps partly just, to which the commissions were exposed, they finished their work conscientiously and presented it to the Main Committee. The Main Committee, under the chairmanship of my brother [Grand Duke Konstantin Nikolaevich], toiled with indefatigable energy and zeal. I consider it my duty to thank all the members of the committee, especially my brother, for their conscientious labors in this matter.

There may be various views on the draft presented, and I am willing to listen to all the different opinions. But I have the right to demand one thing from you: that you, putting aside all personal interests, act not like estate owners but like imperial statesmen invested with my trust. Approaching this important matter I have not concealed from myself all those difficulties that awaited us and I do not conceal them now; but, firmly believing in the grace of God and being convinced of the sacredness of this matter, I trust that God will not abandon us but will bless us to finish it for the future prosperity of our beloved fatherland.

■ Discussion Questions

1. What were Alexander's principal goals in granting the serfs freedom?
2. How did Alexander consider emancipation to be an expression of his power as tsar?
3. In calling for emancipation, did Alexander seek to undermine the existing social hierarchy?

58. Krupa Sattianadan, *Saguna: A Story of Native Christian Life*   (1887–1888)

Along with strengthening state power at home in the late nineteenth century, European leaders expanded their empires abroad and tightened their control therein. Great Britain's decision to assume direct control of India in 1858 provides a dramatic example of this shift in colonial policy. In her autobiographical novel Saguna, *Krupa Sattianadan (1862–1894) illuminates the everyday dimensions of British imperialism. She was born to Christian parents in the Bombay Presidency, an administrative unit of the colonial administration. While in her teens, the death of her beloved brother, Bhasker, gravely affected her physical and emotional health. She was sent to a nearby mission school to recover and in the following passage describes her experiences there. As she recounts, her white teachers strove to mold her according to English tastes, morals, and behavior, thereby exposing the racist attitudes underlying British rule. Her book found a ready audience and was published both in English and in Tamil, a language widely used in southern India.*

My sister paid a visit to the city, not long after Bhasker's death. She noticed my retired ways and my peculiar moods and took me to her home. One day as I was sitting in the hall, puzzling my head over some books that I found in the study, two ladies were announced, and before I had time to run away, they were in the hall. The first grasped my sister's hand in hers and gave her a hearty kiss. Her appearance at once attracted my notice. She seemed fresh coloured, tall, as she looked with a good-humoured smile at me over sister's shoulder. There was a twinkle in her eye, as if she wished every one to be a partaker of her high spirits. She was certainly strikingly different from other ladies, I thought, and I listened with great attention to what she had to say. . . . Then she turned round toward me, and, catching hold of both of my hands, put question after question to me in such a way that I could not but answer. She had large light brown eyes, a fine, full long face, a nose rather blunt, and a broad, high forehead. I liked her. Presently she turned toward my sister and talked aside for a few minutes while her companion smiled to me and drew me toward her. But before we could talk much the other turned toward me, and said, "So that's settled; you are to come next month and stay with me. You will learn to your heart's content there, but mind you are to be very free with me and tell me everything. I mean to quarrel with you very often. Ah! you critical thing. Don't I know what you are thinking?" and with a warm, but rather rough hug and a brushing kiss she left me. My sister said I must go and stay with the two ladies for some time. I liked the idea and made up my mind to go. The first thing that I was told on going to Miss Roberts'—for that was the name of the lady who took charge of me—was that I was a little girl; that in England girls of fourteen and fifteen were considered mere chits, and that I was to lay aside all solemnity of manner and behave as a girl. When it came to the lessons I was asked what I was learning.

I said: "History, geography, etc."

"What in history?"

"I have finished *Landmarks of the History of Greece*, and am reading—"

"Greece! Greece! What have you to do with Greece?"

I had loved this little book. It was like a storybook, and I thought that she would have been pleased, but she only murmured, "Well! I will see. I must get something more suited to you. What about English? Can you read fluently?"

Susie Tharu and K. Lalita, eds., *Women Writing in India: 600 B.C. to the Present*, vol. I, *600 B.C. to the Early Twentieth Century* (New York: The Feminist Press, 1991), 277–81.

Longfellow's poems were put into my hand. The volume opened at "Pleasant it was when woods were green." I read this fast enough.

"Too fast."

"Oh I know it by heart," I exclaimed, anxious to show my cleverness. I shut the book and repeated the whole thing to her. I had once learnt it in a fit of study, and it had given me much pleasure.

"Well! I tell you what," she said, shutting the book, "you know a little too much. When a horse goes too fast, what does his master do?"

I did not know what he did, but I thought the comparison was not a good one, and I exclaimed abruptly, "I am not a horse."

"Well! Well!" she said laughing, "we won't discuss that point. I think you want occupation. You must teach in my little school this afternoon. Now we have done with our lessons for one day."

To my great surprise she shut up the books and put them by. When dinner time came I saw the other lady for the first time. She gave me a smile and pointed to my place by her side, but Miss Roberts never left me alone. She began by saying to her neighbour, "Girls in England never sit at the table with their elders, but of course we shall allow this one." In my sister's house I had learned to some extent how to use spoon and fork, but when I found the lady's eyes fixed on me my fingers trembled, and I thought I was sure to make all kinds of mistakes to her amusement. Already her eyes were twinkling with fun and laughter. I refused many a tempting thing that was offered, while she kept on remarking: "That's right, don't eat if you don't care. Girls in England don't eat these things." At last came curry and rice, of which I took a little, and enjoyed it. . . .

During the day, the school was my delight. This Miss Roberts managed. She instructed me in the art of teaching, in which I found a great delight. I was astonished at the explanations which I was able to give, and the way in which a knowledge of things seemed to spring into existence when it was required. I was in a whirl of delight with the blackboards, the large maps and the pictures, and the new dignity that all these conferred on me. Miss Roberts smiled at my eagerness, and forgot to say that I was only a child. I loved to think myself grown up and important. Miss Roberts used to quarrel with me as impetuously and passionately as if she had been of my own age, and then make it up by giving me a hearty hug and a kiss. She had very peculiar views, and we often had little fights with each other. I can hardly help thinking that she sometimes gave expression to her views for the sole purpose of teasing me. "Oh, Miss D., what made you receive the Bible woman in the drawing room?" she said one day, alluding to a very respectable person, a great friend of our family. "In England we receive them in the kitchen. She is no better than a servant, I assure you."

"In the kitchen?" I said, in amazement and indignation. I was angry, and thought of many grievances that I had heard spoken of. I had also heard that we were the real aristocrats of our country, and that the English ladies who came to India only belonged to the middle class, and I resolved to tell her that, so I boldly added: "What do you think of us? We are real aristocrats of this place." Unfortunately I pronounced the big word wrongly, and she burst out laughing and repeated it again and again, as I had done. "I don't care. Anyhow, you are middle-class people. She is a brahmin, and only takes money from the Mission because she is poor. She is no servant. In your country you are no brahmins. You are sudras." Tears fell from my eyes, and I felt as if I should choke.

"Miss D.," exclaimed the angry lady, now quite beside herself, "do girls ever talk at table like this? I protest against this. I can't have it. I tell you I can't,"—this with so much emphasis that I was quite frightened. Miss D. looked at me and shook her head. The tears that were rolling from my eyes I hastily wiped. "What can I do?" I said, while a shower of words, such as "rude," "bad," "naughty," "disrespectful," etc., fell on my head. Tiffin over, Miss Roberts went with a bounce to her room and I went to mine and began to cry. "Natives," I said to myself, "we are natives. Tomorrow she will say that my mother was a Bible woman too. Oh! I will go away from her," and I began to cry more. About five minutes afterward the door behind me opened, and Miss Roberts rushed in, took hold of me, and kissed me profusely. "Now it is all right," she said smiling and wonderfully changed. "We won't talk about it."

"And you won't send Bible women to the kitchen?" I said.

She shook her head and rushed away from me laughing.

In the evenings we generally sat together in the lobby. It was our free time, and I was told to say anything I liked. I used to sit far back on the deep seat with my hands on my lap, although there was a table in front. I liked to draw my own pictures, with the stars and shadows outside, and often my thoughts were with Bhasker; but I was always disturbed and told to talk. Generally the ladies had some fancy work in their hands; but I never brought any. One day Miss Roberts rebuked me and said: "Why did you not bring some work?"

I felt guilty, but still as I rose I said somehow, "I thought we were expected to be free at this time."

"Yes, but we must not appear so. I hate laziness."

Something in this remark caught my attention. I stood near the table and looked out. All my pictures vanished. I looked into her face and said, "It is only for appearance, is it? What is the good of that? Won't it be acting falsely?"

She flew into a passion, and when I tried to escape to my room, she forced me down. "Falsely! Sit and be lazy," she said, "and let every one of us put you to shame."

The second lady, however, calmed her, saying, "Really I don't do anything. I had better sit quietly too."

"Sit, sit," said Miss Roberts, who had by this time nearly spent her wrath and was in a little pet.

The other lady had on various occasions whispered to me, "She is Irish and means nothing," and now she looked and smiled at me.

My greatest trials always came through my tongue. I had got into the habit of thinking loudly. Bhasker had encouraged it, and the discussions carried on by my other brothers, in which I often took part, had made me quite adept in defending my views. I had had to stand up for my rights from my childhood. I had not then learnt the beauty of silence. One day I was sitting in the lobby in my usual half-sleepy, half-dreamy state, when I heard a visitor announced. As soon as Miss Roberts heard the name, she broke out abruptly, "Oh, how disgusting! What a bore she is! and she wants me, that is true enough." So saying she walked out, and an elderly lady met her near the lobby.

"Oh! I am so glad to see you. How do you do?" Miss Roberts said in a hearty tone as she brought in the visitor. Surely this is somebody else, and I am glad that it is a surprise for Miss Roberts, I said to myself. The talk evidently was cheerful and genial, but as soon as it was over, I was rather taken aback to hear Miss Roberts say, "Oh, what a bore to be sure! How glad I am she is gone! We must really not have visitors at this time."

"She! she!" I said, "was not she a surprise to you?"

"What do you mean?" said Miss Roberts, turning abruptly round on me.

"No! I thought the lady was a surprise to you. You said you were so glad to see her."

"Oh! Oh!" she said, lifting her voice and her hands.

"Miss D., I tell you I can't have this imper—"

"You said free speech was allowed here," I answered, interrupting her.

"Free speech, but not to your superiors, not to me," this with a thump on the table. "You naughty girl."

But it was a little overdone, and there was a burst from the other lady in which Miss Roberts found herself heartily joining.

Later on I came to know that they did not mean anything. It was only the custom, and they used the few set phrases that etiquette compelled them to use. But my readers will understand from this what a boor I was. I loved these two ladies and stayed with them for months, and in spite of little quarrels now and then, I lived very happily with them. Not long after I was attacked with fever, and my sister was compelled to take me away.

■ Discussion Questions

1. How would you describe the attitudes of Sattianadan's teachers toward her, and vice versa?
2. As described by Sattianadan, in what ways did the mission school further advance the goals of British colonial policy?
3. What does this passage suggest about both the benefits and drawbacks of this policy?

59. Charles Darwin, *The Descent of Man* (1871)

As Bismarck and other Realpolitikers *were transforming European political views in the mid- to late nineteenth century, the English naturalist Charles Darwin (1809–1882) was transforming their scientific ones. In 1859, he published* On the Origin of Species, *which argued that animal species evolved over time through a process of natural selection by which the strongest, and most well adapted to any given environment, survived. The biblical story of creation had no place in Darwin's conclusions, and this incited considerable debate. The debate intensified twelve years later when Darwin applied his theory of evolution directly to humans in* The Descent of Man. *The ramifications of this work extended beyond the field of biology when some people began to use evolutionary principles to understand, justify, and perpetuate the social and political inequalities of the day.*

The main conclusion here arrived at, and now held by many naturalists who are well competent to form a sound judgment, is that man is descended from some less highly organised form. The grounds upon which this conclusion rests will never be shaken, for the close similarity between man and the lower animals in embryonic development, as well as in innumerable points of structure and constitution, both of high and of the most trifling importance,—the rudiments which he retains, and the abnormal reversions to which he is occasionally liable,—are facts which cannot be disputed. They have long been known, but until recently they told us nothing with respect to the origin of man. Now when viewed by the light of our knowledge of the whole organic world, their meaning is unmistakable. The great principle of evolution stands up clear and firm, when these groups of facts are considered in connection with others such as the mutual affinities of the members of the same group, their geographical distribution in past and present times, and their geological succession. It is incredible that all these facts should speak falsely. He who is not content to look, like a savage, at the phenomena of nature as disconnected, cannot any longer believe that man is the work of a separate act of creation. He will be forced to admit that the close resemblance of the embryo of man to that, for instance, of a dog—the construction of his skull, limbs and whole frame on the same plan with that of other mammals, independently of the uses to which the parts may be put—the occasional re-appearance of various structures, for instance of several muscles, which man does not normally possess, but which are common to the

Charles Darwin, *The Descent of Man and Selection in Relation to Sex* (New York: D. Appleton and Company, 1896), 606–19.

Quadrumana—and a crowd of analogous facts—all point in the plainest manner to the conclusion that man is the co-descendant with other mammals of a common progenitor.

We have seen that man incessantly presents individual differences in all parts of his body and in his mental faculties. These differences or variations seem to be induced by the same general causes, and to obey the same laws as with the lower animals. In both cases similar laws of inheritance prevail. Man tends to increase at a greater rate than his means of subsistence; consequently he is occasionally subjected to a severe struggle for existence, and natural selection will have effected whatever lies within its scope. A succession of strongly-marked variations of a similar nature is by no means requisite; slight fluctuating differences on the individual suffice for the work of natural selection; not that we have any reason to suppose that in the same species, all parts of the organisation tend to vary to the same degree. . . .

Through the means just specified, aided perhaps by others as yet undiscovered, man has been raised to his present state. But since he attained to the rank of manhood, he has diverged into distinct races, or as they may be more fitly called, subspecies. Some of these, such as the Negro and European, are so distinct that, if specimens had been brought to a naturalist without any further information, they would undoubtedly have been considered by him as good and true species. Nevertheless all the races agree in so many unimportant details of structure and in so many mental peculiarities, that these can be accounted for only by inheritance from a common progenitor; and a progenitor thus characterised would probably deserve to rank as man.

It must not be supposed that the divergence of each race from the other races, and of all from a common stock, can be traced back to any one pair of progenitors. On the contrary, at every stage in the process of modification, all the individuals which were in any way better fitted for their conditions of life, though in different degrees, would have survived in greater numbers than the less well-fitted. The process would have been like that followed by man, when he does not intentionally select particular individuals, but breeds from all the superior individuals, and neglects the inferior. He thus slowly but surely modifies his stock, and unconsciously forms a new strain. So with respect to modifications acquired independently of selection, and due to variations arising from the nature of the organism and the action of the surrounding conditions, or from changed habits of life, no single pair will have been modified much more than the other pairs inhabiting the same country, for all will have been continually blended through free intercrossing.

By considering the embryological structure of man,—the homologies which he presents with the lower animals,—the rudiments which he retains,—and the reversions to which he is liable, we can partly recall in imagination the former condition of our early progenitors; and can approximately place them in their proper place in the zoological series. We thus learn that man is descended from a hairy, tailed quadruped, probably arboreal in its habits, and an inhabitant of the Old World. This creature, if its whole structure had been examined by a naturalist, would have been classed amongst the Quadrumana, as surely as the still more ancient progenitor of the Old and New World monkeys. The Quadrumana and all the higher mammals are probably derived from an ancient marsupial animal, and this through a long line of diversified forms, from some amphibian-like creature, and this again from some fish-like animals. In the dim obscurity of the past we can see that the early progenitor of all the Vertebrata must have been an aquatic animal, provided with branchiae, with the two sexes united in the same individual, and with the most important organs of the body (such as the brain and heart) imperfectly or not at all developed. This animal seems to have been more like the larvae of the existing marine Ascidians than any other known form.

The high standard of our intellectual powers and moral disposition is the greatest difficulty which presents itself, after we have been driven to this conclusion on the origin of man. But everyone who admits the principle of evolution, must see that the mental powers of the higher animals, which are the same in kind with those of man, though so different in degree, are capable of advancement. Thus the interval between the mental powers of one of the higher apes and of a fish, or between those of an ant and scale-insect, is immense; yet their development does not offer any special difficulty; for with our domesticated animals, the mental faculties are certainly variable, and the variations are inherited. No one doubts that they are of the utmost importance to animals in a state of nature. Therefore the conditions are favourable for their development through natural selection. The same conclusion may be extended to man; the intellect must have been all-important to him, even at a very remote period, as enabling him to invent and use language, to make weapons, tools, traps, etc., whereby with the aid of his social habits, he long ago became the most dominant of all living creatures. . . .

The belief in God has often been advanced as not only the greatest, but the most complete of all the distinctions between man and the lower animals. It is however impossible, as we have seen, to maintain that this belief is innate or instinctive in man. On the other hand a belief in all-pervading spiritual agencies seems to be universal; and apparently follows from a considerable advance in man's reason, and from a still greater advance in his faculties of imagination, curiosity and wonder. I am aware that the assumed instinctive belief in God has been used by many persons as an argument for His existence. But this is a rash argument, as we should thus be compelled to believe in the existence of many cruel and malignant spirits, only a little more powerful than man; for the belief in them is far more general than in a beneficent Deity. The idea of a universal and beneficent Creator does not seem to arise in the mind of man, until he has been elevated by long-continued culture. . . .

I am aware that the conclusions arrived at in this work will be denounced by some as highly irreligious; but he who denounces them is bound to show why it is more irreligious to explain the origin of man as a distinct species by descent from some lower form, through the laws of variation and natural selection, than to explain the birth of the individual through the laws of ordinary reproduction. The birth both of the species and of the individual are equally parts of that grand sequence of events, which our minds refuse to accept as the result of blind chance. The understanding revolts at such a conclusion, whether or not we are able to believe that every slight variation of structure,—the union of each pair in marriage,—the dissemination of each seed,—and other such events, have all been ordained for some special purpose. . . .

The main conclusion arrived at in this work, namely that man is descended from some lowly organised form, will, I regret to think, be highly distasteful to many. But there can hardly be a doubt that we are descended from barbarians. The astonishment which I felt on first seeing a party of Fuegians on a wild and broken shore will never be forgotten by me, for the reflection at once rushed into my mind—such were our ancestors. These men were absolutely naked and bedaubed with paint, their long hair was tangled, their mouths frothed with excitement, and their expression was wild, startled, and distrustful. They possessed hardly any arts, and like wild animals lived on what they could catch; they had no government, and were merciless to everyone not of their own small tribe. He who has seen a savage in his native land will not feel much shame, if forced to acknowledge that the blood of some more humble creature flows in his veins. For my own part I would as soon be descended from that heroic little monkey, who braved his dreaded enemy in order to save the life of his keeper, or from that old baboon, who descending from the mountains, carried away in triumph his young comrade from a crowd of astonished dogs—as from a savage who delights to torture his enemies, offers up bloody sacrifices, practises infanticide without remorse, treats his wives like slaves, knows no decency, and is haunted by the grossest superstitions.

Man may be excused for feeling some pride at having risen, though not through his own exertions, to the very summit of the organic scale; and the fact of his having thus risen, instead of having been aboriginally placed there, may give him hope for a still higher destiny in the distant future. But we are not here concerned with hopes or fears, only with the truth as far as our reason permits us to discover it; and I have given the evidence to the best of my ability. We must, however, acknowledge, as it seems to me, that man with all his noble qualities, with sympathy which feels for the most debased, with benevolence which extends not only to other men but to the humblest living creature, with his god-like intellect which has penetrated into the movements and constitution of the solar system—with all these exalted powers—Man still bears in his bodily frame the indelible stamp of his lowly origin.

■ **Discussion Questions**

1. What evidence does Darwin supply to support his theory of human evolution?
2. How does this evidence call into question the relationship between religion and science?
3. In what ways does Darwin voice the concern for realism and concrete facts that marked the general mood of his day?

CHAPTER 19

Empire, Modernity, and the Road to War, c. 1880–1914

The dual phenomena of industry and empire changed Europe and the world profoundly in the late nineteenth century. With domestic industries booming, European leaders looked abroad for new markets and raw materials. The widespread belief that imperial holdings were an indication of a nation's strength and racial superiority also fueled the quest for empire. Industrial growth went hand in hand with imperial expansion, and as the twentieth century dawned, Europeans had cause for both elation and fear. On the one hand, many enjoyed unprecedented prosperity. On the other, domestic and international tensions abounded. At home people struggled to navigate the hazards of modern life, while abroad nation-states faced mounting competition and dissent in their quests for imperial glory. As the following documents reveal, the road of modernity was rocky and uncertain, casting a permanent shadow over Enlightenment faith in the inevitability of progress.

60. Jules Ferry, *Speech before the French National Assembly* (1883)

French politician Jules Ferry (1832–1893) fueled his country's quest to compete in Europe's race to conquer foreign territory in the closing decades of the nineteenth century. While serving two terms as premier during the Third Republic, Ferry took the lead in France's colonial expansion in Africa and Asia. Yet not everyone embraced his imperialist policies, including his conservative and socialist colleagues within the government. In this speech, delivered before the National Assembly in July 1883, Ferry faced his opponents head-on, defending not only the political and economic necessity of French expansionism but also its moral justness. At the same time, his critics voice their views, revealing the basis of their anticolonial sentiment.

M. JULES FERRY: Gentlemen, it embarrasses me to make such a prolonged demand upon the gracious attention of the Chamber, but I believe that the duty I am fulfilling upon this platform is not a useless one. It is as strenuous for me as for you, but I believe that there is some benefit in summarizing and condensing, in the form of arguments, the principles, the motives, and the various interests by which a policy of colonial expansion may be justified; it goes without saying that I will try to remain reasonable, moderate, and never lose sight of the major continental in-

Ralph A. Austin, ed., *Modern Imperialism: Western Overseas Expansion and Its Aftermath, 1776–1965* (Lexington, Mass.: D. C. Heath, 1969), 69–74.

terests which are the primary concern of this country. What I wish to say, to support this proposition, is that in fact, just as in word, the policy of colonial expansion is a political and economic system; I wish to say that one can relate this system to three orders of ideas: economic ideas, ideas of civilization in its highest sense, and ideas of politics and patriotism.

In the area of economics, I will allow myself to place before you, with the support of some figures, the considerations which justify a policy of colonial expansion from the point of view of that need, felt more and more strongly by the industrial populations of Europe and particularly those of our own rich and hard working country: the need for export markets. Is this some kind of chimera? Is this a view of the future or is it not rather a pressing need, and, we could say, the cry of our industrial population? I will formulate only in a general way what each of you, in the different parts of France, is in a position to confirm. Yes, what is lacking for our great industry, drawn irrevocably on to the path of exportation by the [free trade] treaties of 1860, what it lacks more and more is export markets. Why? Because next door to us Germany is surrounded by barriers, because beyond the ocean, the United States of America has become protectionist, protectionist in the most extreme sense, because not only have these great markets, I will not say closed but shrunk, and thus become more difficult of access for our industrial products, but also these great states are beginning to pour products not seen heretofore onto our own markets. . . . It is not necessary to pursue this demonstration any farther. Yes, gentlemen, I am speaking to the economists, whose convictions and past services no one appreciates more than I do; I am speaking to the honorable M. Passy, whom I see here and who is one of the most authoritative representatives among us of the old school of economics [*smiles*]; I know very well what they will reply to me, what is at the bottom of their thoughts . . . the old school, the great school, gentlemen; one, M. Passy, which your name has embellished, which was led in France by Jean-Baptiste Say and by Adam Smith in England. I do not mean to treat you with any irony, M. Passy, believe me.

I say that I know very well the thoughts of the economists, whom I can call doctrinaires without offending M. Passy. They say to us, "The true export markets are the commercial treaties which furnish and assure them." Gentlemen, I do not look down upon commercial treaties: if we could return to the situation which existed after 1860, if the world had not been subjected to that economic revolution which is the product of the development of science and the speeding up of communications, if this great revolution had not intervened, I would gladly take up the situation which existed after 1860. It is quite true that in that epoch the competition of grain from Odessa did not ruin French agriculture, that the grain of America and of India did not yet offer us any competition; at that moment we were living under the regime of commercial treaties, not only with England, but with the other great powers, with Germany, which had not yet become an industrial power. I do not look down upon them, these treaties; I had the honor of negotiating some of less importance than those of 1860; but gentlemen, in order to make treaties, it is necessary to have two parties: one does not make treaties with the United States; this is the conviction which has grown among those who have attempted to open some sort of negotiations in this quarter, whether officially or officiously.

Gentlemen, there is a second point, a second order of ideas to which I have to give equal attention, but as quickly as possible, believe me; it is the humanitarian and civilizing side of the question. On this point the honorable M. Camille Pellatan has jeered in his own refined and clever manner; he jeers, he condemns, and he says "What is this civilization which you impose with cannonballs? What is it but another form of barbarism? Don't these populations, these inferior races, have the same rights as you? Aren't they masters of their own houses? Have they called upon you? You come to them against their will, you offer them violence, but not civilization." There, gentlemen, is the thesis; I do not hesitate to say that this is not politics, nor is it history: it is political metaphysics. ["Ah, Ah," *on far left*.]

. . . Gentlemen, I must speak from a higher and more truthful plane. It must be stated openly that, in effect, superior races have rights over inferior races. [*Movement on many benches on the far left.*]

M. JULES MAIGNE: Oh! You dare to say this in the country which has proclaimed the rights of man!

M. DE GUILLOUTET: This is a justification of slavery and the slave trade!

M. JULES FERRY: If M. Maigne is right, if the declaration of the rights of man was written for the blacks of equatorial Africa, then by what right do you impose regular commerce upon them? They have not called upon you.

M. RAOUL DUVAL: We do not want to impose anything upon them. It is you who wish to do so!

M. JULES MAIGNE: To propose and to impose are two different things!

M. GEORGES PERIN: In any case, you cannot bring about commerce by force.

M. JULES FERRY: I repeat that superior races have a right, because they have a duty. They have the duty to civilize inferior races. . . . [*Approbation from the left. New interruptions from the extreme left and from the right.*]

That is what I have to answer M. Pelletan in regard to the second point upon which he touched.

He then touched upon a third, more delicate, more serious, and upon which I ask your permission to express myself quite frankly. It is the political side of the question. The honorable M. Pelletan, who is a distinguished writer, always comes up with remarkably precise formulations. I will borrow from him the one which he applied the other day to this aspect of colonial policy.

"It is a system," he says, "which consists of seeking out compensations in the Orient with a circumspect and peaceful seclusion which is actually imposed upon us in Europe."

I would like to explain myself in regard to this. I do not like this word, "compensation," and, in effect, not here but elsewhere it has often been used in treacherous way. If what is being said or insinuated is that any government in this country, any Republican minister could possibly believe that there are in any part of the world compensations for the disasters which we have experienced, an injury is being inflicted . . . and an injury undeserved by that government. [*Applause at the center and left.*] I will ward off this injury with all the force of my patriotism! [*New applause and bravos from the same benches.*]

Gentlemen, there are certain considerations which merit the attention of all patriots. The conditions of naval warfare have been profoundly altered. ["Very true! Very true!"]

At this time, as you know, a warship cannot carry more than fourteen days' worth of coal, no matter how perfectly it is organized, and a ship which is out of coal is a derelict on the surface of the sea, abandoned to the first person who comes along. Thence the necessity of having on the oceans provision stations, shelters, ports for defense and revictualling. [*Applause at the center and left. Various interruptions.*] And it is for this that we needed Tunisia, for this that we needed Saigon and the Mekong Delta, for this that we need Madagascar, that we are at Diégo-Suarez and Vohemar [two Madagascar ports] and will never leave them! [*Applause from a great number of benches.*] Gentlemen, in Europe as it is today, in this competition of so many rivals which we see growing around us, some by perfecting their military or maritime forces, others by the prodigious development of an ever growing population; in a Europe, or rather in a universe of this sort, a policy of peaceful seclusion or abstention is simply the highway to decadence! Nations are great in our times only by means of the activities which they develop; it is not simply "by the peaceful shining forth of institutions" [*Interruptions on the extreme left and right*] that they are great at this hour.

As for me, I am astounded to find the monarchist parties becoming indignant over the fact that the Republic of France is following a policy which does not confine itself to that ideal of modesty, of reserve, and, if you will allow me the expression, of bread and butter [*Interruptions and laughter on the left*] which the representatives of fallen monarchies wish to impose upon France. [*Applause at the center.*]

. . . [The Republican Party] has shown that it is quite aware that one cannot impose upon France a political ideal conforming to that of nations like independent Belgium and the Swiss Republic; that something else is needed for France: that she cannot be merely a free country, that she must also be a great country, exercizing all of her rightful influence over the destiny of Europe, that she ought to propagate this influence throughout the world and carry everywhere that she can her language, her customs, her flag, her arms, and her genius. [*Applause at center and left.*]

■ Discussion Questions

1. Why does Ferry consider colonial expansion to be an economic necessity?
2. Aside from its economic benefits, why, according to Ferry, is colonial expansion justified?
3. How does Ferry appeal to nationalist sentiment to defend his imperialist stance, and why?
4. What is the basis of his critics' arguments against imperialism?

61. The I-ho-ch'uan (Boxers), *The Boxers Demand Death for All "Foreign Devils"* (1900)

Despite Europe's domination of the globe, the glow of imperial glory was starting to fade in the late nineteenth and early twentieth centuries. In many places, Europeans' hold on their colonial territories was increasingly tenuous as local resistance to foreign rule and interference mounted. The following placard exposes the beliefs driving one such uprising in China, where Western nations had recently made significant inroads. It was written and circulated by the Boxers at the height of their mass revolt against foreign powers in 1900, during which they burned churches, destroyed telegraph lines and railways, and murdered Chinese Christians and missionaries. As the document reveals, an amalgam of distinctive spiritual values and overt hostility to the trappings of modern "progress" fueled the Boxers' actions. Although brutally repressed, the Boxer rebellion strengthened Chinese nationalist sentiment, which ultimately undermined Western imperialism in China.

The Gods assist the Boxers,
The Patriotic Harmonious corps,
It is because the "Foreign Devils" disturb the "Middle Kingdom."
Urging the people to join their religion,
To turn their backs on Heaven,
Venerate not the Gods and forget the ancestors.

Men violate the human obligations,
Women commit adultery,
"Foreign Devils" are not produced by mankind,
If you do not believe,
Look at them carefully.

Louis L. Snyder, ed., *The Imperialism Reader: Documents and Readings on Modern Expansionism* (Princeton: Van Nostrand, 1962), 322–23.

The eyes of all the "Foreign Devils" are bluish,
No rain falls,
The earth is getting dry,
This is because the churches stop Heaven,
The Gods are angry;
The Genii are vexed;
Both come down from the mountain to deliver the doctrine.

This is no hearsay,
The practices of boxing will not be in vain;
Reciting incantations and pronouncing magic words,
Burn up yellow written prayers,
Light incense sticks
To invite the Gods and Genii of all the grottoes.

The Gods come out from grottoes,
The Genii come down from mountains,
Support the human bodies to practice the boxing.
When all the military accomplishments or tactics
Are fully learned,
It will not be difficult to exterminate the "Foreign Devils" then.

Push aside the railway tracks,
Pull out the telegraph poles,
Immediately after this destroy the steamers.

The great France
Will grow cold and downhearted.
The English and Russians will certainly disperse.
Let the various "Foreign Devils" all be killed.
May the whole Elegant Empire of the Great Ching [Qing] Dynasty be ever prosperous!

■ **Discussion Questions**

1. Why do the Boxers describe foreigners as "devils"?
2. What forces do the Boxers believe are on their side?
3. In addition to killing foreigners, why do you think the Boxers call for an attack on railways, telegraph lines, and steamers?
4. What type of society do the Boxers desire for China?

62. Sigmund Freud, *The Interpretation of Dreams* (1900)

The fast-paced and conflict-ridden nature of life in industrial Europe undermined many people's op-timism about their own and society's future. Austrian doctor Sigmund Freud (1856–1939) developed the method of psychoanalysis to tap into and cure such anxieties. After studying medicine in Vienna,

A. A. Brill, trans. and ed., *The Basic Writings of Sigmund Freud* (New York: The Modern Library, 1938), 183, 188–94, 208–09, 217–18.

in 1886 Freud opened his own practice to treat patients with nervous disorders. His clinical experience was the basis for his lifelong commitment to the scientific study of the human unconscious. He published The Interpretation of Dreams *in 1900. In it, he described dreams as windows into an individual's irrational desires and inner conflicts. Freud believed that by drawing out dreams' hidden meanings, he could expose the roots of his patients' psychological problems. Psychoanalysis was designed to do just that, thereby laying the foundation of modern psychology.*

In the following pages, I shall demonstrate that there is a psychological technique which makes it possible to interpret dreams, and that on the application of this technique, every dream will reveal itself as a psychological structure, full of significance, and one which may be assigned to a specific place in the psychic activities of the waking state. Further, I shall endeavor to elucidate the processes which underlie the strangeness and obscurity of dreams, and to deduce from these processes the nature of the psychic forces whose conflict or co-operation is responsible for our dreams. . . .

I am proposing to show that dreams are capable of interpretation; and any contributions to the solution of the problem which have already been discussed will emerge only as possible by-products in the accomplishment of my special task. On the hypothesis that dreams are susceptible of interpretation, I at once find myself in disagreement with the prevailing doctrine of dreams . . . for "to interpret a dream" is to specify its "meaning," to replace it by something which takes its position in the concatenation of our psychic activities as a link of definite importance and value. But, as we have seen, the scientific theories of the dream leave no room for a problem of dream-interpretation; since, in the first place, according to these theories, dreaming is not a psychic activity at all, but a somatic process which makes itself known to the psychic apparatus by means of symbols. Lay opinion has always been opposed to these theories. It asserts its privilege of proceeding illogically, and although it admits that dreams are incomprehensible and absurd, it cannot summon up the courage to deny that dreams have any significance. Led by a dim intuition, it seems rather to assume that dreams have a meaning, albeit a hidden one; that they are intended as a substitute for some other thought-process, and that we have only to disclose this substitute correctly in order to discover the hidden meaning of the dream.

The unscientific world, therefore, has always endeavored to "interpret" dreams, and by applying one or the other of two essentially different methods. The first of these methods envisages the dream-content as a whole, and seeks to replace it by another content, which is intelligible and in certain respects analogous. This is symbolic dream-interpretation; and of course it goes to pieces at the very outset in the case of those dreams which are not only unintelligible but confused. The construction which the biblical Joseph placed upon the dream of Pharaoh furnishes an example of this method. The seven fat kine, after which came seven lean ones that devoured the former, were a symbolic substitute for seven years of famine in the land of Egypt, which according to the prediction were to consume all the surplus that seven fruitful years had produced. Most of the artificial dreams contrived by the poets are intended for some such symbolic interpretation, for they reproduce the thought conceived by the poet in a guise not unlike the disguise which we are wont to find in our dreams.

The idea that the dream concerns itself chiefly with the future, whose form it surmises in advance—a relic of the prophetic significance with which dreams were once invested—now becomes the motive for translating into the future the meaning of the dream which has been found by means of symbolic interpretation.

A demonstration of the manner in which one arrives at such a symbolic interpretation cannot, of course, be given. Success remains a matter of ingenious conjecture, of direct intuition, and for this reason dream-interpretation has naturally been elevated into an art which seems to depend upon extraordinary gifts. The second of the two popular methods of dream-interpretation entirely abandons such claims. It might be described as the "cipher method," since it treats the dream as a kind of secret code in which every sign is translated into another sign of known meaning, according to an established key. For example, I have dreamt of a letter and also of a funeral or the like; I consult a "dream-book," and I find that "letter" is to be translated by "vexation" and "funeral" by "engagement." It now remains to establish a connection, which I am again to assume as pertaining to the future, by means of the rigmarole which I have deciphered. . . .

The worthlessness of both these popular methods of interpretation does not admit of discussion. As regards the scientific treatment of the subject, the symbolic method is limited in its application, and is not susceptible of a general exposition. In the cipher method everything depends upon whether the "key," the dream-book, is reliable, and for that all guarantees are lacking. So that one might be tempted to grant the contention of the philosophers and psychiatrists, and to dismiss the problem of dream-interpretation as altogether fanciful.

I have, however, come to think differently. I have been forced to perceive that here, once more, we have one of those not infrequent cases where an ancient and stubbornly retained popular belief seems to have come nearer to the truth of the matter than the opinion of modern science. I must insist that the dream actually does possess a meaning, and that a scientific method of dream-interpretation is possible. I arrived at my knowledge of this method in the following manner:

For years I have been occupied with the solution of certain psychopathological structures—hysterical phobias, obsessional ideas, and the like—with therapeutic intentions. . . . In the course of these psychoanalytic studies, I happened upon the question of dream-interpretation. My patients, after I had pledged them to inform me of all the ideas and thoughts which occurred to them in connection with a given theme, related their dreams, and thus taught me that a dream may be interpolated in the psychic concatenation, which may be followed backwards from a pathological idea into the patient's memory. The next step was to treat the dream itself as a symptom, and to apply to it the method of interpretation which had been worked out for such symptoms.

For this a certain psychic preparation on the part of the patient is necessary. A twofold effort is made to stimulate his attentiveness in respect of his psychic perceptions, and to eliminate the critical spirit in which he is ordinarily in the habit of viewing such thoughts as come to the surface. For the purpose of self-observation with concentrated attention it is advantageous that the patient should take up a restful position and close his eyes; he must be explicitly instructed to renounce all criticism of the thought-formations which he may perceive. He must also be told that the success of the psychoanalysis depends upon his noting and communicating everything that passes through his mind, and that he must not allow himself to suppress one idea because it seems to him unimportant or irrelevant to the subject, or another because it seems nonsensical. He must preserve an absolute impartiality in respect to his ideas; for if he is unsuccessful in finding the desired solution of the dream, the obsessional idea, or the like, it will be because he permits himself to be critical of them. . . .

As will be seen, the point is to induce a psychic state which is in some degree analogous, as regards the distribution of psychic energy (mobile attention), to the state of the mind before falling asleep—and also, of course, to the hypnotic state. On falling asleep the "undesired ideas" emerge, owing to the slackening of a certain arbitrary (and, of course, also critical) action, which is allowed to influence the trends of our ideas; we are accustomed to speak of fatigue as the reason of this slackening; the emerging undesired ideas are changed into visual and auditory images. In the condition which it utilized for the analysis of dreams and pathological ideas, this activity is purposely and deliberately renounced, and the psychic energy thus saved (or some part of it) is employed in attentively tracking the undesired thoughts which now come to the surface—thoughts which retain their identity as ideas (in which the condition differs from the state of falling asleep). *"Undesired ideas" are thus changed into "desired" ones.* . . .

The first step in the application of this procedure teaches us that one cannot make the dream as a whole the object of one's attention, but only the individual components of its content. If I ask a patient who is as yet unpractised: "What occurs to you in connection with this dream?" he is unable, as a rule, to fix upon anything in his psychic field of vision. I must first dissect the dream for him; then, in connection with each fragment, he gives me a number of ideas which may be described as the "thoughts behind" this part of the dream. In this first and important condition, then, the method of dream-interpretation which I employ diverges from the popular, historical and legendary method of interpretation by symbolism and approaches more nearly to the second or "cipher method." Like this, it is an interpretation in detail, not *en masse;* like this, it conceives the dream, from the outset, as something built up, as a conglomerate of psychic formations. . . .

When, after passing through a narrow defile, one suddenly reaches a height beyond which the ways part and a rich prospect lies outspread in different directions, it is well to stop for a moment and consider whither one shall turn next. We are in somewhat the same position after we have mastered this first interpretation of a dream. We find ourselves standing in the light of a sudden discovery. The dream is not comparable to the irregular sounds of a musical instrument, which, instead of being played by the hand of a musician, is struck by some external force; the dream is not meaningless, not absurd, does not presuppose that one part of our store of ideas is dormant while another part begins to awake. It is a perfectly valid psychic phenomenon, actually a wish-fulfilment; it may be enrolled in the continuity of the intelligible psychic activities of the waking state; it is built up by a highly complicated intellectual activity. . . .

It is easy to show that the wish-fulfilment in dreams is often undisguised and easy to recognize, so that one may wonder why the language of dreams has not long since been understood. There is, for example, a dream which I can evoke as often as I please, experimentally, as it were. If, in the evening, I eat anchovies, olives, or other strongly salted foods, I am thirsty at night, and therefore I wake. The waking, however, is preceded by a dream, which has always the same content, namely, that I am drinking. I am drinking long draughts of water; it tastes as delicious as only a cool drink can taste when one's throat is parched; and then I wake, and find that I have an actual desire to drink. The cause of this dream is thirst, which I perceive when I wake. From this sensation arises the wish to drink and the dream shows me this wish as fulfilled. It thereby serves a function, the nature of which I soon surmise. I sleep well, and am not accustomed to being waked by a bodily need. If I succeed in appeasing my thirst by means of the dream that I am drinking, I need not wake up in order to satisfy my thirst. It is thus a *dream of convenience.* The dream takes the place of action, as elsewhere in life. . . .

DISTORTION IN DREAMS

If I now declare that wish-fulfilment is the meaning of *every* dream, so that there cannot be any dreams other than wish-dreams, I know beforehand that I shall meet with the most emphatic contradiction. . . .

Nevertheless, it is not difficult to parry these apparently invincible objections. It is merely necessary to observe that our doctrine is not based upon the estimates of the obvious dream-content but relates to the thought-content, which, in the course of interpretation, is found to lie behind the dream. Let us compare and contrast the *manifest* and the *latent dream-content.* It is true that there are dreams the manifest content of which is of the most painful nature. But has anyone ever tried to interpret these dreams—to discover their latent thought-content? If not, the two objections to our doctrine are no longer valid; for there is always the possibility that even our painful and terrifying dreams may, upon interpretation, prove to be wish-fulfilment. . . .

■ **Discussion Questions**

1. How did Freud's theory of dream interpretation reject contemporary views about dreams on the one hand and accept them on the other?
2. What does Freud mean when he describes dreams as "wish-fulfilments"?
3. According to Freud, what is the relationship between a person's dreams and his or her waking state?

63. Emmeline Pankhurst, *Speech from the Dock*   (1908)

By granting working-class men the vote in 1884, the British government hoped to make politics more unified and orderly. Yet the realization of such hopes proved elusive, in part because a new political foe had appeared on the scene: the women's suffrage movement. The founder of the Women's Social and Political Union, Emmeline Pankhurst (1858–1928), was among the most influential voices of the movement. Although women in Britain had long been fighting for rights, the expansion of the male electorate further accentuated their political exclusion. In the following speech before a police court judge, Pankhurst defends the WSPU's tactics, which had become increasingly militant since its inception in 1903. She had been arrested for distributing a leaflet encouraging her supporters "to rush the House of Commons" and, along with two colleagues, faced a prison sentence for refusing to "bind themselves over"—in other words, to promise to behave properly. Her speech reflects her belief that the WSPU's struggle was more than a quest for the vote; it was a war against a patriarchical society.

Ever since my girlhood, a period of about 30 years, I have belonged to organisations to secure for women that political power which I have felt was essential to bringing about those reforms which women need. I have tried constitutional methods. I have been womanly. When you spoke to some of my colleagues the day before yesterday about their being unwomanly, I felt that bitterness which I know every one of them felt in their hearts. We have tried to be womanly, we have tried to use feminine influence, and we have seen that it is of no use. Men who have been impatient have invariably got reforms for their impatience. And they have not our excuse for being impatient. . . .

Now, while I share in the feeling of indignation which has been expressed to you by my daughter, I have lived longer in the world than she has. Perhaps I can look round the whole question better than she can, but I want to say here, deliberately, to you, that we are here to-day because we are driven here. We have taken this action, because as women—and I want you to understand it is as women we have taken this action—it is because we realise that the condition of our sex is so deplorable that it is our duty even to break the law in order to call attention to the reasons why we do so.

I do not want to say anything which may seem disrespectful to you, or in any way give you offence, but I do want to say that I wish, sir, that you could put yourself into the place of women for a moment before you decide upon this case. My daughter referred to the way in which women are huddled into and out of these police-courts without a fair trial. I want you to realise what a poor hunted creature, without the advantages we have had, must feel.

I have been in prison. I was in Holloway Gaol for five weeks. I was in various parts of the prison. I was in the hospital, and in the ordinary part of the prison, and I tell you, sir, with as

Emmeline Pankhurst, "Speech from the Dock [Police Court]," in *Votes for Women,* October 29, 1908, 1.

much sense of responsibility as if I had taken the oath, that there were women there who have broken no law, who are there because they have been able to make no adequate statement.

You know that women have tried to do something to come to the aid of their own sex. Women are brought up for certain crimes, crimes which men do not understand—I am thinking especially of infanticide—they are brought before a man judge, before a jury of men, who are called upon to decide whether some poor, hunted woman is guilty of murder or not. I put it to you, sir, when we see in the papers, as we often do, a case similar to that of Daisy Lord, for whom a great petition was got up in this country, I want you to realise how we women feel, because we are women, because we are not men, we need some legitimate influence to bear upon our law-makers.

Now, we have tried every way. We have presented larger petitions than were ever presented for any other reform; we have succeeded in holding greater public meetings than men have ever had for any reform, in spite of the difficulty which women have in throwing off their natural diffidence, that desire to escape publicity which we have inherited from generations of our foremothers; we have broken through that. We have faced hostile mobs at street corners, because we were told that we could not have that representation for our taxes which men have won unless we converted the whole of the country to our side. Because we have done this, we have been misrepresented, we have been ridiculed, we have had contempt poured upon us. The ignorant mob at the street corner has been incited to offer us violence, which we have faced unarmed and unprotected by the safeguards which Cabinet Ministers have. We know that we need the protection of the vote even more than men have needed it.

I am here to take upon myself now, sir, as I wish the prosecution had put upon me, the full responsibility for this agitation in its present phase. I want to address you as a woman who has performed the duties of a woman, and, in addition, has performed the duties which ordinary men have had to perform, by earning a living for her children, and educating them. In addition to that, I have been a public officer. I enjoyed for 10 years an official post under the Registrar, and I performed those duties to the satisfaction of the head of the department. After my duty of taking the census was over, I was one of the few Registrars who qualified for a special bonus, and was specially praised for the way in which the work was conducted. Well, sir, I stand before you, having resigned that office when I was told that I must either do that or give up working for this movement.

I want to make you realise that it is a point of honour that if you decide—as I hope you will not decide—to bind us over, that we shall not sign any undertaking, as the Member of Parliament did who was before you yesterday. Perhaps his reason for signing that undertaking may have been that the Prime Minister had given some assurance to the people he claimed to represent that something should be done for them. We have no such assurance. Mr. Birrell told the women who questioned him the other day that he could not say that anything would be done to give an assurance to the women that their claims should be conceded. So, sir, if you decide against us to-day, to prison we must go, because we feel that we should be going back to the hopeless condition this movement was in three years ago if we consented to be bound over to keep the peace which we have never broken, and so, sir, if you decide to bind us over, whether it is for three or six months, we shall submit to the treatment, the degrading treatment, that we have submitted to before.

Although the Government admitted that we are political offenders, and, therefore, ought to be treated as political offenders are invariably treated, we shall be treated as pickpockets and drunkards; we shall be searched. I want you, if you can, as a man, to realise what it means to women like us. We are driven to do this, we are determined to go on with agitation, because we feel in honour bound. Just as it was the duty of your forefathers, it is our duty to make this world a better place for women than it is to-day. . . .

This is the only way we can get that power which every citizen should have of deciding how the taxes she contributes to should be spent, and how the laws she has to obey should be made, and until we get that power we shall be here—we are here to-day, and we shall come here over and over again. You must realise how futile it is to settle this question by binding us over to keep the peace. You have tried it; it has failed. Others have tried to do it, and have failed. If you had power to send us to prison, not for six months, but for six years, for 16 years, or for the whole of our lives, the Government must not think that they can stop this agitation. It will go on.

I want to draw your attention to the self-restraint which was shown by our followers on the night of the 13th, after we had been arrested. It only shows that our influence over them is very great, because I think that if they had yielded to their natural impulses, there might have been a breach of the peace on the evening of the 13th. They were very indignant, but our words have always been, "be patient, exercise self-restraint, show our so-called superiors that the criticism of women being hysterical is not true; use no violence, offer yourselves to the violence of others." We are going to win. Our women have taken that advice; if we are in prison they will continue to take that advice.

Well, sir, that is all I have to say to you. We are here not because we are law-breakers; we are here in our efforts to become law-makers.

▪ Discussion Questions

1. In what ways did the WSPU's tactics challenge conventional notions of proper behavior for women at the time?
2. According to Pankhurst, why was the WSPU forced to adopt such tactics?
3. Why did Pankhurst think that women had both a right to and a need for political enfranchisement?

CHAPTER 20

War, Revolution, and Reconstruction, 1914–1929

Contemporaries dubbed World War I the "Great War" with good reason. Over the course of four years, millions died in battle—victims of advanced military technologies, outdated tactics, wretched leadership, and a desire for total victory. The first document allows us to see these horrors through two soldiers' eyes. The second document reveals that civilians contributed to the staggering death toll, for it was they who manufactured the grenades, rifles, and other weapons used on the front with such devastating effects. Yet the war's legacy did not stop there, as the third document attests. Civilian protests against the war unleashed the Russian Revolution, which transformed the world's political landscape. To the west, governments faced their own challenges as they struggled under the weight of postwar reconstruction and popular discontent. Among the people who capitalized on these troubled times was the founder of Italian fascism, Benito Mussolini, who ushered in a new age of violent dictatorship in Europe.

64. Fritz Franke and Siegfried Sassoon, *Two Soldiers' Views of the Horrors of War* (1914–1918)

When the war broke out in August 1914, no one foresaw the years of massive destruction and bloodshed that lay ahead. By late autumn, the two sides were entrenched along a line that extended from France into Belgium, and so the western front was born. Here millions of soldiers like Fritz Franke and Siegfried Sassoon faced unspeakable horrors. In a letter written in the war's first months, Franke, a medical student from Berlin, describes trench warfare as a living hell of shells and corpses. His description also reveals what already had become and would remain the war's defining feature in the west: immobility and stalemate. Franke paid the ultimate price for both: he was killed in May 1915. By contrast, Sassoon, a British officer, survived and became famous for poems like the one following Franke's letter, "Counter-Attack," which describes the war's misery and futility.

FRITZ FRANKE

Louve, November 5th, 1914

Yesterday we didn't feel sure that a single one of us would come through alive. You can't possibly picture to yourselves what such a battle-field looks like. It is impossible to describe it, and even now, when it is a day behind us, I myself can hardly believe that such bestial barbarity and unspeakable suffering are possible. Every foot of ground contested; every hundred yards another trench; and everywhere bodies—rows of them! All the trees shot to pieces; the whole ground

---

A. F. Wedd, trans., *German Students' War Letters* (New York: E. P. Dutton, 1929), 123–25.

churned up a yard deep by the heaviest shells; dead animals; houses and churches so utterly destroyed by shell-fire that they can never be of the least use again. And every troop that advances in support must pass through a mile of this chaos, through this gigantic burial-ground and the reek of corpses.

In this way we advanced on Tuesday, marching for three hours, a silent column, in the moonlight, towards the Front and into a trench as Reserve, two to three hundred yards from the English, close behind our own infantry.

There we lay the whole day, a yard and a half to two yards below the level of the ground, crouching in the narrow trench on a thin layer of straw, in an overpowering din which never ceased all day or the greater part of the night—the whole ground trembling and shaking! There is every variety of sound—whistling, whining, ringing, crashing, rolling . . . the beastly things pitch right above one and burst and the fragments buzz in all directions, and the only question one asks is: "Why doesn't one get me?" Often the things land within a hand's breadth and one just looks on. One gets so hardened to it that at the most one ducks one's head a little if a great, big naval-gun shell comes a bit too near and its grey-green stink is a bit too thick. Otherwise one soon just lies there and thinks of other things. And then one pulls out the Field Regulations or an old letter from home, and all at once one has fallen asleep in spite of the row.

Then suddenly comes the order: "Back to the horses. You are relieved!" And one runs for a mile or so, mounts, and is a gay trooper once more; hola, away, through night and mist, in gallop and in trot!

One just lives from one hour to the next. For instance, if one starts to prepare some food, one never knows if one mayn't have to leave it behind within an hour. If you lie down to sleep, you must always be "in Alarm Order." On the road, you have just to ride behind the man in front of you without knowing where you are going, or at the most only the direction for half a day.

All the same, there is a lot that is pleasant in it all. We often go careering through lovely country in beautiful weather. And above all one acquires a knowledge of human nature! We all live so naturally and unconventionally here, every one according to his own instincts. That brings much that is good and much that is ugly to the surface, but in every one there is a large amount of truth, and above all strength—strength developed almost to a mania!

SIEGFRIED SASSOON

Counter-Attack

We'd gained our first objective hours before
While dawn broke like a face with blinking eyes,
Pallid, unshaved and thirsty, blind with smoke.
Things seemed all right at first. We held their line,
With bombers posted, Lewis guns well placed,
And clink of shovels deepening the shallow trench.
    The place was rotten with dead; green clumsy legs
    High-booted, sprawled and grovelled along the saps
    And trunks, face downward, in the sucking mud,
    Wallowed like trodden sand-bags loosely filled;
    And naked sodden buttocks, mats of hair,
    Bulged, clotted heads slept in the plastering slime.
    And then the rain began—the jolly old rain!

Siegfried Sassoon, *Collected Poems* (New York: Viking Press, 1949), 68–69.

A yawning soldier knelt against the bank,
Staring across the morning blear with fog;
He wondered when the Allemands would get busy;
And then, of course, they started with five-nines
Traversing, sure as fate, and never a dud.
Mute in the clamour of shells he watched them burst
Spouting dark earth and wire with gusts from hell,
While posturing giants dissolved in drifts of smoke.
He crouched and flinched, dizzy with galloping fear,
Sick for escape—loathing the strangled horror
And butchered, frantic gestures of the dead.

An officer came blundering down the trench:
"Stand-to and man the fire-step!" On he went . . .
Gasping and bawling, "Fire-step . . . counter-attack!"
    Then the haze lifted. Bombing on the right
    Down the old sap: machine-guns on the left;
    And stumbling figures looming out in front.
    "O Christ, they're coming at us!" Bullets spat,
And he remembered his rifle . . . rapid fire . . .
And started blazing wildly . . . then a bang
Crumpled and spun him sideways, knocked him out
To grunt and wriggle: none heeded him; he choked
And fought the flapping veils of smothering gloom,
Lost in a blurred confusion of yells and groans . . .
Down, and down, and down, he sank and drowned,
Bleeding to death. The counter-attack had failed.

▪ Discussion Questions

1. Although they fought on opposite sides, what attributes did Franke and Sassoon share?
2. Given Franke's and Sassoon's descriptions of the battlefront, what physical and psychological effects did trench warfare have on soldiers?
3. How does Franke's letter challenge the Allies' propaganda in which German soldiers were depicted as being devoid of humanity?

65. L. Doriat, *Women on the Home Front*   (1917)

Trench warfare was not the only distinctive feature of World War I. The massive mobilization of the home front also made the war like no other fought to date. Across Europe, thousands of civilians poured into factories to manufacture supplies for the troops. With casualties mounting and more and more men leaving to replenish the armed forces, women became particularly vital to sustaining the wartime labor force. Consequently, new employment opportunities arose for them, especially in traditionally masculine domains such as munitions. The following interview of a French factory worker in the city of Saint-Nazaire in Brittany by journalist L. Doriat puts a human face on this aspect of the war's impact beyond the battlefield. In it, the worker, whom Doriat never identifies, reveals her

Margaret R. Higonnet, ed., *Lines of Fire: Women Writers of World War I* (New York: Plume, 1999), 129–31.

sense of patriotic duty mingled with her determination not to lose her femininity amid the din and dirt of her job.

The dwelling I enter is tidy, sun lights up the main room and makes the household objects shine; everything speaks of an orderly woman who likes her home. A few flowers in a vase on the table near which she is working prove to me that I was right about the woman I've come to see. The factory has not destroyed her feminine sense of delicacy. Without a hat she seems to me younger; she is surprised to see me, she confesses, because she doubted I would come. Convalescent, she hasn't worked for a whole month, which is why I am lucky enough to find her.

"The very day after my arrival, I found work, thanks to the foreman of a factory of shells who knew my husband," she hastens to tell me. "There is no comparison between this extremely hard and much more precise work and the little toy-like petards that I was making. Here it's not sheets of white metal but big 120 shells. You must also pay much more attention, a defect is serious. The factory never stops, day and night shifts of eight alternate. It's intensive production; no mawkishness here, we are not women by the arms of the machine. Scarcely any apprenticeship, one or two days and you're set.

"I am in a workshop for tempering the steel, or rather I was—will they give me back my place and my machine when I return to the workshop? At the moment of my accident, which I'll tell you about, I was doing the shop-trial of the steel for the shell, testing or inspecting the casing, of course. Right after the tempering bath, when the steel is still hot and black, the other workers and I had to tap it with a buffing wheel in order to polish the steel on a small surface of the bottom and the ogive of the shell. Doing this we handle at least a thousand shells a day, and as I told you, they are big, very heavy to manipulate. Other workers take these same pieces and make a light mark on the polished area, which must not etch the steel further than a certain depth, in a kind of test; they are equipped with a graduated sheet of metal that lets them evaluate the etched lines. If the mark is too deep, the steel is too soft; if it's too shallow, it is too hard; in either case it can't be used and goes back to be recast. The inspection requires great attentiveness. A final verification is made by a controller and as we are always required to put our number on the pieces that pass through our hands, the imperfections, the errors can be traced to their authors.

"There too you don't talk, you don't even think of it. The deafening noise of the machines, the enormous heat of the ovens near which you work, the swiftness of the movements make this precision work into painful labor. When we do it at night, the glare together with the temperature of the furnace exhausts your strength and burns your eyes. In the morning when you get home, you throw yourself on your bed without even the strength to eat a bite. There are also the lathe workshops, I've never been there; many workers learn quickly to turn a shell without needing to calibrate it; some turners do piece work; they are always the ones who hurt themselves. At the job you become very imprudent, as I told you.

"However, you see, I hurt myself too. Forgetting that my buffing machine does an incalculable number of turns a second, I brushed against it with my arm. Clothing and flesh were all taken off before I even noticed. They had to scrape the bone, bandage me every day, I was afraid of an amputation, which luckily was avoided. Only in the last few days have I been able to go without a sling and use my arm; next week I go back to the workshop. I don't want them to change my job, I'm used to my machine and a fresh apprenticeship would not please me at all. I assure you, the first day I was in this noise, near these enormous blast furnaces, opposite the huge machine at which I had to work for hours, I was afraid. We are all like that, all the more so that we are not given time to reflect. You have to understand and act quickly. Those who lose their heads don't accomplish anything, but they are rare. In general, one week suffices to turn a novice into a skilled worker.

"The foremen scold now and then, but they mustn't count it against us; doesn't everyone know that a man is an apprentice before he becomes a mechanic? But at present, however simplified, however divided up the tasks may be, you become a qualified mechanic right away.

"Yet among us there are women like myself who had never done anything; others who did not know how to sew or embroider; nothing discouraged us. As for me I don't complain, this strained activity pleases me. I can thus forget my loneliness—and not having any children, what else should I do with all my time?

"When the war is over, I will look for a job that corresponds better to my taste. I have enough education to become a cashier in a store. I will then be able to be neater than now, for you can't imagine what care it takes to stay more or less clean if you work in a metallurgy.

"A woman is always a woman; I suffered a lot from remaining for hours with my hands and face dirty with dust and smoke. Everything is a matter of habit; among us there are women who seem fragile and delicate—well! if you saw them at work, you would be stunned: it's a total transformation. As for me, I would never have thought I had so much stamina; when I remember that the least little errand wore me out before, I don't recognize myself. Certainly when the day or the night is over, you go home, the fatigue is great, but we are not more tired than the men are. True, we are more sober because we maintain better hygiene and as a result, our sources of energy are more rational and regular, we don't turn to alcohol for strength.

"Our sense of the present need, of the national peril, of hatred for the enemy, of the courage of our husbands and sons—all this pricks us on, we work with all our heart, with all our strength, with all our soul. It is not necessary to stimulate us, each one is conscious of the task assigned to her and in all simplicity she does it, convinced that she defends her country by forging the arms that will free it. We are very proud of being workers for the national defence."

On that proud phrase, I left this valiant woman, with a warm handshake to thank her and to express my admiration.

■ Discussion Questions

1. What does this account suggest about women's role in the war effort?
2. How do both interviewer and interviewee cast light on people's fears about the war's effects on traditional gender roles?
3. In what ways does this interview reflect the national consensus supporting the war, as fostered by government-directed propaganda campaigns?

66. Benito Mussolini, *The Doctrine of Fascism*   (1932)

Like millions of his fellow Italians, Benito Mussolini (1883–1945) bitterly resented the outcome of War World I. The Allies had reneged on many of their territorial promises, and Italy's economy was in shambles. Mussolini tapped into these waves of discontent when he founded the Fascist movement in 1919, comprised of former socialists, war veterans, and others who embraced the radical right as the new symbol of authority and strength. Blaming the parliamentary government for the country's ills, the Fascists marched on Rome in 1922 to take matters into their own hands. Upon the king's request, Mussolini became prime minister. This marked the beginning of Mussolini's rise to political power. This excerpt from an article by Mussolini, first published in the Enciclopedia Italiana *in 1932,*

Michael Oakeshott, ed. and trans., *The Social and Political Doctrines of Contemporary Europe* (Cambridge: Cambridge University Press, 1947), 164–79.

illuminates the basic ideological contours of fascism as they had developed during the first decade of his authoritarian rule.

FUNDAMENTAL IDEAS

7. Against individualism, the Fascist conception is for the State; and it is for the individual in so far as he coincides with the State, which is the conscience and universal will of man in his historical existence. It is opposed to classical Liberalism, which arose from the necessity of reacting against absolutism, and which brought its historical purpose to an end when the State was transformed into the conscience and will of the people. Liberalism denied the State in the interests of the particular individual; Fascism reaffirms the State as the true reality of the individual. And if liberty is to be the attribute of the real man, and not of that abstract puppet envisaged by individualistic Liberalism, Fascism is for liberty. And for the only liberty which can be a real thing, the liberty of the State and of the individual within the State. Therefore, for the Fascist, everything is in the State, and nothing human or spiritual exists, much less has value, outside the State. In this sense Fascism is totalitarian, and the Fascist State, the synthesis and unity of all values, interprets, develops and gives strength to the whole life of the people.

8. Outside the State there can be neither individuals nor groups (political parties, associations, syndicates, classes). Therefore Fascism is opposed to Socialism, which confines the movement of history within the class struggle and ignores the unity of classes established in one economic and moral reality in the State; and analogously it is opposed to class syndicalism. Fascism recognizes the real exigencies for which the socialist and syndicalist movement arose, but while recognizing them wishes to bring them under the control of the State and give them a purpose within the corporative system of interests reconciled within the unity of the State.

9. Individuals form classes according to the similarity of their interests, they form syndicates according to differentiated economic activities within these interests; but they form first, and above all, the State, which is not to be thought of numerically as the sum-total of individuals forming the majority of a nation. And consequently Fascism is opposed to Democracy, which equates the nation to the majority, lowering it to the level of that majority; nevertheless it is the purest form of democracy if the nation is conceived, as it should be, qualitatively and not quantitatively, as the most powerful idea (most powerful because most moral, most coherent, most true) which acts within the nation as the conscience and the will of a few, even of One, which ideal tends to become active within the conscience and the will of all—that is to say, of all those who rightly constitute a nation by reason of nature, history or race, and have set out upon the same line of development and spiritual formation as one conscience and one sole will. . . .

POLITICAL AND SOCIAL DOCTRINE

Fascism is to-day clearly defined not only as a regime but as a doctrine. And I mean by this that Fascism to-day, self-critical as well as critical of other movements, has an unequivocal point of view of its own, a criterion, and hence an aim, in face of all the material and intellectual problems which oppress the people of the world.

3. Above all, Fascism, in so far as it considers and observes the future and the development of humanity quite apart from the political considerations of the moment, believes neither in the possibility nor in the utility of perpetual peace. It thus repudiates the doctrine of Pacifism—born of a renunciation of the struggle and an act of cowardice in the face of sacrifice. War alone brings up to their highest tension all human energies and puts the stamp of nobility upon the peoples who have the courage to meet it. All other trials are substitutes, which never really put a man in front of himself in the alternative of life and death. A doctrine, therefore, which begins with a prejudice in favour of peace is foreign to Fascism; as are foreign to the spirit of Fascism. . . .

5. Such a conception of life makes Fascism the precise negation of that doctrine which formed the basis of the so-called Scientific or Marxian Socialism: the doctrine of historical Materialism, according to which the history of human civilizations can be explained only as the struggle of interest between the different social groups and as arising out of change in the means and instruments of production. That economic improvements—discoveries of raw materials, new methods of work, scientific inventions—should have an importance of their own, no one denies, but that they should suffice to explain human history to the exclusion of all other factors is absurd: Fascism believes, now and always, in holiness and in heroism, that is in acts in which no economic motive—remote or immediate—plays a part. With this negation of historical materialism, according to which men would be only by-products of history, who appear and disappear on the surface of the waves while in the depths the real directive forces are at work, there is also denied the immutable and irreparable "class struggle" which is the natural product of this economic conception of history, and above all it is denied that the class struggle can be the primary agent of social changes. . . .

6. After Socialism, Fascism attacks the whole complex of democratic ideologies and rejects them both in their theoretical premises and in their applications or practical manifestations. Fascism denies that the majority, through the mere fact of being a majority, can rule human societies; it denies that this majority can govern by means of a periodical consultation; it affirms the irremediable, fruitful and beneficent inequality of men, who cannot be levelled by such a mechanical and extrinsic fact as universal suffrage. By democratic regimes we mean those in which from time to time the people is given the illusion of being sovereign, while true effective sovereignty lies in other, perhaps irresponsible and secret, forces. Democracy is a regime without a king, but with very many kings, perhaps more exclusive, tyrannical and violent than one king even though a tyrant. . . .

8. In face of Liberal doctrines, Fascism takes up an attitude of absolute opposition both in the field of politics and in that of economics. It is not necessary to exaggerate—merely for the purpose of present controversies—the importance of Liberalism in the past century, and to make of that which was one of the numerous doctrines sketched in that century a religion of humanity for all times, present and future. . . . The "Liberal" century, after having accumulated an infinity of Gordian knots, tried to untie them by the hecatomb of the World War. Never before has any religion imposed such a cruel sacrifice. Were the gods of Liberalism thirsty for blood? Now Liberalism is about to close the doors of its deserted temples because the peoples feel that its agnosticism in economics, its indifferentism in politics and in morals, would lead, as they have led, the States to certain ruin. In this way one can understand why all the political experiences of the contemporary world are anti-Liberal, and it is supremely ridiculous to wish on that account to class them outside of history; as if history were a hunting ground reserved to Liberalism and its professors, as if Liberalism were the definitive and no longer surpassable message of civilization. . . .

If it is admitted that the nineteenth century has been the century of Socialism, Liberalism and Democracy, it does not follow that the twentieth must also be the century of Liberalism, Socialism and Democracy. Political doctrines pass; peoples remain. It is to be expected that this century may be that of authority, a century of the "Right," a Fascist century. If the nineteenth was the century of the individual (Liberalism means individualism) it may be expected that this one may be the century of "collectivism" and therefore the century of the State. . . .

10. The keystone of Fascist doctrine is the conception of the State, of its essence, of its tasks, of its ends. For Fascism the State is an absolute before which individuals and groups are relative. Individuals and groups are "thinkable" in so far as they are within the State. The Liberal State does not direct the interplay and the material and spiritual development of the groups, but limits itself to registering the results; the Fascist State has a consciousness of its own, a will of its own, on this account it is called an "ethical" State. In 1929, at the first quinquennial assembly of the regime, I said: "For Fascism, the State is not the night-watchman who is concerned only with the personal security of the citizens; nor is it an organization for purely material ends, such as

that of guaranteeing a certain degree of prosperity and a relatively peaceful social order, to achieve which a council of administration would be sufficient, nor is it a creation of mere politics with no contact with the material and complex reality of the lives of individuals and the life of peoples. The State, as conceived by Fascism and as it acts, is a spiritual and moral fact because it makes concrete the political, juridical, economic organization of the nation and such an organization is, in its origin and in its development, a manifestation of the spirit. The State is the guarantor of internal and external security, but it is also the guardian and the transmitter of the spirit of the people as it has been elaborated through the centuries in language, custom, faith. The State is not only present, it is also past, and above all future. It is the State which, transcending the brief limit of individual lives, represents the immanent conscience of the nation. The forms in which States express themselves change, but the necessity of the State remains. It is the State which educates citizens for civic virtue, makes them conscious of their mission, calls them to unity; harmonizes their interests in justice; hands on the achievements of thought in the sciences, the arts, in law, in human solidarity; it carries men from the elementary life of the tribe to the highest human expression of power which is Empire; it entrusts to the ages the names of those who died for its integrity or in obedience to its laws; it puts forward as an example and recommends to the generations that are to come the leaders who increased its territory and the men of genius who gave it glory. When the sense of the State declines and the disintegrating and centrifugal tendencies of individuals and groups prevail, national societies move to their decline."

11. From 1929 up to the present day these doctrinal positions have been strengthened by the whole economico-political evolution of the world. It is the State alone that grows in size, in power. It is the State alone that can solve the dramatic contradictions of capitalism. What is called the crisis cannot be overcome except by the State, within the State. . . . Fascism desires the State to be strong, organic and at the same time founded on a wide popular basis. The Fascist State has also claimed for itself the field of economics and, through the corporative, social and educational institutions which it has created, the meaning of the State reaches out to and includes the farthest off-shoots; and within the State, framed in their respective organizations, there revolve all the political, economic and spiritual forces of the nation. A State founded on millions of individuals who recognize it, feel it, are ready to serve it, is not the tyrannical State of the medieval lord. It has nothing in common with the absolutist States that existed either before or after 1789. In the Fascist State the individual is not suppressed, but rather multiplied, just as in a regiment a soldier is not weakened but multiplied by the number of his comrades. The Fascist State organizes the nation, but it leaves sufficient scope to individuals; it has limited useless or harmful liberties and has preserved those that are essential. It cannot be the individual who decides in this matter, but only the State. . . .

13. The Fascist State is a will to power and to government. In it the tradition of Rome is an idea that has force. In the doctrine of Fascism, Empire is not only a territorial, military or mercantile expression, but spiritual or moral. One can think of an empire, that is to say a nation that directly or indirectly leads other nations, without needing to conquer a single square kilometre of territory. For Fascism the tendency to Empire, that is to say, to the expansion of nations, is a manifestation of vitality; its opposite, staying at home, is a sign of decadence: peoples who rise or rerise are imperialist, peoples who die are denunciatory. Fascism is the doctrine that is most fitted to represent the aims, the states of mind, of a people, like the Italian people, rising again after many centuries of abandonment or slavery to foreigners. But Empire calls for discipline, co-ordination of forces, duty and sacrifice; this explains many aspects of the practical working of the regime and the direction of many of the forces of the State and the necessary severity shown to those who would wish to oppose this spontaneous and destined impulse of the Italy of the twentieth century, to oppose it in the name of the superseded ideologies of the nineteenth, repudiated wherever great experiments of political and social transformation have been courageously attempted:

especially where, as now, peoples thirst for authority, for leadership, for order. If every age has its own doctrine, it is apparent from a thousand signs that the doctrine of the present age is Fascism. That it is a doctrine of life is shown by the fact that it has resuscitated a faith. That this faith has conquered minds is proved by the fact that Fascism has had its dead and its martyrs.

Fascism henceforward has in the world the universality of all those doctrines which, by fulfilling themselves, have significance in the history of the human spirit.

▪ Discussion Questions

1. According to Mussolini, how is fascism opposed to liberalism, democracy, and socialism?
2. How is this opposition rooted in Mussolini's concept of the individual's role in the Fascist state?
3. What does Mussolini mean when he describes fascism as "totalitarian"?
4. As elaborated here, in what ways were Mussolini's principles rooted in the legacy of World War II?

CHAPTER 21

An Age of Catastrophes, 1929–1945

The Great Depression of the 1930s ushered in an age of unprecedented violence and suffering around the globe. Millions were out of work, hungry, and disillusioned. Authoritarian leaders capitalized on the downhearted, gaining widespread support with their promises to revive the economy and restore national glory. The head of the Nazi Party, Adolf Hitler, was among the most menacing of these political strongmen, as the first document vividly shows. Western democracies responded cautiously to the Nazi menace, hoping to contain Hitler's ambition through a policy of appeasement rather than military force. The second document illuminates this policy in action at a critical juncture in Hitler's march toward war. Once the war began, no one was truly prepared for its horrors. As the last two documents show, the combination of ideology and advanced technology fueling the war was especially cruel to the civilian population, setting a dangerous precedent for the future.

67. Joseph Goebbels, *Nazi Propaganda Pamphlet*   (1930)

Probably no one better personifies the power of authoritarian rulers to manipulate the minds of millions in the 1930s than Adolf Hitler. Among the secrets of Hitler's success was his propaganda chief, Joseph Goebbels (1895–1945). A member of the National Socialist Party since 1922, Goebbels shared Hitler's belief that the masses were easily managed if the message directed to them was simple and repetitive. To this end, Goebbels wrote pamphlets such as the one that follows in support of the Nazi cause. In it, he reveals the virulent anti-Semitism that shaped the Nazis' political program and set them apart from other totalitarian regimes. Goebbels's tactics helped propel Hitler to national leadership in 1933.

WHY ARE WE NATIONALISTS?

We are NATIONALISTS because we see in the NATION the only possibility for the protection and the furtherance of our existence.

The NATION is the organic bond of a people for the protection and defense of their lives. He is nationally minded who understands this IN WORD AND IN DEED.

Today, in GERMANY, NATIONALISM has degenerated into BOURGEOIS PATRIOTISM, and its power exhausts itself in tilting at windmills. It says GERMANY and means MONARCHY. It proclaims FREEDOM and means BLACK-WHITE-RED.

Louis L. Snyder, ed., *Documents of German History* (New Brunswick, N.J.: Rutgers University Press, 1958), 414–16.

Young nationalism has its unconditional demands. BELIEF IN THE NATION is a matter of all the people, not for individuals of rank, a class, or an industrial clique. The eternal must be separated from the contemporary. The maintenance of a rotten industrial system has nothing to do with nationalism. I can love Germany and hate capitalism; not only CAN I do it, I also MUST do it. The germ of the rebirth of our people LIES ONLY IN THE DESTRUCTION OF THE SYSTEM OF PLUNDERING THE HEALTHY POWER OF THE PEOPLE.

WE ARE NATIONALISTS BECAUSE WE, AS GERMANS, LOVE GERMANY. And because we love Germany, we demand the protection of its national spirit and we battle against its destroyers.

WHY ARE WE SOCIALISTS?

We are SOCIALISTS because we see in SOCIALISM the only possibility for maintaining our racial existence and through it the reconquest of our political freedom and the rebirth of the German state. SOCIALISM has its peculiar form first of all through its comradeship in arms with the forward-driving energy of a newly awakened nationalism. Without nationalism it is nothing, a phantom, a theory, a vision of air, a book. With it, it is everything, THE FUTURE, FREEDOM, FATHERLAND!

It was a sin of the liberal bourgeoisie to overlook THE STATE-BUILDING POWER OF SOCIALISM. It was the sin of MARXISM to degrade SOCIALISM to a system of MONEY AND STOMACH.

We are SOCIALISTS because for us THE SOCIAL QUESTION IS A MATTER OF NECESSITY AND JUSTICE, and even beyond that A MATTER FOR THE VERY EXISTENCE OF OUR PEOPLE.

SOCIALISM IS POSSIBLE ONLY IN A STATE WHICH IS FREE INSIDE AND OUTSIDE.
DOWN WITH POLITICAL BOURGEOIS SENTIMENT: FOR REAL NATIONALISM!
DOWN WITH MARXISM: FOR TRUE SOCIALISM!
UP WITH THE STAMP OF THE FIRST GERMAN NATIONAL SOCIALIST STATE!
AT THE FRONT THE NATIONAL SOCIALIST GERMAN WORKERS PARTY! . . .
WHY DO WE OPPOSE THE JEWS?

We are ENEMIES OF THE JEWS, because we are fighters for the freedom of the German people. THE JEW IS THE CAUSE AND THE BENEFICIARY OF OUR MISERY. He has used the social difficulties of the broad masses of our people to deepen the unholy split between Right and Left among our people. He has made two halves of Germany. He is the real cause for our loss of the Great War.

The Jew has no interest in the solution of Germany's fateful problems. He CANNOT have any. FOR HE LIVES ON THE FACT THAT THERE HAS BEEN NO SOLUTION. If we would make the German people a unified community and give them freedom before the world, then the Jew can have no place among us. He has the best trumps in his hands when a people lives in inner and outer slavery. THE JEW IS RESPONSIBLE FOR OUR MISERY AND HE LIVES ON IT.

That is the reason why we, AS NATIONALISTS and AS SOCIALISTS, oppose the Jew. HE HAS CORRUPTED OUR RACE, FOULED OUR MORALS, UNDERMINED OUR CUSTOMS, AND BROKEN OUR POWER.

THE JEW IS THE PLASTIC DEMON OF THE DECLINE OF MANKIND.

THE JEW IS UNCREATIVE. He produces nothing. HE ONLY HANDLES PRODUCTS. As long as he struggles against the state, HE IS A REVOLUTIONARY; as soon as he has power, he preaches QUIET AND ORDER, so that he can consume his plunder at his convenience.

ANTI-SEMITISM IS UN-CHRISTIAN. That means, then, that he is a Christian who looks on while the Jew sews straps around our necks. TO BE A CHRISTIAN MEANS: LOVE THY NEIGHBOR AS THYSELF! MY NEIGHBOR IS ONE WHO IS TIED TO ME BY HIS BLOOD. IF I LOVE HIM, THEN I MUST HATE HIS ENEMIES. HE WHO THINKS GERMAN MUST DESPISE THE JEWS. The one thing makes the other necessary.

WE ARE ENEMIES OF THE JEWS BECAUSE WE BELONG TO THE GERMAN PEOPLE.
THE JEW IS OUR GREATEST MISFORTUNE.

It is not true that we eat a Jew every morning at breakfast.

It is true, however, that he SLOWLY BUT SURELY ROBS US OF EVERYTHING WE OWN.
THAT WILL STOP, AS SURELY AS WE ARE GERMANS.

■ Discussion Questions

1. According to this pamphlet, what do the terms *nationalist* and *socialist* mean within the context of the Nazi party?
2. Why does the pamphlet target Jews as enemies of the German people?
3. What does the pamphlet suggest about the link between the Nazis' racial views and their goals for Germany's future?

68. Neville Chamberlain, *Speech on the Munich Crisis*   (1938)

During the troubled 1930s, a deep longing for peace clouded many Europeans' ability to see the true nature of the Nazi threat. The British politician Neville Chamberlain (1869–1940) was no exception. He became prime minister in 1937 when Hitler's preparations for war were well under way. Upon annexing Austria in March 1938, Hitler turned to his next target, Czechoslovakia. Chamberlain, Benito Mussolini (1883–1945), and French premier Edouard Daladier (1884–1970) met with Hitler in Munich in September 1938 to defuse the situation; their meeting resulted in an agreement that accepted Germany's territorial claims. In his closing speech, delivered during a debate on the agreement in the House of Commons, Chamberlain defended his policy of appeasement toward Hitler as the key to peace. Tragically, it was instead a prelude to war.

War today—this has been said before, and I say it again—is a different thing not only in degree, but in kind from what it used to be. We no longer think of war as it was in the days of Marlborough [John Churchill, first duke of Marlborough, a famed seventeenth-century military commander] or the days of Napoleon or even in the days of 1914. When war starts today, in the very first hour, before any professional soldier, sailor or airman has been touched, it will strike the workman, the clerk, the man-in-the-street or in the bus, and his wife and children in their homes. As I listened I could not help being moved, as I am sure everybody was who heard the hon. Member for Bridgeton (Mr. Maxton) when he began to paint the picture which he himself had seen and realised what it would mean in war—people burrowing underground, trying to escape from poison gas, knowing that at any hour of the day or night death or mutilation was ready to come upon them. Remembering that the dread of what might happen to them or to those dear to them might remain with fathers and mothers for year after year—when you think of these things you cannot ask people to accept a prospect of that kind; you cannot force them into a position that they have got to accept it; unless you feel yourself, and can make them feel, that the cause for which they are going to fight is a vital cause—a cause that transcends all the human values, a cause to which you can point, if some day you win the victory, and say, "That cause is safe."

Since I first went to Berchtesgaden [a town in southeast Germany and the site of Hitler's wartime villa, where Chamberlain traveled to meet with the Nazi leader] more than 20,000 letters and telegrams have come to No. 10, Downing Street. Of course, I have only been able to look

Parliamentary Debates. Fifth Series. Volume 339. House of Commons Official Report (London, 1938), 544–52.

at a tiny fraction of them, but I have seen enough to know that the people who wrote did not feel that they had such a cause for which to fight, if they were asked to go to war in order that the Sudeten Germans might not join the Reich. That is how they are feeling. That is my answer to those who say that we should have told Germany weeks ago that, if her army crossed the border of Czechoslovakia, we should be at war with her. We had no treaty obligations and no legal obligations to Czechoslovakia and if we had said that, we feel that we should have received no support from the people of this country. . . .

As regards future policy, it seems to me that there are really only two possible alternatives. One of them is to base yourself upon the view that any sort of friendly relations, or possible relations, shall I say, with totalitarian States are impossible, that the assurances which have been given to me personally are worthless, that they have sinister designs and that they are bent upon the domination of Europe and the gradual destruction of democracies. Of course, on that hypothesis, war has got to come, and that is the view—a perfectly intelligible view—of a certain number of hon. and right hon. Gentlemen in this House. I am not sure that it is not the view of some Members of the party opposite. [An HON. MEMBER: "Yes."] Not all of them. They certainly have never put it in so many words, but it is illustrated by the observations of the hon. Member for Derby (Mr. Noel-Baker), who spoke this afternoon, and who had examined the Agreement signed by the German Chancellor and myself, which he described as a pact designed by Herr Hitler to induce us to relinquish our present obligations. That shows how far prejudice can carry a man. The Agreement, as anyone can see, is not a pact at all. So far as the question of "never going to war again" is concerned, it is not even an expression of the opinion of the two who signed the paper, except that it is their opinion of the desire of their respective peoples. I do not know whether the hon. Member will believe me or attribute to me also sinister designs when I tell him that it was a document not drawn up by Herr Hitler but by the humble individual who now addresses this House.

If the view which I have been describing is the one to be taken, I think we must inevitably proceed to the next stage—that war is coming, broadly speaking the democracies against the totalitarian States—that certainly we must arm ourselves to the teeth, that clearly we must make military alliances with any other Powers whom we can get to work with us, and that we must hope that we shall be allowed to start the war at the moment that suits us and not at the moment that suits the other side. That is what some right hon. and hon. Gentlemen call collective security. Some hon. Members opposite will walk into any trap if it is only baited with a familiar catchword and they do it when this system is called collective security. But that is not the collective security we are thinking of or did think of when talking about the system of the League of Nations. That was a sort of universal collective security in which all nations were to take their part. This plan may give you security; it certainly is not collective in any sense. It appears to me to contain all the things which the party opposite used to denounce before the War—entangling alliances, balance of power and power politics. If I reject it, as I do, it is not because I give it a label; it is because, to my mind, it is a policy of utter despair.

If that is hon. Members' conviction, there is no future hope for civilisation or for any of the things that make life worth living. Does the experience of the Great War and of the years that followed it give us reasonable hope that if some new war started that would end war any more than the last one did? No. I do not believe that war is inevitable. . . . It seems to me that the strongest argument against the inevitability of war is to be found in something that everyone has recognised or that has been recognised in every part of the House. That is the universal aversion from war of the people, their hatred of the notion of starting to kill one another again. . . .

What is the alternative to this bleak and barren policy of the inevitability of war? In my view it is that we should seek by all means in our power to avoid war, by analysing possible causes, by trying to remove them, by discussion in a spirit of collaboration and good will. I cannot believe that such a programme would be rejected by the people of this country, even if it does mean the establishment of personal contact with dictators, and of talks man to man on the basis that each, while maintaining his own ideas of the internal government of his country, is willing to allow that other systems may suit better other peoples. The party opposite surely have the same idea in mind even if they put it in a different way. They want a world conference. Well, I have had some experience of conferences, and one thing I do feel certain of is that it is better to have no conference at all than a conference which is a failure. The corollary to that is that before you enter a conference you must have laid out very clearly the lines on which you are going to proceed, if you are at least to have in front of you a reasonable prospect that you may obtain success. I am not saying that a conference would not have its place in due course. But I say it is no use to call a conference of the world, including these totalitarian Powers, until you are sure that they are going to attend, and not only that they are going to attend, but that they are going to attend with the intention of aiding you in the policy on which you have set your heart.

I am told that the policy which I have tried to describe is inconsistent with the continuance, and much more inconsistent with the acceleration of our present programme of arms. I am asked how I can reconcile an appeal to the country to support the continuance of this programme with the words which I used when I came back from Munich the other day and spoke of my belief that we might have peace for our time. I hope hon. Members will not be disposed to read into words used in a moment of some emotion, after a long and exhausting day, after I had driven through miles of excited, enthusiastic, cheering people—I hope they will not read into those words more than they were intended to convey. I do indeed believe that we may yet secure peace for our time, but I never meant to suggest that we should do that by disarmament, until we can induce others to disarm too. Our past experience has shown us only too clearly that weakness in armed strength means weakness in diplomacy, and if we want to secure a lasting peace, I realise that diplomacy cannot be effective unless the consciousness exists, not here alone, but elsewhere, that behind the diplomacy is the strength to give effect to it.

One good thing, at any rate, has come out of this emergency through which we have passed. It has thrown a vivid light upon our preparations for defence, on their strength and on their weakness. I should not think we were doing our duty if we had not already ordered that a prompt and thorough inquiry should be made to cover the whole of our preparations, military and civil, in order to see, in the light of what has happened during these hectic days, what further steps may be necessary to make good our deficiencies in the shortest possible time. There have been references in the course of the Debate to other measures which hon. Members have suggested should be taken. I would not like to commit myself now, until I have had a little time for reflection, as to what further it may seem good to ask the nation to do, but I think nobody could fail to have been impressed by the fact that the emergency brought out that the whole of the people of this country, whatever their class, whatever their station, were ready to do their duty, however disagreeable, however hard, however dangerous it may have been.

I cannot help feeling that if, after all, war had come upon us, the people of this country would have lost their spiritual faith altogether. As it turned out the other way, I think we have all seen something like a new spiritual revival, and I know that everywhere there is a strong desire among the people to record their readiness to serve their country, wherever or however their services could be most useful. I would like to take advantage of that strong feeling if it is possible, and although I must frankly say that at this moment I do not myself clearly see my way to any particular scheme, yet I want also to say that I am ready to consider any suggestions that may be made to me, in a very sympathetic spirit.

Finally, I would like to repeat what my right hon. Friend the Chancellor of the Exchequer said yesterday in his great speech. Our policy of appeasement does not mean that we are going to seek new friends at the expense of old ones, or, indeed, at the expense of any other nations at all. I do not think that at any time there has been a more complete identity of views between the French Government and ourselves than there is at the present time. Their objective is the same as ours—to obtain the collaboration of all nations, not excluding the totalitarian States, in building up a lasting peace for Europe. . . .

■ **Discussion Questions**

1. How did Chamberlain justify his policy of appeasement?
2. According to Chamberlain, why did some people oppose this policy?
3. What does Chamberlain's defense indicate about popular attitudes toward war and peace?

69. Sam Bankhalter and Hinda Kibort, *Memories of the Holocaust* (1938–1945)

When Neville Chamberlain detailed the horrors that modern warfare would inflict on civilians, not even he knew how true his words would prove to be. Once the war erupted, one segment of the civilian population in particular was the target of Hitler's fury: Jews. The result was the Final Solution, a technologically and bureaucratically sophisticated system of camps for incarcerating or exterminating European Jews that the Germans put into place between 1941 and 1942. Either inmates were killed on their arrival or were spared to endure a different kind of death: from starvation, abuse, and overwork. The two interviews that follow allow us to see the Holocaust through the eyes of its victims. The first is that of Sam Bankhalter. At fourteen, he was captured by the Nazis in his native Poland and sent to Auschwitz. The second voice is that of Hinda Kibort, a Lithuanian who was nineteen when the Nazis began their assault on the local Jewish population. In 1944, she was deported to Stutthof, a labor camp in northern Poland.

SAM BANKHALTER

Lodz, Poland
There was always anti-Semitism in Poland. The slogan even before Hitler was "Jew, get out of here and go to Palestine." As Hitler came to power, there was not a day at school I was not spit on or beaten up.

I was at camp when the Germans invaded Poland. The camp directors told us to find our own way home. We walked many miles with airplanes over our heads, dead people on the streets. At home there were blackouts. I was just a kid, tickled to death when I was issued a flashlight and gas mask. The Polish army was equipped with buggies and horses, the Germans were all on trucks and tanks. The war was over in ten days.

The Ghetto   The German occupation was humiliation from day 1. If Jewish people were wearing the beard and sidecurls, the Germans were cutting the beard, cutting the sidecurls, laughing at you, beating you up a little bit. Then the Germans took part of Lodz and put on barbed wire, and all the Jews had to assemble in this ghetto area. You had to leave in five or ten minutes or half an hour, so you couldn't take much stuff with you. . . .

Auschwitz   We were the first ones in Auschwitz. We built it. What you got for clothing was striped pants and the striped jacket, no underwear, no socks. In wintertime you put paper in your shoes, and we used to take empty cement sacks and put a string in the top, put two together, one in back and one in front, to keep warm.

If they told you to do something, you went to do it. There was no yes or no, no choices. I worked in the crematorium for about eleven months. I saw Dr. Mengele's experiments on chil-

Rhoda G. Lewin, *Witnesses to the Holocaust: An Oral History* (Boston: Twayne Publishers, 1990), 5–8, 50–55.

dren, I knew the kids that became vegetables. Later in Buchenwald I saw Ilse Koch with a hose and regulator, trying to get pressure to make a hole in a woman's stomach. I saw them cutting Greek people in pieces. I was in Flossenburg for two weeks, and they shot 25,000 Russian soldiers, and we put them down on wooden logs and burned them. Every day the killing, the hanging, the shooting, the crematorium smell, the ovens, and the smoke going out.

I knew everybody, knew every trick to survive. I was one of the youngest in Auschwitz, and I was like "adopted" by a lot of the older people, especially the fathers. Whole families came into Auschwitz together, and you got to Dr. Mengele, who was saying "right, left, left, right," and you knew, right there, who is going to the gas chamber and who is not. Most of the men broke down when they knew their wives and their kids—three-, five-, nine-year-olds—went into the gas chambers. In fact, one of my brothers committed suicide in Auschwitz because he couldn't live with knowing his wife and children are dead.

I was able to see my family when they came into Auschwitz in 1944. I had a sister, she had a little boy a year old. Everybody that carried a child went automatically to the gas chamber, so my mother took the child. My sister survived, but she still suffers, feels she was a part of killing my mother. . . .

Looking Back   Once you start fighting for your life, all the ethics are gone. You live by circumstances. There is no pity. You physically draw down to the point where you cannot think any more, where the only thing is survival, and maybe a little hope that if I survive, I'm gonna be with my grandchildren and tell them the story.

In the camps, death actually became a luxury. We used to say, "Look at how lucky he is. He doesn't have to suffer any more."

I was a lucky guy. I survived, and I felt pretty good about it. But then you feel guilty living! My children—our friends are their "aunts" and "uncles." They don't know what is a grandfather, a grandmother, a cousin, a holiday sitting as a family.

As you grow older, you think about it, certain faces come back to you. You remember your home, your brothers, children that went to the crematorium. You wonder, how did your mother and father feel when they were in the gas chamber? Many nights I hear voices screaming in those first few minutes in the gas chamber, and I don't sleep.

I talk to a lot of people, born Americans, and they don't relate. They can't understand, and I don't blame them. Sometimes it's hard even for me to understand the truth of this whole thing. Did it really happen? But I saw it.

The majority of the people here live fairly good. I don't think there's a country in the world that can offer as much freedom as this country can offer. But the Nazi party exists here, now. This country is supplying anti-Semitic material to the whole world, printing it here and shipping it all over, and our leaders are silent, just as the world was silent when the Jews were being taken to the camps. How quick we forget.

When I sit in a plane, I see 65 percent of the people will pick up the sports page of the newspaper. They don't care what is on the front page! And this is where the danger lies. All you need is the economy to turn a little sour and have one person give out the propaganda. With 65 percent of the population the propaganda works, and then the other 35 percent is powerless to do anything about it.

HINDA KIBORT

Kovno, Lithuania

When the Germans marched in in July 1941, school had let out for the summer, so our whole family was together, including my brother who was in the university and my little sister who was in tenth grade. We tried to leave the city, but it was just like you see in the documentaries—

people with their little suitcases walking along highways and jumping into ditches because German planes were strafing, coming down very low, and people killed, and all this terror. German tanks overtook us, and we returned home.

The Occupation   We did not have time like the German Jews did, from '33 until the war broke out in '39, for step-by-step adjustments. For us, one day we were human, the next day we're subhuman. We had to wear yellow stars. Everybody could command us to do whatever they wanted. They would make you hop around in the middle of the street, or they made you lie down and stepped on you, or spit on you, or they tore at beards of devout Jews. And there was always an audience around to laugh. . . .

The Ghetto   In September all the Jews were enclosed in a ghetto. We lived together in little huts, sometimes two families to a room. There were no schools, no newspapers, no concerts, no theater. Officially, we didn't have any radios or books, but people brought in many books and they circulated. We also had a couple of radios and we could hear the BBC, so we were very much aware of what was going on with the war.

As long as we were strong and useful, we would survive. Everybody had to go to work except children under twelve and the elderly. There were workshops in the ghetto where they made earmuffs for the army, for instance, but mostly people went out to work in groups, with guards. A few tried to escape, but were caught.

We did not know yet about concentration camps.

In 1943 the war turned, and we could feel a terrible tension from the guards and from Germans we worked with on the outside. We could exchange clothing or jewelry for food, but this was extremely dangerous because every time a column came back from work, we were all searched. A baker, they found some bread and a few cigarettes in his pocket. He was hanged publicly, on a Sunday. There was a little orchard in the ghetto, a public place, and we Jews had to build a gallows there and a Jew had to hang him. We were all driven out by the guards and had to stand and watch this man being hanged.

November 5, 1943, was the day all the children were taken away. They brought in Romanian and Ukrainian S.S. to do it. All five of us in our family were employed in a factory adjacent to the ghetto, so we could see through the window what was happening. They took everybody out who stayed in the ghetto—all the children, all the elderly. When we came back after work we were a totally childless society! You can imagine parents coming home to—nothing. Everybody was absolutely shattered.

People were looking for answers, for omens. They turned to seances or to heaven to look for signs. And this was the day when we heard for the first time the word *Auschwitz*. There was a rumor that the children were taken there, but we didn't know the name so we translated it as *Der Schweiz*—Switzerland. We hoped that the trains were going to Switzerland, that the children would be hostages there.

The Transport   On July 16, 1944, the rest of the ghetto were put on cattle trains, with only what we could carry. We had no bathrooms. There was a pail on one side that very soon was full. We were very crowded. The stench and the lack of water and the fear, the whole experience, is just beyond explanation.

At one time, when we were in open country, a guard opened the door and we sat on the side and let our feet down and got some fresh air. We even tried to sing. But then they closed it up, and we were all inside again.

Labor Camp   When we arrived at Stutthof our family was separated—the men to one side of the camp, women to the other. My mother and sister and I had to undress. There were S.S. guards around, men and women. In the middle of the room was a table and an S.S. man in a white coat. We came in in batches, totally naked.

I cannot describe how you feel in a situation like this. We were searched, totally, for jewelry, gold, even family pictures. We had to stand spread-eagle and spread out our fingers. They looked through the hair, they looked into the mouth, they looked in the ears, and then we had to lie down. They looked into every orifice of the body, right in front of everybody. We were in total shock.

From this room we were rushed through a room that said above the door "shower room." There were little openings in the ceiling and water was trickling through. In the next room were piles of clothing, rags, on the floor. You had to grab a skirt, a blouse, a dress, and exchange among yourselves to find what fit. The same thing with shoes. Some women got big men's shoes. I ended up with brown suede pumps with high heels and used a rock to break off the heels, so I could march and stand in line on roll calls.

After this we went into registration and they took down your profession, scholastic background, everything. We got black numbers on a white piece of cloth that had to be sewn on the sleeve. My mother and sister and I had numbers in the 54,000s. People from all over Europe—Hungarian women and Germans, Czechoslovakia, Belgium, you name it—they were there. Children, of course, were not there. When families came with children, the children were taken right away.

As prisoners of Stutthof we were taken to outside work camps. A thousand of us women were taken to dig antitank ditches, a very deep V-shaped ditch that went for miles and miles. The Germans had the idea that Russian tanks would fall into those ditches and not be able to come up again!

When we were done, 400 of us were taken by train deeper into Germany. We ended up in tents, fifty women to a tent. We had no water for washing and not even a latrine. If at night you wanted to go, you had to call a guard who would escort you to this little field, stand there watching while you were crouching down, and then escort you back.

We were covered with lice, and we became very sick and weak. But Frau Schmidt taught us to survive. She was a chemist, and she taught us what roots or grasses we could eat that weren't poisonous. She also said that to survive we have to keep our minds occupied and not think about the hunger and cold. She made us study every day! . . .

By the middle of December we had to stop working because the snow was very deep and everything was frozen. January 20, 1945, they made a selection. The strong women that could still work would be marched out, and the sick, those who couldn't walk or who had bent backs, or who were just skeletons and too weak to work, would be left behind. My mother was selected and my sister and I decided to stay behind with her.

We were left without food, with two armed guards. We thought the guards will burn the tents, with us in them. Then we heard there was a factory where they boiled people's bodies to manufacture soap. But the next day the guards put us in formation and marched us down the highway until we came to a small town.

We were put in the jail there. There we were, ninety-six women standing in a small jail cell, with no bathroom, pressed so close together we couldn't sit down, couldn't bend down. Pretty soon everybody was hysterical, screaming. Then slowly we quieted down.

In the morning when they opened the doors, we really spilled outside! They had recruited a bunch of Polish guards and they surrounded us totally, as if in a box. So there we were, ninety-six weak, emaciated women, marching down the highway with all these guards with rifles.

Then the German guards told us to run into the woods. The snow was so deep, up to our knees, and most of us were barefoot, frozen, our feet were blistered. We couldn't really run, but we spread out in a long line, with my mother and sister and I at the very end. I was near one guard, and all of a sudden I heard the sound of his rifle going "click." I still remember the feeling in the back of my spine, very strange and very scary. Then the guards began to shoot.

There was a terrible panic, screams. People went really crazy. The three of us always hand-held with my mother in the middle, but now she let go of us and ran toward the guards, scream-ing not to shoot her children. They shot her, and my sister and I grabbed each other by the hand and ran into the woods.

We could hear screaming and shooting, and then it got very quiet. We were afraid to move. The guards wore those awesome-looking black uniforms with the skull and crossbones insignia, and every tree looked like another guard! A few women came out from behind the trees, and eventually, ten of us made it out to the highway.

With our last strength, we made it to a small Polish village about a mile away. We knocked on doors, but they didn't let us in, and they started to throw things at us. We went to the church, and the priest said he couldn't help us because the Germans were in charge.

We were so weak we just sat there on the church steps, and late in the evening the priest came with a man who told us to go hide in a barn that was empty. We did not get any other help, whatsoever, from that whole Polish village—not medical help, not a rag to cover ourselves, not even water. Nothing.

Liberation   The next morning there was a terrible battle right in front of the barn. We were so afraid. Then it got very quiet. We opened the door, and we saw Russian tanks. We were free!

The Russians put us into an empty farmhouse. They gave us Vaseline and some rags, all they had, to cover our wounds. Then they put us on trucks and took us to a town where we found a freight train and just jumped on it.

At the border Russian police took us off the train. They grilled us. "How did you survive? You must have cooperated with the Germans." It was terrible. But finally we got identity cards—in Russia, you are nobody without some kind of I.D.—and my sister and I decided to go to the small town where we had lived. We thought somebody might have survived. . . .

Looking Back   I was a prisoner from age nineteen to twenty-three. I lost my mother and twenty-eight aunts, uncles and cousins—all killed. To be a survivor has meant to me to be a witness be-cause being quiet would not be fair to the ones that did not survive.

There are people writing and saying the Holocaust never happened, it's a hoax, it's Jew-ish propaganda. We should keep talking about it, so the next generation won't grow up not knowing how a human being can turn into a beast, not knowing the danger in keeping quiet when you see something brewing. The onlooker, the bystander, is as much at fault as the per-petrator because he lets it happen. That is why I have this fear of what is called the "silent majority."

So when a non-Jewish friend or a student asks, "What can I do?" I say, when you see something anti-Semitic happen, get up and say, "This is wrong" or "I protest." Send a letter to the newspaper saying, "This should not happen in my community," and sign your name. Then maybe somebody else will be brave enough to come forward and say that he protests, too.

■ Discussion Questions

1. What role did the ghettos play in the Final Solution?
2. What was the principal difference between camps like Auschwitz and those like Stutthof?
3. What do these accounts reveal about conditions in the camps and the inmates' strategies for survival?
4. According to these survivors, what lessons does the Holocaust hold for the future?

CHAPTER 22

The Atomic Age, c. 1945–1960

Despite widespread feelings of relief and joy when World War II at last came to an end, an uncertain path lay ahead for the world. With Europe in shambles, two new superpowers emerged from the rubble: the United States and the Soviet Union. Their rivalry, known as the cold war, shaped international affairs for decades to come. The first document illuminates the ideological and political roots of U.S. and Soviet cold war policies. The bipolarization of world politics was not the only sign of Europe's diminished international identity, as the second document shows. War-weary and bitter, colonial peoples from Asia to Africa successfully battled for independence from European rule. The third document points to another campaign for freedom waiting in the wings. As societal and governmental pressures reasserted traditional boundaries between men and women that had been blurred by the war, some women called for change, setting the stage for the women's liberation movement in the 1960s.

70. National Security Council, *Paper Number 68* (1950)

Although he had helped to end World War II, U.S. president Harry S. Truman (1945–1953) had little time to celebrate. Daunting challenges still lay ahead as the fragile wartime alliance between the United States and the Soviet Union collapsed. By 1949, the Soviet bloc in eastern Europe was firmly in place, and the threat of international communism loomed large with the triumph of Mao Zedong in China. In response, Truman set out to devise a coherent strategy for combating the expansion of Soviet power. To this end, he commissioned the State and Defense Departments to compile a report on the subject, which they completed in 1950, on the eve of the outbreak of the Korean War. The classified report, excerpted here, elucidates not only the basis of U.S. cold war tactics but also the fears and perceptions underlying them.

Within the past thirty-five years the world has experienced two global wars of tremendous violence. . . . During the span of one generation, the international distribution of power has been fundamentally altered. For several centuries it had proved impossible for any one nation to gain such preponderant strength that a coalition of other nations could not in time face it with greater strength. The international scene was marked by recurring periods of violence and war, but a system of sovereign and independent states was maintained, over which no state was able to achieve hegemony.

National Security Council, Paper Number 68, *Foreign Relations of the United States* (Washington, D.C.: Government Printing Office, 1977), 235–92.

Two complex sets of factors have now basically altered this historical distribution of power. First, the defeat of Germany and Japan and the decline of the British and French Empires have interacted with the development of the United States and the Soviet Union in such a way that power has increasingly gravitated to these two centers. Second, the Soviet Union, unlike previous aspirants to hegemony, is animated by a new fanatic faith, antithetical to our own, and seeks to impose its absolute authority over the rest of the world. Conflict has, therefore, become endemic and is waged, on the part of the Soviet Union, by violent or non-violent methods in accordance with the dictates of expediency. . . .

On the one hand, the people of the world yearn for relief from the anxiety arising from the risk of atomic war. On the other hand, any substantial further extension of the area under the domination of the Kremlin would raise the possibility that no coalition adequate to confront the Kremlin with greater strength could be assembled. It is in this context that this Republic and its citizens in the ascendancy of their strength stand in their deepest peril.

The issues that face us are momentous, involving the fulfillment or destruction not only of this Republic but of civilization itself. They are issues which will not await our deliberations. With conscience and resolution this Government and the people it represents must now take new and fateful decisions. . . .

Our overall policy at the present time may be described as one designed to foster a world environment in which the American system can survive and flourish. It therefore rejects the concept of isolation and affirms the necessity of our positive participation in the world community.

This broad intention embraces two subsidiary policies. One is a policy which we would probably pursue even if there were no Soviet threat. It is a policy of attempting to develop a healthy international community. The other is the policy of "containing" the Soviet system. . . .

As for the policy of "containment," it is one which seeks by all means short of war to (1) block further expansion of Soviet power, (2) expose the falsities of Soviet pretensions, (3) induce a retraction of the Kremlin's control and influence, and (4) in general, so foster the seeds of destruction within the Soviet system that the Kremlin is brought at least to the point of modifying its behavior to conform to generally accepted international standards.

It was and continues to be cardinal in this policy that we possess superior overall power in ourselves or in dependable combination with other like-minded nations. One of the most important ingredients of power is military strength. In the concept of "containment," the maintenance of a strong military posture is deemed to be essential for two reasons: (1) as an ultimate guarantee of our national security and (2) as an indispensable backdrop to the conduct of the policy of "containment." . . .

At the same time, it is essential to the successful conduct of a policy of "containment" that we always leave open the possibility of negotiation with the U.S.S.R. A diplomatic freeze—and we are in one now—tends to defeat the very purposes of "containment" because it raises tensions at the same time that it makes Soviet retractions and adjustments in the direction of moderated behavior more difficult. It also tends to inhibit our initiative and deprives us of opportunities for maintaining a moral ascendancy in our struggle with the Soviet system. . . .

It is quite clear from Soviet theory and practice that the Kremlin seeks to bring the free world under its dominion by the methods of the cold war. The preferred technique is to subvert by infiltration and intimidation. Every institution of our society is an instrument which it is sought to stultify and turn against our purposes. Those that touch most closely our material and moral strength are obviously the prime targets, labor unions, civil enterprises, schools, churches, and all media for influencing opinion. The effort is not so much to make them serve obvious Soviet ends as to prevent them from serving our ends, and thus to make them sources of confusion in our economy, our culture, and our body politic. The doubts and diversities that in terms of our values are part of the merit of a free system, the weaknesses and the problems that are peculiar to it, the rights and privileges that free men enjoy, and the disorganization and destruction left in the wake of the last attack in our freedoms, all are but opportunities for the Kremlin to do its evil work. Every advantage is taken of the fact that our means of prevention and retaliation are limited by those principles and scruples which are precisely the ones that give our freedom and democracy its meaning for us. None of our scruples deter those whose only code is, "morality is that which serves the revolution."

At the same time the Soviet Union is seeking to create overwhelming military force, in order to back up infiltration with intimidation. In the only terms in which it understands strength, it is seeking to demonstrate to the free world that force and the will to use it are on the side of the Kremlin, that those who lack it are decadent and doomed. In local incidents it threatens and encroaches both for the sake of local gains and to increase anxiety and defeatism in all the free world. . . .

Our position as the center of power in the free world places a heavy responsibility upon the United States for leadership. We must organize and enlist the energies and resources of the free world in a positive program for peace which will frustrate the Kremlin design for world domination by creating a situation in the free world to which the Kremlin will be compelled to adjust. Without such a cooperative effort, led by the United States, we will have to make gradual withdrawals under pressure until we discover one day that we have sacrificed positions of vital interest. . . .

In summary, we must, by means of a rapid and sustained build-up of the political, economic, and military strength of the free world, and by means of an affirmative program intended to wrest the initiative from the Soviet Union, confront it with convincing evidence of the determination and ability of the free world to frustrate the Kremlin design of a world dominated by its will [*sic*]. Such evidence is the only means short of war which eventually may force the Kremlin to abandon its present course of action and to negotiate acceptable agreements on issues of major importance.

The whole success of the proposed program hangs ultimately on recognition by this Government, the American people, and all free peoples, that the cold war is in fact a real war in which the survival of the free world is at stake. Essential prerequisites to success are consultations with Congressional leaders designed to make the program the object of nonpartisan legislative support, and a presentation to the public of a full explanation of the facts and implications of the present international situation. The prosecution of the program will require of us all the ingenuity, sacrifice, and unity demanded by the vital importance of the issue and the tenacity to persevere until our national objectives have been attained.

■ Discussion Questions

1. As described here, how did World War II transform the international distribution of power?
2. According to the report, in what ways did the Soviet Union pose a danger to Americans and all "free peoples"?
3. What solutions does the document set forth to counter this danger?
4. Why does the report describe the cold war as a "real" war?

71. Ho Chi Minh, *Declaration of Independence of the Republic of Vietnam*   (1945)

The devastation wrought by World War II encompassed more than the countless bombed buildings and millions of dead. The war also fatally weakened the European powers' grip on their empires, as colonial peoples around the globe rose up against imperialist rule. French Indochina was no exception.

Allan B. Cole, ed., *Conflict in Indo-China and International Repercussions: A Documentary History, 1945–1955* (Ithaca, N.Y.: Cornell University Press, 1956), 20–21.

In 1939, a small nationalist organization, Viet Minh, had formed, which achieved new prominence in the wake of World War II when the French sought to reassert their control in the region. Less than a month after Japan's surrender, the Viet Minh declared Vietnam's independence from France, reprinted in the following document. It was signed by "President Ho Chi Minh," one of the organization's original leaders who had lived in Paris, Moscow, and China. The document explicitly draws on the language of the French Enlightenment to further the Viet Minh's cause and condemn that of France.

"All men are created equal. They are endowed by their Creator with certain unalienable rights, among these are Life, Liberty and the pursuit of happiness."

This immortal statement was made in the Declaration of Independence of the United States of America in 1776. Now if we enlarge the sphere of our thoughts, this statement conveys another meaning: All the peoples on the earth are equal from birth, all the peoples have a right to live, be happy and free.

The Declaration of the Rights of Man and of the Citizen of the French Revolution in 1791 also states: "All men are born free and with equal rights, and must always be free and have equal rights."

BEFORE THE OUTBREAK OF WAR

Those are undeniable truths.

Nevertheless, for more than 80 years, the French imperialists deceitfully raising the standard of Liberty, Equality and Fraternity, have violated our Fatherland and oppressed our fellow-citizens. They have acted contrarily to the ideals of humanity and justice.

In the province of politics, they have deprived our people of every liberty.

They have enforced inhuman laws; to ruin our unity and national consciousness, they have carried out three different policies in the North, the Center and the South of Vietnam.

They have founded more prisons than schools. They have mercilessly slain our patriots; they have deluged our revolutionary areas with innocent blood. They have fettered public opinion; they have promoted illiteracy.

To weaken our race they have forced us to use their manufactured opium and alcohol.

In the province of economics, they have stripped our fellow-citizens of everything they possessed, impoverishing the individual and devastating the land.

They have robbed us of our rice fields, our mines, our forests, our raw materials. They have monopolized the printing of bank-notes, the import and export trade; they have invented numbers of unlawful taxes, reducing our people, especially our countryfolk, to a state of extreme poverty.

They have stood in the way of our businessmen and stifled all their undertakings; they have extorted our working classes in a most savage way.

In the Autumn of the year 1940, when the Japanese fascists violated Indochina's territory to get one more foothold in their fight against the Allies, the French imperialists fell on their knees and surrendered, handing over our country to the Japanese, adding Japanese fetters to the French ones. From that day on the Vietnamese people suffered hardships yet unknown in the history of mankind. The result of this double oppression was terrific: from Quangtri to the Northern border two million people were starved to death in the early months of 1945.

On the 9th of March 1945 the French troops were disarmed by the Japanese. Once more the French either fled, or surrendered unconditionally, showing thus that not only they were incapable of "protecting" us, but that they twice sold us to the Japanese.

Yet, many times before the month of March, the Vietminh had urged the French to ally with them against the Japanese. The French colonists never answered. On the contrary they intensified their terrorizing policy. Before taking their flight they even killed a great number of our patriots who had been imprisoned at Yenbay and Caobang.

DEMOCRATIC REPUBLIC OF VIETNAM

Nevertheless, towards the French people our fellow-citizens have always manifested an attitude pervaded with toleration and humanity. Even after the Japanese putsch of March 1945 the Vietminh have helped many Frenchmen to reach the frontier, have delivered some of them from the Japanese jails, and never failed to protect their lives and properties.

The truth is that since the Autumn of 1940 our country had ceased to be a French colony and had become a Japanese outpost. After the Japanese had surrendered to the Allies our whole people rose to conquer political power and institute the Republic of Vietnam.

The truth is that we have wrested our independence from the Japanese and not from the French. The French have fled, the Japanese have capitulated, Emperor Bao Dai has abdicated, our people has broken the fetters which for over a century have tied us down; our people has at the same time overthrown the monarchic constitution that had reigned supreme for so many centuries and instead has established the present Republican Government.

For these reasons, we, members of the provisional Government, representing the whole population of Vietnam, have declared and renew here our declaration that we break off all relations with the French people and abolish all the special rights the French have unlawfully acquired on our Fatherland.

The whole population of Vietnam is united in a common allegiance to the Republican Government and is linked by a common will which is to annihilate the dark aims of the French imperialists.

We are convinced that the Allied nations which have acknowledged at Teheran and San Francisco the principles of self determination and equality of status will not refuse to acknowledge the independence of Vietnam.

A people that has courageously opposed French domination for more than 80 years, a people that has fought by the Allies' side these last years against the fascists, such a people must be free, such a people must be independent.

For these reasons we, members of the Provisional Government of Vietnam, declare to the world that Vietnam has the right to be free and independent, and has in fact become a free and independent country. We also declare that the Vietnamese people is determined to make the heaviest sacrifices to maintain its independence and its Liberty.

▪ Discussion Questions

1. How does the document characterize the actions of the French in Vietnam? Why does it describe them as deceitful?
2. In what ways did World War II further the cause of the Viet Minh?
3. Why did the Viet Minh believe that the Vietnamese people had an undeniable right to independence?

72. Simone de Beauvoir, *The Second Sex* (1949)

Like Ho Chi Minh, Simone de Beauvoir (1908–1986) challenged traditional power structures in the postwar era. However, although she watched the growing independence movement in French Indochina with interest, her battle did not center on the plight of colonized peoples. Rather, she dedicated herself to examining the condition of modern women, which, she argued, was similarly marked by injustice and discrimination. She presented her views to the world in her book The

Simone de Beauvoir, *The Second Sex,* trans. and ed. H. M. Parshley (New York: Knopf, 1953), xvi–xx.

Second Sex, *published in 1949. In this excerpt, Beauvoir outlines the fundamental premise of her work: throughout history, women's identities have been defined by men and thus subjugated to them. Only by taking charge of their own lives could women break free from their subservience. Her views would help galvanize the women's liberation movement in the United States and Europe in the 1960s.*

A man would never get the notion of writing a book on the peculiar situation of the human male. But if I wish to define myself, I must first of all say: "I am a woman"; on this truth must be based all further discussion. A man never begins by presenting himself as an individual of a certain sex; it goes without saying that he is a man. The terms *masculine* and *feminine* are used symmetrically only as a matter of form, as on legal papers. In actuality the relation of the two sexes is not quite like that of two electrical poles, for man represents both the positive and the neutral, as is indicated by the common use of *man* to designate human beings in general; whereas woman represents only the negative, defined by limiting criteria, without reciprocity. In the midst of an abstract discussion it is vexing to hear a man say: "You think thus and so because you are a woman"; but I know that my only defense is to reply: "I think thus and so because it is true," thereby removing my subjective self from the argument. It would be out of the question to reply: "And you think the contrary because you are a man," for it is understood that the fact of being a man is no peculiarity. A man is in the right in being a man; it is the woman who is in the wrong. It amounts to this: just as for the ancients there was an absolute vertical with reference to which the oblique was defined, so there is an absolute human type, the masculine. Woman has ovaries, a uterus; these peculiarities imprison her in her subjectivity, circumscribe her within the limits of her own nature. It is often said that she thinks with her glands. Man superbly ignores the fact that his anatomy also includes glands, such as the testicles, and that they secrete hormones. He thinks of his body as a direct and normal connection with the world, which he believes he apprehends objectively, whereas he regards the body of woman as a hindrance, a prison, weighed down by everything peculiar to it. . . . And she is simply what man decrees; thus she is called "the sex," by which is meant that she appears essentially to the male as a sexual being. For him she is sex—absolute sex, no less. She is defined and differentiated with reference to man and not he with reference to her; she is the incidental, the inessential as opposed to the essential. He is the Subject, he is the Absolute—she is the Other. . . .

Thus it is that no group ever sets itself up as the One without at once setting up the Other over against itself. If three travelers chance to occupy the same compartment, that is enough to make vaguely hostile "others" out of all the rest of the passengers on the train. In small-town eyes all persons not belonging to the village are "strangers" and suspect; to the native of a country all who inhabit other countries are "foreigners"; Jews are "different" for the anti-Semite, Negroes are "inferior" for American racists, aborigines are "natives" for colonists, proletarians are the "lower class" for the privileged. . . .

No subject will readily volunteer to become the object, the inessential; it is not the Other who, in defining himself as the Other, establishes the One. The Other is posed as such by the One in defining himself as the One. But if the Other is not to regain the status of being the One, he must be submissive enough to accept this alien point of view. Whence comes this submission in the case of woman?

There are, to be sure, other cases in which a certain category has been able to dominate another completely for a time. Very often this privilege depends upon inequality of numbers—the majority imposes its rule upon the minority or persecutes it. But women are not a minority, like the American Negroes or the Jews; there are as many women as men on earth. Again, the two groups concerned have often been originally independent; they may have been formerly unaware of each other's existence, or perhaps they recognized each other's autonomy. But a historical event has resulted in the subjugation of the weaker by the stronger. The scattering of the Jews, the introduction of slavery into America, the conquests of imperialism are examples in point. In these cases the oppressed retained at least the memory of former days; they possessed in common a past, a tradition, sometimes a religion or a culture.

The parallel drawn . . . between women and the proletariat is valid in that neither ever formed a minority or a separate collective unit of mankind. And instead of a single historical event it is in both cases a historical development that explains their status as a class and accounts for the membership of *particular individuals* in that class. But proletarians have not always existed, whereas there have always been women. They are women in virtue of their anatomy and physiology. Throughout history they have always been subordinated to men, and hence their dependency is not the result of a historical event or a social change—it was not something that *occurred*. The reason why otherness in this case seems to be an absolute is in part that it lacks the contingent or incidental nature of historical facts. A condition brought about at a certain time can be abolished at some other time, as the Negroes of Haiti and others have proved; but it might seem that a natural condition is beyond the possibility of change. In truth, however, the nature of things is no more immutably given, once for all, than is historical reality. If woman seems to be the inessential which never becomes the essential, it is because she herself fails to bring about this change. Proletarians say "We"; Negroes also. Regarding themselves as subjects, they transform the bourgeois, the whites, into "others." But women do not say "We," except at some congress of feminists or similar formal demonstration; men say "women," and women use the same word in referring to themselves. They do not authentically assume a subjective attitude. The proletarians have accomplished the revolution in Russia, the Negroes in Haiti, the Indo-Chinese are battling for it in Indo-China; but the women's effort has never been anything more than a symbolic agitation. They have gained only what men have been willing to grant; they have taken nothing, they have only received.

The reason for this is that women lack concrete means for organizing themselves into a unit which can stand face to face with the correlative unit. They have no past, no history, no religion of their own; and they have no such solidarity of work and interest as that of the proletariat. They are not even promiscuously herded together in the way that creates community feeling among the American Negroes, the ghetto Jews, the workers of Saint-Denis, or the factory hands of Renault. They live dispersed among the males, attached through residence, housework, economic condition, and social standing to certain men—fathers or husbands—more firmly than they are to other women. If they belong to the bourgeoisie, they feel solidarity with men of that class, not with proletarian women; if they are white, their allegiance is to white men, not to Negro women. The proletariat can propose to massacre the ruling class, and a sufficiently fanatical Jew or Negro might dream of getting sole possession of the atomic bomb and making humanity wholly Jewish or black; but woman cannot even dream of exterminating the males. The bond that unites her to her oppressors is not comparable to any other. The division of the sexes is a biological fact, not an event in human history. . . . The couple is a fundamental unity with its two halves riveted together, and the cleavage of society along the line of sex is impossible. Here is to be found the basic trait of woman: she is the Other in a totality of which the two components are necessary to one another.

▪ Discussion Questions

1. What does Beauvoir mean when she describes women as the "Other"?
2. According to Beauvoir, how does women's status both resemble and differ from that of other oppressed groups, such as colonized peoples?
3. Why, unlike some of these groups, have women been unable to change their status?

CHAPTER 23

Challenges to the Postindustrial West, 1960–1980

The 1960s was a decade of turmoil fueled by both optimism and despair. Millions of people across Europe and the United States took to the streets to challenge cold war politics and society. At the same time, technological changes transformed everyday life. The first two documents illuminate the effects of the increasing importance of technology in the postindustrial world. On the one hand, technological advances improved people's lives and enhanced their knowledge of the world and the universe. On the other, technology offered new opportunities for mass destruction and seemed to undermine religious beliefs and values. As the third document shows, for many, nothing was sacred, whether in politics, as the student protesters of 1968 revealed, or in culture, as the popularity of rock music demonstrated.

73. The *New York Times* and Neil Armstrong and Edwin Aldrin, *The First Men Walk on the Moon* (1969)

Along with the rise of civic activism and youth culture, the expanding role of technology in postindustrial society changed people's worldview. Perhaps nothing captures technology's growing importance more dramatically than U.S. astronauts Neil Armstrong and Edwin ("Buzz") Aldrin's walk on the moon in July 1969. Spurred by the United States' desire to demonstrate its technological superiority over the Soviet Union, their moon walk was an unprecedented technological feat. So, too, was the fact that the event was broadcast on television to millions of viewers around the world. These two pieces capture the mood at the time of both the astronauts and their audience. The first is an editorial published in the New York Times *on July 20, the day Armstrong and Aldrin took their momentous steps. In the second, we hear Armstrong's and Aldrin's recollections of their historic lunar landing.*

To Walk on the Moon

In a world long given to marking off its historical progress in periods—the Age of Faith, the Renaissance, the Age of Reason, the Industrial Revolution—language seems too impoverished to encompass so neatly the era that begins with man's first walk on the moon. As a term, the Space Age is grossly inadequate, failing completely to convey the nature of the change that this event portends. For the lunar landing of the astronauts is more than a step in history; it is a step in evolution.

From "To Walk on the Moon," *New York Times* editorial, July 20, 1969. Copyright © 1969 by The New York Times Company. From *The First on the Moon: A Voyage with Neil Armstrong, Michael Collins, and Edwin E. Aldrin Jr.,* written with Gene Farmer and Dora Jane Hamblin (Boston: Little, Brown, 1970), 324, 350–51.

The journey of Neil Armstrong and his companions cannot be viewed in the same perspective as the voyage of Columbus or of any other traveler in recorded time—and the difference is not at all in degrees of courage or individual skill. In truth, Columbus's feat may well have taken more courage than Armstrong's because it was preceded by no unmanned probes and took him to regions unknown to the science of his day, in contrast to the photographed, spectographed and charted terrain of the moon.

What gives the astronauts' expedition a different dimension entirely, what removes it indeed from any venture in the whole history of the human race are two circumstances that stagger the mind: it is man's first step in adapting to an environment beyond this planet's and it is a *willed* step in the evolutionary process, one made deliberately and in the full consciousness of its import.

For the adaptation itself there are comparable precedents in nature, though for one as full of meaning for the future one might have to go back to the first fishy creature that emerged from the Devonian sea to make a feeble try at life on dry land.

For the conscious willing of an evolutionary act there is no precedent. Man has of course taught himself to ride over and under the waves and to fly through space, but what is contemplated now is no such passing accommodation but in time the transfer of human life to other sites in the universe—with ultimate consequences that almost surely must be evolutionary in nature.

It will take years, decades, perhaps centuries, for man to colonize even the moon, but that is the end inherent in Armstrong's first step on extraterrestrial soil. Serious and hard-headed scientists envision, even in the not remote future, lunar communities capable of growing into domed cities subsisting on hydroponically grown food, of developing the moon's resources, and eventually of acquiring a breathable atmosphere and a soil capable of being farmed. What with the dire threats of population explosion at best and nuclear explosion at worst, the human race, as Sir Bernard Lovell warns, may find itself sometime in the 21st century "having to consider how best to insure the survival of the species."

It is not possible to imagine that any such cosmic movement would leave the transported segment of mankind unchanged. Over the centuries and through countless transitions it would adapt biologically and psychologically, following Darwinian law, to existence in an environment differing as much from its earthly ancestors as that of the early mammals differed from the environment in the primeval seas.

Reflections on man's social shortcomings, speculation on what else he might have done instead of sending men to the moon—all this melts away in the moment of awe and wonder.

FIRST ON THE MOON

Neil Armstrong said . . . "The most dramatic recollections I had were the sights themselves. Of all the spectacular views we had, the most impressive to me was on the way to the moon, when we flew through its shadow. We were still thousands of miles away, but close enough so that the moon almost filled our circular window. It was eclipsing the sun, from our position, and the corona of the sun was visible around the limb of the moon as a gigantic lens-shaped or saucer-shaped light, stretching out to several lunar diameters. It was magnificent, but the moon was even more so. We were in its shadow, so there was no part of it illuminated by the sun. It was illuminated only by earthshine. It made the moon appear blue-gray, and the entire scene looked decidedly three-dimensional.

"I was really aware, visually aware, that the moon was in fact a sphere, not a disc. It seemed almost as if it were showing us its roundness, its similarity in shape to our earth, in a sort of welcome. I was sure that it would be a hospitable host. It had been awaiting its first visitors for a long time." . . .

[Buzz Aldrin:] "The moon was a very natural and very pleasant environment in which to work. It had many of the advantages of zero-gravity, but it was in a sense less *lonesome* than zero G, where you always have to pay attention to securing attachment points to give you some means of leverage. In one-sixth gravity, on the moon, you had a distinct feeling of being *somewhere,* and you had a constant, though at many times ill defined, sense of direction and force.

"One interesting thing was that the horizontal reference on the moon is not at all well defined. That is, it's difficult to know when you are leaning forward or backward and to what degree. This fact, coupled with the rather limited field of vision from our helmets, made local features of the moon appear to change slope, depending on which way you were looking and how you were standing. The weight of the backpack tends to pull you backward, and you must consciously lean forward just a little to compensate. I believe someone has described the posture as 'tired ape'—almost erect but slumped forward a little. It was difficult sometimes to know when you were standing erect. It felt as if you could lean farther in any direction, without losing your balance, than on earth. By far the easiest and most natural way to move on the surface of the moon is to put one foot in front of the other. The kangaroo hop did work, but it led to some instability; there was not so much control when you were moving around.

"As we deployed our experiments on the surface we had to jettison things like lanyards, retaining fasteners, etc., and some of these we tossed away. The objects would go away with a slow, lazy motion. If anyone tried to throw a baseball back and forth in that atmosphere he would have difficulty, at first, acclimatizing himself to that slow, lazy trajectory; but I believe he could adapt to it quite readily. . . .

"Odor is very subjective, but to me there was a distinct smell to the lunar material—pungent, like gunpowder or spent cap-pistol caps. We carted a fair amount of lunar dust back inside the vehicle with us, either on our suits and boots or on the conveyor system we used to get boxes and equipment back inside. We did notice the odor right away.

"It was a unique, almost mystical environment up there."

■ Discussion Questions

1. What does the editorial mean when it describes Armstrong and Aldrin's lunar landing as a step in human evolution?
2. How does the editorial link this event to contemporary concerns about the future of humankind?

74. Pope John XXIII, *Vatican II* (1961)

As scientists raced to put a man on the moon and protesters took to the streets, the Catholic church devised its own response to the changes of the day. In 1961, Pope John XXIII (r. 1958–1963) announced his plans in this document to convene an ecumenical council to promote spiritual renewal and reevaluate the place of the church in the modern world. Almost one hundred years had passed since the last council of this type had met. A new council was urgently needed, the pope proclaimed, because the technological and economic advances of the twentieth century posed unprecedented challenges to the church and its faithful. The result was the largest Catholic council ever assembled, known as Vatican II, which met between 1962 and 1965. The decrees, constitutions, and declarations issued by the council established the blueprint for Catholic worship in the postindustrial world.

Walter M. Abbott, trans. and ed., *The Documents of Vatican II: All Sixteen Official Texts Promulgated by the Ecumenical Council* (New York: Herder and Herder, 1966), 703–07.

PAINFUL CONSIDERATIONS

Today the Church is witnessing a crisis under way within society. While humanity is on the edge of a new era, tasks of immense gravity and amplitude await the Church, as in the most tragic periods of its history. It is a question in fact of bringing the modern world into contact with the vivifying and perennial energies of the gospel, a world which exalts itself with its conquests in the technical and scientific fields, but which brings also the consequences of a temporal order which some have wished to reorganize excluding God. This is why modern society is earmarked by a great material progress to which there is not a corresponding advance in the moral field.

Hence there is a weakening in the aspiration toward the values of the spirit. Hence an urge for the almost exclusive search for earthly pleasures, which progressive technology places with such ease within the reach of all. And hence there is a completely new and disconcerting fact: the existence of a militant atheism which is active on a world level.

REASONS FOR CONFIDENCE

These painful considerations are a reminder of the duty to be vigilant and to keep the sense of responsibility awake. Distrustful souls see only darkness burdening the face of the earth. We, instead, like to reaffirm all our confidence in our Savior, who has not left the world which He redeemed.

Indeed, we make ours the recommendation of Jesus that one should know how to distinguish the "signs of the times" (Mt. 16:4), and we seem to see now, in the midst of so much darkness, a few indications which auger well for the fate of the Church and of humanity.

The bloody wars that have followed one on the other in our times, the spiritual ruins caused by many ideologies, and the fruits of so many bitter experiences have not been without useful teachings. Scientific progress itself, which gave man the possibility of creating catastrophic instruments for his destruction, has raised questions. It has obliged human beings to become thoughtful, more conscious of their own limitations, desirous of peace, and attentive to the importance of spiritual values. And it has accelerated that progress of closer collaboration and of mutual integration toward which, even though in the midst of a thousand uncertainties, the human family seems to be moving. And this facilitates, no doubt, the apostolate of the Church, since many people who did not realize the importance of its mission in the past are, taught by experience, today more disposed to welcome its warnings.

PRESENT VITALITY OF THE CHURCH

Then, if we turn our attention to the Church, we see that it has not remained a lifeless spectator in the face of these events but has followed step by step the evolution of peoples, scientific progress, and social revolution. It has opposed decisively the materialistic ideologies which deny faith. Lastly, it has witnessed the rise and growth of the immense energies of an apostolate of prayer, of action in all fields. It has seen the emergence of a clergy constantly better equipped in learning and virtue for its mission; and of a laity which has become ever more conscious of its responsibilities within the bosom of the Church, and, in a special way, of its duty to collaborate with the Church hierarchy.

To this should be added the immense suffering of entire Christian communities, through which a multitude of admirable bishops, priests, and laymen seal their adherence to the faith, bearing persecutions of all kinds and revealing forms of heroism which certainly equal those of the most glorious periods of the Church.

Thus, though the world may appear profoundly changed, the Christian community is also in great part transformed and renewed. It has therefore strengthened itself socially in unity; it has been reinvigorated intellectually; it has been interiorly purified and is thus ready for trial.

THE SECOND VATICAN ECUMENICAL COUNCIL

In the face of this twofold spectacle—a world which reveals a grave state of spiritual poverty and the Church of Christ, which is still so vibrant with vitality—we, from the time we ascended to the supreme pontificate, despite our unworthiness and by means of an impulse of Divine Providence, have felt immediately the urgency of the duty to call our sons together, to give the Church the possibility to contribute more efficaciously to the solution of the problems of the modern age.

For this reason, welcoming as from above the intimate voice of our spirit, we considered that the times now were right to offer to the Catholic Church and to the world the gift of a new Ecumenical Council, as an addition to, and continuation of, the series of the twenty great councils, which have been through the centuries a truly heavenly providence for the increase of grace and Christian progress. . . ..

The forthcoming Council will meet therefore and at a moment in which the Church finds very alive the desire to fortify its faith, and to contemplate itself in its own awe-inspiring unity. In the same way, it feels more urgent the duty to give greater efficiency to its sound vitality and to promote the sanctification of its members, the diffusion of revealed truth, the consolidation of its agencies. . . .

And, finally, to a world, which is lost, confused, and anxious under the constant threat of new frightful conflicts, the forthcoming Council must offer a possibility for all men of good will to turn their thoughts and their intentions toward peace, a peace which can and must, above all, come from spiritual and supernatural realities, from human intelligence and conscience, enlightened and guided by God the Creator and Redeemer of humanity.

■ Discussion Questions

1. Why did Pope John XXIII think that modern society was in a state of crisis?
2. How did the pope link this crisis specifically to the effects of scientific and technological progress on everyday life?
3. How did the pope hope that Vatican II would counter these effects?

75. *Student Voices of Protest* (1968)

College campuses were hotbeds of social activism in the 1960s, and students exploded into action with unprecedented force in the spring of 1968. The year was beset with tragedy, from the mounting number of casualties in the Vietnam War to the assassination of American civil rights leader Martin Luther King Jr. From New York to Paris to Berlin, students rose up in protest, particularly over racial and antiwar issues. They demonstrated, occupied buildings, shut down classes, and went on strike. These excerpts bring students to life in their own words, which convey not only frustration and despair but also a desire to bring about lasting change.

My most vivid memory of May '68? The new-found ability for everyone to *speak*—to speak of anything with anyone. In that month of talking during May you learnt more than in the whole of your five years of studying. It was really another world—a dream world perhaps—but that's what I'll always remember: the need and the right for everyone to speak.—*René Bourrigaud, student at the École Supérieure d'Agriculture, Angers, France*

Ronald Fraser et al., *1968: A Student Generation in Revolt* (New York: Pantheon Books, 1988), 9–12.

People were learning through doing things themselves, learning self-confidence. It was magic, there were all these kids from nice middle-class homes who'd never done or said anything and were now suddenly speaking. It was democracy of the public space in the market place, a discourse where nobody was privileged. If anything encapsulated what we were trying to do and why, it was that. . . . —*Pete Latarche, leader of the university occupation at Hull, England, 1968*

It's a moment I shall never forget. Suddenly, spontaneously, barricades were being thrown up in the streets. People were building up the cobblestones because they wanted—many of them for the first time—to throw themselves into a collective, spontaneous activity. People were releasing all their repressed feelings, expressing them in a festive spirit. Thousands felt the need to communicate with each other, to love one another. That night has forever made me optimistic about history. Having lived through it, I can't ever say, "It will never happen. . . ."—*Dany Cohn-Bendit, student leader at Nanterre University, on the night of the Paris barricades, 10/11 May 1968*

The unthinkable happened! Everything I had ever dreamt of since childhood, knowing that it would never happen, now began to become real. People were saying, fuck hierarchy, authority, this society with its cold rational elitist logic! Fuck all the petty bosses and the mandarins at the top! Fuck this immutable society that refuses to consider the misery, poverty, inequality and injustice it creates, that divides people according to their origins and skills! Suddenly, the French were showing they understood that they had to refuse the state's authority because it was malevolent, evil, just as I'd always thought as a child. Suddenly they realized that they had to find a new sort of solidarity. And it was happening in front of my eyes. That was what May '68 meant to me!—*Nelly Finkielsztejn, student at Nanterre University, Paris*

My world had been very staid, very traditional, very frightened, very middle-class and respectable. And here I was doing these things that six months before I would have thought were just horrible. But I was in the midst of an enormous tide of people. There was so much constant collective reaffirmation of it. The ecstasy was stepping out of time, out of traditional personal time. The usual rules of the game in capitalist society had been set aside. It was phenomenally liberating. . . . At the same time it was a political struggle. It wasn't just Columbia. There *was* a fucking war on in Vietnam, and the civil rights movement. These were profound forces that transcend that moment. 1968 just cracked the universe open for me. And the fact of getting involved meant that never again was I going to look at something outside with the kind of reflex condemnation or fear. Yes, it was the making of me—or the unmaking.—*Mike Wallace, occupation of Columbia University, New York, April 1968*

We'd been brought up to believe in our hearts that America fought on the side of justice. The Second World War was very much ingrained in us, my father had volunteered. So, along with the absolute horror of the war in Vietnam, there was also a feeling of personal betrayal. I remember crying by myself late at night in my room listening to the reports of the war, the first reports of the bombing. Vietnam was the catalyst. . . . —*John Levin, student leader at San Francisco State College*

I was outraged, what shocked me most was that a highly developed country, the super-modern American army, should fall on these Vietnamese peasants—fall on them like the conquistadores on South America, or the white settlers on the North American Indians. In my mind's eye, I always saw those bull-necked fat pigs—like in Georg Grosz's pictures—attacking the small, child-like Vietnamese.—*Michael von Engelhardt, German student*

The resistance of the Vietnamese people showed that it could be done—a fight back was possible. If poor peasants could do it well why not people in Western Europe? That was the importance of Vietnam, it destroyed the myth that we just had to hold on to what we had because the whole world could be blown up if the Americans were "provoked." The Vietnamese showed that if you were attacked you fought back, and then it depended on the internal balance of power whether you won or not.—*Tariq Ali, a British Vietnam Solidarity Campaign leader*

So we started to be political in a totally new way, making the connection between our student condition and the larger international issues. A low mark in mathematics could become the focal point of an occupation by students who linked the professor's arbitrary and authoritarian behaviour to the wider issues, like Vietnam. Acting on your immediate problems made you understand better the bigger issues. If it hadn't been for that, perhaps the latter would have remained alien, you'd have said "OK, but what can *I* do?"—*Agnese Gatti, student at Trento Institute of Social Sciences, Italy*

Creating a confrontation with the university administration you could significantly expose the interlocking network of imperialism as it was played out on the campuses. You could prove that they were working hand-in-hand with the military and the CIA, and that ultimately, when you pushed them, they would call upon all the oppressive apparatus to defend their position from their own students.—*Jeff Jones, Students for a Democratic Society (SDS), New York regional organizer*

Everybody was terribly young and didn't know what was going on. One had a sort of megalomaniac attitude that by sheer protest and revolt things would be changed. It was true of the music, of the hallucinogenics, of politics, it was true across the board—people threw themselves into activity without experience. The desire to do something became tremendously intense and the capacity to do it diminished by the very way one was rejecting the procedures by which things could be done. It led to all sorts of crazy ideas.—*Anthony Barnett, sociology student, Leicester University, England*

■ Discussion Questions

1. What were some of the students' principal targets for criticism, and why?
2. In what ways did the events of 1968 personally transform many of these students?
3. Some historians argue that the student protests of 1968 made governments less inviolable and sacred. What evidence can you find here to support this assertion?

CHAPTER 24

The New Globalism: Opportunities and Dilemmas, 1980 to the Present

After decades of conflict, the cold war virtually came to a halt in 1989 when the Soviet empire disintegrated. The end of superpower rivalries ushered in a new age of global challenges and opportunities. The first two documents pull back the curtain on the opening act of this drama, revealing that an explosive combination of government-sponsored reforms and grassroots political activism fueled communism's demise. The third document, from French president François Mitterrand, illuminates the collaborative efforts of European leaders to redefine Europe's place on the post–cold war stage, just as they had done after World War II. Yet, as Mitterrand's speech to the European parliament in 1995 reveals, the world was now a far different place, where peoples, cultures, and economies were increasingly bound together, as were the problems they faced.

76. *Glasnost and the Soviet Press* (1988)

When Mikhail Gorbachev (b. 1931) became general secretary of the Soviet Communist Party in 1985, the nation's economy was in ruins, and people struggled to meet even their most basic needs. Gorbachev implemented revolutionary policies of economic restructuring (perestroika) and "openness" (glasnost) to confront the crisis. The two articles excerpted here illuminate the crucial role of the Soviet press in this process as a forum for public debate. Never before had Soviet citizens experienced such freedom of speech and expression. Written by Nina Andreyeva, the first article appeared as a letter to the editor on the front page of the prestigious newspaper Sovetskaya Rossiya in March 1988. Politically conservative, Andreyeva attacked Gorbachev's reforms as a violation of socialist ideology. Gorbachev and his supporters countered her assault in an article of their own, published three weeks later in Pravda, defending glasnost and perestroika as the path to a better future.

POLEMICS: I CANNOT WAIVE PRINCIPLES

Nina Andreyeva

I decided to write this letter after lengthy deliberation. I am a chemist, and I lecture at Leningrad's Lensovet Technology Institute. Like many others, I also look after a student group. Students nowadays, following the period of social apathy and intellectual dependence, are gradually becoming charged with the energy of revolutionary changes. Naturally, discussions develop about the ways of restructuring and its economic and ideological aspects. *Glasnost*, openness, the disappearance

---

Isaac J. Tarasulo, ed., *Gorbachev and Glasnost: Viewpoints from the Soviet Press* (Wilmington, Del.: SR Books, 1989), 277–78, 281–85, 290–95, 299–302.

of zones where criticism is taboo, and the emotional heat of mass consciousness (especially among young people) often result in the raising of problems that are, to a greater or lesser extent, "prompted" either by Western radio voices or by those of our compatriots who are shaky in their conceptions of the essence of socialism. And what a variety of topics that are being discussed! A multi-party system, freedom of religious propaganda, emigration to live abroad, the right to broad ·discussion of sexual problems in the press, the need to decentralize the leadership of culture, abolition of compulsory military service. There are particularly numerous arguments among students about the country's past. . . .

In the numerous discussions now taking place on literally all questions of the social sciences, as a college lecturer I am primarily interested in the questions that have a direct effect on young people's ideological and political education, their moral health, and their social optimism. Conversing with students and deliberating with them on controversial problems, I cannot help concluding that our country has accumulated quite a few anomalies and one-sided interpretations that clearly need to be corrected. I would like to dwell on some of them in particular.

Take, for example, the question of Joseph Stalin's place in our country's history. The whole obsession with critical attacks is linked with his name, and in my opinion this obsession centers not so much on the historical individual himself as on the entire highly complex epoch of transition, an epoch linked with unprecedented feats by a whole generation of Soviet people who are today gradually withdrawing from active participation in political and social work. The industrialization, collectivization, and cultural revolution which brought our country to the ranks of the great world powers are being forcibly squeezed into the "personality cult" formula. All of this is being questioned. Matters have gone so far that persistent demands for "repentance" are being made of "Stalinists" (and this category can be taken to include anyone you like). There is rapturous praise for novels and movies that lynch the epoch of "storms and onslaught," which is presented as a "tragedy of the peoples." . . .

I support the party's call to uphold the honor and dignity of the trailblazers of socialism. I think that these are the party-class positions from which we must assess the historical role of all leaders of the party and the country, including Stalin. In this case, matters cannot be reduced to their "court" aspect or to abstract moralizing by persons far removed both from those stormy times and from the people who had to live and work in those times, and to work in such a fashion as to still be an inspiring example for us today. . . .

I think that, no matter how controversial and complex a figure in Soviet history Stalin may be, his genuine role in the building and defense of socialism will sooner or later be given an objective and unambiguous assessment. Of course, unambiguous does not mean an assessment that is one-sided, that whitewashes, or that eclectically sums up contradictory phenomena making it possible subjectively (albeit with slight reservations) "to forgive or not forgive," "to reject or retain." Unambiguous means primarily a specific historical assessment detached from short-term considerations which would demonstrate—according to historical results!—the dialectics of the correlation between the individual's actions and the basic laws governing society's development. In our country these laws were also linked with the answer to the question "Who will defeat whom?" in its domestic as well as international aspects. If we are to adhere to the Marxist-Leninist methodology of historical analysis then, in Mikhail Gorbachev's words, we must primarily and vividly show how the millions of people lived, how they worked, and what they believed in, as well as the coupling of victories and failures, discoveries and errors, the bright and the tragic, the revolutionary enthusiasm of the masses and the violations of socialist legality and even crimes at times. . . .

It seems to me that the question of the role and position of socialist ideology is extremely acute today. The authors of timeserving articles circulating under the guise of moral and spiritual "cleansing" erode the dividing lines and criteria of scientific ideology, manipulate *glasnost*, and foster nonsocialist pluralism, which applies the brakes on *perestroika* in the public conscience.

This has a particularly painful effect on young people which, I repeat, is clearly sensed by us, the college lecturers, schoolteachers, and all who have to deal with young people's problems. As Mikhail Gorbachev said at the CPSU Central Committee February *plenum*, "our actions in the spiritual sphere—and maybe primarily and precisely there—must be guided by our Marxist-Leninist principles. Principles, comrades, must not be compromised on any pretext whatever."

This is what we stand for now, and this is what we will continue to stand for. Principles were not given to us as a gift, we have fought for them at crucial turning points in the fatherland's history.

PRINCIPLES OF *PERESTROIKA*: THE REVOLUTIONARY NATURE OF THINKING AND ACTING

***Pravda* Editorial**

The CPSU Central Committee February *plenum* solidified the party's new tasks in restructuring all spheres of life at the present stage. The *plenum* speech of Mikhail Gorbachev, general secretary of the CPSU Central Committee ("Revolutionary *Perestroika* Requires Ideology of Renewal") made a clear analysis of today's problems and set forth a program of ideological support for *perestroika*. People want to be better aware of the nature of the changes that have begun in society, to see the essence and significance of the proposed solutions, and to know what is meant by the new quality of society we want to achieve. The struggle for *perestroika* is being waged both in production and in the spiritual sphere. And even though this struggle does not take the form of class antagonisms, it is proceeding sharply. The emergence of something new always excites attitudes toward and judgments about the new thing.

The debate itself and its nature and thrust attest to the democratization of our society. The diversity of judgments, assessments, and positions is one of the most important signs of the times and attests to the socialist pluralism of opinions which really exists now.

But it is impossible not to notice one very specific dimension of this debate. It occasionally declares itself not in a desire to interpret what is happening and to investigate it nor in a wish to advance the cause but, on the contrary, in attempts to slow it down by shouting the usual incantations: "They are betraying ideals!" "Abandoning principles!" "Undermining foundations!" . . .

The long article "I Cannot Waive Principles" that appeared in the newspaper *Sovetskaya Rossiya* on March 13 was a reflection of such feelings. . . .

Whether the author wanted it or not, primarily the article artificially sets off certain categories of Soviet people against one another. And this at precisely the moment when the unity of creative forces, despite all the shades of opinion, is more necessary than ever and when such unity is the prime requirement of *perestroika* and an absolute necessity simply for normal life, work, and the constructive renewal of society. Herein resides the fundamental feature of *perestroika*, which is designed to unite the maximum number of like-minded people in the struggle against phenomena impeding our life. Precisely and principally against all of these phenomena, not only or simply against certain incorrigible proponents of bureaucracy, corruption, abuse, and so forth.

In addition, the article is unconstructive. In an extensive, pretentiously titled article essentially no space was found to work out a single problem of *perestroika*. Whatever it discussed—*glasnost*, openness, the disappearance of areas free from criticism, youth—these processes and *perestroika* itself were linked only with difficulties and adverse consequences. . . .

There are, in point of fact, two basic theses running throughout the article: Why all of this *perestroika*, and haven't we gone too far with democratization and *glasnost*? The article urges us to amend and adjust *perestroika*; otherwise, it is alleged, "people in authority" will have to rescue socialism.

It is evident that not everyone has realized clearly yet the dramatic nature of the situation the country found itself in by April 1985, a situation which today we rightfully describe as pre-crisis. It is evident that not everyone is fully aware yet that administrative edict methods are totally obsolete. It is time that anyone who still places hopes in these methods or in their modification understands that all of this has already been tried, tried repeatedly, and it has failed to produce the desired results. Any ideas about the simplicity and effectiveness of these methods are nothing but illusions without any historical justification.

So, how is socialism to be "saved" today?

Should authoritarian methods, the practice of blind obedience, and the stifling of initiative be retained? Should we retain the system in which bureaucratism, lack of control, corruption, bribery, and petty bourgeois degeneration flourished lavishly?

Or should we revert to Leninist principles, whose essence is democratism, social justice, economic accountability, and respect for the individual's honor, life, and dignity? Do we have the right, in the face of the real difficulties and unsatisfied needs of the people, to adhere to the same old approaches that prevailed in the 1930s and 1940s? Has not the time come to clearly differentiate between the essence of socialism and the historically restricted forms of its implementation? Has not the time come for a scientifically critical investigation of our history, primarily in order to change the world in which we live and to learn harsh lessons for the future?

Almost half of the article is devoted to an assessment of our distant and recent history. The last few years have provided graphic proof of the growing interest in the past shown by the broadest strata of the population. The principles of scientific historicism and truth are increasingly the basis on which the people's historical awareness is taking shape. At the same time, there are instances of people playing on the idea of patriotism. Those who loudly scream about alleged "internal threats" to socialism, those who join certain political extremists and look everywhere for internal enemies, "counterrevolutionary nations," and so on, those are not patriots. The patriots are those who act in the country's interests and for the people's benefit, without fearing any difficulties. We do not need contemplative or verbal patriotism, we need creative patriotism. Not nostalgic and backward-looking patriotism, but the patriotism of socialist transformations. Patriotism based not only on love for the area of your birth, but also imbued with pride in the accomplishments of the great motherland of socialism.

Past experience is vitally necessary for the present, for solving the tasks of *perestroika*. Life's demand—"More socialism!"—makes it incumbent upon us to investigate what we did yesterday and how we did it, what has to be rejected and what has to be retained. Which principles and values ought to be considered really socialist? And if today we are taking a critical look at our history, we are doing so only because we want a better and more complete idea of our path into the future. . . .

The best teacher of *perestroika*—the one to whom we should constantly listen—is life, and life is dialectical. We should constantly remember the words of [Friedrich] Engels to the effect that nothing has been unconditionally established once and for all as sacrosanct. It is this continual motion and the constant renewal of nature, society, and our thinking that is the point of departure for and the initial, most cardinal principle in our thinking.

Let us return to the question: What has been done already? How are the party's course and the decisions of the 27th Party Congress and Central Committee *plenums* being implemented? What positive changes are taking place in people's lives?

We have really got down to tackling the most pressing, highest priority problems: housing, food, and the supply of goods and services to the population. A turn toward accelerated development of the social sphere has begun. Concrete decisions about restructuring education and health care have been adopted. Radical economic reform, our main lever for implementing large-scale transformations, is being put into practice. "That is the main political result of the last three years," M. Gorbachev said at the 4th All-Union Congress of *kolkhoz* members.

The voice of the intelligentsia and of all the working people has begun to make itself heard powerfully and strongly in society's spiritual life. This is one of the first gains accomplished by *perestroika*. Democratism is impossible without freedom of thought and speech, without the open, broad clash of opinions, without keeping a critical eye on our life. . . .

There are no prohibited topics today. Journals, publishing houses, and studios decide for themselves what to publish. But the appearance of the article "I Cannot Waive Principles" is part of an attempt little by little to revise party decisions. It has been said repeatedly at meetings in the party Central Committee that the Soviet press is not a private concern, that Communists writing for the press and editors should have a sense of responsibility for articles and publications. In this case the newspaper *Sovetskaya Rossiya*, which, let us be frank, has done much for *perestroika*, departed from this principle.

Debates, discussions, and polemics are, of course, necessary. They lie in store for us in our future, too. There are also many pitfalls in store for us, traps laid by the past. We must all work together to clear these traps from our path. We need disputes that help to advance *perestroika* and lead to the consolidation of forces, to cohesion around *perestroika*, and not to disunity. . . .

More light. More initiative. More responsibility. A more rapid mastery of the full profundity of the Marxist-Leninist concept of *perestroika*, of the new political thinking. We can and must revive the Leninist practice of the socialist society—the most humane, the most just. We will firmly and steadily follow the revolutionary principles of *perestroika*: more *glasnost*, more democracy, more socialism.

▪ Discussion Questions

1. Why is Andreyeva so critical of Gorbachev's reforms?
2. What arguments do Gorbachev's supporters use to counter Andreyeva's criticisms?
3. According to the *Pravda* article, what are the fundamental features of *glasnost* and *perestroika*?
4. In what ways do these two articles reflect different understandings of Soviet history and its role in shaping the country's future?

77. Cornelia Matzke, *Revolution in East Germany: An Activist's Perspective* (1989)

Gorbachev's reforms had a ripple effect throughout the Soviet bloc, sparking an explosion of political debate and civic activism. In the following interview, conducted in 1990, we hear the voice of a young East German activist, Cornelia Matzke, who was caught up in these currents of change. On the one hand, she was an ordinary citizen, leading her life as a physician-in-training in Leipzig, far removed from the activities of well-known dissenters. On the other, people like her were the backbone of the "year of miracles," 1989, which toppled Soviet communism. As she recounts, they were the ones who organized meetings, passed out pamphlets, and successfully urged others to challenge the status quo. Their efforts culminated on November 9, when the Berlin Wall came down.

So much has happened lately that I haven't thought about me and my development for a long time. . . .

I am a woman who has been interested in political issues as far back as I can remember. I always had a desire to have influence. Of course, one would have to reflect on the question as to what it means to "have influence," but it represented a basic motivation to become active politically; otherwise, I could have continued to live a normal life, like most others. . . .

During my training at the university I began to seek contact with grassroots groups here in Leipzig and with the ESG [Evangelical Student Community]. In November of 1985 I organized

Dirk Philipsen, *We Were the People: Voices from East Germany's Revolutionary Autumn of 1989* (Durham, N.C.: Duke University Press, 1993), 69–75, 248.

a presentation on the fortieth anniversary of the victory over fascism within the context of the Protestant Peace Decade that was held in Leipzig at the time. Before that, I had only had sporadic contacts with the church. . . .

My problem had always been to find a way to express myself politically, to find a context or people with whom I could work. . . .

Actually, I was trying to find the women's movement, except that I had not yet quite realized that at the time. . . .

You see, the church was the only possible alternative for any kind of political activism. There was absolutely nothing else. For a while I had considered joining one of the satellite parties, such as the LDPD [Liberal Democratic Party of Germany], but all of them were really the same as the SED [Socialist Unity Party]; they were completely controlled by the SED and followed in every respect the party line. Just the language these people were using was appalling to me. One cannot express oneself in these abstract party-line categories.

So trying to change something from within the party, perhaps with friends who thought along the same lines as you, was never an option for you?

Well, maybe if I had fallen in love with a party member or something like that, but short of that, no. I don't think this would have been possible at all. You see, I always perceived myself as someone from the left, and I had always been very angry about how this party was ruining and corrupting left-wing ideas. I just felt betrayed by this party which claimed to be the bearer of an ideology which they themselves did not live up to at all. But this never resulted in my giving up on left-wing ideas, on the idea of socialism, on a more democratic and egalitarian alternative to capitalism. And I still think that way. . . .

My experiences with working in environmental groups was, on the other hand, that men were always in charge of everything, and they knew they were. . . .

Were women's issues ever debated in any of those groups?

No, not really. It was simply not an issue, mostly because the women's movement was not an issue in the GDR. Women had no support for their grievances or their issues anywhere in the country. Which is, by the way, the main reason why I think women should organize their own groups: so that they can have a support network, a place where their issues and problems are taken seriously, and a forum through which to form some kind of political lobby. Because if women simply join male-dominated groups and parties—and I am not saying they should not do that as well—they will never get this kind of support; they will not be able to identify themselves as women. Women can only achieve some kind of identity by organizing as women, by having a network which allows them to realize that their problems are not individual problems, but rather that many other women have the same problems. . . .

How or when did you realize that you wanted to focus your political activities on women's issues?

The discussions with the men in the environmental group were just dreadful to me. In fact, that was true in all the groups I participated in. One of those was a so-called "discussion group." We met about once a month and talked about certain issues that had been decided upon earlier. Of course, we particularly focused on issues that one could not talk about in public anywhere else. What always bothered me a great deal was that if women came with their partners or husbands, they always ended up not saying anything. I was always drawn to these women in an emotional sense. I just wanted to find out how it would be to have such discussions only with women. . . .

There was an incredible atmosphere in the country during most of 1989, a sort of depression, a feeling of being severely oppressed, a sense that all the things we had put up with and we had suffered could not go on much longer. Everyone felt like that in one way or another.

We had organized a street music festival in June 1989, where I was arrested. I was totally depressed afterward. We simply could not believe that they could be that stupid, that they actually dared to arrest people at a street music festival. They simply went beyond their limits, or at least they did not seem to know anymore where those limits were. If they ever had, they certainly no longer understood where they had to allow some space in order then to be able to crack down on people when it *really* got dangerous for them. They were not even clever as holders of power. They certainly did not belong in the category of "intelligent dictators." In retrospect, it is amazing to see how many blatant mistakes they made from their point of view—in fact, it is astonishing how long they managed to hold on to power.

It was my understanding that this street music festival in 1989 was conceptualized not merely as a cultural event, but rather as a political statement as well. Is that correct?

Well, yes and no. It was not a political rally of any sort. But it was supposed to be a test as to whether the party would in fact react as if it were a political event. We had even tried to get an official permit for this festival, which we did not receive. But we decided to go ahead and invite bands and people anyway. Prior to this, the musicians were put under a lot of pressure from the officials who said that if the musicians participated in the festival, they would lose their licenses. Most of the musicians buckled under this pressure and did not show up. So we mostly had amateur musicians and bands from other cities.

At first, the festival did not really get started, because the Stasi had a lot of agents there who were talking to the musicians, trying to convince them not to play, putting pressure on them and such. A few friends and I walked up to one of those conversations between Stasi officials and musicians and just began to sing—which was difficult, because we didn't really have any songs everyone readily knew.

Well, in the end we found one, and this idea of just beginning to sing and play spread rapidly. So this is how the festival started. Everything was OK until about noon, when the police drove up with trucks and began to arrest people. First, they arrested the musicians, and then others who had played any active role in putting together this festival.

Later on, I got to know quite a few very interesting people in the detention cell, people who had organized the monitoring of the elections in May and who had made public the large-scale election fraud that had been revealed by those members of the grassroots groups who had organized this. It was a very interesting experience.

Why exactly did they arrest you?

Well, at the end they pretty much picked up people at random in front of the Thomas Church. Of course, they were particularly looking for people who they already knew were engaged in "subversive activities" and those who somehow looked conspicuously "alternative." I did not particularly look "alternative," and I could probably have avoided arrest. But first of all I thought that it was time for me to go through this experience as well, and second of all I figured it would be important for them also to arrest people once who did not fit into their preconceptions of who was and who was not opposed to the regime they were serving.

How long did they keep you in detention?

Until about 2:30 at night.

How did they treat you?

Not too badly. The guy who interrogated me was talking about "enemies of the state" and things like that, but that was normal. Surprisingly, I was also not scared at all. We knew, for example, that they were eavesdropping on us, but that did not matter to us at all; we talked to one another completely freely. There was a mood among us—the kind of mood that prevailed until October and, I think, that goes a long way in explaining the mass demonstrations of October—that it did not matter anymore. Things were so bad, it really no longer mattered. Something just *had* to happen, and people were increasingly willing to take risks in order to bring about change. . . .

Many things happened after, . . . the wave of emigration through Hungary and such. What also seemed important to me at the time was the fact that Honecker was sick, and that the entire party leadership simply came across as desolate. They seemed no longer capable of any real decisions. All of this, of course, left the impression that this "power"—this party and state leadership that we had come to know simply as "the power"—that this power had disintegrated so much primarily because Honecker was sick. It was somehow encouraging, because if that was true, it could not be all that great a "power" after all. I at least experienced it that way, and I believe many others did as well. It just signified that such power cannot be infinite.

I well remember a meeting we had in September among opposition activists and church members, and one person said "the whole system is so well organized, so stable, that it will certainly defend itself to the last man." Particularly older citizens, due to all their experiences, thought that this entire party apparatus could never be broken.

Many thought that inertia, or a kind of self-perpetuating dynamic would keep the apparatus in place indefinitely. How wrong everybody was. . . .

How did you experience the period between August and November of 1989?

I was kind of vacillating between doing more within the country and leaving it for good. All of my friends were in this position. We were simply not sure whether it could ever be more than hopeless martyrdom to get involved more openly and actively. It was a very difficult time. . . .

I think many of us would have left as well if nothing had happened until the end of the year. And, don't misunderstand me, not because we ever wanted to leave. Somehow we all felt responsible for this absolutely desolate country.

Let me ask you as someone who perceives herself to be "on the left": did you ever think that socialism in the GDR could be reformed, perhaps along the lines of what was happening in the Soviet Union, or at least that the opposition could be more decisive in determining the future political course, as perhaps it was the case in Czechoslovakia?

Yes, absolutely, that was our goal.

I am asking because you said earlier that you were thinking about emigrating because of how little, if anything, was possible in the GDR. So why did you think that it was more difficult to achieve reforms in the GDR than, for example, in the Soviet Union?

There were many reasons for that. But before I say something more, it is important to point out that what was going on in the Soviet Union was decisive for the entire movement; otherwise nothing would have ever happened here. So this was the basic event. And it was simply terrible how the GDR leadership responded to these openings and changes in the Soviet Union, high-ranking party functionaries like Kurt Hager saying, for example, "just because our neighbor changes his tapestry does not mean we have to do so as well."

■ Discussion Questions

1. What general factors fueled Matzke's political activism?
2. What does Matzke's description of the street festival and its aftermath reveal about the political atmosphere in East Germany in 1989?
3. How did Matzke's gender shape her political identity?

78. François Mitterrand, *Speech to the European Parliament* (1995)

Although the collapse of the Soviet empire brought the cold war to an end, another enemy loomed on the horizon: the economic clout of Asia. European leaders responded by campaigning for the further social, economic, and political integration of Europe. Their campaign bore fruit in 1994 with the creation of the European Union. These extracts from a speech given by French president François

Debates of the European Parliament, 1994–95, no. 4–456/45–51.

Mitterrand (president 1981–1995) to the European parliament in 1995 capture the mood at the time that a truly unified Europe could be achieved. His words reveal that the goals of the EU extended far beyond the concerns of the marketplace; they struck at the heart of Europe's ongoing quest to reshape its identity in the post–cold war age.

Besides the essential coordination of our policies, . . . we must also, in the longer term, build the foundations of a Europe in which renewed—and, I hope, strong, sound and lasting—economic growth can take place. This will be possible, if we prove capable of using three of our major assets to the full. What is the first of those assets? It is the size of our internal market. So far, we have essentially succeeded in removing the administrative, customs and regulatory barriers which partitioned this vast economic area. That is the task that was accomplished by means of the Single European Act. We now have to eliminate or reduce the remaining barriers—which are far from insignificant—including the physical barriers which still restrict the free movement of people, goods and ideas. . . .

Our second major asset is, of course, economic and monetary union, which is the natural and essential complement, in my view, to the single market, and without which the single market—which I and, of course, others were so anxious to achieve, and which was the object of so much hard work—would be a recipe for anarchy and the worst forms of unfair competition.

The monetary tensions which we have witnessed in the past—and which, at least as far as the last few weeks are concerned, we are witnessing today—make clear the need to advance as quickly as possible towards the introduction of a single currency. I know that this is still the subject of discussion, that not everyone has been convinced. In any event, I wish to convey to you my personal conviction—which, I believe, is shared by the majority of people in authority in France; the introduction of a single currency is the only means of ensuring that Europe remains a great economic and monetary power, and it is the best means of ensuring the sustained growth of our economies. . . .

Our third major asset is the European Union's technological excellence. Our research scientists have been responsible for countless innovations. Such capital cannot fail to yield a profit if we prove capable of utilising it properly, and on a European scale. I shall not dwell on this point, but I am sure that the extraordinary number of technological, scientific, inventive and innovative successes which Europe has achieved since the second half of the nineteenth century will come to mind—whilst not forgetting, of course, those elsewhere in the world who have contributed to the general progress. . . .

Let us make no mistake: markets are no more than instruments, no more than mechanisms which are all too often governed by the law of the strongest, mechanisms which can lead to injustice, exclusion and dependence, unless the necessary counterweight is provided by those who can assert their democratic legitimacy. Alongside the markets, there is room for economic and social activities based on the concepts of solidarity, cooperation, partnership, reciprocity and the common interest—in short, public services. So far, we have drawn the outline of a social Europe, but it has no content. And will it not be an exciting, exhilarating venture to provide that content? Will it not be the task of the coming months and years? At that point, I shall be observing the social progress made from the outside and I shall rejoice whenever I see all Europe's leaders coming together—leaving behind their natural divisions and differences of opinion—to ensure that the Europe which is being built does not simply resemble a mechanical or Meccano toy, but is the potent work of men and women who are capable of shaping their own destiny. At present, there are some difficulties, but I hope that in collaboration with the social partners, we shall succeed in taking initiatives in the areas of training, education, the organisation of labour, and the campaign against all forms of exclusion. Indeed, nothing will be possible unless the social partners take their rightful place in the process of European integration.

. . . Such a Europe, our Europe, must be embodied in something more than simply balance sheets and freight tonnages. I would go as far as to say, while not wishing to become too rhetorical, that it needs a soul, so that it can give expression—and let us use more modest language here—to its culture, its ways of thinking, the intellectual make-up of its peoples, the fruits of the centuries of civilisation of which we are the heirs. The expressions of Europe's many forms of genius are rich and diverse; and, as in the past, we must share with the whole world—while not seeking to impose them, somewhat differently from in the past—our ideas, our dreams and, to the extent that they are of the right kind, our passions. . . .

To strengthen our approach, let us rediscover those places and objects which represent our common past. I should like to see the devising and implementation of a vast project to develop the sites of our European heritage. At the same time, let us teach about Europe. Let us educate our children on the subject. Let our schools prepare them for citizenship. Let them develop the teaching of history, geography and culture. Let us encourage the twinning of schools and universities, exchanges of schoolchildren and students. Let us stress the importance of multilingualism. To this end, France will be submitting a draft intergovernmental convention on the teaching of at least two foreign languages. At the same time, let us step up our efforts to promote the translation of written works. I have long observed that the French, my fellow countrymen, frequently complain that their great authors are seldom translated in, for example, some of the countries of Central and Eastern Europe. And I have also observed that in fact, we, the French, do not translate their works either; we complain of a fault of which we ourselves are guilty—because the Europe of cultures is the whole of Europe. . . .

. . . I thank you for the patience and attention with which you have been kind enough to listen to me, and I should like to finish with a few remarks of a more personal nature. Fate would have it that I was born during the First World War and fought in the Second. I therefore spent my childhood in the surroundings of families torn apart, all of them mourning loved ones and feeling great bitterness, if not hatred towards the recent enemy, the traditional enemy. However, ladies and gentlemen, such enemies have changed from century to century, as traditions have always changed. I have had occasion to say to this House before that France has engaged in wars with every European country, with the exception, I believe, of Denmark. We have to wonder why. . . .

But my generation has almost completed its work; it is carrying out its last public acts, and this will be one of my last. It is therefore vital for us to pass on our experience. Many of you will remember the teaching of your parents, will have felt the suffering of your countries, will have experienced the grief, the pain of separation, the presence of death—all as a result of the mutual enmity of the peoples of Europe. It is vital to pass on not this hatred but, on the contrary, the opportunity which we have for reconciliation, thanks—it must be said—to those who, after 1944–1945, themselves blood-stained and with their personal lives destroyed, had the courage to envisage a more radiant future which would be based on peace and reconciliation. That is what we have done.

However, I did not acquire my own convictions in this way by chance. I did not acquire them in the German prisoner-of-war camps in which I was a captive, or in a country which itself was occupied—a situation which many of you will have experienced. I remember that even families who practiced the virtues of humanity, of kindness, spoke with animosity when they talked about the Germans. When I was an escaped prisoner of war—or rather, when I was in the process of escaping—I met some Germans, then I spent some time in a prison in Baden-Württemberg, and I used to talk to the people, Germans, there and I came to realise that the Germans liked the French more than the French liked the Germans.

I say this without wishing to denigrate my country, which is no more nationalistic than any other, far from it. I say this to make it clear that, at that time, everyone saw the world from his or her own viewpoint, and that those viewpoints were generally distorting. We must overcome such prejudices. What I am asking you to do is almost impossible, because it means overcoming our past. And yet, if we fail to overcome our past, let there be no mistake about what will follow: ladies and gentlemen, nationalism means war!

War is not only our past, it could also be our future! And it is us, it is you, ladies and gentlemen, the Members of the European Parliament, who will henceforth be the guardians of our peace, our security and our future!

■ Discussion Questions

1. According to Mitterrand, which assets must Europe use to ensure its economic growth?
2. What other factors does Mitterrand consider to be important to European unity?
3. How did Mitterrand's understanding of Europe's past shape his vision for its future?

Acknowledgments (continued)

Giovanni Pico della Mirandola. *Oration on the Dignity of Man* (1496). From *The Italian Renaissance Reader,* edited by Julia Conaway Bondanella and Mark Musa. Copyright © 1987 by Julia Conaway Bondanella and Mark Musa. Reprinted with the permission of Dutton Signet, a division of Penguin Putnam Inc.

Alessandra Strozzi. *Letters from a Widow and Matriarch of a Great Family* (1450–1465). From *University of Chicago Readings in Western Civilization, 5: The Renaissance,* edited by Eric Cochrane and Julius Kirshner. Copyright © 1986 by The University of Chicago. Reprinted with the permission of The University of Chicago Press.

Chapter 12

Argula von Grumbach and John Hooker. *Women's Actions in the Reformation* (1520s–30s). Excerpt from *The Dissolution of the Monasteries* by Joyce Youings. Copyright © 1971 by Joyce Youings. Reprinted with the permission of HarperCollins Publishers, Ltd.

Henry IV. *Edict of Nantes* (1598). From "The Great Pressures and Grievances of the Protestants in France," Edmund Everand. Saint Ignatius of Loyola. *A New Kind of Catholicism* (1546, 1549, 1553). From *St. Ignatius of Loyola: Personal Writings: Reminiscences, Spiritual Diary, Select Letters including the text of The Spiritual Exercises,* edited and translated by Joseph A. Munitiz and Philip Endean. Copyright © 1996 by Joseph A. Munitiz and Philip Endean. Reprinted with the permission of Penguin Books, Ltd.

Galileo, *Letter to the Grand Duchess Christina* (1615). *From Discoveries and Opinions of Galileo,* translated by Stillman Drake. Copyright © 1957 by Stillman Drake. Reprinted with the permission of Doubleday, a division of Random House, Inc.

Chapter 13

Louis de Rouvroy, Duke of Saint-Simon. *Memoirs* (1694–1723). From *The Memoirs of The Duke of Saint-Simon,* translated by Bayle St. John, Vol. II.

Ludwig Fabritius. *The Revolt of Stenka Razin* (1670). From *Russia Under Western Eyes 1517–1825,* edited by Anthony Glenn Cross. Copyright © 1971 by Anthony Glenn Cross. Reprinted with permission.

British Parliament. *The English Bill of Rights* (1689). From *The Statutes:* revised edition, 1871, vol. II.

Chapter 14

Olaudah Equiano. *The Interesting Narrative of the Life of Olaudah Equiano, Written by Himself* (1789). From *Equiano's Travels: His Autobiography,* edited by Paul Edwards. Published by Frederick A. Praeger, 1966.

Montesquieu. *Persian Letters: Letter 37* (1721). Translated by John Davidson, Vol. I.

Mary Astell. *Reflections upon Marriage* (1706). Excerpt from *The First English Feminist: Reflections Upon Marriage and Other Writings,* edited by Bridget Hill. Copyright © 1986 by Bridget Hill. Reprinted by permission.

Chapter 15

Marie-Therese Geoffrin and Monsieur d'Alembert. *The Salon of Madame Geoffrin* (1765). Reprinted in *Historical and Literary Memoirs and Anecdotes Selected from the Correspondence of Baron de Grimm and Diderot with the Duke of Saxe-Gotha, and Many Other Distinguished Persons between the Years of 1753–1790,* Second edition, vol. III (1815) and from *Memoir of d'Alembert.* Reprinted in *Connection with the Past: The D. C. Heath Document Sets for Western Civilization,* Vol. II.

Jacques-Louis Menetra. Excerpt from *Journal of My Life* (1764–1802). Translated by Arthur Goldhammer. Copyright © 1986 by Arthur Goldhammer. Reprinted with the permission of the publisher.

Frederick II. *Political Testament* (1752). Excerpt from "The Rise of Prussia" in *Europe in Review,* edited by George Lachmann Mosse, Rondo E. Cameron, Henry Bertram Hill, and Michael B. Petrovich. Published by Rand McNally & Company, 1957. Reprinted by permission.

Chapter 16

National Assembly. *The Declaration of the Rights of Man and of the Citizen* (1789). *Readings in European History: A Collection of Extracts from the Sources* by James Harvey Robinson. Published by Ginn and Company, 1906.

Francois Dominique Toussaint L'Ouverture. *Revolution in the Colonies* (1794–1795). Translated by Katharine J. Lualdi, from *Toussaint Louverture a travers sa correspondence* by Gerard M. Lauent, 1953. Reprinted with permission.

Abd al-Rahman al-Jabarti. *Napoleon in Egypt* (1798). From *Napoleon in Egypt: Al-Jabarti's Chronicle of the French Occupation,* 1798, translated by Shumel Moreh. Copyright © 1993 by Shumel Moreh. Reprinted with the permission of E. J. Brill Publishers, Leiden, The Netherlands.

Chapter 17

Factory Rules in Berlin (1844). From *Documents of European Economic History: The Process of Industrialization 1750–1870* by Sidney Pollard and C. Holmes, Vol. I. Copyright © 1968 by St. Martin's Press, Inc. Reprinted with permission of the publisher.

T. B. Macaulay. *Speeches on Parliamentary Reform* (1831). From *Miscellanies,* Vol. 1, by Lord Macaulay. Published by Houghton Mifflin and Company, 1901.

Friedrich Engels. *Draft of a Communist Confession of Faith* (1847). From *Collected Works,* vol. 6, by Karl Marx and Frederick Engels. Reprinted with the permission of International Publishers.

Victor Hugo. *Preface to Cromwell* (1827). From *The Dramatic Works of Victor Hugo,* vol. III. Published by The Athenaeum Society, 1909.

Chapter 18

Alexander II. *Address in the State Council* (1861). From *A Source Book for Russian History* by George Vernadsky, general editor, vol. II. Copyright © 1972 by Yale University. Reprinted with the permission of Yale University Press.

Krupa Sattianadan. *Saguna: A Story of Native Christian Life* (1887–1888). *From Women Were Writing in India 600 B.C. to the Present,* edited by Susie Tharu and K. Lalita, vol. I. Copyright © 1991 The Feminist Press at the City University of New York. Reprinted with the permission of the publisher.

Charles Darwin. *The Descent of Man* (1871). From *The Descent of Man and Selection in Reform to Sex.* Published by Appelton and Company, 1896.

Chapter 19

Jules Ferry. *Speech before the French National Assembly* (1883). From *Modern Imperialism, Western Overseas Expansion and Its Aftermath 1776–1965,* edited by Ralph Austen. Published by D. C. Heath and Company, 1969.

The I-ho-ch'uan (Boxers). *The Boxers Demand Death for All "Foreign Devils"* (1900). From *The Imperialism reader: Documents and Readings on Modern Expansionism,* edited by Louis L. Snyder. Published by D. Van Nostrand Company, Inc. 1962.

Chapter 20

L. Doriat. *Women on the Home Front* (1917). From *Lines of Fire: Women Writers of World War I* edited by Margaret R. Higonnet.

Benito Mussolini. *The Doctrine of Facism* (1932). From *The Social and Political Doctrines of Contemporary Europe,* edited and translated by Michael Oakeshott. Reprinted with the permission of Cambridge University Press.

Chapter 21

Joseph Goebbels. *Nazi Propaganda Pamphlet* (1930). From *Documents of German History,* edited and translated by Louis L. Snyder. Copyright © 1958 by Rutgers, The State University. Reprinted with the permission of Rutgers University Press.

Neville Chamberlain. *Speech on the Munich Crisis* (1938). From *Parliamentary Debates, Fifth Series,* Vol. 339, House of Commons Official Report.

Sam Bankhalter and Hinda Kibort. *Memories of the Holocaust* (1938–1945). From *Witnesses to the Holocaust: An Oral History,* edited by Rhoda G. Lewin. Copyright © 1980 by the Jewish Community Relations Council and Anti-Defamation League of Minnesota and the Dakotas. Reprinted with the permission of The Gale Group.

Chapter 22

National Security Council. *Paper Number 68* (1950). From *Foreign Relations of the United States.* National Security Council reports, Washington, D.C. 1977.

Ho Chi Minh. *Declaration of Independence of the Republic of Vietnam* (1945). From *Conflict in Indo-China and International Repercussions: A Documentary History 1945-1955*, edited by Allen B. Cole. Copyright © 1956 Cornell University Press. Reprinted with the permission of Cornell University Press.

Simone de Beauvoir. *The Second Sex* (1949). Translated and edited by H. M. Parshley. Copyright © 1952 and renewed 1980 by Alfred A. Knopf, Inc. Reprinted with the permission of Alfred A. Knopf, a division of Random House, Inc.

Chapter 23

The New York Times and Neil Armstrong and Edwin Aldrin. "To Walk on the Moon" editorial, July 20, 1969. Copyright © 1969 The New York Times Company. Reprinted with permission. Excerpt from *First Man on the Moon: A Voyage with Neil Armstrong, Michael Collins and Edwin E. Aldrin, Jr.* Copyright © 1970 by Neil Armstrong, Michael Collins, Edwin E. Aldrin, Jr., Gene Farmer and Dora Jane Hamblin. Reprinted with the permission of Little, Brown and Company, subsidiary of Time Warner Trade Publishing.

Pope John XXIII, Vatican II (1961). From *The Documents of Vatican II: All Sixteen Official Texts Promulgated by the Ecumenical Council* published by Herder & Herder, 1966.

Student Voices of Protest (1968). From *Takin' it to the streets': A Sixties Reader*, edited by Alexander Bloom and Wini Brienes. Copyright © 1955 by Alexander Bloom and Wini Brienes. Reprinted with the permission of Oxford University Press, Inc. *A Student Generation in Revolt* by Ronald Fraser. Copyright © 1968 by Ronald Fraser. Reprinted with the permission of Pantheon Books, a division of Random House, Inc.

Chapter 24

Glasnost and the Soviet Press (1988). From *Gorbachev and Glasnost: Viewpoints from the Soviet Press*, edited by Isaac J. Tarasulo. Published by SR Books, 1989.

Cornelia Matzke. *Revolution in East Germany: An Activist's Perspective* (1989). From *We Were the People: Voices from East Germany's Revolutionary Autumn of 1989*, edited by Dirk Philipsen. Copyright © 1993 by Duke University Press. Reprinted with the permission of the publisher. All rights reserved.

François Mitterrand. *Speech to the European Parliament* (1995). From *Debates of the European Parliament 1994/95*. No. 4-456/45-51.